Guide to Gale Literary Criticism Series

For criticism on	Consult these Gale series
Authors now living or who died after December 31, 1959	*CONTEMPORARY LITERARY CRITICISM (CLC)*
Authors who died between 1900 and 1959	*TWENTIETH-CENTURY LITERARY CRITICISM (TCLC)*
Authors who died between 1800 and 1899	*NINETEENTH-CENTURY LITERATURE CRITICISM (NCLC)*
Authors who died between 1400 and 1799	*LITERATURE CRITICISM FROM 1400 TO 1800 (LC)* *SHAKESPEAREAN CRITICISM (SC)*
Authors who died before 1400	*CLASSICAL AND MEDIEVAL LITERATURE CRITICISM (CMLC)*
Authors of books for children and young adults	*CHILDREN'S LITERATURE REVIEW (CLR)*
Dramatists	*DRAMA CRITICISM (DC)*
Poets	*POETRY CRITICISM (PC)*
Short story writers	*SHORT STORY CRITICISM (SSC)*
Black writers of the past two hundred years	*BLACK LITERATURE CRITICISM (BLC)*
Hispanic writers of the late nineteenth and twentieth centuries	*HISPANIC LITERATURE CRITICISM (HLC)*
Native North American writers and orators of the eighteenth, nineteenth, and twentieth centuries	*NATIVE NORTH AMERICAN LITERATURE (NNAL)*
Major authors from the Renaissance to the present	*WORLD LITERATURE CRITICISM, 1500 TO THE PRESENT (WLC)*

ISSN 0276-8178

Volume 75

Twentieth-Century Literary Criticism

**Excerpts from Criticism of the
Works of Novelists, Poets, Playwrights,
Short Story Writers, and Other Creative Writers
Who Lived between 1900 and 1960,
from the First Published Critical
Appraisals to Current Evaluations**

Jennifer Gariepy
Editor

Thomas Ligotti
Associate Editor

GALE

DETROIT • NEW YORK • LONDON

STAFF

Jennifer Gariepy, *Editor*

Thomas Ligotti, *Associate Editor*

Susan Trosky, *Permissions Manager*
Kimberly F. Smilay, *Permissions Specialist*
Steve Cusack, Kelly A. Quin, *Permissions Associates*

Victoria B. Cariappa, *Research Manager*
Michele P. LaMeau, Andrew Guy Malonis, Barbara McNeil, Gary J. Oudersluys, Maureen Richards, *Research Specialists*
Julia C. Daniel, Tamara C. Nott, Tracie A. Richardson, Norma Sawaya, Cheryl L. Warnock, *Research Associates*

Mary Beth Trimper, *Production Director*
Shanna Heilveil, *Production Assistant*

Ninette Saad, *Desktop Publisher Assistant*
Randy Bassett, *Image Database Supervisor*
Robert Duncan, Michael Logusz, *Imaging Specialists*
Pamela Reed, *Photography Coordinator*

Library of Congress Catalog Card Number 76-46132
ISBN 0-7876-2019-X
ISSN 0276-8178

Printed in the United States of America
10   9   8   7   6   5   4   3   2   1

Contents

Preface   vii

Acknowledgments   xi

Preface

Since its inception more than fifteen years ago, *Twentieth-Century Literary Criticism* has been purchased and used by nearly 10,000 school, public, and college or university libraries. *TCLC* has covered more than 500 authors, representing 58 nationalities, and over 25,000 titles. No other reference source has surveyed the critical response to twentieth-century authors and literature as thoroughly as *TCLC*. In the words of one reviewer, "there is nothing comparable available." *TCLC* "is a gold mine of information—dates, pseudonyms, biographical information, and criticism from books and periodicals—which many libraries would have difficulty assembling on their own."

Scope of the Series

TCLC is designed to serve as an introduction to authors who died between 1900 and 1960 and to the most significant interpretations of these author's works. The great poets, novelists, short story writers, playwrights, and philosophers of this period are frequently studied in high school and college literature courses. In organizing and excerpting the vast amount of critical material written on these authors, *TCLC* helps students develop valuable insight into literary history, promotes a better understanding of the texts, and sparks ideas for papers and assignments. Each entry in *TCLC* presents a comprehensive survey of an author's career or an individual work of literature and provides the user with a multiplicity of interpretations and assessments. Such variety allows students to pursue their own interests; furthermore, it fosters an awareness that literature is dynamic and responsive to many different opinions.

Every fourth volume of *TCLC* is devoted to literary topics. These topic entries widen the focus of the series from individual authors to such broader subjects as literary movements, prominent themes in twentieth-century literature, literary reaction to political and historical events, significant eras in literary history, prominent literary anniversaries, and the literatures of cultures that are often overlooked by English-speaking readers.

TCLC is designed as a companion series to Gale's *Contemporary Literary Criticism*, which reprints commentary on authors now living or who have died since 1960. Because of the different periods under consideration, there is no duplication of material between *CLC* and *TCLC*. For additional information about *CLC* and Gale's other criticism titles, users should consult the Guide to Gale Literary Criticism Series preceding the title page in this volume.

Coverage

Each volume of *TCLC* is carefully compiled to present:

- criticism of authors, or literary topics, representing a variety of genres and nationalities

- both major and lesser-known writers and literary works of the period

- 6-12 authors or 3-6 topics per volume

- individual entries that survey critical response to each author's work or each topic in literary history, including early criticism to reflect initial reactions; later criticism to represent any rise or decline in reputation; and current retrospective analyses.

Organization of This Book

An author entry consists of the following elements: author heading, biographical and critical introduction, list of principal works, excerpts of criticism (each preceded by an annotation and a bibliographic citation), and a bibliography of further reading.

- The **Author Heading** consists of the name under which the author most commonly wrote, followed by birth and death dates. If an author wrote consistently under a pseudonym, the pseudonym will be listed in the author heading and the real name given in parentheses on the first line of the biographical and critical introduction. Also located at the beginning of the introduction to the author entry are any name variations under which an author wrote, including transliterated forms for authors whose languages use nonroman alphabets.

●The **Biographical and Critical Introduction** outlines the author's life and career, as well as the critical issues surrounding his or her work. References to past volumes of *TCLC* are provided at the beginning of the introduction. Additional sources of information in other biographical and critical reference series published by Gale, including *Short Story Criticism, Children's Literature Review, Contemporary Authors, Dictionary of Literary Biography,* and *Something about the Author,* are listed in a box at the end of the entry.

●Some *TCLC* entries include **Portraits** of the author. Entries also may contain reproductions of materials pertinent to an author's career, including manuscript pages, title pages, dust jackets, letters, and drawings, as well as photographs of important people, places, and events in an author's life.

●The **List of Principal Works** is chronological by date of first book publication and identifies the genre of each work. In the case of foreign authors with both foreign-language publications and English translations, the title and date of the first English-language edition are given in brackets. Unless otherwise indicated, dramas are dated by first performance, not first publication.

●Critical excerpts are prefaced by **Annotations** providing the reader with information about both the critic and the criticism that follows. Included are the critic's reputation, individual approach to literary criticism, and particular expertise in an author's works. Also noted are the relative importance of a work of criticism, the scope of the excerpt, and the growth of critical controversy or changes in critical trends regarding an author. In some cases, these annotations cross-reference excerpts by critics who discuss each other's commentary.

●A complete **Bibliographic Citation** designed to facilitate location of the original essay or book precedes each piece of criticism.

●Criticism is arranged chronologically in each author entry to provide a perspective on changes in critical evaluation over the years. All titles of works by the author featured in the entry are printed in boldface type to enable the user to easily locate discussion of particular works. Also for purposes of easier identification, the critic's name and the publication date of the essay are given at the beginning of each piece of criticism. Unsigned criticism is preceded by the title of the journal in which it appeared. Some of the excerpts in *TCLC* also contain translated material. Unless otherwise noted, translations in brackets are by the editors; translations in parentheses or continuous with the text are by the critic. Publication information (such as footnotes or page and line references to specific editions of works) have been deleted at the editor's discretion to provide smoother reading of the text.

●An annotated list of **Further Reading** appearing at the end of each author entry suggests secondary sources on the author. In some cases it includes essays for which the editors could not obtain reprint rights.

Cumulative Indexes

●Each volume of *TCLC* contains a cumulative **Author Index** listing all authors who have appeared in Gale's Literary Criticism Series, along with cross references to such biographical series as *Contemporary Authors* and *Dictionary of Literary Biography.* For readers' convenience, a complete list of Gale titles included appears on the first page of the author index. Useful for locating authors within the various series, this index is particularly valuable for those authors who are identified by a certain period but who, because of their death dates, are placed in another, or for those authors whose careers span two periods. For example, F. Scott Fitzgerald is found in *TCLC,* yet a writer often associated with him, Ernest Hemingway, is found in *CLC.*

- Each *TCLC* volume includes a cumulative **Nationality Index** which lists all authors who have appeared in *TCLC* volumes, arranged alphabetically under their respective nationalities, as well as Topics volume entries devoted to particular national literatures.

- Each new volume in Gale's Literary Criticism Series includes a cumulative **Topic Index,** which lists all literary topics treated in *NCLC, TCLC, LC 1400-1800,* and the *CLC* yearbook.

- Each new volume of *TCLC,* with the exception of the Topics volumes, includes a **Title Index** listing the titles of all literary works discussed in the volume. In response to numerous suggestions from librarians, Gale has also produced a **Special Paperbound Edition** of the *TCLC* title index. This annual cumulation lists all titles discussed in the series since its inception and is issued with the first volume of *TCLC* published each year. Additional copies of the index are available on request. Librarians and patrons will welcome this separate index; it saves shelf space, is easy to use, and is recyclable upon receipt of the following year's cumulation. Titles discussed in the Topics volume entries are not included *TCLC* cumulative index.

Citing Twentieth-Century Literary Criticism

When writing papers, students who quote directly from any volume in Gale's literary Criticism Series may use the following general forms to footnote reprinted criticism. The first example pertains to materials drawn from periodicals, the second to material reprinted from books.

[1]William H. Slavick, "Going to School to DuBose Heyward," *The Harlem Renaissance Reexamined,* (AMS Press, 1987); excerpted and reprinted in *Twentieth-Century Literary Criticism,* Vol. 59, ed. Jennifer Gariepy (Detroit: Gale Research, 1995), pp. 94-105.

[2]George Orwell, "Reflections on Gandhi," *Partisan Review,* 6 (Winter 1949), pp. 85-92; excerpted and reprinted in *Twentieth-Century Literary Criticism,* Vol. 59, ed. Jennifer Gariepy (Detroit: Gale Research, 1995), pp. 40-3.

Suggestions Are Welcome

In response to suggestions, several features have been added to *TCLC* since the series began, including annotations to excerpted criticism, a cumulative index to authors in all Gale literary criticism series, entries devoted to criticism on a single work by a major author, more extensive illustrations, and a title index listing all literary works discussed in the series since its inception.

Readers who wish to suggest authors or topics to appear in future volumes, or who have other suggestions, are cordially invited to write the editors.

Acknowledgments

The editors wish to thank the copyright holders of the excerpted criticism included in this volume and the permissions managers of many book and magazine publishing companies for assisting us in securing reproduction rights. We are also grateful to the staffs of the Detroit Public Library, the Library of Congress, the University of Detroit Mercy Library, Wayne State University Purdy/Kresge Library Complex, and the University of Michigan Libraries for making their resources available to us. Following is a list of the copyright holders who have granted us permission to reproduce material in this volume of *TCLC*. Every effort has been made to trace copyright, but if omissions have been made, please let us know.

COPYRIGHTED EXCERPTS IN *TCLC*, VOLUME 75, WERE REPRODUCED FROM THE FOLLOWING PERIODICALS:

The American Political Science Review, v. LXVIII, March, 1974. Copyright, 1974, by The American Political Science Association. Reproduced by permission.—*Critical Inquiry*, v. 10, 1984 for "Secret Languages: The Roots of Musical Modernism" by Robert P. Morgan. Copyright © 1984 by The University of Chicago. Reproduced by permission of the publisher and the author.—*Hispania*, v. 52, 1969 for a review of "Country Judge" by Donald A. Yates. Copyright © 1969 The American Association of Teachers of Spanish and Portuguese, Inc. Reproduced by permission of the publisher and the author.—*Music & Letters*, v. 55, October, 1974 for "Schoenberg and the Crisis of Expressionism" by Alan Lessem; v. 62, January, 1981 for "Schoenberg's Speech-Song" by Peter Stadlen; v. 65, October, 1984 for "The Spiritual and The Material in Schoenberg's Thinking" by Jean Christensen; v. 76, February, 1995 for "'A Survivor from Warsaw' as Personal Parable" by Michael Strasser. © Oxford University Press 1974, 1981, 1984, 1995. All reproduced by permission of Oxford University Press and the respective authors.—*New Theatre Quarterly*, v. 10, February, 1994 for "Two-a-Day Redemptions and Truncated Camilles: the Vaudeville Repertoire of Sarah Bernhardt" by Leigh Woods. Reproduced by permission of the publisher and the author.—*The New York Review of Books*, April 22, 1965: September 18, 1975. Copyright © 1965, 1975 Nyrev, Inc. Both reproduced by permission from The New York Review of Books.—*The New York Times Book Review*, October 31, 1943; June 8, 1944; November 26, 1944; June 2, 1946. Copyright, 1943, renewed 1969, 1944 renewed 1971, 1946 renewed 1971 by The New York Times Company. All reproduced by permission.—*The Opera Quarterly*, v. 6, Spring, 1989. © 1989 The University of North Carolina Press. Reproduced by permission of the publisher.—*Perspectives of New Music*, v. 14, Fall-Winter, 1977 for "Schönberg–Yesterday, Today, and Tomorrow" by Josef Rufner. Copyright © 1977 Perspectives of New Music, Inc. Reproduced by permission.—*The Review of Politics*, v. 29, July, 1967. Copyright, 1967, by the University of Notre Dame. Reproduced by permission.—*The Saturday Book*, v. 27, 1967. © Hutchinson & Company (Publishers) Ltd. 1967. Reproduced by permission of Random House UK Limited.—*Slavic Review*, v. 36, September, 1977 for "Questions of Art, Fate, and Genre in Mikhail Prishvin" by Ray J. Parrott, Jr. Copyright © 1977 by the American Association for the Advancement of Slavic Studies, Inc. Reproduced by permission of the publisher.—*Southwest Review*, v. 24, Spring, 1989 for "San Pietro and the 'Art' of War" by Lance Bertelsen. © 1989 Southern Methodist University. Reproduced by permission of the author.—*Studies in the Literary Imagination*, v. XXV, Fall, 1992. Copyright 1992 Department of English, Georgia State University. Reproduced by permission.—*Time*, July 17, 1944, for "The Guy the GIs Loved (Ernie Pyle's War)." Copyright 1944, renewed 1971 Time Warner Inc. All rights reserved. Reproduced by permission from *Time*.

COPYRIGHTED EXCERPTS IN *TCLC*, VOLUME 75, WERE REPRODUCED FROM THE FOLLOWING BOOKS:

Alexandrova-Schwartz, Vera. From *A History of Soviet Literature: 1917-1964 From Gorky to Solzhenitsyn*. Translated by Mirra Ginsburg. Anchor Books, 1964. Copyright © 1963, 1964 by Vera Alexandrova-Schwartz. All rights reserved. Reproduced by permission of Doubleday, a division of Bantam Doubleday Dell Publishing Group, Inc.—Baring, Maurice. From *Punch and Judy & Other Essays*. Doubleday, Page & Company, 1923. Copyright 1923 by Doubleday, Page & Company. Reproduced by permission A. P. Watt Ltd.—Bellamy, Richard. From *Modern Italian Social Theory: Ideology and Politics from Pareto to the Present*. Polity Press, 1987. Copyright © Richard Bellamy, 1987. Reproduced by permission of Blackwell Publishers. In North America and the Philippine Islands by Stanford University Press.—Bobbio, Norberto. From *On Mosca and Pareto*. Librairie Droz, 1972. Reproduced by permission.—Bradbrook, Muriel. From *Women and Literature 1779-1982: The Collected Papers of Muriel Bradbook, Vol 2*. The Harvester Press, 1982. Reproduced by permission of the Mistress and Fellows of Girton College, Cambridge.—Bradford, Gamaliel. From *Daughters of Eve*. Houghton Mifflin Company, 1930. Copyright, 1931, by Gamaliel Bradford. Copyright renewed 1958 by Sarah Bradford Ross. Reproduced by permission Houghton Mifflin Company.—Brown, John Mason. From *Seeing Things*. Whittlesey House, 1946. Copyright 1946 by the McGraw-Hill Book Company, Inc. Renewed 1974 by Mrs. J. M. Brown, Meredith Mason Brown and Preston Brown. All rights reserved. Reproduced by permission of the Estate of

Sarah Bernhardt

1844-1923

(Pseudonym of Henriette Rosine Bernard) French actress, autobiographer, novelist, dramatist, and nonfiction writer.

INTRODUCTION

Bernhardt is considered one of the greatest actresses ever to work on the French stage, famous in particular for her perfect elocution and the captivating effect she had on her audiences. Offstage, she was known for her independent, extravagant lifestyle, the details of which were publicized around the world and in her memoirs. Not content solely with life on the stage, Bernhardt also gained success as a writer, sculptor, painter, businesswoman, and campaigner for charity. Her fame as a popular culture personality has been compared to the cult-like status of such later performers as Marilyn Monroe and Elvis Presley.

Biographical Information

Bernhardt was born to Youle Bernard, an unmarried Jewish-Dutch seamstress and courtesan, in Paris in 1844. Despite her Jewish background, Bernhardt attended a Catholic convent school as a child. An unconventional woman in her own right, Bernhardt's mother introduced the young girl to the Odéon Theatre in Paris, where Bernhardt would later spend much of her illustrious stage career. According to some accounts, her mother abandoned Bernhardt soon afterward, and the girl subsequently began training at the Paris Conservatoire at the age of thirteen. She made her debut with the Comédie Française in 1862 with a small part in Racine's *Iphigenie*. Bernhardt's work was at the time considered unremarkable, and she left the Comédie Française in only six months after an altercation with another actor. She worked as a burlesque singer until 1869, when she appeared at the Odéon in François Coppée's *Le passant*, a performance that sparked strong interest in both Bernhardt and Coppée. Bernhardt had a child in 1864, Maurice, allegedly the son of Prince Henri de Ligne of Belgium. She and her son were constant companions throughout her life, and managed several successful theatre companies together, although one of their business ventures eventually led to bankruptcy. Around 1870 Bernhardt took up painting and sculpture, and experienced moderate success with her exhibitions. In 1872 she returned to the Comédie Française as the Queen in Victor Hugo's *Ruy Blas*; her performance cemented her reputation as a significant actress, and she rose to prominence in the company. In 1877 Bernhardt appeared in one of the most acclaimed roles of her career, the title character in Racine's *Phèdre*. By this time, she was an international

sensation, with a reputation as a brilliant, temperamental, and sometimes eccentric actress. Bernhardt became frustrated with the scope of the Comédie Française and left the troupe in 1879, moving on to London, where she caused an uproar with her performance of *Phèdre*. She toured the United States for the first time in 1880, keeping company with numerous American celebrities, including Thomas Edison, with whom she made a recording of *Phèdre*. A year later she acted in another of her most famous roles, that of Marguerite in *La dame aux camélias* by Alexandre Dumas *fils*. Bernhardt married a fellow actor, Jacques Damala, in 1882; it was a disastrous union that ended less than a year later. From that point on, Bernhardt devoted most of her time to touring around the world. She began managing her own career, and chose plays largely as vehicles to showcase her talent; she also frequently advised playwrights on their work. In the 1890s Bernhardt took over the Théâtre de Nations, renaming it the Théâtre Sarah Bernhardt. Here, in 1899, she created her most defining role: Hamlet. Bernhardt had not been the first woman to play Hamlet; the tradition of *travesti*–women playing men's roles and men playing women's–dates back to the beginnings of theatre. But her interpretation of the character was considered revolutionary, in particular because she was at the time a fifty-five year old woman playing a young man's part, and because Shakespearean plays had rarely received acclaim in France until Bernhardt's *Hamlet*. Bernhardt continued touring and acting for the rest of her life, even after the amputation of her right leg at the age of seventy. Details of her life–her many liaisons with men, rumors that she slept in a coffin, the wild animals she kept as pets–were pored over in gossip columns even after her death. Known for her charitable work as well as her eccentricities, she had turned the Odéon Theatre into a hospital for soldiers during the Siege of Paris in 1870, and during World War I campaigned to raise money for the wounded. In advanced age, she began a career in the budding film industry, often reviving her stage roles in such silent films as *Tosca*, *La Dame aux Camélias*, *Queen Elizabeth*, and *Adrienne Lecouvreur*. Never able, or willing, to escape the spotlight, she was allegedly filmed on her deathbed in 1923 in Paris, where she was acting in the movie *La Voyante*.

Major Works

Although best known for her commanding performances in such plays as *Hamlet*, *Phèdre*, and *La dame aux camélias* and for her remarkable life, Bernhardt also wrote in a variety of genres. She began her writing career in 1878 with the publication of a children's book: *Dans les nuages; impressions d'une chaise; recit recueilli par Sarah Bernhardt* (translated as *In the Clouds*). As a veteran of the stage, Bernhardt forayed into writing plays beginning in 1888, with the one-act work *L'Aveu*. In 1907 she had much success with her six-act play *Adrienne Lecouvreur*, in which she played the title character; later in life she revived the role in a silent film. She again wrote and starred in a play in 1911, *Un Coeur d'homme*. Bernhardt turned to novel-writing in 1920, when she published *La Petite Idole* (*The Idol of Paris*). Her second novel, *Jolie Sosie*, was published in 1922. Both were romantic adventures featuring, it was assumed, accounts of Bernhardt's own escapades. Throughout her career, Bernhardt wrote theatre criticism, short stories, and essays, which were published in French, American, and English newspapers and periodicals. In 1924 Bernhardt's monograph on the theatre, *L'Art du Theatre*, was published. Although considered a highly individualized study of theatrical techniques, the book was well-received both for its theory and for the insight it provided into Bernhardt's thoughts. But it was her memoirs, first published as *Ma double vie: memoires de Sarah Bernhardt* in 1907, that attracted the most attention. A shrewd handler of the media and of her image, Bernhardt frequently circulated stories about herself to maintain the almost hysterical interest the public had in her. Her memoirs were no exception, comprising as they did a mix of truth and fiction designed to uphold her legend. Bernhardt's memoirs continue to be read both for her reflections on her extraordinary life and talent, and for the glimpse they provide into *fin de siècle* life and culture.

PRINCIPAL WORKS

Dans les nuages; impressions d'une chaise; recit recueilli par Sarah Bernhardt [*In the Clouds*] [illustrated by Georges Clairin] (juvenilia) 1878
L'Aveu (drama) 1888
Adrienne Lecouvreur (drama) 1907 [first publication]
Ma double vie: memoires de Sarah Bernhardt [*My Double Life: The Memoirs of Sarah Bernhardt*] (memoirs) 1907
Un Coeur d'homme (drama) 1911
Petite Idole [*The Idol of Paris*] (novel) 1920
Jolie Sosie (novel) 1922
L'Art du Théâtre [*The Art of the Theatre*] (nonfiction) 1924

    *This work was adapted from the play *Adrienne Lecouvreur* (1852) by Eugene Scribe and Gabriel-Jean-Marie-Baptiste Legouvé.

CRITICISM

George Bernard Shaw (essay date 1895)

SOURCE: "Our Theatres in the Nineties: Duse and Bernhardt," in *Selected Prose*, selected by Diarmuid Russell, Dodd, Mead & Company, March, 1952, pp. 426-32.

[*In the following essay, originally published in 1895, Shaw contrasts performances of Bernhardt with those of Italian actress Eleonora Duse.*]

Mr William Archer's defence of the dramatic critics against Mr Street's indictment of them for their indifference to acting appears to be falling through. Mr Archer pleads that whereas Hazlitt and Leigh Hunt had frequent opportunities of comparing ambitious actors in famous parts, the modern dramatic critic spends his life in contemplating "good acting plays" without any real people in them, and performers who do not create or interpret characters, but simply lend their pretty or popular persons, for a consideration, to fill up the parts. Mr Archer might have added another reason which applies to nearly all modern works: to wit, the operation of our copyright laws, whereby actors and actresses acquire the right not only to perform new plays but to prevent anyone else from performing them. Nevertheless we critics can now at last outdo Hazlitt and Leight Hunt if we have a mind to; for we have just had two Mrs Ebbsmiths to compare, besides a fourth Fedora, and Duse and Sarah Bernhardt playing La Dame aux Camellias and Sudermann's Heimat against one another at Daly's Theatre and at Drury Lane. Clearly now or never is the time for a triumphant refutation of the grievance of the English actor against the English Press: namely, that hardly any critic knows enough about acting to be able to distinguish between an effective part and a well played one, or between the bag of tricks which every old hand carries and the stock of ideas and sense of character which distinguish the master-actor from the mere handy man.

This week began with the relapse of Sarah Bernhardt into her old profession of serious actress. She played Magda in Sudermann's Heimat, and was promptly challenged by Duse in the same part at Drury Lane on Wednesday. The contrast between the two Magdas is as extreme as any contrast could possibly be between artists who have finished their twenty years apprenticeship to the same profession under closely similar conditions. Madame Bernhardt has the charm of a jolly maturity, rather spoilt and petulant, perhaps, but always ready with a sunshine-through-the-clouds smile if only she is made much of. Her dresses and diamonds, if not exactly splendid, are at least splendacious; her figure, far too scantily upholstered in the old days, is at its best; and her complexion shows that she has not studied modern art in vain. Those charming roseate effects which French painters produce by giving flesh the pretty colour of strawberries and cream, and painting the shadows pink and crimson, are cunningly reproduced by Madame Bernhardt in the living picture. She paints her ears crimson and allows them to peep enchantingly through a few loose braids of her auburn hair. Every dimple has its dab of pink; and her finger-tips are so delicately incarnadined that you fancy they are transparent like her ears, and that the light is shining through their delicate blood-vessels. Her lips are like a newly painted pillar box; her cheeks, right up to the languid lashes, have the bloom and surface of a peach; she is beautiful with the beauty of her school, and entirely inhuman and incredible. But the incredibility is pardonable, because, though it is all the greatest nonsense, nobody believing in it, the actress herself least of all, it is so artful, so clever, so well recognized a part of the business, and carried off with such a genial air, that it is impossible not to accept it with good-humour. One feels, when the heroine bursts on the scene, a dazzling vision of beauty, that instead of imposing on you, she adds to her own piquancy by looking you straight in the face, and saying, in effect: "Now who would ever suppose that I am a grandmother?" That, of course, is irresistible; and one is not sorry to have been coaxed to relax one's notions of the dignity of art when she gets to serious business and shows how ably she does her work. The coaxing suits well with the childishly egotistical character of her acting, which is not the art of making you think more highly or feel more deeply, but the art of making you admire her, pity her, champion her, weep with her, laugh at her jokes, follow her fortunes breathlessly, and applaud her wildly when the curtain falls. It is the art of finding out all your weaknesses and practizing on them—cajoling you, harrowing you, exciting you—on the whole, fooling you. And it is always Sarah Bernhardt in her own capacity who does this to you. The dress, the title of the play, the order of the words may vary; but the woman is always the same. She does not enter into the leading character: she substitutes herself for it.

All this is precisely what does not happen in the case of Duse, whose every part is a separate creation. When she comes on the stage, you are quite welcome to take your opera-glass and count whatever lines time and care have so far traced on her. They are the credentials of her humanity; and she knows better than to obliterate that significant handwriting beneath a layer of peach-bloom from the chemist's. The shadows on her face are grey, not crimson; her lips are sometimes nearly grey also; there are neither dabs nor dimples; her charm could never be imitated by a barmaid with unlimited pin money and a row of footlights before her instead of the handles of a beer-engine. The result is not so discouraging as the patrons of the bar might suppose. Wilkes, who squinted atrociously, boasted that he was only quarter of an hour behind the handsomest man in Europe: Duse is not in action five minutes before she is quarter of a century ahead of the handsomest woman in the world. I grant that Sarah's elaborate Mona Lisa smile, with the conscious droop of the eyelashes and the long carmined lips coyly disclosing the brilliant row of teeth, is effective of its kind—that it not only appeals to your susceptibilities, but positively jogs them. And it lasts quite a minute, sometimes longer. But Duse, with a tremor of the lip which you feel rather than see, and which lasts half an instant, touches you straight on the very heart; and there is not a line in the face, or a cold tone in the grey shadow that does not give poignancy to that tremor. As to youth and age, who can associate purity and delicacy of emotion, and simplicity of expression, with the sordid craft that repels us in age; or voluptuous appeal and egotistical self-insistence with the candor and generosity that attract us in youth? Who ever thinks of Potiphar's wife as a young woman, or St Elizabeth of Hungary as an old one? These associations are horribly unjust to age, and undeserved by youth: they belong of right to differences of character, not of years; but they rule our imaginations; and the great artist profits by them to appear eternally young. However, it would be a critical blunder as well as a personal folly on my part to suggest that Duse, any more than Sarah Bernhardt, neglects any art that could heighten the effect of her acting when she is impersonating young and pretty women. The truth is that in the art of being beautiful, Madame Bernhardt is a child beside her. The French artist's stock of attitudes and facial effects could be catalogued as easily as her stock of dramatic ideas: the counting would hardly go beyond the fingers of both hands. Duse produces the illusion of being infinite in variety of beautiful pose and motion. Every idea, every shade of thought and mood, expresses itself delicately but vividly to the eye; and yet, in an apparent million of changes and inflexions, it is impossible to catch any line at an awkward angle, or any strain interfering with the perfect abandonment of all the limbs to what appears to be their natural gravitation towards the finest grace. She is ambidextrous and supple, like a gymnast or a panther; only the multitude of ideas which find physical expression in her movements are all of that high quality which marks off humanity from the animals, and, I fear I must add, from a good many gymnasts. When it is remembered that the majority of tragic actors excel only in explosions of those passions which are common to man and brute, there will be no difficulty in understanding the indescribable distinction which Duse's acting acquires from the fact that behind every stroke of it is a distinctively human idea. In nothing is this more apparent than in the vigilance in her of that high human instinct which seeks to awaken the deepest responsive feeling without giving pain. In *La Dame aux Camellias,* for instance, it is easy for an intense actress to harrow us with her sorrows and paroxysms of phthisis, leaving us with a liberal pennyworth of sensation, not fundamentally distinguishable from that offered by a public execution, or any other evil in which we still take a hideous delight. As different from this as light from darkness is the method of the actress who shows us how human sorrow can express itself only in its appeal for the sympathy it needs, whilst striving by strong endurance to shield others from the infection of its torment. That is the charm of Duse's interpretation of the stage poem of Marguerite Gauthier. It is unspeakably touching because it is exquisitely considerate: that is, exquisitely sympathetic. No physical charm is noble as well as beautiful unless it is the expression of a moral charm; and it is because Duse's range includes these moral high notes, if I may so express myself, that her compass, extending from the depths of a mere predatory creature like Claude's wife up to Marguerite Gauthier at her kindest or Magda at her bravest, so immeasurably dwarfs the poor little octave and a half on which Sarah Bernhardt plays such pretty canzonets and stirring marches.

Obvious as the disparity of the two famous artists has been to many of us since we first saw Duse, I doubt whether any of us realized, after Madame Bernhardt's very clever performance as Magda on Monday night, that there was room in the nature of things for its annihilation within forty-eight hours by so comparatively quiet a talent as Duse's. And yet annihilation is the only word for it. Sarah was very charming, very jolly when the sun shone, very petulant when the clouds covered it, and positively angry when they wanted to take her child away from her. And she did not trouble us with any fuss about the main theme of Sudermann's play, the revolt of the modern woman against that ideal of home which exacts the sacrifice of her whole life to its care, not by her grace, and as its own sole help and refuge, but as a right which it has to the services of all females as abject slaves. In fact, there is not the slightest reason to suspect Madame Bernhardt of having discovered any such theme in the play; though Duse, with one look at Schwartze, the father, nailed it to the stage as the subject of the impending dramatic struggle before she had been five minutes on the scene. Before long, there came a stroke of acting which will probably never be forgotten by those who saw it, and which explained at once why those artifices of the dressing-table which help Madame Bernhardt would hinder Duse almost as much as a screen placed in front of her. I should explain, first, that the real name of the play is not Magda but Home. Magda is a daughter who has been turned out of doors for defying her father, one of those outrageous persons who mistake their desire to

have everything their own way in the house for a sacred principle of home life. She has a hard time of it, but at last makes a success as an opera singer, though not until her lonely struggles have thrown her for sympathy on a fellow student, who in due time goes his way, and leaves her to face motherhood as best she can. In the fullness of her fame she returns to her native town, and in an attack of homesickness makes advances to her father, who consents to receive her again. No sooner is she installed in the house than she finds that one of the most intimate friends of the family is the father of her child. In the third act of the play she is on the stage when he is announced as a visitor. It must be admitted that Sarah Bernhardt played this scene very lightly and pleasantly: there was genuine good fellowship in the way in which she reassured the embarrassed gallant and made him understand that she was not going to play off the sorrows of Gretchen on him after all those years, and that she felt that she owed him the priceless experience of maternity, even if she did not particularly respect him for it. Her self-possession at this point was immense: the peach-bloom never altered by a shade. Not so with Duse. The moment she read the card handed her by the servant, you realized what it was to have to face a meeting with the man. It was interesting to watch how she got through it when he came in, and how, on the whole, she got through it pretty well. He paid his compliments and offered his flowers; they sat down; and she evidently felt that she had got it safely over and might allow herself to think at her ease, and to look at him to see how much he had altered. Then a terrible thing happened to her. She began to blush; and in another moment she was conscious of it, and the blush was slowly spreading and deepening until, after a few vain efforts to avert her face or to obstruct his view of it without seeming to do so, she gave up and hid the blush in her hands. After that feat of acting I did not need to be told why Duse does not paint an inch thick. I could detect no trick in it: it seemed to me a perfectly genuine effect of the dramatic imagination. In the third act of *La Dame aux Camellias,* where she produces a touching effect by throwing herself down, and presently rises with her face changed and flushed with weeping, the flush is secured by the preliminary plunge to a stooping attitude, imagination or no imagination; but Magda's blush did not admit of that explanation; and I must confess to an intense professional curiosity as to whether it always comes spontaneously.

I shall make no attempt to describe the rest of that unforgettable act. To say that it left the house not only frantically applauding, but actually roaring, is to say nothing; for had we not applauded Sarah as Gismonda and roared at Mrs Patrick Campbell as Fedora? But there really was something to roar at this time. There was a real play, and an actress who understood the author and was a greater artist than he. And for me, at least, there was a confirmation of my sometimes flagging faith that a dramatic critic is really the servant of a high art, and not a mere advertiser of entertainments of questionable respectability of motive.

Max Beerbohm (essay date 1899)

SOURCE: "Hamlet, Princess of Denmark," in *Around Theatres,* Alfred A. Knopf, 1930, pp. 46-9.

[*In the following essay, originally published in 1899, Beerbohm finds Bernhardt's* Hamlet *to be a comic spectacle and takes issue with the French prose translation of the play.*]

I cannot, on my heart, take Sarah's Hamlet seriously. I cannot even imagine any one capable of more than a hollow pretence at taking it seriously. However, the truly great are apt, in matters concerning themselves, to lose that sense of fitness which is usually called sense of humour, and I did not notice that Sarah was once hindered in her performance by any irresistible desire to burst out laughing. Her solemnity was politely fostered by the Adelphi audience. From first to last no one smiled. If any one had so far relaxed himself as to smile, he would have been bound to laugh. One laugh in that dangerous atmosphere, and the whole structure of polite solemnity would have toppled down, burying beneath its ruins the national reputation for good manners. I, therefore, like every one else, kept an iron control upon the corners of my lips. It was not until I was half-way home and well out of earshot of the Adelphi, that I unsealed the accumulations of my merriment.

I had controlled myself merely in deference to Sarah herself, not because I regarded the French prose-version of *Hamlet* as an important tribute to Shakespeare's genius. I take that version to have been intended as a tribute to an actress' genius, rather than a poet's. Frenchmen who know enough of our language to enable them to translate Shakespeare know very well that to translate him at all is a grave disservice. Neither into French poetry nor into French prose can his poetry be translated; and, since every element in his work was the direct, inalienable result of his poetry, it follows that any French translation is ruinous. I do not say that this particular translation is unskilful; on the contrary, it seemed to me very skilful indeed. The authors seemed to have got the nearest equivalents that could be got. But the nearest equivalents were always unsatisfactory and often excruciating. "Paix, paix, âme troublée!" for "Rest, rest, perturbed spirit!" is a fair sample of what I mean. Save that it reminds one—an accident which the authors could not foresee—of "Loo, Loo, I love you!" there is no fault to be found with this rendering. It is, I think, as good as possible. But it carries in it no faintest echo nor most shadowy reflection of the original magic. It is thin, dry, cold—in a word, excruciating. The fact is that the French language, limpid and exquisite though it is, affords no scope for phrases which, like this phrase of Shakespeare's, are charged with a dim significance beyond their meaning and with reverberations beyond their sound. The French language, like the French genius, can give no hint of things beyond those which it definitely expresses. For expression, it is a far finer instrument than our language; but it is not, in the sense that our language is, suggestive.

It lacks mystery. It casts none of those purple shadows which do follow and move with the moving phrases of our great poets. In order to be really suggestive, a French poet must, like Mallarmé, deliberately refrain from expressing anything at all. An English poet, on the other hand, may be at once expressive and suggestive. That is a great advantage. It is an advantage which none of our poets has used so superbly as Shakespeare. None of our poets has ever given to his phrases shadows so wonderful as the shadows Shakespeare gave to his. In none of Shakespeare's plays, I think, are these shadows so many and marvellous as in *Hamlet;* and the quality of its theme is such that the shadows are more real to us, and reveal more to us, than the phrases casting them. Cut away those shadows, and you cut away that which makes the play immortal—nay! even that which makes it intelligible. One by one, they were cut away by the two talented Parisians who translated *Hamlet* for Sarah. Reluctantly, no doubt. But I am dealing with the translation as I find it, and (despite my colleagues) I must refuse to regard it as a tribute to Shakespeare. The only tribute a French translator can pay Shakespeare is not to translate him— even to please Sarah.

In England, as I suggested some time ago, *Hamlet* has long ceased to be treated as a play. It has become simply a hoop through which every very eminent actor must, sooner or later, jump. The eminent actor may not have any natural impulse to jump through it, but that does not matter. However unsuited to the part he be in temperament or physique, his position necessitates that he play it. I deplore this custom. I consider that it cheapens both Shakespeare's poetry and the art of acting. However, it is a firmly-established custom, and I must leave it to work itself out. But I do, while there is yet time, earnestly hope that Sarah's example in playing Hamlet will not create a precedent among women. True, Mrs. Bandman Palmer has already set the example, and it has not been followed; but Mrs. Bandman Palmer's influence is not so deep and wide as Sarah's, and I have horrible misgivings. No doubt, Hamlet, in the complexity of his nature, had traces of femininity. Gentleness and a lack of executive ability are feminine qualities, and they were both strong in Hamlet. This, I take it, would be Sarah's own excuse for having essayed the part. She would not, of course, attempt to play Othello—at least, I risk the assumption that she would not, dangerous though it is to assume what she might *not* do—any more than her distinguished fellow-countryman, Mounet Sully, would attempt to play Desdemona. But, in point of fact, she is just as well qualified to play Othello as she is to play Hamlet. Hamlet is none the less a man because he is not consistently manly, just as Lady Macbeth is none the less a woman for being a trifle unsexed. Mounet Sully could be no more acceptable as Lady Macbeth than as Desdemona. I hope he is too sensible a person ever to undertake the part. He would be absurd in it, though (this is my point) not one whit more absurd than Sarah is as Hamlet. Sarah ought not to have supposed that Hamlet's weakness set him in any possible relation to her own feminine mind and body. Her friends ought to have restrained her. The native critics ought not to have encouraged her. The custom-house officials at Charing Cross ought to have confiscated her sable doublet and hose. I, lover of her incomparable art, am even more distressed than amused when I think of her aberration at the Adelphi. Had she for one moment betrayed any faintest sense of Hamlet's character, the reminiscence were less painful. Alas! she betrayed nothing but herself, and revealed nothing but the unreasoning vanity which had impelled her to so preposterous an undertaking. For once, even her voice was not beautiful. For once . . . but why should I insist? The best that can be said for her performance is that she acted (as she always does) with that dignity of demeanour which is the result of perfect self-possession. Her perfect self-possession was one of the most delicious elements in the evening's comedy, but one could not help being genuinely impressed by her dignity. One felt that Hamlet, as portrayed by her, was, albeit neither melancholy nor a dreamer, at least a person of consequence and unmistakably "thoro'bred." Yes! the only compliment one can conscientiously pay her is that her Hamlet was, from first to last, *très grande dame.*

William Dean Howells (essay date 1902)

SOURCE: "A She Hamlet," in *Literature and Life,* Kennikat Press, Inc., 1968, pp.

[*In the following essay, Howells offers a negative review of Bernhardt's Hamlet, arguing that a woman in the title role is a perversion of the integrity of the drama.*]

The other night as I sat before the curtain of the Garden Theatre and waited for it to rise upon the Hamlet of Mme. Bernhardt, a thrill of the rich expectation which cannot fail to precede the rise of any curtain upon any Hamlet passed through my eager frame. There is, indeed, no scene of drama which is of a finer horror (eighteenth-century horror) than that which opens the great tragedy. The sentry pacing up and down upon the platform at Elsinore under the winter night; the greeting between him and the comrade arriving to relieve him, with its hints of the bitter cold; the entrance of Horatio and Marcellus to these before they can part; the mention of the ghost, and, while the soldiers are in the act of protesting it a veridical phantom, the apparition of the ghost, taking the word from their lips and hushing all into a pulseless awe: what could be more simply and sublimely real, more naturally supernatural? What promise of high mystical things to come there is in the mere syllabling of the noble verse, and how it enlarges us from ourselves, for that time at least, to a disembodied unity with the troubled soul whose martyry seems foreboded in the solemn accents! As the many Hamlets on which the curtain had risen in my time passed in long procession through my memory, I seemed to myself so much of their world, and so little of the world that arrogantly calls itself the actual one, that I should hardly have been surprised to find myself one of the less considered persons of the drama who were seen but not heard in its course.

I

The trouble in judging anything is that if you have the materials for an intelligent criticism, the case is already prejudiced in your hands. You do not bring a free mind to it, and all your efforts to free your mind are a species of gymnastics more or less admirable, but not really effective for the purpose. The best way is to own yourself unfair at the start, and then you can have some hope of doing yourself justice, if not your subject. In other words, if you went to see the Hamlet of Mme. Bernhardt frankly expecting to be disappointed, you were less likely in the end to be disappointed in your expectations, and you could not blame her if you were. To be ideally fair to that representation, it would be better not to have known any other Hamlet, and, above all, the Hamlet of Shakespeare.

From the first it was evident that she had three things overwhelmingly against her—her sex, her race, and her speech. You never ceased to feel for a moment that it was a woman who was doing that melancholy Dane, and that the woman was a Jewess, and the Jewess a French Jewess. These three removes put a gulf impassable between her utmost skill and the impassioned irresolution of that inscrutable Northern nature which is in nothing so masculine as its feminine reluctances and hesitations, or so little French as in those obscure emotions which the English poetry expressed with more than Gallic clearness, but which the French words always failed to convey. The battle was lost from the first, and all you could feel about it for the rest was that if it was magnificent it was not war.

While the battle went on I was the more anxious to be fair, because I had, as it were, pre-espoused the winning side; and I welcomed, in the interest of critical impartiality, another Hamlet which came to mind, through readily traceable associations. This was a Hamlet also of French extraction in the skill and school of the actor, but as much more deeply derived than the Hamlet of Mme. Bernhardt as the large imagination of Charles Fechter transcended in its virile range the effect of her subtlest womanish intuition. His was the first blond Hamlet known to our stage, and hers was also blond, if a reddish-yellow wig may stand for a complexion; and it was of the quality of his Hamlet in masterly technique.

II

The Hamlet of Fechter, which rose ghostlike out of the gulf of the past, and cloudily possessed the stage where the Hamlet of Mme. Bernhardt was figuring, was called a romantic Hamlet thirty years ago; and so it was in being a break from the classic Hamlets of the Anglo-American theatre. It was romantic as Shakespeare himself was romantic, in an elder sense of the word, and not romanticistic as Dumas was romanticistic. It was, therefore, the most realistic Hamlet ever yet seen, because the most naturally poetic. Mme. Bernhardt recalled it by the perfection of her school; for Fechter's poetic naturalness differed from the conventionality of the accepted Hamlets in nothing so much as the superiority of its self-instruction. In Mme. Bernhardt's Hamlet, as in his, nothing was trusted to chance, or "inspiration." Good or bad, what one saw was what was meant to be seen. When Fechter played Edmond Dantes or Claude Melnotte, he put reality into those preposterous inventions, and in Hamlet even his alien accent helped him vitalize the part; it might be held to be nearer the Elizabethan accent than ours, and after all, you said, Hamlet *was* a foreigner, and in your high content with what he gave you did not mind its being in a broken vessel. When he challenged the ghost with "I call thee keeng, father, *rawl*-Dane," you would hardly have had the erring utterance bettered. It sufficed as it was; and when he said to Rosencrantz, "Will you pleh upon this pyip?" it was with such a princely authority and comradely entreaty that you made no note of the slips in the vowels except to have pleasure of their quaintness afterwards. For the most part you were not aware of these bewrayals of his speech; and in certain high things it was soul interpreted to soul through the poetry of Shakespeare so finely, so directly, that there was scarcely a sense of the histrionic means.

He put such divine despair into the words, "Except my life, except my life, except my life!" following the mockery with which he had assured Polonius there was nothing he would more willingly part withal than his leave, that the heart-break of them had lingered with me for thirty years, and I had been alert for them with every Hamlet since. But before I knew, Mme. Bernhardt had uttered them with no effect whatever. Her Hamlet, indeed, cut many of the things that we have learned to think the points of Hamlet, and it so transformed others by its interpretation of the translator's interpretation of Shakespeare that they passed unrecognized. Soliloquies are the weak invention of the enemy, for the most part, but as such things go that soliloquy of Hamlet's, "To be or not to be," is at least very noble poetry; and yet Mme. Bernhardt was so unimpressive in it that you scarcely noticed the act of its delivery. Perhaps this happened because the sumptuous and sombre melancholy of Shakespeare's thought was transmitted in phrases that refused it its proper mystery. But there was always a hardness, not always from the translation, upon this feminine Hamlet. It was like a thick shell with no crevice in it through which the tenderness of Shakespeare's Hamlet could show, except for the one moment at Ophelia's grave, where he reproaches Laertes with those pathetic words:

> What is the reason that you use me thus?
> I loved you ever; but it is no matter.

Here Mme. Bernhardt betrayed a real grief, but as a woman would, and not a man. At the close of the Gonzago play, when Hamlet triumphs in a mad whirl, her Hamlet hopped up and down like a mischievous crow, a mischievous she-crow.

There was no repose in her Hamlet, though there were moments of leaden lapse which suggested physical ex-haustion; and there was no range in her elocution expressive of the large vibration of that tormented spirit. Her voice dropped out, or jerked itself out, and in the crises of strong emotion it was the voice of a scolding or a hysterical woman. At times her movements, which she must have studied so hard to master, were drolly womanish, especially those of the whole person. Her quickened pace was a woman's nervous little run, and not a man's swift stride; and to give herself due stature, it was her foible to wear a woman's high heels to her shoes, and she could not help tilting on them.

In the scene with the queen after the play, most English and American Hamlets have required her to look upon the counterfeit presentment of two brothers in miniatures something the size of tea-plates; but Mme. Bernhardt's preferred full-length, life-size family portraits. The dead king's effigy did not appear a flattered likeness in the scene-painter's art, but it was useful in disclosing his ghost by giving place to it in the wall at the right moment. She achieved a novelty by this treatment of the portraits, and she achieved a novelty in the tone she took with the wretched queen. Hamlet appeared to scold her mother, but though it could be said that her mother deserved a scolding, was it the part of a good daughter to give it her?

One should, of course, say a good son, but long before this it had become impossible to think at all of Mme. Bernhardt's Hamlet as a man, if it ever had been possible. She had traversed the bounds which tradition as well as nature has set, and violated the only condition upon which an actress may personate a man. This condition is that there shall be always a hint of comedy in the part, that the spectator shall know all the time that the actress is a woman, and that she shall confess herself such before the play is over; she shall be fascinating in the guise of a man only because she is so much more intensely a woman in in it. Shakespeare had rather a fancy for women in men's rôles, which, as women's rôles in his time were always taken by pretty and clever boys, could be more naturally managed then than now. But when it came to the *éclaircissement,* and the pretty boys, who had been playing the parts of women disguised as men, had to own themselves women, the effect must have been confused if not weakened. If Mme. Bernhardt, in the necessity of doing something Shakespearean, had chosen to do Rosalind, or Viola, or Portia, she could have done it with all the modern advantages of women in men's rôles. These characters are, of course, "lighter motions bounded in a shallower brain" than the creation she aimed at; but she could at least have made much of them, and she does not make much of Hamlet.

III

The strongest reason against any woman Hamlet is that it does violence to an ideal. Literature is not so rich in great imaginary masculine types that we can afford to have them transformed to women; and after seeing Mme. Bernhardt's Hamlet no one can altogether liberate himself from the fancy that the Prince of Denmark was a girl of uncertain age, with crises of mannishness in which she did not seem quite a lady. Hamlet is in nothing more a man than in the things to which as a man he found himself unequal; for as a woman he would have been easily superior to them. If we could suppose him a woman as Mme. Bernhardt, in spite of herself, invites us to do, we could only suppose him to have solved his perplexities with the delightful precipitation of his putative sex. As the niece of a wicked uncle, who in that case would have had to be a wicked aunt, wedded to Hamlet's father hard upon the murder of her mother, she would have made short work of her vengeance. No fine scruples would have delayed her; she would not have had a moment's question whether she had not better kill herself; she would have out with her bare bodkin and ended the doubt by first passing it through her aunt's breast.

To be sure, there would then have been no play of *Hamlet,* as we have it; but a Hamlet like that imagined, a frankly feminine Hamlet, Mme. Bernhardt could have rendered wonderfully. It is in attempting a masculine Hamlet that she transcends the imaginable and violates an ideal. It is not thinkable. After you have seen it done, you say, as Mr. Clemens is said to have said of bicycling: "Yes, I have seen it, but it's impossible. It doesn't stand to reason."

Art, like law, is the perfection of reason, and whatever is unreasonable in the work of an artist is inartistic. By the time I had reached these bold conclusions I was ready to deduce a principle from them, and to declare that in a true civilization such a thing as that Hamlet would be forbidden, as an offence against public morals, a violence to something precious and sacred.

In the absence of any public regulation the precious and sacred ideals in the arts must be trusted to the several artists, who bring themselves to judgment when they violate them. After Mme. Bernhardt was perversely willing to attempt the part of Hamlet, the question whether she did it well or not was of slight consequence. She had already made her failure in wishing to play the part. Her wish impugned her greatness as an artist; of a really great actress it would have been as unimaginable as the assumption of a sublime feminine rôle by a really great actor. There is an obscure law in this matter which it would be interesting to trace, but for the present I must leave the inquiry with the reader. I can note merely that it seems somehow more permissible for women in imaginary actions to figure as men than for men to figure as women. In the theatre we have conjectured how and why this may be, but the privilege, for less obvious reasons, seems yet more liberally granted in fiction. A woman may tell a story in the character of a man and not give offence, but a man cannot write a novel in autobiographical form from the personality of a woman without imparting the sense of something unwholesome. One feels this true even in the work of such a master as Tolstoy, whose *Katia* is a case in point. Perhaps a woman may play Hamlet with a less shocking effect than a man may play

Desdemona, but all the same she must not play Hamlet at all. That sublime ideal is the property of the human imagination, and may not be profaned by a talent enamoured of the impossible. No harm could be done by the broadest burlesque, the most irreverent travesty, for these would still leave the ideal untouched. Hamlet, after all the horse-play, would be Hamlet; but Hamlet played by a woman, to satisfy her caprice, or to feed her famine for a fresh effect, is Hamlet disabled, for a long time, at least, in its vital essence. I felt that it would take many returns to the Hamlet of Shakespeare to efface the impression of Mme. Bernhardt's Hamlet; and as I prepared to escape from my row of stalls in the darkening theatre, I experienced a noble shame for having seen the Dane so disnatured, to use Mr. Lowell's word. I had not been obliged to come; I had voluntarily shared in the wrong done; by my presence I had made myself an accomplice in the wrong. It was high ground, but not too high for me, and I recovered a measure of self-respect in assuming it.

Max Beerbohm (essay date 1904)

SOURCE: "Sarah," in *Around Theatres,* Rupert Hart-Davis, July 9, 1904, pp. 331-3.

[*In the following essay, originally published in 1904, Beerbohm praises Bernhardt's later work, considering her an important cultural institution in her older age.*]

It is our instinct to revere old age. In this reverence, if we analyse it, we find two constituent emotions—the emotion of pity, and the emotion of envy. Opposite though they are, both are caused by one thing. It is sad that so brief a span remains, but it must be delightful to have accomplished so long a span. Any moment may be our last. A flash of lightning, a side-slip, a falling brick—always some imprevisible chance that may precipitate us into the unknown. And how foolish we should look then—we with so little to our account! Certainly, it is enviable to have accumulated so much as have those elders, and to know, as they know, that no power can steal it away. Romantic awe is stirred in us by the contemplation of anything that has been going on for a long time. Ruins are apt to leave us cold; but any upstanding and habitable old building must touch and warm our imagination. Undefeated by time, any old building, however humble and obscure, becomes for us majestic. But greater, of course, and more haunting, the majesty of an old castle or cathedral. To have towered illustriously through the ages, a centre of significance and pomp, and to be towering thus even now! As with buildings, so with human beings. The romantic quality of an old person is intensified in ratio to the prominence of his or her past and present. There has been in our own time one figure that incomparably illustrated this rule. I am glad to have lived in a time when it was possible to set eyes on the aged Queen Victoria. I can conceive no more romantic thrill than I had whenever, in the last years of her reign, I saw her drive past in that old-fashioned barouche, attended not only by that clattering cavalcade of material guardsmen, but also by the phantoms—not less clearly there—of Melbourne and the Duke, Louis Philippe, Palmerston, Peel, Disraeli the younger—of all those many successive sovereigns, statesmen, soldiers, who were but great misty names to us, yet had been sharp little realities to her, in the interminable pageant of her existence. Strange, to see her with my own eyes—that little old lady, in the queer barouche, on her way to Paddington Station. In Queen Victoria I saw always something of that uncanny symbolism which Mr. Pater saw in the portrait of Mona Lisa. Hers, too, surely, was the head upon which all the ends of the world were come, and the eyelids were a little weary. . . . There is no one now to give me that kind of emotion in like degree; but, certainly, the person most nearly filling the void is Madame Sarah Bernhardt, who has played during the past fortnight at His Majesty's Theatre. Year by year, when she comes among us, my wonder and awe are intensified. Seeing her, a few nights ago, in *La Sorcière,* I was more than ever moved by the apparition. The great Sarah—pre-eminently great throughout the past four decades! My imagination roved back to lose itself in the golden haze of the Second Empire. My imagination roved back to reel at the number of plays that had been written, the number of players whose stars had risen and set, the number of theatres that had been built and theatres that had been demolished, since Sarah's début. The theatrical history of more than forty years lay strewn in the train of that bowing and bright-eyed lady. The applause of innumerable thousands of men and women, now laid in their graves, was still echoing around her. And still she was bowing, bright-eyed, to fresh applause. The time would come when our noisy hands would be folded and immobile for ever. But, though we should be beneath the grass, Sarah would still be behind the footlights—be bowing, as graciously as ever, to audiences recruited from the ranks of those who are now babes unborn. A marvellous woman! For all the gamut of her experience, she is still lightly triumphant over time. All this has been to her, as to Mona Lisa, but as the sound of lyres and flutes, and lives only in the delicacy with which it has moulded the changing lineaments, and tinged the hair. Hers is the head upon which all the ends of the world are come, and the eyelids are not at all weary. . . .

Such was my first impression, when Sarah reappeared to me in *La Sorcière.* But presently I had to qualify it. Superficially, it is quite true that Sarah triumphs over time. Her appearance, her voice, her movements are all as ever. But her spirit shows the inevitable signs of wear and tear. Time has succeeded in damping the sacred fire that burnt within her. Gone from her are the passion and sincerity that once held us in thrall. As Phèdre, as Fédora, as any of the characters created by her in her prime, she is as enthralling, doubtless, as in the past, forasmuch as her unimpaired energy and memory enable her to reproduce exactly the effects that she produced then. But when she plays a new part, as in La Sorcière, you are definitely aware that she is not feeling anything—that she is merely urging herself to the performance of certain tricks. Very perfectly she performs

these time-honoured tricks. The lovely voice is always in tune and time, whether it coo or hiss, and the lovely gestures are all in their proper places, and the lovely face is as expressive as ever. But the whole performance is hollow—art without life—a dead thing galvanised. Of course, the play—a play written by the venerable M. Sardou for no purpose but to show Sarah off in the ways in which she likes to be shown off—is itself an utterly dead thing. But there was a time when Sarah could have put life into it. And for her failure to put life into it now we may console ourselves with the implicit revelation that she, too, after all, is mortal, like the rest of us.

Though her genius has been touched thus by Time, all untouched is her love of adventure; and she has given a performance of *Pelléas et Mélisande,* with herself as Pelléas, and Mrs. Campbell as Mélisande. I did not see this performance. I love the play too well, and am loth that my memory of it as performed by Mrs. Campbell in her own language, with Mr. Martin Harvey as Pelléas, should be complicated with any memory less pleasing. I am quite willing to assume that Mrs. Campbell speaks French as exquisitely as she speaks English, and that Sarah's Pelléas is not, like her Hamlet and her Duc de Reichstadt, merely ladylike. But the two facts remain that Sarah is a woman and that Mrs. Campbell is an English-woman. And by these two facts such a performance is ruled out of the sphere of art into the sphere of sensationalism. If Maeterlinck were a sensationalist, that would not matter.

The Nation (essay date 1907)

SOURCE: A review of *Memories of My Life* by Sarah Bernhardt, in *The Nation,* Vol. 85, No. 2209, October 31, 1907, pp. 403-4.

[*In the following essay, the anonymous reviewer praises Bernhardt's* Memories of My Life, *noting that it deftly portrays the actress, but adds that the memoir adds little to common knowledge of Bernhardt's life.*]

If it be the main object of an autobiography to make a complete and merciless exposure of the character of the writer . . . [**Memories of My Life** by] Sarah Bernhardt constitute[s] one of the most successful books ever written—and the revelation is so utterly unconscious, so vivid and so consistent in all its elaborate complexity as to leave no room for doubt or speculation. Herein lies the value of this rhapsodical but interesting *apologia pro vita sua* that it exhibits the true woman in clearer relief than it does the largely mythical superwoman whom it labors to depict. Rich as it is in minor details and vivacious descriptions it adds but little to the common knowledge of the career of the best advertised actress in the world. In fact, it is studiously reticent concerning many essential facts, including those of parentage and pedigree, about which the curious in such matters would like to be better informed. Apparently, there is no foundation for the stories, long prevalent, that her youth was passed in poverty.

Her mother seems to have been amply provided for and she herself wanted for nothing in her childhood except the intelligent guidance and control of which she stood most in need. Concerning the identity and social position of her father a significant silence is observed, although he occasionally appears upon the scene. Her mother, as is generally known, was of Jewish descent, but she herself was reared in the Roman Catholic faith.

Her account of her early years, though crammed with domestic incident and anecdote of an easily credible kind, is so careful in its omissions and so reckless in its exaggeration, that only the most confiding reader would put much faith in its complete veracity. But reading between the lines, it is not difficult to discern in the way-ward, affectionate, wilful, imaginative, and hysterical little girl of the Grandchamps Convent—where she received most of what regular education she had—the miniature copy of the brilliant, paradoxical and unmanageable creature who, a little later on, was to dazzle Paris with her acting and drive successive managers to despair. She furnishes a lively sketch of her convent life, her various escapades, her paroxysms of temper, her triumphs in religious theatricals and her gradual transformation into a religious devotee. At one time, it appears, it was her highest ambition to become a nun, and she draws an imaginary picture of herself as a Carmelite penitent, an idea for which she is indebted to Victor Hugo's *Les Misérables.* Her religious fervor, however, was never strong enough to render her amenable to discipline or to prevent her from indulging in the most caustic comment upon all who opposed or offended her, whether they were nuns, relatives or friends. In her case, the tongue was ever a most unruly member, and her book is highly seasoned with personalities, which, however apt or amusing, are neither polite nor amiable.

It was the Duc de Morny, the favorite of the third Napoleon, who, when her family was fairly at a loss how to dispose of her, suggested that she be put upon the stage. He therein displayed better judgment, than he employed in some weightier affairs. Her recitation of "Les Deux Pigeons" gained her admission to the Conservatoire. She had made no preparation, but the magic of her voice won her judges. Her first engagement at the Français ended ingloriously. Enraged because Madame Nathalie, an old *sociétaire,* had pushed her sister, she slapped her face and resigned rather than apologize. Her unruly temper was also the cause of her leaving the Gymnase, and she ran away, on a wild impulse, to Spain, where luckily she fell into good hands. Returning to Paris, she joined the Odéon, where she rapidly rose to fame. It was there that she made the acquaintance of Prince Napoleon (Plon-Plon)—who offended her hugely by his indifference, but afterward became a good friend—and George Sand. It was there, too, that she achieved one of the most notable of her earlier triumphs in *Le Passant.* After that her popularity, especially among the students, of whom she was ever the favorite, increased apace until it was interrupted by the war.

Her patriotism, as all the world knows, was as practical as it was fervid and vociferous. The Germans, in the present volume are the objects of some of her most vigorous rhetoric. But unlike most of her compatriots she laments the overthrow of the Emperor as well as the national defeat. He had entertained her at the Tuileries and greatly impressed her with his benevolence, gentleness, and wit. She holds that he was the victim of circumstance, and much more sinned against than sinning. Her remarks on political subjects are not profound but her conduct during the siege of Paris is deserving of the warmest admiration. In the emergency hospital which she established at the Odéon she displayed not only energy, endurance, and courage, qualities which she never lacked, but foresight, unselfish devotion, and tenderness. She did not desert her post even when she, with her patients, was driven by the German shells into the cellars, rendered almost uninhabitable by water and rats. Possibly some of her descriptions—that of her visit to a battlefield, for instance—may be colored somewhat too highly, but the reality, doubtless, was horrible enough, and the part she played was at once womanly and heroic.

It is impossible, and unnecessary, to follow her through her long list of triumphs and adventures, her escape from Paris, her descent into the *Enfer du Plogoff* at Finisterre—with its obvious inspirations from *Les Travailleurs de la Mer*—her balloon ascensions, etc. Imagination plays at least as great a part in them as sober fact, but Madame Sarah is a capital *raconteuse.* Nor is it needful to do more than refer to her dramatic achievements, culminating in *Phèdre,* which have made her name a household word from St. Petersburg to San Francisco. It is a pity that her memories are so centred upon herself as to be forgetful of some of her friends who were almost as illustrious. Doubtless, if she had chosen, she could have told many illuminating anecdotes of Gambetta. Thiers (whom she anathematizes), Paul de Rémusat, Canrobert, Macmahon, Hugo, Augier, Bornier, Rochefort, Rostand, and many others. To tell the plain truth, the monstrous egotism of the book greatly weakens the pleasurable impression created by its vivacity, its cleverness, and its abundance of interesting material. It cannot affect, either in one way or the other, the fame of the consummate artist, which is too firmly established ever to be shaken, but it leaves behind it the impression of a woman endowed indeed with many fine qualities, with intellect, ambition, versatility, dauntless courage, and (within certain limits) both generosity and affection, but too much given to self-glorification, to petty animosities and jealousies and unreasonable prejudices to be entirely great.

Max Beerbohm (essay date 1907)

SOURCE: "'Sarah's' Memoirs," in *Around Theatres,* Rupert Hart-Davis, December 7, 1907, pp. 485-8.

[*In the following essay, originally published in 1907, Beerbohm praises the skill with which Bernhardt wrote her* Memoirs of Sarah Bernhardt, *noting, however, that it was typical of Bernhardt to practice all her endeavors with unusual skill and knowledge.*]

I wish I had read this book [*Memoirs of Sarah Bernhardt*] before I left London. In a very small and simple village on the coast of Italy I find it over-exciting. Gray and gentle are the olive-trees around me; and the Mediterranean mildly laps the shore, with never a puff of wind for the fishermen, whose mothers and wives and daughters sit plying their bobbins all day long in the shade of the piazza. In mellow undertones they are gossiping, these women at their work, all day long, and day after day. Gossiping of what, in this place where nothing perceptibly happens? The stranger here loses his sense of life. A trance softly envelops him. Imagine a somnambulist awakening to find himself peering down into the crater of a volcano, and you will realise how startling Mme Sarah Bernhardt's book has been to me.

Hers is a volcanic nature, as we know, and hers has been a volcanic career; and nothing of this volcanicism is lost in her description of it. It has been doubted whether she really wrote the book herself. The vividness of the narration, the sure sense of what was worth telling and what was not, the sharp, salt vivacity of the style (which not even the slip-shod English of the translator can obscure)—all these virtues have to some pedants seemed incompatible with authenticity. I admit that it is disquieting to find an amateur plunging triumphantly into an art which we others, having laboriously graduated in it, like to regard as a close concern of our own. When Sarah threw her energies into the art of sculpture, and acquitted herself very well, the professional sculptors were very much surprised and vexed. A similar disquiet was produced by her paintings. Let writers console themselves with the reflection that to Sarah all things are possible. There is no use in pretending that she did not write this book herself. Paris contains, of course, many accomplished hacks who would gladly have done the job for her, and would have done it quite nicely. But none of them could have imparted to the book the peculiar fire and salt that it has—the rushing spontaneity that stamps it, for every discriminating reader, as Sarah's own.

Her life may be said to have been an almost unbroken series of "scenes" from the moment when, at the age of three, she fell into the fire. "The screams of my foster-father, who could not move, brought in some neighbours. I was thrown, all smoking, into a large pail of fresh milk. . . . I have been told since that nothing was so painful to witness and yet so charming as my mother's despair." The average little girl would not resent being removed from a boarding school by an aunt. She would not "roll about on the ground, uttering the most heart-rending cries." But that is what little Sarah did; and "the struggle lasted two hours, and while I was being dressed I escaped twice into the garden and attempted to climb the trees and to throw myself into the pond. . . . I was so feverish that my life was said to be in danger." On another occasion she swallowed the contents of a large ink-pot, after her mother had made her take some medicine; and "I cried to mamma, 'It is you who have killed me!'" The desire for death—death as a means of scoring off some one, or as an emotional experience—was fre-

quent both in her childhood and in her maturity. When she was appearing as *Zaïre,* M. Perrin, her manager, offended her in some way, and she was "determined to faint, determined to vomit blood, determined to die, in order to enrage Perrin." An old governess, Mlle de Brabender, lay dying, and "her face lighted up at the supreme moment with such a holy look that I suddenly longed to die." Fainting was the next best thing to dying, and Sarah, throughout her early career, was continually fainting, with or without provocation. It is a wonder that so much emotional energy as she had to express in swoons, in floods of tears, in torrents of invective, did not utterly wear out her very frail body. Somehow her body fed and thrived on her spirit. The tragedian in her cured the invalid. Doubtless, if she had not been by nature a tragedian, and if all her outbursts of emotion had come straight from her human heart, she could not have survived. It is clear that even in her most terrific moments one half of her soul was in the position of spectator, applauding vigorously. This artistic detachment is curiously illustrated by the tone she takes about herself throughout her memoirs. The test of a good autobiography is the writer's power to envisage himself. Sarah envisages herself ever with perfect clearness and composure. She does not, in retrospect, applaud herself except when applause is deserved. She is never tired of laughing at herself with the utmost good humour, or of scolding herself with exemplary sternness. Of her sudden dash into Spain she says: "I had got it into my head that my Fate willed it, that I must obey my star, and a hundred other ideas, each one more foolish than the other." And such criticisms abound throughout the volume. It is very seldom that her sense of humour fails her, very seldom that she does not see herself from without as clearly as from within. She seems surprised that people were surprised at her sleeping in a coffin; and it still seems strange to her that a menagerie in a back-garden of Chester Square should excite unfavourable comment. Of this menagerie she gives an engaging description. "The cheetah, beside himself with joy, sprang like a tiger out of his cage, wild with liberty. He rushed at the trees and made straight for the dogs, who all four began to howl with terror. The parrot was excited, and uttered shrill cries; and the monkey, shaking his cage about, gnashed his teeth to distraction." Sarah's "uncontrollable laughter," mingled with that of Gustave Doré and other visitors, strengthened the symphony. M. Got called next day to remind Sarah of the dignity of the Comédie Française; whereupon she again had the cheetah released, with not less delectable results. Can we wonder that there were comments in the newspapers of both nations? Sarah can. "Injustice has always roused me to revolt, and injustice was certainly having its fling. I could not," says she, "do a thing that was not watched and blamed."

Now and again she pauses in her narrative to make remarks at large—to develop some theory of artistic criticism, or to handle some large social problem. And in these disquisitions she is always delightfully herself. She is a shrewd and trenchant critic of art, and in her ideas about humanity she is ever radiantly on the side of the angels, radiant with a love of mercy and a hatred of oppression. Capital punishment she abominates as "a relic of cowardly barbarism." "Every human being has a moment when his heart is easily touched, when the tears of grief will flow; and those tears may fecundate a generous thought which might lead to repentance. I would not for the whole world be one of those who condemn a man to death. And yet many of them are good, upright men, who when they return to their families are affectionate to their wives, and reprove their children for breaking a doll's head." That is the end of one paragraph. The next paragraph is: "I have seen four executions, one in London, one in Spain, and two in Paris." Was Sarah dragged to see them by force, as an awful punishment for lapses in the respect due to the dignity of the Comédie Française? She appears to have gone of her own accord. Indeed, she waited all night on the balcony of a first-floor flat in the Rue Merlin to see the execution of Vaillant, the anarchist, whom she had known personally and had liked. After the knife had fallen, she mingled with the crowd, and was "sick at heart and desperate. There was not a word of gratitude to this man, not a murmur of vengeance or revolt." She "felt inclined to cry out 'Brutes that you are! kneel down and kiss the stones that the blood of this poor madman has stained for your sakes, for you, because he believed in you!'" The wonder is that she did not actually cry these words out. Her reticence must have cost her a tremendous effort. Be sure that she really was horrified, at the time, by the crowd's indifference. Be sure that she really does altogether hate capital punishment. Be sure, too, that she had a genuine admiration for the character of the man whom she was at such pains to see slaughtered. You, gentle reader, might not care to visit an execution—especially not that of a personal friend. But then, you see, you are not a great tragedian. Emotion for emotion's sake is not the law of your being. It is because that is so immutably, so overwhelmingly, the law of Sarah's being that we have in Sarah—yes, even now, for all the tricks she plays with her art—the greatest of living tragedians. If ever I committed a murder, I should not at all resent her coming to my hanging. I should bow from the scaffold with all the deference due to the genius that has so often thrilled me beyond measure. And never has it thrilled me more than through this unusual medium, in this unusual place.

F. G. Bettany (essay date 1907)

SOURCE: "Sarah Bernhardt's Memoirs," in *The Bookman*, Vol. 33, No. 195, December, 1907, pp. 129-30.

[*In the following essay, Bettany praises* My Double Life: Memoirs of Sarah Bernhardt, *but adds that the book contributes no new information on Bernhardt's life.*]

Their serial publication in the French press has robbed [*My Double Life: Memoirs of Sarah Bernhardt*] of most of their freshness. That was only to be expected. Sarah Bernhardt is not only the most popular actress of two continents, she is also a figure of world-wide celebrity,

round whose name has gathered a whole cycle of legends. Hers is one of those commanding personalities that impress themselves on the imagination of the public; like Gladstone, Bismarck, Garibaldi, the Kaiser, the American President, Tolstoi and Patti, to quote a heterogeneous list of famous persons of modern times, she has become a household word, alike in Europe and America. There must be thousands, perhaps hundreds of thousands, of people who have never seen the actress in any of her best-known parts—Phèdre or Fédora, Marguerite Gautier or the heroine of *Frou-Frou,* Magda or Adrienne Lecouvreur—and yet are profoundly interested in Sarah Bernhardt the woman. Her incalculable temperament, her eccentricities and caprices, her violent outbursts of rage, her quarrels and her reconciliations, her travels and her hairbreadth escapes from perils, her coffin and her menagerie, have won her fame, or at any rate notoriety, with hosts of newspaper readers who are quite indifferent to the art of the theatre. These devour greedily any anecdote about Mme. Bernhardt that appears in the public journals, and the press carefully caters for their tastes. No sooner, therefore, was any instalment of the actress's reminiscences published in feuilleton form, than the more piquant portions were straightway copied into every European or American newspaper. Hence it happens that all Sarah Bernhardt's best stories, all her frankest confessions and criticisms, have been made familiar alike to the admirers of her art and to "the man in the street," long before these memoirs were issued to the libraries as a collected volume: Those, however, to whom the book comes as a novelty, will find it entertaining almost from cover to cover; it is only the record of its author's first American tour, forming the last chapters of the volume, that proves rather tedious reading: and on every page of the autobiography, which is sometimes audaciously candid, and nearly always sprightly and chatty, will be discovered some self-revelatory detail.

Yes, Sarah Bernhardt tells us much about herself in her reminiscences. She speaks with an agreeable straightforwardness about her weaknesses and prejudices, her superstitions and her tantrums, her struggles and her triumphs: but though all these reminiscences bear the stamp of Sarah's own personality, in her case, as in the case of every other successful man or woman, it is the early days, before life's battles had been won, which furnish the most interesting chronicles. There is a certain monotony about the history of such an unbroken, series of successes as has fallen to this great artist's lot ever since she conquered Paris and London. This triumphant Sarah we know well, but grateful as we are to her for hours of pleasure in the playhouse, it is not she of whom we wish most to hear. It is rather the lonely little girl who so quickly recognises that the pretty mother she adores has no love for her, but lavishes all her store upon the child's sister. It is the convent-school miss who longs to take religious vows, yet causes the nuns endless anxiety by her alternate fits of mischievousness and temper. It is the timid, hysterical young creature whose career is settled for her without her having a say in the matter, and merely by reason of a few words of the Due de Morny. It is the agonised débutante who, at more than one first night, makes but a half-success and is uncomfortably reminded of her thin arms, her slim figure, and her general lack of plumpness in face and body. It is the actress of promise who has to fight against managerial cabals and cliques which favour her rivals. Happily, it is just of herself in such youthful manifestations that Madame Bernhardt provides the fullest information.

Next to that section of her book which describes her girlhood and her stage novitiate, the most readable chapters of the memoirs are those which contain anecdotes of the distinguished personages the actress has known. All the more famous of her colleagues at the Comédie Française figure in these pages, as well as all the prominent playwrights of the time. Naturally there are many references to Sophie Croizette, Sarah Bernhardt's chief rival, but they are all of them kindly. Apropos of Croizette and *L'Etrangère,* the play of Dumas fils's in which their rivalry at the house of Molière came to a head, Mme. Bernhardt has two amusing stories of her relations with the younger Dumas. One is the story of her going to him after her quarrel with Croizette, and pouring upon him the vials of her wrath, which he took in good part. The other tells how when, through failure of memory, she cut out a whole scene from *L'Etrangère* and afterwards apologised to its author for what she had done. Dumas said, "My dear child, when I write a play, I think it is good; when I see it played, I think it is stupid; and when any one tells it me, I think it perfect, as the person always forgets half of it." For Augier Mme. Bernhardt had no love, but she writes cordially of both François Coppée and Victor Hugo. Hugo it was who sent her, as a tribute to her acting in *Hernani,* a tear she caused him to shed—in other words, a diamond drop; she says she liked to look at Théophile Gautier and to listen to Victor Hugo. Coppée she helped to secure his first hearing in *Le Passant,* and she compares his "handsome face, emaciated and pale," with "that of the immortal Bonaparte." Poets and dramatists, managers and players, were not Sarah's only associates. She met Louis Napoleon both before and after his *coup d'état.* The Emperor once caught her practising a curtsey in the throne-room. Of the Empress Eugénie she declares that no sooner did her Imperial Majesty speak than the spell of her beauty was broken. "That rough, loud voice, coming from that brilliant woman, gave me a shock."

To students of the theatre the quaintest passage in these Memoirs will prove that in which Mme. Bernhardt passes in review the most famous players of her time, and estimates their merits. She begins by remarking that on the stage a man loses his chivalry—the actor becomes jealous of the actress. Then she names four chivalrous actors—Pierre Berton, Worms, Antoine and Guitry. M. Guitry, she says, is both an actor and a comedian, and she adds that she knows few stage artists who are also comedians—whatever the term "comedian" may mean:

> Henry Irving was an admirable artist, but not a comedian. Coquelin is an admirable comedian, but

he is not an artist. Mounet Sully has genius, which he sometimes places at the service of the artist and sometimes at the service of the comedian; but on the other hand, he sometimes gives us exaggerations as artist and comedian which make lovers of beauty and truth gnash their teeth. Bartet is a perfect comedienne, with a delicate artistic sense. Réjane is the most comedian of comedians, and an artist when she wishes to be.

Then follows this pronouncement on the Duse:

> Eleonora Duse is more a comedian than an artist; she walks the paths that have been traced out by others; she does not imitate them, certainly not, for she plants flowers where there were trees, and trees where there were flowers; but she has never by her art made a single personage stand out identified by her name; she has not created a being or a vision which reminds one of herself. She puts on other people's gloves, but she puts them on inside out. And all this she has done with infinite grace and with careless unconsciousness. She is a great comedian, a very great comedian, but not a great artist.

One opens one's eyes at such sweeping generalisations, and recalls Signora Duse's Mirandol na in *La Locandiera* as an example of her creative genius, and her Silvia in *La Gioconda* as an exquisite revelation of her own personality.

Mme. Bernhardt's frank comments on her stage contemporaries make it seem strange, at first sight, that in these Memoirs she should allude so rarely to the technique of her own art. But that, according to a statement she herself is credited with, is to form the subject of a companion volume.

James Agate (essay date 1922)

SOURCE: "Sarah Bernhardt: A Postscript," in *Alarums and Excursions,* Grant Richards Ltd., 1922, pp. 34-61.

[In the following essay, Agate reflects on Bernhardt's body of work and popular reaction to her.]

Those who like myself have cherished a feeling for the actor's art akin to reverence must have rubbed their eyes on seeing a whole front page of a popular newspaper devoted to the personal affairs of little Miss Mary Pickford and a bare half-dozen lines to the announcement that Madame Sarah Bernhardt had appeared in *Athalie:* "The famous actress is in her seventy-sixth year. The rôle may be described as of the recumbent order." Shudder though one may at blithe enormity, it is useless to cavil at the editorial sense of news-values. To the whole uneducated world it really does matter what Miss Pickford eats, wears, and thinks. We were once mountebank-mad; we are now tied to the grimace. Miss Pickford is very pretty and quite a good maker of babyish faces. She brings to many "escape from their creditors and a free field for emotions they dare not indulge in real life." She gives pleasure to millions who have never heard of the great actress, or having heard that she is an old lady of seventy-six, desire not to see her.

Oh, it offends me to the very soul when old age is treated so! The hey-day of a great spirit knows no passing; there is that in this old artist which shall please our children provided they have eyes to see that which is spirit and imperishable. It were idle to pretend that the gesture is as firm, the eye as bright, the voice as liquid as once we knew them. The wonder is in the gentleness of Time which has marred only the inessential. To him who would contribute his quota of good-will this great lady's art is still the quintessence of loveliness. Memory aiding, it is possible to "call back the lovely April of her prime," and looking out upon a later day to see "despite of wrinkles, this her golden time." But you have only to turn to the notices of her latest appearance in *Daniel* to realise the blindness of those who will not look beyond the flesh. "It is a matter for regret," writes one lusty fellow, "that this actress should be driven by circumstance to parade her infirmities before us." Follows a catalogue of departed bodily graces. "I will not bring my critical functions to bear upon the spectacle of an old lady with one leg portraying a paralytic," he concludes. I do not know that I would condemn this blind soul to any darker circle than that of its own sightlessness. The eye sees what the eye brings the means of seeing.

As the artist's physical powers have waned, so her intellectual faculties have ripened. Thirty years ago she had been content to play this foolish little Daniel with "her beauty, her grace, her flashing eye, her sinuous charm"— I quote from the catalogue of departed virtues—gathering him up to heaven at the end in her well-known cloud of fire-works. To-day Madame Bernhardt plays him, as it were, colloquially, informing unreality with a hundred little shades and accents of reality. She is fanciful, wistful, wayward, endowing little things with an actor's interest, with something of the writer's preoccupation with style. I cannot imagine any more delightful grace-note than that of the little blue flames of the rum omelette which shall enliven her loneliness. And when she quotes her line of verse you are made conscious that this is a boy's poem. She lingers over it with the tenderness of all great artists for immaturity. What panting English tragédienne, in the full measure of bodily vigour, may compass the intimacy and interest of the Frenchwoman's lowest tone and slightest motion? In the first two acts Daniel does not appear and the stage is given over to scenes of emotion very creditably portrayed by a leading light of the Comédie Française. We applaud, for the thing seems well done; but when, in the long colloquy with Daniel, the older artist sits motionless at her table, leaving the scene in full generosity to the younger, her very silence it is which holds us, and not the tinkle of less significant speech. What other actress, when it comes to dying, can so let life out of her voice and lineaments, so cease upon the midnight? Add to the glories of such a performance something that I would call a corona of malice, a *gouaillerie,* a Puckish hint that we shall not take this for the sublime car of tragedy but for some workaday vehicle for tears. We are to feel that the rarer gifts of the actress have not been harnessed, and our minds are sent on haunting quest for the greatnesses that once she compassed. As a younger woman she had neither the wit nor strength of mind to make this bargain with our penetration.

A year or two ago a series of performances was announced which was to be determinate and valedictory. Equally looked forward to and dreaded, they did not, as it happened, come off. In the first place the lady declared, in that vigorous way of hers, that the visit would in no way be one of farewell. She was not for epilogising; in any case the time was not yet. She was off to Honolulu, Hong-Kong, Saskatchewan, how did she know whither?—and merely desired to take temporary leave of the polite world. And then she became ill and the engagement was not fulfilled.

Well, there's no harm in this sort of good-bye. May this triumphant lady spend her long winter with her hand at her lips bidding adieu. That's one simile, and I would find another to fit her glory now departing. The shadows may be long; they will be longer yet before the dark, fingers to stir old memories, to set pulses beating at thought of a glamour that never was on earth. Is it our creeping age and recollection playing us tricks? Was it not the artist's acting but our own youth that was the miracle? I wonder!

But there is nothing which does the subject even of avowed panegyric so much harm as lack of discrimination in praise. Let me frankly admit that Sarah Bernhardt was never the mistress of the art of reticence, and that, great show-woman that she is, she has always turned advertisement to commodity. Take the forty-year-old history of her famous tiff with the Comédie Française, ending in the rupture which was the necessary preliminary to those gallivantings over the unacted globe. The story of it all, so far as may be gleaned from the records of the time, is something as follows. The Comédie pays a visit to London, bringing in its train Mademoiselle Bernhardt, a young member whose talents have already been acclaimed by the Parisians. And here we must note that the French, in spite of an excitable temperament, are capable of a rare levelheadedness in their attitude towards artists. They know how to distinguish between the personality of the actor and his talent, and are not swayed by exorbitances outside the scope of the theatre. "Je ne veux connaître de la Comédie Française en ce feuilleton," writes Sarcey, "que ce que l'on peut en voir de sa stalle d'orchestre." The English are quite other. The critic of *The Times* permits himself to write: "Further, all that we have heard of Mademoiselle Sarah Bernhardt, of her various talents and manifold faculties, her character and even her eccentricities, has added to the effect produced by her acting and has made her, indisputably, the centre of our curiosity and interest in the Comédie Française." No Frenchman could have written so. The effect produced by the acting of an artist is, to him, incapable of irrelevant addition or subtraction; he is conquered by the artist and not by the woman. Our race is more phlegmatic, but it is also more naïve.

In the first pages of the *Journal of the Visit of the Comédie Française to London in 1879* Sarcey begins by deploring the coldness of the English public towards the members of the troupe other than Mademoiselle Bernhardt. He recounts for the benefit of his readers in Paris how, in spite of her altogether admirable second act in *Le Misanthrope,* Mademoiselle Croizette failed to please. How, in *Les Caprices de Marianne,* her capriciousness was ravishing but of no avail. How, in *L'Etrangère* the same actress displayed her greatest fascination yet without fascinating; how, after her fine explosion in the fourth act, the audience did, after a fashion, explode in sympathy. "Mais ce n'était pas cela. Le cœur n'y était pas." The only reason he can assign is that the English cannot worship two mistresses at the same time and that their hearts have gone out wholly to Mademoiselle Bernhardt. This is the first mention of her in the *Journal* and is followed by the phrase: "Oh! celle-là.per . . ." "Nothing," he continues, "can convey any idea of the infatuation she has aroused. It amounts to madness. When she is about to appear a quiver runs through the audience; she appears, and an Ah! of joy and rapture is heard on all sides. The house listens with rapt attention, bodies bent forward, glasses glued to their eyes; they will not lose a word, and only when she has finished break into a fury of applause. Outside the theatre they speak of no one else."

It looks very much as though the English on this occasion came to the correct critical conclusion, although, it may be, for the wrong reasons. We must take into account, too, the kind of plays in which Mademoiselle Bernhardt was appearing, and contrast them with our own at the time. In 1879 the English theatre had not yet entirely emerged from the Robertsonian floods of milk-and-water. W. S. Gilbert was still posing as a sentimentalist, Byron's *Our Boys* had been produced four years earlier, the previous year had seen Wills's play of *Olivia.* Concurrently with the Comédie Française at the Gaiety there was running at the Lyceum young Mr Pinero's *Daisy's Escape,* and Mr Burnand's *Betsy* was in rehearsal. London had been melted by the pity of Miss Ellen Terry's Olivia; it was to be purged by the terror of the Frenchwoman's Phèdre. The English of that period were accustomed to see passion garbed as decently as their table legs. What, then, must they have thought of Racine and Sarah in frank exposition of incestuous love! Imagine the Englishman of du Maurier's pencil confronted by Mr Joseph Knight's account, in the respectable columns of *The Athenæum,* of this diversion:

> From the moment she entered on the stage, carefully guarded and supported by Œnone, Mademoiselle Bernhardt realised fully the passionate, febrile, and tortured woman. Her supple frame writhed beneath the influence of mental agony and restless desire, and her postures seemed chosen with admirable art for the purpose of blending the greatest possible amount of seduction with the utmost possible

parade of penitence. This is, of course, the true reading, and the whole shame of Phèdre is due to her ill success. The key-note to her character is struck in a later act, the third, wherein she says:

Il n'est plus temps: il sait mes ardeurs insensées,
De l'austère pudeur, les bornes sont passées.
J'ai déclaré ma honte aux yeux de mon vainqueur,
Et l'espoir malgré moi s'est glissé dans mon cœur.

While, accordingly, she exhausts herself in invective against herself for her crime, she is, in fact, in the very whirlwind of her passion studying, like a second Delilah,

His virtue or weakness which way to assail.

Obvious as is this view, it is not always presented, the cause of absence being, perhaps, the weakness of the actress. In the present case it was fully revealed, and the picture of abject and lascivious appeal was terrible in its intensity.

Add to such a portrayal the personality which was to charm the educated men and women of half the civilised globe, and there is no wonder that the English public lost something of measure in its praise. Incense was offered up, the idol's head was turned. I give what happened next as related by M. Georges d'Heylli:

> It is common knowledge that this great and original artist has a distaste for behaving like the rest of the world and that discipline appears to her mechanical and wearisome. One is not mistress of several arts for nothing. Mademoiselle Sarah Bernhardt did not content herself in England with exhibiting one aspect of her charming personality: to be an actress and nothing but an actress was not enough. She established a studio for painting and sculpture where she could be admired in the delightful costume with which the photographers have made us familiar. Yielding to the numerous requests which her great talents and the general curiosity procured for her, she consented to give performances in the drawing-rooms of the aristocracy. Now this would have been in no way the concern of either her colleagues or the Press, had it not been that the stress of this additional work told so much upon the actress as to render her physically and mentally incapable of giving her best in the theatre. The day arrived when she was unable to fulfil her part in *L'Etrangère.* The bill had to be changed and the money which had been taken for the performance returned. This was followed by recriminations between the artist and the French and English Press. Mademoiselle Bernhardt, annoyed at the general censure, resigned her membership of the Comédie Française, and accepted, or did not accept—the rumour at least was rife—an engagement for a tour in America.

Peace was, however, restored, the artist made a *sociétaire* and granted two months' holiday in the year. She resumed her performances on 17th April 1880. Shortly afterwards a critic of standing complained that she played Doña Clorinde in Augier's *L'Aventurière* in the same manner as Virginie in *L'Assommoir.*

La nouvelle Clorinde a eu, pendant les deux derniers actes, des emportements excessifs de toute manière, d'abord parce qu'ils forçaient sa voix qui n'a de charme que dans le *médium,* ensuite parce qu'ils l'amenaient à des mouvements de corps et de bras qu'il serait fâcheux d'emprunter à la grande Virginie de l'Assommoir pour les introduire à la Comédie Française.

Thus Auguste Vitu in the *Figaro.*

Sarah again resigned, and the great Sarcey was devilish cross about it. "Is it the fault of the Comédie," he asks, "that one of the members has preferred the rôle of star to that of artist? And then, is this so new to us Parisians? Are we not by this time used to the eccentricities of this flamboyant personage? Mademoiselle Bernhardt has resigned and is leaving us. It is unfortunate, it is true, but more particularly unfortunate for her. The Comédie loses a charming actress and must for the time being withdraw a few plays which are now hardly practicable without her. But the number of these plays is small, for her art, divine instrument though it be, has not many notes. Her absence is to be regretted, but we shall get over it, and another artist will arrive, perhaps Mademoiselle Bartet, who with other qualities will turn the public's head in the same way and efface the memory of her predecessor. Actors come and actors go. After Régnier, Coquelin; after Provost, Thiron; after Samson, Got; and others will succeed to the inheritance of Got, Thiron, and Coquelin. Remember the old proverb, *Faute d'un moine l'abbaye ne chôme pas.*" Finally he delivered himself up to prophecy. "Let her make no mistake; her success will not be lasting. She is not one of those who can bear the whole brunt of a play and whose brilliance has no need of a background of mediocrity." Was ever augur more woefully mistaken? Sarcey had tried to bolster up Croizette; the world has long judged between Mademoiselle Bernhardt and Mademoiselle Bartet.

But there is another factor in this character besides wilfulness and caprice—the vacillation in artistic purpose. The Journal of the Goncourts gives a picture of her in mid-career which illustrates this. It is Edmond who writes:

10th October.

Lunch with Sarah Bernhardt at Bauer's, who is kindly using his influence to induce her to play my *La Faustin.*

Sarah arrives in a pearl-grey tunic braided with gold. No diamonds except on the handle of her lorgnette. A moth-like wisp of black lace on the burning bush of her hair; beneath, the black shadow of lashes and the clear blue of her eyes. Seated at the table she complains of being little, and indeed her figure is that of the women of the Renaissance. She sits sideways on the corner of her chair, exactly like a child who has been promoted to the big table.

At once, with gusto, she embarks upon the history of her world-scamperings. She relates how in the

United States, as soon as her next tour is announced, and though it be a year beforehand, orders are sent to France for a shipload of professors in order that the young American "miss" may know what the play is about.

I am placed next to Sarah. She must be nearly fifty. She wears no powder and her complexion is that of a young girl. . . . She talks hygiene, morning exercises, hot baths. From this she goes on to portraits of people she has known. Dumas *fils* among others. She has a natural instinct for affability, a desire to please which is not assumed.

17th October.

Dinner at Sarah's to read *La Faustin.*

The little studio where she receives is not unlike a stage setting. On the floor against the walls rows of pictures, giving the apartment something of the appearance of an auction-room; over the mantelpiece her full-length portrait by Clairin. Furniture everywhere, mediæval chests and cabinets, an infinity of articles of virtu more or less *rasta,* statuettes from Chili, musical instruments from the Antipodes. Only one sign of individual taste, the skins of great polar-bears shedding a lustre on the corner where she sits. . . .

At dinner Sarah is very gracious and full of small attentions. We return to the studio to read the play. There is no lamp and only a few candles. The copy is typewritten and much less readable than it would have been in the usual round hand, with the result that Bauer does not read very well. The effect is cold. After the seventh scene I insist upon reading myself. I, too, do not manage very well, but I get tension into it and Sarah seems impressed by the last scene. Then tea, during which there is no further talk of the play. Finally Sarah comes over to me, says that the piece is full of passion, that the last act seems superb, and asks me to leave the script that she may go through one or two scenes which have been omitted. A few vague sentences which may mean that Sarah will accept the play, and even a phrase as to putting me into touch with her manager, but nothing decisive.

Now there are some things which are not favourable. Sarah is a romantic. At the moment the fuss they are making of Réjane inclines her towards the modern, but her artistic temperament is against it. Further, in my play Sarah has a wretch of a sister, and it so happens that she actually possesses one—a fact of which, until recently, I was ignorant.

26th November.

In reply to my letter asking for the return of my play I have to-day received a telegram from Sarah affirming a wish to act in something of mine, and asking for a further six weeks in which to think *La Faustin* over quietly. My belief is that although she may wish to give the piece she will not do so.

22nd February.

To-day, without a word, the manuscript is returned.

Once free of the Comédie, Sarah envisages her famous world-tours, and embarks upon gallivantings innumerable. And once definitely on the rampage candour compels me to admit, as it compelled Joe Gargery, that she was indeed a Buster. So began the long period of trumpeting vagabondage, and with it the history of "Sardoodledum." The actress tore about the habitable globe piling whirlwind upon earthquake and littering the stages of half-a-dozen countries with the pasteboard wreckage of Fédoras, Théodoras, Toscas, Sorcières. There was probably not more than one English critic who kept his head in all this welter of popes, princes, cardinals, Russian Grand Dukes, Austrian Archdukes, German counts, cantatrices, Inquisitors, gaolers, nihilists, poisoners and assassins. Amid the general delirium Mr Shaw alone was heard to declare himself unimpressed by the sight of an actress "chopping a man to death with a hatchet as a preliminary to appearing as a mediæval saint with a palm in her hand at the head of a religious procession." "Her charm," he declared, "could be imitated by a barmaid with unlimited pin-money and a row of footlights before her instead of the handles of a beer-machine." Her voice he likened to the *voix céleste* stop, "which, like a sentimental New England villager with an American organ, she keeps always pulled out."

But this was not criticism's general temper. Even Mr Shaw admitted that when the actress was engaged "not in stabbing people with hat-pins, but in the normal straightforward business of acting she could do it completely enough." Then came the great day of Wednesday, 9th December 1896. A grand fête was organised by a Mr Henry Bauer, "to mark the apogee of Mademoiselle Bernhardt's artistic career." This gentleman invited Sarah to sit herself down for an hour or two and, recalling her early struggles and her present triumphs, let the readers of the *Figaro* into her soul-state on the occasion of a ceremony which was to be in every way remarkable. Nothing daunted, the great artist replied "Mais c'est un examen de conscience que vous me demandez, cher ami," and with characteristic aplomb continued: "Et cependant, je n'hésite pas une seconde à vous répondre." The affair was a combination of luncheon and theatrical performance; sonnets specially composed were read by François Coppée, Edmond Haraucourt, André Theuriet, Catulle Mendès and one, inaudibly, by Heredia. And then the great Rostand gave tongue:

En ce temps sans beauté, seule encor tu nous
　restes
Sachant descendre, pâle, un grand escalier clair,
Ceindre un bandeau, porter un lys, brandir un
　fer.
Reine de l'attitude et Princesse des gestes.

En ce temps, sans folie, ardente, tu protestes!
Tu dis des vers. Tu meurs d'amour. Ton vol
　se perd.

Tu tends des bras de rêve, et puis des bras de
　chair.
Et quand Phèdre paraît, nous sommes tous
　incestes.

Avide de souffrir, tu t'ajoutas des cœurs;
Nous avons vu couler—car ils coulent tes
　pleurs!—
Toutes les larmes de nos âmes sur tes joues.

Mais aussi tu sais bien, Sarah, que quelquefois
Tu sens furtivement se poser, quand tu joues,
Les lèvres de Shakespeare aux bagues de tes
　doigts.

Our own Wilson Barrett sent a silver crown with the names of her rôles on the leaves, and Sarah was duly overcome.

But then Sarah could always be overcome at will. It is said that when, many years later, she rehearsed the English of her reply to the address to be publicly presented to her by Sir Herbert Tree, she paused in the middle and said: "Here I shall cry a little." And, on the day, in that place she did cry a little.

There is a strange account of the actress by the Roumanian, de Max, which the curious will not desire that I should omit:

Il y a deux Sarah—au moins. Il y a celle qu'on voit de la salle. Et il y a celle qu'on voit des coulisses. Le malheur est que, des coulisses, on voit quelquefois la même que dans la salle, la plus belle. C'est un malheur, parce que ces jours-là, on n'est plus maître de soi; on arrive avec de la haine, de la fureur. On veut se venger d'elle, et puis on devient spectateur en jouant; quand le rideau se ferme, on lui baise les mains, avec des larmes. . . . Acteur, je connus l'actrice Sarah. Je commus aussi à son Théâtre une petite fille, qui s'appelait, par hasard, Sarah. Ai-je détesté, ai-je aimé cette insupportable petite fille? Je ne sais plus. C'est si loin. J'ai vieilli. Pas elle. C'est toujours une petite fille, une insupportable petite fille, qui a des caprices, des cris, des crises. Ah! les crises de cette petite fille!

And yet this *petite fille* is the artist from whom "speech fell, even as her dress, in great straight folds, fringed with gold." It is the artist with the soul of Clairon's "I am eighty-five; my heart is twenty-five."

It is now a good many years since Madame Sarah, as she likes to be called by people who have a real affection for her, came to lunch at my mother's house at Manchester. My mother managed, throughout her long life, to superimpose upon an outlook not unlike Jane Austen's a great sympathy with all artists. This may have been through her descent from Edward Shuter, the comedian, of whom Doran says that his life was one round of intense professional labour, jollification, thoughtlessness, embarrassment, gay philosophy and addiction to religion as expounded by Whitfield. My mother's grace and wit were, however, entirely her own. She accepted Madame

Sarah's proposal that she should come to lunch graciously and without commotion of spirit. There was some discussion, I remember, as to what ceremonies were to be observed, and what eaten and drunk. We tried to imagine what Charles Lamb would have set before Mrs Siddons. Could we rely upon our guest "counting fish as nothing"? Our old nurse it was who clinched the matter. "I suppose the poor body eats like everyone else," she said, "her stomach will be none the worse for a good warming." There was some question as to who should hand the great lady out of her carriage and help her up the steep slope of the path. It was decided that the gardener, who for many years had performed this office for my mother, should not now be denied. If there had ever been sincerity in Adrienne's passages with the old servitor, she would, we felt, understand. You see we were not unmindful of the fiasco of the seaport Mayor. The story goes that many years ago the great actress was to descend upon a town which boasts of a fine council-chamber, situated at the top of a flight of forty-six steps. Here, when the time came, were to be ensconced the Mayor in his robes, the town clerk, the beadle and other dignitaries. It was up these steps that the great actress was to toil. The train draws in, a state carriage with postillions and outriders is at hand. A huge crowd. A delighted Sarah sets forth, only to catch sight, after a few yards, of the stairway at top of which, perched in his eyrie, Bumble-surrounded, awaits her the Mayor. "Ah, mais non! mais non!" she cries "J'ai assez grimpé dans ma vie! A l'hôtel."

Well, Madame Sarah came, and she came in state. She wore a wonderful mantle of misty grey like the breasts of sea-birds. It was in the first chill of autumn, and I like to think that the bowed trees of the garden bent still lower to touch with the tips of their branches the radiance as it passed. It was a moment or two before the presentations were over; she had brought her granddaughter and a woman friend. And the lunch, of which we could persuade our guest to touch only a quarter of a wing of chicken and some toast fingers dipped in milk. Horribly I found myself thinking of Tilburina and her confidante. But almost at once, to put us at our ease, she began to talk. The smallest of small talk, conventional inquiries as to what we did, a declaration that if my brothers became great men or my sister a great actress, we should not, the whole lot of us, amount to the value of our mother's little finger. About the theatre she would say very little and it was a subject we naturally avoided. I had a feeling that one of us might suddenly, out of sheer nervousness, ask her to recite.

And then, after a time, Sarah fell to talking about actors and acting, and this I take to be the finest politeness I have experienced. First she had some handsome things to say of English players. Of Henry Irving, whom she called a great artist and a bad actor. She admired his temperament, but his oddities, his uncouthness, his queerness of technique perplexed her, and I should certainly not have trusted her to appreciate Benson. Of Forbes-Robertson, whose Hamlet she considered a jewel to be worn on the finger of the poet himself. She talked affectionately of

Coquelin, "ce bon Coquelin," and admiringly of Réjane. A very great comedian she called her, but rather resented my suggestion that she had great tragic gifts. "Non," she replied, "elle a la voix canaille." And then the conversation turned upon her interpretation of a part which she was then playing. This was Lucrecia Borgia, of whom I thought then, and still think, her conception wrong. Her idea of Lucrecia—and in this it must be admitted that she followed Hugo's lead—was of a perfectly good woman with a poisonous kink. She held that even if Lucrecia did entertain a passion for murder she would not show her vice except when viciously engaged. One remembered Charles Peace fiddling between thefts, but without succeeding in thinking this an apt reinforcement for her. One thought, too, of the provincial lady who was accustomed to give a lecture to schoolgirls on the occasion of the annual Shakespearean revisal. Confronted with *Antony and Cleopatra* the lecturer evaded the difficulties of her subject by announcing that she proposed to confine her considerations of the heroine's character to her aspect as a mother. This, again, did not seem a very suitable remark, and frankly, we did not shine.

Actors are always difficult to talk to. They will not realise that all that matters is the impression the spectator actually receives and that he is not influenced by what the actor thinks or hopes he is conveying. If only actors knew how much of the interpreting is done by the spectator and how little by themselves! We experienced, of course, extreme difficulty in putting it to Sarah that what she thought about Lucrecia was of no importance, that it was only what she made us think that mattered. In fact we could not put it at all. We could only say that she turned Lucrecia into a good-natured goose with unaccountable moments. However, she came to the rescue with a happy "Eh bien, je vois que ça ne vous plaît pas. Qu'est-ce qui vous plaît donc?" And we tried to get her to talk about her Pelléas, which is the one perfect thing that not Mademoiselle Mars, not Mademoiselle Clairon, not ten thousand Rachels could ever have accomplished. She had singularly little to say about this, but we put it down to our not having proved ourselves worthy to be talked to. The thing we would most have instilled into our guest was that our admiration was critical. Youthfully we had long settled the order of her parts. First Pelléas, the butt and sea-mark of her utmost sail, then the world-wearied Phèdre; next the Jeanne d'Arc of inviolate ecstasy, and last the Marguerite, patchouli'd, but still incredibly lovely. We wanted her to realise something of this. Well, we failed.

We would have read to her the whole of that passage on art and the artist which I have given in an earlier part of this book. "There!" we would have said. "That's what we think of the actor's art, and of the heights to which only the very few are capable of rising. It's just because art is as fine as all this that you can be so fine." I think we would have lectured her in our young enthusiasm, but for the impossibility of throwing off so tremendous a creed at a moment's notice. "Mais, qu'est-ce qu'ils me chantent, ces enfants?" she would have exclaimed.

She declared that she never read dramatic criticism: "Les critiques ne savent rien." It was then that I wanted to do something violent, to induce in that august head some perception of the discernment of which she had been the object. But she was, I thought, a little like some intolerant goddess bored by her worshippers and disinclined for nice distinctions.

I tried to get her to understand something of the overthrow of my small soul when first I saw her act. It was on an evening in July in the early nineties. From my place in the queue I could see a long poster in mauve and gold, spangled with silver stars. The ineffability was that of Marguerite Gautier. It was not for some years that I was to hear how such a commonplace sentence as "On nous abandonne, et les longues soirées succèdent aux longs jours," could be set to such music that it should vibrate in the memory for ever. I had yet to hear these phrases dropped like stones into some golden well of felicity. The play that evening was *La Tosca.* The wait was long. At the hour of her coming my heart began to beat. I remember as though it were yesterday the opening of the door, the dark, silent theatre, the second long wait, the turning up of the lights, the going up of the curtain, the exquisite tenderness of the opening scene. I remember the setting of the candles round the body of Scarpia, and that is all. I next saw the actress in *Fédora,* and shortly afterwards in *Frou-frou* and **Adrienne Lecouvreur.** *La Dame aux Camélias* followed about 1898. All these were in Manchester; and then came the time when I went to Paris frequently and saw her often. There was always great difficulty in getting a glimpse of her Phèdre. The actress seemed wilfully to prefer rubbish, and both Phèdre and Pelléas were difficult birds to bring down. When, finally, one saw it there was the further difficulty of finding any French critic up to writing adequately about it. Once more I turn up my little hand-book and read again what the late W. T. Arnold wrote forty years ago:

> Could anything have been more deliciously poetical than that kindling eager eye, the hand slowly stretched out, and the finger pointing into space, as Phèdre sees before her half in a dream the chariot "fuyant dans la carrière"? The great Phèdre has hitherto been that of Rachel. It is useless to dilate upon Rachel's tragic power. Her performance alike in the second and in the fourth acts is declared by all competent critics to have been all but perfection. The doubtful question is rather whether she was capable of rendering the tenderness and the infinite piteousness of the hapless woman as she rendered her transports of passion. We can conceive Rachel as having been better than Madame Bernhardt in the denunciation of Œnone, and, indeed, M. Sarcey, in his notice of the performance of *Phèdre* by the Comédie Française intimates that she was so; but we should like to know how Rachel said such passages as this:
>
> Œnone, il peut quitter cet orgueil qui te
>   blesse;
> Nourri dans les forêts, il en a la rudesse.
> Hippolyte, endurci par de sauvages lois,

Entend parler d'amour pour la première fois:
Peut-être sa surprise a causé son silence;
Et nos plaintes peut-être ont trop de violence.

The inexpressible tenderness with which those lines were sighed rather than spoken was all Madame Bernhardt's own. This line again:

> Et l'espoir malgré moi s'est glissé dans mon cœur.

And this, when she has discovered the love of Hippolyte and Aricie, and contrasts their affection with her own guilty passion:

> Tous les jours se levoient clairs et sereins
>   pour eux.

These were the passages Madame Bernhardt marked with the most personal and enduring charm, and in these we cannot believe that she has not surpassed her forerunners.

And then came the time, about 1908, when I was first privileged to write about her. I have written elsewhere all that I ever intend to write What more is there to be said of that quick and frenzied diction, that foam and spate of speech alternating with pools of liquid bliss? What more of those plumbed depths of abasement, those scaled yet unimaginable heights of remorse, that fury of immolation tearing its own flanks as the tiger "rends with those so awful paws the velvet of the breeding hind"? Where earlier actresses have been content with a molten and brassy horror, Bernhardt's passion has taken on the fragrance of bruised violets. None other could suffer as she did. Rachel may have exceeded her in terror; she cannot have surpassed her in inviolacy and immaculacy, in rapt and mystical purity. Bernhardt did not use to die so much as to swoon upon death. "Combien sont morts qui, moins heureux que vous, n'ont pas même donné un seul baiser à leur chimère!" Her beloved Rostand asks the same question:

> Combien,
> Moins heureux, épuisés d'une poursuite vaine,
> Meurent sans avoir vu leur Princesse lointaine.

And Mélissinde replies:

> Combien, aussi, l'ont trop tôt vue, et trop
>   longtemps,
> Et ne meurent qu'après les jours désenchantants!

Yet none of this is true of Bernhardt. She has embraced the glory and the dream. She has measured herself with destiny and touched the lips of her desire. Her acting is now an affair of the spirit, the victory of the incorruptible. For victory it is, victory over the fraying scabbard, victory in the dauntless survival of the soul of steel, the will to persist, *quand même.* One picture springs to the mind. It is the transfiguration of Lear:

> I will do such things—
> What they are, yet I know not; but they shall be
> The terrors of the earth.

Substitute for terrors, wonders; then picture this valiant woman still wresting a last late secret from her art. Can we not see the trust put in us here to read by the spirit those ardours, perils, and adventures which may no longer be expressed save by the spirit? Yet be sure of this, that as no quarter is asked so none will be given. If this acting of to-day mislikes you, you must be prepared to say that at the player's hey-day you had also been displeased; for of genius it is the spirit and not the body which matters. Of this artist all that is left is spirit. She has bent her will to battle with doom and death. She has, to echo Charlotte Brontë, fought every inch of ground, sold every drop of blood, resisted to the latest the rape of every faculty, has *willed* to see, has *willed* to hear, has *willed* to breathe, has *willed* to live up to, within, and even beyond the moment when death to any less fiery spirit had said: "Thus far and no farther!"

Can it not be realised that it was something of all this that we wanted, and failed so lamentably to say? We wanted to tell her that we *knew*. Did she know, I wonder? As she drove away she said something to my mother which we did not hear. The carriage receded and she waved her flowers. There was a look of grave amusement in her eyes, something of the memory and the kinship of youth.

Lytton Strachey   (essay date 1923)

SOURCE: "Sarah Berhardt," in *Characters and Commentaries,* Harcourt, Brace and Company, 1933, pp. 255-60.

[*In the following essay, originally published in 1923, Strachey comments on Bernhardt's natural genius for acting, noting that she did not necessarily understand either great drama or the craft of theatre, but was instead primarily concerned with her extraordinary ability to create and develop memorable characters.*]

There are many paradoxes in the art of acting. One of them—the discrepancy between the real feelings of the actor and those which he represents—was discussed by Diderot in a famous dialogue. Another—the singular divergence between the art of the stage and the art of the drama—was illustrated very completely by the career of Sarah Bernhardt.

It is clear that the primary business of the actor is to interpret the conception of the dramatist; but it is none the less true that, after a certain degree of excellence has been reached, the merits of an actor have no necessary dependence upon his grasp of the dramatist's meaning. To be a moderately good actor one must understand, more or less, what one's author is up to; but the achievements of Sarah Bernhardt proved conclusively that it was possible to be a very good actor indeed without having the faintest notion, not only of the intentions of particular dramatists, but of the very rudiments of the dramatic art.

No one who saw her in *Hamlet* or in *Lorenzaccio* could doubt that this was so. Her *Hamlet* was a fantastic absur-

dity which far, far surpassed the permitted limits even of a Gallic miscomprehension of "le grand Will." But perhaps even more remarkable was her treatment of *Lorenzaccio. Hamlet,* after all, from every point of view, is an extremely difficult play; but the main drift of Musset's admirable tragedy is as plain as a pikestaff. It is a study in disillusionment—the disillusionment of a tyrannicide, who finds that the assassination, which he has contrived and executed with infinite hazard, skill, and difficulty, has merely resulted in a state of affairs even worse than before. Sarah Bernhardt, incredible as it may seem, brought down the final curtain on the murder of the tyrant, and thus made the play, as a play, absolutely pointless. What remained was a series of exciting scenes, strung together by the vivid and penetrating art of a marvellous actress. For art it was, and not mere posturing. Nothing could be further from the truth than to suppose that the great Frenchwoman belonged to that futile tribe of empty-headed impersonators, who, since Irving, have been the particular affliction of the English stage. Dazzling divinity though she was, she was also a serious, a laborious worker, incessantly occupied—not with expensive stage properties, elaborate make-up, and historically accurate scenery—but simply with acting. Sir Herbert Tree was ineffective because he neither knew nor cared how to act; he was content to be a clever entertainer. But Sarah Bernhardt's weakness, if weakness it can be called, arose from a precisely contrary reason—from the very plenitude of her power over all the resources of her craft—a mastery over her medium of so over-whelming a kind as to become an obsession.

The result was that this extraordinary genius was really to be seen at her most characteristic in plays of inferior quality. They gave her what she wanted. She did not want—she did not understand—great drama; what she did want were opportunities for acting; and this was the combination which the *Toscas,* the *Camélias,* and the rest of them, so happily provided. In them the whole of her enormous virtuosity in the representation of passion had full play; she could contrive thrill after thrill, she could seize and tear the nerves of her audience, she could touch, she could terrify, to the very top of her astonishing bent. In them, above all, she could ply her personality to the utmost. All acting must be, to some extent, an exploitation of the personality; but in the acting of Sarah Bernhardt that was the dominating quality—the fundamental element of her art. It was there that her strength, and her weakness, lay. During her best years, her personality remained an artistic instrument; but eventually it became too much for her. It absorbed both herself and her audience; the artist became submerged in the divinity; and what was genuine, courageous, and original in her character was lost sight of in oceans of highly advertised and quite indiscriminate applause.

This, no doubt, was partly due to the age she lived in. It is odd but certainly true that the eighteenth century would have been profoundly shocked by the actress who reigned supreme over the nineteenth. The gay and cynical creatures of the *ancien régime,* who tittered over *La Pucelle,* and whose adventures were reflected without exaggeration in the pages of *Les Liaisons Dangereuses,* would have recoiled in horror before what they would have called the "indécence" of one of Sarah Bernhardt's ordinary scenes. Every age has its own way of dealing with these matters; and the nineteenth century made up for the high tone of its literature and the decorum of its behaviour by the luscious intensity of its theatrical displays. Strict husbands in icy shirt-fronts and lovely epitomes of all the domestic virtues in bustles would sit for hours thrilling with frenzied raptures over intimate and elaborate presentments of passion in its most feverish forms. The supply and the demand, interacting upon one another, grew together. But by the end of the century the fashion had begun to change. The star of Eleonora Duse rose upon the horizon; Ibsen became almost popular; the Théâtre Antoine, the Moscow Art Theatre, introduced a new style of tragic acting—a prose style—surprisingly effective and surprisingly quiet, and subtle with the sinuosities of actual life. Already by the beginning of the twentieth century the bravura of Sarah Bernhardt seemed a magnificent relic of the past. And the generation which was to plunge with reckless fanaticism into the gigantic delirium of the war found its pleasures at the theatre in a meticulous imitation of the significant trivialities of middle-class interiors.

Fortunately, however, Sarah Bernhardt's genius did not spend itself entirely in amazing personal triumphs and the satisfaction of the emotional needs of a particular age. Fortunately the mightier genius of Jean Racine was of such a nature that it was able to lift hers on to its own level of the immortal and the universal. In this case there was no need on her part for an intellectual realisation of the dramatist's purpose; Racine had enough intellect for both; all that she had to do was to play the parts he had provided for her to the height of her ability; his supreme art did the rest. Her Hermione was a masterpiece; but certainly the greatest of all her achievements was in *Phèdre.* Tragedy possesses an extraordinary quality, which, perhaps, has given it its traditional place of primacy among all the forms of literature. It is not only immortal; it is also for ever new. There are infinite implications in it which reveal themselves by a mysterious law to each succeeding generation. The *Oedipus* acted yesterday at Cambridge was the identical play that won the prize two thousand years ago; and yet it was a different *Oedipus,* with meanings for the modern audience which were unperceived by the Athenians. The records show conclusively that the Phèdre of Bernhardt differed as much from that of Rachel as Rachel's differed from Clairon's, and as Clairon's differed from that of the great actress who created the part under the eyes of Racine. But each was Phèdre. Probably the latest of these interpretations was less perfect in all its parts than some of its predecessors; but the great moments, when they came, could never have been surpassed. All through there were details of such wonderful beauty that they return again and again upon the memory—unforgettable delights. The hurried horror of

Mes yeux le retrouvaient dans les traits de son père;

the slow, expanding, mysterious grandeur of

Le ciel, tout l'univers, est plein de mes aïeux;

the marvellous gesture with which the words of Oenone, announcing the approach of Thésée, seemed to be pressed back into silence down her "ill-uttering throat"—such things, and a hundred others, could only have been conceived and executed by a consummate artist in her happiest vein. But undoubtedly the topmost reach came in the fourth act, when the Queen, her reason tottering with passion and jealousy, suddenly turns upon herself in an agony of self-reproach. Sarah Bernhardt's treatment of this passage was extremely original, and it is difficult to believe that it was altogether justified by the text. Racine's words seem to import a violent directness of statement:

Chaque mot sur mon front fait dresser mes cheveux;

but it was with hysteric irony, with dreadful, mocking laughter, that the actress delivered them. The effect was absolutely overwhelming, and Racine himself could only have bowed to the ground before such a triumphant audacity. Then there followed the invocation to Minos, culminating in the stupendous

Je crois voir de ta main tomber l'urne terrible.

The secret of that astounding utterance baffles the imagination. The words boomed and crashed with a superhuman resonance which shook the spirit of the hearer like a leaf in the wind. The *voix d'or* has often been raved over; but in Sarah Bernhardt's voice there was more than gold: there was thunder and lightning; there was Heaven and Hell. But the pitcher is broken at the fountain; that voice is silent now for ever, and the Terror and the Pity that lived in it and purged the souls of mortals have faded into incommunicable dreams.

James Agate (essay date 1923)

SOURCE: "Sarah Bernhardt," in *Fantasies and Impromptus,* E. P. Dutton & Company, 1923, pp. 33-52.

[*In the following essay, Agate offers a critical assessment of Bernhardt's body of work on the occasion of her death.*]

I

For some whose business it is to write of the theatre it is as though Beauty had veiled her face; so determinate, so utterly beyond repair is the sense of loss. It is not that the stock of loveliness is diminished for a time, as the blossoming earth is subdued by winter: there will be other flowers, but the rose is gone for ever. Those who would charge me here with phrase-making can have known nothing of Bernhardt; she can have meant little to them, and their praise was lip-service. To them such a line as—

Elle avait un petit diadème en dentelle
    d'argent

brings up no picture the like of which they will not see again; for them *Ruy Blas* can find other Queens, and to spare. Our worlds are different, that is all; those who have not known our ecstasy cannot know our loss. Beauty, in her remainder catalogue, has nothing by which Bernhardt can be measured or imagined.

Even so, I hear it objected that this great actress has been dead, in all that matters, these twenty, thirty years; that she outlived even the memory of her splendours. They would have her dead whose old age and infirmity hurt them so. A writer in the *Manchester Guardian* shows a finer temper: "Latterly she had not been able to realise her heroines for those whose test is realism. Yet the fragments of her art have been more stimulative than others' perfections." To know not only bravery in the maimed presentment but also the imperishable soul of beauty, to recognise the heart bound with triple brass, the spirit scorning an end in sandy deltas—this, the pain of others, was our privilege. I say without hyperbole that, for those to whom the art of Sarah Bernhardt was their most intimate communion with Beauty, her bodily passing leaves a gap in Nature.

I could never have believed that a Requiem Mass at Westminster Cathedral could have been so little impressive. The stage was set at least as magnificently as Irving's church scenes in *Becket* and *Much Ado;* the eye was rested by the humility of brickwork raised to grandeur by its ordering, offended only by the scalloped edging of the giant crucifix. The cathedral seemed to wait for some more imposing celebrant, for Sarah herself, and then one asked oneself, curiously, what the great actress had to do with that company of dingy saints—Simon and Thaddeus, Linus, Clitus, Clement, Xystus, Cornelius, Cyprian, Lawrence and Chrysogonus. *Ces gens-là ne sont pas son affaire!* One had read something of the fortitude of those last hours. How little of Sarah was conveyed by that mediæval wail of the "guilty, suppliant, and groaning!" God's creatures do most honour to God when they face Death with as high a heart as they faced Life. This Bernhardt did. If there is a Heaven, then it is not groaning and suppliant that she comes, but as a warrior carving rightful entry like the good man in Bunyan, giving and receiving many wounds.

II

This essay is a critical look round, a note of what our cleverest have said in the past, and stressed recently; a suggestion of where, as an actress, Bernhardt may finally be placed.

In Mr. Desmond MacCarthy's judgment, the best criticism of Sarah Bernhardt, and the finest tribute to her in English, are to be found in Mr. Maurice Baring's *Puppet Show of Memory.* The most perverse, as also the most stupid criticism emanated from the self-sufficiency of Mr. Shaw. "She was not an author's actress. The only character she gave to the stage was her own." Judging from the whole article I assume that this is meant to be

derogatory. In that Shaw is wrong, for to be an author's actress is inevitably to be second-rate. It is only the actor of the domitable personality who changes his mode of being as he would his shift. The fact that Ristori could so alter her features, walk and voice, that it was impossible to believe the Mary Stuart of one night could have been acted by the same woman who played Elizabeth the next, marks her as strictly second-rate. The same applies to Coquelin, whose Cyrano and M. Jourdain were never credibly made out of the same flesh. Or shall I put it that the Ristoris and the Coquelins are the first-rate actors, and that those who put their indomitable selves upon the stage are, strictly speaking, not actors at all? Irving was always Irving; upon that we are all agreed. Bernhardt, says Mr. Shaw, was always Bernhardt. Agreed again; that is her glory. Will Mr. Shaw affirm that Mrs. Campbell was ever anybody except Mrs. Pat? I have the greatest admiration for the genius of that lady—the only actress on the English stage possessing something more than talent—and yet confess that I never saw a pin's weight of difference between her Paula, Hedda, Magda, Agnes. She was always the same glorious Stella Patrick Campbell in circumstances of differing wretchedness. Did she, on this account, fail to be Ibsen's, Sudermann's, Pinero's actress? Yes, and the greater player she. But I do not remember that Mr. Shaw ever made complaint on this score. Can it be that "Joey's" passion put out the eyes of "G. B. S."? As Mrs. Campbell, so Bernhardt, and so, too, Duse. No violence to play or author has ever been too great for the Italian actress, who would have bestowed her own quality of irony, resignation and dignity upon a leg of mutton. When Duse played Marguerite Gautier, a farded courtesan, she persisted in her refusal to make-up and insisted upon her own grey hair. As though Dumas's Armand, Varville, Saint-Gaudens—none of whom exhibits so much as a *souteneur's* intelligence—would have lost their little of heart and wit to so grave and distinguished a monitress, an Egeria, as Sir Arthur Pinero would put it, a trifle "dusty at the hem." Hear what Lemaître says of Duse's Marguerite.

> Elle en fait dès le début une douce et tendre amoureuse, à qui elle prête l'aspect, comment dire? . . . d'une grisette extrêmement distinguée et un peu préraphaélite, d'une grisette de Botticelli. On ne se la figure pas un instant riant faux dans les soupers, allumant les hommes, s'appliquant à leur manger beaucoup d'argent, ni faisant aucune des choses qui concernent son état. Presque tout de suite, sans combat préalable, sans défiance, sans étonnement de se sentir prise, et prise de cette façon-la, elle donne son cœur à Armand. Elle a même trouvé pour cela un beau geste symbolique, un geste adorable d'oblation religieuse, que Dumas fils n'avait certainement pas prévu. Bref, elle joue les deux premiers actes délicieusement, mais comme elle jouerait Juliette ou Françoise de Rimini: elle est, comme Françoise et comme Juliette, "sans profession"; elle est la Duse amoureuse; et voilà tout.

A "Duse amoureuse" is all for Mr. Shaw's delight. How would he not have inveighed against a Marguerite who was nothing but "Sarah amoureuse"! In the Italian text the story of the courtesan is softened. There is no more question of prostitution. "Ce n'est plus que l'aventure très touchante de deux amants très malheureux, séparés on ne sait plus bien par quoi. . . ." Some members of the Paris audience took this Marguerite "pour une pensionnaire grondée par un vieux monsieur très imposant." The character, as played by Duse, had nothing to do with Dumas's *cocotte*. Her Adrienne Lecouvreur had as little to do with Scribe's heroine. Both were pure Eleonora Duse. But we do not find Mr. Shaw objecting against this artist that she is not an author's actress.

Bernhardt, Mr. Shaw goes on, "found something in Maeterlinck that jumped with her fancies and made her touch me by her Pelléas as she never touched me in any other part." To put it that way is the very venom of prejudice. As well say that something in d'Annunzio jumped with Duse's fancies so that her Gioconda, etc., etc. No, Mr. Shaw has reached an unripe old age without realising that the great actors are those who count greatness in the number of facets which a single personality can show.

Duse's supreme distinction, says Mr. Arthur Symons, "comes from the kind of melancholy wisdom which remains in her face after the passions have swept over it. Other actresses seem to have heaped up into one great, fictitious moment all the scattered energies of their lives, the passions that have come to nothing, the sensations that have withered before they flowered, the thoughts that have never quite been born. The stage is their life; they live only for those three hours of the night; before and after are the intervals between the acts. But to Duse those three hours are the interval in an intense, consistent, strictly personal life; and, the interval over, she returns to herself, as after an interruption." But great acting is more than an interruption, and that which I have just quoted seems to me only a pretty way of saying that Duse is a greater artist off the stage than on.

Let us thrash out this matter. Duse's greatest moments, Mr. Symons also tell us, are the moments when she does least. He admits that "she does not send a shudder through the whole house, as Sarah Bernhardt does, playing on one's nerves as on a violin." The very expression of emotion with Duse is "the quieting down of a tumult until only the pained reflection of it glimmers out of her eyes, and trembles among the hollows of her cheeks." But should not great acting be more than a melancholy residuum, a banking of fires and hollow, trembling cheeks? To my mind Bernhardt made it more.

But I must return to Mr. Shaw. "When I first saw Sarah, forty years ago, she had strength and temper enough to make a super-tigress of Doña Sol in *Hernani* for an unforgettable moment in the last act; and although this feat reappeared later on as a mechanical rant introduced *à tort et à travers* to bring down the house once in every play it was very astonishing at first." This is unoriginal nonsense. To rant is to make a noise without suggestion of a reserve of power, and Sarah's apparent reserve was very

great. Her *justness* of emotion was equally remarkable; it was the most French of her qualities. She did nothing *à tort et à travers,* and the fact that once in each evening she let off steam simply means that those who wrote her plays took care to provide at least one such opportunity. But to say that she opened the valves without reason is untrue. "She had some natural disadvantages to struggle against; the famous *voix d'or* was produced by intoning like an effeminate Oxford curate; and its monotony was aggravated by an unvarying mask of artificial sweetness, which would have been exasperating in a ballet dancer; yet she forced the public to accept both these faults as qualities." Mr. Shaw will not force me to accept his estimate of Bernhardt as anything except a gap in his sensibility.

The Press as a whole acquitted itself badly in its obituary columns. Alone Mr. Lytton Strachey was exquisite. Mr. Arthur Symons, Mr. Max Beerbohm, Mr. Montague were silent; Mr. William Archer was sober and judicial; Mr. Walkley, if, indeed, it was he who wrote in the *Times*—a matter of which one cannot be sure since that paper's relapse into anonymity—was faintly facetious. Ignoring alike her Marguerite Gautier and her Pelléas, the *Times* memorialist re-hashed a good deal of the old nonsense about coffins, horsewhippings, black-whiskered Brazilians and alligators killed by champagne. Mr. Archer did better; at least he declared his position in the famous Bernhardt-Duse controversy. "Bernhardt's finest period as an actress lay between the years 1875 and 1885. She had then attained full artistic maturity, and had not yet coarsened her talent by the reckless overwork of her European and American tours. During her last years at the Théâtre Français she was certainly an exquisite creature. In such parts as Doña Sol in *Hernani,* the Queen in *Ruy Blas,* Berthe in *La Fille de Roland,* Mrs. Clarkson in *L'Etrangère,* and another Berthe in *Le Sphinx,* her lithe and slender figure and her insinuating, caressing voice produced an unforgettable effect. Her diction was always consummate, and though she lacked the physical resources to carry her to the utmost heights of such a character as Racine's Phèdre, her rendering of most of the scenes, and especially of the opening passages of languorous and hectic despair, was the perfection of purely poetic acting. Here, and in all characters demanding tragic elevation, she was far superior to her great rival Eleonora Duse; but in modern parts the Italian's sincerity and depth of passion produced effects unattainable by the more factitious art of the Frenchwoman. At the same time there can be no doubt that Sarah Bernhardt's range was much wider than Duse's. If Duse carried the palm (as in my judgment she certainly did) in such parts as *La Dame aux Camélias, Magda,* and *La Femme de Claude,* she was distinctly inferior to Sarah Bernhardt not only in tragic parts but in those characters of frenzied, nervous excitability, such as Fédora, which Sardou manufactured for world-wide exportation." This is worthy of respect.

And then the contradictions! Throughout Sarah's career these were never conspicuously lacking. One great critic calls her Hamlet merely lady-like; Mr. Baring says that it was "one of the four greatest achievements of her career"; and that, "with the exception of Forbes Robertson's Hamlet, it was the only intelligible Hamlet of our time." Mr. Baring's criticism is detailed and elaborate, and I quote only one passage here.

> Perhaps the most poignant scene of all, and what is the most poignant scene in the play, if it is well played, was the conversation with Horatio, just before the final duel when Hamlet says: "If it be not to come, it will be now." Sarah charged these words with a sense of doom, with the set courage that faces doom, and with the underlying certainty of doom in spite of the courage that is there to meet it. It made one's blood run cold.

As, I presume, a merely lady-like performance would not have done.

The *Times* writer, forbearing comment, says simply that Sarah gave us the chance of seeing her as Hamlet himself—"a weak and violent prince, whose character she thought 'perfectly simple.'"

"What is there to add?" he asks, looking round to see which of her parts he has not mentioned. And remains blind to Pelléas.

It is significant that these full-dress accounts of Sarah give no hint of the quality or qualities which differentiated her from all other actresses. They teem with inessentials; the portraits bring her before us as little as the mere statement of her age gives the sense of time. Perhaps there is no direct method, and we must go to the artist rather than the journalist for some sidelight that shall bring truth. Some glint of what Sarah was comes to me in an article written by Mr. Max Beerbohm in the *Saturday Review* twenty years ago.

> Year by year, when she comes among us, my wonder and awe are intensified. Seeing her, a few nights ago, in *La Sorcière,* I was more than ever moved by the apparition. The great Sarah—preeminently great throughout the past four decades! My imagination roved back to lose itself in the golden haze of the Second Empire. My imagination roved back to reel at the number of plays that had been written, the number of players whose stars had risen and set, the number of theatres that had been built and theatres that had been demolished, since Sarah's début. The theatrical history of more than forty years lay strewn in the train of that bowing and bright-eyed lady. The applause of innumerable thousands of men and women, now laid in their graves, was still echoing around her. And still she was bowing, bright-eyed, to fresh applause. The time would come when our noisy hands would be folded and immobile for ever. But, though we should be beneath the grass, Sarah would still be behind the footlights—be bowing, as graciously as ever, to audiences recruited from the ranks of those who are now babes unborn. A marvellous woman! For all the gamut of her experience, she is still lightly triumphant over time.

All this has been to her, as to Mona Lisa, but as the sound of lyres and flutes, and lives only in the delicacy with which it has moulded the changing lineaments, and tinged the hair. Hers is the head upon which all the ends of the world are come, and the eyelids are not at all weary. . . .

Two decades were to pass, and still Sarah was to remain preeminently great. And now it is she whose hands are folded and immobile for ever, whose eyelids are closed against the possibility of weariness. For me the genius of this passage lies in the reiterant "bowing and bright-eyed lady." There was that in her acceptance of welcome and tribute which was more exquisite than whole acts of other players.

Just as I find in the carefully moulded periods of this meticulous artist a sense of Sarah's will to conquer not only our hearts but Time itself, so in the phrase of one who is not a professional writer I get the best glimpse of what Sarah looked like. Ellen Terry's "like a cloud, only not so thick"—gives what whole volumes have failed to say. There is something more, which I forget, about azaleas and smoke from a burning piece of twisted paper; the cloud simile is the essential Sarah. To the end she could lean back in her carriage bedizened like Mrs. Skewton, her eyes two burned-out holes of lamp-black in a dead face, and remain the embodiment and parade of loveliness. This was Sarah *quand-même.*

Let me quote a "great moment" by Mr. Desmond MacCarthy. "When Hamlet runs his sword through the arras and, hearing a body fall, thinks he has accidentally killed the king, she stood suddenly tiptoe, like a great black exclamation mark, her sword glittering above her head, and a cry, 'C'est le Roi!' rang in our ears, so expressive of final triumph and relief, that for a tingling second it seemed the play itself must be over."

Here the quintessential Bernhardt stands before me, and satisfies the mind's eye.

It is become a commonplace that in physical resources her immediate predecessor was superior to Bernhardt. So much has been written about Rachel's tragic power that I have the uneasy suspicion that she may not altogether have lacked the Kemble fudge. Was she, I wonder, something like our own Siddons, with a dash of Ada Crossley in *The Messiah?* Yet Rachel is always supposed to have been the only actress who ever coped successfully with those frenzied sixty lines ending with the wrenching of the sword from Hippolyte.

> Voilà mon cœur: c'est là que ta main doit
>   frapper,
> Impatient déjà d'expier son offense,
> Au-devant de ton bras je le sens qui s'avance.
> Frappe, ou si tu le crois indigne de tes coups,
> Si ta haine m'envie un supplice si doux,
> Ou si d'un sang trop vil, ta main serait
>   trempée,
> Au défaut de ton bras prête-moi ton épée;
> Donne.

The great Clairon frankly confessed that she could never deliver this passage to her satisfaction. The difficulty, of course, is to attain the human passion and preserve the classic grandeur. Rachel may have achieved this; Sarah threw compromise, and Racine, and classic grandeur, and the Théâtre Français overboard, and played the woman as though she were of our own day. But her frenzy and feverishness were of the spirit as well as of the body. And I cannot believe that any actress can ever have surpassed the pathos of her Phèdre. Let us grant, however, that Rachel was greater than Bernhardt in purely classic tragedy. And, if you like, that Duse outdid her in modern "sincerity." But there were two "lines" of Sarah's which, I am persuaded, Rachel could never have approached, and in which Duse, I am certain, failed. One was romantic rubbish, the other pure poetry. Quite how Rachel would have tackled Sardou and his kind we cannot know; it is improbable that she could have given us the tender banter of the church scene in *La Tosca*. In *Fédora* Duse found nothing that she could act; in the rôle of Cleopatra she peak'd and pined. I saw her in **Adrienne Lecouvreur** and, as I have said elsewhere, in that one performance Sarah took full revenge. Duse is a greater artist than she is actress; her talent must be deemed less than supreme in that it needs masterpieces to feed on. She is not one of those great players who, in Stendhal's phrase, "donnent un sens charmant à ce qui n'en a pas." Duse has not the power to recreate at the bidding of Sardou's fustian the spirit of the Middle Ages and the Renaissance, in the delineation of pasteboard heroics to bring before us Byzantium and Rome. Half the function of the great player is to make bricks without straw. Sarah did this, and the mortar between the layers was of molten gold.

In poetry be sure Bernhardt had no peer. Note how even Mr. Shaw puts his finger on her Pelléas, though, as we have seen, he would meanly minimise the passion for beauty by that nonsense about jumping with her fancies. How, in this part, can Sarah not have been Maeterlinck's actress? I remember one scene in particular—a tower in Golaud's castle, and the roadway beneath. At the window Mélisande is combing her hair and chanting. The words are:

PELLEAS. Holà! Holà! ho!

MELISANDE. Qui est là?

PELLEAS. Moi, moi, et moi! Que fais-tu là à la fenêtre en chantant comme un oiseau qui n'est pas d'ici?

It is not possible that anything lovelier was ever heard than that cry from the wings, "Holà! Holà! ho!" or that happiness can ever again so flood the spirit as it did with that onrushing "Moi, moi, et moi!" The whole performance was in a key of beauty as if not of this earth, of ecstasy like that of a child singing. Mark how all reputable critics proclaim Sarah to have excelled in those parts where verisimilitude was of the least value. To see Pelléas raise that face to Mélisande and bathe and drown in those black tresses, to behold the passion of Jeanne d'Arc burn like a flame swaying in the wind, to gaze

upon rapt inviolacy, pity and ruth—this was to know the most shining facet of a supreme artist. To sum up, consider this: that in classic drama Bernhardt ranked next to Rachel, that in modern, realistic plays she was within measurable distance of Duse. In romantic rubbish, which she galvanised into semblance of life by personality alone, she was admittedly unrivalled; in pure poetry she achieved heights which no other actress has even begun to scale. In other words, whatever Rachel and Duse could do Sarah did almost as well; that which she did supremely they could not attempt. There is no question of other rivalry. Take Bernhardt for all in all, it is, in my humble opinion, rank nonsense to pretend that the world has ever looked upon her like.

III

If I were asked to name my most exquisite recollection of Sarah, I think I should choose that moment in *La Dame aux Camélias* when the dying Marguerite, kneeling on the sofa and looking up at Armand, would say, "Tu ne sais pas? Nichette se marie. Elle épouse Gustave ce matin. Nous la verrons. Cela nous fera du bien d'entrer dans une église, de prier Dieu et d'assister au bonheur des autres." The joy which she used to put into that "Nichette se ma-rr-ie!" cut the heart to ribbons. They say that Duse's Marguerite died among her pillows—a wistful little creature blotted in the folds of the huge bed, pathetically withdrawn from the world and into her frail, wan self. It must be confessed that Sarah's choice in parting was more spectacular. Once I saw Marguerite die seated on the sofa, her mouth laid on Armand's and her arms round his neck. You could see nothing save the tangled mop of red hair and the exquisite hands. Marguerite's last words had been "Ah! que je me sens bien!" You might have thought her asleep. And then the handkerchief which she carried fell from her hand. I never saw Sarah die in that exquisite way again.

I remember a performance in London of *La Tosca*. The actress was grown too old to care about jumping into the Tiber, and it was arranged that the platoon of soldiers which had shot Cavaradossi should shoot her too. But on this occasion something went wrong. No soldiers appeared, and the curtain came down upon a Sarah baulked of her agonising. And then from behind the curtain proceeded not, as Mr. Symons has put it, an obscure sensation of peril such as one feels when the lioness leaps into the cage, but a sense of very real danger, and a commotion like that of a hundred forest-bred in conclave. The curtain drew up and Sarah was discovered in a fury the like of which cannot be described, beating her breast, lashing her flanks and roaring with open mouth: "Mais tuez-moi donc! Tuez-moi! Tuez-moi!" And, sheepishly, the platoon appeared, lined up, and killed her.

IV

It was on my eleventh birthday that I first saw Sarah Bernhardt. I remember how small yet how important I felt as I jostled the grown-ups in the pit queue. I remember the exact shape and colour of the sunset on that hot September evening, how it changed from blood-red to mauve, and a single star came out. I remember that the poster on the theatre wall showed a delicate lady in a dress of the same mauve posing wistfully against a background of white camellias and silver stars. I remember the long wait in the dingy theatre, the growing tension, the blood which seemed to bubble in my temples, the fever-heat of expectancy. And then Sarah came. At once, by her mere aspect, she opened the door to a world hitherto unknown. Consider that up till then all that I knew was Manchester, its mean, bowler-hatted men of business and their dolman-swathed, grotesquely-bonneted wives. Here was a creature half sylph, half rainbow. I believe that I cried "Oh!" and I know that I waited for her to speak in a state of overthrow not far removed from anguish. The applause stopped. La Tosca had begun that long, teasing colloquy, and I knew that just as my eyes had never before beheld vision so strangely troubling, so my ears were drinking in sounds the like of which I had never heard. It is a little difficult to disentangle what I thought then from what I have thought since. I can only say that when, later, I was to read such lines as

> . . . thy body packed with sweet
> Of all the world, that cup of brimming June,
> That jar of violet wine set in the air,
> That palest rose set in the night of life,

to listen to the ache in Wagner's *Tristan and Isolda,* or to marvel before the glory of Shakespeare's *Antony and Cleopatra*—I can only say that these experiences had all been forestalled. Let me admit that Bernhardt is but one page in the never-ending book of beauty, yet declare that I have known none more shining. Her acting on that evening unveiled for me the ecstasy of the body and the torture of the mind. My small world had not up till then held cause for pity like this poor lady. For days after I was unhappy, not because of Tosca, but because the play was over, and the world had become empty.

It was many years later that I came to know Sarah. She had lived down old legends then. Emperors, they once said, waited upon her, and Popes failed of an audience. Her chariot was horsed by captive kings. She loosed none too tame cheetahs upon unwelcome visitors . . . Of all this I saw nothing. The actress whom I knew was an old lady of infinite dignity. I used to watch her give lessons on the stage of her Paris theatre to pupils who were either artists of repute or humble students. Those who had no capacity were dismissed with a gracious smile; upon such as showed a vestige of talent Sarah would bestow first a scolding and then an infinity of pains. To the younger pupils she was a veritable Mother Superior, and often the theatre took on the aspect of a convent. I remember Sarah, on her seventieth birthday, seated over the fire in my mother's drawing-room, telling stories and in manner and spirit as young and fresh and radiant as a girl of twenty. I remember her now as she left, gathering round her that mantle of misty grey and filling the October garden with a seabird's splendour. I remember the look of affection

which she threw to my mother as the carriage rolled away. I remember how we gazed after it, and that presently, from the window, a bunch of flowers was waved.

That this great figure who has stirred all my life should, in delirium at the end, recite passages from the plays in which I first saw her, moves me as for many years I have not been moved. Even now, as I think of that flower-filled room, still figure and quiet face, of that rosewood coffin and gold mountings, it seems to me more bearable to reflect not upon the pathos of transcendent glory and imperishable fame, but upon my childish wonder and that vision which forty years have not dimmed.

Maurice Baring (essay date 1923)

SOURCE: "Sarah Bernhardt," "Sarah Bernhardt in Phedre," and "Pelleas and Melisande," in *Punch and Judy & Other Essays,* Doubleday, Page & Company, 1923, pp. 25-42; 322-6

[*In the following essay, Baring provides an overview of Bernhardt's career.*]

I

"Sans doute il est trop tard pour parler encor d'elle." So Alfred de Musset began his beautiful poem to La Malibran, in which he said almost all there is to be said about the death of one of the queens of the stage. Only, in the case of La Malibran, the world's regret, which found so lovely an echo in the song of the poet, was all the more poignant because La Malibran died in the flower of her youth.

Sarah Bernhardt, according to standards which we should apply to any one else, was an old woman when she died; old, and full of glory, "having seen, borne, and achieved more than most men on record," and yet when the news of her death flashed through the world it seemed an incredible thing, and the blackness and the void that the disappearance of her presence left behind were felt by the whole world. The world seemed a duller and a greyer place without her:

> She, she is dead; she's dead: when thou knowst this,
> Thou knowst how wan a ghost this our world is.

That was the feeling we had when the news of her death came. It came with the shock, as of something living, vital, and actual leaving us, and not as the final vibration of an echo of the past. For Sarah Bernhardt never grew old. She remained young because her spirit was able to serve the novitiate which, La Rochefoucauld tells us, awaits the human being at every stage of his life, and she was ready at each revolution to face the possibilities of the new phase. So that death caught her acting for the cinematograph.

Many years ago, in 1882, after her first performance of Sardou's *Fédora,* Jules Lemaître, bidding her farewell as she was starting for America, in one of the most graceful tributes to her genius ever written, advised her, when she was weary of travel, adventure, and struggle, to come back and find a final home at the Théâtre français and to rest in the admiration and sympathy of "ce bon peuple Parisien," who, he said, would forgive her anything, as it owed her some of its greatest pleasures. And then, he added: "Un beau soir, mourez sur la scène subitement, dans un grand cri tragique, car la vieillesse serait trop dure pour vous." No doubt he was right, if he thought of Sarah retiring, as others have done, to some quiet suburb, living in the company of a parrot and an old servant, and weeping over old Press cuttings, a living ghost, and only a name to the present generation. Only that was just what did not and what could not happen. Although she had lost a leg, and though she was over seventy, she was still finding new things to do, and things which she, and she only, could do, and till the hour of her death she continued to adjust new means to a fresh end, and never gave the world the chance of saying "What a pity!"

Indeed, one of the triumphs of her career was the twelve performances she gave of *Athalie* after the war, for one of which all the theatres of Paris closed to give the whole theatrical profession the chance of witnessing this example of her incomparable art.

II

What remains of it all? What idea will future generations have of the art and the power of Sarah Bernhardt? What will they believe? Will they just think of her as an old-fashioned catchword brandished to check the enthusiasm of the young as they swing their censers to a new idol? No, she will be more than that: the very photographs that exist of her, from her early days at the Comédie française, when she was as slender as a sylph, and a puff of wind seemed sufficient to blow her away, until the other day, when she embodied the sumptuous malignity of Athalie, bear witness to the feline grace, the exotic poetry, the electric power, the enigmatic expression, the strange splendour, as baffling to analysis as the scent of an aromatic herb, that emanated from her personality.

I believe there are cinematograph films which reveal at least some of the most telling of her gestures, some of the most poignant of her silences, and I used myself to have a gramophone record which held a poor ghost of her voice; but all that is nothing, for Sarah Bernhardt's art was a complex whole, a combination of rhythmical movement, gesture, look, speech, hands, hair, body, and spirit; and those who never saw her will only be able to guess at it, but it will be one of the beautiful and permanent guesses of mankind; one of the lasting dreams of poets, one of the most magical speculations of artists and of all smokers of "enchanted cigarettes," like the charm of Cleopatra, the voice of the masters of the *bel canto*, the colours of Greek paintings and the melodies of Greek music. The record of her struggles, her efforts, her achievements, and her triumphs, exists in full and analytical detail. We can find it in the collected writings of Sarcey, Jules Lemaître, T. T. Weiss, and in the articles of

Jacques de Tillet, Faguet, and others. I have lately been reading a number of the articles that Sarcey wrote on the various plays in which Sarah Bernhardt appeared, from the outset of her career, and I feel as if I had been watching the long and crowded panorama of her artistic destiny.

It was a difficult career from the start. She did not want to be an actress. She once told me herself, that her ambition had been to be a painter, but since she was forced to go on the stage she decided that if she had to be an actress, she would be the first. *Aut Cæsar, aut nullus.* There should be no question about it. I enjoyed her friendship for many years, and that was one of the few remarks I ever heard her make on the subject of acting or the stage. She never theorised about her parts, or the plays she acted in. They were to her, I think, so much plastic material that she kneaded and moulded and shaped with all the skill and force at her command. In kneading them she was guided by instinct, and she made herself perfect in execution by unremitting, relentless practice.

When, as a little girl, she was taken by her mother to face the entrance examination for the Conservatoire before a jury headed by Auber, she recited, instead of a tirade from Corneille or Racine, La Fontaine's Fable, "Les Deux Pigeons" (just as Trilby sang, "Au clair de la Lune").

Scarcely had the lines, so says a contemporary record,

> Deux pigeons s'aimaient d'amour tendre,
> L'un d'eux s'ennuyant au logis,

passed her lips, when Auber interrupted her, spoke to her and told her she was admitted. The story has often been told, but it has always struck me that the recitation of those two lines probably contained, as in a microcosm, the whole of Sarah Bernhardt's genius, just as in some early lines of a poet written in the April of his genius you sometimes find the blossom that foretells the whole majesty and all the golden fruits of the tree. Such a poem is the short sigh written by the boy D'Annunzio and beginning:

> O falce di luna calante,

or Keats's sonnet on Chapman's Homer.

When Sarah Bernhardt played Adrienne Lecouvreur she used to recite the opening of that fable, and one felt as one heard it that for the perfect utterance of beautiful words this was the Pillars of Hercules of mortal achievement, that it was impossible to speak verse more beautifully.

III

The sighing of La Fontaine's Fable by this little girl at the Conservatoire was the prelude, the prophecy, and in one sense the epitome of all her long and glorious career; but the career was far from being one of roses, roses all the way. The whole of Sarah Bernhardt's artistic life was a fight against apparently insurmountable difficulties—

obstacles from the moment when she was handicapped by her frailty, the delicacy of her constitution, the weakness of her lungs and her vocal organs, until the moment she had to face, first the inability to move, owing to invading rheumatism, and then the loss of a leg. She prolonged the wrestle until she was on her death-bed. It was a long time before she won the suffrages of the critical. She made her début at the Théâtre français in 1862, but all that Sarcey, who as a conscientious and hard-working critic expressed for so many years the opinion of the play-going world of Paris, said of her on this occasion was that she held herself well and spoke her lines distinctly.

It is interesting in following her career as it is revealed in his articles to note the gradual crescendo of his appreciation. When she played *Le Passant,* by Coppée, at the Odéon in 1869, he noted the delicate charm with which she spoke the verse. The performance made her famous. In 1872 she left the Odéon, returned to the Théâtre français and played in *Mademoiselle de Belle-Isle.* Sarcey notes her delicious diction, but doubts whether she will ever find those strong and vibrating accents that carry an audience away. Nature had, he said, denied her that, otherwise she would be a complete artist, and such a thing, he added, did not exist on the stage. She followed this up by playing the part of Junie in Racine's *Britannicus.* Sarcey notes that she has "Je ne sais quel charme poétique, elle dit le vers avec une grâce et une pureté raciniennes." In 1873 she plays the small part of Aricie in *Phèdre,* and Sarcey says of her voice that it is music itself and of an unimaginable purity and transparency. In 1876 she had belied Sarcey's prophecy that she would never have the strength to move an audience, by her performance of the Roman Vestal's mother in Parodi's tragedy, *Rome Vaincue.* In this tragedy she played an old woman, Posthumia, who is blind, and who, at the end of the tragedy, stabs her daughter to save her from being buried alive; the daughter is bound and cannot stab herself, and the mother, being blind, has to fumble for the place of her heart.

> " . . . Elle était admirablement costumée et grimée," wrote Sarcey, "un visage amaigri, ridé, et d'une majesté extraordinaire; des yeux vagues et ternes, un manteau qui, tombant des deux côtés quand les bras se soulevaient, semblait figurer les ailes immenses de quelque gigantesque et sinistre chauve-souris. Rien de plus terrible et de plus poétique ensemble . . . ce n'était plus là une comédienne; c'était la nature même, servie par une intelligence merveilleuse, par une âme de feu, par la voix la plus juste, la plus mélodieuse, qui jamais ait enchanté les oreilles humaines. Cette femme joue avec son cœur et ses entrailles. Elle hasarde des gestes qui seraient ridicules chez tout autre et qui emportent une salle. . . ."

No completer criticism of the art of Sarah Bernhardt is to be found than in these lines. Many have thought her rendering of this old woman, Posthumia, one of the two greatest triumphs of her career, and it is doubtful whether she ever excelled it; she chose an act of this

play together with an act of *Phèdre* for the celebration of her jubilee in Paris.

It must have been about this time that she first appeared in *Phèdre,* for in 1877 Sarcey talks of her success in *Andromaque* as exceeding that of her *Phèdre,* and he notes the number of shades she can indicate by the simple modulation of her voice in three lines of verse, without any seeming search after effect or time-taking effort, and also the continuous tremor that thrilled the audience as she spoke her lines; she was interrupted by unstiflable bravos, as happens sometimes to great singers.

In the same year, she played Doña Sol in *Hernani,* and from that time forth she was recognised not only as an actress of genius, but as a personality that counted not only in the life of the world of art, but in life in general. She became henceforth to France something as well known as the Arc de Triomphe, and more than that, an object of unceasing interest and curiosity, the theme of poets, the godsend of gossips and paragraph makers, the centre of a legend.

In 1879 she went to London with the Comédie française and she appeared in *Phèdre, Hernani, Andromaque, L'Etrangère, Le Sphiux,* and *Zaïre.* The London public went mad about her, and Sarah Bernhardt having tasted blood, in the shape of the conquest of London, determined on the conquest of the world. She abandoned the Théâtre français after a quarrel, and went to America.

That was the first great break in her career.

— — IV

All this time, her travels, her adventures, her extravagances, her tantrums, her quarrels, her facile successes, her cheap victories, never prevented her from continuing, at the same time, as if on a parallel line, her personal battle and wrestle with the angle of art, and from every now and then discovering and achieving a new victory, conquering a fresh province.

In 1880, she plays Adrienne Lecouvreur for the first time, and in London, and reveals to Sarcey, who goes to London to hear her, what were to him unsuspected stops of pathos and passion. In the same year she plays *Froufrou* in London, and she has to compete with memories of Aimée Desclée. She must succeed or die. "Eh, bien!" says Sarcey, comparing them in the scene which was Desclée's greatest triumph, "elle en est venue à bout. C'est tout autre chose et c'est aussi puissant. . . . Au quatrième acte, il n'y a pas de discussion possible, Mad^elle Sarah Bernhardt s'est montrée supérieure à sa devancière."

Then came more journeys and more world-tours, and, in 1882, the beginning of her association with Sardou, her production of *Fédora,* the first of those ingenious and powerful melodramas which were cunningly constructed in order to bring out her especial qualities, garments which were cut tightly to her measure, and which no one else has been able to wear since. *Théodora, La Tosca, Gismonda, La Sorcière*—she toured the world with these, and no plays brought her louder applause, and in no plays could she produce a more certain and sometimes a more stunning effect. But although her performance in them was certainly a unique phenomenon, which nobody since has been able to imitate or to emulate, they were for her easy triumphs, and it was not in them that she reached anywhere near the high-water mark of her art. She could sometimes content herself by merely imitating herself in them, and by letting the strong situations do the business, with the minimum effort on her part, although I can bear witness that there was often a vast difference between Sarah Bernhardt playing listlessly in a part of Sardou's, and any one else playing the same part with all their might.

The wrestle with art went on in spite of Sardou. Again she moved Sarcey to an ecstasy of surprise when she first plays in *La Dame aux Camélias* in Paris in 1883: "I have seen something perfect!" he exclaims. She continues to experiment. She plays Lady Macbeth. At one time she has the idea of playing it in English, and takes lessons from Madame de Guythères, an inhabitant of Versailles, who told me of the first lesson. When she arrived for the second lesson, Sarah Bernhardt was selling her furniture and starting for America. The facts of life had intervened. She plays in Richepin's *Nana Sahib;* she plays Cleopatra in an adaptation of Shakespeare by Sardou; she plays Joan of Arc. She visits London every year. She still tours the world. Then there comes to her a moment when she instinctively feels that the public is tired of her repertory and irritated by her producing stuff that is inferior to her, so on her return from a prolonged tour in South America she turns over quite a new leaf. She takes the Renaissance Theatre in Paris, either in 1892 or 1893, and produces a delicate play by Jules Lemaître, *Les Rois.* "The Sarah of the 'seventies has come back to us," said the critics. In 1893 she plays Phèdre, and Sarcey says that in the part she is younger and more beautiful than she was at the Théâtre Français in the 'seventies, when her powers were not quite ripe enough for the part.

"Chose étrange, inouïe, inexplicable, mais qui est vraie cependant, Mme Sarah Bernhardt est plus jeune, plus éclatante et, tranchons le mot, plus belle qu'elle n'a jamais été, d'une beauté artistique qui fait passer dans tout le corps un frisson d'admiration comme à l'aspect d'une belle statue." Lemaître speaks in the same note. With one voice the French critics agreed that never was anything finer seen. It was here she reached the high-water mark of her genius. She does not stop; she brings into prominence Rostand, and produces *La Princesse Lointaine, La Samaritaine,* D'Annunzio's *Ville Morte,* and Sudermann's *Magda.* She takes a theatre of her own. She plays in *Hamlet* and *L'Aiglon,* and from this moment till the day of her death her artistic career alternates between hazardous experiments likely to be caviare to the general, such as Tristan Bernard's *Jeanne Doré,* and revivals of popular plays such as *La Dame aux Camélias,* or new productions calculated to please the crowd. She

injures her leg, and her leg has to be amputated. No matter, she will appear in plays where it is not necessary for her to walk. The European war breaks out, she plays to the *poilus* in the trenches. And still the experiments continued; still the wrestle with great art continued, and culminated in her production of *Athalie* in 1920. Finally, while she was rehearsing a new play by Sacha Guitry, she fell ill from the malady from which she was destined never to recover. But she spent her last illness in rehearsing for the films, until, after the long contention, the moment for the final *recueillement* came and she received the last Sacraments.

V

She spent her life in making discoveries and in surprising the public and her critics by finding out what she could not do, and in immediately doing it. She began by surprising herself in 1873 when playing in *Zaïre;* she thought she was dying, and she determined to die in real earnest, to spite the manager, with whom she had quarrelled. She gave a cry of real pain when the stage dagger struck her, and she thought she could never recover; but to her astonishment she found herself, after the tremendous effort, exertion, and nervous expenditure, as fresh as a daisy. After this experience she knew she could draw when she liked on her physical resources. Her energy, the amount of hard work she accomplished, were frightening to think of. Her recreation was change of work. She could command sleep when she wished, but she never rested. Yet she was fundamentally sensible. She made the best of the inevitable, and from the beginning to the end of her career she turned her limitations into virtues.

She had a weak voice by nature and a delicate constitution, yet she succeeded by self-training, practice, management, and tact, in achieving so great a mastery of modulation, pitch, and tone that she could express anything from the fury of the whirlwind to the sigh of a sleepy stream.

VI

What was the secret of her art, and what were the main characteristics of her genius?

I believe that the secret of her art was that of all great art: that she was guided by an infallible instinct, and that whatever she did she could not go wrong. When what she did was done, it seemed simple, inevitable, and easy; and so swiftly accomplished, that you had no time to think of the *how;* nor was your sense sharp enough, however carefully you watched, to detect the divine conjury. It was the same whether she spoke lines of La Fontaine and Racine, or whether she asked, as she poured out a cup of coffee, as she did in one play: "Du sucre, deux morceaux?" She was artistically inerrant. It is this gift which was probably the secret of the great actors of the past: Garrick, Siddons, Talma, and Salvini. It is certainly to be seen in the work of the great singer of the present, Chaliapine, whether he is portraying Satan holding his court on the Brocken, or a foolish, good-natured Chinovnik, half-fuddled with drink after a night out. When such a gift is at work, the greater the material it is interpreting, the greater, of course, the effect.

The greater the play Sarah Bernhardt appeared in, the greater the demand on her instinct, which *was* her genius; the swifter and the fuller the response. As the occasion expanded, so did her genius rise to it.

Her Hamlet was and is still hotly discussed, and quite lately several eminent English writers have expressed opinions that are completely at variance with one another on the subject. But every critic when he reads *Hamlet* creates a Hamlet in his own image, and when he sees it acted, the more vivid the impersonation, the more likely it is to be at variance with his own conception. One critic finds her Hamlet an unpardonable Gallic liberty to take with Shakespeare; another, that she electrified Hamlet with the vigour of her personality. I remember a culti-vated philosopher, who was a citizen of the world, telling me that he thought her Hamlet the only intelligible ren-dering he had seen of the part, just because it rendered the youthful inconsequence of the moods of the moody Dane. But whether you thought it justifiable or unjustifi-able, true or untrue to Shakespeare, in witnessing it you were aware of the genius of the interpreter answering the genius of the dramatic poet. Deep was calling to deep.

When Hamlet looked into the guilty King's face at the end of the play within the play, or thought for one second that the King and not Polonius had blundered into death behind the arras; when Hamlet concealed his forebodings from Horatio, and when Hamlet looked at Laertes during the duel and let him know that he knew the swords had been exchanged and that one of them had been poisoned, all thought of the part—the rendering, tradition, the lan-guage, the authorship—went to the winds: you knew only that something which had been invented by one great genius was being interpreted by another great genius, and that the situation had found an expression which was on its own level. That, at least, was the impression of many.

A brilliant Irish essayist (whose essays appeared during the war) arrived at just such a conception of Hamlet as Sarah Bernhardt did, and it should always be remem-bered that she was the first to give to the French stage a plain and accurate translation of *Hamlet* in which the play was allowed to speak for itself, and was neither "adapted" nor dislocated by being put into romantic French verse.

A French friend of mine, an English scholar, who was a friend of M. Marcel Schwob, the translator of this ver-sion of *Hamlet,* assisted at some of the rehearsals, and once or twice, he told me, Sarah Bernhardt consulted him as to the meaning of a passage. He said what he thought, and she answered in a way which showed she had com-pletely misunderstood him, had perhaps not even lis-tened. Then, he said, she went on to the stage and played the passage in question, not only as if she understood the

words that he had explained, but as if she had had access to the inner secrets of the poet's mind. This, again, was an instance of her instinct at work. If you pressed her for a theory about any part or passage she might invent something ready-made to please you, but it would have been an afterthought and not a precon-ceived plan. She acted by instinct and left the theory to others.

Her performance in Musset's *Lorenzaccio* was thought by some to be the most subtly interesting of all her achievements—nothing she ever did received greater praise from the critical in Paris (it received but little in London). M. Camille Mauclair speaks of "ce magnifique 'Lorenzaccio' dont elle faisait une des merveilles de sa carrière." It is true that Musset's work was mangled to make an acting play, but as it was written it would prob-ably be unactable, and given the nature of Sarah Bernhardt's performance it was worth it. But there was one part which, great as it was, needed no readjustment or alteration when she assumed it, and that was the part of Phèdre.

Of all the parts she played it demanded the greatest effort and exertion, and that is why, during her long career, she played it comparatively seldom. Here, at any rate, she was beyond discussion. When she played it for the first time in London in 1879 she was so overcome with ner-vousness that she had to be pushed on to the stage, and as she began to speak she pitched her voice too high. Whenever she played it afterwards, she told me herself that she went through an agonising period of anguish, wondering whether she could bear the heavy load, and I remember seeing her between the acts of one perfor-mance in London, reading over her part, which was cop-ied out in a large copy-book, murmuring the lines and saying to herself, with tears in her eyes: "Quel rôle, quel rôle," fearful even then of succumbing!

In reading the play again and conjuring up the visions, the sounds, of the harmonious, rhythmical, architectural symphony which was her Phèdre, the moments I remem-ber most vividly were firstly her look, as of a frightened hunted animal suddenly caught in a trap, when in the first act Oenone first mentions the name of Hippolyte and Phèdre cries out, as if stabbed by a poisoned arrow, or feeling the fangs of a steel trap close:

C'est toi qui l'as nommé!

Then I see her sitting rigid with horror on her golden throne as she reflects that her Father is Judge in Hell and there is no refuge for her, the guilty, either on the earth, in the sky, or under the earth:

Minos juge aux enfers tous les pâles Humains.

As she said the line her eyes reflected the visions of Virgil and Dante:

Terribiles visu formae! Letumque, Labosque!

There was a line she charged with so great a sorrow and so grave a load of beauty that one thought Racine must have stirred in his tomb as she said it:

On ne voit pas deux fois le rivage des morts.

And the note of pathos was almost unbearable when she said:

Est-ce un malheur si grand que de cesser de vivre?

But perhaps most beautiful of all, and as striking in its restraint as the explosions of the preceding acts were formidable by their fury, was her utterance of Phèdre's final speech.

J'ai voulu, devant vous exposant mes remords,
Par un chemin plus lent descendre chez les morts.
J'ai pris, j'ai fait couler dans mes brûlantes veines
Un poison que Médée apporta dans Athènes.
Déjà jusqu'à mon cœur le venin parvenu
Dans ce cœur expirant jette un froid inconnu.
Déjà je ne vois plus qu'à travers un nuage,
Et le ciel, et l'époux que ma présence outrage.
Et la mort à mes yeux dérobant la clarté
Rend au jour qu'ils souillaient toute sa pureté.

After all the passion and the paroxysms, the storm and stress, the exultations and the agonies, she breathed out her final confession with that calm and harmonious unity of tone and absence of gesture and of facial expression which the quiet close of a great tragedy demands. She spoke as if she were already dead, with the impersonality and aloofness of what was no longer mortal. Her voice seemed to come from a distance, from the sunless regions; the chill of Cocytus was upon it, and as her head fell on the shoulder of the attendant slave, visions of the masterpieces of Greek sculpture were evoked, and all that the poets have said so briefly and so sweetly about the mowing down of beautiful flowers, and broken blossoms and ruined rhymes.

It was in moments such as these that Sarah Bernhardt enlarged rather than interpreted the masterpieces of the world. But praise of her now is no longer a living thing that might prove an incentive to others to go and see and hear for themselves. It is only a dirge of regret and a procession of melancholy shadows. Nevertheless, it is fitting to weave a few words, however idle and inadequate, and to honour her imperishable name with a perishable wreath.

VII

When in the future people will say, "But you should have heard Sarah Bernhardt in the part!" the newcomers will probably shrug their shoulders and say, "Oh, we know all about that!"

But they will not know, nor will anybody be able to tell them or explain to them what Sarah Bernhardt could do with a modulated inflexion, a *trait de voix,* a look, a gesture, a cry, a smile, a sigh, nor what majesty, poetry and music she could suggest by the rhythm of her movements and her attitudes, what it was like to hear her speak verse, to say words such as:

Songe, songe, Céphise, à cette nuit cruelle,

or,

Si tu veux faisons un rêve.

Nobody will be able to tell them, because, in spite of the gramophone and the cinematograph, the actor's art dies almost wholly with the actor. It is shortlived, but only relatively shortlived; and nobody understood that better than Sarah Bernhardt, one of whose mottoes was "Tout passe, tout casse, tout lasse."

(It was tempered by another: "Quand même.")

On the loom of things the poems of Homer are only a little less ephemeral than a leading article, and the art of a Phidias is, after all, as perishable as the sketches of a "lightning" music-hall artist.

Le temps passe. Tout meurt. Le marbre même
    s'use.
Agrigente n'est plus qu'une ombre, et Syracuse
Dort sous le bleu linceul de son ciel indulgent.

The most enduring monuments, the most astounding miracles of beauty achieved by the art and craft of man, are but as flotsam, drifting for a little while upon the stream of Time; and with it now there is a strange russet leaf, the name of Sarah Bernhardt.

Frank Harris (essay date 1924)

SOURCE: "Sarah Bernhardt," in *Contemporary Portraits,* Grant Richards Ltd., 1924, pp. 294-302.

[*In the following essay, Harris eulogizes Bernhardt and provides a personal recollection of her.*]

Sarah, *la divine,* as the French called her, is dead, and the authorities have given her a gorgeous funeral: to tell truth, the finest funeral I've ever seen, even in Paris, except perhaps the funeral given to Victor Hugo some forty years ago.

But even at Hugo's funeral there were not such masses of flowers as at Sarah's: two huge van-loads, besides wreaths uncountable.

The poet had made an immense reputation: judge him how you will, condemn his rhetoric here and his theatrical effects everywhere, and there yet remains a residuum of astonishing poetry. He was a singer like Swinburne; and just as Swinburne brought new cadences, unknown harmonies, into our English verse, so did Hugo into French verse: a verbal magician of the first rank. But what had Sarah Bernhardt done to be honoured in like fashion? Nothing, it seems to me; nothing whatever of enduring value. Very early Matthew Arnold said of her that Rachel began where Sarah Bernhardt left off; and, if one can explain this by noting that Arnold saw Rachel as a young man and Sarah in his maturity, still he suggests a doubt of Sarah's power, which I feel was justified. I thought more could be made even of *Phèdre* than she made of it, and she never gave me the unearthly thrill that Duse gave in *La Femme de Claude*.

Now that Sarah is dead, I can only think of her in a personal way; for it is as a personality, rather than as an actress, that she always impressed me most. To write of her at all makes me feel as if I were fallen into anecdotage. It is so long since I first saw her play *Doña Sol* in Victor Hugo's *Hernani* in the Comédie Française in Paris—further off than far away.

It must have been in the year '77 or '78, when I was in the early twenties, and Sarah already in the thirties. She won a prize at the Conservatoire of Paris in '62, and entered the Comédie Française shortly afterwards. I cannot help thinking that, when she said she was born in '45, she must have forgotten to count some Sundays.

When I saw her first she was at her best as a woman, though perhaps not as an actress—the Jewish type with grey eyes and lissome figure, a *fausse maigre,* as the French call those who look thin, but are really of rounded outline. She was wonderful as *Andromaque,* but her Phèdre was better, sixteen years later, when she had reached the full maturity of her talent; to me, it was always talent she possessed, and not genius. She had a beautiful voice, and, as long as she kept to the middle register, it really deserved to be called a voice of gold, so lovely were the mellow contralto tones in it. Who that ever heard her in *Doña Sol* can forget how she declared her love: "Je vous aime, je vous aime encore, et je vous aime toujours"? But, when she went on to the greater phrases in which Victor Hugo sought to realize passion, I thought her declamation hardly more than admirable recitation. She did not realise the feeling in its intensity, though the house rose to her in wildest enthusiasm and cheered and cheered again. She gave no indication of how life left her as her lover's steps died away, and there was no gasp of renewed life when she felt her soul revive with his returning:

> "Quand le bruit de vos pas s'efface
> Je crois que mon cœur ne bat plus
> Mais dès qu'enfin ce pas que j'attends et que
>   j'aime
> Vient frapper mes oreilles, alors il me souvient
>   que je vis
> Et je sens mon âme qui revient."

Mounet Sully played *Hernani,* and he was certainly a most splendid stage lover, with quite as great a power as she had of beautiful recitation. His voice, too, was most melodious.

When I came to myself, after seeing them both a dozen times, I felt that all Victor Hugo had written was really

good rhetoric, and all Sarah Bernhardt and Mounet Sully had given was superb declamation.

Once in the old Burg Theatre in Vienna I heard a young actress—I forget even her name—but she was greater than Sarah Bernhardt, just as Adelaide Neilson in Juliet made a deeper impression on me than Sarah did, to say nothing of the incomparable Duse, who surely was head and shoulders above her. I honestly think Mimi Aguglia as great an actress as Sarah Bernhardt; but then I am not taken by mere beauty of voice or reciting. I look, if I can, for the moment in which the soul is bared with intensity of realisation.

I was introduced to Sarah Bernhardt in the foyer of the Thêâtre Français by Marguerite Durand, but Sarah paid scant attention to me at that time, taking me, evidently for an admirer of Mlle. Durand, and not considering me in any sense a foeman worthy of her steel. I admired her as much as she deserved to be admired, I thought. I remember visiting her at her home, and seeing one or two of her sculptures; but her sculptures, like her painting, only confirmed my impression that she had no understanding of genius or the diabolical discipline it imposes.

I knew her husband, Jacques Damala, better than I knew Sarah. He was a very good-looking man, five feet eight or nine in height, and well-built, with long, dark brown eyes, regular features, and olive complexion. If I remember rightly, the family had gone from Marseilles to Athens; at any rate, it was in Athens and at the Hotel d'Athènes that I got to know them—the handsome mother and a lovely daughter; Jacques had just left the Corps des Pages. They all spoke French as if it had been their mother tongue—as well, of course, as modern Greek.

I was in Paris for a year, a little later, and met Damala again and again. He dined with me three or four times, and once I remember his taking me to some Cercle in Paris where baccarat was being played for pretty high stakes, and where he lost four or five thousand francs without turning a hair. "La guigne," he remarked, carelessly, "me poursuit." But the proverb held good with him: "Unlucky in play, lucky in love," for later I heard in London that he was on the best of terms with Sarah Bernhardt. When I next visited Paris I joked him about it, but he met my poor attempts at raillery with portentous earnestness, declaring that he admired Mlle. Sarah enormously, and that he was thinking of becoming an actor.

A few weeks later the world was startled with the news that the pair had crossed to London and been married. A year or so later I saw them acting together, and was astounded at the mastery of the art shown by Jacques Damala. I have forgotten all about the play, but he had to say "I love you" to Sarah in it, and I thought he said "I love you" better than I had ever heard it said on any stage. He was really a remarkable *cabotin,* fitted to play almost any part in life with assured mastery, or masterly assurance.

With all gravity he told me that they were ideally happy, and the halcyon weather lasted almost exactly as long as his wife's savings—which ran into millions of francs, I believe.

The next winter they went on a *tournée,* and when in eastern Europe somewhere—I think at Trieste—the end came. Sarah, it appears, even before this had reason to doubt M. Damala's fidelity. At Trieste she found out that he was deceiving her with one of the younger actresses of her own company. She was furious, and told him what she thought of him on the stage at a rehearsal, before everyone. One of the company declared that it was a great scene. Damala listened to her calling him names in perfect silence, with all the appearance of patient courtesy. When she had screamed herself hoarse, he bowed to her and assured her that she would never be troubled by him again. He went out of the theatre, ordered his valet to pack his boxes, and took the first train back to Paris.

A really great gambler, who knew when to leave—the table.

He was a curious nature, Jacques Damala; though very simple when you came to know him. He had got the ideal of "the perfect gentleman" into his head, and really tried to live up to it. A debt of honour was to him sacred, yet he would give you a "stumer cheque" for your good *billets de Banque,* as if he were conferring a favour. He had excellent manners, dressed in quiet style, and made his ideal the companion of his acts and thoughts. He resented Sarah's slanging him in public passionately. As soon as I heard of it I knew he would not forgive her easily.

When I saw Damala in Paris, many months later, he did not talk much about his matrimonial adventure. He regretted suavely that a bad temper and the tongue of a fishwife usually went with great talent in an actress, but he had no wish to enter into details. He regarded the incident as closed. "One should never marry a celebrity," was his final man-of-the-world's comment on the affair.

Sarah, I learned, had taken the matter desperately to heart. For a day or two after Damala's departure she went on acting as if nothing had happened; but within a week she cancelled all further engagements in Moscow and Petersburg, paid all the penalties, and returned hotfoot to Paris, to meet Damala and bring about a reconciliation; but he would not see her.

One day in the Avenue de l'Opera I almost ran into her as she got out of her brougham. To my astonishment, she caught me by the arm. "The very man I wanted to see," she cried; "give me Jacques's address. Take me to him!"

"I regret I cannot," I replied.

"How do you mean?" she exclaimed; "you must know where he lives and how to find him."

"Yes," I replied, "but I've promised him not to give his address to anyone."

"You won't deny it to me," she cried; "you wouldn't if you knew how I have suffered. Oh, I want to meet him again; I must win his forgiveness! Oh, can't you realise how terrible it is to have thrown away what you most desire in the world? As soon as he left me, I realised how foolish I had been, how mad. What did it matter to me whom else he kissed, so long as I had him? What fools jealousy makes of us all, what insane fools! I beg you to give me his address; even if you won't speak for me, tell me where I can see him. I love him!"

She found even deeper words, but first she made me get into the brougham and go home with her. There she pleaded as I've never heard a woman plead—or a man either, for that matter.

"Miserable creatures, we women are," she flung out; "we love more and more, give ourselves more and more completely, whereas the man loves most at first. What an irony of the gods to make us, the weaker, suffer the more intensely. The tragedy of life, it is all in that; the bitterness and the shame."

I never heard her plead on the stage with a tenth part of the persuasiveness lent her by passionate feeling. I simply could not refuse her. Who was I to judge between them? I said: "Madame, I won't give you the address, but I am going there now. If you choose, come with me. I will write him a little note asking him to dine, and leave it for him if he's not at home."

I wrote the note; we went downstairs, got into a sapin, and went to Damala's apartment. I begged her to wait till I came out, to wait at least a short quarter of an hour if he were in and I didn't return immediately. I meant to give him the note asking him to dine with me, say a word or two, and come away; but he insisted on coming to the door with me, and, as I opened it, there was Sarah. She had not waited, as she had promised. She held out her hands to him imploringly and passed into the room, and I shut the door; but I had seen him draw back, and heard the contemptuous word—*cabotine.*

Much later, Marcel Schwob, the excellent French writer, asked me to help him with some translations out of English, especially *Hamlet.* One night he insisted on taking me round to Madame Bernhardt's theatre, and, as my luck would have it, the manager came into our box in the second act and told us that he had the worst of news—M. Damala was dead.

I had not even known he was ill.

"What are we to do?" cried the manager.

"Don't tell it to Madame Damala till after the play," advised Schwob. And when the curtain fell, he asked me to go round with him to Sarah's dressing-room, so that the news might be broken to her as carefully as possible.

Sarah was in her dressing-room, with her hat on, but only half dressed: in fact, she was in her corset, and a little bit of linen stuck out of her drawers behind, giving her the air of a hen. She said: "I hope you don't mind seeing me like this; I'll be ready in a moment," and went on putting some carmine on her lips, when the knock of the stage manager came to the door.

"Qui est-ce?" she asked imperiously; and then: "entrez."

The stage manager came in.

"Vous!" she cried in astonishment; then "que voulez-vous?"

"Madame," he said, "j'ai de bien tristes nouvelles à vous donner!" (I have sad news for you!)

"Ah, what?" she said, looking at him.

"M. Damala est au plus mal." (M. Damala is very ill.)

Sarah turned and went on reddening her lips, and then:

"Vous voulez dire qu'il est mort." (You mean he's dead?)

"Oui, Madame."

She turned again to the glass to finish her lips, and then suddenly "Tant mieux!" (so much the better), she tossed out, disdainfully.

A moment later she repeated it impatiently as a dismissal. "Tant mieux, tant mieux!" bidding the manager go. I thought Damala deserved a better requiem; but then I was judging him by his exquisite sister.

Alexander Woolcott (essay date 1924)

SOURCE: "Bernhardt," in *Enchanted Aisles*, G. P. Putnam's Sons, 1924, pp. 10-8.

[*In the following essay Woolcott eulogizes Bernhardt and remembers his last encounters with her.*]

It was to "pauvre Rachel" that Bernhardt's thoughts flew as her boat pulled away from these shores after her first glittering tour more than forty years ago. A generation before that her forerunner in the French theater had, in a humiliating and grotesquely disastrous tour, found us a less hospitable, less civilized and less understanding land and had known the agony of playing her great scenes of tempest and woe to the whirr and rustle of a thousand turning pages, each head in the audience bent earnestly but disconcertingly over a translation of the play. "Pauvre Rachel" and the "Divine Sarah" are in the same company to-day—the illustrious company that lies in Père Lachaise, the sloping crowded cemetery, marooned now in a dreary part of Paris where elevated trains roar by and there is an unending rattle of trucks and trams on the streets all about.

It had been Bernhardt's plan to lie buried in a tomb cut deep into the seawashed rock of her own Belle Ile, that little, white edged island which lies just off the ugly port of Saint Nazaire and which, in the morning sunlight, was the first glimpse of France that greeted the soldiers from America who sailed in the first contingent in the half forgotten excitement of June, 1917. But, in the juggling of her moneys which distracted all her later years, she lost the island, so that, after all, it was to Père Lachaise that Paris carried her. She is in the company not only of Rachel, whose grave is in the older and leafier corner close to the twin tomb of Abelard and Heloïse, but in the company, too, of others who, like herself, had had their day in the theater. Talma is there and Molière. Playwrights like De Musset, Beaumarchais, Oscar Wilde and Scribe; painters like Corot, Ingres, Daubigny, Gustave Doré and David. Dr. Hahnemann is there. So is August Comte and Balzac and Marshal Ney and La Fontaine. It is a great troupe—the company of Père Lachaise.

We saw her in her last June. There she sat in her little, cheerful sitting room up in the musty, frowsy, old house in the Boulevard Pereire, which belongs, they say, to some South American government, but from which, since the day when an infatuated Minister had grandly placed it at her disposal, she had never been ousted. She was resplendent in a dressing gown of white satin with a saucy, fur edged overjacket of blue Indian silk and there were blazing rings on the ancient fingers which now and again adjusted the jacket so that there should always be a good view of the scarlet Legion of Honor badge on her breast. It had taken her so many years and so much trouble to get it. Her face was a white mask on which features were painted, but no craft of makeup could have wrought that dazzling smile which lighted the room. Just as in the glory of her early years, she had never suggested youth but seemed an ageless being from some other world, so now, in her seventy-eighth year, it was not easy to remember that she was old.

There she sat, mutilated, sick, bankrupt and, as always, more than a little raffish—a ruin, if you will, but one with a bit of gay bunting fluttering jaunty and defiant from the topmost battlement. There she sat, a gaudy old woman, if you will, with fainter and fainter memories of scandals, ovations, labors, rewards, intrigues, jealousies and heroisms, notoriety and fame, art and the circus. But there was no one in that room so young and so fresh that this great-grandmother did not make her seem colorless. She was nearly fourscore years of age and had just finished a long, harassing season. But she was in no mood to go off to the shore for her rest until she had adjusted her plans for this season. There were young playwrights to encourage with a pat on the head, there were scene designers and costumiers to be directed, there were artists to be interviewed and there was need of some sort of benign intervention in behalf of a new play struggling along in her own theater.

Above all, there were plays to be selected for the following season and, if none appeared, then there were playwrights to be lectured or cajoled into writing them for her. She had one hand on the younger Rostand, son of the finest imagination harnessed by the French theater in half a century, son of the Rostand who had written for her the very play that was halted at the Théâtre Sarah Bernhardt in the Place du Chatelet the night she died. This son of his, surely, could be depended on. And in case he couldn't she had her eye on the younger Guitry. Indeed, she had just had herself carried around to his house and had dazzled him all through luncheon for no other purpose. Out of this was born a project for a play about 'Adam and Eve,' which Sacha Guitry, reluctant but helpless, forthwith began to write. Bernhardt would play *Eve*, of course, and the elder Guitry, *Adam*. This prospect, at first encounter, seemed alarming and the author was questioned. Surely, he was not thinking of writing for them the drama of Eden nor blandishing Bernhardt into thinking that she could suggest *Eve* before the Fall.

"I am not a fool," he replied, tartly. "When my play opens, *Eve* is 650 years old."

"And *Adam?*"

"*Adam* is 750 years old."

"But how did you know there was just that difference?"

"He read it," put in Guitry, *père*, "*dans la Gazette de Milton.*"

And America. Of course, she was full of shrewd questions about America. She wanted to know what new playwright might be dug up there, what this O'Neill was like and if business was good at the box offices in New York. She asked after *la petite Taylorrr,* whose great success, *Peg de mon Cœur,* was even then playing in Paris and who had had, Bernhardt always knew, *beaucoup de talent.* She was planning, she confessed, to visit us in the winter.

"Not a long tour this time," she added a little ruefully and then went on in the exceptionally earnest tone of one who expected to be doubted, "I am too old and too frail to undertake one of those exhausting tours. Not a long one this time. Just Boston, New York, Philadelphia, Baltimore, Washington, Cleveland, Chicago and a few places like that." This program was proffered without a suggestion of humor. She meant it. She was magnificent.

There are many portraits of her, none lovelier nor more discerning than the slim, serpentine Claretie painting, so often reproduced. The original hung at the far end of the long, ground floor salon in the Boulevard Pereire, a room rich in the elegance of the eighties and crowded like the Cluny Museum with relics of a past civilization, a thousand and one trophies of triumphs from Moscow to Valparaiso. But there is no portrait probably which so catches the essential thing in her as the word portrait by Rostand which Forrest Izard has reproduced in his excellent book, *Heroines of the Modern Stage*. It runs thus:

All these things that I have known only in the telling—all these journeys, these changing skies, these adoring hearts, these flowers, these jewels, these embroideries, these lions, these one hundred and twelve rôles, these eighty trunks, this glory, these caprices, these cheering crowds hauling her carriage, this crocodile drinking champagne—all these things, I say, astonish, dazzle, delight and move me less than something else I have often seen: this—

A brougham stops at a door; a woman enveloped in furs jumps out, threads her way with a smile through the crowd attracted by the jingling bell on the harness and mounts a winding stair; plunges into a room crowded with flowers and heated like a hothouse, throws her little beribboned handbag, with its apparently inexhaustible contents, into one corner and her bewinged hat into another, takes off her furs and instantaneously dwindles into a mere scabbard of white silk, rushes onto a dimly lighted stage and immediately puts life into a whole crowd of listless, yawning, loitering folk; dashes forward and back, inspiring every one with her own feverish energy; goes into the prompter's box, arranges her scenes, points out the proper gesture and intonation, rises up in wrath and insists on everything being done over again; shouts with fury; sits down, smiles, drinks tea and begins to rehearse her part; draws tears from case hardened actors who thrust their enraptured heads out of the wings to watch her; returns to her room, where the decorators are waiting, demolishes their plans and reconstructs them; collapses, wipes her brow with a lace handkerchief and thinks of fainting; suddenly rushes up to the fifth floor, invades the premises of the astonished costumier, rummages in the wardrobes, makes up a costume, pleats and adjusts it; returns to her room and teaches the figurantes how to dress their hair; has a piece read to her while she makes bouquets; listens to hundreds of letters, weeps over some tale of misfortune, and opens the inexhaustible little clinking handbag; confers with the English perruquier; returns to the stage to superintend the lighting of a scene, objurgates the lamps and reduces the electrician to a state of temporary insanity; sees a super who has blundered the day before, remembers it and overwhelms him with her indignation; returns to her room for dinner; sits down to table, splendidly pale with fatigue; ruminates her plans; eats with peals of Bohemian laughter; dresses for the evening performance while the manager reports from the other side of the curtain; acts with all her heart and soul; discusses business between the acts; remains at the theater until after the performance and makes arrangements until 3 o'clock in the morning; does not make up her mind to go until she sees her stage manager respectfully endeavoring to keep awake; gets into her carriage; huddles herself into her furs and anticipates the delights of lying down and resting at last; bursts into laughter on remembering that some one is waiting to read her a five act play; returns home, listens to the piece, becomes excited, weeps, accepts it, finds she cannot sleep, and takes advantage of the opportunity to study a part. This is the Sarah I have always known. I never made the acquaintance of the Sarah with the coffin and the alligators. The only Sarah I know is the one who works. She is the greater.

Of this passion and capacity for work—what Shaw in his essay on Cæsar describes as "the power of killing a dozen secretaries under you, as a life or death courier kills horses"—the wanderer back stage in our own theater will find some stray examples. Maude Adams had it—a tireless general. Margaret Anglin has it. And Jane Cowl. Bernhardt had it supremely, and even as a sick and crippled woman of seventy-eight she could do more work any day than half the inert young people who litter up the French theater as they do ours. It has been said that she died in harness. That expression of a plodder overtaken by death is inadequate for so gallant, so defiantly twinkling an exit. She was a boat that went to the bottom with its orchestra playing gayly. In her final year she was aflame with that spirit which lighted the despondent blackness of the North Sea one ghastly and terrifying night when a transport carrying some American doughboys to the French battlefields was sunk many miles from shore. They went over the side into the rowboats, not chanting in the approved heroic vein but humming with incorrigible and facetious cheerfulness: "Oh, boys, say, boys, where do we go from here?"

A. B. Walkley (essay date 1925)

SOURCE: "Sarah," in *Still More Prejudice*, Alfred A. Knopf, 1925, pp. 7-10.

[*In the following essay, Walkley contrasts the Bernhardt he knew with the "legend" of Bernhardt.*]

We say Sarah as our forefathers said Rachel. It is a tribute to greatness, as you call a pope Innocent or a king George. There have been greater actresses, but Sarah was without peer as a great institution. Her prestige was world-wide and, as her countrymen say, legendary. Too much of it was bluff and claptrap—pet panthers, coffins to sleep in, and the rest of the Sarah caprices—but these things the legend exaggerated; they were the touch of romance which popular imagination expects from great institutions. Doubtless, however, she was capricious by nature. There is corroboration of this in Daudet's sketch of her girlhood in one of his novels. There is further evidence in her behaviour during the visit of the Comédie Française to London in 1879, when she was no longer a girl. It is from this year that her prestige dates. There was a sort of rivalry between her and Croizette. The London public took sides and Sarah became first favourite. Soon afterwards she became the institution that we have all seen and admired, or, at any rate, marvelled at.

It was not done single-handed, but was a collaboration between Sarah and Sardou. The author wrote, or rather, manufactured, plays "round" the actress. These were destined chiefly for foreign consumption; showing violent situations that would be understood without knowing the language and exhibiting the actress in her celebrated postures, accompanied by her celebrated "golden" tones or by her no less celebrated shrick. She coiled sinuously round Ipanoff in *Fédora*, shrieked when Searpia was torturing Mario in *La Tosca*, lolled voluptuously in *Cléopâtre* and *Théodora*, and languorously in *Gismonda*. A foreigner could follow all this as well as any Frenchman, who, indeed, would be more likely to detect the flimsiness of the play which served as a background to the attitudes. But the actress did create, with Sardou's help, a new type—the embodiment of Oriental exoticism; the strange, chimæric idol-woman; something not in nature, a nightmarish exaggeration, the supreme of artifice.

This type and Sarah became one. She wandered all over the world with it, and no wonder that it became in the end somewhat travel-stained. Perhaps the author, too, wearied of supplying perpetually the same article of exportation. At any rate, by the time *Gismonda* was reached it was generally felt that the type had become a bore. This is the penalty of repeating the same attitudes before all the nations of the earth. Another is the inevitable development of mannerisms or tricks. For example, Sarah had three favourite styles of delivery, each of which became a trick. First, there was a rhythmical chant, or intoning, a melody of "linked sweetness long drawn out." This was delightful when she played Phèdre or Andromaque; it was the very delivery for the smooth, sweet verse of Racine; delightful, again, when she played the Queen in *Ruy Blas*. By the time she had got to *Théodora* it had become burlesque. Second, there was the metallic hammering out of her words; the most notable use of *staccato* I think the stage has ever heard. Of this the great instance was the passage in Act III. of *La Dame aux Camélias*, in which Marguerite describes to Armand the seamy side of her life: the passage ending with "ruine, honte, mensonge." (I can hear those three words ringing out, as I write, like the strokes of a bell.) Well, this beautiful grace of elocution became in time an obviously calculated "effect," too, a mere trick. Third, there was her rapid patter. The words tumbled out, one after the other, at such a helter-skelter pace that one was simply left to gather their sense from the context or the accompanying gesture. This went very well in the earlier acts of *Frou-Frou*, say, where, moreover, it was artistically right because it illustrated the character. But when you heard the same trick in the first act of *La Tosca* it seemed to you merely irritating gabble.

When at last Sarah got away from the idol-woman she made her greatest success in what our forefathers called a "breeches part," the hero of Rostand's *L'Ailgon*. That was a notable achievement for a woman already over sixty. Since she lost her leg, the only part I have seen her play was the eponymous hero of *Daniel,* and that was wonderful, too, though more wonderful still was the intense emotion of the whole house while waiting for the curtain to go up on the great actress, who, for the majority, must have been merely a name.

I have spoken of her caprices, but really only by hearsay, because they were a part of the famous "legend." It is, however, a duty to speak of people as one finds them, and I am bound to say that Mme. Bernhardt (one naturally goes back to that, when one is speaking of the woman in private life), as I knew her off the stage, showed no caprice. She struck me as a sensible, shrewd, kind-hearted woman, with a keen sense of humour, and modest, for all her fame.

Gamaliel Bradford (essay date 1930)

SOURCE: "Eve in the Spotlight: Sarah Bernhardt," in *Daughters of Eve,* Houghton Mifflin Company, 1930, pp. 241-82.

[*In the following essay Bradford surveys Bernhardt's life and works.*]

I

Sarah Bernhardt's superbly characteristic motto was, *Quand même*—Even if—What if it does—No matter. Take the sweet of life, crowd it full of beauty and splendor, make a tumultuous riot and revel of it. No matter if disasters come, and diseases, and decay, no matter if crooked fortune does her spitefulest, you will have had your hour and made the most of it—*Quand même.*

Assuredly no career could be more startling or more picturesque. Born in Paris, in 1844, of dubious paternity, Jewish in origin, Catholic and conventual in training, sometimes fondled and petted by her mother, sometimes neglected and abandoned for months together, the child was finally flung into the whirlpool of the Parisian theater. For years she struggled perilously, escaping disaster by miracle, but her genius and her magnificent courage and persistence brought her to the top, not only of Paris, but of the world, and made her one of the most known and notable figures of her day. When she died, at eighty, she was still a superbly creative spirit, capable of weaving life out of her vitals with a gorgeous sheen of silken splendor.

My concern is not so much with Sarah Bernhardt's art in the abstract as with her human personality and characteristics, but it should be recognized and established at the beginning that, however different critics may estimate her various impersonations, she was a most important factor in the dramatic life of her day. She had an immense influence on the art of acting, on the methods of playwriting, on the forms of stage production, and the history of the theater for the last fifty years could hardly be written without her. Above all, it is necessary, in connection with her art, to take into account the peculiar elements of her material personality, her extreme slenderness, giving an ethereal quality to everything she did, her mobility, her sensibility, her subtlety and power of adaptation. To some of us it appeared that there was just the suggestion of something hard and cynical about her, even of something common, but many of her admirers do not seem to have felt this, and in any event the drawbacks

were lost in the charm, a charm summed up and epitomized in the voice, the voice of gold, which has been eulogized by so many critics and sung by so many poets. We do not generally consider Mr. Lytton Strachey inclined to excessive enthusiasm, but even he breaks out into lyrical raptures over the voice of Sarah Bernhardt, whether in its sweetness or still more in its power: 'The secret of that astounding utterance baffles the imagination. The words boomed and crashed with a superhuman resonance which shook the spirit of the hearer like a leaf in the wind. The *voix d'or* has often been raved over; but in Sarah Bernhardt's voice there was more than gold, there was thunder and lightning, there was heaven and hell.'

When we turn from the abstract artist to the human being, we are on more tangible ground. In the first place Sarah was a worker, a tremendous, natural worker, who set out to do things, and did them, and got them done. The instinct of work may have been somewhat whimsical and erratic, especially in the earlier days. When George Sand is trying to get a play produced at the Odéon, during Sarah's apprenticeship, she complains that the actress 'does not work and thinks only of amusing herself.' Again, there was a furious rush, a sense of constant hurry and pressure, about the woman's life at all times, which sometimes suggests that there may have been more bustle than actual labor. What a vivid picture does Claretie give of that driven, crowded, breathless existence: 'When she returned from the theater, doing a bit of sculpture, a bit of painting, receiving her friends, posing for a painter or a photographer, giving literary advice to the unpublished poets who brought her manuscripts.' Or again, there is the single illuminating incident of the English teacher, who was engaged in haste because Sarah wanted to act Shakespeare in his own language. 'But I can give you only a half-hour a day,' said the actress. 'Will that be enough?' And when told it would be, she casually explained that it would have to be at half-past two in the morning, as every other minute was filled.

Yet, for all this apparent superficial confusion, good observers insist upon the enormous power of accomplishment. Take memory. Sarah could learn any part in a few rehearsals, and she never forgot it, when she wanted it. So with everything. When tremendous, concentrated, intelligent, even systematic effort was called for, it was always forthcoming, and the results were both surprising and permanent. As Mr. Maurice Baring puts it: 'Her energy, the amount of hard work she accomplished were frightening to think of. Her recreation was change of work. She could command sleep when she wished, but she never rested. Yet she was fundamentally sensible.' The last comment is one never to be lost sight of with Bernhardt.

One asks oneself how much abstract, theoretical thinking she did about her art. In the rush and tumult of her life general ideas somehow seem to find little place. At least I get little suggestion of them. It does not appear that she ever had much formal education, or that she ever read at all widely or thought on general subjects of any kind, as for example Charlotte Cushman did. I am not sure that she even speculated much on the general principles of acting. Her little book on *The Art of the Theatre* is extraordinarily acute in detail, but does not show the larger movement of psychological analysis. On the other hand, everything that keen perception, instinctive and subtle sympathy and comprehension, imaginative penetration, could do, was done immediately and with complete and finished effect.

For her art was essentially an art of instinct and sympathy. 'This woman acts with her heart and her whole vitality,' says Sarcey. Her theory would not have been exactly that of Joseph Jefferson, who said, 'For myself I know that I act the best when the heart is warm and the head is cool.' Sarah could keep her head cool enough when she chose. But she wanted to be aroused, stirred, excited, fired, inspired, by the situation and the circumstances, and then she could throw herself into the character with all the power and the energy that were in her. As she puts it, in *The Art of the Theatre:* 'Whatever I have to impart in the way of anguish, of passion, or of joy, comes to me during rehearsal in the very action of the play. There is no need to cast about for an attitude, or a cry, or anything else. You must be able to find everything you want on the stage in the excitement created by the general collaboration. Actors who stand in front of a mirror to strike an attitude or try to fall down on the carpet of the room are fools.'

Sarah Bernhardt had in a high degree the artist's peculiar combination of sensibility to the beautiful with the eager desire to create it. The ordinary person, even when richly endowed with such sensibility, is content to let beauty come to him, to open his senses to it, to absorb it and appreciate it and forget it. But such perception at once and at all times stimulates the artist to assert his own power and personality in the production of beauty of his own. So it was with Bernhardt. This desire even took varied artistic forms. Sometimes she was determined to paint, busied herself with lines and colors till it seemed as if the theater was forgotten. Again, it was all sculpture, and curiously enough, another great tragic actress, Sarah Siddons, also in her old age developed a passion for working with clay. In the later Sarah the passion was very real and very lasting, witness her own account of her absorption: 'I kept no clock, not even a watch with me. I wanted to ignore the time of day altogether. . . . How often I neither breakfasted nor dined, having simply forgotten all about it.' It is characteristic of her that when she began a work of this kind, she finished it. She may have destroyed it afterwards, as the bust of Rothschild, which she smashed before his face, just when he had drawn her a check for ten thousand francs. But, good, bad, or indifferent, the work had to be done.

After all, however, these things were avocations and side issues. And her real life, her real existence, was on the stage. It is probably true of all artists that in a sense they do not live for themselves at all, that is, they do not give

themselves up to pure, simple, intense, natural living for itself. There is always the sense of the 'double life,' which Sarah suggests in the subtitle of her Memoirs, always the consciousness of standing apart and observing oneself, of getting out of every passion and experience something to enlarge and enrich and develop the permanent artistic production that is all you care for. As Goethe put it, 'whenever I had a sorrow, I made a poem.' The result of this is a curious blend of reality and artificiality, varying in its proportions with the type of artist and with the individual, but probably most intense and most complicated of all with the actor, whose everyday life is so fleeting and uncertain and whose artistic life is so dominating and so pervasive. This quick and constant and complicated interchange of life and art is admirably suggested in Mrs. Siddons's confidence, as recorded in the Diary of Moore. 'Among other reasons for her regret at leaving the stage was that she always found in it a vent for her private sorrows which enabled her to bear them better; and often she got credit for the truth and feeling of her acting when she was doing nothing more than relieving her own heart of its grief.' But certainly no artist, theatrical or other, ever effected a more complete intermingling and reaction of art and life than did Sarah Bernhardt. When she was off the stage, she always seemed to be acting; she always seemed to be living when she was on it.

II

Which does not mean that she did not live at all times with passionate veracity, and most of all the veracity was evident in the variety of her human relations. The temperament of the artist appears again I think especially in these, because I do not find that she really lived very much for any one but herself, or ever much lost her identity in that of any one else. But human beings were immensely necessary to her, in all possible connections, and if she did not give to them, she took from them, enormously, which, after all, involves a certain amount of giving.

Her family relations were curious. Her father was little more than a phantom. But her mother and her two sisters she was very close to at times, close to, yet worlds remote from. For they were all much like butterflies—when they were not like cats: they flitted, and quivered, and kissed, with sudden, astonishing propensities to scratch, as in Sarah herself. Nothing can be more significant than the little touch of Sarah's mother forgiving her sister on her deathbed. 'You do forgive me? The priest has bidden you to forgive me. You do forgive me?' 'Yes—camel!' Such was Madame Bernhardt, and it can hardly be wondered that Sarah never got much satisfaction out of her.

Did she get much more out of her son, Maurice? Madame Berton, who has narrated Sarah's career with such minute, if not always very amicable, fidelity, insists that mother love was an overpowering and developing motive, and that the necessity of providing for her child was the mainspring of Sarah's devotion to her art. This is absurd, and all the children in the world would not have made her an actress, or prevented her being one. No doubt she was attached to Maurice. No doubt she was proud of him. No doubt she made sacrifices for him, after her fashion. The risk of her life to get him out of her burning apartment, as she did, in spite of her inborn horror of fire, was just the sort of thing that would have appealed to her at any time. But I do not gather that Maurice's companionship or sympathy really meant much in her existence. Perhaps she got as much out of him as parents usually do.

In the same way with Sarah's innumerable love-affairs, it does not appear that she ever really gave herself, or lost herself. There was infinite curiosity, eagerness, the sense of adventure, the desire to probe, to investigate, to explore, other thoughts, other hearts, other souls; there is no suggestion of complete abandon or self-forgetfulness. Perhaps to the very end Sarah retained something of the cynical childish impression that she imbibed from her mother's very promiscuous establishment: 'My mother's house was always full of men, and the more I saw of them, the less I liked them.'

Even the eccentric marriage to the Greek actor Damala in 1882 does not seem to be any marked exception to the rule. It was simply a *toquade,* a wild, erratic fancy. Sarah took a notion to run off with the man to England, broke all her engagements, and paid a huge forfeit on her contract. She sent two telegrams to Sardou. The first ran: 'I am going to die and my greatest regret is not having created your play. Adieu!' The second followed: 'I am not dead, I am married.' And when Sardou asked her later why the devil she married, she replied: 'Why? Because it was the only thing I never had done.' She stuck to her drug-besotted husband till his death seven years later, with obstinate racial loyalty that was very impressive. But the whole affair seems to have been mainly a conflict of sex-vanities, in which Sarah got rather the worst of it.

The two things that are really significant about Sarah's amorous connections are first that she loved for love or for character or for position, but not for money: her lovers were not idle sons of wealthy men. And secondly, her love appears to have inspired, ennobled, enriched life, instead of degrading it. As Madame Berton puts it, admirably: 'The influence she exerted on her century in matters of art was incalculable. To painters she would say: "If you love me, then paint a masterpiece and dedicate it to me." To poets she would say: "If it is true that you love me, you will write a poem about me that will live when we both are dead."' And Alexandre Dumas fils once summed up the same thing: 'She drives me mad when I am with her. She is all temperament and no heart; but when she is gone, how I work! How I *can* work!' While the larger quality of Sarah's influence is well indicated in Maurice Baring's enthusiastic statement of the trace she left in all the art aspects of her time: 'Eliminate these things and you eliminate one of the sources of inspiration of modern art; you take away something from

D'Annunzio's poetry, from Maeterlinck's prose, from Moreau's pictures; you destroy one of the mainsprings of Rostand's work; you annihilate some of the colors of modern painting and you stifle some of the notes of modern music; for in all these you can trace in varying degrees the subtle, unconscious influence of Sarah Bernhardt.'

So, in all the human relations, more intimate or more remote, it is the same story, always the artist, stimulating, inspiring, but infinitely curious, gathering, not giving, needing, and using, and absorbing, and throwing aside, not so much from deliberate selfishness or cruelty, as from immense, unbroken preoccupation with the one, huge, engrossing object of life. Sarah had, it appears, at all times the power of attaching, devoting human beings to her service with an unreasoning, animal devotion. 'Even the stage hands adored her,' says Claretie. When an old maid left her, worn out with service, she assured her mistress, 'If madam is ever in difficulties, we shall remember that we owe her everything: she shall have our best chamber at her disposal.' And the faithful attendant, Madame Guérard, who appears to have been bullied and browbeaten without much mercy, yet stuck to her friend with a fidelity, an assiduity, and a discerning tenderness that nothing could shake or break.

Through it all, for good, bad, or indifferent, you feel that with Sarah the human element was the one thing that counted. If it was lovers, she must have the best, and as many as possible. If it was admirers and spectators, let them throng to her in untold thousands. If the War came, in 1870, or in 1914, still there were human beings to be thought of and dealt with and appealed to, and in 1870 she gave up her art and threw herself into hospital work with the same furious ardor that she brought to the stage.

The human zest is so constant and so keen and so besetting that you wonder whether it left her time for anything else, whether the woman had any inner, solitary life at all. When she was alone, if she ever was, apparently she slept. To be sure, in one irritated moment, she cries out, in her **Memoirs**, 'I detest frequented walks, I adore deserted regions and solitary places.' But this is only to make an effective antithesis, and I gravely doubt whether she ever relished solitude in her life. So with the things that go with solitude, for example, God. She had queer attacks of religion in her childhood, both in the convent and out of it. For a time she vibrated between the cloister and the stage. The stage instinct was probably at the bottom of both inclinations, and she herself frankly admits that there was little real devotion about her conventual fancies. She continued a devout Catholic, after her fashion, all her life, and died as one. But what the Almighty thought of her as an adherent, it may be easy to conjecture. And on the spiritual side her career hardly merits extensive study.

No, she was human, always intensely, passionately, collectively, extensively human, and all her wildest freaks and vagaries, her extraordinary whims and fancies and eccentricities, have some bearing on her human interest and are best understood in their human connection.

In a sense all these extravagances were genuine and spontaneous: they were native in the complicated tangle of Sarah Bernhardt's inheritance; but, whether trivial and insignificant or profound and far-reaching, they were always calculated to impress and startle and bewilder the human beings about her. If she went on a sleigh-ride in Canada, she would suddenly call to the driver to stop, rise in her place, throw off the robes, and fling herself out into a snowdrift, to stamp the image of her face and figure, like a child. Of the same order was her balloon ascent, which astonished Paris and shocked the staid director of the Théâtre Français. So again the whole world was told of the coffin, which she had made and carried about with her everywhere, sometimes sleeping in it or even celebrating an elaborate funeral service. And, like Circe, she always had her strange herd of animals, lizards, leopards, alligators, monkeys, lions, not to speak of dogs and cats, which she cherished and petted, partly from genuine love of the creature life and partly to torment and perplex everybody who had to come into contact with her.

All these actual facts of extravagance were amplified into a mad halo of fiction and legend, like the story that Sarah set her own apartment on fire, to get the insurance and make publicity, and endless others. And where she did not invent or encourage these tales, she at any rate reveled in them, as is clearly indicated in the confession of her *Memoirs:* 'Although I had then fully reached the age of reason, I took pleasure in this mischievous childishness, which I always regret afterwards, and always renew, since even to-day, after the days, the weeks, the months, the years that I have lived, I take infinite pleasure in playing tricks.' The notable point is that through all this mad, freakish frolic the one thing that is always taken seriously is Sarah herself. There is not a trace of the subtle dissolution of self, of the vast sense of personal insignificance, which haunted, for example, Charles Lamb, or Sarah's contemporary on the stage, Joseph Jefferson. Self is the one thing that is not laughable under any circumstances. The universe is Bernhardt, and Bernhardt is the universe: there is absolutely nothing else.

III

What is most interesting and significant about all these freaks and extravagances of Sarah's is their value for publicity and advertising. As it happened, her career ran side by side with that of Barnum, the great wizard of notoriety creation, and with the enormous development of newspaper activity that characterized the middle of the nineteenth century. Certainly no actor ever before had had a tithe of the general printed notice that fell to Sarah Bernhardt, and it was said that if the newspaper comments she received were placed end to end, they would have reached around the world. The peculiar characteristics of her personality were registered and trumpeted and enlarged, till it seemed as if Barnum could have done no more for his most cherished monstrosity.

Yet all the time it must be remembered that Sarah was not only a popular phenomenon, but an artist of real genius, a great actress, a creator, and a poet. That is what gives her case its importance and curiosity. Every possible use was made of ingenious advertising, but the thing advertised was worth while and of enduring value. Of course Whistler offers a somewhat similar instance. The genius was undoubted, but the methods of getting it before the public were sometimes startling, to say the least. Perhaps one may adduce Mr. Bernard Shaw in the same line. Mr. Shaw's genius is as real as Bernhardt's or Whistler's, but neither of them was a more skillful artist in drawing public attention. And one wonders sometimes what would have been Shakespeare's attitude towards such procedure. Shakespeare was a shrewd man of business and the hard experience of life had taught him the value of coin and the difficulty of getting it. Would he have utilized publicity to the full and developed unheard-of resources in it? If he had, we may at least be sure that he would have done it with a smile at himself, like Whistler and Mr. Shaw, and unlike Bernhardt.

There are various interesting questions in regard to Bernhardt's attitude in this connection. First, how far were the eccentricities cultivated and developed with a consciousness of their publicity value? I have already insisted that they were native and inborn. So they undoubtedly were. At the same time, human nature, Sarah's human nature above all, being what it is, when the profit of such things became increasingly obvious, it was hardly to be supposed that the tendency to them would diminish: it certainly did not. Just the working of the tendency is delicately suggested in the remark of Arsène Houssaye: 'She has her enemies and her critics, but the more of her statues you break, the more there are made for her. Moreover, she takes a hand in the matter herself.'

Again, one asks not only how far did Sarah deliberately supply the material for the notoriety, but how far did she encourage and support it? She knew perfectly well that the newspapers and the world rang with her oddities and vagaries. Just how far did her hand in the matter reach? It is difficult to say exactly. In her Memoirs she of course denies any interference whatever. What had she to do with it? 'When you think that my first title to publicity was my extraordinary slenderness and my fragile health! . . . Was it simply to be notorious that I was so slight and so thin and so weak?' The same plea is frequently urged in varying forms. Yet it is hard to believe that the publicity would have flourished without the artist's connivance and one inclines to think that, like Shaw and Whistler, she was quite as much of an artist in getting her work known as in creating it.

Again, there is the question, how far she not only stimulated publicity but enjoyed it. No doubt there were times when the boredom was intolerable. Reporters, especially in America, were silly and intrusive and wearisome. Absurd stories, like that of her adventure with the whale, were repeated and exaggerated to the point of nausea. Publicity carried with it its necessary burden not only of tediousness but of actual hostility and spite: 'Ah! success! With what a strong chain it rivets one and how painful it sometimes is. How many times the noise made around me, the good said in my favor, the bad written against me have invaded my tranquillity and created an atmosphere of battle. Jealous friends, secret or open enemies, into what turmoil have you not often thrust me! And how many times have I not been accused of an immoderate liking for advertisement.' But it has not yet been discovered that these drawbacks of glory were sufficient to induce any one to throw it away.

The final question is, how much Sarah profited practically by the huge notoriety, and the answer is that her financial gains were constant and very considerable. She was clear-headed and cold-blooded, when it suited her, and she knew just when, just where, and just how the francs and the dollars came. Madame Berton asserts that 'altogether she brought back considerably more than six million dollars' from the United States, and if this is somewhat fantastic, the actual product must have been large enough. The figures given by one of her managers, Schurman, are most impressive, and equally so is one little financial scene narrated in her *Memoirs:* 'In the saloon of my car Abbey and Jarrett show me the balance-sheet for the sixty-two representations, given since we left home, amounting to 225,459 dollars; that is to say, one million, one hundred and thirty-seven thousand francs, or an average of eighteen thousand, three hundred, and forty-three francs for each performance.'

And every bit of the money was needed and spent, for, earn as vastly as she could, her outlay was usually in excess of her earning. To be sure, her personal tastes were not in all ways extravagant. She was temperate in eating and drinking, all her life was a strict vegetarian and attributed her enduring vigor largely to this regimen. But she could not hold on to money, did not care to. She lavished it on whims of all sorts, took a pride and pleasure in doing so. She lent and gave as freely as she spent for herself, so that finally, in a crisis she murmured, 'All my life, it seems, I have been making money for others to spend.' Always she was piling up obligations and then discharging them and then piling up more. How vivid is the picture that Claretie gives of these financial comings and goings. 'She laughed at everything, with the utmost cheerfulness. In her dressing-room the money that she daily received evaporated like the solution of gold under *aqua regia.* During the entr'acte there was, as it were, a hand-to-mouth distribution of her daily receipts in all sorts of fractions, by hundred francs, by twenty francs. Fifteen hundred francs was paid her. Quick! the distribution, the pillage, the slaughter! Poor woman! "Here, you, take this! Carry it to the coiffeur." "Ah! Something on account for X.—something for Z.—Well, what is it now? T. wrote this morning. I'll send him this, and he will be patient a little longer." Then, laughing still, "What have I got left? Fifteen francs. Bah! With fifteen francs you don't die of hunger. But just go and change this five franc piece for me. I've got to have some change to pay the cabman." So it went every night.'

It was not exactly that she did not have the making of a business woman in her. It is curious to think how much of that woman there was in these great tragic actresses. Mrs. Siddons was a hard money-maker, who had the keenest eye for a bargain. You have only to read Charlotte Cushman's manuscript letters in the Shaw Collection to see what her business habits were. And Sarah was as keen as either of them to know a good trade and follow it up. But her Bohemian training made her incurably erratic, and still more, she took a pride in her financial indifference. The training and the pride both show in her careless account of her own carelessness: 'I promise everything with the firm intention of executing my promise and two hours after I have forgotten everything. If some friend recalls it to me, I tear my hair and make up excuses to patch up my neglect. I complicate my life with all sorts of useless frets. So it has been since—always, and so it will be to the end.'

And this woman undertook to manage theaters, just as a somewhat similar dreamer, Edwin Booth, did, but curiously enough, she was far more successful than Booth. The erratic habits always seemed destined to wreck her. As Claretie puts it, of an early venture: 'Directress of La Porte Saint-Martin, this magnificent lunatic, who never knew how to direct her own life! In eight days she accepted eighteen plays, all sublime, and all to be played by Sarah Bernhardt, each three hundred times running. All this to end in a situation which reeked with bankruptcy and the odor of disaster.' What saved her, what enabled her to do what she wanted in the world was her power over people. She got the actors she wanted, she got the managers she wanted, she got the authors she wanted, and she made them all do what she wanted. That was perhaps her greatest gift and the richest instrument of her financial as of other success. I don't know anything in this line that has impressed me more than her conquest of Roosevelt. Naturally there was no sex in the matter, at least not directly, it was simply a case of one soul of power recognizing another. But she had a letter from Roosevelt which she treasured, and with reason: 'I have altered my plans so as to arrive in Paris after you return from Spain. I could not come to Paris and miss seeing my oldest and best friend there.' And when she showed the letter to her friends, she murmured, perhaps with a certain reason also: 'Ah! but that man and I, we could rule the world!'

With this magic gift of dominating and swaying hearts, it was natural that fortunes should come to her as lightly as they departed. It seemed as if she had but to hold out her hand and money would flow into it. Only, as often as not, the hand was held out the wrong side up.

IV

But let no eager aspirant for dramatic success imagine that Sarah's career was an unbroken triumph or a shadowless course of easy felicity. It was far, far the contrary, and no doubt she often pictured it to herself as a series of struggles and difficulties and obstacles that had to be eluded or surmounted or blown or blasted away. As Maurice Baring describes it: 'The whole of Sarah Bernhardt's artistic life was a fight against apparently insurmountable difficulties.'

There was health, and in the early years this seemed to be an insuperable obstacle to success. Sarah's voice was weak, and her extreme physical tenuity appeared to be incompatible with stage impressiveness. She was always fainting, or collapsing, or giving out in some way at inopportune moments. But she showed a superhuman skill in turning her very defects to excellences, and her own account of the triumph of spiritual resource over fleshly weakness is most extraordinary, above all, in just the touch of melodrama which is peculiarly characteristic. It seems that, in desperation over her failures and the disgust of Perrin, the director of the Français, she had made up her mind that she never could succeed, and one day, when she was playing the tragic rôle of Zaïre, she decided to throw herself into it with such fury of passion as in her exhausted state would necessarily be fatal. She carried out her suicidal determination to the full, pouring into the part a tempest of excitement which she thought she could not possibly survive. What happened? Not only did she achieve a sudden and immense success, but she found herself physically—or spiritually—remade. 'I hopped up lightly for the recall, and greeted the public without exhaustion, without weakness, quite ready to begin the play all over again. And I marked this performance with a white stone, for from that day on I understood that my vital forces were at the service of my brain. I had tried to follow the impulse of my intelligence, all the time believing that this impulse would be too violent for my physical energy to sustain it. And when I had done everything I tried to do, I found that the balance of mental and physical was perfect. Then I began to see the possibility of realizing what I had dreamed.'

Again, there was the obstacle of stage fright, which haunted Sarah from the beginning to the end of her career. This took one of the most hampering and annoying forms for an actress, it affected her voice. As Sarcey expressed it, 'her teeth set sharply by a sort of unconscious contraction, and the words left her lips cut short and tense, with a harsh sonority. She recovered her natural voice only when she had succeeded in mastering her emotion.' Sarah's own account of her experiences is much the same, though she distinguishes curiously between her early fear of simply not making herself heard at all in public and the later nervousness that overcame her when she began to be conscious of all the possibilities of failure. Once more curiously characteristic, however, is the fighting spirit in which she met this difficulty as well as others. Mrs. Siddons speaks of the peculiar resolution which came to her in exceptional crises, 'one of what I call my desperate tranquillities, which usually impress me under terrific circumstances.' So with the other Sarah; when she had a struggle to face, she faced it, and never gave way: 'I who am so liable to stage fright had no fear, for with me stage fright assumes a curious form; in front of a public which I feel to be hostile for

one reason or another, I am free from all stage fright; I have only one idea, one resolve: to subjugate the refractory audience. In front of a benevolent public, on the other hand, I am alarmed lest I should not come up to expectations and stage fright grips me imperiously.' But the strain of the battle was exhausting, all the same: it was hard to say which took more out of you, the public that was benevolent or the public that was not, and the path to glory, whether it led to the grave or elsewhere, was one of incessant struggle and war.

There was war with the human elements about you, also, at all times, and of all human elements undoubtedly the most vexing and distracting was yourself, at any rate for one constituted as was Sarah Bernhardt. There was the petulant, devouring fury of her inborn temper, which she inherited from her mother. In her childhood her fits of frenzy developed into absolute collapse, and listen to her own account of one outburst of provocation with her sister in later years: 'When once we were in the carriage, I struck my little sister with such rage that Madame Guérard, terrified, covered her with her body and herself received my blows with my fists, my feet, with everything, for I rushed at her all over, mad with rage, with fury, and with shame.' She not only had the fury of temper, she had a native quickness of tongue and a burning outspokenness, which fostered hostility even where she had no intention of doing so. As to whether she was fundamentally jealous of her fellows, there may be more question. She herself would never admit it, not having the charming candor which made Joseph Jefferson confess, 'In this case my rival was a good actor, but not too good to be jealous of me, and if our positions had been reversed, the chances are that I would have been jealous of him.' Her bitter enemy, Marie Colombier, insists that 'she proved herself jealous of all her comrades, jealous even of her sisters.' Probably she was not less inclined than others to dislike the success of her rivals and even to belittle it, for in this as in everything, she was constantly and enormously human.

In any case, with her temperament as it was, she had her difficulties with humanity, plenty of them, at all times and in all varieties. Perhaps the most of these were with her fellow actors. It must be admitted that in some cases she cherished long and loyal friendships. Her relation with Croizette, for years perhaps her most prominent competitor, seems to have been in the main friendly and even affectionate. And Sarah herself makes a very curious comment, that she finds much more pettiness and hostility and mean jealousy and spite from the men actors than from the women, who she says are in the main inclined to be friendly to her and to get along well. This was not always true, however, for it was an actual slap in the face, given to an older fellow actress, which drove Sarah from the Français in the early days, and long, long afterwards the same tendency to physical violence would break out when her nerves got too strained and the provocation too desperate. Also, there was the unseemly war of words and pamphlets between her and Marie Colombier, in which probably everybody was wrong and certainly everybody was unfortunate and indiscreet.

The relations with managers were no less complicated and difficult than with actors. But to keep well with managers was essential to one's bread and butter, and Sarah had always a shrewd sense of the importance of bread and butter as the first essential of life. Therefore her managerial history, though checkered by all sorts of flaws and breaks and disasters, was eminently practical. All the same, to have to rehearse her must have been an ordeal for any manager. She had her inspirations of genius, but to meet and deal with her whims and fancies was a task that at times assumed the proportions of nightmare.

If it was bad for the managers, it was much worse for the authors, since the manager has at least the power of his contract and his forfeit behind him. The poor author could hardly even suggest, he could only obey. How vividly does Claretie sum up the tragedy that rehearsal meant, after narrating various harrowing incidents in one particular case: 'These rehearsals, calculated to drive an author mad, achieved a real celebrity. With interpreters like this woman, who is nevertheless a great artist and in no sort of way a spiteful creature, the author's business becomes a torment. I had rather break stone on the roads than put Sarah Bernhardt through a rehearsal.'

Yet was there ever an actress who made the reputation and fortune of more dramatic authors than Sarah Bernhardt did? Coppée and she first soared into glory together. Richepin and Lemaître owed their chief success to her. Dumas thought nothing of *Camille* till she remade it and made it the triumph of two continents, and it was through her that *Frou-Frou* became Meilhac and Halévy's masterpiece. Sardou gladly recognized that it was the adaptation of her genius to his that gave him wealth and credit and Rostand was almost her child as well as her lover.

With the critics the story is something the same. Newspaper criticism is the plague, the bane, the horror of every artist, but of the actor most of all, for with the actor it is always most cursory and generally least intelligent. Great actors are apt to proclaim their indifference to it, and also to devour every word of it with tortured curiosity. On the whole, Sarah Bernhardt was more fortunate than some others. Heaven knows, she got abuse and vilification enough, of her art, of her characters, of her extravagances and oddities. But the greatest critics of Paris were usually kind to her. Some were her lovers, some were her personal friends without being lovers, and the long, devoted, unloverlike attachment of the greatest genius among them, Jules Lemaître, is the best testimony to the finer qualities of Sarah's heart. All the same, criticism is a misery at the best. The artist could not flourish without it, but sometimes he feels that he can hardly exist with it, and what appears most fretting is the utter unintelligence of it. You could forgive these people anything, if only they would make the least effort to understand what you are trying to do.

So the life of the artist, especially of the dramatic artist, is a long struggle, and that of Sarah Bernhardt was no exception, rather a most vivid illustration, of the rule.

There are times when the struggle seems intolerable, when the wisest falter and the bravest are ready to give up. Even the self-centered and self-assured Charlotte Cushman was overcome at moments and cries: 'Often, as I left the theater and compared my own acting with Rachel's, despair took possession of me and a mad impulse to end life and effort together.' If we can accept her own accounts and those of others, Sarah was repeatedly at the point of suicide, and there is no more effective description of such a crisis than that given by George Sand, all the more important because it deals with Sarah's early, formative years and has a larger bearing on her character as well as on the special point involved: 'One evening *L'Autre* was being given at the Odéon. I looked in at Duquesnel's office and I found the whole theater in commotion. I was told that Sarah Bernhardt, who played Hélène with exquisite grace, had tried to poison herself. I went up to see her. I reasoned with her. I spoke of her son to whom she owed all her care and tenderness. I said everything that a woman and a mother could say in such a case. Sarah burst into tears. She assured me that she had a horror of the existence she had been leading hitherto, that nobody had ever spoken to her as I had done, and that my advice would never pass from her memory. A few days after this I got to the theater a little late. I met Sarah Bernhardt and her sister Jeanne on the staircase, both dressed like men and starting for the Bal Bullier. And this is all my remonstrances and my sermon came to. Let me repeat, look out for the women of the theater: they are at once more fascinating, more perverse, and more dangerous than any others.'

The fascination and the perversity and the danger were certainly unlimited, and also the misery running to any point of despair and even suicide. What carried Sarah Bernhardt through it all to a triumphant consummation was the magnificent, vital energy and persistence of her character. You could not really discourage her, or dishearten her, or beat her, or kill her. From the beginning she was determined to succeed. 'Madame Sand,' she said, in the early days, 'I would rather die than not be the greatest actress in the world.' Not only a great actress, you see, but the greatest actress in the world. And on the whole, for her day, she certainly was, and it was sheer will that did it, or at any rate will was the driving force, the same superb will that attracted her in Theodore Roosevelt and made her see herself and him as ruling the world.

It is impossible to give a more vigorous and telling picture of what this driving force was than her own, in association with the careless motto, *Quand même*: 'They knew that my device, *Quand même*, was not a matter of accident, but the result of deliberate reflection. My mother explained that at nine years old I adopted this device, after a mad leap over a ditch that no one could cross and to which my young cousin had challenged me. I had scratched my face, broken my wrist, bruised my whole body. And while they were carrying me home, I shouted, beside myself: "I will do it again, I will do it again, if he dares me again, and I will do all my life just what I will to do."' So she did, as far as a human being may. What gave more than mere erratic violence, more than mere chaotic tumult, to such furious exertion of the will for itself, was a certain pervading, if obscure, sense of the ideal behind it: 'My ideal?' said Sarah. 'My ideal? But I am still pursuing it. I shall pursue it until my last hour, and I feel that in the supreme moment I shall know the certainty of attaining it beyond the tomb.'

v

The result of this determined ambition and prolonged ideal effort was a career of triumph and success hardly paralleled by any other artist either on the stage or off it. And the peculiar quality of Sarah Bernhardt's success was its inexhaustible novelty, its endless series of developments and surprises and renewals. She did not attain one great climax and stay there or gradually fade away from it. She did not identify herself with one great part and remain identified with it till she died, like Joseph Jefferson. She was vital, spontaneous, creative, to an extraordinary extent, was always attempting new things and achieving them. As Mr. Baring expresses it admirably: 'She spent her life in making discoveries and in surprising the public and her critics by finding out what she could not do and in immediately doing it.'

This element of surprise, of perpetually revealing herself, even to herself, is notable all through her life, in the later years just as much as in the earlier. At the Odéon the managers thought nothing of her. She discovered Coppée, and triumphed. She went to the Français, and repeated the story. She went to London and became the star of the company. She left the Français in 1880. Everybody thought it was her ruin. Instead, she went to America and became the star of the world. When she came back to Paris, the critics thought her head would be turned and she would be no longer capable of serious art. Yet when she played *Phèdre,* in 1893, at nearly fifty, Sarcey and Lemaître raved over her and declared that she was younger and more beautiful than she had ever been. Then she began all over again with the creations of Sardou, a new drama and a new style of acting. When this wore thin in Paris, she carried it to America and to Australia, and came back to France to develop a new author and a new art with the romantic plays of Rostand. She lost a leg, and an ordinary actress would have dropped into the infirmary and the invalid chair. Not Sarah. She acted with her voice and her soul, not with her legs, and she went right on. When she produced Racine's *Athalie,* in 1920, after the War, every theater in Paris was closed, so that her fellow actors might see her perform once more. On the very eve of her death, when she was nearly eighty, she acted for the movies. The doctors said it would kill her. Perhaps it did. What did she care? She was bound to die fighting.

The priceless privilege of this element of perpetual renewal in Sarah's life was that she escaped the decay and self-survival that disfigure the old age of so many artists, actors, and others. Hear what Mrs. Kemble writes of her aunt, Mrs. Siddons: 'What a price my Aunt Siddons has paid for her great celebrity! Weariness, vacuity, and utter deadness of spirit. The cup has been so highly flavored that life is absolutely without sorrow or sweetness to her now, nothing but tasteless insipidity. She has stood on a pinnacle till all things have come to look flat and dreary, mere shapeless, colorless, level monotony to her. Poor woman! What a fate to be condemned to! and yet how she has been envied as well as admired!' There was nothing of this decay about Sarah, nothing but superb, mature power and exuberant energy to the very end. Again, there is no trace in her of the haunting melancholy that clung to Edwin Booth even in his days of greatest triumph, or of the subtle sense of dreamy emptiness that Jefferson found in the greatest successes of the stage. Just because she took herself and all her effort so seriously there was no sense of hollowness or emptiness in it at all. You have to look long and closely for even a suggestion of the satiety that almost always follows great spiritual strain and unalloyed success, as in her brief beautiful phrase, 'Tout passe, tout casse, tout lasse, all fails, all stales, all pales,' or in Claretie's story of her stopping in the midst of a triumphant rehearsal to complain of the unsatisfactoriness of her lot. To be sure, she had everything. 'But the end, the end! It is the end that counts. It is the finish that ought to be dramatic and enthralling. Take Rochefort—killed by a ball at the moment of his escape. What an admirable death! That was a climax. Drama! Mystery! Tell me, how do you think I shall end?'

Yet even here, in the touch of disgust, you get the vitality, the mystery, the suggestion of the unknown that gave a thrill to it all. As she herself puts it, most effectively, in her ***Memoirs:*** 'Always, when circumstances arise to disturb the current of my life, I at first have an impulse of shrinking. For a second I cling to what actually is; then I fling myself headlong into what may be. . . . All at once what is becomes for me what was, and I cherish it with a tender emotion, as if it were something dead. But I adore what is to be. It is the unknown, the alluring, the mysterious. I believe always that it will be the unheard of, and I shudder from head to foot, with a delicious surmise.' Always adventure, discovery, experiment, always probe the unknown and reach out for its deepest secrets, *Quand même, Quand même,* no matter what happens, and make it your highest pride to go out of life with the same magnificent zest that you brought into it.

Muriel Bradbrook (essay date 1982)

SOURCE: "Paris in the Bernhardt Era," in *Women and Literature 1779-1982: The Collected Papers of Muriel Bradbook,* Vol 2., The Harvester Press, 1982, pp. 69-80.

[*In the following essay, Bradbrook examines Bernhardt's social and artistic standing in Paris during her time.*]

At the service of thanksgiving for 'the greatest actress whom I have called friend'—Edith Evans—her biographer told how he, seeing that she was rapidly failing, took aside his little daughter and prepared her by telling her that Dame Edith was very old and was going to die. The child paused in deep thought, then confidently replied, 'No, I don't think she's going to die. She's not the sort!'

Sarah Bernhardt's words to Ellen Terry, 'There are two people who will never be old. You and I, darling', were echoed when Maurice Rostand wrote her epitaph

> Ci-gît Sarah
> Qui survivra.

Sarah Bernhardt, like Edith Evans, was not classically beautiful; the stage self is something that comes when their craftsmanship, so exact and scrupulous, flowers; and 'the god was there', as Sarah said. They served.

> I know what wages beauty gives
> How hard a life her servant lives,

sang Yeats, who fell in love with beauty, and married a plain woman. Even Sarah's detractors conceded that she knew her craft. It seems to me that before great playwrights can make their innovations there must be a high level of craftsmanship among the actors of the 'painted scene'. Those geniuses of the theatre, Shakespeare, Molière, Ibsen, were all craftsmen themselves, but they needed acting material to build on. The actor's art survives on stage.

Throughout the nineteenth century the dominance of Europe—indeed the world—by the Parisian theatre meant that at Paris the great practical experiments were initiated. Playwrights sent their work to Paris, from whence it travelled on to the rest of the world; Paris was the manufacturing centre. The nineteenth century saw the arrival of international theatre, as the old national traditions merged. Up to then, the ancient centres of theatre in Europe—Paris and London, Italy and Spain—had developed in relative independence their individual styles. The Comédie Française, the Theatre of Molière, safeguarded the French classical tradition by its monopoly of performance. Italy, home of the most continuous formalist tradition, of the *commedia dell'arte,* carnival and marionettes, made its contribution in the form of opera. England's great Shakespearean tradition existed alongside historical spectacular dramas, based largely on Walter Scott; burlesque and pantomime offered a form of entertainment which, even in a Puritan society, Tories could accept; this culminated in Gilbert and Sullivan's operas, the most successful venture of the later Victorian period. After the Lyceum triumphs of Henry Irving and Ellen Terry came the polemical theatre of Shaw and, in the late 1890s, the beginnings of Irish drama at the Abbey Theatre.

To track the French influence would entail a survey of every European capital and parts of the near East also, for it was Napoleon's invasion of Egypt that evoked the first tentative drama in Cairo and Beirut. Like other actresses, Sarah Bernhardt visited Egypt; but all round the perimeter of French hegemony, the French model prevailed in theatres, whilst from the perimeter appeared the new dramatists who were to transform the theatres they served. Great men came from little countries—Norway, Sweden, Ireland—and brought their plays to Paris before they could be more widely known. Ibsen, Strindberg and, of course, Turgenev had to be given in translation; in France, Hauptmann and Suderman were played in French. Wherever Bernhardt played, it was in the tongue of Racine and of Sardou.

The three phases of development on the French stage might be summarised as the advent of a Romantic freedom, of which the *Bataille d'Hernani* in 1830 was the symbol; the gradual growth of contemporary 'realism' during the Second Empire, with Montigny as director, Augier as dramatist; the advent of naturalism in the mid-1880s, and later of symbolism (Théâtre Libre, 1887; Théâtre de l'Oeuvre, 1895).

At the age of twenty-five, Sarah enjoyed her first dazzling success in *Le Passant* of Coppée, whilst in the same year (1869), at the age of forty-one, Ibsen produced his first realist drama, *The League of Youth,* and attended the opening of the Suez Canal. For Sarah, as for Ibsen, the 1860s had provided the 'run-up'; the 1870s brought achievement, culminating at the end of that decade. In 1879 Sarah Bernhardt, with her first visit to London, broke with the Comédie Française; and began that international career which was to liberate her from French theatrical tradition, and to break up the old repertory system in favour of the 'star vehicle' spectacularly produced. The same year, with the appearance of *A Doll's House,* Ibsen inaugurated the drama of the modern age.

The 1880s saw the consequences of these two events. In 1880 Sarah went to New York, where her most famous role, *La Dame aux Camélias,* was played and in the course of her tour, repeated sixty-five times. Sarah *was* Marguerite Gautier, the victimised and virtuous courtesan; Adrienne Lecouvreur was another such role, but historically distanced. Hereafter increasingly she appeared in plays written specifically for her, mainly by Sardou, though she also tried her own hand at composition. Through the 1880s she alternated foreign tours with Parisian triumphs. The counter-move began in the little amateur theatres; by 1888 Paris had seen *Ghosts,* and the Meininger troupe had paid a visit. *Ghosts* and, in 1890, *The Wild Duck,* did not succeed yet soon Lugné-Poë was staging Strindberg's *Lady Julie* and Hauptmann's *The Weavers* (both 1892), followed by *The Father* (1895).

From world tours (her special trains symbolised the age of new communication), Sarah moved into management (financed by her foreign earnings), first in the theatres run by her son Maurice, then in 1899 at the Théâtre Sarah Bernhardt.

By this time the Théâtre de l'Oeuvre had inaugurated the new wave of the symbolists. Whilst Sarah had acquired a new Romantic poet, Rostand, who supplied her latest famous roles in his plays *Cyrano de Bergerac* and *L'Aiglon* (1900), Maeterlinck was supplying puppet plays for the *avant-garde* theatre of Paris (in 1905 Sarah was to play Pelléas in *Pelléas et Mélisande*). She once (1905) essayed the part of Ellida in *The Lady from the Sea* also; it was not a success, although it had been a triumph for the Théâtre des Escholiers. But what matter if the *avant-garde* production of *An Enemy of the People* was taken as an image of the Dreyfus affair? There was room for more than one theatrical tradition in Paris, and indeed before the end of the century some of the *avant-garde* were writing for the Comédie Française. By 1900, however, the separate establishments of the classical theatre, the popular theatre and the *avant-garde* stage had each its well-defined clientele. If France, the most powerful theatre centre, had expanded its eclecticism to produce plays in other national traditions (in itself an important change) yet these had gained recognition only by the lead given in Paris. Plays were imported, but theatre exported.

Paris still experiments—the ruinous theatre, open to the sky, where Peter Brook furnished his stage with bits of old junk, represented the *avant-garde* of the 1970s. Nowadays if there is no such absolute French predominance, the group of writers drawn from all countries who led the revival of the 1950s resided in Paris— the Irishman Beckett, the Romanian Ionesco, the Russian Adamov, the Spaniard Arrabal.

. . . . .

For the stage and for her public life Sarah developed both a self and an anti-self. Some years ago *The Three Faces of Eve* presented in a case of split personality the initial face of a very meek, good, complaint little girl out of whom burst an unruly, boisterous tomboy with delinquent tendencies. The mature person who integrated and supplanted both was occasionally troubled by the resurfacing of one or other of the previous selves.

Sarah's style was refined and elegant, her golden voice— so christened by Hugo at the hundredth performance of *Ruy Blas*—a soprano, whose effects were lyric; a very rapid recitative interspersed with her *cri sauvage*. The delicate pathos of her instrument, which at first suited the roles of *jeune princesse*—Monime or Aricie—later displayed a use of the vibrato which her arch-enemy, Shaw, compared to the organ's *voix céleste*. She played boy's parts also. In the role of the victimised lover—Marguerite, Adrienne Lecouvreur, and the rest—the plangency grew till even Andromaque and Athalie became seductive. But she had, of course, been trained in declamation at the Conservatoire as she describes in her **Art du Théâtre,** being taught by Provost, Samson and Regnier. The last was her most admired master. In gesture, however, from the first she showed herself an innovator and she recounts her altercation with her professor about the right, in a very minor role, to turn her back upon the audience:

> Mademoiselle, it is disrespectful of you to turn your back upon the audience . . . But, sir, I was

accompanying an old woman to the rear door, and I could not very well escort her backwards . . . Your predecessors, Mademoiselle, whose talents were equal, if not superior to yours, have managed to walk upstage without turning their backs to the audience . . . As he angrily turned to leave, I wasted no time in stopping him. Excuse me, sir, do you think you can reach that door without turning your back to me? . . . He attempted to do so, but then left in a violent temper, turning his back and slamming the door.

The 'theatre of Molière' held her only for a year. As Sarah left the Comédie (after, as a mere student, slapping the face of the leading lady) she developed her art in the freer theatre of the boulevards. Her most celebrated piece of choreography was the death scene in *La Dame aux Camélias* (although all her death scenes became celebrated, and she was required to die in every play). In seduction scenes she used her whole body in a manner as compelling as it was unclassical; she was also a mistress of attitudes, discoveries, as the famous painting by Clairon testifies.

Off-stage she was demonic, flamboyant, and subject to such alarming rages as the one which caused her to horsewhip the woman who had libelled her as Sarah Barnum. She terrified her managers by venturing out on to the ice floes of the St Lawrence River at Montreal. Her vitality drove her to live round the clock, exhausting all her colleagues; she delighted in shooting, in keeping a menagerie of wild animals. She ventured boldly into the arts of painting and sculpture, as well as play writing.

Yet on the stage she was plaintive, elegant, mournful, and wholly feminine, though also essaying transvestite roles. Physically, in some respects, she was frail. She suffered from stage nerves. But when in 1872 she re-entered the Comédie Française as Chimène, Théodore de Banville wrote:

> Very tall, thin, [actually she was *not* tall], endowed with that slimness which we find in so many theatrical heroines, even though it gives such ready ammunition to wit, Mlle Sarah has one of those expressive yet delicate heads that medieval artists painted . . . From Provost she learnt pure, elegant, scrupulously exact diction, but nature gave her a far rarer gift—the quality of being totally and unconsciously lyrical in whatever she attempted. Her voice captures the rhythm and music of poetry as naturally as a lyre . . . this makes her quite the opposite of other actors and actresses. They, as Talma so rightly explained, are always troubled by poetry, which locks them in an inexorable bond of words. They are at their best when they obtain the sort of scripts which they can turn to their own ends, a play with lively and well developed situations, in which the style is of no importance . . . Mlle Sarah on the other hand receives all her inspiration and force from poetry, and the nearer she approaches the purely lyrical, the greater she is and the more she is herself. Make no mistake, the engagement of Mlle Sarah Bernhardt at the

Comédie Française is serious and violently revolutionary. It is poetry entering the realm of dramatic art; it is the wolf in the sheepfold.

When after eight years she resigned for a second time from the Comédie Française, Sarah moved towards just the sort of plays de Banville had rejected for her. Scribe supplied her with *Adrienne Lecouvreur,* the opening play of her New York visit. *Frou Frou* was less tragedy than a fashion show, and the strong melodramas which Sardou wrote for her from 1881 (the date of *Fédora*), with their profusion of jewels, crowds and historic depiction of exotic times and places were combined with the pathos of the virtuous courtesan, with violent deaths, with tortures and triumphs.

Perhaps without the undeviating standards of the Comédie Française there would have been nothing to rebel against, nothing to test the muscles. It is still possible for the older classical roles to be transformed, as for instance Hecht transformed the role of Néron in *Britannicus.*

The London public was unprepared for Sarah's combination of delicate lyricism and erotic boldness. One reviewer spoke of her 'orchidaceous air', Matthew Arnold of 'a fugitive vision of delicate features under a shower of hair and a cloud of lace'. As she first landed at Folkestone quay, a young actor, Johnston Forbes Robertson, presented her with a modest bunch of violets; but Oscar Wilde carpeted her path with lilies. Later she studied the part of his *Salome,* which the censor refused to license, and once he said: 'The three women I have admired most in my life are Sarah Bernhardt, Queen Victoria and Lily Langtry. I would have married any one of them.' The first two had in common at least a golden voice—the most outstanding charm of the Queen as of the actress.

According to some, the endless tours caused a hardening of Sarah's style; playing to audiences who could not understand her speech must have had an effect on gesture and led her to spectacle. Sardou, it is said, perfected the clockwork play; he was 'a mere set of fingers with the theatre at the tips of them'.

. . . . .

The apex of Sarah's classical reputation came between 1869, when she achieved her first great success as Zelotto (a transvestite part) in *Le Passant,* and her departure on her first world tour in 1880. The theatrical-spectacular years that followed, the years of Fédora, Théodora, La Tosca, Cléopatre, Gismonde, La Sorcière, coincided with the arrival of the naturalist and then the symbolist theatres. The prophet of the naturalists was Zola, who declared that art should aspire to the condition of journalism. The real furniture, real trees, real rabbits and even real Sèvres china, introduced by Augier at the beginning of the Second Empire gave way to *A Doll's House,* then to the Théâtre Libre (1886) and, in less than a decade, to Strindberg's *Lady Julie* (1888).

The foremost of the English Ibsenites, Bernard Shaw, consistently mocked with deadly praise the art of Sarah Bernhardt, as part of the attack on what he termed Sardoodledom. In the *Saturday Review,* 1 June 1895, he nostalgically recalled the Sarah who had not sold out 'to a high modern development of the circus and the waxworks',

> I confess I regard with a certain jealousy the extent to which this ex-artist, having deliberately exercised her unquestioned right to step down from the national theatre in which she became famous, to posture in a travelling show, is still permitted the privileges and courtesies appertaining to her former rank . . . Miss Bernhardt has elected to go round the world pretending to kill people with hatchets and hairpins and making, I presume, heaps of money. I wish her every success, but I certainly shall not treat her as an artist of the first rank unless she pays me well for it. As a self-respecting critic, I decline to be bought for nothing.

A fortnight later, comparing her with Duse, even more maliciously he links the art of her excessive make-up with her cult of fine art.

> Her dresses and diamonds, if not exactly splendid, are at least splendacious; her figure, far too scantily upholstered in the old days, is at its best; and her complexion shows that she has not studied modern art in vain. Those charming rosette effects which French painters produce by giving flesh the pretty colours of strawberries and cream and painting the shadows pink and crimson are cunningly reproduced by Miss Bernhardt in the living picture. She paints her ears crimson and allows them to peep enchantingly through a few loose braids of her auburn hair. Every dimple has its dab of pink; and her finger tips are so delicately encarnadined that you fancy they are transparent like her ears, and that the light is showing through their delicate blood vessels. Her lips are like a newly-painted pillar box and her cheeks right up to the languid lashes have the bloom and surface of a peach. She is beautiful with the beauty of her school—and entirely inhuman and incredible . . . She adds to her own piquancy by looking you straight in the eye and saying in effect; 'Now who would ever dream that I am a grandmother?'

Shaw did not spare the golden voice his damning praise, as her recitative, 'monotonous chanting on one note', was compared with Duse who 'immeasurably dwarfs the poor little octave and a half on which Sarah Bernhardt plays such pretty canzonets and stirring marches'. Again, comparing hers with Duse's interpretation, 'The coaxing suits well with her acting, which is not the art of making you think more highly or feel more deeply, but the art of making you admire her, champion her, weep with her, laugh at her jokes, follow her fortunes breathlessly and applaud her wildly when the curtain falls.' In 'Sardoodledom' he said of *Fédora* ('one of the claptraps which Sardou contrives for her') that it offers 'the whole Bernhardtian range of sensational effects . . . effects so enormously popular and lucrative that, though their production is hardly more of a fine art than lion-taming, few women who are able for them can resist the temptation to devote their whole lives to them.'

There is no doubt that Shaw himself was the most thoroughgoing showman and lion-tamer; he resented in Sarah arts which in his own fashion he cultivated. It was his habit to attack the favourite of the hour, a publicity stunt which by now is well attested, if the attacker has sufficient talent. When the Théâtre Libre came to London Shaw attacked the leading actress for playing Rebecca 'à la Bernhardt'.

Yet Sarah was to essay Hamlet; and l'Aiglon, her 'white Hamlet', represented her genuine patriotism, often displayed in ordinary life, from the hospital at l'Odéon, during the Siege of Paris, to the melodramatic pieces of the First World War. Her boyish pathos in l'Aiglon combined with the spirit that had led her on her first international campaign for French theatre (as she explained in her old age to her grand-daughter).

. . . . .

The development of the French *avant-garde* theatre in the last two decades of the nineteenth century is one of the most well documented subjects in theatrical history. Antoine's acting team was not gifted, but his method was copied. The talented actor Lugné-Poë had indeed opened an amateur theatre before Antoine, and at his Théâtre de l'Art had played *The Cenci;* Mallarmé, Verlaine and others supported him in his reaction against the Théâtre Libre. At his new Théâtre de l'Oeuvre settings were sparse, movements evocative, costumes unrealistic. A marionette *Tempest,* Marlowe and Ford represented the exotically antique, but reacted in favour of the playwright against the absolute predominance of the star.

Shaw had summed up the view of many playwrights when he declared that Sarah substituted personality for characterisation. 'She does not enter into the leading character, she substitutes herself for it.' If she grounded her emotions in technique, Sarah was, in Jouvet's terms, an *actrice* not a *comédienne,* whereas Lugné-Poë subjected himself to the rich, varied material which such playwrights as Ibsen and Strindberg were supplying.

For these playwrights, the Paris stage remained an ideal. In *Ghosts* (1884) Ibsen represented the city as the home of all joy and artistic freedom and of perfect purity to boot. The hero, Osvald, returning to his gloomy Northern fjord describes that artist's life there to his mother and her pastor. The young artist 'can't afford to get married' but lives in a 'proper and comfortable home' in complete decorum 'with his children and his children's mother'. Only model husbands and fathers, in Paris for a spree, 'were able to tell us of places and things we'd never dreamed of'. For bachelors the models ('There are plenty of fine types among the models which you wouldn't see up here') came of an evening to partake of a slice of ham and a bottle of wine before beginning to dance.

Ibsen, in spite of his emancipated views, was extremely Puritan (Strindberg was to term him 'the celebrated Norwegian male blue-stocking') and himself did not visit Paris. He allows a vigorous girl like Régine to dream of it, the equally vigorous and ruthless Rita to offer her Alfred 'champagne' with pink lighting. By 1899, in his last play, Irene has posed as a model, naked, on a turntable, evidently in some kind of show. She has travelled all over the world, and claims to have killed her husband with a pin from her hair. The hero regrets not having seduced her when young.

By the time Ibsen wrote this play, the 'new wave' which he had started with *A Doll's House* was succeeded by a third wave; Strindberg was parodying Ibsen, and whilst Shaw was still learning from the naturalism of Brieux (translated into English by Mrs Shaw), the two lines of development had separated. The varied drama of the twentieth century descends from both. Ibsen's world became that of the German naturalists, who went on to contribute to the next great movement, the expressionism of Kaiser and Toller. The 'world within' descended through the later plays of Strindberg and through Pirandello to the modern theatre of the absurd. Polarised, the two produced Beckett at one point, Brecht at the other.

The playwrights had certainly taken the initiative over from the players. That Ibsen had learnt his craftsmanship in the theatres of Norway, dominated by France through Copenhagen, and given to the works of Scribe, provided him with a training that he exercised far from the living stage; but Strindberg married an actress, and after the calamitous break with her, came to Paris where his plays had already been staged. He resided there during the years 1894-6. In Sweden his works were banned but, although the shadows of his 'Inferno' crisis were closing on him, in France he enjoyed success, and this he dramatised in a play set in Paris, *Crimes and Crimes* (1899). It deals with a young playwright whose new drama has made him the toast of the city but who, drawn into a love affair with a beautiful sculptress, Henriette, leaves his mistress Jeanne and their child Marion. He is even heard to say it would be better if the child had not been born; shortly after she dies, and he is suspected of killing her. Although found innocent, he still feels remorse for 'the murder in the heart', and confesses himself to an old Abbé. He goes back to the theatre, absolved.

The setting in Paris is unusually precise for Strindberg; the beautiful cemetery at Montparnasse where Jeanne is chilled by foreboding, recalls Strindberg's actual encounter with a woman mourner in this place. The story is a reflection as always of his own inner conflicts, but in spite of the elements of fantasy, Paris gave Strindberg the impulse for his most 'theatrical' play. He is said too to have met Bernhardt herself in the Montparnasse cemetery, where they engaged in some spiritualist experiments.

With the plays of Strindberg and others, the Paris theatre began to reflect a surrealist view of drama before the end of the century. Twenty years before Dada, Alfred Jarry's plays were staged by Lugné-Poë, and with his work this survey may conclude. What Sarah would have thought of it defies comment. Although she expressed goodwill towards the Théâtre Libre, on Jarry she might have pulled a gun. But on 11 December 1896 she had just enjoyed her great Day of Glorification and was otherwise occupied.

On 10 December Sardou, Coppée, Rostand, Jules Lemaître and others organised a day of tribute, beginning with a banquet in the Salle du Zodiac of the Grand Hotel. Five hundred guests gathered for lunch, a theatre ticket, a medal and a Golden Book of the Gala. Sarah appeared on a balcony in a white dress embroidered in gold and trimmed with sable. It was reported that as she descended

> Her long train followed her like a graceful tame serpent. At every turn she bent over the railing and twined her arms like an ivy wreath round the velvet pillars whilst she acknowledged the acclamations with her disengaged hand. Her lithe and slender body scarcely seemed to touch the earth. She was wafted towards us in a halo of glory.

For the feast she sat between the Minister of Fine Arts and the personal representative of the President of the Republic. Afterwards the star appeared in the third act of *Phèdre* and the fourth of *Rome Vaincue;* then was staged the Apotheosis of Sarah Bernhardt. The poets came on to read their tributes. Rostand opened as follows:

> En ce temps sans beauté, seule tu encore nous restes,
> Sachant descendre, pale, un grand escalier clair,
> Ceindre un bandeau, prêtre un lys, brandir un fer,
> Reine de l'attitude et princesse des gestes.

At the end Sarah dissolved in tears, whilst showers of camellias rained down on her from the flies.

At the other end of the spectrum, on the following night, history was being made in the Théâtre de l'Oeuvre. The past and future touched each other here; this sustaining relationship makes the story of Sarah Bernhardt part of the continuing life of the theatre, and ensures that she survives through the living currents of the actor's art.

10 and 11 December 1896 epitomised the struggle between the theatre of the star-actor and the theatre of the poets. Whether playing the great classic roles—Sarah was always comparing herself with Rachel—or the made-to-measure part of a spectacular melodrama, the actor resisted the new theatre until it had become more familiar. The *avant-garde* theatre was the counter-assertion of the writer; if Sarah reduced the playwright to a puppeteer, Jarry reduced the actor to a puppet. His *Ubu-Roi* was closely based on Shakespeare's *Hamlet*—which Sarah was to play—indeed the author claims Ubu turns into Shakespeare:

> Then Father Ubu shakes his speare, who was afterwards yclept Shakespeare by the English, and you have from under his own hand many lovely tragedies by this name.

11 December, the opening night of *Ubu Roi,* saw one of the great French theatrical riots—perhaps the most sig-

nificant since the *Bataille d' Hernani.* Again it was the language that roused the audience—the curtain rose on Ubu's cry of 'Merdre!' Among the crowd were W. B. Yeats and Arthur Symons. Yeats wrote,

> I go to the first performance of Jarry's *Ubu Roi* . . . The audience shake their fists at one another and my friend whispers to me 'There are often duels after these performances', and he explains to me what is happening on the stage. The players are supposed to be toys, dolls, marionettes, and now they are all hopping like wooden frogs, and I can see for myself that the chief personage, who is some kind of King, carries for Sceptre a brush of the kind we use to clean a closet. Feeling bound to support the most spirited party, we have shouted for the play but that night at the Hôtel Corneille, I am very sad, for comedy, objectivity, has displayed its growing power once more. I say 'After Stephane Mallarmé, after Paul Verlaine, after Gustave Moreau, after Puvis de Chavannes, after our own verse, after all our subtle colour and nervous rhythm, after the faint mixed tints of Corot, what more is possible? After us, the Savage God.'

As it happened, Mallarmé approved. Symons describes the painted scene, representing both indoors and outdoors, even the torrid and arctic zones simultaneously. At the foot of a bed stood a tree, snow-laden; there were also palm trees, a boa constrictor, a gallows with pendant skeleton. Changes of scene were announced by placards. Among the artists cited as inspiration was Gauguin.

Here is the polarisation of Sarah's theatre, but the French theatre was strong enough to tolerate these opposites; indeed, only in so strong a setting could they appear. Revolt did not induce collapse—only counter-movements. Contraries are more positive than mere negation; the *avant-garde* theatre was sustained by the opposing power of the establishment. Together they provided a force that held society magnetised. True classicism is that which can tolerate change, and without changing its identity, can modify itself to accommodate the new works. This kind of confidence gave to the French theatre the power to radiate its art, as well as absorb changes.

So, a week after witnessing the Ubu riot, Yeats met the shy young student who lived on the top floor of the Hotel Corneille, and invited John Millington Synge to come back to Ireland. From that encounter on 16 December came Synge's new life on Aran, his one fine tragedy, the kind of comedy that in a few years produced riots in Dublin. He fell in love with an actress, and died at the height of his powers, leaving a legend to the Abbey. To that legend, France had contributed.

J. C. Trewin (essay date 1984)

SOURCE: "Bernhardt on the London Stage," in *Bernhardt and the Theatre of Her Time,* edited by Eric Salmon, Greenwood Press, 1984, pp. 111-31.

[In the following essay, Trewin discusses London's reaction to Bernhardt and her reaction to the city.]

1

I would like to move selectively across Sarah's visits to a city that—in spite of Bernard Shaw—she loved; and midway, to unveil (for a moment only) a personal King Charles's Head.

May I begin by dropping into poetry?—not my own, but that of the nearly forgotten Stephen Phillips, dramatist of the golden shuttle and the violet wool, the dreaming keels of Greece, the souls that flashed together in one flame. The year was 1912. Sarah Bernhardt, aged sixty-five, was appearing at—of all theatres—the London Coliseum, today an opera house, then the most celebrated music-hall in Britain. Hardly, I would say, a citadel of the classical stage—though that may not have troubled Sarah, with her admiration for Marie Lloyd: two rather different splendours of the Theatre Theatrical (it is a phrase that, in such a book as this, the reader will surely forgive me for repeating).

A distant cousin of Frank Benson, and trained as an actor in Benson's touring university of the stage—the supreme company of what, in my part of England, we call "the pomping folk"—Stephen Phillips was the shooting-star of verse dramatists. At the turn of the century he had been ranked incautiously with Sophocles, Shakespeare, Dante, Marlowe, Webster and—according to that usually restrained Scot, William Archer—"the elder Dumas speaking with the voice of Milton". It was rather a lot for one man. In spite of those early intimations of immortality, the critics soon regretted their rapture. After three ornate productions—and the *Nero* which came a few years later—Phillips and his neo-Elizabethan verse (all revival, no begetting) swiftly declined. Even so, twelve years after his first outbreak, he was still about, still ready with the kind of glib ceremonial verse he wrote for Sarah Bernhardt, the actress who had ruled the world's stage, the rival of the Italian Duse. Phillips's ode, zoological and ornithological, began like this:

> O myriad-minded child of France
> That still canst half the earth entrance!
> Now panther stealing on its prey,
> Now waking lark in breaking day,
> Now tigress crouching in her lair,
> Then dove afloat on summer air,
> Enchantress of the voice of gold. . . .

And so on, and so on, to the last invocation, presumably the Phillippine voice of Milton:

> Temple with classic phantoms tread,
> Thou resurrection of the dead!
> Here we salute thee from a shore
> From France divided now no more;
> No longer sundered by the brine,
> But lightly, strongly, bound to thine.

Yes, dreadful . . . but the poem was printed in the old *Westminster Gazette*. And the *Gazette* did have a genuine literary reputation. We must suppose that Sarah's protean fame, lark, panther, tigress, and dove, and the remembered fame of Phillips, echoing in a vault, had between them overpowered the editor. The simple fact was that Sarah had overpowered everyone since she first landed from the sundering brine at Folkestone pier. She was then, in the early summer of 1879, on the way to London for the visit of the Comédie Française—forty-three performances, in eighteen of which she would appear—at the Gaiety Theatre by the Strand. This was John Hollingshead's theatre, devoted to extravaganza, burlesque, the "lighter lyric stage". Not that Sarah minded: Gaiety, Adelphi, Coronet, Coliseum—through life she never troubled about her theatres; whatever they were she made them her own. She was thirty-four when she landed that May morning: looking taller than she was, very thin, neither fair nor dark, her eyes deep and dark brown, her face the "delicate features" that Matthew Arnold would see under a shower of hair and a cloud of lace.

As (if we may change again) this orchid of the French theatre appeared on the Folkestone landing-stage, she heard a cry of "Vive Sarah Bernhardt!" Next, a tall, pale young man "with the ideal face of Hamlet"—it was Johnston Forbes Robertson, not yet with a hyphen in his name—came up to present her with a tribute about which there is a slight difference of opinion. It could have been a bunch of violets. Sarah, typically, preferred to call it a gardenia. One of her companions and rivals said, with a certain spite: "They'll be making you a carpet of flowers next." And, on the word, the carpet arrived. A young man with long, flowing hair, who always doubled and redoubled any gesture—his name was Oscar Wilde—scattered at Sarah's feet an armful of lilies. Sarah had no wish to trample on them. But there they were. It was, on the whole, a complicated beginning, and it must have been something of an anti-climax to arrive later in a London drizzle at Charing Cross Station, with no noticeable welcome and no flowers, either in the hand or underfoot. Indeed, even the promising red carpet in the station was not for the French company but for the Prince and Princess of Wales, Edward and Alexandra. Tactlessly, they had left that afternoon for Paris: not in itself the most heartening news.

Never mind. Half an hour later Sarah was handed down from her carriage at the wide-open door of the house in Chester Square where she would lodge. Within she found an immense bouquet inscribed simply "Welcome! Henry Irving." It was a semi-regal salute from the English stage, though Ellen Terry would murmur, much later, that "of [Sarah's] superb powers as an actress, I don't believe Henry ever had a glimmering notion". One great idiosyncratic player unable to recognise another.

Sarah was to open at the Gaiety on June 2, 1879. This, in its various ways, was quite a year in international stage history: a major event, the appearance of Ibsen's *A Doll's House;* a minor one (at the time), the inauguration of the Shakespeare Memorial Theatre at Stratford-upon-Avon. We must decide for ourselves where Sarah's début in

London can be placed. Though Sarah came to love London, that summer it depressed her. She wrote:

> Those tall houses with sash windows uncurtained; ugly monuments in mourning with dust and grime; flower-sellers at the street corners, faces sad as the rain, bedraggled feathers in their hats, and lamentable clothing, the black mud of the streets; the low sky; the funereal mirth of drunken women hanging on to men just as drunken; the wild dancing of dishevelled children round the street organs as numerous as the omnibuses—all this caused a curious indefinable suffering to a Parisian.

That was the London of a century ago. She would find that it was, in fact, a special city; slowly its charms were revealed, the "beauty of the aristocratic women", the "dizzying movement of Hyde Park", the generous hospitality, the men's wit which compared favourably with that of Frenchmen: "Their gallantry—much more respectful and so much more flattering—does not make me regret the gallantry of the French."

The first Gaiety programme was an ample triple bill, its centrepiece (in which Sarah would appear) the second act of *Phèdre* where Phèdre owns to Hippolyte her fierce and incestuous love. London playgoers, excited by the news from Paris (a city regarded as a kind of blissful and perpetual orgy) waited for Sarah as they had always waited for some mysterious and exotic foreigner. True, some—like the obstinate Yorkshireman in quite another context—refused to yield to rumour. "*Show* me!" the man had said; that night at the Gaiety many were saying "*Show* us!" as they waited in the elaborate scarlet and gold theatre. Outside were the six lamps that, ten months before, had lit the Strand with electricity for the first time.

Sarah herself would electrify any doubters. A single night established her in London. In effect, it would establish her there through forty-two years. It was the more remarkable because Rachel was still remembered, and comparison can be the deadliest form of criticism, something Dogberry said better and more briefly. Moreover, Sarah was what the French know as a *traqueuse,* subject to stage fright. That evening, in her hot Gaiety dressing-room, she was almost afraid to go on:

> Three times over I put rouge on my cheeks and darkened my eyes. Three times I took it all off again with a sponge. I thought I looked ugly, and it seemed to me that I was thinner than ever, and not so tall.

Then she closed her eyes and listened to her voice, which sounded to her off-key. Distraught now, she was warned that the second act of *Phèdre* was about to begin. She had put on neither veil nor rings; her cameo belt was unfastened; she felt that the words were escaping her. The actress, Thénard, who was playing the Nurse, said soothingly: "Calm yourself, Sarah! All the English have gone to Paris. There are only Belgians in the house."

"How silly you are!" Sarah cried. "You know how frightened I was in Brussels."

"All for nothing", said Thénard, who gets more and more like someone out of *Alice in Wonderland.* "There were only *English* people in the theatre that day!"

With this, Sarah Bernhardt, pardonably bewildered, found herself for the first time on an English stage. In desperation she pitched her opening speech on too high, too hysterical a note. She suffered acutely, and the suffering intensified her performance. She herself described what happened:

> I wept, I implored, I cried out; and it was all real. . . . My tears were flowing, burning and bitter. I implored Hippolyte for the love that was killing me, and the arms I stretched out to Mounet-Sully were the arms of Phèdre, tense with cruel longing for his embrace. The inspiration of "the god" had come.

The "god" never left her. At the end she fainted and was carried to her dressing room, though when the audience, in a prolonged standing ovation, insisted upon seeing her again, she did return to take a call, supported in the arms of Mounet-Sully. Always, Sarah Bernhardt was a child of the Theatre Theatrical; as London knew her first, so she went on. That second act of *Phèdre* had decided her future. She would be an actress-manageress.

2

The Gaiety season was astonishing, Sarah's success more than that of the great national company. On her nights the guinea stalls were often re-sold for five guineas. The critic Francisque Sarcey wrote back to Paris: "Nothing can give any idea of the craze Sarah is exciting. It's a mania." Undeniably it was, though on only her second night she had fainted three times as she dressed for the play, the *L'Etrangère* of Dumas *fils,* and managed in the third act to cut her big scene entirely. I may be forgiven for remembering an old actor in the West-Country city of Plymouth, who flourished at about the same time as Sarah (whom he would never have heard of) elsewhere. When his memory went, as it did frequently, he was accustomed to say to anyone on stage with him, in any play of any period at any time: "Hold! Thou weariest me! Take thou this purse of gold, furnish thyself with richer habiliments, and meet me at my lodging straight." Whereupon he would leave the stage and let the other actors get on with it. (They did: provincial "stock" was a training that fortified them against any disaster.)

During her second Gaiety performance Sarah should have told to her fellow-actress an interminable and important story—important, at least, to the plot. Instead, she said quite calmly: "The reason I sent for you here, Madame, is that I wished to tell you why I have acted as I have. I have thought it over and have decided *not* to tell you today." It seemed to her and to the rest of a startled company that she had ruined the piece, but apparently neither audience nor critics—they can behave like this even now—noticed anything wrong. An influential Frenchman, who later read the text, exclaimed to Sarah: "So much the better! Very dull, that story, and quite useless!"

Anyway, after this sub-editorial adventure, all was triumphantly well. Sarah completed a double event by exhibiting some of her pictures and pieces of sculpture in a Piccadilly shop. She made enough money to run up to Liverpool, on one of her days off, to buy a cheetah and a wolfhound, and to receive a present of six chameleons. "I would have liked", she sighed wistfully, "to have a dwarf elephant."

It had been a startling visit. During the following summer, 1880, she came back to London, but without cheetah, wolfhound, dwarf elephant or, for that matter, the support of the Comédie, with which she was at war and to which she would have to pay substantial damages for breaking her contract. Sarah was a permanent Declaration of Independence: she had to have her own company. A. B. Walkley, a young man then, who one day would be a principal drama critic, said long afterwards: "The extraordinary, the exaggerated, the unreasoning fuss that was made over her in London in 1879 suggested to her soul to become like a star and to dwell apart. It was the Gaiety French season of 1879 that turned Sarah Bernhardt into Sarah Barnum."

Extraordinary, exaggerated, unreasoning: those are harsh words. Agreed, London audiences lost control: a "mania", as Sarcey put it; but the mania would endure in varying degrees through four decades. As he showed when he became a drama critic, Walkley—quiet, fastidious and, with reservations, an admirer of Sarah—was not a man for the theatre's more tumultuous acclamation, today's fan-worship. Still, there seems to have been a certain mild discomfort among practising drama critics in the season for 1879. Joseph Knight of *The Athenaeum,* for one. He began with a ponderously-expressed cheer:

> What in most members of the company is true and highly cultivated talent is in Mlle. Bernhardt genius. We are not disposed to plunge into the sea of troubles that awaits those who attempt a definition of the quality. We content ourselves with a bare assertion that the powers of dramatic exposition possessed by this lady reach this point.

And yet:

> The present generation attests, maybe too warmly, certainly with something of fanaticism, its delight in a class of acting which seemed to have been lost to the stage, and in so doing contrives to spoil what it so profoundly admires and enjoys. Prudential considerations are not likely to weigh with the public, nor can they be expected to do so.

They seldom did. Thenceforward, Sarah would usually be a storm over London; a disciplined frenzy; on her night—for her performances could be a sierra—a technician who watched herself acutely through the whirlwind and the tempest of passion. As for the "seductive Sarah", *Punch* had hailed her as early as 1879:

> Mistress of Hearts and Arts, all met in you!
> The picturesque, informed by soul of passion!

> Say, doest thou feed on milk and honey-dew,
> Draining from goblets deep of classic fashion,
> Champagne and nectar, shandy-gaff sublime . . . ?

She brought back her champagne and nectar, and not a little shandy-gaff, sublime or not, when in 1880, again at the Gaiety Theatre, and within a few breaths of Irving and Ellen Terry at the Lyceum, she roused her audience with the death scene—death from poison—in *Adrienne Lecouvreur* (naturally, she collapsed in the dressing room afterwards: "I die quite well", she said). She was also the social butterfly in *Frou-Frou,* a part Ellen Terry acted later in the English provinces. Bernhardt had developed a true affection for London and Londoners, though she was never sure of the physical aspect. She once wrote:

> I prefer our pale mud to the London black mud, and our windows opening in the centre to the horrible sash windows. . . . Ours open wide: the sun enters the heart of the dwelling. . . . English windows open only half-way, either the top half or the bottom half. One may even have the pleasure of opening them a little at the top and a little at the bottom, but not at all in the middle. The sun cannot enter openly, nor the air. The window keeps its raffish and perfidious character. I hate the English window.

3

In spite of the "perfidious windows", she never failed to return on these flamboyant visits, the sun entering the heart of the dwelling, her London audiences carried through what Henry James called an "agglomeration of horrors" and John Gielgud, in a preface to Dr. William Emboden's *Sarah Bernhardt,* has summarised as "the great procession of queens, princesses, adventuresses, and courtesans, as well as some of her strange transvestite excursions". Through the years (and again Gielgud speaks) she would glow as Théodora, coquette as Tosca, yearn and swoop as Marguerite Gautier. Or, in the words of Bernard Shaw, who never liked her, she would come every season with a new play in which she killed someone with any weapon from a hatchet to a hammer.

In London she was married, during April 1882, to an actor, Ambroise Aristide Damala (the marriage lasted less than a year). One by one, through the seasons, she played all her parts, fierce, seductive, orchidaceous, not invariably with complete critical approval (William Archer, whatever he thought of Phillips, could be unsure of Sarah), but keeping throughout her tireless personal power and her life-long death-wish. No actress was happier in her dying, and her audiences expected it, at any length. The theatre would change about her. She cared nothing for that, nothing for the day's social and ethical variations. She went on being herself, through the 'nineties, through the Edwardian era, Sarah Bernhardt insulated in her own world. Her most fervent English admirer was Maurice Baring, who combined a passion for the romantic Theatre Theatrical with a milder homage to the

Theatre of Ideas. Sarah had little to do with the second of these. It did not worry Baring, who would write of the actress's caressing voice in the first act of *La Tosca,* and of her foreshadowing glance when she caught sight of the knife on the supper table in the fourth act; of Théodora, walking on like a Burne-Jones vision come to life in the glories of Byzantium; of La Samaritaine, evoking the spices, the fire, the vehemence, of the Song of Solomon; mediaeval Gismonda, with orchids in her hair. He remembered Sarah's movements and how a Frenchman, describing her descent of a hotel spiral staircase, said that, as she came down the steps, the staircase seemed to turn and she to be motionless. Baring remembered her voice, "so soft, so melting, so perfectly in tune and in time, with so sure a rhythm, and so perfectly clean-cut that one never lost a syllable, even when the words seemed to float from her lips like a sigh". We can add to this the memory of May Agate, whom Sarah taught, and who remembered her simile for final consonants. Sarah likened the actor to a fisherman casting his line. "It's all very well to throw it out, but you must bring it back again. Don't let your final sound go floating away, but be sure of a good, cleancut finish."

In 1895, there was the unpremeditated "contest" between Bernhardt and Duse when Shaw insisted that they were playing *La Dame aux camélias* and Sudermann's *Magda* against each other, one actress at Daly's Theatre, one (Duse) at Drury Lane. Shaw, of course, championed the quieter Duse; he insisted that Sarah, instead of first-class acting, offered only her reputation: "She does not enter into the leading character; she substitutes herself for it." Very well; but let me quote also a younger critic, James Agate (May was his sister), who, through life, was at Bernhardt's feet. He wrote in 1917: "Her art has been subject to a thousand comparisons: to a summer's day, to tropical lightning, to a wild beast ravening upon prey, and by one gifted writer, C. E. Montague, to four such dissimilar things as the view of Florence from Fiesole, a pheasant's neck, Leonardo's Mona Lisa, and ripe corn with poppies in it. . . . Admittedly, it is a tedious and thankless task to translate fine acting into fine phrases. Those who have never seen Sarah will wonder at the tiresome excess of her critics' raptures; those who remember her acting at its best will marvel at the panegyrist's ineffectual poverty."

At the end of the 'nineties, for a while leaving Sardou and her usual repertory (now hardly from the quick forge and working-house of thought), Sarah played Hamlet. No half-measures: simply Hamlet. Baring was sure that she was the first to give to the French public an exact idea of the part, which she saw as a passionate, highly-coloured portrait of a young man of unclouded intellect. It was a less improbable choice than one might have imagined; after all, she had acted men before, Lorenzaccio for one, and she would come to L'Aiglon. In a previous *Hamlet,* several years earlier, she had cast herself as Ophelia without much success: not, I think, a Bernhardt rôle (death-scene off-stage). Now in 1899 she opened in Paris, in the Place du Chatelet by the river, her new the-atre under her own name—the name, alas, has recently been changed—and during May of that year she put on *Hamlet* in a new and contentious prose version. Aged fifty-five, she went over to London during the following month to appear at the Adelphi in the Strand.

Female Hamlets were by no means rare. Sarah Siddons occasionally played the part in the provinces. During 1864, Shakespeare's tercentenary year, an actress named Alice Marriott, who (not that it mattered) would be Edgar Wallace's paternal grandmother, sought to make her audiences liegemen to the Dane at Sadler's Wells, a theatre she had managed for six years. Apparently, it was quite a competent performance if (as with all woman Hamlets) the onlooker could once suspend disbelief: not altogether easy. There were other aspirants (according to the *Referee's* critic, old Chance Newton) of "all shapes and sizes". They included Clare Howard at the Pavilion in Whitechapel, an actress "addicted to music cues": her Hamlet was presented in the melodramatic fashion, with illustrative "chords" and "crashes" when needed—and they were needed a great deal. There was also Mrs. Bandmann-Palmer, who took the first half of her name from her husband, a German Actor, Daniel Bandmann. A short, squat woman, she did much of her playing on the dark circuits of the manufacturing north of England during the 'nineties and the early years of this century. Offstage she usually wore tweeds and hob-nailed boots, carried an oak walking stick, and had an insensate passion for watercress at all times. She is said to have played Hamlet with some tragic force, though because of rheumatism she had difficulty in rising from her knees. Baliol Holloway, afterwards a renowned Shakesperian, was in her company as a youth. One day, entering our house in Hampstead like a gentle whirlwind—he was well over seventy at the time—he exclaimed: "This is Mrs. Bandmann-Palmer's doing. At my first rehearsal with her she said: 'Advance boldly, young man, and do not lurk, I will not have lurkers in my company.'"

This was the odd regiment of Hamlets that Sarah Berhardt joined. No one would have called her a lurker. It was bad luck that in that summer of 1899 she had in her audience Max Beerbohm, "the incomparable Max". Aged twenty-seven, he had followed Shaw on *The Saturday Review* only twelve months earlier. Elsewhere he could admire Sarah—he called her "volcanic"—but on this occasion, Hamlet was a challenge he could not resist. Heading his notice "Hamlet, Princess of Denmark"—we assume that it was his own title and not a sub-editor's—he began by marking the polite solemnity of the night. He objected to the translation by Marcel Schwob: "The French language, limpid and exquisite though it is, affords no scope for phrases [that are] charged with a dim significance beyond their meaning, and with reverberations beyond their sound." Then he turned to Sarah:

> Her friends ought to have restrained her. The native critics ought not to have encouraged her. The custom-house officials at Charing Cross ought to have confiscated her sable doublet and hose. I, a

lover of her incomparable art, am even more distressed than amused when I think of her aberration at the Adelphi. Had she for one moment betrayed any faintest sense of Hamlet's character, the reminiscence were less painful. Alas! she betrayed nothing but herself, and revealed nothing but the unreasoning vanity which had compelled her to so preposterous an undertaking.

And he added:

One could not help being genuinely impressed by her dignity. One felt that Hamlet, as portrayed by her, was, albeit neither melancholy nor a dreamer, at least a person of consequence and unmistakably thoroughbred. Yes! the only compliment one can conscientiously pay her is that her Hamlet was, from first to last, *très grande dame.*

Mischievously amusing though he was, Max could be dangerous (thus, he did great harm to the Benson company by a silly and distorting notice of *Henry V*). Presumably Sarah had read his dismissal. No doubt she would have preferred Clement Scott, who thought that she was imaginative and poetical: though that does tell us little, at least he omitted "convincing" which, of all critical words, is the least helpful and should by this time have been ground into powder. Whatever Sarah felt, she appears to have kept it to herself. Certainly she was not prevented from making a journey to Stratford-upon-Avon as the only female Hamlet that had appeared, or ever would appear, in the first Memorial Theatre.

Nothing at all like the severe Royal Shakespeare Theatre that guards the Avon today, the Memorial was an eccentric, much-abused, much-loved building by the river: a "striped sugar-stick" built of brick with dressings of stone and some half-timbering, and with gables, turrets, a tall, fussy central tower and an assortment of sham-gothic decoration. Its architect, a Mr. Unsworth, protested that, on the whole, he had brought in everything pretty well. He had. Ultimately, his masterpiece was opened on the drenching night of April 23, 1879, Shakespeare's Birthday, with a *Much Ado About Nothing* in which Helen Faucit, once Macready's leading actress and the First Lady of the mid-Victorian stage, left her retirement to play Beatrice to Shaw's favourite, Barry Sullivan. This was just five weeks before Sarah's first appearance in London.

Presently, the Memorial grew into the home of the Frank Benson festivals. Benson was a remarkably winning man who could coax "great leviathans to dance on sands". Besides his own guests, heads of the London stage, there would frequently be extra-Festival visitors who wanted to play at Stratford simply because it was Shakespeare's parish. The American actress Ada Rehan came as both Rosalind and the Shrew (who seems now to leap from her portrait in the Picture Gallery); and about mid-day on June 29, 1899 Sarah Berhardt arrived at the town in state to end her visit to England with a flying matinée of *Hamlet.*

Certainly in state. Sarah's appearance caused intense excitement in what was still a secluded Warwickshire market-town. Its decorated streets were filled with people who waited to cheer the great actress on her way to Waterside. The High Steward of the borough met her special train—for Sarah could have no less—with the Mayor and the entire Corporation behind him; Marie Corelli, the novelist, not a retiring personage, and owner of the old house that today is the Shakespeare Institute (she would have liked this) presented Sarah with a bouquet tied in tricolour ribbon. Then—in the circumstances it was quite natural—Sarah drove down in the Corelli carriage through Wood Street and Bridge Street (but not by Shakespeare's Henley Street birthplace), and along by the river, to a theatre close-packed to the roof. (The members of Sarah's company managed to get there as well.) Stratford had never known higher-priced seats. People paid a guinea each, which was vastly expensive in those days, for either stalls or places in the front row of the circle. Even the gallery was five shillings. The reception was frenzied ("mania", Sarcey would have said). Bernhardt, dressed like pictures of the young Raphael, was called again and again. Years afterwards, Beerbohm forgotten, she was still saying: "I shall always remember my pilgrimage to Stratford. It is one of my heart's memories."

Critics less ironical than Max had spoken of this as an always-practical Hamlet who realised his task and his own danger in performing it. Maurice Baring, calling it the only intelligible Hamlet of the time except Forbes-Robertson's, put it among the finest achievements in Bernhardt's career:

What is perhaps the most poignant scene, if it is well played, is the conversation with Horatio just before the final duel when Hamlet says, "If it be not to come, it will be now." Sarah charged these words with a sense of doom, with the set courage that faces doom, and with the underlying certainty of doom in spite of courage that is there to meet it.

We can think also of Desmond MacCarthy. He remembered the moment when Hamlet ran his sword through the arras and heard the body of Polonius fall. "Sarah stood for a moment, tiptoe, like a great black exclamation mark—her sword glittering above her head." That was indeed Hamlet of the Theatre Theatrical. Max had not responded to it. Neither had *Punch,* which unkindly suggested Irving for Ophelia.

4

Richard Findlater has named the other player queens of Sarah's time: none of them true rivals, and none likely for half a moment to consider a Hamlet. I have never been able to believe wholly in Mrs. Patrick Campbell—who seems to be a kind of theatrical folk-myth—but I once saw Madge Kendal, claimed by some critics to be the supreme English actress of her day. In later life, she seldom created any specially challenging part. (Who now remembers *The Likeness of the Night?*) Over eighty, and in retirement for nearly twenty years, Dame Madge had come down to the West of England to open a church bazaar. She looked like an angry Volumnia. The staff at the church hall shivered before her, and the chairman was in visible distress. She made her opening speech in tones that would have been heard across the estuary of the river Plym outside the doors, and the summer-heavy woods of Saltram beyond. When someone asked her what she thought of the city, she replied in a voice as steely as Dickens's Miss Murdstone: "It has changed greatly—for the worse". I disliked her intensely; but I could see, even then, that she must have been a remarkable actress—to Sarah as the Arctic to the tropics. They would never have understood each other. In life and art they were irrevocably sundered by the brine; and I cannot begin to imagine what Dame Madge would have made of the near-operatic Queen Elizabeth film Sarah made in her final years. Certainly I cannot imagine Baring writing of her as he did (before the preservative devices of our own period) in one of his most familiar tributes to Sarah:

> She will always be one of the permanent and beautiful guesses of mankind, one of the lasting dreams of poets, one of the most magical speculations of artists, like the charm of Cleopatra, the beauty of Mary Stuart, the voice of the masters of the *bel canto,* the colours of Greek painting, and the melodies of Greek music. But it will be only a guess; because the actor's art dies almost wholly with the actor.

I said I would unveil my King Charles's Head. So much depended in Sarah's time, and indeed depends now, upon the drama critics of the period. It has been so since drama criticism began. In a sense, we might say that Edmund Kean (who, at his worst, must have been a really bad actor) was a superb romantic invention by Hazlitt. In the London of our own time Donald Wolfit's Lear, impressive but certainly not the best of its period (he was better as Kent in a Stratford production years before) entered history largely on the evidence of one man, James Agate. Fairly recently—a minor example—the British National Theatre has staged *Julius Caesar.* I happened to meet half-a-dozen people who had not seen the play, but who had read (between them) half-a-dozen reviews. Every reader had taken his or her opinion from his or her favourite critic and was prepared to defend it more or less to the death. Now, though (as it chanced) the reviews of John Gielgud's Caesar were unanimous, other opinions were sharply diverse. Those diverse opinions, read in various households over the country, will harden into fact. The fact will become legend; and that, in time, will become irrefutable. What will theatre historians do, a century on, when they seek to explain just what happened on the Olivier stage of the National Theatre on March 22, 1977?

Who, for that matter, can really say now what Sarah's Hamlet was like? We can guess, but it can be only a guess. Are we with Beerbohm or Baring?

We know a great many things about Sarah, yet it remains uncommonly difficult to see and hear her in the mind as she was in her prime. Every major artist was once the creation, for the public, of a single observer, or a small group of observers. Release the snowball of the written word, and presently, reinforced by narrative, rumour, interview, reminiscence, it swells to an avalanche. When, years ahead, the historian picks his way among the moraine of evidence, he can be alarmed . . . by the conflicts of opinion, the contradictions, the repetitions: B borrowing from A, C from B and so on through the alphabet. Who was A? What was his authority? As the dying Alexander says in Rattigan's least typical play, "Where did it all begin?" Who is to be trusted, and why? Where would Sarah be if we had only the testimony of Bernard Shaw? There are hypnotic players. There have also been over-hypnotic drama critics. Over and over, in our mosaics, we return to the same names; and sometimes, I think, all credentials should be more closely examined. Minor critics have held major appointments. We examine the status of the player, but do we always examine the status of the witness?

5

Sarah seemed to flower again with the new century. When she wanted to take lessons to play Lady Macbeth in English, the teacher said: "I would gladly do it, but I can spare only half an hour a day." "Very well", Sarah replied, "You must try to let me have the half-hour from two to two-thirty a.m., for it is the only time I am not engaged." During each successive May and June she rarely failed to come to London. In 1905, when no West End theatre was empty, she went out to the semi-suburban Coronet (which is now a cinema) in Notting Hill, and in Maeterlinck's tragedy played Pelléas to the Mélisande of the comparably temperamental Mrs. Patrick Campbell. A Dublin critic said that they were both old enough to know better, but W. L. Courtney wrote in the *Daily Telegraph,* arguably, I think: "When criticism has nothing to say, one may be sure something has been seen rare and strange and beautiful." Courtney did not know—and it was lucky he did not—that at one of the performances Sarah took Mélisande's hand during a tender love scene and gently squeezed into it a raw egg.

Though she was unfaltering, her mid-Edwardian audiences and critics were a trifle less responsive. They were responding to her less as a sensation-drama in herself than as a guide showing them expertly round an ancient monument. Then, once more, there was fresh life. Some of the most tingling of her later appearances were on the immense prairie-stage of the Coliseum, the variety house where Sir Oswald Stoll booked her on five occasions, the first in 1910. Originally, she had cabled back the resolute refusal: "After monkeys, not", but she was persuaded to change her mind, and she arrived in St. Martin's Lane during the autumn of the year when she was sixty-six. That dignified figure, Sir Squire Bancroft, with the inevitable silk hat, morning coat, and dangling monacle, met her at Folkestone; this time the only lilies were from an unknown little girl who had bought them herself. Sarah first acted at the Coliseum in the second act of *L'Aiglon,* and during a further fortnight, as Tosca. She was paid a thousand pounds a week, the houses were reverent and rapt, and people stood five deep at the back of the circle.

In 1912—thirty-three years after her English début—it was Arthur Bourchier, burly and authoritative, on the familiar damp pier at Folkestone. Sarah played some of Lucrezia Borgia, Phèdre, and Queen Elizabeth; and the Coliseum's publicity manager, Arthur Croxton, said: "In a great democratic house she got right into the heart of people to whom hitherto she had been a name." The management, over-awed, was not particularly democratic. From her dressing-room to an immaculately clean stage Sarah would walk for nearly eighty feet over a Turkey red carpet: it was laid so that her feet would not touch the boards that possibly performing elephants (even dwarf ones) had trod. Her manager would support her on her right and the leading man on her left; other members of the company would be in attendance. The passages Sarah chose were invariably the most florid; reeling, writhing, and fainting in coils, but always in the grand manner. If she felt the house was restless, she would cut as she went on (in the manner of *L'Etrangère* long before, but not for the same reason). There were occasional problems. I cannot resist mentioning the kind of triviality familiar in most stage autobiographies. On the first night, the Coliseum's official black cat, a little bored with the plate-spinners who had preceded *Phèdre,* had been washing herself in the wings; when the scene from *Phèdre* was ready to begin, the cat walked gravely across the stage—a long and arduous journey—inspected the audience, highly disliked what she saw and walked off by the opposite prompt entrance. Mercifully, a roar from the audience was obliterated at once by cheering for Sarah, who had seen nothing. Neither, we presume, had A. B. Walkley of the *Times.* "From the moment Phèdre tottered across the stage in the Nurse's arms, unpacking her heart, not so much with words as in a low, wailing melody, we were spellbound" (the customary phrase).

On this visit Sarah said to a London interviewer: "What you need is a real National Theatre with substantial aid from public funds. Every nation ought to have such a theatre." In its way, this might have been a gesture to the Comédie Française from an actress who, for British audiences, seemed to be herself the national theatre of France.

In 1913 she was back, now in scenes from Sardou's *Théodora,* Barbier's *Joan of Arc* and, inevitably, Marguerite Gautier. All, with their various arias and tirades, were from many years earlier or, as Agate said, the postscripts and codicils to masterpieces that were conceived and perfected long ago. Finally, in 1916, after her right leg had been amputated, she continued to act with an artificial limb: "I accept being maimed, but I refuse to remain powerless." She had to play everything seated; her most dramatic part was as the Cathedral of Strasbourg from a poem in which nun-like figures represented the cathedrals of France exhorting the country's youth to vengeance:

> Pleure, pleure, Allemagne,
> L'aigle, l'aigle allemand, est tombé dans le Rhin!

It was in a half-hour sketch she had written herself in a morning's work (though anonymous, most people knew it was hers) that John Gielgud saw her for the only time. He was thirteen years old, and, in his preface to Dr. William Emboden's book, he remembered the experience like this:

> She played the part of a young French *poilu* lying mortally wounded on a bank in the wood near the battlefield. I remember so well how she looked in her short brown wig, her horizon-blue tunic open at the neck, and the lower half of her body covered with a rug. In her right hand she grasped a tattered flag, and during the course of the action she recited some patriotic verses, after which she fell back dead. I understood very few of the words she spoke, but there was a magical stillness in the big auditorium, and her voice rang out, throbbing with energy and varying modulations of rhythm and colour. The curtain fell, but rose again almost immediately to reveal her standing proudly upright on one leg, leaning her hand on the shoulder of one of her fellow-actors. I was spellbound.

(Hear how the word recurs.)

Gielgud wrote this in March 1974. I was curious enough to look up what his mother, the enchanting Kate Terry Gielgud, had written twenty-one years earlier about the same performance. Not much. "Sarah", she said, "played a most poignant death scene, and I saw her for the last time as the stretcher-bearers lifted her inanimate form." Kate Terry Gielgud had watched Sarah in the theatre for nearly forty years. She had seen her in 1880 as Adrienne Lecouvreur, and the description takes us back from the crippled tragedienne of the last brave years to a "tiny, pale face cut by scarlet lips, reddish-gold hair, a long thin neck swathed to the ears in soft white material, long thin arms and hands, and nails cut to sharp points and very much polished". One of the only parts Kate Gielgud (as good a critic as any professional) disliked, was Hamlet: "No sense of awe, no sense of humour, no fatalism, no self-pity."

6

We near the end. It was on April 6, 1921, when she was seventy-six, that Sarah Bernhardt began her last engagement in London, at the cavernous Princess Theatre (since re-named) at the top of Shaftesbury Avenue. Here she was "a noble-hearted gentleman aged about thirty, addicted to morphine" in *Daniel* by Louis Verneuil, shortly afterwards her grandson-in-law. It was the first full-length play she had given in London for many years. There had been mishaps on the journey from Paris two days before. She had been held up for a night; she had had a rough Channel crossing; her car broke down while they were travelling up from Dover; and she was suffering from a cold. But Sarah was set to keep faith with her English impresario, C. B. Cochran. The performance itself was uncanny. She appeared at the beginning of the third act, an unhappy lover dying of a broken heart. (Again, Sarah's Angel of Death.) We have the critic Archibald Haddon's picture of the night straight from the theatre: the picture of a young man in a high-backed chair, wearing a plum-coloured dressing-gown, his feet on a crimson footstool and a rug over his knees. He was deathly pale; there were black rims to his sunken eyes; he coughed distressingly. Sarah acted with her old command. May Agate recalled a small piece of miming when the man spoke of a rum omelette he had enjoyed, and the little sparkling flame that would light it up—something Sarah suggested with a slight quivering gesture of her fingers. At the end she died upon the stage, a fading away during the reading of a letter. The death took a full five minutes, Sarah's own theatre of silence: and the ultimate cheering, Haddon said, "swelled into a mighty roar as the curtain rose and fell a dozen times". That was the final first-night sound in London of what Sarcey called the "mania": a salute profoundly affectionate and admiring: a farewell to the supreme professional, the most formidable actress of her world. She never appeared in London again. Within two years she lay still in her Paris room, her bed covered in flowers—roses, lilacs and forget-me-nots. It was four decades since the bleak noon of Folkestone, the gardenia (or violets) and the lilies, the journey to a lost London, Henry Irving's flowers, the despair in that hot dressingroom before the scene from *Phèdre* and the night's thrust into an excitement sustained across the turbulent years.

We began with Stephen Phillips. We can end with a finer mind, that of Baring, who had adored Sarah from his playgoing childhood and who remembered her in the sonnet that begins: "Her gesture is the soaring of a hymn". It closes with these lines:

> A sorceress, the victim of her snare;
> A wounded eagle, struggling to be free,
> Whose kingdom was the sunlight and the snows—
> More queenly than all empresses is she,
> Discrowned albeit, defeated and in despair;
> The stricken lily puts to shame the rose.

Laurence Senelick (essay date 1984)

SOURCE: "Chekhov's Response to Bernhardt," in *Bernhardt and the Theatre of Her Time,* edited by Eric Salmon, Greenwood Press, 1984, pp. 165-79.

[*In the following essay, Senelick discusses Bernhardt's acceptance by critics and Anton Chekhov's opinion of the actress.*]

Biographers of Sarah Bernhardt spend little time on her three Russian tours (1881, 1892, and 1908). For the most part, they are taken to be stations of the triumphal procession through barbaric provinces that followed her success at the Odéon. The American tours have been productive of the most anecdotes; the English tours have been exhaustively covered by memoir literature. But Bernhardt's first visit to Russia in 1881-1882 may be worth closer examination than it has received, both for what it tells us of the development of Russian taste a decade before the founding of the Moscow Art Theatre, and because of the comment made upon it by Antosha Chekhonte, a young

journalist who was to become better known under his real name, Anton Chekhov.

In seeking a new audience in Russia, Bernhardt was following a long tradition of European artists who saw in that exotic hinterland illimitable largess waiting to be tapped. Politically, Franco-Russian relations were growing more cordial and would result, at the height of the entente, in a mass purchase of Russian bonds by French capitalists, an investment that they would rue well before 1917. Culturally, the Russian aristocratic fashion for speaking and reading French had been maintained, despite the unmannerly intrusions of Napoleons I and III. The critic Pavel Annenkov recalled in the 1850s that all men of taste of his generation had cut their teeth on Corneille, Racine and other classics of the *grand siècle.* Abroad, Russians were reputed to be munificent and enthusiastic in the welcomes extended to distinguished foreign performers. After all, had not Rachel managed to make 300,000 francs in a few weeks?

Bernhardt's expectations were not disappointed, and both her vanity and her bank balance were gratified by the results of the venture. Russia proffered her what Louis Verneuil was to call "une réception grandiose".

> Every day, for some hours, the crowd waited for her to leave the hotel to give her an ovation. Every night, when she reached the theatre, a wide red carpet was swiftly unrolled on the pavement so that in getting out of her sleigh she needn't put her foot in the snow. Special trains from Moscow had been laid on to allow the residents of that city to attend her performances [in St. Petersburg]. The Grand Dukes, all the members of the Imperial family, were daily in the auditorium where all whom Petersburg deemed most illustrious congregated.
>
> Twice she was commanded to the Winter Palace, home of the Tsar, before whom she played first *Le Passant* and the death scene from **Adrienne Lecouvreur,** and the next time two acts of *Phèdre.* The evening that she was presented to Alexander III, whom she had positively bowled over, he hastily halted her in her curtsey and said, in the presence of all the Court: "No, Madame, it is for me to bow to you!"

Whether or not such stories are to be ranked as *haute* press-agentry, it is noteworthy that they are set in St. Petersburg, seat of the government and most Westernized of Russian cities. In the Russian mind, Petersburg acted as its founder Peter the Great had intended, as a "window on Europe". Its tastes, amusements and predilections were, in the upper echelons of society, French, German, and English. Since the eighteenth century, it possessed a French theatre with its own company, a kind of Comédie Française East; its audiences were familiar with the standard Gallic repertoire, fluent in the language and rather given to that reverse chauvinism that believed that art is best when imported from the West. Moreover, St. Petersburg had been the climax of Bernhardt's Russian tour, the excitement generated by reports of her appearances elsewhere. As usual, her arrival had been heralded by a carefully and lavishly laid train of publicity.

Less cosmopolitan centres were more erratic in their reception. In Odessa, crowds shouting "hurrah" had thrown pebbles into her carriage, hitting a member of her troupe in the eye with a shard of window glass. Moscow blew hot and, mostly, cold. Priding itself on being the mother of Russian cities, Moscow was more impatient with foreign foppery, and steadfastly loyal to its own heritage of purely Russian acting and play-writing. The advance publicity campaign had disgusted many critics, who supposed that the public's delight in the French star was more the result of pre-conditioning than of any inherent excellence in her abilities. A leading newspaper, *Russkie Vedomosti (The Russian Intelligencer)* did not even bother dedicating a special article to her touring activities, but simply carried items in its gossip column. On the whole the items were favorable, but they hardly suggested that a marvel was in their midst.

Bernhardt opened at Moscow's Bolshoy Theatre, a house primarily devoted to opera, ballet and spectacle, on 26 November 1881 in *La Dame aux camélias,* and the first reports were temperate and measured. *Russkie Vedomosti* benignly declared, "Yesterday instead of a pompous heroine we saw the living image of a deeply loving, deeply suffering woman from a notorious milieu—who grappled to herself the audience's sympathy and attention with irresistible force." The perfection of her technique, the flexibility of her voice and the careful plotting of the rôle's details were all noted with favour. But other papers were not so charmed. S. Vasil'ev, the influential critic for *Moskovskie Vedomosti (The Moscow Intelligencer),* after granting that Bernhardt's Marguerite Gautier had something of the eternal feminine about her, even if she was "a Parisienne from top to toe", went on to complain: "everything is deliberate, everything is accurate, everything is typical; all the intonations are in place; all the gestures and movements are truthful. But truthfulness [*pravlivost'*] is not truth [*pravda*], eternal truth". His later reports emphasized the same deliberate sophistication of Bernhardt's acting and its accompanying lack of candour. A viewing of her other rôles revealed that her vocal tricks and poses were constantly repeated, well-wrought gimmicks. Bernhardt, Vasil'ev summed up, "is very talented, but not an actress of genius. She gives us remarkably clear, so to speak really palpable, almost chiselled types. They are splendid statuettes, which one would gladly place on one's mantelpiece. But a statuette, not a statue"*: Similar opinions were echoed by the *Russkiy Kur'ër (Russian Courier), Sovremennye Izvestie (Modern Tidings)* and *Novoe Vremya (New Times),* whose critic V. P. Burenin remarked that Bernhardt's affected gesticulation, pseudo-tragic sobs, and cardboard romanticism made her moments of truth and power all the more surprising for being unexpected.

Among those who found Sarah Bernhardt grist for their journalistic mills was twenty-one-year-old Anton Chekhov, a medical student who had begun to contribute squibs and anecdotes to various humour magazines solely with a view to increasing his income. From childhood, Chekhov had been stage-struck, first performing in various amateur productions at home and in school, later religiously attending the Taganrog Civic Theatre, a solid provincial company with a broadly-based repertoire. In Moscow, Chekhov mingled with the Bohemian world of the greenroom and the pressroom: he rapidly became *au courant* of the latest scandals, knew the ins and outs of backstage intrigue, and avidly followed the fluctuations of the box-office.

The two articles that Chekhov devoted to Bernhardt are written in the flippant, know-it-all style that "Antosha Chekhonte" practised in those post-adolescent days: the writer's tongue is firmly lodged in his cheek and one eyebrow is permanently cocked. But for all that, the aesthetic concerns that lie behind these grimaces both reflect the serious connoisseur's interest in acting and strike a chord that can be heard throughout Chekhov's later, important work—the question of an artist's integrity and diligence in the creative act.

His first article, "Sarah Bernhardt", appeared in *Zritel' (The Spectator)* on 30 November 1881, before he had seen her perform. His piece is in the nature of a news item *cum* potted biography, derivative of the sketches by Sarcey and others, that had already appeared in the Moscow press; the others included Evgeniya Tur' who wrote under the elegant *nom-de-plume* of Saliasse de Tournemire. Chekhov intends to inform his readers of the diva's arrival, her impact on the average Muscovite, and her background; but, because his essay is satirical, he dwells on the hyperbole of her publicity campaign. With sardonic deadpan, reminiscent of Mark Twain, he begins with the astonished discovery that the divine Sarah has, after traversing all the world, deigned to call in at Belokammenaya Street.

> Two days ago Moscow knew only four elements; now it won't stop talking about a fifth. It knew seven wonders; now a fraction of a second doesn't go by without it discussing an eighth. Those who had the luck to get even the worst ticket are dying with impatience for nightfall. Forgotten are foul weather, poor roads, expenses, mothers-in-law, debts. Not a scurvy coachman sitting on his box but will give lectures about the new arrival. The reporters forget to eat and drink, they run around and make a fuss. In short, the actress has become our *idée fixe.* We feel that something is going on in our heads much like the onset of *dementia praecox.*

> A frightful amount has been written about Sarah Bernhardt and is still being written! If we were to pile together everything that has been written about her and were to sell it by the ton (at 150 rubles per ton), and if we were to dedicate the receipts from the sale to the "Society for the Protection of Animals", then—we swear by our quills!—we could at least give dinner and supper to the horses and dogs at Olivier's and the Tatar's [a very exclusive and a very seedy restaurant, respectively: L. S.]. Much has been written and, of course . . . many lies have

been told. She's been written about by Frenchmen, Germans, blacks, Englishmen, Hottentots, Greeks, Patagonians, Indians. . . . We'll even write something about her, we'll write and try not to lie.

This last statement is followed by a footnote which remarks, "It's incredible, gentlemen! No sooner does one begin to write about Sarah Bernhardt, than one has a desire to tell a few lies. The respected diva, it must be stated, has bewitched the loveliest of human passions." Chekhov then proceeds to recount some of the celebrated incidents in Sarah's early life, her intention to take the veil, her recitation of a La Fontaine fable which procured her admission to the Conservatoire. "Had she not recited a fable with feeling, had she flunked," Chekhov surmises sarcastically, "she probably would never have got to Moscow." Obviously following the standard press release, Chekhov continues to chronicle her career: the fiasco of her début at the Comédie, her abandonment of the Théâtre de Gymnase and flight to Spain, her return to Paris and obscurity, and her eventual success at the Odéon. At this point, the humourist gets the upper hand over the reporter, and despite his avowed intent, Chekhov begins to spin yarns after the fashion of Sarah's advance agents.

"Her success was so spectacular," he proclaims, "that the commander-in-chief of literature, Victor Hugo, wrote the rôle of the queen in *Ruy Blas* specifically for Sarah Bernhardt. . . . Hitherto-microscopic dramatists began, thanks to Sarah's acting, to creep forward and attain visibility." As he expatiates on her motto, "Quand même", and her passion for publicity, Chekhov's prose accelerates and his exaggerations burgeon, as if the legend of Bernhardt impels him willy-nilly to hysteria. "Sarah's 'Quand même' is straightforward and urgent. With it Sarah Bernhardt rushed headlong into the sort of ghastly messes that only an extraordinary mind and a will of, at least, iron could break through. She strode, as the saying goes, through fire, water and copper pipes." After touching on her skill at sculpture, painting and literature, which make her the rival of all the muses, he moves on to her recent trips to England and America:

> In America she performed miracles. . . . She flew on her journey through a forest fire, fought Indians and tigers, and so forth. There she visited, among others, the professor of black magic, the wizard Edison who showed her all his telephones and phonophones. According to the French artist Robidà, the Americans drank up all of Lake Ontario in which Sarah had swum. . . . In America she gave (horribile dictu) 167 performances! The total sums of the box-office receipts were so long that no professor of mathematics could read them. . . .

He congratulates her on ignoring the Germans on her European tour, but notes that "'tis an ill wind blows nobody good, an extra hundred thousand rubles will remain at home in German pockets, and the little children can use the hundred thousand for milk money." Finally, Chekhov promises his readers to keep them impartially informed of Sarah's exploits in Moscow. "We shall com-

pliment her as a guest and criticise her up and down as stringently as we can as an actress."

Clearly, Chekhov, like his colleagues, had been put off by Bernhardt's fondness for *réclame,* and could hardly believe that any performer could stand up to claims made so extravagantly. "More about Sarah Bernhardt", his second article, published in *Zritel'* on 6 December 1881, after he had seen her on stage, begins on a note of exasperation.

> What the hell is going on! We wake up in the morning, trick ourselves out, draw on our swallow-tail coat and gloves and round about twelve we head for the Bolshoy Theatre. . . . We return home from the theatre, gulp down lunch without chewing it and do some scribbling. At eight at night, it's back to the theatre; from the theatre back home and more and more scribbling till about four. And it's like this every day! We think, speak, read, write about nothing but Sarah Bernhardt. O Sarah Bernhardt! All this folderol will end with our straining our reportorial nerves to the maximum, our catching, thanks to irregular mealtimes, a most virulent stomach catarrh, and sleeping soundly for two straight weeks as soon as the eminent diva departs.

The reason for all this theatre-going is to discover whether the actress in any way corresponds to the rhetoric used to describe her, but, Chekhov confesses, he can find in her no resemblance to the Angel of Death or any other epithet bestowed on her by her admirers.

In amusing detail, Chekhov limns the crush at the theatre for ***Adrienne Lecouvreur,*** the boxes filled to bursting with families sitting on one another's laps. He observes the curious phenomenon of an audience made up not only of the regular playgoers, the *aficionados* of acting, but the sensation-seekers, who do not know the difference between the Bolshoy and the Salamonsky Circus, the businessmen who ordinarily have no time for the theatre, the deaf and paralytic who have not been seen in public since 1848. Astutely, he recognises that the attraction of beholding a sacred monster is only part of the explanation; it is the fact that the entertainment smacks of Paris that has drawn this audience together. The three knocks that announce the show (in lieu of the Russian bell), the eighteenth-century décor familiar from reproductions of salon paintings in illustrated magazines, the luxurious costumes and the incomprehensibly guttural language conjure up for Chekhov all the clichés about Paris.

> You dream, and before your eyes flash one after the other, the Bois de Boulogne, the Champs Elysées, the Trocadéro, Daudet with his long hair, Zola with his round beard, our Turgenev and our "heartthrob" Mme. Lavretskaya, carousing, tossing Russian gold-pieces hither and yon.

> The first act ends in silence, no applause even from the gallery.

> In the second act Sarah Bernhardt herself appears. She is handed up a bouquet (it can't be called a

bad one, but it's not exactly, no offence meant, a good one either). Sarah is nothing like the postcards you bought. . . .

The curtain falls—and the audience applauds, but so listlessly! Fyodotova and even Kochetova are applauded far more energetically. But the way Sarah Bernhardt takes her bow! With her head cocked somewhat to one side, she comes out the door centre, walks slowly and grandly down to the apron, looking in no particular direction, much like the *pontifex maximus* at a sacrificial offering, and with her head describes an arc in the air not visible to the naked eye. "Here you are, take a look!" seems to be written all over her face. "Take a look, wonder, marvel, and say thank you for being allowed the honor of seeing 'the most original of women', 'notre grande Sarah'!"

The coolness of the Muscovite audience, Chekhov imagines, may provoke in the minds of the French actors the belief that it is composed of brute beasts, insensitive to the subleties of refined performances and ignorant of French. But this would be a misconception: for the most part, the audience is made up of experts ready to debate heatedly every nuance of an interpretation and quite fluent in French. No, declares Chekhov, this audience has been spoiled by the mellow acting of Sadovsky, Zhivokini, Shumsky, Samarin and Fyodotova, sensitized by the socially responsible writing of Turgenev and Goncharov, and keenly attuned to real emotion and pathos on the stage. "No wonder," he concludes, "it doesn't fall into a swoon the moment that Sarah Bernhardt lets the audience know a moment before her death by the most energetic convulsions that she is now about to die."

His summing-up of Bernhardt as an actress is worth quoting at length, because it distills the general opinion in Moscow while underlining certain important features of Russian critical thought on the subject of acting:

We are far from worshipping Sarah Bernhardt as a talent. She has none of the stuff that makes our most respected audience love Fyodotova; she has none of the spark that alone is capable of moving us to bitter tears or ecstasy. Every sigh Sarah sighs, every tear she sheds, every antemortem convulsion she makes, every bit of her acting is nothing more than an impeccably and intelligently learned lesson. A lesson, reader, and nothing more! As a very clever lady, who knows what works and what doesn't, a lady of the most grandiose taste, a lady deeply read in the human heart and whatever you please, she very deftly performs all those stunts that, every so often, at fate's behest, occur in the human soul. Every step she takes is profoundly thought out, a stunt underscored a hundred times. . . . She remakes her heroine into exactly the same sort of unusual woman she is herself. . . . In her acting, she goes in pursuit not of the natural but of the extraordinary. Her goal is to startle, to amaze, to dazzle. . . . You watch **Adrienne Lecouvreur** and you see not Adrienne Lecouvreur in her but the ultra-clever, ultra-sensational Sarah Bernhardt. . . . What shines through all her acting is not talent, but tremendous,

strenuous hard work. . . . That hard work comprises the whole key to this enigmatic artiste. Not the slightest trifle exists in any of her rôles great or small that has not been put through the purgatory of that hard work a hundred times. Extraordinary work. Were we as hard-working as she is, what wouldn't we write! We would scribble all over the walls and ceilings just in revising the most paltry scrawl. We envy and most respectfully kowtow to her hard work. We have no objection to advising our first- and second-rate artistes to learn how to work from our guest. Our artistes, no offence meant, are dreadfully lazy! For them, study is harsher than horseradish. We deduce that they, the majority of our actors, work at practically nothing from the simple fact that they are at a standstill: they go neither forward nor . . . anywhere! Were they to work as Sarah Bernhardt works, were they to know as much as she knows, they would go far. . . . We watched Sarah Bernhardt and derived indescribable pleasure from her hard work. There were brief passages in her acting which moved us almost to tears. But the tears failed to well up only because all the enchantment is smothered in artifice. Were it not for that scurvy artifice, that premeditated tricksiness, that over-emphasis, honest to goodness, we would have burst into tears, and the theatre would have rocked with applause. . . . O talent! Cuvier said that you are at odds with facility! And Sarah Bernhardt is monstrously facile!

These remarks come as the climax of a century of tension within the Russian theatre between native impulses and foreign examples. The first great Russian actor, Ivan Dmitrevskiy (1734-1821) had founded his technique on Western models: personally acquainted with Garrick and Lekain, he had introduced the declamatory mode back home. Dramatists and actors were hard pressed to warp Slavonic sounds and rhythms into the formal diction and constraints of the hexameter, and to pare down generous emotions to suit histrionic decorum; but they tried. To the unconditioned observer, however, the results were often ludicrous and out-of-keeping; French modes sorted ill with the growing nationalism of writers, popular interest in Russian culture and mores, and the development of self-taught native actors. A sharp distinction developed between the state theatres in Petersburg and those in Moscow. The Petersburg company aped its French colleagues: the accepted manner in tragedy was cool, restrained and, in its opponents' view, punctiliously bureaucratic. Karatygin (1802-1853), for many years the city's leading tragedian, playing his tortured heroes with chill precision; "he commits suicide by numbers", complained the radical writer Herzen. The polished technique of Petersburg actors was exemplary and mirrored the manners of its aristocratic audience.

Moscow, on the other hand, considered its theatre to be "the second Moscow University": the audience was variegated, a mixture of officials, merchants, students and artisans. Its star tragedian Mochalov (1800-1848) has been characterized as the Russian Kean, erratic and impulsive, uneven in his performances because dependent on inspiration steeped in vodka, but always genuine and always exciting. The Moscow theatre's actors had, in many cases, received irregular training; some of them were even of serf origin. They knew life better than they knew the rules of art. Chief among these was Mikhail Shchepkin (1788-1863), who had been redeemed from serfdom by his admirers after he had become the most famous actor in the provinces. Realism and naturalness were Shchepkin's keywords, and he propagandized tirelessly, through his teaching in the dramatic academy, his correspondence and his own sedulously prepared performances, for emotional truth on stage. Shchepkin was no naturalist insistent on the photographic reproduction of everyday details, but he demanded observation of life and the selection of general traits from it that would harmonize with a playwright's conception. Subordination to character was a prime desideratum.

The years that the French tragedienne Mlle. George had spent in Russia at the beginning of the nineteenth century (1802-1812) had imprinted the neo-classic style of declamation on her epigones, a style which Shchepkin strove to uproot. When Rachel arrived in 1853, playing classical tragedy and romantic melodrama in Petersburg and Moscow, she offered a later generation the opportunity of contrasting an accepted European style, executed by a specialist, with the home-grown approach. Pavel Annenkov, the dean of Petersburg critics, devoted three lengthy and detailed essays to Rachel's performances, concluding that her finest moments were those outbursts of passion which owed least to art, and that her failures came when she embroidered most. In a correspondence with Annenkov, Shchepkin considered the question of Rachel's natural talents, and suggested that, had she not been corrupted by the French school of artificial acting, her genius and understanding of human nature might have preserved her from mechanical gimmickry. Both Annenkov and Shchepkin were convinced that Russia was following the right path in forgoing the French elocutionary manner, and in pursuing goals of emotional authenticity. (However, it should be pointed out that the French artists who visited Russia were luminaries of the Comédie, wedded to the academic style and, as *prime donne,* to self-aggrandizement. Had Shchepkin encountered Frédérick Lemaître, he might have revised his negative appraisal of French actors.)

The same dichotomy between French craftsmanship and Russian values was apparent in the repertory that Chekhov beheld in the early 1870s as a boy in Taganrog. The local theatre alternated the neatly-tailored melodramas of Scribe and Dennery with comedies and dramas of Russian life, accurate in reproducing real dialogue and recognizable types. Because dramatists like Ostrovsky and Potekhin viewed the theatre as a means of educating and reforming public opinion, Russian actors in their rôles sought to move the audiences by touching their hearts. And the audiences responded in kind by favoring those actors who displayed the greatest depth of feeling. It was axiomatic that any actress worth her salt could cry real tears. The actors whom Chekhov mentions as Muscovite favorites—Sadovsky, Zhivokini, Shumsky and Samarin—

were distinguished by the realism of their impersonations and the ability to create a character from within. Their own identification with the character aroused an empathy in the audience.

Bernhardt's opposite numbers at the Moscow state theatre, Mariya Ermolova and Glikeriya Fyodotova, excelled at this. Ermolova (1853-1928), a *grande dame* not much liked by Chekhov, was apportioned the heroic parts, such as Laurencia in *Fuente ovejuna* and Schiller's Maria Stuart and Jeanne d'Arc, in addition to flashy rôles in an undistinguished repertoire, which she was able to endow with considerable nobility. She combined the highly-colored romanticism of Mochalov with the emotional authenticity of Shchepkin to work upon the spectator's loftier feelings; young audience members would leave the theatre aglow with revolutionary fervor after one of her classical renditions, illustrating once again the performer's importance in Russia not simply as an entertainer but as a social impetus. (This function was of special significance in the politically repressed 1880s, when outright protest and criticism were stifled.) Those close to Ermolova recalled that she had no private life, but dwelt in the lives of the characters she incarnated, retiring into the rôles she created.

Fyodotova (1846-1925), whom Chekhov greatly admired, had an even wider range than her colleague, playing in tragedy, drama, romantic spectacle and comedies of manners; a student of Shchepkin, she was noted for the warmth and pathos with which she imbued her characters. The novelist Pisemsky stated that in his travels throughout Europe, visiting all the best theatres and seeing all the most celebrated actresses, nowhere had he found anyone with the emotional range and depth of Fyodotova.

These women, of unimpeachable moral character, profoundly involved in the progressive social and literary movements of the time, held in affectionate esteem by their public, were the yardsticks by which Bernhardt was measured. It was natural, then, that the enlightened Muscovite impression was of a mountebank and an exhibitionist whose behaviour on stage bore little correspondence to life as it is lived. What must be emphasized, however, is that the Russians were not asking for the kind of true-to-life behaviorism sought by Zola and Antoine. A certain M. N. R. writing in *Gazeta A. Gattsuka (Gattsuk's Gazette)* after Bernhardt's departure sharply criticized her depictions of Marguerite Gautier's demise from consumption and Adrienne Lecouvreur's death by poison. "The essence of dramatic art," he opined, "is to show and interpret what causes a person's death, what spiritual and not what corporeal motions accompany his removal from life." Curiously, the same charge of sensational naturalism had been levelled by Annenkov at Rachel a generation earlier, when her writhing and hysteria in Adrienne's death throes sent women screaming from the auditorium; in his opinion, such melodramatic devices made no statement about the character. Rather, the Moscow public hoped that Bernhardt would drop the mask of star and let the woman appear; wielding the upper hand on stage at every moment, in complete control of each vocal modulation, Bernhardt lacked vulnerability. "Let me whisper my general impression in your ear", confided Spectator in *Sovremennye Izvestie:* "It is all clever, pretty, detailed, with forceful and appropriate expression, but . . . but not once did any of it make my heart beat any the faster, not in the least."

Along with Chekhov, several critics advised young actresses to ignore Bernhardt's example, except in regard to her firm grip on the rôle in all its details, her disciplined work habits and her ability to listen on stage. Chekhov's friend, the powerful editor Suvorin, suggested that Russian actors pay close attention to her pauses, for "she performs her rôle like a piece of music [for] she knows that certain mimic moments on stage should be more pronounced than they are in life". It may be that the famous Moscow Art Theatre pause derives in part from Bernhardt, filtered through Maeterlinck to Chekhov and Stanislavsky. But the consensus remained that Sarah Bernhardt was less the product of genius than of puffery. For the Moscow *cognoscenti,* the press campaigns had resulted in overkill. Chekhov, returning to his analysis of *Adrienne* at last, finally bursts out:

> Or else, look here, reader! You're fed up reading my gibberish, and I want awfully to go to bed. The clock is striking four, and the cock is bawling at my pretty neighbor-lady's place. . . . My eyelids are sticking together as if smeared with glue, my nose is grazing my writing-d. . . .
>
> Tomorrow, back to Sarah Bernhardt . . . ugh! However, I won't write any more about her even if the editor pays me fifty kopeks a line. I'm written out! I quit!

He meant it. One can examine Chekhov's writings and letters from this point on and find very few references to Bernhardt, except as a commonplace for an internationally known actress. His full-length portrait of a spoiled, capricious leading lady, Arkadina in *The Seagull,* was modelled after Russian stars with whom Chekhov was better acquainted, among them his mistress Lidiya Yavorskaya, whose favorite rôle was Marguerite Gautier. Arkadina, her son Konstantin tells us, cannot stand being compared to Bernhardt or Duse; but this is vanity, not criticism.

Actually, Duse was the foreign actress who, ten years later, attracted Chekhov at a time when his outlook on the Russian stage had been soured by first-hand involvement in it. After he had seen her in Petersburg in *Antony and Cleopatra,* he wrote to his sister (March 17, 1891): "What an actress! I've never seen anything like her. I watched Duse and worked myself into agonies thinking that we have to cultivate our temperaments and tastes through the medium of such wooden actresses as Ermolova and her ilk, whom we consider great because we haven't anyone better. After Duse I can understand why the Russian theatre is so boring." Once again, the moral uplift provided by art, the refining influence of a sensitive performance, are the main criteria for aesthetic evaluation.

Such an attitude, which somewhat parallels that of Bernard Shaw and Max Beerbohm in their contrasting of Duse and Bernhardt, was not uncommon among experienced judges in Russia, who found it revealing to compare visiting stars in the same rôles. Speaking of the scene in act three of *La Dame aux camélias,* in which Armand flings his packet of banknotes in Marguerite's face, the Baron Drizen, an official of the Petersburg state theatre, recalled that;

> Sarah Bernhardt at that moment hid her face in her hands and sobbed deeply. Tina di Lorenzo automatically fell into an armchair and simply gnawed her lips in silence. Duse reacted quite differently. She could not believe her eyes. What, was this her Armand? He who had sworn eternal love to her, pleaded and wept at her feet? No, it is some other. And with half-closed eyes and outstretched arms, she repeats in different tones but one word: "Armando! Armando!" . . . I have never experienced a keener sensation in the theatre.

The Baron's impressions are seconded by the shrewd critic A. R. Kugel' ("Homo Novus") who was unimpressed by Bernhardt's emotional grasp of the rôle. He considered Marguerite Gautier to be her masterpiece in many ways; he admired the feminine tenderness of the first act, the sophisticated style of the interview with Armand's father, the expressiveness of her hands and her moaning. But Kugel' was left utterly cold by any scene that required of her "inner life and great sorrow". These were the very qualities that the Russians esteemed most highly in an actor. The word I have translated as "inner life"—*perezhivanie*—actually means "experiencing, reliving, living *through* an emotion" and was to become the touchstone of Stanislavsky's approach to acting. For him, the performer had to exploit his emotional memory and re-create, within himself, the feelings of the character he undertakes to impersonate. Stanislavsky codified and formalized what was already the common direction and predilection of the Russian theatre. So it is little wonder that Sarah Bernhardt, ultimate exemplar of the cult of personality, past mistress of *métier,* should have seemed to the informed Russian spectator an irrelevant throwback to an obsolete and superseded form of exhibitionism.

Leigh Woods (essay date 1994)

SOURCE: "Two-a-Day Redemptions and Truncated Camilles: the Vaudeville Repertoire of Sarah Bernhardt," in *New Theatre Quarterly,* Vol. 10, No. 37, February, 1994, pp. 11-23.

[*In the following essay, Woods analyzes Bernhardt's roles on the American vaudeville stage, contending that her portrayals of complex and conflicted women produced a significant marriage of high and low cultures and allowed Bernhardt to continue performing despite illness and advanced age.*]

Sarah Bernhardt's forays into American vaudeville came in lengthy tours while the form was at its height, in 1912-

13 and 1917-18, essentially at the same time as the heyday of the British music hall—in which Bernhardt also toured half a dozen times between 1910 and 1920. For her, these tours involved escapes, of a sort, from a legitimate theatre that could no longer easily accommodate her advancing age and worsening health.

Bernhardt's repertoire in vaudeville, although borrowed in part from her legitimate career, is striking for its departure from the generally light tone which the producers and audiences of vaudeville typically favoured. In aggregate, her vaudeville productions offered a grim view of female experience in reiterated and, as time went on, increasingly ritual-like images of masochism and self-destruction.

In what follows, I shall first examine several contexts around Bernhardt's appearances in vaudeville. I shall try to suggest the nature of her appeal in vaudeville, and the appeal of the actress's unconventional repertoire, by vaudeville's standards, to an audience used to making merry. What I hope to unfold here are some of the exactions made on famous actresses in the nineteenth century which were carried over and in some ways intensified in vaudeville until the final years of the First World War.

To some degree, Bernhardt can be seen to have colluded in the processes by which her fame and her notoriety were penalized. She seems to have done so because she knew it was good business, because her options were narrowing, and because marketing bits of her stageworn suffering struck her as the logical and perhaps inevitable extension of her previous career.

THE BILL AND ITS FORMAT

Vaudeville was willing to compromise its roots in popular culture to accommodate the glittering if generally rather coy luminaries it drew away from the legitimate stage. It paid large amounts of money to stage stars, often in excess of what they could have made in 'legit'—and more, too, than all but a handful of the most versatile entertainers trained up in vaudeville could expect to earn. In its taste for stage stars, vaudeville traded something of its reputation as an egalitarian form for the more distinguished profile it displayed while gripping noted actors in its embrace. It also sacrificed something of its trademark in brisk pacing to a group of actors accustomed to more leisurely appearances in generally more gracious and 'respectable' circumstances.

Vaudeville bills after the turn of the century generally comprised between seven and nine elements. Opening acts were called 'doormats' and closing acts 'chasers'. These often consisted of dumb or non-speaking performers whose main function was the utilitarian one of easing audiences into and out of the theatre as part of the quick turn-around dictated by multiple shows daily. The performers in doormats and chasers knew that, because of their placement, they could never expect the audience's full attention, or for that matter any attention at all when the hour was late or the preceding entertainments laggard.

Black performers were often stationed next-to-last, though rarely as 'headliners', because many chasers consisted of animal acts and only the animals could be guaranteed not to complain about following African-Americans on the bill. There was a class system in vaudeville, and stage stars stood at the very top of it, at a great remove from performers who inhabited the levels below them. The stars' very appearances in vaudeville elevated the bills they headed well above the range of standard fare.

These stars found themselves sharing bills with a motley assortment of performers. There were street acts that had developed some kind of specialty; ethnic acts featuring dialect humour to capture Jewish, German, Irish, and Italian immigrants; other ethnic acts in blackface, sometimes African-Americans but more often whites; acrobats, jugglers, aerialists, skaters, and animal-trainers with feats of skill or daring; and supporting players and chorus members appearing in larger and showier vaudeville productions, but lacking stars of magnitude. Song-and-dance acts were common, often including a performer of each sex. After 1910 or so, non-dialect comedians became vaudeville staples, too, often in double acts of laugh-getter and straight man (or woman).

All headliners from the stage found themselves either in the spot just before intermission or next-to-last on their vaudeville bills. The next-to-last act fell after the audience returned from the intermission, and had usually seen another filler act to settle them back into their seats. After the traditional headliner's slot, then, the audience was primed to leave the theatre either during the chaser or just after it.

THE ROLE OF THE STAR

Stage stars like Bernhardt with heavy sets always played in the next-to-last slot because the time needed to arrange the stage could only come during the intermission. The slot following just after intermission was a particularly tough one, sandwiched as it was between the two most prestigious acts on the bill. This act fulfilled a function in some ways like the opening and closing acts before an audience that was restless, distracted, and looking forward to the headliner.

All acts were short. Doormats and chasers often ran ten minutes or less. Longer acts lasted between twenty and thirty minutes, and fell in the featured slots—usually four, five, and seven. Occasionally, a stage star's play would last longer than half an hour, but given vaudeville's brisk and insistent rhythms, such a length could carry risks. In fact, the most common criticisms of stage stars in vaudeville damned them for action that took too long in getting under way.

Vaudeville audiences also expected that a star would be on stage when the play began, or enter very soon afterwards. This expectation either accelerated or erased entirely a practice prevalent in the legitimate theatre of the day, that had the star's character discussed at length by the other characters before that star made her triumphal appearance.

Slots in the less prominent parts of the vaudeville bill were often juggled by local managers after the first weekly matinee on Monday. When changes were made in a stage star's bill, this often took the form of shuffling the acts on either side of the star, so as to manipulate the audience into the proper frame of mind just before or after the headlined act appeared. A performer doing a dumb act to open for Bernhardt might well have been a headliner many times at a smaller theatre, sometimes only the week before.

Nevertheless, the class and salary system in vaudeville related very directly to slots on the bill, and to the prestige of the theatre where the bill was playing. There was truth in Channing Pollock's jest, written in 1911, that when it came to vaudevillians, 'By their numbers ye shall know them.' Performers grew accustomed to thinking of themselves as numbers in their slot on the bill, in the minutes that their acts took up, and in their weekly salaries. Vaudeville showed a passion for quantification that affected all levels of the enterprise.

A kind of mechanized quality that seemed brisk and efficient to vaudeville audiences did not always seem so to stars accustomed to the legitimate theatre. Mrs. Patrick Campbell, famed from legit in A. W. Pinero's *The Second Mrs. Tanqueray,* complained of the trials she suffered during her single short tour of vaudeville in 1910: 'Oh, those two [daily] performances. . . . I had to kill a man twice a day and shriek—and it had to be done from the heart—the Americans see through "bluff"—and I was advertised as a "Great tragic actress"!' Ethel Barrymore found touring difficult at a time when she had young children. But she remembered her tours later for the way that, in vaudeville, 'Things ran as systematically and efficiently as in a large business concern', training up an 'audience . . . so used to perfection that they are tough.'

Jessie Millward, a British actress who specialized in melodrama, grew frazzled by the travel and the mechanized vaudeville routine. In her case, though, her first tours were short ones—only the several blocks between F. F. Proctor's Fifth Avenue and his Twenty-Third Street theatres in New York City in 1904. Then again, Millward played two shows in each theatre for a total of four shows daily, racing from one theatre to another for both matinee and evening performances in order to fill spots on the two different bills:

> When the first week of it was over, I caught myself jumping out of bed in the middle of nights and rushing to the door mechanically as if I were going to take another car to somewhere or other. It was an experience that I certainly shall never go through again. Hereafter, I shall be content to appear in one theatre at a time, giving two performances, of course, each day, but not in places several miles apart [*sic*].

Millward's nightmare resembles what performers in small time vaudeville experienced routinely, doing as many as five or six shows per day. On the other hand, Millward became the first actress to make $1000 a week in vaudeville in a development which in some ways presaged Bernhardt's interest and eventual appearance in the form. But Millward's salary and her mode of travel would both find themselves outstripped eight years later, when Bernhardt entered the field.

BERNHARDT ENTERS VAUDEVILLE

Extensive travel was built into vaudeville, with large circuits of its theatres coming under the control of a handful of monopolistic producers during the dozen years that followed the turn of the century. Extensive travel suited Bernhardt, part of whose celebrity derived from popular images of her itinerancy and rootlessness as an artist, and from the grand manner in which she travelled with her entourages. She made several world tours during her legitimate career, and the one that began in 1891 lasted over two years, taking her across the United States and Canada, to Hawaii, Samoa, New Zealand, and Australia, then back to the United States, off to France and London, to Belgium, the Netherlands, Luxembourg, Switzerland, Czechoslovakia, Poland, Russia, Austria, Italy, Monaco, the French Riviera, on to a jaunt that included Hungary, Romania, Turkey, Greece, and Portugal, and then to a final leg with stops in Brazil, Argentina, and Senegal.

Lacking the model domestic life that drove and at the same time confined the American star Ethel Barrymore's stints in vaudeville to locations mostly in and around New York City, Bernhardt may even have welcomed the prospect of entering its farthest reaches at such a late stage in her career. She certainly welcomed the $7000 a week she earned during her first tour and (with a war on) the $5500 a week she made during her second vaudeville engagement.

Because vaudeville offered cheap daily matinees and relatively low prices for its evening shows, women were often more heavily represented in its audiences than they were in legitimate theatres of the time. This element of vaudeville seems to have suited it to female performers in general and ageing actresses in particular. The spectacle of the late-sixtyish and then finally seventyish Bernhardt on two long marches through vaudeville recalled that offered by the not-quite-so-matronly Lillie Langtry. Langtry was also internationally famous from a long touring career and the days of her earlier attachment—shared later by her friend Bernhardt—to the Prince of Wales, Queen Victoria's son Albert Edward, who later became Edward VII of England.

In the legitimate theatre, Langtry had specialized in worldly-wise, bejewelled characters in comic or satiric pieces. Her vaudeville offerings, however, located themselves much more firmly in a retrograde morality. *Between Nightfall and the Light* and *The Test* were both excerpted from her legitimate success in the 1880s in Victorien Sardou's *A Wife's Peril,* and during her first and second vaudeville tours respectively each play had Langtry's character dying at the hands of her would-be-seducer after having been tempted to infidelity by him with the news of her own husband's philandering. On her third and final vaudeville tour, Langtry alternated in *Ashes* and *The Eleventh Hour,* in both of which she featured as an erring and anxious wife. Here, her characters did not die, but were chastened rather—and determined to expiate their lapses from domestic propriety.

Bernhardt's vaudeville repertoire showed even greater licence—and greater severity. She had first played Marguerite Gautier, the Camille in *La Dame aux Camélias* by Alexandre Dumas *fils,* in the United States during her first tour there in 1880. When originally in America, Bernhardt had been amused to learn that schoolchildren were forbidden to see her as Camille; in France, though she had still not played the role there, she knew that children attended matinees of Dumas' play as a rite of passage in their educations. In any case, her characterization of Camille made a sensation in the United States, only later becoming one in Europe. Over time, it came to stand as the prototype of an undomesticated and therefore rootless woman falling victim to the tortures of love.

Vaudeville thus afforded Bernhardt and Langtry outlets for their notoriety in ways the legitimate stage did not. And in its hypocritical and self-serving attempts to serve up 'family' entertainment, vaudeville offered an arena where a sort of confused and titillating Victorianism prevailed. Such values permitted sexual reference and erotic innuendo—never more so than when these could be instantly juxtaposed, in plays lasting only about half an hour, with suffering and very often death.

BERNHARDT'S FIRST REPERTOIRE

More than thirty years after she first played the role, Bernhardt made Camille, the only part she played on both her tours, her most durable attraction in vaudeville. Furthermore, during her first tour no fewer than four of the other five pieces she played portrayed women victimized by the strength or expression of their love. The fifth role was from her own son's play, *Une Nuit de Noël sous la terreur,* in which romantic love did not figure prominently. On the other hand, Maurice, as Bernhardt's illegitimate son, was the living emblem of the actress's much-publicized erotic history.

Besides *Camille* and Maurice's, her other plays included Jean Racine's seventeenth-century classic *Phèdre,* Victor Hugo's *Lucrèce Borgia,* and Sardou's *La Tosca* and *Théodora.* Bernhardt had played all of these at full length in the legitimate theatre: indeed, the roles in Sardou's plays had been written for her in the first place. In choosing portions of the full-length pieces for her brief appearances in vaudeville, Bernhardt fixed on the climactic episodes of plays which—like *Camille* but excluding *Phèdre,* where she played the first two acts only—included her characters' deaths. Even her extract from *Phèdre,* though, included her spurned character's invitation to her beloved stepson to kill her with his sword.

Such plays and such outcomes stood squarely in line with notions of gender in the late nineteenth century. Here, Bronson Howard describes a scenario common on legitimate stages during the last two decades of the century, and his sense of poetic justice would extend itself in vaudeville in the hands of Bernhardt and some of the other female stage stars who entered it. According to Howard, himself a playwright of note:

> In England and America, the death of a pure woman on the stage is not 'satisfactory', except when the play rises to the dignity of tragedy. The death, in an ordinary play, of a woman who is not pure, as in the case of *Frou-Frou* [*by Meilhac and Halévy, in which Bernhardt had also created the title role*], is perfectly satisfactory, for the reason that it is inevitable. . . . The wife who has once taken the step from purity to impurity can never reinstate herself in the world of art on this side of the grave; and so an audience looks with complacent tears on the death of an erring woman.

Bernhardt chose a sequence of roles for herself in vaudeville modelled on a formula rooted thirty years earlier, when she had first played Camille, having also taken many similar roles in her earlier and later legitimate career. In vaudeville, however, the permutations these parts found in bills through the course of several weeks, and the compression in suffering they assumed by being cut to conform to vaudeville's exacting time limit, rendered their cautionary qualities the more conspicuous.

Bernhardt was unique among the serious actors who entered vaudeville in alternating several different pieces there. Other stars lacked her repertoire of short pieces and her skill in playing them, perfected over the previous thirty years of her career from the continental practice of touring in several pieces rather than in one. Other actresses of note also lacked her skill in putting over (and varying) outcomes involving loving too much or 'wrongly', and the consequent suffering and death.

Alternating in a number of pieces gave Bernhardt and the vaudeville producers a strategy for drawing more spectators to see her—one night as Camille, the next as Phèdre, and so on; but this cycle was transformed through the course of vaudeville's fourteen weekly shows into a litany of womanly love's most dire consequences.

THE REPERTOIRE FOR THE SECOND TOUR

This same pattern fell out during her subsequent tours in vaudeville, even when her repertoire changed. In 1917-18 Bernhardt often doubled Camille with Alexandre Bisson's *Madame X* within single weeks and, sometimes, even on single bills during the legitimate engagements she sometines interspersed with her appearances in vaudeville. *Madame X* treated a wife who had deserted her husband and young son only to be reunited years later with that son, who comes by chance to defend her against a murder charge. Madame X, like Camille, dies morally absolved and quite ecstatic at the end of her play.

In 1915—the year after the First World War began and two years after her first tour of vaudeville ended—Bernhardt's right leg was amputated. Not only did this confine her to the brief *tours de force* she had been refining as her staple for English music halls since 1910, but it forced her to change an acting style which had been marked for many years by a quality of movement some had called feline, some serpentlike, and which all agreed was heavily charged with erotic associations.

Having to perform under this limitation seems only to have enlarged her taste for the heroic and the sacrificial. On her final tour, with the First World War raging, she paired 'a French Countess who refused to leave her chateau during the German invasion and gave shelter to wounded French and American soldiers', from *Arrière les Huns,* with the role in another patriotic vehicle, *Du Théatre au champs d'honneur,* of a mortally wounded young man on the battlefield, 'a former actor and poet . . . determined to save his battalion's flag from enemy hands.'

At other times, Bernhardt doubled on vaudeville bills as the doomed son of Napoleon in the last act of Edmond Rostand's *L'Aiglon* and as the title character in Maurice Bernhardt's *La Mort de Cléopâtre.* At still others, she paired the dying Cleopatra with the martyr in Emile Moreau's *Le Procès de Jeanne d'Arc.*

Thus, Bernhardt brought into vaudeville for her final tour two male roles plus a third, Joan of Arc, with masculine qualities. She had done this earlier in her career, even playing Hamlet in one controversial engagement that took her to both Paris and London. Far from escaping the prototypical suffering woman's experience in such roles, though, Bernhardt suffered and died—or in the case of her Joan saw herself railroaded toward death—in all of them.

Thus, in a theatrical femininity that had by this time become emblematic, Bernhardt on the one hand applied herself to suffering in a universal way, with warfare as the male equivalent of her female characters' martyrdoms to romance; on the other, her male characters and Bernhardt's Joan of Arc were ennobled by a heroism seen to benefit entire nations. The roles were consequently imbued with a kind of altruism that departed in some ways from what in Bernhardt's time were often called 'soiled doves', so willing to die for the men they loved.

The 'Weekly Laugh Bulletin' of the *New York Star* anatomized Bernhardt's performance as Joan of Arc at the Palace Theatre, New York, for the week ending 6 January 1918, pinning down the actress and her produc-

tion in its customarily clinical and quantified way. Under 'Reception' it noted that Bernhardt's had been 'Big'; under 'Applause', 'Good'; under 'Laughs', not surprisingly, '0'; under 'Finished', again 'Big'; and under 'Acting Time', '31 minutes'.

Sandwiched between a song-and-dance act and a comedian at the Wednesday matinee, Sarah's initial reception took top honours, but Rooney and Bent before her and Harry Fox following her gathered twenty-one and twenty-two laughs respectively, and Rooney and Bent finished 'excellent', according to the *Star.* Their exit in *Up Town* surpassed and set up the less conventional and more equivocal vaudeville 'finish' that Bernhardt offered her audiences. Vaudeville's passion for quantification seems to have set the actress's suffering as Joan at a comfortable distance—and perhaps was what made it tolerable. Furthermore, her Joan had been only one element on the bill, complemented and in some ways compromised by the laughs that came before and after it.

THE LEGEND APPROPRIATED

In one respect, Bernhardt seems to have mined a vein in her vaudeville pieces which already existed in her legitimate repertoire—and which she did not need to look very hard to find. More surprisingly, though, vaudeville seems to have furnished her with a climate that suited the suffering characters in her repertoire. And so sisters-in-pain to her Camille were taken up by other actresses who toured in vaudeville before and after her.

Valerie Bergere, another French actress, tailored Camille for American consumption in her vaudeville sketch called *A Bowery Camille.* Camille was played on the legitimate stage by Virginia Harned, Nance O'Neil, Clara Morris, Olga Nethersole, Mrs. Leslie Carter, and Ethel Barrymore—to list only those most noted among the actresses like Bernhardt who came to vaudeville from the stage. But none chose to play Camille in vaudeville—the role was too strongly associated with Bernhardt after the late 1880s—though all but Barrymore moved into the form with the savour of this kind of role around her.

Vaudeville marketed Bernhardt's profile and her line of suffering women in other ways, too. Thus, when Olga Nethersole came into vaudeville in 1913-14, the year after Bernhardt's first tour, she was billed as 'the British Bernhardt'. A certain derivative quality showed itself in the way Nethersole took her curtain calls after playing Sapho, another libidinous and subsequently repentant character. *Variety* derided Nethersole for her numerous 'unnatural Bernhardt bows' in vaudeville. Earlier, Mrs. Leslie Carter had been labelled 'the American Bernhardt', after her turn-of-the-century success as the loose-living music hall artiste, Zaza. She later took Zaza, or as it might have been called, 'the American Camille', into vaudeville with her.

David Warfield, subsequently a star in his own right, came up in vaudeville in the late 1880s. He confessed many years afterward that his early appearance at The Wigwam, a vaudeville house in San Francisco, had included, among other things, 'imitations of Bernhardt, Irving, and Salvini. Bernhardt I had never seen, but that did not bother me—I created a burlesque of her in *Camille.*' Warfield's resourcefulness prefigured Bernhardt's appearances in vaudeville, while those of Nethersole and Carter were in some ways predicated on Bernhardt's, suggesting the multifarious ways her most famous role was appropriated by public and peers alike.

Perhaps anticipating the audience's sure interest in her storied appearance, Bernhardt joked about the weight she had put on prior to her first tour in vaudeville. At the age of sixty-eight, she knew she would be playing several women jeopardized by love on the tour besides Camille. Her bantering with interviewers suggests that she took it as her strategy to prime her first vaudeville audiences to be pleasantly surprised at her appearance.

She certainly used the clever costuming and lighting for which she was known to enhance her appeal. She took pains over the look of her shows far in excess of vaudeville's customary expectations, with one critic praising her productions for their ability 'to create illusion and to banish the vaudeville atmosphere'.

As her later vaudeville appearances began to assume the tone of valedictories, creating 'illusion' appears to have become even more crucial. Bernhardt had been playing Camille for nearly forty years by 1917, and observers of some of her later performances noticed her using her leading man's arm to break her final death-fall—a sensible choice for an ailing and finally one-legged actress.

ROLES OF EMBLEMATIC SUFFERING

The cutting for vaudeville prefaced Camille's death perfunctorily, with only enough music and dialogue to set the moment up. But Bernhardt's Camille lent itself to abbreviation in its familiarity to many audience members and in her long association with the role—including a filmed appearance in Dumas *fils'* play prior to taking Camille into vaudeville.

It was as though Bernhardt was finally able to serve up her Camille in a kind of shorthand, taking for granted her audience's knowledge of the story and her own history in the role. In this way, she used Camille and her long tenure in it as emblems of suffering and, paradoxically, of the transcendence of her acting. Of course, her suffering in Camille and similar roles was precisely what rendered them transcendent in Bernhardt's eyes and, to judge the matter from a steady demand for such roles in vaudeville, in the eyes of her audiences as well.

Furthermore, the magnitude and longstanding nature of Bernhardt's celebrity lent her acting considerable transparency by the time she hit vaudeville. This left her, in many minds as well as her own, indistinguishable from the most recurrent among her roles. She had figured

prominently in no fewer than five *romans à clef* over the years, including Alphonse Daudet's *Le Nabab* (1876), Edmond de Goncourt's *La Faustin* (1881), Félicien Champsaur's *Dinah Samuel* (1880s), Jean Lourain's *Le Tréteau* (1906), and most sensationally in *Les Memoirs de Sarah Barnum* (1883) by her fellow-actress and former friend, Marie Colombier.

It is fitting that Colombier should have conflated Bernhardt with America's circus master and huckstersupreme, P. T. Barnum, the analogy anticipating Bernhardt's huge appeal in vaudeville three decades later. By then, American press agentry had been grafted onto 'vaudeville'—the very term borrowed, for the sophistication and respectability it carried with it, from the French, in something of the way vaudeville, in Francophilic fashion, deployed Bernhardt's prestige for its own cultural aggrandisement.

Perhaps the most famous fictional realization of Bernhardt fell in writing of a much higher order than the *romans à clef*—in Marcel Proust's *The Remembrance of Things Past,* through the character of the actress Berma. Bernhardt's loftier cultural associations lent her presence even greater appeal in vaudeville, ever eager as it was to offer something for everyone—and, in Bernhardt's case, to raise its ticket prices in the process. Still the most famous performer in the world, Bernhardt legitimated a new scale when she commanded a top price of $2.50 for her three and a half weeks at the Palace in May 1913, furnishing testimony of the more monied kind of patron she succeeded in drawing into vaudeville in her capacious wake.

ACTING OUT MORTALITY

Circumstances perhaps gave Bernhardt more powerful grounds for the conflation of her life with her art as that life drew to its close. A young anaesthetist who assisted at the actress's amputation—which fell between the two vaudeville tours—kept notes of the event:

> At 10 A.M. the great artist was wheeled into the operating room. She was dressed in a white satin peignoir and swathed in pink crepe-de-chine veils. She seemed very calm. . . . Turning to [*the surgeon*] Denucé she said: 'My darling, give me a kiss.' Then to me, 'Mademoiselle, I'm in your hands. Promise you'll really put me to sleep. Let's go, quickly, quickly.' In all this one could not help see the tragedienne putting on an act. I felt I was at the theatre except that I myself had a role in the painful drama. . . . The wound is dressed and the great tragedienne, crowned by her peignoir and satin-lined sheepskin, is wheeled back to her room. When she is in bed she screams: 'I want my beloved son, my Maurice, my darling child!' He kisses her, saying: 'Maman, you look just fine, you're all right, all right.' 'Where is Denucé and the young woman who put me to sleep?' 'Madame, I am here', I said. 'Ah, darling, you're nice. Come here. I want to see you.' I try to leave but she detains me. 'Darling', she says, 'I like you, stay a

bit longer.' I tell her to be calm and not to talk. 'I'm talking because I must speak a little. Oh, I'm suffering, suffering.' The drama continues. One feels she is always acting, playing the role of someone who has just undergone a grave operation.

The anaesthetist, like the vaudeville audience, was aware of Bernhardt's standing and eager to preserve it so as to lend value to her own presence at a significant event. The actress's mortality is the background against which both Bernhardt as its possessor and purveyor, and her portable audience as its morbid consumer, judges the significance of the performance. Bernhardt was acting out her own death, after a fashion, as she did in vaudeville both before and after her operation in anticipation of a real death which did not come until 1923. She seems also to have been casting her surgeon, Denucé and even her own son, Maurice, as operating room Armands to her stricken Camille.

Bernhardt had great gifts as a comic actress, but this was clearly not the expressive idiom she developed as she aged, nor the mode that her later audiences preferred. Comedy was, on the other hand, precisely the vocabulary taken up by 'the American Bernhardt', Mrs. Leslie Carter, when her Camille-like Zaza took her through her first vaudeville tour in 1915-16. In her vaudeville version of Zaza, she was criticized for doing 'considerable "comeding" that would put [the low comedienne] Marie Dressler or Charles Chaplin to shame.' Then, in the 'twenties, Mrs. Carter played a series of character roles on the legitimate stage, such as Lady Kitty in Somerset Maugham's *The Circle* in New York, in which she could lampoon her earlier glamour and sensuous allure.

Lillie Langtry also ventured into comedy in vaudeville during her second tour in 1912-13—seeking, perhaps, to avoid overt comparisons with Bernhardt, whom she knew would be touring at the same time. Langtry took roles as suffragists and independent women, first in *Helping the Cause,* and later, after returning to her staple errant wife in *The Test,* in *Mrs. Justice Drake,* a play according to one critic, 'full of prankish situations arising from the regime of the suffragettes.'

Her success in this piece on the western part of her tour in some ways redeemed Langtry's dismal failure in *Helping the Cause,* which was received 'coldly' at the Brooklyn Orpheum and was later closed down in mid-run by the manager of Pittsburgh's Grand Theatre. For her final tour in 1915-16, Langtry went back to erring wives, although she avoided fatal endings, and then retired after one more engagement at English music halls in 1918.

Olga Nethersole, 'the British Bernhardt', retired at the end of her only vaudeville tour in 1914. Bernhardt might have done the same, but instead she did one more tour in England, including some music halls there after her last stint in vaudeville in America. She was acting in a film in France, at a studio fashioned in her own lodgings within days of her death. Produced by a Hollywood company, *La Voyante,* with Bernhardt as the title character, was about a clairvoyant who told the future from Tarot cards.

THE IRONY OF 'INDEPENDENCE'

Although Bernhardt ended her career playing a character looking into the future, her vaudeville phase referred in more ways to the past. Jean Cocteau wrote that 'by her extraordinary power of swooning she filled the arms of the world'. Unconsciousness or death, with its savour of vulnerability, was the only release for most of the characters she played in vaudeville. Such extreme conditions proved to be Bernhardt's only release from acting, too— the career that gave her much freedom, but only, it would seem, of a certain sort. In this regard, her time in vaudeville and the conclusion to her career stand distinct among her contemporaries and fellow actresses.

Bernhardt's appearances in vaudeville suggest that a popular entertainment, in a way not unrelated to its escapist tendencies and more malleable cultural presence, can reaffirm values at risk of unravelling—even, and perhaps especially in the person of such a negative exemplar as Sarah Bernhardt. Vaudeville did not always fill a recuperative function, particularly when employing the younger, jazzier entertainers it had itself trained up: but it joined in a reactionary stance with the renowned Bernhardt to recommend, through a series of admonitory outcomes for otherwise highly attractive characters, a narrow morality for women and the mortal penalty for deviations from such morality.

With the plays she chose to present in vaudeville, Bernhardt seems to have referred her audiences quite wittingly to her own romantic past, chequered with affairs with actors, men of letters, statesmen, members of the nobility, and occasionally, it was rumoured, other women. Her personal life lent her a certain allure, but it seems also to have engendered an expectation that she would redeem such licence on the stage and pay for it in some way later in her life.

The valedictory appearances Bernhardt made in vaudeville, gauged in the context first of her growing incapacity, and finally of the amputation of her leg, represented a sort of public repentance even while they offered her huge financial rewards. By acting in a larger touring repertoire than any other actor to come into vaudeville, she was able to capitalize on the image of 'variety' that had marked vaudeville from its inception—and, perhaps, on her own sense of acting as 'a feminine art'.

On the other hand, she found herself late in her career speaking a language that few among her audiences could understand—even while invoking moral assumptions around women, in their freedom and capacity to express love, that appear to have been so ingrained and transcultural as to have been taken for granted by all parties concerned. In this connection, her vaudeville repertoire was not as liberating or as liberated as it might have seemed in the 1880s.

It is ironic that this process should have depended on an actress whose career and personal life were viewed by so many of her contemporaries as models of personal initiative and independence. This dramatizes the degree to which Bernhardt found herself captivated—and in her later years driven—by a repertoire that held such appeal to audiences in vaudeville. Indeed, Bernhardt's vaudeville repertoire was even more striking, set into fare that magnified even while it trivialized the actress's virtuosity in suffering and pain.

None of the most famous male stage actors to enter vaudeville played death scenes. Among the women, only Virginia Harned, a minor star, who played the title role in an adaptation of Tolstoy's *Anna Karenina* in vaudeville, and the Russian expatriate Alla Nazimova, who played a character who committed suicide at the end of Marion Craig Wentworth's *War Brides,* could approach the gravity of Bernhardt's scenarios.

In short, only women—and foreign ones at that among the major stars—were qualified to enact death on the vaudeville stage. Their ignorance of the American form's prevailing escapism may have been conceded, or they may have been granted the right to perform their heavy pieces in deference to their international stature. Even more broadly, suffering unto death may have seemed to vaudeville's producers, and to many among its audiences too, the proper expressive preserve of women.

Nazimova was only thirty-six when she appeared in *War Brides,* though, and so the impact of her character's death seems to have signified something quite different than it did in the venerable Bernhardt's battery of doomed characters. In Bernhardt's case, vaudeville audiences seem to have taken voyeuristic fascination in a famous actress's willingness to expose her body as a simulacrum of her state in life, and in a kind of public penance for the life she was known to have led. The frankness of this exchange defined vaudeville as a more 'popular' form in its day than the legitimate theatre was or than it wanted to be.

Gerda Taranow (essay date 1996)

SOURCE: "The Context: Literary, Theatrical, Cultural," in *The Bernhardt Hamlet: Culture and Context,* Peter Lang Publishers, Inc., 1996, pp. 67-111.

[*In the following essay, Taranow provides a critical overview of the literary and theatrical influences and historical background of Bernhardt's* Hamlet.]

Following the *première* of May 20, 1899, at the Théâtre Sarah Bernhardt, a number of comments appeared in the press affirming the originality of the Bernhardt *Hamlet.* To Catulle Mendès, the evening represented the first production of *Hamlet* ever to have taken place in France; to Robert de Flers, it seemed like the first production of *Hamlet* anywhere; and to A.-Ferdinand Herold, it became the initial performance in Paris, not merely of *Hamlet,* but of any Shakespearean play. The originality of Bernhardt's approach explains the critical euphoria for, according to Herold, Sarah Bernhardt recognized that "Shakespeare was not a writer from the 1830's and that the characters in his plays could not be interpreted as if they were heroes in romantic drama." In place of the procrastinator that dominated the nineteenth-century stage, Bernhardt presented an avenger with his roots in the Elizabethan and Jacobean theatre of his origins.

As the revenge play developed in the Elizabethan theatre, it represented a type of drama to which *Hamlet* belonged and with which it shared many characteristics. Fredson Bowers enumerates some of these characteristics: "the ghosts of the murdered urging revenge, hesitation on the part of the avenger, a delay in proceeding to his vengeance, his feigned or actual madness; . . . the wearing of black; reading in a book before a philosophical soliloquy; . . . and the melancholy of the revenger. . . ." So integral a characteristic of the revenge play was the delay of the avenger that the dramaturgy hinged upon it. As Fredson Bowers observes, "For there to be any play at all, the revenger must delay." What to Coleridge, in romantic terms, represented the protagonist's "aversion to real action" was, in Elizabethan terms, a technique of dramaturgy characteristic of the revenge type. From its inception in the late 1580's with Thomas Kyd's *The Spanish Tragedy* and the no longer extant *Ur-Hamlet,* Elizabethan revenge tragedy continued to adhere to a formulaic conception which, throughout the Jacobean and Caroline periods, included hesitation, delay, melancholy, violence, ghosts, madness—simulated and real—and revenge. *Hamlet* belongs to a large group of plays written over a period of more than half a century which share many of these characteristics and which have as their principal concern the theme of private revenge. Notable among these plays are *Antonio's Revenge* (John Marston), *The Revenger's Tragedy* (Cyril Tourneur), and *The Revenge of Bussy d'Ambois* (George Chapman). It is Bernhardt's emphasis on what are now recognized as the Elizabethan aspects of *Hamlet* that links her production with the tradition from which the play sprang and that imbued it with its freshness and vigor.

Sarah Bernhardt's comments on *Hamlet* indicate that she regarded both play and protagonist in traditional revenge terms. In a letter she wrote, in French, to the London *Daily Telegraph,* responding to certain criticisms of her interpretation, she presented an argument diametrically opposed to romantic principles still in vogue in the English theatre. Countering the accusation that her Hamlet was "too spirited and too manly," she observed that the English seemed to regard Hamlet as a "woebegone professor of Wittenberg," but that she played him as the "student" Shakespeare intended. She rejected the prevalent attitude that the contemplative temperament precluded virility: "What people are determined to see in Hamlet is a feminized, hesitating, bemused creature. What I see, however, is a person who is manly and resolute, but nonetheless thoughtful. As soon as Hamlet encounters the spirit of his father and grasps the nature of the crime, he decides to avenge him. But since he is the opposite of Othello, who acts before he thinks, Hamlet, characteristically, thinks before he acts, a trait indicative of great strength and great spiritual power." Her defense of her treatment of the prayer scene also involves a strong rejection of the irresolute procrastinator so often seen in the nineteenth-century theatre: "In the prayer scene I am criticized for approaching the King too closely, but if Hamlet wishes to kill the King, he must be close to him. And when he hears the King speaking words of repentance in prayer, he thinks that if he kills him, he will send him to heaven. He avoids killing the King, not because he is hesitant and weak, but because he is firm and logical. He wishes to kill him in a state of sin, not of repentance, for he wants to send him to hell and not to heaven." Bernhardt responded with indignation to the charge that in her performance she did not follow tradition. "But where is tradition to be found?" she queried and, in so doing, raised the larger issue involving the romantic-hamletic tradition compatible with nineteenth-century sensibility and the revenge tradition compatible with the Elizabethan context of the play.

In her histrionic treatise *L'Art du théâtre,* Sarah Bernhardt sustained her interpretation of *Hamlet* as a revenge play. Here she maintains that in spite of the complexity of Hamlet's character, he was impelled by a single dominant purpose: avenging his father's murder. He was, however, unable to carry out his intentions until he ascertained the integrity of the Ghost. Since a diabolical spirit could have provoked unwarranted suspicion of murder, the words of the Ghost, until confirmed by the consequences of *The Mousetrap,* remained contestable. Exhibiting the interdependence of revenge and delay, her explanation reinforces her previously stated attitudes. Bernhardt further emphasizes revenge by comparing Hamlet with the protagonist of Alfred de Musset's *Lorenzaccio,* the first play in her cycle of three Hamlet plays. Both Hamlet and Lorenzo, she asserts, are impelled by revenge, but in the case of Lorenzo, the vengeance is political. Although both are avenging the death of parents, for Lorenzo, the parent is metaphoric, as the mother whose slaughter he seeks to avenge is his native city Florence. The adaptation of *Lorenzaccio* by Armand d'Artois which Bernhardt produced, moreover, placed increased emphasis upon the revenge motif through the replacement of the hamletic ending with decisive vendetta. Musset's ending had focused not only upon the perpetuation of tyranny, but upon the futility of idealistic action, themes integral to the philosophy of Hamletism. The adaptation that Bernhardt performed concluded with the triumphal revenge of the protagonist. It is clear that what Bernhardt intended by her comparison of the adapted *Lorenzaccio* and of *Hamlet* was an emphasis in both plays upon thematic vendetta.

When an English scholar asked Sarah Bernhardt who it was that initiated her into the mysteries of Hamlet, she answered with surprise, "Why, Hamlet himself did!" There can be little doubt that a close reading of the text, without inherited preconceptions, would yield fresh insights into the tragedy. Sarah Bernhardt, however, may have had additional sources of orientation. Inevitably, one thinks of her translator, Marcel Schwob, who was steeped in the *Hamlet* scholarship of the period. In referring to the origins of Hamlet in his introduction to the translation, Schwob cites such scholars as Frederick Fleay, Gregor Sarrazin, Edward Dowden, and Edmund Malone. Sources such as these would have contributed little to Bernhardt's understanding of *Hamlet* as an Elizabethan revenge play. Dowden, for example, accepts Goethe's "oak tree" passage from *Wilhelm Meister,* although not as a total interpretation. He does refer to the inheritance from an older and more primitive play, but he fails to connect *Hamlet* with the revenge tradition. In 1899, of course, limited information was available concerning *Hamlet* as part of the tradition of revenge. Ashley Thorndike's study "The Relation of *Hamlet* to the Contemporary Revenge Play" did not appear until 1902; Charlton M. Lewis' *The Genesis of Hamlet* would not be available until 1907; and other studies, such as those of E.E. Stoll, Lily Bess Campbell, and Fredson Bowers, were to be written many years in the future. It remains a matter of conjecture as to whether Marcel Schwob, who knew of the *Ur-Hamlet* and who was familiar with *The Spanish Tragedy,* discussed these plays with Sarah Bernhardt. It is less conjectural to propose that Bernhardt's grasp of the revenge tradition was derived from exposure to other sources.

By 1899, the 54-year-old Sarah Bernhardt had spent most of her life in the theatre. She was therefore familiar with a vast repertoire, initially through performance, but later through directing and producing as well. Having played such Racinian roles as Andromaque (*Andromaque*), Junie (*Britannicus*), Iphigénie (*Iphigénie en Aulide*), Monime (*Mithridate*), and Aricie as well as Phèdre (*Phèdre*), she possessed an intimate knowledge of classical dramaturgy with its observance of the unities, its use of reported action, its usual avoidance of death scenes, its long and intricately structured *tirades,* its finely wrought alexandrines, its formality, its decorum, and its statuesque elegance. Having performed such Sardovian roles as Fédora (*Fédora*), Théodora (*Théodora*), Floria Tosca (*La Tosca*), Gismonda (*Gismonda*), and Cléopâtre (*Cléopâtre*), she acquired an equally impressive knowledge of the techniques of Boulevard dramaturgy with its emphasis on plot, peripeteia, and strong central conflicts; its preference for action acted rather than action reported; its long, sometimes extended death scenes; its use of prose rather than poetry; and its opulent scenographic effects. She approached *Hamlet* from a background of two traditions—classicism and the Boulevard—and undoubtedly recognized that although Shakespeare's dramaturgy had points of contact with both, it had greater affinities with the popular tradition of the Boulevard. While the soliloquies of the Prince of Denmark could satisfy any classicist who savored the *tirades* of Corneille and Racine, the Ghost, the mad scene, the graveyard scene, the fencing match, and the death scene must have seemed like indigenous fare to audiences at the Théâtre Historique where the Dumas-Meurice *Hamlet* was performed in 1847 and to those at the Porte Saint-Martin where the Cressonnois-Samson *Hamlet* was performed in 1886. Boulevard dramaturgy, however, could also be encountered in the romantic repertory of the Comédie-Française and the Odéon, for romantic playwrights such as Victor Hugo were acknowledged borrowers of popular techniques. Through the romantic influence, too, Shakespeare, free from the alterations of Ducis, had been introduced, first at the Odéon, then at the Théâtre Français. Indeed, Sarah Bernhardt's first experience with Shakespeare occurred at the Odéon when she assumed the role of Cordelia in an adaptation of *King Lear*. Ten years later, she appeared as Desdemona together with Mounet-Sully in the fifth act of *Othello* at a benefit performance at the Comédie-Française. After her break with classicism, Bernhardt appeared at the Porte Saint-Martin on May 21, 1884, as Lady Macbeth in Jean Richepin's translation of the tragedy. Two years later she again appeared at the Porte Saint-Martin, this time as Ophelia in the Cressonnois-Samson *Hamlet*. Bernhardt assuredly learned a great deal about *Hamlet* from this initial encounter with the play. When thirteen years later she returned to Shakespeare's tragedy, she had already performed Musset's *Lorenzaccio* and had assimilated a knowledge of dramaturgy—classical, Boulevard, and romantic—acquired through thirty-seven years of theatrical experience. Her perception of *Hamlet* as a revenge play was not a result of extensive reading in unavailable Elizabethan scholarship. It was rather a combination of inherent perspicacity supported by wide and varied exposure to all types of drama. The result was an interpretation of the tragedy that was intrinsically Elizabethan in its vibrant portrayal of revenge.

The question inevitably arises as to whether Sarah Bernhardt had any nineteenth-century predecessors for her treatment of *Hamlet* as a revenge play. In attempting to determine precursors, one must examine the interpretations of those who, consciously or unconsciously, contested the prevailing romantic-hamletic view of the tragedy. The closest one might come to precursors would then be Philibert Rouvière, Charles Fechter, and William Poel.

At first glance, Philibert Rouvière (1809-1865), the romantic actor who created the role of Hamlet in the Dumas-Meurice translation, seems an unlikely possibility. His playing showed the influence of the English actors Charles Kemble and William Charles Macready, whose performances at the "soirées anglaises" at the Odéon had left no cultured person in Paris untouched, but whose interpretations of the Prince of Denmark were completely unrelated to the revenge tradition. His playing also showed the influence of Delacroix, whose lithographs presented a distillation of those same English *Hamlet* performances at the Odéon. Rouvière's playing, however, showed still another influence: that of the performing tradition of the Boulevard, which emphasized physical energy and emotional intensity. The combination of influences produced a fiery interpretation of Hamlet that in appearance was deceptively hamletic. Rouvière's costume, designed by Bonhommé, had been modelled on Delacroix' prints. Baudelaire, who admired Rouvière's

Hamlet, did so despite the fact that the actor deviated so strongly from the Prince of Delacroix, whose appearance he resembled. According to Baudelaire, Rouvière's Hamlet was "angry," "high-strung," "active," and "Latin" in conception. The author of the Spleen Poems considered Rouvière's Prince "bitter," "ill-fated," and "hot-tempered," qualities he attributed to the actor's bizarre romantic orientation. Théophile Gautier was in agreement with Baudelaire, insisting that there was not enough of the dreamer in Rouvière's Prince and that, instead of alternating meditative moments with those of impetuosity, the actor continually emphasized emotional outbursts and madness. Gautier nevertheless affirmed that Rouvière retained enough of the characteristics of Hamlet to make him recognizable "'to poets and to the general public.'" In imbuing the role with exaggerated romantic characteristics, Rouvière was interpreting the Prince in the dominant style of the Boulevard where romantic drama had its roots. The performing tradition of the Boulevard, however, differed markedly from the romantic-hamletic interpretation current among the literati. Despite Rouvière's interpretation and despite the original ending of the Dumas-Meurice adaptation which kept the Prince alive at the end, the productions of the play in which Rouvière appeared—at Saint-Germain-en-Laye in 1846, at the Théâtre Historique in 1847, at the Odéon in 1855, and at the Théâtre Beaumarchais in 1861—were never discussed in terms of the revenge tradition. If Rouvière can indeed be considered a precursor of Bernhardt's *Hamlet*, it would be only in terms of his spirited acting.

Charles Fechter (1824-1879) comes more immediately to mind as a precursor of Sarah Bernhardt's *Hamlet*. An Anglo-French actor born in London to French-speaking parents, Fechter was a bilingual performer exposed at an early age to English theatre, but trained in the French traditions of classicism and the Boulevard. In Paris he established a considerable reputation as a stage lover and in 1852 created the role of Armand Duval in *La Dame aux camélias*. Initially appearing in London in 1847 with a French troupe, he returned in 1860 to perform in English. Fechter eventually became associated with the English theatre, but in intonation and selected pronunciations retained his French accent. On March 20, 1861, Fechter appeared at the Princess Theatre in *Hamlet*, the first of his three productions of the tragedy. The other two took place at the Lyceum Theatre (May 21, 1864) and Niblo's Garden, New York (February 14, 1870). All three productions were considered innovative, but only one would have special significance for Bernhardt's *Hamlet*.

In all of his *Hamlet* productions, Fechter brought to the title role experience derived not from English theatrical practice, but from the French tradition of the Boulevard. When his Hamlet was called unconventional and even revolutionary, it was largely attributable to the fact that English critics did not find in his playing the performance traditions of the English theatre. In his London productions, his interpretation of the Prince was in keeping with contemporary expectations, for he, too, modelled his

Hamlet on key passages from *Wilhelm Meister*. Adding a detail also suggested in *Wilhelm Meister*, he surprised English audiences by appearing in the blond wig which Goethe had considered appropriate for a Danish Prince. What made his *Hamlet* productions so unconventional, however, was not merely the blond wig, but the use of a performance style of the French Boulevard theatre. In Bernhardt's histrionic treatise *L'Art du théâtre,* she reveals a formula for the pantomimic style of Boulevard acting: glance, gesture, word; the progression beginning with facial acting, continuing in gestural expression, and culminating in the spoken word. The style she learned at the Conservatoire, on the other hand, was based upon a two-step formula of gesture's preceding speech. The addition of facial expression to the method ingrained in classical practice created a pronounced difference between the styles of classicism and the Boulevard. One of the reasons that Fechter's Hamlet seemed so unconventional to English audiences is that, in spite of the familiar reliance upon *Wilhelm Meister,* his performance represented a style of acting totally foreign to the English tradition of playing Shakespeare.

Fechter's interpretation of *Hamlet* in his two London productions had little in common with the revenge tradition. The blond, conversational, pantomimic Hamlet of a great stage lover, influenced, moreover, by the "oak tree" passage from *Wilhelm Meister,* would scarcely seem representative of the tradition from which the play sprang. Fechter, however, produced *Hamlet* a third time, and it is the third production, which took place in New York in 1870, that possesses characteristics linking it with the older tradition. Retaining the attributes of the Boulevard style, the actor appears to have dispensed with *Wilhelm Meister* in all matters except the blond wig. Critical evaluations disclose a rejection of the standard Goethe-Coleridge vocabulary. When, for example, the Boston critic Henry Austin Clapp argued with Fechter about his interpretation, the actor insisted that Hamlet "'did not procrastinate, but pursued his task with vigor.'" Furthermore, Fechter's biographer Kate Field, who describes the American production in detail, sustains the actor's pronouncement. "Fechter's *Hamlet,*" she states, "was restrained by reasonable doubt, not vacillation of purpose. . . ." To substantiate the determination of Fechter's Prince, Kate Field cites his treatment of the Queen in the closet scene. "Killing the *Queen,*" she asserts, "was not impossible to the *Hamlet* of Fechter, who was convinced of her complicity in his father's murder." Here, however, Fechter reveals his roots in the French tradition, roots which extend directly to the *Hamlet* of Jean-François Ducis. In Ducis' *Hamlet,* the Queen's complicity is integral to the text, leading to the once highly prized urn scene. So strongly were the French influenced by the idea of Gertrude's participation in the murder that even Mounet-Sully, whose Hamlet was modeled on *Wilhelm Meister* and whose meticulous study of the text was well-known, maintained that the Queen was guilty of complicity in the murder of her former husband. What Fechter did in this scene was blend the Ducis inheritance with his newly developed awareness of revenge. Such an awareness also led him to make a notable restoration in the fourth act where he included the interchange between Hamlet and Claudius regarding the disposal of Polonius' body. Kate Field asserts that in this act Hamlet treated his uncle with "undisguised contempt" and that if the Prince had not been under guard, he would immediately have sent his uncle to the place referred to in his quip, "If your messenger find him not there, seek him in the other place yourself." Fechter's reasons for altering his interpretation of Hamlet in his third production remain a matter for speculation. Troubled by the shift in interpretation, John Mills considers, and rejects, the possibility that Fechter's New York Hamlet seemed robust only in comparison with the then current "irresolute, brooding, sensitive, intellectual" Hamlet of Edwin Booth. Whatever his reasons for changing interpretations, it is clear that Fechter's New York production of *Hamlet* contained a sufficient number of revenge elements to be regarded as a precursor of the Bernhardt *Hamlet.*

William Poel's conspicuously Elizabethan production of the First Quarto of *Hamlet* on April 16, 1881, at St. George's Hall in London should also be included as a precursor even though it represents the staging of a variant text. Of the three texts of *Hamlet* that have come down to us from Elizabethan times—the First Quarto, the Second Quarto, and the First Folio—the First Quarto possesses great historical and theatrical interest. The nature of the text is such, however, that it has generated controversy about its composition and authorship. It is chiefly in terms of language that the First Quarto has been held suspect of a host of literary ills, including several varieties of Elizabethan piracy. The text of the First Quarto, 1600 lines shorter than that of the authoritative Second Quarto, contains many lines recognizable as Shakespeare's, and others that seem like garbled and unrhythmic paraphrases of the two reliable Elizabethan *Hamlet* texts. "To be or not to be—ay, there's the point" is probably the best known and most startling line from the First Quarto, but others are equally characteristic of its verbal structure. "O that this too much griev'd and solid flesh/ Would melt to nothing" and "Why, what a dunghill idiot slave am I!" are typical of the jarring verbal effects found throughout the First Quarto. It is this text that William Poel produced in Elizabethan staging and as an Elizabethan revenge play. According to Robert Speaight, Poel approached *Hamlet* first as a drama of revenge, then as a "puzzle in psychology." Forty-one years after his initial production of the First Quarto, Poel wrote an article entitled "The Elizabethan 'Hamlet,'" and there he justified Hamlet's delay in Elizabethan terms. With the prayer scene in mind, Poel asserts that Hamlet refrained from killing the King because he wished to avoid the possibility of his attaining salvation: "He would have no Divine mercy granted the man who has murdered his father." Three years later, Poel wrote another article concerning *Hamlet,* and once again he rejected the then current notions of delay and irresolution, insisting that Shakespeare's tragedy was a play of revenge. Poel, moreover, admired Sir Barry Jackson's modern dress production of *Hamlet* at the Kingsway in 1924 because it approached the play as a tragedy of revenge. When in 1881 Poel initially produced the First Quarto, he boldly revived the Elizabethan emphasis on revenge and, despite the fact that the text was not a standard one, his production should be regarded as a precursor of the Bernhardt *Hamlet*.

Prior to the nineteenth century, one cannot truly speak of precursors, for the traditions of the Elizabethan revenge play were less affected by neoclassicism and sentimentalism than they would be by the romantic movement. Carol Jones Carlisle points out that the predominant interpretation during the eighteenth century was a "heroic" one. An inheritance from the Restoration, the heroic Hamlet prevailed on the English stage until replaced by the irresolute hero of romanticism. The interpretations of Betterton and Garrick had little in common with those of Goethe, Schlegel, and Coleridge. Although Garrick's Hamlet was more sentimental, delicate, and melancholy than the robust Prince of Betterton, his protagonist remained essentially energetic and resolute. Romantic attitudes, however, began to surface even in the eighteenth century. Carlisle cites the views of Thomas Sheridan as foreshadowing those of romanticism. Thomas Sheridan (1719-1788), father of Richard Brinsley Sheridan and a significant interpreter of Hamlet, discussed his conception of Hamlet with James Boswell. Preserved by Boswell in his *Journal* (April 6, 1763), the conversation represents "the earliest recorded interpretation" of Hamlet as a forerunner of the thought-sick procrastinator who appears so often in criticism and performance during the nineteenth century. Sheridan's vocabulary serves as a harbinger not only of the conceptions of Goethe and Coleridge, but of Schlegel and Hazlitt as well. As a result of his "'studious contemplative life,'" Sheridan explains, Hamlet became "'delicate and irresolute.'" He lacks the "'strength of mind to execute what he thinks right and wishes to do. . . .'" His failure to act in the prayer scene, moreover, is attributed to his making "'an excuse for his delay.'" Thomas Sheridan's words were to reverberate in nineteenth-century criticism. Supplementing Goethe's "oak tree" passage in *Wilhelm Meister* was August Wilhelm von Schlegel's interpretation of Hamlet as a man whose weakness is apparent in the resolutions he "'so often embraces and always leaves unexecuted.'" Having influenced the thinking of Coleridge, Schlegel's views emerge as an essential part of English *Hamlet* criticism. Furthermore, the reflective procrastinator of Goethe, Schlegel, and Coleridge was reinforced by William Hazlitt's interpretation of the Prince as one whose "ruling passion" was "to think, not to act." With the diffusion of romantic sensibility, the revenge tradition was expunged, and the heroic Hamlet replaced by a brooding and vacillating Prince who, in Coleridge's pronouncement, possessed "enormous intellectual activity" counterbalanced by an "aversion to real action." It was this Hamlet that Sarah Bernhardt's audiences on both sides of the Channel were accustomed to seeing.

When Bernhardt opened her *Hamlet* in Paris in 1899, audiences for the past thirteen years had been exposed to the romantic Prince of Jean Mounet-Sully. Permeated by hamletic influences, Mounet-Sully's Prince appeared to Francisque Sarcey to be a living embodiment of the Hamlet figure from the lithographs of Delacroix. He was also an embodiment of the literary figure emerging from the pages of *Wilhelm Meisters Lehrjahre*. In his memoirs, Mounet reveals that among the many books on Hamlet he had read was *Wilhelm Meister*, and criticism repeatedly calls attention to the fact that his Hamlet was modeled on Goethe's. "Hamlet," Mounet asserts, "represents irresolution." Employing the now familiar comparison with Fortinbras, he regards Hamlet as hesitant and Fortinbras as determined. From Jean Jacquot's reconstruction of Mounet's interpretation of Hamlet, it is clear that his performance was interspersed with such intense emotional responses as sighs, sobs, tears, tears in the voice, trembling, kneeling, and even simulated fainting. When, for example, the Ghost first appears to Hamlet on the battlements, the Prince's line "Angels and ministers of grace, defend us" elicited a strategically placed sigh from Hamlet. In the English theatre, the line possesses a rich heritage of histrionic responses, and Mounet's own response adds another approach to one of the "points" of the performance tradition of *Hamlet*. Preceding the line, Hamlet stood on the battlements, trembling from head to toe as the clock struck midnight. Then at the appearance of the Ghost, he called out, "Anges du ciel," paused, "heaved a deep sigh of anguish," and continued with "Protégez-nous." During the Ghost scene, his expressions of emotion were still more intense. When the Ghost identified himself—"Je suis l'esprit/De ton père"—Mounet's Hamlet sobbed and knelt. The kneeling is called for in a stage direction of the Dumas-Meurice text, but the sobbing is an interpretive addendum. Rising at the revelation of the murderer, he sank to both knees as he learned of his mother's adultery, covering his face with his hands, his torso wracked with sobs. At the Ghost's call for vengeance, he rose vehemently, only to kneel again, his arms outstretched in a gesture of supplication and farewell when the Ghost wished to depart. At the Ghost's disappearance, he fell into a simulated faint and, after remaining motionless for a while, gradually revived. The emotional emphasis found throughout Mounet-Sully's interpretation was in keeping with the "beautiful, pure, noble, extremely moral being" lacking in "heroic fortitude" set forth in *Wilhelm Meister* and with the pallid, sensitive, melancholy, and contemplative Prince of Delacroix. Mounet's Hamlet was filled with original insights, all of them romantic in nature and all of them supporting the already romantic adaptation of Alexandre Dumas père and Paul Meurice. Speaking the rhyming couplets in a flexible baritone voice and wearing the black plume of tradition, Mounet-Sully executed with skill and suppleness the greatly admired fan scene and sustained the sensibility of his age in presenting an interpretation of Hamlet so romantic that a former member of the Comédie-Française commented on its resemblance to Verdi.

In comparison with Mounet-Sully's *Hamlet*, Bernhardt's earlier production of the Cressonnois-Samson text with Philippe Garnier as the Prince had little impact upon the aesthetic perceptions of audiences. Although it preceded the production of the Dumas-Meurice text at the Comédie-Française by seven months, the Porte Saint-Martin *Hamlet* failed to develop into the cultural phenomenon that Mounet's *Hamlet* would become. In his review of the Mounet-Sully *Hamlet,* Sarcey predicted that "no one in Paris with literary or theatrical propensities could do without seeing Mounet in Shakespeare's masterpiece." No such review accompanied the earlier production. Despite the fact that it was directed by the distinguished Félix Duquesnel; designed by the outstanding talents of Rubé, Chaperon, Robecchi, and Amable; costumed by the gifted Thomas; and despite the fact that Sarah Bernhardt played Ophelia, the production never rose to the status of intellectual event of the season. The translation of Lucien Cressonnois and Charles Samson is partially at fault, for though based on the Dumas-Meurice text and written in alexandrines, it lacks the felicitous phrasing of the earlier adaptation. The main reason that the production remained without literary effect, however, was the Hamlet of Philippe Garnier. A strikingly handsome actor of only respectable talent, Garnier was Sarah Bernhardt's lover at the time, and it is believed that she produced *Hamlet* in 1886 in order to provide him with a role of distinction. Garnier had previously created the role of Andréas in Sardou's *Théodora,* but the interest he brought to the part of a Sardovian lover was lacking in his Prince of Denmark. He was criticized for the monotony of his delivery, a monotony which he augmented through his use of *déblayage.* When a performer employs *déblayage,* he delivers his lines rapidly and in a monotone, without accentuation. In English stage terminology, he is said to be "throwing away his lines." Although the critic of *Les Annales du théâtre* partially forgave Garnier for resorting to *déblayage* because of the length of the role, he was less charitable in commenting on the raucous quality his voice assumed when he increased its volume. Garnier's overall performance, too, was lacking in variety and, as a result, he quickly lost his audience. Jules Lemaître had little patience with Garnier's conception of Hamlet. Reviewing Mounet's Prince, he extolled the classical actor's interpretation because it was tailored to the specifications set forth in *Wilhelm Meister.* Goethe is never mentioned in connection with Garnier's interpretation, possibly because there was no influence, but also because his performance was so undistinguished that critics concentrated upon pointing out its many flaws. In contrasting the Hamlets of Mounet and Garnier, Lemaître rejects Garnier's interpretation as that of a "completely mediocre actor" who converted Hamlet into "an affected and malevolent madman." Reviews of the production record praise for the scenery, especially the graveyard scene; praise for the costumes, for the directing, and for Sarah Bernhardt's vocal interpretation of the songs in the mad scene. They even take note of the fact that Garnier played Hamlet in a blond wig, an influence stemming from either Goethe or Fechter, or both. The Porte Saint-Martin *Hamlet,* however, provided no competition for the Comédie-Française version. The differences between the two productions were many, but the distinguishing characteristic was the actor who played the role of the Prince. It would be thir-

teen years before Sarah Bernhardt challenged the interpretation of the reigning Hamlet of the day.

While French audiences had been conditioned by the Prince of Jean Mounet-Sully, English audiences had been exposed to the performances of several respected contemporary Hamlets: Henry Irving (1838-1905), Johnston Forbes-Robertson (1853-1937), and Herbert Beerbohm Tree (1853-1917). Each of these performers illuminated the text with his unique insights, but all of them remained essentially romantic. Taken as a whole, their performances provide the theatrical context in which Bernhardt performed her Hamlet in England.

An actor possessing great stage presence, Henry Irving appeared in two of his own productions of *Hamlet* at the Lyceum in 1874 and 1878, with revivals as late as 1885. His performance grew in stature over the years, but his underlying conception remained a sentimental one. G.C.D. Odell maintains that Irving stressed Hamlet's love for Ophelia so forcibly that it dominated his entire interpretation. As a result, the revenge motif was relegated to the background. Performing in a style that Bertram Joseph regards as "romantic realism," Irving rejected traditional point-making and instead, in his soliloquies, seemed to be thinking aloud. His stated purpose, to present Hamlet "'as a man, not as a piece of acting,'" encapsulates the realism he imparted to performance. With his "black, disordered hair" and eyes so intense they seemed "burning," he looked twice his age in his "very pale" make-up which, Ellen Terry recalls, "made his face beautiful when one was close to him, but at a distance . . . gave him a haggard look." When Hamlet made his initial entrance during the first court scene, "the lights were turned down . . . to help the effect that the figure was spirit rather than man." The spiritual quality of his appearance was coupled with speech that placed character and thought above elocution. In an age that emphasized fine speaking voices, a contemporary, Eden Phillpotts, maintained that Henry Irving's voice possessed none of the "resonance and mellow purity of diction and intonation" of such performers as Tommaso Salvini, Johnston Forbes-Robertson, and Edwin Booth. Indeed, Irving's voice, as preserved on two cylinder recordings—a section of a soliloquy from *Richard III* and a speech from *Henry VIII*—does not possess the qualities of range, richness, and elegance preserved on recordings of Salvini, Forbes-Robertson, and Booth. With his love of theatrical effects and spectacle, Irving in 1878 offered a production of *Hamlet* containing striking processions and tasteful sets designed by Hawes Craven. At the heart of both the 1874 and 1878 productions of *Hamlet,* however, was the Prince of Henry Irving: intellectual, realistic, theatrical, charismatic, and above all, romantic. It is therefore understandable why the eminent critic of the *Daily Telegraph* Clement Scott cites the "oak tree" passage from *Wilhelm Meister* in connection with what he regards as the "irresolute" character of Irving's Prince. Since at that period the Lyceum was considered "the centre of metropolitan culture," Irving's interpretation of Hamlet was thoroughly ingrained in the perceptions of contemporary English audiences.

Although Henry Irving's Prince of Denmark dominated the Hamlet consciousness of his age, Johnston Forbes-Robertson's protagonist acquired considerable prestige. Opening on September 11, 1897, at the Lyceum in Henry Irving's "scenery," "properties," and costumes for the "subordinate characters," Forbes-Robertson's production of *Hamlet* was completely redirected in the light of the new interpretation of the protagonist. According to Clement Scott, then considered dean of the London drama critics, Forbes-Robertson's Hamlet was well-bred, courtly, graceful, pensive, facially expressive, and lovable, possessing a keen but subtle sense of humor. His mind, moreover, was "deeply sensitive to religious impression," and his pervasive conception was that of a man who had "thought very deeply" on "the life to come." Forbes-Robertson's voice, as preserved on recordings, substantiates the descriptions of both Clement Scott and Bernard Shaw. Scott noted that the voice was reminiscent of "the moan and wail of a '*cello*," and Shaw compared it to the chalumeau, or lower register, of a clarinet in A. Recordings reveal that Robertson's voice is that of a resonant baritone, rich and sonorous, exhibiting wide range and elegant sound. The articulation is precise, the breathing so well controlled that it is scarcely audible. According to his niece Beatrice Forbes-Robertson, who acted with him, her uncle's power of vocal projection was so accomplished that "'he could be heard at the back of the top gallery of Drury Lane when apparently speaking in a whisper.'" Forbes-Robertson's recordings disclose the technical polish for which he had been admired. Interpretively, however, they remain bland. The critic of the *Athenaeum* observed as much concerning Robertson's overall performance as Hamlet, remarking that he was "'gratefully pleased and stirred,'" that he received new insights from the interpretation, but that he was not "'fired'" by a performance he regarded as "'too statuesquely faultless.'" Perhaps the best known aspect of Robertson's production of *Hamlet* is the innovative ending. For the death scene Hamlet was seated upon the throne of Denmark while Horatio placed the crown upon his knees. The play did not end with "The rest is silence" or "Good night, sweet prince, . . ." but with a scene dependent upon the appearance of a character who, other than in William Poel's production of the First Quarto, had not been seen in the English theatre since the Restoration. Bernard Shaw had suggested to Forbes-Robertson that he restore Fortinbras to the play, and although Robertson did not include the scene of "quiet pass" in the fourth act, he brought the Norwegian Prince back to the ending of *Hamlet*. When the actor Whitworth Jones made his entrance as Fortinbras, a contrast immediately arose between "death and life" as "all that is left of the dreamer and philosopher" was borne off upon a shield. Despite his admiration for Forbes-Robertson's Hamlet, Clement Scott points out that the actor's good breeding robbed several scenes of their "vigour and intensity." Among these, he mentions the scenes which were most powerful with Henry Irving, those involving Gertrude and Ophelia, that is, the closet scene and the nunnery scene. Robertson also failed to speak Hamlet's soliloquy in the prayer scene, "Now might I do it pat," possibly because the theme of vengeance, irascibly evident in the speech, might have been too vehement for so courteous a Prince. "Dreamy and metaphysical" were the words used to characterize Robertson's Hamlet by a critic making a comparison with Bernhardt's "bright" and "dramatic" protagonist. Forbes-Robertson began performing Hamlet in 1897 when he was 44 years old, and he would continue to appear in the role until he was 64. When in 1899 Bernhardt brought her *Hamlet* to London, playgoers had fresh remembrances of the well-mannered, well-spoken, gentle, and metaphysical Prince of Johnston Forbes-Robertson.

Playgoers' remembrances of Herbert Beerbohm Tree's *Hamlet* would doubtless have focused principally on his embellishments of the text. Preceding the great Shakespearean spectacles that characterized Tree's direction of Her Majesty's Theatre from 1897 to 1914, the production of *Hamlet* on January 21, 1892, at the Haymarket served as a harbinger of his future emphasis upon all aspects of mise en scène. In a production designed by William Lewis Telbin, Tree cut the play more heavily than any of his contemporaries or predecessors. The missing lines were replaced by a series of theatrical effects: scenographic, musical, and pantomimic. The settings were numerous and opulent, and audiences eagerly anticipated the visual splendour of his Shakespearean revivals. Especially praised in his *Hamlet* production were the décors for the nunnery scene and the graveyard scene. In addition to its scenographic emphasis, Tree's *Hamlet* included more extensive use of music than the productions of his contemporaries. Employing George Henschel's score, Tree readily substituted music for deleted text. At the conclusion of the play, for example, Tree used a traditional cut and brought the curtain down on Horatio's couplet "Good night, sweet Prince / And flights of angels sing thee to thy rest!" He then replaced the excised text with an operatic curtain, for at the moment Horatio finished his couplet, an "angelic choir" was heard "to faintly echo" his words "Good night, sweet Prince." According to Clement Scott, the firstnight audience, "with hearts full and nerves a little overstrained," was "visibly affected" by the ending. Tree's use of pantomimic effects represents still another of the theatrical techniques that dominated his production. In his book *Thoughts and Afterthoughts,* the actor maintains that in order to emphasize Hamlet's deep love for Ophelia, he introduced a pantomimic effect at the conclusion of the graveyard scene: "Hamlet has departed, followed by the King, Queen, Laertes, and the courtiers. In the church close by, the organ peals out a funeral march. Night is falling, the birds are at rest, Ophelia's grave is deserted. But through the shadows, Hamlet's returning form is seen gathering wild flowers. He is alone with his dead love, and on her he strews the flowers as he falls by her grave in a paroxysm of grief. And so the curtain falls." Beerbohm Tree took special pains to achieve strong curtains, but he was by no means the only actor-manager to employ them. Henry Irving made such frequent use of the well-built curtain that William Poel complained of his habit of working up a scene to a "'striking picture upon which the curtain may fall.'" Indeed, the strong curtain is so characteristic of the pictorial realism associated with the nineteenth-century picture-frame stage that Sarah Bernhardt, who broke completely with romanticism in her intellectual interpretation of *Hamlet*, employed the same kind of emphatic curtains as did her English colleagues across the Channel.

In retrospect, when one thinks of Beerbohm Tree's production of *Hamlet*, one is apt to concentrate almost exclusively on the mise en scène. To Tree's contemporaries, however, his production was more than scenography, music, pantomimic interpolations, and strong curtains. In the midst of an elaborate production of Shakespeare's tragedy was the refined and gentle Prince of Herbert Beerbohm-Tree: wearing "reddish hair" and a "slight unobtrusive beard"; possessing expressive eyes and mobile features; and appearing "so soft and sentimental . . . that one critic called . . . [him] a 'Werther Hamlet.'" In his book, Tree speaks with the anticipated Goethe-Coleridge vocabulary. He is convinced that Hamlet really does not wish to do the deed and that he seeks excuses for not carrying out his duty. The overbalance of intellectuality, moreover, is the true impediment to action. That he admires Goethe's comparison with the oak tree is by no means unexpected. The Hamlet orientation of the London public at the turn of the century was therefore shaped by still another performer whose interpretation of the Prince of Denmark continued the traditions established by romanticism.

Henry Irving, Johnston Forbes-Robertson, and Herbert Beerbohm Tree were the key figures who shaped the Hamlet consciousness of the time in London. Remembrances of Fechter were also present, but by 1899 they were beginning to belong as much to history as did the accounts of the Hamlet performances of Betterton, Garrick, Edmund Kean, Macready, and Phelps. In Paris, Jean Mounet-Sully was the key Hamlet figure, with Philibert Rouvière's receding into history and François-Joseph Talma long established in memory as the great classical interpreter of Ducis' adaptation. In Paris as in London, however, there were also remembrances of actresses who, with varying degrees of distinction, had attempted the role of Hamlet.

In France, recollections were chiefly of Mme Judith, who, 32 years prior to the Bernhardt *Hamlet*, had performed an abridged version of the Dumas-Meurice text at the Théâtre de la Gaîté. Little is known of those 1867 performances beyond some negative critical comments. Still less is known of the single performance by Émilie Lerou as the Prince of Denmark. Buried in obscurity, too, are the Hamlet performances in 1898 by Adeline Dudlay and Mme Derigny. Dudlay had initiated her provincial tour in Toulouse by appearing as Hamlet, and Mme Derigny had performed the Prince at the Théâtre des Bouffes du Nord in Paris. What is significant about all these Hamlet performances is that they emerged from a theatrical tradition that for centuries had nurtured the conventions of *travesti*.

By the year 1899, three types of *travesti* had evolved in the French theatre. The first, that of a man's assuming the role of an older woman or duenna, belongs to the comic repertoire and stems largely from the theatre practice of Molière. The second, that of a woman's assuming the role of a boy or young man, also has its roots in the theatre of the past and is mainly, but not exclusively, associated with the comic repertoire. The third type of *travesti*, that of the transformation of a significant male, or *premier rôle*, into a female *travesti* role, is an outgrowth of the woman-as-boy type and appeared with increasing frequency in the theatre of the nineteenth century.

The first type of *travesti* role, that of a man's assuming the role of an older woman, or duenna, stems from the early French theatre and extends from pre-seventeenth-century stage practice to the age of Corneille. According to Arthur Pougin, the practice fell into temporary disuse, only to be reintroduced by Molière, who trained certain actors to perform the roles of older women in the comic repertoire. As a specialist in the acting category of *travesti*, André Hubert (c. 1634-1700) created such roles as Mme Jourdain (*Le Bourgeois gentilhomme*), Philaminte (*Les Femmes savantes*), Mme de Sotenville (*Georges Dandin*), and Lucette (*Monsieur de Pourceaugnac*). The role of Nérine in *Les Fourberies de Scapin* was created by Edmé Villequin de Brie (1607-1676). After the death of Molière, these *travesti* roles were assigned to women, a custom that has persisted into the present. In such modern productions as that of *Les Femmes savantes* at the Théâtre Récamier in 1960, however, Georges Wilson undertook the role of Philaminte with great success. The advantage of reverting to Molière's practice is similar to the one derived from the traditional performance by a man of the "dame" role in English pantomime and of such a male *travesti* role in ballet as Mother Simone in *La Fille mal gardée*. In these roles, the comedy is enhanced by the exaggeration of features, limbs, stature, movements and, in the case of spoken roles, by the disparity between disguised sex and undisguised voice as well. Despite occasional performances containing Molière's male *travestis*, one is apt to become more familiar with them in the study than on the stage.

The second type of *travesti*, that of a woman's assuming the role of a young man or boy, existed in the French theatre long before Beaumarchais was to codify the practice. Jeanne Ausoult (1625-1662), the first wife of Michel Baron's father, for example, was greatly admired for her performances in *travesti*. So substantially did the use of the female *travesti* role increase in the eighteenth century that Beaumarchais saw the need to offer an explanation for his own as well as contemporary practice. In his play *Le Mariage de Figaro*, Beaumarchais specified that an actress, not an actor, perform the role of the page Chérubin since, he maintained, the theatre no longer possessed young actors with sufficient technique to "penetrate the subtleties of the role." Doubtless other dramatists who called for women to perform the roles of young men were motivated by the same practical approach as Beaumarchais.

The nineteenth century saw so great an expansion in the use of *travesti* that Beaumarchais' explanation can only partially account for the newly awakened interest in the role. In his book *Shakespeare on the American Stage,* Charles Shattuck devotes an entire chapter to the "extraordinary intensification of woman-worship" in the nineteenth century. Discussing the preoccupation with augmented female sexuality, Shattuck is especially concerned with women's roles to which erotic interest had been newly imparted. In connection with augmented female sexuality, he mentions the expanded use of *travesti* that occurred in an all-female production of *As You Like It.* Indeed, both types of roles are relevant to the climate of feminization that prevailed. In women's roles a feminine emphasis was introduced where previously none had been. The newly introduced sexuality of Lady Macbeth, as interpreted initially by Sarah Bernhardt in 1884 and subsequently by Ellen Terry in 1888 and Lily Langtry in 1889, provides a striking example of the feminine emphasis in women's roles. For female *travesti* roles, the feminizing was achieved through means that were distinctly different: the audience was continually aware that a male character was being presented, in stylized fashion, through the body, voice, and gestures of a woman. Only movement was given the freedom that masculine costume permitted, but that, too, was subject to stylization. Masculine costume, moreover, exposed the actresses' legs, an effect not invariably emphasized, but one that was by no means ignored at a time when women's costumes were ankle-length. Considering the artistic ambiance of the performing arts in the nineteenth century, it would be misleading to characterize the then popular *travesti* roles as androgynous. The roles did not seek to intermingle opposite sexualities, but to emphasize, with delicate insistence, the feminine presence that by the nineteenth century had become a stage preoccupation.

The expanded use of *travesti* occurred both on the Boulevard and in the classical theatre. The soubrette of the popular theatre, Virginie Déjazet (1798-1875), was so successful in performing *travesti* that the roles in which she appeared in vaudeville came to be regarded as a major acting category which bore her name, the *Déjazet* role. Virginie Déjazet created over one hundred *travesti* roles at such Boulevard theatres as the Variétés, the Gymnase, and the Gaîté. Déjazet's roles were not exclusively comic. She appeared, for example, as the young son of Napoleon in *Le Fils de l'homme,* a play that preceded Rostand's internationally known *L'Aiglon.* According to Théodore de Banville, Déjazet possessed the kind of undefined sex found in such creatures of fantasy as Puck and Ariel, roles that in the nineteenth century had become the province of actresses. The term "undefined" employed by Banville is less elusive than it initially appears, for Déjazet was clearly successful in presenting her young men not through realism, but through stylized feminization.

Unlike the male *travesti,* which concentrated on the *grime,* or character role, the female *travesti* sought to lend a feminine aura to masculinity. This feminine aura was to be found not only in theatre, but in ballet and opera as well. Déjazet was the most famous theatrical performer of *travesti* in her day, and her techniques were constantly imitated by other actresses appearing in similar roles in the theatres of the Boulevard. With the demise of vaudeville, much of the style and substance of that semi-musical genre were integrated into the Opéra-Comique where the *Déjazet* roles, performed by soubrettes specializing in *travesti,* were known as *Dugazons.* The *travesti* role, moreover, became as essential a part of classicism in the nineteenth century as it did of the Boulevard. Sarah Bernhardt therefore conformed to custom when she began performing *travesti* in her student days at the Conservatoire. At that time she appeared at the little Théâtre de la Tour d'Auvergne as Edouard V in *Les Enfants d'Édouard* by Casimir Delavigne and as Richelieu, one of Déjazet's most successful roles, in *Les Premières armes de Richelieu* by Bayard and Dumanoir. She continued appearing in *travesti* at the Odéon and Comédie-Française, performing such *ingénu-travesti* roles as Zanetto in François Coppée's *Le Passant,* Zacharie in Racine's *Athalie,* and Chérubin in Beaumarchais's *Le Mariage de Figaro.* Once she even appeared at the Comédie-Française as the 18-year-old Racine in Émile Moreau's verse drama *Parthénice.* The female *travesti* role was available to all young actresses at the two citadels of classicism, providing, of course, they had the physical qualifications to perform them. Indeed, at the time, it was regarded as a compliment to be able to wear "the jerkin and the wig."

Given such theatrical orientation, it might have been anticipated that classically trained actresses would embark upon the third type of *travesti* role, the transformation of a significant male *premier rôle* into a *premier travesti rôle.* Such was the case when Mme Judith, Émilie Lerou, and Adeline Dudlay assayed the role of a young Prince who, in the romantic tradition of the Dumas-Meurice adaptation, acts with the delicacy, sentimentality, and irresolution that would have suited the quality of feminized masculinity characteristic of the female *travesti* in the nineteenth century. When Sarah Bernhardt attempted the role of Hamlet, she, too, through performance practice, followed a traditional pattern of feminized masculinity. Through interpretation, however, she departed from the romantic-hamletic mode of both predecessors and contemporaries in presenting an avenger compatible with the Elizabethan tradition of the play.

Hamlet became attractive to French actresses in the nineteenth century not simply because the *travesti* orientation of the theatre provided a natural background for their performing the role, but also because romanticism had discovered a feminine strain in Hamlet's character. Indeed, a substantial number of critics went so far as to believe he possessed the soul of a woman. A dichotomy then arose between the feminine soul and the masculine body. So convinced were many nineteenth-century critics that such a body/soul dichotomy existed in Hamlet that the concept is recurrent in criticism of the period. Derived from suggestions scattered throughout the pertinent chapters of *Wilhelm Meister,* the idea of the disparity between soul and body in the young Prince was quickly assimilated into French Hamletism. Delacroix's series of Hamlet lithographs, though based upon the performances of Charles Kemble and the English actors at the "soirées anglaises" at the Odéon in 1827, was clearly influenced by Mme Pierre, the female model Delacroix himself had chosen as the Prince of Denmark. The pale and delicate Prince that emerges from the Delacroix lithographs could easily have suited the type of feminization found in the best interpreters of female *travesti.*

Paradoxically, it was precisely the feminization of Bernhardt's Hamlet that made some of the propounders of the body/soul dichotomy object to her Prince. Less than a week before the *première,* the playwright Emile Bergerat wrote an article in *L'Éclair* in which he denounced the Hamlet Bernhardt was about to perform. Citing Goethe as his authority, he insisted that a *travesti* Hamlet was a misconception because it deprived the public of the contrast between "a masculine body and a feminine soul." He asserted that an actor was as necessary to the role of Hamlet as an actress to Molière's Célimène in *Le Misanthrope,* and he refused to take seriously what he was certain would be the androgynous creation he labeled "Hamlette." The comments of Hippolyte Lemaire partially sustain Bergerat's romantic misgivings. Reviewing *Hamlet* after the *première,* Lemaire himself was unctuously complimentary about Bernhardt's performance, but he pointed out that there were those who questioned the validity of *travesti* for Hamlet because, in their words, "'It is the soul of Hamlet that is feminine and not the body.'" A similar type of objection in a somewhat modified vocabulary surfaced across the Channel, for some English critics regarded Hamlet's soul as only partially feminine. Both A.B. Walkley and Max Beerbohm complain about Bernhardt's Hamlet in concepts inherited from romanticism. To Walkley, Hamlet's feminine strain did not provide an excuse for a woman's undertaking the role. Apparently forgetting the by no means undistinguished tradition of women Hamlets in England, the critic dismissed Bernhardt's Hamlet as a "curio." He maintained that Hamlet possessed what he considered such feminine attributes as "the fragility and mobility of a woman" in addition to a "touch . . . of hysteria." After reconciling Balzac's observation "'les artistes sont un peu femmes'" with Robert Burns' "'a man's a man for a' that,'" he concludes that "a woman can no more present the partly feminine Hamlet than a man can present the partly masculine Lady Macbeth." Like his colleague, Max Beerbohm emphasized Hamlet's feminine traits and, as a consequence, he, too, regarded Bernhardt's "Princess of Denmark" as an "aberration." In Hamlet he found such purportedly feminine qualities as "gentleness and lack of executive ability." He was nevertheless distressed that Sarah, "unmistakably 'thoro'bred'" though she was, would have attempted to perform the role of a man despite the fact that he was not "consistently manly." A variation on the romantic dichotomy then follows: "Sarah ought not to have supposed that Hamlet's weakness set him in any possible

relation to her own feminine mind and body." In their responses to Bernhardt's Hamlet, both Beerbohm and Walkley articulated ideas that were derived from those of Bergerat and the followers of the romantic contrast between the masculine body and feminine soul of Hamlet.

No such contrast would have been necessary for Edward P. Vining, for his research led him to the publication in 1881 of a book in which he claimed Hamlet possessed so many feminine traits that in what he regarded as the final version of the play the Prince actually had become a woman. In Vining's definition of femininity, the following major qualities are given as specifically feminine: weakness, vacillation, gentleness, finesse, and the use of "indirect means" rather than "straightforward acting." Minor traits are also considered, including Hamlet's "small and delicate" body, derived from his comparison of himself with Hercules; his "sensitiveness to weather and perfumes," derived from his comment on the platform ("The air bites shrewdly; it is very cold."); and from his olfactory reaction to Yorick's skull. Vining maintains that Shakespeare, during his revisions of the play, kept increasing the number of feminine traits until Hamlet finally developed into a woman. He traces this progression from the First Quarto, which he considers genuine Shakespeare, to the First Folio, which he regards as the final version of the play. Although that progression was widely accepted at the time, no critic other than Vining expressed the theory of the Prince-as-woman. Not only is Hamlet a woman to Vining, but a woman in love as well. The object of his affections is Horatio who, for his part, shared an intimacy with Ophelia of which Hamlet was aware. Hence the Prince's brutal treatment of Ophelia. Vining suggests that the play is filled with hints of Hamlet's feminine sexuality, including his youthful beauty which was "far greater than is natural in a man of thirty years of age." Together with Hamlet's "maturity of mind," his physical appearance offers "strong proof" that he was a woman "masquerading" as a man. At Hamlet's birth, moreover, the Queen, for reasons of succession, was responsible for the perpetration of the original deception. Furthermore, the Ghost never addresses Hamlet as "son," as he does in *Der bestrafte Brudermord,* the German play closely linked with the First Quarto. Of all the hints of gender with which the play abounds, the "most remarkable" is given in Hamlet's dying words, for Vining maintains that "the rest is silence" is a direct reference to the clandestine sex of the protagonist.

How seriously Vining's book was taken in its day can be inferred from Edwin Booth's comments. Booth read *The Mystery of Hamlet* and wrote about it in two separate letters to William Winter. In both letters, he rejects Vining's central thesis that Hamlet was a woman, but nevertheless asserts that he agrees with much that the critic "urges." Booth, moreover, believes that the secret of his own success in the role lies in the fact that he has "always endeavored to make prominent the femininity of Hamlet's character." He seriously questions whether a "robust and masculine treatment of the character" will ever be so widely accepted as "the more womanly and refined interpretation." Making a clear distinction between the feminine and the effeminate, he confesses that he does frequently "fall into effeminacy," but only because he "can't always hit the proper key-note." Booth's objection to the "absurdity" of Vining's theory did not preclude his giving serious consideration to a number of the arguments, and not surprisingly, since they reflected his own stage practice. The book, moreover, was taken with sufficient seriousness to warrant its translation into German two years after its American publication. Although a sampling of then contemporary reviews does not indicate a favorable reception of Vining's book, it does reveal that the reaction towards his theory was more tolerant than one might anticipate. Only the reviewer of the *Shakespeare Jahrbuch* vehemently rejected it as one of several "transoceanic" offerings providing food for scholarly amusement. C.M. Ingleby, on the other hand, became so incensed with peripheral matters that he did not deign to penetrate the "mystery" with which Vining was concerned. The critic of *The Literary World* took a more moderate course. Admitting that he was not "converted" to Vining's theory, he nevertheless reviewed the book with dispassionate indulgence. The significance of *The Mystery of Hamlet,* however, is unrelated to its impact upon reviewers. As Edwin Booth's response indicates, the book arose from an intellectual climate that had been feminizing Hamlet for almost a century.

In such an intellectual climate, the terms *curio* and *aberration* used by Walkley and Beerbohm to characterize Bernhardt's Hamlet seem incongruous, especially from the pens of English critics who, unlike some of their French counterparts, regarded Hamlet as only partially feminine. Furthermore, they had as much familiarity with the English tradition of *travesti* in the popular theatre of pantomime, burlesque, and extravaganza as the French had in their tradition of the Boulevard. In addition to their exposure to popular forms, they could scarcely have been unaware of the trend, in England and elsewhere, during the nineteenth century, of women's performing not only the role of Hamlet, but other male Shakespearean roles as well. All of the performing arts in the nineteenth century were permeated by the female *travesti,* for the tendency to feminize the arts was a ubiquitous inheritance from romanticism.

When Sarah Bernhardt took her *Hamlet* to London, most, if not all of those who filled the seats at the Adelphi had seen performances in *travesti* since their childhood. Doubtless most had been taken at an early age to Christmas pantomimes. Had they attended the Drury Lane pantomime during the eleven years prior to Bernhardt's visit in 1899, they would have seen the celebrated Dan Leno performing his specialty, the role of "an over-ripe, middle-aged woman" known as the "dame." They might have seen him as the Widow Twankey in *Aladdin,* Sister Anne in *Bluebeard,* the Stepmother in *Cinderella,* or some other role of a "comically absurd woman." The 5'4" Leno, a product of the British music halls, was one of the most beloved performers of dame roles in pantomime at the turn of the century. As the "masculine" coun-

terpart to the dame roles were the women who performed such "principal boy" roles as Aladdin, Prince Charming in *Cinderella,* or Robin Hood in *Babes in the Woods.* With its roots in the theatre of the past, the principal boy role was a descendant of the "breeches part" which stemmed from the Restoration. At the time, breeches parts in heroic drama as well as comedy were for the most part based upon sexual disguise which was eventually revealed. Some breeches parts, however, such as Young Fashion in Vanbrugh's *The Relapse,* require that the performer, originally Mrs. Kent, remain in masculine character throughout the play. Others, such as Sir Harry Wildair in Farquhar's *The Constant Couple,* were originally written for a man (Robert Wilks) and were later assumed by women (Peg Woffington and Dorothy Jordan). One of the attractions of the breeches part in the Restoration was its overtly sexual appeal, for in an age when ankle-length dresses prevailed, the revealing of the feminine leg was regarded as highly sensual. Begun in the Restoration, the breeches part continued in the eighteenth century in burletta as well as the standard repertoire, and it flourished in the nineteenth, especially in burlesque and pantomime. In the first half of the nineteenth century, the "spritely, graceful" Madame Vestris, with her rich contralto voice and the "'symmetry'" of her legs, attracted audiences in droves to the Olympic Theatre when she appeared, initially in W.T. Moncrieff's burlesque of *Don Giovanni, Giovanni in London,* and thereafter in a series of burlesques that included Orpheus in *Olympic Revels* and Perseus in *The Deep, Deep Sea.* It was, in fact, Madame Vestris' success in breeches parts that brought about the integration of the role of principal boy into pantomime during the 1840's. By the end of the century, the principal boy became "an identifying characteristic" of pantomime. The costume of the principal boy indicated that the role's attraction for Victorian audiences was similar to that possessed by Madame Vestris and by such historic predecessors as Nell Gwynn, Peg Woffington, and Dorothy Jordan. It made possible the presentation of "a shapely woman in closefitting man's attire." Although, according to David Mayer, interest in sexual humor was rare in pantomime, the genre was obviously geared to adults as well as children. Sarah Bernhardt's audiences at the Adelphi thus had many years of exposure to the *travesti* of the popular theatre.

Bernhardt's *Hamlet* audiences at the Adelphi also had knowledge, either directly or indirectly, of the numerous women interpreters of Hamlet in the English-speaking tradition. Beginning with Mrs. Furnivall in Dublin in 1741, the tradition would actually take root when Sarah Siddons (1755-1831) performed the role in Worcester in 1775. It grew to such proportions in the nineteenth century that by the time Bernhardt took her *Hamlet* to London, the distinguished Elizabethan scholar W.J. Lawrence observed that in old world and new there had now been "fully fifty women Hamlets." It is historically suggestive that both Mrs. Furnivall and Mrs. Siddons, the first women Hamlets to appear on the English-speaking stage, did so in the approximate chronological period of Thomas Sheridan's 1763 conversation with Boswell, a conversation which heralded the romantic conception of the Prince as the possessor of many character traits soon to be regarded as feminine. Although Siddons appeared in Hamlet over a period of twenty-seven years—in Manchester and Liverpool in 1777, in Bath in 1778, in Bristol in 1781, and in Dublin in 1802—she had "an innate dislike to the donning of male apparel," and possibly because of her attitude, never performed her Prince of Denmark in London. The performer who established the tradition in London was Mrs. William Powell. She appeared as Hamlet at Drury Lane on May 12, 1796.

The number of women Hamlets increased, and included such actresses as Alice Marriott, who was known for her melodious delivery and elocutionary precision and who wore a variation of the traditional black plume; Julia Seaman, who modeled her Hamlet on that of Fechter and who was highly commended for her rendering of the play scene; and Millicent Bandmann-Palmer, who, like her husband Daniel Edward Bandmann, wore the black plume of tradition and who was, moreover, the reigning woman Hamlet of the day in the provincial theatres of England when Bernhardt appeared as Hamlet in London. The popularity of these women Hamlets is not to be underestimated, for Julia Seaman recalls having played Hamlet at least two hundred times, and Mrs. Bandmann-Palmer had appeared as Hamlet 270 times by 1899 and over a thousand by the end of her career. Alice Marriott, moreover, included it as a standard part of her repertoire for many years. Furthermore, Marriott chose the role for her American debut in New York in 1869, as did Julia Seaman for her initial American appearance at Booth's Theatre in New York in 1874. In the United States, both actresses assuredly discovered that the custom of performing Shakespeare in *travesti* was even more extensive than in England. Charlotte Cushman, whose Romeo was as famous as her Lady Macbeth, had played Hamlet, as did a long list of actresses, beginning with Mrs. Bartley in 1819 at New York's fashionable Park Theatre and including such performers as Mrs. Charlotte Connor, who "could play nothing tolerably save the Prince"; Charlotte Crampton, whose make-up was in imitation of Edwin Forrest's and who was "one of the finest fencers of the day"; and Fanny Wallack, who was considered "the reigning transatlantic woman Hamlet." *Travesti* Hamlets took on international proportions in the nineteenth century, with Australia's contributing three women Hamlets (Mrs. Cleveland, Mrs. Evans, and Miss Louise Pomeroy), Italy's one (Giacinta Pezzana), and Germany's one (Felicitas Vestvali). Actually Vestvali, who first performed Hamlet in 1869, was preceded by the first woman Hamlet on the German stage, Felicitas Abt, who played the Prince with great success in Gotha, possibly as early as May, 1779. Bernhardt's Hamlet therefore fits into a pattern that had been developing since the second half of the eighteenth century. In 1899, audiences could not have been unaware of what by that time had developed into a tradition.

The tradition, as applied to Shakespeare, was wide-ranging and included many of the great male Shakespearean roles from tragedy, comedy, and history. Actresses who came from theatrical families and performed Shakespeare as children usually began their careers in *travesti*. Ellen Terry, for example, recalls that the Shakespeare roles of her childhood were Mamillius, Puck, Arthur, and Fleance. Her sister, the young Kate Terry, played Ariel as had Sarah Siddons in her youth. It was also customary for mature actresses to perform the role of Ariel, a convention that survived many of the changes of the first half of the twentieth century. The tradition of a woman Ariel stems from the eighteenth century when Kitty Clive played the part at Drury Lane in 1746, and it extends well into the twentieth century with Margaret Leighton's performing Shakespeare's airy spirit at Stratford in 1952. *A Midsummer Night's Dream* also provides creatures of fantasy who were played by women. In the nineteenth century, it was standard procedure to perform not only Puck in *travesti*, but Oberon as well. Notable Oberons included Madame Vestris, who had played the role in her own production in 1840, and Julia Neilson, who appeared in Beerbohm Tree's 1900 production in which live rabbits were used in the forest scenes. The twentieth century generally preferred male Oberons, but the tastes of the previous era persisted from 1933 to 1940 at the Open Air Theatre in Regent's Park where Phyllis Neilson-Terry regularly acted Oberon until she relinquished the role to Jean Forbes-Robertson who, in turn, relinquished it to Gladys Cooper. In addition to playing supernatural beings, women in the nineteenth century performed the usual male Shakespearean roles. Other than Hamlet, tragedy was represented by Othello, Iago, Romeo, Lear's Fool, and possibly Macbeth and Macduff. Roles from the history plays that were taken by women were Richard III, Richmond, and Tressell; Hotspur, Prince Hal, and Falstaff; and Cardinal Wolsey. Roles from the comedies were Shylock and Petruchio. Of these parts, the most popular by far was Romeo, with approximately 26 actresses assaying the role. Beginning in 1810 in Plymouth when Mrs. Freeman played the young Montague to the Juliet of her 12-year-old daughter, the convention was established and then continued by actresses such as Ellen Tree, who played Romeo to Fanny Kemble's Juliet at Covent Garden in 1829; Charlotte Crampton, whose Shakespearean *travesti* roles included Hamlet, Iago, Richard III, and Shylock, and who may well be the only female Hotspur on record; and Charlotte Cushman, the outstanding American actress who played many *travestis* throughout her career, including Hamlet and Cardinal Wolsey, and whose Romeo to her sister Susan's Juliet became one of the signature pieces of nineteenth-century theatre in England and America. Three years prior to Bernhardt's visit to England, Esmé Beringer had appeared in London as Romeo to her sister's Juliet at the Prince of Wales Theatre, and she won critical acclaim for her performance. "'It was not a woman at all!'" observed Clement Scott; "'it was a boy. . . . A more ideal Romeo has seldom been seen.'" Her "picturesque and impassioned" Romeo was therefore fresh in people's minds. The use of *travesti* in Shakespeare was so extensive that W.J. Lawrence records the all-woman performance of not only *As You Like It*, but *The Winter's Tale* as well. *As*

You Like It in *travesti* was performed, initially in New York in November, 1893, and three months later, at the Prince of Wales Theatre in London; *The Winter's Tale* was performed at Copley Hall in Boston in 1896. Clearly, Shakespearean performance in the nineteenth century was permeated by the *travesti* role.

Sarah Bernhardt's own experience with *travesti* was extensive. Although most of the roles with which she became identified were not in the *travesti* category—Doña Sol (Victor Hugo, *Hernani*), Doña María (Hugo, *Ruy Blas*), Phèdre (Racine), Marguerite Gautier (Dumas, fils, *La Dame aux camélias*), Fédora, Théodora, and La Tosca (Sardou)—several of her most distinguished creations were those of young men, including the protagonists of the three plays in her Hamlet cycle, *Lorenzaccio, Hamlet,* and *L'Aiglon.* During the course of her career, she appeared in 27 *travesti* roles, 18 of which were performed in the latter part of her career when repertorial needs became pressing and when the age-concealing make-up of *travesti* was more than welcome. Beginning with *Lorenzaccio* in 1896, she converted the *travesti* category from the customary *ingénu* of Chérubin to the *premier travesti rôle* of her Florentine Hamlet. In her treatise, she insisted that a woman could play *travesti* only if the intellectual dominated the physical, but in true nineteenth-century fashion, she planned to play Romeo to the Juliet of Maude Adams if she were able to learn the role in English. Linguistic difficulties apparently were insurmountable, for the production never progressed beyond a meeting of the two actresses in Paris. The hundred performances projected for the United States followed by a tour of England and the Continent therefore did not materialize. According to a letter printed in the New York *World,* Bernhardt was said to have given up the role of Romeo not so much because of language, but because of her unsympathetic response to Romeo's character. How much credence can be given to the letter, however, is questionable. Supposedly written to Henry Irving in English, without the aid of her "teacher," the letter consists of the type of Franglais that the readership of a popular newspaper might well find amusing. In the letter, she admits that the task of memorizing Romeo seems "desperating," but that the assertion made in some newspapers doubting her ability to act Shakespeare in the original text is very disturbing to her. Nevertheless, there is a problem: "The most main trouble . . . is because I am not fond of Romeo's character. I do not believe in it. I love Juliet more of the two, despite she is not very humanly correct either." She continues by admitting she admires "small pieces" of the play, but not the characters. She then extends her comments to other characters in other plays of Shakespeare and makes a statement about Hamlet that, considering her dedication to the play, is nothing short of horrendous: "All Shakespeare's personages do me the same effect—uncouth, unreal, disgustingly emphatic. Hamlet most than all." The author of the unsigned article claims that Bernhardt allowed him to have a copy of this letter to Henry Irving, yet the authenticity of the letter appears so dubious that one cannot help regarding it as spurious. Although Sarah Bernhardt did not play Romeo, she did undertake another Shakespearean role in *travesti* in Boston when in 1916 she alternated the role of Portia in Edmond Haraucourt's translation of the trial scene from *The Merchant of Venice* with what became the *travesti grime* of Shylock. During the course of her career Sarah Bernhardt appeared in seven Shakespearean roles: Cordelia, Ophelia, Portia, Desdemona, Lady Macbeth, Shylock, and Hamlet. Since she played Shylock in but a single scene, her only significant Shakespearean *travesti* remained Hamlet.

The nineteenth century's fondness for *travesti* was by no means confined to Shakespeare. Charlotte Crampton played a number of non-Shakespearean breeches parts, including the title role in an adaptation of Byron's narrative poem *Mazeppa.* There were seven interpreters of that Byronic role in the United States alone, among whom was the versatile and notoriously sensual Adah Isaacs Menken. Charlotte Cushman assumed at least seven non-Shakespearean *travesti* roles, one of which was the noble and romantic youth Claude Melnotte in Bulwer-Lytton's *The Lady of Lyons.* The *travesti* roles were many and varied and were performed by every type of actress, from those like Madame Vestris, who in their private lives were promiscuously feminine, to those like Charlotte Cushman, who was unquestionably masculine.

Sarah Bernhardt's personal life was dominated by a lengthy series of heterosexual liaisons which, though less multitudinous than some of her unreliable biographers have proposed, were nevertheless substantial in number. As the illegitimate child of a fashionable *cocotte,* she was reared in a home in which her two half-sisters, by different fathers, were similarly illegitimate and in which her mother's protectors were frequent visitors. Her mother's sister, her Aunt Rosine, also belonged to the frivolous society of the Parisian *demi-monde.* After graduation from the Conservatoire, the young Sarah Bernhardt entered the Comédie-Française, and sometime during that period, took her first lover, Émile, comte de Kératry. He was followed by the Belgian aristocrat, Henri, prince de Ligne, who was the father of her illegitimate child Maurice, born in December 1864 when the actress was 20 years old. According to Ernest Pronier, Sarah Bernhardt's only scholarly biographer, Ligne abandoned her during her pregnancy and refused to recognize the expected child. Those who succeeded Ligne were the kind of affluent, usually aristocratic, men-about-town who often provided the women they kept with lavish sums of money and who were regarded as protectors. Under the Second Empire, they became one of the distinguishing features of the private lives of actresses. Sarah Bernhardt's protectors, at different times, were Robert de Brimont, a rich industrialist; the marquis de Caux, who eventually married Sarah's friend Adelina Patti; and Jacques Stern, a banker who ultimately married Sarah's colleague Sophie Croizette. Succeeding the liaisons with protectors were those with men of the theatre, many of whom were her acting partners: Pierre Berton, Jean Mounet-Sully, Édouard Angelo, Philippe Garnier, Albert Darmont, and possibly, in the latter part of her career,

Lou Tellegen. To this list of actors should be added the name of the playwright Jean Richepin, the painter Georges Clairin, the critic Jules Lemaître, probably Edmond Rostand, and possibly Gustave Doré. During her affair with Mounet-Sully, which occurred while both were appearing at the Comédie-Française, there was talk of marriage, but nothing materialized. Bernhardt did marry a Greek diplomat named Aristide (Jacques) Damala, but separation was not long in ensuing because of Damala's many infidelities as well as his incurable morphine addiction. In her amorous involvements, Bernhardt showed herself to be a true child of her environment, both societal and theatrical.

Despite Bernhardt's manifest heterosexuality, the claim has been made that the actress had a liaison with a woman who was a close friend. Surfacing in a novel written in 1882, the claim has been repeated, with variations, in disparate publications, none of them scholarly, and some, flagrantly pornographic. The friend in question, Louise Abbéma, was the great-granddaughter of Louise Contat of the Comédie-Française and was an artist who specialized in theatrical portraits. Bernhardt met the openly homosexual Abbéma when she herself became interested in art and began to paint and sculpt. Ernest Pronier, whose biography of Sarah Bernhardt remains authoritative, discusses the relationship of the two women in terms of a devoted and long-lasting friendship. Cornelia Otis Skinner adds that Bernhardt was not disturbed by Abbéma's sexual preference. Mention of a possible liaison with Abbéma can be attributed to Félicien Champsaur who, at the age of 20, penned in *Dinah Samuel* a fictionalized account of Sarah Bernhardt that is noteworthy for its sexual preoccupation, its anti-Semitism, its scatology, and its oftentimes purple prose. The thinly disguised Dinah is shown as not only bisexual, but unfaithful to lovers of both sexes. Continually dressed in her "costume d'atelier," she betrays her lover Alice Penthièvre (Louise Abbéma) when she seduces her own model Berthe Paradis, a woman of such flexible morals that she claims to have as many lovers, presumably heterosexual, as there are days in the year. The model addresses Dinah as "joli garçon." *Dinah Samuel* was obviously intended as a fictionalized attack on Sarah Bernhardt since the author, who, in the course of the book, exhausts the synonymy for *prostitute* as applied to the title heroine, shows Dinah, in public, dallying amorously with Francisque Sarcey. A respected and respectable drama critic, Sarcey was recognized for his integrity and impartiality, and the implication that Sarcey's customary, but by no means inevitable, praise of Sarah's acting was the result of sexual favors would have been rejected by the reputable Parisian press.

Although *Dinah Samuel* was reprinted as late as 1925, it appears to have had no influence until assimilated by Philippe Jullian over half a century later. Jullian mentions the Bernhardt-Abbéma relationship in three of his publications, two on the popular aspects of nineteenth-century art history and one on the life of Sarah Bernhardt. Initially stating in his *Dreamers of Decadence* that Bernhardt's "liaison with Louise Abbéma . . . was an open secret," he takes a different though not necessarily opposite approach in his book *Montmartre*. In speaking of lesbianism in Montmartre, he mentions that Abbéma had a studio there which Bernhardt frequented and that young actresses flocked to the studio for two reasons: "to be painted by Louise Abbema [*sic*] and to meet Sarah Bernhardt, who permitted the lady to worship her." In his biography of Sarah Bernhardt, Jullian returns to his original claim concerning the relationship with Louise Abbéma, in support of which he states that Bernhardt had many feminine admirers and that her predilection for *travesti* roles "underlined her sexual ambiguity." Jullian provides no documentation here or in his other relevant publications. The biography, moreover, is beset with factual errors and is interspersed with graphic anecdotes concerning the genitalia, male and female, of the literary and theatrical. From the context of the biography, Jullian's source concerning the putative liaison with Louise Abbéma was clearly Champsaur's novel *Dinah Samuel* which he often mentions and from which he quotes passages pertinent to his sexual conclusions.

The chain begun by Champsaur and continued by Jullian has two additional links: a catalogue accompanying an exhibit on Sarah Bernhardt and an imaginary interchange of letters between Sarah Bernhardt and a contemporary French novelist. In 1984, Georges Bernier wrote the catalogue for an exhibit on Sarah Bernhardt which he both conceived and organized. Here he chose to follow and embroider Jullian's statements, noting that the liaison between Abbéma, a "militant lesbian," and Sarah was "notorious," adding, however, that the relationship eventually changed into an enduring and devoted friendship. Bernier, too, offers no documentation for his assertions, but his source, from content to wording, is obviously Jullian. The final link in the chain was provided by Françoise Sagan. In a fictional exchange of letters between the author and Sarah Bernhardt, Sagan receives a letter from Sarah concerning lovers, friends, and gossip. In this letter Sarah says that Louise Abbéma adored her to the point of offering her life in exchange for a night with the actress. Bernhardt's observation is that she found "this price absolutely excessive." At this point, one must conclude that assumptions based upon non-existent sources yield insubstantial conclusions.

What is substantial is the knowledge that Sarah Bernhardt, like Ellen Terry, "attracted passionate loyalty from women as well as men." After Bernhardt had experienced international success, moreover, she began to cultivate a "court," and Louise Abbéma became one of its faithful adherents. Other members of the court were the artist Georges Clairin, a former lover; Arthur Meyer, editor of *Le Gaulois;* Edmond Haraucourt, poet and playwright; Suzanne Seylor, an actress in Sarah's company who served as companion and first lady-in-waiting; the composer Reynaldo Hahn; and Bernhardt's other devotees, Dr. Samuel Pozzi, Édouard Geoffroy, and the comtesse de Najac. Many of these courtiers accompanied Sarah to Belle-Isle during the summer, and for some, such as

Louise Abbéma and Georges Clairin, she had a special villa built, complete with atelier.

Possibly related to previous assertions, although only tangentially, is Maurice Rostand's analysis of Sarah Bernhardt's personality. As the son of Edmond Rostand, the young Maurice had been introduced to the *tragédienne* in his childhood. When Edmond Rostand married the poetess Rosemonde Gérard, the couple took up residence not far from Bernhardt's *hôtel particulier* on the Boulevard Péreire, and a close friendship developed between the Rostands and Sarah Bernhardt. At the end of her career Bernhardt appeared in two plays which the young Rostand had written specifically for her: *La Gloire* and *La Mort de Molière*. In his book on Sarah Bernhardt, Maurice Rostand maintains that Sarah was a combination of two people, one "extraordinarily virile," the other "extremely feminine," and that her composite personality had both professional and personal consequences. From a professional point of view, he maintains that such sexual completeness provided her with the ability to assume either masculine or feminine roles. As seen through the lens of nineteenth-century theatre practice, this segment of the analysis falls short of accuracy, for actresses of pronounced femininity, such as Virginie Déjazet in France and Madame Vestris in England, built a substantial part of their reputations upon their accomplishments in *travesti*. Rostand's belief, moreover, that only women were attracted to her Hamlet, and men to her Marguerite Gautier, cannot be substantiated on the basis of then contemporary audience responses, since it is known that her artistic accomplishments and her intense personal magnetism attracted audiences of both sexes to both types of roles. From a personal point of view, Rostand continues, her own blend of opposite sexualities prevented her from becoming part of any enduring relationship with another person. Other people, however, were attracted to either the feminine or the masculine aspect of her personality. In this regard, he mentions two feminine members of the Bernhardt court, Suzanne Seylor and the Comtesse de Najac, both of whom idolized the actress. Rostand recognizes that adulation was involved in the entire concept of court and courtiers, furthermore that Sarah, "sublime and charming monster" that she was, encouraged the cult of adoration. His belief that she was "Romeo and Juliet" as well as "Tristan and Isolde" nevertheless remained steadfast.

Whatever the merits of Rostand's analysis, he does not raise the issue of a homoerotic relationship between Bernhardt and any of her feminine admirers, an omission that fails to surprise, since adulation does not necessarily result in sexual intimacy. Furthermore, Bernhardt had many ardent masculine admirers with whom she never entered into a relationship other than that of diva and devotee. Whether or not during the course of her lifetime Sarah Bernhardt ever had a liaison with Louise Abbéma or any of her feminine admirers remains unknown. Available evidence, however, points strongly in the direction of a heterosexual preference. What Bernhardt did have in common with other performers of *travesti* relates not to their personal lives, but to the nineteenth-century tradition of actresses' including *travesti* roles in their repertoires.

Repeatedly in descriptions of the interpreters of *travesti,* one finds praise of their vocal abilities. Indeed, three of the performers—Charlotte Cushman, Madame Vestris, and Felicitas Vestvali—began their careers as singers. Charlotte Cushman made her début not in Shakespeare, but in Mozart, in the vocally demanding role of the Countess in *The Marriage of Figaro.* Madame Vestris' contralto voice was originally used in a number of *travesti* roles in opera, among which was the title role in Arne's *Artaxerxes* and several Rossini roles, including Pippo the village youth in *La Gazza Ladra,* Malcolm in *La Donna del Lago,* and Edoardo in *Mathilde di Shabran.* Vestvali, also a contralto, made her American début in February 1855 in the *travesti* role Arsace in Rossini's *Semiramide,* and two years later sang the baritone role of the King, Carlo, in Verdi's *Ernani.* Since none of them experienced the kind of success in singing that suggested the exclusive pursuit of an operatic career, each adapted her vocal talents to different aspects of theatre. All three, however, shared the common experience of appearing in Shakespeare. Other performers of *travesti* who are not credited with operatic backgrounds, but were known for their outstanding vocal performances in Shakespeare, were Charlotte Crampton, Rebecca Deering, Alice Marriott, and Julia Glover. From the petite, dark-haired Charlotte Crampton with her "exquisitely modelled form" and "handsome face" to the full-figured Julia Glover who appeared as both Hamlet and the Falstaff of *The Merry Wives of Windsor,* the critics' comments reveal that vocal interpretations contributed significantly to the success of the *travesti* performances. Charlotte Crampton was praised for her "wonderfully strong and sweet voice" and, while Julia Glover's "'noble figure, handsome and expressive face'" were duly commended in *Hamlet,* it was the "'finished elocution'" of her soliloquies delivered in a "'rich and powerful voice'" that brought forth "'continued bursts of applause'" from her appreciative audiences. The American-born Rebecca Deering experienced similar success with the title role of Richard III. Her powerful and flexible voice undoubtedly stood her in good stead for her approximately two hundred performances of that role. Alice Marriott's accomplishments were greater still, for, according to the Liverpool *Daily Post,* she did for Hamlet what Charlotte Cushman had done for Romeo: she made it "'a thing of beauty.'" Much of her success was attributable to her "'admirable elocution'" and to her "'fine, sweet, melodious mezzo-soprano voice.'" In an age that cultivated great theatrical voices and that often described them in a vocabulary today employed for singers, it is not unusual to find that performances were appreciated in terms of vocal beauty, power, flexibility, and projection.

Together with the aesthetic pleasure derived from listening to fine vocal instruments, audiences responded to performances in terms of the actor's ability to speak with precision, variety, and elegance, that is, with what they called good elocution. One of the earliest women Hamlets, Sarah Siddons, was a superb elocutionist and a great vocal musician, with an instrument capable of portraying majesty and subtlety alike. In 1899 the current woman Hamlet, Sarah Bernhardt, possessed an instrument that was the spoken equivalent of a lyric soprano, silvery and crystalline in quality and capable of expressing a wide range of emotions. With her mastery of breathing and her use of punctilious articulation, Bernhardt, like her English predecessor Siddons, brought to Hamlet the virtuosity of speech and voice which has always been essential to the creation of a great Shakespearean role. Even lesser performers relied heavily upon their vocal resources to present the role of the Prince of Denmark. From Sarah to Sarah, and even beyond, the major *travesti* Hamlets have been successfully undertaken only by actresses with outstanding vocal qualifications.

Sarah Bernhardt's audiences on both sides of the Channel knew *travesti* not only from theatre, but from opera as well. Opera possesses numerous roles of young men and boys whose musical demands are best negotiated by the trained voices of women. Pages, such as Cherubino in Mozart's *Marriage of Figaro*, Oscar in Verdi's *Ballo in Maschera*, and Smeton in Donizetti's *Anna Bolena;* children, such as Yniold in Debussy's *Pelléas et Mélisande;* the young shepherd in Puccini's *Tosca;* the young servant Niklausse in Offenbach's *Contes d'Hoffmann;* and the young lover Romeo in Bellini's *I Capuleti ed i Montecchi*—all were intended for women's voices, most sung by mezzo-sopranos, but one, Oscar, by a soprano. The dramatic soprano role of Leonore in Beethoven's *Fidelio* also belongs in this category even though the audience is aware that the use of sexual disguise is a means of Leonore's gaining access to her imprisoned husband. With the passing of the castrato tradition, moreover, many roles written for male sopranos and male altos fell to women. The best known of these today is the title role in Gluck's *Orfeo*, originally written for the alto castrato Gaetano Guadagni and generally sung by a mezzo-soprano or contralto. Others include a substantial number of roles from Händelian opera, in which such heroes as Rinaldo (*Rinaldo*), Julius Caesar (*Giulio Cesare*), Bertarido (*Rodalinda*), and even the comic Xerxes (*Serse*) were intended for castrati; and from such *opera seriae* as Mozart's *Idomeneo*, with the role of the young lover Idamante written for a castrato, and *La Clemenza di Tito*, with two castrato roles. Although the French never evinced any fondness for castrati, they showed a strong predilection for the sung *travesti*. Niklausse in *Les Contes d'Hoffmann* is but one of many *travesti* roles in the Offenbach *oeuvre*. So hospitable throughout Europe was the artistic climate to the *travesti* or trouser role (pants part, as it is often called in opera) that when Bellini composed his opera *I Capuleti ed i Montecchi* in 1830, he wrote the role of Romeo for the mezzo-soprano Giuditta Grisi. Undoubtedly Prince Orlovsky in Johann Strauss' *Die Fledermaus* (1872) arose from the same sympathetic ambiance. Rossini contributed several *travesti* roles, including the florid Arsace in *Semiramide* sung in Paris and London by the "coloratura contralto" Maria Malibran. The trend became so extensive that

some women even attempted tenor roles, including Tamino in Mozart's *Die Zauberflöte*, Belmonte in his *Die Entführung aus dem Serail*, and the title role in Rossini's *Otello*. Felicitas Vestvali had ventured still further when she sang the baritone role Carlo in Verdi's *Ernani*. Given such a theatrical environment, it was certainly not extraordinary that Massenet's opera *Cendrillon*, which had its *répétition générale* at the Opéra-Comique on the same evening as the *première* of Bernhardt's *Hamlet*, contained the role of Prince Charmant in *travesti*. Of all the operatic *travestis*, the most sophisticated appeared in the twentieth century with Richard Strauss' *Rosenkavalier*, for in the course of the opera the young lover Oktavian, written for a mezzo-soprano, has the demanding task of disguising himself as a young woman. Oktavian is, of course, an outgrowth of Cherubino, who is, in turn, a musical version of Beaumarchais' Chérubin. In opera houses, therefore, one continues to experience the various currents of the previous century in the numerous *travesti* roles that remain an essential element of the standard repertoire.

If theatre and opera were permeated by the female *travesti*, it may be said that ballet was saturated with it, so much so that outside of Russia and Denmark, male dancing was seriously impaired in the nineteenth century. With the exception of a few greatly admired male dancers, such as Jules Perrot and Arthur Saint-Leon, the *danseur* was for the most part relegated to partnering the ballerina. It is true that Théophile Gautier regarded Jules Perrot as the greatest dancer of his time, but he had little patience with male dancers in general, finding their muscularity, massive frames, and "red necks" more suited to mime roles than to the ethereal substance that romantic ballet had become. Lucien Petipa, brother of the great choreographer Marius Petipa and creator of the role of Albrecht in the quintessentialy romantic ballet *Giselle*, was actually praised for knowing how to keep himself in the background. The opportunities for technical display on the part of male dancers became increasingly limited, with only an occasional *pas de trois or pas de quatre*, with national dances, and with the male variation in the adagio. The influential critic Jules Janin rejected the male dancer, and his very manner of rejection reveals once again the feminizing tendency of the nineteenth century. To Janin, the *danseur* was "'a frightful *danseuse* of the male sex.'" The rejection of the masculine presence on the ballet stage led to the proliferation of *travestis*, first in the *corps de ballet*, but by the 1870's, in principal male roles as well. According to Ivor Guest, so intense a "revulsion" against the male dancer had developed by the 1840's that whenever possible women were substituted for men in the *corps de ballet*. Hence the female hussars in *Paquita* and the female "shipboys and sailors" in *Betty*. Such substitutions were as common in London as in Paris. The female *corps* was followed by the hero in *travesti*, who first appeared during the 1860's. When *Coppélia* was created at the Théâtre Impériale de l'Opéra in Paris on May 25, 1870, Swanilda was danced by Giuseppina Bozzacchi, and Franz in *travesti* by Eugénie Fiocre, a dancer known for her physical beauty.

Franz continued to be danced in *travesti* at the Paris Opéra until after World War II, at which time it was performed by Paulette Dynalax. According to Clive Barnes, the Opéra did not relinquish the tradition of a *travesti* Franz until the 1950's. At the Palais Garnier one could therefore have seen in mid-twentieth century a continuation of the sensibility of a previous age that sought to feminize all its performing arts: dance, opera, and theatre.

As part of the feminizing tradition, Bernhardt performed her Hamlet in *travesti,* not, however, as a man with a feminine soul, but as a boyish young man with a masculine soul; not as the vacillating procrastinator of romanticism, but as the determined and purposeful avenger of the Elizabethan theatre. Ellen Terry observed in her memoirs that Bernhardt's acting in all roles was stylized rather than realistic. "No one plays a love scene better," affirmed the great English actress, "but it is a picture of love that she gives, a strange exotic picture rather than a suggestion of the ordinary human passions as felt by ordinary people." On stage, Ellen Terry maintains, Sarah always seemed "more a symbol, an ideal, an epitome" than a woman. To *travesti* roles she brought a similar stylization for, according to the English actress, in the title role of *L'Aiglon* Bernhardt did not offer a realistic representation of the boyish King of Rome, but "a truth far bigger than mere physical resemblance." Ellen Terry's pronouncement elucidates the nature of the idealized type that Bernhardt presented in Hamlet and her other *travesti* roles: stylized masculinity performed through a feminine presence.

That French critics would praise Bernhardt for her naturalness and elegance in wearing the costume of *travesti* is by no means unusual, for she had been performing such roles since her student days at the Conservatoire and she was, moreover, as accomplished in the subtleties of movement as in those of voice. Indeed, the dancer Alexandre Sakharov (1886-1963), who as a young man had come to Paris to study painting, decided to become a dancer after seeing Bernhardt in the third play of her Hamlet cycle, *L'Aiglon.* He said that in observing her performance, he had discovered "'the magic of movement.'" Bernhardt's advice to the young Mary Marquet, to whom she taught the role of L'Aiglon in 1915, indicates just how meticulous she was in determining movement that is characteristically masculine. It also reveals the close relationship between costume and movement. Sarah had been coaching Marquet for two weeks but, exhausted from her performances in *Les Cathédrales,* she left Paris for Andernos. Apparently she had seen Marquet in rehearsal before leaving and was dissatisfied with several matters relating to masculine movement. In a letter to Marquet, she sent some suggestions for improvement: "I am extremely upset that you are rehearsing *L'Aiglon* from the perspective of a woman, not a man. You must wear your costume in rehearsal, either the black one or the white one. It is essential for generating relaxed movements and for endowing your performance with naturalness. You should also carry a riding whip in Acts I and II. . . . Don't let your body sway. When you are standing, keep your legs widely spaced, as men do." Essentially practical, the advice concerning Rostand's "white" Hamlet yields an insight into Bernhardt's methods of creating the illusion of masculinity in her "black" Hamlet.

Bernhardt's costume for Hamlet, a version of which she undoubtedly wore at rehearsals, was tasteful, elegant, princely and, in color, traditional. With its black tunic of brocaded silk extending to mid-thigh, its black silk tights, and its black cloak suspended over the left shoulder, the costume might have been equally appropriate for a male Hamlet, but it was eminently suited to *travesti.* Only the elevated heels of her black velvet shoes were specifically feminine, though short actors have been known to increase their stature by similar means. The tunic was trimmed with fur at the hem and had brocaded sleeves which were tight-fitting from the elbow to below the wrist and widely puffed from elbow to shoulder. Beneath the tunic, which in pictures was worn unbuttoned from waist to neck, a white blouse with a high white ruff was visible. A chain linking two jeweled ornaments on either side of the modified mandarin collar held the top of the tunic in place. The costume also contained a jeweled belt to which was attached "a rapier, steel-hilted, in a black scabbard, with an ornamental chain." A significant part of the costume was the wig: long, almost shoulder-length, blond, and with bangs "brushed loosely over the forehead." Although the wig was suitable to *travesti,* it was, in fact, a direct inheritance from the suggestion in *Wilhelm Meister* popularized by Fechter. The wig enhanced the youthfulness of the character. For a theatre steeped in the romantic-hamletic tradition, the most daring part of the costume was the hat. Worn in the graveyard scene, it might, out of context, appear simply as a tasteful and well-fitting piece of headgear, suiting admirably with the costume. In the context of *fin-de-siècle* art, however, the absence of the black plume was revolutionary, for the plume had become emblematic of the irresolute dreamer of nineteenth-century Hamletism. Apart from its potential for controversy, the hat, like the entire costume, would have been as appropriate to a male Hamlet as to a Prince in *travesti.* It therefore served as another means of fostering, in a feminine presence, the illusion of masculinity.

In an interview with the New York *World* given prior to her London opening, Bernhardt maintained it was precisely an illusion of masculinity she sought to create. Countering the argument that it was absurd for a woman to assume the role of a man, she responded affirmatively:

> I see no more absurdity in a woman playing a man's part than in a man playing a woman's. Less, for it is easier for a woman to pretend to be a man than for a man to pretend to be a woman. There is no absurdity. The question is, does the actor produce the illusion? Does she make the audience forget the actor in the character? If she does, where is the absurdity?

In another interview which Bernhardt granted, she elaborated upon the technique required for creating the illusion of masculinity. Having been extolled throughout her career for her feminine magnetism, and having herself insisted upon the importance of such magnetism, she now explained how, without the presence of a strong characteristic of her acting, she could perform the role of a man. Her response yields further insights into her technique:

> Much of the success of the usual woman's role . . . lies in the feminine charm and magnetism with which the actress is capable of investing the part. It is contended that in assuming a man's role she is obliged to part with her strongest weapons, and that therefore more skill is required to achieve success. This is only partially true. Skill is undoubtedly demanded. But it is the skill which can assume and depict the masculine charm and magnetism which exists just as surely as does the feminine. It is not sufficient to look the man, to move like a man and to speak like a man. The actress must think and feel like a man, to receive impressions as a man, and to exert that innate something which, for want of a better word, we call magnetism, just as a man unconsciously exerts it.

That such masculine behavior was achieved through technical means rather than metamorphosis can be substantiated by Bernhardt's style of performance. A fervent believer in the emotionalist school of acting, Bernhardt maintained in her treatise that she identified with her role to the extent of becoming the character she was portraying. Contrary evidence, however, gathered from critics—French, English, and American—and from the actress May Agate, who was her former student, is so overwhelming that one cannot help concluding Bernhardt was primarily a personality actress. The phrase encountered most frequently in critical writing is, "She is always Sarah," or as Jean-Jacques Weiss, encapsulating years of commentary, observed, "Sarah she is and Sarah she remains." In Louis Jouvet's now classic distinction between Protean actor and personality actor, the former is defined as a *comédien,* the latter as an *acteur.* The *comédien,* Jouvet states, relies upon metamorphosis; the *acteur,* upon personality. He adds that a tragedian will always be an *acteur,* for his personality is too distinctive to be expunged. In Jouvet's terms, Sarah Bernhardt would emerge an *actrice.* The illusion of masculinity that Bernhardt created in her Hamlet, then, was attained not through character identification, but through sophisticated technical achievement.

Possibly because of her dominant personality, Bernhardt became an irresistible target for the caricaturist. In London, *Punch* rose to the anticipated occasion of the opening of the Bernhardt *Hamlet* by publishing a caricature of Sarah Berhnardt and Henry Irving in what is clearly the nunnery scene. Bernhardt is shown as the black-clad Prince, legs widely spaced, as she instructed the young Mary Marquet, Fechterian wig in mild disorder, and arms and hands conveying anger and reproach. Around her neck is a chain with the miniature of the dead King which, in practice, was not part of her costume, but of Henry Irving's. Irving, frequently caricatured because of his height and his spindly legs, is here shown as Ophelia.

He is shown, moreover, as the "wispy, willowy" figure the *Daily Telegraph* would soon praise Sarah Bernhardt for creating in the Prince. His height is greatly diminished by the concern he expresses for Hamlet's behavior, indicated by the bent knee, the leaning on a chair, and the placing of the opposite hand on the cheek. The distinctively Irvingesque face, with its dark, heavy, masculine eyebrows, is surrounded by an adaptation of the long, bound tresses Marthe Mellot wore as the Ophelia of the Bernhardt production. The flowered headband has clear reminiscences of the mad scenes many an Ophelia had performed in the English and French theatre, including those of Irving's acting partner Ellen Terry. The caricature is rich in overtones, especially for English theatregoers, for Clement Scott had declared that Irving's "finest acting" occurred in the nunnery scene where his love for Ophelia dominated all other emotions. In a caption to the drawing, the suggestion is offered that perhaps Madame Bernhardt, having had "so conspicuous a success" as Hamlet, should join forces with "our Leading Tragedian" when she comes to London, for "Sir Henry's *Ophelia* would be sure to attract more than passing notice." The caricature became so popular that the *Athenaeum* quoted from the caption and Alan Dale, who echoed the caption in one of his New York articles, embroidered it in a second. Insisting that despite the beauty of her vocal performance, it was not Hamlet but Sarah he had observed, Dale went on to wonder what France would say "if Irving went to Paris to play Phèdre" or Mansfield to appear there as Camille. The caricature itself is whimsical, subtle, delightful, and imaginative. Its success, however, lies in the fact that there is no metamorphosis in either of the principals and that Irving looks like Irving and Sarah like Sarah.

The inventiveness of the caricaturist notwithstanding, Bernhardt was eager to foster, in a feminine presence, the illusion of masculinity in her Hamlet, and one of her principal means of doing so was in making the Prince a young man. Rejecting the 30-year-old Hamlet which her translators questioned but felt obliged to retain, she created a character distinguished by his youth. An American critic even called him "the most youthful Hamlet of recent years." When an interviewer from the New York *World,* reflecting the attitudes of some contemporary critics, went so far as to call her Hamlet a boy, she objected, insisting that he was a youth and that his behavior throughout the play—towards Ophelia, the King, and the courtiers—indicated as much. The distinction between boy and youth requires clarification. The American actress Elizabeth Robins called Bernhardt's Hamlet a "spirited boy" with "quick boyish gestures" and "little runs and jumps"; the critic of the *Daily Telegraph* spoke of the Prince's "boyishness and effervescent youthfulness"; Béatrix Dussane observed that her Hamlet had not yet emerged from adolescence; and John Hansen, in praising the "sinuous grace" of her movement, spoke of her "faithful simulation of a youth's body, whose actions are agile and youthful." From comments such as these, it can be inferred that her Hamlet was the youth she intended, but one who possessed many boyish traits.

Bernhardt's insistence upon the Prince's youth led her to an explanation of a *travesti* Hamlet that is a direct outgrowth of the Beaumarchais type:

> A boy of twenty cannot understand the philosophy of *Hamlet,* nor the poetic enthusiasm of *L'Aiglon,* and without understanding there is no delineation of character. There are no young men of that age capable of playing these parts; consequently an older man assays the role. He does not look the boy, nor has he the ready adaptability of the woman, who can combine the light carriage of youth with the mature thought of the man. The woman more readily looks the part, yet has the maturity of mind to grasp it.

All of Sarah Bernhardt's explanations about *travesti* concern some aspect of the artistic credibility of the type. It is consequently understandable that she would question the appearance in the Prince of broad-shouldered health which, she says, she found so often in foreign Hamlets. In her opinion, such an appearance contradicts Hamlet's "despondent sleeplessness" and his many "inner conflicts." The stylization of *travesti* would, of course, eliminate such concerns.

Bernhardt's Hamlet was stylized not only in movement and appearance, but in voice as well. It is evident from a variety of comments in the press that instead of creating a special voice for her young Prince, she used the natural sound of her lyric instrument, delivering most of her lines and soliloquies in the combination of middle and upper register she employed for most roles, but alternating occasionally with the lower register. Both Elizabeth Robins and Béatrix Dussane affirm that her voice remained that of a woman, but Theodore Stanton contributes a significant addition to the description of her vocal performance: "If it were not for the high pitch of the voice and its occasional thinness, you would never imagine that this Hamlet was a woman. And even this slight reminder of the fact disappears after the first few minutes, when you get accustomed to it. And in the violent passages even this slight fault is wholly removed, for then Bernhardt's voice is as manly as one could wish." Bernhardt's vocal technique in *Hamlet* appears to have been similar to the one she used in her 1909-1910 recording of a speech from the *travesti* role Jacasse in *Les Bouffons* of Miguel Zamacois in which she delivered most of the speech in her middle and upper registers, but reserved her lower register for a passage of jealousy. The voice, however, remains the silvery instrument for which she had become renowned.

The youthful masculinity that Bernhardt achieved in her *travesti* Hamlet was a blend of stylizations: voice, movement, and appearance. Critical comments descriptive of the masculinity of her *travesti* invariably point to its nonrealistic attributes. To John Hansen, her creation was "sexless if not altogether masculine." To the critic of *The World,* she achieved "the manner of masculinity" with a residual "feminine tincture." To Béatrix Dussane, the sex of her *travesti* was, in a sense she insists is by no means pejorative, "undetermined." Such comments sustain Ellen Terry's observation concerning Bernhardt's attainment of artistic truth, not through realism, but through stylization. It was through such stylization that Bernhardt achieved her own version of the feminine presence in a resolute and purposeful avenger.

English audiences were immediately attracted to Bernhardt's *Hamlet,* possibly because of the uncommon blend of circumstances it represented: an internationally renowned performer who spoke French rather than English; a play that was heavily layered with English theatrical tradition; and an interpretation of the title role that had been heralded in the press as untraditional. Tickets for the Bernhardt *Hamlet* sold so rapidly in London that even before the production opened Sarah Bernhardt had to increase the number of performances originally announced from eight to sixteen. Prices at the Adelphi were unusually high, ranging from a half crown, or two shillings sixpence, for standing room, to a guinea, or 21 shillings, for a place in the stalls. According to the standard of ticket prices J.C. Trewin had compiled for Edwardian theatre, prices for the Bernhardt performances did indeed reach the "almost prohibitive" level of which Alan Dale complained. Trewin states that ticket prices, which remained the same for some years, ranged from 10S/6d for the stalls to a shilling for the gallery. Although he does not list the price of standing room, a half crown would have entitled a spectator to a place in the pit, at that time the rear of the stalls. Similar prices were charged a year and a half later in New York when Bernhardt performed her Hamlet with Coquelin in the role of the First Gravedigger. At a time when for 75 cents one could have had an excellent seat at the Academy of Music for a performance by James O'Neill in *The Count of Monte Cristo* or when for $2.50 one could have paid top price at Carnegie Hall for the "Farewell Song Recital" of Marcella Sembrich, Bernhardt's *Hamlet,* as well as the other plays in her New York repertoire (*L'Aiglon, Cyrano de Bergerac, La Tosca,* and *La Dame aux camélias*) were commanding prices of $3.00, $4.00, and $5.00. A complaint in *The New York Dramatic Mirror* reflected the reaction to the inflated scale of prices: "Five dollars for an orchestra chair is too steep even in New York, and with both Bernhardt and Coquelin in the cast." The critic adds that scarcely any good seats were available at the box office of the Garden Theatre, for many of the best tickets were in the hands of "hotel and street speculators," who added an additional fee. With or without speculators, the inflated ticket prices in London and New York never compensated for the expense of the production. Despite the fact that the Bernhardt *Hamlet* toured extensively—to London, the French provinces, Switzerland, Austria, Hungary, South America, and the United States—and that it was performed another 50 times in Paris beginning December 16, 1899, Sarah Bernhardt lost money on a production that was both innovative and popular.

The popularity of the Bernhardt *Hamlet* in London was reflected by the cross-section of society it drew to the

Adelphi. Among the standees, "everybody studied 'Hamlet' out of little old books." There were undoubtedly others in different parts of the theatre who consulted their well-worn copies of the play, for by 1899, it had become a custom among serious London playgoers to attend performances of Shakespeare with their literary libretti in hand. The chic and gossipy *Vanity Fair* assures us that fashionable society was also well represented, Lady Gosford having "brought a party one night last week, which almost filled a long row of the stalls"; Cecil Rhodes appearing another night in a box with Lady Chesham "and a party"; and countless others, titled and untitled, to be seen on many evenings "in various parts of the house." London was alive with theatrical activity but, according to *Vanity Fair,* the "French plays" were, "of course, the thing." The French plays included *La Tosca* and *La Dame aux camélias,* both of which were as popular as the perennially popular Sarah. *Hamlet,* however, had special significance, since it was not only Sarah, but Shakespeare as well.

Although the competition Bernhardt offered her English colleagues was appreciable, the competition they offered her should not be underestimated. At the Lyceum, Henry Irving and Ellen Terry were appearing in *Robespierre;* at Her Majesty's, Beerbohm Tree appeared initially in a double bill including *Captain Swift,* then as D'Artagnan in *The Musketeers;* at the Prince of Wales, the romantic Martin Harvey assumed the role of Sydney Carton in *The Only Way: A Tale of Two Cities;* and at the Savoy, a revival of *H.M.S. Pinafore* was in progress. Popular playwrights, such as Henry Arthur Jones (*The Manoeuvres of Jane*), Arthur Wing Pinero (*The Gay Lord Quex*), and the now totally forgotten Haddon Chambers (*Captain Swift* and *The Tyranny of Tears*) were well represented. Popular performers, such as Cyril Maude, George Alexander, and Charles Wyndham, were ensconced in fashionable plays. The music halls were thriving, and at the London Pavilion Dan Leno and George Robey appeared on the same bill. On June 12th, the opening night of the Bernhardt *Hamlet, Rigoletto* was being performed at the Royal Opera with Nellie Melba, Antonio Scotti, Fernando de Lucia, and Marcel Journet; *Halves,* a new play by Arthur Conan Doyle, was at the Garrick; and *Sweet Lavender* with Edward Terry and Ben Webster was at Terry's Theatre. Madame Tussaud's, of course, was open from ten to ten and, to the accompaniment of "delightful music all day," one could, for a shilling, see "accurate and realistic Portrait Models of Mr. Rudyard Kipling." With the exception of the waxworks, a number of the theatrical offerings could be regarded as genuine competition for the Bernhardt production. It is of more than marginal interest that the only Shakespeare performed in London at the time was represented by Bernhardt's French *Hamlet.*

Alas! It was precisely the Frenchness of the Bernhardt *Hamlet* that caused consternation among some English critics. Part of the reaction was directed against the translation, not so much against the Schwob-Morand version, which was generally found acceptable, but against the idea of experiencing Shakespeare in any language other than English. To the critic of the *Daily Telegraph,* the initial encounter in the program with a French cast of characters caused "a slight shiver to run through Anglican limbs." Reading of the Ghost as "Le Spectre" and the gravediggers as "Fossoyeurs" was, he continued, "unquestionably droll because it forced in upon us the essential differences of rival tongues." The critic of the *Standard* admits that the translation is accurate, but he insists that locutions such as "Le spectacle—voilà la chose!" do not "sound like Shakespeare." He adds that "other still quainter renderings might be quoted," and they would all "demonstrate the fact that *Hamlet* in French—and more particularly with a lady for Hamlet—is inadmissible." Irritated also by Bernhardt's avoidance of a "pathetic" interpretation of the Prince, the critic concludes that if English audiences wish to see Shakespeare, "it is absolutely essential that they should see it in English." Chance Newton, critic of the *Referee,* takes the matter a step further, for he finds the translation so literal that if it were retranslated into English, it would set "the teeth on edge." If, for example, "le siècle est disloqué" and what follows ["O maudit ennui d'être né, moi, pour le remettre en ordre!"] were rendered into English, the result would be "The age is dislocated, and cursed am I that I was born to put it in order." Clearly, no one would quarrel about the superiority of "The time is out of joint;—O cursed spite,/ That ever I was born to set it right!" Under circumstances of such clumsy retranslation, one might even be sympathetic to the implications of the critic's queries, "Is it the language of a poet? Or is it the language of a plumber?" The retranslation, however, was not made by Schwob and Morand, nor was it the text spoken by Bernhardt.

In comparison with Chance Newton's comments on the translation, the complaint of the American actress Elizabeth Robins initially seems of minor significance. She protests the verbal inadequacy of Hamlet's response to Polonius' question, "What do you read, my lord?" Of the translation of Hamlet's "Words, words, words" into "Des mots, des mots, des mots," she comments, "Those little clogging particles have prevented the point from going home." The fact that the Schwob-Morand translation is at this point identical with the Dumas-Meurice version would have been meaningless to Robins or to any member of an English-speaking audience. What is surprising, however, is that Bernhardt's acting of the scene, considered one of the high points of her performance at the *première* in Paris, went completely unnoticed by Robins, who was herself an actress of considerable talent. According to Maurice Baring, when Polonius asked the question, Hamlet was "lying on a chair" reading a book. He spoke the first "des mots" with "absent-minded indifference"; the second, as if his answer "seemed to catch his own attention"; and the third, "accompanied by a look" and charged with the intensity that conveyed his attitude that everything in the world consisted of nothing more than words. Baring was so impressed by the philosophical implications of the delivery that he failed to comment, favorably or unfavorably, upon a translation which at this point he accepted without question. Max

Beerbohm was not of the same opinion and denounced not only the translation, but the idea of ever translating Shakespeare into French. Although he regarded the current rendering as "skilful," he remained convinced that any translation into the French language would be "ruinous." As an example of the "excruciating" quality of some of the current translation's "nearest equivalents," he offers "Paix, paix, âme troublée!" for "Rest, rest, perturbed spirit." Not only does it remind him of a line which, he admits, the translators could not have foreseen—"'Loo, Loo, I love you!'"—but it lacks the "original magic" and is, in addition, "thin," "dry," and "cold." He assures his readers that "for expression" French is a "far finer instrument" than is English, but that it does not possess the "suggestive" qualities characteristic of English which are capable of endowing it with "mystery." He concludes that "the only tribute a French translator can pay Shakespeare is not to translate him—even to please Sarah." While there were other critics who had varying reactions to the translation—praise, indifference, or even lack of awareness—the substantial number of comments hostile to anything but English Shakespeare seems paradoxical when centered on a playwright admired for his universality. As the reviewer of the *Stratford-upon-Avon Herald* observed, Shakespeare could not be regarded as an international dramatist unless he were performed in languages other than English.

The response towards a French text was supplemented by a variety of reactions towards the French temperament. English and American critics agreed that the Bernhardt *Hamlet* was "Gallic" rather than "English," and "Latin" rather than "Gothic." Although some welcomed the interpretation of a player "fired by French blood," others regarded a production starring a "volatile, nervous, excitable" Prince as "little less than an invasion of national property." Comments such as these point as much to the revenge emphasis of the production as to the national temperament of the performer. John Hansen determined another aspect of what was considered French temperament. He explained that in the recitation of "To be or not to be," the sentiment among French and English actors would have been the same, but the manner of expression, different. While an English actor would deliver the soliloquy with tears in the voice, a French performer would utilize a more subtle, hence deceptively frivolous, smile. It may well have been Bernhardt's often used smile as well as her expression of revenge that caused many English critics to place so much emphasis upon the difference between an Anglo-Saxon and a French Hamlet. To Clement Scott, the difference in temperament was welcome. In an article on Bernhardt's *Hamlet* which he wrote for the *New York Herald,* Scott began by stating his agreement with Constant Coquelin that the French temperament as well as the English should be exhibited in *Hamlet.* He added that one should not stop at this point, since Shakespeare, as "the poet of humanity," wrote "for all men, all times, all ages, all nations."

Connected with temperament was the Paris Conservatoire, for it was held responsible for a "special national ca-

dence" suiting "every character" and "every dramatic representation." The critic of the *Pall Mall Gazette* seriously questioned "whether anyone of French nationality, trained in their school of declamation and gesture, to say nothing of the long training Mme. Bernhardt has of late years undergone in the lower school of Sardou, could ever successfully present so purely English, or at least, Scandinavian, a figure as Hamlet's." The critic's views were supported by those of A.B. Walkley, for he regarded Bernhardt's French "temperament and training" as an "insuperable obstacle" to performing a role that was "English to the backbone." The critic of the *Globe* was more favorably disposed towards a French *Hamlet.* Observing that Bernhardt was received by her audience "with rapture" and with curtain calls "too numerous to be counted," he noted that in the past English audiences had not been predisposed to accepting a French Hamlet, but that the success of Fechter had "removed some illusions." The attitude towards Fechter's two productions of *Hamlet* in London in 1861 and 1864, however, differs markedly from that expressed about Bernhardt's *Hamlet.* Despite the fact that Fechter performed in the style of French Boulevard theatre, he did so in an English text, in English productions, and with English casts. Bernhardt, on the other hand, performed in French, in a French production, and with a French cast. Fechter also modeled his London productions of *Hamlet* on fashionable interpretations derived from *Wilhelm Meister* while Bernhardt rejected romantic attitudes in favor of revenge. In presenting himself in London, Fechter was able to win considerable critical favor because his distinctly foreign acting style was surrounded by readily apprehended familiarities: linguistic, theatrical, and cultural. Bernhardt offered the London public a blend of the uncustomary, the unfamiliar, and the unknown. Given such circumstances, it is remarkable that she won the admiration of audiences and the support of a respected critical minority.

In many reviews of the Bernhardt *Hamlet* that appeared in London and New York, the French attributes of the protagonist were linked with what became the issue of *travesti.* John Hansen maintained that despite his own appreciation of Bernhardt's Hamlet, he recognized the inability of the English to grasp "the woman of it and the French of it." Repeatedly in criticism, *travesti* is discussed in relation to its Frenchness. Chance Newton admired the "original Hamlet" produced by "an actress of genius," but he went on to make a direct connection between the role's being "outside a woman's nature" and "foreign to the French temperament." The critic of the *Daily Graphic* also had great respect for the art of Sarah Bernhardt and regarded her Hamlet as a *tour de force.* His orientation is that of the nineteenth century, for he states that Bernhardt's interpretation "casts a flood of feminine revelation upon a character that has some feminine aspects." He is furthermore a follower of the romantic school that was deeply concerned with the Prince's "hesitancy." The critic's attitude towards a French *travesti,* however, is that it is both "courageous and eccentric" for a "Frenchwoman . . . to undertake to teach us how to play Hamlet." A woman, moreover, is "no more fit to play

Hamlet than she is to command the Channel fleet." The most extreme expression of this view expands the linkage still further to include a prejudice vaguely hinted at by A.B. Walkley. When Bernhardt took her *Hamlet* to New York she encountered a special enmity in the attitude of William Dean Howells. Sarah Bernhardt, who was Catholic by upbringing, but half-Jewish by birth, found that the eminent man of letters dismissed her Hamlet as triple impertinence: not merely French and feminine, but Jewish as well. The parochialism of such objections was finally put in perspective by Edward A. Dithmar, critic of the *New York Times*. Devoting two articles to his contentions, he defended both the artistic integrity of *travesti* and the universality of Shakespeare. "I hope I have no prejudices," Dithmar states. "I do not object to seeing a woman in a male role if she can act it. Sarah Bernhardt certainly can act Hamlet well enough to justify her attempt to act that character. One is glad to have seen her in it." Concerning Shakespeare's universality, Dithmar wonders how English-speaking people could at the same time praise Shakespeare's genius as belonging "to all ages and the whole world" and question the ability of a foreigner to comprehend it: "If he belongs to all the world, he belongs to the French; if to all ages, to the present age! Surely, then, we ought to respect the French interpretation of him and, if it differs from ours, 'as a stranger, give it welcome.'" Dithmar does not respond directly to the anti-Semitic comment of Howells, possibly because such hostility was not widespread, possibly because his rejection of prejudice would tactfully include a dismissal of anti-Semitism as well. The most significant aspect of Dithmar's reviews is his insistence upon critical standards not always adhered to in theatrical evaluations. Ahead of his time by many a decade, the New York critic thus presents a climate for responding to the Bernhardt *Hamlet* and evaluating its contribution to the history of Shakespeare's tragedy in the theatre.

FURTHER READING

Biography

Agate, May. *Madame Sarah*. London and Edinburgh: Home & Van Thal, Ltd., 1945, 223 p.
  Biography of Bernhardt by an English actress trained by her; includes personal reflections of time spent with Bernhardt.

Baring, Maurice. *Sarah Bernhardt*. New York and London: D. Appleton-Century Company, Inc., 1934, 163 p.
  Personal reflections on Bernhardt's life and work.

Brandon, Ruth. *Being Divine: A Biography of Sarah Bernhardt*. London: Secker & Warburg, 1991, 466 p.
  Biography that seeks to analyze the wider impact of the

"phenomenon" of Sarah Bernhardt on acting, popular culture, and the changing place of women in society.

Emboden, William. *Sarah Bernhardt*. New York: Macmillan Publishing Co., Inc., 1975, 176 p.
  Biography of Bernhardt that includes an introduction by Sir John Gielgud.

Gold, Arthur, and Robert Fizdale. *The Divine Sarah: A Life of Sarah Bernhardt*. New York: Alfred A. Knopf, 1991, 352 p.
  Biography of Bernhardt focusing on the spell she was able to cast on her audiences and the impression she created of herself.

Richardson, Joanna. *Sarah Bernhardt and Her World*. London: Weidenfeld and Nicolson, 1977, 232 p.
  Biography that examines the "cult and legend" of Bernhardt.

Verneuil, Louis. *The Fabulous Life of Sarah Bernhardt*. Translated by Ernest Boyd. New York and London: Harper & Brothers Publishers, 1942, 312 p.
  Biography of Bernhardt by her friend and fellow actor.

Criticism

Beerbohm, Max. "Incomparables Compared." In *Around Theatres*, pp. 201-205. New York: Alfred A. Knopf, 1930
  Compares the acting craft of three early twentieth-century stage actresses: Sada Yacco, Réjane, and Bernhardt.

Isherwood, Christopher. "Vivekananda and Sarah Bernhardt." In *Vedanta for the Western World*, pp. 268-72. London: George Allen & Unwin, Ltd., 1948.
  Recounts a meeting between the Indian mystic Swamiji Vivekananda and Bernhardt.

MacCarthy, Desmond. "Duse and Bernhardt." In *Theatre*, pp. 157-59. London: MacGibbon & Kee, 1954.
  Contrasts the acting techniques of Eleonora Duse and Bernhardt.

Stokes, John; Michael R. Booth; and Susan Bassnett. Bernhardt, Terry, Duse. The Actress in Her Time. Cambridge, England: Cambridge University Press, 1988, 192 p.
  Examines the professional lives of Bernhardt, Ellen Terry, and Eleonora Duse.

Taranow, Gerda. *Sarah Bernhardt: The Art within the Legend*. Princeton, N.J.: Princeton University Press, 1972, 287 p.
  Attempts to separate Bernhardt's art and acting technique from her life and legend, focusing on her training and "histrionic theory."

Additional coverage of Bernhardt's life and career is contained in the following source published by Gale Research: *Contemporary Authors*, Vol. 157.

Vilhelm Ekelund

1880-1949

Swedish poet, aphorist, and essayist.

INTRODUCTION

Ekelund is considered Sweden's leading aphorist and among its most influential modern poets. His career is generally divided into two phases. Prior to 1909 Ekelund focused exclusively on poetry, producing highly personal verse in the romantic mode. Later he abandoned poetry altogether in favor of prose, taking cues from classical models and the thought of such individuals as Friedrich Nietzsche, Johann Wolfgang von Goethe, and Ralph Waldo Emerson. The at times cryptic style of his aphorisms and essays betoken Ekelund's visionary quest in search of beauty and truth in an abstract or Platonic sense. Nevertheless, his writings—in both the symbolic imagery of his poetry and compact, philosophical musings of his prose—are acknowledged among the most enduring in twentieth-century Swedish literature.

Biographical Information

Ekelund was born in Stehag in the Skåne district of southern Sweden, son of a village blacksmith. He attended the University of Lund—his father had moved to the larger town when Ekelund was in his early teens—but never obtained a degree. In 1908 he left Sweden to avoid some minor legal entanglements after engaging in a public altercation and simultaneously cast aside poetry, opting instead to write essays and aphorisms. He lived in Berlin until 1912, then relocated to Denmark, which he preferred to Germany, though he became seriously ill for many of the years he spent there. He eventually returned to live in Sweden in 1921, hoping to provide a spiritual voice to the younger generation in his native country, but instead found himself alienated from all but a small, devoted following of readers. Ekelund died in Salsjobaden, Sweden in 1949.

Major Works

Ekelund's earliest poetic efforts are represented by his collections *Vårbris* and *Melodier i skymning*, which contain a variety of rhymed lyrics on personal subjects and introspective meditations inspired by the natural landscapes of his native Skånia. Ekelund's later poems, contained in *In candidum, Dithyramber i aftonglans,* and other volumes, represent developments in form, such as Ekelund's resonant use of free verse, as well as his passionate adoption of the ideals and precepts of classical antiquity. After forsaking poetry in favor of prose, Ekelund sustained his exploration of classical themes in a modern idiom, while breaking away fully from the romantic origins of his early verse. Inspired by his admiration for the thought of Friedrich Nietzsche, *Antikt ideal* includes an impassioned praise of the German philosopher's concept of the indomitable will. A later, less strident collection of essays *Veri similia* represents the more moderate side of Ekelund's thought and betrays the influence of Emerson and Goethe among its models. The ideal of moderation is the ruling force in the essays of *Metron* and *Attiskt i fågelperspektiv,* both of which contain Ekelund's thoughts on the world's preeminent thinkers and artists since the classical era. In *På hafsstranden* Ekelund equates the Nordic and classical ideals of bravery, fortitude, and sobriety. Among his later works, *Plus salis* offers Ekelund's thoughts on the synthesis of idea and reality in life.

Critical Reception

Ekelund's poetry, essays, and aphorisms never reached more than a modest popularity during his lifetime, and drew consistently negative criticism from many of his contemporaries. Influenced in his style and thought by the German classicists, notably Friedrich Hölderlin and August Graf von Platen, Ekelund placed his passionate longing for the philosophical ideal of beauty before all other concerns, leading to what critics have observed are highly personal and at times abstruse writings. Still, Ekelund's passionate appeal in favor of the classical ideals of balance, moderation, beauty, and ultimate truth, coupled with his prophetic and experimental use of language, proved influential on the succeeding generation of poets in Scandinavia. Likewise, his bold style and mastery of the aphorism have made him one of the most highly regarded prose writers and versifiers in his native Sweden.

PRINCIPAL WORKS

Vårbris (poetry) 1900
Syner (poetry) 1901
Melodier i skymning (poetry) 1902
Elegier (poetry) 1903
In candidum (poetry) 1905
Dithyramber i aftonglans (poetry) 1906
Grekisk bukett (translated poetry) 1906
Havets stjärna (poetry) 1906
Antikt ideal (essays and aphorisms) 1909
Böcker och vandringar (essays and aphorisms) 1910
Båge och lyra (essays and aphorisms) 1912
Tyska utsikter (essays and aphorisms) 1913
Agenda (essays and aphorisms) 1913-14

Nordiskt och klassiskt (essays and aphorisms) 1914
Veri similia (essays and aphorisms) 1915-16
Metron (essays and aphorisms) 1918
Attiskt i fågelperspektiv (essays and aphorisms) 1919
På hafsstranden (essays and aphorisms) 1922
Sak ock sken (essays and aphorisms) 1922
Lefnadsstämning (essays and aphorisms) 1925
Västöstligt (essays and aphorisms) 1925
Passioner emellan (essays and aphorisms) 1927
Lyra och Hades (essays and aphorisms) 1930
Spår och tecken (essays and aphorisms) 1930
Båge och lyra 1932 (essays and aphorisms) 1932
Valda sidor och essays 1908-1930 (essays and apho-
   risms) 1933
Det andra ljuset [*The Second Light*] (essays and apho-
   risms) 1935
Elpidi (essays and aphorisms) 1939
Concordia animi (essays and aphorisms) 1942
Atticism-humanism (essays and aphorisms) 1943
Plus salis (essays and aphorisms) 1945
Dikter (poetry) 1951
Prosa (essays and aphorisms) 1952
Nya vakten (essays and aphorisms) 1953
Ars magna (essays and aphorisms) 1954
Saltet och helichrysus (essays and aphorisms) 1956
In silvis cum libro (essays and aphorisms) 1957
Skoltal (essays and aphorisms) 1961
Själens tillflykt (essays and aphorisms) 1962
Campus et dies (essays and aphorisms) 1963
Brev (essays and aphorisms) 1968-70
Hjärtats vaggvisor (essays and aphorisms) 1970
Hemkomst och flykt (essays and aphorisms) 1972
Den ensammes stämningar (essays and aphorisms) 1985

CRITICISM

Lars Gustafsson (essay date 1936)

SOURCE: "Vilhelm Ekelund," in *Forays into Swedish Poetry,* translated by Robert T. Rovinsky, University of Texas Press, 1978, pp. 65-71.

[*In the following essay, Gustafsson analyzes Ekelund's poem "The First Spring Rain," noting the particular Swedishness of Ekelund's work.*]

"Det första vårregnet"

Som ett nät av svarta spindelvävar
hänga trädens våta grenar.
I den tysta februarinatten
sjunger sakta, klingar, svävar
fram ur däldens snår och stenar
suset av en källas vatten.

I den tysta februarinatten
gråter himlen stilla.

—Syner, 1901

"The First Spring Rain"

Black, like webs from spinning spiders playing
branches, moisture-heavy, bend
In the silent February night
singing slowly, ringing, swaying
out of rock-strewn, brushy glen
sounds of wellspring, watery delight.

In the silent February night
cry the heavens softly.

—Visions, 1901

For the average Swede, Ekelund's poetry can occasionally take on an exotic quality, which comes about quite simply because his Scanian landscape truly *is* a foreign landscape. Our everyday experiences mean more to our relationship with a poem than we would normally imagine.

I remember how, while teaching Tomas Tranströmer to students at the University of Texas, I came to the well-known line that reads: "like a sun-warm stone in my hand" ("som en solvarm sten i handen").

"That can't be," one of the students said immediately. "If somebody were to hold a 'sun-warm stone' in his hand, he'd get blisters. And he'd toss that stone away as fast as he possibly could."

Undoubtedly, this is how stones and men behave in the parched regions around Texas' Colorado River. Of course, that did not prevent the student from understanding what Tranströmer meant. I think the poem even became more interesting to him when he understood that this brief picture contained a wholly alien climatic experience.

For a reader from central or northern Sweden, February is a period of deep snow and dryness; arctic-clear days, when bullfinches and silktails come out from the deep woods in search of food; ice-cold nights, when contraction brought on by the chill causes a moaning and groaning in wooden houses, and shoes crunch on unplowed roads.

For Ekelund, "the silent February night" is the time when the landscape begins to shed silent tears. I think that a northern Swedish reader would more readily associate this experience with the beginning of April.

Differences which do not mean anything and, yet, most profoundly *do* mean something. They compel us to make an extra effort, and in this small exertion there is always a gain, a small electrical charge. I know of no more sterile an idea than that poetry should sneak up as close to its reader as possible, make itself as accessible as possible to him. The little difference in electric potential itself—the one that makes it possible for the spark to leap between anode and cathode—will, of course, be lost in that way.

Ekelund's February night, then, is not our February night. It belongs to central Europe; spring nights in Berlin parks are like this: he must have seen such branches, felt that kind of wetness, countless times during his lengthy exile.

I do not think there is any Swedish poet who manifests such firmly rooted opposition, antipathy, obstinate refusal, heightened loathing toward lightly flowing, melodic poetry as does Vilhelm Ekelund. All his contempt for the stale Establishment poetry which dominated the Swedish scene in his youth is present, concealed, in his rhythms.

Nowadays, when free verse is frequently but an expression of the fact that the poet has never learned, or even become acquainted with, any other poetic technique, such verse, in the happiest cases, is created by coincidence.

Among now-living Swedish poets there are precious few who actually take pains to write free verse which is, at the same time, *rhythmically interesting*. In Göran Sonnevi one can recognize such an endeavor, but he is an exception. On the whole, one must go to the great Finland-Swedish poets, to a Diktonius or a Björling, to find anything similar to this.

"The First Spring Rain" begins quite monotonously with two long series of trochees, almost like a ticking clock; even better, like drops—yes, of course, drops falling from branches:

  dá-dit-dá-dit-dá-dit-dá-dit-dá-dit
  dá-dit-dá-dit-dá-dit-dá-dit

Note that there is one trochee less in the second line. Ekelund is poet enough to know what Petrarch and Dante also knew; *regularity* does not necessarily preclude *irregularity*. It is precisely in the monotony that one can prepare the real surprises. From this uniform, discreetly rhymed trochaic verse the words *February night* free themselves like great beings, slowly and silently advancing creatures.

What occurs in the next line is very typical of Ekelund's entire poetic technique:

  singing slowly, ringing, swaying

One *adjective* is seldom enough, and here one *verb* is not enough. Ekelund takes his time, he specifies exactly, through a series of words, the sensation he wishes to encircle. Because of this, it would be easy, even if we did not know when or by whom it was written, to see that this is a poem written on the threshold of Swedish poetic modernism.

From a classical point of view—that is to say, proceeding from the poetics which have their roots in the French classics—in Boileau's poetic theory there is always one word which is the correct one, and the trick consists in finding that word. Poetry becomes a kind of sharpshooting at reality, with the help of words.

In order for such a poetic technique to appear practicable and reasonable and effective, one must be convinced, naturally, that language really coincides with reality, and it is precisely upon this condition that French classicism builds.

The dissolution, the dejection, begins with romanticism and reaches its culmination during the second half of the nineteenth century, when a succession of philosophers—such as Nietzsche, Fritz Mauthner, and Alexander Bryan Johnson—state plainly that language is not simply approximative: it has nothing at all to do with reality.

This linguistic pessimism penetrates deep into literature during the second half of the nineteenth century. We can already see it in Henrik Ibsen's *The Wild Duck* (1884), with its conviction that human beings cannot possibly live without their illusions, without the "life lie."

And it forms one of the deepest roots for what is usually termed literary modernism. What language can best do with reality is not to reproduce it but, rather, to encircle it through circuitous operations.

This is exactly what is occurring when Ekelund writes:

  singing slowly, ringing, swaying

The line produces an enormously effective intensification, but it also evokes an uncertainty, and nature becomes spiritual. It is impossible to differentiate between the state of one's soul and the landscape in **"The First Spring Rain,"** and this is the second characteristic of the poem that obviously connects it with poetic modernism. It is even possible that at bottom it is *exactly the same thing* as saying that the essential element seems to lie between the words rather than in them, but to explain why would take us too far.

The poem is a story about a landscape, but it is at once and in the same context a story about a human being who, after disappointments, impoverishment, and bitterness, suddenly discovers that there are new, life-giving forces in the very midst of the impoverishment and the nakedness. There is a wellspring in the leafless February forest. The rain is not merely rain, it is a crying, exactly as the rain cries in the great French symbolists and, above all, in Paul Verlaine. In all stillness, a change is being readied, the soul is awakening from a period of bitterness, and this must of necessity change the landscape in its entirety. Image and eye coincide. We are what we see, and thus we are changed.

"The First Spring Rain" fits into a great European tradition which, having become a reality, will not permit itself to be forgotten.

Leif Sjöberg and Niels Lyhne Jensen (essay date 1982)

SOURCE: "Early Scandinavian Symbolism by Leif Sjöberg (Stony Brook) and N. L. Jensen (Aarhus)," in

The Symbolist Movement in the Literature of European Languages, edited by Anna Balakian, Akadémiai Kiadó, 1982, pp. 580-84.

[In the following essay, Sjöberg and Jensen discuss how Ekelund was influenced by early Swedish avant-garde poets.]

While *avant garde* Symbolist and Decadent coteries were forming in Paris after 1880, August Strindberg (1849-1912) and Ola Hansson (1860-1925) made great headway in developing an *avant garde* in Sweden, where by 1900 there were several counterparts to Parisian groups. Students at Uppsala University joined to form *Les quatre diables,* to which belonged Sigfrid Siwertz (1882-1960) and Sigurd Agrell (1881-1937). This group exhibited their predilection for French poets, Arthur Rimbaud in particular, after he had been introduced in *Svenska Dagbladet* by Oscar Levertin (1862-1906). The poetic production of this period was later resolutely rejected by the poets themselves, which, as Gunnar Brandell put it, "has been a contributing factor to the disrepute of all Swedish Symbolism". *Tuakretsen* (The Tua-group) at Lund, led by Bengt Lidforss (1868-1913), cultivated the *avant garde* approach and kept up contacts with other international-oriented coteries, especially those in Berlin. Their favorites were Dehmel, George, Hofmannsthal and Rilke. In this group, Vilhelm Ekelund (1880-1949), then a young student and budding poet, was influenced significantly.

When Ekelund made his debut as a poet with *Vårbris* (1900, *Spring Breeze*) in a verse "of extraordinarily sensitive musical quality", he described the nature of his native Scania in the manner of A. U. Bååth (1853-1912) and Ola Hansson, rather than in that of more established poets such as Werner von Heidenstam (1859-1940), whose tendencies towards national romanticism and pomposity Ekelund did not care for.

According to Algot Werin, the Ekelund scholar whose comprehensive research is followed here, a new orientation in Ekelund's writing is noticeable in *Syner (Visions,* 1901) where the names of Dehmel, Verlaine and Verhaeren occur. When visiting Berlin in 1902 Ekelund met Dehmel, who later sent Ekelund his collection *Zwei Menschen* (1903). For some time it appears as if Ekelund chose Dehmel as his master above all others. Verlaine, whom Dehmel and George had introduced in Germany, appears in a motto to Ekelund's poem *"En februarimorgon"* (**"A Morning in February"**). The motto is from Verlaine's *"Il pleure dans mon cœur"*. "While in Verlaine his heart's quiet crying is accompanied by the song of the rain, in Ekelund the happy exultation of spring is contrasted with the melancholy and darkness of his soul. However, this is naturally not as heavy in the twenty-year-old poet, whose poem is more brightly accentuated than that of the thirty-year-old Verlaine, whose health was in decline . . .". If Ekelund has made the mood of the Verlaine poem his, or, if he identified with it as he met it in *Romances sans paroles* is hard to determine.

Ekelund's poem, *"Verlaine stämning,"* (**"In the Manner of Verlaine"**) also has a motto from *Il pleure:*

Pour mon cœur qui s'ennuie
O le chant de la pluie!

Ekelund's poem is, as Werin points out, a variation on Verlaine's theme:

Det regnar öfver staden,
det regnar tyst och sakta
på gatans tysta hus.

Från mjukt beslöjad himmel
igenom skymningen silar
ett mildt och dämpadt ljus.

O denna veka, stilla
vårkvällsmelankoli!
och regnets sakta sus—

Mitt hjärta gråter tyst . . .

(Translation: It rains over the city, / it rains quietly and softly / on the quiet houses of the streets. // From a gently darkened sky / through the dusk filters / a mild and dimmed light. // Oh this tender, quiet / spring—evening—melancholy! / and the low tapping of the rain—// My heart cries quietly . . .)

For some time Verlaine's verse music enchanted Ekelund, as is especially noticeable in his poems of 1900-1901. However, in many of these poems he also comes close to Ola Hansson's *Notturno* poetry, which may or may not have been influenced by the French Symbolists. A nature scene as a state of the soul, the gently gliding verse, the vague moods and the undefined sentiments—all of this Ekelund could find in *Notturno* (1885) as well as in Verlaine's *Romances sans paroles* (1874) and *Sagesse* (1880).

It was in the last portion of *Syner* that Verlaine's influence (and that of Ola Hansson) was felt most strongly. Ekelund followed Verlaine even in his next collection of poetry, *Melodier i skymning (Melodies in Twilight,* 1902). In November, 1902, Ekelund in a literary chronicle in *Svenska Dagbladet* reviewed a German Verlaine anthology. He suggested that among the French poets of the past century, Verlaine was the one who might have the greatest appeal to Germanic sympathies whereas Baudelaire (like Platen) had as yet failed to gain recognition there.

In the spring of 1902, Ekelund wanted to translate Baudelaire's *Petits poèmes en prose* and the same spring he wrote a brief essay on **"Baudelaire—Przybyszewski"** published in *Majgrefven (Lund).* Ekelund finds many similarities between Baudelaire and Przybyszewski; both are *Rauschkünstler,* a term borrowed from Przybyszewski's book of essays, *Chopin und Nietzsche* (1892). Of the two, the Swedish poet feels closer to Baudelaire. Pure contemplation, the ecstasy of beauty gave him, too, moments of a higher life.

Ekelund finally presented his version of the little introductory poem of *"Petits poèmes en prose, L'Étranger."* The stranger recognizes neither relatives, friends, nor fatherland; his love he wishes to offer to Beauty, but he is without hope. Ekelund put the last few words as the motto of his essay:

> But what do you love, you unusual stranger?
> —I love
> the skies—the skies that wander—up there—
>   the strange skies!

Melodier i skymning is considered the greatest and also the most complex of Ekelund's collections of poems. It is a book in which he freely acknowledges his sources and influences, and contains celebrations of the romantic Stagnelius (1793-1823), of Platen, Hölderlin and Mallarmé, as well as translations of Theodor Storm and Stefan George. One poem is entitled *"Des Esseintes"* after the main character in Huysmans' novel *A Rebours* (1884; Eng. tr., *Against Nature,* 1959). It is characteristic of Ekelund's attitude during this phase of dependence on Symbolism that thought of the sea in *"Afsked"* (**"Farewell"**) make for a death poem, and that *"Till hafvet"* (**"To the Sea"**) becomes a love poem:

> O Haf, när skum af ångst min syn förblindas
> och själen våndas i sin onda dröm,
> är du den arm jag känner sakta lindas
> omkring mitt hufvud älskande och öm.

(Literally: Oh Sea, when my eyes are blinded by dark anguish, / and the soul endures its evil dream, / you are the arm I feel, lovingly / and tenderly, encircling my head). As it was perceived by many at that time, the sea here is both a death symbol and one filled with erotic content.

Ekelund's *"Den hemliga liljan"* (**"The Mysterious Lily"**) becomes the symbol of the growth and flowering in his soul. He is moved to speak of the *underblomma,* the wonder-flower living in his soul, which raises its perianth from a dark well. Above this is an arched room from which resounds a wordless melody that fills his soul:

> ack! som en öfverfylld skål,
> högt buren på rädda händer,
> bär dig min själ,
> o du min käraste!
> Du min hemliga lilja—
> Du min ofödda melodi!

(Literal translation: Like an overflowing cup / borne high on fearful hands, / my soul carries you, / oh you my dearest! / you my mysterious lily—/ You my unborn melody!) "As no other Swedish poet after Tegnér (1782-1846) Ekelund has celebrated the sublime effect of Song and the redeeming power of Beauty".

After *Elegier* (*Elegies,* 1903), *In Candidum* (1905), and *Hafvets stjärna* (*The Star of the Sea,* 1906) influenced by Hölderlin, Platen and Nietzsche, Vilhelm Ekelund's poetry takes a characteristic line, stressing the heroic in the lifestyle of antiquity (Pindar, Heraclitus, Plato, etc.). This development away from Symbolism is foreseen in Ekelund's seventh and final collection of poetry, *Dithyramber i aftonglans* (*Dithyrambs in Evening-luster,* 1906) in which the poem *"Lunaria"* appears.

The following discussion is based on Carl-Erik af Geijerstam's essay on *"Lunaria"* In Lindman's treatise on the species of plants, *Lunaria* is called "moon violet" (*månviol*), a three-foot plant with large purple petals; when the valves (*valvlerna*) fall off and the broad, silvery intermediate wall is laid bare, the plant acquires a rather strange appearance. In the poem it is emphasized that in its splendor the plant is *alone* (l. 1.). Lunaria has a brightness of its own, is "a flame". This brightness is sharply contrasted to the shadowy place from which it strives upwards. "It is the quality of being carrier of an inner light source which is celebrated in the dithyrambic second strophe". In the third strophe Lunaria is placed in relation to the surrounding world. Outwardly the flower is "alien and quiet" (l. 17) and its look (*blick*) is "rare and cold". In its vicinity, the *collective* life (of the other flowers) flourishes, but it is mindless, characterized largely by carelessness or indifference. No one ever bothers to pay attention to the moon violet, which is thus, literally, left *alone.* Only at night, when the buzz of the day is no more, Lunaria can break out of its isolation—by speaking to the stars. The poet clearly identifies with the flower.

The solitary feeling so clearly expressed in *"Lunaria"* and common among the poets around the turn of the century gradually becomes acceptable to Ekelund as a sign of his distinctive character. Does he not indicate in his poem that *the solitary* is also the unique, and that precisely *the unique* gives the opportunity for personal growth, for the fulfillment of personality? The "coldness" of Lunaria's beauty must be seen as representing Ekelund's detached, high-brow attitude, his Nietzschean contempt for sentimentalism.

To be sure, Nature becomes—in Ekelund's later work even more than before—*a symbol of the state of the soul,* but the appropriation of nature's beauty breeds struggle and requires the *active* participation of all mental powers. There is an ever-present longing for the moment when the pain and the oppressive conditions of life can be conquered and the spirit raised to a higher and richer life, and finally pain itself to Ekelund becomes a stimulating means and a precondition of reaching the sublime.

"The dreamlike in the description of reality and the *passive* in sentient life, so typical of Symbolism, was dominant for only a few years in Vilhelm Ekelund". It is one of the considerable achievements of Symbolism that it made Ekelund into *the* great liberator and pioneer of free verse in Sweden.

Dithyramber i aftonglans was Ekelund's last collection of poetry. He went abroad (to Germany) in 1908 and gave up poetry as unsuited to his type of temperament. He wrote twenty-five books of aphorisms, essays, and criticism. He returned to Sweden in 1921, admired by a few loyal friends and supporters.

FURTHER READING

Criticism

Gustafson, Alrik. "Two Early Fröding Imitations: Vilhelm Ekelund's 'Skördefest' (1900) and 'I pilhäcken' (1901)." *Journal of English and Germanic Philology* 35, No. 4 (October 1936): 566-80.
　　Notes considerable stylistic affinities between two of Ekelund's early poems and the works of Gustaf Fröding.

Shideler, Ross. "'The Glassclear Eye of Dreams' in Twentieth-Century Swedish Poetry." *World Literature Today* 51, No. 4 (Autumn 1977): 530-34.
　　Traces Ekelund's contribution to the tradition of poetry as dream-vision in Swedish literature.

Francis Jammes

1868-1938

French poet and novelist.

INTRODUCTION

Francis Jammes was a French poet whose early work exemplified nineteenth century romanticism's fascination with the natural world. At their best, his poems and novels, which included *Le Roman du lièvre* (*The Romance of the Rabbit*) exhibited a spontaneity and unself-conscious joyousness which brought Jammes friends and admirers among such noted literary figures as André Gide and Stephane Mallarmé. However, the work that followed his 1905 conversion to Catholicism tended toward self-consciousness and a didactic quality that diminished his legacy among succeeding generations.

Biographical Information

Jammes spent most of his life in the Pyrenees foothills, where his father held several successive government posts. His father died when Jammes was 20, and Jammes continued living with his mother for many years afterward. Always a lackluster student, he studied law briefly and worked for a time as a notary's assistant, but generally he spent his time in peaceful and pastoral pursuits, taking long walks and observing the natural world in a precise detail which he translated into his later poetry and prose poems. His first poems appeared in 1891, when he arranged to print 50 copies of *Six Sonnets*. A second volume attracted the attention of Mallarmé, Gide, and others, and Jammes began a series of interactions with leading literary figures that included a lengthy correspondence with Gide. Thereafter he published various poems, books, and articles. His friendship with another leading poet, Paul Claudel, led to his conversion to Catholicism in 1905. In 1906, when he was 38 and still living with his mother, Jammes married and eventually fathered seven children. He continued to write during the three remaining decades of his life, but commentators have maintained that his best work lay behind him. He died in 1938.

Major Works

Jammes first established himself with such poetic works as those collected in *Six Sonnets* and *Vers*. Within a few years, he was moving into narrative with *Un jour*, which depicted a day in the life of a poet. There was not much activity in *Un jour*, though in the companion pieces *La Naissance du poète* (*The Birth of the Poet*) and *La Mort du poète* (*The Death of the Poet*), he dramatized stages of the poet's life. In 1897 he published a short manifesto in the literary journal *Mercure de France*, wherein he

sketched a model for a poetic style that incorporated naturalistic and sensual elements. His best-regarded poetry appears in the collection *De l'Angelus de l'aube à l'Angelus du soir*, published in 1898, wherein he explored a variety of themes, always according to the rubric of naturalism—or "Jammism," as his style would come to be called. Around the turn of the century, he entered the last fruitful phase of his career with the publication of several novels depicting young girls in often tragic circumstances. The title character of *Clara d' Ellébeuse*, for instance, is obsessed with a mystery surrounding a deceased woman named Laura who had become pregnant by her uncle. Ultimately Clara, swept up in the drama of people she has never met, finds herself succumbing to a possible seducer of her own, the poet Roger. She poisons herself and dies on Laura's grave. The most famous of Jammes's novels is the more lighthearted *The Romance of the Rabbit*. In it, the Hare goes through numerous adventures on earth and winds up in heaven, where he finds that he misses the dangers of his earthbound existence. The quantity of Jammes's output in the next decades was high, but his writings were not well-regarded. His only other noteworthy works were his three-volume *Mémoires*, published from 1921 to 1923.

PRINCIPAL WORKS

Six Sonnets (poetry) 1891

Vers (poetry) 1892

Un jour [*A Day*] (poetry) 1895

La Naissance du poète [*The Birth of the Poet*] (poetry) 1897

La Mort du poète [*The Death of the Poet*] (poetry) 1898

De l'Angelus de l'aube à l'Angelus du soir (poetry) 1898

Clara d' Ellébeuse; ou, L'Histoire d'une ancienne jeune fille (novel) 1899

Almaïde d'Etremont; ou, L'Histoire d'une jeune fille passionée (novel) 1901

Le Roman du lièvre [*Romance of the Rabbit*] (prose poem) 1903

De l' âge divin à l' âge ingrat (memoirs) 1921

L'Amour, les muses et la chasse (memoirs) 1922

Les Caprices du poète (memoirs) 1923

CRITICISM

Robert Vallery-Radot (essay date 1914)

SOURCE: "The Renascence of Catholic Lyricism," in *The Constructive Quarterly*, Vol. 2, June, 1914, pp. 384-402.

[*In the following essay, Vallery-Radot includes Jammes in a discussion of French-Catholic poetry.*]

While politicians are persisting in serving up to the masses, in the name of the laïc spirit and of Progress, the pernicious puerilities of the *Encyclopédie* now superannuated, while certain professors of the Sorbonne are madly bent upon ruining our worldwide reputation for straight thinking and clear speaking, while the fashionable stage and fashionable fiction are rehashing in senile fashion their tiresome physiologies, while the reviews are leading opinion astray upon fictitious glories, and the magazines are exalting stage-players, mountebanks, dancers and courtesans, it is good to turn aside for a moment from all this din and grimacing and, entering into the silence that is within, to give ear to the new and mysterious sounds which are awakening from out of the very depths of the French soul.

It is indeed true that the atmosphere in the intellectual regions of our country is becoming purer and lighter; literature, in particular, seems to be shaking off the stifling yoke of naturalism, and aspiring to some sort of heroic state, which is transfiguring it. We must go back to romanticism to find such an effervescence, principally in lyrics, such an ebullition of restless, ardent forces. Now lyric verse is the very soul of a literature, its secret love. Thus may we say to a given epoch: "Tell me your company, and I will tell you who you are."

We find in the *Traité de la Vraie Contemplation* these words of Ruysbroeck:

> The sons of nature are those who give themselves up to the elements and obey the movements of the firmament; as for the children of God, they dominate the course of the firmament and the planets, and all things obey them.

In the strange crowded, tumultuous medley of sounds which rise from the lyres of our time we can distinguish two choirs: on the one hand, that of the sons of Nature, prostrate before Life, Love and all the idols named with capitals which can be engendered by the pestilent mythology of the Unconscious; on the other hand, the sons of God, for whom the universe is not at all a matter of chance, but ruled and protected in every detail by its Creator, for whom every being is sacred, the glorious reflection of its eternal Beginning. Before giving our attention to the latter, even before separating the cockle from the good grain, we may assert without fear of contradiction that on every side rationalism is in headlong flight, that even among unbelievers the religious forces are awaking from their long sleep, and that, astonished at feeling as hungry for spiritual life as they were before, and with intuitions a thousand times more fertile than all the dialectics cut off short from an emancipated reason, they are asking themselves if those intuitions are not the very roots of the human tree, and whether cutting them away was not effectively drying up all the sap of that tree. And resting upon the world which for them has again become unknown, somewhat intoxicated with the new wine that is turning their heads, not measuring their language and yet well expressing by it their state of utter confusion, they repeat the strange cry of Zarathustra: "Deep is the night, deeper than the day thought." To avoid all misunderstanding let us say at once that this obscure and feverish exaltation conceals many dangers.

> "The love of God," Angela da Foligno admirably says, "is above everything an object of suspicion to me. If it is not armed with discernment it goes to death and illusion; if not discreet, it runs to a catastrophe: *that which begins without order cannot issue in anything.*"

Far be it from us, then, to rejoice unreservedly in this vaguely mystical current which runs through the lyricism of today. What we would first of all clearly deduce from it is, once more, that the religious realities, far from being contemned and ignored as they were forty years ago, are again becoming the primordial concern of all minds. Men are ranging over Catholic dogma, sometimes with sympathy, sometimes with fear, but always with respect. Already such phrases as "unconscious," "intuition," "the will to live" have been abandoned for another—very much perverted from its sense, indeed, but so very symptomatic. That other phrase is "faith," simply that; "faith," the word so discredited but yesterday, considered so unscientific! Here is M. Romain Rolland, a free-thinker, naming one of his works *Tragédies de la Foi* and, for the purpose of incarnating the hero of religious faith, choosing St. Louis. It is a faith evidently besmirched with errors, but after all it is interesting to note that the word is coming back upon the lips of men, that it has reconquered its right of citizenship. M. G. Hanotaux, in his turn, does not hesitate to affirm, in his *Jeanne d'Arc:*

> Between reason and faith there is neither contradiction nor necessary conflict. It belongs to the highest reason to accept faith, and faith incessantly appeals to reason. According to the scholastic formula, faith seeks understanding, and understanding finds faith.

It is no longer fashionable to laugh at mysticism, to regard it as dreams. It attracts and holds men; they seek to derive heroic inspirations and wise lessons from its boldest flights. A Francis of Assisi is surrounded with fervent homage. M. Barrès seeks of St. Teresa and St. Ignatius lights for the discernment of the most complex spiritual states, and, while he transposes, only applies their methods in his *Homme libre.* Such a pagan as d'Annunzio is moved by the profundity of insight of a Catherine of Siena, by the manner, at once lyric and prudent, in which she draws on the most hesitating souls; the works of Ruysbroeck demand a Maeterlinck. An Angela da Foligno, a Tauler, are translated and read with avidity. A great publishing house has commissioned M. Henry Bordeaux to present to the public, in a series in which famous romances are chiefly to be found, the *Introduction à la vie dévote,* and has issued thousands of copies of it. The rival house has this year (1913) countered with an *Imitation de Jésus-Christ.*

Undoubtedly, the mass of readers interpret the mystics in their own way—that is, understand them very badly. To comprehend them, they lack the spiritual tradition of the Church. But are not these promptings of sympathetic curiosity indubitable evidence that at the end of its inductions contemporary reason finds itself obliged to see that there is an infinite reality which surrounds it, engulfs it, supports and nourishes it, and outside of which it cannot but fade away in unsubstantial visions? Is it not a way of confessing after all that to reason is not to create—that in presenting to us only the idea of things, whilst all our being urges us to embrace the reality itself, Kantian idealism gives us but stones instead of bread? Yes, reason understands that abstract metaphysics could never afford any nourishment, and that man must have a kind of revelation which shall place him in intimate relation with beings; reason confesses itself impotent to construct from the ground up a religion, a morality, a system of politics, and, remorseful at having ruined the whole heritage of mankind by laying down the most fantastic laws, it seeks its lost God, ranging through the most obscure manifestations of His will as to being and duration, manifesta-

tions which it names heredity, race and society. Once more, this is the bankruptcy of rationalism. *Reason no longer seeks the pure idea, it seeks pure Being.* It no longer cries out for an ideology, but for an ontology. It calls aloud for *Him who is.* How pathetic is the moment in which it is our lot to live! To whom is reason going to open the gates of the city? What God is it going to recognize as its sovereign?

Its salvation depends on this and on nothing but this. Now it would be foolish to deny the prodigious power of the modern false god who moves forward *more terrible than Moloch.* He is the son of the far-off dreamers of India, and the philosophers of Jena have but dressed him in their own fashion. He has a complete theology and a complete lyric poetry at his service: he is called the Unconscious. This dark and dangerous god has no personal life; he is the weird flower of the human soul, its limitless desire that wanders in all directions; it is the pride of man who believes himself deified because he is mad, and mistakes the vapours of the instinct which leads him astray for the inspiration of the spirit; it is he whom Baillard, in Maurice Barrès' *Colline Inspirée,* strives to possess by communicating with the creative forces which rise up from the fields, when he hugs only his own shadow; it is he, again, whom reason invokes when, failing to possess the true God, it gives itself over to a blind necessity which it calls by turns Progress, the Universe, Nature, Humanity, Justice, Liberty, Life, Love, and which attracts to its worship a religious feeling that has strayed away from its legitimate end. Read Romain Rolland's *Tragédies de la Foi* and you shall see how that lyric, carried away by its revolutionary mysticism, is led into parodying every sacred phrase, every rite, and dedicating sacrifices and whole burnt offerings to its idols. His speech quite naturally employs the terms *Messiah, expiatory victim, martyr, cross, crown of thorns,* and the like.

Such parodies scandalize, at first sight, every soul that loves Christ and His Church. But we must remember the dying words of Jesus: "Father, forgive them, for they know not what they do." Without their knowing it, thinking to advance the evolution of the human soul, as they say, poor things, they are simply beginning over again the eternal rebellion of the fallen archangel. It is the supreme temptation, to wish to attain Being, the first principle of our essence, of our acts, and of all things—even Him whom we call the Father—without any intermediary or mediator; the temptation to be one's own Redeemer, to be the incarnation of God. It is a doctrine full of sorceries, seducing the best. It is not only Romain Rolland who bows before this phantom, there is Maurice Barrès, who speaks to us

> of that admirable vision of the Divine in the world which, under the most modern name, the Unconscious, Philip found in *Le Jardin de Bérénice.*

It is Maeterlinck who in his latest book, *La Mort,* delights in hiding himself from death in the fog of this most barbarous of names, which they call the most modern; it is the Comtesse de Noailles who, in her *Les Vivants et les Morts,* a work so unspeakably moving, cries out with magnificent ingenuousness to what she thinks to be God:

> I cannot explain it, but Thy supreme brightness seems like my reflection in the lake of a Paradise. One evening I saw Thee like myself, on the road where my body was grown large through the shadow. . . . It is ever oneself that one seeks when one thinks to escape oneself; one would wish to repose in its blessed arms . . .

A terrible annihilation, at the end of which one would but hug death! But there precisely is the stumbling block of the lyricism of the Unconscious, the wall against which it is fated to dash itself to pieces. After reaching the extreme point of its desire, it will have to define its object; there remain but two alternatives for it: either a mortal doubling-back upon itself, the raving, anarchic delirium of all the powers of humanity, or the cry of deliverance to the God of Abraham, of Isaac, and of Jacob, Whom Pascal invoked, the personal God, the eternal Being distinct from us, Who frees us from ourselves. This dilemma our generation is actually living. It is the pathetic drama which has been enacted in all of us, and which is still being enacted in thousands of young minds. Happy are they who have slowly but surely freed themselves, through Catholic theology, from the horrible slavery in which this doctrine of shadows holds us—those who have already turned to the pure, true voices which rise swelling, and who will in the end, we are certain, dominate all the other voices. It is such as Claudel, Jammes, Le Cardonnel, Péguy that give back in the face of the astonished century imperturbable testimony to the Incarnate Word, unsealing our eyes to the abyss that yawns at our feet. The whole of their work proclaims that Christ alone can save us from ourselves and make us live, that He alone can pronounce over the tomb of Lazarus the liberating words: "Come forth, come forth from the cult of your Ego, and come to us, the Father and Son in the unity of the Spirit." Their work proclaims that Christ is the light that enlighteneth every man that cometh into this world, that he who thinks himself wise apart from Christ, he who thinks to find the truth outside of Him *through whom all things were made,* he who refuses Him His real, incarnate, eucharistic existence,—he repulses all the light, extinguishes all understanding in himself, and annihilates himself in a pantheism from which there is no issue.

In presence of this sublime hymn, some are disconcerted by the new technic employed in its interpretation, smile and shrug their shoulders. Nevertheless, the young, who go deep into things, for whom literature is no simple, banal display of elegance—those who lean over their books eager for, and unsatisfied by, the teaching or, rather, the absence of teaching, that falls from the official chairs—the young hasten to listen to these voices with inexpressible emotion; they feel their purer infancy reawakening in them, and as it were the eternal youth of the world. This lyricism persuades them, it gives them the orientation of their hearts which have for so long been lost in inextricable shadows. Here they find, for the first time, lyrics which offer them no disquieting potions, no deadly philters, but the bread and wine of the family table.

It is not difficult to find—in Lamartine or Hugo, for example—beautiful religious inspirations, but they come as it were by accident; at one moment their lyre vibrates to the wind from the everlasting hills, but the next moment they will be singing, with just as much earnestness, of passion or of pantheistic dreams; their prayers and meditations are often directed to a perfectly abstract Infinite; God is an idea of perfection, of goodness, of justice, not a living being present in us. They sing of God from outside the temple. On the contrary, open the *Magnificat* of Claudel, listen to these new accents or, rather, these revived accents:

> O my God, you have called me by my name, as one who knows it, chosen me amongst all those of my age. You know, my God, how full of affection is the heart of the young, and how they are not obstinate in their impurity and their vanity. And, behold, on a sudden you are someone!

Here is the great revelation. God is no longer a vague, uncertain spiritualistic conception, He is *someone who speaks to us, and we to Him;* He is the Father and the Friend; He has made with us an alliance which nothing can undo; we have His promise for it; He has repeated it without ceasing to His faithful, and His words are recorded in the Book of His Covenants. "All that is," Ruysbroeck had exclaimed, "is God or creature;" there is, therefore, nothing outside of these relations between the uncreated Being and creatures. Everything else is entity, abstraction, nothingness. There is no real metaphysics outside of theology, and the true name of that is mystical theology. Such is the philosophy of Claudel, and his aesthetics is only the natural flowering of his faith.

We must go back to Dante to find a poet possessing in so rare a degree the profound feeling and the touch, as it were, of the Divine Presence. In his work the visible worlds are penetrated and impregnated with, and lifted up by the invisible virtues; matter is forever groaning with Providential thought. And the eternal order shines forth in it; at every moment we plunge into the heart of Divine love. Christ is not summarily and confusedly the just man charged with the sins of the world, the Son made an oblation to the offended Father; He is, even antecedently to the mystery of redemption, the firstborn Man, the new Adam from among the dead, in whom we are all of us, substantially, crucified. To be united to Christ is to be deified, because in Him, and in Him alone, at once God and Man, the marriage of Being and His creatures can be consummated. In Him alone, and through Him alone, we rise to our Beginning, the Father, the *actus purus.* A sublime system of metaphysics, very far removed indeed from modern philosophy! It is the great drama of creation, the pursuit of the lost sheep, the call of the Spouse from beyond the hills; it is the groaning of the outraged Beloved, His anger, His mercy. It is the incomparable dialogue between God and man—"And, behold, on a sudden you are someone!"—behind the vain phantoms born of the sophists' imaginations and those that make systems! The world, the world of bodies and spirits, is restored to us in its integrity. And the poet intones his canticle, which is truly the symbol of Catholic poetry and of all truly sacred poetry.

> Blessed be Thou, my God, who has delivered me from the idols, who makest me to adore only Thee, and not Isis and Osiris, or Justice, or Progress, or Truth, or Divinity, or Humanity, or the laws of Nature, or Art, or Beauty; and who hast not suffered all these things to exist, which are not, or which are the void left by the absence of Thee. Even as the savage that buildeth himself a canoe and from what is left of the same piece of wood fashions Apollo, thus do all the speakers of words; from the surplus of their adjectives they have made insubstantial monsters more hollow than Moloch, devourers of babes, more cruel and more hideous than Moloch. A sound they have, but not a voice; a name, and there is no person. And there is the unclean spirit that filleth the waste places and all the things that are empty. Lord, Thou has delivered me from books and from ideas, from the idols and their priests, neither hast Thou suffered Israel to serve under the yoke of the effeminate. I know that Thou art not the God of the dead, but of the living. I will not pay honour to the phantoms and the puppets, neither Diana, nor Duty, nor Liberty, nor Apis the ox. And your 'geniuses' and your 'heroes,' your great men and your supermen, the same horror of all these formless things; for I am not free among the dead, but I exist among the things that are, and I force them to hold me indispensable, and I desire not to be superior to anything, but to be a just man—just as Thou are perfect—just and living among the other real spirits.

Here then is the man, the just man, such, that is, as he should be and where he should be; here is the true hero, no longer the useless, sickly dreamer, the being of caprice linking us with romanticism, but the conqueror and the apostle, the priest or cathedral-builder, cultivator or tamer of the multitudes, who has scorned enjoyment and never lingers, but ever plunges into the most burning current of life and bravely throws the weight of his will into the balance of events. In him he has a power of life which he wishes to dispense, which only the absolute will satisfy. This is man in his majesty as a predestined creature, as David evokes him in the eighth Psalm:

> Thou hast set him a little lower than the angels. Thou hast given him the empire over the works of Thy hands. Thou hast crowned him with glory and honour.

He that will grow into the infinite perpetually feels in him that secret being which Claudel calls "the germinal means, the innermost grain, the seed of our own proper name." And again, in another place: "This life of mine, this thing not married, not born, the function which is above myself." Woe betide him if he turns it aside from

its end and aim, which is God, and makes it but a food to nourish his own pride; he shall die miserably, like *Tête-d'Or,* and all his labour shall disappear in nothingness. On the contrary, if, like Violaine, one's soul murmurs, "Behold the handmaid of the Lord," in answer to the angel's announcement, it shall know the ineffable joy of possession; it shall receive, as Violaine expresses it:

> More than an answer, the drawing forth of all my substance. Like the secret shut up in the heart of the planets, the due relation of my being to a greater being.

Here below we have but one rôle to play: to accomplish the task assigned to us, to take the part which is assigned us by the office that is incessantly sending for us. Let us set out for our Father's house, considering each advancing day the messenger of God; all brings us to Him, sorrow as well as joy; it is not for us to choose the road. Let us follow the Son of Man, who tells us, as of yore He told Peter: "I will lead thee whither thou wouldst not." The essential here below is, to be in God's hand, to leave ourselves there in order that we may co-operate in the Redemption by crucifying ourselves, in imitation of Jesus Christ, upon the cross of our miseries. In this state is no shame, no night, no death, only a continual exaltation in the eternal Being from Whom nothing can separate us.

> Hail to thee, O world so bounteous in my eyes. I know by what thou comest to be present. It is because the Eternal is with thee, where the creature is the Creator has nowise left it.

Such is Claudel in his great lyric passages. Here we are at the first sources of all poetry. It is Claudel's magnificent gift to be incessantly bringing us thither, to set us, according to his own expression, "on the very pulse of Being."

Where Claudel is of the kindred of St. Thomas, Francis Jammes is related rather to St. Francis. We already owed him much. He it was who, just when poetry was mad with the extravagancies of symbolism, caused the voice of the child to be heard, a fresh voice that sang with the greatest simplicity about things that are. It did not invoke the gods, boasted of no aesthetic theories; it told the adventures of the everyday walk abroad, of the little donkey going to market, of the cart with the sheep bleating in it because its feet were hurt by the ropes that tied it, of the geese trooping along the road and cackling as they went, the sparrows strung out along the telegraph wire, the kitchen garden that knows the sun. This note seemed so new, in an age accustomed to bookish verse, that people thought a new Rousseau had come into existence, that nature was once more given to us in her entirety, with her sap and her smells, her lights and her greenery. This poet, not at all touched by the pantheistic atmosphere which at the time impregnated all the sensitive faculties, as far removed from the romantic overflowing of the personality as from Parnassian annihilation in the great All, he alone considered creatures as having a distinct life, an individual being, beautiful every one of them, and all worthy of love and admiration because they all showed forth this miracle—*being.*

It was his daily joy to see them, and he could never tire of telling us about it: the commonest stone on the road, the poorest weed by the roadside, held his attention. For him the universe was an immense Noah's ark, with flowers, fruits, plants, beasts and men, all painted and articulated; and above all this was the sky, like a canopy embroidered with clouds, or with smooth blue and a great sun in the middle, during the day, and a white moon and thousands of stars during the night. Jammes is full of astonishment at all this; he does not describe, he sings; the commonest words become ennobled in passing through his mouth and take on a splendid gravity of which we had been unaware, an unknown and venerable sense, the sense that God Himself gave them.

Let us go with this poet along the village street, its pavement cluttered. with dirty children, between dark, stuffy cottages, such a street as he has described in an immortal elegy, *Deuil des Primevères:*

> The scene was so humble, where you were so fair.

The whole of Jammes is in that line, all the great gift of love that he has given to the earth, all the humble outpouring which we had not heard in such tones since Francis of Assisi.

This love,—let us call it by its true name—this charity was quite the best way to go to God. And no one was astonished to learn that Jammes, walking with his dog along the road, had, like a shepherd of primitive times, gone into the *Eglise habillée de feuilles;* the swallows of course had made their nest there, and the blind man at the door was of course shaking his tin cup. He had not to change his voice or raise its pitch; with his rosary in his hand, he had knelt, had confessed his sins and gone up to the holy table with the servant-girls and the old women. And as he had admired the visible universe, he admired just as simply, with the same great humility, the invisible universe; he did not go wandering among intellectual subtleties, but looked in silence, weeping with love, as the work of grace and the mystery of the Eucharist purified his heart and ripened in him magnificent fruits. With docility he surrendered himself, only listening to those unspeakable groanings of which St. Paul speaks, and faithfully expressing them, thus giving us utterances of the deepest and most wholesome mysticism. His eyes saw farther than they had seen; they saw as far as God Himself, not the abstract, distant God, but a God in whom all things live, and move, and exist, a God who is careful of his creature, who keeps account of the sparrow's feathers and the hairs of our heads, a God whose glory he read every moment in the face of the sun and the opening of the flower, whose love he read in the roadside crosses, in the silence of the churches, at the bedsides of the people, and in the downcast eyes of poor women. His vision was not changed, it was enlarged and transfigured, it saw as far as the glorious resurrection, it saw as far as the new

heavens and the new earth foretold by Scripture, and inspired by this certitude, he cried out to the creatures he had so loved:

> Blessedness for you, O rose-bedecked hedges, O gilded Junes, O balmy odours and sombre verdures of the shy woods! For love shall touch you with its eternity.

And after that time Francis Jammes lived only in this transfigured love.

In his last poem, *Géorgiques chrétiennes,* we find him offering up to God the brilliant and robust work of his maturity. It has by no means deceived our expectations, but on the threshold of the century bears witness to the wonderful Catholic revival manifesting itself in the domains of art. Less than thirty years after Zola's *La Terre,* he reconsecrates the soil to its Creator. Whether under the veil of figurative speech or in reality, it is indeed the Eucharist that this poem of the Bread and the Wine celebrates, and there is not a verse of it but brings us the presence of God felt and savoured in the humblest daily task. The reader will pardon us if we quote the invocation to Bernadette:

> On the seventh of January, year eighteen hundred and forty-four, Bernadette brought light to the most obscure of creatures. She was born of the Soubirous, in a mill that fell short of affording them bread. Timid, patient, intelligent and good, from eight years of age she went to watch in the pastures. Grotto of Massabielle! Forever do flocks, but human flocks, take the place of the lambs. Where a hundred thousand tapers burn today, there was a corner lifted of the curtain of heaven; this child saw the Virgin. What God denies to the most powerful here below with it He dazzled this soul of but fourteen years. The eglantine clasped beneath the feet we honour. Bernadette turned pale, her eyes fixed upon this outburst of light. Thereupon all the nations, their voices broken with sobs, fall down with arms extended in prayer; and the groans of human sorrow have taken the place of the bleatings of pastured sheep; and the mother shows to the Mother her dying son; leprosy is healed in the pellucid stream; and the inmost sorrow hidden in us is poured forth in the holy fragrance of the valley; and the artist, escaping his last peril, lays down all his pride in presence of an artless art. There in the solemn grandeur of night I have seen a population encamped, sleeping on the grass; that night I saw a bishop officiating at the altar beneath lights which the heavens carried as they moved in their course, and I saw that population rise like one man turning to the God in whom death is for ever ended. It was you, Bernadette, poor girl on bended knees, you who, being dead, in your turn revealed yourself to us.

One would wish, for the sake of its teaching, that a book like the *Géorgiques chrétiennes* might be scattered broadcast through our schools and our homes. In its splendid simplicity it has all the quality of the popular song: variety of episodes, abundance and brilliancy of images. Far removed from rhetorical vanities, it blooms like a flower of the fields in which there burns all the fire of summer.

In Charles Péguy's books we get the same Catholic vision, still infinite love, the God of the Catechism loved in the heart of each man, felt and tasted in every one of His creatures. Of small importance are all the objections which may be raised in detail about the misuse of repetitions, a rather artificial and, indeed, puerile practice which the author could justify in many places. Those brusque repetitions, that obstinate, awkward insistence, that greedy dwelling upon words, all contribute to impart an impression of homespun roughness to the charm of which, I must admit, I am not insensible. But let us pass over these questions of literary taste and stick to the intimate strength of the work, its singular power in a sceptical and emasculated age, a power that seems to spring straight from the Middle Ages—from the soul of some Villon inspired with a Dantesque vision to reveal to us the invisible worlds in the simple, everyday language of a child playing hop-scotch, or a servant-girl sweeping out her kitchen, or a shepherdess spinning, the lowly language of old time cottages where the pot steamed, where duty was always apparent, tangible, imperious, in the mean, repellent, monotonous, truly heroic task.

In the presence of Jeanne's bitter sorrow, little Hauviette exclaims:

> You see, you see what all the rest of us know. You see it. You see what they are telling us. Catechism, the whole Catechism, and Church, and Mass, you don't know it, you see it, and your praying you don't do it, you only see the prayers. There's no weeks for you. There's no days. There's no days in the week, and no hours in the day. All the hours strike for you the same as the Angelus bell. All the days are Sundays—more than Sundays,—and Sundays more than Sundays, and more than Christmas Sunday and Easter Sunday, and Mass more than Mass.

It seems to me that we shall have to thank Claudel, Jammes and Péguy for curing our sensibilities of their feverish disorder, for they alone, reawakening our innermost energies, the most secret recess of our being, our very substance engendered by God, and by thus binding together again the great Catholic tradition of the Middle Ages, have known how to give back to us something beyond all the pantheistic efflorescence—the reality of Being and of that providential order which is traced here below and realized beyond this life in the integrity of all substance. And for this reason, leaving the many to linger before the stages upon which the favourites of the hour are strutting, a whole generation is being carried away after them and is singing the hymn that Jammes set ringing last year on the boards of the Théatre de l'Oeuvre in the *Brebis égarée:*

> You will not be happy if you live away from God. Too long have we been afraid to mention Our Lord's name. I will take it out of the shadow, even if I do it alone, before the crowd. For it is always alive, and it speaks to us at this moment. Younger than youth itself, it gives us nourishment at Mass. And here, on the horizon, behold a generation. It knows where is strength, and it is coming out of its bark. And it bursts into flower and comes back to you, O Lord! It is coming back with its eyes upon Your Cross. For You are, we know, He who is. It has conquered its pride, and, behold, it stands already at the threshold.

Yes, here is the threshold—our Father's house at last. It is the threshold of no superb palace, one of those proud monstrous monuments in which one is so cold and so lonely; *it is the threshold of a stable;* but in that stable radiates the glory of Him who has overcome the world; and this generation that has set out to go thither, guided by the star and the singing of angels, you can see it. As in the old pictures of the Nativity, shepherds and kings of the Magi are bringing their gifts. The generation "has conquered its pride, and, behold, it stands already at the threshold." One brings myrrh and balsam; another, bread, wine and the fruits he has taken from the rustic table of his dwelling; another, the flowers of his Christian childhood, gathered by the paths of the family domain, on the steps of the altar, by the college walks, when, in the enchanting silence after Vespers were ended, the incense was still mingling its smoke with the odour of extinguished tapers; another lays down branches of oak, moist with sap, freshly plucked from its native forests, another runs from the deserts of Africa to offer his sword—they come without end. And all these youthful forms prostrate themselves before the Emmanuel, the newborn child in whom they behold the eternal purity of Being, the Divine Infancy radiating beyond all the systems of men, and they sing the old Noël of bygone days:

> *Il est né, le divin Enfant.*
> *Chantez hautbois; résonnez musettes. . . .*

Yes, He is born at last, He for whom we waited; He is born in our French literature, in our lyric poetry; the freshening dew has fallen. He has been given to us who knows not evil and sees the truth. He is born, the Divine Child who triumphs over our old doubts and our desiccated argumentations. He is born, the Child who knows not how to lie, the Child who knows how to repose in peace in the tranquillity of the eternal order. He is born, the Child who proclaims life, who proclaims hope, who proclaims Being. He is born, the Divine Child, and that not only in time and space, but in us ourselves forever, and merely by opening his blessed eyes he drives out of us old age, and scepticism, and doubt, and darkness, and death.

Madame Mary Duclaux (essay date 1919)

SOURCE: "Francis Jammes," in *Twentieth Century French Writers,* W. Collins Sons & Co. Ltd., 1919, pp. 98-114.

[*In the following essay, Duclaux discusses Jammes's conversion to Catholicism and its influence on his writing.*]

Francis Jammes is a Faun who has turned Franciscan Friar. As we read his early poems, his delicious rustic prose, we seem to see him sitting prick-eared, in some green circle of the Pyrenees, with brown hands holding to his mouth a boxwood flute, from which he draws a brief, sweet music, as pure as the long-drawn note of the musical frog, as shrill as the plaintive cry of some mountain bird who feels above its nest the shadow of the falcon.

And then he met Paul Claudel and was converted.

After all, little was changed, for his innocent paganism had been tinged with natural piety, and in his religion he might say, like the Almighty, in the **Roman de Lièvre,**—

> J'aime la terre d'un profond amour. J'aime la terre
> des hommes, des bêtes, des plantes et des pierres.

Only henceforth we see him, in our imagination, like Saint Francis, with a monk's hood drawn over his brow, sandals on his feet, his brown gown cinctured with a knotted cord, a couple of doves hovering over his shoulders, and, at his side, fawning and faithful, a converted wolf. . . .

I met M. Jammes at Madame Daudet's house one winter, and, in fact, his appearance was not wholly unlike this fancy portrait. The gown was a brown woollen suit, but just the Franciscan colour. Above the ruddy, jocund, rustic face, a crown of grizzling curls, behind which Nature had provided the tonsure. Neither dove nor wolf, but, in their stead, all the young Catholic poets of Paris, pressed in serried ranks to meet the Master who, for a few days, had consented to quit his belovèd solitude of Orthez.

We can remember a different Francis Jammes. The poet has said of himself, 'My soul is half the soul of a Faun, and half the soul of a young girl.' But let me quote an admirable strophe from his **'Le Poète et sa Femme':**—

> Il est de ceux qui voient les parfums et il sent
>   Les couleurs. Et il s'intéresse
> Au scarabée cornu, au hérisson piquant,
>   Et aux plantes des doctoresses.
> Mais le voici, avec sa figure camuse
>   Et son sourire de sylvain,
> Fatigué par l'amour bien plus que par les muses
>   Qui aiment son cœur incertain . . .
> Lui-même est un Silène, on le voit au jardin
>   Veiller au légume, à la treille. . . .

This gentle Francis Jammes recalls sometimes the charming La Fontaine, and also Verlaine. A La Fontaine bereft of his philosophy, his deep knowledge of human nature; a Verlaine from whom the taint of corruption has been washed and therewith his terrible sincerity. And if we can imagine these two great poets mulcted so utterly in their essential substance, the residue in them, too, might re-

mind us of a Faun and a young girl—a mischievous, experienced rustic maid, yet holding in her arms a bunch of lilies. The first prose study of our poet—which still remains one of his most exquisite pages—is the story of a young girl, **Clara d'Ellébeuse.** What a delightful book! It is the sort of little story one can read a dozen times in a dozen years, and find it as affecting the last time as the first.

If any attentive student should feel inclined, having read these pages, to fill a shelf with some selected volumes of these modern French writers—with *Colette Baudoche,* for example, from among the novels of Barrès, and *Antoinette* from Romain Rolland; with *La Jeune Fille Violaine* from Paul Claudel; with *La Porte Etroite* from André Gide; to which he might add *La Jeune Fille Bien Elevée* from the works of René Boylesve; *L'Ombre de l'Amour* by Madame Tinayre; *Marie-Claire* by Marguerite Audoux; and the young girls of Francis Jammes, especially **Clara d'Ellébeuse,**—what an idea, what an admirable, unconventional idea such a reader would get of the young French girl! What a gift, at once instructive and delightful, he could make to some young English girl on, say, her five-and-twentieth birthday!

Francis Jammes has spent nearly all his life in or near that little town of Orthez (in the department of the Lower Pyrenees), where he was born about 1869. In that part of France, almost as much as in Ireland, Protestants and Catholics divide society pretty equally. Our poet was born and baptized a Catholic, but many of his nearest relations were Huguenots, and, seeing so much of both sides, he does not seem to have taken either very seriously. He showed no particular precocity and, though he began to write poetry, like most people, in his twentieth year, he made his real debut only in 1898, with a volume called **De l'Angelus de l'Aube, à l'Angelus du soir.**

A certain langour mixed with fervour ran in his blood. He had inherited Creole traditions. His grandfather, the doctor, and his grand-uncle had emigrated from Béarn to Guadeloupe, and had settled there, had died there; his father was sent back to France to be educated at seven years of age; his dim memories of the Antilles, his stories of the cousins in Martinique, and the little chair in rare colonial wood that the child had used on the passage, were, a generation later, to set a-dreaming another child, our poet, whose first heroine will belong, like him, to a family dispersed among the Atlantic Islands and the Pyrenees.

I suppose that a doctor would describe Clara d'Ellébeuse as a victim of the *maladie du scrupule.* She is a girl of sixteen; a dear little old-fashioned girl, living in a dear little old-fashioned manor, sheltered among the foothills of the Pyrenees, towards 1848. She has that dread of sin, of impurity, as a sort of quagmire into which one may fall unawares and be lost for ever, which the practice of confession may exaggerate, or palliate, according to the wisdom of the confessor. (Our poet Cowper was no Catholic.) Poor Clara d'Ellébeuse, because one day the young poet she secretly adored had wiped away her nervous tears and laid upon her bowed nape a pitiful, respectful hand, imagines that she has fallen into the sin of unchastity and that she is with child! (And we think of Renan who, in his twelfth year, I think, accused himself in confession of 'the sin of simony.')

The mischief with Clara is that she does not confess; she tells no kind elder of her secret fear; she lets concealment feed, like a worm in the bud, upon her damask cheek. And we know how that ends. Clara does not pine away. One day in March, overcome by horror and remorse for her imaginary crime, she drinks a dose of laudanum and quits this unkind world.

In telling the pathetic history of Clara d'Ellébeuse, Francis Jammes left unhampered that half of his soul which is that of a young girl; but in narrating the fate of *Almaïde d'Etremont, jeune fille passionnée,* that other half (which belongs to a Faun) shows the cloven foot. More tenderly does he commemorate the sad life of *Pomme d'anis, jeune fille infirme.*

But it is not to be supposed that a poet who, by his own showing, partakes so largely of the nature of Silenus and his Sylvans, should frequent exclusively the society of virgins. Some of his earlier poems betray an ardent sensuality. One cannot read either these or the *Notes* printed in the volume called *Le Roman du Lièvre* (or even, perhaps, that most touching idyll of a play: *La Brebis Egarée*) without feeling that the poet's experience has lain also among the lost sheep . . . among the lost sheep, and perhaps among the swine; for there was a moment when he was even as the Prodigal Son!

In 1913, making a general confession of those past errors (oddly enough) to a reporter of *Le Temps,* Francis Jammes recalled their bitterness. Nothing except a love story is so interesting as the true history of a conversion—I give this one therefore without apology, though it appeared for the first time in a newspaper (November 3, 1913).

> 'Je me suis converti le 7 juillet, 1905, commence M. Francis Jammes lorsque je lui demande s'il n'est pas indiscret que je cherche à savoir comment sa pensée évolua de l'indifférence à la ferveur.'

> 'Vous n'étiez pas catholique?'

> 'De baptême? Si. Mais pas davantage, avec des sympathies pour les beaux motifs littéraires du catholicisme, avec beaucoup de dédain pour ce que j'appelais, pour ce que je n'appelle plus le catholicisme des vieilles femmes. J'étais un païen, un véritable faune. Les fleurs, les bois, les femmes! J'avais la passion de tout ce qui existait; il n'y avait pas dans toute la nature de gamin plus déchaîné; j'aimais tellement la vie que la seule pensée de la quitter un jour me paraissait un épouvantable blasphème.'

> 'Et vous ne l'aimez plus?'

> 'Plus de la même manière.'

> 'Ce fut un coup de la grâce?'

> 'Non. Avant la grâce, il y eut les épreuves et il y eut Claudel. . . . Claudel, dont, par l'intermédiaire d'un de ses anciens camarades de classe, Marcel Schwob, je devins l'ami à l'époque faunesque où je battais les buissons . . .

Claudel! Le poète prononce ce nom avec une émotion et une admiration touchantes.

> 'Claudel! Je n'oublierai jamais, raconte M. Francis Jammes lyrique, ma première entrevue avec lui; il était déjà grand pour quelques-uns d'entre nous. Je vois encore cette petite chambre où l'on nous introduisit, mon camarade et moi. C'était une sorte de cellule nue; trois choses attirèrent mon regard, les seules: un chapelet, l'*Appel au soldat* de Barrès, et un paroissien de vieille femme. Il parut. Le marbre romain allait parler. Il avait de l'antipathie pour la personne qui m'accompagnait: j'entends le son sec et tranchant de ses brèves réponses. Le lendemain je déjeunai avec Schwob et lui. Le marbre, resté glacial la veille, s'anima: ce fut pour moi un émerveillement. Le catholicisme entrait dans ma vie.'

> 'Le faune avait des inquiétudes?'

> 'Le faune était tenace. Mais insensiblement je commençais à me demander: où est la vérité? Et de ne pas la connaître, de sentir une limite à l'homme, j'éprouvais une impression pénible, je découvrais un ver dans la pomme. Je m'apercevais qu'il y avait une force dans la vie et que cette force je ne la possédais pas.'

> 'J'étais dans cet état de désillusion et de doute quand je fus la victime d'une crise morale affreuse. Je tombai dans le désarroi le plus complet. J'avais demandé à un des mes amis de Bordeaux l'hospitalité et je m'abandonnai à ma détresse; c'est alors que par un bienfait de Dieu une lettre de Claudel nous parvint, une lettre admirable de consolation et d'enseignement. Je fus frappé, je réfléchis. Si cette vie que j'aime tant, me disais-je, ne me donne pas son explication, elle n'est qu'une horreur, nous sommes dans un hôpital de fous; j'allai à la cathédrale, longtemps je pleurai: le travail de la grâce s'opérait en moi.

> 'Je rentrai à Orthez. Ce que la lettre de Claudel avait commencé, la parole de Claudel devait le finir. J'eus bientôt le bonheur de le voir arriver; il me parla du catholicisme en grand philosophe, en savant. Ensemble nous priâmes. J'étais au fond du fossé, mourant, anéanti. Je me relevai guéri, suavé. Le 7 juillet, 1905, je me confessai, je communiai; Claudel, mon ange gardien, servait la messe. Depuis lors j'ai retrouvé tout ce qui me manquait, j'ai récupéré la joie. Après avoir traversé d'âpres solitudes, j'ai la joie de la certitude, l'explication de ma vie. Je suis catholique!'

Dans l'espace, M. Francis Jammes lance cette profession de foi comme un cri de triomphe.

'Catholique pour de bon, insistai-je, pratiquant? La foi totale, absolue, obéissante?

'La foi du dernier savetier. Je ne suis pas un néo-chrétien. Je pratique, comme vous dites, j'observe tous les préceptes de l'Eglise, ma mère. . . . Je sais: on rit, vous riez des dévotionnettes. J'en ai ri jadis moi-même. Je me les suis expliquées. L'Eglise ne les aurait peut-être pas imposées si tous les hommes étaient des Pascal et des Claudel. Mais l'humanité n'est pas composée que de Pascal et de Claudel. Ces pratiques, ces observances sont comme des nœuds au mouchoir, elles constituent, en quelque manière, un rappel à la vertu et à la piété. L'Eglise les a jugées nécessaires ou utiles. Je m'incline sans discussion. Cette attitude a déconcerté certains hommes qui n'ont rien de catholique mais qui veulent exploiter le catholicisme au profit d'un système politique. Quand on a la flamme de la foi, comme je l'ai, on trouve humiliante cette exploitation. Nous, nous sommes catholiques foncièrement, par-dessus tout.

'Vous parlez comme si vous étiez certain de posséder la vérité.'

'Je la possède. Je suis dans la vérité puisque la sécurité où je suis est si bonne! Il n'y a rien dans le monde à quoi je puisse comparer le bonheur que ma foi me donne. J'y tiens davantage qu'à la vie elle-même. J'ai été comme un verger où le vent a passé, maintenant je suis un verger doré avec de beaux fruits.

'Et comme j'esquissais un discret sourire de scepticisme, M. Francis Jammes me regarda avec infiniment de générosité.

'Je vous souhaite le bonheur que j'ai.'

'I was converted on the 7th of July, 1905,' began M. Francis Jammes, when I asked him if I were not indiscreet in seeking to trace the progress of his mind from indifference to fervour.

'You were not always a Catholic?'

'I was christened a Catholic, but that was about all: that, and a sort of sympathy for the fine literary themes afforded by the Church, mixed by much disdain for what I no longer call the "churchiness" of old women. I was a Pagan, a veritable Faun! Flowers, forests, women—I was in love with all that lived! In all Nature there was not a merrier young vagabond alive. Life was so delightful in my eyes that the very idea of one day quitting all that, seemed to me a frightful blasphemy.'

'And you are no longer so much in love with Life?'

'Not in the same way.'

'You were changed by a sudden flash of grace?'

'No; there were trials before the Grace of God touched me; and there was Claudel, too, . . . Claudel with whom I made friends (through one

of his old schoolfellows, Marcel Schwob) when I was still a Faun, haunting the thickets.

(Claudel! The poet pronounces the name with a touching admiration and emotion.)

'Claudel! I shall never forget our first interview. He was already a great writer in the eyes of a little clan. I still see the small room into which we were shown, my friend and I. It was a sort of bare cell: three things attracted my attention, a rosary, an old woman's prayer-book, and Barrès's *Appel au Soldat*. And then Claudel came in. It was as if a Roman bust were to move its lips and speak. He disliked the person who accompanied me, and I remember the harsh cut-and-dry tone of his short answers. But the next day I lunched with him and Schwob; and the icy marble softened into flesh and blood. I was lost in wonder, a sort of happy astonishment. Catholicism had entered into my life. . . .'

'The Faun began to feel anxious?'

'The Faun stood firm! But, little by little, I began to ask myself: Where lies the Truth? And the sense of my ignorance, that feeling of a limit to what man can do and be, was the canker in the fruit. I felt there was a force in Life—a force that I did not possess.

'And while in that state of doubt and disillusion, I was overtaken by a cruel moral crisis. I wallowed in the Slough of Despond. One of my friends lived at Bordeaux; I went to stay with him, and it was there that, by God's grace, I received a letter from Claudel. Such an admirable letter, full of consolation and instruction! I was struck by it. And I pondered it in my heart. "If this dear life," said I, "that I so love, remains a riddle, if there is no answer to our questions, then away with it! Life is a horror, a madhouse!" I went to the Cathedral, and for a long while I wept; the miracle of grace began to operate in my soul.

'I returned to my home at Orthez. That which Claudel's letter had begun, speech with Claudel was to effectuate. He came; he spoke to me of religion like a great philosopher, like a man of science, too; and we prayed together. I was in the bottom of the pit, dying, dejected. On the 7th of July, 1905, I went to confession, I received the Communion; Claudel, my guardian angel, served the Mass. Since then I have found all that I missed in life; I have recovered my delight. After the harshest solitudes I have come to a place of certainty: I am a Catholic!'

(And M. Jammes flings this cry forth into space, like a chant of triumph.)

'A real thorough-going Catholic?' said I; 'absolute, obedient faith?'

'The faith of a cobbler! I am no neo-Christian; I practise all the precepts of the Church I know. You smile (I used to smile) at certain observances.

The Church would not have enjoined them if all the faithful stood on the intellectual level of a Pascal or a Claudel. But humanity is not made up of Pascals and Claudels. These minor practices are just knots in our handkerchief, lest we forget! The Church thinks them necessary; I bow to her decision. I know this attitude seems disconcerting to certain persons, who really are not Catholics at all, but would like to exploit the Church in favour of a political system. But, when the flame of faith is lit in our hearts, we scorn to be the catspaw of a politician. We are just Catholics.'

'You speak as though you were sure of possessing Truth itself!'

'So I am; Truth is my heritage, since I find my security so good! Nothing in Life is comparable to the happiness which I derive from my religion; it is dearer to me than life itself! I was as an orchard harassed by the wind; and now I am an orchard golden with ripe fruit.'

So spake Francis Jammes. I smiled the slight smile of the sceptic. The poet glanced at me with an infinite generosity.

'I wish you the same happiness!' he said.

–Elie-Joseph Bois, *Le Temps,* Nov. 3, 1913.

But this conversion has not greatly changed the nature of the poet. His verse is still fresh with the fragrance of wild thyme newly wet with dew. He continues to sing his happy valley, with the mountain towering up behind, right into the blueness of the sky. Only, in his landscape, he gives more prominence to the village church, garlanded with yellow roses: **'L'Eglise habillée de Feuilles.'**

> Par cette grande paix que l'homme cherche en soi;
> Par les jours finissants aux vieux balcons de bois
> Où le cœur noir des géraniums blancs s'attriste;
> Par l'obscure douceur des choses villageoises;
> Par les pigeons couleur d'arc-en-ciel et d'ardoise;
> Par le chien dont la tête humble nous invite
> A lui passer la main dessus; par tout cela:
> Chapelle, sois bénie à l'ombre de ton bois!

His verse has still its candour, its ingenuous freshness, its Franciscan simplicity:—

> Je prendrai mon bâton et sur la grande route
> J'irai, et je dirai aux ânes, nos amis:
> Je suis Francis Jammes et je vais au Paradis.
> Car il n'y a pas d'enfer au pays du Bon Dieu.

And yet so great a change has necessarily had its repercussion in the very form of the poet's art: Francis Jammes is no longer a *ver-librist.* Having accepted a discipline for his soul, he may well admit one for his muse. He would no longer write:—

> J'avais été assez éprouvé pour connaître
> Le bonheur de finir ses jours dans la retraite;

and think he had done his duty by the rhyme. He would not now content himself with the loose and lazy assonance of a verse (a beautiful verse) like the following:—

> Accablé, je m'étais assis, tant les ajoncs
>   Étaient impénétrables.
> Quand j'eus équilibré mon fusil contre un arbre,
>   Je relevai le front.

His last charming volume of Bucolics, **Les Géorgiques Chrétiennes,** is written in rhymed Alexandrines, which differ only from those of classic French poetry in a few innocent and agreeable liberties—a plural and a singular being allowed to rhyme together, the mute E not counting where it is not pronounced. It is a pleasant form of verse. The picture of the harvesting angels whirling in the sky, which opens the poem, has the rich colour and the large facility of a fresco by Correggio—say, the Assumption at Parma. It is beautiful with a calm beauty:—

> De temps en temps l'un de ces anges touchaient terre
> Et buvait à la cruche une gorgée d'eau claire.
>
> Sa joue était pareille à la rouge moitié
> De la pomme qui est l'honneur de compotier.
>
> Il reprenait son vol, et d'abord sa faucille.
> Quelque autre alors foulait l'ombre qui fait
>   des grilles.
>
> Ou tous ils descendaient ensemble, ou bien encor
> Ensemble reprenaient avec calme l'essor.
>
> Chacun avait passé le bras à sa corbeille
> Dont les tresses formaient comme un essaim
>   d'abeilles
>
> Clarté fondue à la clarté, ces travailleurs
> Récoltaient du froment la plus pure des fleurs.
>
> Ils venaient visiter sur ce coin de la Terre
> La beauté que Dieu donne à la vie ordinaire.

One of my friends, who is Professor of Rhetoric (Modern Literature) in a High School, tells me that the enthusiasm of her scholars for Francis Jammes is a thing touching to behold—for we of a bygone generation can never quite attain their diapason. Michelet and Renan leave them cold; Claudel and Francis Jammes fire their imagination. If I were a teacher, certainly I should profit by the experience; by all means let the young learn from the young!

Les Géorgiques Chrétiennes is full of the most delightful episodes of country life told in beautiful (if rather free-and-easy) French. There is no particular tale in it. It is rather a series of pictures; the daily life of a family of husbandmen on a farm. It is a sort of rural *Christian Year.* But what candid and happy pictures! What a sense of rustic cheer and frugal abundance! What primitive poetry in the labourer's account of the creation of his daily bread; the chestnut, the maize, the vine! And the betrothal of the little farm servant! And the vocation of the farmer's daughter who takes the veil.

There is but one thing in the whole volume which I find displeasing. It is the short certificate of orthodoxy which the poet delivers to himself on the first page and on the last. He is at great pains to assure us that he is not a reformer, a philosopher, a modernist, or a free-thinker. We should never have suspected this gifted and ingenuous singer of being any kind of thinker! He is a poet, a most indubitable poet, and that is enough.

Joseph Warren Beach and Gustave Van Roosbroeck (essay date 1920)

SOURCE: "Francis Jammes, Primitive," in *The Sewanee Review,* Vol. XXVIII, No. 2, April, 1920, pp. 172-85.

[*In the following essay, Beach and Van Roosbroeck discuss Jammes's use of pastoral imagery.*]

Francis Jammes is the poet of Orthez, as closely associated with that little village in the mountains as Wordsworth with Grasmere or Robert Frost with his "North-of-Boston". He has always in his view the cold peaks of the Pyrenees, yellow and threatening on the approach of winter, and in the rainy spring showing their blue veins, which make them more luminous than glass. Every year, in the season of love, he may witness the departure of "the great severe shepherds" for their cabins by the lakes of Barèges, where they shall see the jonquils, the prairies,—"where the water silvers, froths, and leaps, and laughs." Along the slopes are the woods where he hunts the wild duck; lower down is the mountain stream, the *"gave",* overflowing its banks in spring; "between the shining woods and the racing stream are the wheat, the corn, and the twisted vines." And here are "the black door-sills where the blue smoke hovers." Orthez, "humble village, of rude and sibilant sound", is so characterized by the poet, Charles Guérin, in his account of a visit to the home of his friend; and he goes on to describe the house in which Francis Jammes was living with his mother, a one-story, cedar-shaded, ivy-grown farmhouse, with the grass pushing up between the stones of the courtyard about the laurel and the well of blue water. Here it is, in his *"Elegy"* addressed to the poet Samain, that Jammes invited his dead friend to make him a visit as in the old days:—

> Viens encore. C'est Orthez où tu es. Bonheur est
>   là.
> Pose donc ton chapeau sur la chaise qui est là.
> Tu as soif? Voici de l'eau de puits bleue et du vin.
> Ma mère va descendre et te dire: 'Samain. . . .'
> Et ma chienne appuyer son museau sur ta main.

Here it is that he has been content to pass the unambitious days of life, overseeing the work of the farm, "assisting" at the vintage, driving to market on a Tuesday.

I.

This rural poet seems to have little of the traditional appetite for literary glory. His dog, his pipe, his grain-fields, and his little church in the fields, limit his outlook and content him. He prays in his poems to be of as little account as a donkey or a poor beggar-man. But the humble shall be exalted, and the poet of Orthez is celebrated far beyond the bounds of his own land. He has been translated into Spanish by the Mexican poet, Enrique Martinez; a chapter was devoted to him in his *Frank Poesi* by Christian Rimestad, the Dane, and one by Miss Lowell in her pioneering study, *Six French Poets.* His latest biography, by the Flemish poet, Jan van Nÿlen, was recently published in Holland. He had been the subject of laudatory articles in various countries, and in France he is acknowledged as one of the purest talents of the "modern school". He has had a great influence on the later developments in French poetry; and in Belgium there is a distinct school of Christian poets *à la* Jammes.

It is, at first blush, the more surprising to find him thus promoted to literary kingship, inasmuch as he has never undertaken to produce 'literature'. And yet this is a familiar phenomenon,—this turning back from 'literature' to poetry. Literature is forever tending to become a polished and pleasing rhetoric, the creation of a sensitive intelligence and a strong will-to-art rather than of simple unsophisticated feeling. Hardly a greater effort is conceivable for a poet than the effort to erase all second-hand impressions from his mind, to contemplate life again in its original simplicity. To do this is to discover his 'originality'; and such an achievement is welcomed sooner or later by a world of readers weary of echoes. His verse is dewy with that mysterious beauty of freshness which is wanting in so many poets of far greater technical perfection. He gives us candidly his impressions of his daily life, with little concern to please the public or the critics, without torturing his words to fit the forms prescribed by theorists. "I could have imitated the style of Flaubert or of Leconte de Lisle," he says in the preface to his early *Vers,* "and I could have repeated like others a stamped pattern. I have written irregular verses, disdaining, or nearly so, all rules of form and metre. My style stammers, but I have spoken according to my own truth."

This disdain of theories and schools is the more pleasing when one recalls how modern French poetry has gone on producing, by a process of fission, an ever-increasing number of "cénacles". One historian of recent literature has listed seriously—or was it with extreme irony?—no fewer than sixty or seventy of them, the mushroom growth of twenty-five years, each with its obscure-illustrious leader. Each one of them has announced, with wide exorcising gestures for all that went before, the advent of the only great Art—and each has joined its predecessors and competitors in the graveyard of oblivion: naturism, impulsionism, futurism, unanism, synthetism, intensism, paroxysm, and all the other banners in the motley pageant of late French literature. To the earlier ambition of the seventeen-year-old French youth—to write an historical tragedy in alexandrines and in six acts—has succeeded the ambition, it would seem, of founding a new literary school. The faith and energy of these restless founders is touching, indeed, but why "toujours penser en bande"? Why substitute for the tenets and narrowing rules of an older school an equally narrowing set of new rules? Jammes claims the right to complete freedom of personal feeling, to originality of vision and of diction.

Among modern French poets Jammes is remarkable for his simplicity. Since the time of Mallarmé and Rimbaud, many poets of intellectual distinction (Jules Laforgue, René Ghil) have indulged in a kind of grandiose and apocalyptic obscurity of thought, and a tortuousness of expression, which largely exclude the non-initiated from the enjoyment of their refined art. The super-subtlety of many symbolists, their generally abstruse mysticism (Edouard Schuré), their artificiality, their hair-splitting acuteness in self-analysis, stamp their work as exceptional and individualistic, the art of intellectuals, and largely for intellectuals. They stand aloof from the multitude, even from humanity itself. But Jammes disdains the pride of the intellect. He is no analyst of the ego in its fluctuations, its impalpable shades of thought and feeling, noting in rare and jewelled verse, like de Gourmont in his *Litanies,* all the subtle, wavering changes of his delicate 'soul'. He is even a little proud, it seems, of his intellectual naïveté: "and I, I do not know what my thoughts think"—

> Et moi, je ne sais pas ce que mes pensées pensent.

He might be a disciple of Thoreau. He has freed himself from the non-essentials of existence in order to live life for its own sake, to be simply man. He has cast off all the burdens of fashion, wealth, pride, even of thought, doubt and learning—all that makes our lives so nervously tense and distracting, and turned to the things which are essential, vital, primitive. A sharpening of enjoyment results from such a finely tempered asceticism. The fullest life lies in simplicity.

II.

Poetry, for such an one, is not invested with the sacerdotal glamor and awe of the symbolists. It is humble work, humble as a stonemason's, to which, indeed, Jammes compares it. It is a patient transcription of nature, like that of the old masters in painting, who, he tells us, spent a long while on the eyes, and on the lips, and the cheeks and the ears, of those who were happy enough to be their subjects. His is the humility, or the proud democracy, of nature herself. Nature, he thinks, may be presented with no adornment but her own, and without the apology of elaborate personification, Horatian epithet and classic allusion.

It is of the essence of his religious sentiment to feel that nothing is too humble for art, there being none of God's creatures which he must not approach with reverential wonder. He mentions in verse plants, animals, and objects in general, humble, forgotten things, or things despised, which seemed forever excluded from the language of poetry, although Chaucer and Villon might serve as

reminders of an earlier, pre-Victorian order of things. We were still under the spell—not long since—of the neoclassics, still bowing more or less to their injunction not to mention in verse any 'base' objects, such as animals of the lower kind, and in any case to prefer the general to the particular, as more refined. We still prefer 'fish' to 'herring', and the democratic 'bloater' is altogether excluded. Jammes has undertaken in French poetry what Wordsworth undertook, with considerable success in English,—to do away with the tradition of 'poetical' subjects. As with Wordsworth, too, this breadth in the choice of subject-matter is associated with, is perhaps rooted in, a religious mysticism; but in both cases it shows itself in many observations little connected with religious feeling, and in his claim to freedom in this matter the modern poet makes no appeal to other principles than those of poetic naturalism. This poet writes of fish and fishing with distinctions as precise as those of Izaak Walton himself. In **"Jean de Noarrieu,"** it was a delightful invention of the story-teller to have the infidelity of the girl revealed to her lover by the mountain flowers she carries,—gentians and edelweiss and pale pink laurel. They had been sent her by the shepherd from his airy cabin; but she says they are a present from a girl friend, who gathered them on the near-by hillside. Jean de Noarrieu knows better, and he replies in a voice low and dry: "Lucie, these flowers are mountain flowers."

> Et elle dit: 'Il y en a aussi
> sur le coteau où est la métairie
> dedans laquelle habite mon amie.'
> Et en mentant, encore elle rougit
> —'Ce sont des fleurs de montagne, te dis-je!
> Elles ne mentent jamais à leur pays.'

Jammes writes, then, with his eye on the object, as Wordsworth prescribed; and he writes with a Wordsworthian joy in the unvarnished facts of nature. Every hour of the day and night, every change of the seasons is recorded, is literally sung, with lingering tenderness, with the joy of fresh discovery, with brooding melancholy, or with positive rapture, according to the mood of the poet. His naturalism is not incompatible with the most graceful action of the fancy. What could be more 'poetic' than the description of the song of the nightingale—

> ses trois appels suivis d'un rire en pleurs de source?

The love of nature as she is in literal truth does not prevent the poet from suggesting those intimate and haunting correspondences between the material and the spiritual fact. In his mood of prayerful and humble resignation to the divine order, he finds the most touching analogies for his spirit in the aspect of nature.

> Je me laisse aller comme la courbe des collines.

He does not even disdain the use of language of much more symbolistic flavor. In the thirteenth of his *Elegies,* which is in the symbolist manner throughout, he tells his mystical fiancée that he has prepared for her the green freshness of his dreams, where lambs sleep, and he invites her to the cell of his contemplations, "whence one can hear running the living water under the mints which the white sun consumes"—

> d'où l'on entend courir l'eau vive sous les
> menthes
> que le soleil blanc consume.

III.

More direct and obvious is the reading of nature in religious terms, once more after the fashion of Wordsworth, but with a greater naïveté of anthropomorphic realism. The sense of natural objects as living in the breath of God is present throughout all his work, even the most secular. In the love-chronicle of Jean de Noarrieu, in the moonlit night of love, "the garden prays; one feels the heart-beat of the peaches in the silence of God." Over and over again, in the **Fourteen Prayers,** one returns to this pantheistic feeling of the immanence of God and the divine joy in the most insignificant of creatures. The fields and pastures "lie there like a great ocean of goodness over which fall light and serenity, and, to feel their sap in the sunlight bright with joy, the leaves sing as they stir in the woods."

It is in this ocean of divine goodness that the poet would plunge his sick soul to find oblivion of self. He would like to "come back down into his simplicity," to watch the wasps work in the sand, to be wise like them, and accomplish without pride the work God has given him to do. He has not always lived the life of simple piety which is his ideal. He has thought himself a genius, has desired fame; he has craved love and sought for happiness; he has indulged in himself "the learned reason that makes mad." But now he has had enough of the "complicated and learned life." He will no longer set himself apart from other men, or from the meaner creatures of God. He will let himself go, as readily compliant to the will of God as a butterfly to the breath of the wind. Sorrow will make him as gentle as the laborer patiently following the plough in the midst of the horned cattle.

Most of this has a natural enough sound to an English ear, even when falling in the cadences and among the associations of poetry. Rather more surprising, in its somewhat conscious naïveté, and most charming and original in conception, is the **"Prayer"** "to go to heaven with the donkeys." He says he will choose a day and a way to suit himself, and then—"I will take my stick and on the highroad I will go, and I will say to my friends the donkeys: 'I am Francis Jammes and I'm going to Paradise, for there is no hell in the land of the Good-God.' I will say to them: 'Come along, sweet friends of the blue sky, poor dear beasts who, with a brisk movement of the ear, drive away flies, blows and bees.'. . . . O God, grant that I may appear before you in the midst of these beasts whom I love so much because they lower their heads gently, and in stopping join their little feet in a way so sweet and pitiful. I shall arrive followed by their thousands of ears, followed by those who used to carry baskets at their sides," etc., etc. "Grant that, resting in this sojourn of souls, by your divine waters, I may be like the asses who shall mirror their sweet and humble poverty in the limpidity of the eternal love."

> Je prendrai mon bâton et sur la grande route
> j'irai, et je dirai aux ânes, mes amis:
> Je suis Francis Jammes et je vais au Paradis,
> car il n'y a d'enfer au pays du Bon-Dieu.
> Je leur dirai: Venez, doux amis du ciel bleu,
> pauvres bêtes cheríes qui, d'un brusque
> mouvement d'oreille
> chasses les mouches plates, les coups et les
> abeilles. . . .
>
> Que je vous apparaisse au milieu de ces bêtes
> que j'aime tant parce qu'elles baissent la tête
> doucement, et s'arrêtent en joignant leurs petite
> pieds
> d'un facon bien douce et qui yous fait pitié.
> J'arriveral suivi de leurs milliers d'oreilles,
> suivi de ceux qui portèrent au fianc des
> corbeilles. . . .
>
> . . . . .
>
> et faites que, penché dans ce séjour des âmes,
> sur vos divines eaux, je sois pareil aux ânes
> qui mireront leur humble et douce pauvreté
> à la limpidité de l'amour eternel.

This may seem to smack rather of *simplesse* than of *simplicité,* as Arnold distinguishes them,—this religious democracy *à la* St. Francis. But the suggestion of artifice lies in the dramatic presentation, in the somewhat fanciful picture of the poet, with his walking-stick, arriving in Paradise with his nimbus of asses' ears; and there is no reason to question the genuineness of feeling that underlies the poem. His work overflows with unaffected sympathy and brotherly feeling for the lower animals,—for lambs, dogs, sparrows, as well as for beggar-men and the unfortunate and despised of our species. And there is a medicinal virtue for him in the exercise of putting himself on a level with these fellow-charges of Providence. We all know the feeling: and we unconsciously assume an attitude of humility, a lower stature, that shall make us a less shining mark for the arrows of fortune, and bring us under the indulgence of Him who notes the fall of a sparrow. The sensitive heart of the poet, having experienced the "irony of love," hopeless of happiness and tired of self-dissection, longs to return to the state of the brute, of the patient wretch so low in the scale of fortune that he has neither hope nor fear, nor even the direction of his own course. He loves particularly to rest the tired eyes of his soul with the thought of night, figuring a mental darkness. "I feel the night upon me as it is upon the fields when the sun goes out like a lamp in the evening. I see no longer within myself. I am like the evening that hides from sight the gleaners of azure across the prairies of the thoughts of my soul."

Such is the meditation to which he summons himself in his prayer; the concentration of mind, or *recueillement,* which shall simplify his spirit. It is not a matter of enlarging his thought; it is partly, indeed, an inhibition of thought in its logical ranges. It is very much a matter of sensation, and very much a matter of sentiment. It is, in short, revery, dream.

> Je songe. J'ai souffert. Je ne sais plus. Je songe.

In such a state the dreamer lets himself float luxuriously upon the stream of sensation, of feeling only pleasantly tinged with thought, of thought guided by feeling. Thought and effort divorce one from that common life of things with which it is the desire of the mystic to identify himself. In the ecstasy of love, worldly or spiritual, he cries: "I can no longer think. I am nought but things."

It is a return to the great undifferentiated consciousness—a descent into the subliminal. This is what the poet means when he bids himself "come back down into thy simplicity."

> Redescends, redescends dans ta simplicité.

IV.

If he reminds us of St. Francis, he reminds us quite as much of that more sophisticated "fratello," Jean Jacques. With St. Francis he shares the humble renunciation, the mystical love of all created things. But his mysticism is not visionary and ecstatic like that of St. Francis; it is tempered with a sensuousness, even a naïve sensuality, and sounds a pastoral note more like Rousseau's wistful cornet than the jubilant cry of the friar of Assisi. In his renunciation Jammes is not ascetic; he loves all that makes his simple life joyful,—his pipe, his glass of wine, the dancing maids on the village green; it is even to enjoy them more relishingly that he has renounced the heart-poisoning ambition for 'success'. His solitude is filled, like Rousseau's, with a thousand simple but stirring emotions. He has Rosseau's sense of the soul in things. There is the old sideboard smelling of candle-grease and jam, a faithful servitor that will not steal. There is the old linen-chest, "which has heard the voice of my grand-aunts, which has heard the voice of my grandfather, which has heard the voice of my father, and is faithful to these memories. It is wrong to think that it knows only how to be silent, for I talk with it." Jammes loves to dream over in Arcadian revery the days of his early childhood, making much of the grandfather who went to the West Indies, and dwelling upon certain female figures in the tenderest manner of the great Doctor of Sentiment. His favorite author is Rousseau; and his favorite book is the **Reveries,** "whose sweetness blends with the sad quiet charm of the prairies, of river-banks haunted by the angelica, of deep woods where the oaks decay and mushrooms flourish. . . ."

In his early **Elegies** Jammes has produced a peculiarly appealing and romantic type of revery,—in which love and grief, gentle faith and memory, and the dreamy contemplation of nature, blend in a kind of general solution of wistful serenity, as of a restless and suffering heart fallen into peace at the sunset hour. The note of them all is sounded in the tenth of the series, in which the poet, tortured by the very intensity of love, and the suffering which lovers cause one another, yet comforts his beloved with a view of the grave beauty of life.

> Ne pleure pas, amie. La vie est belle et grave.

The first **"Elegy"** is addressed to his dead friend, Albert Samain. It is in no sense a lament for the departed poet. "Je ne regrette pas ta mort. Ta vie est là." The friend who remains takes pleasure in inviting the other to make him a visit in happy Orthez and in reviewing the simple joy they have shared there. He refers to his beautiful and enduring songs. And he *dreams*. He dreams of his friend, and of the twilight hour together at Orthez; he dreams of his native mountains, and of their walks at Versailles; he dreams of sheep and the pure void of the sky; of endless water and the clarity of fire; he dreams of his friend, he dreams of himself, and he dreams of God.

> Je songe à toi. Le jour baisee comme le jour
> où je te vis dans mon vieux salon de campagne.
> Je songe à toi. Je songe aux montagnes natales.
> Je songe à ce Versaille où tu me promenas,
> où nous disions des vers, tristes et pas à pas.
> Je songe à ton ami et je songe à ta mère.
> Je songe à ces moutons qui, au bord du lac bleu,
> en attendant la mort bêlaient sur leur clarines.
> Je songe à toi. Js songe au vide pur des cieux.
> Je songe à l'eau sans fin, à la clarté des feux.
> Je songe à la rosée qui brille sur les vignes.
> Je songe à toi. Je songe à moi. Je songe à Dieu.

The religion of the **Elegies** and the **Fourteen Prayers** is not very specifically Catholic, not perhaps even Christian. Their philosophy is, like that of his still earlier poems, a kind of broad and vague humanism, in the school of Rousseau and Bernadin de Saint-Pierre, whom he resembles in his naïveté, his vague goodness and loving tenderness for all of God's creatures,—his God being at that time very much the God of the "Confession de foi du vicaire savoyard." Slowly, however, he drew nearer the strict Catholic faith, partly under the influence of Charles Guérin, author of *Le Coeur solitaire* and *L'Homme intérieur.* Domestic sorrow, the betrayals and disillusionments of life, may have made him feel how little of a consoler in pain is the eloquent humanism which prays to a vague and impersonal God, omnipresent and yet elusive. In 1905, he submitted definitely to Roman Catholicism, and the immediate fruit of his conversion was a series of intimate religious poems, **L'Église habillée de feuilles,** in which the orthodox note is very clearly sounded. Much is made of the church and its exercises. The poet suffers now from a "nostalgic des cieux" of which we did not hear in his earlier poems; he feels that his body separates him from God, and that he must leave this flesh to be made free. He calls upon his guardian angel, whom he had neglected in the summer of his joy, in the pride of his body, in the days of his sweet dreaming. "I have lost the art of dreaming. Take my hand in thy hand!" One is reminded of Wordsworth's *Ode to Duty,* in which the English religious poet acknowledged that he had no longer felt strong enough to guide his life by the sole light of nature, but must resort to some external stay.

V

Is he a modern? Is he a man of our times? Does he have something to say to us in a certain dialect, with a certain inflection, which we may recognize as ours and serving our need? Different readers will answer differently these extremely delicate questions, involving such difficulties of definition and classification. If one considers his technique, the deliberate freedom of his verse—his assonances for rhyme, his syllables left uncounted, his lines uncapitalized—one will answer at once: he *must* be a modern of the moderns, an innovator, a *révolté.* The same answer will probably be made in view of his daring naturalism, and even of the directness of his manner, his extreme informality. He is modern, and ultra-modern, in his avoidance of the 'literary'.

But then one begins to think of his return to the Middle Ages. After all, one says, he has nothing different to tell us from what good Catholics have always had to tell. He has renounced—in so far as he ever had it—the critical unrest of our time. Scientific facts do not disturb him. Will the flower be more beautiful because it has been classified in a system, or because we have studied the structure of its roots and leaves? Will that help us to understand the more essential question, *why flowers?* And philosophies? What philosophy gives peace? And social theories? What more can one demand of society than that it should give one a house, a mother, a dog, and blue water of the well? However modern in its form and manner, we say, his poetry reproduces, in spiritual content, the emotional states of an age when religion was in fullest flower. He is like one of those anonymous troubadours, with their simple canticles to the Virgin. Up they looked through all the circles of heaven, to God himself, bejewelled Emperor, in mantle of purple and gold, enthroned among all His orders of holy beings. And since the mediæval vision of life was a mystical synthesis, well-ordered in its complexity, since heaven and earth were spiritually interwoven, they showed a naïve familiarity with all things divine: the saints and the Holy Virgin were real protectors against material enemies and the assaults of the devil, needed intercessors at the court of the Eternal. Nature was a symbol, and the objects of this world were veils through which the eternal truths were felt and seen. The mediæval artists loved nature intensely, and pictured it minutely—witness the sculptured doorways of cathedrals or the paintings of Rogier van der Weyden—but it was a nature glorified by the mystical meaning which their piety read into it, their vision of what lay beyond. In his simple but intense mysticism, in his love for sanctified nature in all its forms, in his familiarity with things divine, Francis Jammes reminds us of some artist of the twelfth century.

But there again something pulls us up. What! we say, a twelfth-century vision of life at the end of the nineteenth, the beginning of the twentieth? What! in the twelfth century, a *prayer* "to be simple"! A prayer, even of St. Francis, "to go to heaven with the donkeys"! Does it not almost smack of the satirist, Anatole France, and his court of heaven bewildered with the problem of baptized penguins? We do not have to go so far back as the Middle Ages for this cultivation of a democratic humility, this *tendre* for the underdog. Is it not quite recently that Vachel Lindsay of Illinois has sung the praises of the Negro and the grasshopper, and has shown us the social outcasts of our cities "entering into heaven" with General William Booth and his big bass drum?

And this mysticism of the unconscious, their escape into the subliminal, this soul-bath of revery, have we not found it in many profane writers throughout the past century, in the *Journal* of Amiel, in Richard Jefferies's *The Story of My Heart,* far enough removed from the spirit of the middle age? Is it not indeed one manifestation of the "maladie du siècle"? And, not confined to the nineteenth century, we find it in the poets characteristic of the present moment, in Carl Sandburg, who prays the mysterious "Bringers" to—

> Cover me over
> In dusk and dust and dreams;

who, in words that might be straight out of the mouth of the French poet, prays the Lord:—

> To-day, let me be monosyllabic. . . . a crony of
> old men
>   who wash sunlight in their fingers and
>   enjoy slow-pacing clocks.

The passion for simplifying art is but one phase of the passion for simplifying life,—which is modern enough in all conscience. We have met it in more and more striking guise in each of the successive schools of painting which have followed the Impressionists. In the very beautiful description, in **"Jean de Noarrieu,"** of the return of the shepherd with his sheep from the mountains, one is strongly reminded, in sentiment and detail, of various Post-Impressionist pictures:—

> Sous le troupeau ennuagé du ciel,
> il conduisait le troupeau de la terre.
> D'un geste large et rond il étenduit
> son long bâton, comme s'il bénissait
> les brebis donneuses de laine et de lait.
>
> . . . . .
>
> Et Jean pleura. Et les brebis boiteuses
> penchaient la tête, sous le souffle de Dieu,
> dans l'âcre automne aux rivières brumeuses.

Is it primitive art? Was Gauguin primitive in his return to Tahiti? Is Vachel Lindsay primitive in his return to the Congo? Were Matisse and Picasso really primitive?

What one recognizes in Jammes, as in these others, is the *cult* of the Primitive. And is not that the latest thing in all the arts?

William A. Drake (essay date 1928)

SOURCE: "Francis Jammes," in *Contemporary European Writers,* The John Day Company, 1928, pp. 243-51.

[*In the following essay, Drake praises Jammes's early works, but laments a decline in his later writing.*]

When one speaks of a poet as "well loved" or as a "favorite bard of simple things and homely virtues," one is not always seeking to condone a particular type of mediocrity which happens to appeal to him. Despite the thriving, if modest, school of Robert Frost, we have somewhat lost sight, in this day of neurotic exacerbations, of the proved truth that verse does not have to be tormented to be beautiful. The idyllic scenes of Whittier have in them more of pure loveliness than many of the most rapturous clamors of the sadistic school of English poetry; and there are also the classic examples of Hesiod's *Works and Days* and the *Georgics* of Vergil, which contain more essential poetry than the *Æneid* or the *Eclogues.* So we have no need to apologize for Francis Jammes when we say that, in our discordant age, there is no voice as sweet and tender, as utterly homely as his has been.

"Let us give to men, to be their judges, Irony and Pity," says Anatole France, in *Le Lys Rouge.* These are the judges that Jammes gives, not to men alone, but to all the creatures of the earth—to the infinite advantage of the latter. He loves the skies and the waters, the asses and the dogs, the kingfishers, the periwinkles, and the long tresses of the fields, better than any poet since the Greeks has loved them. They have rewarded him, as only love can reward a poetaster, by making him a poet. An indifferent student, a botanist, zoölogist, and ornithologist with more enthusiasm than learning, Jammes has become, so to speak, the Thoreau of France. "My style stammers, but I have told my truth," he says, in the dedication of his first volume of *Vers,* published privately in 1893, at Orthez, the little village in the Basses-Pyrénées which is still his home. That is the important thing; and despite the faults of his style, this simple quality of expressiveness of his particular truth has made Francis Jammes a poet certain to be remembered beyond his generation: an original, and an originator.

Jammes's intense sensitiveness to every feature of pastoral life, his profound apprehension of visible Nature, his spiritual and physical perceptions, his healthy sensuousness, his deep contentment with his lot, the simplicity of all his emotional responses, and his extraordinary faculty of objective and ironical, yet sympathetic, observation, brought this more or less untutored French provincial, from his first scribblings, to an attitude of mind and spirit perfectly designed for the utterance of poetic truth. If the sentiment of love finds its most sublime utterance in poetry, every line that Jammes has written is filled with love—with the love of life, the love of every tree and flower and blade of grass, the love of every animal, the love of every man, except, perhaps, the apothecaries of Orthez. These sentiments he feels spontaneously; and he records them spontaneously, without affectation, without obedience to, or revolt from, the precept of any existing school—although the perfect naturalness of his verse was the last blow to the Neo-Parnassian revival of 1895, and although the benefits of his influence are clearly perceived in such dissimilar productions as *Le Coeur Solitaire* and *Le Semeur de Cendres* of Charles Guérin and *Le Cocur Innombrable* of Madame de Noailles. In his rich, playful humor, Jammes has had neither inheritors nor predecessors. The French have had wit in plenty, but they have never before produced humor as delicious and earthy as his.

Jammes has told much of himself in his books—in *Un Jour, La Naissance du Poète* and *La Mort du Poète,* in the volume *De l'Angélus de l'Aube a l'Angélus du Soir;* in *Le Poète et sa Femme,* in *Clairières dans le Ciel,* and in scores of his shorter poems. But he has not explained his genealogy as an artist. There is no need to do that, for he is a natural singer; and it was clearly the irrepressibility of his gift alone that transformed the young solicitor's clerk of Orthez into the beloved sexagenarian of French poetry. Jammes was born, on the 2d of December 1868, at Tournay, in the Hautes-Pyrénées, of a substantial bourgeois family of that region. His great-grandfather had been a notary in the town of Albi; his grandfather, a physician, had migrated to the West Indies, where he had married a Creole woman of good family, and was eventually ruined by the earthquake of La Pointe-à-Pitre. Jammes has inscribed a poem to this ancestor, whose far wanderings beckoned the poet toward the enchanting course made luminous and delectable by the imaginary peregrinations of his great similar, Bernardin de Saint-Pierre:

> Tu écrivais que tu chassais des ramiers
>   dans les bois de la Goyave,
> et le médecin qui te soignait écrivait,
>   peu avant ta mort, sur ta vie grave.
>
> Il vit, disait-il, en Caraïbe, dans ses bois.
>   Tu es le père de mon père.
> Ta vieille correspondance est dans mon tiroir
>   et ta vie est amère.
>
> Tu partis d'Orthez comme docteur-médecin,
>   pour faire fortune là-bas.
> On recevait de tes lettres par un marin,
>   par le capitaine Folat.
>
> Tu fus ruiné par les tremblements de terre
>   dans ce pays où l'on buvait
> l'eau de pluie des cuves, lourde, malsaine, amère . . .
>   Et tout cela, tu l'écrivais.
>
> Et tu avais acheté une pharmacie.
>   Tu écrivais: "La Métropole
> n'en a pas de pareille." Et tu disais: "Ma vie
>   m'a rendu comme un vrai créole."

Tu es enterré, là-bas, je crois, à la Goyave.
  Et moi j'écris où tu es né:
ta vieille correspondance est très triste et grave.
  Elle est dans ma commode, à clef.

Upon the death of his mother and father, the son of this man, then a child of five years, was sent to Orthez, to be cared for by his aunts. This was the father of Francis Jammes, who married a good woman of the province and removed to Tournay, where he earned a modest livelihood as a notary until his appointment as Keeper of Records at Bordeaux made it possible for him to go to that city, where his son might enjoy the advantages of the University. But Francis Jammes proved only a languid scholar, and, instead of studying his Roman Code, he haunted the wharves and picked up odd bits of botanical lore at the public parks. When his father died, young Jammes forgot the legal career that had been planned for him and returned, with his mother, for whom he cherished a tender sentiment, to the ancestral cottage at Orthez, which Charles Guérin has celebrated in his poem:

O Jammes, ta maison ressemble à ton visage.
Une barbe de lierre y grimpe, un pin l'ombrage
Eternellement jeune et dru comme ton coeur . . .

There he has remained ever since, anxiously preserving himself from the contaminations of the city. He was married about 1906, and his poems to his wife and to his young daughter are inexpressibly tender. His prose record of this daughter's daily life, *Ma Fille Bernadette,* is one of the most charming modern contributions to the literature of childhood.

The literary accomplishment of Francis Jammes is divided sharply into two periods by his reconciliation with the Roman Catholic Church, which occurred about 1902, a short time after the return of Paul Claudel from his sojourn in the Orient. With his second conversion, Jammes began to mistrust the healthy sensuousness and the whimsicality which had made his earlier work particularly cherishable and unique. In curbing these native impulses, and in turning his quest from the love of life and visible beauty to the love of God, he lost an element of natural vigor and a robust earthy tang which his work has not compensated in the contemplation of higher excellences. This is the false note which renders insipid *Les Géorgiques Chrétiennes,* the work which he, as the only poet of contemporary France competent to essay such a theme, ought to have made his masterpiece.

We may not pause here to discuss Jammes's contribution to the Neo-Catholic revival in France, but we may observe, with some abstract justice, that the poet's early devotion to Rousseau—whose *Confessions* he formerly called "son livre ami"—was a more invigorating influence in his art than his later devotion to the doctrines of Catholicism. What Jammes lost in vitality, however, he more than gained in spiritual beauty; and if one would seek for a Saint Francis of Assisi in the modern world, one would find the humble counterpart of the saint in his French name-son. One cannot read the poems collected

in *Clairières dans le Ciel,* for example, without being aware of the moral greatness of their author; but where has vanished the simplicity and the humanity of *Quatorze Prières?* We cannot resist the temptation to translate one of them, the **"Prière pour Aller au Paradis avec les Anes":**

When my time comes, O God, to go to thee,
Upon a festal day then let it be,
When fields are filled with dust; I wish to go
By any road I please, as I go here,
To Paradise, where stars shine all day long.
Taking my stick, I'll seek the broad highway,
And to my friends, the asses, I shall say:
My name is Jammes; I go to Paradise,
Because there is no hell in God's good land.
I'll say: Come, gentle friends of azure skies,
Poor, precious beasts, whose twitching ears brush off
The silver flies, the bees, the cruel blows . . .

Grant I may come to thee among these beasts
That I so love, because they hang their heads
Gently and, halting, put their little feet
Together thus, so pitiful and sweet.
Let me approach amid their million ears,
Followed by those with baskets on their flanks,
By those who draw the carts of acrobats,
Or bear a huckster's truck upon their backs;
She-asses, full as gourds, with halting steps,
And those who wear quaint breeches, made to stanch
The ooze of blue sores bit by stubborn flies.
Grant that these asses come with me, my God,
Grant that in peace the angels may conduct
Both me and them to tufted streams where trees
Tremble like laughing flesh of tender maids;
And grant that, as I then shall bend above
The heavenly waters of that place of souls,
I may become as these same patient beasts,
Who mirror humble, gentle poverty
In the clear waters of eternal love.

Yet, the spirit of his later poems is as noble and admirable in the consciousness of a destiny. In the dedication of a late edition of the most personal of his books, *De l'Angélus de l'Aube a l'Angélus du Soir,* the poet writes: "My God, you have called me among men. Here I am. I suffer and I love. I have spoken with the voice which you have given me. I have written with the words that you taught my father and mother, and which they have transmitted to me. I pass upon the road like a laden ass at whom the children laugh, and who lowers his head. I will go where you will, when you will." For Jammes has two magnificent gifts, which nothing can take away from him. These are courage and, above all, love.

It is a common observation that most superior poets are deprived of the gift of writing fine prose, but that the occasional exceptions to this rule produce prose of exceptional beauty and power. While the prose of Francis Jammes is by no means to be compared with that of the English poets, some observation of this nature may certainly be made of it, for Jammes has carried into his prose many of the finest qualities of his exceedingly orderly and provocative verse. Jammes had been occupied with the idea of metrical romance since his first appearance as a poet, and his early self-revealing narratives had been somewhat in this character. In 1899, he wrote *La Jeune Fille Nue,* and the two long narrative poems in *La Triomphe de la Vie,* "Jean de Noarrieu" and "Existences," record his finest development of this genre. He early began to write prose, and his first prose romance, *Clara d'Ellébeuse ou l'Histoire d'une Ancienne Jeune Fille,* first appeared in 1899, to be followed, two years later, by *Almaïde d'Etremont ou l'Histoire d'une Jeune Fille Passionnée,* both of which were later republished, with additional stories and with Jammes's sensitive essay on Rousseau, in the volume entitled *Le Roman du Lièvre.* This series of romances was completed in 1904 by the publication of *Pomme d'Anis ou l'Histoire d'une Jeune Fille Infirme,* which was reissued in 1913, in the volume in which the poet's best prose is to be found, *Feuilles dans le Vent.* Most of Jammes's writings, as age has come upon him and as he has drifted out of the current of his times and closer to the sheltering bosom of the Church, have been in prose; and his achievements in what may be termed lyrical fiction constitute, in a sense, a third and final phase of his work.

The recent work of Francis Jammes has declined lamentably. The reticences of strict religious obedience, the disturbances of the war, and the sad ravages of advancing age, have combined to relegate this once renowned poet to the limbo of those anachronistic reputations respected but unread. Jammes, having given the coup de grâce to a school of pernicious artificiality, having written better bucolic poetry than any Frenchman except Mistral, having influenced the art of scores of poets, one (Madame de Noailles) even greater than himself, and having been proclaimed the inspirer of a group with which he had nothing in common, has fallen upon the same misfortune as many other French poets of his generation—he has become religious, and religion has confined his spirit, diluted his style, and taken the poetry out of him. He is happier in his desuetude, perhaps, although he was happy before, when his God lived for him in the smile of the skies and the blue of the periwinkles; but he is less readable, and he is no longer Jammes. And, since we loved that very human Francis Jammes, our brother and friend, we may be forgiven if we refuse commerce with his pious shadow.

François Mauriac (essay date 1938)

SOURCE: "To Frances Jammes - An Obituary Tribute," in *Poet Lore,* Vol. XLIV, No. 4, 1938, pp.

[*In the following essay, Mauriac eulogizes Jammes.*]

Those of us who do not believe that the affairs of men are governed by pure chance, rejoice at the honor which Our Almighty Father has bestowed upon his faithful poet in welcoming him with solemn acclaim into the glorious and eternal Company of His Saints.

The end came while Jammes was listening to the Services appropriate to that day, namely, to that part of the Gospel which we term the "Beatitudes," of which all are intrinsically applicable to him, but especially that one which promises that the meek shall inherit the earth. For, apart from occasional and purely superficial outbursts of violence, Jammes was meek; his was that inner meekness given only to those who truly love the poor, and to whom Poverty is the Godhead incarnate. As his reward, it was vouchsafed him to pass on to others in his poems the spirit of all the breezes and of all the floating clouds of the provinces of Bearn and of Biscaye; and his verses are redolent of the sweet fragrance of peasant gardens when the sun shines through the last drops of a passing shower.

There are those—happily only a few—who feel that he overestimated himself. After all, is not the reason easily defined? All great poets fail of recognition during their lives: even the greatest. Hugo, was as little recognized as was Jammes; and in his case it was not his poetry to which, in general, he owes his outstanding position. Fortunately, in Paris, some devices still exist, which allow a poet to forget that others, besides himself, evaluate his book. At Orthez and at Hasparen, daily, almost from moment to moment, there came to Francis Jammes a sensation approaching the physical in its poignancy, of having been forgotten, overlooked, unrecognized. Is not this, perhaps, the explanation of those outbursts of irritation; of those stinging words; of those moments of unwarranted pride?

And yet, as each next morning broke, he was to be found kneeling with bowed head among the crowd of devout peasant women, before the altar; and, humbly, on bent shoulders, he accepted the yoke which the Almighty decreed was his to bear.

So now, to-day, when there actually appears before his eyes what he had so steadfastly believed; when at last to his poetry has been awarded the crown of enduring fame, it can matter but little to him that he is about to take his proper place in the front rank of contemporaneous French poets. And that pre-eminence he shares with none; unless it be that he stands chosen from among the many with Claudel and with Valéry. Even so, his niche is somewhat removed, since that niche is consecrated to men who have kept themselves from the world apart; who have eschewed all worldly power, all social honors, all secular distinctions. Except for the Cross of the Legion d'Honneur, none has he accepted save only that Cross which he loved and to which he clung when his Last Hour came upon him.

For many years I believed that he had reached the peak of his glory in those earlier anthologies: *De l'Angélus de l'Aube à l'Angélus du Soir; Le Deuil des Primevères; Clairières dans le Ciel.* I now bow to the judgment of his young disciple. Jean Labbé, who maintains that of all his poems, the recently published collections, *Les Poèmes Mesurés* and *Sources* are his finest work.

Francis Jammes, my beloved, of all my masters, you are the one for whom I have felt the greatest admiration and the deepest love. I am proud to belong to a generation which has never given aught but respect to its elders; of whom we, its members, are but the humble successors. And yet it was you who opened my eyes that they might see the beauties of this world. It was you who achieved in a manner utterly beyond my unworthy comprehension, the transmutation of Satyrs into Angels, and of the Great God Pan into the living Christ. You, in your work, established the bond between Nature and the Grave Divine. And in those Heavenly Regions where to-night you are, near unto Maurice and Eugénie de Guérin and to André Lafon, pray, I beseech you, unceasingly for those of us who in this world have loved you and who, until they die, in hushed tones and solely for their own pleasure, will re-tell your poems into their listening ears.

Sister Mary Jerome Keeler (essay date 1938)

SOURCE: "Chapter IX: Frances Jammes," in *Catholic Literary France: from Verlaine to the Present Time,* Books for Libraries Press, 1969, pp. 123-38.

[*In the following essay, originally published in 1938, Keeler provides an overview of Jammes's major works.*]

The year 1935 saw the publication of *De tout temps à jamais,* by a poet who had been for a time silent. Though Francis Jammes is an old man now, we find in this latest volume of poems all the charming freshness and artless beauty of his early work. He ever remains the simple, humble poet of country life, who lives and writes far from Paris, in his beloved country of the Hautes-Pyrénées. He belongs to an old Creole family and many of the traits of his ancestors appear in his books which emit a perfume of exoticism, a fragrance of bygone days.

In his three volumes of memoirs, he tells us the story of his life up to his thirty-eighth year. *Ma Fille Bernadette* and *Le Testament de l'auteur,* also contain autobiographical material. In fact, all of Jammes' works reveal much about himself, external and internal. He was born on December 2, 1868, at Tournay, where his father was receiver of records, and he lived there six years and six months. His mother, nee Anna Bellot, was from the Basses-Alpes of a family of merchants and nobles. His only sister, Marguerite, three years his elder, went to live at Pau with the maternal grandparents, who took care of her education.

Jammes has an astonishing memory and relates many interesting incidents of his childhood. He recalls distinctly that the water of his favorite stream was *sucrée,* that his first illness made him realize the devotion of the "tenderest of mothers," that Marie, the servant, used to save him cream from the fresh milk, and that his aristocratic grandfather showed some annoyance when he saw his grandson getting off the train like "Jeannot-lapin, or the country rat."

In 1875 his father was transferred to Sauve-terre-de-Gironde, and he left his wife and two children with the grandparents at Pau. While here, Francis often visited Orthez, where his two great-aunts, Clémence and Célinaire, dwelt in the old home. At night he slept on an ancient trunk of camphor wood brought from the Indies, and during the day he attended the school of three old maids. On occasion he would visit his rich uncle from Mexico in his sumptuous villa. In 1876 the family was reunited at Saint-Palais, an agreeable little city watered by the Bidouze and the Joyeuse, and not yet spoiled by railroads. Here Francis' teacher was M. l'Abbé Duc, and a distrust of schools and schoolmasters, which was to last many years, took birth. It is true that the boy was sometimes misunderstood, and consequently treated with apparent injustice both by professors and students, but Jammes himself acknowledges that he was often lazy and rebellious, neglecting everything but botany and poetry.

It was at the primary school of M. Sabre that his "poetic initiation," as he calls it, began. It came quite unexpectedly; "A book is open before me. Suddenly, without any warning, I see and realize that the lines are living. . . . I had just received from Heaven this reed, shrill and dull, humble and sublime, sad and joyful, sharper than the dart of a savage, sweeter than honey. I exercised it a few days after. My father was astonished at my attempts, and showed me more tenderness than he had ever before evinced." Later Francis stayed with his grandparents and attended the lycée at Pau, but he was no more successful than before, so his father undertook to give him private instruction in his office, and obtained better results than any of the schoolmasters.

In 1871, owing to a disagreeable change of situation imposed upon him, M. Jammes resigned his position, and the family went to Orthez to live with the Huguenot aunts, one of whom (Clémence) was "thin and long, and could have been one of the Sisters of the primitive Church who followed Paul of Tarsus." The other (Célinaire), though angular, was quite different from her sister, without mysticism, but with housewifely instincts well developed. The family moved to Bordeaux in 1880, and they would have wished to see Francis enter the polytechnic school there, but unfortunately, it was his sister and not he, who manifested talent for mathematics. He had developed at thirteen or fourteen, what he calls a "malady, odious especially for the associates of the one who is attacked by it, and which becomes more manifest in early adolescence, *l'âge ingrat.*" Nevertheless the boy was doing more satisfactory work in school. He was delighted with his discovery of Jules Verne and charmed with his studies in natural history under M. Dabas. Another teacher, "who belonged to that class of professors who displeased him least," was Professor Ducasse. Francis studied botany with him, and was even punished because he was caught examining flowers during history class! In fact, he failed in his examinations and left the lycée at seventeen without his degree.

Early in 1888 the family made a sojourn at Béarn with the Mexican uncle and his wife, but soon returned to Bordeaux. The father's health had been poor for some time, and on December 3, 1888, at the age of fifty years, he died and was buried at Orthez. Francis, his mother, and sister decided to live in this city with one of the aunts. He was spared military service, being the only son of a widow and in poor health, the result of a state of nervous depression. He went into the office of a notary for a time, but hated it and abandoned it to become a poet. Stéphane Mallarmé, Henri de Régnier, and André Gide, who had read some of his verses, encouraged him to publish them, and **"Un Jour"** appeared shortly after. He says of it: "It was in the heart of April, 1895, that I was *invaded*—I can find no other word to express my meaning. A simultaneous outburst of all my lyrical powers took place in me. I do not know why I did not die from the breath, as it were, of a violent wing which seemed to strike me, and of which my poem **"Un Jour"** was born." Alfred Vallette edited it and Raymond Bonheur set it to music.

In March, 1896, a friend invited him to accompany her to Algeria, where she was to visit André Gide. Jammes made quite an extensive trip, going on from Touggourt through the desert to Biskra. Later he describes his journey in his *Notes sur des oasis et sur Alger.* He begins his third book of Memoirs (*Les Caprices du poète*) with the words: "*Mon Dieu,* how young I was at that time [1897] when I was nearly thirty!" He and his mother were living in a cottage near the road between Bayonne and Pau. Jammes loved this house, of which Charles Guérin wrote: "O Jammes, your home resembles your face." He was still much disturbed mentally and spiritually, and continuously speaks of his *mal.* Nature always had power to soothe him, however, and a trip to Normandy, which he took in the autumn of 1898, ameliorated sensibly the crisis of sadness in which he was plunged.

About this time he published *De l'Angelus de l'aube à l'Angelus du soir,* which drew from Hérédia this comment: "It is certain that this fellow is a poet." *Clara d'Ellébeuse* followed in March, 1899. Jammes calls this novelette a *folie de pureté* and says that Claudel wrote him an admirable letter about it. The following summer he and his mother visited the Basses-Alpes where she had been born, and on their way saw the country where Jean Jacques Rousseau passed his adolescence. His poem to Madame de Warens, one of the best Jammes ever wrote, was composed at this time. It begins:

> *Madame de Warens, vous regardiez l'orage*
> *plisser les arbres obscurs des tristes Charmettes,*
> *ou bien vous jouiez aigrement de l'épinette,*
> *ô femme de raison que sermonnait Jean Jacques.*

> [Madame de Warens, you used to watch the storm bend the dark trees of dreary Charmettes, or in a sour mood you played the spinet, O woman of sense, whom Jean Jacques used to lecture!]

In 1900 he spent several days at Paris on his way to Belgium, where he gave a series of lectures. From there he went on to Holland, and during the return trip he made the personal acquaintance of Paul Claudel. M. Schwob

had written to Jammes: "This poet [Claudel] is the only one besides you who moves me." *Almaïde d'Etremont* appeared in 1900, and not long after, that strange poem, **"Existences."** Jammes himself says it is "burlesque and satiric, an act of madness," in which he maliciously ridiculed the Orthezians. Soon after he wrote **"Jean de Noarrieu,"** an idyll full of paganism. Later these two long poems were united in one volume entitled *Le Triomphe de la vie.* The next years were troubled ones for Jammes, and he gave expression to his dejection in a volume, *Tristesses.* This is an "interior drama in three acts and in three years." It was followed in 1903 by a more normal and readable book *Le Roman du lièvre.*

His life glided by peacefully at Orthez, with occasional visits to Bordeaux where he had many literary friends, or to Estang where his married sister was living. He and his mother passed the evenings reading favorite authors, among whom he numbers Homer, Vergil, Cervantes, La Fontaine, Rousseau, Victor Hugo, and Eugénie de Guérin. In 1905 Claudel came to Orthez to visit Jammes. The latter was going through a moral and religious crisis at the time, and though very unlike Claudel in every way, he was greatly impressed by the rugged Catholicity of his illustrious contemporary. The following year he returned to the faith of his childhood and recovered peace of mind and heart.

Jammes tells us nothing of his marriage, but in his book *Ma Fille Bernadette,* he relates the story of the babyhood of his little girl, who was born at Orthez in August, 1908. Her first smile, her first tear, her first Christmas, her first illness, are all of paramount importance to the loving parents. He gives a portrait of the child's father (himself at forty years), and describes his bushy eyebrows, his strong curved nose and sensual mouth. He declares that his only beauty is in his hair turning gray, and in his green, catlike eyes, sometimes hard in expression and again very gentle. He makes no mention of his beard "big and black like that of Robinson Crusoe," which he may have grown later. He gives us a glimpse of his wife at twenty-six with well-formed features and beautiful teeth, singing the baby to sleep in true motherly fashion. In a poem entitled **"La Vie"** he tells Bernadette,

> You will understand how dear is the little house;
> The house on the path in which there is nothing
> 　　extraordinary,
> But where four hearts live: your father, your
> 　　mother, your grandmother and you.

From *Le Testament de l'auteur* we learn that Jammes had four other daughters (Emmanuèle, Marie, Anne, and Frances) and two sons (Paul and Michel). This last testament was drawn up and signed in March, 1928, at Hasparren, where Jammes moved about 1919. Here, far from the capital, which attracts him no more than does literary fame, he still lives in the midst of his family, presiding over his humble hearth "more sonorous with crickets than with gold pieces," praying much, writing occasionally, dreaming always, surrounded by his beloved flowers and animals.

Critics usually stress the difference between Jammes' earlier and later manner, making 1905 the point of division. Before this date, his work is more pagan and lyric, and he writes in free verse. After 1905, the date of his conversion (or reversion) to the faith of his early years, his poems are more religious and didactic, and he uses regular verse. As he grows older, we notice that his poetry is somewhat less original, more mature and studied.

His first publication, *Vers,* which appeared in 1893, created quite a sensation. It was a volume of poems about the common things of everyday life, written in a simple, direct style, without pretension to poetic diction. He says in the preface to this volume: "I have written irregular verses, disdaining or nearly so, all rules of form and meter. My style stammers, but I have spoken according to my own truth." *Un Jour,* mentioned previously, followed in 1895. This outlines a typical day in the life of a poet, with three scenes, morning, afternoon, and evening, and seven characters, the Poet, his Soul, his fiancée, his mother, his father, his servant, and his dog. Later this was printed in the same volume with *De l'Angelus de l'aube à l'Angelus du soir* (1898), a collection of poems, humorous, sensual, descriptive, romantic, malicious, sad, or gay, according to the mood of the author. He writes of the blue mountains, of the shepherd with his big umbrella and dirty sheep, of his favorite animals (the donkey, dog, and cat), of his house full of roses and of wasps. The lines

> *. . . je pleurais, ô mon Dieul sans savoir pourquoi,*
> *et sans savoir sur qui, et cans savoir de quoi*

> [I was weeping, my God, without knowing why,
> and without knowing for whom, or wherefore.]

remind us of the more famous *Il pleure dans mon coeur* of Verlaine.

Quatorze prières (1898), *La jeune fille nue* (1899), *Le Poète et l'oiseau* (1899) and *Élégies* were published in one volume with *Le Deuil des primavères* in 1901. The fourteen prayers are interesting, in fact astonishing at times, but not very pious. In one the author begs God for a star, in another for a simple wife; again, he prays to go to Paradise with the donkeys; in another he asks to love sorrow:

> *Je n'ai que ma douleur et je ne veux plus qu'elle.*

> [I have only my grief and I wish nothing more.]

La Jeune fille nue is a poetic drama with three characters and three scenes in which the poet relates a dream and gives full play to the caprices of his imagination. *Le Poète et l'oiseau* is a dialogue between the Poet and a very philosophic bird, which displays more wisdom than do most men.

Le Triomphe de la vie, including the two narrative poems mentioned before (**"Jean de Noarrieu"** and **"Existences"**), also belongs to his first manner. The former is a Hesiodic poem, divided into four cantos. The hero is a gentleman farmer of thirty years, who is enamored of his servant, the peasant, Lucie. She, however, has lost her heart to Martin, the shepherd. At first Jean is jealous, but finally plays the part of the magnanimous master and marries the two. A hint at the end gives us to understand that he did not die of a broken heart, but immediately turned his eyes toward Jeanne, a lass "with red and laughing lips." More important than the love story is the picture of country life—the harvest, vintage, fishing, and hunting. **"Existences"** chronicles everyday happenings in a village, and has no plot, but is merely a series of incidents. They are entertaining and realistic, but vulgar and salacious at times. The keynote is given at the beginning: *Et c'est ce qui s'appelle la vie.*

Besides these books of verse, Jammes published four volumes of prose before 1905: *Clara d'Ellébeuse* (1899) *Almaïde d'Etremont* (1901) *Le Roman du lièvre* (1903) and *Pomme d'Anis* (1904). Three of them are stories of young girls, lovely, graceful, and unreal, but fascinating just the same. Clara d'Ellébeuse is a pious, scrupulous, convent girl, who worries so much over a slight fault which her ignorance exaggerates, that she commits suicide. Almaïde d'Etremont is an orphan of much the same type, and would probably have ended her life like Clara, a victim of her shame and remorse, had she not been saved by the sound advice of a kind old gentleman, a friend of the family. Pomme d'Anis is more mature and worldly-wise than her two antecedents. She is a cripple, and realizes too late that it is rather pity than love which has attracted Johannes to her. *Le Roman du lièvre* stands out alone in Jammes' work. It pictures as no other French story does, the frail animal protecting itself from man. Jammes catches La Fontaine's manner, especially in the opening pages of the book:

> Between the thyme and the dew of Jean de La Fontaine, Lièvre listened to the hunters, and climbed to the path of soft clay, and he was afraid of his own shadow, and the heather fled behind him, and the blue belfries arose from valley to valley, and he redescended and mounted, and his leaps bent the grass where hung dewdrops, and he became the brother of the larks in his rapid flight, and he crossed the high-ways and hesitated at the finger-post before following the connecting road, which, pale with sun and sonorous at the cross-roads, is lost in the dark and silent moss.

The hare is a living person, and never once does Jammes lose the sense of proportion and balance so vital in this attempt to merge the human and animalistic.

It is usually granted that the prose of Jammes in these early works is superior to his poetry. The probable reason for this is that the simplicity and naïveté of his verse is apt to degenerate into triviality or affectation. It is extremely difficult for a writer to treat at any length the humble things of life in a familiar and natural manner, especially in poetry where the form is more or less arbitrary. When Jammes writes spontaneously the freshness and originality of the verse delight us. But as soon as the creative impulse seems forced, when preciosity mingles with candor, we can pick out verses which either repel us by their banality or amuse us by their ingenuous affectation. The last lines of **"La Salle à manger"** exemplify this:

> *Il est venu chez moi des hommes et des femmes*
> *Qui n'ont pas cru à ces petites âmes.*
> *Et je souris que l'on me pense seul vivant*
> *Quand un visiteur me dit en entrant—*
> *Comment allez-vous, monsieur Jammes?*

> [Men and women came to my house, who did not believe in these little souls. And I smile because they think I am living alone, when a visitor says to me on entering, "How are you, M. Jammes?"]

The principal volumes of poetry published by Jammes since his conversion are *Clairières dans le ciel* (1906), *Les Géorgiques chrétiennes* (1912), *La Vierge et les sonnets* (1919), *Le Tombeau de Jean de la Fontaine* (1921), *Les Livres des quatrains* (4 books, 1923-25), *Brindilles pour allumer la foi* (1925). With the exception of the first-named, all of these are inspired by faith and piety and are written in classic prosody. They contain beautiful verses, full of "sweetness and light" and if they are more restrained and at times more monotonous than his earlier ones, still there is an added charm which comes from religious fervor. We agree with Amy Lowell that "his Catholicity is a very sweet and lovable thing." His attraction to nature is as strong as before, but now he turns more quickly to the God of nature. *Clairières dans le ciel* contains **"En Dieu"** (a poem on the death of Eugénie de Guérin), the pessimistic **"Tristesses,"** the poetic drama **Le Poète et sa femme, "Poésies diverses,"** and the long poem **"L'Église habillée de Feuilles."** This last is an allegory which relates the author's return to Catholicity. Pilon remarks that the church Jammes describes is not the cathedral of Huysmans but a little rustic chapel. *Les Géorgiques chrétiennes* is a lengthy, bucolic poem, giving a series of kaleidoscopic pictures of rural life, and treating nature from the Christian point of view. Critics judge the poem differently. Some praise it highly while others speak of it as a long accident to be deplored. It is true that the Alexandrine doublets are rather monotonous, but they are well suited to convey the idea of the peace and calm of country life.

La Vierge et les sonnets is fresher and more buoyant. For instance, Sonnet VII relates how, when out walking with an old servant, he caught a gay and gaudy butterfly and brought it home in a box. But it did not seem nearly so pretty in its cage as it did flitting through the air, and the poet ends:

> *. . . O mes frères en poésie!*
> *Il n'avait plus autour des ailes la prairie*
> *Qui me l'avait fait croire aussi grand que le ciel.*

> [O my brothers in poetry! It had around it no longer the wings of the prairie, which had made me believe that it was as large as the sky.]

Clouard says that the sonnets contain "incomparable harmonies, worthy of the beautiful evening of life of an inspired poet." *Le Tombeau de Jean de la Fontaine* is a collection of short, clever poems, in which the different animals in La Fontaine's fables appear to lodge complaints against the author for the way in which he misrepresents them. *Brindilles pour allumer la foi* is, as the title indicates, and the preface explains, a small collection of devout thoughts, simple explanations of Catholic doctrines, short meditations, and bits of pious admonition with no pretense at style or art.

The principal volumes of prose written after his conversion are: *Feuilles dans le vent* (1914), *Pensées des jardins* (1906), *Ma Fille Bernadette* (1910), *Le Rosaire au soleil* (1916), *M. le Curé d'Ozeron* (1918), *Le Poète rustique* (1920), *De l'âge divin à l'âge ingrat* (1921), *Le Livre de Saint Joseph.* (1921), *L'Amour, les Muses, et la chasse* (1922), *Les Caprices du poète* (1923), *Le Mariage Basque* (1926), *Trente-six Femmes, La Divine Douleur* (1929), *La Vie de Guy de Fontgalland, L'Arc-en-ciel des amours* (1930), *L'École buissonière* (1931). His three volumes of memoirs have already been mentioned, as also *Ma Fille Bernadette*. In this latter book, the dedication to "Mary of Nazareth, Mother of God," and the passage in which the watchful care given to Bernadette by her guardian angel is described, are exquisite. *Le Poète rustique,* the tale of a poor poet and his family living in a small village, also contains much autobiographical material, though not avowedly so. *Le Rosaire au soleil* and *M. le Curé d'Ozeron* are both idealistic novels. The first is divided into fifteen chapters, each representing a mystery of the rosary. This rather artificial framework does not help a novel which is almost too nice in itself, and in which the heroine, Dominica, is a beautiful but bloodless character. *M. le Curé d'Ozeron* is somewhat better, for the curé is a living, lovable old priest. In both, however, the mixture of fiction and piety is rather labored and displeasing. Calvet calls them "paradisiac novels, the color of angels' wings." *Pensées des jardins* is a book in both poetry and prose, full of insects and animals, of flowers and vegetables, of snow and wind, and of humble folk. It was written during the period between the old and the new manner of Jammes. *Feuilles dans le vent* contains twenty meditations (many of them on Scripture texts), *Quelques hommes* (biographical notes on friends of Jammes), *Pomme d'Anis,* and *La Brebis égarée*. This last is a prose drama which relates how Françoise, wife of Paul, goes off with Pierre Denis, a friend of her husband. They are punished and brought to a sense of duty by poverty and misfortune. *La Divine douleur* is an exposition of all types of human suffering which result from death, mourning, separation, injustice, poverty, sickness, and humiliation. *L'Arc-en-ciel des amours* is a collection of little love idylls, prose poems with the verses numbered. **"La Declaration d'amour acceptée"** from *L'Idylle de la palombière* may serve to illustrate:

> 1. *Onze ans après Pierrech a vingt-cinq ans et Kattalin les a auusi;*

2. Dans la même palombière;

3. Dans la même cuisine;

4. Seul à seule, de même;

5. Avec les réjouissantes escalopes de veau qui, à chaque fois, l'emportent de fort loin, dans le goût du jeune homme, sur la reste de menu.

6. Kattalin regarde ce beau garçon de tout son coeur et de tous ses yeux qu'elle a bleus et en amande, d'un bleu sauvage qui n'est que basque, le bleu d'un certain dur calcaire lorsque la pluie a passé dessus.

7. Précisément le soleil de l'amour les fait luire.

8. Rompant, vis-à-vis d'elle un silence de toute sa vie.

[1. Eleven years later Pierrech was twenty-five years old and so was Kattalin; 2. In the same dove cot; 3. In the same kitchen; 4. Alone, just the same; 5. With the heartening pieces of veal which, each time, according to the taste of the young man, were by far the best thing on the menu. 6. Kattalin looks at the handsome lad with all her heart and with all her eyes which are blue and almond-shaped, a savage blue which is only basque, the blue of a certain hard limestone when the rain has fallen on it. 7. It is the sun of love that makes them shine. 8. Breaking, opposite her, the silence of a lifetime.]

L'École buissonière contains selections from Jammes' earlier prose works with a few unpublished sketches.

The characteristic that strikes us most in Jammes is his love of nature. The different epithets applied to him by critics indicate this. He has been called *"le fils de Virgile," "Coppée bucolique,"* "the Catholic rustic," "brother of La Fontaine," "the Theocritus of his native Béarn." Though, as we have pointed out, there is some difference between his early and late manners, his devotion to nature remains the same. Humble creatures seem to be full of mystery for him, still he treats them with a familiarity and fraternal love that recalls St. Francis. He loved all animals, and they march through his books in an endless procession: dogs, cats, rabbits, butterflies, wasps, larks, swallows, doves, goats, sheep. . . . He seems to be partial to donkeys, however, as he wrote a whole series of poems to them in *Pensèes des jardins.* His descriptions of landscapes, plants, and trees show first-hand knowledge, and prove that he heard the story of Mother Earth from her own lips. Amy Lowell says that "all his books are cool and white like snow, and threaded with the blue of skies, of snow-shadows, of running water." He also writes of those human beings who are close to nature, shepherds, villagers, and peasants. He is especially attracted to young girls, frail, innocent, and graceful like sweet flowers; old-fashioned girls with musical names. Jammes has been compared to Wordsworth for his effort to do in French poetry what the latter did in English (interpret nature's soul), and also to A. E. for his close communion with the lowly beings of earth. But there is more faith and humility in Jammes than in either the British or the Celtic poet, both of whom are tinged with pantheism.

All Jammes' books are full of himself. As Lalou remarks, "Jammes recounts Jammes abundantly." Besides his three books of memoirs, the story of his daughter Bernadette, and his testament, we have *Un Jour, Le Poète et sa femme, La Mort du poète,* and *Le Poète rustique,* in all of which he is the protagonist. He has related his conversion in verse and in prose. In his prefaces he explains his motives and intentions copiously. Often this personal note is pleasing, and lends a flavor of veracity to his work, but at times it jars upon the reader.

The outstanding quality of Jammes' style is its simplicity. His language is pure and sober. He has an extraordinary ability to write of simple things in a simple way, to see poetry in the commonplaces of life, and to transfer his impressions to paper without any flourish of language or straining after effect. Moreover, he has the soul of a child and he speaks like a child in a direct, spontaneous manner, unmindful of form and order. This naïve ingenuousness sometimes degenerates into affectation and absurdity. In fact, the word *Jammisme* connotes just this excess of simplicity. But Francis Jammes usually saves himself from this fault, however, by his ability to convey swiftly the humor of the situation. We feel that he writes with a twinkle in his eye and thus he prevents others from laughing at him.

We must admit that, although Jammes is to be admired for his love of nature, his simplicity, and his power of imagination, there is something lacking in his poetry. We read his verses and enjoy them, but we are never profoundly moved. Somehow they fail to awaken thoughts "that do often lie too deep for tears." Jammes is a charming, lovable writer, but the sublimity of Claudel, the tenderness of Verlaine, the psychology of Bourget, and the vigor of Huysmans are unknown to him. He believes that when a poet looks at the sky and says that it is blue, he has said all, and everything else would be vain epithets. There were vaster and more extended literary domains, to be sure, but he consciously avoided them, likening himself to the poor faun. He deliberately chose "the way of spoliation of the primitives, who have not sacrificed sentiment to form." Perhaps this realization of his limitations is one of the greatest proofs of his genius. How many failures there are in life because men neglect what they can do and attempt what they cannot! Jammes caught a glimpse of the hidden beauty in the Creator's work, and he celebrated it in free verse admirable for its rhythmic variety, or in musical prose adapted to the manifold moods of the author. He is an anonymous troubadour, wandering through the twentieth century, content to sing his humble canticles to God and His Virgin Mother.

François Mauriac (essay date 1961)

SOURCE: "Letter to Frances Jammes," in *Second Thoughts: Reflections on Literature and on Life,* The World Publishing Company, 1961, pp. 128-31.

[*In the following essay, presented as a letter to Jammes, Mauriac praises Jammes's poetry and sensibilities.*]

Dear Jammes: I have followed a shaft of moonlight down through the black arbors to this terrace from which I look out toward you. We are separated only by the vineyards, heavy now with grapes, and by a thirty-league accumulation of fields and pine groves, of simple churches where God keeps watch, and sleeping farms. This is what you called in one of your elegies an *océan de bonté,* but it is really you, your heart and your love that break at my feet like a wave in the darkness.

You have given us this world, this murmurous night that surrounds the bed on which you lie stretched out in pain. The suffering poet, man's one benefactor, his one friend! A little while ago, before I came to join you out here on the terrace, the *Radio Journal de France* was thundering like the voice of destiny through the house, stilling even the laughter of children. The boys stared at the floor as they listened. I watched the bowed heads of my sons and the face of their friend, which was like a sorrowing angel's. Suddenly the invisible voice uttered the terrible words announcing the hecatomb: "Liberty, Law, Justice. . . . " When it paused, one of the young boys near me murmured, "Just the same . . . it would be a pity. . . ." Of what projects, what interrupted loves was he dreaming?

Dear Jammes, great and gentle poet, your work is the river rushing between the alders, springing without end from a hallowed heart. In you and in all men of vision, who are your brothers, I pay honor to one image of the goodness of God visible in this world. Presently, when I shall have joined you who lie ill beyond the countless pines, I will be alone in a deserted living room, in the heart of a house that shelters many sleeps. From all over Europe music will flow into the old room, as if it were emboldened by solitude and the immobility of all creatures and things to offer itself freely. Seldom does an oboe or a clarinet fail to bring out of the air from somewhere the consolation that Mozart lavishes on a world that stands today condemned. A line of Jammes, a melody of Mozart—nothing more is needed to reassure us that, if mankind is plunging into the shadows where the blood of Abel has never ceased to flow, the light and joy of which you are both witness and hero none the less exist. Only in you and in your poems and in the poems of your brother poets do we sense and seek and finally discover this light, like lilacs blooming in the night.

What Frenchman is not divided against himself today? Who among us is not filled with indignation, torn between anger and shame? But you are my certitude, Jammes, you from among the very few who have not deceived us. Even in the terrible hours we are sentenced to live through, you wring from us the cry Rimbaud uttered between two blasphemies: *Le monde est bon, je bénirai la vie. . . .* Yes, the world is good, even if men kill each other! Yes, we will be strong enough to bless life, even as we dangle at the mercy of the whim or pleasure of a clutch of murderers.

The mighty lament that has risen from the churches and from ancient Israel, the tears and blood shed in concentration camps, the curse that has rung out from the charnel houses of Spain and Ethiopia and China, and the silence of our sons, more tragic than any outcry—these are covered, Jammes, by the piping air of your eternal song. It covers them, not to drown them nor to distract us from awareness of them but as a sign that we have not been created for cataclysm or for submission to the law of evil.

Once again I see the Bible that lies on your bed table at Hasparren. Of all those many words, these sound new and strange in our dreadful world: "Blessed are the meek, for they shall possess the earth!" It is you, O poet, who must have possessed it, for you have given it to us. You are the mild master of Béarn and the Pays Basque, of Landes and Guyenne; you reign for all time over the hills and the meadows, the streams and the springs. Fearlessly you push open the doors of old abandoned houses in farms where no one now lives; you make yourself at home in the chimney corners of dead kitchens. Your name is carved on a *prie-dieu* in the poorest village church. All that is enfolded within this night in which I write to you, all that it holds of living brooks and plants and wild hares, all the countryside that this moon bathes with light sings as it sleeps in your work, until I feel as close to you this evening as I was on a certain spring day when I opened your bedroom door.

FURTHER READING

Criticism

Aldington, Richard. "Recent French Poetry." *Poetry*, Vol. XV, No. 1 (October 1919): 42-48.
    A comparative review of Jammes's *La Vierge et les Sonnets* and works of other French poets published after the end of World War I, all of which the reviewer finds lacking in originality and energy.

Caws, Mary Ann. "*Correspondance de Francis Jammes et de Francis Vielé-Griffin (1893-1937)*." *L'Espirit Créateur* Vol. IX, No. 1 (Spring 1969): 58-59.
    An unfavorable review of the collected correspondence, in French, of Jammes and his friend Francis Vielé-Griffin.

O'Brien, Justin. "Gide and Antigide." In *Contemporary French Literature*, edited by Leon S. Roudiez, pp. 229-32. New Brunswick, NJ: Rutgers University Press, 1971.
    O'Brien surveys letters exchanged between Jammes and Gide.

Redman, Ben Ray. "Weaker Wings." *The Nation*, Vol. 115, No. 2986 (September 27, 1922): 311-12.
    A comparative review of works by several European writers, including Jammes's *Romance of the Rabbit*, all of which the reviewer treats unfavorably.

Symons, Arthur. "A Pastoral Poet." *Saturday Review*, Vol. 86, No. 2242 (October 15, 1898): 510.

A review of *De l'Angelus de l'aube à l'Angelus du soir* which is favorable with much qualification, including a suggestion that the reviewer may have been influenced by reading the poems in a setting much like that in which Jammes wrote them.

Van Slyke, Berenice K. "The Poet and Inspiration." *Poetry*, Vol. XXI, No. 1 (October 1922): 47-51.

A favorable review of Jammes's *Le Poète et l'Inspiration*, which includes his "beatitudes of the poet," describing the function and reactions of the poet.

Gaetano Mosca

1858-1941

Italian political scientist.

INTRODUCTION

Mosca is most often credited with bringing modern political science to Italy with the publication of his *Elementi di scienza politica* (*The Ruling Class*) and for developing the theory of democratic elitism. Along with the writings of such other notable Italian political thinkers as Vilfredo Pareto and Benedetto Croce, Mosca's works are considered to have been a major impetus to Italian fascism, although this result was both unforeseen and unintended on his part.

Biographical Information

Mosca was born in Palermo, Sicily, in 1858. During his childhood, Italy, and the region of Sicily in particular, experienced one of the most turbulent periods in its political history, and some critics speculate that Mosca's later repudiation of parliamentary governments may have been a reaction against the unrest he witnessed as a young man. Mosca earned his law degree at the University of Palermo in 1881, where he went on to lecture beginning in 1885. Despite his work at the university, Mosca experienced little success in academia, which he blamed on his rejection of the popular political ideologies of the time. In response to what he considered his academic failure, Mosca accepted the position of editor of the proceedings of the Chamber of Deputies in 1887, where he remained for ten years. The publication of his *Elementi di scienza politica* (*The Ruling Class*) in 1896 won him the chair of constitutional law at the University of Turin. In 1908 Mosca became active in politics for the first time, with his election to the Chamber of Deputies. In 1914 he served as undersecretary for the colonies, and in 1919 he became a senator. During this time, fascism was gaining popularity in Italy, and Mosca initially took a distant but tolerant position on it. Eventually his stand changed to one of unqualified rejection. In 1923 Mosca published an updated edition of *The Ruling Class*, which earned him a position at the University of Rome, where he assumed Italy's first chair of the history of political institutions and doctrines. Mosca remained at the University of Rome until he reached Italy's mandatory retirement age in 1933. He died in 1941.

Major Works

Mosca's first publication, *Teorica dei governi e governo parlamentare* (1884) was an antiparliamentary polemic aimed against the Italian politics of Mosca's time. In this work he began to formulate his differentiation between what he considered democratic "myths" and genuine liberty, which would become an integral part of the development of his later theories on democratic elitism and the myth of the ruling class. In 1896 Mosca published the first edition of *The Ruling Class,* his most important work; the second, expanded, edition appeared in 1923. In *The Ruling Class* Mosca delineated his contention that in all forms of government the organized minority is always in a position of power over the majority. This ruling class justifies its power by developing for itself a "political formula," which is a guiding principle that follows the common ideals of the community. The majority, or those being ruled, are thus implicitly in compliance with their rulers, and order is maintained. The political formula propagated in any given society is the "myth of democracy" according to Mosca, wherein the image of rulers and ruled working together toward a common moral or legal goal is offered as democratic freedom. Mosca also posited that two opposing social forces are always in action in any governmental situation: the desire to keep power within a particular, aristocratic group who inherited it by virtue of their ancestors, and the desire to bring new leaders up from the majority class to renew the political process (the latter was known as the "circulation of the elites"); Mosca favored a balance between the two political courses.

Critical Reception

Mosca's work did not generally receive much attention during his lifetime. Although many fascist intellectuals at the time credited him as one of the seminal ideological fathers of the movement, critics today believe that this was due to a misunderstanding of Mosca's theories, which are now considered to lean toward classical European liberalism because of his emphasis on representative rather than parliamentary governments, and his preference for the circulation of the elites. After World War II, Mosca's theories took on new life as Marxism moved to the world political forefront and class awareness became a major intellectual issue.

PRINCIPAL WORKS

Sulla teorica dei governi e sul governo parlamentare: Studi storici e socialia (political theory) 1884; also published as *Teorica dei governi e governo parlamentare,* 1925
Questioni costituzionali (political theory) 1885
Sulla libertà di stampa: Appunti (political theory) 1885

Elementi di scienza politica (political theory) 1896;
  revised edition, 1923; published as *The Ruling Class*
  [edited by Arthur Livingston], 1939; published as *La
  classe politica* [edited by Norberto Bobbio], 1966
Questioni pratiche di diretto costituzionale (political
  theory) 1898
"Il principio aristocratico ed it democratico nel passato e
  nell'avvenire" (lecture) 1903
Appunti di diritto costituzionale (political theory) 1908
Sui provvedimenti per l'istruzione superiore (political
  theory) 1909
Italia e Libia: Considerazioni politiche (political theory)
  1912
Sulla riforma elettorale politica (political theory) 1912
Sul Tratto di Losanna (political theory) 1912
Sulla riforma della legge elettorale politica (political
  theory) 1919
Per l'assetto della Tripolitania (political theory) 1920
Sulle cause degli ultimi fatti avvenuti in Tripolitania
  (political theory) 1920
Sulle comunicazioni del governo (political theory) 1920
*Sui disegno di legge relativo alle "Attribuzioni del Capo
  Governo"* (political theory) 1925
Sul dilancio delle colonie (political theory) 1926
Saggi di storia della scienca politica (political theory)
  1927
Lezioni di storia della istituzioni e delle dottrine politiche
  (political theory) 1933; revised and published as
  Storia delle dottrine politiche, 1937; revised and pub-
  lished as *A Short History of Political Philosophy*,
  1972
*Histoire des doctrines politiques depuis l'antiquité jusq'à
  non jours* (political theory) 1936; revised edition,
  1966
Partiti e sindacati nella crisi del regime parlamentare
  (political theory) 1949
*Ciò che la storia proebbe insegnare: Scritti di scienza
  politica* (political theory) 1958
Il tramonto della stato liberale (political theory) 1971
Scritti sui sindacati (political theory) 1974

CRITICISM

Sidney Hook (essay date 1939)

SOURCE: "The Fetishism of Power," in *The Nation*, Vol.
148, No. 20, May 13, 1939, pp. 562-3.

[*In the following essay, Hook reviews the English translation of* The Ruling Class.]

Not so many years ago the conquest of power was the
central theme of all left-wing social theory oriented to
political activity. Today, in the light of the consequences
of totalitarian rule, concern with power is primarily with
its abuses, its destruction of life and corruption of the
spirit. The naivete of the messianic reformer has given

way to weary skepticism. The Young Davids of radicalism seem to have laid aside their slings for the Book of
Ecclesiastes—or for a safe berth with the New Deal. For
most of the disillusioned the main political task is conceived as preventing fascism from coming to power, not
by winning power for socialism, but by strengthening liberal capitalism. Suspicion of the excesses of all power
makes easier the acceptance of the customary abuses of
existing power.

This new attitude toward power is revealed more in
moods than in explicit argument, though theoretical formulations have not been lacking. But it is to books of an
earlier day that we must turn to find the weightiest critiques of political power. Mosca, Pareto, Michels, writing
in an age when optimism was as general as pessimism is
today, raised all the crucial problems which have now
come to the fore. They fortified their conclusions on the
nature of political power with a mass of historical material and a nicety of analysis which commands respect
even when it does not elicit agreement.

The translation into English of Gaetano Mosca's **The
Ruling Classes** offers an opportunity to evaluate both the
strength and the weakness of this recurrent philosophy of
political power. Like most doctrines that catch hold easily, the basic thesis is simple and recommends itself with
a high initial plausibility to anyone who has had some
political experience. It asserts that political power never
rests upon the consent of the majority, that irrespective of
ideologies or leading personalities all political rule is a
process, now peaceful now coercive, by which a minority
gratifies its own interests in a situation where not all
interests can receive equal consideration. As Mosca himself puts it: "Political power always has been, and always
will be, exercised by organized minorities, which have
had, and will have, the means, varying as the times vary,
to impose their supremacy on the multitudes." In peaceful
times, the means are public myths and secret frauds; in crisis—force. Whichever side wins, the masses who have
fought, bled, and starved are made the goat. Their saviors
become their rulers under the prestige of new myths. The
forms change, but the essential content remains. This is put
forth as a "law" of all social life which can be demonstrated
to the satisfaction of everyone except the dull, the pious, and
candidates for political leadership. It is a law accepted by
every political partisan as obviously true for other organizations but as a slander when applied to his own.

The reactions to this position in recent discussion have
been astonishing. They tend to confirm some corollaries
Mosca has drawn from his thesis about the distribution of
political intelligence. One group does not argue the truth
of the theory on the evidence but asserts that since its
acceptance makes for defeatism it must be wrong. Another group applauds Mosca's theory or some variant of
it and deduces therefrom the comforting view that revolutions are never justified; this despite Mosca's contention that revolutions do not depend upon any theory of
political power. Some contest the truth of his findings on
the nature of political power because on some other unre-

lated points he is clearly mistaken. The most sophisticated opponents of the thesis first state it in such a way as to suggest that according to it all power is necessarily evil and should never be employed. They then have little difficulty in showing that this leads to a *reductio ad absurdum,* for men must act, and this involves a choice between alternatives all of which demand implementation by some power.

In the interests of clear analysis we must distinguish between Mosca's descriptive generalizations of the actual uses and abuses of political power in the past and present, and the theoretical explanation he offers of them. As descriptive generalizations, Mosca's conclusions are valid, once differences in the form of political rule have been properly noted. It is true that every political organization is in effect run by a minority. It is true that vital illusions, chicanery, and naked force have been three important props of all political rule. It is true that every successful mass movement—even with a democratic ideology—has compromised some of its basic principles, on occasions all of them. The history of Christianity, of German Social Democracy, of the Russian Communist Party indicates in a dramatic and focal way all this and more. But in explaining these phenomena and in predicting that the future must always be like the past Mosca falls back upon a psychological theory of human nature considered independently of its social context. Almost every one of his explanations and predictions involves an appeal to an original nature conceived as essentially unalterable despite its varying expressions. Mosca's antiquated terminology can be brought up to date by translation into the language of dynamic psychology or psychoanalysis. But the controlling assumptions are the same no matter what the terms. The laws of political power are frankly characterized as psychological. They flow from fixed and unchangeable elements in the nature of men. Mosca has no hesitation in sometimes referring to them as "wicked instincts." It is from this conception of original sin that Mosca's dire prophecies flow.

The fact that the argument from human nature must be invoked to support the thesis is *prima facie* evidence that the entire position is unhistorical. Everything Mosca says may be granted except when he speaks in the future tense; for the genuine problems of power are always specific, are always rooted in the concrete needs of a particular people at a determinate time. Any conclusion based on his findings about the futility of social change and struggle is therefore a non-sequitur; it betrays political animus, and if grounded at all, is derived from other considerations. The belief that there is an invariant core of properties which constitutes the "essential" character of human nature rests on gross data drawn from history and on a faulty technique of definition. Habits, traditions, and institutions play a much more important role in political behavior, and are more reliable in predicting the future, than any set of native impulses. By isolating the latter from their objective cultural setting, selecting from among them an alleged impulse to dominate, fight, love, or flee, the pattern of human nature can be cut to suit any current political myth.

Despite the fact that Mosca's "laws," when presented in psychological dress, have no empirical warrant, they can be reformulated so as to bear relevantly on particular situations in which intelligent choice between different modes of power is possible. They then function as "cautions" or "guides" to possible dangers that attend transference of power from one group to another. The task then becomes one of devising safeguards—an occasion for experiment not for lamentation. And most safeguards do not make accidents impossible; they make them less frequent. Sufficient evidence has been assembled which indicates the probable sources of future corruption and oppression. It would require a treatise to explore this theme, but in a preliminary way we can indicate the spheres of social life in which conflicts will arise, necessitating safeguards against oppression.

The first sphere of conflict and possible oppression is obviously economic. Most socialists grant this readily enough for the past but deny that it holds for collectivist society. Yet it is apparent that under no system operated by finite creatures in a finite world can all men be equally served in everything and, what is just as important, equally served at once. That there will probably be some differences in standards of living, no matter what the level of productive forces, none but a utopian will deny. But there are differences and differences. Conflicts there will be, but their kind, generality, and intensity will depend upon the specific mechanisms adopted to reflect and negotiate the interests of different groups of producers and consumers. Socialists have always asserted that there is no genuine political democracy without economic democracy. In a collectivist economy the converse is even more emphatically the case.

The second sphere of possible abuse of authority is administrative. Every administrator intrusted with responsibility for making decisions that may affect the jobs, pleasures, and life careers of other human beings may function as a tyrant. The greater the area of administration, the greater the danger. Especially when efficiency is the goal is it easy to palm off injustice as a necessary evil. Here too the situation is one that must be met, for better or for worse, by contriving checks and reviews with a maximum of publicity.

Finally there is the undeniable fact that many people love the exercise of power. For some it is a compensation for frustration; for others it is a way of acquiring prestige, glory, a sense of vitality or importance; for almost everybody it is a temptation to prefer those we like and to overlook those we despise. Everyone has his own list of people whose absence he thinks would be a boon to the world. But what follows from all this? Nothing that need dismay anyone who is not a saint or a fool. Here as everywhere else, once we surrender the dogmas of an unalterable human nature or inevitable laws of organizational progress or corruption, we can do something to mitigate and counteract, and to establish moral equivalents.

Whether we are talking of pain or injustice or power, there is no such thing as *the* problem of evil except to a supernaturalist. There are only evils. The more we know about the pathological lust for power, the conditions under which it thrives, the instruments it uses, the myths behind which it hides—and the more public we make that knowledge—the better can we cope with the problem of taming it. Skepticism is always in order; but no more than in science need it lead to paralysis of activity. More knowledge is always desirable, but we know enough to make at least a beginning. And if we are interested in democratic socialism, by keeping our eyes on both Germany and Russia we certainly know what to avoid. Despite the swelling chorus of disillusion there still remain alternatives to the insanity of uncontrolled myth and the inhumanity of uncontrolled power.

Thomas I. Cook (essay date 1939)

SOURCE: "Gaetano Mosca's *The Ruling Class,*" in *Political Science Quarterly,* Vol. 54, No. 3, September, 1939, pp. 442-7.

[*In the following essay, Cook reviews* The Ruling Class, *disputing the common interpretation of Mosca as a supporter of totalitarian rule.*]

The prime task of a reviewer is normally to discuss the contents and viewpoint of an author's work. In the present instance, however, it is perhaps not less important, as a preliminary thereto, to insist on what the work is not, particularly in view of the title given to this translation and edition [*The Ruling Class* (*Elementi di Scienza Politica*)], the nationality of the author, and a quotation on the jacket from Charles A. Beard to the effect that the book is important for an understanding of "the modern trends toward Fascism, Communism and other types of 'strong government'." For there seems a real danger that the unwary may infer that this is an apologia (or at least a foundation, since the first Italian edition appeared in 1895) for fascism and an attack on the democratic way. Nothing could be further from the truth, and, whatever the gains in emphasis in the English title, one feels that the Italian is more justly descriptive. For, while Mosca's central theme is, no doubt, that in any society there will be a ruling class, his essential objective is to analyze the various ways in which men are governed, to demonstrate methods by which ruling classes are created and preserved and by which they exercise their authority, and to give an account of the dangers to such classes, the means of their transformation, and the techniques of judicious coöption by which they attain stability.

The idea, indeed, that Mosca is a defender of doctrines of the absolute state is readily dispelled by a consideration of his very first chapter, which is at once one of the most moderate and, by reason of its very restraint, one of the most mordant attacks on various exaggerated and oversimple approaches to political science that have recently been used, many of them as defenses of absolutism of one sort or another. He denies with real insight the doctrine that the superiority of certain civilizations depends upon climate, and in particular argues that it is absurd to believe in the moral superiority of those who come from the cool climes of northern lands; and he insists, too, that the ability to preserve and profit from free institutions cannot be ascribed to those living in any particular area. *Mutatis mutandis,* the same considerations apply to topography. In both instances, however, Mosca recognizes fully that geography is a conditioning factor, though not a causative one, and that its significance changes with changing knowledge and technology.

Even more thoroughgoing is his attack on the doctrine of racial determinism and the superiority of certain peoples; and here it is particularly worth while noting that he rejects the idea of the Jews being a special people, discusses their real assimilability, and points out to how large an extent the Jewish problem is a consequence of enforced isolation. Indeed, his analysis of the fallacies of racial interpretation is as thoroughgoing as that of, say, Professor Boas, and far less emotional. Similarly, he attacks the whole organismic doctrine and the idea of social evolution as it has been used both by Spencerians and by the advocates of the organic state. That he is also skeptical of any pure doctrine of economic determinism, though admitting the significance of economic factors as part of the problem, and the fact that he cautions us against any facile application of the findings of anthropological study of primitive peoples to the modern state, do not lessen the effectiveness of his criticisms. His own approach seems to be largely historical, though he carefully insists that the historical method may be perverted by an undue emphasis on biography or by an unwise narrowing of the scope of history.

The dominant characteristic of Mosca's position is his awareness of the complexity of the human being and his sad, but probably just, disillusion. Indeed, his essential argument is that naïve idealists who, Icarus-like, endeavor to reach the sun destroy themselves and, more important, undermine that organization without which men are unable to exist. Man is a finite animal; and, while he may aspire to perfection, he cannot hope to attain it. Certainly the great mass of mankind are unregenerate and tainted with irrationality; they must be governed, and, while governing involves giving satisfaction, it involves no less the creation of effective stereotypes and catchwords which will command attachments to a prevailing, though not static, order. The plea, therefore, is for gradualness, and is at once conservative and liberal. Its basis no doubt is temperamental, but it seems to involve a rational temper whose conclusions are documented and justified by vast learning used with discrimination and with insight.

Dr. Mosca's chief prejudice is indeed revealing as to his bias, and that in two senses. For he condemns utterly what he calls social democracy, a term which apparently would embrace all change brought about by governmental action in the economic sphere, from the moderate policies of English pre-war liberalism and the techniques of intervention in the business world developed and established by the New Deal, to thoroughgoing state socialism and the practices of dictatorship of the proletariat. He is, that is to say, basically a defender of laissez faire; and, while this is doubtless anachronistic and would in the present age prove ruinous to any governing class that endeavored to practice it even in moderate purity, it is inimical no less to fascist theory and practice.

Secondly, however, Mosca's work is in a definite way a wholehearted plea for a government which governs and adapts itself to the needs of the civilization within which it functions; and, outside the context of the struggle against laissez faire, Mosca shows an extraordinary awareness of the dangers to a ruling class that arise from an inability to create an effective basis for consent and to insure adequate routes by which the abilities that are useful and appreciated in a particular age may enter it in sufficient numbers. His essential fear of social democracy rises, it is worth while to note, from a feeling that the extension of governmental functions means the extension of administration and administrators; and he seems to believe that, once one embarks on this undertaking, one is bound to end up, in one way or another, with government by a bureaucracy that becomes top-heavy, rigid, and lacking in comprehension of the feelings of the governed, to the final destruction both of itself and, in all probability, of the civilization which has produced and suffered from it.

Yet Mosca makes a strong case for republican as against autocratic government, and condemns the excessive extension of so-called democratic techniques on the very ground that these lead to dispersal of authority and responsibility, and so open the way for an arbitrariness that may indeed restore order, but by reason of its narrowness cannot itself be stable. If, therefore, one discounts his particular prejudice and recognizes that it is the inconsistency of one who, while normally scientific, is in that particular area a doctrinaire liberal of the school of classical economics as popularly interpreted, one finds in the whole ethos of his work a powerful argument for the positive social welfare state under republican institutions, and with an ultimate judgment in the electorate, as the essential and desirable alternative to dictatorship. This becomes the more clear when one considers his attacks on hereditary aristocracy and his long analysis of the evils of *a priori* individualistic rationalism on the one hand and facile, unilinear theories of social determinism on the other.

The difficulties and seeming inconsistencies of Mosca's analysis are, nevertheless, real. They are, indeed, clarified, though not, in the present reviewer's judgment, solved in the final chapter, which constitutes part of Mosca's revised edition of 1923, from which the present edition is made, and embodies his reflections on the postwar world. That chapter is a renewed plea for representative government, for something closely approaching Madison's republican government. Mosca urges that, while a wide electorate exercising the suffrage is necessary and even desirable under modern conditions, it is especially dangerous to social solidarity in times of stress unless its function is narrowly and precisely confined to the selection and judgment of leadership. Secondly, he insists with renewed vigor that a ruling class disintegrates under the attacks of its own skepticism as to its right to rule and its lack of awareness of calling and duty. It is therefore necessary for it to develop a unity of feeling (though *not* a rigidity of structure and an exclusiveness in membership) and a strong sense of public obligation. Mosca is frankly skeptical as to whether either of these developments will take place. Thirdly, however, he sees a ray of hope: the present ruling class has a wide base, being created by the beneficent coalescence of a bureaucracy and a political leadership created and elected by reason of talents valued in the current order. Thus it becomes clear that Mosca finally approves, rather than deplores, the growth of a class of administrators as such. What he fears is that such a class may become first dominant in the ruling class, and then synonymous with it.

Yet it is just at this point that we encounter the essential question which he does not answer—a question unanswerable indeed in his terms. Bureaucracy, sound in moderation and under restraint, becomes the ruling class of a socialist state, itself created by a false pursuit of equality, and involves a suppression of liberty. Yet the participating bureaucracy of which Mosca approves is, surely, the outcome of a positive state, endeavoring to undo the consequences of an excessive inequality—an inequality he, as a defender of a strong middle class and a lover of the Aristotelian mean, formally condemns. Indeed, without the development of such a state to redress the balance of laissez faire, modern bureaucracies created under representative government would have no *raison d'être*. But, Mosca argues, the policy of gradualness, of progressively diminishing inequality by political techniques, is unsound and does not lead to stability or harmony—and this for political reasons. For such a policy does not please, but does give aid and comfort to the endeavors and convictions of the proponents of absolute socialism and of communism, while at the same time weakening the allegiance to the existing régime of considerable parts of the governing classes. Yet this is surely to argue (a) that, political and administrative leadership apart, there is in the ruling class a group of great wealth possessed of predominant economic and political power, and commanding the allegiance of a considerable section of the bourgeoisie, and (b) that class struggle is inevitable. The ruling class, he has urged, must be intelligent, must coöperate and concede. But, under conditions of representative government and industrial civilization, as produced in the nineteenth century, the very essence of that undertaking is the social welfare state. Mosca does not want absolutism, fascist or communist. Now, granted that pure justice and complete rationality do not characterize human affairs, it is none the less true that, unless the economic powers that be can be persuaded that concession is wiser than fascism—a difficult but not unreasonable inference, in view of the sufferings of business enterprise where it has put its confidence in fascistic leadership—and unless communists lose appeal, in so far as they are revolutionary, by the progressive removal of causes of extreme discontent, the adventure of representative government is doomed, since it becomes static, and is hence impotent.

Mosca, condemning socialism, and particularly the orthodox Marxian form, ends by giving away his case through unwitting agreement with his avowed opponents. He weakens scientific support, painstakingly built, for a governmental system suited to current needs, and capable of realizing a type of society which many of us, on ethical and rational grounds, would concede to be the best attainable in the world of the second-best.

A word should perhaps be added as to Professor Livingston's Introduction and as to the translation. The latter, as Professor Livingston stresses in the former, is not literal, while the material has been rearranged. Broadly, the work is readable and has continuity, though on occasion a section ends with a sentence opening new vistas not subsequently surveyed. The elimination of Mosca's discussion of Labriola's ideas is, in the reviewer's judgment, debatable, while one must, in view of recent events and of probable developments in the near future, deplore Mosca's insistence that his treatment of the Roman question be deleted.

Livingston's introduction is an excellent summary of the genesis and development of Mosca's ideas, with a very useful discussion of his debt to Taine and his parallelism with Pareto. It includes a significant analysis of Mosca's life, stressing both his habitat and his activities—though one fancies its emphasis on biographical explanation might not be completely acceptable to its subject. It clarifies his seminal concepts, and in particular emphasizes his first-rate contribution to an analysis of the rôle of the military in different types of society, pointing out the general and unwise neglect thereof by most republican and democratic writers—a warning made especially timely by the problems and issues of these last months.

Arthur Livingston (essay date 1939)

SOURCE: An introduction to *The Ruling Class: Elementi di Scienza Politica* by Gaetano Mosca, translated by Hannah D. Kahn, McGraw-Hill Book Company, Inc., 1939, pp. ix-xxxvi.

[*In the following introduction to Mosca's* The Ruling Class, *Livingston provides an overview of Mosca's theory of elites.*]

I. TAINE AND MOSCA: THE *TEORICA*

Gaetano Mosca's theory of the ruling class was evolved in its first form during the years 1878-1881, while Mosca was a student under Angelo Messedaglia at the University of Palermo. It occurred to him at that time to generalize the method which Taine had used in the *Ancien*

régime. There, it will be remembered, Taine sought the origins of the French Revolution in the decadence of the groups of people that had ruled France during the golden age of the old monarchy, a class which he considered and analyzed under three headings, the crown, the clergy and the nobility.

The first thought of the student Mosca was that perhaps any society might be analyzed the way Taine had analyzed monarchical France; and his second was that, in view of the vogue that doctrines of majority rule had had in the nineteenth century, he had hit upon a most fertile and suggestive hypothesis. If one looks closely at any country, be it commonly known as a monarchy, a tyranny, a republic or what one will, one inevitably finds that actual power is wielded never by one person, the monarch or head of the state, nor yet by the whole community of citizens, but by a particular group of people which is always fairly small in numbers as compared with the total population. Taine had shown, also, that the traits of the brilliant French civilization of the age of the Great King were the traits less of the French people at large than of the same French aristocracy and, in fact, seemed to be connected with the special conditions under which that aristocracy had functioned during the seventeenth and eighteenth centuries. That principle, too, could be generalized into the thesis that the dominant traits of the civilization of a given society during a given period will be the traits of the group of people who govern it (politicians, rulers).

Today Mosca is eighty years old; but at no time in the course of his long life has he ever been quite able to forget the thrill of discovery that he experienced away back in the seventies as he found himself in possession of what he thought to be a golden key to the arcana of human history. To tell the truth, the originality of his discovery has not seldom been a subject of dispute among his colleagues and competitors; and during the fifty years that have intervened since those days, many writers have busied themselves compiling lists of thinkers who have explicitly noted a fact which has always been perfectly apparent to everybody, *viz.,* that in all human groups at all times there are the few who rule and the many who are ruled.

The maxim that there is nothing new under the sun is a very true maxim; that is to say, it covers about half the truth, which is a great deal of truth for a maxim to cover. All human beings who have lived on earth have lived, by and large, on the same earth. They have all beheld, at least out of the corners of their eyes, the same realities; they have all experienced the same emotions; they have all thought, we may imagine, the same thoughts. But what the history of human civilization shows is the unending variety with which individuals evaluate the various things that everybody sees. Probably no human being since Adam has been without an approximate knowledge of the law of gravity; but no one till Galileo's day thought of centering his whole attention upon the falling object and making it the pivot of a scientific revolution. No human being since the day of Cain and Abel has been unaware that people preach moral principles and then use such power as they have often, if not always, without regard to moral principles. Yet no one before Machiavelli ever thought of taking that fact and founding upon it a scientific politics which would eliminate ethical considerations. I believe Croce has said it somewhere: The originality of thinkers lies not always in their seeing things that nobody else has ever seen, but often in the stress they give now to this commonplace and now to that. I consider it useful to make this little digression for the benefit of an ever-lengthening roster of source hunters who spend their time drawing literary and scientific parallels without considering questions of stress or the uses that men of genius make of commonplaces. The medieval Venetians or the ancient Romans were so much in possession of the concept of class and of the concept of ruling classes that they devised meticulous legislation to cover class relations and even the movement of social atoms from class to class. All the same, no Venetian and no Roman ever formulated Mosca's theory of the ruling class. Class is a visible external fact of everyday life in Europe, and few European writers have been able to discuss social problems at any great length without eventually encountering the fact of class, of class struggle, of class circulation, in some form or other. None of them, however, not Guicciardini, not Marx, not Taine, made the use of the fact of class that Mosca made. And conversely, one may say the same of those who have paralleled or utilized Mosca—of Michels, of Sorel, of Pareto.

Why do individual thinkers come to stress certain relations and facts which everybody observes and takes for granted? Usually these problems of personal evolution are beyond recovery by history. We shall never know why Voltaire became a mocking skeptic while his brother remained a pious "enthusiast." We know, indeed, that, in periods of intense and free cultural activity, if a certain number of intellectuals are placed in one general environment in the presence of the same general problems, certain numbers of them will evolve the same solutions. This fact is ordinarily taken account of in the remark that at certain periods certain concepts, certain manners of thinking, seem to be "in the air." Sorel developed the concept of the political myth in the first decade of the twentieth century. Mosca had developed his concept of the "political formula" twenty years before. Sorel was not a methodical scholar. He knew nothing of Mosca. Evidently the concept was "in the air." For two generations before Mosca's time, socialism had been emphasizing the conflict of classes, and in Italy in particular the educated classes had become explicitly aware of their duties and responsibilities as "leading" or "directing" classes (*classi dirigenti*). One should not be surprised, therefore, at such evident parallels as exist between Mosca and many other thinkers before him or after him.

While the details of individual evolution most often remain undiscoverable, apart from individual memoirs or confessions which are themselves not too trustworthy in such regards, one is usually able to note certain general environmental circumstances that seem to influence individual choices of stress in certain directions. When we find Mosca in possession of Taine in 1878, we should not forget that Mosca was an Italian while Taine was a Frenchman. I find it very French in Taine that he should never have been interested in the general bearings of the method that he was using. So true is this that, as he proceeds to rear his intellectual structure about the old regime, he is continually led into the fallacy of assigning particular causes (associated with the fact of the exclusion of the French aristocracy from their feudal functions) to phenomena that are general and worldwide—preciosity, for instance, rationality, politeness, display, all of which recur in times and places where ruling classes are situated far otherwise than was the French aristocracy of the golden age. I find it also very French in Taine that he should never free himself, in the *Origines,* from the preoccupation with good citizenship. Aspiring indeed to a stern and rigorous historical method, Taine can think of history only as at the service of certain high moral ideals.

Mosca instead was an Italian, to whom the analytical method of thinking came naturally. He leaped upon Taine's method as a tool for straight thinking and sought to be, and, to a surprising extent in one still so young, succeeded in being "objective." I find that very Italian. Italians do easily and as a matter of course what other human beings do rarely, if at all, and then only with great effort and after hard and sustained discipline: they think by processes of distinction. While the rest of the world is hunting for ways to show that the true is good and the good true, and that both are beautiful, the Italians are busy keeping virtue, truth and beauty separate and in the heart as well as in the mind. Perhaps that is the great Italian "contribution to civilization," which Italian nationalists are always trying to discover.

One may as well add that Mosca is a Sicilian (born at Palermo in 1858). That too is a determining factor in his individuality which Americans especially should bear in mind. Americans as a rule stand at an opposite pole to the run of Sicilians in their manner of approaching life through thought. Americans are impatient of theory and suspicious of philosophies and general principles. We study history and almost never the philosophy of history. Few American lawyers will have anything to do with the philosophy of law. Let an American show a definite propensity for theoretical generalizing and he will be barred from public life as an impractical menace. It is amazing, on the other hand, with what a dearth of theoretical discipline certain famous Americans can get along through life and go far. To that deficiency we partly owe the reputation for ignorance and naïveté that we enjoy, as a nation, in a more sophisticated Europe. The level of theory in the United States is much lower than the level of theory on the Continent. The Continent in its turn is, on the whole, in the rear of Italy in this respect, and the great Italian theoreticians tend to be southerners. In a charming "confession" with which he prefaced the 1884 edition of the *Teorica,* Mosca tells of his great interest as a boy in history and boasts of his retentive memory. But what strikes one in Mosca, the historian, is the fact that history has no meaning whatever to him until it has become general principle, uniformity, philosophy. So it was with Vico and Bruno, and so it is with Croce—all men of the Italian South.

Two other determinations, one professional, the other Sicilian, have perhaps a more direct bearing upon Mosca's development of the vision he owed in the first instance to Taine. In the *Teorica* of 1884, Mosca kept strictly to problems of government, and that interest is paramount even in the *Elements.* This narrowing of his field is all the more striking as one contrasts the uses to which the concept of class, or of the ruling class, has been put by thinkers all the way from Marx to Pareto. The reason undoubtedly is that Mosca began life as a student of constitutional law and of political theories. He became an unsalaried lecturer on those subjects, first at Palermo (1881-1886), then at Rome (1887-1895). From Rome he went on to be a professor of constitutional law at Turin (1895-1923), returning to Rome (1923-1931) as professor of political theories. Now it is clear that government proper is only one phase of social life, while the implications of the theory of the ruling class as Taine had applied that theory in the sixties and as Mosca had conceived it in 1881, lead out into society as a whole and beckon toward a general sociology. Mosca was never to follow them in that direction beyond the limits reached in the *Elements.* Perhaps in a spirit of professional specialization, perhaps for practical reasons, he always kept turning backward and inward upon the strictly constitutional or political problem, leaving some of his richest and most suggestive ideas in the form of hints, assertions, or casual observations, but at any rate undeveloped.

Sicilian again one may call the political bent which Mosca's placid biography shows. Not all Sicilians are politicians, but when a Sicilian is a politician he is a good one. The Sicilian takes to politics as a duck to water. North Italians, too, of course, have been seen in Italian public life. But they make a great to-do about it. They shout and wave their arms from soap-boxes, they fill the newspapers with their publicities, their polemics, their marches on Rome, they fight libel suits and duels; and finally they get into the government, only to be upset, as likely as not, at the next turn of the wheel. The Sicilian, instead, simply takes the train and goes to Rome, where a coach-in-four is waiting to drive him to what Carducci called "the summit of the Capitol." That, more or less, was Mosca's experience in public life. Editor of the journal of the Chamber of Deputies from 1887 to 1895 (a bureaucratic post—it maintained him during his unpaid lectureship at the university), he became a deputy himself in 1908, and sat with the Liberal Conservatives during two legislatures till 1918 (those included the war years), serving also as under-secretary for the Colonies under the Salandra ministry (1914-1916). And there he was, in 1918, senator for life by the usual royal appointment, and all without any great clamor, any boisterous quarrels or exposures, without even any particular public fame.

Prezzolini and Papini tried to publicize Mosca in 1903-1904—"to valorize him as a public asset," as the language went in those days. Prezzolini made a second effort in his *Voce* series in 1912 (see *Il nuovo nazionalismo*). One need mention this aspect of Mosca's career, always eminent yet never prominent, simply as reinforcing the mental attitudes that inclined him to leave his work permanently in a somewhat embryonic form, and even to subordinate it, in some few respects, to the outlook of a political party.

The Italian and Sicilian background, the professional outlook, the political talent, which are revealed by this forward look from Mosca's student days, help us to understand the developments that Mosca gave to his theory of the ruling class in the years 1881-1883. At that time he was in possession of three or four simple concepts which he thought he could use for the construction of an outline history of the rise of the modern state. Contrary to theories of majority rule, he perceived, societies are always ruled by minorities, by oligarchies. The current classification of governments, therefore—Aristotle's (monarchies, aristocracies, democracies), Montesquieu's (absolutisms, limited monarchies, republics), Spencer's (militant and industrial states)—could be dispensed with in favor of a classification of oligarchies. Essaying this classification, Mosca distinguished a number of types: military and priestly aristocracies, hereditary aristocracies, aristocracies of landowners, aristocracies of liquid wealth (money), aristocracies of merit (allowing, that is, free access to power to all elements in society and notably to people of the poorer classes). Now the various political theories that have prevailed in history—"chosen people" theories based on conceptions of race or family, divine-right theories or theories of popular sovereignty—by no means reflect the realities underlying this classification. Mosca, therefore, went on to develop his theory of the "political formula." There is always a ruling minority, but such minorities never stop at the brute fact of holding power. They justify their rule by theories or principles which are in turn based on beliefs or ethical systems which are accepted by those who are ruled. These "political formulas" contain very little that could be described as "truth," but they should not be regarded as deliberate deceptions or mystifications on the part of scheming rulers. They express, rather, a deep need in human nature whereby the human being more readily defers to abstract universal principles than to the will of individual human beings.

Mature in 1881, these ideas were formulated in the *Teorica dei governi e governo parlamentare,* which was complete in 1883 and published in 1884 (2d ed., 1925). In spite of its age and the writings of Mosca that have followed it, this book still has its interest and its points of originality. Eleven years later, 1895, Mosca completed and published his *Elements (Elementi di scienza politica,* 1896).

As compared with the *Teorica,* the *Elements* presents the theory of the ruling class in more rounded form, along with a series of new concepts that are exceedingly suggestive.

II. THE CONCEPT OF HISTORY

In the *Elements,* in line with an outstanding preoccupation of European scholarship during the nineties, Mosca confronts the problem of constructing a political science (which he prefers to keep distinct from sociology). The content of that science will be the discovery of the constant tendencies or laws that determine the behavior of the human masses and regulate the organization of political authority. These tendencies or laws can be discovered only from a study of "social facts," which in turn can be found only in the history of the various nations: "It is to the historical method that we must return."

Actually, Mosca's practice is better than this incomplete statement would indicate. He will of course take the facts about society from any source or method that can supply them, only so they are facts—from economics, from anthropology, from psychology, or any similar science. He does explicitly reject for the politico-social field any absolute or exclusive acceptance of climatic or north-and-south theories, anthropological theories based on the observation of primitive societies (the question of size is important), the economic interpretation of history (it is too unilateral), doctrines of racial superiorities and inferiorities (many different races have had their moments of splendor), and evolutionary theories (they fail to account for the rhythmical movement of human progress—biological evolution would require continuous improvement). However, apart from some keen remarks (as, for instance, those on the limitations of the experimental method or on the applicability of science to the control of social living), the main interest in this statement of the problem of scientific sociology lies in the fact that it undoubtedly influenced the penetrating and altogether novel discussion of the same problem in Pareto's *Trattato* (chap. I), which, in turn, is the final enlargement of an essay by Pareto written in 1897.

The interest of Mosca's view comes out if we consider it not from the standpoint of social science, but from that of historical science. Now if one were to say that this view is new and original, a host of scholars would appear with no end of citations to show that Mosca says nothing that has not been known to everyone since the days of Herodotus. Historians have always felt more or less vaguely that their work ought somehow to enrich human experience, that one can, after all, learn something from the fact that billions of human beings have lived out their lives on earth before us. Historians as metaphysical and theological as Bonald have always contended that history confirmed their arbitrary creeds. On the other hand a very respectable list of authorities could be quoted to show that history can teach us nothing; that life is always new; that where there is a will there is a way; that no impulse of the present need be checked in the light of analogies from the past. If one examines the present outlook of historical science in the United States, one observes a

considerable variety of attitudes and practices. Of the routine and elementary task of the historian, the construction of the historical record, there is general awareness, and one notes many distinguished performances in this field. As to the meaning of the record, its utility—why "to know all about Poussin" is any more important than to know how many cigarette butts are thrown daily on the subway stairs—the greatest bewilderment prevails. There is the anecdotic interest in history, the sentimental titillation that comes from reliving exciting episodes in the past or retraversing the lives of unusual or successful individuals (the common rule in literary or freelance productions). There is the propaganda history, where the writer is meticulous about the accuracy of the record and even makes contributions to it, but then feels it necessary to give the record an apparent meaning by saucing it with reflections which amount to saying, "I am a pacifist"; "I am a socialist"; "I am a Catholic"; and so on. There is the pseudoscientific or semi-artistic history where the record is again accurate and fairly complete, but where the writer gives it an arbitrary meaning by organizing the facts around more or less unconscious sentimental attitudes borrowed from his environment, now ethical, now romantic, now optimistic, now (if the author is unusually intelligent) ironical or cynical. Finally, there is the Robinsonian history, the most scientific of these various types, where the past is taken as the explanation of the present, and, to a certain extent, the present is taken as the explanation of the past, but where the matter of choosing ideals is regularly left hazy and doubtful.

Into this atmosphere Mosca's conception of history should come as a clarifying breeze. The record of human experience is now from three to ten thousand years old. It is probable that during that time human nature has been able to make a fairly complete revelation of its general traits, its basic tendencies and laws. What are those tendencies, those laws? It is the business of the historian to tell us, and history is a mere amusement, a purposeless activity, unless its record is made to contribute to knowledge of tendencies and laws. To complete this theory a remark or two may be necessary. The construction of the historical record, the determination of facts in their sequence, motives or causes is a research by itself. In itself it has no purpose and envisages no utility. It has its own methods, its own technique, which reign sovereign over the research. As regards what can be learned from history, it is clear that the latter can supply only the general forms of human behavior—the specific situation will always be new, without exact precedent or analogy in the past.

Mosca feels that history is probably better able to tell us what not to do than what to do in the given case. But, really, it always remains a question of tendencies, of psychological, social forces which man may conceivably learn to master some day, the way he has learned, and marvelously learned, to master and utilize the material forces of nature. At any rate, Mosca's conception of history suggests the proper attitude to take toward his various theses. "Human societies are always governed by minorities"; "Rapid class circulation is essential to progress"; "Human societies are organized around collective illusions"; "Level of civilization corresponds to grade of juridical defense"; "Human societies show a tendency to progress toward higher and higher levels of civilization"; "Over-bureaucratization facilitates revolution." These and the others like them would be so many tentative statements of general laws. They are subject to objective scientific criticism, emendation, refutation.

III. SOCIAL FORCES AND BALANCE OF SOCIAL FORCES

The concept of social forces was already present in Mosca's early *Teorica.* In the *Elements* it is amplified, and its implications are more fully perceived.

A "social force" is any human activity or perquisite that has a social significance—money, land, military prowess, religion, education, manual labor, science—anything. The concept derives from the necessity of defining and classifying ruling classes. A man rules or a group of men rules when the man or the group is able to control the social forces that, at the given moment in the given society, are essential to the possession and retention of power.

Implicit in the theory of the ruling class is the law (I like to call it "Mosca's law") that "type and level of civilization vary as ruling classes vary." Ruling classes will vary in respect to the number and grade of the social forces which they control, tolerate, stimulate or create. The internal stability of a regime can be measured by the ratio between the number and strength of the social forces that it controls or conciliates, in a word, represents, and the number and strength of the social forces that it fails to represent and has against it. Progressive, and one might even say "successful," regimes regularly create social forces which they find it difficult to absorb; governments often fall because of their virtues, not their defects (a drastic emendation to Taine and to ethical interpretations of history in general). Struggle is one of the continuous and never-failing aspects of human life. Social forces, therefore, regularly manifest themselves in aspirations to power. Soldiers want to rule, and they are a hard group to control since they hold the guns and know best how to use them. Money wants to rule and it is hard to control money because most people succumb to the glamour and influence of wealth. Priests want to rule, and they have the weight of the ignorant masses and the majesty of the mysteries of life in their favor. Scientists want to rule, and, from Plato to Comte and from Comte to Scott, they have dreamed of dictators who will establish their technocracies and their "rules of the best." Labor wants to rule and would rule did it not always encounter the law of the ruling class and fall into the hands of its leaders. Public officeholders want to rule, and they might easily do so for they already sit in the seats of power.

When we have Mosca safely ensconced among the immortals, a mystery will confront the historian of social theories: Why, having reached this point in his medita-

tions, did Mosca not throw his political research away and set out to write a sociology? The answer will probably be found in the professional and temperamental determinations to which we have alluded. Mosca was thinking primarily of the political aspects of society and could never wholly divest himself of that interest.

Montesquieu had supplied him, already in his student days, with the concept of balance—with Montesquieu it was a balance of powers, of which the American constitution was eventually to supply an impressive example. Mosca transfers the concept to social forces.

In certain cases we see social forces that do succeed in usurping power, and one symptom of the usurpation is their imposition by force of the political formula that they happen to hold as an absolute principle to which everyone must bow and which everyone must believe or pretend to believe. That means tyranny, and it also means a reduction in the number of active social forces and, therefore, a drop in level of civilization. In other cases we see, for example, military power checked and balanced by money or by religion; or money, perhaps, checked and balanced by taxation imposed by land; or an obstreperous religious hierarchy checked and balanced now by superstitious sects which grow up within itself, now by coalitions of external forces of enlightenment. At certain moments—they are the heavenly interludes in history—we see fairly stable balances of forces where nearly everyone can do as he pleases and have his say so that the whole infinite potentialities of human nature burst into bloom.

IV. JURIDICAL DEFENSE: THE IMPORTANCE OF POLITICAL ORGANIZATION

This beneficent balance is attained, Mosca decides, at times and in people where it has become law, where, that is, the aggressiveness of social forces, or of the individuals who embody them, is checked, not by the sheer manifestation of force applied case by case, but by habit, custom, acquiescence, morals, institution and constitution—in a word (his word), juridical defense (government by law with due process). Contrary to Marxist, evolutionary and other materialistic or sociological interpretations of history, Mosca holds that the problem of political organization is paramount. If ruling classes can be appraised by noting the number and grade of social forces which they recognize, the governments which various ruling classes manage can be appraised by the grade of juridical defense which they provide. This Mosca seems sometimes to regard as very largely a technical problem of government. A blossoming Mohammedan civilization first became stationary and then declined because the caliphs failed to solve the problem of the army. The armies in the provinces followed their generals, the generals became independent and arbitrary despots; social forces contracted in numbers and then languished. There is no reason to assume that the evolution of the Mohammedan peoples was any more predetermined than that of the Christian peoples. The fact is that at certain moments in their history they, or rather their ruling classes, must have made wrong political decisions that headed them toward decline instead of toward higher levels of civilization. In the case of the Mohammedan world one mistake, according to Mosca's system, would have been the failure to separate church and state, since that separation he regards as one of the basic essentials for a proper balance of social forces.

A high grade of juridical defense depends also, Mosca contends, upon a sufficient division of wealth to allow of the existence in fairly large numbers of people of moderate means; in fact, the numbers of such people will probably supply the gauge for measuring the effectiveness and stability of the balance of social forces. The presence of a strong middle class in a society means that education is discovering and utilizing the resources of talent which, quite independently of race and heredity, are forever developing in the human masses at large (resources which backward societies somehow fail to use; that is why they are backward). It also means that the ruling classes always have available materials with which to restock and replenish themselves as their own personnels deteriorate under pressure of the multiple forces that are always edging aristocracies toward decline. Middle classes represent the variety and the intensity of a society's activities and the maximum variety in types of wealth and in distribution of wealth. Standing apart from the daily clash of the more powerful interests, they are the great repositories of independent opinion and disinterested public spirit. One hardly need say it: In developing these postulates and their many corollaries, Mosca has written the classic of Italian conservatism, which functioned as an influential minority in Italy's political life just before the war.

But supposing we bring these arguments back to the strictly objective plane. We have spoken of "mistakes" and of choices as though the lawgivers of Mosca, like those of Rousseau or of the many writers who antedated the rise of deterministic theories, were free agents who could do with society just as they pleased. Suppose it be conceded that the separation of church and state and a distribution of wealth that allows the existence of a strong middle class are essential in a society if it is to attain a high level of civilization. How is science to obtain the recognition and application of those "laws" in the face of the religious interests which will in all pious enthusiasm continue to strive for uniformity of dogma and for control of education and the state, and in the face of the greed of human beings, who will go madly on amassing great fortunes and then using them to acquire power and dominion? Mosca leaves us no hope except in the enlightened statesmanship of those who wield power over the nations. Instructive in this connection is the distinction he draws between the politician and the statesman, the former being the man who is skilled in the mere art of obtaining power and holding it, whereas the latter is the man who knows how to manipulate the blind instincts of the human masses in the direction of conformity with the laws of man's social nature, much as the

navigator manipulates the brute forces of tide and wind to the advantage of his ship and its passengers. Mosca has little confidence in the inborn good sense of the masses and despairs of ever bringing any great number of people to a rational and scientific view of public problems. History shows not a few ruling classes, on the other hand, the Venetian and English aristocracies, for instance, which have been able to lay interests and sentiments aside to a very considerable extent and to govern scientifically and objectively.

V. STANDING ARMIES

Ampler consideration of the problem of juridical defense leads Mosca to one of the most brilliant and original investigations in the *Elements.* From the standpoint of struggle, military power is the best equipped of all social forces to assert itself and claim dominion. Why then is the military dictatorship not the normal form of human government? The peoples of the western world have for some generations now been familiar with systems where armies and navies are rigidly subject to civil authorities, and they are wont to regard the military rebellion as something exceptional and monstrous. Actually the human beings who have lived on this earth in security from the brutal rule of the soldier are so few in number, on the background of the whole of human history, as hardly to count. The military tyranny in some form or other is in fact the common rule in human society; and even in the best-ordered societies, as we are only too easily able to observe after the experience of the nineteenth and twentieth centuries in Europe, any serious disturbance of an established order of a nonmilitary type is likely to result in a reversion to the military dictatorship. The process by which the modern civilized nations have escaped from this grievous law of man's social nature Mosca rightly regards as one of the most interesting in history. Paradoxically enough, and contrarily to the modes of thinking of those liberals who dream of total disarmaments, Mosca finds the solution of the secret in the growth of the standing army.

Croce, somewhere in the *Ethics,* classifies human beings into four types, corresponding to the stresses of the four "forms of the spirit" which he makes basic in his system: the artist, the scientist, the statesman, the saint. That classification overlooks the adventurer, the warrior, the man who instinctively resorts to violence in his relations with his fellow men and prefers dangerous living to any other mode of existence. The antics of this individual on the stage of history are so conspicuous and withal so fascinating that a virtual revolution in historical method has been required in order to win some attention from the thoughtful for the types whom Croce recognizes. Give the adventurer a good brain, a good education, a supply of genius and an historical opportunity, and he becomes a Napoleon or an Alexander. Give him a great ideal and he becomes a Garibaldi. Give him a chance and he becomes a Mussolini. Give him a job and he becomes a soldier and a general. Ignore him and he becomes the gangster and the outlaw. A believer in final causes might soundly assert that the man of violence was invented by a wise Creator as a sort of catalyzer for human progress. The adventurer is never in the majority. The majority of human beings prefer peaceful orderly existences, and, when they dream, they dream of heavens where there is only light and music and no sorrow or toil, where the lion lies down with the lamb, where manna falls now from the sky and now from the government, where, in short, we are free from the competition of our neighbors and from the wearying struggle of life. Eras of prosperity are continually recurring in human history when the dream of security and idleness seems almost realizable; then, just as regularly, the man of violence comes along and sets the wheels to grinding again. So in our day, the citizens of the prosperous democracies had referred the movement of history to the social workers and the lawyers at Geneva in order to settle back in the night clubs to enjoy the nobility of their peaceful sentiments and the dividends of science. But a Hitler, a Mussolini, a Japanese general rises and tells them that to win or retain the right to drink and dance and be self-complacent they have to get out and fight.

On the other hand, the man of violence is not much more than that. The world that he creates is a pretty wretched affair. Give him the power and he regularly enslaves the rest of men, leaving them only the bare means of subsistence. Quite regularly he stultifies thought into hypocrisy and flattery, and the stimulating lift of organized public spirit he replaces with some form of mob fanaticism.

Mosca conceives of the standing army as a device automatically arrived at by the modern world for disciplining, canalizing and making socially productive the combative elements in the peoples. In loosely organized societies violence concentrates around a large number of different focuses and differing interests, and the anarchy of the Middle Ages and of feudal societies at large results. In our own day, in Russia, Italy, Germany, Spain, we have seen that as soon as the stability of a society wavers power recreates itself in small centers, and periods of rule by local gangs ensue for greater or lesser lengths of time. The standing army, instead, tapers up to control by the state and therefore becomes part and parcel of the social order. Strong enough to enable the state to master local or sporadic manifestations of violence, it is itself under the direct control of all those mighty social forces which create and maintain the state itself. Recent history again confirms this conception of the status and objective role of the standing army. The national army of our time is an organism of incalculable might. The human forces which it embraces, the weapons and other material agencies of which it disposes, are incredibly powerful. Yet we have seen two revolutions take place in great and highly civilized countries in the face of the army and against the army. Certain observers of the rise of Fascism and National Socialism in Italy and in Germany looked to the loyally monarchical or republican armies to crush those movements, and undoubtedly they could have with a mere show of force. But the submersion of the German and Italian armies in the established order was complete, and, lacking the impulse from the apex of civil authority,

they did not move. Not only that: Once new rulers were established in the seats of power, the armies responded obediently to their new orders.

What is the secret of the amazing subordination of the armies of the West? Mosca finds the answer in the aristocratic character, so to say, of the army, first in the fact that there is a wide and absolute *social* distinction between private and officer, and second that the corps of officers, which comes from the ruling class, reflects the balance of multiple and varied social forces which are recognized by and within that class. The logical implications of this theory are well worth pondering. If the theory be regarded as sound, steps toward the democratization of armies—the policy of Mr. Hore-Belisha, for instance—are mistaken steps which in the end lead toward military dictatorships; for any considerable democratization of armies would make them *active* social forces reflecting all the vicissitudes of social conflict and, therefore, *preponderant* social forces. On the other hand, army officers have to be completely eliminated from political life proper. When army officers figure actively and ex officio in political councils, they are certain eventually to dominate those councils and replace the civil authority—the seemingly incurable cancer of the Spanish world, for an example.

VI. SOCIAL TYPE AND POLITICAL FORMULA

The concept of social type is basic in Mosca's thought, and, since the phenomenon of the social grouping is one of the facts that the historian encounters at the most superficial glance at society, there is nothing remarkable in that. An elementary discussion of what Mosca calls social type is already present in Machiavelli. Mosca's analysis of the elements that constitute the greater social groupings was complete in the nineties. It is interesting that at that early date he was discounting race as a factor in the sense of nationality and emphasizing the greater importance of the myth of race. But he was also, with remarkable insight, foreseeing an intensification of nationalisms in the twentieth century as a sort of compensation for the decline of faith in the world religions which, under the pressure of experimental science, were losing their utility as cohesive forces in society. Quite original and too much neglected, I believe, is Mosca's conception of the modern sense of nationality as a product of the world religions, to the extent that those religions, with their doctrines that transcend race and nationality, came to embrace the most diverse groups within the same social type and so inclined those groups to coalesce individually around political formulas of a nonreligious character. That doctrine throws light upon the conflict of church and state in the Middle Ages in the West, a conflict that was essential to the growth of secular civilization which rescued Europe from the fossilization that settled upon the Mohammedan and eastern worlds. In this regard Mosca, one may say, has formulated rather than prosecuted the research into the complicated interplay of group instincts within each separate society. His conclusions, at any rate, are susceptible of almost indefinite elaboration.

The methodological advantages of Mosca's concept of social type are very considerable. In the first place it points the way to sound scientific solutions of conflicts that cannot be solved by ethical methods. For instance, the United States prohibits the immigration of Asiatics. Whenever our diplomats go prattling about democratic principles or even Christian principles they expose themselves to devastating rejoinder from the Japanese diplomats, who can quite properly observe that democratic or Christian principles would require unlimited Asiatic immigration. It is well to note, therefore, that the questions at issue are not questions of democratic theory or Christian ethics, but questions of social type, which latter are always settled either by force or by accommodation and reconciliation of apparent interests.

To complete our examination of conscience we might go on and ask what, then, we are to do with our democratic principles and our Christian ethics? The answer is that these latter are formulas which have a very limited scientific validity and function as guides of conduct within strictly limited fields. What those limits shall be, just how and where they shall be drawn, are problems for statesmen, not for pastors or for professors of ethics. Our civilization subsists only so long as our social type subsists. Whether or not certain social types "ought" to vanish in the interests of civilization is a cosmic question that could be answered only by some neutral divinity looking at our planet from afar off. What we know is that social types good and bad insist on existing and that the measure of that insistence is a measure of force (or of accommodation as a substitute for force). So it is with any conflict between a universal ethical ideal and the instincts and the interests of social type.

The extent to which political formulas of universal pretension are serviceable for specific groups is an interesting and important one which the events of our time have raised to a critical prominence. Hitler's Germany seems to have concluded that a national myth in which only Germans can believe is of stronger cohesive potency than universal myths such as Christianity, democracy or socialism. Apparent to the eye is the advantage of ease of enforcement, in that such a myth makes a direct appeal to group instincts without mitigations or attenuations from rationality. But equally apparent are the disadvantages. Strictly national myths, like the "chosen people" myths of the Jews or Greeks, tend to sharpen international antagonisms unduly. Hitler is building up the same universal detestation that the pan-Germanism of the first decade of the century aroused. Such myths, besides, have in the past been effective only on very low planes of civilization where they have had very few social forces to fuse or coordinate. One may wonder whether German civilization will not in the end be oversimplified by the long inculcation of an exclusively national myth.

Fascist Italy is working on the theory that the universal myth can be subordinated to the national myth (subjugation of church to state) and then used as a channel of influence upon the countries that accept or tolerate it.

Says Mussolini (to Professor Starkie, *The Waveless Plain*): "The Latin tradition of Imperial Rome is represented by Catholicism. . . . There are in the world over 400,000,000 men [i.e., human beings] who look towards Rome from all parts of the earth. That is a source of pride for us Italians." Soviet Russia is using a universal political formula, communism, and explicitly claims leadership over the minorities which accept the myth in other countries. The myth intrinsically has considerable potency, as resting on powerful combative sentiments (hatred of the poor for the rich), reinforced by humanitarian sentiments of aversion to suffering (poverty can be abolished). In this sense it has its analogies with early democratic theory, which rested on those same sentiments. It is less fortunate than democratic theory in respect of the sentiments of property. These it openly flouts, whereas democratic theory takes full advantage of them. It is curious that Russian nationalism has grown in intensity under the communist political formula much as the western nationalisms grew up inside the Christian and democratic formulas. However, all such formulas are absolute and strive to achieve uniformity of acceptance. When their universal character is taken too seriously, believed, that is, with too great ardor, they suck the life blood from the social type, either by absorbing too much of the type's combative energy or by oversimplifying its structure and so lowering its civilization level.

Mosca's concept of social type has another methodological advantage in that it supplies the general form and, therefore, emphasizes the common nature of many varied phenomena. Two men see each other at a distance in Hong Kong. They meet in Cairo, and the fact that they had seen each other at a distance in Hong Kong constitutes a bond between them that justifies closer contacts. They form thereby an embryonic social type, which rests upon a single, inconsequential fact. At another extreme we find millions of people bound together by millions of ties, memories, interests, common experiences. It is the same phenomenon but with a differing inner structure. Mosca's concept of the social type supplies a tool for severing the common from the differing elements. It stops, however, one step short of Pareto's concept of group-persistence—persistence of relations between persons and things, which would be an hypothesis for investigating the basic psychological phenomena involved in human associations of whatever type. Parties, sects, religions, movements, nations, states, are still often regarded as separate phenomena. "Nationalism began with the French Revolution," writes an American historian. Actually nationalism began with Adam, in the sense that it rests upon a fundamental law of human nature, which can be seen at work in thousands of other manifestations.

Mosca repeatedly emphasizes the historical utility of the social type as coordinating a multiplicity of wills and efforts for the achievement of common ends. On that basis it can be seen that history will be a play of two contrary forces, a trend toward unity and expansion, and a trend toward diversity and concentration. The Abyssinians, the Armenians and the Californians are Christians, and humanity surely profits in many ways from that advance toward world solidarity—group and even class isolation seem regularly to be elements in social fossilization and decline. On the other hand, the world has profited even more from particularity of social type—the existence of separate and powerful groups, all on the offensive and on the defensive, each struggling first for independence and then for domination, each living in a fever heat of life and death struggle in which the talents and moral traits of its individual members are stimulated and utilized to the utmost. Even within particular types a very considerable play of subtypes is an advantage, as implying multiplicity of social forces. This is just the reverse of the doctrine of Bossuet who viewed multiplicity of social types (or rather of political formulas) as disastrous. Bossuet wanted Europe to fossilize at the level of the Council of Trent. The prosperity, rising civilization level and world dominion of the Protestant countries after Bossuet's time refute his thesis. Obviously questions of proportion are involved: The social type must be large enough and compact enough in structure to survive in the struggle of types; it must be diversified enough, that is, tolerant enough, to utilize all its social forces and increase their number. The western world today threatens to fly to pieces from the violence of its antagonisms. It would gain by a little more unity which a hackneyed democratic formula, with its disastrous doctrine of minority determinations, seems unable to supply. The eastern world would surely gain, as it is in fact gaining, from more diversity. The great civilizing force in Asia at present is nationalism.

In dealing with the relations between social type and political formula, Mosca halts on the brink of a great research. The external manifestation of the existence of a type, at least of the larger types, will be the acceptance of a given formula. Does the type create the formula or the formula the type? Mosca answers quite soundly with a theory of interdependence: The type partly creates the formula in that the latter is usually a dogma put forward by some seer or prophet—now Mahomet, now Rousseau, now Marx—in response to certain "demands" of the given era. Once the formula exists and is accepted, it helps powerfully in molding the type by formulating maxims and precepts to which individuals more or less necessarily and successfully conform. The formula normally contains a large amount of nonsense mixed in with a certain small amount of verifiable truth. Observing the same facts Bentham considered in some detail the specific case where politicians talk the nonsense involved in the formula for the purpose of swaying mobs (scientifically, one should say, for the purpose of utilizing the social type for a given purpose). Making this difficulty the center of a research and centering all his interest upon it, Pareto evolved his epoch-making theory of residues and derivations.

VII. LEVEL OF CIVILIZATION

Mosca is one of the few (if any) political theorists to take level of civilization frankly and squarely as a criterion of evaluation. In not a few passages in the *Elements* he seems to assume that the desirability of high levels of civilization is self-evident, and that would be a very venial departure from the objective standpoint that he strives to maintain in his work. As a matter of fact relatively few people care very much about level of civilization—the great majority are interested in achieving some ideal—communism, democracy, peace, "happiness," "spirituality," "the salutary captivity of the faith," to quote Monsignor Moreau—regardless of the level at which civilization will find itself when those ideals are achieved or as a result of the effort to achieve them. The "nostalgie de la boue" is an organized human sentiment that snipes at the outposts of every free society when it is not slinking into the inner fortress under the guise of idealism and love of "higher things."

But subjective or metaphysical as this preference on Mosca's part may be, the concept of level of civilization nevertheless contributes, almost more than anything else, to maintaining the objective attitude in the *Elements*. It is a criterion that is definable to a high grade of approximation as multiplicity of activities; grade or quality of achievement in each; size and stability of social cohesion and, therefore, offensive and defensive power; standard of living and distribution of wealth; control of nature and utilization of that control; and so on—so on even to the "higher things" themselves. (Why be so disheartened over the number of our airplanes, telephones or bathtubs, when in addition to them we are producing humanists, neo-Thomists and even saints in fair abundance?)

The methodological advantages of the concept are enormous: and prime among them is the need which the concept creates, and the analytical method which it supplies, for viewing the given historical phenomenon or appraising the given proposal in the light of the total social picture. The literature of science and the literature of opinion suffer continually from their very virtues of specialization. In restricting the field of fact with which they deal they often develop unilateral methodologies which end by establishing arbitrary relations between facts. If we consider the Christian unity, so called, of the Middle Ages and linger on the metaphysical or logical implications of medieval political formulas, we may get a very distorted view of the importance of Christian unity or even of unity itself. Any consideration of the general level of civilization in the Middle Ages would certainly correct that view. So, for that school of writers which magnifies Greek thought and art as though those were manifestations of a heavenly state which mankind has lost forever. So, for those orientalists who propound the sublimities of the wisdom of the East without remembering that the eastern peoples have for ages been a sort of herring on which the sharks of the world, domestic and foreign, have feasted at their will and leisure. So, also, for those who regard literature, the arts, and philosophy as the distinctive representatives of level of culture. It is certain that arts, letters and metaphysical thinking can flourish among limited numbers of individuals in civilizations of very low level. It is also certain that when any great proportion of a nation's energies are devoted to arts, letters and metaphysics, its cultural level will decline. To be sure, it is just as certain that no highly diversified and intensely cultivated civilization will fail to show eminence in those activities.

Level of civilization is a dynamic, not a static, level, and in no civilization are all activities at the same level, or even at a level where they can automatically meet all the needs of the given historical moment. The ancient world needed more physical science than it possessed, if it was to perpetuate its achievements in the political and social fields. As Mosca points out, the great political upheaval at the end of the eighteenth century became more drastic through a lag in historical science. Napoleon's empire collapsed for the reason, among others, that transportation was in arrears both of industry and of military science—the steamboat and the railroad came a generation too late for the united Europe of which Napoleon dreamed. In our own time one may wonder whether the economic and social sciences will have attained a level to meet the great crises which our highly geared civilization periodically produces. One clings the more willingly to Mosca's concept of level of civilization in that, on a subjective plane, it is optimistic as to man's future on earth. In spite of the tremendous forces of inner expansion and disgregation that are continually rocking the societies of our day, Mosca very soundly feels that, in view of the scientific and moral resources that our time has at its disposal, the man of the present is far better placed than any of his historical predecessors have been to deal with the destructive material, social and psychological influences that have wrecked civilization so many times in the past and are threatening to wreck our own.

VIII. DEMOCRACY AND REPRESENTATIVE SYSTEM

Mosca's theory of the ruling class enters a third stage of development with the 1923 edition of the *Elementi,* which was enlarged by a "second part" (chaps. XII to XVII of the present translation). This second part contains a tentative history of the theory of the ruling class. It contains an outline of the rise of the modern state from the standpoint of types of ruling classes and types of political organization. Interesting here especially is the essay on the rise of the bourgeoisie and the origins of the French Revolution. As for the classification of governments, which in Mosca's earlier works had been reduced to two types, the feudal and the bureaucratic, Mosca now tries out another order of distinctions— autocratic and liberal principles, democratic and aristocratic tendencies. This discussion gives him occasion to add some interestingly objective reflections on class or social circulation in its bearing on the prosperity and decadence of nations.

But the most significant portions of the "second part" are a clarification, and first of all in Mosca's own mind, of the import of the criticism of democracy that he had made in the past and his impassioned appeal for a restoration of the representative system in Europe.

Mosca was on safe ground in asserting that great human masses can be organized and utilized for the attainment of specific purposes only by uniting them around some formula that will contain a large measure of illusion. He was also right in asserting that one element in that fact is the further fact that human beings more readily defer to abstract principles that seem to have an abiding validity than to the will of individual persons, which not seldom functions capriciously, may be valid only case by case, and, in any event, may shock the self-respect of the plain man who has a right to feel that he is being overridden by brute force. But in this regard all systems of political metaphysic are in the same boat: The "will of God," the "will of the people," "the sovereign will of the State," the "dictatorship of the proletariat," are one as mythical as the other. Perhaps of the lot, the least mythical is the will of the people, if by it one agree to mean that resultant of sentimental pressures, beliefs, habits, prejudices, temperaments (the general will of Rousseau or MacIver), on which common action can be based, and almost always is based, in tyrannies as well as in republics. In refuting a metaphysical thesis, one may be left in a metaphysical position oneself if one attaches any great importance to the refutation, on the assumption that political action must be based on formulas that are "true." Mosca is well aware of that. He repeatedly emphasizes the fact that the historic role of Christianity is there, whatever the scientific soundness of its dogmas. More directly to the point he urges that statesmen should beware of trying to enforce all the apparent implications of metaphysical formulas. The Church would not last a week if it tried to live up to its doctrine of poverty. No democracy would endure if it followed the "will" of the ignorant peace-loving masses instead of the aggressive leadership of the enlightened few. So, he argues in the *Teorica* and again in the *Elements,* the mere fact that universal suffrage follows from the premise of majority rule or the will of the people is in itself no recommendation for universal suffrage as a practical measure. Other considerations of a utilitarian character have to be introduced. Democratic metaphysics would require that the voting of budgetary expenditure be in the hands of the people's representatives, of Congress, let us say. In practice, it might easily be more satisfactory to have the budget in the hands of a responsible minister or president than in the hands of an irresponsible Congress. At least the sense of responsibility will be more active and effective in one conspicuous individual than in six hundred less conspicuous individuals.

But in spite of this very considerable consistency and objectivity, Mosca, in the *Teorica* and in Part I of the *Elements,* was undoubtedly swayed by certain prejudices of nationality, region and party and so lapsed into metaphysical errors. It is an error to argue that a limited suffrage is any sounder, theoretically, than universal suffrage (an error arising in sentiments of liberal conservatism). It is an error to argue that the history of a social system which is based on universal suffrage will necessarily follow the apparent logical implications of the theory of majority rule. Between the publication of the second and the third editions of the *Elements* the political equilibrium was upset in Europe—in Russia, in Italy, in Germany and Austria. In none of those cases did the upset occur because of the application of universal suffrage and the growth of the demagoguery required for governing by universal suffrage. The Fascist and communist regimes have come into being and have governed in joyous indifference to universal suffrage. The upset in Italy in particular did not come either from socialism or from the church. It came from those public-spirited young men whom Mosca was inclined to laud for their attacks on socialism, and those young men were working on a myth, not of democracy, but of nationalism. Far more fortunate were Mosca's prophecies when he stuck close to his theory of social forces and foresaw, in Russia, all the anarchy and horror that would follow from the attempt to establish communism by force, and in Italy all the consequences of the establishment of a single absolute formula to which absolute adherence would be forcibly required—and the end is not yet.

On the basis of the *Teorica* and the first form of the *Elements* it was easy to classify Mosca among those many Italian writers who have combatted the theory of democracy. The democratic system always had a stronger hold on the Italian head than on the Italian heart. Strong in all classes in Italy was the sense of social subordination (the sense of equality is more characteristic of France and the Protestant countries). Especially in rural Italy and on the Italian latifundia one still encounters many of the phenomena of class dependence that went with the older feudal world and, as Stendhal in his day perceived with a homesick yearning for old times, were not without their charm. The Italian intellectual and upper classes never embraced democracy wholeheartedly. They never applied the theory of mass education with any real conviction. One may therefore explain the antidemocratic intonation of Mosca's earlier works as partly a matter of fashion and partly a matter of youth. Democratic theory was generally accepted—it was original, therefore, to attack it. Democracy was unpopular, especially in south Italy. One was therefore swimming with the current in overstressing the corruption and inefficiency of parliamentary politicians and in waving the menace of socialism in the face of those who were eager to strengthen popular education and extend the suffrage.

All the same, the defense of the representative system in the second part of the *Elements* is not a mere case of the "jitters of '22," nor is it exactly a palinode. It is a bona fide return to the implications of Mosca's theory of social forces, freed of metaphysical divagations. "A maturer contemplation of history" has convinced Mosca that, of all forms of political organization, the representative system has shown itself capable of embracing the largest social units at incredibly high levels of civilization; and that, as compared with competing systems today, it gives promise of allowing freest play to increasing numbers of social forces and of providing more readily for that rapid social circulation which is essential to the stability of ruling classes and to reinforcing culture with tradition.

James Burnham (essay date 1943)

SOURCE: "The Machiavellian Tradition, The Ruling Class, Composition and Character of the Ruling Class, and Tendencies in the Ruling Class," in *The Machiavellians: Defenders of Freedom,* The John Day Company, Inc., 1943, pp. 81-115.

[*In the following essay, Burnham analyzes Mosca as a neo-Machiavellian.*]

I. THE MACHIAVELLIAN TRADITION

Machiavelli livied and wrote during a great social revolution, through which feudal society, its economy, political arrangement, and culture, were being replaced by the first stage of capitalist society. This revolution occupied a long period of time, and its boundaries cannot be given exact dates. Nevertheless, we may consider that it reached a decisive turning point during Machiavelli's own life, with the discovery of the New World, the rise of the first international stock exchanges, the Protestant religious revolution, the consolidation of the English national state under the Tudors, and the first appointment of bourgeois representatives—by Henry VIII—to the chief political offices of a great kingdom.

We also live during a great social revolution, a revolution through which capitalist society is being replaced by what I have elsewhere defined as "managerial society." It is, perhaps, the close analogy between our age and Machiavelli's that explains why the Machiavellian tradition, after centuries during which it was either neglected or misunderstood or merely repeated, has, in recent decades, been notably revived. Through the thought and research of a number of brilliant writers, Machiavellism has undergone a profound and extensive development.

The crisis of capitalist society was made plain by the first World War. With a far from accidental anticipation, much of the chief work of the modern Machiavellians was done in the period immediately preceding that war. Gaetano Mosca, it is true, had formulated many of his ideas as early as 1883, when he finished his first book, *Teorica dei governi e governo parlamentare.* However, his mature and finished thought is presented, with the war experiences close at hand, in the revised and expanded 1923 edition of *Elementi di scienza politica,* which is the basis of what has been translated into English as *The Ruling Class.* Georges Sorel's active career went on through the war, and ended with his death in 1922. Robert Michels and Vilfredo Pareto were writing their major books when the war began.

In a revolutionary transition, the struggle for power, which, during years of social stability, is often hidden or expressed through indirect and undramatic forms, becomes open and imperious. Machiavellism is concerned with politics, that is, with the struggle for power. It seems natural, therefore, that its first appearance as well as its revival should be correlated with social revolution. The revolutionary crisis makes men, or at least a certain number of men, discontent with what in normal times passes for political thought and science—namely, disguised apologies for the status quo or utopian dreams of the future; and compels them to face more frankly the real issues of power: some because they wish to understand more clearly the nature of the world of which they are a part, others because they wish also to discover whether and in what way they might be able to control that world in the furtherance of their own ideals.

Modern Machiavellism has, needless to say, weighty advantages over Machiavelli himself. Mosca, Michels, and Pareto, heirs—as all of us are who wish to be—of 400 years of scientific tradition, have an altogether clear understanding of scientific method. Machiavelli wrote at the beginnings of science; he was scientific, often, by instinct and impulse rather than design. Many of Machiavelli's insights are only implicit in his writings—indeed, I have done him perhaps more than justice in making explicit much that was probably not fully so to himself. Machiavelli mixed together an art and a science of politics; his scientific conclusions are frequently the by-products of an attempt to lay down a rule for securing some particular kind of political result. The modern Machiavellians are fully conscious of what they are doing and of the distinctions between an art and a science. They have, moreover, the incalculable advantage of that great treasury of historical facts which the patient and accumulating research of post-Renaissance scholars has put at our disposal.

. . . . .

Gaetano Mosca, like all Machiavellians, rejects any monistic view of history—that is, any theory of history which holds that there is one single cause that accounts for everything that happens in society. From the days, in the early centuries of Christianity, when the first philosophies of history attributed all that happened to the Will of God as sole causal principle, there have been dozens of examples of such monistic theories. Mosca examines three of them in some detail: the "climatic theory," the "racial theory," and the "economic materialist theory," which maintain, respectively, that differences in climate, in race, or in methods of economic production, are able to explain the course of history. He rejects all of these theories, not because of any prejudice against monism, but for that simple and final reason that seems to have no attraction for monists: because these theories do not accord with the facts.

Mosca is acquainted with the history of the nations not only of Europe but of the world. He has no difficulty in showing that the supposed invariable influences of hot or cold or dry or rainy climate on the fate of peoples and nations do not operate; that huge empires or democracy or courage or sluggishness or art or slavery have arisen in North and South, in the cold and the hot, in dry and in humid territories. So, too, in the case of different races, besides the initial difficulty in all racial theories to be found in the fact that the concept of "race" has no biological precision.

Both the racial and the climatic theories were popular when Mosca first was writing, in the last years of the 19th century. Nowadays they have few adherents, outside of the Nazi racial school, but theories of "economic materialism" or "economic determinism" are still influential. However, these, also, are unable to meet the test of the facts. Social and political events of the very greatest scope and order—the collapse of the Roman Empire, the rise of Christianity, the advance of Islam—have occurred without any important correlated change in the mode of economic production; consequently the mode of production cannot be the sole cause of social change.

The critique of these monistic views does not mean that Mosca wishes to substitute some similar view of his own, or, on the other hand, to deny that such factors as climate, race, or mode of production have causal influences in history. Climate, obviously, can change the course of events: some regions of the earth are literally uninhabitable, others so unhealthy or so arid that a high level of civilization cannot be supported by them (though a vigorous society learns to conquer unfavorable natural conditions); a drop in rainfall might lead to a migration. Changes in the mode of economic production must unquestionably be recognized as one of the chief factors entering into the historical process: the invention of new tools or machines, new ways of organizing work, new relationships of economic ownership, may have vast repercussions throughout the social order. Even racial differences may conceivably affect political and social organization. For that matter, still other circumstances can influence history—new types of armaments or ways of fighting, to take an important example, or shifts in religion and social beliefs.

Mosca himself holds what is sometimes called an "interdependence" theory of historical causation: the view that there are a number of important factors that determine historical change, that no one of these can be considered solely decisive, that they interact upon each other, with changes in one field affecting and in turn being affected by changes in others. He makes his critique of historical monism in order to break down abstract approaches to history, to do away with preconceptions of how things ought to be, and to force a concrete examination of the facts in each specific problem rather than an adjustment of the facts to fit the requirements of some schematic theory. Monistic theories of history, he believes, are a great obstacle to a recognition of the facts.

His particular field is politics. He thinks that by a comparative and historical approach to the facts of political life it is possible to have a science of politics, though he is very modest in his hopes about what political science can at the present time accomplish, either in reaching general conclusions or in providing guides for action:

Man neither creates nor destroys any of the forces

of nature, but he can study their manner of acting and their interplay and turn them to his advantage. That is the procedure in agriculture, in navigation, in mechanics. By following it modern science has been able to achieve almost miraculous results in those fields of activity. The method surely cannot be different when the social sciences are involved, and in fact it is the very method that has already yielded fair results in political economy. Yet we must not disguise the fact that in the social sciences in general the difficulties to be overcome are enormously greater. Not only does the greater complexity of psychological laws (or constant tendencies) that are common to all human groups make it harder to determine their operation, but it is easier to observe the things that go on about us than it is to observe the things we ourselves do. Man can much more easily study the phenomena of physics, chemistry or botany than he can his own instincts and his own passions. . . . But then, even granting that . . . individuals can attain scientific results, it is highly problematical whether they can succeed in using them to modify the political conduct of the great human societies. (*The Ruling Class*)

Since the primary purpose of Machiavellians is to discover the truth, they do not feel required to make demagogic claims even about their own accomplishments.

2. THE RULING CLASS

It Is characteristic of Machiavellian political analysis to be "anti-formal," using "formal" in the sense which I have defined in the discussion of Dante's *De Monarchia.* That is, Machiavellians, in their investigations of political behavior, do not accept at face value what men say, think, believe, or write. Whether it is the speech or letter or book of an individual, or a public document such as a constitution or set of laws or a party platform, Machiavellians treat it as only one fact among the larger set of social facts, and interpret its meaning always in relation to these other facts. In some cases, examination shows that the words can be accepted just as they stand; more often, as we found with *De Monarchia,* a divorce between formal and real meaning is discovered, with the words distorting and disguising the real political behavior which they indirectly express.

This anti-formal approach leads Mosca to note as a primary and universal social fact the existence of two "political classes," a ruling class—always a minority—and the ruled.

> Among the constant facts and tendencies that are to be found in all political organisms, one is so obvious that it is apparent to the most casual eye. In all societies—from societies that are very meagerly developed and have barely attained the dawnings of civilization, down to the most advanced and powerful societies—two classes of people appear— a class that rules and a class that is ruled. The first class, always the less numerous, performs all political functions, monopolizes power and enjoys

the advantages that power brings, whereas the second, the more numerous class, is directed and controlled by the first, in a manner that is now more or less legal, now more or less arbitrary and violent, and supplies the first, in appearance at least, with material means of subsistence and with the instrumentalities that are essential to the vitality of the political organism.

> In practical life we all recognize the existence of this ruling class. . . . We all know that, in our own country, whichever it may be, the management of public affairs is in the hands of a minority of influential persons, to which management, willingly or unwillingly, the majority defer. We know that the same thing goes on in neighboring countries, and in fact we should be put to it to conceive of a real world otherwise organized—a world in which all men would be directly subject to a single person without relationships of superiority or subordination, or in which all men would share equally in the direction of political affairs. If we reason otherwise in theory, that is due partly to inveterate habits that we follow in our thinking. . . .

The existence of a minority ruling class is, it must be stressed, a universal feature of all organized societies of which we have any record. It holds no matter what the social and political forms—whether the society is feudal or capitalist or slave or collectivist, monarchical or oligarchical or democratic, no matter what the constitutions and laws, no matter what the professions and beliefs. Mosca furthermore believes that we are fully entitled to conclude that this not only has been and is always the case, but that also it always will be. That it will be, follows, in the first place, from the univocal experience of the past: since, under all conditions, it has always been true of political organization, it must be presumed that it is a constant attribute of political life and will continue to hold for the future. However, the conclusion that there will always be a minority ruling class can be further demonstrated in another way.

By the theory of the ruling class Mosca is refuting two widespread errors which, though the opposite of each other, are oddly enough often both believed by the same person. The first, which comes up in discussions of tyranny and dictatorship and is familiar in today's popular attacks on contemporary tyrants, is that society can be ruled by a single individual. "But," Mosca observes, "the man who is at the head of the state would certainly not be able to govern without the support of a numerous class to enforce respect for his orders and to have them carried out; and granting that he can make one individual, or indeed many individuals, in the ruling class feel the weight of his power, he certainly cannot be at odds with the class as a whole or do away with it. Even if that were possible, he would at once be forced to create another class, without the support of which action on his part would be completely paralyzed."

The other error, typical of democratic theory, is that the masses, the majority, can rule themselves.

If it is easy to understand that a single individual cannot command a group without finding within the group a minority to support him, it is rather difficult to grant, as a constant and natural fact, that minorities rule majorities, rather than majorities minorities. But that is one of the points—so numerous in all the other sciences—where the first impression one has of things is contrary to what they are in reality. In reality the dominion of an organized minority, obeying a single impulse, over the unorganized majority is inevitable. The power of any minority is irresistible as against each single individual in the majority, who stands alone before the totality of the organized minority. At the same time, the minority is organized for the very reason that it is a minority. A hundred men acting uniformly in concert, with a common understanding, will triumph over a thousand men who are not in accord and can therefore be dealt with one by one. Meanwhile it will be easier for the former to act in concert and have a mutual understanding simply because they are a hundred and not a thousand. It follows that the larger the political community, the smaller will the proportion of the governing minority to the governed majority be, and the more difficult will it be for the majority to organize for reaction against the minority.

Nor is this rule at all suspended in the case of governments resting in form upon universal suffrage.

What happens in other forms of government— namely, that an organized minority imposes its will on the disorganized majority—happens also and to perfection, whatever the appearances to the contrary, under the representative system. When we say that the voters "choose" their representative, we are using a language that is very inexact. The truth is that the representative *has himself elected* by the voters, and, if that phrase should seem too inflexible and too harsh to fit some cases, we might qualify it by saying that his friends *have him elected*. In elections, as in all other manifestations of social life, those who have the will and, especially, the moral, intellectual and material *means* to force their will upon others take the lead over the others and command them.

The political mandate has been likened to the power of attorney that is familiar in private law. But in private relationships, delegations of powers and capacities always presuppose that the principal has the broadest freedom in choosing his representative. Now in practice, in popular elections, that freedom of choice though complete theoretically, necessarily becomes null, not to say ludicrous. If each voter gave his vote to the candidate of his heart, we may be sure that in almost all cases the only result would be a wide scattering of votes. When very many wills are involved, choice is determined by the most various criteria, almost all of them subjective, and if such wills were not co-ordinated and organized it would be virtually impossible for them to coincide in the spontaneous choice of one individual. If his vote is to have any efficacy at all, therefore, each voter is forced to limit his choice to a very narrow field, in other words to a choice among the two or three persons who have some chance of succeeding; and the only ones who have any chance of succeeding are those whose candidacies are championed by groups, by committees, by *organized minorities.*

Few who have paid attention to the political facts, rather than to theories about these facts, in the United States, will disagree with the account as it applies to this country.

Within the ruling class, it is usually possible to distinguish roughly two layers: a very small group of "top leaders," who among themselves occupy the highest and key positions of the society; and a much larger group of secondary figures—a "middle class," as it could properly be called—who, though not so prominent nor so much in the limelight, constitute the day-by-day active directors of the community life. Just as Mosca believes that the individual supreme leader is unimportant to the fate of a society, compared to the ruling class, so does he believe that this secondary level of the ruling class is, in the long run at least, more decisive than the top.

Below the highest stratum in the ruling class, there is always, even in autocratic systems, another that is much more numerous and comprises all the capacities for leadership in the country. Without such a class any sort of social organization would be impossible. The higher stratum would not in itself be sufficient for leading and directing the activities of the masses. In the last analysis, therefore, the stability of any political organism depends on the level of morality, intelligence and activity that this second stratum has attained. . . . Any intellectual or moral deficiencies in this second stratum, accordingly, represent a graver danger to the political structure, and one that is harder to repair, than the presence of similar deficiencies in the few dozen persons who control the workings of the state machine. . . .

From the point of view of the theory of the ruling class, a society is the society of its ruling class. A nation's strength or weakness, its culture, its powers of endurance, its prosperity, its decadence, depend in the first instance upon the nature of its ruling class. More particularly, the way in which to study a nation, to understand it, to predict what will happen to it, requires first of all and primarily an analysis of the ruling class. Political history and political science are thus predominantly the history and science of ruling classes, their origin, development, composition, structure, and changes. The theory of the ruling class in this way provides a principle with the help of which the innumerable and otherwise amorphous and meaningless facts of political life can be systematically assembled and made intelligible.

However arbitrary this idea of history as the history of ruling classes may seem to be, the truth is that all historians, in practice—even such historians as Tolstoy or Trotsky, whose general theories directly contradict it— are compelled to write in terms of it. If for no other reason, this must be because the great mass of mankind leaves no record of itself except insofar as it is expressed or led by outstanding and noteworthy persons. Nor does this method result in any falsification of the historical development. The account of a war cannot nor need not cover what all or a most part of the soldiers did, nor need the accounts of a school of art or the formation of a constitution or the growth of a religion or the progress of a revolution tell everything about everyone. Even if theory were to decide that ultimately the movements of the masses are the cause of what happens in history, yet these movements attain historical significance only when they alter major institutions and result in shifts in the character and composition of the ruling class. Thus, the analysis of the ruling class, if not directly, then indirectly, will produce an adequate history and an adequate political science.

There is an ambiguity, which is noted by Professor Livingston, in Mosca's concept of the "ruling class." Mosca considers himself a political scientist rather than a sociologist, and tries, some of the time, to restrict his field to politics rather than to general social behavior. If literally translated from the Italian, his phrase would usually be "political class," or "governing class," rather than "ruling class." In his writings his meaning seems to shuttle between the narrower concept of a "governing class"—that is, the class directly or indirectly concerned with the specific business of government—and the more general concept of a "social élite"—that is, the class of all those in a society who are differentiated from the masses by the possession of some kind of power or privilege, many of whom may have no specific relation to government.

However, this ambiguity does not affect Mosca's argument to any considerable degree; and if we judge by the context, the general concept of an "élite" is usually more appropriate to his meaning. What seems to have happened is that Mosca began his work in the narrower field of politics, with the narrower concept in mind. His political inquiries then led him outward into the wider field of social action, since the political field could not be understood apart from the background of the whole social field. The idea of the political class expanded its meaning into the idea of a social élite without an explicit discussion of the change. In later Machiavellian thought—in Pareto, particularly—the wider meaning of "élite" is consistently employed.

We should further note that in stating the theory of the ruling class, Mosca is not making a moral judgment, is not arguing that it is good, or bad, that mankind should be divided into rulers and ruled. I recently read, in a review by a well-known journalist, that "this country will never accept a theory of the élite"—as if it is wicked to talk about such things, and noble to denounce them. The scientific problem, however, is not whether this country or any other will accept such theories, but whether the theories are true. Mosca believes that the stratification of society into rulers and ruled is universal and permanent, a general form of political life. As such it would be absurd to call it good or bad; it is simply the way things are.

Moral values, goodness and badness, justice and injustice, are indeed to be found, and Mosca does not try to avoid making moral judgments; but they are meaningful only within the permanent structure of society. Granted that there are always rulers and ruled, then we may judge that the societies of some ruling classes are good, or more good, just, or less unjust, than others.

3. COMPOSITION AND CHARACTER OF THE RULING CLASS

Mosca rejects the many theories which have tried to apply the Darwinian theory of evolution directly to social life. He finds, however, a social tendency that is indirectly analogous to the process of biological evolution:

> The struggle for *existence* has been confused with the struggle for *pre-eminence,* which is really a constant phenomenon that arises in all human societies, from the most highly civilized down to such as have barely issued from savagery. . . .
>
> If we consider . . . the inner ferment that goes on within the body of every society, we see at once that the struggle for preeminence is far more conspicuous there than the struggle for existence. Competition between individuals of every social unit is focused upon higher position, wealth, authority, control of the means and instruments that enable a person to direct many human activities, many human wills, as he sees fit. The losers, who are of course the majority in that sort of struggle, are not devoured, destroyed or even kept from reproducing their kind, as is basically characteristic of the struggle for life. They merely enjoy fewer material satisfactions and, especially, less freedom and independence. On the whole, indeed, in civilized societies, far from being gradually eliminated by a process of natural selection so-called, the lower classes are more prolific than the higher, and even in the lower classes every individual in the long run gets a loaf of bread and a mate, though the bread be more or less dark and hard-earned and the mate more or less unattractive or undesirable.

The outcome of this "struggle for pre-eminence" is the decision who shall be, or continue to be, members of the ruling class.

What makes for success in the struggle? or, in other words, what qualities must be possessed by individuals in order that they may secure or maintain membership in the ruling class? In answering a question like this, it is above all necessary to avoid the merely formal. Spokesmen for various ruling classes have numerous self-satisfying explanations of how superior morality or intelligence or blood or racial inheritance confer membership. But Mosca, like all Machiavellians, looks beyond the verbal explanations to the relevant facts.

He finds that the possession of certain qualities is useful in all societies for gaining admittance to the ruling class, or for staying within it. Deep wisdom, altruism, readiness at self-sacrifice, are not among these qualities, but, on the contrary, are usually hindrances.

To rise in the social scale, even in calm and normal times, the prime requisite, beyond any question, is a capacity for hard work; but the requisite next in importance is ambition, a firm resolve to get on in the world, to outstrip one's fellows. Now those traits hardly go with extreme sensitiveness or, to be quite frank, with "goodness" either. For "goodness" cannot remain indifferent to the hurts of those who must be thrust behind if one is to step ahead of them. . . . If one is to govern men, more useful than a sense of justice—and much more useful than altruism, or even than extent of knowledge or broadness of view—are perspicacity, a ready intuition of individual and mass psychology, strength of will and, especially, confidence in oneself. With good reason did Machiavelli put into the mouth of Cosimo dei Medici the much quoted remark, that states are not ruled with prayer-books.

The best means of all for entering the ruling class is to be born into it—though, it may be observed, inheritance alone will not suffice to keep a family permanently among the rulers. Like Machiavelli here also, Mosca attributes not a little to "fortune."

> A certain amount of work is almost always necessary to achieve success—work that corresponds to a real and actual service to society. But work always has to be reinforced to a certain extent by "ability," that is to say, by the art of winning recognition. And of course a little of what is commonly called "luck" will not come amiss—those unforeseeable circumstances which help or seriously harm a man, especially at certain moments. One might add that in all places at all times the best luck, or the worst, is often to be born the child of one's father and one's mother.

These qualities—a capacity for hard work, ambition (Machiavelli's *virtù*), a certain callousness, luck in birth and circumstances—are those that help toward membership in any ruling class at any time in history. In addition, however, there is another group of qualities that are variable, dependent upon the particular society in question. "Members of a ruling minority regularly have some attribute, real or apparent, which is highly esteemed and very influential in the society in which they live." To mention simple examples: in a society which lives primarily by fishing, the expert fisherman has an advantage; the skilled warrior, in a predominantly military society; the able priest, in a profoundly religious group; and so on. Considered as keys to rule, such qualities as these are variable; if the conditions of life change, they change, for when religion declines, the priest is no longer so important, or when fishing changes to agriculture, the fisherman naturally drops in the social scale. Thus, changes in the general conditions of life are correlated with far-reaching changes in the composition of the ruling class.

The various sections of the ruling class express or represent or control or lead what Mosca calls *social forces,* which are continually varying in number and importance. By "social force" Mosca means any human activity which has significant social and political influence. In primitive societies, the chief forces are ordinarily war and religion. "As civilization grows, the number of the moral and material influences which are capable of becoming social forces increases. For example, property in money, as the fruit of industry and commerce, comes into being alongside of real property. Education progresses. Occupations based on scientific knowledge gain in importance." All of these—war, religion, land, labor, money, education, science, technological skill—can function as social forces if a society is organized in terms of them.

From this point of view, it may be seen that the relation of a ruling class to the society which it rules need not be at all arbitrary; in fact, in the long run cannot be. A given ruling class rules over a given society precisely because it is able to control the major social forces that are active within that society. If a social force—religion, let us say—declines in importance, then the section of the ruling class whose position was dependent upon control of religion likewise, over a period, declines. If the entire ruling class had been based primarily upon religion, then the entire ruling class would change its character (if it were able to adapt itself to the new conditions) or would (if it could not adapt itself) be overthrown. Similarly, if a new major social force develops—commerce, for example, in a previously agricultural society, or applied science—then either the existing ruling class proves itself flexible enough to gain leadership over this new force (in part, no doubt, by absorbing new members into its ranks); or, if it does not, the leadership of the new force grows up outside of the old class, and in time constitutes a revolutionary threat against the old ruling class, challenging it for supreme social and political power. Thus, the growth of new social forces and the decline of old forces is in general correlated with the constant process of change and dislocation in the ruling class.

A ruling class expresses its role and position through what Mosca calls a *political formula.* This formula rationalizes and justifies its rule and the structure of the society over which it rules. The formula may be a "racial myth," as in Germany at the present time or in this country in relation to the Negroes or the yellow races: rule is then explained as the natural prerogative of the superior race. Or it may be a "divine right" doctrine, as in the theories elaborated in connection with the absolutist monarchies of the 16th and 17th centuries, or in Japan at the present day: then rule is explained as following from a peculiar relationship to divinity, very often in fact from direct blood descent (such formulas were very common in ancient times, and have by no means lost all efficacy). Or, to cite the formula most familiar to us, and functioning now in this country, it is a belief in the "will of the people": rule is then said to follow legitimately from the will or choice of the people expressed through some type of suffrage.

> According to the level of civilization in the peoples among whom they are current, the various political formulas may be based either upon supernatural beliefs or upon concepts which, if they do not

correspond to positive realities, at least appear to be rational. We shall not say that they correspond in either case to scientific truths. A conscientious observer would be obliged to confess that, if no one has ever seen the authentic document by which the Lord empowered certain privileged persons or families to rule his people on his behalf, neither can it be maintained that a popular election, however liberal the suffrage may be, is ordinarily the expression of the will of a people, or even of the will of the majority of a people.

And yet that does not mean that political formulas are mere quackeries aptly invented to trick the masses into obedience. Anyone who viewed them in that light would fall into grave error. The truth is that they answer a real need in man's social nature; and this need, so universally felt, of governing and knowing that one is governed not on the basis of mere material or intellectual force, but on the basis of a moral principle, has beyond any doubt a practical and real importance.

Since the problem of such formulas (ideologies, myths) will occupy us at length later on, I shall note here only two further facts concerning them. First, the special political formula employed within a given nation is often related to wider myths that are shared by a number of nations, so that several political formulas appear as variations on similar basic themes. Conspicuous among these wider myths are the great world religions—Christianity, Buddhism, Mohammedanism—which, unlike most earlier religions or still-continuing religions of the type of Japanese Shintoism, are not specifically bound up with a single nation or people; the myth, probably best expressed by Rousseau, which is built out of such ideas as the innate goodness of man, the will of the people, humanitarianism, and progress; and the contemporary myth of collectivism, which, in Mosca's opinion, is the logical extension of the democratic Rousseau myth.

Second, it may be seen from historical experience that the integrity of the political formula is essential for the survival of a given social structure. Changes in the formula, if they are not to destroy the society, must be gradual, not abrupt. The formula is indispensable for holding the social structure together. A widespread skepticism about the formula will in time corrode and disintegrate the social order. It is perhaps for this reason, half-consciously understood, that all strong and long-lived societies have cherished their "traditions," even when, as is usually the case, these traditions have little relation to fact, and even after they can hardly be believed literally by educated men. Rome, Japan, Venice, all such long-enduring states, have been very slow to change the old formulas, the time-honored ways and stories and rituals; and they have been harsh against rationalists who debunk them. This, after all, was the crime for which Athens put Socrates to death. From the point of view of survival, she was probably right in doing so.

4. TENDENCIES IN THE RULING CLASS

Within all ruling classes, Mosca shows that it is possible to distinguish two "principles," as he calls them, and two "tendencies." These are, it might be said, the developmental laws of ruling classes. Their relative strength establishes the most important difference among various ruling classes.

The "autocratic" principle may be distinguished from the "liberal" principle. These two principles regulate, primarily, the method by which governmental officials and social leaders are chosen. "In any form of political organization, authority is either transmitted from above downward in the political or social scale [the autocratic principle], or from below upward [the liberal principle]." Neither principle violates the general law that society is divided into a ruling minority and a majority that is ruled; the liberal principle does not mean, no matter how extended, that the masses in fact rule, but simply gives a particular form to the selection of leadership. Moreover, it is seldom, probably never, that one of the two principles operates alone within a ruling class. They are usually mixed, with one or the other dominant. Certain absolute monarchies or tyrannies show the closest approximation to a purely autocratic principle, with all positions formally dependent upon appointment by the despot. Some small city-states, such as Athens at certain times in its history, have come very close to a purely liberal principle, with all officials chosen from below—though the voters were at the same time a restricted group. In the United States, as in most representative governments of the modern kind, both principles are actively at work. The greater part of the bureaucracy and much of the judiciary, especially the Federal judiciary, is an expression of the autocratic principle; the President himself, as well as the members of Congress, are selected according to the liberal mode.

Each principle in practice displays typical advantages and defects. Autocracy has been by far the more common of the two, and of it Mosca remarks:

> A political system that has been so widely recurring and so long enduring among peoples of the most widely various civilizations, who often have had no contacts material or intellectual with one another, must somehow correspond to the political nature of man. . . . Autocracy supplies a justification of power that is simple, clear and readily comprehensible to everybody. There can be no human organization without rankings and subordinations. Any sort of hierarchy necessarily requires that some should command and others obey. And since it is in the nature of the human being that many men should love to command and that almost all men can be brought to obey, an institution that gives those who are at the top a way of justifying their authority and at the same time helps to persuade those who are at the bottom to submit is likely to be a useful institution.

Autocracy, moreover, seems to endow societies over which it operates with greater stability and longer life than does the liberal principle. When autocracy is functioning well, it can bring about the deliberate selection of the ablest leadership from all strata of society to perform the various tasks of the state.

However, in compensation, autocracy seems unable to permit a free and full development of all social activities and forces—no autocracy has ever stimulated so intense a cultural and intellectual life as have developed under some of the shorter-lived liberal systems, such as those of Greece and western Europe. And in the selection of leaders by the autocrat and his immediate clique, favoritism and personal prejudice easily take the place of objective judgment of merit, while the method encourages sycophancy and slavishness on the part of the candidates.

The liberal principle, conversely, stimulates more than the autocratic the development of varied social potentialities. At the same time, it by no means avoids the formation of closed cliques at the top, such as are usually found in autocracies; the mode of formation of such cliques is merely different. "In order to reach high station in an autocracy it is sufficient to have the support of one or more persons, and that is secured by exploiting all their passions, good and bad. In liberal systems one has to steer the inclinations of at least the whole second stratum of the ruling class, which, if it does not in itself constitute the electorate, at least supplies the general staffs of leaders who form the opinions and determine the conduct of the electing body." When the liberal system is broadly based (that is, where suffrage is widely extended or universal), the candidates for high office must proceed by exploiting the backward sentiments of the masses:

> Whatever their origins, the methods that are used by the people who aim to monopolize and exploit the sympathy of the masses always have been the same. They come down to pointing out, with exaggerations, of course, the selfishness, the stupidity, the material enjoyments of the rich and the powerful; to denouncing their vices and wrongdoings, real and imaginary; and to promising to satisfy a common and widespread sense of rough-hewn justice which would like to see abolished every social distinction based upon advantage of birth and at the same time would like to see an absolutely equal distribution of pleasures and pains.

> Often enough the parties against which this demagogic propaganda is directed use exactly the same means to combat it. Whenever they think they can profit by doing so, they too make promises which they will never be able to keep. They too flatter the masses, play to their crudest instincts and exploit and foment all their prejudices and greeds.

. . . . .

The distinction which Mosca makes between the "aristocratic" and "democratic" tendencies is independent of his distinction between the autocratic and liberal principles. Aristocratic and democratic, as Mosca uses the terms, refer to the sources from which new members of the ruling class are drawn.

> The term "democratic" seems more suitable for the tendency which aims to replenish the ruling class with elements deriving from the lower classes,

and which is always at work, openly or latently and with greater or lesser intensity, in all political organisms. "Aristocratic" we would call the opposite tendency, which also is constant and varies in intensity, and which aims to stabilize social control and political power in the descendants of the class that happens to hold possession of it at the given historical moment.

In terms of this definition, there can be, as there have often been, in spite of common opinion to the contrary, autocracies which are primarily democratic in tendency, and liberal systems which are largely aristocratic. The most remarkable example of the former is the Catholic Church, which is almost perfectly autocratic, but at the same time is always recruiting new members of its hierarchy from the masses. Hitler, in *Mein Kampf,* observes that the rule of celibacy compels the Church to remain thus democratic in its policy of recruitment, and he concludes that this is a principal source of the Church's strength and power of endurance. On the other hand, modern England, during many generations, was in many respects liberal, but, by various devices, preserved an aristocratic continuity in the membership of its ruling class. This was also the case in many of the ancient city-states which had liberal extensions of the suffrage to all citizens, but restrictions on eligibility to office which kept rule in the hands of a small group of families.

Since all of us in the United States have been educated under democratic formulas, the advantages of the democratic tendency are too familiar to need statement. We less often discuss certain of its disadvantages, or some possible advantages of aristocracy. To begin with, so long as the family remains, and in some form it is likely to remain as long as we can foresee, the aristocratic tendency will always be asserting itself to some degree at least; it too accords with ineradicable human traits, with the fact that, since a man cannot help all other men equally and since all cannot prosper equally, he will prefer as a rule that those should be favored toward whom he feels some special attachment. A revolutionary movement ordinarily proclaims that its aim is to do away with all privileges of birth, but invariably, once it is in power, the aristocratic tendency reasserts itself, and a new ruling group crystallizes out from the revolution.

> It is not so certain, meantime, Mosca adds, that it would be altogether beneficial to the collectivity to have every advantage of birth eliminated in the struggle for membership in the ruling class and for high position in the social hierarchy. If all individuals could participate in the scramble on an equal footing, struggle would be intensified to the point of frenzy. This would entail an enormous expenditure of energy for strictly personal ends, with no corresponding benefit to the social organism, at least in the majority of cases. On the other hand, it may very well be that certain intellectual and, especially, moral qualities, which are necessary to a ruling class if it is to maintain its prestige and function properly, are useful also to society, yet require, if they are to develop and exert their

influence, that the same families should hold fairly high social positions for a number of generations.

The fact of the matter, however, is that both of these tendencies, aristocratic and democratic, are always operative within every society. The heavy predominance of one of them is usually the occasion or the aftermath of a period of rapid and often revolutionary social change.

5. THE BEST AND WORST GOVERNMENTS

Mosca, like Machiavelli, does not stop with the descriptive analysis of political life. He states plainly his own preferences, his opinions about what types of government are best, what worst. Naturally, as is the case with all Machiavellians, his goal is not anything supernatural or utopian; to be the best, a government must be first of all possible. He does no dreaming about a "perfect state" or "absolute justice." In fact, Mosca suggests what I had occasion to mention in connection with Dante: namely, that political doctrines which promise utopias and absolute justice are very likely to lead to much worse social effects than doctrines less entrancing in appearance; that utopian programs may even be the most convenient of cloaks for those whose real aims are most rightly suspect. The impossibility of attaining absolute justice, however, does not render useless an effort after what measure of approximate justice is possible in the actual social world that we inhabit.

> Human sentiments being what they are, to set out to erect a type of political organization that will correspond in all respects to the ideal of justice, which a man can conceive but can never attain, is a utopia, and the utopia becomes frankly dangerous when it succeeds in bringing a large mass of intellectual and moral energies to bear upon the achievement of an end that will never be achieved and that, on the day of its purported achievement, can mean nothing more than triumph for the worst people and distress and disappointment for the good. Burke remarked more than a century ago that any political system that assumes the existence of superhuman or heroic virtues can result only in vice and corruption.

> But even if there is never to be an absolute justice in this world until humanity comes really to be molded to the image and likeness of God, there has been, there is and there will always be a relative justice in societies that are fairly well organized. There will always be, in other words, a sum of laws, habits, norms, all varying according to times and peoples, which are laid down and enforced by public opinion, and in accordance with which what we have called the struggle for pre-eminence—the effort of every individual to better and to conserve his own social position—will be regulated.

Again following Machiavelli, the dominant element in Mosca's conception of that "relative justice" which he thinks possible as well as desirable is liberty. The meaning of "liberty" he makes more precise by defining it in terms of what he calls "juridical defense."

The social mechanisms that regulate this disciplining of the moral sense constitute what we call "juridical defense" (respect for law, government by law). . . . It will further be noted that our view is contrary to the doctrine of Rousseau, that man is good by nature but that society makes him wicked and perverse. We believe that social organization provides for the reciprocal restraint of human individuals by one another and so makes them better, not by destroying their wicked instincts, but by accustoming them to controlling their wicked instincts.

> Guicciardini defines political liberty as "a prevalence of law and public decrees over the appetites of particular men." If we take "particular men" in the sense of "individuals," meaning "single individuals," and including individuals who have power in their hands, it would be difficult to find a more rigorously scientific definition. . . . A corrupt government, in which the person who commands "makes his will licit in his law"—whether in the name of God or in the name of the people does not matter—will obviously be inadequate to fulfilling its mission in regard to juridical defense. The freest country is the country where the rights of the governed are best protected against arbitrary caprice and tyranny on the part of rulers.

Juridical defense, then, means government by law and due process—not merely formally, in the words of constitutions or statutes, but in fact; it means a set of impersonal restrictions on those who hold power, and correlatively a set of protections for the individuals against the state and those who have power. The specific forms of juridical defense include the familiar "democratic rights":

> In countries that have so far rightly been reputed free, private property cannot be violated arbitrarily. A citizen cannot be arrested and condemned unless specified rules are observed. Each person can follow the religion of his choice without forfeiture of his civil and political rights. The press cannot be subjected to censorship and is free to discuss and criticize acts of government. Finally, if they conform with certain rules, citizens can meet to engage in discussions of a political character, and they can form associations for the attainment of moral, political or professional ends.

Of all these rights, Mosca considers the right of public discussion—of free speech, as we usually call it—the most important, and the strongest foundation of juridical defense as a whole.

A firm juridical defense is required for the attainment and maintenance of a relatively high "level of civilization." Level of civilization is measured, according to Mosca's definition, by the degree of development and number of social forces: that is, the more social forces there are and the more fully each is developed, the higher the level of a given civilization. A civilization that has an active art, an active literature and commerce and science and industry, a strong army, and a progressive agriculture, is higher than one that concentrates on only one or two of these, or one that is mediocre in most or all of them. Thus, the conception of "level of civilization" can serve as a rough standard for evaluating different cultures.

But what is it that makes possible a high level of juridical defense and of civilization? With the answer to this question we come to what is perhaps the most profound and most important of all Mosca's ideas, though it, also, has its source in Machiavelli. Mosca's answer, moreover, is sharply at variance with many accepted theories, and particularly opposed to the arguments of almost all the spokesmen of the ruling class.

The mere formal structure of laws and constitutions, or of institutional arrangements, cannot guarantee juridical defense. Constitutions and laws, as we certainly should know by now, need have no relation to what happens—Hitler never repealed the Weimar Constitution, and Stalin ordered the adoption of "the most democratic constitution in the history of the world." Nor can the most formally perfect organizational setup: one-house or two- or three-house legislatures, independent or responsible executives, kings or presidents, written or unwritten constitutions, judges appointed or elected—decisions on these formalities will never settle the problem. Nor will any doctrine, nor any reliance on the good will of whatever men, give a guarantee: the men who want and are able to get power never have the necessary kind of good will, but always seek, for themselves and their group, still more power.

In real social life, only power can control power. Juridical defense can be secure only where there are at work various and opposing tendencies and forces, and where these mutually check and restrain each other. Tyranny, the worst of all governments, means the loss of juridical defense; and juridical defense invariably disappears whenever one tendency or force in society succeeds in absorbing or suppressing all the others. Those who control the supreme force rule then without restraint. The individual has no protection against them.

From one point of view, the protective balance must be established between the autocratic and liberal principles, and between the aristocratic and democratic tendencies. Monopoly by the aristocratic tendency produces a closed and inflexible caste system, and fossilization; the extreme of democracy brings an unbridled anarchy under which the whole social order flies to pieces.

More fundamentally, there must be an approximate balance among the major social forces, or at the least a shifting equilibrium in which no one of these forces can overpower all the rest.

> Even granted that such a world [the world of so many utopians, where conflicts and rivalries among different forces, religions, and parties will have ended] could be realized, it does not seem to us a desirable sort of world. So far in history, freedom to think, to observe, to judge men and things serenely and dispassionately, has been possible—always, be it understood, for a few individuals—only in those societies in which numbers of different

religious and political currents have been struggling for dominion. That same condition . . . is almost indispensable for the attainment of what is commonly called "political liberty"—in other words, the highest possible degree of justice in the relations between governors and governed that is compatible with our imperfect human nature. . . . History teaches that whenever, in the course of the ages, a social organization has exerted such an influence [to raise the level of civilization] in a beneficial way, it has done so because the individual and collective will of the men who have held power in their hands has been curbed and balanced by other men, who have occupied positions of absolute independence and have had no common interests with those whom they have had to curb and balance. It has been necessary, nay indispensable, that there should be a multiplicity of political forces, that there should be many different roads by which social importance could be acquired . . .

Freedom, in the world as it is, is thus the product of conflict and difference, not of unity and harmony. In these terms we see again the danger of "idealism," utopianism, and demagogy. The idealists, utopians, and demagogues always tell us that justice and the good society will be achieved by the absolute triumph of their doctrine and their side. The facts show us that the absolute triumph of any side and any doctrine whatsoever can only mean tyranny.

> The absolute preponderance of a single political force, the predominance of any over-simplified concept in the organization of the state, the strictly logical application of any single principle in all public law are the essential elements in any type of despotism, whether it be a despotism based upon divine right or a despotism based ostensibly on popular sovereignty; for they enable anyone who is in power to exploit the advantages of a superior position more thoroughly for the benefit of his own interests and passions. When the leaders of the governing class are the exclusive interpreters of the will of God or of the will of the people and exercise sovereignty in the name of those abstractions in societies that are deeply imbued with religious beliefs or with democratic fanaticism, and when no other organized social forces exist apart from those which represent the principle on which sovereignty over the nation is based, then there can be no resistance, no effective control, to restrain a natural tendency in those who stand at the head of the social order to abuse their powers.

By 1923, when Mosca revised his major book (the English translation is made from this revised version), he had come to the conclusion that the great parliamentary-representative governments of the 19th century had reached the highest level of civilization and juridical defense so far known in history. In many ways, this was a remarkable opinion for Mosca to have held. The chief theme of his entire work is a devastating attack on the entire theoretical basis of democratic and parliamentary doctrine. He gives not a little space to a withering exposure of concrete abuses under modern parliamentary government. In his critique of collectivism, he states: "The strength of the socialist and anarchist doctrines lies not so much in their positive as in their negative aspects—in their minute, pointed, merciless criticism of our present organization of society," and he holds that the criticism is largely justified.

Nevertheless, Mosca does not expect utopia or absolute justice. Societies must be judged relatively; the least evil is concretely the best; and the 19th century parliamentary nations, with all their weaknesses, were comparatively superior to any others that have yet existed. In their governmental structures, the autocratic principle, functioning through the bureaucracy, balanced the liberal principle, expressed in the parliaments. The aristocratic tendencies of birth and inheritance were checked by a perhaps unprecedented ease with which vigorous new members were able to enter the ruling class. Above all, under these governments there occurred an astounding expansion not of one or a restricted few social forces, but of a great and rich variety, with no one force able to gain exclusive predominance over the rest. Commerce as well as the arts, education and science, technology and literature, all were able to flourish. His judgment on these governments thus follows from his general principles; he does not praise parliamentary government for its own sake, but because, under the specific circumstances of the 19th century, it was accompanied by this relatively high level of civilization and juridical defense.

From his favorable judgment, however, Mosca did not conclude that the 19th century form of parliamentary government was necessarily going to last. It is the habit of utopians, of those who, like Dante, interpret politics as wish, not of scientists, to confuse their desires with what is going to happen. Mosca, on the contrary, believed that it was almost certain that parliamentary governments, as the 19th century had known them, were not going to last very much longer.

The War of 1914, he believed, marked the end of an age that could be considered as having begun with the French Revolution, in 1789. The parliamentary governments were the great social achievement of that age; but the age was ending. In the new age, just beginning, these governments would be displaced. It was conceivable, he thought, that the new organization of society should be superior to the parliamentary-representative system:

> If Europe is able to overcome the difficulties with which she is struggling at present, it is altogether probable that in the course of another century, or even within half that time, new ideas, new sentiments, new needs will automatically prepare the ground for other political systems that may be far preferable to any now existing.

But the depth of the crisis into which he understood that Europe had, with the first World War, irrevocably entered, suggested the probability of attempts at extreme and catastrophic solutions. These, he believed, could lead only toward the destruction of liberty and a decline in the level of civilization. Though a small reserve of optimism was permissible, pessimism was on the whole called for by the facts.

> The feeling that springs spontaneously from an unprejudiced judgment of the history of humanity is compassion for the contradictory qualities of this poor human race of ours, so rich in abnegation, so ready at times for personal sacrifice, yet whose every attempt, whether more or less successful or not at all successful, to attain moral and material betterment, is coupled with an unleashing of hates, rancors and the basest passions. A tragic destiny is that of men! Aspiring ever to pursue and achieve what they think is the good, they ever find pretexts for slaughtering and persecuting each other. Once they slaughtered and persecuted over the interpretation of a dogma, or of a passage in the Bible. Then they slaughtered and persecuted in order to inaugurate the kingdom of liberty, equality and fraternity. Today they are slaughtering and persecuting and fiendishly torturing each other in the name of other creeds. Perhaps tomorrow they will slaughter and torment each other in an effort to banish the last trace of violence and injustice from the earth!

H. Stuart Hughes (essay date 1954)

SOURCE: "Gaetano Mosca and the Political Lessons of History," in *Teachers of History: Essays in Honor of Laurence Bradford Packard,* edited by H. Stuart Hughes with the collaboration of Myron P. Gilmore and Edwin C. Rozwenc, Cornell University Press, 1954, pp. 146-62.

[*In the following essay, Hughes contrasts the theories of Mosca and Pareto, arguing that their differences stemmed from Mosca's view of history as an "experienced reality."*]

Among American students of political science and history, Gaetano Mosca is usually considered as a kind of second-class Pareto. The leading ideas ascribed to the two thinkers are similar—the theory of elites, of the role of force and deception in history, in short, of a neo-Machiavellianism derived from a common Italian heritage. As sharp critics of parliamentary democracy and socialism, Pareto and Mosca appear to occupy similar places among the precursors of fascism—half-unconscious, perhaps, of what they were doing, but still in some ultimate sense responsible for the collapse of Italian democracy and the advent of Mussolini. From this standpoint, Pareto looms as the larger figure. His range is wider, his books are longer, his "scientific" apparatus is more impressive, and his criticism cuts deeper. Moreover, the Fascist chief himself honored Pareto and was happy to number him among his intellectual inspirers; apparently he never mentioned Mosca. Conversely, the latter's eventual opposition to Mussolini's regime was too quiet to attract much attention: the sweet notes of reasoned dissent reached the outside world through Croce alone, and other voices sounded muffled and ineffective. On all counts, then, Mosca has seemed a lesser figure; he wrote more gracefully than Pareto and his views were more moderate—but those were the only respects in which his work ranked higher.

The accidental circumstance that Pareto's *Trattato di sociologia generale* appeared in English translation five years earlier than Mosca's **Elementi di scienza politica** partly explains the greater prestige the former work enjoys. But even in Italy, where the two books were equally available to the reading public, Mosca's took second place. Although his theory of the "political class" quite obviously antedated Pareto's formulation of the "elite" concept, Mosca experienced the greatest difficulty in maintaining his claim to priority. The result was a polemic that went on for two decades to the eventual weariness of both the contestants and the other learned figures who were drawn in. There was no doubt that Mosca was the injured party. Pareto affected a lofty disdain for the whole controversy and simply "erased Mosca's name even from his footnotes." But at the same time there must have been something profoundly irritating to the sage of Lausanne about the pertinacity with which a less-well-known scholar ten years his junior kept insisting on his title to an idea that was by no means totally original and that could plausibly be regarded as no more than the product of the general intellectual atmosphere in Western Europe just before the turn of the century.

It is not the purpose of the present essay to argue against the prevailing impression and to give Mosca his due. It is rather my intention to point out once again the obvious—if frequently overlooked—difference between the practical conclusions in which the two theories terminate, and in so doing to suggest that this contrast is due in great part to a different attitude toward history—an attitude that in Mosca's case was the product of a longer personal experience. Mosca's sense of history as an experienced reality, even against his expressed intention, worked gradual and subtle changes not only in his political ideas but even in the presuppositions behind them.

I

The difference between Pareto's and Mosca's practical conclusions is too well known to require elaboration. Pareto died, as he had lived, the sworn foe of parliamentary democracy. He had experienced only the first year of Mussolini's new government; he had expressed his reservations about it—but these were on matters of emphasis rather than principle. Mosca lived nearly two decades longer, virtually through the whole of the Fascist dictatorship. He had ample time to see what was happening, and he early came to a negative judgment, although once the regime was consolidated, he prudently kept his opinions to himself. This difference in age, however, was not decisive. Mosca had reached his new conclusions even before Pareto's death; the second edition of his **Elementi,** published a few weeks after Mussolini came to power, already shows his transformation from a critic of parliamentary democracy into its defender—a sceptical defender, indeed, but an extremely effective one. The difference lies, rather, in the divergent experience of the two writers during the quarter century preceding the March on Rome; while Pareto was living in scholarly seclusion and enjoying his self-imposed exile in Switzerland, Mosca was actively participating in Italian political life. The day-to-day contact with political reality was insensibly modifying his theoretical judgments and even the concept of history on which they were based.

Mosca's original idea of history closely resembled Pareto's. It was a simple, straightforward view, reflecting both the heritage of the Enlightenment and the more recent teachings of French positivism. In its didactic emphasis, it recalled the Enlightenment. Like Voltaire or Gibbon, Mosca set out to ransack the records of past ages for instructive examples that would yield general truths on the political behavior of mankind. He had read widely and thoroughly both in the classics and in the published literature of European history. And he seemed able to remember nearly everything he read; as a young man of twenty-five, in the introduction to his first political work, he somewhat naïvely congratulated himself on the advantages he owed to his unusually retentive memory.

Mosca was not only looking for examples. He was also seeking "laws." Here his debt to Taine was manifest and amply recognized. Like his French master, Mosca was radically dissatisfied with the methods and categories ordinarily employed by political writers. He found them imprecise, emotionally grounded, and generally unrelated to the recorded facts of political behavior. And the result had been that the study of politics and sociology had lagged far behind the other scholarly disciplines. It had not yet become a "science." Mosca implied, although he refrained from making too flat-footed a claim, that his own works would rank as the founding documents of this new science.

This was positivist thinking with a vengeance. Mosca's scientific self-confidence, his cold disdain for sentimental ideologies, and his emphasis on force as the basis of human society were strictly in consonance with the prevailing temper of the post-Darwinian age. From this standpoint, he was by no means the innovator that he claimed to be—he was simply the typical bright scholar of his time. Yet he was too open-minded to allow himself to become imprisoned in his own formulas. He did not rest content with the materialist, mechanical explanations that to contemporary readers make the work of Taine so repellent. And he was careful to avoid the trap of historical determinism. The "political classes" whose role in history he was charting he subjected to no inexorable law of degeneration and fall from power. Their fate lay in their own hands. As Mosca's American editor has pointed out, it was simply "wrong political decisions that headed them toward decline instead of toward higher levels of civilization." Hence Mosca's theory of society, as opposed to that of his leading predecessors and contemporaries, was "open" rather than "closed." It would have satisfied the rigorous requirements of the great living theorist of the "open society." Like Karl Popper, Mosca in effect argues that "we must learn to do things as well as we can, and to look out for our mistakes," and further, that "progress rests with us, with our watchfulness, with our efforts, with the clarity of our conception of our ends, and with the realism of their choice."

Moreover, proud as Mosca was of his theory of the political class, and stoutly as he defended it from all competitors and detractors during more than half a century of catastrophic political changes, he never seems to have taken it with the deadly seriousness characteristic of most discoverers of new ideas. Mosca's mature work, despite the dogmatism of its major premise, is far from dogmatic in tone. It flows along pleasantly and easily in a style that combines the old-fashioned, piled-up periodic sentence with great simplicity and clarity of expression. It is full of sly asides, tantalizing hints of ideas that will never be developed, quiet jests—in short, of an ebullient Mediterranean good humor. The dominant tone is one of urbane scepticism. His own theory, Mosca implies, while it is doubtless the best produced to date, is, after all, only a theory. And all theories should be taken rather lightly. It is probable that Mosca never expected his ideas to have much effect—as indeed they did not—or to be taken to heart too literally by his contemporaries. It would be enough if he had planted in their minds the suspicion that the contrasting political ideologies they so vociferously supported were essentially fantasies—pious frauds of widely varying social usefulness. Subsequently, when Mosca entered politics himself, his conduct was far from doctrinaire. Untroubled by apparent contradictions, he serenely permitted himself to be guided by his naturally pragmatic temper. Thus, although unconvinced of any practical advantage accruing to Italy from the Tripolitan War, he declared himself a colonialist and even consented to serve as under-secretary of state for colonies during the First World War. "It is frequently better," he is reported to have remarked, "to make a bad deal than to cut a poor figure."

The same good-humored disclaimer of infallibility cannot be found in Pareto. About many aspects of human behavior, Pareto was deeply sceptical—witness the conventional charge of cynicism brought against him. But about his own mental processes, his own conclusions, he permitted himself little doubt; in this respect he remained closer than Mosca to the original positivist faith. Pareto was content to respect the ultimate mystery of human motivation—but he was convinced that he had at least discovered enough about the laws of social mechanics to provide an adequate guide to mass manipulation. Hence his writing has a rigidity of categorization and an asperity of tone that are found only in Mosca's earliest work. Moreover, Pareto's sociological writings are all of one piece. Only seventeen years elapsed between the publication of the first volume of the *Systèmes socialistes* and that of the final volume of the great *Trattato*. And during this period the author's ideas underwent no significant alteration. He simply reworked them to give them a more "scientific" terminology and presentation. Once Pareto

had retired to the shores of Lake Geneva, his attitude was fixed for all time; distinguished visitors came and conversed with the master, but the reverberation of the earth-shaking storms beyond the borders of Switzerland did not alter Pareto's fixed ideas any more than they upset the ordered, if rather eccentric, routine of his daily living. Even the advent of Mussolini and the award of a seat in the Italian Senate could not induce him to return to Italy.

In Mosca's case the gap between the youthful moment of discovery and the ultimate retouches applied to his theory for the last edition of the *Elementi* published during his lifetime was a matter of fifty-seven years. In the interval the political configuration of Europe had changed utterly. For Mosca this was no particular source of dismay, either theoretical or practical. Serene in his conviction that most political leaders were garrulous fools, he was not surprised by what had happened. On balance, he concluded, his theory had stood up well. There was little he wished to retract or alter. Even where he confessed that youthful intrepidity had led him to overstate his case, he noted "with a certain satisfaction" that the "fundamental principles" did not "need many corrections." And "several of the most important predictions" that he had made had been "confirmed by events" either "in whole or in part." Nevertheless the passage of time had left its mark. Under the stress of enlarged experience, the "open" element in Mosca's thinking began to predominate over what was merely positivist and doctrinaire.

To many of us today, Mosca's basic notion of history may seem profoundly unhistorical. The problem of historical knowledge never troubled him; he never questioned the credentials of his data. They were simply given "facts," transferable blocks for the political theorist to build with. To the end of his days the concept of history as a drama taking place in the mind of the historian never seems to have occurred to him—despite the fact that he was the contemporary, the countryman, and presumably (as a fellow senator) the acquaintance of Benedetto Croce. On the surface, Mosca retained his positivist allegiance. But somewhat deeper down, a more refined feeling for historical change gradually asserted itself. Despite his own professions, despite his denials of subjectivity, his essential historical-mindedness broke through. This is part of what Croce had in mind when he found a great deal of good sense in a book like the *Elementi* that rested on "philosophical presuppositions" so radically different from his own.

II

This paradox is already apparent in Mosca's first published work. In a little treatise entitled *Teorica dei governi* (1884) that was intended to define the permanent truths of political behavior—derived from historical observation, it is true, but themselves timeless and unchanging—Mosca revealed how deeply his thought was anchored in his own historical situation. With a lordly scorn for his predecessors, Mosca dismissed their theories as based on faulty "historical preconceptions." He alone had discovered the "key to the great secrets of history."

All the political history of mankind in all times, in all nations, and in all civilizations can ultimately be summarized under two major points of view: on the one hand, the degree of coordination of the various political classes, the number of resources that they are able to gather in their own hands, and the force of their collective action; on the other hand, the various elements that make up these classes, their different methods of imposing their rule, their rivalries, their struggles, their compromises and "combinations."

And so he went on to elaborate in their first and most dogmatic form the basic theories associated with his name—the doctrine of the necessary predominance of an active minority in all times and under all forms of government, even those that call themselves the rule of one man or of all the citizens, and the parallel concept of the "political formula," the convenient myth that conceals the harsh realities of class rule under the respectable cloak of religious or ideological legitimacy.

This emphasis on class considerations in politics already begins to locate Mosca in a specific historical situation. As Karl Mannheim has pointed out:

> It is almost possible to establish a sociological correlation between the type of thinking that appeals to organic or organized groups and a consistently systematic interpretation of history.... A class or similar organic group never sees history as made up of transitory disconnected incidents.

Thus it appears to be no accident that during the past century the great integrated views of history have been associated with the aspirations and fortunes of fairly well-defined social classes. They have expressed the struggle of the urban working classes for economic improvement and social equality, as in the case of Marxism. Or, as with the theories of Pareto and Spengler, they have been phrased as last-ditch appeals to a tottering oligarchy to "shore up its fragments" of prestige and authority by infusing new life into the traditional aristocratic values. Finally—as in the case of Toynbee, or, in our own country, F. S. C. Northrop—they have been efforts to restore self-confidence to a great middle class, structurally unintegrated and unsure of its own political allegiance, by lifting to a higher plane of spiritual contemplation and extra-European validity, the somewhat shop-worn credo of liberalism inherited from the Enlightenment. In this schematic arrangement, Mosca's theories fall somewhere between the second and third categories. They began by more closely resembling the former and ended as a vigorous reaffirmation of liberal principles.

Thus Mosca, as a discerning and clear-headed anti-Marxist, confronts Marx with his own terminology. Unlike the conventional American refutation of Marxism, which denies the whole class interpretation of history, Mosca's theory accepts it but redefines it in such a way as to reverse its implications.

> The existence of a political class does not conflict

with the essential content of Marxism, considered not as an economic dogma but as a philosophy of history. . . . There is no essential contradiction between the doctrine that history is the record of a continued series of class struggles and the doctrine that class struggles invariably culminate in the creation of new oligarchies which undergo fusion with the old.

But in Mosca's hands, the classes cease to be historical actors in their own right. They become simply a series of passive audiences, disciplined claques pathetically anxious to applaud the posturings of narrower groups drawn from their own ranks. History, Mosca assures us, cannot be the story of the political vicissitudes of classes conceived as entities—a moment's reflection shows this to be a technical impossibility. It can only be the record of the rise and fall of oligarchies. And if this is the case, then the whole apocalyptic vision of the new world of classless harmony simply vanishes into thin air. The new world will be very much like the old one. Mosca does not deny the possibility of human progress: the word occurs frequently in his writings, and the great ethical purpose behind his work is to confirm the progress that has already been made and to preserve the conditions essential to further advances. His own era—the last quarter of the nineteenth century—Mosca feels to be superior in nearly all respects to its predecessors. But this superior level of civilization is precarious and desperately threatened. A new political class is striving by methods of fraud and violence to displace the old oligarchy whose leadership has brought the European world to its current position of eminence. Under these circumstances, a revolution—the displacement of one oligarchy by another—far from opening up glittering vistas of further progress, would imperil and perhaps destroy the progress that has already been made.

Redefined in this fashion, the class interpretation of history is transformed from a revolutionary into a conservative doctrine. It becomes a vehicle for restoring the self-confidence of the European ruling classes, whose will to govern has been sapped by the Rousseauist dogmas of democracy and social equality. In effect, Mosca's teaching gives back to them a good conscience about their privileges. If history is simply a succession of oligarchies, it tells them, and political equality a mirage, then it is foolish to worry about one's own position as an oligarch. The democratic gestures inspired by such scruples will be worse than futile; they will pave the way to power for a new oligarchy—far inferior in talent, in ethical standards, and in respect for individual rights to the political class that is currently governing the European parliamentary states. Rather than pursuing the will o' the wisp of democracy, it would be better to take thought for the strengthening and improvement of the existing class regime.

Such was the final lesson of Mosca's neoconservative theory. In the 1880's, after a century of ideological debate, it brought a refreshing breath of realism and practical sense into a political atmosphere stale from the passionate repetition of conflicting slogans and credos. It is only in this context that Mosca's thought can properly be understood. As with the work of so many other political writers, it must be read as an answer to something that has been said earlier. It is neoconservatism—or, to use a contemporary term, sophisticated conservatism—in the sense that it is both postdemocratic and postsocialist. Like the majority of nineteenth-century conservatives, like Tocqueville or Burckhardt or Metternich himself, Mosca considered democracy no more than a brief halt on the way to socialism; the latter was already implicit in the Rousseauist "political formula." But unlike De Maistre and the original theorists of the counterrevolution, in repudiating democracy Mosca did not simultaneously reject the whole liberal tradition of the Enlightenment. On the contrary, he accepted the Enlightenment in its broadest emphasis on rationalized procedures, personal freedom, and limited government. At the same time he sought to free this tradition from the democratic accretions that had drastically altered its original outlines and that threatened eventually to destroy it. In the light of the experience of two generations of parliamentary government, he argued, one could at last locate precisely where liberalism had gone astray.

It was as a young but already self-conscious member of the liberal upper middle class, then, that Mosca composed his first treatise on politics. This class, which had figured in recent history both as the bearer and as the beneficiary of the liberal tradition, was in the 1880's the dominant group in the economic and political life of the three great parliamentary states of Western Europe. In all of them, it was true, the upper-middle-class oligarchy shared power with the old aristocracy—but with each year that passed the balance seemed to incline more heavily in favor of the former. When Mosca wrote his *Teorica,* this happy state of affairs was still of recent origin. In England it had existed at the most for half a century, in France and Italy for perhaps a decade. And yet it was already threatened with disruption. It was threatened not merely by the assaults of democracy and socialism. It was also being undermined by the malfunctioning of the very parliamentary institutions that had served as the vehicles of upper-middle-class supremacy.

In this historical situation, it was not surprising that Mosca should have devoted the whole second half of his little book to a critique of parliamentarism. After defining the eternal laws of political behavior, the intrepid young theorist quite logically turned his attention to the specific institutions through which these laws manifested themselves in his own time. One might study them, he noted, in England or in France, in the United States, in Austria, in Germany, in Spain, or in Italy. The reasons he gave for using his own country as his test case were not particularly convincing. Presumably he chose it simply because he knew it best.

This choice of Italy, however, and the fact that Mosca was an Italian, were not merely incidental to what he had to say. They profoundly affected the character of his judgments on parliamentary institutions. For Italy in the 1880's was by no means the typical parliamentary country that Mosca claimed. On the contrary, it was an extreme and somewhat eccentric example of the general phenomenon. Still more, Mosca was a southerner, a Sicilian, and it was from southern Italian experience that he drew his most damaging instances of parliamentary malfunctioning. It was already enough that Mosca was writing from an Italian vantage point; the fact that he was a Sicilian compounded the distortion.

In fact if one were deliberately to choose a time and a place that would display parliamentary institutions to their maximum discredit, it would be hard to find a more telling example than southern Italy in the 1880's. Ever since the fall of the "old Right" in 1876—an event which liberal conservatives of Mosca's type regarded as an unmitigated calamity—Italy had been ruled by a "Left" that was leftist only in name and that in practice represented little more than the replacement of the oligarchy of birth and talent that had founded the new Italian kingdom with a less respectable "political class" of professional parliamentarians and officeholders. The franchise has just been extended to include a million and a half new voters—but still only about one out of every three adult male Italians was even theoretically entitled to participate in elections. And as a practical matter merely a fraction of those enfranchised actually exercised their privilege. Devout Catholics scrupulously refrained from participation in public life; thousands of other citizens shunned the polls through political apathy or distaste for the upstart regime that had overthrown their traditional allegiance. In Rome the parliamentary chambers had become the scene of an unabashed trading of votes against local favors. Under the supple manipulation of Agostino Depretis—prime minister for nearly a decade—party lines had dissolved and old oppositionists had been lured into the governmental majority. The word *trasformismo* had been added to the Italian language to epitomize all that was wrong with the country's parliamentary life.

It was quite obvious, then—and it took no great discernment on the young Mosca's part to detect it—that Italy was being ruled by a fairly narrow governing class. This was particularly the case in the South and Sicily, where quasi-feudal class relations persisted, where the bulk of the population was still illiterate, and where one or two "great electors"—a large landholder or other local potentate—could sometimes swing the vote of an entire constituency. Tightly knit cliques controlled the nomination of candidates and not infrequently called on the local *mafia* or *camorra* to enforce their will. What wonder that Mosca concluded—to cite his most celebrated thrust at the parliamentary system—that "it is not the electors who elect the deputy, but ordinarily it is the deputy who has himself elected by the electors."

Presumably this was necessarily the case; under what Mosca's admirer Robert Michels has called "the iron law of oligarchy" no elective system could function otherwise. But in Mosca's early work the distinction between what is merely the normal condition of any political activity and what an abuse is not always made clear. The spirited polemical tone of the young author's writing frequently carries him beyond his expressed intention. At times he keeps rigorously to his professed position of detachment. As opposed to most other political commentators of the period, he is not shocked by the interference of the prefects in elections; indeed, he argues that in a majority of cases this may actually be a good thing, since it produces better candidates than those ordinarily chosen by the local political cliques. At other times, however, Mosca gives way to his natural polemical bent and makes statements that sound like an unqualified condemnation of the whole parliamentary system. At such times he betrays what is obviously a deep personal annoyance.

One source of this annoyance is theoretical. Mosca is exasperated by what he regards as the hypocrisy of political rhetoric, and he is out to expose how shamelessly the "democratic" politicians violate the principles they profess. At all costs, he wishes to set the record straight. Beyond this, however, the careful reader can detect a class grievance. As a member of the educated upper middle class, Mosca understandably regards himself as belonging to the natural elite of the new Italian kingdom. Properly this class should be managing the affairs of the state. And to a large extent such is still the case. But through a cynical manipulation of the parliamentary system, the natural elite of the country is being displaced by a new and unsavory class of politicians and profiteers. Mosca protests against this state of affairs and looks around for a way to change it. An Italian Henry Adams, he resents being defrauded of his birthright.

It comes as no surprise, then, when at the end of his *Teorica* he predicts the end of the parliamentary system. Even the apparent stability of Britain, he notes, rests less on its parliamentary institutions than on the continuity of its governing class. But here Mosca's theoretical difficulties begin. It is one thing to expose the deficiencies of parliamentary government. It is something far more difficult to devise a new system to replace it. Mosca is too acute a political observer to imagine that a return to a frankly aristocratic regime is possible. The idea of representative government—however fallacious the reasoning behind it—is far too deeply rooted to permit that. And so when he comes to outline his remedies, he appears somewhat at a loss. After all the vigor of his condemnation, he has few concrete changes to offer. A return to the letter of the Italian constitution, with executive authority again in the hands of the King, and a new method of appointing senators so as to make them truly independent of political considerations—this is virtually all he proposes. And he advances it somewhat lamely and diffidently, as though conscious that it is actually a reactionary proposal, unrealistic and impossible of attainment. He seems already to suspect that this is not a practicable way to attain his highest goal—"a true renewal of the whole political class . . . on the basis of personal merit and technical capacity."

Such is the direction in which Mosca's theory is actually heading. And his second great desideratum is even more revealing—a "reciprocal control among all the members [of the political class] so as to avoid, so far as is humanly possible, the arbitrary and irresponsible action of a single individual or group of individuals." In this statement Mosca leaves open the way for his eventual reconciliation with the parliamentary regime itself.

III

In its original form the *Elementi*—published in 1896, twelve years after the *Teorica*—did not depart very far from the main principles embodied in the earlier work. It was longer, more detailed, more systematic in organization, and more moderate in tone. The theories of the political class and the political formula, however, were still its central features. And the windy abstractions of democracy and socialism remained the chief targets of Mosca's quiet scorn.

Nevertheless the emphasis had changed. Partly this change reflected the author's altered circumstances of life. In 1885, after the publication of the *Teorica,* Mosca became an unpaid lecturer on constitutional law at the University of Palermo. He was still at the bottom of the academic ladder and still confined to a Sicilian horizon. In the following decade he virtually severed his connections with Sicily. Although remaining a junior lecturer, he transferred to the University of Rome, where he could study national political life at the center rather than on its eccentric periphery. And, in addition to his university work, he had found a paying position that gave unequaled opportunities for observing politics at close hand. As editor of the journal of the Chamber of Deputies, Mosca occupied a unique vantage point for acquiring an education in the realities of parliamentarism.

The day-to-day view of a parliament in action, as opposed to merely observing electoral abuses in the local constituencies, seems to have mollified the uncompromising critic of representative institutions. In 1896 Mosca was not prepared to retract anything that he had said earlier; he still regarded the conventional justifications of parliamentary rule as largely fictitious. But from the practical standpoint he was more prepared to see the advantages of representative government and less eager to point out its failings. Parliamentarism—in the sense of a regime that concentrates in the parliament "all prestige and all power"—he still considered "one of the worst types of political organization"; it was simply the "irresponsible and anonymous tyranny of the elements that prevail in the elections and speak in the name of the people." But properly controlled and limited in their powers, representative bodies offered at least two great advantages. They permitted public opinion—or, as Mosca more sceptically phrased it, "certain sentiments and certain passions of the crowd"—to find an echo "in the highest spheres of government." And they guaranteed the "participation of a certain number of socially valuable elements in the rule of the state." In this fashion, representative institutions could help in attaining what Mosca still regarded as the prime desiderata of good government—a system that would permit "all the elements that have political value in a given society to be used and specialized to the best advantage, and to be subjected to reciprocal control and the principle of individual responsibility for what they do in their respective spheres of action."

All this was familiar to readers of the *Teorica*. At the same time the original version of the *Elementi* shows Mosca already beginning to shift his emphasis from the first to the second of his requirements for good government. He still speaks of the importance of recruiting and maintaining the best possible political class. He is still the technician striving to lay the theoretical foundations for a more competent oligarchy. But now he emphasizes more frequently than he did before the necessity of checking the oligarchs in the exercise of their functions. The danger of "arbitrary and irresponsible action" looms larger in his thought. "The true moral guarantee of representative governments," he finds, "is the public discussion that takes place in the assemblies."

Necessarily, then, Mosca is led to re-examine his theory of the political formula. He reiterates his contention that all such formulas are equally mythical, but he is now more ready to distinguish between those of them that are socially useful and those that are dangerous. Specifically, he separates the two main "intellectual currents" that have produced the parliamentary formula. The democratic doctrine of Rousseau he finds almost wholly noxious. But the theory of limited government associated with the name of Montesquieu he considers "not fundamentally mistaken." Actually Mosca might have gone much farther. Had he been less anxious to assert his own originality as a political writer, he might have been more generous in recognizing his debt to the great French theorist. He might have granted that on all essential points he and Montesquieu are in agreement. For, like Montesquieu, the Mosca of the *Elementi* draws "a sharp dividing line between despotism and all other forms of government." And, though an uncompromising foe of despotism in all its guises, he is too sceptical to "elaborate any radical solution" as a substitute for it. He lacks faith "in the capacity of men to effect and maintain a radically new society. . . . His awareness of the ambiguous character of progress, his insistence on slowness and caution in legislative changes—all this makes for a conservative but not necessarily reactionary attitude toward life." These conclusions of a contemporary writer on Montesquieu describe with amazing accuracy the position that Mosca had reached midway in his career as a political theorist.

IV

The two decades following the publication of the first edition of the *Elementi* completely altered Mosca's circumstances of life. In 1896, just after the *Elementi* appeared, he had been made a professor at the University of Turin. This event established him as a man who had ar-

rived in life—just as it shifted his orientation from Sicily to the northern part of the country. By 1908 he had attained a position of sufficient eminence so that he could "have himself elected" a deputy. And from that point on the highest public honors followed in regular succession. From 1914 to 1916 he served as an under-secretary in the government, and in 1919 he was appointed a senator of the realm. Mosca's ambition evidently reached no higher. His elevation to the Senate automatically made him an elder statesman, and it was in that capacity that in 1923, the year following Mussolini's accession to power, he accepted a chair at the University of Rome.

Such substantial success in the realm of public life is almost unique in the biographies of political thinkers. In itself it may have had something to do with the increasing mellowness of Mosca's writing and the more favorable attitude he came to adopt toward the parliamentary system. But his experience as a deputy and senator also entered in; he was participating in the activity of the chambers during a period when talent and devotion to the public service were perhaps more conspicuous in those quarters than they had been during the last decades of the previous century. He was experiencing as a historical reality the advent of universal suffrage and the shaky beginnings of Italian electoral democracy. And he did not condemn the new developments in the unrestrained terms that he might have used in the past. This was the more noteworthy since the period immediately following his appointment to the Senate witnessed a further historical change that might well have destroyed his whole new-found tolerance toward the parliamentary system—the virtual breakdown of that system during the three years preceding the March on Rome.

It would have shown a superhuman restraint on Mosca's part if he had refrained from reminding his fellow countrymen that they were now experiencing what he had predicted nearly forty years earlier. This is doubtless what he had in mind when in 1924 he congratulated himself on the accuracy of his foresight. In an essay on the "crisis in parliamentarism" published four years later, he stressed the gravity of the current breakdown in representative institutions. It had come about, he argued, largely through the "mistake" of conceding universal suffrage—a mistake, however, "which had become more or less necessary through the mentality of the times in which it was conceded." Once again he had little to offer in the way of a remedy. He simply gave his implied endorsement to a system of weighted suffrage "in which the vote of the poor and ignorant" would not count "exactly the same . . . as that of the educated person and of the person who has had the ability to acquire honestly a certain well-being."

Yet at the same time he remained faithful to the basic principles of limited, representative government. He surprised a number of his intellectual disciples by refusing to rally to the new Fascist regime. More than that, the very advent of the dictatorship reinforced his tendency to take a more charitable view of parliamentary institutions.

In the first edition of the *Elementi,* he had stated that "the only practical criterion for judging . . . political regimes is . . . by comparing them . . . with those that have preceded them and, when possible, with those that have followed them." The coming to power of Mussolini gave him a chance to apply this criterion—to judge the parliamentary system in the light of what had succeeded to it. Mosca's verdict was unqualified. In December 1925, during the debate on the bill that in effect ended the responsibility of the prime minister to the Parliament, Mosca rose from his seat in the Senate to make the following declaration:

> I who have always sharply criticized parliamentary government must now almost lament over its downfall. . . . Certainly representative parliamentary government must not and can not be immutable. As the conditions of society change political organizations are changed. But should the change have been rapid and radical, or should it have been slow and wary? This is the very grave question which vexes my soul. As an old adversary of the parliamentary regime, I believe that this problem must be solved in the most moderate and prudent manner.

Beneath the cautious phraseology, the implication was unmistakable. Mosca rejected Mussolini's brutal solution of the parliamentary crisis. In the showdown, his loyalty to personal freedom and limited government took precedence over his elitist yearnings, which the Fascists had actually gone far to satisfy. Moreover, the tone of his retrospective judgment on the parliamentary system indicated a revised attitude toward history. The elderly senator, now in his late sixties, was far less confident than he had been as an intrepid young theoretician of twenty-five. He was now less sure that his "key" to history had unlocked all its secrets. Nearly half a century before, he had discovered the theoretical formulas that seemed to explain both the political systems of past ages and the course that would be followed by the representative institutions of his own day. And the formulas had worked. They had indicated the crisis in the parliamentary system that in fact had come to pass. But still something had been lacking. The positivist-minded syllogisms in which Mosca had tried to imprison the variety of human political experience had failed to embrace all contingencies. The elusive stuff of history itself had slipped through the theoretician's deftly shaping fingers.

In four decades of lived history, all the elements of his problem had altered. The institutions had changed, but the change had not merely been one of degeneration, as Mosca had earlier predicted. Electoral democracy had come to Italy, but its coming had not been quite the unmitigated catastrophe that he had expected. The virtual universal suffrage extended to the Italian people in 1912 had not destroyed the country's representative institutions. In some ways it had actually strengthened them, by bringing a number of "socially valuable elements" into the Parliament and by adding to it new deputies of unquestioned talent. After all, Mosca himself had been re-

elected to the Chamber under the new extended suffrage. It was true that the postwar years had seen the collapse of Italian parliamentary government. But its overthrow had come not from the forces of socialism and syndicalism, as Mosca had long predicted, but from a new and unexpected radicalism of the Right. As late as 1925 it was difficult to determine the precise nature of the Fascist regime. But the old political theorist understood it well enough to know that it was even less to his taste than the system of government that had preceded it. An elitist reaction against democracy had come—but not in the form he had hoped for. Or was it perhaps that his theories themselves had changed? Was it perhaps that the shift from emphasizing the mythical character of all "political formulas" to an insistence on their qualitative differences that caused him to render a negative judgment on the new Fascist regime? If something similar had come in the 1880's, might he have been willing to accept it? Or was it the theoretician himself who had gradually accommodated himself in practice to the characteristic institutions of his time? It was impossible to say—there were too many variables. In place of the old clear-cut lessons of history, the flux of human experience itself had taken over.

This new feeling for historical change is apparent in the second edition of his *Elementi,* published early in 1923. For this revision of a work that had already become a political classic, Mosca adopted an unusual and extremely honest approach. Aside from adding a few explanatory notes, he simply left the original text exactly as it stood. His later ideas and reflections he appended to it as a somewhat shorter second volume. While this arrangement makes for rather curious reading, it has the advantage of displaying the young and the old Mosca side by side. The leading ideas are the same—again it is simply the emphasis that has altered.

Although this second volume must have been written almost in its entirety before the March on Rome—since its publication followed so soon thereafter—it already reveals Mosca's new attitude toward parliamentary institutions that we have seen embodied in his statements of 1925 and 1928. And in some respects this new version of the *Elementi* goes even farther. It praises representative government as the form of rule that "has succeeded in coordinating a maximum sum of energies and of individual activities for the benefit of the collective interest." And it includes a qualified endorsement of "the democratic tendency" as "in a certain way indispensable to . . . the progress of human societies." Mosca adds a characteristic justification for this rather surprising change of front:

> The democratic tendency, so long as its action does not tend to become excessive and exclusive, represents what in vulgar language would be called a conservative force. For it permits a continual addition of new blood to the governing classes through the admission of new elements that have innately and spontaneously within them the attitude of command and the will to command, and so prevents that exhaustion of the aristocracies of birth that is wont to bring on the great social cataclysms.

This, then, is the message of the *Elementi* in their final form—a tentative recourse to "the democratic tendency" to revive the European elites that have so signally failed in their task of holding off the forces of despotism. And it is the youth that must accomplish the fusion of the old and the new elements in the political class. Mosca's second volume closes on a note of warm supplication—an appeal for political "vision" to the "noblest part of the youth" of his country, in the hope that they will rise to the responsibilities that the new age imposes upon them.

v

The second volume of the *Elementi* represents the completion of Mosca's work as a political thinker. In the last two decades of his life, he felt himself too old to do much further writing. The period between 1923 and his death in 1941 saw the publication of two relatively minor studies and of the few notes he added to his *Elementi* for the third edition, which appeared in 1938. It is on the final version of this work that Mosca's reputation rests and that the contemporary relevance of his ideas may best be judged.

To a sceptical age that has seen the destruction of so many hopes and the blasting of so many illusions, Mosca's theory of society may well have a peculiar appeal. For it seeks in one formulation both to explain the revival of despotism that has characterized the past half century of Western history and to establish on a more solid basis the permanent validity of free government. The theory of the political class and the political formula cuts both ways: it exposes what is abstract and unrealistic in the doctrine of popular sovereignty at the same time as it insists on the supreme importance of preserving a liberal, constitutional regime. In drawing a sharp distinction between the liberal and the democratic traditions, it clarifies much that is imprecise and sentimental in contemporary historical writing and the contemporary discussion of political issues. And in establishing the priority of the former, both in time and in importance, it seeks a way out of a dilemma as old as Aristotle—the dilemma of a democracy that freely chooses to abdicate to tyranny. This ancient problem has reappeared with renewed force in our own time. The collapse of Italian, German, and French democracy in the period from 1922 to 1940 and the present precarious situation of the restored parliamentary regimes in those countries, have brought home to men's minds once again the age-old danger that democracy may degenerate into despotism.

Mosca's answer to this question was aristocratic, conservative, and largely ineffective. To check the excesses of democracy, he had nothing more promising to offer than a weighting of the suffrage in favor of education and property and a strengthening of the powers of nonelective officials. The very hesitation with which he advanced these remedies suggests that he half suspected how unrealistic they were; democracy, he admitted, "had become more or less necessary through the mentality of the times." Hence his specific proposals have little relevance for the contemporary world. It is rather his insight into the functioning of representative government that is useful to us—that and his insistence that the talent and ethical level of the political class can alone guarantee the preservation and progress of a free society. This teaching is only superficially inapplicable to a modern democracy. It is "undemocratic" only under a definition of democracy that seeks to add to an equality of rights an equality of attainments and ideas. The latter definition is widely held today, particularly in the United States. But it is coming under increasingly heavy attack from those who see the dangers to a free society that such a leveling of talents implies. For them Mosca's warnings carry a note of particular urgency. In a democracy—subject as it is to gusts of popular prejudice and passion—the systematic cultivation of talent, the persistent fostering of the higher-than-average individual, are indispensable to the proper functioning of free institutions.

We have seen how under the influence of a long experience of history itself, Mosca's concept of the political lessons of history gradually altered. We have seen how as an old man he was willing to grant what in his youth he would never have admitted, that under proper circumstances "the democratic principle" could actually function as a stabilizing force in society. Had Mosca lived a decade longer, he might have seen that a new turn of history had necessitated still a further revision in his theories. He might have recognized that in a country like the United States, with a standard of living unparalleled in history and the majority of its population assimilated in habits and attitudes to a vast middle class, his theory of a "political class" is no longer strictly applicable. It is too rigid to embrace the realities of our current society. In a situation in which the locus of political influence is almost impossible to establish, in which authority is diffused among a wide variety of mutually interacting pressure and "veto" groups, it is idle to speak of a clearly defined political class. In practice the rule of minorities still obtains; but their influence is exerted in so shifting and amorphous a fashion that it cannot be described any longer in terms of a specific ruling group. Once more a loosening and reinterpretation of Mosca's categories is in order.

Nevertheless, even in such a society, the problem of the recruitment of political and administrative talent remains. It is perhaps the crucial problem that faces the United States today. Here the historical lessons taught by Mosca—for all their quaint conservatism—can still be studied with profit.

Ferdinand Kolegar (essay date 1964)

SOURCE: "The Elite and the Ruling Class: Pareto and Mosca Re-examined," in *The Review of Politics*, Vol. 29, No. 3, July, 1967, pp. 354-69.

[*In the following essay, originally presented at the fiftieth annual meeting of the American Sociological Association in Montreal, Canada, in 1964, Kolegar argues against the prevailing view of Mosca and Pareto as anti-democratic, claiming instead that their theories ushered in a significant modern sociological concept.*]

Mosca's and Pareto's elite conceptions have had a curious fate. Mosca's work, in many ways an anticipation of Pareto's, has been overshadowed by his more brilliant and renowned antagonist from the very beginning, and perhaps only the circumstance that his American editor chose as the title for his *Elementi di scienza politica* the two words which fairly epitomize his theory ("the ruling class") enables many a student of sociology to associate Mosca's name with at least a vague notion about the nature of his contribution. Pareto himself, the skeptically disinterested "maître de Céligny," whose only ambition was to "tell the complete truth and nothing but the truth," has generally come to be regarded as a "Karl Marx of bourgeoisie," an intellectual precursor of Fascism, and worse. Both are seen, unjustifiably, as enemies of democracy and detractors of the "new belief in the common man."

After a brief flurry of interest in Pareto's work, attendant upon the publication of the English translation of his *Trattato di sociologia generale* in the nineteen-thirties, Pareto today is seldom acknowledged as one of the *magni parentes* of modern sociology and his elite theory has been underplayed even by his most thoughtful American interpreters.

Labeled as neo-Machiavellians, both Pareto and Mosca are uncritically and almost automatically stereotyped as "protosociologists" par excellence, addressing themselves to problems of an earlier, more deferential and hierarchy-conscious age and advancing, if not complete inanities, then at least hasty generalizations based on a superficial study of social structures typical of an era loosely identified as preindustrial or premodern.

Mosca and especially Pareto themselves vastly contributed to the confusion which attaches itself to their work. Although both of them paid lip service to the institutional norm of personal humility expected of a scientist and cite their "predecessors," the very vigor, even bitterness with which they waged the polemic over the originality and priority of their writings on the elites betrays, to my mind, that they both regarded their theories as innovative achievements of the first order. And, as is the wont of all pioneers and discoverers, they could not resist the temptation to exaggerate the significance of their contributions and to overstate their claims.

The incidence of phrases such as "classe politica" and "l'élite gouvernementale"; the fascination of both writers with the role of force and deception in society; the choice of illustrative material from political history and contemporary political scene; the unmistakable animus against the equalitarian propensities of modern democratic regimes and the almost inevitable political implications of their ideas: all these things have conspired to lend a rather one-sided emphasis to Mosca's and Pareto's elite models.

Hence, the common interpretation has been to view Mosca's and Pareto's theories as constructions of a *political* elite model pure and simple and to assert that it was an ideological reflection of, or at best an attempt to master conceptually, a political regime antithetical to representative democracy, applicable perhaps to the analysis of oligarchic or autocratic remnants and tendencies afflicting democratic systems of government and democratically organized corporate bodies, but wholly unsuited for a sociological analysis of the overall stratification system of modern society.

It would be superfluous to present a detailed exposition of the two elite conceptions, of the parallels and dissimilarities between the various versions of these theories, although a historian of ideas finds this tracing of elective affinities of particular interest. However, at the risk of being expository, we should like to remove one widespread misunderstanding, namely: the deriving of Pareto's theory of elites from his conception of residues. The theory of elites represents in Pareto's overall analytic scheme a fundamentally independent part and as such was formulated, in all its essentials, in his early works, *Cours d'économie politique* (2 vols., 1896-97) and above all *Les systèmes socialistes* (2 vols., 1902). It was only later, in the *Trattato,* that it was integrated with the other components of Pareto's analytic frame of reference, that is, the residues.

The theory of elites as expounded in the *Systèmes socialistes* is predicated on the incontrovertible and universal fact of human differentiation. The graphic representation of this fact, used by Pareto, is a "social pyramid" (*in concreto:* a pyramid of wealth), whose vertex is composed by the rich few and whose wide base consists of the poor.

Pareto hypothesizes that this socioeconomic gradation or ranking "depends probably on the distribution of men's physiological and psychological characteristics" and asserts that the general shape of this pyramid is virtually unchangeable, although the individuals composing it ("les molécules dont se compose l'agrégat social," is Pareto's scientist way of putting it) are never at rest, moving up and down, becoming rich and poor. Since social stratification then depends on the distribution of physiological and psychological characteristics in a given population, Pareto suggests the need to construct a number of such pyramids, all of them roughly alike in form, based on the distribution of such traits or qualities as intelligence, musical or literary talent, mathematical ability, moral character, and the like. It is most unlikely for identical individuals to occupy identical places in several of these pyramids, but there will be considerable amounts of overlapping between the pyramids of social and political influence and power. Yet, Pareto does not deny that "the so-called upper classes are generally also the richest. These classes represent an elite, an *'aristocracy'* (in the etymological sense of the word)."

Pareto, we note, does not operate with the concept of a single unitary elite but explicitly recognizes the existence of several elites in society. He insists repeatedly that his elite concept is neutral and nonevaluative and may be applied with equal justification to an elite of saints just as well as an elite of brigands, an elite of scholars as well as of thieves. Or, as he puts it later in *Trattato,* an elite is "a class of people who have the highest indices [of talent or achievement] in their branch of activity," irrespective of the nature of that activity.

In other words, Pareto's elite is an essentially statistical, classificatory concept comprising persons with specified characteristics, that is, generally persons who excel others in a determinate activity. As such, it is a social category rather than a genuine group, and Pareto makes no attempt to prove that it does operate as a group. Justified as this procedure is, it raises a serious problem when Pareto, having divided the elite into a governing elite ("comprising individuals who directly or indirectly play some considerable part in government") and nongoverning elite (= the rest of the population), tries to account for the actions of the governing elite *stricto sensu,* it would have to be assumed to constitute a more or less cooperating and cohesive group of individuals acting in concert, possessing at least a modicum of "class consciousness." In any case, Pareto's work, although full of suggestive allusions, is singularly devoid of concrete propositions about how the governing elite goes about its job.

Pareto's silence regarding this crucial problem of cooperation and consensus and of the *modus operandi* of elite rule may be due to several things. It may be attributed to his failure to specify a key term of his discourse or his failure to recognize the cohesive group character of political elites. Or it may be explained from a hypothesis, never made explicit by him but entirely plausible, that a "governing elite" is not to be construed as a "power elite," and that power, rather than being a monopolized facility in the possession of a more or less unified elite (or of several coalescing elites), is a variable attribute of certain elite positions. This would, of course, imply that individuals occupying elite positions do not need to operate as a group in order to get what they want but can function separately or even individually.

The elites do not last forever; they decline, degenerate and die, sometimes at a fast rate, sometimes slowly. History, in Pareto's phrase, is a "graveyard of aristocracies." They decay not only in numbers but also in quality, making room for the entry of new elements from the other parts of the social aggregate and setting in motion the "circulation of elites," of varying degrees of intensity and amplitude.

The question raised but unanswered by Pareto is: What accounts for the decay of elites, composed as they are of the fittest, the strongest, the best elements of society? He admits that the causes of this phenomenon are "obscure," objects to the simple explanation by the factor of heredity, and intimates that the main source of the decay of elites is the fact that they co-opt, in an increasing measure, subjects of mediocre qualities, their loss of vigor

and *élan,* and the concurrent growth of a new elite in the other strata of society.

The abstract description of the process of circulation of elites, chosen by Pareto in order to eliminate all possible bias that might stem from the discussion of a concrete case, may serve as the best thumbnail sketch of his theory:

> Let A stand for an elite in power, B for an elite which tries to unseat and replace it, C for the rest of the population. . . . A and B are the leaders (*chefs*) who regard C as their tools in the struggle. C alone, an army without leaders, are powerless and gain importance only when led by A or by B. Very often, nearly always, it is B who place themselves at the head of C, whereas A are lulled by a false sense of security. . . . Besides, B are in a better position to lure C, precisely because—having no power—they can tempt them by vague promises. At times, however, A and B try to outbid each other, in hope of satisfying C by seeming, but not real, concessions. As B gradually replace A, by slow infiltration . . . C are deprived of leaders who could incite them to a revolt. . . . As a rule, A try to counteract this infiltration, but their opposition may be inefficient and amount to a mere sulking. . . . In order to succeed, B must have C as their allies in battle. Once they succeed and seize power, a new elite D will be formed and will play the same role that B played with regard to A, and so on.

Pareto criticizes historians for failing to see, for the most part, this process of circulation:

> They describe this phenomenon as if it were a combat of an aristocracy or oligarchy, always the same, against the people, also always the same. But in reality (1) it is a struggle between two aristocracies, and (2) the aristocracy in power is constantly changing. Aristocracy in power today will be after a certain lapse of time replaced by its adversaries.

Some historians give credit for successful political changes to the people (C) but do not comprehend that it was the work of a new elite which led the people (C) or acted in its name. Similarly, many members of the elite B believe that their action will not benefit them personally or their own elite and think that it is in the interest of the people (C). This illusion is shared by the old elite (A) as well.

Illustrations adduced by Pareto in support of his theory cover the entire range of history from classical antiquity to his own day. As he sees it, the ruling class of his time, composed largely from bourgeoisie and the remnants of the old aristocracy, is proving increasingly less able to defend its positions. A new, determined and energetic elite, represented especially by the trade union leaders, is gradually emerging and will replace the old decadent ruling groups which have succumbed to egalitarianism and humanitarian illusions and which are on their way down and out.

Pareto's theory of elites is in essence a bold and simplified generalization of the fact that all organized societies have superordinate and subordinate groupings and strata. We know of no modern society without a definite system of imperative control and without a system of authority. But Pareto seems to ignore the immense variability of the types of authority, the distribution and functioning of administrative personnel and the "decision-makers," of political ideologies and legitimation of coercive decisions, and the like. Untenable also is Pareto's view that the distribution of the ruling minority is a simple function of the distribution of psychophysical qualities. Pareto's reasoning on this matter is dangerously close to the kind of "monistic" explanation which he so sharply criticizes in the methodological passages of his work. Social and political change and the changes in the structure of authority clearly cannot be adequately understood if they are seen as a mere consequence of a change in the composition (or biological and psychological equipment) of the elite, or the result of a sudden appearance of a set of desirable attributes in the nonelite, but must be seen in the context of a far wider range of social phenomena.

The conception of elites outlined thus far bears unmistakable traces of the social and intellectual atmosphere of the period which we now, in retrospect, see as the beginning of a far-reaching reorientation of European thought and a crisis of bourgeois liberalism, a period which reached its peak in the quarter of a century preceding the beginning of the First World War.

There can be little doubt that Pareto and Mosca alike were heavily influenced by the idea of competition and of the survival of the economically fittest which was one of the main tenets of the nineteenth-century liberal ideology. As an economist *a fortiori,* and a vigorous advocate of free-trade policies to boot, Pareto especially was bound to notice the "disturbances" resulting from interference with the free play of the market and to adopt the vivid imagery of this economic mechanism to his sociology of elites. Indeed, Pareto argues that the liberal society (or laissez-faire economic system) ensures maximum social mobility and unhampered circulation of elites. All obstacles to this circulation represent so many limitations upon the creation of new cultural values, an upsetting of the delicate social "equilibrium," and with it an increased danger of revolutions and social crises. The circulation of elites thus becomes the same kind of *perpetuum mobile* as is, in the free capitalist market, the equilibrating automatism of supply and demand. That this should be so is due, in the main, to the fact that the closed estates and legal barriers to mobility characteristic of the preindustrial phase of development have been removed.

There is really no empirical society with absolute mobility or circulation of elites. Indeed, if in the selection of members of the elite there existed a condition of perfectly free competition so that every individual could rise just as high in the social scale as his talents and ambition permit, the elite would consist exactly of those persons who are best fitted for membership in it, and the society

would be automatically correcting its own defects and weaknesses. In reality, even in the liberal (open-class) society competition is not entirely free, and, as the institution of private property in the bourgeois liberal society, so in other societies there are other obstacles that interfere with the free circulation of individuals on the mobility ladder. The impossibility of an entirely free circulation of elites is particularly true of Pareto's "governing elite."

Later, in his *Trattato,* Pareto ties this conception of elites in with his theory of residues. There are essentially two types of elites corresponding to two main classes of residues: speculators, that is, those who, endowed with strong and numerous residues of combinations, tend toward daring innovation and speculation in economic matters. Rentiers, in whom the residues of the persistence of the aggregates predominate, represent psychologically the conservative type with a strong sense of duty and a narrow but determined will. Social development, in effect, is nothing but oscillation between these two elites and the corresponding forms of government.

If we look closely we discover that what Pareto enunciated as a general rule valid in all societies is actually based on observation of a rather limited segment of empirical reality, namely Italian society and government in the latter part of the nineteenth century. In Italy, a short period of genuine laissez-faire liberalism was followed by the policy of economic interventionism, and the regime of "speculators" was replaced by new forms of economic life and economic thought. Pareto himself aptly illustrates his conception by analyzing, in terms of his frame of reference, the succession of Italian governments of this period.

The regime of speculators began with Depretis, who "made many speculators rich men by protective tariffs, railway deals, government contracts" and the like. The cabinets of Crispi and Giolitti continue but modify somewhat this policy. The Libyan War and the resurgence of nationalism are symptoms of a coming change. Premier Sonnino, "lacking either the ability or the inclination to act as a faithful agent of the band of speculators," is helpless in coping with the new economic problems. The rule of speculators is undermined and new men appear on the political and economic scene. It is conceivable that Pareto's scheme provides a fitting explanatory tool when applied to political and economic changes in this circumscribed period (roughly 1876-1914), but it is doubtful that it could be applied without substantial modifications to other eras and other cultural contexts.

Coming at the heels of this cycle, which he called the cycle of "demagogic plutocracy," Pareto foresaw a new type of political elite, diminution of freedom and ascendancy of "planning," in a word: an epoch of new, rigid and restrictive "Byzantinism."

The elite of the "foxes" (= speculators) will be unable to withstand the onslaught of the "lions," for it will have lost the courage and determination to use force in the defense of its rule, which alone could postpone its downfall.

Mosca's theory was first published in the **Teorica dei governi e governo parlamentare** in 1883. It has undergone several revisions and emendations but its scope was consistently narrower than Pareto's, focusing mainly on the structure of political organization.

In essence, it posits the necessary predominance of an active minority under all forms of government. Simpler and narrower, it is at the same time more "functional." In no way constrained by Pareto's premise of a direct quantitative correspondence between the distribution of capabilities and the distribution of elites, Mosca avers that there always has to be an organized minority in order to discharge the functions of government, that is, not because there exist persons with an irresponsible *libido dominandi* but because all societies are in need of management and ordering and consequently in need of a "classe dirigente."

Mosca's later work, especially the four successive editions of his **Elementi di scienza politica** (1895, 1922, 1938 and 1947, the edition of last hand), contain a number of qualifications and modifications of his original contraposition of the ruling minority and the subject class, reflecting the changes in social structure and approximating more adequately the complex power relationships.

Whatever prompted these changes, they made Mosca's conception resemble Pareto's in some important respects. He insists on the sharp dichotomy between the ruling class and the lower classes, but admits that, "as a consequence of their isolation," there comes into existence within these lower classes another ruling class, or directing minority, which is often antagonistic to the legally constituted government.

Furthermore, he came to see that below the highest level of the ruling class, below the clique of "perhaps two or three dozens of persons, or even as many as a hundred, according to the case," there is another "stratum" comprising all those with capacities for leadership, without whose operation the stability of any political system would be impossible. The concept of the "mid-elite" as developed in the writings of Harold Lasswell is a close parallel of this latter "stratum" of Mosca.

The conceptions of Pareto and Mosca discussed here contain errors, ambiguities and oversimplifications. Those who look in Pareto's and Mosca's work for an easy operational index of elite membership will be disappointed. But to dismiss their elite model just because it is not an operational model would be premature, and so would be any interpretation holding that the Mosca-Paretian model is a mere conceptualization of autocratic rulership, out of tune with the times.

A more careful scrutiny of the elite conceptions inaugurated by Mosca and Pareto will reveal them to be modern conceptions *kat' exochén*. It is not without significance that both theories were formulated towards the end of the nineteenth century and at the beginning of this century, and not at an earlier date. It has been rightly suggested that the elite concept is a *historical concept* which has arisen together with the object it was chosen to denote, and not an *instrumental concept* created artificially in order to label something yet to be discovered by subsequent research.

One need not be reminded that the history of social thought is strewn with ideas extolling or justifying the rule of the enlightened few. The charisma of the "best," and the belief that the "best" (*hoi aristoi*) should rule, with its corollary that people are unequal and the masses benighted, is one of the most persistent themes of the utopian writings reaching as far back as Plato.

In modern times, this idea is persuasively expounded by writers who contributed to the "rise of sociology from the spirit of restoration": de Bonald, Saint-Simon and Comte. It is at the heart of the conceptions of the early socialists (such as Saint-Simon himself), the Saint-Simonians, and an assortment of social Darwinists, romantic totalitarians and utopians of the most diverse provenience. Whether as an aristocracy of administrators, or a "pouvoir spirituel," a "positivist clergy" of scholars, or a technocratic elite, all of these conceptions are purely *utopian* constructions, of great visionary power and insidious appeal but little analytic value. The same is true of the conceptions of Georges Sorel (and his revolutionary syndicalist elites), Marx and Lenin (envisioning the group of professional revolutionaries acting as a vanguard of the proletariat), and Roberto Michels, representing what might be called the *ideological* formulation of elitism, typically arising at a time of increasing massification of modern society and a breakdown of the established society of the "honoratiores" and an increasingly felt precariousness of certain parliamentary institutions of liberal democracy. Michels, a pupil of Mosca's, especially is concerned with the consequences of this general process of democratization, evidenced among other things in the transformation of the structure of political parties from the liberal middle-class parties to modern mass parties and their consequent bureaucratization and formation of oligarchies of top party functionaries.

Viewed against this background, Pareto's theory, in spite of some ideological elements, represents truly the first relatively objective attempt to explore the effects of these modern developments upon the nature of social elites. After the utopian and ideological versions of the concept, his is the first one to be conceived as a scientific, *sociological* category. It is revealing of his intention that his discussion of the elites in the *Trattato* is prefaced by an assurance that he will "eliminate everything that sounds like counsel, admonition, or preaching, or is designed to encourage this or that practical conduct."

For Paretian elite is not an aristocracy in the hereditary sense, nor is it confined to the ruling group in a particular society. Built into Pareto's approach to the elite phenomenon, and thus reflecting the changes which European societies were undergoing during his active life, is the emphasis on the norm of *achievement,* in conscious contradistinction to the ascriptive basis of the positions of privilege and authority characteristic of the (preindustrial) *estate* society, as well as, to some extent, to the criterion of property which constituted the main key to high status positions in the ideal-typical *class* society as it evolved in the period of consolidation of capitalist economy following the phase of early industrialization.

Pareto's insight into this process enabled him to take cognizance of the high degree of dependence of continued industrial growth upon functional specialization and differentiation of skills. We recall that his conception implies the existence of a plurality of elites and that an individual's "capacity" is viewed by him as the chief criterion of selection, stressing the necessity "to take into account the actual, not the potential achievements of a person."

Mosca, on the whole more impressed by the tenacity with which the "political class" maintains itself in power and transmits its privileges and power to its descendants, is less outspoken in his recognition of the criterion of achievement, but his discussion of the two types of political organization (aristocratic and democratic) reveals his awareness of the implications of the historical tendency toward democratization and the concomitant tendency to the "restocking of the ruling class" from the lower strata of society.

And Mosca recognizes that whatever advantages the inherited social position, family background and education may have, they are not enough to make up for some fundamental deficiencies in more important qualities: capacity for work, energy, knowledge of men, etc.

In order fully to understand the link between elites and social structure that we postulated, it is necessary to realize that modern industrial society, contrary to those who would see it as one of unmitigated uniformity and equalization, is a richly diversified society with highly differentiated occupational structure and with a large number of separate hierarchies of prestige. It is a society in which the ascriptive criteria of status, although not altogether abandoned, are becoming progressively attenuated and to some extent replaced by more exacting criteria of competence and achievement, especially in the functionally most significant areas of life (for example, economy). The professionalization of most of the major modern occupations and the proliferation of bureaucratic structures with their characteristic mechanisms of evaluation and promotion are but two examples of this overall trend. In this society, perhaps for the first time in history, men's universal tendency to enhance themselves and to improve their station in life is not only openly recognized and positively sanctioned but is institutionalized and reinforced by the functional requirements of the economic-industrial complex.

A society which puts such a high premium on efficiency, productivity and economic growth cannot do without specialists and a technically increasingly qualified labor force. Hence, it must, in a way, forever try to fulfill the promise with which it has set out to conquer the world, a century and a half ago: *carrière ouverte aux talents!*

Growing more and more complex and technically efficient, modern society faces increasingly difficult problems of coordination in its public realms as well as problems of management in the areas of private consumption, distribution of goods and services, recreation and entertainment. This enhances the importance and enlarges the scope of activities in the areas of politics, public administration and planning, education, cultural pursuits, leisure, and the like. Within each of these branches of activity there is, of course, further differentiation on the basis of individual talent, adaptability, inventiveness, achievement, and success. It is entirely appropriate to refer to those who rose to the top in each of these branches of activity as an *elite,* with the individual achievement serving as the paramount classifying or stratifying criterion. We may indeed speak of *elites of achievement* and presume that these were the elites which prompted Pareto's inquiry.

Each elite of achievement, or even simply individuals occupying certain positions of advantage and prominence, tend to perpetuate these positions and perquisites to a greater or lesser extent. It is almost axiomatic that a high position achieved by one individual will be a stepping-stone for those of his family who will follow him. But the peculiar quality of modern industrial society is that what is inherited are, for the most part, the advantages (and handicaps) of status, not status as such. High status position, or more generally elite membership, has to be ratified and reconfirmed, as a rule, in every generation, and sometimes several times during a single lifetime.

Viewed in this light, Pareto's conception of elites, contrary to the view of most interpreters of Pareto's contribution, is eminently applicable to modern society. It provides a good general explanatory principle which will be found particularly useful by those who are engaged in studying the emergence and development of the pluralistic elite structure characteristic of the modern industrial society. Pareto's notion of the multiplicity of the elites and their circulation, his implicit stress on the principle of achievement, his functionalization of the elite concept and its extension to the entire network of social institutions deserve to be singled out as the most relevant for the analysis of the social structure of advanced societies.

This is not to say that Pareto's work absolves us of the need to go on probing into the problem of elites and their function in contemporary society. Pareto offers hints rather than solutions. He, who vociferated against unproved assumptions, moralizing and speculation, did not himself proceed in the most rigorous scientific manner when it came to adducing empirical evidence for his theories and conclusions. Too often, to prove his point,

Pareto resorts to a high degree of abstraction and leaves out all qualitative differences. Instead of dealing with concrete types and specific elites, and instead of putting forward empirically testable propositions, his approach prompts him to view people only as "human molecules" whose behavior towards society differs only quantitatively, for example, innovating or clinging to established patterns to a varying degree. Most of his examples cited in support of his theory of the circulation of elites seem to be suggestive illustrations rather than strict empirical proofs.

The alternation of the periods of prosperity and stagnation, periods of quick accumulation of new cultural values and periods of conservatism, or "undulations in social facts" (to use Pareto's expression) do exist but their character is so varied that they defy any attempt at being subsumed under an abstract scheme such as Pareto's.

And above all, Pareto did not completely escape the Machiavellian or Hobbesian connotations of his conception, especially so in its later version (in the *Trattato*). Concern with power led him to an excessive preoccupation with the "governing elite" and the stratagems with which it monopolizes its power.

Nor did he clearly see all the structural changes wrought by the process of industrialization and democratization, and particularly its effect in the direction of an increased influx of new elements into the elite and the consequent increase in their size and number, as well as their loss of exclusiveness, tendencies so convincingly analyzed by Karl Mannheim. Skeptical as he was of all "derivations," Pareto for instance failed to take into account the existence of "value-shaping elite" (Carl J. Friedrich), or of intellectuals, whose influence on the process of government is great but who seldom coincide with the "governing elite" in the narrow sense.

The intrusion of his passions and fears into his writings, although strenuously held in check by him, cannot escape any careful reader of Pareto. He seemed to have shared the pessimistic attitude of such writers as Gustave Le Bon and similar critics of the "age of the masses," and their apprehension that their cherished cultural values are disintegrating under the blows of new barbarians and their leaders. But it was his great merit to have fastened his attention on an important element of modern social structure and to have adopted a relatively objective sociological point of view in his study of it.

Norberto Bobbio (essay date 1972)

SOURCE: "Gaetano Mosca and the Theory of the Ruling Class," in *On Mosca and Pareto,* Librairie Droz, 1972, pp. 11-31.

[*In the following essay, Bobbio attempts to create a systematic "exposé" of Mosca's theory of elites in order to explain the contemporary relevance of the theory.*]

1. Gaetano Mosca's fame is based on his theory of the ruling class. This fame is certainly not on the wane, to judge from the attention paid to this concept by a distinguished American scholar, James H. Meisel, in a recent work which, next to the book by the Italian writer Delle Piane, is the most complete survey of the question.

Mosca remained true to the theory of the ruling class all his life. He enunciated it in his first work of any importance which was written when he was twenty-six, *Sulla teorica dei governi e sul governo parlamentare* (1884); he worked out the theory more fully in a book of his later period, the *Elementi di scienza politica* (1896). He corrected and completed it in the *Parte Seconda* which he added to the *Elementi* in the second edition (1923). And he gave a telling summing up of it in his last work, the *Storia delle dottrine politiche* (1937). Pareto had formulated a similar theory of the *élites,* first in an article in 1900, and later in his *Systèmes socialistes.* Mosca insisted with some feeling on having been the first to make the discovery. But, despite his long meditation on this subject and subsequent revisions, Mosca never provided a systematic, properly articulated exposé of his doctrine, in which the various components were logically arranged and examined from all points of view. He dealt with it on various occasions. He made no distinction, except casually and incompletely, between the various headings under which methodical investigations of the subject could have been carried out, and contented himself with an elementary classification. It was only when he discussed it for the last time that he made a clear distinction between two types of problems, those regarding the *recruitment* of the ruling class and those regarding its *organization.* But he did not feel the need to gather together the scattered members of his theories into an organic whole.

For this reason, an exposé of Mosca's theory should begin by arranging the material in proper order. If only to avoid interpretations which are either oversimple or oversubtle, I have felt it useful to group this material in a sequence of subjects which may serve to give the reader an immediate and fairly precise idea both of the complexity of the research, that is, of the various levels involved, and of the gaps in it, that is, of the unfinished state in which the author left it. The aspects of the ruling class which I propose to illustrate by passages drawn freely from his various works are as follows: 1) composition and formation; 2) extension; 3) renewal and replacement; 4) organization and means of exercising power. I need hardly say that the line of demarcation between these aspects is not always sharp, but this is an observation which will undoubtedly occur to the reader himself.

2. A few observations on terminology are called for. Right from his first book, Mosca chose the expression "ruling class" to indicate the phenomenon with which he was so much concerned. In the *Teorica,* after having described the phenomenon of the ruling minority, he concludes: "This special class will from now on be referred to as the ruling class." Although the expression "élite" used by Pareto finally prevailed (with the result

that the expression "theory of the élites" was used in such a wide sense as to include Mosca's theories of the ruling class as well), the expression "ruling class", as Mosca himself rightly observed in the *Parte Seconda* of the *Elementi,* has the advantage over "élite" that it does not imply a positive judgment on the members of that class. "Elite" in common parlance is a value expression and, as such, unsuitable for scientific language, in which preference should be given to neutral expressions such as "ruling class". The expression "ruling class" is used nowadays in everyday language and by historians (we cannot yet speak of a language of political science in Italy, as there is no tradition of studies in this field), not so much in the sense of an organized minority group as of the total of those who habitually engage in politics. It refers not so much to the phenomenon, which is specially stressed by the theory of the élite, of the ruling minorities, as to the phenomenon, equally important and deserving of study, of the professional or almost professional nature of politics in modern parliamentary systems.

Although Mosca adopted right from the start the expression "ruling class", he often liked to use synonymous expressions without giving too much thought to the need to define them clearly. This may be regarded as a first sign of the rather rough state in which Mosca left his theory, even though he returned to it on a number of occasions. In the *Teorica* we find "dominating or ruling class." Elsewhere he uses "upper classes" (*Elementi,* I); "governing class" (*Elementi,* I); "the ruling clique" (*Elementi,* I); "organized minority" (*Teorica*; *Elementi,* I); "governing minority" (*Elementi,* I). One's immediate reaction to a concept to which so many different names are indiscriminately applied is that it has not yet been very strictly defined, but the use of expressions other than "ruling class" is usually to be explained by Mosca's need of two antithetical expressions to define the basic distinction in any society between those who govern and those who are governed. Whereas the expression "ruling class" does not enable him to define the rest of the population by antithesis, the other expressions lent themselves to a description of that section as "dominated, directed, lower or governed class" or as the "unorganized or governed majority".

3. The first point which I have termed the composition of the ruling class includes the study of the qualities which members of a given social group possess or should possess in order to belong (or aspire to belong) to the ruling class. By studying this question, we can say whether there are qualities which distinguish those forming the ruling class, and what they are.

Mosca's reply to the first question is in the affirmative. "The ruling minorities are usually formed in such a way that the individuals composing them can be distinguished from the mass of the governed by certain qualities which give them a certain material and intellectual or even moral superiority . . . ; in other words, they must have some prerequisites, real or apparent, which are highly respected and can be effectively applied in the society in which they live". These qualities are not always the same ones; they may change with history. As a result, it is possible to distinguish various types of ruling classes according to the different qualities which characterize their members. Replying to the second question, Mosca distinguishes, both in the *Teorica* and in the *Elementi,* three qualities which, in varying degrees, give access in different societies to the ruling class—martial ability, wealth, membership of the priesthood. From these qualities or status flow the three forms—military, money and priestly aristocracy. Less prominent among the characteristic qualities of a ruling class, according to Mosca, is culture. To be precise, he makes two reservations to this statement: 1) culture may become an important political force "only in a very advanced stage of civilization"; 2) what has political value "is not so much knowledge in itself as the practical applications which may be made of it to the general advantage". However, when Mosca took off his scientific hat and put on his political and moralizing one, he expressed a longing for a society in which culture would prevail over the other qualities in the composition of the ruling class to the point of regarding the ideal scientific policy as one which could obviously be worked out only by a class of scientific politicians working hand in hand with experts on politics.

It is possible to belong to a ruling class not only because of one's qualities but also of one's birth and because one is born into a family in which those qualities were possessed by one's forebears. Indeed, where hereditary castes have been formed, Mosca observes, birth is the only criterion which governs entry into a class or exclusion from it. Here, the problem of the composition of the ruling class converges with that of its formation and transformation. For the time being, we need only ask what is the relation between membership of a ruling class as a result of birth and the possession of the allegedly superior qualities. Mosca rules out the more extreme theory which links the two factors so closely as to imply that anyone born into the ruling class thereby automatically possesses superior qualities. In this connection, he quotes the theories of Gobineau and Gumplowicz, but it is only to reject them. However, he admits that members of an aristocracy possess certain special qualities peculiar to the ruling classes to a greater extent even if they have obtained these qualities not through blood but through upbringing, which tends to develop certain intellectual and moral gifts rather than others.

4. It would seem that Mosca never attributed great importance to the problem of how far the ruling class extended. He merely repeated that the ruling class constituted a minority, but he did not and could not go beyond vague references to this minority, as for example when he spoke of "those few dozen people who control the levers of the state machine". But there are minorities and minorities. Even in a democratic state, the ruling class is a minority, but it is a bigger minority than that in an autocratic regime, and we may well ask whether in such a case the difference of quantity does not also imply a difference of quality. The size of the minority in a democratic system

depends on various factors: 1) the existence of several political classes in mutual competition, with the result that, side by side with an existing élite, there is always a potential or reserve élite; 2) the multiplication of the organs of the central authority (parliament as well as the privy council, two chambers instead of one, etc.); 3) the creation of local government bodies side by side with those of the central government.

What attracted Mosca's attention in his later period was another phenomenon. As the state extended its territory in the transition from the small city state of ancient times to the large Roman State, or else strengthened its structure in the transition from the medieval feudal State to the modern bureaucratic one, the "few dozen persons" became insufficient to win and retain power. This observation led Mosca to widen his approach and study the ruling class's auxiliaries, what he called the second most numerous stratum of the governing class, or the middle class, and he termed it "the backbone of all the great political organizations". In primitive autocratic regimes, this second stratum is almost always formed of priests and warriors. In organized autocratic regimes, it is formed by the bureaucracy (hence the identification between streamlined autocracy and bureaucratized autocracy); in electoral regimes, it is identified, or rather should be identified, with the electorate. (At this point, Mosca passes from a scientific observation to a political proposal).

This recognition of the existence of a second stratum of the governing class should have impelled Mosca to work out a more precise definition of the concept of ruling class in the strict sense of the word and of the relations between the first and second stratum. It may be asked whether the discovery of the second stratum embracing the whole of the middle class in the widest sense of the word does not end up by distorting the real significance of the theory of the ruling minorities? It docs not seem that Mosca was concerned about this difficulty. On the contrary, in the only section in which he dwells on the nature of the relation between these two strata, he gives the impression, in the examples cited, that the ruling class in a narrow sense of the word, has now, in order to make way for the second stratum, shrunk so far as to be synonymous with the one supreme head (the Roman Emperors, George III of England, Louis XIV and so on). The second stratum thus includes the first, or at least cannot easily be distinguished from it.

5. Any ruling class has a different life-span. Heredity, election and cooption are the normal procedures by which it perpetuates itself and renews itself (it can perpetuate itself without renewing itself or it perpetuates itself by renewing itself or renews itself purely and simply).

Mosca deals at length with and devotes particular attention to the first of these processes. He singles out two tendencies. On the one hand all ruling classes have a tendency to become, *de facto* if not *de jure,* hereditary. So much so that, when a certain *de jure* state has been consolidated, it has certainly been preceded by a *de facto* state. On the other hand, there are always new forces, tending to replace the old ones. According to whether the first or the second tendency prevails, the ruling class becomes closed and rigid or renews itself with varying degrees of rapidity. In the second volume of the **Elementi,** Mosca calls the first tendency aristocratic and the second one democratic, and examines at length the value and advantages of both possibilities. He is opposed both to the pure aristocratic tendency (perpetuation without renewal) and to the revolutionary democratic tendency (renewal without perpetuation). Both are extreme cases. He repeatedly expressed his sympathy with the type of society in which there is a certain equilibrium between the two tendencies. He recognizes the need for the ruling class to have a certain stability and not to have to be "substantially renewed with each new generation", but he also sees that it would benefit by drawing new blood from the lower classes, provided this does not take place too rapidly and too extensively. As between the two fundamental tendencies, Mosca showed clearly that he considered the former the most important of the two, at least to make possible a correct understanding of the course of history. The latter was merely a useful corrective.

He never speaks explicitly or in detail about cooption, but from his ideas as a whole it is clear that he regarded it as the normal method (and the most useful one socially) for the renewal of the ruling classes. On several occasions, he returns to the question of the continuity of the aristocracy and of its decadence as a result of its gradual isolation from the other classes and also its gradual transformation into a closed caste. Hence his positive judgment on those aristocracies which have been able to renew themselves by drawing fresh energy from the lower classes. In putting forward ideas for reforms which will correct the main defects of the parliamentary system (the interference of members of parliament in civil service matters), he proposes that new men be coopted from outside the official circles. These men must not "expect to be confirmed in their appointment by begging for votes, by obtaining the approval of a committee or of an electoral boss".

On the other hand, Mosca does discuss the electoral method in several passages not only of his works on political science but also of his writings on constitutional law and militant politics. But he discusses it in connection not so much with the problem of the renewal of the ruling class as with that of its organization, and hence we will defer consideration of it to the next section.

6. Of all the problems regarding the ruling class, the one to which Mosca reverts most often is that of its organization. Right from the start, as we have already observed, he regarded the ruling class as "an organized minority". He thought that, although it was a minority, it was in a position to keep in power only because it was organized. "A hundred people who always act in harmony with each other will be triumphant over a thousand individuals who cannot reach agreement among themselves. And at the

same time it will be much easier for the former to act in harmony and to reach an understanding because they are a hundred and not a thousand". By "organization" he meant the sum total of the arrangements made by the upper class in order to maintain its cohesion and to exercise its power. This enabled him to distinguish between the various forms of the state according to the different ways in which the different political classes in different times and places had organized themselves and hence exercised their power. Having abandoned the old distinction of governments into monarchies aristocracies and democracies, he regarded four forms of political organization as specially characteristic, from classical antiquity down to our own time—the city state of Greece and of the oldest part of Roman history; the bureaucratic state, of which the Roman Empire was an early example, and which was represented by the absolute monarchies of the 17th and 18th centuries; the feudal state peculiar to the barbarian societies of the middle ages; and the modern parliamentary state born in 17th century England and then transplanted with varying success to the Continent.

In a later synthesis, Mosca thought he could identify two basic principles in the welter of historical forms of government. These he called the autocratic and liberal principles according to whether authority was transmitted from above down to the lower officials or whether on the contrary it was delegated from below to higher authority. In the modern parliamentary state which was derived from the grafting of the liberal principle on the bureaucratic state of the absolute monarchies, both principles were present in a blend which was not always completely successful. It should be noted that this distinction between the two typical forms of political organization or of the transmission and exercise of power by the ruling class must not be confused with the distinction, set out in the previous section, between two methods of renewing the ruling class. The combination of the two distinctions may thus give rise to four ideal types of state: 1) aristocratic-autocratic; 2) aristocratic-liberal; 3) democratic-autocratic; 4) democratic-liberal.

The liberal principle is characterized by the relatively perfect organization of an electoral system. But a distinction must be made between the case in which the electorate coincides roughly with the ruling class (as in the Republic of Venice and in that of seventeenth-century Poland) and the case where the electorate is greater than that class. In the former case, the elective method is not used to achieve the renovation of the ruling class but to provide an internal rotation (and hence it does not work in favour of the democratic tendency but in favour of the aristocratic one). In the second case, it might be useful for the renewal of the ruling class if the class holding powers of direction and compulsion did not have at its disposal a variety of means of coercing the electors. In other words, where the electoral method may be useful it does not contribute to renovation, and where it might help renovation it is at most a pretence. In Mosca's study of the electoral principle, it is never possible to distinguish clearly between scientific judgments and political

appreciations. He used to repeat that it was not the electors who chose the members of parliament but the members who got themselves chosen. It is hard to say whether this observation, which he regarded as strictly scientific, fortified his anti-democratic attitude or whether his firmly rooted conservative instinct induced him to dwell on the negative aspects of the electoral system.

7. True, it has often been objected that Mosca's theory is an ideology and more precisely that it is an ideology masquerading as a scientific theory. We all know that Mosca had his own political ideas, those of an incorrigible conservative. And he himself never made any bones about it. He had the conservative historian's bitter realization of human vices and wretchedness. He was, or he claimed to be, a realist, a man who has no faith in the power of ideals in history and who regards history only as a perpetual clash of ambitions, interests and passions. And yet, if one takes a closer look at the matter, the theory of the ruling class represents the beginning, or, if one prefers, the first outline of modern political science conceived of as objective research into political phenomena.

Political science could not be born except from a realistic attitude (the fact that a realistic attitude is usually linked with a conservative ideology is a point which we need not go into here). By "real" we mean the opposite of "ideal" and "apparent". In the antithesis between "real" and "ideal", historical realism means the devaluation of ideals as propellant forces in history, and the concentration of attention solely on what men *are* instead of what they *believe* they are. In the antithesis between "real" and "apparent", historical realism means the devaluation of the great figures and of the institutional forms as significant historical data, and the search for the collective forces which move beneath the surface.

In order to assert itself, political science needed to discover some constant in the evolution of political societies which would provide a broad initial generalization, however provisional. The existence of a ruling class, composed of an organized minority which holds power against the unorganized majority appeared to satisfy this need more than any other datum which had been ascertained until then. There are frequent passages in which Mosca draws attention to the value and scientific interest of his discovery, and implies that only by basing itself on the study of the ruling class can research clear the ground of the deeply rooted prejudices which had hitherto hampered the development of politics as a science. In the very first pages of the early *Teorica,* he put forward the new theory as the correction of a "scientific error" (*i.e.,* the traditional distinction between the forms of government). In the first volume of the *Elementi* he recognized explicitly the superiority of the ruling class as a "basis for scientific research". In the second volume, he talked of a "new doctrine", the novelty of which consisted in scholars concentrating on an enquiry into the formation and organization of the various ruling classes. The ruling class for Mosca was a firm starting point for the development of political science because, unlike other theories which had been irrefutably disproved by the progress of historical studies, this concept was not deduced from *a priori* principles but was derived exclusively from an unprejudiced and ruthless observation of the facts. Criticizing the distinction made by Spencer between military and industrial states, he reiterated the proposition that this distinction rested "on utterly *a priori* suppositions which did not stand up to a realistic examination". The theory of the ruling class, having met this test, could be adopted as the first chapter of a scientific study of politics.

8. The concept of the ruling class was not only the expression of an ideology but the core of a scientific theory of politics. This is confirmed by the fact that, as has been repeatedly observed, it was accepted as a useful tool for historical analysis and doctrinal adjustments even by democratic and progressive writers. The difference between a conservative attitude and a progressive one does not consist in the acceptance or rejection of the concept of the ruling class, but in the different way of solving the problems regarding the four points to which we have reduced the analysis of Mosca's thought, that is, the composition, extension, replacement and organization of the ruling class.

As regards the first point, what distinguishes a democratic ideology from a conservative one is the rejection of any form of hereditary transmission of power. The democratic ideal, if taken to its logical extreme, calls for the total exclusion of the so-called privilege of birth from every sector of social life and not only from that of the training of the ruling class. In other words, it is the substitution of the value of merit for that of rank. To be democratic, it is not necessary to disavow the theory of the ruling class. It is sufficient to admit it and to claim that a ruling class may be formed by other than hereditary means. As to the second point, it has already been observed in the fourth section that a democratic society is distinguished from an aristocratic one by the greater number of the people forming the ruling class, even if this expansion will never be sufficient to transform the minority into a majority and to make the definition of democracy as government by the people, by everyone, by the majority, a very convincing one. As to the third point, that is, renewal, Mosca noted two main tendencies on the part of the ruling class. There was either a tendency to seal itself off with a consequent hardening of the arteries, or to open its doors and hence initiate a process of renovation. He called the first one aristocratic and the second democratic. Here the democratic attitude is shown by the desire for a society in which the abolition of the privilege of birth, accompanied by an economic policy which aims at equality of opportunity, facilitates the constant and rapid access of new blood to the ruling class. From the institutional point of view, a democratic regime, according to a common formula, is the one in which the replacement of even the whole of the ruling class can be effected without bloodshed, or, to put the point somewhat less dramatically, without revolutionary upheavals. In other words, the change is effected by the method of legal opposition and by the substitution of a government

crisis, which is within the constitution, for a revolutionary break which is outside it. Lastly, as regards the fourth point (the organization of power), Mosca again recognized two alternatives, which, while retaining the ideal of a ruling class as an organized minority, help to establish another difference between a conservative and a progressive ideology. This minority, which in any regime is always a minority, may justify its power as coming from above (theory of divine right of sovereigns, theory of traditional power or of historical prescription) or as derived from below (contractual theories). One of the most common formulae of democratic ideologies is that of power founded on the general consensus where it appears obvious that the role of the majority is not that of exercising power but of agreeing to others exercising it. At most, it should be added that an occasional consensus is not sufficient to stamp a regime as democratic but that the periodical confirmation by this consensus is essential.

9. I have tried to clarify the point that what distinguishes a conservative ideology from a progressive one is not the acceptance or refusal of the concept of a ruling class but the different attitude towards the problems of its composition, extension, renewal and organization, because this helps us to understand Mosca's political conservativism. For he was not a conservative *qua* theorist of the ruling class but *qua* defender and advocate of conservative ideas in almost all those situations in which it becomes permissible and useful, as we have seen in the previous section, to distinguish between a conservative attitude and a progressive one.

To take the first point first, Mosca's political ideal was certainly not that of a hereditary aristocracy. But, right from his first book, he contrasted the privilege of birth with that of merit and longed for a society in which intelligence and culture would be the basic virtues of the ruling class. But he never went as far as to desire or propose that the privileges of birth should be completely abolished. He realized that this privilege tends to be reconstituted in every society as soon as it rests on a stable basis and as a ruling class has power firmly in its hands. And even the electoral system does not succeed in doing away with privilege. He was therefore led to stress the advantages as well as the disadvantages of a hereditary system; the former consisted principally in the fact that the offspring of the upper classes find it easier to assume attitudes of authority if only because of their upbringing, and are more disposed to produce men willing to dedicate themselves to those disinterested activities on which the cultural and scientific progress of mankind depends. At this point, the concept of ruling class, which is lacking any value connotation, was transformed into that of the aristocracy (or hereditary upper class). And Mosca gravitated from the "scientific" theory (or what purported to be so) of the ruling class, imperceptibly or at least inexplicitly, to a favourable assessment of the function of aristocracies in history which was the reflection of a political ideal.

As regards the extension of the ruling class, Mosca always gave the impression, as pointed out in section 4, that it was formed of a very restricted group, and, even when he came to considering the so-called middle class, especially prominent in bourgeois society and in the democratic state, he considered it as a subsidiary class (or second stratum) or a kind of nursery of the ruling class. But it must at once be added that, when he analysed the problem not as a scientist but as a politician, he fully realized its importance. Among the most infallible remedies against the evils of the parliamentary system he included decentralization, and he regarded it specifically as the best way of enabling citizens to take part in public affairs, who would otherwise have been excluded from them, in short, as a widening of the scope of the ruling class. However, he did not concern himself with the other aspect of the problem, that is, the division of the ruling class into two parts—one in power and one in opposition. He continued to conceive of the ruling class as a monolithic group. It was for Dorso to correct the master's doctrine on this point with the observation that, in democratic regimes, the very nature of the political struggle tends to divide the ruling class into two opposite classes, whereas the ruling class as a monolithic group is an institution specifically confined to authoritarian regimes.

On the third point, that is, on the renewal of the ruling class, Mosca's conservativism was revealed by his fear of excessively violent upheavals which would ruin the old structure without preparing the ground for the emergence of a better one. As we have seen, a definitely favourable appreciation of the function of aristocracies in history went hand in hand, in his thinking, with a rooted distrust of too abrupt changes in the course of politics. He did not deny the need for renewal. Indeed, he regarded that as necessary in order to avoid the decadence of the ruling class, but he wanted it to be slow, gradual, and controlled from above. He was certainly not an incorrigible *laudator temporis acti,* and he ended up in the second part of his life, notwithstanding many reservations which were by no means unjustified, by accepting the democratic system. But he was and remained all his life a man who refused to capitulate to the advent of the mass regime which would have profoundly renewed the Italian ruling class (as in fact it did) with effects which were not always salutary. He was one of the most unbending of those prophets of doom who could never resist the temptation to see in the extension of political rights to the plebs one of the factors making for the final catastrophe.

Perhaps the point where he reveals his ideals most transparently, or perhaps it would be more exact to say his fears as a conservative, was over the organization of the state and the way in which a ruling class exercises its power. This was also the occasion of several of his most memorable political battles. The reason for his concern is simple. He placed no trust in elections, especially in popular elections. He accepted the principle with the greatest reluctance; he accepted the elections themselves, but with great reservations as to the accuracy of their results; he energetically rejected universal suffrage at all stages of his thinking, even in the less polemic ones when

he seemed to moderate his anti-parliamentary fury. The great bogey of his life was the elevation to the dignity of a nation of electors of the plebs whom he denounced as ignorant, credulous and easy to corrupt.

In combating universal suffrage, he challenged the type of mind, which, so he said, had made it unavoidable. In fact, the democratic mentality which, once the dogma of the sovereignty of the people had been accepted, had been obliged to draw all the consequences thereof. The extension of the franchise had, in his opinion, resulted in the decline of the ruling class in a period of crisis (his diagnosis of the crisis, at the end of the second edition of the *Elementi,* refers to the post-war period), and a long adjustment (Fascism?) which would lead to a regime even worse than its predecessor.

10. I do not believe that anyone would nowadays be inclined to confuse the theory of the ruling class with the ideal which accompanied it, at least when it was originated. But, once this confusion has been cleared up and the origin of the theory has been brought out, the question remains whether this seed was destined to sprout. What is the place of the theory of the ruling class in contemporary political science? If I were to express a judgment solely on the basis of the recent volume called *Politische Forschung* which contains essays on recent developments in political science in a number of countries, my reply would have to be that the theory of the ruling class can be written off. Only one of these essays mentions the "ruling class" as analysed in recent studies. But the reference appears in the article on political science in Italy written, as it happens, by the author of the present article. This judgment, however, is decidedly partial. At the last International Congress on Sociology, held at Stresa in September 1959, a special session was devoted to the problems of the élite and elicited intense interest, as was shown by the number of people taking part in it, even if they were not all agreed as to the merit and topicality of the theory. Behind that remarkable discussion there loomed, even when not specifically mentioned, Wright Mills' book, *The Power Elite* (1956), which had so strikingly drawn the attention of scholars in different countries to the existence in the classical country of democracy, of a ruling class in the very sense in which it had been conceived by Pareto and Mosca (even if Mosca is quoted only once in the whole book). And I will leave aside the particular success in Italy of the theory of the ruling class which calls for a separate essay.

If the discussion on the ruling class now seems to have come to a dead end, this is because the main aspects of the theory are now clear to everyone, but it has proved difficult to move on from theory, as a working hypothesis, to field research which alone can verify and correct this hypothesis. The aspects of political science which are most assiduously cultivated today and which figure most prominently in the reviews and bibliographies of the last fifteen years are precisely those in which research has pounced in its eagerness for data to collect and classify. The main topic is that of electoral behaviour. True, in order to supply a useful model for research, the theory of the ruling class must get over the hump formed by the difficulty of demarcating its field. Who are the people who belong to the ruling class? Or, more precisely, what is the criterion, which can be reliably and easily controlled, by which those who belong to the ruling class can be distinguished from those who do not? The difficulty in finding a criterion has led some writers to reject this theory outright as a useful hypothesis for research. The difficulty exists, even if I do not feel able to draw the conclusion from it, which has, however, been drawn, of the non-existence of a ruling class.

11. As we have seen, Mosca's criterion for determining whether an individual belongs to the ruling class was the possession of certain qualities which varied according to the different historical periods (wealth, valour and so on). A criterion of this kind is obviously too vague to delimit a field of empirical research.

On the contrary, the only criterion that can be used is one which takes account of the exercise of a certain function for a certain period of time, regardless of the personal qualities possessed. In a democratic state, probably the most important functions are those discharged by the members of the government, the upper or lower house, certain consultative bodies at the summit, the administrative bodies of large cities, and so on.

If this criterion is accepted, the starting point for research on the ruling class should be restated as follows: "All those should be regarded as belonging to the 'ruling class' who during the period $x\ y\ z$ have exercised functions $a\ b\ c$". It will be understood that we are dealing rather with the class of politicians, that is, the group of individuals which is more and more clearly identified, in states with an increasingly tentacular and rigid organization, with the class of professional politicians, and not the ruling class in the sense of a group of persons who in a specific society exercise the real power. Whether the class as thus defined is the one which really exercises power is another question which would call for further analysis. For one thing, it could be necessary to study (as is now so fashionable) the centres of hidden power (pressure groups) and the relations between those centres and politicians, but, as Sartori rightly observes, "there is only one way of ascertaining whether, and if so to what extent, it is true that an invisible power controls the visible power; that of ascertaining what the visible ruling élite does or does not do, and, to begin with, who belongs to it and does not".

Once an easily applicable criterion has been accepted which can determine whether a person belongs to the ruling class, at least two of the four subjects, into which, for convenience sake, I have divided my description of the theory, may lead to research conducted with the techniques which are now practised by the empirical science of politics. I mean the first subject, that of the composition and formation, and the third, that of renewal. I exclude the second subject, i.e. extension, because this is

one rather for historical investigation, and the fourth, i.e. organization, because this is half way between history of institutions and constitutional law. Besides, it is a classical part of the theory of the state (under the heading of forms of government). We must classify partly under the first subject, and partly under the third, the research already carried out or under way in Italy and elsewhere on members of parliament or of the government in a specific country for a certain historical period chosen to that end.

In conclusion, I have no hesitation in saying that the validity of the theory of the ruling class has not yet been undermined. Indeed, it has, if anything, been confirmed by authoritative writers, even if its fertility has not yet been demonstrated for lack of specific research.

However, there is one point in which the theory appears to me to be no longer acceptable. Mosca was constantly of the opinion that every ruling class constituted a very restricted and monolithic group—in contemptuous terms, a clique; and, in expressing this idea, he never omitted to add the adjective "organized" to the noun "minority". The strongly ideological attitude, which continually underlay the working out of the concept, cannot have been extraneous to its origin. This attitude led him to pass a not entirely favourable judgment on the parliamentary regime in his later days. We now know that in the party state (and perhaps even in the one-party state) there are different centres of power, which are at times in alliance, at times in open or concealed hostility. If we may borrow a concept from economic theory, it is an oligopoly rather than a monopoly. The point we are making is that, in addition to the relation between minority and majority which alone roused Mosca's interest, there are no less complex relations between minority and minority. This suggests that only if we go more thoroughly into these new problems will it be possible for the theory of the ruling class to make further progress.

Dante Germino (essay date 1974)

SOURCE: A review of *The Ruling Class: Elementi di scienza politica,* in *The American Political Science Review,* Vol. LXVIII, No. 1, March, 1974, pp. 261-2.

[*In the following essay, Germino reviews the paperback edition of* The Ruling Class, *noting that even the book's publishers erroneously claim Mosca to have provided the "theoretical foundation" for fascism in Italy.*]

Gaetano Mosca's classic, **Elementi di scienza politica,** originally published in 1896, with successive revisions until 1923, is here reprinted in paperback from the hardback translation first published by McGraw Hill in 1939. While the decision to make available a less expensive paperback edition deserves to be welcomed, it is unfortunate that the publishers did not commission someone (James Meisel, whose magisterial study of Mosca, *The Myth of the Ruling Class,* Ann Arbor, 1958, provides a much needed corrective of earlier impressions of the

Sicilian's political thought, immediately comes to mind in this connection) to add an introduction more relevant to the concerns of contemporary students of politics than that composed in the 1930s by Arthur Livingston. It is further to be lamented that the publisher's description on the cover of the paperback edition erroneously states that Mosca's "conception of social forces and of the rulers who acquire power to control them served as a theoretical foundation for Italian fascism." Even if one accepts the arguable proposition that Fascism had a "theoretical" (as opposed to an ideological) foundation, it has never been convincingly demonstrated that Mosca's work served as a major intellectual basis for Fascist thought. On the contrary, Mosca himself, as Meisel shows, opposed Italian fascism and retired from the Senate in 1925 after courageously denouncing Mussolini's regime for destroying parliamentary democracy. As early as 1904 Mosca had offered a reasoned defense of the *practice* (as opposed to the rhetoric) of parliamentary democracy (Mosca, ***Partiti e sindacati nella crisi del regime parlamentare,*** Bari, Laterza, 1949 ed. pp. 334-335. For a general discussion of Mosca and elite theory see Germino, *Beyond Ideology,* New York, 1967 Chapter 6). To "link" Mosca to fascism in this way is, therefore, fundamentally to distort his teaching; yet one all too frequently comes across this kind of attribution by careless interpreters.

The heart of Mosca's political theory is the concept of the *classe dirigente,* usually translated as "ruling class," although the Italian means literally "leading class" and "leading" sounds less "authoritarian" than "ruling." The term "class"—a political sociologist's nightmare—also has a static, fixed ring about it which is quite foreign to Mosca's view of the permeability of elites to accession from below in any but the most rigid and repressive society. For Mosca, as for Machiavelli before him, context was all, and his achievement as a political theorist consists in his extraordinary capacity for evoking the flavor and vitality of the concrete political struggle, coupled with his unrelenting drive to free himself and his readers from the self-serving illusions of the conventional wisdom and its typically mushy analytical categories. Despite frequent claims to the contrary, political theory is an *empirical* enterprise, concerned with illumining through critically clarified symbols man's participation with his fellows in the drama of existence. The differences between theorists (e.g., Aristotle vs. Plato, Machiavelli vs. Hegel, Mosca vs. Voegelin) have to do, not with whether one is "empirical" and the other "normative," but with the accent of their analysis. To speak metaphorically, if we conceive of political reality as an immense canvas, theorists may be divided into those whose gaze is concentrated on the foreground, with the larger existential background at the periphery of their observation, and those whose intellectual priorities are the reverse. Mosca is clearly a "foreground" theorist: the immediate political and electoral struggle in all its aliveness and vitality is clearly at the center of his concern.

Mosca is at his best when "demythologizing" current political clichés, and he can be devastating when he comes upon reductionist theories which seek to explain all in terms of "race" or economics. Ever puncturing self-righteousness, ethnocentrism, and complacency, he acidly reminds allegedly "superior" societies of their weaknesses. An example of his salubrious acerbity in this regard is his remark that the belief that all non-Western societies "—the Egyptian, the Babylonian, the ancient and modern Chinese—have been, and still are, uniformly stationary seems . . . to be due to nothing less than an optical illusion arising from the fact that we view them from so far away."

Mosca's concept of the "ruling class," "social forces," "juridical defense," and the "political formula" have become part of our cultural inheritance. Nothing would be served here in attempting briefly to recapitulate them, for their original exposition in all its complexity and subtlety continues to be worth reading and pondering. Nor has "elite theory" stood still since the days of Mosca and of his more verbose, pretentious, and less interesting fellow countryman, Pareto. Guido Dorso, Norberto Bobbio, and Giovanni Sartori (to speak only of Italian scholars) have quietly and perceptively made refinements, elaborations, and revisions to Mosca's famous theory about the predominance of elites. Mosca deserves continued study by political scientists not only for what he wrote but also because of the creative reflection which he helped to inspire.

Robert A. Nye (essay date 1977)

SOURCE: "Mosca," in *The Anti-Democratic Sources of Elite Theory: Pareto, Mosca, Michels,* SAGE Publications, 1977, pp. 14-20.

[*In the following essay, Nye discusses the evolution of elite theory in Italy, focusing on Mosca's understanding and interpretation of Italian political thought.*]

The Italian *postrisorgimento* provided fertile soil for the nurturing of elite theory. For Gaetano Mosca and Vilfredo Pareto the melancholy years following Italy's unification were the context for the characteristic personal disillusionment that invariably figures in the biographies of the men who contributed to elite thought. By the mid-1860s the words and deeds of the *Risorgimento* had taken on a nearly mythical significance in Italian cultural life. The glorification of personal courage and the principles of idealized liberalism associated with the tortuous process of national unity were so entrenched in Italian intellectual life that they continued to serve as an ideal touchstone for Italians of all political convictions until the First World War. In contrast to those poetic inspirations, the prosaic reality of Italian political life after 1870 provoked a mood of bitter recrimination that took for its object the failings of the parliamentary system and its leadership. The reputation of the lower chamber as 'a fetid place where all virtue languished in an atmosphere of accommodation' (Thayer, 1964) was well-established by the mid-1880s, and the successive parliamentary epochs of Depretis, Crispi, and Giolitti appeared to surpass one another only in their ability to efficiently manage majorities, rig electoral campaigns, and benefit the private fortunes of deputies.

In the eyes of the generation weaned on the romantic philosophical pap of Risorgimento achievements but too young to actively participate, it was a simple matter to identify the failures of the political system with its gradual extension of political rights to the masses. In Italy as in Victorian England the same dialectical relationship prevailed between the political ambitions of the parliamentary left and their advocacy of the admission of newer classes of voters to the franchise. The franchise was enlarged from 600,000 to 2,000,000 in 1881 and increased piecemeal (with some temporary setbacks) until universal manhood suffrage was finally voted in 1912. In 1884 Gaetano Mosca was a recent law graduate and an unsuccessful aspirant for an academic post in the capital; for him the issue resolved itself into an analysis of the means by which the 'political class' gains and holds power. An uncompromising liberal political outlook, worthy of a Cavour or a Guizot in their heyday, sustained him throughout a career that only ended on the eve of Mussolini's fall from power.

Mosca first enunciated his principle of the 'political class' in his 1884 work *Teorica dei governi e governo parlamentare.* As Pareto was to do in his earliest work, the young Mosca generously acknowledged his intellectual debts. Chief among these is Hippolyte Taine, whose 'stupendous volumes on the *Origins of Contemporary France*' Mosca confessed to have picked over for facts and ideas. If one can judge from the internal evidence, it would appear that it was Mosca's intent to reach an audience with sufficient knowledge to appreciate his detailed examination of Italian political institutions, but which also harbored reservations about the developments in national politics since the advent of the *Sinistra* in 1876. His message was not, however, couched in terms calculated to appeal to the reactionary clerico-aristocratic cabal which had governed Italy briefly after 1870, but spoke the language of positivistic 'political science', more certainly intended for those politicians and informed men of affairs who believed with Mosca that only the 'scientific study of social laws' by men of 'merit' and 'technical ability' could ensure truly effective government. For the benefit of those members of the *political class* who did not share his love of social science, Mosca included some blunt warnings on the dangers of continuing the trend toward democracy.

In the *Teorica,* Mosca described the emergence of 'the strong, the domineering' leadership from the state of primitive anarchy that all contemporary social scientists assumed had prevailed in prehistoric times. This disaggregated body of men ruling their class by force eventually learned to pool their authority and rule by a combination of guile and consensus through a 'political formula'. At this stage of evolution their authority resided in a rather vague 'superior moral character' and the 'incalculable prestige' and 'inherent superiority' that derives from the advantage of organization enjoyed by the political class over the disorganized masses. Most recent commentators have chosen to interpret Mosca's comparatively 'neutral' argument on superior organization as the central 'sociological' insight to which other sources of political authority were merely 'auxiliary'. Mosca takes care to point out, however, as do all the later contributors to elite theory, that authority stems as much from the *appearance* of power which the political class 'must have, or in any case be presumed to have' by virtue of the prevailing criteria for the bestowal of 'prestige' and 'respectability' in a given time or place. Mosca's psychological realism, often downgraded despite his own protestations to the contrary, deserves a much closer examination.

At base, I would argue, Mosca is interested in exploring the psychosocial mechanisms of command and obedience that his historical survey indicates have always figured in human societies between the rulers and 'the plebians' who undergo the rule. Once he clarified the objective nature of political authority, it was his desire to offer his insights to Italian politicians and would-be politicians. Though he had originally chided his readers about the absurdity of seeing 'innate rights' as anything more than 'hypotheses of our minds', he saw a certain danger in their use of political formulas for governing the masses. In this connection he employed an historical metaphor which drew heavily on his mentor Taine and expressed his opinion of the use of 'equality' as a political formula by the French ruling class in 1789. This class was 'like an armed man in the middle of a hostile but unarmed crowd; he is able, up to a certain point to restrain them and keep them at a distance: but to use such a weapon with success, or with any power, it is an indispensable condition that one have resolution and energy; this was the very point that the nobles and privileged Frenchmen were lacking'.

Failing to perceive the self-serving nature of Mosca's 'historical' examples, Meisel wonders why Mosca did not treat the Jacobins as a political class in the *Teorica* when he acknowledged their ready ability to stir up the masses. In fact Mosca hoped to make the point that there is no room for frivolousness or irresponsibility within the ruling classes. Ability to move the masses is not a condition of wise leadership, only an aspect of the exercise of power by leadership. Thus, by inviting the masses into the political arena to share political power the Jacobins forfeited their own 'moral superiority' and rapidly abandoned the field first to anarchy, then despotism. This is history as polemic, meant to indicate the resources at the disposal of the political class, and the pitfalls of agitating 'the hopes and cupidity of the ignorant and poor masses' by holding out the promise of political equality. Though a mere 'hypothesis', democratic ideas, like an intoxicating beverage, stir in the plebes the 'most base passions' and 'most bestial instincts' which could only end in government 'by the ignorant crowd'.

While acknowledging the relatively narrow historical limits within which certain political formulas may be effectively employed, Mosca is urging the Italian parliamentary regime to draw the line on further enlargement of the franchise. The 'envy' and 'hatred' instinctively felt by the mass toward its masters proved the folly of democratic regimes and threatened the disappearance of quality, distinction and individualism in the levelling that would surely follow. Mosca had no cause for optimism between 1884 and the 1896 publication of his famous *Elementi di scienza politica (The Ruling Class),* but he had sharpened his arguments with information drawn from collective theory.

By 1895 the same conditions that were encouraging the development of anti-democratic collective psychology in Italy were prompting Mosca as he completed his *Elementi.* The franchise had been expanded further, providing the social base for Italy's first mass socialist party (PSI), founded in 1892. Giolitti's first premiership began the same year with Giolitti's friendly overtures to reformist socialism; but his government ended the following year amidst the humiliating circumstances of the Bank of Rome scandals. None of these events was calculated to please Gaetano Mosca, who had spent much of the decade in Rome as editor of the Chamber's parliamentary journal closely observing political activities. They merely added a new urgency to his warnings about the dire consequences of democratization.

It is important to understand that for Mosca, as later for Pareto, socialism was the natural extension of the logic of democratic sovereignty. The more immediate enemy, therefore, was Rousseau, not Marx, and Mosca wastes little time in polemics that would be appreciated only by Italy's tiny knot of Marxist intellectuals. Instead, as in the *Teorica,* he addressed his arguments to those members of the Italian ruling class who he felt would benefit from an exposure to the history of elite-mass relations and a deeper knowledge of their nature.

Mosca is at pains to discredit purely racial or biological theories of social evolution, not simply because their insistent determinism leaves the practical politician helpless before events, but because they overlook or minimize the psychic factors in human affairs. He advances, in a rather vague way to be sure, a theory of historical change which is fundamentally psycho-social in nature and depends on the dynamic interaction of mass and elite. Far from being strictly sociological in nature, Mosca's *Elementi* may be more usefully considered a variety of what Morris Ginsberg has called 'differential social psychology'. A successor to simplistic biological theories of race, this body of theory sought to identify and evaluate the psychic natures of ethnic populations and races. Accordingly, Mosca concentrates heavily on the 'ideas, beliefs, customs, prejudices' that define historical peoples and exhibits a tendency to reduce social phenomena to psychological ones, and vice versa, in a way that was endemic to this mode of analysis. In this framework changes are brought about when new beliefs are introduced by men of genius or vision and universalized by a process identical to Gabriel Tarde's 'laws of

imitation'. Citing Tarde's work, Mosca variously describes this process as 'suggestion, imitation or mimetism', working on man's 'sentimental and affective faculties'.

Mosca understandably pays particular attention to the growth and expansion of the great world religions, especially the capacity of their leaders for 'instilling his own convictions and especially his own enthusiasms into others . . .'. What is perhaps less obvious is Mosca's conviction that 'political-social' ideologies are 'religious too, though shorn of strictly theological elements'. They are similar in other significant ways. First, they are both 'illusions' (measured against empirico-scientific standards), the first of a supernatural order, the second cloaked in the guise of rational discourse, but nonetheless 'true' insofar as 'illusion is a need for almost all men, a need that they feel no less strongly than their material needs'. A generally unappreciated fact is that Mosca understood this need to believe as a psychological characteristic of collectivities. Thus, human sentiments 'taken individually, may be imponderable, hard to analyze and harder still to define, but . . . in sum are very powerful and may contribute to bringing on the most important social phenomena'. This tendency to merge social and psychological phenomena, already noted above, serves to give Mosca's conception of 'social forces' responding to 'political formulas' a firmer basis in contemporary theories of collective behavior than commentators have heretofore acknowledged.

Here and there Mosca sheds light on his conception of the nature of the masses under the sway of collective beliefs. They may be virtuous and self-sacrificing or cowardly and have 'lust for blood'; appeals to their 'loftier sentiments and low passions' will not be, therefore, without some success. These characteristics are in turn based upon what Mosca calls the 'herding and fighting instinct' which is 'the most primitive and, so to say, the most animal of the instincts'. Therefore, though the proselytes of a new dogma are 'the stronger element numerically . . . [they represent] the most negligible factor intellectually and morally'. Conversely, the elite leadership has a moral and intellectual superiority.

This non-rational and exaggeratedly passionate behavior of the masses suggested to Mosca certain postulates about contemporary politics which he was eager to pass on to his peers. First, electoral politics in a system of universal suffrage encourages the representatives to pander to the base 'sentiments and passions of the common herd' and therefore exposes them to the reciprocal suggestions of the mass which would end by jeopardizing their moral superiority and capacity to lead. Moreover, as political participation is made more universal, political leaders must adapt their ideas to 'a fairly low moral level' to 'play upon all the sensitive springs of conduct . . . [and] take advantage of all their weaknesses . . .'. In this infernal dialectic the least scrupulous, those who lie most persuasively, dissemble most effectively and pitch their appeals to the lowest passions will gain ascendancy. The only foreseeable result of this process, says Mosca, is the utter triumph of Rousseau's fantasy of the general will, for in the democratic arena victory goes to the most vulgar ideology: 'Collectivism and communism, like all doctrines that are based on the passions and the blind faith of the masses, tend to destroy multiplicity of political forces.' Thus, for Mosca, as for Pareto, it is democracy which leads inevitably to socialism and threatens the roots of modern civilization.

This is not to say that Mosca felt the ruling class would cease to exist; indeed, as its political and economic power grew in the wake of a dissolution of political 'multiplicity', the new leaders of the masses would prove all the more overbearing. Hence the inevitable futility of allowing the masses a legal expression of their profound hatred for their betters. The issue for Mosca, then, seems to have been one of seeking the improvement of 'juridical defense', which he understood to be those institutions and political processes that operated to protect personal liberty and defend a stable and orderly rule of law. Among these was resistance to further extension of the franchise, and a return of parliamentary initiative to the monarch, undertaken seriously on more than one occasion by the parliamentary right between 1895 and 1901. Over thirty years later, with Mussolini at the height of his power, Mosca was still arguing that the adoption of universal suffrage was the greatest error made by European parliaments. By lowering intellectual and moral standards, it had helped bring on the victory of socialist regimes with their diabolical tendency to make man 'according to the situation, an abject automaton or a ferocious beast'.

Much has been made of Mosca's 'horror' at Mussolini's fascism and his valiant defense of parliamentary prerogatives. This reputation rests largely on one rather mild speech (his last) made as a senator in 1925 and some scattered remarks in his later writings (Hughes, 1954; Meisel, 1958; 1965). It can be just as cogently argued that Mosca contributed to the pathetic liberal capitulation to Mussolini between 1920 and 1922 by his diehard position that the left was the 'greater' danger, his tacit endorsement of a manipulative conception of elite political authority, and his essentially pragmatic definition of the political utility of popular 'illusions'. As an example of the latter instance, a passage of the 1895 *Elementi* anticipated Mosca's later endorsement of the ameliorative social effects of the Libyan war of 1911 in *L'Italia e Libia* (1912):

> Just as we do not combat a religion because its dogmas seem far-fetched, so long as it produces good results in the field of conduct, so the application of a political doctrine may be acceptable so long as they result in an improvement in juridical defense.

As in the case of Pareto's treatment of ideology as a 'derivation' of residues of collective behavior, Mosca's assimilation of the fundamental perspectives of collective psychology with its invidious distinctions between the disproportionate quantity of reason in elite and mass, helped perpetuate a 'myth of the ruling class' as much as any other influence.

Edward C. Hansen and Timothy C. Parrish (essay date 1983)

SOURCE: "Elites versus the State," in *Elites: Ethnographic Issues,* edited by George E. Marcus, University of New Mexico Press, 1983, pp. 257-76.

[*In the following essay, Hansen and Parrish examine the anthropological organization of elites in modern capitalist societies using the theories of Mosca and Pareto.*]

This essay is concerned with retooling an old concept—that of *elite*—with a view toward making an anthropological contribution to the eternal debate over who rules in capitalist societies. To this end, we hope to revive and recast those of Pareto's and Mosca's original ideas about the nature of elites and society that we feel have been stripped of their epistemological value by generations of scholars subsequent to Pareto and Mosca. As anthropologists, we are particularly interested in their suggestions that elites are organized by kin and connections, in opposition to formal institutions of power, such as states, corporations, or political parties. Especially intriguing to us is that such elites still exist at hegemonic levels of power in advanced capitalist societies, in spite of the marked evolution of institutional forms of power in such societies. It saddens us that the persistence of hegemonic elites has been discussed and documented principally by political journalists (not to mention novelists) rather than by social scientists. Part of the explanation for social scientists' neglect of the higher levels of power lies within the intellectual history of the various disciplines involved, and falls beyond the scope of this work. For now, we are content to restore the Pareto-Mosca elite concept to its rightful position as a critical tool in the analysis of hegemonic power in capitalist society. We will argue below that one problem in this debate is that the elite concept—when used at all—has been employed to describe what C. Wright Mills (1956) dubbed the middle and lower levels of power, an intellectual development that would make Pareto and Mosca turn over in their graves.

Central to the debate over who rules in capitalist societies is the question of the dominant form of power organization at the apex of such societies, the issue of ultimate hegemony. Has the panoply of institutionalized expressions of political power—the state, the corporations, the political parties—evolved to the point where it has definitively eclipsed the power of upper-class kindreds, their friends, their connections? Do the Rockefellers get no respect these days? A modern version of this longstanding debate appears in a 1975 interchange in the *New York Review of Books* between Andrew Hacker and William Domhoff, seconded by Maurice Zeitlin. Domhoff's book *The Bohemian Grove* advances the position that elite watering holes such as the Bohemian Grove are the crucibles in which the class cohesion necessary for the continuity of the ruling class is forged. That is, although the ostensible functions of such exclusive clubs or spas may be camping, wenching, performing skits, and so on, their most vital function is providing a suitable informal milieu well outside of the public view where members of the elite may come to know each other in order to unite for grand political purpose. Zeitlin, defending Domhoff from an attack by Hacker, argues that the ruling class has largely escaped scrutiny because it is organized by kinship, to the extent that if we wish to discover the nature of control over corporations "we must discover the most effective kinship unit" (1975). For Domhoff and Zeitlin, the real stuff of hegemonic power is to be found in upper-class kin and connections, well outside of the formal institutional apparatuses of power.

Hacker's critique of Domhoff presents the opposite position: hegemonic power rests in institutional structures staffed by the socially obscure. Thus, "it has to be demonstrated how deeply one can hate American Cyanimid or Rockwell International. The class struggle is easier with an enemy of flesh and blood, as we know from China and Cuba, where local landlords were an everyday sight. Our own capitalism's demise seems slated for yet another postponement until its attackers find ways of rousing class anger against an edifice whose power depends neither on the personal qualifications of those who hold it nor on their membership in a ruling class . . ." (Hacker 1975). Executive positions are staffed not by the scions of blue-blooded families, but by the offspring of people anonymous enough "to send their children to freshwater colleges such as Lehigh and Wesleyan and Iowa State" (Hacker 1975). For Hacker, the structure of hegemonic power in the contemporary United States represents a Weberian apotheosis; for Domhoff and Zeitlin, it is a ruling class politically constituted along the clandestine lines suggested by Pareto and Mosca.

The interchange between Hacker and Domhoff-Zeitlin has its antecedents in the original formulations offered by Marx, Weber, and Pareto-Mosca about the nature of power in capitalist societies. Each of these three positions offers a distinct epistemology of capitalism, society, or both, and each is inextricably linked to the political activism of its respective authors to a degree that is inconsistent with the presumed neutrality of contemporary social science. Critical to this debate is the visionary character of each position which stems from the radically different political orientations of its key proponents. In essence, the authors of each position advocate an ideal typical vision of what type of hegemonic power organization we should find at the political apex of society. These positions are proffered as salutary alternatives to what is actually at the top. The problem for contemporary social science is that it has consistently confused these visions with empirical realities. In short, the *should be*'s have been reified to become the *is*'s, or at least the *was*'s. A very live question is to what extent old prophecy has become a new reality, not to mention the issue of whatever happened to the old realities, assuming that we understood their nature in the first place.

Marx and subsequent Marxists have long sought to identify in society a politically coherent ruling class, but they have not found one. The capitalist class is notoriously factionalist in its political comportment, then and now (Marx 1952). The Orleanists, Decembrists, et al., of the *18th Brumaire of Louis Napoleon* have given way to the modern class fraction (Poulantzas 1975, 1978), or kin and connection group (Miliband 1969; Zeitlin 1974). For Weber, the capitalist class should have come to embrace legal bureaucratic rationalism, in business, in legislative assemblies, and in the civil service. But it has preferred in practice patronage, monocratism, and personalism (Weber 1946; Wright 1979). Pareto and Mosca felt that the real elite—defined by a curious mélange of archaic class standing and morality—should reassert itself in the face of the growth of the state, which represented to them the decline of civilization (Mosca 1939; Pareto 1968). The failure of the elite to get its act together was a source of theoretical and political disappointment for Pareto and Mosca, as we shall argue in some detail below.

Disparate as these three positions may be, all of them posit the existence of two different forms of power—real and imagined, actual and potential—at the apex (hegemonic level) of capitalist society. All anticipate the emergence of institutional forms of power while recognizing that there is in fact another form of power already in place. In the rush to prophesy the new order, the structure and ideology of the old order are left relatively unexplored. The possibility that non-institutional forms of political organization might have enduring structural relevance to the organization of hegemonic power—and thus coexist with the newer forms of institutional power—is not entertained by any of these theorists. Lost in the classical formulations is the question of the relationship of these forms to each other, which we contend is one of the most important dialectical relationships in the political life of all capitalist states in any historical period.

As we will argue below, only Pareto and Mosca suggest that kin and connections—the organizational matrices of elites—are antithetical to institutional political life. We suggest that if their conception of elites were removed from the realm of psychology and morality and linked to the political-economy visions of Marx and Weber, then the elite concept might help us resolve the ancient debate over who rules in capitalist societies.

If there is utility in the elite concept, it depends upon demonstrating that much critical behavior at the apex of capitalist society (e.g., the making of critical decisions) requires informal (rather than institutional) organization for reasons of flexibility.

Simply stated, major political issues at hegemonic levels of power—which we see as generated by the changing circumstances of capital accumulation—are not very susceptible to institutional resolution. Institutional power is rational bureaucratic in character, and can only deal effectively with problems that are sufficiently well understood to have routine solutions. Such is not the case with issues involving the changing requirements of capital accumulation, which are frequently confusing to major capitalists themselves. We believe that it is the chaotic and crisis-ridden nature of the accumulation process that has selected for informal politics as a permanent structural feature of hegemonic power organization in capitalist societies.

Testing the validity of this hypothesis requires actual behavioral data on the performance of elites in the critical moments of capitalist evolution. The role of elites cannot be inferred from merely positional criteria—who holds what positions, who is married to whom, who belongs to what club, and so on. Their behavior must be observed directly over the course of time. This is precisely the proper domain of ethnography, a key reason why we believe that anthropology has a critical mission to fulfill in resolving this debate, and that systematic ethnographic inquiry into the nature of elite families and networks would go a long way toward resolving a stalemated issue.

PARETO AND MOSCA REVISITED

Our insistence that the study of elites should be the examination of the internal anatomy of the capitalist ruling class draws upon an interpretation of the works of Pareto and Mosca that is contrary to views generally held. In current usage, the term *elite* has been applied to such a wide range of individuals standing at the apex of an equally large number of hierarchies that the term has lost any analytical utility. Perhaps most distressing is the tendency to identify the elite as the holders of governmental or institutional positions. While some early studies of this type, most notably C. Wright Mills's *The Power Elite* (1956), studied people who actually exercised power—corporate executives, military general staff, and the executive and congressional leadership—these studies are increasingly lost among studies of the middle or lower levels of power, and in some cases, simple studies of bureaucratic hierarchy. Thus we are treated to accounts of the big man in the firm, the bureaucracy, the union, and so on right down to small town or village government. Some good work continues to be done on the upper levels of power in capitalist society (Stanworth and Giddens 1974), but this work remains heavily dependent upon conceptions that define the elite in terms of its institutional position.

For Pareto and Mosca, most of the institutional power holders studied by contemporary social science would not only not be an elite but would be nobodies. Elite theory was written in reference to something different from the advanced capitalist state, and indeed, it can be seen as an argument against the emergent modern interventionist "welfare" state. Indeed one of the minor intellectual errors of contemporary elite theory is a failure to realize the snobbishness and moralizing tone that pervades both Pareto's and Mosca's writings. This snobbishness and moralizing were part of a plea for a real elite to step forward and redeem itself and society from the depredations of the masses and the liberal state. It is Pareto's and Mosca's insistence on the exclusivity and autonomy

of the elite that endows their concept with a measure of analytical coherence lacking in contemporary elite literature.

The history of elite theory has been examined elsewhere (Heyl 1968; Gouldner 1971). Here, the three most common errors of interpretation will be discussed without reference to this fascinating and revealing history in the sociology of knowledge. The first error is a confusion of Pareto's discussion of hierarchy with the concept of elite. The second is a confusion of the elite with institutional and governmental position: these are separate and even antithetical entities in Pareto's and Mosca's writings. The final error, which in some senses includes the first two, is a confusion about the nature of the state, both historically and theoretically, and about the relationship in classic elite theory of the elite-ruling class to the state. These misinterpretations result both from the climate of ideological and academic bias in which these theories were received, and from Pareto's and Mosca's claims to a universal theory of power and government.

The first of these errors stems from Pareto's discourse on how human groups develop hierarchical organization. Pareto argues that any individual in the hierarchy can be assigned a rank position between one and ten depending upon the relative merit, prominence, or skill that he or she displays. As opposed to Marx's classes determined by capitalism, hierarchy is universal and transhistorical, and it is the nature of the hierarchy itself that determines merit and rank or the lack of it. Here, Pareto discusses what constitutes merit and hierarchy among thieves, prostitutes, and politicians (Pareto 1935), and it is a small conceptual leap to find elites in every human grouping imaginable. But this tendency is peripheral to Pareto's main thrust, and neglects his distinction between governing and nongoverning elites. Pareto is not interested in the organization of bandits and tarts, but in the organization of the class that controls the state apparatus. Social science would have been better served if Mosca's term *the ruling class* had been adopted in place of Pareto's *elite*. But whatever the term, both elite theorists are concerned with the study of who rules, and the organization of this power in a particular class.

The second misinterpretation, the identification of the elite with institutional and governmental position, even more seriously dilutes the elite concept of Pareto and Mosca. This is not to argue that those who hold certain positions in government or institutions may not be elite members, but that elites are organized separately from the state apparatus. In both Pareto and Mosca, the state is, by definition, controlled by the elite or ruling class which provides a moral principle (Mosca 1939); or in more modern terminology, it was the hegemony of that class which was to control the repressive machinery of the state, the masses, and the bureaucracy. Both authors considered the growth of the institutional power of the state to be detrimental and feared that increasingly the state would be despoiled by either the bourgeoisie or the masses. The elite for both men would provide the "enlightened" leadership for the parliament and the moral purpose to resist these depredations and to save civilization itself.

The third common misinterpretation of Pareto and Mosca results from a neglect of the realities of the state, both historically and theoretically. On the historical side, it is important to note that both men were involved in politics, Mosca for most of his adult life and Pareto for a brief, but intense, period at the end of the nineteenth century (Hughes 1952; Finer 1966). In the end both were disillusioned and shocked by the course of Italian politics, from unification to fascism, and finally they watched the failure of the very system of elite politics they had sought to define. Their hopes were ruined when no elite emerged as the defender of national development, and the liberal state was increasingly drawn into mass politics. The growth of the state and the failure of the bourgeoisie to form the desired elite hegemony were intimately linked for Mosca:

> So a vicious circle of reciprocal causes and effects is closed: the impoverishment of small capitalists and holders of medium-sized properties makes it almost necessary to increase taxes still more: and the very elements of society that in more prosperous countries would remain independent citizens, and constitute a most effective balance to bureaucratic influence are themselves transformed into professional bureaucrats (Mosca 1939).

Pareto likewise grew pessimistic and bitter over the liberal state, and laid the blame squarely upon the bourgeoisie.

> Whom do I call the bourgeoisie? All those who live comfortably and enjoy protective tariffs, get government jobs for their children, make gains through contractors, and when the occasion arises, despoil the banks: and besides these many wealthy and well-to-do persons, honest in their private lives, but who think it necessary in order to support their class and so as not to dry up the well springs of money for their friends to support any knavery on the part of the government (Letter from Pareto to Pantaleoni, 23 December 1896, cited in Finer 1966).

The state for Pareto and Mosca was the classic liberal nation-state: its principal function was to protect property, particularly from the claims of the dispossessed classes for redistribution. To them, the principal danger of the liberal state was that it might degenerate into a bureaucratic entity dedicated to satisfying the illegitimate claims of the rabble. To counteract this danger, the elite or ruling class was charged with providing a body of public-spirited and financially independent citizens for the executive and parliament, and perhaps most important of all, with providing the morality or ideology that was defined by a later Italian political analyst, Gramsci, as hegemony. There is a very incomplete and scattered analysis in Pareto and Mosca that shows their disappointment in the failure of the bourgeoisie to form an elite, their fears about mass politics, and their doubts about the

modern bureaucratic state. Gone were the great aristocratic politics of Cavour, and in their place was an increasingly institutionalized bureaucratic state controlled by the middle class who used both bureaucratic position and corruption for personal gain. Eventually, this would lead to major state crises during downturns in the economic cycle, which the "new feudalism" of the trade unions and employers would be unable to resolve. The rise of mass politics, and particularly of fascism, made impossible a return to the elite politics that Pareto and Mosca had desired, and in the decline of elite influence both saw the decline of morality, order, and progress (Mosca 1939; Meisel 1962; Finer 1966; Pareto 1968).

Historically, the nation-state that Pareto and Mosca wrote about was in the process of change. The first part of this century saw the rise of bureaucratic institutionalized states, mass politics, and in the case of Italy, fascism. Theoretically, Pareto's and Mosca's concept is plagued by an instrumentalist definition: they have "the tendency to assume that the state as an instrument is neutral and can be used with equal facility and equal effectiveness by any class or social force" (Jessop 1977). In spite of their strong sense of morality and strong notions of what a proper elite should be, both authors consider the group or alliance that controls the state machinery to be by definition the elite or ruling class. Hence, even Mussolini, whom both Pareto and Mosca personally and politically abhorred, could claim elite status when he and his fascists seized the Italian government. Italian fascism marked the bankruptcy both of elite politics and theories and of the classic liberal capitalist state, which was inundated by fascist bureaucratization.

Obviously, our revisionist examination of elite theory is concerned with what these theories can provide for the examination of power in modern capitalist societies. Before turning to the relationship of contemporary elites to the advanced capitalist state, it is necessary to condense what ideas remain in Pareto and Mosca into a solid analytical core that can serve as a guide for future research and theory. Perhaps the most central of these notions is the independent organization of the elite through family, clientage, and network, as opposed to its identification with the institutional framework of the state. Another useful idea concerns the relationship of this elite and the state to capital accumulation. Finally, there is the importance that both Pareto and Mosca attach to class ideology.

At the core of elite organization is the family or some notion of a hereditary class. Pareto himself used *aristocracy (aristocrazia)* and *dominant class* interchangeably before settling upon the term *elite* in his later works (Pareto 1935, 1968; Finer 1966). Mosca, who particulary approved of the English gentry (Mosca 1939), was even more specific in his justification of hierarchy and privilege: he held "that certain intellectual and especially, moral qualities, which are necessary to a ruling class if it is to maintain its prestige and function properly, are useful also to society, yet . . . if they are to develop and exert their influence . . . some families should hold fairly high social position for a number of generations" (Mosca 1939).

Both writers emphasize that this class should be foursquare against the abuses of parliamentarianism and the dangers of mass democracy. Hence, this class must also be organized not only through family, but through network and alliance, even reaching into other classes to draw support and talented recruits.

Capital accumulation is necessary for the maintenance and development of elites. Both authors were concerned by the growing tendency of the middle classes to seek professions in the state and to obtain their wealth through bureaucratic favoritism, nepotism, corruption, and other means not related to economic development. In the rise of the bureaucratic state, Pareto and Mosca saw the impoverishment of the potential bourgeoisie elite through taxation (Mosca 1939; Pareto cited in Finer 1966) and as a result of attempts by the bourgeoisie to buy off the working classes and reward themselves instead of forming elites. Venality is antithetical to elite formation. These attempts were doomed to failure as the cost of such policies could not be borne except in periods of economic prosperity, as became clearly evident in Italy during the post-World War I depression. In this analysis there are also indications of the potential lines of cleavage and alliance in the ruling class, as in Pareto's discussion of rentiers and speculators (Pareto 1935; Finer 1966) or Mosca's discussion of feudal remnants, latifundism, and mafia (Mosca 1935, 1939).

Finally, there is in both Pareto's and Mosca's work a concern with ideology which raises important issues of ruling-class hegemony and the actual mechanism of class domination. For Mosca, it was the notion of a "political formula" which provided a justification for class rule (1939). Pareto's emphasis on the role of ideology can be found in his discussions of nonrational action and "derivations," and specifically in his discussion of socialism, nationalism, and patriotism as religions (1968). It is an important theme neglected in many studies, for the state and the ruling class have not only repressive but persuasive means. An ideological focus provides grounds for the investigation of a capitalist class which is not united conspiratorially into a single "committee" but is divided into factions in search of the cross-clan constituencies that are so essential for success in capitalist electoral politics. From the division along elites, we would expect to find specific competing ideologies embodying the strategies of the factions participating in hegemonic struggle. Yet because all elites ultimately form a single class, we would also expect to find a general ideological justification for capitalist rule held in common by members of otherwise opposed factions.

Having isolated some critical aspects of Pareto's and Mosca's conception of elites, it remains to reformulate this concept into a theory of advanced capitalist society.

ELITES IN CONTEMPORARY CAPITALIST STATES

In order to clarify the concept of an elite, it is necessary to have a theory that examines the complex interwoven relationship between elites and the modern capitalist state. Both the instrumental definition—that the state is the instrument of the "executive committee" of the bourgeoisie—and the pluralistic conception fail to provide an understanding of this relationship. Clearly, our notions about the state need rethinking, a matter beyond the scope of this paper (Jessop 1977). For our immediate purpose we will adopt the following conception, modified as indicated: "The [capitalist] state should not be regarded as an intrinsic entity: like 'capital,' it is rather a relationship of forces, or more precisely, the material condensation of such a relationship among classes and class factions, such as this is expressed within the state in a necessarily specific form" (Poulantzas 1978). The advantages of this definition will become clearer in the following discussion, but most importantly it provides a starting point which avoids those either-or discussions that have bogged down research and theorization about power in complex societies.

If the elite and the state are not separate intrinsic entities but inhere each within the other, then conceptualization can begin by specifying their contradictions and complementarities. To this end we propose to examine four major areas of this relationship—capital accumulation, state policy, organization, and hegemony—which we feel represent the major axes of elite-state opposition and conjuncture. This is primarily an analytical and conceptual exercise and although some American examples are presented, there is a real lack of concrete data.

Both elites and the state accumulate capital, but they do so in different ways and for different ends. States accumulate capital through taxation and through revenues derived by publicly owned resources. While both taxation policies and the definition of what constitutes the public domain vary widely in developed capitalist societies, the state redistributes public capital between public and private sectors. State fiscal policy in developed capitalist countries since the depression of the 1930s has been universally characterized by deficit spending, rather than the progressive accumulation sought by the private sector's aggressive elites, or the maintenance of previous accumulations sought by less dynamic elites. Profit turning is not the stuff of the modern state; fiscal probity remains an ideological utopia for political conservatives.

Capital accumulation for elites is another matter entirely. For us, one defining characteristic of elites is their accumulation of capital sufficient to become a market factor in at least one sector of economic endeavor. By market factor, we mean that the accumulated capital is substantial enough to influence decisively the outcome of sectorial competition in the marketplace. In earlier phases of capitalist development, influence of this kind might be confined primarily to a single sector, as was the Carnegies' in steel, or the first-generation Rockefellers' in oil (Collier and Horowitz 1976). At present, transnational corporations dominate many sectors of an international economy simultaneously; thus contemporary capitalist elites should be found as major shareholders and/or on the boards of directors of such entities (Barnett and Muller

1974). We have selected the market factor as a definitional benchmark for elite standing on the grounds that such levels of accumulation indicate economic power sufficient to permit individuals or families to enter the struggle for hegemonic power in the political arena. If, as we have suggested earlier, hegemonic struggles in capitalist societies have to do with the accumulation process, then the power of our restrictive definition rests in its ability to indicate which capitalists have the economic ante to be contenders in the game. Our betting hypothesis is that lesser capitalists cannot successfully constitute political elites; their political expression will take the form of voluntarism, which is in turn linked to institutional politics in what C. W. Mills (1956) referred to as "the middle levels of power."

A second definitional criterion of elite capital accumulation is that it is a transgenerational phenomenon. That is, while initial fortunes are generated within one lifetime, elite economic goals entail the maintenance and enhancement of the original accumulation in perpetuity. The Rockefellers and the Fords were with us then and they are now (Collier and Horowitz 1976; Conot 1975), to cite but two well-known examples. Of particular interest to us as anthropologists is that a primary organization in the accumulation process, initially and over successive generations, is the family. At the risk of sounding waggish, we suggest that elite accumulation represents a domestication of capital, insofar as wealth serves family ends and vice versa. Small wonder that elite family kinship relations are so extensive and intense; the deployment of family members in strategic economic and political positions is probably as crucial to the maintenance of capital accumulation over time as Zeitlin (1974) suggests.

The capitalist state has increasingly become the focus of efforts to maintain capital accumulation and reproduction on a general level, and in addition has increasingly become a mediator of the class struggle (Jessop 1977). What this means for various elite families or networks can be very contradictory. On the one hand, there are massive government subsidies, loans, and bailouts, favorable legislation and tariffs, and, as will be discussed later, an increasing role in the organization of class hegemony for the elites. On the other hand, there is the price of peace in the class struggle, primarily through regulation and redistribution. Each of these factors creates certain dynamics within the elites.

The essentially positive side of state intervention does have its drawbacks and dangers for the elites. Some have argued that the state could be seen as a sort of ideal "collective capitalist," but this is a mistaken and dangerous notion (Jessop 1977). As the state and the elites are organized quite differently, there is no solution that will ultimately satisfy the demands and needs of various factions of both the elite and the state. In particular this can be seen in the problems surrounding the internationalization of capital and a developing split between interests of national and international sectors of the capitalist class (Barnett and Muller 1974).

The process that is much more dangerous for the elites is that of redistribution and the mediation of class conflict. Elites obtain some indirect rewards from state intervention in these processes; they are provided with a better-trained and -educated work force, and the demands of the dominated classes are redirected toward the state and away from the elite (Poulantzas 1978; Wright 1979). But on the whole this process has increasingly impinged upon elite autonomy and presents a constant threat to the continuity of established elite families. Perhaps the two most obvious examples of this process are taxes levied on either income or inheritance, and antitrust legislation directed toward corporations that are major elite holdings (Myers 1906; O'Connor 1974; J. Smith 1974).

Yet in spite of the fact that the state has increasingly been seen as redistributive and "welfaristic" since the New Deal, there are questions about how successful it has been (Kolko 1962).

This brings us to the problem of state policy and its effects upon the elite. Obviously there are potential conflicts of interest in the general areas of capital accumulation and reproduction, of redistribution, and of mediation of class conflict. Perhaps it is best to look at the policies of the contemporary capitalist state as crisis management. The state is not the perfect collective capitalist but responds to problems and struggles within capitalism. It does not always act in the best interests of particular elites and in fact imposes upon them in its attempts to mediate class antagonism (Poulantzas 1978).

Elites must bear some of these policies, as the price of peace in the class struggle, and as necessities for the continuation of capitalism, but ultimately they are inclined to act subversively. This is not to resurrect justly discredited theories of the elite conspiracy, but to point out that the state apparatus is itself crosscut by the elites. Policies that hinder elite capital accumulation, or attempt to redistribute wealth at the expense of elite interests must be structurally subverted, while at the same time policies that encourage capital accumulation and offset the tendencies of capitalist stagnation and declining rate of profit must be promoted (Wright 1979). The processes by which this is done are quite clear. Not only do elite members serve in public office, bankroll candidates, maintain extensive lobbying apparatuses, and serve on a variety of influential committees and commissions, such as the Council on Foreign Relations, the Trilateral Commission, or various other "blue ribbon" panels, but they are quite willing to engage in corrupt practices, bribery, and influence peddling should these other methods fail (Collier and Horowitz 1976).

Elites are able successfully to subvert the state, in part because they are organized differently. Elites are, as Pareto and Mosca realized, organized by kinship and network and are the bane of the institutionalized state. Kinship forms the basis for bonds of moral obligation through which members of an extended kindred can maintain control over capital and over each other. It is possible to see through several examples in American life how the Rockefellers (Collier and Horowitz 1976), the Fords (Conot 1975), the Mellons, and others . . . have gained control over substantial amounts of capital and domesticated this capital over several generations. Throughout the contemporary United States there continues to be an enormous public fascination with economically, socially, and politically prominent families, but this interest seems to stop at the doors of the university. With few exceptions, academic debate has been preoccupied with the issue of whether there is or is not a ruling class, and has not focused on the specific internal dynamics of elite families and networks.

This blindness to family and network is not at all surprising. In fact, it has followed from the conventional sociological wisdom concerning the relationship between the rise of industrial capitalism and the nuclear family. Briefly stated, the conventional view has been that modern society with its requirements of geographic and occupational mobility makes keeping a family together increasingly difficult, and at the same time the "welfare" state increasingly takes over the former functions of the family. What is left eventually are single-family households, husband-wife dyads, and single-parent households primarily ordered by the state and in minimal communication with each other. In short, the functions of kinship diminish as industrial capitalism becomes increasingly developed.

There is increasing criticism of this view of the United States family structure from both anthropological and feminist perspectives. Some of these critics argue that kinship continues not only to serve as a defense of the state but is central to the reproduction of patriarchal capitalist relations (Zaretsky 1976; Rapp 1978). In America, even the poorest individuals continue to form extended kin-groupings as an alternative to having their lives organized by the state (a point brilliantly illustrated by Carol Stack in *All Our Kin* [1975]), and the family has become an increasingly politicized issue. It is evident that elites also use this source of flexible organization.

If a group of families forms the core of an elite then their extension through networks and clientage should be studied as well. Through networks and clientage many of the connections of the elites within themselves, to institutions, and to clients who are aspiring elites can be drawn. From just the simple juxtaposition of names and connections, such as Domhoff's "List of Heavies" (1971), one can discover a surprising amount of overlap and linkage. While clearly factionalized, these networks may be the source of the flexible organization and consensus that allow the elites to promote their form of corporate capitalism.

One of the more difficult areas to discuss is the role of the state in hegemony and ideology, for increasingly the ruling class has abandoned efforts to justify publicly its separateness, and now finds its protection in democratic ideologies. It has long been observed that the bourgeois nation-state has been the best shell for capitalism (Jessop 1977; Poulantzas 1978), and has increasingly organized the propaganda of corporate capitalism. The state, particularly in America, has come to occupy a dual role, representing, on the one hand, the living proof of the success of democracy and "free enterprise" and, on the other, the target that is attacked when the failings and the political repercussions of advanced capitalism become evident. This is particularly propitious for the elites, for not only does the nation-state provide them with an arena for organization but ultimately it takes the blame for the consequences of this organization onto itself.

Yet if the elite no longer needs a grand ideological justification, which is in part what Pareto and Mosca were trying to provide, it still can and does make use of a particularly potent ideological device—the manipulation of established cultural codes. The very exclusiveness and closure that are implied by an elite are maintained by manipulation of the larger American value system which claims to value openness and mobility. The entire system of clubs, education, residence, social registers, and the like may make entry into the elites, like the domestication of capital, a transgenerational phenomenon. Even language can mark the boundaries of an elite (Baltzell 1958, 1964). Through the manipulation of cultural codes the elite can all but vanish behind a screen of institutions and images that provides privacy and security and conceals the extent of their power, influence, and holdings.

Manipulation of culture is also embedded in the very institutions of "high culture" and public service, which are in turn often creations of elite philanthropy. Looking at the foundations, charities, and funds created and supported by elite families, one finds a pattern which denies any sense of disinterested giving, in which the ideological and political aims of such giving are often quite clear. Rockefeller philanthropy, in the form of educational institutions such as Rockefeller University and of various cultural institutions, has created a different image than that of the "Trust" and the Ludlow massacre, but its influence has not stopped there. For in addition Rockefeller money has created a host of agencies which have defined "overpopulation" and "population control" as major problems in the Third World (Horowitz 1972; Collier and Horowitz 1976) and most recently has provided the seed money for the creation of the Trilateral Commission, whose work on the problems of advanced capitalism has already given us the spectre of "excess democracy." These institutions are also useful in recruiting a "second stratum" (Mosca 1939) of intellectuals, state functionaries, and celebrities who not only provide ideological justifications and personnel, but also mask or mark as needed the boundaries and the centers of power within the elite.

The results of elite manipulation are extremely clear in the practice of the American free enterprise democratic myth. The right to freedom and private property becomes a defense of the unlimited accumulation and concentration of capital. The individualism, the social mobility, and the "Protestant ethic" of Americans become part of the denial of the existence of this concentration and are appealed to in efforts to justify the existence of the rich, the wellborn, and the powerful. The state itself and the alternation of the two political parties, although both are heavily interpenetrated with elite politics, became the living proof of democracy itself.

All of these factors—capital accumulation, policy, organization, and ideology—must be viewed in the larger, historically specific framework of capitalist development. Just as Pareto and Mosca's theories must be understood in reference to a particular period in state formation and capitalism, so must contemporary elite theory view its subjects in their historical context. There is considerable evidence that large modifications are taking place in the structure of elites in America, associated with geographic north-to-south movements and the rise of different elites, and reflecting the increasing internationalization of capital and changes in the nature of the state.

Satisfactory studies of elites must reckon with these changes and account for them.

CONCLUSIONS: THE CASE FOR ETHNOGRAPHIC INQUIRY

In the preceding pages we have argued that a revised version of Pareto's and Mosca's elite concept might be useful in resolving the ancient controversy over who rules in capitalist society. We hope that the revised elite concept may be useful in Marxist analysis by clearing away theoretical preconceptions about the existence of a politically unitary ruling class, and may help to inject both social-structural and political content into the notion of class fraction in vogue among some modern Marxists (Poulantzas 1978). Class fractions may not derive from sectorial clashes; indeed it may be hard to argue that there is overall unity of interest within elites based in single economic sectors—witness finance and energy at the moment—but they could possibly reflect the limits of elite organization itself. That is, there are finite, perhaps even mathematically predictable, limits to the optimum effective size of any organization based on kinship and network. These limits must be very finite indeed when we consider that kin and network have to generate trust among people of a class whose economic activities render them untrustworthy even to themselves. There is the possibility that the modern capitalist class poses an interesting anthropological paradox: while often considered to be the perpetrator of the modern "individualistic" social order, this class remains relatively "primitive" in terms of its own social organization, insofar as kinship performs more manifold and critical functions among elites than in other classes. The revised elite concept should also help us to resolve the question of who rules by refocusing the issue of hegemony entirely. We suggest that hegemony is not an either-or proposition, as in either the state or the ruling class, either the institutional order or the elite (or oligarchy, etc.). Instead we posit a struggle between contending elites on the one hand, and the state and the elites on the other. We see these struggles as stemming from

permanent structural features of the capitalist political order, that is, elites and the institutional order. Hegemonic issues are resolved in elite-elite struggles, and in struggles between elites and parts of the institutional order that they do not effectively control. Elites, the state, and the nature of hegemonic struggle itself are continually redefined by the transformations of the capitalist economy. But profound though these transformations may be, they do not result in the replacement of elite politics by institutional politics, a point argued at length by one of us elsewhere (Schneider, Schneider, and Hansen 1972).

Our redefinition of the elite concept should help clear up a major analytical problem in the debate, namely the lack of critical data on hegemonic elites, past and present. Currently, even those scholars who insist upon the existence of a ruling class held together by kin and network (or class fractions similarly constituted) (e.g. Miliband 1969; Domhoff 1975; Zeitlin 1974, 1975) argue their case on the basis of positional data alone. That is, they start from the knowledge that there are indeed wealthy and prominent families in advanced capitalist countries, and that members of these families, their friends, and/or retainers demonstrably occupy critical positions in corporations, the government, political parties, and so on. Having located these individuals at key positions in the institutional matrix, these scholars rest their case, or worse, attempt to infer the nature of elite behavior from these data alone. Small wonder that such studies have been criticized as speculative conjuring acts, mystifications, or reifications (Hacker 1975).

If we view hegemonic elites as familistic entities defending accumulated capital over time through the mobilization of kin and connections, then the limitations of analysis based on positional data become obvious. Given that both the accumulation and the maintenance of capital occur over time and require shifting strategies to meet changing conditions, any form of analysis that locates individuals at one point in time is limited, since it cannot possibly tell us empirically, in a behavioral sense, why such individuals are found in these positions at any given time. Simply stated, positional analysis has static and ahistorical qualities that render it inappropriate to the analysis of hegemonic elites. While data gathered from this method are useful in establishing interrelationships between elites and the institutional order, they can tell us very little either about the quality of such interrelationships or about how they came to exist in the first place. Ultimately, positional analysis cannot possibly be used to analyze the dynamics of elites, much less the dynamics of interelite relationships, or the dynamics of relationships between elites and the order. At best, it only suggests what is to be researched and analyzed.

Our conception of hegemonic elites implies a methodological solution to the analytic problems which arise from lack of critical data. We feel that straightforward ethnographic inquiry, particularly the taking of genealogies and family histories, might definitively solve these problems, and go a long way to resolving the debate over who rules. Detailed family histories can provide the missing temporal dimension of positional analysis, but their advantages go much further. Such accounts can provide a history of alliances forged, and decisions taken over generations, that are critical to the survival of such groups. Such data cannot possibly be gleaned from public records, which are the principal sources of data for positional analysis. Almost by definition the history of elites cannot be accurately documented in public records, which are generated largely from within the institutional sector, and thus come to represent ideology rather than history. Ethnography conducted through network analysis, and participant observation should do much to reveal the dynamics of elite behavior, which appears to depend so heavily upon the dynamics of interpersonal relationships forged in an atmosphere of mistrust.

It strikes us that this task is a vital one for anthropologists to perform, in an era when the rationale for the discipline is increasingly under question with the shrinkage of the primitive world, held together as it was by kinship. Hegemonic elites may be the last of the primitive order that we could profitably study. Perhaps there is continuing justification for the existence of our discipline to be found in Stanley Diamond's (1974) prophetic statement that the basic struggle in human history is "the struggle between the state . . . civil authority—and the constituent kin or quasi kin units of society."

Richard Bellamy (essay date 1987)

SOURCE: "Gaetano Mosca," in *Modern Italian Social Theory: Ideology and Politics from Pareto to the Present,* Polity Press, 1987, pp. 34-53.

[*In the following essay, Bellamy contends that Mosca's and Vilfredo Pareto's respective theories of elites were based on differing "personal political preferences"— Mosca's on moderate conservatism, and Pareto's on classical liberalism.*]

Mosca is habitually obscured behind the shadow of Pareto. Both are lumped together as the founding fathers of elite theory, and Pareto praised for his more rigorous and 'scientific' approach. This characterization misleads in several respects. Mosca developed his concept of the 'political class' from a quite different ideological standpoint to Pareto—that of the moderate conservative, rather than the classical liberal. As a result, in spite of a similar methodological commitment to create a science of society on the model of the natural sciences, his theory evolved in a manner divergent from his Swiss colleague's, and they reached opposing conclusions about the future of democracy and the nature of fascism. The contrast between the two provides a vivid illustration as to how personal political preferences can completely transform the character of a purportedly neutral social theory. Moreover, it renders senseless the largely sterile debate, carried on by Mosca, as to whether Pareto had or had not derived the notion of the elite from his earlier writings on the same subject.

Unlike Pareto, Mosca did not construct a system of general sociology. His work is far more impressionistic and often contradictory. Although he too appealed to history for proof of the validity of his ideas, he openly addressed the problems of contemporary politics and subtly changed his thesis accordingly. Thus what he lost in logical rigour was amply compensated for by the flexibility and richness of his analysis of political life.

The changes in his thinking are easily traced. Mosca was something of a monomaniac, and essentially wrote three versions of the same book. He gave his first account in the youthful *On the Theory of Governments and Parliamentary Government: Historical and Social Studies* of 1884. Twelve years later he expanded and added to the argument in the first edition of his most famous work, the *Elements of Political Science,* which was later translated into English as *The Ruling Class.* Finally, in 1923, a second edition of this book appeared, with a new volume appended, and this version essentially constituted a third rendering of his famous theory. Formally Mosca only admitted to amendments and additional refinements; taken as a whole, however, they provided a transformation of the original theory. In this [essay] I shall give an account of each successive version, and show that the constant factor behind each extension of his thesis was the changing social and economic situation of the upper middle class in Italian society, whose political role he sought to define and defend.

THE POLITICAL CLASS I

Mosca was born in Palermo, Sicily, in 1858, and his political vision exemplified the southerner's distinctive perspective on Italian politics. . . . [The] southern question came to epitomize all that was wrong with the new state. The *Teorica* was conceived at a crucial time, when the upper middle-class elite who had ruled Italy since the Risorgimento—the Historical Right—had lost their parliamentary majority. Mosca's work shares the general condemnation felt by intellectuals for the corrupt practices of the so-called Left. However, he linked his criticism with a direct appeal for a return to government by the ousted political class of 'disinterested' men of the middling rank.

Mosca's diagnosis of the situation follows on from a particular line of thought prominent at the time amongst fellow *meridionalisti.* They laid the decline in the standards of public life at the door of parlimanetary democracy. The enlargement of the electorate to include members of the largely unlettered masses had, they claimed, simply increased the powers of landowners and other influential groups to manipulate the government. Whilst the landlords' economic hold over the peasants remained complete, the notion of free elections was a farce. Worse, it provided a spurious legitimacy for their political ascendency. The only solution was the creation of a middling class of independent proprietors, who were free from the influence of quasi-feudal landlords.

The following two examples of Sicilian electoral practice amply demonstrate the accuracy of this analysis:

> In 1881 communal elections were held at Villalba . . . and the Marchese of Villalba, supported by the Mafia, took his precautions ten days in advance. The 214 citizens possessing the qualifications entitling them to vote were locked up in a granary from which they were released, eight at a time, and escorted by the Marchese's armed guards to the polls. The Marchese was elected.

By 1900 new methods of democratic persuasion had been perfected to cope with the enlarged electorate. One observer, Alongi, provided a vivid description of the new voting arrangements:

> Some short distance from the polling station the road was barred by a group of sinister figures. Here each voter as he approached was seized, thoroughly bastinadoed and forced to drink a huge glass of wine. There followed a thorough search of his person, after which the government candidate's voting slip was put into his hand and he was led or dragged to the ballot box, where the president took the slip from him and put it in.

Cynicism about the virtues of democracy is hardly surprising, given the novel application of its procedures prevalent in the Italian south. The studies of Sonnino, Villari and Fortunato were largely empirical. Mosca provided a theoretical dimension to their work, although still in the positivist mode. However, he also sought to undermine their contention that democracy was in principle workable once the sources of economic and physical coercion available to certain minority interests had been abolished. In this respect he aligned himself with the conservative wing of southern analysts, like Pasquale Turiello, who maintained that only rule by a restricted group of public-spirited citizens could prevent 'a violent return to barbarism.'

Mosca's intentions were plain in the very organization of the *Teorica,* which had three main sections. First, a criticism of the Aristotelian division of polities into tyrannies, aristocracies and democracies, and the assertion that all political systems are products of elite rule. Second, a historical survey of past states in order to prove this thesis. Third, the application of his theory to the conditions of parliamentary democracy, a discussion which significantly concluded with an analysis of the 'social question', more or less identified with the problems of the south. The main thrust of his argument is plain—the democratic aspiration of government by the people for the people was an illusion, since all rule was by a minority over a majority. However, the details of his discussion led to a slightly different conclusion, namely the justification of the rule of a particular type of minority political class.

Like Pareto, Mosca aspired to ground the study of politics in certain constant laws of human psychology. As

many commentators have remarked, the methodology adopted to arrive at this result was underdeveloped and inadequate. The main difference between the natural and the human sciences, he believed, was that the latter required an infinitely greater wealth of detailed data to arrive at its laws. However, once historians and anthropologists had gathered together a vast store of solid facts 'it is a case of saying to ourselves: who has eyes to see, sees'. Fortunately for Mosca's subsequent reputation, nothing like this crude empiricism guided his studies. Whilst he was intent on showing that all societies had and would be ruled by a minority, he did not, in Paretian fashion, assume a set of uniform human traits which could explain all the resultant social patterns. Indeed, he damned as a prioristic the racial, evolutionary and materialist schemes put forward by Gumplowicz, Spencer and Comte respectively—thinkers whom he largely admired. Mosca's implicit awareness of historical change, both material and cultural, may have been at odds with his methodological premises, but it gave his thought an extra dimension. In particular, he acquired the ability to appreciate the new conditions of modern society and adapt his ideas to meet them, a virtue noticeably lacking in the system of his rival in Lausanne.

Mosca attributed elite rule to the 'indisputable properties of the social nature of man':

> [i] that a superiority of moral character usually prevails in the long run over a superiority of numbers and brute force . . .

> [ii] more important and less observed . . . that an organized minority, which acts in a co-ordinated manner, always triumphs over a disorganized majority, which has neither will, nor impulse, nor action in common.

This passage suggests that Mosca thought the political class was necessarily composed of 'inherently superior persons', and that they shared a common purpose and acted in unison. However, it soon emerged that he appreciated that this was not always the case, and that it merely represented his ideal.

He claimed that we do not generally know how political classes come into being. However, he did admit that the two features he had isolated varied over time. In particular, he noted that in modern industrial societies there is a far greater accumulation of power in the hands of government than ever before. The revenue generated through taxes, the presence of a standing army and a bureaucracy that entered into every aspect of public life, gave the contemporary political class an unprecedented accumulation of economic and political power, rendering their organized action irresistable. The qualities of the ruling elite were correspondingly different too. In the middle ages military prowess led to wealth and political success. However this was rarely required, apart from exceptional periods of social unrest when force again became important, and the strong leadership associated with 'Caesarism' was called for. 'Very civilised societies', however, 'which have arrived at a notable degree of maturity', laid the greatest stress on 'personal merit'. This arose not only because such societies valued equality and social justice more, but

> principally because the technical and scientific element is more developed in them, and, as in other departments of a civilised society, finds its applications in public life. Where a special culture, for those who are called upon to rule the destiny of the country, has been formed, and it necessarily is formed in any cultured and civilised nation, it becomes an indispensable quality which every member of the political class must possess to a greater or lesser degree.

Mosca maintained that the requisite degree of culture was most likely to obtain when accompanied by a moderate degree of wealth. Great riches reduced the will to work, whilst poverty did not provide the necessary leisure time for study. Men of moderate means were less effected by private interest and were both more able and more prepared to devote a large part of their time to the common weal. This was Mosca's model public servant—a modern equivalent of the Aristotelian 'great-souled man'. A man of slightly higher rank than the independent peasant proprietor advocated by his fellow *meridionalisti,* yet below the status of the aristocratic landowner—in sum, a member of the professional middle classes like himself. The class which in his opinion came closest to this ideal was that of the English country gentlemen, who performed the duties of J. P. and Alderman, not as elected representatives or career bureaucrats, but because 'they are called to exercise certain offices by virtue of the social position they occupy. It would appear', he went on, 'that with this system one has functionaries who are the most independent influences.'

The argument outlined so far constituted Mosca's core thesis. Different renderings of it appeared in all three versions of his theory. However, it was all too evident to him that the natural ascendency of the upper middle class no longer pertained. The bourgeoisie had had their brief moment of glory during the Risorgimento, and declined thereafter. Mosca appreciated that quite a different kind of elite now ruled. He therefore turned to an examination of how democracy encouraged corruption and a decline in public standards, as a preliminary to suggesting reforms which would bring about a political revival of the middle classes. A Paretian aspiration to produce a universal law which merely described practices operating in all social systems was therefore superceded by an overtly prescriptive argument for a particular type of rule. Instead of asserting that the rulers were always composed of the best, he was forced to argue that rule should be by those who possessed 'personal merit'.

Mosca began his explanation of the rise and acceptance of democratic practices by offering an account of why political classes, and the moral justification they offered for their rule, changed. As Meisel and others have noted, his thesis was remarkably Marxian for a committed critic of socialism:

> [T]he political elements in a society, he wrote, are never very stable; they continually change with changes in the level of culture and of the general social and economic conditions of a people. As a result there are always new elements in a position of entering into the political class, and usually entering it under the aegis of a new formula, which replaces the old.

Each new class justified its position according to certain 'abstract principles' or 'political formula'. This did not necessarily correspond to the real reasons for a class's success—indeed it rarely did so. However, it had to be attuned to the dominant mores of the age. Thus 'from changes in the formula we can easily infer the changes which occur in the political class, and from the examination of the abstract principles, which inform the first, we can divine the real elements which enter into the composition of the second.' Mosca contended that a political class which did not alter with the times could not maintain its rule indefinitely. Another elite would form amongst the ruled, which in the fullness of time would replace them, if necessary by force. Nor did he believe that a given social and economic situation required a certain ideology—rather the political class chose the 'formula which best suits them' from a number of possibilities.

He did not claim he had discovered an inevitable process of 'elite circulation'. He had merely provided an understanding of the factors militating in favour of alterations in the ruling strata of society. Despite superficial similarities with Marxism, he did not argue that changes in the composition of the rulers indicated the substitution of a whole social class by another; in his view only the men in power varied. This enabled him to explain the apparent paradox of elite manipulation of democracy. Industrialisation had produced new social conditions and increased social mobility so that new political elements had to be satisfied: namely, the masses. This meant that the legal and political superstructures of power had to be altered. Moreover new, largely intellectual, qualities were demanded of rulers. But the true nature of government remained the same—only the appearance, the type of justification, the 'formula' and procedures needed to maintain it, were different. The reality was still rule by an elite. Mosca proceeded to push home his views via an analysis of the practices of modern Western democracies; concentrating his study on Italy. He aimed to show that first, although the French and industrial revolutions had necessitated a new 'political formula', democracy had no substantive basis as majority rule and second, that democracy actually corrupted the elite.

He argued that 'whoever has assisted at an election knows perfectly well that *the electors do not elect the Deputy, but usually the Deputy has himself elected by the electors*', or more accurately, 'his friends have him elected'. The electoral system favoured the prime factor leading to elite rule: the advantage of an organized minority over a mass of isolated individuals. Voters could not pick at will candidates from amongst themselves, but were presented with a very limited number of parties to choose from. Given the 'artificial' environment created by representative democracy, victory went to those elements best able to impose themselves, and the notion that elections reflected the decision of the popular masses *'is a lie'*.

The choice of candidates, he continued, was really made by one of three different sources of power. Prefects, 'grand electors', and 'political and workers' societies in all their infinite subdivisions and variety'. The influence of the first, Mosca warned, had progressively increased with the growth and acceptance of state interference in local affairs. Once deputies were elected and formed part of the government, ministers could use their control of the bureaucracy to manipulate elections. This power largely derived from the vast sources of patronage available to them from the dispensing of state jobs, finance and contracts. By this method the strength of the 'political class' could in theory grow indefinitely. The 'grand electors' were those individuals whose personal social position and wealth allowed them to impose their will on voters dependent upon them for their livelihood. Mosca had southern landowners chiefly in mind, but factory owners in particular circumstances would fit just as well. As in the first example of malpractice in Sicily cited above, the system added to the 'grand elector's' already considerable local power political influence at a national level to protect his interests. *Trasformismo* consolidated their power, Salvemini pointedly remarking that the 200 deputies elected by the south from 1880 to 1900 had been 'eternally ministerial'. As long as they could reliably get their candidates chosen, governments which sought to cultivate their votes were unlikely to pass measures which might ameliorate the condition of the oppressed. Democracy had thus considerably worsened the peasant's lot. Finally, the influence of political and workers' associations was predominately an urban phenomenon. Mosca seemed to be primarily concerned with the trade unions and employers' associations, which collectively acted—through their links with political parties—in much the same fashion as the 'grand electors'.

The upshot of these different methods for buying the electorate had been a general decline in the standards of both political practices and of deputies. The independent men of the Right no longer had the stomach for politics, for 'one can no longer use only honest and legal means, one must act like a gangster (*camorrista*) if one does not want to be a victim of a gangsterly attack (*atto di camorra*)'. The system was prone to an infinite degeneration, as everyone, 'from the Minister to the voter, finds their private interest in betraying the public interest which is entrusted to them'. The 'precious qualities' of 'independence of character, boldness and impartiality . . . which constitute the true moral force of . . . political organisms, are increasingly sacrificed', excluding from office the men who possessed them. In parliamentary democracies ' . . . moral cowardice, lack of a sense of justice, cunning, intrigue, which are precisely the qualities which bring peoples and states to ruin, are best suited, [and] lead to the advancement of their practitio-

ners, and therefore develop and become increasingly evident'. Mosca argued that democracy was inherently bad, and that the desire to rectify these problems via reforms aimed at instituting 'true democracy' were totally misconceived. They would only make matters worse. He similarly rejected the notion that a genuine two-party system would produce beneficial effects by preventing any one group obtaining a monopoly of power. No genuine competition would take place, he argued, because the parties would always collude together to keep important issues off the electoral agenda, thus protecting their common interests as rival members of the same political class. Anticipating one of his later arguments, he identified the problem in the already quasi-universal authority of the elected chamber. Although constitutionally both King and Senate acted as countervailing forces, they could not realistically perform this function. They lacked an alternative 'political base', representative of 'political elements different and independent from those which create and compose the Chamber of Deputies.' This was the role Mosca carved out within the democratic system for the middle classes. The ministers, the top echelons of the civil service, and the Senate should be royal appointees, and not those designated by the majority party in the lower house. Independent of both popular elections and government patronage, these positions would be formed from 'the most cultured and independent elements of the nation; to which class would be confided the whole provincial administration, and a wide participation in the work of the provincial bureaucracy'. If these reforms were effected '[t]hen King and Senate would indeed have both great prestige and great power, and the Chamber of Deputies would be not only counter balanced, but also effectively braked . . .'.

Mosca readily admitted that such measures would only seem desirable, let alone practicable, if one had 'entirely left the orbit of ideas and the spirit which inform the parliamentary system'. However, he was adamant that this was the only path to take. He likened his project to the 'admirable [English] system of self-government; by which almost all the administrative duties and a good part of the judicial ones, are performed by gentlemen, who serve the country gratis, who are neither dependent on Ministers nor the electorate, and do not have to conform to any other regulations than those proscribed by the common law.' Ideally, he believed, this role could have been performed in Italy by a new aristocracy of merit, a utopian goal whilst differences in economic wealth and power brought such great political advantages. In the present situation of near anarchy, a simple return to respect for law and order took precedence over idealistic schemes from whatever quarter. Reform must therefore occur within the paradigm set by the current political formula.

This last pronouncement appears to contradict the whole gist of Mosca's earlier contention that democracy could never be reformed from within. However, he was clearly moving towards his later position where he re-conceptualized democratic theory away from the notion of popular majority rule and towards modern-day doctrines of pluralism. This revision did not entail dropping the 'political formula' of democracy, although it departed dramatically from the ideals of classical theorists such as Mill or Rousseau. I will give fuller consideration of this development when examining the later versions of his theory, since Mosca expounded it at greater length in the two volumes of the *Elementi*.

The concluding section of the *Teorica* addresses the crucial problem of the social question, presenting a synthesis and application of the analytical instruments developed in the body of the book. This is hardly surprising, given that it had provided the original impetus behind the entire project. The nub of the problem, according to Mosca, were the great inequalities of political leverage arising from disparities in wealth. He rejected both the liberal contention that they were the natural result of free competition, and the socialist belief that they could be abolished in an egalitarian communist future. Government intervention was needed to redistribute the grosser discrepancies between rich and poor. The chief drawback in this scheme arose from the domination of government by the wealthy, who 'to better the condition of the poor will never damage their own interests'.

The solution lay, therefore, in the introduction of non-economic elements into the political class. Whilst riches were an important requisite for membership, other criteria should count as well, particularly 'technical expertise and a high level of cultural attainment', qualities which 'daily acquire ever greater importance' in modern society, 'such that someone who is totally ignorant cannot perform the tasks of high office for long', or as Mosca somewhat naively stated:

> It does not seem possible to us, that a political class, in which a superior culture was obligatory . . . and to which the children of all social classes can come to be admitted, could then have such base, egoistic and mean aims to subordinate every government action to the interests of gross capital and the big landowners . . . Thus that government is in the hands of the most educated class, and that it takes resolutely the initiative for the betterment of the lower classes, such according to us is the sole means which can lead to a peaceful solution to the so called social question.

Mosca provided two applications of his theory. Elite rule as a description of contemporary politics revealed the manipulation of democratic procedures by economic interests—a view similar to Pareto's. To remedy this, Mosca invoked the prescriptive side of his theory—rule by a disinterested educated elite, serving the common good. Without their countervailing influence, Mosca intimated in the conclusion, a 'new barbarism' would arise in Europe, in which the 'feudal barons' of capitalism and landed property would hold unlimited sway. Maintaining this double perspective involved Mosca in a number of potential contradictions. After all, if the masses were as base as he believed, and greed a universal human charac-

teristic, why should the persons of merit who rose from the ranks of the people devote their superior talents to the common interest, rather than their own? When writing this first version of *The Ruling Class,* Mosca could still hark back to the ideals of the Historical Right. However, without debating the validity of his (inordinately) high estimate of their merits, it was increasingly evident that as an economic and social group their days were numbered. The new elite would have to be drawn from the masses. This led Mosca to see democracy in a new perspective and try to unite the formation of an educated political class with the procedures and even ethic of democratic government. As the two subsequent sections will show, his continued attachment to the rule of the nineteenth century gentleman class doomed this scheme to failure.

THE POLITICAL CLASS II

The first edition of the *Elementi* appeared in 1895. In the intervening twelve years since publishing the *Teorica,* Mosca had had ample opportunities to observe the parliamentary system at work as Revisore, from 1886, at the Chamber of Deputies. He had obtained this post through the patronage of his friend and protector, the Sicilian politician Antonio Di Rudini. Along with Sonnino, Di Rudini led the right wing of the liberal party and was Prime Minister in 1891 and 1896. His stance sheds light on Mosca's political allegiances during this period. An opponent of Crispi, whose Abyssinian adventures and financial scandals he criticized, Di Rudini also oppressed the socialists and the Catholics—a policy which did not endear him to anybody. However, in his last administration he attempted a moderate conservative parliamentary reform, which sought to counterbalance the power of universal suffrage at the centre by a considerable degree of administrative decentralization, precisely what Mosca had proposed earlier. The additions to Mosca's theory clearly reflected the political concerns of the times. As in his first book, the presentation of principles is followed by their explicit application to contemporary parliamentary politics.

The first two chapters read like a succinct restatement of the methodological criteria and the theory of the political class elaborated in the opening chapter of the *Teorica.* The 'constant element' in all political organisms was still the presence of 'two classes of persons: the one that governs and the other that is ruled', the former consisting of an organized minority which imposed its will by 'manipulation and violence', even, indeed especially, in a democracy.

Mosca both clarified and extended other aspects of his earlier work. In particular, he elaborated upon his explanation of elite circulation. All ruling groups had, he maintained, to become hereditary. Yet when 'there is a shift in the balance of political forces' and new talents are called for, then the ruling class must adapt or (more likely) topple:

> If a new source of wealth forms in a society, if the practical importance of knowledge grows, if the

old religion declines or a new one is born, if a new current of ideas spreads, then, simultaneously, powerful dislocations occur within the ruling class. One might say, indeed, that the whole history of civilised humanity can be summed up in the conflict between the tendency of dominant elements to monopolise political power and transmit possession of it by inheritance, and the tendency . . . towards a dislocation of old forces and an insurgence of new forces, which produces an unending ferment of endosmosis and exosmosis between the upper classes and certain portions of the lower.

He reasserted the link between changing social forces as society became more civilized, and the rise of a new political class from amongst the governed. He also noted, in a later passage, that the split could even occur within the ruling class itself, and that the different sections of the minority would appeal to the masses for support. As in the *Teorica,* he is vague about the relations between the 'political formula' adopted and the prevailing social and economic conditions, suggesting it was to some extent autonomous. Like Pareto, he was clearly impressed by the effect ideas could have no political processes, and was deeply troubled by the increasingly ideologized nature of contemporary politics. However, he was less cynical than his rival. Whilst opposed to religion, he recognized it as a legitimate need of human nature, impossible to replace with secular 'rational' modes of thought. He did hope, though, that a liberal moral ethic would emerge, adapted to the needs of the modern age.

Unlike the cynic of the Villa Angora, Mosca only flirted briefly with the discovery of a 'universal psychological law' to link the role of ideas with the circulation of elites. If he elaborated his thesis less rigorously, however, it was largely to his advantage in this instance. Mosca made two general observations about the influence of ideas. First, he distinguished 'social' and 'national' types. The former, as in the great religions, could command universal allegiances which cut across or even opposed duties to the state deriving from the latter. A political class would therefore be ill advised to deny the religious aspirations of a people, but should seek to increase the ties to the state as much as possible. Such Machiavellian advice, rare in Mosca's writings, clearly emanated from his traditional anti-clericalism, fuelled at the time by Di Rudini's recent struggle with the Catholics, who still denied the authority of the newly-formed state over former Papal territory. Second, he argued that whilst 'feudal' governments could impose a 'universalistic' political formula, 'bureaucratic' organizations are necessarily pluralistic.

At this point, Mosca's supposedly 'neutral' categories clearly emerged as aspects of a normative theory. Whilst bureaucratic government increased the scope for central control of social life, its functions were dispersed amongst a plurality of officers. The feudal lord may have ruled over few people and had less power over their lives, but he filled all the functions of judge, general and tax man. He had a direct and personal relationship with his subjects, and could impose a unified moral code upon

them. Contemporary life, in contrast, was much more atomistic due to the division of labour and the concomitant specialization of work and leisure. Mosca, as we shall see, was well aware of certain drawbacks arising from this situation. However, he saw a possible solution in 'bureaucratic' organization. Certain norms of behaviour and attitude emerged from the procedures of administration itself, both products of a progressive rationalization of social life. Unlike Weber he did not fear humanity risked entrapment in an 'iron cage' of bureaucratic uniformity, since he maintained somewhat illogically that it could never be extended to the whole of society, denying even its applicability to the production and distribution of wealth.

The reasoning behind Mosca's additional thoughts on the links between the political class, social change and systems of belief became clearer in the fifth chapter, entitled 'juridical defence'. His remarks here provided preliminary clarifications for a major development of his theory. By broadening the political class to include both 'in' and 'out' groups, which needed to woo different sections of the lower classes, and who had to appeal to a variety of ideological viewpoints to do so, Mosca had laid the groundwork for a theory of elite rule adapted to the conditions of modern society. The increased organization of society, by joining people together in greater mutual dependence rendered

> moral discipline indisputably greater, and the overly egoistical acts, which by the control and reciprocal restraint of the individuals, who make up society, are prohibited or prevented, are more numerous and more clearly defined. . . . The social mechanisms which regulate this disciplining of the moral sense form what we call the 'juridical defence.'

Mosca noted that his scheme did not have recourse to any altruistic or virtuous instincts—'we believe instead, that as social organisation has the consequence of the reciprocal restraint of human individuals, it makes them better, not by destroying their wicked instincts, but by accustoming the individual to tame them.' Quoting Guiccardini, he argued that a government of law and authority established political liberty by curtailing the selfish appetites of particular men.

So far Mosca appeared to be tracing the development of a natural process within a civilized nation. However, as we have seen, he was all too aware that it did not reflect current Italian experience. Instead he was advocating a particular constitutional reform, similar to Di Rudini's, which he had been developing in a number of legal writings. 'The degree of perfection that juridical defence can attain in a given people' was, he observed, denoted by the 'political arrangements, which establish the character of the relations between the governing class and governed, and between the various levels and the various sections of the ruling class. Should a single political force ever manage to monopolize and exploit the advantages of power totally for its own benefit, then despotism would result. This danger existed in representative democracies, where deputies could claim supreme power. The remedy, implicit in his very definition of a political organization, was to have competing groups within the political class, which would balance each other out. One might have expected him to develop this into a theory of indirect democracy, whereby competing elite groups would curry favour with the electorate. Although all the elements were there, he still cherished a place in the sun for his cultured class, so instead he made the following two proposals. First, drawing on Montesquieu, he advocated separating the functions of government. The church, army, judiciary and bureaucracy must all be autonomous, and not under the control of elected representatives. Second, economic and political power must be kept apart—'There is no use in cherishing illusions about the practical consequences of a regime, in which the management of economic production, and the distribution of political power, are linked and conferred upon the same persons. Like Pareto, Mosca applied this criticism even-handedly to corporate socialism and monopoly capitalism alike. The danger of the former though, was that democracy appeared to give these procedures some legitimacy—it provided for the complete hegemony of a single 'political formula' as a cover for particular interests. Its humanitarian pretensions were only a veneer, for

> when all the moral and material advantages depend upon those who hold power, there is no meanness that people will not do to please them; just as there is no act of violence or deception which will not be resorted to to attain power, or rather to belong to the number of those who distribute the cake, rather than remaining amongst the many others who must be content with the portion given them.

Socialism therefore constituted a double danger, combining a universalistic religious appeal with the concentration of absolute political and economic power in the hands of a party cadre. To criticize the particular measures of socialism did not suffice to undermine its impact—*'to a complete metaphysical system one must oppose a complete positivist system'*.

Mosca clearly offered his own work as filling this role. But his neutral political science was obviously ideological too. Mosca followed Pareto in making two main objections to socialism. First, he contended that the abolition of private property would not solve the problem of inequality. Relations of subordination were based on a variety of factors in different societies, such as the ability to fight or intellectual skills in Military and Bureaucratic societies respectively. Second, he elevated present attitudes into a universal law of human nature, denying *a priori* the possibility for altruism to win over egoism. However, unlike his rival, and in contradiction with his basic thesis, he saw one class whose position fitted them for public duty and were able to transcend self-interest. By now we are no longer surprised to learn that society can be saved by an economically independent group

> Who are sufficiently comfortable, to be able to dedicate a part of their time to perfecting their

culture and acquiring that interest in the public good—that quasi-aristocratic spirit—which alone can induce men to serve their country with no other satisfactions than those stemming from self-respect [*amor proprio*].

The gentry ideal surfaces again, and with it the renewed hope of replenishing their ranks to form a meritocracy from a new educated elite: the professional men—lawyers, scientists and technicians—required to service the needs of modern industrial society. A note to the third edition of 1939 reveals the dream to have been no more substantial than that. He claimed:

> This passage corresponded in great part to the truth of the epoch in which it was written, that is 1895: after the war the middle classes of almost all nations were, if not destroyed, more or less decimated . . . This decline of the middle classes has been one of the principal causes of the major difficulties affecting the functioning of the representative system in most of Europe and America.

Preparing a third version of his thesis after the First World War required substantial revisions to cope with this harsh reality.

THE POLITICAL CLASS III

Twenty-seven years separated the first and second editions of the *Elementi*. In the Preface he said it had been conceived over the past two or three years to take into account both new facts, occasioned by the changed times, and the effect recent events had had on his way of seeing things. He chose not to update the first edition, but to add instead a second volume written from his new perspective.

The critical approval of parliamentary democracy is the most striking aspect of this version. Two factors no doubt contributed to this. First, although he secured an academic post in 1896 at Turin University, and from 1902 taught constitutional law and the history of political thought at Bocconi University in Milan as well, he did not desert the active world of politics. After the death of Di Rudini in 1908 he became a deputy. He remained in the lower house until 1919, serving as under-secretary in the colonial office from 1914 to 1916, during Salandra's administration. In 1919 he became Senator. Although he continued to attack the actual working of democracy, by which 'any party label, conservative or clerical, radical or socialist, only serves to cover up purely personal ends', he did come to believe in the spirit which animated them—namely the ideal of 'free discussion, and the limitation of the exercise of sovereign powers' by governments. Democracy, he now argued, produced bad effects as an abstract ideal, but not if it corresponded to the 'real conditions' of a society—'According to this criteria the best electoral system would succeed in drawing on all the political values that a nation contains and uniting within an assembly the representatives of all the sentiments, and the ideas and all the interests of a people.' In other words, he saw the possibilities the system offered as an arena for different interests to meet and debate and mutually control each other.

The second factor working towards this appraisal of democracy, was his anxiety about the social divisiveness of the unions. As interest groups operating outside the parliamentary system, he believed they cut workers off from any sense of the general interest. The dependency of the modern economy on certain specialized groups gave miners or steel workers, for example, tremendous economic power, which did not necessarily operate within a legal constitutional framework. The unions acted like feudal barons, disputing the authority of government and the state. He was perceptive enough to appreciate that fascism offered no solution to this problem. Its violent methods took it outside the legal matrix, which he now regarded as vital to political liberty, whilst its proposed system of corporate representation perpetuated people's concern with the narrow economic interests of their group.

Mosca's reconciliation with representative government was nonetheless far short of wholehearted acceptance. In two parliamentary speeches on 7 and 14 May 1912 he opposed Giolitti's proposal for universal male suffrage and the further extension of the vote to women respectively. He remained firm in his belief that democracy only worked if the precondition of an independent middle-class electorate obtained. His attempt to incorporate this elitist element into the democratic system was, I shall argue, fraught with contradictions, which ultimately doomed the project to failure. Unlike contemporary theorists of democratic elitism, Mosca had the presence of mind to realize this.

Mosca's notion of 'juridical defence' offered a constitutionalist solution to the conflict of interests, but was inadequately related to their origins within society. The new edition of his work sought to remedy this defect. The central chapter here is the fourth on 'the principles and diverse tendencies which affect the formation and organisation of the political class.' Mosca began by broadening this class to include more than just those who wielded political or economic power. 'Below the ruling class', he now noted, 'there is another much more numerous, which comprises all the capacities for government of the country', and without which the upper strata could not manage. The stability of a political organism ultimately depended on the level of morality, intelligence and activity attained by this lower strata, and increased in proportion to 'the degree of pressure that the sense of the collective interests of the nation or the class, succeeds in exerting upon the selfishness of the individuals who make it up.' The qualities of this second stratum were crucial therefore, and Mosca's attention turned to the principles and tendencies regulating its recruitment.

The two tendencies were the aristocratic and the democratic, the two principles the autocratic and the liberal. The tendencies referred to the means by which the ruling class was replenished, either by hereditary transmission or from the lower classes respectively. The principles denoted the system of authority in vogue; autocratic rule being of a single person or small group for their personal ends, liberal governments sharing power with other citizens and expressing the general will of the people. Although the aristocratic and the autocratic, and the democratic and the liberal generally went together, this need not occur. China, for example, mixed autocratic rule with the democratic tendency to recruit the mandarins from the best candidates amongst the masses. The Venetian republic, on the other hand, was governed by a liberal aristocracy. The health of a society depended upon having the right balance appropriate to the prevailing social conditions. The ideal was a mixture of both tendencies and both principles, so that the political class did not atrophy, nor become unstable through a lack of continuity, and the efficacy of government was combined with a certain accountability to the interests of the people as a whole.

Having provided a sociological account of how to ensure a healthy political class, Mosca integrated it into his constitutional scheme for a perfected 'juridical defence'. He achieved this by constructing a system of indirect democracy. Rival groups for office formed in the second stratum of the political class, and competed for the vote of both their peers and members of the lower classes. Mosca argued that if the second stratum was sufficiently large, so that not everybody could hope for office, this would prevent collusions between the different factions to manipulate the electorate for their collective interest. There would remain a large number of independent voters capable of enjoining responsible government. However, a difficulty arose if universal suffrage was granted too soon, so that the ignorant masses could outvote this middle group. By appealing to the basest sentiments, the ruling groups could gain the support of the masses for their self-serving policies. Thus, whilst the democratic tendency was beneficial in rejuvenating the political class, it was disastrous if adopted integrally and the aristocratic virtues dropped altogether. Similarly the liberal principle of free debate should always be tempered by a respect for authority, and vice versa.

This conclusion placed Mosca in a quandary, since he freely admitted that the balance he desired had only obtained during the brief 'belle epoch' of the late nineteenth century. Mosca's reflections had come full circle, irrevocably wedded, throughout all their different versions, to a view of society which was anachronistic even in 1884, at the start of his career. Unlike recent advocates of democratic elitism, Mosca was aware of the interrelationship of political organization and social forces. In turn of the century Europe there was a large enfranchised middle class, whose ranks could be joined by upward social mobility from the working classes. Whether the system worked quite as well as Mosca's encomium made out may be doubted. Yet even he had to admit that 'the greatest and most magnificent of all the eras that humanity has traversed' came indisputably to an end with the First World War.

Only the confrontation with the autocratic rule of fascism finally reconciled Mosca to the representative system. Democracy at least offered a modicum of control over the government, providing 'a regime of liberty' in the only manner possible at the time 'given the extent of modern states and the complexity of their structure'. However, to be totally consistent, Mosca would have had to drop the exclusivity of the political class *vis à vis* the masses. He was unwilling to do so because he realized that only if education and increased prosperity had turned all the electorate into middle-class voters would democratic elitism be a plausible option. Its champions of the 1950s, like Dahl and Lipset, clearly believed this had occurred. A presupposition of pluralist theories, evident in the companion thesis of 'the end of ideology', consisted in an assumed general and fundamental agreement on values in society. If there were no such agreement, then the clash between diverse interests would foreclose the possibilities for conciliation and accommodation between rival groups. Pluralists claimed that the diffusion of power creates the necessity to respect the needs and demands of others. However, unless the forces involved were really equal, a highly unlikely event, arbitration between the two would always reflect the prevailing balance of power. For impartial government to result, there must exist certain ground rules and principles of justice or equity commonly accepted by all parties.

Mosca had realized early on that the capacity of a political class to govern depended upon the degree of acceptance of its political formula. His theory of 'juridical defence' was not a substitute for this notion, but built upon it. He assumed a 'collective moral sense' as the key to the successful operation of a political organism. Adopting the elitist model of democracy posed a real difficulty. Classical theorists of participatory democracy argued that it was intrinsically good, and that involvement in decision making together with others transformed the individual into a citizen. Proponents of indirect democracy, in contrast, regarded the masses as self-interested and essentially inactive. Mosca appreciated that paradoxically this system of government would not work either, unless the electorate had attained the same degree of cultural and moral awareness that classical theorists regarded as the product of participation alone. Mosca maintained that this posed an insuperable dilemma: liberalism and democracy presupposed a common cultural and moral base, yet, contrary to what Mill and Rousseau believed, they undermined the consensus necessary for them to function. Both doctrines were based on the belief that 'the good sense of the people suffices to distinguish truth from error and to bring to justice anti-social and harmful ideas.' Mosca contended that this notion was defeasible, and far from producing 'a better and more moral system of social and political organisation in the future, is certainly well suited to destroy that presently existing. The problem was that the world which had pro-, duced a healthy balance between the two principles and the two tendencies no longer existed, for the First World War had destroyed the younger generation, which would have renewed the ranks of the middle classes, and created deep social and moral divisions. He despaired of a new class arising amongst the masses, as he lacked faith in the practicality of the ideals of liberty, equality and fraternity espoused by democrats. As a result, his liberalism no longer had a foundation, and his stoic defence of it lacked conviction. Patriotism, which he feebly clutched at as the basis for a new secular religion, had already revealed its destructive side in the rampant nationalism of the First World War. Instead he feared a return to a new barbarism, 'which this time will be without God, and hence without the observation of oaths, and will have at its disposition in exchange the aeroplane, asphyxiating gasses and dynamite'. The basis of the modern state would be force alone.

The attempt to rebuild a community, based on a common faith, from the ruins of the war, was one of the prime considerations of the idealist school, and in particular the two thinkers Mosca most influenced—Croce and Gramsci. Similarly preoccupied by the existence of two classes within the new nation, they rejected positivism as inadequate for the necessary task of creating a moral framework for political action. . . .

FURTHER READING

Criticism

Bachrach, Peter. "The Precursors: Mosca and Schumpeter." In *The Theory of Democratic Elitism: A Critique*, pp. 10-25. Boston: Little, Brown and Company, 1967.
> Explores the place of Mosca and economist Joseph Schumpeter in the theoretical question of the problem of democracy, and their subsequent development of democratic elitism.

Bobbio, Norberto. "Liberalism Old and New." *Confluence* 5, (Fall 1956): 239-51.
> Examines the major figures, including Mosca, in the social and political shift away from classical European liberalism in the early twentieth century.

Hoover, Calvin B. Review of *The Ruling Class* by Gaetano Mosca. *The Journal of Political Economy* XLVII, No. 6 (December 1939): 877-79.
> Reviews Arthur Livingston's revised edition of *The Ruling Class*, noting the book's growing importance alongside events in Europe at the time, and offering high praise for Livingston's analytical introduction to the book.

Meisel, James H. *The Myth of the Ruling Class: Gaetano Mosca and the "Elite."* Ann Arbor, Mich.: The University of Michigan Press, 1958, 432 p.
> Uses Mosca's lesser-known works to follow the development of his thought.

Meisel, James H., ed. *Makers of Modern Social Science: Pareto and Mosca.* New Jersey: Prentice-Hall, Inc., 1965, 184 p.
  Collection of essays on Pareto and Mosca by major political theorists.

Wilson, Francis G. Review of *The Ruling Class* by Gaetano Mosca. *The American Political Science Review* XXXIII, No. 3 (June 1939): pp. 521-23.
  Reviews Arthur Livingston's revised edition of *The Ruling Class,* noting the book's significance in the search for an alternative to the "eighteenth-century metaphysics of democracy."

Pedro Prado

1886-1952

(Also wrote under the pseudonym Alvaro J. de Credo) Chilean poet, novelist, and essayist.

INTRODUCTION

Prado is acknowledged as one of the most important and innovative modernists in the Latin American literary tradition. He is credited with extending the boundaries of poetry and fiction in his native Chile, notably by introducing free verse there. In addition, his later experiments in the sonnet form are thought to demonstrate not only his technical expertise, but also his elegant use of both philosophical idealism and skepticism in celebration of the human spirit. In his fiction Prado is said to have argued for an elevation of hope and meaning in an age of social and philosophical crises. His novel *Alsino* (1920), in particular, has been singled out as his masterpiece for its blending of regionalism, realism, and allegory in a sustained appeal for human salvation.

Biographical Information

Prado was born on 8 October 1886 in Santiago, Chile. He received his secondary education at the Instituto Nacional in Santiago and later enrolled in the engineering school of the University of Chile. He never completed his studies at the university, but instead worked for a time as an architect; the structure that now houses the United States Consulate in Santiago was designed by Prado. In 1905 he published his first work of fiction, a short story entitled "Cuadro de estío: el inválido" under the pseudonym Alvaro J. de Credo, and several more of his stories appeared in the journal *Zig-Zag* over the course of the next few years. He published his first collection of free verse *Flores de cardo* in 1908. In early 1910 he married Adriana Jaramillo Bruce, and later that year founded the short-lived literary and intellectual journal *Revista Contemporánea*. Meanwhile Prado continued to produce more volumes of poetry, mainly free verse and prose poems, and in 1914 published his first novel *La reina de Rapa Nui*. The following year he founded a small artistic society known as Los Diez (The Ten); he also published a collection of poems and a review under the same name. The community flourished for a short time, while Prado continued with his individual pursuits, including the composition of his second and most widely acclaimed novel *Alsino*. As he continued to write Prado also became more involved in public life. Between 1921 and 1925 he served as director of the Museo del Bellas Artes in Santiago, later, in the years 1927 and 1928, he was employed as a university lecturer on aesthetics and art history. During this same period Prado acted as the Chilean diplomat to Colombia as well,

serving for approximately eighteen months. In 1933 he experienced a serious bout of illness. His declining health appears to have been an important factor in his conversion to Roman Catholicism in 1936. His literary output from this period onward was largely concentrated in his production of verse in sonnet form, notably in the collection *Esta bella ciudad envenenada* (1945). In 1949 Prado was honored with the Chilean National Prize of Literature. He died at his home in Viña del Mar on 31 January, 1952, after suffering a severe cerebral hemorrhage.

Major Works

A gifted writer in multiple genres, Prado's literary reputation rests equally between his poetry and his fiction. His early volume of poetry *Flores de cardo* represents his experimentation with free verse in a series of mostly nostalgic and romantic poems. This collection was followed by *La casa abandonada: Parábolas y pequeños ensayos* (1912), which contains both prose poems and several parables. Critics note the Prado's most enduring verse appears in his later, more philosophical sonnet collections, particularly in *Camino de las horas* (1934) and *Esta bella ciudad envenenada*. As for Prado's fiction, interest in it has generally been focused on his three novels. Though largely overshadowed by his later works, *La reina de Rapa Nui* (1914) is still considered a fictional tour de force. Set on Easter Island, Prado's first novel is made up of many stories relating to a former queen of Rapa Nui (the native name for the island) and the first-person narrative of an outside journalist covering a severe drought there. Prado infuses his story with a sense of approaching cataclysm as he details a civil war and the ultimate destruction of this mysterious civilization. Considered his finest fictional achievement, *Alsino* reflects Prado's skilled blending of social realism and mythological symbolism. The allegorical novel presents the world of an unfortunate Chilean peasant boy named Alsino who shatters his back during an attempt to fly. From the resulting hump Alsino magically sprouts wings, only to become the victim of fear, hatred, and prejudice. Critics note that the work not only contains an inquiry into the appalling living conditions endured by Chile's rural poor, but also represents a sustained examination of human alienation in its imaginative rendering of the classical Icarus myth. His final novel *Un juez rural* (1924; *Country Judge: A Novel of Chile*) was thought by some Chilean readers to be an autobiographical account of a period Prado spent as a district judge. The work is generally viewed as a critique of prejudice and injustice. Its protagonist, a judge without a law degree or any formal judicial training, uses common sense, his conscience, and a simple belief in what is just to resolve disputes, but finds himself viciously attacked for his views. Rather than being a narrow, denunciatory work, however, *Un juez rural* manifests a sense of humor and optimism.

Critical Reception

Although considered a modernist, Prado has been said to surpass much of the intellectualizing formalism of his contemporaries in works that ultimately seek to apprehend truth and find beauty. While recognition of his works has been in large part limited to the Spanish-speaking world, his influence has been considerable in Latin America, with critics noting the effects of his writings on authors of wider international reputation, such as Gabriela Mistral and Pablo Neruda. His position in the development of Latin American literature in the first half of the twentieth century is considered unique. Alexander Coleman has summarized it as follows, "No writer of his time, and possibly no writer since, at least in Chile, has more successfully combined philosophy, aesthetic good sense, fiction, and poetry."

PRINCIPAL WORKS

Flores de cardo (poetry) 1908

La casa abandonada: Parábolas y pequeños ensayos (poetry) 1912

El llamado del mundo (poetry) 1913

La reina de Rapa Nui (novel) 1914

Los Diez: El claustro, La barca (poetry) 1915

Los pájaros errantes: Poemas memores y breves divagaciones (poetry) 1915

Ensayos sobre la arquitectura y la poesía (essays) 1916

Alsino (novel) 1920

Las copas (poetry) 1921

Karez-I-Roshan [with Antonio Castro Leal] (prose) 1922

Bases para un nuevo gobierno y un nuevo parlamento (political essay) 1924

Un juez rural [*Country Judge: A Novel of Chile*] (novel) 1924

Androvar, poema dramático (poetry) 1925

Camino de las horas (poetry) 1934

Otoño en las dunas (poetry) 1940

Esta bella ciudad envenenada (poetry) 1945

No más que una rosa (poetry) 1946

Antología: Las estancias del amor (poetry) 1949

Viejos poemas inéditos (poetry) 1949

La roja torre de los Diez: Antología de Pedro Prado (poetry) 1961

El llamado del mundo . . . Flores de cardo, Karez-I-Roshan y textos inéditos (poetry and prose) 1971

Pedro Prado: Antología (poetry) 1975

Cartas a Manuel Magallanes Moure (letters) 1986

CRITICISM

G. Dundas Craig (essay date 1934)

SOURCE: "Pedro Prado," in *Modernism in Spanish-American Poetry,* University of California Press, 1934, pp. 313-5.

[*In the following essay, Craig analyzes Prado's best-known poem, "Lázaro," contrasting it with Robert Browning's treatment of the same subject.*]

Between the work of González Martínez and that of Pedro Prado there is very little resemblance. They have in common only their seriousness of purpose. González Martínez, thanks to his early devotion to the study of French and Italian models, was a master of all the arts and artifices of the Parnassian school. The very limpidity of his style is evidently the fruit of much patient labor. With Prado it is different. His writing seems more spontaneous, and it would almost seem as if he deliberately eschewed any form of ornament, and depended for his emotional effect on his subject-matter alone. Yet his comparative plainness of statement may arise from lack of imagination—an inference to some extent borne out by the general vagueness of impression produced by his *"Lázaro."* In the same way he seeks freedom from the restrictions of the conventional verse-forms by discarding rhyme and writing in free verse, or (as in *"Pájaros errantes"*) in a kind of elevated prose in which he has caught successfully the cadence of the Hebrew Psalms.

Though discarding rhyme, Prado makes free use of assonance, as in **"Las manos"**; and, as assonance is little favored in the practice of English poets, the translator is faced with an awkward choice: he must either use rhyme, and lose some of the fluidity of the original; or have recourse to blank verse, and lose some of the musical effect that Prado intended to produce. In this poem I have used rhyme, though I feel that the rhymes are rather too obtrusive.

"Lázaro" is generally regarded as Prado's best poem. It describes Lazarus rising or just risen from the tomb, and relating to the bystanders his experience of death and the transformation through which he was passing when recalled to life by the command, "Lazarus, come forth!" This poem, read alongside of Browning's *"Epistle, Containing the Strange Medical Experience of Karshish, the Arab Physician,"* supplies a measure by which we may compare a highly reputed Spanish-American poet with an acknowledged master in English poetry. Such a comparison reveals striking differences, not only in the outlook of the two poets on life and death, and on the life beyond death, but also in their powers of presentation, description, and characterization. For Prado, body and soul are one, and death is a change of state in which the elements of the body and the soul alike are transformed, and return to life in the sparkle of the rivers and the perfume of the flowers. There seems to be some inconsistency in the

poem; for, though Lazarus declares that an impenetrable wall separates the states of life and death, and that death blots out the memory of life, as life the memory of death (that is, of our existence before birth), yet he is able to give a vivid account of his sensations while lying dead in the grave. In contrast with this materialistic view, Browning lays emphasis not on the purely physical changes, which indeed he hardly mentions, but on the deeper sense of moral and spiritual values attained by one who has passed within the veil.

Equally striking is the difference in descriptive power. There is nothing in Prado to compare with Browning's

> A black lynx snarled and pricked a tufted ear,
> Lust of my blood inflamed his yellow balls;
> I cried, and threw my staff, and he was gone;

nor with his description of the rocky pass from which the physician looked down on Bethany:

> I crossed a ridge of short, sharp, broken hills,
> Like an old lion's cheek tooth. . . .

Compared with these, Prado's references to the "ardiente paisaje de Judea," or to the "suaves colinas de Bethania" over which Lazarus rambled as a boy, are pale and ineffective. So also, the writer of the epistle in Browning's poem is a vivid personality, with a keen eye for everything that might interest his correspondent. In *"Lázaro,"* the speaker is a vague figure, apparently one of the spectators. He tells us, *"Quedamos* con la luminosa y húmeda mirada de los vivos"; but toward the end of the poem we read:

> Entre las yerbas, Marta y María yacían agotadas;
> estremecidos los Apóstoles veían llorar a los
> judíos. . . .

Evidently, therefore, the speaker was not one of these. Who then was the speaker? This may seem rather niggling criticism, but it points to an important difference between the work of a conscientious artisan and that of a poetical genius, in whose imagination the whole poetic conception rises complete and finished at the touch of a single suggestion from the outside.

We find the same difference between Browning's Lazarus, who is a very human figure, going about his daily work though haunted by the vision of splendor he has seen, and Prado's Lazarus, who is little more than a phantom, a mouthpiece for the materialistic monism of the poet.

Arturo Torres-Ríoseco (essay date 1942)

SOURCE: "The Spanish American Novel," in *The Epic of Latin American Literature,* Oxford University Press, 1942, pp. 204-6.

[*In the following essay, Torres-Ríoseco discusses Prado's place among Spanish-American novelists.*]

[Pedro Prado], . . . who is also a poet of distinction, has passed most of his days in the peaceful family life of his spacious country villa on the outskirts of Santiago. Here, from 1915 to 1916, he presided over the celebrated group of 'The Ten,' an association of painters, poets, musicians, and architects. Chile's leading stylist, if not the leading stylist of all Spanish America, Prado is known for his essays, parables, and poems in prose, but especially for his novels, of which the most celebrated are *A Rural Judge* (1924) and *Alsino* (1920), and for his prose tragedy *Androvar* (1925). These books are studies of remarkable characters, but their purpose is less psychological than philosophical, and they stamp Prado as a philosophical novelist of great distinction—a title that can be claimed by few other writers of Spanish America.

In Prado's work one hardly knows which to admire more, the moral elevation of the thought or the limpid perfection of the style. His writing frequently reaches the level of poetry, yet at the same time he is fond of realistic bits of description, which give a strangely Chilean atmosphere to his symbolic stories. In *Alsino,* for instance, he describes a farmhouse kitchen, sooty and dim with the vapor of cooking food, and smelling of the garlic and onions hung from the rafters.

Yet it is never the background or even the characters themselves that preoccupies Prado; his chief concern is always with ideas and the building of a personal philosophy. Thus in *A Rural Judge,* Prado analyzes the dilemma that confronted him as a district judge who tried to administer justice by the dictates of his conscience. The judge's decisions are shown as clashing with the rigid legal code; his moral interpretations of justice are wasted on rascals and rogues; he finds it impossible to do individual justice, for if you punish a man for a crime, you punish at the same time his mother, his wife, and his children; to be just, he feels that he should reward good at the same time that he punishes evil. Finally, unable to satisfy his own conscience, he resigns. The problem here is the tantalizing one of human limitations, which Prado has explored still further in *Androvar.* In a strange combination of fancy and reality, he has created the parable of the master Androvar, his wife, and his disciple Gadel—an extraordinary triangle, in which three souls are supernaturally fused and penetrate the mysteries of death itself.

Prado's masterpiece is *Alsino,* which some critics have classified as a fairy tale, some as an allegory, and some as a work of transcendent symbolism. *Alsino* is the simple saga of a Chilean country boy who longs to fly, and by his efforts to do so falls from a tree and becomes a hunchback. In time, however, his hump grows into a real pair of wings; Alsino flies under the blue sky, over valleys, mountains, and rivers; he descends to earth and comes into contact with ugly and cruel reality; he is mistaken for an angel, he is arrested, his wings are clipped and he is exhibited in a cage, and finally he is blinded by a girl who tries to win his love. He starts to fly once more, only to fall wounded into the bottom of a ravine, where he hears the voices of the springs and the trees; the fox comes to lick his wounds, the wild creatures bring flowers, fruits, and meat, and the wild doves lull him to sleep. In his death agony, Alsino feels one last impulse to fly; at a terrific altitude, he folds his wings and his body ignites:

> A league before reaching the earth, there remained of Alsino only impalpable ashes. Lacking the weight to continue falling, they floated like snowflakes till dawn. The breezes at daybreak set about scattering them, and at length they fell—but the slightest wind blew them upwards again. And so, dispersed and imponderable, they have remained for a long time now, and will continue to remain, floating like mist in the invisible air.

The symbolism of *Alsino* is clear: the little hunchback with wings is man, longing to soar above the ugliness of life into the regions of the infinite, and yet fatally bound to earth.

Alsino is unquestionably the highest expression of the psychological and philosophical trend in Spanish American fiction—a trend which, next to the rural novel, has attracted the greatest number of writers. . . .

Arturo Torres-Ríoseco (essay date 1968)

SOURCE: A foreword to *Country Judge: A Novel of Chile* by Pedro Prado, translated by Lesley Byrd Simpson, University of California Press, 1968, pp. v-vii.

[*In the following essay, Torres-Ríoseco provides a brief overview of* Country Judge.]

Country Judge (*Un Juez Rural*) is an autobiographical novel. As the story opens we find the protagonist Solaguren (Prado) surrounded by his family, just as I described the author's home in 1932:

> Pedro Prado, with his wife and children, lives in a large country house in a remote suburb of Santiago near the railroad station. It is a peaceful house: many trees, fountains, a tower, old storerooms—a house that for more than 250 years has belonged to the family. The rooms are spacious and tastefully furnished with old pieces, modern paintings, rare and curious books, books everywhere. The house has many rooms, all of which have windows facing the Andes, to admit the mountain air and the light the poet loves. The fountains murmur, a few leaves fall, and the silence is broken only by the brief and nervous song of a *diuca*. In the evening the poet and his friends stroll in the garden to watch the moon rising over the wall of the patio, its light shining through the leaves of the grape arbor. (*Novelistas contemporáneos de América,* 1939).

It was in this house that Prado wrote *Country Judge,* which, despite its modest length, is a significant landmark in the literary history of Chile. Solaguren, like Prado an architect, is a melancholy and thoughtful man.

He feels himself smothered in the cotton-wool of his too-peaceful life, and to escape it he accepts a judgeship in a rural suburb of Santiago. An equally compelling motive is a romantic urge to put into practice his own notions of justice, or, perhaps, of esthetics. Like Sancho Panza on his Island, Solaguren knows nothing of the law, but, again like Sancho, his sense of fitness and his humor lead him to pronounce sentences which appeal, not only to his pedantic little Secretary (who, incidentally, is one of the most incisively drawn figures of the book), but certainly also to the reader.

Prado squeezes the last bit of juice out of the courtroom scenes. The odd assortment of litigants and their foolish cases gives him a broad canvas on which to depict humanity in all its depravity and occasional nobility. Many of the scenes are hilarious, others are poignant, and all are drawn with sharpness and economy. The dialogue is equally spare and equally effective. In a word, Prado is a writer.

As time goes on, Solaguren makes the inevitable discovery that the administration of justice is a very complex matter and that it is quite beyond his power to interpret and solve the human problems brought to his court. Indeed, he has been assailed by doubts since the first day of his tenure. He is, moreover, depressed by the general sordidness and ugliness of the courtroom. Luckily, he has a friend, the painter Mozarena, with whom he escapes to the country in between sessions. These excursions supply a kind of counterpoint to the main theme. The two friends, the painter and the poet-philosopher, see the landscape in its great beauty, its delicacy, its rawness, and its macabre contrasts. And they talk. They talk about everything and they talk exceedingly well, in the Cervantean tradition. Nothing is too trivial, nothing too vast, for their exploring minds. But they solve none of Solaguren's problems, and one gets the feeling that they are thrashing about in a vacuum.

The judge returns to his courtroom in a deepening melancholy. He sees himself, not as a judge, but as an arm of the police, his sole function being to mete out punishment. This is so at odds with his original purpose that he resigns his post in a letter to the governor, in which he examines the nature of justice itself and admits his defeat. This letter (in Chapter 19) is the high point of the book and the best of Prado's writing.

After his crisis Solaguren slips off into a kind of dream world, a flight into unreality. He runs away to the seaside, where he is driven frantic by the vapid life of the vacationers. Two months of this, and he escapes again, this time back to the city. Needless to say, he finds no peace there either. On the contrary, its dust, dirt, and hurly-burly are as unendurable as life at the beach. Even his friend Mozarena deserts him and retreats into domesticity. So the judge makes a final flight to his empty house and utter loneliness.

Donald A. Yates (essay date 1969)

SOURCE: A review of *Country Judge,* in *Hispania,* Vol. 52, 1969, pp. 163-4.

[*In the following essay, Yates reviews a translation of* Country Judge, *finding the novel "sincere" and "thought-provoking," but "not a great or especially significant novel."*]

In *Country Judge,* a short, episodic novel first published in 1924, Chilean writer Pedro Prado (1886-1952) endowed his title character with several of his own characteristic attitudes: a deep love for Santiago and its environs, a longing for order and justice in the affairs of men, and a quiet resignation to loneliness and melancholy. In the Foreword to this new translation of the work, critic Arturo Torres-Ríoseco, who knew the author in Chile, states that the novel is frankly autobiographical. So it appears to be.

Solaguren, a bored, restless, reflective architect, is the Prado-like protagonist who decides at the story's beginning to accept a judgeship in a suburban district of Santiago. Perhaps foremost among his reasons for taking on the job, for which he has no formal training, is his ambition to put into practice his personal concepts of wisdom and fairness. (His insights into the task of dispensing justice have come to him over the years solely as the fruit of his meditative readings in philosophy.) What Solaguren undertakes to do, in effect, is to project into the questions of conflict arising in his rural jurisdiction a type of ideal and perfect order that he has not been able to impose on his own life. For this reason, and for others easily imagined, the new judge is destined eventually to come face to face with disillusionment and defeat. *Country Judge* is, quite simply, the brief and poetic account of how all this comes about.

When, after two months of instructive and saddening experience with the humble people and perplexing human problems paraded before him, Solaguren finally feels compelled to submit his letter of resignation, he pens a pair of sentences that contain true wisdom and constitute the only moral one might draw from this tale of frustrated idealism. He writes: "Everything I have done leaves me with a bitter taste in my mouth and a contempt for myself. Such is the penalty incurred by one who has not mastered his subject by study, or who does not remain in blissful ignorance by avoiding it altogether."

Pedro Prado began his career in the early years of this century as a poet and only later shifted to prose. However, the rigor of his poetic apprenticeship obviously carried over into his narrative works, and in the best of these he produced memorable cameos of essentially poetic prose. Many sections of *Country Judge* merit this designation. An example is the chapter entitled "The Cabbie," describing a country outing enjoyed by Solaguren in the company of his grand painter friend Mozarena, which rivals the delicate pastoral charm achieved by the Spanish Nobel Prize-winning poet Juan Ramón Jiménez in his celebrated volume of sketches, *Platero and I.*

Country Judge is not a great or especially significant novel, but it is a sincere, thought-provoking, and readable one. The sympathetic translation by Lesley Byrd Simpson is intelligently executed and has very few flaws. However, somewhere we should have a word of explanation of how and why the original novel has been "edited."

John R. Kelly (essay date 1974)

SOURCE: "Prado, the Novelist and Short Story Writer," in *Pedro Prado,* Twayne Publishers, Inc., 1974, pp. 73-114.

[*In the following essay, Kelly offers an extensive survey of Prado's fiction.*]

Prado's fame as one of Latin America's principal novelists rests solidly on three very different types of novels. His first endeavor, *La reina de Rapa Nui (The Queen of Rapa Nui)*, published in 1914, displays the persistence of Modernism in his writing. *Alsino,* his longest, most ambitious novel revealed a symbiosis of *Criollismo* with Modernism, of lyric poetry with the allegorical novel. It appeared in 1920. His last novel, *Un juez rural (Country Judge)*, a thinly veiled autobiography, was published in 1924.

Prado's short stories form parentheses around his major prose and poetic works. They have been totally ignored by literary critics and historians. **"Cuadro de estío: el inválido"** (**"A Summer Picture: The Invalid"**), published in 1905, represented his first attempt at writing. The following year brought two more short stories, **"La reina maga"** (**"The Wise Woman"**) and **"Cuando se es pobre"** (**"When You Are Poor"**) to the pages of the new *Zig-Zag* magazine. In 1907 the twenty-one-year-old Prado wrote **"Luz lunar"** (**"Moonlight"**) for the readers of *Zig-Zag.* All of these stories reflect the uncertain literary direction of their young author. His last two stories, **"La risa en el desierto"** (**"The Laugh in the Desert"**) and **"El pueblo muerto"** (**"Ghost Town"**), both originally appearing in 1925, continue the psychological and realist vein of his last novel, *Country Judge,* and reveal Prado's firm control of the genre.

I *LA REINA DE RAPA NUI (THE QUEEN OF RAPA NUI)*

Prado's plot, simple and linear, concerns the youthful adventures of a man whose name he does not want to reveal: "I do not wish to give the name of my friend because he could be a relative of the reader and perhaps his adventures and his attitude and way of thinking may bother you. . . . His family was and is related to almost every Chilean family, therefore I believe it prudent to keep silent." (No quiero dar el nombre de mi amigo, porque puede ser pariente del lector, y quizás sus aventuras y su modo de ser y de pensar le molesten. . . . Su familia estaba y está relacionada con casi todas las familias chilenas; por esto creo prudente callar). After his friend's death, Prado learns of the adventures on Easter Island (Chile's remote, exotic, and only colony) in an old manuscript. As a young journalist, his friend departed from Valparaíso for the oceanic possession ostensibly to do a feature on it. He records his impressions of the island and its inhabitants—the history, customs, and art of Rapa Nui—in thirteen chapters. The young man meets the native queen and soon has a love affair with her. A complication arises in chapter five which causes the initial signs of impending tragedy to emerge. The island is completely dependent upon rainfall for its water supply, but no rains are predicted to fall in the appropriate season. The forecasted drought becomes a fact, and the end result is the queen's death. Somewhat anti-climactically, the desired rains begin shortly after the queen's demise. The young man, matured by his experiences on the island, returns "to [the] sad and tortured peoples" of civilization. At the novel's conclusion, we see him sailing away but looking nostalgically back at the island. He recalls in the final paragraph the happy life of its inhabitants, who live "far from the fever and ambition of modern men," whose happy and wise existence was led "among harvest and love feasts, and only subject to the rains from heaven."

The novel's episodic structure depends for its unity on the characterization of the unnamed narrator and the love affair with the queen. Prado, in an explanatory prologue, first describes his close, lifelong friendship with this "strange and solitary man" whom we will call "X" and next how he learned of his friend's voyage to Easter Island. Prado explains the circumstances surrounding the discovery of an old, yellow manuscript, which "back at my home, I could see . . . was incomplete and full of erasures and corrections. I have carefully done it over. The title, *The Queen of Rapa Nui,* is of my invention. The scenes which he recounts waver, it seems to me, between 1870 and 1874, give or take a year." (De vuelta en mi casa, pude ver que estaba incompleto y lleno de borraduras y tachas. Con gran cuidado lo he rehecho. El título, *La Reina de Rapa Nui,* es de mi invención. Las escenas que relata me parece que fluctúan entre los años 70 y 74 poco más o menos). This time-honored structural device, the manuscript, permits a smooth transition in narrative point of view from Prado to X in the remainder of the novel or, in his words, in the text of the "done over" manuscript. The change from viewing X as he to I more forcefully convinces us of X's existence and reliability.

In reality Prado only develops this single character, X. We see him first as a mature man through Prado's eyes in the prologue. We learn that he was a vagabond type who over the years had been a sailor, journalist, businessman, military man, smuggler, farmer, and judge, among other things. At times, in fact, Prado's mysterious character bears an uncanny resemblance to himself. In a statement that seems to come directly from the *Ensayos . . . ,* X declares, "My reading is not a passive act. I do not read for knowledge; I read in order to think." (Mi lectura no es un acto pasivo. No lo leo para saber; leo para pensar). His consciousness, distracted by the first lines, begins to follow thoughts that have their origin in those lines. He too forms philosophical maxims based on ob-

servation and meditation. While lunching with a painter on his farm, he explains that for him, "painters are the true philosophers. They love what they see, reality first, and although it may not be truth, everything else is still more vague and uncertain." (Los pintores son los verdaderos filósofos. Aman lo que ven, la realidad primera, y aunque ni ella sea verdad, todo lo otro es aún más vago y más incierto). Like the principal character of the last novel, *Un juez rural* (*A Country Judge*), he was the judge of his local district who soon had to resign, "because he never sentenced anyone and he had a boundless taste for the picturesque." (porque las sentencias no las dictaba nunca y tenía una afición desmedida por lo pintoresco). One of X's sentiments anticipates a prose poem from *Los pájaros errantes,* **"The Nameless Wish"** (**"El deseo sin nombre"**). X explains that he has a desire or a wish, "that I do not know how to define and I do not know what it is seeking and what it wants, but it is eating away at me." (que no sé definir y que ignoro lo que busca y lo que quiere, me va taladrando como una carcoma). This same vague desire is amplified and poeticized in **"El deseo sin nombre,"** where the poet writes: "Once more here I am, stopping and asking myself what do I want? Because there is a constant desire that endures after our easy wishes have been fulfilled; because there is an endless yearning that surpasses any vain ambition. Nameless wish, formless object, limitless finality, you take root like a monstrous tree that grows and grows ceaselessly, and dies without ever blossoming." (Una vez más, hé aquí que me detengo y me pregunto ¿qué deseo? Porque hay un deseo constante que perdura, cumplidos nuestros fáciles anhelos; porque hay una ansia infinita que supera a toda vana ambición. Deseo sin nombre, objeto sin forma, finalidad sin límites, tú arraigas como un árbol monstruoso que crece y crece sin cesar, y muere sin que alcance a florecer jamás).

It is perhaps one of the flaws of the novel that we learn more about X from Prado in the prologue than we do from X's own words in the manuscript. X records his reactions to the climate, the new experiences, and the landscape surrounding him, but he does not reveal anything significant about himself nor his relation to the other secondary characters. What X describes seems convincing, but he fails to grow in roundness. His few thoughts and feelings are interspersed between long descriptive passages.

The other characters delineated in the book are: Coemata Etú, the queen; Bornier, the French exploiter; Coturhe Uruiri, the island's sage; and Adams, the wandering Dane and subordinate of Bornier. Coemata Etú's existence is vital to the progression of the plot, but to say that she is developed as a character is false. We know she is beautiful: "Her eyes were large, dark, and moist; her face smooth and tranquil; her well-formed nose, opened its sensual nostrils to the sea breeze, and her large mouth of fine, caressing lips, her white teeth . . . ; her yellowish hair was lightly tanned, like the skin of her long and flexible neck; . . . her muscles fine and her skin smooth and velvety. . . ." (Sus ojos eran grandes, negros, y húmedos; su frente, tersa y tranquila; la nariz perfilada, abría las ventanillas sensuales a la brisa marina, y en la boca grande, de labios finos y acariciadores, los dientes blancos . . . ; su cabellera amarillenta era ligeramente tostada, como la piel de su pescuezo largo y flexible; . . . los músculos finos y la carne suave y aterciopelada . . .). Coemata Etú is also inquisitive and intelligent: "curious about customs we call civilized, she had opinions so original that they made me admire her tranquil and free intelligence." (Curiosa de las costumbres, que llamamos civilizadas, tenía sobre ellas juicios tan originales que me hacían admirar su inteligencia tranquila). Unfortunately very little of this intelligence is conveyed in the several dialogues she has with X. She seems only to link the various episodes together. X becomes infatuated with her after the first meeting, but as the novel progresses he becomes very physically attracted to her. In a scene that consummates their nascent love affair, we see the couple climbing over sharp rocks. The queen hurts her ankles and X sits her upon his lap, "with a handkerchief I soaked up the blood. Her weight was no greater than an armful of flowers, and the warmth of her body going through her tunic and my clothes disturbed my senses. Crimson dragonflies flew in pairs playing at love. Silently we contemplated their undulating course. From time to time the ardent buzz of their wings reached us." (Con un pañuelo enjugaba su sangre. Su peso no era mayor que el de una brazada de flores, y el calor de su cuerpo, al atravesar su túnica y mis ropas, turbaba mis sentidos. Libélulas encarnadas volaban de a pares jugando al amor. Silenciosos contemplamos sus giros ondulados. De vez en vez llegaba hasta nosotros el zumbido ardoroso de sus alas). Prado delicately implies the logical sexual progression in their relationship by panning to the flight of the dragonflies. No genuine love is ever expressed by X, only erotic sensualism; and his expression of grief at her death is more perfunctory than heartfelt.

Bornier, Adams, and Coturhe Uruiri are very minor characters, but contribute to the plot's movement. Bornier actually did exist and his real, historical role as villain and exploiter is very similar to the one he plays in the novel. Adams serves as a necessary vehicle of information and communication. He recounts the island's past and X reveals his thoughts and feelings to this fellow civilized man. Coturhe Uruiri, the product of Prado's imagination, augurs the tragic drought which indirectly causes the queen's death and resolves the novel's conclusion for Prado. Coturhe also illustrates certain of the exotic beliefs and practices of the Easter Islanders. He tells X of the annual competition where the young men swim to a neighboring islet to find and return safely with the egg of the shearwater. The one who survives the strong currents and dangerous surf rules as chief, subservient only to the king. According to Coturhe, war is good and comes in the springtime. X explains that spring is the season of love in his land, Coturhe replies that "Love and war are brothers; but love on Rapa-Nui is sad" (El amor y la guerra son hermanos; pero el amor en Rapa-Nui es triste). He clarifies the last comment by explaining the

epidemic of venereal disease that once assailed the island. Sex brought death, and "fear spread and the men feared the women, and the women feared the men, and since they all wanted each other, Rapa-Nui went mad because it could not love without death." (Cundió el miedo y los hombres temían a las mujeres y las mujeres temían a los hombres, y como todos se deseaban, Rapa-Nui se volvió loca de no poder amar sin caer en la muerte). The wise man stoically concludes that ultimately love and sickness will not matter since they are all going to die soon of thirst. Coturhe's ominous prophecy closes the chapter, and the next opens with the news of his suicide, "a frequent thing among the islanders." X witnesses the incredible joy, singing, and celebration surrounding the suicide. Those who take their own lives, he learns, are not to be mourned because it was their decision and they should be respected for it. Those who die naturally and unwillingly, of course, deserve weeping, sorrow, and mourning because death was imposed on them.

The natives prepare for a feast; courtesans and other women appear near the funeral bier; and X is soon joined by Coemata Etú. The funeral is converted into a love feast. The queen draws X into an embrace and the sons of Coturhe amuse the women and soon the other men form a circle around them. "Little by little the dancing stopped and then only ardent words of love could be heard." (Cesaron poco a poco los bailes y luego sólo se oyeron las palabras ardientes del amor). Coturhe becomes twice identified with sex and death.

Adams sheds additional light on the natives' penchant for suicide: "they are not as savage as those who are ignorant of their ways believe. They have a very developed nervousness and many times their desperation is born from reasons that I have been unable to comprehend. Quite to the contrary of primitive peoples, they give the impression of a simple race, but worn smooth by the centuries." (no son tan salvajes como los ignorantes los creen. Tienen una nerviosidad muy desarrollada y muchas veces la desesperación nace por motivos que yo no he podido comprender. Muy por el contrario de un pueblo primitivo, da la impresión de una raza sencilla, pero trabajada por los siglos). Adams also explains the natives' peculiar lack of religion. Their ancient priesthood died without leaving any initiates and soon they found no need for a religion. Attempts at conversion by French missionaries were only partially successful. Adams provides the necessary balance between the civilized man and the native. He can furnish X the opportunity for a degree of objectivity. X through Adams, is permitted to have a wider view of things and to know facts that would not normally be accessible to him through the natives.

Prado's most successful accomplishment in the novel is the establishment of a credible setting. Setting provides Prado with ample opportunity to display his imaginative virtuosity as a creator of verbal landscapes, vague sensations, and philosophical musings. The precise descriptions of the exotic natives, geography, legends, and customs led more than one reader to believe that Prado based his novel on an actual visit to the island. Gabriela Mistral, commenting on the book's merit, honestly thought that the novel was the direct result of Prado's extensive travels. The real origin of Prado's inspiration and information came from the pages of so pedestrian a source as the *Anuario hidrográfico chileno (Chilean Hydrographic Annual)*.

Prado, in the prologue, first establishes a very Chilean setting. He describes a declining but picturesque estate where X lives out his remaining years. Everything described is recognizable and easily assimilated by his Chilean readers. He makes a smooth transition from this familiar setting to the more exotic, island one in the opening paragraphs of the manuscript. Prado beautifully and effectively communicates Chile's intimate bonds with the sea when X writes:

> It has been said that Chile is an island, and I believe that there are few islands as insular as our territory. In reality, we only possess one long beach. The Andes push us to the sea, and if we contemplate them at a distance, blue and snowcrested, they seem to us a giant wave flourishing its foam; and if we climb them we see, on clear days, an immense ocean.
>
> In the southern region, the waters move inland into the narrow valleys and they form millions of islands. I see in it an invitation, and I see in the beautiful archipelagos little squadrons of ships making for the sea.
>
> Se ha dicho que Chile es una isla, y yo creo que hay pocas islas tan islas como nuestro territorio. En realidad, sólo poseemos una extensa playa. La cordillera nos empuja al mar, y si la contemplamos a la distancia, azul y empenachada de nieve, nos parece una ola gigante floreciendo su espuma; y si trepamos por ella vemos, en los días claros, un océano inmenso.
>
> En la región austral las aguas se internan en los valles estrechos y forman millones de islas. Veo en ello una invitación, y veo en los hermosos archipiélagos escuadrillas de naves haciéndose a la mar.

He continues to demonstrate the influence of the sea on Chile and on himself. The sea is a constant invitation to escape and he, in the guise of X, follows adventure. X describes the enigmatic statues of Easter Island, the isolated inhabitants, the frequently tragic events as retold to him by his various informants. Prado exhibits a painterly style in his lyrical descriptions of the sea, the mountains, and the landscapes of the island. His intention to paint with words is implicit in the novel's dedication to the Impressionist painter Juan Francisco González, although Impressionist (of the pictorial type) is not an inappropriate label for the contents of this work.

The novel does not neatly fit into Modernist escapism. A nagging sensation that true contentment or happiness is unattainable pervades the book from prologue to penultimate chapter. Easter Island is far from idyllic. Man's folly, cruelty, and selfishness exist everywhere. Prado's melancholy theme on man's loss of innocence may have some relationship to the gathering war clouds in Europe and the deplorable social conditions in Chile. The book, however, stands as a warning that even a remote, uncivilized island is not without its natural and manmade perils. Prado destroys the impact of his message by his concluding paragraph cited earlier. He indulges in a sentimental and Romantic nostalgia for the primitive and the past when he compares the "happy" islanders to the "sad and tortured peoples" of civilization. His islanders, albeit victims of the evils of European exploitation and diseases which are alien to their natural environment, lie, steal, and make war. They exhibit no moral, artistic, or material development. Their art, for example, simply repeats something they have ceased to understand. It has descended from art to handicraft. The island's magnificent and mysterious statues and megalithic temples were the products of another, long-disappeared race and have no significance for them.

The novel, in spite of the last chapter, has more virtues than defects. The apparent Modernist exterior should not obfuscate Prado's comment on human conduct and society. *La Reina de Rapa-Nui* is successful fiction. It contains no stylistic or structural innovations nor experimental language, but it does attract and maintain the reader's interest. Prado, nevertheless, has much to learn in the art of fiction and he will not attempt to publish his next novel, *Alsino,* until six years have passed.

II *ALSINO*

Prado's international reputation as a novelist stems from the enthusiastic reception accorded to his allegorical novel, *Alsino.* Criticism of the work from its first edition up to the fifties, mostly Chilean, has tended toward hyperbole. Arturo Torres Rioseco was one of the first critics to discover and discuss Prado, in 1942 proclaiming *Alsino* one of South America's greatest novels. This work generally is considered Prado's masterpiece, and most criticism concentrates on it.

The genesis of the novel seems to be specified in a letter of Prado dated 1915, to a friend: "For the moment, all my concerns and energies are attached to a novel that I have been working on for three years. If it responds to my enthusiasm, it will be the best thing that I have done up to now." It is not inconceivable that Prado devoted from five to eight years to the elaboration of *Alsino.* The direct inspiration for the work seems to have been provided initially by his own children, who were querying him about a hunchback boy they had seen. In response to their insistent interrogation, Prado fabricated a story on the spot. The dedication to *Alsino* seems to corroborate this anecdote.

Alsino, divided into forty-one chapters and grouped into five general sections, recounts the adventures of the eponymous adolescent hero. The five subdivisions could be titled the fall, flight, song, captivity, and the second fall. These headings suggest the tone or the content of each section. In the first section, Alsino, the older son of two alcoholic peasants, passionately wants to fly. Alsino's grandmother succinctly explains his exacerbated nature in deterministic terms: "Since you are the son of drunks, you are sad, Alsino, and since you are sad, you think. . . . Your brother sleeps off your parents' drunkenness. When they begat you, they were at the beginning of that bad life and perhaps they might still have the strength to be ashamed. I remember that between them they used to blame each other and their anger was due to desperation. They wanted to be something other than what they came to be. You inherited their sadness and their desire to get away and to change. Don't you, Alsino, continually want to be like the birds? Poor child, in your mother's bad milk you drank the visions of her drunkenness." (¡Como hijo de borracho eres triste, Alsino, y como eres triste, te quedas pensando! Tu hermano duerme las borracheras de sus padres. Cuando a ti te engendraron, ellos estaban en el comienzo de esa mala vida y quizá todavía tuvieran fuerzas de vergüenza. Recuerdo que entre sí se culpaban, y la ira de ellos era por desesperación. Querían ser otros de los que iban siendo. Tú heredaste su tristeza y los deseos de salir y de cambiar. ¿No andas, tú, Alsino queriendo ser como los pájaros? ¡Pobre niño; bebiste en la mala leche de tu madre las visiones de sus borracheras!)

This passage, besides providing the necessary details of Alsino's humble origins, is noteworthy for illustrating the serious problem of alcoholism among the lowest classes in Chile. Alcoholism, symptomatic of the severe social injustice, not only dulls the pains of the poorest, the *rotos,* but keeps them, conveniently for the elites, in their miserable condition. This section becomes one of the few, although quite attenuated, overt social criticisms made by Prado.

The idea of being able to fly like the birds, subject to his own whims, obsesses his sleeping and waking hours. In recurring dreams he is able to soar and glide, understanding the secrets of human flight. One day, after several previous unsuccessful attempts, he tries to fly but falls, injuring his back. For some time he remains paralyzed. Due to the ministrations of his grandmother he is able to walk again, but not without the outward sign of his failure, a large hump. Soon after Alsino's recovery from his accident, he flees from his increasingly unbearable existence.

In the second section Alsino passes through several experiences, but the most important one is his first successful flight. The hunchback in Latin America is both a source of derision and of supposed good luck (if one rubs the deformed back). It is during an incident of goading and jeering that the frustrated Alsino, trying desperately to flee his tormentors, sheds his clothing, and in halting motions, begins actually to fly. At first he runs in extended jumps; and then, to the shock and bewilderment of his antagonists, he climbs in an amazing ascent into the sky.

Alsino's joys, adventures, and closeness to nature are given lyrical vent through the third section. Alsino is twice mistaken for an angel. The first time, early in the section, an old hermit takes him to be the answer to his prayers. The second occasion, at the end of this section, Alsino's aged and dying grandmother believes Alsino has come for her in order to lead her to heaven. Between these two incidents, Alsino sings the glories of flight, song, and Chilean nature. He also rapes a young country girl "in the silent summer," an incident contrived to convince us of his human tendencies toward lust and passion.

The fourth part of the book narrates his capture and confinement on a large Chilean *fundo* (estate). The existence of this bird-man creates awe and fear in the superstitious country people who are so well portrayed in these chapters. But his captor, Don Javier, views Alsino as a possible business venture which could save him from pressing financial reverses; and his daughter Abigail at first shows curious affection and then genuine love for this fantastic being. He is content to stay until Abigail dies from a long unspecified illness, after which he flees. Abigail's love made Alsino like other men. Alsino, weeping at her bedside, cries out in anguish "Wretched me! Not only others took me for a being alien to them; I too felt that way! Only when love came, did I know I was like everyone else . . . !" (¡Miserable de mí! ¡No sólo los demás me tuvieron por extraño a ellos; yo, también, así lo sentía! ¡Sólo cuando el amor llegó, supe que era igual a todos . . . !).

Overcome by grief for the loss of Abigail, Alsino escapes from his captors and hides in the neighboring mountains in the fifth and final section. There he lives with a family of an ailing father, his two daughters, and young son, Cotoipa. Rosa, the younger daughter, falls in love with Alsino, but her love is not reciprocated. Rosa seeks a love philter from the local healer. This woman, already jealous of Alsino's own healing powers, decides to destroy his influence in this area. She gives the unsuspecting girl a liquid which she guarantees will make Alsino "follow her everywhere like a dog." The old woman instructs the girl in the proper use, pouring the liquid "into both eyes at the same time." Alsino, asleep, becomes the victim of love and jealously. The philter blinds him forever.

Alsino's earlier melancholy is exacerbated now by the blindness and helplessness. He seems only to exist, not to live. His blindness permits him oracular, apocalyptic visions. His fame grows and he is sought out by pilgrims seeking cures for themselves or their loved ones. One day, in the company of Cotoipa, he realizes or senses that his power of flight has returned, but he needs eyes to guide his take-off. He convinces the small boy to help him, but the child becomes frightened when, indeed, Alsino ascends higher and higher. Alsino, struggling with the boy, loses control and both fall to the ground. Cotoipa escapes raving; Alsino lies bleeding and unconscious. Nature's secret voices come to his aid: "'Stretch your arm out, I am near you. Wash your wounds.' It was the birds, the trees, and a brook that spoke like that to him." ("Estira tu brazo, estoy cerca de ti. Lava tus heridas." Eran los pájaros, los árboles, y una vertiente los que así hablaban). Even the fox at night "silently approached Alsino and carefully began to lick his leg and side wounds." (Silencioso se acercó a Alsino, y púsose a lamer, cuidadosamente, las heridas de la pierna y el costado).

The reflections of Alsino on his plight and his past reveal new self-knowledge and a discovery of God. His human limitations nevertheless overwhelm him, and his condition worsens. Deliriously he flies upward into the highest atmosphere. We see him "blind and feverish, climbing straight up into the high, black night, moving his enormous wings in a powerful and tragic flight." (ciego, y febril, recto hacia la alta noche negra, asciende agitando sus alas enormes en un vuelo poderoso y trágico). Delirium, dream, and lucidity alternate. Alsino, attempting to awaken from his nightmare, clutches his wings with his arms and "suddenly he falls with frightening speed"; and then "before the sense of reality returns to him, the contact of his body with the increasingly denser air, begins by igniting his wings, and rapidly, like a vertigo, the fire seizes him and consumes him." (Antes de que a él vuelva el sentido de la realidad, el roce de su cuerpo con la atmósfera, cada vez más densa, comienza por encender sus alas y, rápido, como un vértigo, el fuego se apodera de él y lo consume). Only Alsino's ashes filter down to earth, and these become "fused forever with the invisible, wandering air." (para siempre, fundidas en el aire invisible y vagabundo).

Setting predominates over plot and character throughout the pages of the novel. *Alsino*'s structure is mainly a pretext to entone the beauties of the sea, the Andes, the stars, and the landscape. Many whole chapters and portions of most of the others seem extensions of Prado's earlier use of the prose poem, certain pages can even stand as independent poetic units. This emphasis on the poetic is confirmed in the label that Prado applied to *Alsino,* "poema novelesco" (novelized poem). This description convinces us that Prado's intention was not simply to narrate the adventures of a flying youth but to poeticize, through his selective omniscient narrator, the Chilean land.

Alsino mixes attitudes in addition to genres. Prado blends concrete, realistic observations of life with the fantastic quasi-abstract nature of his hero. The alternating zig-zagging movement from reality to fantasy to reality succeeds in destroying the reader's own perception of the limits between them. Alsino's impossible power of flight becomes progressively more plausible with the precise unfolding of his environment. Prado's narrator pinpoints specific geographical places and uses exact local names of the flora and fauna that compose his landscapes. We see many regions of Chile, many seasons, and many hours of the day painted in this work. No other Chilean writer has so completely and successfully combined and synthesized so many various elements of nature into one lyric, cohesive sum. Prado has used nature not only as setting but also as a poetic theme and as a protagonist.

The development of character is relegated to a minor role in the novel. Only Alsino's thoughts and feelings are described. Prado's hero incarnates his own philosophical concept of *naturaleza-hombres* (nature-men), the fantastic blend proposed in his earlier ***Ensayos . . . (Essays)*** and sketched in a few of his earlier prose poems. There is no lack of comprehension between Alsino and nature's components, no artificial or prescribed limits between them. Alsino addresses nature directly and expresses both his terror and joy at discovering that nature and he can understand each other: "'during a long, a very long time everything has been confused for me, but now it finally is clear and it was you leaves; it was you rocks, waters and flames; and it was you wind, and perhaps it was the things of the earth, and perhaps of the world, which were making that noise in me.'" ("Durante largo, muy largo tiempo, todo ha sido confuso para mí, mas ahora él, por fin, se aclara, y erais vosotras, hojas, erais vosotras rocas, aguas y llamas; y eras tú, viento, y eran acaso todas las cosas de la tierra, y quizás del mundo, las que hacían en mí ese ruido"). Nature's elements proceed to talk openly and unhesitatingly to him, to comfort him, to shelter him, and to lull him gently to sleep.

The other characters form a backdrop or become a part of the landscape. The narrator describes them and records their conversations. He develops them only to move the plot along or to contrast them with Alsino. The cast of characters represents a parade of Chilean types. These men and women, mostly poor country folk, are given to superstition, drink, and cruelty. The narrator generally shows an aloof attitude toward them. The arrival of the first airplane to Vega de Reinoso provides an excuse for a fiesta. After the pilot landed everyone went to greet him, "but there were not lacking those who, tired or uncertain of their legs due to their drunkenness, remained where they were, incapable, besides, of neglecting the big meal and the thick mountain wine." (pero no faltaron algunos cansados o inseguros de piernas, por lo borrachos, que se quedasen donde estaban, incapaces, además, de desairar la comilona y el grueso vino de la montaña). Some of the celebrants, hearing about Alsino's presence in the vicinity, seek him out and mistake an idiot for him: "Some gathered around the cretin and since the latter did not want to fly, in a flash they undressed him and beat him." (Reuniéronse algunos en torno del cretino y como éste no quisiese volar, en un dos por tres lo desnudaron y diéronle de golpes). Finding Alsino at last, they proceed to strip him and are pleased to see his mutilated clipped wings.

On occasion, the narrator sympathizes with the plight of these humble people, as in the case of Margarita, a servant girl. Margarita, the unwed mother of a "baby that rained from heaven" (una guagua que . . . le ha llovido del cielo) is barely eighteen, "but her youth is so withered that only when she laughs, does it sparkle. . . . She doesn't know what she wants. Perhaps her dream would be to become another Miss Abigail. Since she clearly understands that that will never be, she zealously dedicates herself to caring for her young mistress. . . . She looks weak and pale. Her hands are red and rough. Everything that she contemplates with her air of a sleep walker is reflected clearly in her very dark, big eyes, like two tiny mirrors." (pero su juventud está tan tan ajada que sólo cuando ríe, brilla. . . . No se sabe lo que quiere. Tal vez su sueño sería convertirse en otra señorita Abigail. Como bien comprende que eso no será nunca, se dedica a cuidar con celo a su joven patrona. . . . Está débil y pálida. Tiene las manos rojas y estropeadas. En sus ojos grandes y muy negros, se reflejan claramente, como en dos pequeñitos espejos todo lo que ella, con ese su modo de sonámbula, contempla).

Although beneficent paternalism exudes from this touching portrayal, the selection illustrates an important stylistic element. Prado has individualized the girl, especially contrasting her general appearance with her hands. He has compressed an accumulation of pathetic events or rather non-events into a few lines, delicately suggesting her life story. In contrast to the *Criollistas* he does not phonetically transcribe the peasants' speech nor clinically detail their lives.

He describes Candelaria, the cook, with imagery that depicts the closeness of the people to the soil: "A little old woman, dark, dry, and wrinkled like a dried peach. She still has her alert mind and a quick answer. She is short-tempered and, although she has been the cook for fifty-five years, she has angered everybody. . . . Her dark face, furrowed by infinite wrinkles, where her two ash-gray eyes shine brightly, brings to mind the tilled fields of farm land of the fallowing season, when the clear, small puddles of water sparkle with the first rains on the dark, plowed earth. (Una viejecita morena, seca y arrugada como un huesillo. Tiene el genio vivo y la respuesta pronta. Gasta escasa paciencia, y, aunque hace cincuenta y cinco años que es cocinera, ha rabiado todos. . . . Su rostro moreno, surcado por infinitas arrugas, donde brillan claros sus ojos cenicientos, trae el recuerdo de los trabajados campos de labranza, llegada la época de los barbechos, cuando brillan, con las primeras lluvias, entre la oscura tierra arada, las claras y pequeñas pozas de agua). Candelaria's cranky, bossy spirit is tolerated because of her great age. She commands the same awed respect that the peasant holds for the plowed fields.

Florencio, the keeper of the wine cellar, is "good company, happy, not funny for what he says but for his attitudes. Clean shaven, with bulging eyes and gesturing like a good stutterer, he owns an enormous Adam's apple in his long neck which, when he drinks, goes up and down and attracts everyone's glances. . . . The truth is that you suffer looking at the poor man who never finishes swallowing that exasperating bump. He is happy with his lot. Perhaps the secret resides in the fact that he takes care of the wine." (buen compañero, alegre, no gracioso por lo que dice, sino por sus actitudes. Lampiño, posee en el largo cuello una nuez enorme que, al bajar y subir, cuando bebe, atrae sobre sí todas las miradas. . . . La verdad es que nunca termina de tragarse ese bulto desesperante. Está contento con su suerte. Quizá el secreto resida en que tiene el vino a su cuidado). Again Prado returns to the theme of alcoholism as the poor man's escape from harsh reality.

These concise, realistic portraits of the pathetic people surrounding Alsino demonstrate the narrator's remote compassion for the common people, and perhaps even that Prado's own affection for them was platonic and distant. His intellectual and economic aristocracy no doubt hindered any genuine understanding of their character. His portrayal of Don Javier, the owner of the *fundo,* and his daughter, Abigail, shows more penetration, more perception of their motivations. Don Javier is very realistic and Abigail incarnates an ideal, a symbol of human love. This explains why the representation of Abigail falls into the idyllic, sentimental mold of the Romantic heroine, such as the Colombian archetype in Jorge Isaac's nineteenth-century novel *María.* We first see Abigail as "she advanced, svelte and graceful; she was white, with golden brown hair." (Avanzaba esbelta y graciosa; era blanca, de dorados cabellos castaños). Somewhat later we observe her nervous and restless before Alsino, who has already revealed his love to her, and "in her moist, open, and imploring eyes, some luminous dots shone, perhaps the reflection of the distant stars." (En sus ojos húmedos, abiertos e implorantes, brillaban unos puntos luminosos, acaso el reflejo de las remotas estrellas). Alsino is paralyzed by her beauty and Abigail, in order to hurry him, extends "one of her small, soft, cool hands" (una de sus pequeñas manos suaves y frescas). Alsino's aroused passion is very effectively conveyed when his "fingers gradually closed around those of the young girl, like the flames of a bonfire when they seek to burn the fragrant wood that falls among them." (Los dedos de Alsino fueron cerrándose en torno de los de la joven, como las llamas de una hoguera cuando buscan encender la olorosa madera que cae entre ellas). Abigail's death, reminiscent of María's in Isaac's novel, is indirectly revealed when Alsino hears a penetrating lament fly through the night, "like a black, fateful bird" (como una negra ave fatídica). He runs to the house to be with her, only to find her lying dead, surrounded by flowers, flickering candles, and the drone of prayers for the dead.

Abigail and Alsino were kindred spirits. Alsino could understand her thoughts just as he could understand the voices of nature. Abigail introduces the theme of human love into the novel. Alsino's recognition of this love marks the climax of the book. Abigail, however, intuited the impossible nature of their love. At the beginning of her illness Alsino frequently related his many adventures, after one of which she exclaimed, "Oh if I could have wings, what adventures we would have together. . . . We would marry, right, Alsino? (she asked jokingly). Because otherwise, me without wings and you with them, a fine pair we would make! You would feel like flying and there I would be planted on the ground. If you flew with me on your back, you would not climb high or go far. If you resigned yourself to staying always at my side among people you could not go around half-naked, and if you covered your wings, what a hump it would make, my God! Little kids would follow us throwing stones." (— Ah! si yo tuviese alas, qué de aventuras no correríamos juntos. . . . Nos casaríamos ¿verdad, Alsino?—preguntó burlesca—. Porque así, yo sin alas y usted con ellas, bonita pareja. . . . Que le venían ganas de volar; pues yo a quedarme plantada. Si volaba conmigo a cuestas, no subiría alto ni llegaría lejos. Si se resignaba a permanecer siempre a mi lado, entre la gente no podría ir medio desnudo, y si se cubría las alas, ¡qué joroba! ¡Dios mío! ¡Los chiquillos nos seguirían, lanzándonos piedras!).

This conversation has a great deal of social significance within the context of the symbolism of the novel. Abigail, the daughter of the land owner, belongs to a class that is at the opposite pole from Alsino's origins. This passage points out the obvious impossibility of social mobility. They have their love to unify them, but society would make their existence together unbearable. Prado also uses the conversation to hint at Abigail's approaching death, which handily resolves a potentially difficult situation.

The exact meaning of the allegory of **Alsino** is subject to various interpretations. Some critics, among them Torres Rioseco and Silva Castro, view the novel as the Chilenization of the Icarus myth; others such as Arriagada and Goldsack consider it as social allegory. According to the latter critics, Alsino is a symbol of the plight of mankind and, more specifically, of the oppressed Chilean lower class. As a universal symbol, he represents the struggle of man to overcome the limitations of his existence, to better his human condition, to strive, even if unsuccessfully, towards higher goals of achievement and knowledge. The story of Alsino, they feel, has special meaning for the Chilean poeple. Prado's purposeful selection of a member of Chile's most abused class as hero becomes an intellectual vehicle for Prado's criticism of Chilean society's long neglect of the needs of its people. They comment that "the failure and death of the hero involves a bitter criticism of the entire society."

In reality, Alsino represents a composite allegorical figure, embodying several of Prado's earlier themes. This connection will bring the problem into clearer focus. He is a man in ideal harmony with nature, he is an example of Prado's pantheism, particularly when his ashes forever blend with the air, and he is the symbol of the poet. It is the latter thematic function which is most clearly developed throughout the novel. Prado's use of the destitute peasant was not actually so much to convey social criticism as it was to show that the poet is not the exclusive product of an educated, urban background. There is no connection, for Prado, between intelligence and artistic inspiration or between rational knowledge and poetic knowledge. The deprived rural boy, therefore, serves as an excellent example of the poet and his inspiration. Flight, first identified with poetry and poetic knowledge in **Los pájaros errantes,** here permits Alsino to transcend

his human and intellectual limitations. Alsino's flights produce poetry in him and he joins his voice with that of nature. Society does not understand the poet who suffers at its hands. This idea, clearly established in **La casa abandonada,** influences Alsino's relationship with other men. When Alsino flies through the air, he is viewed as a beautiful creature endowed with the magic of song; on earth, satisfying his human necessities or urges, he is awkward, and "when he walks along searching for wild fruits, the weight of his great wings bends him slightly to the ground, his steps take on the sway of stevedores." (cuando marcha buscando frutos silvestres, el peso de sus grandes alas lo inclina ligeramente a tierra, y toman sus pasos el vaivén de los cargadores). These lines, reminiscent of Baudelaire's own winged symbol of the poet in "L'Albatros" (The Albatross), reminds us of the poet's very human needs and his very human origin. Alsino's knowledge is not intellectual or rational. He derives the source of knowledge from his instincts and from flight which is poetic knowledge. This explains Alsino's wisdom and his understanding of men.

Prado's most extensive work has suffered over the years. For 1920, **Alsino** represented a break with the conventional novel. Prado, by introducing the winged youth, became an early practitioner of fantastic literature which in the past two decades has produced some of Latin America's best fiction. The earlier inflated opinions of its value and place in Prado's production and its significance in Chilean literature have changed toward a more realistic appraisal of its importance. Reading **Alsino** now we are still very much impressed with Prado's beautiful style, his lyric natural descriptions of Chile, and his interesting philosophical concepts, but at the same time we are struck by the impression that we are confronting a lovely period piece of literature.

III UN JUEZ RURAL (COUNTRY JUDGE)

Country Judge is the anguished, desperate story of a man questioning the meaning and direction of his life. Early in the novel we learn that Solaguren, the protagonist, is suffering some kind of nervous strain. An architect by profession, he accepts the duties of a judgeship in the suburbs of Santiago where he lives. His acceptance seems to him an opportunity for change and, possibly, escape from his routine responsibilities. Ironically, the result is quite different. He deems the administration of justice to his fellow men a humanitarian duty. In the course of six chapters we watch Solaguren render unconventional verdicts in a series of cases which expose the colorful, very human foibles of the litigants. These people are generally the poor or the lower middle class of the surrounding district portrayed by Prado with sympathy and honesty. Solaguren suffers bouts of insecurity in his new position and flees to the neighboring countryside on weekends with an intimate friend, Mozarena. They paint, they talk, and they reveal their thoughts on a variety of subjects. Due to a serious illness in his family and a painful interview with the mother of a young man he has sentenced to prison, Solaguren resigns his post, convinced of his inability to judge human actions. The letter of resignation that Solaguren writes concisely summarizes Prado's own theories on the nature of justice first discussed in the pages of *Los Diez* in 1916. The letter contained in chapter nineteen marks both a turning point in Solaguren's development and the end of the first half of the novel.

In the second part Solaguren escapes, this time packing his family and self off to the coastal resort, El Tabo. He hopes to regain a perspective of things, to find peace of mind, and to understand himself. His emotional state corrodes any former tranquility. The atmosphere of the resort tends more to depress him and increase his anxiety rather than to relieve it. He finds another pretext to escape back to Santiago, but this time alone. He seeks out Mozarena and tries to communicate something of what is happening inside of him. They attempt to solve the problem by first toying with flirtations and then by indulging their senses in food and heavy drinking. Mozarena, after their repast, suggests a brothel as a good remedy to dissipate their boredom. In the concluding pages of the novel, the two friends regretfully part company. Solaguren is once more alone with his thoughts and vague feelings. The disconcerting, inconclusive end of the novel finds Solaguren completely alone in his room, groping with his own dark image reflected in a mirror.

Prado, as the synopsis of the plot indicates, has chosen to develop a strong, clearly delineated character. No other work prior to this one manifests such an effort. He convinces us of Solaguren's reality through the gradual, poignant unfolding of his psychology and philosophy. Prado relates a spiritual crisis with no specific remedy; he poses questions and provides no answers.

Solaguren, as a fictional creation, undergoes no real, essential change in the novel, but our understanding of him does change. At the conclusion of the first chapter, we see Solaguren "in the silent house and the enveloping calm oppressed him, as if his soul were alone in the world." (el silencio de su casa y la quietud de todo lo que le rodeaba lo turbó desagradablemente, como si en el vasto mundo su alma estuviese solitaria). The novel's conclusion finds him four months later engulfed in the same oppressive silence of his house. The nearly identical beginning and end of the novel effectively conveys the futility of the character's quest for a meaning to existence.

The protagonist's spiritual quest provides the basic unity through the novel's twenty-seven chapters. We see Solaguren at first as a man who faces life and its consequent responsibilities. He is married, the father of an unspecified number of childen, an architect, and an idealist. The daily routine of many minor crises and problems both at home and at work nibbles at his mind and soul, leaving him an unsatisfied desire for something different. This frame of mind leads him to accept the local judgeship as a form of escape from monotony.

The gravity and nature of Solaguren's nervous condition is forcefully revealed after his first day in court. That night, plagued by sleeplessness "from which he had been suffering since spring," we see him as "panting and breathless in the torture of insomnia, he suddenly sat up in bed, struck a match with trembling fingers, and in its feeble and flickering glow saw the furniture and the objects in his room stand out in unreal immobility, as spoiled and worthless as the debris of a shipwreck. Even so at that late hour they were his only firm support in the surrounding shadows, and he clung to them in the palpitating and ocean-like night." (Jadeando, inquieto, cogido en la tortura del insomnio, de un salto sentábase en el lecho, raspaba, trémulo, un fósforo, y a esa luz naciente, débil y temblorosa, veía surgir los muebles y los objetos de su cuarto, erguidos con una inmovilidad irreal, todos mermados de valer como restos de un naufragio. Y sin embargo, a esa hora, constituían el único apoyo real entre las sombras circundantes. Asiéndose de ellos, sentía en torno el palpitar de la noche oceánica). Prado's choice of imagery, reminiscent of **"Oración al despertar"** (**"Prayer on Waking"**) in *Los pájaros errantes,* insinuates an underlying cause of Solaguren's nervous state. The ocean, associated in Prado's other works as a symbol for eternity as well as death, and night as a symbol for death, markedly contrasts with Solaguren's material achievements, values, and reality in the symbol of the furniture seen as flotsam.

The second contact with the root of Solaguren's problem emerges one day on an outing with Mozarena. Sitting on the bank of a stream Solaguren "watched the vast cumulus clouds that crowned the Andes. He remembered how, on summer afternoons, he used to watch these same eternal clouds pile up over the mountains. And now, as he observed the dark and turbid waters of the river—waters always different and always the same—and when he saw the trees that reminded him of the infinity of other trees, and the light of that day identical with the light of the innumerable days of all the summers of his life, he felt oppressed by a feeling of darkness, poverty, littleness, and loathing." (divisó grandes cúmulos que encimaban la Cordillera de los Andes. Recordó Solaguren que en las tardes de verano, año a año, veía agruparse sobre la mole andina esas mismas eternas nubes. Y al observar las aguas turbias y oscuras del río, aguas cambiantes y siempre iguales; al ver los árboles que traían el recuerdo de árboles incontables, la luz de ese día, claridad sorda, idéntica a la de los días innúmeros de todos los estíos que viviese, le trajo una sensación de oscuridad, de pobreza, de pequeñez y de hastío). The author deftly displays Solaguren's despair at the passage of time by the passing clouds and flowing waters, while painfully emphasizing the sameness and the smallness of his life. The contemplation of nature does not dissipate his depression. Reacting against this mood, Solaguren looks for Mozarena whom he finds flirting with a sensuous peasant girl. A ripple of lust passes over him quickly, but it is summarily dismissed.

The two men, on the road again, wistfully evoke the life of the free vagabonds which leads Mozarena into an anecdote about a local, rural Don Juan he once knew. The man, "Calienta-la-tierra," represents a type of hero for he was truly free from responsibility and concerns. He lived and loved as he pleased, subject only to his own whims. However, the atmosphere once more becomes somber when the two companions come upon an old cemetery, very similar in aspect to the one described in the prologue to *La reina de Rapa Nui*. They confront the specter of death when the caretaker opens one of the coffins, revealing the disintegrating skeletal remains of its occupant. The caretaker supplements her meager income by emptying and reselling old coffins to the poor. The whole day's outing reminds Solaguren of his mortality where even the coffins, bones, and earthly trimmings decay and disappear in the wind.

Solaguren, after serving two months as judge, resigns and flees to the seaside. A change of scene, he hopes will dispel his personal crisis. At first the funereal air of the town before the onslaught of vacationers and later the rhythm of the sea and the vapid personalities of the holidayers deeply disturb him. After two months he returns to the capital "on business." The last three chapters, covering the day and night of his arrival in Santiago, build to his climactic confrontation with himself in the mirror.

Solaguren's encounter with his likeness in the mirror, described in the last pages, is the fourth and culminating instance of life seen as a reflection. The first time occurs during the train ride to the coast, "the windows became murky mirrors, in which the cross and tired passengers in the dim cars were reflected, passengers silently navigating a river of restless shadows. None of them noticed the mirror of the night itself, or the blurred image that each one projected into the dark country side." (los cristales transformábanse en borrosos espejos. En ellos aparecían otros viajeros deslizándose arrebatados sin ruido a través de un río de sombras intranquilas. Nadie reparaba en el espejo que ofrecía la oscuridad; nadie, en la imagen desvanecida que cada cual arrojaba sobre las sombras de los campos). Prado uses this scene to illustrate man's passage through life seen in the reflections of time's murky mirrors. No one, but Solaguren, notices its quick passage and no one can grasp its substance.

The second reflected image occurs in chapter twenty-two. Solaguren's family is in the living room of their coastal vacation home. With the children asleep around their mother,

> Solaguren, withdrawn and wrapped about in the shadows of a dark corner, stands before the black panes of the great window that looks out over the sea, and there sees the intimate tableau reflected in the air or upon the dark waters. . . . Isabel carries the children off to bed and Solaguren remains gazing through the black window. Time passes. His thought dissolved in the rhythm of the light and the song of the sea among the shadows, Solaguren sees a dim glow on the rim of the horizon; he sees it take form and advance toward him. A woman is gliding silently over the waters; she enters the circle of light and kisses the brow of the man reflected in the window, who clasps her yielding body and buries his mouth in her smooth and fragrant hair. Solaguren gazes out upon the floating and unreal scene beyond the window, and there sees two human shadows in the night and the solitude of the sea, tenderly embracing.

> (Solaguren, ratirado y envuelto en las sombras de un rincón oscuro, vecino a los negros cristales de la amplia ventana que da hacia el mar, ve reflejarse en ellos, como en el aire y sobre las aguas oscuras, ese cuadro íntimo. . . . Cuando Isabel lleva los niños a acostarse, él queda mirando, siempre mirando hacia los negros cristales. Pasa el tiempo, y deshecho todo pensamiento en el ritmo de la luz y el canto del mar entre las sombras, Solaguren ve surgir vagamente una claridad en el horizonte marino; la ve concretarse y venir hacia él: es una mujer que se desliza silenciosa sobre las aguas, roza el círculo de la luz, y a la imagen de un hombre allí reflejada la besa en la frente. Y mientras él siente que también unos labios acarician su rostro, que sus brazos estrechan un blando y tibio cuerpo femenino, y que su boca se hunde en una suave y olorosa cabellera, vuelto siempre sus ojos hacia la escena suspendida e irreal, allí tras los cristales, ve cómo aquellas sombras humanas, cercadas por la noche y la soledad marina, se estrechan dulcemente.)

Again Solaguren perceives life through its reflection. The brevity of life powerfully contrasts with the night and the eternity of the sea. Love, physical love, provides him an illusory hold on life's substance, but life still seems floating and unreal as it did in his insomnia. Love and sex assert his existence, his material self over the vast sea of death and eternity.

The third reflection appears in the very next chapter, entitled "Escape" ("Alta Noche"). Solaguren takes his horse on a late night ride along the beach:

> The tide was ebbing, the wide sheet of sand invited him, and he galloped through the last delicate bits of the floating gauze of the waves. As he rounded a point he was astonished by a great light shining on the wet sand, while far below, in an unfathomable abyss that opened before him, shone another moon broken into a thousand mad and glistening fragments that were struggling to reassemble themselves. . . . The waning moon, as deformed as a dying planet about to plunge into the dark sea, the sheet of burning silver that covered the sand, sand rendered invisible by its faithful reflection of the stars, and the smell of the ocean flowing in from its vastness to overwhelm the weak air of the earth, transformed the prideful sea into a single wave born of the measureless night. Solaguren contemplated his own puniness with something like horror. . . . He paused at the edge of the foam and then spurred his horse at a furious gallop into the abyss at his feet, into a never-ending falling, into a flight among the planets, a mad gallop over the gigantic looking glass of the beach. . . . Solaguren thought, as he left the unforgettable night behind

him, that he must look like a man returning from among the dead.

(La marea comenzaba a descender, y gran parte de la inmensa sábana de arena se ofrecía como un camino ideal. Puso su caballo al galope y lo hizo internarse hasta romper los últimos y delgados velos flotantes de las olas. Al torcer una puntilla, una gran luz, emergiendo de las negras y húmedas arenas, le hirió de asombro: remota, en un abismo insondable abierto allí a sus pies, otra luna inmensa resplandecía deshecha en mil fulgores enloquecidos que buscaban unirse. . . . ¡La luna, menguante deforme como un mundo en agonía próximo a desaparecer en el oscuro seno de las aguas, los cendales de plata hirviente que se extendían sobre las arenas, arenas invisibles, a fuerza de reflejar con nitidez el fulgor de los astros, el aroma de infinito que venía de la inmensidad a oprimir los débiles aires de la tierra, hacían de todo el orgullo del mar una simple ola nacida en el océano de la noche inconmensurable! Solaguren sintió hasta el horror su infinita pequeñez; disparó sus pensamientos hacia la última fantasía, y, como si ese fuera el comienzo de un viaje a la eternidad, apoyándose un instante en las últimas espumas, lanzó su caballo al abismo que allí parecía abrirse en un galope sobrenatural: ¡un caer siempre suspendido, un vuelo entre los mundos! ¡La carrera enloquecedora sobre el gigante espejo de las playas! . . . Solaguren pensó, al salir de esa noche inolvidable, que él también debía tener el aspecto de alguien que vuelve de entre los muertos.)

This passage, among the most beautiful and forceful that Prado ever wrote, casts Solaguren's finiteness against the cosmos' infinity and mystery. The vocabulary of death pervades the entire chapter from the first to last lines. Prado's surreal description begins placidly enough but then gallops to a desperate frenzy. The earlier associations of night and death imperceptibly blend with the mirror images. Life, death, sea, and night fuse in Solaguren's mind. All of his anxieties, anguish, despair, and loneliness culminate in this moonlight ride between two nightmarish worlds.

Among Prado's other characters Solaguren's wife and his court secretary are very effectively drawn. The presence of the wife is felt through all but the last four chapters. She is tender, loving, understanding, and firm when necessary. She is not an extraordinary or idealized woman. She is totally credible in her role as wife and mother. Her normalcy adds to the effect that Prado is trying to construct in the novel. The delineation of Galíndez is more circumscribed. He is the perfect, petty bureaucrat, completely at home among his forms, papers, and procedures. He offers a humorous contrast to the naïve comportment of the novice judge. In spite of his bustling officiousness, he eventually gains our sympathy. Mozarena, the friend, in contrast to what we might presume, is less well rendered because he is too much an alter-ego of Solaguren. Their thoughts and sentiments, although certainly not identical, are very compatible.

Many other characters pass through the courtroom or cross Solaguren's path. Chapter three introduces "a long string of plaintiffs: a shy woman of greenish hue, suing to recover the rent on a piece of property . . . ; a man, his head swathed in dirty bandages stained with dried blood, seeking the punishment of his assailants; two women, the younger of whom complained that she was the object of amorous attentions; a heavy, overdressed woman, exuding vigor and authority, loudly demanding damages . . . in the sale of some onion sets." (siguió el desfile de los que imploraban justicia. Una mujer enteca y verdosa, querellándose por ciertos útiles de su propiedad . . . ; un hombre, la cabeza con lienzos sucios manchados de sangre seca en busca de castigo para sus asaltantes; dos mujeres, la menor de ellas diciéndose víctima de una continua persecución amorosa; emperejilada y presumiendo juventud y señorío, una vejancona . . . pedía se castigase a un chacarero que le engañara en la venta de cierto almácigo de cebollas). These same people will provide the colorful basis for subsequent chapters occuring within the confines of the courtroom.

Setting occupies a secondary role in *Country Judge* in contrast to the other novels. Prado has not forgotten nature or the Chilean landscape, but they have ceased to exist as a purely lyrical or didactic element. Nature accents a psychological or philosophical development in the characters. For example on one occasion Solaguren and Mozarena go off to paint the picturesque countryside. Both men choose to paint the same scene of a house and landscape, much to Solaguren's irritation. They are absorbed in their sketching for nearly two hours, after which they examine each other's works. Their canvases were identical in size, their subject and proximity to it are also, but the results are quite different. Mozarena had filled his painting with the house; Solaguren had made the house only a part of the surrounding landscape. The observation and rendering of the landscape move him to record in his diary that evening that "all things . . . became fused together as they reflected each other, and each merges with its surroundings as if seeking its true and full meaning. But what are the limits of those surroundings? Well, each observer fixes them according to his whim. To see, therefore, is to create, and no law determines its limits." (Todas las cosas se entrelazan con sus mutuos reflejos, y cada una de ellas se prolonga en el ambiente que la circunda como para alcanzar su verdadero y pleno significado. Pero ¿cuáles son los límites de ese ambiente? Cada observador lo fija a su antojo. Ver resulta ser, así, arbitrariedad de limitación!). The original landscape becomes the departure point for a discussion of one of Prado's favorite themes, the limits of things. The landscape begins a chain of ideas which eventually ties into his questioning of human justice. The title of the chapter, "Prueba de testigos" ("Test of Witnesses"), although the action occurs almost entirely outdoors and ends in Solaguren's home, implies its relationship to the questioning of justice. Solaguren senses that the subjectivity of the perception of reality becomes one more obstacle in the rendering of justice.

During another sketching session, Solaguren simply observing the landscape and Mozarena painting, bathed in the sun's golden light, thinks "in the vast open landscape his was only one figure, possibly the most arresting one, but there were so many others! So many others which, being registered, so to speak, on a lower octave of consciousness, or on one higher than the ordinary half-octave of man, were at first glance unperceived, like colors beyond the limits of the spectrum." (En el vasto espectáculo abierto en contorno era ese hombre un simple episodio, por momentos el más apasionante; ¡pero había tantos otros! Tantos que por ofrecerse como a una octava de sensibilidad más baja, o más alta que la media y más constante del hombre, quedaban, en una primera impresión, insospechados, como colores prolongándose más allá de los límites del espectro luminoso). Man's fragility against this backdrop prompts Solaguren's personification of the earth. Sitting on the edge of a ditch he touches the grass, almost as if he were affirming his own existence, and reflects that "the hair of his own children was not more beautiful than the green hair of the ditch. . . . Beneath its incomparable skin, how the transparent blood seemed to pulsate! The sap, still so akin to water, the living water, was identical with the stream flowing through the ditch: a lapping of the waves of life, a pure essence!" (la cabellera de sus propios hijos no valía más que la verde cabellera del foso! ¡Qué frescura! qué humedad contenida al acariciarla; qué sensación de palpar, tras el velo incomparable de la piel vegetal, esa sangre transparente: la savia . . . savia tan próxima aun del agua, agua alzándose en vida, idéntica a la mansedumbre del arroyo que allí, en el fondo del foso, era sólo un cabrilleo de luz y un hálito puro!). The earth is alive and life-giving. It can and should be loved as one loves his own children. Imperceptibly nature has implanted a philosophical mood in its observer. Solaguren has progressed from mere enjoyment and repose to serious meditation on man's temporal nature and the earth's vital, eternal force. Other similar descriptions of nature or the landscape lead Solaguren into deeper, more disturbing contemplation and create or abruptly change his mood. Nature no longer has the same didactic function that it did in *La casa abandonada* or *Los pájaros errantes* and certainly no longer has the power to console and solace its observer. Pessimism infects nature.

Prado follows a conscious plan in *Country Judge*. The alternating pattern of reality and fantasy that he followed in *Alsino* appears again modified by the theme and content of this novel. The twenty-seven chapters proceed chronologically, shifting from chapters of exterior reality and social responsibility to chapters of escape and psychological and metaphysical probing. Prado uses subtle foreshadowing and effective repetition of images and symbols to develop his themes. There is a circular design to *Country Judge* which allows us to follow the full cycle of Solaguren's anguish and despair. He ends where he began and we are all the more devastated by his failure to resolve his plight.

Country Judge concentrates themes and imagery of his earlier works. In addition to the metaphysical theme of a man's search for a meaning to his life, three others of importance are woven into the fabric of the main theme. The theme of death obviously forms an integral part of the search theme. It lies just under the surface of most of the chapters of the novel, occasionally it surfaces as it did in the cemetery scene or in the beach ride. This pervasive aura of death and mortality is evident in the last chapter. Walking the empty streets to his home, Solaguren's footsteps "sounded as hollow as if he were walking over gravestones." (sus pasos sonaban huecos como sobre lápidas). Reaching the door of his house, "he fingered the knocker, a little bronze hand, which looked as limp and cold as that of a dead man." (Acarició el golpeador, una pequeña mano de bronce, colgada y fría como la de un muerto). In the novel's very last sentence Solaguren touches his reflection in the dark looking glass, "but their hands, separated by a cold and impenetrable wall, would never clasp each other." (¡pero las manos, sin poder estrecharse, quedaron separadas por algo frío e infranqueable!). All of these lines typify the novel's vocabulary and imagery of death.

Prado investigates the concepts of justice. The required imposition of rational thought in rendering verdicts is examined and criticized in chapter four, "O Socrates" ("La razón derivada"). Attempting to vanquish insomnia, he begins to read Socrates, but his ideas wander off the page as he contemplates:

> "To think, to deduce, to derive a conclusion—O Socrates! . . . Thought is like water. Give me a slight difference in level and I will carry your thought wherever you wish. We think we reason by a rigorous and logical process, and all we do is to fill up the space, *a posteriori,* which links the case at hand with our immediate intuition about it. He deceives himself, or lies, who thinks to build up an argument unconnected with the spontaneous conclusions he has held from the very beginning, which are not the less present for being unperceived. Then, feigning an apparent continuity that will strengthen our argument, or free us from the guilty consequences thus deduced, we fill the empty space with logical and hollow connectives."

> ("Pensar, derivar, obtener una conclusión ¡oh! Sócrates. . . . El pensamiento es como el agua: dame un ligero desnivel, y llevo el pensamiento donde tú quieras. Creemos juzgar por riguroso razonamiento lógico, y no hacemos sino rellenar *a posteriori* el espacio que media entre el caso que se nos presenta a examen y nuestra intuición inmediata sobre él. Se engaña o miente quien cree construir razonamientos como algo ajeno a la conclusión espontánea que entrevió desde el primer instante. No por quedar oculta a los que no saben observarse, desde el primer momento, ella deja de estar menos presente. Después, para fingir una aparente continuidad que dé vigor a lo que decimos, o que nos libre de culpa por las consecuencias al parecer deducidas, rellenamos el espacio en blanco con huecas trabazones lógicas.")

These anti-rational thoughts reassert the views that Prado sustained in his *Essays on Architecture and Poetry* and represent Solaguren's initial inquiry and suspicion of justice. After some direct juridical experience, he proceeds to question semantics. In one case two men have claimed a lost horse as theirs. They each describe the horse accurately and the judge is hard-pressed to render a decision. Due to the good, personal recommendation by Galíndez on behalf of one of the claimants, the judge awards the horse accordingly. It happens, however, that when the man goes to take the horse he discovers it is not his. The other claimant is recalled, but he too finds that the horse is not his. Some days later the true owner comes for the animal and ironically he cannot clearly recall or describe its distinctive features. Solaguren wonders, "words that described a given animal, a given object, did they agree in appearance only, useless for a positive recognition?" (Palabras que coincidían con un animal dado, con un objeto preciso, ¿coincidían en una apariencia inútil para el reconocimiento real?). Solaguren, distressed by the inadequacy of words, feels that they are a "false representation of things." The judge cannot depend on what he sees nor now what he hears. His distrust of logic and the inadequacy of mere words further weaken the basis of justice in his mind.

One day the mother of a thief whom he has convicted appears at his door. She pours out her grief and troubles to the perplexed judge. She understands the guilt of her son, the sole support of their large family, but punishing him punishes them: "He's guilty, and the innocent are paying the penalty." Confusion sweeps over Solaguren. Her argument is valid in his mind, but he is powerless to act, according to the law, in any other way. That night, disillusioned by the practical concept of justice, he writes his letter of resignation.

Solaguren, in the letter, first reveals his own character and then his idea of justice. He notes that, "I have not been a judge, but only half a one, the melancholy and thankless half. Of the exalted dignity, which for me was its greatest attraction and the lure that induced me to accept the honored duties of judge, I was given only the cruel and somber part. . . . The truth is, Your Excellency, that I am confused to the point of anguish." ("No he sido un juez; he sido sólo la mitad de un juez, la mitad ingrata y triste! De aquella decantada dignidad que constituyó el atractivo, el lazo que me hizo aceptar honrado el desempeño de juez, sólo me fue dada la parte cruel y sombría. . . . La verdad es, señor Intendente, que estoy confuso hasta la angustia.") "Late, too late, and with much suffering," Solaguren concludes that "justice is . . . a desire, a longing, beyond our grasp and remote from human comprehension." He confesses that gradually he came to judge the very principle that had moved him, justice itself. He reflects, in lines echoing from *La casa abandonada, Los pájaros errantes,* and the *Essays,* that

> "since men do not live in isolation, the punishment of any individual, guilty or not, is shared by the infinity of people who surround him. . . . My despair, Your Excellency, arises from my inability to isolate the guilty individual and punish him

alone. . . . Our laws are based upon a concept of the individual, and I am beginning to question that concept. An unlimited individual, what kind of individual is that? We are deceived by the illusory independence of his body. Upon what foundation does one erect true justice? I am too confused to say. I see nothing clearly. This post has induced in me a vast uneasiness about life, and because of it I understand life less."

("como no hay hombres aislados, el castigo de cualquier individuo, culpable o no, trae una repercusión sobre infinidad de seres que le rodean. . . . Mi desesperación, señor Intendente, proviene de que no puedo aislar un individuo, el culpable, y castigarlo sólo a él. . . . Nuestras leyes se basan en el concepto de individuo, y ese concepto se me hace sospechoso: un individuo que no limita ¿qué individuo es? Su cuerpo aislado nos engaña con su apariencia independiente. ¿Sobre qué base fundar la verdadera justicia? Estoy demasiado confundido; no veo cosa alguna con claridad. Me ha traído este cargo una inquietud mayor ante la vida; por su causa, ahora la comprendo menos.")

The themes of justice and limits blend imperceptibly in this personal confession of failure. The same concern with arbitrary limits that motivated the prose poem **"Where Does the Rose Begin"** is restated this time in direct application to men and justice.

Prado overtly criticizes the existing social order for the first time in his fiction or poetry. Implied in the theme of justice is an awareness of the plight of the poor. At an early point in his chapter, "O Socrates," Solaguren concludes, in legal phrases oozing sarcasm, that the death penalty would be too light for the richest landowner and biggest taxpayer, Don Juan Crisóstomo Urquieta. He reasons that the inequitable distribution of wealth is the basis for the social injustices inflicted upon the poor. Solaguren does not, however, advocate revolution although he does mention it. Revolution "would perplex them with its pitiful results, the real causes being always out of sight and hidden. . . ." (una revolución que por sus frutos mesquinos los desconcierte, ocultas siempre las causas reales . . .). Prado's social preoccupation emerges a few pages later when Mozarena and Solaguren come across some poor country women on one of their outings. Solaguren, touched by the emaciated and prematurely aged appearance of one, gives her some money. He explains his sudden charity to his friend: "What misery! The old woman was actually afraid of me. That insignificant bill was for her more money than she could count in her amazement. . . . All that merely to live! What is this poverty business all about? Since I was appointed judge I understand these things even less than I did before. Why does the sight of poverty affect me like an insult screamed in my face? As if I were being called a thief!" (¡Qué miseria! La vieja me miraba con un susto. . . . Ese billete insignificante fue para ella tanto dinero que no supo en su asombro qué decir. . . . ¿Y qué es esto de la miseria? Desde que soy juez, comprendo menos que nunca todas las cosas . . . ¿Por qué la vista de la miseria me subleva como un insulto que se me hace? es como si me gritaran: ¡ladrón!). In response to Solaguren's outburst of social conscience and guilt, Mozarena replies that he is a poor man himself. Solaguren, picking up the threads of his tirade, tells him, "your poverty is relative. To those women you are a Croesus! I was speaking of real poverty." (tu pobreza es relativa; para esas mujeres eres un Creso. ¡Hablo de la miseria!). This brief exchange describes the gulf that separates the lower and lower-middle classes from the truly disinherited and indigent of Chile, by graphically illustrating the difference between *pobreza* and *miseria*.

The realistic style and content of **Country Judge** set it quite apart from his other lyrical novels and sentimental early short stories. Philosophy still present vies with psychology for importance and the fusion of the two produces a sensitive portrait of a man on the threshold of middle age. Solaguren's ideals have been destroyed. Despair replaces hope. His body and mind have become his enemy and only decline, age, and death await him.

Pablo Neruda, discussing the novel, commented that Prado was "delving into his well and its waters become increasingly murky. At the bottom of the well he will not find the sky, nor [the] splendid stars, but rather the earth again. . . . The last chapters of his great book, **Country Judge,** have already entered into this well and are darkened not by the flowing water, but by the nocturnal earth." Perhaps of all of Prado's works, **Country Judge** will endure the longest because of its universal themes, its precise characterization and setting, and its concise style.

IV THE EARLY SHORT STORIES

Prado launched his literary career as a short story writer. He had published four short stories before any of his poetic experimentation. In all four of these earliest stories, Prado describes the plight of the poor or contrasts them with the rich, but he does not really seem to understand them or their real social problems. He is obviously no social revolutionary, but then the interest of writers and poets in the urban poor was just beginning. He does not choose to disregard the poor and their misery as many of the Modernists tended to do. Prado's literary attitude toward the humble is sympathetically paternalistic and misguided. Chilean society and artists were just awaking to the new ideas of social justice and Prado's timid approach to these problems is reflected in them. These stories, despite their youthful flaws, are historically interesting and important for an understanding of Prado's development. There is, strangely enough, no hint of the poet of *Flores de cardo* (*Thistle Flowers*) in any of them.

The first story, **"Summer Picture: The Cripple"** (**"Cuadro de estío: el inválido"**) dated October 1905 when he was only nineteen abounds in long adjectival and qualifying phrases. The story is quite short, occupying only one page. One third or more of the story sets the

scene. The young narrator describes a drowsy summer garden in a small resort near Valparaíso. The monotony of the heat and the morning is interrupted by the arrival of the crippled gardener. The narrator's attention then focuses on the gardener at work. The young man becomes more enthralled as "that splendent blue, that verdure sprinkled with red flowers, with white flowers, with yellow flowers; those murmuring waters and fluttering insects, that fragrant mixture of perfumed flowers, all that harmony of the summer softly and sweetly caresses my senses and draws me closer, makes me more intimate with the worker, with our unfortunate brother, disinherited from material and spiritual wealth." (Ese esplendente azul, esa verdura espolvoreada de flores rojas, de flores blancas, de flores amarillas; esos murmullos de agua y de aleteos de insectos, esa fragante mezcla de olorosas flores, toda esa armonía del estío acaricia mis sentidos suave, dulcemente y me acerca, me hace intimar con el trabajador, con nuestro infeliz hermano, desheredado de los bienes materiales y del espiritu). His patronizing attitude turns into indiscretion when he asks the gardener how he lost his leg. The gardener's "face reflects a mixture of pain and joy, as happens to any one who is asked to stir up the past." The gardener relates that he lost his leg in the civil war of 1891. He was forcibly recruited by some soldiers on the street, trained for five days, sent into battle near Concón, where he was wounded. In spite of his swollen, black leg he had managed to find his way to the present resort town where a doctor, seeing his condition, amputated. The narrator comments that, "It is curious—they recruit you by force, they put a rifle in your hands, they lead you into combat where you receive a bullet wound and as a consequence you lose a leg and all that without knowing even the name of your regiment and much less, of course, the causes of the war." This sad, sentimental story is somewhat mitigated by the gardener's ironic reply, "it was just like that, sir . . . and would you believe, sir, that they didn't even pay me for the eight working days in which all that happened?"

This comment, however, does not conclude the story, because Prado, even in this first story, draws a moral lesson from the event and the natural setting, "upon seeing that young and crippled man led by circumstances of existence to other regions, where he only found the aid of a piece of wood which the earth, grateful for his attentions, grants him in exchange for his leg lost in the savage struggle of brothers."

"When You Are Poor" (**"Cuando se es pobre"**) is unrelenting in its pathetic description of an impoverished school teacher. An omniscient narrator describes the twenty-year-old teacher working with a group of laborers. Waiting for his pupils to finish on a cold winter night, he begins to recall his past. His promising future terminated with the news of his father's death. He inherited only the responsibilities of an ailing mother and his sister so he had to find work in order to support them all. His schedule now permits him no more time for his studies or for his sweetheart. Suddenly the wind blows open the window of the cold classroom and the young man goes to close it. There in the cold, wet night, he discovers his sweetheart whom he has not seen for sometime standing, observing him from the street. Surprised she begins to run away, "his love, his poor love, who upset by so long an absence came to see him, perhaps to talk to him. And the workers would see him. . . . Already some laughs were heard. A deep, immense grief came over him." (su amor, su pobre amor, que inquieto por tan larga ausencia venía a verle, a hablarle, quizás. Y los obreros le verían. . . . Ya se escuchaban algunas risas. Una pena honda, inmensa, lo invadió).

The narrator reveals an inner conflict in the young man. He feels that perhaps his mother would not be so seriously ill if only he had spent more time earlier with her than with this girl. His indecision between love and duty briefly tears at him, but then "resisting the impulse that came from outside, fleeing the light of those eyes, he slowly closed the shutter, pushing, separating from him forever hopes and illusions, dreams of love and happiness. And the window moaned. . . ." (Contrarrestando el impulso que venía de fuera, huyendo la luz de esos ojos, cerró lento el postigo, empujando, alejando de sí y para siempre anhelos e ilusiones, ensueños de amor y de alegría. Y la ventana gimió . . .). This story of unadulterated pathos from the first depressing description of the classroom to the moaning window maintains a high level of tension and suspense in spite of the sentimental tone.

"The Wise Woman" (**"La reina maga"**) continues the pathetic vein of the second story. Lucia, a child of well-to-do parents has just heard the story of the Magi who leave presents in good children's shoes from her English nursemaid. When her parents return from shopping, Lucia pleads with them to leave her shiny, new shoes out for the three Wise Men. Later that Christmas Eve night an old street sweeper finishing her work, comes upon the shoes, "she remains undecided for a moment and then, in a gust of past reminiscence she recalls having heard many years ago, she knows not where, the eternal story of the Wise Men." (Queda indecisa un momento y entonces, en una ráfaga de evocación pasada recuerda haber oído, no sabe donde, hace ya mucho tiempo, la eterna historia de los Magos). She takes the shoes to a little girl she has unofficially adopted whom the *barrio* residents call the "little virgin" because of her likeness to church statues of the Virgin Mary. The grief of the rich child on Christmas morning quickly vanishes when she is handed a lovely new doll left in the place of her missing shoes; and the unbelievable joy of the slum child with her new shoes completes the miracle of the Magi: "And so it was that an old street sweeper, on Christmas Eve, became a Wise Woman to a rich little girl, and when she put the shoes on the naked feet of an orphan she left a dream of peace take root in her white soul." (Y fue así como una vieja barrendera, en una noche de Navidad, hizo de Reina Maga para con una personita rica, y como al calzar los pies desnudos de una huérfana dejó prendido en su alma blanca un ensueño de paz!). This sentimental story of rich and poor undoubtedly appealed to the bourgeois public served by *Zig-Zag* because **"La reina maga"** was

selected as the best Christmas story submitted to *Zig-Zag* in its seasonal competition. The misery of slum people is realistically described, but it recedes into the background, creating a sensation that this is the way things are and, indeed, the "little virgin" was truly blessed by a Christmas miracle.

The last of these early short stories, **"Luz lunar"** (**"Moonlight"**), is a sketch of another pitiful character, "Catapún," the village drunk. Prado re-creates the cold, lonely atmosphere of a small Chilean town. The title seems to indicate a story whose tone and content are very different from what really is offered. The story, less sentimental than the others, succinctly describes "Catapún," and his chronic alcoholism. Deserted first by his burro, then by his wife, he began to drink, "since then he lost his job and, now his faculties dulled by alcohol, he is the source of derision for the boys of the town who follow him in the day and throw stones at him when he comes to the station. Here he makes a commotion while the trains pass, on one of which his wife, who took everything from him, ran away. . . ." (Desde entonces perdió su empleo, y ahora, embotadas por el alcohol sus facultades, es el escarnio de los muchachos del pueblo que en el día le siguen y arrojan piedras cuando viene a la estación y hace aspavientos mientras cruzan los trenes, en uno de los cuales fuésele la mujer que le llevó todo . . .). The rural setting, the pervasive melancholy, and the problem of alcoholism make of this story an embryonic prototype for the line of characters which pass through the pages of *Alsino* and *Country Judge.*

V THE DESERT STORIES

Prado finished his prose career by returning to the short story genre. His last prose works, **"El pueblo muerto"** (**"Ghost Town"**) and **"La risa en el desierto"** (**"The Laugh in the Desert"**), reveal a strongly realistic and psychological turn, quite disassociated from philosophy and lyricism. In a sense they continue the psychological probing found in *Country Judge,* but otherwise they are completely unlike anything that Prado had done before. Originally the stories appeared in the pages of the Buenos Aires daily, *La Prensa,* and **"El pueblo muerto"** reappeared ten years later in the pages of *Zig-Zag.*

Prado traveled frequently to the Atacama region. These stories are either a result of these personal journeys or of his official diplomatic mission to Bolivia in 1925. Prado's close familiarity with the area is reflected in the strong rendering of character set against the harsh backdrop of the desert.

The first and longest story, **"El pueblo muerto"** relates an ironic change in the principal character, Juan Otamendi. Prado uses a selective omniscient narrator to follow Otamendi from his arrival at Chañaral to his intended destination, the "Manto Verde" mine. The story opens with a somber description paralleling Otamendi's psychological state with the oppressive atmosphere of the little coastal port. Little by little we learn that he is on the verge of a nervous collapse, but only in the second part of the story are we shown Otamendi's past and the reason for his being in Chañaral. He is a "mining engineer, lacking enterprise, ambition, and optimism, he had lead the life of a professional man who feels himself vegetating between the windows of his office, like a plant squeezed in the heavy air of a green house. . . . He had grown old in his youth." (ingeniero de minas, falto de empuje, de ambición y de optimismo, había llevado la vida de un profesional que se siente vegetar entre las vidrieras de su oficina, como una planta oprimida en un conservatorio de atmósfera pesada. . . . Había envejecido en plena juventud). Only two events have affected his life, his unsuccessful marriage and the loss of his job, both viewed by him as accidents. He wanders listlessly from job to job until one day, on a chance encounter, an old classmate offers him the opportunity to investigate the possibility of reopening a mine in the North. Then Otamendi, "in a moment of keen insight, accepted. Yes, a sea voyage, a little of the true solitude of the desert, a month of a rough and different life from the one he led, unknown lands and faces, and then, perhaps, a few thousand pesos would not be bad at all." (en un momento de clarividencia, aceptó. Sí, un viaje por mar, un poco de la soledad verdadera del desierto, un mes de vida ruda y distinta de la que él llevara, tierras y hombres desconocidos, y luego, tal vez, algunos miles de pesos, no vendrían mal).

His proposed destination, "Manto Verde" mine, requires him to pass through Las Animas (souls), an appropriately named ghost town. It is there that Pascual Cerezo, the sole inhabitant, will eventually effect Otamendi's change. Solidly rooted in practicality because of the desert environment, Cerezo has become pragmatic and devoid of any supernatural beliefs. He has adjusted to his environment and learned to be self-sufficient. Cerezo explains his quiet life and the Engineer asks him if he considers living alone in the middle of the desert as life. Ironically Otamendi accuses him of pessimism, not realizing his own. He sees the other man's life as death, not understanding that his own existence in Santiago was more so.

The fourth part of the story contains the climax. The two men, the morning after Otamendi's arrival, climb to the cemetery where Cerezo's wife and two children lie buried among his friends and acquaintances of many years past. These dead and buried people, mute testimony of the mining town's heyday, are very much alive in the vivid memory of Cerezo, who goes along relating stories about those whose names are still legible on the tombstones. Suddenly Otamendi comes across the grave of Juan Otamendi, dead May 17, 1895, in Las Animas, an unpleasant suggestion of his own mortality. Cerezo, however, is more interested in revealing his own surprise, bones and skulls completely covered in oxidized silver. He has discovered, after a recent earthquake, that the cemetery lies above an incredibly rich vein of silver ore. He has already filed a claim for it, but has been undecided about developing the mine since he lacks the necessary capital to start operations. Otamendi offers to join

efforts with him, the first active step taken by him so far in the story and the first sign of optimism for his future. This promising discovery appears ironically to be the third accident in Otamendi's life.

The conclusion of the story shows Otamendi on his way to the "Manto Verde" mine, obsessed by the idea of the silver, the cemetery with his namesake, the ghost town, and Cerezo. Looming abruptly before him is "a calm lake of tremulous transparency. In the center of the lake, a large rocky island is seen which is reflected in the imaginary water." (un lago dormido, con una transparencia trémula. Al centro del lago se ve una gran isla rocosa, que se refleja en el agua imaginaria). These closing lines make us wonder if Otamendi's hopes and recently revived optimism are as illusory and evanescent as the mirage. Regardless, Otamendi has come alive and changed from our first introduction.

"La risa en el desierto" ("The Laugh in the Desert"), at first seems an apparent sequel to **"El pueblo muerto,"** but the similarities exist only in the names. We find a Juan Otamendi at the "Manto Verde" mine, confronting Menares, another solitary desert dweller, quite different from Cerezo. This Juan Otamendi, although only summarily sketched, seems to possess a different personality. The principal character is Menares. With the device of the story within a story, Prado uses an omniscient narrator to move from Otamendi and his reaction and relationship to Menares to the latter's narration of events of his youth. Prado in the telling of his story is less dependent on setting than in **"El pueblo muerto"** and is more effective showing the relationships of his characters to one another. The interplay of personalities is more complex and more truly revealing than in the first story.

Otamendi avoids Menares' company, "the man inspired him with a feeling of vague discomfort," but he has no other alternative since they are the only two at the mine. The narrator describes Menares in the first sentence as "a fat man starving for company and conversation." The ironic metaphor strikes the first of a series which reveal that surface impressions are only that. Menares' "pockmarked face, decayed teeth, bristly brows, and bloodshot eyes filled Otamendi with morbid loathing." (resultaba en extremo desagradable contemplar un rostro picado por la viruela, ver dientes podridos, cejas peladas y ojillos rojos y pitañosos). In spite of this repulsive exterior, Otamendi senses a "considerable delicacy of sentiment in his rough and vulgar host." (ese hombre vulgar y repulsivo revelaba en sus frases rasgos originales acusadores de una rara sensibilidad). At first the wily Menares avoids any personal revelations, always eluding questions about his past. The narrator remarks that "in the same way we wrap up fragile articles in cotton batting until they make big parcels, so Menares seemed to have wrapped up a subtle and sensitive spirit in his gross and enormous body." (Del mismo modo que para trasportar aparatos delicados se les envuelve en algodón basto, Menares envolvía en blanda gordura y gruesa apariencia un espíritu sutil). This image effectively insinuates that there is more to Menares than what we have witnessed so far. The unfolding of his enigmatic character occurs on one particular day "when the heat weighed like lead on the galvanized roof, when the shadow of the boulders outside shrank and shrank and finally vanished, when the sun's shafts were so intense that they seemed almost to collide in a sort of dazzling darkness . . .". (Es un mediodía que gravita a plomo sobre la calamina que cubre la casa. . . . Es la hora en que hasta las sombras de las piedras se recogen y desaparecen, y queda, de tanto sol, cierta disminución de la luz que entre sí choca, se equilibra y agota). Menares tells Otamendi that he can understand the Engineer's aversion for him and that it does not bother him so long as Otamendi will at least listen to him. After some clever maneuvering, he manages to capture Otamendi's unwilling attention and, between gulps of wine and nervous laughter, he commences his story. He feels certain that Otamendi will understand the significance of what he has to say.

As a young cadet, Menares was sent out to reconnoiter a tract of desert in the company of his lieutenant, Casares, and a corporal. Casares, known for "his rudeness and brutality," causes them "through his oversight, miscalculation, or obstinacy" to exhaust the provisions for themselves and their horses. Besides suffering from heat, fatigue, and hunger, Menares is the victim of all the abuse and insult that Casares can heap on him. A mad idea of murder seeps into his head and he is about to shoot the lieutenant in the back when the corporal spots a house with smoke, a sure sign of life. Menares' murder plans are abruptly substituted by hopes for food, water, and rest. After an agonizing climb to the house, they are greeted by a young man, a mine guard, who caters to their every need, all the while unceasingly commenting, questioning, and laughing.

The men, half starved, are hard pressed to answer the unending stream of chatter. Casares, in irritation, shoves the young man across the room. Not understanding or feigning not to understand, the young man proceeds to fill their glasses and offer them cigarettes, "without interrupting his hysterical giggle." The three men only return icy silence. He changes tactics by employing a calmer, quieter tone and begins to tell them ancient jokes. Casares, his patience exhausted, draws his gun and threatens to kill him if he is not silent at once. The young man continues laughing and reading aloud and the lieutenant fires his gun into the air. Banging his head to the table in hysterical sobs, he tells them that he only wants to talk and laugh a little, that he is starved for company having been alone there for so long. He breaks off his words with "a long, shrieking laugh so violent that the tears ran down his cheeks and he fell twitching to the ground." (dió una carcajada terrible que le hizo saltar las lágrimas, una carcajada que no concluía nunca, algo que fue cundiendo por todo su cuerpo y que le hizo caer al suelo con un temblor de locura).

When fully recovered from his seizure, the youth said nothing, got up, and walked outside to sit on a rock.

Casares ordered the other two men to mount up and offered the young man money for the food. His words are ignored. The mine guard merely watches them leave in stony silence. On the trail into the valley Menares thinks he hears a shout, but he no longer can see the house or the young man. At this point the lieutenant passes, his eyes full of tears, and rhetorically asks if he is not some sort of savage. The episode complete, Menares, in the concluding lines of the story, sardonically offers his guest, Otamendi, another glass of wine to help him sleep better.

Prado's exposition of the theme of loneliness and the very necessary, physical need of communicating thoughts to another being are sharply etched in this brief story. Each man reacts differently to the desert and the solitary life, but every man needs some one to talk to as much as he needs food or drink in order to survive in the hostile environment. Menares, of course, indirectly tries to convey a measure of his own loneliness and need for communication by relating his story to Otamendi, who obviously begrudges him every moment. Our understanding of Menares is deepened and our sympathy for him grows, in spite of our first unfavorable exterior impressions of him. Menares' relationship to Otamendi is similar to the lonely young man's relationship to the three men in his story. Menares is warning Otamendi not to be like another Casares or like himself as a youth.

Prado creates a wealth of psychological detail and insight in this last story. His gift for concise realistic expression was never better. It is strange, considering the considerable talent for the short story exhibited in these last two prose works, that he never pursued the possibilities further. Instead he was shrouded in a literary silence lasting almost ten years. We can only wonder if the deep psychological probing evident in *Country Judge* and these desert stories was too irritating to his increasingly delicate nervous and physical condition.

John R. Kelly (essay date 1974)

SOURCE: "Conclusion: Prado's Role and Influence on Chilean and Latin American Literature," in *Pedro Prado,* Twayne Publishers, Inc., 1974, pp. 133-37.

[*In the following essay, Kelly considers Prado's place among and influence on other Latin-American writers.*]

I PRADO'S HISTORICAL ROLE

Pedro Prado was the first important poetic voice heard in Chile in the twentieth century. From 1915 to 1924 he held the enviable status of undisputed leader of an entire generation of poets, painters, and critics. He became the pivotal figure in the general artistic renaissance in Santiago. His literary preeminence was due to both formal and thematic innovations. He initiated the use of free verse in Chile in his first book *Flores de Cardo*. The work, published in 1908, clearly broke with all prior poetic traditions. Prado first demonstrated in this slender volume, and subsequently in *El llamado del mundo* of 1913, that a poem could be something other than a vehicle of Romantic sentimentality or Modernist *preciosité*. A poem, he believed, need not adhere to any pre-established systems of rhythm and rhyme. This stance opened the way for later poetic experimentation by others.

In 1912 Prado was the first Chilean to utilize the hybrid genre of the prose poem in *La casa abandonada*. This significant, but neglected, early work developed through its very plastic form the poetic and thematic possibilities of metaphysical concerns and Chilean nature. Prado introduced the *peumo, boldo, patagua,* and *litre* trees into poetry. To this literary arboretum, he added a Chilean aviary of humble *chercanes, diucas, raras,* and other common native birds. He awakened Chileans to the poetic and esthetic values of the surrounding landscape and continued the metaphysical inquiry that he initiated in *El llamado del mundo.*

By 1915 Prado had defined the prose poem form and combined it with philosophy in one of his major works, *Los pájaros errantes.* From this book came the first clear manifestations of the anti-lyricism and anti-rationalism of modern Chilean poetry, particularly in the works of Pablo de Rokha, Pablo Neruda, and Vicente Huidobro. That same year Prado organized the group "Los Diez," composed of luminaries of the period, among whom Eduardo Barrios, novelist; Augusto d'Halmar, novelist and short story writer; Armando Donoso, critic; Gabriela Mistral, Nobel poet laureate, were a few (the best known perhaps outside of Chile's narrow frontiers) of the changing decimal membership. "Los Diez" brought artists together to exchange ideas, to enjoy the mutual support of similarly oriented people, and to encourage creative activities by implementing, in their subsidiary role as publishers, the establishment of a review devoted to all the arts.

Prado's publishing activities commenced in a short-lived review, *Revista contemporánea,* which he founded and financed in 1910. He intended it to be a serious vehicle of communication for the multiple aspects of Chile's art, thought, and culture. The noble attempt failed, but the impetus provided by his "brothers," "Los Diez," led him to establish once more a publishing enterprise. This time, however, "Los Diez" represented a self-supporting effort where poets and writers not necessarily members of "Los Diez" could find an outlet for their works without financing their own publication. This was a commercial novelty at the time which indicated to Chilean publishers that a portion of the reading public would actually pay for literary works of Chilean authorship.

Prado acquired an international reputation after the publication of *Alsino* in 1920. He had begun his novelistic career with a pleasant, escapist work, *La reina de Rapa-Nui,* in 1914. *Alsino* and *Un juez rural* established him among the best of the Latin American novelists and earned him a firm place in the histories of the novel of Spanish America. The psychological realism of *Un juez*

rural carried over to his last short stories **"El pueblo muerto"** and **"La risa en el desierto"** which have merit for their concise structure and their thematic impact.

At the end of his literary peak Prado, still experimenting, ventured into a hybrid dramatic form in *Androvar* which in some ways resembles a play, but is under his own classification a dramatic poem. The play was innovative in its concept of philosophy presented as drama.

The actual conclusion of Prado's long literary career came in four volumes of sonnets published from 1934 to 1947. The sonnets represented another kind of innovation for Prado since he had assiduously avoided traditional forms and genres throughout most of his life. The sonnets began as personal, lyric revelations and ended in hermetic, awkward expressions of philosophy. These poems hold little interest for the general reader. Even the most serious students and admirers of Prado's many talents come away saddened and disillusioned by their quality.

II PRADO'S INFLUENTIAL ROLE

Among the direct influences on individual writers, we must mention Prado's significance to Pablo Neruda, one of Latin America's principal poets and another Chilean Nobel laureate. The initial impact on Neruda was Prado's early and active encouragement of the adolescent poet. *Crepusculario,* Neruda's first book published in 1921, contained a woodcut of a drawing by Prado, a tacit *imprimatur.* Vocal approval came in the pages of *Zig-Zag.* Neruda tells us that Prado, "wrote before anyone else a quiet, masterly page, charged with meaning and foresight, like a dawn at sea." Neruda's poetic form in *Anillos,* published in 1926, clearly imitated Prado's earlier prose poem form. This book represented the young man's first endeavour in this genre, a genre synonymous with Prado. The older poet's imprint is palpably evident in Neruda's "El otoño de las enredaderas" ("Autumn of the Vines"), "Imperial del Sur" ("South Imperial"), and "Primavera de agosto" ("August Spring"). The imagery of these three poems resembles Prado's in **"La esperanza"** (**"Hope"**) and **"El guijarro"** (**"The Pebble"**) from *Los pájaros errantes.* Both men had recourse to images of leaves, birds, flight, the wind and its voice, and of the ocean's restless, eternal movement forever reminding man of his own fleeting existence. Neruda's poetic lexicon, syntax, and rhythm in the first two prose poems reflect those of **"La esperanza"** (**"Hope"**) and **"El guijarro"** (**"The Pebble"**) in *Los pájaros errantes,* but **"Primavera de agosto"** finds its echo in Prado's even earlier *La casa abandonada* in **"Las patatas"** and **"El bosque"** where Chilean trees are described and sung. Prado used his descriptions to form didactic symbols; Neruda sang of his unbridled joy, almost passion at the arrival of spring, of "time's return."

Prado's deep, poetic love for Chile, first revealed in *La casa abandonada,* does not wane until after 1924 when he becomes more preoccupied with death. The birds, the trees, the plants, the Andes, and especially the sea are integral parts of Prado's best poetic works. The same aspects of nature are projected in Neruda's *Anillos,* in his *General Song,* particularly that portion known as the "General Song of Chile," and in *Elemental Odes.* For both poets, the close observation and rendering of nature and the landscape have as their end the celebration of instinctual, telluric, and poetic knowledge over inferior logic and reason.

The single most important and enduring force exerted on Neruda was Prado's intellectual stimulation and inspiration. This meaningful, intangible influence received eloquent public recognition in Neruda's autobiographical speech, "Mariano Latorre, Pedro Prado, and My Own Shadow." This speech, read in 1962, pointed out the immense debt that writers of his generation owed to earlier masters. He confessed that "noting in my own book of accounts, I owe no small amount to three great men of our literature" (the critic "Alone," Eduardo Barrios, and Pedro Prado). In Neruda's recollections, Prado's gift of intelligent conversation most clearly stands out. He recounts that "suddenly one summer afternoon I felt the need of Prado's conversation. . . . His stock of direct observations on people and nature was prodigious. Perhaps this is what is called wisdom and Prado most approaches what in my adolescence I could call a wise man. . . . But no one since has given me that sensation of the supreme power of intelligence received at my young age, not even André Malraux who crossed more than once with me . . . the roads between France and Spain, giving off the electrical sparks of his extremist Cartesianism." Neruda adds two other famous European literary names, but hastens to clarify that "among my wise friends this Pedro Prado of my youth has remained in my memory like the tranquil image of a great blue mirror in which might have been reflected, in an extensive way, an essential landscape made of meditation and light, a serene cup always brimming with reasoning and balance."

Gabriela Mistral echoes and corroborates Neruda's observations on the magic effect of Prado's conversation. She wrote that his "conversation will have to be called the most substantial in Chile, which is wise and restless at the same time, so pithily original this talk and so manly in the real virtues of manhood (of creating, of teaching, and of illuminating), that he who enjoyed it has eaten of the ox of Ulysses sprinkled with spices and he will seek a similar conversation his whole life. There are days, days of strong hungers and months of shivering in foreign lands, when I look for that lost conversation the same way as my deluded eyes look for the Andes."

Apart from his historical, innovative role in Chilean literature and his intellectual influence on two Nobel laureates, Prado continues to interest, if he no longer directly influences, contemporary Chilean writers. It is notable that in a 1970 poll of the reading preferences of 250 Chilean writers, Prado was fourth in esteem after Pablo Neruda, Gabriela Mistral, and the novelist Manuel Rojas among national authors. Even though most of Prado's works and reputation have been confined to Chile, his novels and the original, unique prose poems of *La casa abandonada* and *Los pájaros errantes* have justifiably earned him a place of honor in the evolution of Latin American literature. No writer of his time, and possibly no writer since, at least in Chile, has more successfully combined philosophy, esthetic good sense, fiction, and poetry.

FURTHER READING

Criticism

Adams, Robert Martin. "Fiction Chronicle." *The Hudson Review* XXI, No. 1 (Spring 1968): 225-31.
    Includes a review of *Country Judge* that observes, " Señor Prado manages the quiet naïvetés of his story with a kind of wise openness which has been in the Spanish tradition since *Don Quixote.*"

Craig, G. Dundas. "Pedro Prado." In *The Modernist Trend in Spanish-American Poetry*, pp. 154-67, 313-15. New York: Gordian Press, 1971.
    Overview of Prado's poetic themes, with selected translations of his poems.

Kelly, John R. *Pedro Prado.* New York: Twayne Publishers, 1974, 154 p.
    Full-length study of Prado's works, life, and influence on Chilean and Latin-American literature.

The following source published by Gale contains additional coverage of Prado's life and works: *Contemporary Authors,* Vol. 131.

Mikhail Prishvin

1873-1954

(Full name Mikhail Mikhailovich Prishvin) Russian essayist, short story writer, novelist, agronomist, naturalist, and ethnographer.

INTRODUCTION

Prishvin is primarily known as a nature writer whose works evoke in realistic, lyrical detail the birds, animals, and plants of the Russian countryside, and its people, folklore, and language. While his career spanned several decades of a tumultuous period in Russian history, his writings remained largely unaffected by the revolutionary politics of Bolshevism or the socialist realism of Stalinist Russia. Instead, his sketches, short stories, and novels chronicle the life of the common people and their relationship to nature, treating in symbolic fashion universal themes of good and evil and the place of human beings in the cosmos. Although Prishvin's work influenced subsequent Russian artists, it has not been widely studied in Russia or abroad.

Biographical Information

Prishvin was born on an estate near Elets in Oryol province, the son of a well-to-do merchant who provided him with an upper-class education at Elets High School and Riga Polytechnicum. While at Riga, which he attended from 1893-1897, Prishvin's education was interrupted when he was jailed for his support of Marxist doctrines, a common occurrence among students of that era. He finished school at Leipzig University in Germany, where he graduated with a degree in agronomy. By 1904, Prishvin had returned to Russia to work in his chosen field. It was during this time that he began to write stories and sketches for children, and developed an interest in folk speech. In 1905, he was advised by an acquaintance to study folklore in northern Russia, and his first collection of sketches describing animal life and nature, *V Kraiu Nepugannykh Ptits* (*In the Land of Unfrightened Birds*), was written on this trip. Published in 1907, the sketches were well received, and Prishvin was invited to join a circle of writers that included the symbolist poet and novelist Alexei Remizov, whose neorealist work influenced his own. Prishvin continued to travel throughout Russia as a naturalist, hunter, and writer, recording people's stories and describing the beauties of the countryside. Although he wrote a number of other works before the revolution of 1917, including *Za Volshebnym Kolobkom* (*The Bun*), a folk tale with autobiographical detail, and *Adam and Eve*, a sketch based on the biblical story, he first attained prominence with the publication of his folkloric, autobiographical novels *Kurymushka* and its continuation published in serial form, *Kashcheeva*

Tsep' (*The Chain of Kashchey,*). Prishvin's reputation grew steadily during the 1930s and 1940s with such works as *Crane's Birthplace,* sketches depicting unfulfilled love, *Zhen'-shen', Koren'zhizni* (*Jen Sheng: The Root of Life,*), a novel describing a man's search for a legendary Chinese plant, and *Lesnaya Kapel'* (*Drops from the Forest*), a series of lyrical prose poems on nature. By the 1950s, he had achieved widespread popularity and literary influence in his country, despite remaining outside mainstream Soviet politics. He died in Moscow on 16 January 1954.

Major Works

Prishvin's major works evolved from the lyrical sketch form, a type of poetic, philosophical essay that he developed in such early works as *In the Land of Unfrightened Birds* and *The Bun*. Using realistic, colorful detail and folklore motifs, these works explore such themes as the loss of childhood innocence, the nature of good and evil, unfulfilled love, the healing powers of work and creativity, and humans's link with nature. Mikhail Alpatov, nicknamed Kurymushka ("Little Rabbit"), a man of the common people, is the hero of Prishvin's first novel, through whom he gives a fictionalized account of his own early life and initiation into the sometimes frightening world of adults. Alpatov's story continues in *The Chain of Kaschey,* a cycle of ten tales that describe the young man's encounters with the evils of poverty, injustice, and greed. Such characters from Russian folklore as the wizard Kaschey, who enslaves humans in his chains of evil, and the fairy-tale maiden Marya Morevna, who must be rescued from Kaschey, symbolize for Alpatov the state of contemporary society. As had Prishvin, Alpatov tries and rejects a totally political solution to these universal problems. Later, after losing his first great love, he finds solace and hope in the creative forces of life and in such important but mundane work as draining swamps for the Russian people. In *Crane's Birthplace,* a cycle of sketches, Prishvin expands on this theme of lost love, and through a depiction of life in the country, delineates his philosophy of the place of humans in the cosmos.

Critical Reception

During his lifetime, critics deemed Prishvin the best writer on nature to emerge from prerevolutionary and Soviet Russia, citing the abundance of natural detail in his works. Later critics acknowledged the influence on subsequent Russian artists of his simple, concrete language and syntax derived from folk speech, his origination of the lyrical sketch form, and his cosmic themes. While Prishvin is relatively unknown today, the critic Marc Slonim states that the writer's "whole outlook is so very Russian, his stories and fairy tales are so akin to folklore, his descriptions convey so strongly the smell of Russian fields and forests, and he gives his reader such a perfect image of the country's vastness and its inexhaustible vitality, that he must be ranked as high as . . . Remizov and be considered a worthy follower of Tolstoy."

PRINCIPAL WORKS

V Kraiu Nepugannykh Ptits [*In the Land of Unfrightened Birds*] (sketches) 1907
Za Volshebnym Kolobkom [*The Bun*] (folk tale) 1908
Adam and Eve (sketch) 1909
Kurymushka (novel) 1924
The Springs of Berendey (short stories) 1925
Kashcheeva Tsep' [*The Chain of Kashchey*] (novel) 1930*
Crane's Birthplace (sketches) 1932
Zhen'-shen', Koren' zhizni [*Jen Sheng: The Root of Life*] (novel) 1932
Facelia (sketches) 1940
Undressed Spring (sketches) 1940
Lesnaya Kapel' [*Drops from the Forest*] (prose poems) 1943
Collected Works. 6 vols. (sketches, novels, short stories, folk tales) 1956-57

*First published in serial form, 1923-1928.

CRITICISM

Vera Alexandrova (essay date 1963)

SOURCE: "Mikhail Prishvin (1873-1954)," in *A History of Soviet Literature: 1917-1964, From Gorky to Solzhenitsyn,* translated by Mirra Ginsburg, Anchor Books, 1964, pp. 222-35.

[*In the following essay, which was first published in Russian in 1963, Alexandrova offers an overview of Prishvin's life and works.*]

Among the writers of the older generation who had won their literary fame before the revolution of 1917, but had later become an organic part of Soviet literature, we must name, first and foremost, the late Mikhail Prishvin.

In his autobiography, written for the anthology *Writers* (edited by V. Lidin, Moscow, 1928), Prishvin relates only a few basic facts about his life:

> Out of my childhood, adolescence, and early youth I fashioned a tale which I have not yet altogether finished living, and which gives me great joy. The title of this autobiographical tale is *Kurymushka.* It would be tedious now to talk again about that period. My youth was revolutionary—the customary youth of the Russian intellectual. I belonged to the circle of the archaic Bolshevik, the well-known Vassily Danilovich Ulrikh. After serving a prison term in Riga, I went to Leipzig, where I studied agronomy at the university. Returning to Russia, I engaged in agronomic work for a year and a half. The special literature in this field still retains from that period [1904] a bulky work on *Potatoes in Field and Garden Culture* and several pamphlets and articles. At the same time I devoted myself to the study of folk speech. In 1905 I abandoned forever the profession of an agronomist and went north, where I wrote the book *In the Land of the Unfrightened Birds.*

In this autobiographical sketch Prishvin does not speak of his first story, "Sashok," published in a children's magazine, *Rodnik,* in 1906. We might also have omitted to mention it if the writer had not used its plot again in the story **"At the Burnt Stump,"** which appeared in the magazine *Apollon* in 1910. Later the same plot—about the hunter and dreamer Gusyok—was developed for a third time in the opening part of the long autobiographical epic *The Chain of Kashchey,* which began to appear in print in 1923.

Prishvin's first story, **"Sashok,"** went unnoticed by the critics. The writer won recognition only after the publication of his book of sketches *In the Land of the Unfrightened Birds* (1906). This book has its own curious history. When he was still working as an agronomist, Prishvin began to write stories and sketches for children. Soon afterward he went to live in Petersburg. Here he met the future academician and ethnographer, N. Onchukov, who advised him to go north to study and record folklore. Prishvin went to Vyg Lake, in the province of Arkhangelsk. When he returned, he brought with him the manuscript of the book of sketches. The book was not merely noticed; it produced a great impression.

Soon afterward the writer Alexey Remizov brought Prishvin into a circle of young decadent writers, who influenced him to some extent. Inwardly, however, they remained alien to him. Among the writers who exerted a lasting influence on him, he mentions only Lermontov, Tyutchev, Aksakov, and Lev Tolstoy.

Prishvin's second book, *The Bun,* utilizes for its plot the famous Russian folk tale about a bun (*Kolobok*). Out of a handful of flour, an old woman bakes a bun and puts it on the window sill. The bun jumps down from the window, rolls across the house and into the street, and begins to wander over the world, becoming a symbol of free and footloose wandering. Prishvin's bun encounters on its way many other folk-tale characters—Marya Morevna, Kashchey the Deathless, Baba-Yaga. *The Bun* begins in the spirit of a fairy tale; written on two levels—fairy tale and autobiography—it is imbued with fine lyricism. In this book Prishvin introduces himself for the first time as a lyrical hero. His goal is to realize his dreams of a new, happy, and beautiful world, where the childhood vision may be reborn within the hero himself in all its unspoiled freshness and integrity. And foremost among Prishvin's dreams is the desire for freedom of thought and for creative freedom.

It was of this book that Alexander Blok said that it was not poetry, but added a moment later: "No, it is poetry, and something else as well." Prishvin refers to this comment in his essay **"Baring the Method,"** in the book *Crane Homeland.* After long reflection on the meaning of Blok's "something," Prishvin came to the conclusion that a sketch or an essay always contains two elements: the writer begins with direct observation of people and nature; some of this he succeeds in condensing into poetic images, the rest is presented as direct material, interwoven with his comments and ideas. Prishvin started out on his literary path by combining elements of the folk tale with original philosophic lyricism. Such a synthesis of two entirely different genres in the essay had never been attempted in Russian literature before.

Among the works published by Prishvin before the revolution of 1917, one must name *Adam and Eve* (1909), *The Black Arab* (1910), *At the Walls of the Unseen City* (1907), *Nikon Starokolenny* (1907), and *The Beast of Krutoyarsk* (1907).

In contrast to other writers, who are loath to offer autobiographical data, Prishvin willingly and even joyously talks about his life. In addition to the brief essay written for the anthology *Writers,* we know of four other autobiographical sketches, each of them containing pages of incomparable freshness and perfection. In **"The Hunt after Happiness,"** (included in the book *Crane Home-*

land), the writer tells of the mistake he had made shortly before the revolution in building a house on the plot of land he had inherited from his mother. In the eyes of the peasants Prishvin was a *pomeshchik,* a "landowner." After the revolution, for a time, they did not molest the writer, respecting his mother's memory. Later, however, "strangers" arrived from "other parts," and soon Prishvin received an official order to vacate the premises. At the meeting which passed the resolution to evict him, a friend of the writer attempted to intervene in his behalf: "One day we may raise a monument to him, as we did to Pushkin." But others cried: "There you are! That's why we should throw him out now, so that we wouldn't have to bother raising monuments afterward."

In his essay **"Baring the Method,"** Prishvin tells in detail how he arrived at his own literary genre and how it was, generally, that he chose such a "slow road to literature, through ethnography, by horsecart, as it were":

> I came to literature at an age when a man no longer has any need to strike a pose, and without any thought of gaining a position in society. . . . I began to write in the era of superfluous people, of Chekhov characters. The absence of a way of life in which an artist's personality develops thoughtlessly, like a flower, was about to condemn me also to impotent meditation about the problem of moral reconciliation of life with one's childhood vision. . . .

Prishvin first described how he overcame this "impotent meditation" in his *Adam and Eve* (1909), in which he made use of the Biblical legend of the two Adams. According to this legend, the second Adam came into the world long after the first had sinned and suffered exile from Paradise, after he had multiplied, and his children had populated the earth. This second Adam became *the Landless Adam;* he took up the work of cultivating a narrow strip of land. The *ocherk* or "sketch" form developed by Prishvin was just such a "narrow strip of land." And one of the most characteristic qualities of his sketch is its rich suggestiveness, its wealth of "subtextual" content.

The introductory chapter of Prishvin's autobiographical prose epic *The Chain of Kashchey* sheds a good deal of light on Prishvin, the writer. In this chapter—"The Rabbit"—Prishvin describes a walk he took one autumn day, which led him past the country house where he had spent his childhood. As he looked at the house and the surrounding landscape, Prishvin was struck by the picture of "triple dying": everything around seemed to be dying— the house, the day, and the year, with its golden falling leaves. And in the midst of this, at the end of a long avenue strewn with maple leaves, on the ivied terrace, sat a rabbit. At first the presence of this rabbit seemed to the writer almost a deliberate mockery. He was at that time struggling with the idea of a novel in which he hoped to describe the house and the years of his youth spent in it. Many of the pictures were already formed in his mind, but he still had no central hero. And he asked himself:

"Can it be that my beloved native land will not provide me with a hero? I thought of the many remarkable men born on this land. There, not too far away, lay the fields once plowed by Tolstoy; here were the woods where Turgenev had hunted; here Gogol had come to seek advice from the extraordinary old monk Amvrosy. How many great men had sprung from this black-earth region, but they seemed, indeed, to have come and gone like spirits, while the land was left all the poorer—exhausted, gutted with clay ravines, covered with dwellings unworthy of man, resembling heaps of manure."

It occurred to the writer that some little old peasant, who had done nothing in his lifetime beyond the humble planting of orchards in the ravines to hold down the soil, was perhaps a worthier hero for his novel than many of the great men who had left this land. Presently another idea came to Prishvin: it was not necessary to have a hero; the novel could do very well without him—"he can simply come out, like the rabbit, to sit for a few moments on the terrace, and the most grandiose events will follow."

When he reached this conclusion, Prishvin ceased to torment himself and began to write a story, told in the first person by his alter ego, Alpatov, whose childhood nickname was Kurymushka, a local expression meaning "Little Rabbit." *Kurymushka* was first published as a children's book. At the same time Prishvin began his major novel, *The Chain of Kashchey,* the separate parts of which he called "links."

The Chain of Kashchey was conceived as a cycle of *povesti* or "tales," linked by the events in the life of his principal character, Mikhail Alpatov, beginning with the period of Czar Alexander II and ending with the overthrow of Nicholas II. In a certain sense *The Chain* is a parallel to Gorky's *Klim Samgin,* and it helps us, to some extent, to see where Gorky had sinned in his work against the pre-revolutionary intelligentsia.

Prishvin is right, of course, in saying that *The Chain of Kashchey* grew out of sketches and essays. It is reminiscent of an antique patch-quilt, in which a multitude of pieces are sewn into one large fabric. It is not by chance that the narrative abounds in lyrical digressions addressed to the contemporary reader. Each digression is rich in allusions, which heighten the modern reader's interest in the tale of the distant past. Thus, in "The Green Door" (the sixth link), the author says that, in the days of Alpatov's youth, "there was a law for men of conscience in our land, which said: 'one cannot live like this.' The prison cell seemed the only possible dwelling for the man of conscience, a temporary ordeal to be suffered until the day of the world catastrophe, after which it would become permissible to live well, because the terrible inequality would then be a thing of the past."

In another passage of this link the writer speaks again to the contemporary reader, explaining:

> My friend, this reference to our age gives me still

greater courage to yield to my imagination, for I have become convinced that our fathers have not transmitted to their children any ready-made forms of marriage; that, in these revolutionary times, mothers have bartered their daughters' dowries for bread; and in this emptiness of life, Alpatov's dreams are real and will find their own interpreters.

The first link of the epic—"**Azure Beavers**"—describes Alpatov's early childhood and his father's death. Kurymushka's father, a man of ready enthusiasms, has reduced his family to financial ruin. When he dies, he leaves his wife, Marya Ivanovna, and their five children without means. Fortunately, Marya Ivanovna, like the writer's mother, is a descendant of an old merchant family and possesses considerable business acumen, which helps her to cope with her difficult situation.

Feeling the approach of the end, his father calls Kurymushka and gives him a slip of paper with a drawing of some strange "azure beavers"—as if trying to bequeath to him the gift of imagination and the hunger for the "unknown." The leitmotiv of this first link is the dream of something extraordinary, a dream intensified by the meeting with Marya Morevna, the fairy-tale maiden. To Kurymushka, this maiden is reincarnated in the young daughter of the general from whom his parents had bought their estate. Like a true little knight errant, Kurymushka is fired with the idea of saving Marya Morevna from captivity in the land of the evil wizard Kashchey. And, in his imagination, Kashchey is the old man he heard about in a conversation among adults, who had spoken of some old man who "arranged things" for young women.

The second link—"The Little Cain"—describes the shattering of illusion, the first failure, complicated by an episode first sketched by Prishvin in *The Bun.* This theme—the search for a forgotten or still unknown land—plays an important part in Prishvin's work. The second link, like the sketch **"The Hunt after Happiness,"** relates how Kurymushka attempts with several schoolmates to escape to a certain mysterious country called "Asia." On the third day the fugitives are captured by a district policeman. The young adventurers are the butt of many jokes, and a little ditty is composed for the occasion: "They went to Asia, and came to the gymnasium." All of Kurymushka's life seems to flow through two irreconcilable worlds: the childish world, full of mysteries, illusions, and dreams, and the frightening world of adults who hide their secrets from children. The childish world is inhabited by oppressed children and hapless paupers like the penniless dreamer and passionate hunter Gusyok, whom we first met in the guise of Sashok in Prishvin's earliest published story (1906).

When Kurymushka discovers for himself the terrifying world of adults, he is filled with animosity toward it. The longing to free himself of the dreadful "chain of Kashchey" is born and grows stronger in the young hero under the impact of this menacing dark world, governed by "adults."

Prishvin describes Alpatov's youth in the third link; and Kurymushka's return to his mother and his desire to continue his education in the fourth.

The fifth link—"State Criminal"—tells about the birth of his great love, for Ina Rostovtseva, whom Alpatov meets during his imprisonment for revolutionary activity. At that time a number of young women who sympathized with the revolutionary movement posed as sisters or fiancées of prisoners without families in order to obtain permission to visit them in prison. Ina becomes Alpatov's "prison fiancée," but he falls in love with her in earnest, and searches for her all over Petersburg after his release.

Most of the links of the second part of the *Chain* are devoted to Alpatov's love for Ina, his search for her, their brief meetings, their friendship and alienation, and his final break with her. This theme of the great love which remains unfulfilled became the central theme of many of Prishvin's later works, particularly of his book *Ginseng* (1933), his remarkable cycle of sketches *Undressed Spring* (1940), and *Facelia* (1940).

Among the links of the second part of *The Chain of Kashchey,* the sixth—"The Green Door"—is especially important for insight into Prishvin's creative world. Against the background of his search for the elusive beloved, the writer sketches in his impressions of prewar Germany and his reflections on the great and little truth of ordinary people. While he describes the German worker Schwarz and his peasant wife with warmth and respect, Alpatov finds that many people of their circle aspire to little more than honest service to that "brief truth" which in Russia is called the philistine way of life. But it is also in Germany that Alpatov becomes aware of his own inconsonance with the world of his revolutionary comrades. He makes this discovery during one of his visits to the Dresden Art Gallery, where he often comes to admire the Sistine Madonna. One day he meets at the gallery his friend and comrade Nesgovorov. A short, but intensely charged dialogue follows. The blunt and direct Nesgovorov, who has no interest in art and no understanding of it, asks:

> "What has happened to you? Why are you sitting here, among the bourgeoisie, all dressed up and staring at the Madonna like an owl?"

Alpatov tries to explain why the Sistine Madonna moves him so deeply (her face reminds him of a Russian reaper he once saw in a field). But his words fail to reach Nesgovorov. With perhaps a deliberate exaggeration of his rejection of art, Nesgovorov says that his one wish as he looks at the Madonna is to hide under one of the seats until evening, when the guards go home, and then destroy the picture. He is convinced that the visitors to the gallery are "idlers," who find in the Madonna "an escape, a blessed refuge to help them forget their obligations to mankind." Alpatov replies that he could "kill" any man who destroyed the Madonna. Nesgovorov reminds Alpatov once more that revolutionaries are "midwives"

who must cut "the umbilical cord that ties people to God." And Alpatov feels more poignantly than ever that he can never accept Nesgovorov's blunt and simple philosophy.

In the seventh link ("The Young Faust") Prishvin describes his hero's life at the German university, his study of German philosophy, and his encounters with other Russian students abroad, who are shown in a number of fascinating portraits, some of them reminiscent of the heroes of Dostoyevsky's *The Possessed.* This link also indicates the direction of Alpatov's future work. With the diploma of "Torfmeister," he plans to return to Russia and devote himself to draining its many swamps.

The final links of *The Chain of Kashchey* deal with the developing relationship between Alpatov and Ina. But the brief episodes of friendship alternate with new periods of alienation. Soon after his return to Petersburg, Alpatov comes to the conclusion that his great love does not evoke a genuine response in Ina, a young woman of another, privileged world, and they part. With his diploma as Torfmeister, Alpatov-Prishvin soon finds work in the provinces. His life there, illuminated by his inner experiences and meditations, provides material for the cycle of sketches collected in the book *Crane Homeland* (1929), which, in a way, is a sequel to *The Chain of Kashchey.* Significantly, it is subtitled "The Story of an Unsuccessful Love."

To collect material for this book Prishvin made a number of visits in the course of several summers to the Dubny district and Moscow Polesye. The stories of his meetings with the local residents, his reflections on life, and his descriptions of nature, astonishing in their perfection, place *Crane Homeland* and *Berendey's Kingdom* among the finest achievements of the newest Russian literature. There is, perhaps, no other writer with such an ear for folk speech, with such talent for seizing and conveying the sly uniqueness of the man of the people. Prishvin never strove for sensational material or striking plots. He merely gathered what lay in the path of his many wanderings, with gun in hand, over the forests, swamps, and fields of the wide expanses of central Russia. Yet, seen through the prism of the writer's "loving attention," the trifles gathered in this way became transformed into glittering jewels of enchanting beauty.

Here are a few illustrations. One day the writer hears about a chief of militia in an out-of-the-way village, with the incredible name of Schopenhauer. Prishvin takes a trip to the village and finds Schopenhauer, no longer a chief of militia, but a pensioned invalid. Making his acquaintance, Prishvin soon learns the secret of his name. His former name was Aslenkov. As a private in World War I, Aslenkov was wounded and taken prisoner. In the German hospital he was under the care of a nurse called Luiza Schopenhauer. Returning to Russia after the revolution, Aslenkov found all his relatives leaning toward the old way of life; one of them had even become a kulak. But Aslenkov himself sympathized with the revolution and joined the Communist Party. And so he wanted to shake off "all the Aslenkov dust" from his feet. When he learned that it was now possible to change one's name, he recalled Luiza Schopenhauer. To him, she remained an incarnation of all that was brightest and most beautiful in life, and he decided to adopt her name. Of course, he knew nothing of the existence of a famous German philosopher of that name, or of the remoteness of his philosophy from that of Karl Marx.

Prishvin seems to be most fascinated by episodes and encounters in which the old and new in the life of the people are fantastically intertwined. Describing a geological excursion into the depths of the Pereyaslavl district (*Secrets of the Earth*), Prishvin draws a remarkable portrait of Father Filimon, a former priest now working as a ferryman on Pleshcheev Lake. At first Father Filimon continued even after the revolution to perform the ritual duties of a priest at the ancient little church in his village. Soon the deacon and the caretaker left, and the priest took over their work as well. Meantime, his family suffered great hardship, and his wife went to work in a factory. But it was not until he lost the last member of his flock that Father Filimon locked up the church and became a ferryman, soon developing a great love for the lake. And the local people coined a new expression for ferrying across the lake: they called it "crossing with the priest."

Despite the folk character of his topics and language, Prishvin had no illusions about the speedy acceptance of his works by the people. "The best I can hope for," he wrote in *Crane Homeland,* "is the popular success of some love ditty of my composition. But *Crane Homeland* and *Berendey's Kingdom* would evoke nothing but mockery. . . . *Crane Homeland* will come here many years later, and then only in fragments, included in some school-books. . . ."

The same idea is wonderfully illustrated in the incident with the writer's little friend, the shepherd boy Vanyushka. Vanyushka did not read the story Prishvin gave him. He began it, but it bored him and he says, as if to justify himself: "If you were writing the truth! But I'll bet you made it all up yourself. . . ." And Vanyushka boasts that he can write a better story. When Prishvin asks him to tell it, the boy's story, about a night on the swamp, turns out to consist of but a dozen words: "It's night. There is a huge, huge bush by the water. I sit under the bush, and the ducklings keep going—swee, swee, swee." The writer remarks that the story is very short, but Vanyushka is undaunted: "Why short? They kept on with their 'swee, swee' all night long. . . ." After this conversation Prishvin reflects for a long time "about the great creative power and sense of freedom" inherent in every living being and vividly expressed in Vanyushka's rebuff to the writer and the boy's own story.

In the early days of the war Prishvin wrote two cycles of sketches, *Undressed Spring* (first published in the magazine *Oktyabr,* April-May 1940) and *Facelia* (published in *Novy Mir,* September 1940), and collected fragments of his **"Writer's Diary"** in a book under the title of *The Spring of the World.* In all these works we find the same Prishvin, with an undiminished feeling for the truth of life and the truth of art, telling many stories of his encounters with people, often with matchless artistry. One of these stories tells of the writer's encounter with a coachman, a man of heroic proportions, called Pcholka, or Little Bee.

> We saw before us a giant with a long blond beard, sitting in the coachman's seat of an ancient sleigh, such as one rarely sees today. There was a pride in the giant's carriage that seemed to flow from an exuberance of strength and freedom, as if he were not a mere driver, but the unchallenged master of the entire Volga region. Maxim Gorky had this quality, and another, too, a great singer, also born on the Volga. It was as if they drew it from the Volga herself. She spreads in flood, but these men are ready to spread with their whole souls, paying no more attention to trifles than to the dust under their feet.

Prishvin began a conversation with Pcholka, in which some nearby fishermen joined in. When the writer used the word "fine-pored," a small man, with a gray, sharp, and clever face, who also turned out to be a fisherman, remarked to him that he was speaking to "dark, ignorant men of Nekrasov's day; to them, a simple word like 'fine-pored' is less intelligible than Chinese." To Prishvin's astonishment, another member of the group turned to the skeptical citizen, crying out: "You're pretty small-holed yourself!"

It is not easy to be an independent writer in a country held in the rigid grip of a dictatorship. Prishvin did not always succeed in retaining his independence. It is enough to recall his resignation from the literary group Pereval at a time when it was under fire from the official critics. But in his work itself, Prishvin succeeded better than many of his contemporaries in remaining free and independent—a writer with his own creative "meridian."

A wealth of material on this problem may be found in the writer's *Literary Diary,* which he kept for fifty years. Some of the entries were used by the writer himself during his lifetime, in works like *Undressed Spring, Facelia, The Storeroom of the Sun* (1945) and *The Eyes of the Earth* (1945-46). But most of the *Diary* began to appear posthumously. Some of Prishvin's ideas about the nature of creativeness are closely akin to the thinking of Boris Pasternak in *Doctor Zhiyago.* "I have left far behind me," remarks Prishvin in one of his entries, "any proud attempts to govern my creative work as if it were a mechanism. But I have made a thorough study of the conditions under which I can produce sound works: the first of these is the integrity of my individuality. And so, recognition and protection of the conditions necessary for maintaining this integrity have become my guiding principles in relation to creative work. I do not direct my creative activity as if it were a mechanism, but I conduct myself in such a way as to assure that durable works will come out of me."

During the celebration of Prishvin's seventy-fifth birthday in 1948, the writer confessed in an interview with a reporter for the *Literary Gazette* that he had not the slightest desire for the fame of a "master" or "singer"; what he wished most of all was to be a "contemporary." In one of his diary entries in 1952 (published after his death), Prishvin dwells on this theme in greater detail:

> I look at some people and think of how they follow time and will pass, with all that is temporary. But contemporary men are those who are the masters of time. Thus, Shakespeare is far more contemporary to us than N., who watches the trend of the time so closely that yesterday he argued for plays without conflicts, but today he has heard something new, and now is all for conflict. . . .

And, as we review his extensive and uniquely original literary heritage, we see that Prishvin truly succeeded in being a "contemporary" writer in the most dramatic epoch of Russia's history. But what renders him "contemporary" is not so much his lyrical comments and descriptions, as the images of ordinary people he has recorded in his work, with their spiritual wealth, independence, and profound sense of innate freedom. Truly, Prishvin was not only the singer of the "land of unfrightened birds." In the years of Russia's deepest bondage, he was able to portray the *unfrightened soul of the man of the people.*

Marc Slonim (essay date 1964)

SOURCE: "Mikhail Prishvin: The Nature Lover," in *Soviet Russian Literature: Writers and Problems,* Oxford University Press, Inc., 1964, pp. 105-11.

[*In the following essay, Slonim discusses Prishvin's treatment of nature in his works.*]

The main slogan of the industrial revolution promoted in Russia by the Communists was "the conquest of nature by man." The Party, repeating the statement of Bazarov, the nihilist hero of Turgenev's *Fathers and Sons,* that "nature is not a temple but a workshop, and man is a toiler in it," hailed the struggle against elemental forces, and saw mankind's historical aim as changing and shaping the face of the created world according to the rational designs of organized human beings. In an agricultural country such an ideology was bound to generate many contradictions. The conquerors of nature were linked to nature by a thousand bonds, they loved it and often felt that true happiness could be found only in its motherly womb. Though they built cities and power stations, harnessed rivers and bored through mountains, they frequently wondered whether supreme wisdom was not hidden in the serenity of the sky and the silence of the forest.

This contradiction was directly or obliquely reflected in fiction, and it explains the survival of a Rousseau-Tolstoy-back-to-nature trend in Soviet literature—even though such a tendency was condemned by official ideology. In the 'twenties and 'thirties its strength was proven by the growing popularity of Mikhail Prishvin. Acknowledged by Gorky as a first-rate writer, Prishvin was loved by millions of readers, and Communist critics had to make dialectical somersaults in order to explain why this "investigator of nature" was overshadowing the laudators of the Five-Year Plan and the social realists.

Prishvin was born in 1873 into a family of rich merchants. His father owned the estate Khrushchevo, near Elets, in Oryol province, and Mikhail's childhood was similar to that of the noblemen of Central Russia. His father died when he was 7. A few years later, while a student in Elets gymnasium he "escaped to America," but was duly caught and brought home. He had the typical upbringing of a radical intellectual, and since his family was connected with Populists, Mikhail became involved in revolutionary circles, was arrested, and subsequently went to Germany to finish his education. An agronomist by profession, he was an ethnographer, a folklorist, and a hunter by avocation, and began to write by the turn of the century. He wandered all over Russia, particularly in the north, with his rifle and notebook, listening "to the voice of forest, rock and water," talking to old peasants and young huntsmen, and gathering a tremendous amount of first-hand information about birds, beasts, plants, and human beings. Although his first books, such as *In the Land of Unfrightened Birds* (1907) and *The Little Round Loaf* (1908), which won him an award from the Geographical Society, were appreciated by nature lovers, he did not acquire a general public until after the Revolution, and he did not emerge as a mature and original artist until the 1920s. He was 50 when he began to play an important role in Soviet letters. His collections of tales, such as *The Springs of Berendey* (1925), and his vast autobiographical novel *The Chain of Kashchey,* serialized between 1923 and 1929 and published in book form in 1930, made him widely known, and his popularity kept growing. Other books, such as *Crane's Birthplace, The Calendar of Nature, Root of Life—Ginseng* (1932), *Forest Drip-Drop* (1940), *The Larder of the Sun* (1943), have been reprinted countless times.

Prishvin's work has a strong personal note: a wanderer and a sportsman, he wrote masterly sketches about nature which can be linked only with Aksakov's classic *Notes of a Rifle Hunter* (1852). "I do not know any other Russian writer," said Gorky, "in whom the knowledge and the love of the earth are so harmoniously united." For authors like Turgenev or Bunin nature is either a background or a frame and is conceived as a force hostile to man, but for Prishvin it is the main theme, and man's communion with it brings him wisdom and happiness. To him there is no rift between the "thinking reed" and the rest of the world; in contrast to Tiutchev, he affirms that man swims in the great cosmic stream, and that the life of the individual fits perfectly into the universal order of things. He speaks of animals, seasons, and men as equal manifestations of one and the same vital essence, but his outlook has no mystical vagueness, and his pantheism is free from overgeneralization. With the precision of a naturalist he gives the results of his observations; he has a horror of shallow talk about "the beauty of nature or the miracles of the creation," preferring to describe the exact coloring of a heathcock during mating time or the activity of bees on a summer day (*Honey from Beyond the Pale*, 1951). What makes the writing of this poet-scientist so captivating is his genuine love for everything that exists. He is forever making discoveries, and the thrill he feels in seeing and hearing, smelling and tasting, touching and thinking is infectious—it fills the reader with the joy of being alive and of detecting something new every moment. Fundamentally he is a moralist and a philosophical lyricist, and he talks of life with serenity and extraordinary insight. His own statement—"like autumn leaves, words of wisdom fall effortlessly"—can be fully applied to his writing. The wisdom of Prishvin derives from his "endless joy of constant discovery": beneath the phenomenal world he sees a "second world" of harmony and beauty, and his fiction becomes a poetization of nature. When readers and critics spoke of Prishvin's "spell and witchcraft," they actually meant his capacity to transform externals into meaningful images and to extract inner order from the diversity of impressions.

Gorky said to Prishvin: "You are a man's friend." And it is true that Prishvin's humanism is wholesome and simple, and devoid of sentimentality or sophistication. He has a delightful sense of humor and often chuckles over human foibles—the ridiculous grimaces of vanity and stupidity; the pretentious posturing of *Homo sapiens* are to him as funny as the caperings of monkeys. His approach, nevertheless, is not a purely biological one: he always looks for man's idealistic aspirations and tries to reveal in every individual that creative streak which, in his opinion, is "the essential thing in life." What is most important in man, he said, is the dream everyone keeps in his heart—be it the dream of a wood-cutter, a shoemaker, a hunter, or a famous scientist. In his peculiar and symbolic manner Prishvin gives the name of Berendey to those who are aware of this quality in themselves and have therefore found their own path and their own philosophy; most of them are doers and creators, from the simple peasants who display the wisdom of the earth and possess an infallible instinct of life, to artists and builders for whom every instant is a stimulus to creativeness. Those who search for the miraculous Ginseng or Gen Shen, the Chinese root of life which resembles the mandragora of the Renaissance, believe that this rare plant is a universal panacea; so does Louven, the hero of Prishvin's beautiful tale *Root of Life.* But their striving acquires a highly symbolic meaning, since men yearn for plenitude of being and for liberation from all the entanglements caused by social aberrations and false values.

This use of symbolism is Prishvin's usual device: his subject matter is strictly realistic and he is a student of concrete facts; but observation and inquiry lead him to general concepts and symbols that explain and hint at the secret order of the universe. As a writer he is akin to neo-realists like Remizov or Zamyatin, who absorbed and transformed in their work the heritage of Russian symbolism. What differentiates him from Remizov, however, is that his vocabulary is more simple, his sentence structure clearer, his syntax more condensed. One of the best post-revolutionary stylists, he declared that a good writer "has to use terms that are absolutely necessary and to compress words into units endowed with physical force." In fact his writing has a surprising quality of solidity. His prose is rhythmic and smooth, drawing from the sources of popular speech. He often makes use of miniatures that form some sort of literary mosaic, and his main themes are disclosed through metaphors which compare human feelings and social events with animal behavior. His images derive from a kind of animism that pervades his descriptions of seasons, plants, rocks, and rivers. It is more than anthropomorphism—he humanizes natural phenomena, but man in his work always belongs to the universal whole.

Although many Soviet writers learned a great deal from this "pagan rationalist," he refused to be considered a teacher. "It is useless to ask a writer about the mysteries of his creativeness," Prishvin answered when interviewed on "the secret of his art." "One must put his question to life, one must live and stop asking the artist who is in love with the world: 'how could I, too, fall in love?'"

In *The Chain of Kashchey,* Prishvin tells how he became a lover of life and nature and how his road went "from loneliness to people." His hero Alpatov has heard in his childhood, which is described in masterly fashion, the popular Russian fairy tale about the evil sorcerer, deathless (and death-like) Kashchey, who cast his chain about the earth and tangled all human beings in it. When Alpatov grows up, he understands that Kashchey's chain is forged of injustice, greed, malice, slavery, and poverty. It prevents men from leading decent, happy lives—so the chain must be broken. In the same way that Tolstoy, as a child, had sought for the little green magic wand that would unite all men in the great Brotherhood of the Ant, Prishvin's young man searches for means to break the chain. He does not quite understand what will bring him closer to the great goal; he sympathizes with revolutionaries and is arrested, yet at the same time feels that political activity is not the whole answer. With experience he comes to understand that each creative effort, each enterprise, each worthwhile deed is a blow against the hateful chain.

Finally he gets absorbed in the practical task of draining swamps in the Moscow region and discovers the formula of "blessed work." To work for others is the highest achievement of mankind, since the fullest blossoming of the individual, of his creative qualities, of his vital functions, is possible only in an activity that fits into the general pattern of a common cause. The personal and the collective efforts merge into a creative one; creativeness means giving to others, it is an organic, natural part of life, as important as mating and child-bearing, and it strengthens the ties among human beings. It also brings man closer to the ever-producing, generating, breeding, blossoming nature. To do, to build, to work, to create, to give birth to somebody and something—these are the primeval laws of life, and only in fulfilling them does man attain satisfaction and inner peace. Thus Prishvin's religion of nature and creative activity assumes moral overtones that are not surprising in a writer whose ideological growth was determined in its early stage by Tolstoy, and, in succeeding stages, by ethical and revolutionary Populists. Later, Prishvin said that he admired Lenin because the great leader talked about the "commune" which will always be the goal of mankind. But although Prishvin did not accept Tolstoy's "non-resistance to evil by violence" and his ascetic and religious preaching, he could not support the Bolshevik practice of terror and compulsion, and remained outside the political struggle of his era. He avoided taking part in social activities, lived in the country according to his heart's desire, and his way of life was in perfect accord with his convictions.

The Chain of Kashchey consists of ten separate tales, called links. The first or Kurumushka link, dealing with the hero's childhood, is still very popular in the Soviet Union (as are Prishvin's various books for children). The other links are filled with charm and wisdom, particularly those describing Alpatov's university years in Germany and his adventurous search for a girl who had visited him once in a Russian prison, pretending to be his betrothed so that she could see him. He pursues this unknown girl even as a male bird flies for miles after its mate, but when he finally overtakes her he realizes that there is no real hope for him, and his first love turns into his first great disillusionment. Alpatov is crushed and desperate, yet he is strong enough to sense that this is only the beginning in his long pursuit of happiness, and that passion and frustration, ecstasy and bitterness are still awaiting him on this marvelous and cruel earth.

This ending is, however, by no means sad or depressing. Prishvin's acceptance of life is unlimited and his optimism is never marred by melancholy. He does not complain about the brevity of earthly existence or the frailty of human illusions. His serenity in the face of death matches his consecration of vital instincts. His is not the primitive, biological optimism of brawn and bravado; he hails all the manifestations of being and the exuberance of the life force, but he also asserts the priority of an enlightened conscience that strives to unite reason and instinct, wisdom and intuition, man and nature. In one of his most meaningful books, *Crane's Birthplace,* Prishvin wrote: "The world could be saved not by humanism, which degenerates into man's boasting about his civilization being superior to life, but by a harmonious accord of conscience and of creativeness of life through a single act of wedlock." To what extent this view expresses the mentality of an agricultural country is debatable. Some critics, at any rate, regard Prishvin as a typical representative of the peasant way of thinking. But even those, who find him old-fashioned and aloof from the issues of the day, concur in acknowledging "the deeply national

characteristics of his writing." His whole outlook is so very Russian, his stories and fairy-tales are so akin to folklore, his descriptions convey so strongly the smell of Russian fields and forests, and he gives his reader such a perfect image of the country's vastness and its inexhaustible vitality, that he must be ranked as high as his teachers Leskov and Remizov and be considered a worthy follower of Tolstoy.

In turn he became the head of a literary group. Several writers, such as Ivan Sokolov-Mikitov (b. 1892), author of *Tales of the Motherland* (1947), continued Prishvin's tradition and in their descriptions of the Russian landscape stressed the feeling of nature they inherited from their master. Others learned from him the art of the lyrical sketch, a genre that had and still has a tremendous vogue in Soviet literature. But they lacked Prishvin's "cosmic sense" and imitated only his technique. By stressing the proud role of man as conqueror and master of nature they betrayed the very essence of his philosophy. Much closer to Prishvin's spirit was Konstantin Paustovsky, but he overcame the influence of the master and achieved his own place in Soviet letters.

Ray J. Parrott, Jr. (essay date 1977)

SOURCE: "Questions of Art, Fate, and Genre in Mikhail Prishvin," in *Slavic Review,* Vol. 36, No. 3, September, 1977, pp. 465-74.

[*In the following essay, Parrott describes Prishvin's use of various traditional Russian literary genres as sources for the new literary forms embodied in his works.*]

It is customary in Soviet criticism of Mikhail Mikhailovich Prishvin (1873-1954) to speak of the unique blend of fact and fantasy, of science and art in his work. In fact, this view is not restricted to Soviet discussions of the writer's art. It is a reasonable view, if cautiously considered as no more than a convenient generality. Something of the same generalizing nature operates in discussions of the literary forms which Prishvin most often employed in his narrative art: the *ocherk,* the *rasskaz,* and, less frequently, the *povest'.* Scholars and critics speak of the writer's inimitable mastery of these forms, but rarely in definitive terms. Briefly summarized, Prishvin's preferred forms are the half-sketch and half-tale, or the novelette-sketch; his pieces represent an amalgam of fact and fiction. They are, above all, lyrical and poetic, but they are also "scientific." They are the one and the other, but their specificity seems almost too elusive to capture and define.

It is interesting in this respect to note the kinds of epithets which have most often been applied to Prishvin in the attempt to generalize succinctly about the nature of his craft. These epithets contribute little to a thorough understanding and appreciation of his work, but they are suggestive of the dual impulse behind his creativity and broadly indicative of the special character of his preferred genre. Most critics begin with the assertion that Prishvin is a *lyrical poet-philosopher;* they then proceed to qualify this tag with a wide variety of "scientific" epithets. Among Prishvin scholars, for example, it is axiomatic to speak of the writer as a *poet-fenolog,* a *poet-fol'klorist,* a *poet-puteshestvennik,* a *poet-etnograf,* a *poet-kraeved,* a *poet-geograf,* a *poet-okhotnik,* a *poet-pedagog,* a *poet-sledopyt,* a *poet-agronom,* a *poet-estestvoispytatel',* or even a *poet-rybolov.* The few commentators who do disdain such inclusive tags seldom fail to speak of Prishvin's manner as one of "poetic scientism" (*poeticheskaia nauchnost'*). The writer's widow, V. D. Prishvina, accounts for the double impulse in his work:

> It is common knowledge that Prishvin began his creative life working in science. Thereafter the school of scientific thought doubtlessly affected his artistic work. To the end of his days he constantly sought to combine both methods: the scientific and the artistic. For Prishvin they are both *essential.* . . .

Prishvin himself in a letter to a friend, Iu. Saushkin, wrote:

> My imaginative literature ("belles-lettres") was formed during the transition from scientific (for which I prepared myself for a period) to artistic (poetic) activity. That is most likely why a great deal of my writing bears the character of "research" devoted to describing the features of a region.

Clearly, the writer's own remarks substantiate the comments of the critics about the dual character of his creative work. It remains to examine these general genre characteristics in more detail and to attempt a more satisfactory statement of their distinguishing features.

Prishvin's own comments are not too helpful. Even though he was wont to state that "belles-lettres, for example, does not interest me: the *ocherk* interests me because it overlaps with science," there still appears to be a considerable lack of rigor in his understanding of the nature and definition of genre forms. One scholar has correctly noted that "at one time or another Prishvin designated all his pieces as sketches, folk tales, or narrative poems, depending on which genre fascinated him at the time." More often than not, he labeled all his literary pieces as *ocherki,* including even the large-form *Kashcheeva tsep'.* This has occasioned considerable confusion among Prishvin scholars and critics, particularly with regard to the distinction between the writer's *rasskazy* and *ocherki.* In fact, one critic is inclined to include most of the writer's work under the category of the narrative tale (*rasskaz*), asserting that this is his basic genre form. Others are closer to the mark when they note that Prishvin's basic literary forms lie outside of, or violate, commonly accepted genre categories:

> All this only says that his creative work does not fit into the customary bounds of a traditional genre, that he destroys all genres and creates his own new, unprecedented, inimitable . . . genre. . . .

> Therefore much more important for Prishvin are not the limits of a genre—he continually violates them—but rather genre definition, or what it is in a given genre that he considers essential for himself.

Nevertheless, such statements are scarcely definitive. It is one thing to say what something is not; it is considerably more difficult to define what something is. The studies by A. K. Tarasenkov and I. P. Motiashov, therefore, have been steps in the right direction. While not pretending to thoroughness, these studies do suggest the point from which any literary analysis of Prishvin's genre forms ought to proceed. They suggest that Prishvin's primary form is the *ocherk* and that all his work *basically* derives from this literary type.

Prishvin himself frequently acknowledged that it was difficult to define his *ocherk* precisely. In his essay **"Moi ocherk,"** presented to a gathering of local folklorists in 1933, he discussed this particular problem: "As we understand the term *ocherk,* it has to do with a particular, specific relation that the author has to his material in the sense of submission to it, as well as, say, *possession* [by it]." He then recollects the response of the poet Alexander Blok to his ***Za volshebnym kolobkom:*** "This is poetry, of course, but something else too." Tacitly acknowledging the poetic component of his work, Prishvin proceeds to define this "something else" as the critical determinant of his conception of the *ocherk:*

> [I have] now solved this problem: in each *ocherk* there is something not of the poet; there is something of the scholar and, perhaps, of the truthseeker in the sense of what Turgenev said about Gleb Uspenskii's *ocherki:* "This is not poetry but it may be greater than poetry." In general, this something of the *ocherk* is like a residue of material that has not been artistically worked; it springs from an authorial relation to the material that is more complex than the workings of art alone. From this, however, arises yet another question: is it artistically possible to polish this something in the *ocherk* and if yes, then can the finished piece be called an *ocherk?* Answering this question [I] . . . can say that such *ocherki* . . . as ***The Black Arab. The Chain of Kashchei,*** and countless small tales can be designated *ocherki* only by a special effort if the author's actual relation to the material is intensified so truthfully and forcefully that students of local lore, ethnographers, pedagogues, and hunters consider his works to be like ethnography, local lore, hunting stories, children's literature, and so on.

The crucial points being made in these remarks are the following: First, the material of Prishvin's *ocherki* is processed with a scientific fidelity and exactness. Second, Prishvin has a special relation to his material. Third, the *"chto-to"* of his work arises out of the mutual relation between this authorial attitude and the natural phenomena being presented. It constitutes, in varying proportions, a blend of authorial lyricism, factual scientific data and phenomena, and cognitive "truth": perceived moral and aesthetic qualities. The authorial personality is tripartite:

the poet, the scholar-scientist, and the truth-seeker. Natural phenomena, coupled with autobiographical material, are presented through a lyrical authorial prism of microscopic clarity and precision (*"mikrogeografiia"*), ultimately yielding a poetically transformed, cognitive representation of reality. Artistic and scientific "truth" merge into an evocation of cognitive "truth." It is this complex interrelation that has prompted Soviet critics of Prishvin to speak of the coexistence in his work of a moralizing philosophy, objective "knowledge," lyricism, and the "baring" of a personal relation to the world.

Fidelity to this "objective" material was important to Prishvin, who preferred the designation *writer-researcher* (*issledovatel'*) to that of belletrist; he strove rigorously to preserve the integrity of the facts in his artistic *ocherki*. His narrative was designed not to subvert a documentary quality, but to channel it:

> In my experience the ideal *ocherk* . . . results if I don't discard any of the documentary material, if I don't change a single feature in it, and if I give it artistic significance exclusively by arranging it correctly in the course of my artistic experience.

It is generally agreed that in addition to the central importance of the author-narrator's direct role in the *ocherk,* the representation of real facts—documentary details—is crucial to the genre. Real events and people are to provide the factual basis on which the *ocherk*'s plot (*siuzhet*) is organized and developed. Moreover, this factual basis is to be founded upon *primary* details; materials only tangentially related to the central movement of the narrative are to be avoided or discarded. The informational demands of the genre require a faithful presentation of perceived material, that is, the material may be organized around the principle of artistic generalization or typification, but it is not to be altered by "fictional invention" (*vymysel*). On the other hand, a certain admixture of *vymysel* is necessary in the interests of narrative and thematic direction. Broadly speaking, the *ocherk* represents a form of "fictionalized factuality"; yet, the fictional quality of the form must be subordinated to the documentary quality. The "factuality" of any given *ocherk* must be perceived as such, and not as the result of fictional invention.

In a recent essay on the genre, Deming Brown has noted that there is an artistic obligation upon the author-narrator of an *ocherk* to inform his reader as to what is factual and what is fictional in a given sketch. The writer of *rasskazy* and *povesti* can be expected to employ primarily *vymysel* in his craft, but the *ocherkist* has a moral obligation to "label" clearly the difference between fact and fiction in his work. He must distinguish between what is a product of his imagination, and what is the factual representation of real-life phenomena. For a work to be definitively labeled an *ocherk,* this authorial responsibility must be exercised.

A major problem confronts the *ocherkist* in determining the appropriate admixture of "fact" and *vymysel*. There is little agreement among literary theorists, critics, and writers with respect to the problem. Although all agree that an admixture is imperative, the relative proportion of *dokument* and *vymysel* continues to be a moot point. However, there is unanimity of agreement on the principle that the representation and analysis of facts—*dokumental'nost'*—is a primary feature of the *ocherk,* whereas the element of fiction (*vymysel*) plays an organizational role. *Vymysel* is employed to structure the element of "fact," to assist in the interpretation of this "fact," and to make it accessible to the average reader. In the terms of the Russian Formalists, the element of "fact" in the *ocherk* roughly corresponds to the *fabula* of a literary piece, *vymysel* to the *siuzhet*. But the analogy is not perfect or complete. Studies of the *ocherk* stress that the element of *siuzhet* is usually slight, that "plot" does not play a determinative role in the literary form.

In any case, the factual material in Prishvin's narratives is customarily called the surface text; the subtext marks a subjective, usually metaphorical interpretation of this material, which may or may not be infused with a significant admixture of "verisimilar *vymysel*." Thus, when Prishvin speaks of the verisimilitude of his narratives, one must understand this epithet as a result of the interrelation between his surface text and subtext. It would be more correct to speak of his *lyrical fidelity* to his material. There *is* a scientific precision and factual exactness in Prishvin's surface texts. However, the special quality of his narratives stems from the necessary interrelation between this surface text and the subtext. The lyrical authorial attitude derives equally from his personal empathy with the material and his desire to give a lyrical and ethical interpretation to these factual data and phenomena.

The special authorial relation to the material is partially suggested by a number of qualifying phrases: *samosblizhenie s materialom, sliianie s materialom,* or, to employ Prishvin's favorite term among these, *rodstvennoe vnimanie* to the phenomena being presented. The terms stress the author's physical, intellectual, and affective proximity to these phenomena. Prishvin strives to fuse artistically his authorial personality with his material. The author-narrator "submits" to his material; he is "possessed" by this material, merging with it completely. Alexander Tvardovskii also discerned a similar relation between an author and his material in his discussion of the lyrical *ocherk.*

Soviet scholars and critics generally agree that an intimate, subjective, and sympathetic connection must exist between author and material in the *ocherk* genre. In addition, the authorial "I" serves both an *editorial* and *narrative* function; it is the focal point of the *ocherk* form, for which it supplies both narrative perspective and a thematic center. Consequently, the point of view in the *ocherk* is typically that of an editorial, first-person narrator, who is usually an alter ego of the author. More often than not, the first-person narrator will assume a participatory role in the narrative, intellectually and affectively if not "physically." The author-narrator in an *ocherk* perforce acts as an eyewitness re-corder: "First-person narration in the *ocherk* is perceived not as a hero's speech about himself (the principle of the lyric tale), but rather as the author's speech about what he has personally seen, felt, and experienced."

Prishvin himself recognized that his *ocherki* could be viewed as such only by stretching the concept of the genre. For some Soviet scholars the lyrical coloration of his narratives, the special perspective from which he engages the reader's response to his artistic sketches, represents an excessive reliance upon personal experi-ence and the lyrical interpretation of "fact." This is an exaggeration of the importance of the author's personal response, a slighting of the necessity to be essentially "objective" and "informative." However, most Soviet discussions of the genre minimize this objection.

Prishvin intended and realized the vast majority of his *ocherki* as both informative and lyrical pieces, as poetic evocations of real-life phenomena. Elements of scientific "knowledge" are organically woven into all of his *ocherki;* yet, in many of his pieces the relative proportion between "fact" and *vymysel,* or "poeticization," appears to be weighted in favor of the latter. This is especially the case in his best collections of lyrical miniatures, **Fatseliia** (1940) and **Lesnaia kapel'** (1940). The genre impulse behind these works is the *ocherk;* on the other hand, the lyrical subtexts in these works, and others, ultimately tend to dominate.

Prishvin also recognized that many of his *ocherki* were dissimilar, that his work as an *ocherkist* was not of a piece. Looking back over a forty-year career in 1947, he attempted to identify the two basic strains in his creative life as an *ocherkist:* the *sluzhebnyi* and the *prazdnichnyi ocherki,* or, roughly, the "everyday" and the "holiday" sketches. Of the two, it was clearly the latter for which he felt a special affection. The "everyday" *ocherk,* as he complained in his correspondence with Maxim Gorky, provided him with a livelihood, but it could not afford him *artistic* pleasure and satisfaction. Certainly, his "holiday" (artistic) *ocherki* are his best literary creations.

Prishvin's artistic *ocherki* conform to all the intrinsic features which have been established to date by Soviet and Western scholarship. For example, as Deming Brown notes in summation:

> a *xudozestvennyj ocerk* must be provided with both an "eye-witness" quality and an explicit analysis of the things it depicts, and . . . although it contains *vymysel,* it must have a means of discriminating between facts and fiction. The only source from which these elements can come is the *narrator,* whose (direct) commentary upon and intervention in the events depicted provide interpretations, verification and *dokumental'nost'.* What is most essential, however, is that the narrator be identified closely with the author himself.

Soviet sources enumerate identical norms for the *ocherk,* they also develop a lengthy list of quasi-literary features.

An example of this kind of norm would be the assertion that the *ocherk* must meet the demand of *operativnost':* a socio-political informational or agitational function. If judged by this or similar extrinsic features, Prishvin's *ocherki* do not conform to established standards. In fact, the one real criticism that consistently has been leveled by Soviet commentators at Prishvin's artistic sketches—indeed, nearly all of his imaginative literature—is his lack of *operativnost'.*

Two basic tendencies can be observed in the writing of *ocherki* during the 1930s, the period in which Prishvin wrote his most accomplished pieces: (1) a tendency to-ward writing journalistic, publicistic ("everyday") *ocherki* on economic, political, and technical themes; and (2) a tendency toward "artistic" sketches with either well-developed plots (*siuzhetnost'*) or a considerable amount of psychologizing. The journalistic *ocherki* for the most part are descriptive pieces re-creating the progress of socialistic transformation in the Soviet Union. The narra-tive interest focuses upon social, economic, agricultural, and industrial problems encountered and overcome by the "builders of socialism." In general, Prishvin wrote very few journalistic sketches in the 1930s. The artistic *ocherki* of the period, on the other hand, tend to focus on the problem of the individual faced with the reality of this transformation. A major theme is the dichotomy be-tween new and old values occasioned by the country's sociopolitical upheaval. Often this dichotomy is explored through a psychological analysis of the individual con-fronted by a choice between these values; at other times the dichotomy is presented not so much as a choice be-tween two systems of values but as a matter of their rec-onciliation. A number of Prishvin's works from these years develop this theme, including his masterpiece **Zhen'-shen': koren' zhizni** (1933).

The artistic *ocherki* of this second tendency at times come very close to qualifying as *rasskazy.* Their focus upon plot (*siuzhet*) and the author-hero's psychological conflict inevitably lead to an increase in artistic *vymysel* at the expense of the principles of *dokumental'nost'* and *poznavatel'nost'* ("objective" informational role). This tendency undoubtedly accounts in large part for the des-ignation of Prishvin's (and others') genre as "half-sketch and half-tale." As we have seen, however, it is the *ocherk* that serves as the basis of his art.

Another feature of Prishvin's *ocherk* which brings it in close proximity to the *rasskaz* is the *personalism* of his authorial-narrative response to the world about him. He does not seek to typify, to generalize his response in accord with customary Soviet practice in the genre; rather, he seeks to individualize this response. Thus, the informational impact of his *ocherki* is restricted in terms of the Soviet standard; his works appeal to a limited readership, an audience which, as Poe would have noted, brings to his work a kindred spirit. In the words of Prishvin's widow, the writer requires a special kind of empathy from his reader. The reader has to *desire to read Prishvin on the writer's terms.* This is a far cry from an activist, Soviet theory of the publicistic and informational function of the genre which stipulates a literary response accessible to the broad masses of the reading public. Prishvin's appeal is limited and was intended as such:

> I know that my "drop" will not interest every reader, and in particular it will offer little to those seeking deception in verbal art, escape from active life. But what's to be done, you can't please everyone. I write for those who sense the poetry of passing moments in everyday life, and who suffer because they themselves do not have the power to seize them.

The lyricism of this personal response to reality tends to overshadow the more "objective" informational role of the *ocherk* demanded by most Soviet literary theoreticians and critics. Consequently, Prishvin's *ocherki* represent for this critical persuasion an impure form, a blend of the *ocherk* and the *rasskaz.* On the other hand, it would appear that the lyrical *ocherk* as such is gradually achieving independent literary rights in the present-day Soviet Union.

Prishvin scholars are also in general agreement that the *metaforichnost', inoskazatel'nost',* and *nedoskazannost'* of his *ocherki* incline them toward the *rasskaz.* These qualities also detract from the genre's informational function, not to mention its *operativnost',* but they are integral features of Prishvin's lyricism. The writer's metaphors, allegorical or otherwise, are the basis of his natural imagery. They serve to illustrate the fundamental unity between natural and human phenomena through the principle of *analogy:* nature is the mirror of the human soul. Thus:

> An analogy which is drawn from the life of nature, and which acquires a figurative, metaphorical meaning in the writer's work proves to be an instrument of cognition and an explanation of the author's thoughts or the hero's (authorial image's) spiritual impulses.

The lyrical interest is always foremost in Prishvin, and the primary means to this lyricism are his *metaforichnost'* and lyrical digressions on man and nature. Although he recognized the informational requirements of the genre, he preferred to frame them within his own lyrical perception. A Soviet critic of kindred spirit expressed it this way: "as an *ocherkist* Prishvin does not separate his informational tasks from his tasks as a writer, and that is why in his hands the *ocherk* acquires the force of a lyric verse or even a narrative poem." Put somewhat differently, Prishvin's means to express the informational role of his *ocherki* was his *poetic prose.* The communicative function of his language and work is inseparable from its expressive function.

Prishvin scholars generally agree that the *dnevnik* (diary) form provided a major impetus to the writer's craft. Prishvin frequently acknowledged his diary to be a requisite part of his equipment as a writer. In fact, the daily entries that he made in his diary formed the basis of all his literary pieces. While there is not an inherent, literary connection between the diary and *ocherk,* for Prishvin a direct correlation existed between the two forms. T. Khmel'-nitskaia asserts not only that Prishvin's diaries were the basic source of his creativity, but that they were his favorite and primary literary activity. His diary entries constitute, in fact or in effect, the rough first drafts of his literary pieces. As such, they are above all an expression of his authorial personality and his unique perception of the world. The diaries also help us understand why Prishvin's alter-ego narrators occupy such a central position in his work.

We see, then, that Prishvin used diary entries as a kind of rough draft; he also employed snapshots in a similar fashion. He was accustomed to equip himself with a camera in his daily pursuit of local lore and natural phenomena. Having noticed some object, situation, or event—plant, animal, or human—Prishvin would record that *momentary impression* of the phenomenon on film. Later, he often would create a verbal representation of that moment, using his photographs as a form of shorthand. Essentially, he would *animate* the still life captured on film. He would not attempt to re-create the entire photograph, because he preferred to focus his artistic resources on one central aspect which, for him, caught the essence of the captured, "beautiful" moment and phenomenon. Concentrating on this central image, object, or situation, he would slowly record his lyrical impression(s) in a manner similar to that of *time-lapse photography.* He even entitled one of his collections *Fotosnimki* (1936).

Prishvin's use of the camera has played an important role in recent discussions of his work that seem contradictory. One set of critics stresses the concentrated exactitude (*"mikrogeografiia"*) of his work and its affinities with time-lapse photography. The other group of critics stresses his paramount interest in the general "contours" of his material. The two interpretations appear to be incommensurate and, in fact, incompatible.

The appearance of incompatibility is deceptive, however. One must remember that Prishvin's narrative manner has much in common with literary impressionism—specifically, with the impressionists' propensity for charging their work with suggestive detail and their belief in the importance of capturing the creatively significant moment. A similar propensity underlies both seemingly incompatible interpretations of his work. The desire to re-create lyrically the momentary impression of a given phenomenon is central to both interpretations. Their seeming difference can be translated in terms of the dual planar constructions of Prishvin's *ocherki:* the surface text charged with everyday realistic details, the subtext lyrically evoking the central impression (*kontur*) perceived by the author-narrator. In other words, in the two-planed mosaic composition of Prishvin's work, the surface text represents specific features or details, whereas the subtext strives to create not particulars, but the *distinctive feature,* or features, lyrically emblematic of the total representation. This is a synecdochic manner, with the significant part representing the whole. It is a product of the unique interrelationship between Prishvin's surface and subtexts, an interrelationship predicated upon evoking a "lyrical echo" in the reader identical to that experienced by the writer.

Prishvin's synecdochic manner springs directly from his understanding of the character of the universal order. As the critic Ivanov-Razumnik perceptively noted early in the writer's career, at the base of Prishvin's art lies a pantheistic interpretation of and response to the universe. Reality, for Prishvin, consists of a single essence; every component part of the whole is but a microcosm of the single, macrocosmic essence or being. Moreover, the microcosmic parts are equivalent to the macrocosmic whole; a hierarchical order of values is foreign to his perception of reality, as well as to his conception of the universal order. All of reality consists of, and is expressed in, a single creative process of the "organic whole":

> understand life as the creative process of an organic whole, then in its sense the significance or quality lies not in the large or small part, but only in the coordination of this or that part with the whole. Thus the small part must recognize itself in the whole and then it will disappear as a small part and enter into an equal relation with all the parts . . . each phenomenon, be it the appearance of a sparrow or the sparkling of a dewdrop on the grass . . . all these are features of the whole; everything is visible in every feature and *it is perfect and understandable*. . . .

The significant detail, the significant part synecdochically represents the whole; microcosmic phenomena express and define the macrocosmic whole. The measure of *significance* rests completely upon the writer's personal values. In this lies the potential for Prishvin's unique contribution to the artistic interpretation and ordering of the universal experience of Man.

FURTHER READING

Criticism

"Flower Deer." *The Times Literary Supplement*, No. 1796 (4 July 1936): 557.
> Plot summary of *Jen Sheng* emphasizing its mysticism.

Huxley, Julian S. Foreword to *Jen Sheng: The Root of Life,* by Mikhail Prishvin, translated by George Walton and Philip Gibbons, pp. v-vii. 1936. Reprint. Westport, Conn.: Hyperion Press, Inc., 1973.
> Appreciation of *Jen Sheng*.

Parrot, Ray J., Jr. "Evolution of a Critical Response: Mixail Prisvin." *Russian Language Journal* 31, No. 109 (Spring 1977): 101-23.
> Comprehensive survey of Soviet critical reception of Prishvin's works.

Review of *Drops from the Forest*, by Mikhail Prishvin. *Soviet Literature* 11, No. 3 (March 1944): 64-5.
> Labels *Drops from the Forest*, "a kind of hunter's diary."

Struve, Gleb. "Pre-revolutionary Writers after 1924," in *Twenty-five Years of Soviet Russian Literature (1918-1943)*, pp. 1-22. London: George Routledge & Sons, Ltd., 1944.
> Contains a short description of Prishvin's works that focuses on *The Chain of Kashchey*.

_____. "Prishvin (1873-1954)," in *Russian Literature under Lenin and Stalin, 1917-1953*, p. 146. Norman: University of Oklahoma Press, 1971.
> Brief discussion of Prishvin's work.

Tompkins, Lucy. "Green Mansions in Manchuria." *The New York Times Book Review* (1 November 1936): 2.
> Favorable review of *Jen Sheng*.

Ernie Pyle

1900-1945

(Full name Ernest Taylor Pyle) American journalist.

INTRODUCTION

A career newspaper man, Pyle is best remembered as a populist war correspondent who documented the experiences of the regular soldier. Unlike his contemporaries, who reported the war in terms of broad strategic events, or by profiling generals and political leaders, Pyle focused on the many small struggles of infantrymen and tried to give the war a human face. His compassion earned him great popularity in the United States, and his death in battle elevated him to the status of war hero.

Biographical Information

Pyle was born on his parents' small farm outside Dana, Indiana, on August 3, 1900. He enlisted in the navy immediately after graduating from Helt Township High School in 1918, but he was never sent overseas. The following year he enrolled at the University of Indiana in Bloomington, where he took his first post as a reporter, working for the school newspaper, *The Student.* He eventually rose to become editor-in-chief of both *The Student* and the campus humor magazine, *The Smokeup.* Without completing his senior year, Pyle left college to take a job reporting for the *La Porte Herald.* During his three-month tenure there he placed an article in the paper describing a Ku Klux Klan rally, despite attempts to intimidate him. Pyle left Indiana to work for the *Washington Daily News,* first as a reporter and later at the copy desk. In 1925, Pyle married Geraldine Siebolds. They settled briefly in New York, but Pyle was back at the Washington *Daily News* by 1927. He was made a full-time aviation columnist in 1929, and managing editor three years later. Pyle wrote a popular column about his travels throughout America, criss-crossing the country a number of times in the process, and in 1939 Scripps-Howard syndicated the column. By this time, Pyle determined to go to Europe to cover the war first-hand. He left for London in late 1940 and his dispatches were a great success back in the United States. The columns were collected and published by Scripps-Howard in 1941 after Pyle had returned. During his absence, Geraldine had become increasingly depressed and alcoholic, and they divorced in 1942. Pyle returned to Europe, then moved on to North Africa, but he remained in contact with Geraldine and eventually remarried her by proxy in 1943. In the months that followed, Pyle traveled to Italy and then back to England. He was one of the twenty-eight correspondents who covered the D-Day invasion of Normandy on 6 June 1944 and followed the Allied armies to Paris. His distinguished correspondence dur-

ing this period won him the Pulitzer Prize in 1944, as well as two honorary degrees. After a brief sojourn in the United States, during which Geraldine suffered a relapse and was hospitalized, Pyle went to cover the war in the Pacific in 1945, landing with the troops at Okinawa. There, on the island of Ie Shima, he was shot in the head by a Japanese sniper. President Truman awarded him the Medal of Merit posthumously, and his remains were moved from Ie Shima to the National Memorial Cemetery in Punchbowl Crater, Hawaii.

Major Works

Pyle's most famous single column, describing the death of Captain Henry T. Waskow at San Pietro, appeared on front pages across the country in 1943, filling the entire front page of the *Washington Daily News.* Scripps-Howard released a number of compilations of his columns; his London visit is documented in *Ernie Pyle in England;* the collection of his African correspondence, *Here is Your War,* became a bestseller and was adapted for the screen as "The Story of G.I. Joe." Around this time the U. S. Congress passed "The Ernie Pyle Bill," raising combat pay by ten dollars a month. His account of D Day and the European war was released in 1944 under the title *Brave Men*. Pyle's Pacific dispatches were posthumously collected in *Last Chapter*. His prewar writings were assembled and published by Scripps-Howard in the 1947 collection, *Home Country*.

Critical Reception

Pyle wrote columns that met with popular approval. One of his earliest columns, reporting the death of pilot Floyd Cox in a plane crash, brought in a flood of letters from readers across the country; this was the type of success Pyle enjoyed. He avoided polarizing political questions, and he did no historical evaluation of the events he covered. Modern historians regard him more as a contemporary source of information about public opinion than as a critical observer.

PRINCIPAL WORKS

Ernie Pyle in England (journalism) 1941
Here Is Your War (journalism) 1943
Brave Men (journalism) 1944
Last Chapter (journalism) 1946
Home Country (journalism) 1947
Ernie Pyle's Southwest (journalism) 1965
Ernie's War: The Best of Ernie Pyle's World War II Dispatches (journalism) 1987
Ernie's America: The Best of Ernie Pyle's 1930s Travel Dispatches (journalism) 1989

CRITICISM

Edward Streeter (essay date 1943)

SOURCE: "Ernie Pyle's Story of G. I. Joe," in *The New York Times Book Review,* October 31, 1943, pp. 1, 34.

[*In the following essay, Streeter praises Pyle's "deeply human portrait of the American soldier in action."*]

Ernie Pyle has drawn a graphic and absorbing picture of the fighting in Tunisia. [in *Here Is Your War*]. He has also achieved something far more difficult and important—a full length, deeply human portrait of the American soldier in action.

This ability to disclose the individual beneath the war-stained uniform of the soldier is what has made Pyle one of the most popular of the war correspondents. He writes only of what he sees, and he sees the things that those at home want most to know: what their boys eat, where they

sleep, what they talk about, and how they react to the fatigue, dirt and danger of a fighting front.

Pyle spent most of his time in North Africa with the men who were shooting and being shot at. He sees them not as "soldiers," but as boys from the farms and the cities, the plains and the uplands of forty-eight States. He sees them as ex-storekeepers, soda jerks, truck drivers, clerks, cowpunchers, farmers and gas station attendants—dumped into a small segment of North Africa, called upon to perform dangerous and unaccustomed tasks—yet still civilians at heart.

From the general staff point of view, a military campaign consists of a carefully worked-out plan, executed with precision and skillfully timed. A campaign is also composed of myriads of incidents, small in themselves but vitally important to those who take part in them. History is written as much by the reaction of individuals to the impact of relatively trivial things as it is by the leaders.

It is this phase of war which interests Ernie Pyle:

> I haven't written anything about the Big Picture, because I don't know anything about it. I only know what we see from our worm's-eye view, and our segment of this picture consists only of tired and dirty soldiers who are alive and don't want to die; of long darkened convoys in the middle of the night; of shocked, silent men wandering back down the hill from battle; of chow lines and atabrine tablets and foxholes and burning tanks and Arabs holding up eggs and the rustle of high-flown shells; of jeeps and petrol dumps and smelly bedding-rolls and A rations and cactus patches and blown bridges and dead mules and hospital tents and shirt collars greasy-black from months of wearing; and of laughter, too, and anger and wine and lovely flowers, and constant cussing. All these it is composed of; and of graves and graves and graves.

These are the materials from which the story is woven; innumerable strands which, when drawn together, disclose the magnitude of the over-all accomplishment. It is the story of thousands of bewildered, frustrated and very human beings, who through their daily actions and reactions merged into an irresistible fighting machine.

There is no embellishment, no fine writing. This is not a book of memories, revived and polished on a sunny terrace in Connecticut. It was written behind rocks scarred by snipers' bullets, in pup tents, foxholes and dugouts, in freezing cold and cruel heat, in the midst of dust and dirt and unnamed crawling things which shared the common quality of being repulsive.

It concerns only what came within the range of Pyle's vision. He wrote of what he saw—whether or not it fitted with preconceived notions of how men behaved in battle. If man chooses to appear ridiculous when he is supposed to be sublime that is no fault of the reporter. In fact, Pyle seems to enjoy letting the greatness in men manifest itself through their weakness.

This book is going to be of particular interest to thousands of old gaffers all over the country who, twenty-five years ago, fought the battle of Quarante Hommes and Huit Chevaux. They will discover here that the American soldier, 1943 model, has not changed in the least from the one they knew in 1918. His reactions to jeeps, tanks, mines, dive bombers and 88s are the same as those of a former generation to quads, artillery horses, duck boards, French freight cars and 77s. None of them liked any of them.

An American army is once more fighting on foreign soil and its attitude to foreigners is the same as that of its predecessor. Language barriers meant nothing in 1918. They mean nothing today. The Yanks' amazement at the inability of other races to understand pidgin English (especially if shouted) is as great as ever and equally tinged with indignation.

The interest of the 1943 fighting man in the post-war readjustment of international problems continues to remain at zero. His chief concern is to get the show over with and get home to the family, the girl and the land of hamburgers, flivvers, name bands, Coke and movies—just as it was with the men of 1918.

When aroused, these Yanks are fierce and determined fighters. But the bitterness which fighting generates disappears as it always has like morning mist when the shooting stops. When called on for a real battle job they will burst their hearts to accomplish their objective, getting shot in the attempt if need be. Put them on a fatigue detail behind the lines, however, and they will go to just as much trouble to duck it as their brothers-in-arms of a quarter-century ago.

"Taking things as they find them. Only vaguely understanding. Caring less. Grumbling by custom. Cheerful by nature. Ever wanting to be where they are not. Ever wanting to be somewhere else when they get there. Sacrificing without thought of sacrifice. Serving as a matter of course. Content to leave the flag waving to those at home." Those words were written twenty-five years ago. They are apparently equally true today.

The backdrop is new, but the actors appear to remain the same. Perhaps this is only to be expected. For in spite of the difference in equipment and techniques the bond between the men of 1943 and 1918 is a close one in view of the fact that a majority of the boys now on the battlefronts or in training are the sons of those who cussed and groused through World War I. It is a sort of father and son tournament on a global scale.

Ernie Pyle's book is easier to discuss than to describe, for it makes no pretense of being a connected narrative. Rather it is a series of candid camera shots beginning on a transport in an English harbor and continuing through the day when Rommel's war-weary army seated itself on the Tunisian plain and waited stolidly for someone to cart it away to an internment camp.

The thousands who have followed his dispatches from North Africa as they appeared daily in *The New York World-Telegram* are already familiar with the style. Bit by bit he builds a cross-section of a life without roots or reason, lived in a fantastic country, by men many of whom had never been farther than a day's automobile ride from the old home town until war picked them up and deposited them on the other side of the world.

Man is an adaptable creature, however. Gradually the transition from civilian to soldier is taking place. The naive optimism of the training camps is being forged by reality into tougher and more enduring metal. Pyle sums it up in his final paragraph.

> This is our war, and we will carry it with us as we go on from one battleground to another until it is all over, leaving some of us behind on every beach, in every field. We are just beginning with the ones who lie back of us here in Tunisia. I don't know whether it was their good fortune or their misfortune to get out of it so early in the game. I guess it doesn't make any difference once a man has gone. Medals and speeches and victories are nothing to them any more. They died and others lived and nobody knows why it is so. They died and thereby the rest of us can go on and on.

Time Magazine (essay date 1944)

SOURCE: "The Guy the G.I.s Loved (Ernie Pyle's War)," in *This Was Your War: An Anthology of Great Writings from World War II,* edited by Frank Brookhouser, Doubleday & Company, Inc., 1960, pp. 434-41.

[*In the following essay, originally published in 1944, the writer argues that Pyle's success at capturing the often mundane realities of war sprang from his own averageness.*]

From Hollywood: I had a long talk last night with Chris Cunningham of the United Press, who was with Ernie in England and North Africa. He is here advising the United Artists studios on the production of a movie based on Pyle's book, *Here Is Your War*. He says that the studio is sticking faithfully to Ernie's stipulation that the picture must be dedicated to the infantry and tell a true story of the G.I.s. But the movie will be full of Ernie. And it will stress his frailties throughout. It will admit his fear of battle, his apprehension about his work, his latest quirk—the conviction that now he is in France, he is going to be killed.

From Normandy: It was the afternoon that Cherbourg fell, and the fighting was still pretty hot. We went a little way and a 20-mm. began shooting at us from behind. Most of the G.I.s hit the dirt behind a wall. Ernie, who was talking to a couple of them, kept standing and kept his hands in his pockets. I watched his face as he went down the street and he was scared all right. A little later we got mixed up in a tank-v.-pill-box duel and the pill-box knocked the tank out right outside of the house where we were. I said, "Let's get out of here," and Ernie said, "O.K., you get a start and then I'll follow you." I ran about 25 yards, didn't see Ernie, and stopped in another house. Presently he came along. When he reached me he said: "Some of those fellows that jumped out of that tank knew me from my picture so I had to stop and talk."

From Indiana: I spent Sunday at Ernie's old home with his father, "Pop" Pyle, and his Aunt Mary Bales. It is a comfortable old white farmhouse on a dusty road three miles north of Dana. Several relatives and neighbors dropped in, and as usual the conversation turned toward Ernest [as his father and aunt call him, not Ernie]. Aunt Mary got to talking about how Ernest on his last trip home told her that he didn't feel above any of them when she asked him how it felt to be a celebrity, and Hazel Frist put in: "There just ain't a bit of that in him, Aunt Mary." Aunt Mary said Ernest was born with a wanderlust, that she knew it all along. Mr. Pyle said: "He liked to ride horseback but he didn't like to work with them. Horses were too slow for Ernest. He always said the world was too big for him to be doing confining work here on the farm."

The subject of these reports received from *Time* correspondents last week is—as they demonstrate—well on his way toward becoming a living legend. Four years ago he was an obscure roving reporter whose syndicated column of trivial travelogues appeared in an unimpressive total of 40 newspapers. At that time almost any class of war correspondents would have voted him least likely to succeed. Aged 40, small and skinny (5 ft. 8 in., 115 lbs.), perpetually sick or worrying that he was about to be, agonizingly shy, he was completely lacking in the brash and dash of the Richard Harding Davis tradition. He had a great gift of friendship, but it was always an effort for him to meet new people and he especially disliked crowds. Neat in his habits, he hated dirt, disorder and discomfort. Above all, he hated and feared war. Except for a few months of naval R.O.T.C. during World War I, he knew nothing about it. He stood in awe of professional war correspondents and firmly believed himself incompetent to become one.

Yet now, four years later, he is the most popular of them all. His column appears six days a week in 310 newspapers with a total circulation of 12,255,000. Millions of people at home read it avidly, write letters to him, pray for him, telephone their newspapers to ask about his health and safety. Abroad, G.I.s and generals recognize him wherever he goes, seek him out, confide in him. The War Department and the high command in the field, rating him a top morale-builder, scan his column for hints. Fellow citizens and fellow newsmen have heaped honors on him.

What happened to Ernie Pyle was that the war suddenly made the kind of unimportant small people and small things he was accustomed to write about enormously important. Many a correspondent before him had written of the human side of war, but their stories were usually about the heroes and the exciting moments which briefly punctuate war's infinite boredom. Ernie Pyle did something different. More than anyone else, he has humanized the most complex and mechanized war in history. As John Steinbeck explained it:

"There are really two wars and they haven't much to do with each other. There is the war of maps and logistics, of campaigns, of ballistics, armies, divisions and regiments—and that is General Marshall's war.

"Then there is the war of homesick, weary, funny, violent, common men who wash their socks in their helmets, complain about the food, whistle at Arab girls, or any girls for that matter, and lug themselves through as dirty a business as the world has ever seen and do it with humor and dignity and courage—and that is Ernie Pyle's war. He knows it as well as anyone and writes about it better than anyone."

One reason that Ernie Pyle has been able to report this little man's war so successfully is that he loves people and, for all his quirks and foibles, is at base a very average little man himself. He understands G.I. hopes and fears and gripes and fun and duty-born courage because he shares them as no exceptionally fearless or exceptionally brilliant man ever could. What chiefly distinguishes him from other average men is the fact that he is a seasoned, expert newsman. His dispatches sound as artless as a letter, but other professionals are not deceived. They know that Ernie Pyle is a great reporter. Young would-be journalists could search far for a better textbook than his life and writings—a profitable study both of skills acquired and handicaps overcome.

Young Ernie, nicknamed "Shag" for his pinkish, shaggy hair, was a born listener. Too small and bashful to play much with the other kids, he liked to sit around and hear the grown-ups talk. What he heard he remembered. Observant and curious, he pasted in a scrapbook every picture postcard that came to the Pyle house. And he had a solid respect for facts. As a schoolboy, assigned to write a composition about a visit to the country courthouse, he reported: "Many interesting statistics were brought out in the examination of the assessment sheets. It was found that Old Dobbin has completely succumbed to the invasion of the automobile. The total value of horses listed in the county is $297,096, while that of automobiles is $398,322. The average horse is worth a fraction less than $72 and the average auto is slightly above $330. Dobbin still has the advantage of numbers, however, as there are four horses to every automobile."

These were sound journalistic groundings. But when he entered Indiana University in 1919, "Shag" Pyle had not decided much about his career except that he did not want to spend his life "looking at the south end of a horse going north." He signed up for journalism because he had heard it was a snap course. The high spot of his college career was a trip to Japan with the Indiana University baseball team. No athlete, he thumbed his way to the coast, worked his passage across the Pacific as a cabin boy. A few months before he was to graduate, his restlessness grew too much for him. He quit school and went to work for the La Porte, Ind. *Herald-Argus.* Four months later he moved on to Washington and a job on the *News.* There he stayed, except for a brief interlude in New York on the late *Evening World* and *Post,* until 1935.

"He was a hell of a good copyreader," recalls his friend Lee Miller, who now, as managing editor of the Scripps-Howard Newspaper Alliance, sometimes refers to himself as "vice president in charge of Ernie Pyle." Editor Lowell Mellett, who still calls Pyle "one of the best desk men anybody ever saw," promoted him to be managing editor in 1932. But other *News*men in the dingy city room on New York Avenue never dreamed that quiet, competent, friendly Ernie Pyle would ever be famous. "A good man, but not much drive," is the general recollection now.

Ernie himself was never happy at a desk. Despite his shyness, something drove him on to move around, meet new people, see new things, get his facts firsthand. For a while he wrote a successful column of aviation chitchat. In 1935, after a severe attack of influenza, he went to the Southwest to recuperate and wrote a dozen travel pieces about his trip. "They had a sort of Mark Twain quality and they knocked my eyes right out," remembers Scripps-Howard's Editor in Chief George B. ("Deac") Parker. When Ernie proposed that he become a permanent roving reporter, Mellett and Parker agreed.

For the next five years, with "That Girl" by his side (small, pert, blond Geraldine Siebolds Pyle was a Government girl when he married her in 1925), Columnist Pyle roved the highways and byways of the Western Hemisphere. He crisscrossed the continent 35 times, wore out three automobiles. He wrote about anything that took his fancy: soap, dogs, doctors, the art of rolling a cigaret, hotel bellhops, hotel rooms, how to build a picket fence, his troubles with a stuck zipper in his pants. He went to Alaska and wrote about being shaved by a woman barber in the mining camp of Platinum, near the Arctic Circle. He went to Molokai and wrote about the lepers. He flew around South America. And for most of the five years he worried.

He worried about his health ("I claim to have been sick in more hotel rooms than any man on earth"). He worried himself into repeated attacks of nervous indigestion over approaching interviews, finally got so he never made an appointment more than a few hours ahead. He grew moody and morose when some Scripps-Howard papers failed to print his column every day. Time and again he decided that his stuff was no good, that he should have stayed on the farm in Dana.

But at the same time Ernie Pyle, the professional, was shrewd enough to capitalize on most of these same worries. In his column he kidded himself, dramatizing every

little frailty, foible and misadventure. Gradually he created a sort of prose Charlie Chaplin, a bewildered little man whose best intentions almost always led to pratfalls. His readers loved it. People who recognized a fellow spirit, people who wanted to mother and protect him, wrote to him by the hundred. By 1940 he probably knew more people at firsthand or by mail than any man, with the possible exception of Jim Farley, in the U.S. And he had become a master of the art of putting people at their ease and drawing them out, observing and remembering the significant detail, and reporting his findings in vivid, folksy, readable language. However little he himself may have suspected it, he was ready now for his great assignment.

Ernie himself was a little slow to recognize the nature of the new assignment. At first he tried to be a more or less conventional war correspondent, covering the news as others did. The change began one day in Africa when the press corps was invited to meet Admiral Darlan. Scripps-Howard cabled him to be sure to attend. He was hurrying across an airfield to the interview when a swarm of *Stukas* swooped down, began splattering bullets around him. He dived into a ditch just behind a G.I. When the strafing was over he tapped his companion on the shoulder and said, "Whew, that was close, eh?" There was no answer. The soldier was dead.

Pyle sat through the interview in a daze, went back to his tent and brooded for hours. Finally he cabled his New York office that he could not write the Darlan story. Instead he wrote about the stranger who had died in the ditch beside him. For days he talked of giving up and going home. But when the shock wore off, he knew for sure that his job was not with the generals and their stratagems but with the little onetime drugstore cowboys, clerks and mechanics who had no one else to tell their stories.

The G.I.s were slow to reciprocate the Pyle devotion. In the field Ernie, abnormally sensitive to cold, wraps his skinny frame in as many thicknesses of nondescript clothes as he can lay hands on, makes himself look like a ready-made butt for jokes. At first the G.I.s plagued the funny-looking little man unmercifully, "scrounging" (*i.e.,* swiping) his blankets and water, knocking off his helmet to reveal the wad of toilet paper always kept there, ridiculing his passion for orderliness and his perpetual puttering, pouncing on him in howling droves when he modestly retired behind a bush to relieve himself. Then the letters from home began to arrive, mentioning the Pyle column or enclosing clippings of it. Slowly it dawned on the G.I.s that they had acquired a champion, a man who really understood and cared what they—not as regiments or armies but as individual men— were like and were trying to do. Their affection grew as, time and again, they saw Pyle force himself to share their dangers and keep on sharing them, despite the increasing fears that sometimes made him scream in his sleep, despite the fact that he could go home any time he wanted.

And they also learned that, on the human side, he is somewhat less and more than the sort of super-chaplain he appears to be. Old Newspaperman Pyle cusses with the best of troopers, enjoys a good dirty joke, takes a drink when he feels like it. He also loves to sneak up on fellow reporters in the dead of night, scare the daylights out of them with a belch which has been favorably compared with the bark of a French 75. There are probably still some G.I.s who would not give their last cigaret or blanket to Ernie Pyle. But nothing that any G.I. can scrounge from another is too good for him.

Columnist Pyle, still genuinely humble yet not unaffected by his new fame, is particularly worried lest the forthcoming Pyle-based movie portray him dashing around with pad and pencil, eagerly asking questions and making notes. Actually, the only notes he ever takes are of the names and addresses which stud his column (occasionally accompanied by such messages as "Corporal Charles Malatesta of Malden, Mass. asks me to tell his wife that he loves her"). His usual practice is to attach himself to one small unit for several days (in last week's columns it was an ack-ack gun crew), and live just as they live, doing no writing at all. When he has learned enough, he goes back to the rear and spins out as many columns as the experience is good for. Sometimes he gets as much as three weeks ahead.

When he writes, he yearns to be alone; the normally easy-going Pyle can be extremely short with tentmates who distract him while he is composing. His homespun, sometimes corny, sometimes eloquent style comes natural to him, but it does not come easy. He writes slowly at best, often rewrites a column three or four times.

Last week, after a breather at a Normandy press camp in the rear, Ernie Pyle—who will be 44 on Aug. 3—was preparing to go up to the battle line again. He dreaded it more than ever. To a fellow correspondent he confided: "The thought of it gives me the willies. Instead of getting used to it, I become less used to it as the years go by. With me it seems to have had a cumulative effect. I am much more afraid of a plane overhead now than I was during the London blitz, or even during our early dive-bombing days in Africa. With those four narrow squeaks at Anzio [where a bomb blew in two walls of a room where he was sleeping] coming after a year and a half of sporadic squeaks, I have begun to feel I have about used up my chances."

But to "That Girl" who was waiting for him back in their small white house at Albuquerque, N. Mex. (they were divorced in 1942, remarried by proxy the next year), he wrote: "Of course I am very sick of the war and would like to leave it and yet I know I can't. I've been part of the misery and tragedy of it for so long that I've come to feel a responsibility to it or something. I don't know quite how to put it into words, but I feel if I left it it would be like a soldier deserting."

With the premonition of death that haunts him now, Ernie Pyle is not doing much personal postwar planning. But if he lives to resume his U.S. roving, as both he and his wife hope to do, he will be one man with a future clearly cut out for him. Everywhere he goes he will find old friends of the foxholes, and it will be his job to report to the nation how justly and successfully they are being received back into civilian life, how they feel about the America they have come back to, what they think of the way the people who stayed home are carrying on the fight for lasting peace and freedom which they began.

Thus, in his unique way, he is almost sure to be a sort of national conscience. He may be that even if he is killed in battle. For if Ernie Pyle should die tomorrow, as well he may, it would still be a long time before Americans forgot Ernie Pyle's war.

EDITOR'S NOTE: This article on Ernie Pyle was published in the July 17, 1944 issue of *Time*. Ernie Pyle did not die "tomorrow," but he did die "in battle" less than a year later, when the long war he had covered so magnificently was almost at an end.

On April 16, 1945, American troops assaulted the tiny (10 square miles) island of Ie Shima off the coast of Okinawa in the Pacific. It was there, two days later, that death finally found the beloved correspondent. He was killed by a Japanese machine gunner in a ditch after fleeing a jeep the gunner had placed under fire.

Bill Mauldin, who had become the most famous cartoonist of World War II, as Pyle had been its most famous correspondent, made this comment, quoted by Pyle's biographer, Lee G. Miller:

"The only difference between Ernie's death and the death of any other good guy is that the other guy is mourned by his company. Ernie is mourned by the Army."

Pyle is buried in the new National Memorial Cemetery of the Pacific in Punchbowl Crater, near Honolulu.

At the conclusion of his biography, *The Story of Ernie Pyle,* Miller quotes the words on the crude marker put up at the site of his death. They were as simple and meaningful as many of the words Pyle had written. They were:

> At This Spot
> The 77th Infantry Division
> Lost A Buddy
> ERNIE PYLE
> 18 April 1945

Bruce Rae   (essay date 1944)

SOURCE: "America as Ernie Pyle Observed It," in *The New York Times Book Review,* June 8, 1944, pp. 4, 28.

[*In the following essay, Rae praises Pyle's depiction of the diversity of American life in* Home Country.]

Before he left on his last journey to the Pacific, Ernie Pyle said to his publishers: "I hope some day you people will publish the book of mine that I like best myself. That's the book with all the stuff I wrote before the war, the book about my own country. About home. I think that's the best writing I've ever done."

Home Country is that book. It tells the story of five years of wandering across the continent, and throughout its pages the gentle spirit and keen perceptions of the author are constantly manifest. It combines autobiography with topical comment. It is full of folklore and Americana. With a simple approach Pyle at times becomes impressive in his descriptive passages, but he seems most at home when writing about people—the odd types which he seemed to find in every State he visited.

The prairie winds sweep through the book. The desert dust clings to the pages. The deadness of Death Valley is invoked in a few telling strokes. The majesty of Glacier Park, the tumbling icy streams of the Northwest, the desolation of the drought bowl, all fall into focus in the framework of Pyle's simple prose. The book has a nomadic sweep, but the author's zest for picturesque detail gives it a homely flavor.

In specific terms Pyle crossed the country twenty times, visited every State in the Union at least three times, and every country in the Western Hemisphere except two, stayed in more than 800 hotels, flew in 66 airplanes, traveled in 29 ships and in five years turned out enough daily columns to fill twenty books. He did not have a Christmas at home in four years. He spent one Fourth of July in hipboots, sheepskin coat, mittens and stocking cap. The steepest hill he ever climbed was on the Gaspé Peninsula in Quebec, and it was "like driving up over the roof of a barn." The most frightening road he ever traveled was a mountain trail in Idaho, right after a cloudburst. It was the width of a car, and hung over an abyss. The outside was caving off in washouts; the inside was banked up with landslides.

Pyle found Oklahoma one of the friendliest States in the Union. He came to the conclusion that the people of Portland, Oregon, "mixed their New England soundness with a capacity for living the freer, milder Northwest way, and it made a pretty highclass combination." He found western Kansas in the middle Nineteen Thirties the saddest land he had ever seen. He wrote of its terrific desolation:

> Following the horizon around, as you sometimes gaze out from a ship at sea, I saw not a solitary thing but bare earth, and a few lonely, empty farmhouses. As far as the eye could see there was not a tree, or a blade of grass, or a fence, or a field; not a flower or a stalk of corn, or a dog or a cow, or a human being—nothing at all but gray raw earth and a few farmhouses and barns, sticking up like white cattle skeletons on the desert. There was nobody in the houses; the people had given up and gone. It was death, if I have ever seen death.

He drove nearly 2,000 miles around the drought bowl in 1936, and in that same year ran into a grasshopper plague in South Dakota. He fled from the snakes in the cactus country and failed to find freaks in Santa Fe. "They all must have been out picking huckleberries," he commented. "All the writers and artists seemed to be as fine people as you'd ever wish to see—intelligent, serious, good."

In Memphis he talked to Sim Webb, the Negro fireman who rode the cab with Casey Jones. He was the first man to be shaved by Alaska's woman barber—in the town of Platinum. In Idaho he learned from a one-armed man how to roll his cigarettes with one hand. He journeyed to Four Corners, to stand on the spot where Colorado, Utah, Arizona and New Mexico all touch one another briefly. He visited George Washington Carver at Tuskegee and brought happiness to William Andrew Jackson, an old ex-slave in Knoxville, who was received by President Roosevelt as the result of a column written about him by Pyle. He flew 16,000 feet over the Andes, visited the Central American ruins, ate guinea pig in Peru and iguana in Guatemala and went through an earthquake in Nicaragua. One of the best sections of the book is devoted to the leper colony at Molokai, which Pyle was permitted to visit. With his usual close attention to detail, he gives a clear and moving picture of life among the lepers.

In this, the last of his books, there are glimpses of Pyle's early life at Dana, Ind. He worked "like a horse from the time he was nine." His father was a farmer, carpenter and handy man. His mother was the best chicken raiser and cake baker in the neighborhood. She would rather stay at home and milk the cows than go to the State Fair. She was a devout Methodist, a prohibitionist and had quite a temper. Among Ernie's strongest recollections of his farming days was the summer wind in the Midwest—"one of the most melancholy things in all life, it comes from so far and blows so gently and yet so relentlessly."

He first saw Washington in the soft spring of 1923 and walked with the world ahead of him that day. After trying Washington and New York, he came to the conclusion that Washington had the "personal liberty of that most cosmopolitan of all cities, New York, without its cruelty and lonesomeness."

Ernie Pyle lies in Ie. But his voice, with its old beguiling note, is heard through the pages of *Home Country*.

C. L. Sulzberger (essay date 1944)

SOURCE: "World War II—The Human Side," in *The New York Times Book Review*, November 26, 1944, pp. 1, 22.

[*In the following essay, Sulzberger reviews* Brave Men, *suggesting that Pyle's main contribution to wartime journalism was "a more concrete recognition of GI Joe's services."*]

A skinny little fellow with weather-beaten face, querulous expression and thinning gray hair is not only without doubt the best-known American war correspondent reporting to the United States public, he is also far and away the best known to the United States armed forces serving in the general European area. His name is Ernie Pyle.

The first category of popularity results from the enormously widespread circulation of Ernie Pyle's daily columns syndicated through the Scripps-Howard papers and of his first book compiled from these and called *Here Is Your War*. The second category is, however, still more important. Not only does Pyle know hundreds of GI's personally as friends. Thousands of others know him—and tens of thousands feel they do. He has a knack for getting around, and he makes the very best of his opportunities.

Finally, not only by recognizing that the doughfoot in the infantry (which only more ponderous military writers call the "Queen of Battles") is the key man in this as other wars, but by harping on this fact, and continually depicting his trials and tribulations as well as his heroism, Ernie has done a considerable service. He has not only made the infantryman realize that he is far from being the forgotten man; he has paved the way for further popularization by such other students of the GI as Sgt. Bill Mauldin, whose cartoons, originally drawn for the *Forty-fifth Division News,* are now widely known back home. Also, Ernie Pyle through his influence on readers has helped obtain more concrete recognition of GI Joe's services.

Ernie Pyle's new book, *Brave Men,* is like his last one; that is to say, it is excellent and will unquestionably be at least as widely read. Like the last one it reads like a rambling but acutely written series of letters to the folks back home—telling them what the armed forces have been doing in Europe, from the invasion of Sicily through the Italian campaign, the landing in France and finally the fall of Paris.

It's exactly the same as *Here Is Your War* in its general make-up. The only difference in the plot is that this time it's about what the American armed forces did in Europe instead of in Africa; General Marshall draws up the plot and Ernie writes about it. The main character is the same in both cases—GI Joe—and, incidentally, he is the same character Ernie used to write about on Main Street before he himself got to be quite such a well-known guy.

Time Magazine once described Ernie Pyle's war as "the war of homesick, weary, funny, violent, common men who wash their socks in their helmets, complain about the food, whistle at Arab girls, or any girls for that matter, and lug themselves through as dirty a business as the world has ever seen and do it with humor and dignity and courage." That not only goes for Ernie's myriad sergeants, corporals and privates but for Ernie himself. He is not nor does he try to be an analytical reporter describing trends politically or strategical concepts. Ernie's job is to tell what the GI smells, feels, hears, sees and thinks day after day in battle and during the dull routine waiting, often in mud or dust or heat or cold.

That is the meat of this book and Pyle accomplishes his task skillfully. *Brave Men* contains some fine individual anecdotes and accounts such as those included in what were perhaps the two finest single columns Pyle ever wrote: that describing the calm, heart-breaking courage of an English pilot dug out of the wreckage of his shot-down night fighter eight days after it crashed; and the terrible yet magnificent story of how they brought the body of Capt. Henry Waskow down from the battlefield one moonlit night on muleback and what the soldiers said as they stared at the dead hero's face. "God damn it," they said. And "God damn it to hell anyway." And one of them said just simply: "I'm sorry, old man."

Ernie Pyle knows the infantry and the artillery and the engineers and the air force and the ordnance outfits. He knows C rations and K rations and the particular value of a scrounged bottle of vino. He knows what mosquitos can be like when they come in clouds. He knows intimately the permeating smell of death. . . . He knows what squalor, discomfort, unease, fear and homesickness are—not merely because he can feel them all himself but because in his unassuming way he can get other fellows who feel these things to tell him about it. His particular and special gift is that he can put this down in cold type and have it sound just as it really is; neither too mawkishly sentimental nor uncomfortably restricted and embarrassed but simple, factual and human.

Added to all this, Ernie has a nice, easy way of making the reader feel he is simply turning the page of a letter from an old friend whose reactions to strange things he can almost guess. Says Ernie: "The American soldier has a fundamental complex about bodily cleanliness which is considered all nonsense by us philosophers of the Great Unwashed, which includes Arabs, Sicilians and me." Ernie says he feels "a little shame at the average soldier's bad grammar and lack of learning." He expresses a viewpoint which certainly was widely held, at least until France was well-entered, when he says "actually most of us felt friendlier toward the Sicilians than we had toward the French."

His reports on GI observations concerning some problems of international importance have value. Describing the reaction of an artillery gun crew to the rumor some Russian officers might be around on an inspection trip: "One of the cannoneers said: 'Boy, if they show up in a fighting mood I'm taking out of here. They're fighters.' Another one said: 'If Uncle Sam ever told me to fight the Russians I'd just put down my gun and go home. I never could fight people who have done what they have.'"

Or this revealing interlude, important in the light of a lot of hogwash which has not illumined the recent political campaign:

> I was riding in a jeep with an officer and an enlisted man who was of Italian extraction. The officer was saying that there were plenty of girls in Naples— most of the soldiers there had girls.

"Not me," said the driver. "I won't have anything to do with them. The minute they find out I speak Italian they start giving me a sob story about how poor and starved they are and why don't the Americans feed them faster.

"I look at it this way—they've been poor for a long time and it wasn't us that made them poor. They started this fight and they've killed plenty of our soldiers, and now that they're whipped they expect us to take care of them. That kind of talk gives me a pain. I tell them to go to hell. I don't like 'em."

Ernie records for posterity some of the finest linguistic expressions which war's hardness can squeeze out of the ingenious American brain. "It was at that early morning moment when one soldier looked for a long time at another one and then said, 'Cripes, you look like a tree full of owls.'" His book not only describes the bravery of the men in the armed forces, but their endearing qualities: how they managed to get their laundry done by the Italian peasantry; how they acquired innumerable pets; how they adopted dozens of homeless children and dressed them in cutdown uniforms (Pyle doesn't mention this, but he himself is a member of the "Uncles' Club," helping a young major to care for an orphan youngster named Mario); the odd characters of the Army, such as Pfc. James McClory and his friend "Alfred the Ape" in the Cleveland zoo.

There is some first-rate writing. ("The smell of death washed past us in waves as we drove on. There is nothing worse in war than the foul odor of death. There is no last vestige of dignity in it.") Or, describing that unhappy moment in France when our own bombers pounded American troops (the time General McNair was killed): "We stood tensed in muscle and frozen in intellect, watching each flight approach and pass over, feeling trapped and completely helpless. And then all of an instant the universe became filled with a gigantic rattling as of huge ripe seeds in a mammoth dry gourd."

But this book cannot be picked apart and analyzed any more easily than can the history or experience of war itself. In a nutshell, ***Brave Men*** is the account of the American soldier during the campaigns of Sicily, Italy and France. It is an account written from the bottom of the hierarchical pyramid, not the top. It is sort of an inside-looking-out job; an emotional history of the war in terms of the man who does the hardest fighting under the worst conditions—the front-line combat soldier. And there is a deep point, one that cannot be over-emphasized, which is included in a brief last chapter that Ernie wrote in France just for this volume and not for his columns. The point is this (in Ernie's words):

The end of the war will be a gigantic relief, but it cannot be a matter of hilarity for most of us. Somehow it would seem sacrilegious to sing and dance when the great day comes—there are so many who can never sing and dance again.

Charles Fisher (essay date 1944)

SOURCE: "Ernie of the Warm Heart," in *The Columnists,* New York Publishers, 1944, pp. 296-317.

[*In the following essay, Fisher discusses Pyle's World War II journalism, noting that Pyle's concentration on the details of soldiers' lives and experiences made him an exceptional war correspondent.*]

Ernie Pyle is a columnist only in the sense that he has available each day a certain amount of newspaper space which he may fill with such matter as seems proper to him at the time. By the Big Think standards, he is no columnist at all.

After a couple of years on virulently active battle fronts, he has neglected to evolve seven better ways to win the war. Heads of nations look to him in vain for an approving word or a line of kindly criticism. He is more concerned with the current problems of the soldier in an adjoining fox hole than with the peace to come. When he discusses the millennium it is likely to be one where dry socks are available, where there is an occasional slug of Bourbon whisky, and where a sniper isn't offering him personal attention from a tree ahead on the left.

He has muffed the larger opportunities quite badly. He is only a passenger in the world, riding it in fear and pity and pride, instead of carrying it around handily in his hip pocket.

In his work during World War II, Pyle has not even been the familiar type of reporter or war correspondent. That is, he has not covered the lead story. He does not deal with the official communiqués, tactical movements, and ground gained or lost. He is a feature writer, doing what the papers used to call side-light stuff. But he has been doing it with such superb simplicity and skill that he is probably the best-known American writer of the war. He is certainly the one whom newspaper readers regard with deepest affection. He has never tried to tell them where mankind is going. He tells them instead where young Joe slept last night, and how many blankets the boy had, and was his food good. Sometimes he tells them how he died.

The simplicity isn't professional dress. Pyle is, of course, a man of normal sophistication: product of many news rooms, responsible jobs and much travel. No untrained writer could step as surely as he along the line which separates honest feeling from mawkishness when the tale is of great and terrible events.

The genuine simplicity in him is so constant that it has been known to drive his editors to walking the floor at nights and snapping at their loved ones. Ernie, for example, might have had his great success two full years before he did. He was in London during the blitz of 1940-41. Until then he had been a moderately popular roving reporter, doing a daily series of pieces on the back roads of America. But the bombing of London moved him to a few columns of great beauty and sensitiveness. His sales to papers around the United States increased by fifty percent.

Some column features grow slowly over the years and some succeed almost instantly. The Scripps-Howard papers and the United Feature Syndicate, which handle Pyle, felt in early '41 that he was the war writer of whom all syndicates had dreamed. He was riding a skyrocket, they said. A few more pieces like that and. . . .

While they were discussing it, Ernie came home. He was tired and nervous, he said. He was going to take a rest.

Syndicates are accustomed to columnists who clutch at success, or at least accept it gratefully. There are writers who watch added papers hungrily and who, upon learning that their column has been dropped by one, will travel halfway across the country to plead with the dissatisfied editor. Men argued with Ernie and told him he was a fool to throw away his big opportunity.

No, he said, he was tired and nervous. He was going to take a rest.

The rest cost him all his new buyers and it obscured his new fame. When he went abroad again in 1942, he was down to 40 papers, most of them small and unprofitable. He spent some time with American troops in Ireland and then sailed with them when the invasion of Africa began late in that year.

His stories of what the fighting meant to individual soldiers caught the public mood once more. Thirty new papers were added to his string with unusual speed, and most of them were large. The boom grew as Ernie moved with the Army from Africa to Sicily. At the end of fifteen months of constant action, however, returning correspondents began dropping in at Scripps and United Feature's offices in New York.

"Maybe you'd better bring poor little Ernie home for a rest," they said. "He's had tough going."

He was, accordingly, summoned home. His friends at the office awaited him uneasily. Although he is a man of medium height—five feet, seven and one-half inches—he usually weighs only 110 pounds, and so looks smaller. In addition, although he is springy as a buggy whip and normally in health, he is by nature of an anemic countenance and generally frail appearance. No one was at all certain what sort of wraith to expect.

Ernie came in looking better than he had ever looked in his life. His color was good, he had discarded a life-long slouch. It appeared that hardship had agreed with him astoundingly.

"He'd put on two pounds." George Carlin, managing editor of United Feature explained later, "He looked all filled out."

Plans for the stay in America were discussed. In the syndicate field, Ernie was Hot. He could write of America, tell of contrasts, perhaps re-hash material the censors had banned and, in general, keep the pot steaming until his return overseas.

"No," said Ernie slowly, "I'm tired. I'm going to take a rest."

There was, once again, no way of changing him. Perhaps he had seen things which made celebrity and affluence unimportant. He set forth for Albuquerque, New Mexico— where his wife had built in his absence the first home the wandering Pyles ever knew—leaving Scripps and United wondering moodily what to tell the customers.

In one western city there were two papers which had persistently turned down salesmen offering the Pyle column for years. Now they wired in for it within twenty minutes of one another. That pleasant sort of thing was happening all the time. Moreover, the early part of the trip had not been particularly profitable in the syndicate's eyes. Ernie's personal expenses overseas are reported to be moderate, averaging only about $15 a week, even though they are paid by his employers. But cable tolls are high.

Someone, casting around, thought of the uncertain experiment of re-printing columns Ernie wrote long before the war, when his beat was no larger than America. They were sent out with large ceremony, but with a good deal of inner diffidence.

There was never any doubt about their reception. The public told Ernie to go home and rest and God bless him, and meanwhile read with relish old pieces about the farm where he grew up; the mother, lately dead, whom he had adored; and bell-hops and old men with wooden legs and all the places he had seen, and the unimportant people he had met and liked. As it happened, the final wonder was the fact that sales increased while he was away. They kept increasing when he went abroad again and, at the time of this writing, the Pyle pieces were being sold to 206 newspapers, with a circulation of over 10,000,000. New orders were still arriving, sometimes at the rate of six a day, and there was a feeling that the boom had not yet reached its peak.

Pyle established another record in his field, with no effort and little attention to the mechanics of it. *Here Is Your War,* a book of his articles, was published at about the time of his return. It sold 70,000 copies within the first two months. The pieces appeared unedited, as they were first published. Ernie's only chore was writing a final chapter. No other book of columns, including those of Westbrook Pegler or the late Heyward Broun, ever approached the Pyle sales figure.

In addition to his income from the book royalties, Pyle is reported to receive $25,000 a year from Scripps-Howard, which sends his column to the 18 papers in its chain, and half of the gross income from all sales to other newspapers. Selling expenses, like transmission expenses, are paid by the syndicate. In the case of Pyle, as in those of Pegler and Raymond Clapper, Scripps-Howard is the employer and editor; United Feature simply sells the material around the country.

Pyle has never displayed any sign of being afflicted by a sense of authority as a result of his success and fame. Most people familiar with the trade believe he has suffered less from that ailment than any of his fellow columnists. It is only infrequently that his dispatches deal with matters of state, and then they are held within the bounds of first-hand knowledge.

One was rather a celebrated beat. In the beginning of 1943, before the Tunisian battle was decided, correspondents in North Africa were not permitted by censors to send home an accurate picture of political conditions. But on January 4th, Ernie startled his editors and readers with a flat statement that pro-Axis French officials were still in power in some offices and that our policy in Algeria was one of "soft-gloving snakes in our midst."

The manner in which the story passed the censors has not been made publicly clear. It is believed, though, that some censorship officer who was accustomed to Pyle's warm and innocuous dispatches, simply looked at his by-line and let the piece through half-read.

Ernie, having filed what he knew from personal observation, went on to other matters without troubling to argue the significance of his report or to do a series of essays on political philosophy. But in America, his paragraphs furnished material for a week's speculation by other writers.

Pyle's work has usually had a quiet realism. He has reported many ugly and distressing things. He may have passed more of them through the censors than more pretentious writers. But if he saw a tank go up in flames early in the war, or fell in with an outfit suffering from lack of equipment, he made his report in accordance with the facts he knew. He did not extend it to speculations upon American industrial and labor relations, the international shipping situation and the science and history of warfare. That is a rare quality in a columnist newly come to the peak of adulation. It comes out of a newspaper background and Pyle's insistence that he is still primarily a reporter. He has said frequently that he dislikes the habit of some correspondents of withholding from dispatches material which they sell later to magazines or other sources.

"I believe," he says, "that what I get should go into the column."

He is as interested in names and addresses as a well-trained kid on his first police beat. A very strong sense of responsibility to readers who buy his stuff to see if their own son's name is there impels him to use as many names as he can. A characteristic column said that the most freakish victory he knew had been accomplished by "Lieutenant Cowell Vandeventer, 6028 Clemens Ave., St. Louis," and then having made certain that the hero's home town would know whom they were reading about, went on with the story.

Ernie Pyle has known too many towns not to honor the individuality of each. It would not occur to him to deliver a pretentious sermon on the virtues of ordinary people, because he has never bothered much to determine which people are ordinary and which are not. He just makes sure that in dealing with generals and privates he spells the names with the same care.

The itching foot which took him around the country and then to war was a strange heritage on the Indiana farm where he was bred. He was born three miles from the town of Dana on August 3, 1900, the son of William and Maria Taylor Pyle. He was christened Ernest Taylor Pyle.

"I wasn't born in a log cabin," he explained apologetically when the interviewers first began to look him up, "but I did start driving a team in the fields when I was nine, if that helps any."

He went through the grade and high schools and then to the University of Indiana. He took the journalism course there, not because he was interested in newspaper work at the time, but because it was a cinch course, charmingly disassociated from farming. He tried playing football but found the 100 pounds he carried weren't adequate and settled for the manager's post on the team. He worked summers. Once he got down to Kentucky and got a job in the oil fields. Once he shipped as bell-hop on a liner and went to Japan with the university baseball team making one of those sporting good-will junkets which were discontinued as of December 7, 1941. He managed the baseball team too.

He quit college after three and a half years, served a hitch with the Naval Reserve during World War I, and then, more or less casually, went to work as a reporter on the *Laporte, Indiana, Herald-Argus*. He only stayed three months; at the end of that time he moved on to the *Washington News*.

He liked Washington, married there, and stayed three years. His wife is, of course, "that girl who rides around with me . . . ," a lady who appeared in so many peacetime columns that she became as familiar to readers as her husband. She was Geraldine Siebolds, of Hastings, Minnesota, a Government employe when Ernie met her. He had gone around with only one other girl before her.

In the third year in Washington, there developed in Ernie that urge to be on his way which seems to be almost pathological, and which has never abated. He quit his job and went to New York. For a time he worked on the evening *World* and then moved to the *Post*.

The *Post* was at that time edited by Ralph Renaud, whose staff was recruited for its originality and for editorial freshness. The head of the copy desk kept a couple of special chairs on the rim where, from time to time, he sat bright young reporters, with a view to training them in unhackneyed editing. Ernie was one of them, and the now-doddering editor still remembers the first head he wrote.

The story concerned a citizen who was waylaid by foot-pads on the footpath of Brooklyn Bridge and pushed over the rail in the struggle. The head said:

THIEVES ROB MAN;
THROW HIM AWAY

It so delighted his superior that Ernie might have remained a copy-reader to this day. It is an occupation regarded by some as moderately genteel and desirable, and by others as a fate worse than death. In 1928, though, Ernie quit and went back to the *News* in Washington.

Air travel was still novel and his city editor assigned him to the airplane beat. The job was supposed to consist of a listing of travelers using the Washington airport. Ernie filled it with humor and humanity and anecdote and, in consequence, was made aviation editor of the Scripps-Howard chain in 1928. (The *News* is a Scripps paper.)

He was a memorable aviation editor, quite possibly because he saw in every plane the apotheosis of travel. He gave it up to become managing editor of the *News*. He was a good one, until the day in 1934 when Bruno Richard Hauptmann was arrested for the kidnaping of the Lindbergh baby.

"Hell," said Ernie, "they're always arresting somebody in that case."

And he buried the story.

It was one of those errors which shake American journalism to the roots every hundred years or so. Ernie was far too good a man for the bounce, however, so it was suggested that he take a vacation for a while. He had been ill and needed one anyway.

He headed for Arizona with That Girl. On the way, when he thought of it, he wrote discursive and informal letters to Lowell Mellett, editor of the *News*. The Scripps people are very good at discerning unorthodox talents. Mellett read the letters, passed them around the office and then began to use a few in the paper.

The Pyles returned at a time when Heywood Broun, then the ranking Scripps columnist, was on vacation. Mellett turned Broun's space in the *News* over to Ernie. His vacation anecdotes aroused enough mild interest to induce the Scripps chain to give him what was, all in all, probably the most charming assignment ever turned over to a newspaperman. He was to get into his car and go where he pleased, stay as long as he pleased and then move on to wherever he pleased, sending back a column

a day. Ernie accepted it, groggy with delight, and with every newspaperman in the country envying "that Scripps guy who all he's got to do is drive around on the expense account and write one lousy little piece a day." He and his wife, who is called Jerry and who is as blonde and as slight as Ernie, filled up the gasoline tank and got going.

Large events never engaged Ernie's attention, nor were they supposed to. According to Scripps' idea, and to his own, he was traveling by proxy for a good many people of restive heart who were never able to travel themselves. His life work was writing home to Aunt Bessie and Uncle Ben. He took it seriously.

A columnist is a man who, having put all his eggs in one basket (which may not be quite substantial enough to hold them, at that) naturally keeps the basket with him day and night. The column is the pay-off; any energies or gifts which might be spread over a hundred incidents or details of another job have got to be concentrated in some thousand words a day. Every day.

Each columnist regards his column according to his nature. To Walter Winchell, it is more intimate a part of himself than his underpants. Miss Dorothy Thompson finds hers a vehicle for high and erratic flight. Westbrook Pegler delights in his as a club with which to clout the world. But it is doubtful if any of them spend many minutes completely detached in mind from the blank piece of paper waiting for them the next day.

The first Pyle article, as part of his permanent job, appeared in August of 1935 and within less than a year he was discussing that "one lousy little piece a day" with the classic columnist's complaint:

"The job would be wonderful, if it weren't for having to write the damned column."

But the traveling was a delight which never ended. The Pyles became the only couple in America who quite literally had no home. Their life was lived in a diverting abyss between the last town and the next town. Just before his trips to the wars began, Ernie summed it up in this way:

> We have traveled by practically all forms of locomotion, including piggyback. We have been in every country in the western hemisphere but two. We have stayed in more than eight hundred hotels, have crossed the continent exactly twenty-four times, flown in sixty-six different airplanes, ridden on twenty-nine boats, walked two hundred miles, gone through five sets of tires and put out approximately $2,500 in tips. In the past six years, these columns have stretched out to the horrifying equivalent of twenty-two full-length books. Set in seven point type they would make a newspaper column three-quarters of a mile long. The mere thought of it makes me sick at my stomach.

> Of all the places we've been, we'd rather pay another visit to Hawaii. In the states we are partial

to New Mexico. My most interesting long trip was through Alaska, although I wasn't crazy about it at the time. . . . We have worn out two cars, three typewriters, and pretty soon I'm going to have to have a new pair of shoes. I love to drive and never get tired of it, but on long days I do get to hurting on the bottom.

The most serious predicament we've ever been in was when an airplane motor went dead as we were 10,000 feet over the Andes in northern Peru. But we flew for an hour on one motor, and it turned out just like all good short stories. Sure, we were scared. . . . For four years straight we have got our last Christmas presents in April.

But the story of the perpetual vacation was not a big success, as columnar successes go. United Feature began trying to sell it outside the Scripps chain in 1938. Only four papers bought it during the next six months. The others came almost as slowly.

Syndicated columns are sold—as are barrels of flour, shoes and case lots of peppermint chewing gum—by traveling salesmen. Prices are flexible and subject to bargaining, bidding and the general relationship between syndicate and newspaper. Some syndicates make up "budgets," offering virtually every feature they handle at a flat rate. The paper buying a budget uses what it pleases and salts the rest away with the pleasant feeling that at least the opposition can't get it.

Budget prices vary, naturally, with the circulation of the buyer. In extreme cases, a syndicate has been known to offer a very small country weekly the entire output for $12 a week. A paper accepting, and demanding the lot, would receive some 300 features—a wild hodge-podge of comic strips, jokes, capsule philosophies, picture pages and various sorts of filler—in a load of mats weighing a full ton. (Mats are the thin fibre molds into which type metal is poured.)

When the war began only 22 papers aside from the 18 in the Scripps-Howard chain had become Pyle customers. They were for the most part in small towns and small cities.

But there was something noticeable about the trade. Pyle was a stable commodity. Once a paper started him it was unlikely to drop him later. His readers were singularly devoted. Aunt Bessie and Uncle Ben got into the habit of looking forward to the daily letter. The things that interested Pyle interested them: the size of the policemen's feet in Camel's Hump, Mo., so to speak; the modern comfort station in some Iowa county seat; the look of mountain snow and the way the wind felt at night on the prairie.

He rode a freight truck from Denver to Los Angeles and a bus from New York to San Francisco. He drove to Canada to see the Quintuplets and then down to Mexico to get warm (he hates cold). He is by nature a shy man, but he talked endlessly with everyone he met: gas station men by the thousands, traffic cops, farmers, ranchers, bank clerks, storekeepers, bartenders, bankers and bums. Half the time he told of the places where they lived. The other half, he told about the people themselves. It is significant that in the five years preceding the war Ernie, who must have known more of America and his fellow Americans than any living man, never followed his colleagues in announcing dogmatically that the national mood was—or should have been—thus and so.

When the war began he saw no reason to change his method. Going abroad, he found that the people about whom he used to write were still around him, except that they were in uniform. He kept on relaying their stories home.

When the bombs fell on London in 1940 and Ernie was there, there were some professional misgivings back in New York. The gentle tone of his column had never altered from that of the first letters to Mellett on the *News*. But there was something in the magnitude of the new kind of war which might induce over-writing in the most careful craftsman.

"Ernie," a friend said recently, "didn't lose his simplicity when the big thing came up."

His first piece on the blitz appeared in America on January 1, 1941. He watched the attack from the roof of the Savoy Hotel and wrote:

> Some day when peace has returned again to this odd world, I want to come to London again and look down the peaceful silver curve of the Thames with its dark bridges. And I want to tell somebody who has never seen it how London looked on a certain night in the holiday season of 1940. It was a night when London was ringed and stabbed with fire. . . .
>
> The closest fires were near enough for us to hear the crackling flames and the yells of firemen. Little fires grew into big ones even as we watched. . . . The sky was red and angry, and overhead, making a ceiling in the vast heavens, there was a cloud of smoke. . . .
>
> And now and then, through a hole in the pink shroud, there twinkled incongruously a permanent, genuine star—the old-fashioned kind that has always been there. . . . These things all went together to make the most hateful, the most beautiful scene I have ever known.

After the piece appeared in America it was cabled back to British newspapers, so that Londoners might see how their city had looked.

Later, Pyle visited the early public bomb shelters. He found them as makeshift "as our own makeshift depression camps at home." But, he wrote:

> When you see a church with a bomb hole in its side and 500 pretty safe and happy people in its

basement, and the girls smoking cigarettes inside the sacred walls without anybody yelling at them, then I say the church has found a real religion.

When he came back after the blitz, to ignore the editors and his new readers, and to rest, it was to find that his first home had been built in his absence. It was at Albuquerque, New Mexico. He had approved rough plans before he left and his wife had supervised the building job.

Perhaps the house jinxed the Pyles. At any rate, in April of 1942, a mid-western newspaper printed an effusive advertisement about Ernie and "That Girl" on one of its inner pages. On the first page was an announcement of their divorce, on grounds of incompatibility, after sixteen years of marriage.

Eleven months later they were re-married. The move was initiated by Pyle. He had gone back overseas shortly after the divorce, but the wedding was performed by proxy in March of 1943. A special ruling of the Judge Advocate of the Army in North Africa was necessary to permit the ceremony.

Ernie had worked out his own method of covering his part of the war by then. He'd go out and live with a front-line outfit for a time, talking to everyone he could find, from the ranking officers down, taking what they took in the way of enemy attack. (For months he was bombed, strafed, shelled, machine-gunned and sniped at.) Afterward he'd go a distance to the rear and hole up for days, writing what he had seen.

He'd make seven copies of his stuff. One went to the Army paper, *The Stars and Stripes*. Five were started back to the Scripps-Howard office by cable. He started five, by various channels, because in the confusion of war there was no certainty about which one would get through. He'd keep the seventh copy himself in case, as he explained it, "everything else went wrong."

Afterward, exhausted, he'd sleep for a whole day or more.

His success swelled at home mostly because American families knew he was going through the same thing their sons were enduring. His pictures—notably a line drawing done by George Biddle on the edge of some battlefield—showed him as a frail and not too significant-looking fellow. His columns had humor in them at times, but they were full of death as well, and the fear of death. As they came in day after day over the months, they added up to what is perhaps the most accurate, detailed and skillful picture of the life of combat troops this war has known.

In an article about Pyle written for the *Saturday Evening Post* in October of 1943, under the dateline "Somewhere in Africa," Frederick C. Painton said that Ernie had, in the days of his peacetime columns, "made of himself a character who lived in a daily installment of a serial adventure which people read smilingly 'to see what Ernie's up to now.'"

The serial was continuing, but they didn't read smilingly during the African and Sicilian campaigns, for they were reading about their own boys as well as Ernie. But they read eagerly and in the thousands of letters sent him each year, the names of mothers began to predominate. They said they felt a little as if he were their own son. An astounding number began to pray for him. He is, most likely, the only columnist of record who has ever been prayed for with any degree of enthusiasm.

Some of his material was disconcerting to a startling degree. Thus, he informed a nation dedicated to the habit of incessant bathing, that after a while one felt no hardship in missing a bath at the front, and, indeed became quite likely to skip the opportunity to take one if much trouble was involved.

He told of the terror that lay in scrambling for fox holes when enemy planes came in close and of the continuing misery of wet clothes. He told of the simple practicality of life in combat areas; a chaplain, who had been obliged to do the chaplain's job of going through the effects of a group of ten men killed in action, told Pyle that the most commonplace article carried was toilet paper.

And once in Tunisia, weary to death of the desert, he wrote humorously that if someone would just send him a little sack of sand for Easter, everything would be wonderful. The Charlotte, N.C., Civitan Club promptly dispatched one to him.

The National Press Club at Washington, a tolerably cynical organization not un-used to war correspondents, took up an anonymous collection among members and dispatched it to Scripps-Howard with a request that they "send a little something to Ernie Pyle, cigarettes, or nickel chocolate bars," for he was the only one who had made the war real to them. Uncounted other packages went his way, so that he had scores of thousands of cigarettes to distribute to the troops.

The National Headliners Club of Atlantic City gave him its award for the best foreign feature writing of 1942. Army generals called his material helpful to morale and the *Infantry Journal* praised his reporting. Thousands of soldiers came to know him by sight, and Painton reported that Pyle knew at least a thousand by name.

Toward the end of the Sicilian campaign he became ill. He recovered, writing a piece on the thing he called Battlefield Fever. You don't die of it, he said, but you think you're going to. He described it:

> It's the perpetual dust choking you, the hard ground wracking your muscles, the snatched food sitting ill on your stomach, the heat and the flies and dirty feet and the constant roar of engines and the perpetual moving and the never settling down and the go, go, go night and day, and on through the night again. Eventually it works itself into an emotional tapestry of one dull, dead pattern . . . yesterday is tomorrow and Troina is Randazzo and when will we ever stop and, God, I'm so tired!

When he got back to America a little while later, in September of 1943, he apologized for not going on into Italy. He knew that the soldiers were more weary than he, he said. And he wrote:

> I was fed up and bogged down. Of course you say other people are too and they keep going on. But if your job is to write about the war, you're apt to begin writing unconscious distortions and unwarranted pessimisms when you get too tired. I had come to despise and be revolted by war out of any logical proportion. I couldn't find the Four Freedoms among the dead men. Personal weariness became a forest that shut off my view of events about me. I was no longer seeing the things that you at home want to know about the soldiers.

He went back to the house at Albuquerque for his rest, while Scripps and United Feature searched through files and pulled out his old columns.

The radio and lecture people came after him with stupendous offers: $25,000 advance guarantee for a personal tour, $1,500 for a single radio appearance, $1,000 a night for other programs. His friends estimate that he might, in his two months at home, have earned an extra $60,000. He rested instead, playing a little poker and snooker pool, throwing darts and fanning over things with old friends whilst Lee Miller of Scripps—whose special title is Vice President in Charge of Ernie Pyle—tried to keep the visitors away.

He traveled to New York to pick up some special equipment at Abercrombie & Fitch shortly before he went overseas again. George Carlin took him to lunch at the Yale Club and, one thing leading to another, the shopping went undone.

So he left for Italy on his third trip to the war traveling light, as usual. He had made no speeches about the sort of peace he preferred, had written no essays on what is wrong with America. He had endangered his whole columning franchise for a few games of pool and now, letting others talk of the significance of things, he was going back to see how G.I. Joe was getting along in the mud.

Graham B. Hovey (essay date 1944)

SOURCE: "This is Ernie Pyle's War," in *The New Republic,* Vol. III, No. 24, December 11, 1944, pp. 804-06.

[*In the following essay, Hovey attempts, through a review of* Brave Men, *to explain why Pyle was the most popular war correspondent in America during World War II.*]

Like Franklin Roosevelt and the Brooklyn Dodgers, Ernie Pyle is the people's choice. They elected him their favorite war correspondent for the duration shortly after Americans first began to fight Germans in this war, and his popularity has steadily increased. The explanation, I think, is simple: Ernie Pyle consistently has contributed the best job of reporting and writing about the Americans who have to fight the war. Pyle's popularity puzzles our British friends, who concern themselves more with articles on strategy and the political aspects of the conflict. But Americans have been most interested in the human side, and that side is Ernie Pyle's war.

Ernie's columns on the battle for Tunisia were collected in a book called *Here Is Your War*. It was so popular that his dispatches on the campaigns in Sicily and Italy, the Normandy invasion and the break-through which liberated Paris have been incorporated in a new volume, *Brave Men*. Pyle's best columns, such as the one in *Brave Men* on Captain Henry T. Waskow, wear well. In addition, the books tell the reader far more about what war is like than he could ever glean from histories or military texts. For Pyle writes about the whole army—the doughboys, tankers, artillerymen, engineers, bomber pilots, aerial gunners, the soldiers of ordnance and the quartermaster corps. As one reviewer said, when future generations of Americans seek to know what kind of army fought for them in this war they will be thankful for Ernie Pyle.

As a correspondent who campaigned with Ernie Pyle in Africa and Italy, I have profound respect for this little man who hates war so passionately and writes about it so well. I also envy him. That envy increased as I read *Brave Men*. I constantly asked myself why Ernie had done a better job than the rest of us; how he had gotten closer to the American soldier and his thoughts, hopes, fears and reactions; why he had been able to portray better the tragedy of war.

Most war correspondents envied Ernie the freedom his job afforded, and we liked to think that was a major reason why he was more successful than we. Most of us had daily deadlines to meet. We had to go to the front each day; dip briefly into the war, then drive back to base and file "spot" stories on developments. Ernie could remain in the field with one unit for five days at a time; get to know many soldiers, then come back and write enough columns for a week. But that does not explain his effectiveness. Not at all. Apart from any advantage his job gives him, Ernie Pyle is a great reporter.

A recent New Republic advertisement said, correctly, that our soldiers overseas do not yet know why they are fighting; that they understand few implications of the struggle between democracy and fascism, and they look on war only as a job they must do and get done with quickly. Many of us tried to write that effectively in dispatches from the Mediterranean. But the one who did it best was Ernie Pyle. Early in *Brave Men,* he describes assault ships nearing Sicily:

> Then darkness enveloped the whole American armada. Not a pinpoint of light showed from those hundreds of ships as they surged on through the night toward their destiny, carrying across the

ageless and indifferent sea tens of thousands of young men, fighting for . . . for . . . well, at least for each other.

Later, he writes that he has "been around long enough to know that nine-tenths of morale is pride in your outfit and confidence in your leaders and fellow fighters." And after listing the incredible hardships of infantry fighting in Normandy hedgerows, he observes that soldiers continually went back to them "because they were good soldiers and they had a duty they could not define."

It is tragic but true that American soldiers fight "at least for each other"; that morale generally is not based on an understanding of the war, but on pride in one's unit, and that men do return to the lines because they are "good soldiers," not because they can define their mission in Europe.

Pyle writes informatively about all branches of the service. His detailed "plugs" for such unadvertised units as ordnance, the quartermaster corps, anti-aircraft and the combat engineers are deserved and they help bring one's perspective of the army into focus. His best writing, however, is reserved for the infantry. That is natural, for Ernie Pyle, like anyone who has seen infantry fighting close up, is prejudiced on the side of the doughboy. In my opinion, a writer who can help make the nation "doughboy conscious" is helping to win the war. Ernie Pyle has stimulated this process more than anyone else.

If I were asked to select one column from **Brave Men,** I would choose the one on Captain Waskow, a Thirty-sixth Division company commander from Texas, who was worshiped by his men. It is the article one newspaper ran boldface across its entire front page, explaining that the editors believed it would give readers more real information about the war than communiqués from the various fronts. It describes a scene at the foot of an Italian mountain trail the night the body of Captain Waskow is carried down on the back of a mule. At the foot of that trail were several soldiers and Ernie Pyle. In simple, powerful writing, Pyle reveals the feelings of the men at the loss of their leader.

Other notable chapters describe the vicious fighting to win the Normandy beaches, the incredible courage of an RAF pilot, pinned in his crashed plane in no-man's land for eight days with a broken leg, and the liberation of Paris. But one of the most unforgettable passages for me is the one summing up the author's thoughts on the discouraging campaign in Italy, where "the enemy had been hard and so had the elements. Men had had to stay too long in the lines. A few men had borne a burden they felt should have been shared by many more. There was little solace for those who had suffered, and none at all for those who had died, in trying to rationalize about why things had happened as they did."

It was terribly difficult for anyone to acquire "the long view" in Italy during that bitter last winter. It was terribly difficult for our soldiers to convince themselves they were not fighting the war practically by themselves. Ernie Pyle explains why.

A last word about the brave man who wrote **Brave Men.** Describing the job of an officer who had to spend every day in a landing craft in Anzio harbor, checking ship cargoes "with shells speckling the whole area," Ernie asserts, "I wouldn't have had his job for a million dollars." But in the next paragraph, Ernie says, "I rode around with him one day. . . ."

Perhaps that furnishes a clue to Ernie Pyle's popularity.

John Mason Brown (essay date 1945)

SOURCE: "Brave Man," in *Seeing Things,* Whittlesey House, 1946, pp. 46-53.

[*In the following essay, which was first published in 1945, Brown provides a personal remembrance of Pyle, commenting on Pyle's motivation in writing about "the common front-line soldier."*]

"Hi-ya, Ernie?" That's what they used to cry when they saw him. In their throats this was more than a salutation. It was also a question; a question which came from their hearts, and brightened their eyes. They really cared. They wanted him to be feeling "fine."

No other military figure held a higher place in their affections than did this unmilitary little man. They knew that in Ernie they had a friend. I say "Ernie" because the fact that he was known as Ernie was part of his character. A stranger would no more have thought of referring to him as "Mr. Pyle" than he would have dreamed of calling Bismark "Otto," or Will Rogers "William." Although I knew Ernie slightly, I felt I knew him well. So did everyone who read him. He was that kind of man. I wish I had know him intimately.

I saw him several times in Europe. First, in Naples, when he had just returned from Cassino and I was headed that way. Next, in London, when the spring was there and all of us were waiting impatiently for the Invasion. Later, on the *Augusta,* where, when he came aboard to file his copy, excitement swept through that cruiser like a monsoon. Finally, in Normandy. The last time I saw him was when, early one morning, several of us went in with him to that littered beach known as "Omaha" about which he was to write one of his finest stories.

When I met Ernie in Naples, his flat may have had furniture in it, but that furniture did not show. All I remember in the way of furnishings are people; young G.I.'s, airmen, and Army nurses. No canteen was ever more crowded than these small rooms. There was a difference, however; a sense of veneration, a centering of interest, such as no canteen knows. Ernie was that center.

These young people hovered about him like priests around an altar. He sat there like some benign god who refused to admit that he was being worshiped. More than hanging upon his words, these youngsters chinned themselves upon them. It took only a minute or two to realize how much Ernie meant to them, and how much they meant to him. He treated them with the solicitude most people reserve for Brass Hats. He showed them the same courtesy and respect which they showed him. He was more than a host. More than a wise uncle. More than an oracle, too. He was their friend and confidant; a person who palpably shared their interests and seemed to share their age. In his case age created no barrier. It did not lessen their affection for him; it merely increased their respect.

The strain of what he had undergone told heavily upon Ernie in Naples. He was so frail and thin that on the way home Bill McDermott, who had been as impressed by him as I was, likened him to Gandhi with his clothes on. Ernie was disturbingly pale. He was fighting not only against the enemy and for the G.I. with his typewriter; he was also fighting against anaemia. There was something of the blueness of his bright blue eyes even in the ivory whiteness of his skin.

When I saw Ernie again, it was, as I say, in London during those final suspensive months which preceded D-Day. He looked made over. His color was no longer white. He told me he had been pinkened by red meat and rest.

We were having drinks late one afternoon in the crowded bar of the Dorchester. Two young airmen from a nearby Bomber Command came in and sat next to us at the corner table. Men in uniform were always recognizing Ernie.

Ernie happened to be looking straight ahead of him when one of the young pilots spotted him. "Isn't that Ernie Pyle?" he whispered across tables to me. When I signaled a "yes" with my head, he nudged his companion. The two of them were as excited as if they had just completed a successful mission over Berchtesgaden.

I told Ernie what had happened, and he asked them both over. Long after I had left, he remained with them. His friendship did not stop with that chance meeting. He visited them at their Command, as any reader of **Brave Men** remembers. He wanted to talk to any man in uniform, especially if he wasn't too highly placed. What is more surprising, every man in uniform wanted to talk to him.

The last time I saw Ernie was when we climbed down the *Augusta*'s net into a small boat, and headed for the beaches. With us was the Navy's Charles E. Thomas, Pho. M. 1/c. As is the way of photographers, Thomas was not traveling light. He was freighted down with a large movie camera, while I was carrying his no less sizable still camera. When we waded ashore, Ernie was next to me. Half way in, he said, "Come on, give it to me now. It's my turn." I hesitated because he looked so frail and the camera was so heavy. I soon realized, however, that Ernie meant what he said. Not to have given him the camera would have been to hurt his feelings. His carrying it was a point of pride; a principle of behavior also. When he took it, there was a moment when I thought that both he and the camera were lost for good. But, though he sagged uncertainly for an instant, he managed to get both it and himself safely ashore.

His insistence upon sharing the burden was typical of him. It made me understand all the more fully why, as we trudged down those improvised roads, dusty and traffic-jammed, one tired G.I. after another would smile upon seeing him, saying either, "Jeez, there's Ernie Pyle," or the inevitable, "Hi-ya, Ernie. Glad to see ya."

Ernie was more than a little bundle of nerves and perceptions, of high courage and deep sympathy. He was the G.I.'s walking delegate to history. If he shared their feelings, it was because he shared their dangers. In the past there may have been a girl known as the daughter of the regiment. But Ernie was a fellow who had been adopted by the whole Army to serve as its spokesman; by the Navy, too, at least when it could tear him away from a foxhole. No one in this war has been able to do as much as he did to transform the blood and sweat of battle into printer's ink. Or brought the war with such intimacy into more distant homes.

When, in **Brave Men,** he wrote, "I'm a rabid one-man movement bent on tracking down and stamping out everybody in the world who doesn't fully appreciate the common front-line soldier," Ernie was only stating a credo which explained his unique strength as a war writer. Although the common cause was his, he had a cause of his own. He did not want the forgotten men who were making history to remain forgotten.

In physical appearance and mental attitude, Ernie had no connection with either the Richard Harding Davis type of war correspondent or the tough swaggerers so dear to Hollywood. With his balding forehead and his fluffy gray hair, he looked more like a character actor than a lead.

Heroics were as foreign to him as tenderness was natural. He did not glorify battle; he admired the men who could endure it. He hated war as heartily as do most of the sailors and soldiers who fought beside him. His hatred of it colors many of his best passages. Yet he never wrote about it as an observer; always as a participant. He was a new kind of war correspondent—democracy's perfect symbol in a democratic war.

What was exceptional about him was his *seeming* averageness; his ability to enclose every man's war within the parentheses of his own personality. Scores of correspondents have had his courage, but none has had his heart. Ernie remained the small-town boy in a big-time war. He was one Little Man writing about all the others in this Little Man's war. Writing for them, too. Again and again he proved himself their equal in bigness and in gallantry.

He was different from them mainly because he was articulate. This is why the typewriter was his weapon, and one that, in the midst of battle, he could use superlatively.

A few of Ernie's readers (a few, because they are the ones who sneered at his simplicities) have tried to suggest that Ernie's columns were on a par with the letters the G.I.'s might have written home, had they been allowed to send them. These scoffers, I believe, have flattered the G.I.'s, and done Ernie a serious injustice. They might as well have been saying what Charles Lamb said when, after discussing Shakespeare with Wordsworth one night, he stuttered gleefully, "W-W-William says he could have written *H-H-Hamlet* if only he had had the m-m-mind to."

There are millions of G.I.'s, thousands of whom write extremely well, and some of whom, in this letter or in that, have done the best writing to have come out of the war. There are countless professional correspondents, too. But there was, and will be, only one Ernie Pyle. He may have been no Pater. Which was all to the good. Yet he had a neat, clean, driving style of his own, and a beagle's eye for details.

He could stipple a paragraph with these details. He advanced them in short sentences, rich in color. He made these details do their full emotional duty. He stabbed with them, too. The only deceptive feature of his style was the ease with which he could persuade the reader that he could have written like Ernie. Part of Ernie's skill was his adroitness in hiding it.

Ernie may have been as careful to write down the names and home-town addresses of all the sailors and soldiers he met as if he were covering a meeting of the Rotary Club. He was, however, able to endow the telephone book with a heart. He did not do this as a cheap reader-getting stunt. It was part of his kindness, and a proof of his understanding. It was one of the many ways in which he bridged the wide chasm separating those overseas from those here.

He knew what these names and addresses meant to the men at the front no less than to their families and friends back home. Soldiers and sailors always remained to Ernie citizens in uniform, anxious to get home. To him they were local boys making good in their living, their dying, and their enduring. He was anxious to get them home again, if it was only in print. Ernie did this as no other person writing about this war has been able to do.

His books, **Here Is Your War** and **Brave Men,** may be hard, if not impossible, to read continuously. They suffer, as all newspaper reprints do, when encountered within the covers of a book. This does not lessen their value, or mean that their individual entries are not excellent. It is only one measure of their high virtues as journalism. When it comes to a day by day record of the struggles for Africa, Sicily, Italy, and Normandy, Ernie's books will always remain the G.I.'s Bible.

He could tell a story as movingly as his remarkable account of the passage by muleback on a moonlit night of Captain Waskow's body down an Italian mountain. He could describe a scene as unforgettably as he did when he recorded what he saw as he strolled along the Normandy beaches. He could capture the feeling of a convoy, the agony of a hospital tent, or the emotions of men moving into battle, no less graphically than in a dispatch from the Pacific he recorded the pantomime of the signalmen on a carrier. As a writer, Ernie was no less good than as a man.

The only columns by Ernie which distressed me were those he wrote before he headed for the Pacific. I have in mind those embarrassing "fillers" about the burdens of being famous. They seemed to me in the worst of bad taste. Instead of adding to his legend, I thought, and feared, they might subtract from it. They made me worry about Ernie. They worried me until I realized they were the final indications of his ingenuousness and his honesty. He *was* famous, and his fame bothered him. He wrote about it without affectation, exactly as he had written about all the other unpleasant things he had survived.

Ernie had run more risks and seen more fighting than most. Even before Normandy, he told me he thought his number might be up. He did not want to go to the Pacific. "I am going," wrote he, "simply because there's a war on and I am part of it. And I have known all the time I was going back. I am going simply because I have got to go—and I hate it."

Immediately after the report of Ernie's death on Ie had reached this country, President Truman issued a statement at the White House. It was the second of this kind he had issued since Franklin Roosevelt's passing. "The nation," began Mr. Truman, "is quickly saddened again by the death of Ernie Pyle." The notable word in that statement, the word which stands out almost as if printed in capitals, is the "again." Surely no fancy adjective ever paid so high a compliment as that simple adverb which linked the sadness felt because of a correspondent's passing with the grief we had all known because of President Roosevelt's dying.

Randall Jarrell (essay date 1945)

SOURCE: "Ernie Pyle," in *Kipling, Auden & Co.: Essays and Reviews 1935-1964,* Farrar, Straus and Giroux, 1980, pp. 112-21.

[*In the following essay, originally published in 1945, Jarrell praises Pyle's ability to evoke in his writing the experience of war.*]

He wrote like none of the rest. The official, press-agent, advertising-agency writing that fills the newspapers, magazines, and radio with its hearty reassuring lies, its mechanical and heartless superlatives; the rhetorical, sensational, and professional pieces of ordinary *Time-Life* journalism—the same no matter what the subject, who the writer; the condescending, preoccupied work of "real writers" officially pretending to be correspondents for the duration: all this writing about the war that by its quality denies the nature and even the existence of the war, he neither competed with nor was affected by. He was affected by, obsessed with, one thing—the real war: that is, the people in it, all those private wars the imaginary sum of which is the public war; and he knew that his private war, his compulsive obligation, was to write what he had seen and heard and felt so that neither those who had felt it nor those who had not could ever again believe that it was necessary for anyone to be ignorant of it. He was their witness; and he looked not to find evidence for his own theories or desires, to condemn, to explain away, to justify, but only to *see,* and to tell what he saw. What he cared about was the facts. But facts are only facts as we see them, as we feel them; and he knew to what a degree experience—especially in war—is "seeing only faintly and not wanting to see at all." The exactly incongruous, the crazily prosaic, the finally convincing fact—that must be true because no one could have made it up, that must be Pyle because no one else would have noticed it—was his technical obsession, because he knew it was only by means of it that he could make us understand his moral obsession: what happens to men in our war. (A few reporters cared almost as much and tried almost as hard; but their work is hurt by emotional forcing, self-consciousness, the hopeless strain between their material and their technique. To the reporter's trained consciousness there is something incidental, merely personal, almost meretricious, about his exact emotions or perceptions or moral judgments; these things are not part of "the facts," and he professionally supplies only as much of their generalized, familiar equivalents as his readers immediately demand and immediately accept. These things, for many years, had been the only facts for Pyle.) Pyle did not care how he told it if he could make us feel it; there is neither self-protectiveness nor self-exploitation in his style. What he saw and what he felt he said. He used for ordinary narration a plain, transparent, but oddly personal style—a style that could convince anybody of anything; but when his perceptions or emotions were complex, far-reaching, and profound, he did his utmost to express their quality fully—at his best with the most exact intensity, at his worst with a rather appealingly old-fashioned spaciousness of rhetoric. It is easy to be critical of some of these last passages, and of the flat homeliness of others: he possessed few of the unessential qualities of the accomplished writer but—at his rare best—many of the essential qualities of the great writer. It was puzzling and disheartening to read some of the reviews of his books: the insistence that this was not "great" reporting, the work of a "real" writer, but only a good reporter, a good man—nobody missed *that*—reproducing what the "G.I. Joes" felt and said. (Some writers seemed compelled to use about him, as they do about all soldiers who are at the same time enlisted men, the words *simple, plain,* or *little*—so disquieting in their revelation of the writers' knowledge and values.) And yet all of us knew better. We felt most the moral qualities of his work and life; but

we could not help realizing that his work was, in our time, an unprecedented aesthetic triumph: because of it most of the people of a country *felt,* in the fullest moral and emotional sense, something that had never happened to them, that they could never have imagined without it—a war.

In war the contradictions of our world, latent or overt, are fantastically exaggerated; and what in peace struggles below consciousness in the mind of an economist, in war wipes out a division on atolls on the other side of a planet. So in Pyle war is the nest of all contradictions; the incongruous is the commonplace homogeneous texture of all life. All of them know it: a cannoneer, playing poker by two candles in a silent battery, says to him "as though talking in his sleep," *"War is the craziest thing I ever heard of."* A man builds a raft to float on the water of his foxhole; another goes to sleep, falls over in the water, and wakes up, until he finally ties himself by a rope to a tree; four officers of a tank company fix themselves a dugout with electric lights, a pink stove, an overstuffed chair, and "a big white dog, slightly shell-shocked, to lie on the hearth." Men in shallow foxholes under severe strafing, try to dig deeper with their fingernails, are commonly "hit in the behind by flying fragments from shells. The medics there on the battlefield would either cut the seats out of their trousers or else slide their pants down, to treat the wounds, and they were put on the stretchers that way, lying face down. It was almost funny to see so many men coming down the hill with the white skin of their backsides gleaming against the dark background of brown uniforms and green grass." Pyle "couldn't help feeling funny about" fighter pilots who had just strafed a truck convoy, and who, "so full of laughter . . . talked about their flights and killing and being killed exactly as they would discuss girls or their school lessons." Soldiers pile out of their jeeps for an approaching bird, thinking it a Stuka ("I knew one American outfit that was attacked by Stukas twenty-three times in one day. A little of that stuff goes a long way"); and a digger testifies, with utter magnificence: "Five years ago you couldn't have got me to dig a ditch for five dollars an hour. Now look at me. You can't stop me digging ditches. I don't even want pay for it; I just dig for love. And I sure do hope this digging today is all wasted effort, I never wanted to do useless work so bad in all my life. Any time I get fifty feet from my home ditch you'll find me digging a new ditch and, brother, I ain't joking. I love to dig ditches." And yet it is a war where "few ever saw the enemy, ever shot at him, or were shot at by him"; where "physical discomfort becomes a more dominant thing in life than danger itself"; where everything is so scarce that passing soldiers stop Pyle six times in a day to borrow a pair of scissors to cut their nails—"if somebody had offered me a bottle of castor oil I would have accepted it and hidden it away."

Pyle is always conscious of the shocking disparity of actor and circumstance, of the little men and their big war, their big world: riding in a truck in the middle of the night, so cold he has to take off his shoes and hold his toes in his hands before he can go to sleep, he feels shiveringly "the immensity of the catastrophe that had put men all over the world, millions of us, to moving in machine-like precision through long nights—men who should have been comfortably asleep in their warm beds at home. War makes strange giant creatures out of us little routine men that inhabit the earth." And, flying from the Anzio beachhead to D-Day in the Channel, passing at sunset over the peaks of the Atlas, he thinks longingly of the worlds inside the world: "Down below lived sheep men—obscure mountain men who had never heard of a *Nebelwerfer* or a bazooka, men at home at the end of the day in the poor, narrow, beautiful security of their own walls." His column describing the apotheosis of another world, the debris of the Normandy beachhead, is so extraordinary in its sensitivity, observation, and imagination that I wish I could quote all of it; but, taken at random from "this long thin line of personal anguish": from the sleeping, dead, and floating men; from the water "full of squishy little jellyfish . . . in the center of each of them a green design exactly like a four-leaf clover"; from the ruined tanks, trucks, bulldozers, half-tracks, typewriters, office files, steel matting, and oranges—a banjo and a tennis racket; from the dogs, Bibles, mirrors, cigarette cartons (each soldier was given a carton of cigarettes before embarking), and writing paper of that universe where "anything and everything is expendable," here are two objects:

> I stooped over the form of one youngster whom I thought dead. But when I looked down I saw that he was only sleeping. He was very young, and very tired. He lay on one elbow, his hand suspended in the air about six inches from the ground. And in the palm of his hand he held a large, smooth rock.

> I stood and looked at him for a long time. He seemed in his sleep to hold that rock lovingly, as though it were his last link with a vanishing world. . . .

> As I plowed out over the wet sand, I walked around what seemed to be a couple of pieces of driftwood sticking out of the sand. But they weren't driftwood. They were a soldier's two feet. He was completely covered except for his feet; the toes of his G.I. shoes pointed toward the land he had come so far to see, and which he saw so briefly.

Yet their war's grotesque unnaturalness finally becomes for them a grotesque naturalness, all that they have known or done—except for that endlessly dwelt-on fantasy that was before and may be after the war, their civilian lives and families and home. Pyle one night—back in one world after weeks in the other—"never wide awake, never deeply asleep," thinks fitfully: "One world was a beautiful dream and the other a horrible nightmare, and I was a little bit in each of them. As I lay on the straw in the darkness they became mixed up, and I was not quite sure which was which." From his long experience of front-line troops, divisions used steadily for months or years, he creates calmly and objectively and prosaically—under their jokes and addresses and grammatical errors, the speech of the farms and garages of America—

their extraordinary suffering: the "endlessness of everything," their "state of exhaustion that is incomprehensible . . . past the point of known human weariness . . . one dull, dead pattern—yesterday is tomorrow and Troino is Randazzo and when will we ever stop and, God, I'm so tired." He and an officer look at some muddy, exhausted troops and decide "they haven't been up in the line at all." They don't have "that stare" of front-line troops. Pyle continues: "It's a look of dullness, eyes that look without seeing, eyes that see without conveying any image to the mind. It's a look that is the display room for what lies behind it—exhaustion, lack of sleep, tension for too long, weariness that is too great, fear beyond fear, misery to the point of numbness, a look of surpassing indifference to anything anybody can do." Nobody else makes you feel so their *long* dreary suffering, everything going on past not only their own lives but the lives of their replacements, until a whole division is "only a numbered mechanism through which men pass"; you remember Mauldin's bearded and filthy soldier, so exhausted he looks middle-aged, staring at his rifle and saying to it slowly: "I've given you the best years of my life."

And these are not professional soldiers but only ordinary people: we feel behind every word the ironic pathos of what they are doing and what they are, of the threadbare shiny scraps that are all that remain to them of the old life they hope their way back to, from this dream where they lie "shooting at the darkness from out of the dark." These scraps—jobs, families, and states—repeated with the same perpetual heartbreaking plainness to the listening Pyle, are a bridge pushed back shakily to their real lives; and he understands and puts down what they tell him, always; and the foolish think it a silly habit of his. Even his generals seem human, as he tells how one is waked: the sentry kneeling beside the general, asleep on the ground in his long underwear, repeating softly, "General, sir, general, sir." The desperate antinomies of war are held together by their common ground, the people who endure them: in the foreground, overshadowing the great convulsions, the appalling strengths, are always "the individual cells of that strength"—their stubbornly and precariously stable commonplaceness, their wonderful pathetic persistence in all they can keep of their old understanding and lives and world. If there are few of the regular heroes, there are many of Pyle's: men chosen by chance, sent out "across the ageless and indifferent sea," doing determinedly and unwillingly what they have to do, heroic if they have to be, and not for a public cause but for their own private moral obligations—fighting "for . . . for . . . well, at least for each other." So Pyle stays with them year after year and finally dies with them, because of them—the lives that, with their pets, their dreams of after and before, their pictures of their children and wives and girls, their intermittent unending exhaustion and suffering and despair, inch out their marginal existence under the 88's.

Nobody else in the world but Pyle makes you feel so intensely *sorry* for them, makes you feel how entirely against their will and aside from their understanding it all happens. The terrible particulars of their misery, of this catastrophe beyond anything they could have deserved or even imagined, drive home to anybody who can understand anything the final moral contradiction of such a war: that though from it come, along with suffering and brutality and death, courage and stubborn endurance and sacrifice, people's real love for one another—*all these things have their price;* and this price is so much too great that it is absolutely incommensurable. Though our victory in this war is better than our defeat, though there is a difference between the two sides that is essential, still what has to be done, the actual substance of the war, is almost entirely evil. The sergeant says to Pyle about the replacements: "I know it ain't my fault they get killed, and I do the best I can for them. But I've got so I feel like it's me killing 'em instead of a German. I've got so I feel like a murderer." For Pyle, to the end, killing was murder: but he saw the murderers die themselves.

His condemnation of war seems to the reader more nearly final than any other, because in him there is no exaggeration, no hysteria, no selection to make out a case, no merely personal emotion unrecognized as such; he has nothing to prove. He has written down all that is favorable or indifferent—his readers have noticed this most, the commonplace courage and endurance and affection of his soldiers; but after all this his condemnation is so complete, detailed, brought home to us so absolutely, that it is unforgettable and unarguable. This proper evaluation of things, his calm, detachment, and objectivity (some of his most humorous and equable columns were written while he himself was in the depths of frustration and revulsion) help to give his work its serious truth.

Here are the soldiers of this war:

> I was sitting among clumps of sword grass on a steep and rocky hillside that we had just taken, looking out over a vast rolling country to the rear. A narrow path wound like a ribbon over a hill miles away, down a long slope, across a creek, up a slope, and over another hill. All along the length of that ribbon there was a thin line of men. For four days and nights they had fought hard, eaten little, washed none, and slept hardly at all. Their nights had been violent with attack, fright, butchery, their days sleepless and miserable with the crash of artillery.
>
> The men were walking. They were fifty feet apart for dispersal. Their walk was slow, for they were dead weary, as a person could tell even when looking at them from behind. Every line and sag of their bodies spoke their inhuman exhaustion. On their shoulders and backs they carried heavy steel tripods, machine-gun barrels, leaden boxes of ammunition. Their feet seemed to sink into the ground from the overload they were bearing.
>
> They didn't slouch. It was the terrible deliberation of each step that spelled out their appalling tiredness. Their faces were black and unshaved. They were young men, but the grime and whiskers and exhaustion made them look middle-aged. In their

eyes as they passed was no hatred, no excitement, no despair, no tonic of their victory—there was just a simple expression of being there as if they had been there doing that forever, and nothing else.

This is how they die:

> When a man was almost gone, the surgeons would put a piece of gauze over his face. He could breathe through it but we couldn't see his face well.
>
> Twice within five minutes chaplains came running. One of those occasions haunted me for hours. The wounded man was still semi-conscious. The chaplain knelt down beside him and two ward boys squatted nearby. The chaplain said, "John, I'm going to say a prayer for you."
>
> Somehow this stark announcement hit me like a hammer. He didn't say, "I'm going to pray for you to get well"; he just said he was going to say a prayer, and it was obvious to me that he meant the final prayer. It was as though he had said, "Brother, you may not know it, but your goose is cooked." Anyhow, he voiced the prayer, and the weak, gasping man tried vainly to repeat the words after him. When he had finished, the chaplain added, "John, you're doing fine, you're doing fine." Then he rose and dashed off on some other call, and the ward boys went about their duties.
>
> The dying man was left utterly alone, just lying there on his litter on the ground, lying in an aisle, because the tent was full.

There are many passages in Pyle that, in their extraordinary intensity and exactness of observation and presentation, seem to the reader to have reached a pure truth of statement. (When we read his famous column about the dead Captain Waskow we are no longer separated from the actual event by anything at all.) In the hospital tent he sees that all the wounded and dying look alike, their faces reduced to a "common denominator" by dirt and suffering and exhaustion—except for any extremely fair soldier, who looks like "a flower in a row of weeds." As the bombs from hundreds of our heavy bombers were falling toward Pyle (by that mistake that killed General McNair and hundreds of other Americans), he heard how "the universe became filled with a gigantic rattling as of huge ripe seeds in a mammoth dry gourd"; he and a stranger wriggled desperately under a farm wagon, and waiting for the bombs already exploding around them, he saw that "we lay with our heads slightly up—like two snakes—staring at each other." Is there any imaginable way in which the next quotation could be altered?

> Our fighters moved on after the enemy, and those who did not fight, but moved in the wake of the battles, would not catch up for hours. There was nothing left behind but the remains—the lifeless debris, the sunshine and the flowers, and utter silence. An amateur who wandered in this vacuum at the rear of a battle had a terrible sense of loneliness. Everything was dead—the men, the machines, the animals—and he alone was left alive.

I do not need to write about Pyle's humor and honesty and understanding, all the precious and "human" qualities—this use of *human* seems an inexorable rationalization, a part of the permanent false consciousness of humanity—that no reader has missed. Along with them there is the charm of those frailties which he insisted on so much. He told beautifully, and often, how scared he was (*Lord, but I felt lonely out there*); but his extraordinary courage—no, his ordinary courage, the courage which, as he showed endlessly, had to be ordinary for millions of men—his readers could only guess, from the long voluntary succession of those situations he was so scared in. His steady humility and self-forgetfulness—without any of the usual veneration of the self for what it is forgetting—were reinforced by his peculiarly objective amusement at his own relation to the world. (When he landed on Okinawa he borrowed a combat jacket with "U.S. Navy" on the back. Later a marine told him: "You know, when you first showed up, we saw that big Navy stenciled on your back, and after you passed I said to the others: 'That guy's an admiral. Look at the old gray-haired bastard. He's been in the navy all his life. He'll get a medal out of this sure as hell.'") His affectionate amused understanding and acceptance of all sorts and levels of people come from his imaginative and undeviating interest in, observation of, these people; he is as unwilling to look away from them because they do not fit his understanding of them as he is to reject them because they do not satisfy the exacting standards he keeps for himself.

He was very much more complex than most people suppose; and his tragedy—a plain fatality hung over the last of his life, and one is harrowed by his unresigned *I've used up my chances*—was not at all that of the simple homogeneous nature destroyed by circumstances it is superior to. People notice how well he got along with people and the world, and talk as if he were the extrovert who naturally does so; actually he was precisely, detailedly, and unremittingly introspective, and the calm objectivity of his columns is a classical device—his own confused and powerful spiritual life always underlies it, and gives it much of its effect. This contradictory struggle between his public and private selves, between the controlled, objective selectivity of the pieces and his own intense inner life, one must guess from fragments or the remarks of those who knew him best; it is partly because this one side of him is incompletely represented in his work that one regrets his death so much.

His writing, like his life, is a victory of the deepest moral feeling, of sympathy and understanding and affection, over circumstances as terrible as any men have created and endured. By the veneration and real love many millions of people felt for him, their unexplained certainty that he was *different* from all the rest, and theirs, they showed their need and gratitude for the qualities of his nature, and seemed almost to share in them. He was a bitter personal loss for these people. Most of his readers could not escape the illusion that he was a personal friend of theirs; actually he was—we meet only a few people in our lives whom we ever know as well or love as much. There are many men whose profession it is to speak for us—political and military and literary representatives of that unwithering estate which has told us all our lives what we feel and what we think, how to live and when to die; he wrote what he had seen and heard and felt himself, and truly represented us. Before his last landing in the Ryukyus, he felt not only fear and revulsion but an overwhelming premonition that he would die there: "repeatedly he said he knew he would be killed if he hit another beachhead. Before he finally settled the question of whether or not to go ashore in his own mind, he spent three sleepless days and nights. Then on the fourth day he made up his mind." He told a good friend, "Now I feel all right again"; to other people he said merely that he didn't want to go there, but he guessed the others didn't either. He had to an extraordinary degree the sense of responsibility to *the others,* the knowledge of his own real duty, that special inescapable demand that is made—if it is made—to each of us alone. In one sense he died freely, for others; in another he died of necessity and for himself. He had said after visiting the lepers in the Hawaiian Islands: "I felt a kind of unrighteousness at being whole and 'clean.' I experienced an acute feeling of spiritual need to be no better off than the leper."

After he died I saw, as most people did, a newsreel of him taken in the Pacific. He is surrounded by marines trying to get his autograph, and steadies on the cropped head of one of them the paper he is signing. He seems unconscious of himself and the camera; his face is humorous, natural, and kindly, but molded by the underlying seriousness, almost severity, of private understanding and judgment. I remembered what the girl in *The Woodlanders* says over another grave: "You were a *good* man, and did good things." But it is hard to say what he was or what we felt about him. He filled a place in our lives that we hardly knew existed, until he was there; and now that he is gone it is empty.

Charles Angoff   (essay date 1945)

SOURCE: A review of "Brave Men," in *The American Mercury,* Vol. LX, No. 254, 1945, pp. 244-46.

[*In the following essay, Angoff reviews* Brave Men, *distinguishing Pyle from the "political philosophers" whose less emotional understanding of war distances them from its true tragedy.*]

Among the hopeful things about contemporary American journalism are the wide popularity of Ernie Pyle and the recognition of his excellence, at long last, by the "serious" arbiters of literary taste. Some of these arbiters still speak of him with a bit of condescension, claiming that his pieces are merely "reporting of a special kind," very good, of course, but rather deficient in the understanding of "underlying forces." There is, indeed, much truth in this claim. Ernie Pyle does not understand "underlying forces," as the more intellectual journalists think they do.

He is a more modest man. His reporting is really "of a special kind." He does not indulge in ideological acrobatics or hand out hunches as inside information. He only tries to tell us how millions of young Americans grapple with loneliness and despair and fear and intense heat and bitter cold and boredom and pain and death every minute of the day and night in every conceivable climate and environment on this planet. He does not write about these things "philosophically," as if he were above them; he writes about them personally, intimately, and he is not ashamed or afraid to express his feelings.

Brave Men is a collection of his Scripps-Howard columns from July 1943, when the Allies landed on Sicily, to the liberation of Paris thirteen months later. It is an even better book than his *Here Is Your War,* because it is even less "objective" and more "sentimental." Ernie Pyle can never forget that a dead soldier or sailor is not just a "casualty," but a colossal tragedy, a disgrace to creation, an enduring catastrophe to his family and friends. And he can never forget that every living soldier or sailor is not merely a serial number, a possible expendable, but someone who was sent off to war with heartbreak and dreadful foreboding. And in writing about soldiers and sailors from these standpoints he often displays more "understanding of underlying forces" than the political philosophers do.

Ernie Pyle was on a warship in the armada approaching the Sicilian shores:

> The night before we sailed the crew listened as usual to the German propaganda radio program which featured Midge, the American girl turned Nazi, who was trying to scare them, disillusion them and depress them. As usual they laughed with amusement and scorn at her childishly treasonable talk.

> In a vague and indirect way, I suppose, the privilege of listening to your enemy trying to undermine you—the very night before you go out to face him—expresses what we are fighting for.

Pyle's favorite fighting men are the common front-line soldiers, "the fabulous infantry." His most moving pages are devoted to them. Some of them make such stylists as Hemingway seem very poor stuff indeed. There is the magnificent section on the death of the beloved Captain Henry T. Waskow, of Belton, Texas, who "had a sincerity and a gentleness that made people want to be guided by him." A few specimen lines:

> Dead men had been coming down the mountain all evening, lashed onto the backs of mules. They came lying belly-down across the wooden packsaddles, their heads hanging down on one side, bobbing up and down as the mules walked.

> The Italian mule skinners were afraid to walk beside dead men, so Americans had to lead the mules down that night. Even the Americans were reluctant to unlash and lift off the bodies when they got to the bottom, so an officer had to do it himself and ask others to help.

> I don't know who that first one was. You feel small in the presence of dead men, and you don't ask silly questions. . . .

> The unburdened mules moved off to their olive grove. The men in the road seemed reluctant to leave. They stood around, and gradually I could sense them moving, one by one, close to Captain Waskow's body. Not so much to look, I think, as to say something in finality to him and to themselves. I stood close by and I could hear.

> One soldier came and looked down, and he said out loud, "God damn it!"

> That's all he said, and then he walked away.

> Another one came, and he said, "God damn it to hell anyway!" He looked down for a few last moments and then turned and left. . . .

> Then a soldier came and bent over, and he too spoke to his dead captain, not in a whisper, but awfully tenderly, and he said, "I'm sorry, sir."

II

Pyle knows the soldiers as probably no other one man knows them. He seems to sense their every dream, yearning, dread. He knows what makes them laugh and suddenly grow somber. He knows what commands their respectful silence and what draws a gag out of them. He can describe them fully in a few words. "The men of Oklahoma are drawling and soft-spoken. They are not smart-alecks. Something of the purity of the soil seems to be in them. Even their cussing is simpler and more profound than the torrential obscenities of Eastern city men." Sgt. Buck Eversole's grammar "was the unschooled grammar of the plains and the soil. He used profanity, but never violently. Even in the familiarity of his own group his voice was always low. It was impossible to conceive of his doing anything dishonest. He was such a confirmed soldier . . . that he always said 'sir' to any stranger. . . . Buck Eversole had no hatred for Germans, although he had killed many of them. He killed because he was trying to keep alive himself. The years rolled over him and the war became his only world, and battle his only profession. He armored himself with a philosophy of accepting whatever might happen." Pfc. James Framis McClory "was crazy about apes" and was so loyal to his commanding officer that when "Captain Kennedy's mother was very ill, McClory took the last money he had and telegraphed home to his own parish to have a Mass said for the Captain's mother."

These men and the millions of other American soldiers and sailors, united by "the powerful fraternalism in this ghostly brotherhood of war," are less afraid "of the physical part of dying. That isn't the way it is. The emotion is rather one of almost desperate reluctance to give up the future." And what is the future for these men? It includes

> things such as seeing the "old lady" again, of going to college . . . of holding on your knee just once your own kid whom you've never seen, of again being champion salesman of your territory, of driving a coal truck around the streets of Kansas City once more and, yes, even of just sitting in the sun once more in the south side of a house in New Mexico.

This sort of honest reporting has been absent from American journalism since our reporters decided that it was more important to write personal histories and philosophize on world affairs than to write simple, heart-felt accounts of how ordinary men and women manage to maintain their self-respect in this life. One hopes that Ernie Pyle's *Brave Men* will show these journalists the error of their ways.

David Dempsey (essay date 1946)

SOURCE: "Ernie Pyle's Last Stories of GI Joe," in *The New York Times Book Review*, June 2, 1946, pp. 3, 20.

[*In the following essay, Dempsey reviews Pyle's last book,* Last Chapter, *published thirteen months after the author's death, commenting that while its fragmentary nature may disappoint some readers,* Last Chapter *continued Pyle's effort to make the experience of the American soldier in battle real to civilians.*]

Ernie Pyle is the greatest and best loved of all that army of camp followers who traded green eye shades for tin helmets and fought the war with typewriters. The publication of this brief volume [*Last Chapter*], thirteen months after his tragic death on Ie Shima, reminds us again how much we owe to the man who told us—and who will tell the historians of the future—what war was like to the common soldier in the fifth decade of the twentieth century.

Pyle's books were something of a war phenomenon, about on a par with the invention of radar. *Here Is Your War* has sold 1,320,000 copies, including a 25-cent reprint edition. *Brave Men* chalked up a staggering sale of 1,300,000 copies, without benefit of reprints but including a book club distribution. Another half million copies of each book was distributed free to the armed forces.

Such popularity is no accident, but the result of two revolutions which Pyle pioneered in war reporting. He brought war home to the people, who found the traditional news dispatches too remote from their own experience; and he took it away from the generals and gave it to the enlisted men and junior officers. This is so obvious in retrospect that it seems almost impossible to believe that wars were not always reported in such fashion. But they were not and Ernie was the first to discover the kind of war that the average soldier was fighting—the intimate war of the company and platoon—and to make it real to millions of people for whom it had become too vast and remote to comprehend. He was one of the first to ask the GI's themselves how war felt, and in so doing to shift the perspective of war from the command post to the foxhole. And in a war that increasingly glorified its mechanized branches, Pyle rediscovered the infantry—the "solemn, bearded, dirty, drooping old men of the infantry."

Actually, Ernie's primary interest was not the war itself but the people who fought it. It was not logistics and strategy that constituted battle but the sadness and loneliness of men. He was fond of saying that for the average soldier the war extended about 100 yards on either side of him and it was on this small sector that he took up his own position; it was not the machine but its parts that he set himself the task of understanding. Even when this brought him in contact with all the technical paraphernalia of war, it was the individual's human, rather than functional, relationship to his weapon that interested him.

As war became more and more technical, Ernie's constant reminders that it was men and not machines who did the fighting were increasingly important. He became a sort of nexus between the remote and unimaginable world of the foxhole and that equally (to the soldier) incomprehensible world of civilians. Ernie's popularity at home is well known. His popularity among the troops was just as great and his books, where obtainable, were avidly read. For the men found in them a conception of themselves as something more than a piece of Government property. Ernie wrote of them as human beings, with a home town, a street address, a family, and a claim on the good things of life. He gave them personality in an impersonal Army. Even after other correspondents had adopted the Pyle technique, Ernie remained the symbol of the "GI" war. There were as many preparations made to receive him at an Army headquarters as if General Eisenhower himself were coming, and it is no exaggeration to say that in his own way he was as important to the war.

It was a supreme bit of irony that Pyle's career should have been made expounding this dirty business that he hated so much. To him, war was a violation of all civilized values; the miracle was that in all its waste and despair and suffering men not only held on to these values but that there were moments when war quickened in them a sense of comradeship and purpose seldom experienced in peace. All the intimate and homely details that fill his books point this up; and although this was probably not a conscious conviction, they gave his books a sense of war's tragic ambiguity and kept him from either glorifying or debunking it. War was something to be endured and, because our values were right, to be won.

It is this attitude, expounded with the simplicity and restraint that mark his style, that gives his books a sentimental quality. Ernie's style, like all good styles, was a mode of feeling and Ernie was a sentimental man. His books, too, are sentimental, but they are not sentimentalized. The test of true sentiment is whether the lump comes back in the throat on second reading. With Pyle's books it does.

Last Chapter is but a fragment of Ernie Pyle's war. To many it will be a disappointing fragment. Pyle's Pacific assignment was cut short before he had really gotten started. At best, he had missed the pioneering days of Guadalcanal, New Guinea and Bougainville. Except for a few weeks, almost all his time was with the Navy and you feel that he never really was at home in an officer's stateroom after so many years in a foxhole. The whole tradition in which he found himself was different, and Ernie was just beginning to get the feel of it when he was killed. *Last Chapter,* as the publishers tell us, is essentially a "brief, brave little book to complete the record."

Because Pyle's influence was so enormous, it is easy to make him out a greater writer than he was. The aim he set for himself was simple—to discover the common denominator of the common soldier, that part of him by which he was remembered at home, and which enshrined, beneath his calloused surface, the nostalgic humanity of small kindnesses and hopes. Ernie cared little for the intellectual abstractions of the struggle and everything for the men who were its victims. He was, first and last, a reporter, and it was the way he saw the fight, not what he thought about it, that gives his facts a sort of compassionate and wistful truth. Compare his writing with much of the ballyhoo that passed for war reporting and you understand how intrepidly he cut through the conventions of his profession to get at the heart and soul of war.

Many of Ernie's stories were gotten at the risk of never living to write them. The whole Army, to him, was a sort of Lost Battalion which he rescued from the No-Man's-Land of the communiqué to bring as close to home as the written word can do. And it is not unfitting that out of all this Army he should have stayed with those who will not come back. He did not choose this—no soldier ever does. In his own words: "They died and others lived and nobody knows why it is so. They died and thereby the rest of us can go on and on."

Bill Mauldin (essay date 1946)

SOURCE: "Ernie Pyle's Last Book," in *The Nation,* Vol. 162, No. 25, June 22, 1946, pp. 754-56.

[*In the following essay, Mauldin, a fellow journalist during World War II, offers praise for Pyle's last book,* Last Chapter.]

It is standard operating procedure to find someone who knew Ernie Pyle to write reviews about his books. In the hundreds of reviews, each tried to be original, but it was hard because Ernie was not a man you kick up controversies over—if you knew him you loved him. He didn't hurt any feelings, follow any party lines, accuse any generals, nor were his personal feelings or motives a mystery. As far as I know not a single review was unfavorable to him.

Most of them said, "The last time I saw Ernie, he was sitting on a cot in his long-handled G.I. drawers, with a haunted look on his face, expecting to be killed. . . ." and they went on to say he was a gnomish, generous, real little guy you regarded as a father or a brother—depending on the writer's age—upon first sight. Well, he was a gnomish, generous, real little guy, susceptible to hard-luck stories and hangovers, and he often was found in long-handled drawers with a haunted look on his face, expecting to be killed.

And the last time *I* saw Ernie, he was sitting on a folding chair giving me hell for getting an agent. He told me how well he got along without one, and since I already knew what I wanted to do in civilian life after the war, why did I need advice? Shortly afterward, a Hollywood producer, noted for his enterprise and thrift, secured the movie rights to Ernie's then current book, got the blessing and cooperation of the War Department, and turned out a picture which was a Hollywood war picture. It contains such box-office attractions as an oversexed American soldier of foreign parentage. This was an insult to the memory of many very fine and very dead guys of foreign extraction, as well as to Ernie, who did not believe in selling his column by portraying soldiers as childish delinquents with funny accents. One of Ernie's great heroes was a captain named Waskow, and he wrote one of the most touching stories of any war about Captain Waskow's death. The producer, perhaps afraid that the name Waskow might not appeal to certain customers, changed it to Walker in the movie.

The agentless Ernie received $10,000 for the right to produce this epic—about 5 per cent of what a more agent-minded author of so popular a best-seller would have received from other thrifty and enterprising producers. I don't see how Ernie could have liked the movie, but he still would advise me not to get an agent.

Since reviews about Ernie must contain a personal anecdote, that was mine.

I think *Last Chapter* is mostly a meandering beginning to what would have been as great a story of people in war as *Brave Men*—but the foxhole stuff didn't start until the last part of the book, where he made an invasion with the marines and spent some time with the infantry which he had done so much to glorify in the days when the only glory they saw was at the Pearly Gates. I hope it is not irreverent to mention that one time after Ernie's death I thought of him on a cloud being pointed out by a couple of infantrymen on another cloud—one of them saying, "There's the guy who made Congress raise our pay."

The first parts of the book are mostly about the navy. The Navy Department, hurt because it hadn't any Boswells, wanted Ernie to come stay with them for a while. Ernie, who respected what he had seen of the navy, and who didn't want anybody to be hurt, went along with them. Possibly the only trouble was that the navy, which has very set ideas about rank and prestige, couldn't quite adjust itself to the idea of a man of Ernie's stature, with the rank of war correspondent to boot, chumming with ordinary sailors.

Anyway, most of the book's navy section is about officers. To Ernie Pyle's everlasting credit, he loved everybody alike, and he considered officers every bit as good as enlisted men. So when he found himself among officers, he wrote interesting things about them. In fact, although I had always known that gentlemen with officers' rank had a pretty hellish time in companies and battalions, and usually distinguished themselves and got killed as regularly as gentlemen of enlisted rank—it wasn't until I read Ernie's columns regularly in Europe that I discovered officers of higher rank were often human beings with halitosis and homesickness just like everybody else.

Ernie's naval officers did a highly complex, difficult, and dangerous job, and they deserved his publicity. He mentions often that the ship was well stocked with sailors, and I gather they were necessary to the successful operation of the voyage, but they seemed mostly background. I don't intend this as a crack at the book. Ernie was bunked with officers, but he would have been equally at home among the sailors, and would have made them just as interesting. But I can't help wondering if the Navy Department ever wonders why the hell it never had a Boswell.

If a simple, honest man ever had reason to become neurotic and anti-social, Ernie did during his last stay in America. Our good citizens overwhelmed him with love, and among the citizens were those with business interests at heart. He bit once, a full-color cigarette ad displayed him smoking the service man's favorite brand—I forget which—and he resisted successfully after that.

I'm sure he would have gone to the Pacific war anyway, but I have often thought the trip was possibly hurried somewhat by all the love that was showered upon him. I know, I know, thought five hundred thousand mothers throughout the land, I know he's awfully tired, but it wouldn't hurt to phone him and ask why Johnny's in the guardhouse.

But he kept on loving people right back in his worried way, and he kept simple and honest. It sounds very trite, but there it is. Here's real honesty, in my opinion, from a page in *Last Chapter*:

> We hadn't been in the room two seconds when one Seabee called through the window: "Say, aren't you Ernie Pyle?" I said, "Right," and he said, "Whoever thought we'd meet you here? I recognized you from your picture." All the others stopped work and gathered outside the window while we talked through the screen. . . .

Look, dear reader, let's put you out there on an island in his place. You're writing a column which is being eagerly awaited by millions, and you have a reputation which is causing statues to be erected. Senators are suggesting

your birthday become a national holiday. You gotta play your cards right. The public likes to knock heroes off pedestals. One wrong word can queer you. If you're the clever type, you write, "One of the Seabees looked in my window and said, 'Hey, mugs, they're sendin' a sideshow to build our morale!'" Or if you're the quiet type, you say, "They looked at me like any other replacement." Or else you forget the incident and go looking for other copy.

But Ernie put it down, because it happened, and it was an experience. Nobody else could have got away with it, but then there was nobody like him.

David Nichols (essay date 1986)

SOURCE: An introduction to *Ernie's War: The Best of Ernie Pyle's World War II Dispatches,* edited by David Nichols, Random House, 1986, pp. 5-37.

[*In the following essay, Nichols provides an overview of Pyle's life, focusing on his relationship with his wife.*

Ernie Pyle was born August 3, 1900, on a farm a few miles outside Dana, Indiana, the first and only child of Will and Maria Pyle. He was a senior in high school when a neighbor boy went off to World War I. Pyle wanted to go, too. Bored with the steady rhythms of farm life and enamored of men of action, he found the prospect of marching off to war in storied Europe irresistible. He shared with countless other Americans a love of parades and boisterous song. His parents, however, insisted that he finish high school, a big disappointment for a young romantic. Upon graduation he enrolled in the Naval Reserve, but the Armistice was signed before he made it to advanced training.

He entered Indiana University at Bloomington in the fall of 1919. Shortly after he arrived, he met Paige Cavanaugh, a war veteran several months his senior. Both were Indiana farm boys anxious to make as solid a break with the farm as possible. Soon they became good friends, Cavanaugh telling of his wartime experiences in France and Pyle wishing he had been so blessed. "He thought the war was a great experience for me," Cavanaugh has said, "and he regretted that he'd not been able to be a part of it—the risk, the romance, the adventure of it, perhaps." Cavanaugh, both in his urge to travel and in his contempt for the conventional, was to deeply influence Pyle.

In January 1923, just short of completing his journalism degree, Pyle left the university to take a general-reporting job on the *La Porte Herald* in La Porte, Indiana. His parents were strongly opposed to it (the graduation issue again), but Pyle had deferred to their wishes once and missed a war for it. He was not about to pass up a real newspaper job.

Pyle left La Porte after a few months to become a reporter for the Scripps-Howard *Washington Daily News,* a one-cent tabloid of generally twelve pages, competing against three more established publications, including the *Washington Post.* Pyle, his bosses discovered, had a knack for writing punchy headlines, and soon they made him a copy editor. Only a few months short of twenty-three when he arrived in Washington, Pyle began what would be a long association with Scripps-Howard, the only employer of any duration he would ever have. He met Lee Miller, also an Indiana native, who would steadily promote his career, encourage him when depression overcame him, edit his copy (leniently, for the most part), and, when fame arrived, handle his business matters. Miller would also write a posthumous Pyle biography.

In college, Pyle had written a windy editorial entitled "The Ideal Girl," in which he described the kind of young woman a young man ought to marry. She would be "the type who is willing to share your troubles, sympathize with you in your periods of adverses, and makes your interests her interests." Ernie believed he had found such a woman in Geraldine Siebolds, to whom he was married on July 7, 1925, by a justice of the peace in Alexandria, Virginia. Jerry, twenty days her husband's junior, was a civil-service worker who had moved to Washington from her native Minnesota shortly after graduating from high school. She was an extremely bright, attractive woman, willing to share Ernie's troubles and sympathize with him in his "periods of adverses." For the most part, she was also willing to make his interests her interests. But she had little use for marriage. Jerry was stubbornly nonconformist and agreed to marriage only if the deed were kept hidden from their Washington friends. Ernie, whose only concern in the matter was his parents' feelings, agreed, and "for years," Miller wrote, "they made a fetish of insisting they weren't really married."

They fancied themselves bohemians and were not model housekeepers. When they socialized, it was with the newspaper crowd, including Lee Miller, who described the floor of their downtown apartment as tobacco covered, the window sills stained by party drinks, the furnishings limited to army cots, wicker chairs, and a breakfast grill.

In the summer of 1926, the Pyles quit their jobs and left Washington to drive around the United States. They traveled nine thousand miles in ten weeks. The trip ended in New York, where Ernie got a job on the copy desk of the *Evening World* and later the *Post.* In December of 1927, the *Washington Daily News* invited him to return as its telegraph editor, and Pyle, never fond of New York, readily accepted. Although it was another desk job, he was soon able to compensate for the long, hectic hours of editing wire-service stories and writing headlines by carving out a beat all his own, the first daily aviation column in American journalism.

Pyle undertook the aviation column about a year after Charles Lindbergh's celebrated transatlantic flight. Lindbergh's feat and the attendant hero worship in the press must have profoundly touched him: even as an adult he was fascinated with men of action, much as he had marveled at Indianapolis 500 drivers as a student.

His work on the copy desk completed by early afternoon, Pyle would hunt for material at the several airports in and around Washington. The writing he did on his own time, in the evenings at home. Soon his apartment became a gathering place for flyers and assorted hangers-on.

Two things germane to Pyle's later success emerged from his dealings with aviators. He found that total immersion in his subject matter yielded the best results, that he had a gift for becoming a member of a group while retaining his ability to explain it to outsiders. Just as important, Pyle discovered that he could mix with all kinds of people. Inherently shy, he was a democratizer in a group. Meeting him, even reading his column, people felt at ease and were inclined to open up.

Scripps-Howard eventually made Pyle aviation editor for the entire chain. Aviators were the heroes of the hour, and he was their scribe. Yet Pyle was not an altogether happy man. Paige Cavanaugh was routinely indulging his wanderlust by traveling to Europe, and it's likely that Pyle wanted some of that for himself. Cavanaugh, however, was single and perfectly content to drift from job to job, abandoning any pursuit he found even marginally dull. Pyle cared about financial security. It was one thing to live a pared-down existence, mock middle-class aspirations, drink bootleg liquor, and listen to Jerry read poetry aloud, but it was quite another to be unemployed, and Pyle feared being out of work. Even so, what others might have taken for ambition—working on his own time at the aviation writing, for example—was mostly a flight from boredom, a lifelong affliction for Pyle.

Much to the disappointment of aviators and readers alike, Pyle quit the aviation column in 1932 to become managing editor of the *Washington Daily News.* He didn't want the position, but he didn't think he could turn it down, either. While Pyle did a good job in his three years as managing editor, neither inside work nor politics appealed to him. In one picture taken near the end of his managing editor term, Pyle looks fifty years old. He was only thirty-four, just beginning the hectic period of his life.

In the winter of 1934, Pyle developed a severe and lingering case of influenza. His doctor ordered him to seek a warmer climate, and the *News* granted him a leave of absence. With Jerry, he traveled by car to Los Angeles, where they boarded a freighter and sailed six thousand miles to Philadelphia in three weeks. It was an arduous convalescence that suggested a new career. Back in Washington, he wrote a series of articles about his vacation. The pieces were well received, and soon Pyle talked his bosses into giving him a try as a roving columnist. Now officially employed by Scripps-Howard Alliance, he was to write six columns a week for distribution to the twenty-four Scripps-Howard papers, including the *Washington Daily News.*

" . . . I will go where I please and write what I please," he told a friend, and for the next six years he did just that. Thirty-five times he crossed the American continent, dipping into each state at least three times. He reported from Alaska, Hawaii, and Central and South America, moving by car, truck, plane, boat, horse and muleback.

It was Pyle's habit to travel for a week or so, collecting material as he went, then hole up in a hotel room to write. If the week had gone well, he might have, say, four interviews with which to work. These he would write as reports, almost always including himself. They revealed a man who enjoyed a tall tale and the company of rugged individualists—Alaskan gold miners or a squatter who painted pictures in his shack behind the Memphis city dump. Thus readers met a variety of interesting characters whose personalities were revealed in apposition to Pyle's. The balance of the week's pieces would be personal essays on his own foibles and illnesses (which were legion), or on curious things that happened to him as he puttered across country at speeds rarely exceeding forty-five miles per hour.

The latitude the job offered was far from liberating, however. Ernie and Jerry were free enough to follow their own inclinations, but there was a purpose to it all, and that weighed heavily. Both were often discontent with their traveling life. Paige Cavanaugh had married and settled in Inglewood, California, and though he still regularly changed jobs, Cavanaugh was becoming more rooted. "Many times on this trip, Mr. Cavanaugh," Pyle wrote from Guatemala, "I've envied you—just thinking of you sitting there . . . with every comfort in the world. . . ." Pyle had in Cavanaugh a friend whose light-hearted approach to life offered respite from the wearisome routine of travel and from his concern for Jerry, who, early in their travel days, had begun to show signs of the depression that would later twice cause her to attempt suicide.

It's impossible almost forty years after her death to offer anything but conjecture about Jerry's unhappiness. A mystery to Ernie, as well as to his friends and associates, it was likely a mystery to Jerry herself. She was an emotional chameleon, capable of change at a moment's notice. Column readers knew her as "that Girl who rides with me," though she was a vague figure, never well developed. She lived out of suitcases, retyped his copy, offered praise and criticism of his work, her life revolving around Ernie and his restive disposition. Life on the road held very little for Jerry, whose pleasures—reading, playing the piano, working crossword puzzles—were largely sedentary. More than ever before, Pyle's college description of the "ideal girl" applied to her: she shared in his troubles and sympathized with him in his "periods of adverses." Even sex was denied her.

Ernie and Jerry probably never wanted children early in their married lives, but later on—just when is unclear— the question was moot. Ernie had become impotent. He often joked about the problem in letters to Cavanaugh and eventually sought treatment for the condition in San Diego, but he apparently never recovered. Later, in desperation, Jerry would want a child.

Beginning with Ernie's extended trip to Alaska in April of 1937, they began spending more time apart, carrying on their marriage by correspondence. Their letters were full of the superlatives of endearment, but something was amiss. Jerry's depression, slowly building for two years, was now virtually unchecked; she drank heavily and used sedatives and Benzedrine. While Pyle toured Alaska and the Aleutian Islands, Jerry closed their Washington apartment for good. For three years, until they built a house in Albuquerque, she was a woman without a home, living variously with her mother in Minnesota or with friends around the country.

Ernie, meanwhile, was in demand and carried along by the pleasure he took in his new-found popularity, but in these years, he surrendered the only intimate relationship he had ever had—that with Jerry—to the pressures of a largely unseen audience. He was aware of this—aware, too, that the more successful the column became the harder it would be to quit. Still, he pushed ahead toward syndication outside the Scripps-Howard chain, often chafing when the results were meager.

In September 1938, the Pyles began a tour of Central and South America. They parted in French Guiana so that Ernie could visit the penal colony at Devil's Island; Jerry ended up in Miami, alone in a hotel and drinking heavily. Ernie later found her incoherent, emaciated, and unable to eat. Outwardly, she recovered quickly, and they resumed their travels.

When the war that would make him a national hero was breaking out overseas, Pyle was mostly uninterested. Not until September 3, 1939, when Great Britain and France declared war on Germany, did he take serious notice. Eight days after the declaration, he wrote to Cavanaugh: "Personally, I'm just about to bust. I want to get over there as a war correspondent or something so bad. However, there is an unspoken stalemate on between Miss Geraldine and me as regards that subject. The matter has never been discussed openly, but we know how each other stands. I'll probably win in the end, however. Pacifism is fine as long as there ain't no war around. But when they start shooting I want to get close enough just a couple of times to get good and scared."

At the age of thirty-nine, Pyle still had a schoolboy's vision of battle, an untutored conception of war that recalled his disappointment over not accompanying his neighbor friend to World War I twenty-two years before. He was restless. He had avoided doing pieces on serious topics for so long that now, in the face of world crisis, his work seemed trivial. "For the last two weeks I've been so goddam bored writing silly dull columns about Mt. Hood and hop ranches that I think I'm going nuts," he wrote Cavanaugh. But relief was slow in coming.

It was a little over a year later, in mid-November 1940, that Ernie sailed to England to report on the Battle of Britain. He left Jerry in Albuquerque to oversee the construction of their new house, the first and only house they would ever own. Though Jerry eventually came to love the little house, she hardly found it compensation for her husband's decision to go to war. She wrote to friends of her fears for Ernie's safety, which, she said, she was learning to live with. She added: "But to pretend that I give one single solitary good goddamn about a shack or a palace or any other material consideration in this world would be to foist upon everybody at all interested the greatest gold-brick insult a low mind could conceive."

Frightened but animated after waiting twenty-three years for his first taste of war, Pyle arrived in England in mid-December for a three-month stay. Shortly thereafter, London received a particularly brutal pounding by Luftwaffe fire bombs, which Pyle watched from a balcony. He described the city as "stabbed with great fires, shaken by explosions, its dark regions along the Thames sparkling with the pinpoints of white-hot bombs. . . ."

Pyle soon found that he liked England and the English. His columns, flavored by their persistence and understated humor, the copy chatty and somewhat glib, were well received in the States. He wrote about life in the subway shelters, about the firemen who worked through the night and the spotters who enforced blackout provisions and watched for roof fires. He took a long tour of England's industrial midlands and stood in the ruins of Coventry. Now marginally familiar with one aspect of war, Pyle had yet to shed his dilettante's view of it. He was a tourist, a visitor sharing his hosts' misery in a cursory way. When Pyle next went to war—almost two years later—he would not be on a balcony looking down; he would be in a foxhole, looking up. And what he would see then would dispel forever his adolescent view of the romance of war.

Since he had begun his travel work five years before, it had been cruelly true that for every gain Pyle made professionally, he had suffered a personal setback. As his popularity increased, his marital happiness declined. Privacy was a thing of the past: in the spring of 1941, tourists began driving past his house in Albuquerque at all hours, hoping to get a glimpse of him. Even his stay in England had been marred by word of his mother's death in Indiana.

Much as the new house delighted him, Pyle had little time to enjoy it because he had to travel frantically to keep the column going. Jerry's unhappiness had deepened during his months abroad, partly out of concern for Ernie's well-being, and now her troubles took a new turn: she tried to take her life, apparently by closing herself off in the kitchen and turning on the gas jets. Ernie took her to Denver for a thorough physical, but the doctors found nothing wrong.

He was on a tour of Canadian air bases in late August when friends summoned him back to Albuquerque. A friend had found Jerry near death, hemorrhaging at the mouth. An ulcer had eaten through a blood vessel in her stomach. Her doctors predicted a slow recovery. Jerry

had been "drinking colossally for days," Ernie wrote Cavanaugh. "Will stay here until she gets completely back to normal, and may have to completely reshape our lives to prevent her ever doing this again." He offered Scripps-Howard his resignation, but the company flatly refused it. They settled on a three-month leave of absence—with no pay, at Pyle's insistence.

Calling Jerry a "psychopathic case," he explained her condition to his bosses: "Because of her futility complex (I suppose) she is not permanently interested in anything. And without any interest, she frequently gets to wallowing in boredom and melancholy and hopelessness, and that leads her to progress from normal drinking to colossal drinking. . . ."

Jerry made a remarkable recovery. By mid-fall, Ernie was proposing a three-month trip to the Orient, but when his plans fell through, he had to make do with resuming the column stateside. Jerry, meanwhile, turned again to heavy drinking. That December the Japanese attacked Pearl Harbor, and the United States declared war on Japan and the other Axis powers.

The year 1942 was the low point of Pyle's life. In the year's first six months, he began and ended a love relationship, apparently platonic, with a woman in San Francisco. He traveled relentlessly to rebuild circulation lost during his three months of leave, concentrating mainly on the West Coast so that he could undergo a series of painful (and nonproductive) treatments for impotence in San Diego. All the while, Jerry's condition steadily worsened. She was in and out of the hospital, "doping and drinking to excess again," eventually coming to believe that having a baby would help her right her life. " . . . I *can't* give you a child, as you know," Ernie told her. "I haven't been lying when I've told you that the power of sex had gone from me."

Finally, with the concurrence of Jerry's doctors and family, Ernie reluctantly divorced her on April 14, 1942, hoping the shock would force her "into a realization that she [has] to face life like other people." He left open the possibility of remarriage, assuming that Jerry would "get to work and cure herself. . . ." Ernie signed the house over to her, divided their savings equally between them, and provided her with a weekly income.

Scripps-Howard, meanwhile, wanted Pyle to prepare for a foreign trip, something interesting to give the column the impetus it lacked after his frequent absences over the last year. He flew to Washington and quickly concluded that Great Britain was his best bet. The law required that he register for the draft, and he did so, discovering in the process that his classification was 1-A. He requested and was granted a six-month draft extension.

Shortly before he left the United States for Britain, Jerry's mental health slipped sufficiently that Ernie found the courage to do what he said he should have done long before. He committed her to a sanitarium at Pueblo,

Colorado, for six months. When she pleaded to be released and remarried to him, Ernie refused, admitting that his comments seemed cold. " . . . I'm coming back (permanently I mean) when you are so far along the road of cheerfulness and normal outlook and usefulness to yourself and other people, that there can be no doubt about our future, and not until then. . . ." Emotionally unstable himself, Ernie in his dealings with Jerry had assumed more the outlook of a foster parent than that of an ex-husband. That he urged her to make herself useful to others is significant. For years, Ernie and Jerry had dismissed middle-class American life as unworthy of their aspirations. They had lived a rootless existence, clung to the bohemian pretensions of their Washington days, and traveled at Scripps-Howard's expense, liberally dispensing tips at a time when most Americans their age were struggling to raise families in the Depression.

"Stability cloaks you with a thousand little personal responsibilities, and we have been able to flee from them," Ernie had written of their traveling life. Blind as he was to the fact Jerry desperately needed his steady company to overcome her problems, Ernie was quicker than she to apprehend that service to others in a time of national need was a potential antidote to their troubles. With the country mobilized for war and the government enjoining everyone to do his part, Pyle felt the tug of usefulness. He was not certain how to act upon those sentiments, but he closed the travel-writing phase of his career on a note of chagrin, sure only that what lay ahead would be preferable to the strain of the preceding twelve months.

Before Pyle flew from New York to Ireland during mid-June 1942, he wrote his ex-wife, "I am all alone. Be my old Jerry when I come back. I love you."

Americans were already at war in the Pacific as Pyle began writing about the training of American troops in Ireland and England. By studying the men he wrote about, he picked up on their longings and away-from-home habits and sent back the kind of detail no other reporter bothered with. His circulation figures steadily improved, and slowly his frame of mind did, too, though mail from Jerry was infrequent, and this bothered him. In late summer, he received word from her that she had left the Colorado sanitarium and was living in Albuquerque, in a house on the grounds of a Catholic hospital. (She had prevailed upon her sister to authorize her release.) Perplexed, Ernie urged her to find a job, something congenial to get her mind off her problems.

Living close to his subjects worked an insidious change in Pyle, the one-time bohemian outsider. He found himself in the unlikely position of chronicling the daily lives of the conscripted soldiers of what was becoming a very middle-class nation. Pyle's subjects were men whose backgrounds were often strikingly "normal," even boring, and whose postwar dreams called for more of the same. Many a Pyle subject wanted nothing so much as a little white house with a yard bordered by a white picket fence—precisely the sort of house Pyle and Jerry had

built in Albuquerque, which he had sardonically described to Cavanaugh as a "regular little boxed-up mass production shack in a cheap new suburb."

Though some days he believed induction into the Army would be a relief, by late September Pyle had guardedly decided to stay with column writing. Homefront reaction to his pieces was favorable, so he asked Lee Miller to file with the draft board for another six-month extension. The board promptly granted it, but soon thereafter the government stopped drafting men thirty-eight and older. By month's end he had come to equate writing with service. He told Jerry, "As much as I would like to come home, I don't see any point in getting home for a few days and then spending the rest of the war as a private when I can do more good—if any at all—by sticking to what I'm doing."

Visiting Air Corps bases consumed most of his time in October. There were rumors that a second front would be opened soon, and Pyle concluded that he would go along, not with the forces actually making the landings, but a little later. From London, in late October, he wrote Jerry a long, introspective letter. "My future without you is unthinkable," he said, "and I hope you feel the same way. We have both suffered so much that surely there is peace waiting for us ahead. . . . I too look at things much differently than I did; I have sobered a great deal, and I see now that I was bad in so many ways. I've finally realized that I unconsciously had the German attitude—that everything I did was right just because I did it. . . . I don't waste any time reproaching myself for the past, but somehow I feel that my character and my mind have deteriorated so terribly; I don't have any spiritual stability within myself at all. . . all purpose seems to have gone out of life for me (except the one of hope) and I've no interest in anything."

His spirits continued to sag. The column had become "something I don't love anymore," he wrote Jerry on November 3, 1942. "I would do almost anything to abandon it forever. I have no interest in it, and I'm weary almost unto illness of thinking for a living."

Shortly after that, he boarded the *Rangiticki,* a British transport ship carrying troops to replace those wounded or killed in the Allied invasion of North Africa. He had shared several months of agreeable companionship in Ireland and England with the American men quartered in the ship's hold. By traveling with them through hostile waters to a foreign place, he was beginning to share their future in a serious way. Yet he had no intention of becoming their spokesman in this war; he planned, rather, to take a quick look at Africa, then travel to India or China. Had he been in a better frame of mind, he might have seen that he had already found a new outlet for his ability to capture the human side of events great and small, a talent previously diluted for want of focus.

Pyle went ashore in Algeria on November 22, 1942, and spent the balance of the year in and around Oran. From his column, readers got a sense of how massive an effort the war was, of how diverse were the duties of its participants.

A few days after he landed in North Africa, Ernie, depressed and lonely, wrote Jerry a letter asking her to be remarried to him by proxy. He got an Army judge to draw up the papers, which he forwarded to Albuquerque. Bedridden with influenza over the Christmas holidays, he was horrified by a dream in which Jerry had married someone else. It was their third straight Christmas apart.

Shortly after the holidays, Pyle was ready for a look at the front. In January 1943, he flew from Oran to a desert airfield called the Garden of Allah. He planned to write a series of columns on the bomber crews and fighter pilots stationed there, take a look at how the infantry was faring, then resume the travel column. Thus far, his portrait of the American soldiers in North Africa was instructive but incomplete. In this next phase of his introduction to war, Pyle would come face to face with what most people understand intellectually but that only the combatant or his astute observer comes to know emotionally—that battle demands of its participants a suspension of the peacetime moral sense that killing is wrong. Pyle would see nothing of the sublime in this moral transformation, necessary as it was.

He spent a week with a group of P-38 Lightning pilots who generally flew escort for the bombers but who delighted in an occasional strafing mission. After one such mission, during which they had blown a German truck convoy to pieces, the pilots laughed as they told their story of Germans flying out of the trucks "like firecrackers." It bothered Pyle to see men so young kill so readily—and with such relish. He "couldn't help having a funny feeling about them. . . they were so casual about everything. . . they talked about their flights and killing and being killed exactly as they would discuss girls or their school lessons."

The column on the fighter pilots and their strafing marked the emergence of a more serious Pyle voice, at the core of which was an engaging tension: the enormous moral difference between life at home and life at war. Pyle was well acquainted with offbeat behavior from offbeat people; he had spent years tracking down such characters and writing their stories. Now he found so-called normal men doing bestial things, and he was both intrigued and repelled.

Pyle left the relative comfort of the Garden of Allah in late January 1943 and joined the infantry of General Fredendall's (later General Patton's) II Corps, headquartered at Tébessa in Algeria, near the Tunisian border. By jeep he traveled to the Tunisian front lines, getting to know the commanders and their men. His unobtrusive style of reporting—mingling, listening, rarely taking notes—ingratiated him with nearly everyone he encountered. He shared in the soldiers' tight-knit company, endured the same privations, subjected himself to the same dangers, and thus began his

most significant body of work—describing for those at home the daily lives of the infantrymen who fought the war at its dirtiest level. Reporting the actual news of the war— "the big picture," in the parlance of the time—was the job of numerous other reporters; Pyle was free to seek his own line of inquiry. He could spend a week or two living at the front before withdrawing to write his pieces.

Pyle soon rejected the notion of resuming his travel work, preferring to cover the story unfolding before him. For the first time in his life, he had become morally connected to an undertaking of great moment. His nerves were smoothing out; he had virtually stopped drinking—admittedly for lack of supply—and the combination of the tan he had picked up at the Garden of Allah and the windburn from the front gave him a ruddy look of health and well-being.

Ernie's pleasure in his work was diminished in early February 1943 by a letter from Albuquerque: Jerry had refused his offer of remarriage, perhaps because she still resented him for having committed her to a sanitarium. "It was just dusk when I got the letter," he wrote her, "and I sat on a stump all bundled up against the cold, and read it. I was so disappointed I almost felt like crying."

On February 14, German tanks and infantry under the command of General Erwin Rommel startled the inexperienced Americans by driving fifty miles through their positions at Kasserine Pass in Tunisia. The Americans retreated, Pyle with them. The retreat was for the Army what Pearl Harbor had been for the Navy, and Pyle's front-line description of it was radioed back to the United States for immediate distribution to subscribing papers.

"I've been at the front for seven solid weeks, and although you may not believe it, I like it up there because life becomes so wonderfully simple—even a lot simpler than you've got yours arranged," he wrote Cavanaugh from Algiers, to which he had fled after the retreat. "There are only four essentials—clothes, food, cigarets, and whatever portion of safety you can manage to arrange for yourself."

For the first time in over a year, Pyle was optimistic. Life at the front was invigorating. A letter to Jerry was confident, good-humored, and full of pride in his own capacity. "If anybody had ever told me I could stand to sleep right out on the ground and wake up with snow on my bedroll I'd have called him nuts; but I have and you find you can stand almost anything." While Pyle spent ten days in Algiers writing about what he had seen in the last seven weeks, Jerry sent a cable informing him that she was working as a civil service clerk at Kirtland Field in Albuquerque and that she was moving back into the house. This pleased him. He was elated when, on March 12, during a few weeks' break from the front lines, he received notice that Jerry had reconsidered his offer of remarriage and exercised the proxy on her lunch hour. This made him feel "some peace with the world again. . . ."

There was also evidence of his quickening stateside popularity. More papers now ran the column, which increased his earnings. Accepting an offer from Henry Holt & Company to reprint his North Africa work in book form was the happy coincidence of two good fortunes—an upswing professionally and personally.

What's more, Pyle had finally resolved the question of what to do with himself. He was committed to staying with the men whose blooding he had only begun to describe. His dilettante's sense of war had evolved into a more mature outlook. He hated the "tragedy and insanity" of war, but "I know I can't escape and I truly believe the only thing left to do is be in it to the hilt."

When Pyle returned to the front lines in early April 1943, he found he had become inured to carnage—"somehow I can look upon mutilated bodies without flinching or feeling deeply"—but not to fitful sleep after a day of watching men kill and be killed; then "at last the enormity of all these newly dead strikes me like a living nightmare. And there are times when I feel that I can't stand it all and will have to leave."

As the Tunisian war wound its way northward toward the Mediterranean port cities of Bizerte and Tunis, Pyle lived and traveled with the 1st Division. It was here that he wrote his most memorable columns of the North Africa campaign, reflecting his new maturity and, as always, his keen eye for detail. What was most engaging was the fusion of Pyle's documentary impulse with his heightened moral sense. He now celebrated true character traits versus absurd ones; gone was the juvenile admiration of race-car drivers and Air Mail pilots who brazened it out in the face of quick and violent death. The infantrymen with whom he now spent his time lived decidedly unromantic lives. They fought, they waited, they endured dive bombings and heavy-artillery shellings—they were the ultimate victims. To Pyle, they were heroes, not dashing or even particularly brave, but men who persisted in the face of great fear and discomfort because they had to. By sharing their lives, Pyle was becoming one of them in spirit if not in age, in practice if not by force of conscription.

By mid-May, the Tunisian war was over. While the troops practiced for the invasion of Sicily, Pyle and the other correspondents retreated to a press camp on the shore of the Mediterranean near Algiers. Lee Miller suggested that he return home for several weeks, but Pyle declined, fearing guilt pangs. Perhaps by fall he could take a leave "with a clear conscience." Meanwhile, he turned his attention to the long essay that would be the last chapter of his book *Here Is Your War*.

It was a remarkable piece. The war in North Africa had been a testing ground for American men and equipment, Pyle wrote. The men had been well cared for, their food and medical care were good, their equipment less so but getting better. Because Pyle was "older and a little apart," he could see the changes in the soldiers, and he emphasized that no one could undergo what these men had without being permanently affected. War had made them rougher, more profane, and prone to taking what

they needed when and where they could find it. "The stress of war puts old virtues in a changed light," he wrote. "We shall have to relearn a simple fundamental or two when things get back to normal. But what's wrong with a small case of 'requisitioning' when murder is the classic goal?"

Six months after Pyle had arrived in North Africa—confused, sickly, and depressed—his fortunes had reversed themselves. He had proved to himself that he could endure. He had found pleasure and purpose in his renewed union with Jerry, and he had forgotten about the woman in San Francisco with whom he had fallen in love. His indecision of six months before had given way to commitment, his lack of interest to singularity of purpose. Battle had brought a terrifying focus to his life, and the clarity that attached to front-line existence was exhilarating, drawing him back whenever he was away. He had yet to prove himself over the long haul, but he was prepared to do so.

On June 29, 1943, a year and ten days after he had arrived in Ireland, Pyle flew to Bizerte in Tunisia. There he boarded an American ship, the USS *Biscayne,* and settled in for his second invasion voyage in eight months.

The invasion of Sicily marked for Americans and their allies the beginning of the long assault on Axis Europe, and it was with the war in Europe that Pyle would come to be most identified. Even so, his beginning there was slow and unhappy, his work disconnected.

The Sicilian campaign was a short one, lasting only five weeks, from July 10 to August 17. During it Pyle displayed none of the exuberance that had marked his months in Africa. He was tired, sick, and fearful that redundancy would rob his copy of the vitality it had had in North Africa. "I'm getting awfully tired of war and writing about it," he told Jerry. "It seems like I can't think of anything new to say—each time it's like going to the same movie again."

After General George Patton's victory at Palermo two weeks after the invasion, Pyle drove to 45th Division headquarters at Cefalù, where he settled in with the 120th Engineers Battalion. He became ill and spent five days in a tent hospital amidst the "death rattle" of dying men. In the campaign's closing days, Pyle rejoined the 120th Engineers, then the 10th Engineers.

He wrote Jerry, "I find myself more and more reluctant to repeat and repeat the same old process of getting shot at." He added that "the war gets so complicated and confused in my mind; on especially sad days it's almost impossible to believe that anything is worth such mass slaughter and misery; and the after-war outlook seems to me so gloomy and pathetic for everybody."

Ten days after his forty-third birthday, the campaign ended, and Pyle decided to go home for a break. In a wrap-up piece on the Sicilian campaign, he explained:

I had come to despise and be revolted by war clear out of any logical proportion. . . . Through repetition, I had worn down to the nub my ability to weigh and describe.

Pyle arrived exhausted in New York at four A.M. on September 7, 1943, four days after the Allies had invaded Italy. Within twenty-four hours, he endured several newspaper interviews, countless phone calls from wives and friends of soldiers, requests from the Office of War Information and the WAC recruiting office for radio recordings, and one from Treasury Secretary Henry Morgenthau to appear on the war-bond radio program *We the People*. Two radio networks engaged in a bidding war for Pyle's services. He turned both down.

Washington wasn't any better. Pyle had to see the dentist, his lawyer, his tax accountant, and there were more interviews with reporters, more picture-taking. A Pentagon panel of fifty officers questioned him. He had a private talk with Secretary of War Henry Stimson. For a thousand-dollar fee, Pyle agreed to be photographed for a Chesterfield cigaret advertisement. A movie producer, Lester Cowan, came down from New York to talk about basing a movie on Pyle's forthcoming book.

After a short visit with his father and Aunt Mary (his mother's sister) on the family farm in Indiana, Ernie flew to Albuquerque, where Jerry met him at the airport. But his stay there was chaotic, too. Cavanaugh flew over from Los Angeles for a visit, and Lester Cowan arrived for more movie discussions. Mail from all over the country arrived by the bagful. The telephone rang constantly. Everyone, it seemed, wanted something from him, including Jerry, who by this time was hardly able to articulate anything of her tortured inner life.

Jerry's condition was tentative, Pyle told friends. Even as she slept, there was "horrible anguish in her face." He knew she loved him, but he was ambivalent toward her: on the one hand, "my normal feeling of love for her has been sort of smothered in an academic viewpoint," and on the other, "she is the only thing in the world that means anything to me. . . ." In his months of leave from war, Pyle avoided spending much time alone with Jerry—perhaps out of guilt over their prolonged separations (which she abhorred), perhaps because his sexual dysfunction troubled him, perhaps because he had little need of true intimacy, preferring his associations light and cursory.

Jerry broke down shortly before his stay ended, and Pyle admitted her to the hospital. He told Lee Miller that Jerry was depressed about his forthcoming departure and under a great deal of pressure on her job. Pyle feared that his leaving would be too much for her to bear. "But," as he explained in the column a few weeks later,

> what can a guy do? I know millions of others who are reluctant too, and they can't even get home. . . . [At home] you feel like a deserter and a heel—not so much to the war effort, but to your friends who are still over there freezing and getting shot at.

Pyle spent three weeks in Washington before traveling to Italy. *Here Is Your War* had been published to laudatory notices. He autographed books, went to tea with Eleanor Roosevelt and to film conferences with Lester Cowan. He commented in the column on his own popularity. If, as Lee Miller wrote, Pyle had a "boyish curiosity" about his fame when he had arrived in New York, he now saw celebrity for what it was: an all-consuming claim on his time and a diversion from the things and people who really mattered.

Before he left Washington for Italy in late November, Pyle completed his income-tax return for 1943: he had made about sixty-nine thousand dollars, twenty-nine thousand of which he paid in taxes.

Unlike their German and Italian opponents, who were fighting on or close to native soil, the American soldiers Pyle wrote about saw home as a continuum, a place fixed in the imagination that would stay the same, possibly even improve, in their time away. Before his vacation, Pyle, too, had sustained himself with mildly idealized thoughts of Jerry and the house in Albuquerque. As he began to cover the war in Italy, however, any sense of home as an emotional buffer was gone. What remained was Pyle's ever-growing compulsion to tell the story of the American fighting man from firsthand experience. But that compulsion was now largely a reflex action, a commitment bereft of pleasure.

The winter of 1943-1944 was the worst Italy had seen in years. For soldiers the misery of the cold and mud compounded the confusion of fighting in mountainous terrain. The distant objective was the conquest of Rome, the immediate goal to survive what Pyle called "this semi-barbarian life."

What had been exciting in North Africa, and to a much lesser extent in Sicily, was now debilitating. But even with the chaos of battle and its awful cost wearing on him as never before, his "ability to weigh and describe"—the faculty he said he had lost by the end of the Sicilian campaign—was unimpaired. And the columns he produced in Italy served to further boost his stateside circulation and consolidate his popularity among the troops. Pyle still feared redundancy in his copy, still was reluctant to subject himself to battle, but by Christmas he had already made two extended trips to the front and had written his best piece ever.

The column was an account of the affection an infantry company felt for its commander, young Captain Henry Waskow, who had been killed in the mountain fighting near San Pietro, and whose body had been brought down a mountain on the back of a mule. The column's emotional content was implicit, revealing both the intimate personal waste of war and the depth of Pyle's growth as a writer and observer.

Pyle failed to see the achievement for what it was, but few stateside were so obtuse. The column was a coast-to-coast sensation. The *Washington Daily News* gave over its entire front page to the Waskow piece and sold out the day's paper. If there were any doubts about who was in the ascendant as America's premier war correspondent, the Waskow column laid them to rest. Pyle was on his way to becoming a central figure of the era, a living, high-profile symbol of the fighting man's displacement from ordinary life and of his sacrifice. He had become the focus of his audience's good will toward the soldiers; assigned to him were many of the same idealized sentiments the public assigned to them. The *Saturday Evening Post* noted that Pyle "was probably the most prayed-for man with the American troops. . . ."

At home, just eight weeks before, Pyle had complained that Americans stateside "haven't had anything yet, on a national scale, to burn and crucify [them] into anything greater than [they] were to begin with." His heroes were different because they had suffered and endured and found strength in adversity. Just as Pyle had been drawn away from self-involvement by what he had seen at war, so, too, had the infantrymen. Pyle saw redemption in this collective action, a redemption unavailable to some statesiders who were concerned with the war only insofar as it affected their personal comfort.

After seeing on his vacation how untouched Americans at home were by events overseas, Pyle had arrived in Italy all the more intent upon getting across to his readers the magnitude of the infantryman's sacrifice. While his work in North Africa and Sicily had been largely descriptive reporting, in Italy it became more essay-like. Pyle was not a religious man, but he had been raised in a conservative Christian community, and increasingly he called on the Christian themes and language of his childhood to confer upon his subjects a peculiar brand of secular beatification. He admitted that his admiration for the infantry was obsessive and that to him "all the war of the world has seemed to be borne by the few thousand front-line soldiers here, destined merely by chance to suffer and die for the rest of us." He had found in his heroes an unusual degree of selflessness, of duty perceived and performed, and was deeply moved.

Having acquired a more sophisticated, more fluid, sense of good and evil, Pyle realized the men he wrote about were battling an evil enemy by engaging in murderous behavior themselves—and that, ironically, this often brought out noble characteristics in them. Living with an infantry company of the 34th Division, Pyle encountered Sergeant Buck Eversole, a platoon leader who had been at the front for over a year and who was now "a senior partner in the institution of death." Pyle's pieces on Eversole were the best expression of those characteristics he most admired in the fighting men; Eversole was a killer by necessity, but at core he was a moral man, thoughtful and capable of great feeling in the midst of moral contradictions. "I know it ain't my fault [green replacement soldiers] get killed," Eversole told Pyle.

> And I do the best I can for them, but I've got so I feel like it's me killin' 'em instead of a German.

> I've got so I feel like a murderer. I hate to look at them when the new ones come in.

Pyle filed his last reports of the Italian campaign in March 1944 from the Anzio-Nettuno beachhead, which was subject to constant shelling and bombing. He was nearly killed when a five-hundred-pound bomb landed near the building in which he lived, blowing a wall into his room, shattering windows, and ripping doors off their hinges. Other correspondents assumed Pyle was dead, but he emerged from the rubble with only a slight cut on his cheek. Despite the constant danger, Pyle told Jerry he was glad he had visited the beachhead; it wouldn't have been "right" for him to have avoided it.

He left Anzio on April 5 "in the clasp of a strange new safety" aboard a hospital ship bound for Naples. From Naples Pyle flew to North Africa, and thence to London. Something big was afoot—he was sure of that—but only later would he learn that the long-awaited invasion of France was imminent.

Shortly after Pyle arrived in London during mid-April 1944, word came that he had won a Pulitzer Prize for "distinguished war correspondence" in 1943, an unexpected but relished honor.

Ernie had received only a few letters from Jerry during his time in Italy and France, but now mail from her was more frequent. He was glad to learn that she was set to undergo a series of hospital treatments. She asked him if he was tired of war, and he replied, "Of course I am very sick of the war, and would like to leave it, and yet I know I can't. I've been a part of the misery and tragedy of it for so long that I've come to feel a responsibility to it or something. I don't quite know how to put it into words, but I feel if I left it, it would be like a soldier deserting."

Later, when Jerry returned home from the hospital in the company of two nurses and reported that she was abstaining from alcohol, Ernie's mood was still somber, and he explained to her his fear that "I'm going to be so torn up inside and maladjusted by the time [the war] is over that I'll take a lot of 'doin' with, so your mission in life is to get well and ready to take care of me when I get back!"

While Pyle fed Scripps-Howard and United Feature copy on invasion preparations and Air Corps crews, Lee Miller saw to plans for a second compilation of Pyle's columns, ***Brave Men***.

Pyle set foot on French soil on June 7, 1944, the day after the Normandy invasion began, at Omaha Beach, one hundred twenty miles to the southwest of Brest, where Paige Cavanaugh had landed with the 36th Division twenty-seven years before. By now, Pyle's post-adolescent fascination with Cavanaugh's war tales was an attitude so remote that a reminder of it would surely have embarrassed him. Intense weariness and a spooky sense of the fragility of life would thread throughout his columns from France. A week after the landings, he told Lee

Miller he was "beginning to feel that I've run my last race in this war and can't keep going much longer."

Pyle resumed the advocate's role he had taken on in Italy, writing from the beachhead a description of the effort it took to open a second front so that his audience could "know and appreciate and forever be humbly grateful to those both dead and alive who did it for you." After writing a series on the ack-ack gunners on the beachhead who provided ground troops protection from enemy planes, he spent time with the 1st Division and the 29th Division, then accompanied the 9th Infantry Division in its assault on Cherbourg.

Pyle had gone far toward making what A. J. Liebling of *The New Yorker* later called "a large personal impress on the nation" during the biggest war in its history, and now the inevitable American myth-making apparatus, keyed to perfection in this war, took over. As Pyle became ever more weary, the press increasingly lionized him, often turning the facts of his life to its own ends and casting him in the mold of greatest social utility. Pyle was pleased to learn that *Time* magazine was preparing a cover story on him, but when the article appeared in the July 17, 1944, issue, he was disappointed, then angry. "Some of it of course was swell," he wrote Jerry, "but some was so completely distorted."

Time portrayed Pyle as an anemic Everyman, stumbling willy-nilly into war, all the while suffering silently his sense of inferiority among his fellow correspondents. Moreover, *Time* said, Pyle had early on been the object of many practical jokes and other indignities perpetrated by the soldiers whose stories he sought. Later, the magazine reported, they had let up on him because he shared their miserable lives and wrote such fine things about them. The forthcoming movie based on Pyle's book **Here Is Your War,** from whose scriptwriters *Time* reporters got much of this fictional nonsense, would, the magazine said, "admit his fear of battle, his apprehension about his work, his latest quirk—the conviction that now he is in France, he is going to be killed."

Pyle told Jerry that he had never been the victim of soldiers' scorn or practical jokes, that the article left him "without any dignity, and I believe I do have a little," and that he didn't "have any premonition of death, as they claim." He added, "In fact I certainly plan and dream way ahead all the time about what we'll do after the war." He told Lee Miller the *Time* story "created a legend that makes me a combination of half-wit and coward, and it'll grow and be perpetuated."

Three days after his invective against *Time,* Pyle underwent his most horrifying experience of the war, the climax of his combat reporting from the European Theater.

On July 25, 1944, the American First Army began its breakout from the beachhead toward Saint-Lô. Two hours' worth of heavy bombing and shelling were to precede tank and infantry attacks. But before the ground forces could move forward, a bombing error killed hundreds of Americans. Pyle, who had been assigned to an infantry division, was standing in a farmyard when "all of an instant the universe became filled with a gigantic rattling," and bombs began falling all around him. He and an officer scrambled under a farm wagon for shelter, Pyle remembering afterward "an inhuman tenseness of muscle and nerves." He was "grateful in a chastened way I had never experienced before, for just being alive." In the column, he forgave the flyers their mistake on behalf of the infantry, telling them the "chaos and bitterness" of that afternoon had passed. This equanimity in the aftermath of the bombing was great public relations between service branches, but privately Pyle said he would go crazy if he had to endure anything like it again.

Pyle entered Paris with French troops on August 25, 1944. The pleasure of the newly liberated Parisians and the rich symbolism of the event momentarily eased his fatigue, but within two days he was making preparations for a stateside leave. He was proud of not having taken a break for so long, but now he had to go home. "I have had all I can take for a while," he told his readers.

> I've been immersed in it too long. My spirit is wobbly and my mind is confused. The hurt has finally become too great. All of a sudden it seemed to me that if I heard one more shot or saw one more dead man, I would go off my nut. . . .

When Lee Miller met Pyle's ship in New York on September 18, 1944, he handed Pyle a letter from Jerry. She wrote that she was "humbly—and numbly, thankful" he was back, hastening to add that she was eager to see him, and, knowing his propensity for dawdling, jocularly adding that she would try to be patient. But, "if you linger in the East until frost takes the flowers—and nips the lawn—well! Love, darling." The letter's disjointed syntax held a clue to the instability of Jerry's condition. Like thirteen million other Americans, she read Ernie's column, and if she had experienced "real terror—simply stark terror" while he covered the London blitz four years before, it requires little imagination to sense what she had felt when she read of his narrowly escaping death at the Anzio beachhead and at Saint-Lô.

Jerry understood Ernie's devotion to the American troops he wrote about, but she had argued against his going to war from the start, and she suffered each time he ventured out. He was, after all, her only link to a happier past. Childless, living at great distance from her family in Minnesota, alone save for the impersonal attentions of doctors and private nurses, Jerry needed to be engaged emotionally. Sexual intimacy was out of the question, but the emotional intimacy she had enjoyed with Ernie in their youth wasn't—or so her plaintive letter hopefully implied.

As it turned out, it was. Ernie's capacity for intimacy, never highly developed in the first place, was now severely strained. (After the liberation of Paris, he had written that war had so "wrung and drained" his emotions that they "cringe from the effort of coming alive again.") As Jerry doubtless sensed in her more lucid moments, Ernie had abandoned her years before to marry his audience, with which he had a stylized intimacy that neatly suited his emotional needs. He phoned Jerry and told her he intended to remain in New York for several days so that the sculptor Jo Davidson could make a bust of his head. After that, he would spend a few days on the farm in Indiana, then fly to Albuquerque.

With millions of appreciative readers anxious for his every utterance, the pressures on Pyle had redoubled from those of a year before. So many people wanted so many things! *Editor & Publisher* wanted an interview. People on the street wanted his autograph. Helen Keller wanted to run her hands over his face; John Steinbeck wanted to talk. The mayor of Albuquerque wanted to throw a welcome-home dinner with five hundred guests. Wives and mothers wanted information about their husbands and sons. Roy Howard of Scripps-Howard wanted to have dinner. Lester Cowan wanted to confer about problems with his movie, *The Story of G.I. Joe.* Photographers wanted to take his picture. Scripps-Howard competitors wanted him to work for them.

Jerry, Paige Cavanaugh, and Jerry's private nurse met Pyle's plane at Albuquerque in late September, and within the week Lester Cowan and his director William Wellman arrived to discuss the movie. Shortly thereafter Pyle flew to Hollywood for more film conferences. Back in Albuquerque he spent mornings at the dentist's, while at home two secretaries worked to keep up with the mail and the constantly ringing telephone.

One day Ernie returned home and found Jerry's nurse in hysterics in the front yard. Jerry had locked herself in the bathroom after repeatedly stabbing herself in and about the throat with a pair of scissors. When Ernie broke open the bathroom door, he found Jerry standing expressionless before the wash basin, bleeding profusely. He held her until a surgeon arrived. Jerry neither spoke nor flinched while the doctor stitched her wounds. Luckily, she had not done mortal damage, but her wounds were severe. Ernie wrote to Cavanaugh: "On the right side of her neck, just below the jaw and just ahead of the ear, she had gouged a hole an inch and a half deep. There was a similar hole, though a little smaller, in the same place on the other side. Right square in front, just above the collar bone, she pounded the scissors straight into her neck nearly two inches, and got her windpipe. Then hacked her left wrist. She cut her left breast about 15 times with the razor blade, apparently stabbed with the corner of it."

He sent a long account of Jerry's suicide attempt and her subsequent confinement in an Albuquerque sanitarium to Lee Miller. It was a narrative remarkable chiefly for its documentary coolness and gross insensitivity. The moral sensibility so sharply present in Pyle's war reporting was absent here. Pyle told Miller he had feared for ten years that Jerry might try to kill herself but had decided "that

her indirect threats were all part of her act. She had tried it a couple of times in the past but botched them up so badly they were almost laughable and convinced us she was acting. . . . But brother this one was no act. . . ."

While Jerry underwent thirty days of shock-therapy treatments, Ernie accepted honorary doctorates from the University of New Mexico and Indiana University and traveled to Washington to plan his trip to the Pacific Theater and to have his income taxes figured. (His tax bill for 1944 totaled one hundred five thousand dollars.) He had returned to Albuquerque by the time Jerry came home from the hospital, her memory fractured and her behavior erratic. She had learned of Ernie's plans to go to the Pacific and was depressed.

The procession of houseguests resumed. A writer came to prepare a profile of Pyle for *Life,* and Cavanaugh flew in from Los Angeles to sit in on the interviews. A photographer arrived to take pictures. One was of Pyle, Jerry, and their dog Cheetah in the living room of their house. Jerry sat semi-reclined in a dayseat, half smiling as she read a biography of Samuel Johnson. Pyle sat on a hassock, his hands pensively clasped, his jaw set, his eyes fixed on the wall opposite. Between them was the needle-nosed dog, staring in yet another direction. It's a lonely photograph; one can't avoid the sensation that all three were caught in the midst of supreme discomfort.

Pyle and Jerry saw each other for the last time at the railroad station in Los Angeles on or about Christmas Day 1945. They had spent a week or so with the Cavanaughs while Pyle visited the set of *The Story of G.I. Joe.* On their last night together, Lester Cowan took them to Ciro's, the Hollywood nightclub, where they danced together, after which Jerry and her nurse took the train back to Albuquerque. On the evening of New Year's Day, Pyle left Los Angeles for Camp Roberts, near San Francisco, on the first leg of his long journey to the Pacific. He resumed the column in San Francisco by dissembling about his vacation. "Despite all the frenzy, I've felt almost pathetic in my happiness at being home," he told his readers. "I've had a wonderful time." He spoke of Jerry, emphasizing her devotion to him, and ending on a rueful note:

> That Girl has been burdened by recurring illnesses, and has had to revolve between home and hospital. But she has succeeded in keeping the little white house just as it always was, which she knew is what I would want. . . .
>
> She lives only for the day when war is over and we can have a life together again. And that's what I live for too. . . . I hope we both last through until the sun shines in the world again.

Pyle had doubts about his surviving the war, despite his protests to Jerry after *Time* magazine had reported that he feared he would die in France. He had recently drawn up a will, laughingly telling Cavanaugh and Lee Miller, "I want you bastards to know that if I'm knocked off in the

Pacific, you share in ten percent of my estate." He had arranged with an Albuquerque banker to handle Jerry's immediate financial needs, while his will provided her an income for life. And he told a reporter: "Well, you begin to feel that you can't go on forever without being hit. I feel that I've used up all my chances. And I hate it. . . . I don't want to be killed."

Jerry continued to plead with him to stay home. "I'm sorry darling," he wrote her, "but it's too late now to back out on this trip. You know that I don't want to go any more than you want me to, but the way I look at it it's almost beyond my control. If I stayed I'm afraid that would defeat both of us, for I'd probably gradually work up a guilty feeling that would haunt me. I hate it, but there's just nothing else I can do." Ernie told her, as he had countless times before, that he wanted her to be her old self again. This was not only a futile wish, it utterly ignored the changes Jerry had undergone. He failed to see that Jerry's old self was in part a product of his steady companionship, a commodity she had gone without for ten years.

In her loneliness, Jerry had begun to approach a spiritual understanding of herself and her condition. She wrote Ernie, "I'm a long way from reaching the honest humility I should have—but I see it clearly enough in moments to long for it. . . . I don't know the way—but hope and believe I may find it, dear. . . ." Jerry wanted to learn to pray, but Ernie frowned on the notion. "That has to be up to you, of course," he wrote her, "but it is so different from anything you or I have ever felt. I want you to get better but I wouldn't want you to become pious—for then you wouldn't be *you*." No, Ernie told her, the solution to her troubles didn't reside in any "mystic device," nor was there any value in what he considered undue contrition. Calmness and a full routine would be her salvation—that and accepting things that made her unhappy, by which he surely meant his again subjecting himself to dangers he publicly admitted frightened him.

Shortly before he left San Francisco, Ernie mailed Jerry a wedding ring. She had never worn one before because she considered such overt symbols of union too conventional for her. Of late, though, she had changed her mind.

Hawaii was to be Pyle's first stop on his way to the Pacific Theater. Shortly before he left San Francisco, he told Jerry, "I think it's the lack of opportunity for calmness in America that has whipped me as much as anything; aboard a ship or in the islands I won't be such a public figure and can get back to normal routine."

It's hard to conceive of covering a war as "normal routine," but for Pyle it was, and he knew that re-establishing his work rhythm was his one hope of regaining peace of mind. But just as he had begun his vacation weary from war, he returned to war weary from home. He never overcame that emotional fatigue, even though Jerry wrote him frequently and at length, and even though her condition seemed improved. Nor did he ever recapture the

pleasure work had represented for him. His coverage of the Pacific would be interesting enough, but missing would be the emotional and moral engagement so readily apparent in his European work. Pyle got a bad start in the Pacific, partly because his unyielding loyalty to the European Theater impaired his judgment, and partly because his celebrity forever got in the way.

At San Francisco, the Navy, delighted to have him, presented Pyle his naval insignia—a gold anchor and a gold-braided war correspondent's badge. On a tour of the Port of Embarkation, Pyle was greeted by a thousand cheering soldiers and a fifty-piece band. Newspapers reported that Pyle's presence in the Pacific would be a boost to servicemen's morale, but his comments in San Francisco hardly set the stage. "Ernie is a bit dubious about the prospects of doing a good job covering the Navy," one reporter wrote. "He says it's tougher to dramatize the life of a sailor." In this account, as in many others, Pyle was quoted as saying his time with the Navy would be short and that he would rejoin the infantry as soon as possible.

In Hawaii he told a reporter for a service newspaper that he couldn't "go overboard on sympathy" for men suffering so-called "island complex in the Pacific—not after I've seen the misery and cold and mud and death in Europe." From the Marianas he wrote, "Now we are far, far away from everything that was home or seemed like home. Five thousand miles from America, and twelve thousand miles from my friends fighting on the German border."

Pyle boarded an aircraft carrier, the USS *Cabot,* in a convoy carrying planes that would bomb the Japanese mainland and heavy artillery that would support landings on Iwo Jima. The *Cabot*'s sailors were an amicable bunch, "just as friendly as the soldiers I'd known on the other side," but Pyle believed they talked "more about wanting to go home than even the soldiers in Europe [did]." The sailors lived well—good food, daily baths, clean clothes, a bunk to sleep in, a locker to store things in. Their work was hard but the hours were regular. "The boys ask you a thousand times how this compares with the other side. I can only answer that this is much better. . . ." Most could see his point, but

> others yell their heads off about their lot, and feel they're being persecuted by being kept out of America a year. I've heard some boys say "I'd trade this for a foxhole any day." You just have to keep your mouth shut to a remark like that.

This was not sterling public relations; Pyle knew better than anyone how intensely service branches competed for attention. Moreover, he had lost sight of the fact that his audience comprised not only stateside readers but also servicemen overseas, many of whom received Pyle clippings from home. Pyle's comments did not go unanswered. In Honolulu, the editors of an Air Corps magazine severely rebuked him for his ignorance of the Pacific war and for his generally dismissive attitude.

Part of Pyle's irritation lay in his trouble with Navy censors, who wouldn't allow him to use sailors' names in his copy. Frustrated, Pyle threatened to clear out for the Philippines, where he might have a better chance of writing his sort of material. (The censorship restrictions were eventually lifted.) Here, too, the remoteness of one Pacific outpost from another injected a note of discontinuity into Pyle's writing. His erratic movement was reminiscent of his travel days in the 1930s. It wasn't until the invasion of Okinawa that Pyle returned to his "normal routine"—and that was only seventeen days before his death.

Traveling from Ulithi, near Guam, to Okinawa with units of the 1st Marine Division, Pyle was sure that this time he would be killed. "There's nothing romantic whatever in knowing that an hour from now you may be dead," he wrote of the landings. Ninety minutes after the invasion began, Pyle went ashore with the 5th Marine Regiment and was relieved at the lack of resistance in his sector. He spent two days with the Marines, then returned to the ship to write.

Pyle had always been squeamish about foreign cultures, particularly in matters of personal hygiene, but his comments on the Okinawan civilians were scathing, out of character for him and an indication of his fatigue. The Okinawans were "pitiful" in their poverty, "not very clean"; their houses were "utterly filthy." Certainly their standard of living was low, but Pyle couldn't understand "why poverty and filth need to be synonymous." The Okinawans "were all shocked from the bombardment and yet I think rather stupid too, so that when they talked they didn't make much sense."

Ironically, Pyle had found peace in the chaotic sounds and sights that filled his first night on Okinawa; they constituted the "old familiar pattern, unchanged by distance or time from war on the other side of the world." These were soldier verities, and with them he was comfortable. They were "so imbedded in my soul that, coming back . . . again, it seemed to me as I lay there that I'd never known anything else in my life. And there are millions of us."

Pyle returned to shore and spent a few days with the Marines, then boarded the command ship *Panamint*. So relieved was he to be alive that he promised Jerry this would be his last landing. Short of an accident, he wrote his father, he believed he would survive the war. There was another cause for optimism, too: Jerry's recent letters pointed toward some of the normalcy he had hoped for.

Ernie was pleased with the abundance of mail from her, and he vowed that his next trip home would be for good. She wrote him asking not just for reports on what he was doing, but for an indication of what he was thinking and feeling as well. This was an extraordinary departure from the desperately closed tone of the few letters he had received from her in Europe. When Ernie wrote her about his postwar vision of sitting quietly with no demands on him, she took pleasure in it. She wasn't beyond her

troubles, she wrote, but things *were* better. She now saw as "faulty" her contempt for convention; she had revised her youthful notion that appearances were meaningless, and she regretted she had been remiss in keeping up the house and yard. Now she wanted the looks of the place "to fit in with the honor" bestowed on him when New Mexico had designated his birthday Ernie Pyle Day. She wanted to be worthy of being his wife, and she promised she would be useful to him when he came home to stay. "My love reaches out to you—strongly—and wants so much for you—Bless you my Ernie."

Pyle was killed by a Japanese sniper's machine-gun bullet on April 18, 1945, two days after American Marines landed on Ie Shima, a ten-square-mile island west of Okinawa. He had honored his commitment to make no more landings and had gone ashore a day later.

Spending the night in what had been a Japanese soldier's dugout, Pyle was affable and relaxed, glad to be with the infantry again. Shortly after ten the next morning, Pyle set off by jeep with four soldiers to find a command-post site for the 305th Regiment of the 77th Division. When the jeep was fired upon near the village of Ie, Pyle and the others took cover in ditches on either side of the road. Pyle raised his head to look for a companion and died instantly when a bullet pierced his left temple.

Several infantrymen who recovered his body under fire found in his pocket a draft of a column intended for release upon the end of the war in Europe, which Pyle had known was imminent. In it, Pyle urged the living, in their joy, not to forget that the price of victory had been paid by the dead. For his part, Pyle would never forget

> the unnatural sight of cold dead men scattered over the hillsides and in the ditches along the high rows of hedge throughout the world.
>
> Dead men by mass production—in one country after another—month after month and year after year. Dead men in winter and dead men in summer.
>
> Dead men in such familiar promiscuity that they become monotonous.
>
> Dead men in such monstrous infinity that you come almost to hate them. . . .

Pyle was buried on Ie Shima in a crude wooden coffin a soldier constructed.

In death as in life, Pyle was a democratizer. Reaction to his death was swift and effusive. The news followed by six days that of President Roosevelt's death, and everyone responded to it, from the newly sworn-in President of the United States to GIs all over the world, from General Eisenhower to a blacksmith in La Porte, Indiana. The tone of the comments was unanimous: Pyle's death was a personal loss for everyone. Official comments were no less sincere for their being steeped in press-release sentiment.

"The nation," said President Harry Truman, "is saddened again by the death of Ernie Pyle." War Secretary Henry Stimson felt "great distress," and Navy Secretary James Forrestal said America owed Pyle its "unending gratitude." "I have known no finer man, no finer soldier than he," said General Omar Bradley. Cartoonist Bill Mauldin, for whom Pyle had helped arrange stateside syndication, said, "The only difference between Ernie's death and the death of any other good guy is that the other guy is mourned by his company. Ernie is mourned by his army."

At Albuquerque, Jerry's doctor brought her the news, and newspaper headlines told the public "'That Girl' Takes News Bravely." Paige Cavanaugh was at home in Inglewood, California, when a friend called with the sad message. (He immediately flew to Albuquerque to be with Jerry.) Lee Miller was shaving in the Philippines when he heard a bulletin on Armed Forces Radio. At Dana, a neighbor told Pyle's father and Aunt Mary.

It soon became clear that Pyle's demise meant more than the loss of a personal friend; it also represented the loss of a potent symbol. Because, as one newspaper noted, there was "no vice president to take Ernie Pyle's place," in the weeks following his death Americans sought to reclaim his symbolic value as the perfect embodiment of a democracy at war; and the expression of this reclamation, like the immediate reaction to the loss of him, ran from the eloquent to the bombastic. The poet Randall Jarrell wrote in *The Nation:*

> There are many men whose profession it is to speak for us—political and military and literary representatives . . . ; [Pyle] wrote what he had seen and heard and felt himself, and truly represented us.

Others sought to canonize him. In their eyes, Pyle was a martyr, and the popular conception of a martyred saint admits no moral ambivalence, much less moral failing. These comments were published in the *Congressional Record:*

> A brave man, a courageous man, a modest man, with the whole world as his assignment, Ernie Pyle looked out on the field of light and life with eyes that were kind and charitable and understanding. . . . It has been said that the dead take with them clutched tightly in their hands only the things they have given away. . . . Ernie Pyle took much with him in death, because he had given . . . [of] the best that was in him every day of his adult life.

Meanwhile, news items appeared in papers nationwide detailing the provisions of Pyle's will, President Truman's wish that Pyle be honored with a special Congressional medal, and the christening of a new troop transport with Pyle's name.

The Story of G.I. Joe was approaching release when Lester Cowan hit a snag with the Hays Office of the Motion Picture Producers and Distributors of America. This was to be the movie that faithfully portrayed the roughness of infantry life, including the coarseness of soldier talk. Nonetheless, the Hays Seal of Approval could not be granted the film because "certain lines of dialogue . . . are regarded as profanity under the Production Code. . . ." Cowan protested that the dialogue was spoken with "such deep feeling and conviction that it could not be construed as blasphemy," but eventually he changed the lines, and the Hays Office passed on the picture.

On July 4, Jerry and her sister flew to Washington for an advance showing of the film at a meeting of the National Press Club, after which an Army general and a Navy admiral jointly presented her a posthumous Medal For Merit for Pyle on behalf of their service branches and the State Department. Present were the British ambassador, war correspondents, members of Congress, and several Supreme Court justices.

The Scripps-Howard *Indianapolis Times* had engineered an auction of Pyle's last manuscript ("bearing his own pencilled corrections"), with the proceeds going to war bonds. The bidding had lasted several weeks, with each bid duly reported in the paper. Finally, American United Life Insurance Company had come through with the fantastic sum of ten million five hundred twenty-five thousand dollars, and the company's treasurer accepted the manuscript at the world premiere of *The Story of G.I. Joe* on July 6. That evening, two thousand people viewed the film, including three hundred wounded veterans whose ten-dollar tickets had been paid for by civilians.

The citizens of Dana, meantime, had decided that a thirty-five-thousand-dollar library named for Pyle would be a suitable way to honor a celebrated native son. A New York public-relations firm got wind of the idea and formed a company, Ernie Pyle Memorial, Inc., through which to promote a grander scheme: a multi-million-dollar, one-hundred-acre, "landscaped, lake-studded park and cemetery, to which [Pyle's body] could be moved from Ie Shima. . . ." Pyle's tomb was to be surrounded by "honored dead of all states, [and] symbolic scenes of allied nations. . . ."

The proposal enraged Jerry, who told reporters her late husband would have been "horrified and indignant" at such an ostentatious undertaking. It was "entirely out of keeping with everything that Ernie ever did, or said, or thought, or was," she said. Moreover, she would never "consent to having his body moved," because "Ernie is lying where he would wish to be, with the men he loved." Editorial writers applauded Jerry's comments; Chicago columnist Sydney Harris thought she should be awarded a prize equivalent to the Pulitzer for her "magnificent blast at the press agents and promoters who have attached themselves like body lice to Ernie's well-deserved fame." Harris aptly dismissed the memorial park as "vulgar" and, with Jerry, endorsed "living memorials," like the Dana town library, in honor of Pyle and the other war dead.

Jerry's health steadily declined in the months following Pyle's death. In mid-November, she contracted influenza.

Her weight dangerously low, she checked into St. Joseph's Hospital in Albuquerque, where she died of uremic poisoning the morning of November 23, 1945. One of her sisters told reporters Jerry had lost all interest in living in the seven months since Pyle's death. Paige Cavanaugh flew to Albuquerque to close out the Pyles' house. He retrieved bundles of letters Pyle had written Jerry over the years—"reams and reams of lovely lovemaking by mail," he called them.

Jerry was buried November 27 on a snow-covered hill near Afton, Minnesota. Pyle's body was later moved to Hawaii and buried in the National Memorial Cemetery of the Pacific in Punchbowl Crater. That they are buried forty-five hundred miles apart befits the physical and emotional distance at which they lived in the last decade of their lives. But the burial place of each is ironic in its own right.

Jerry had sung in the church choir and been active in the Christian Endeavor Society in her native Minnesota; but she had departed from the conservatism of her upbringing in 1918, when she moved to Washington, hopeful, in a girlish way, of finding excitement and freedom in the nation's capital. She found some of both, but she had spent the better part of her short life rebelling against what she had left behind.

Pyle had accepted the possibility that he would die in a war zone, but he would certainly have preferred to have been buried in Europe, where, after so many years of rootlessness, he had found a home and a sense of purpose with the infantry. Still, there is a curious bit of circularity about his having been buried in the Hawaiian Islands.

On a 1937 trip there, Pyle had visited the Kalaupapa leper colony on Molokai made famous by the Belgian priest Father Damien. His walk into "the foothills of martyrdom" bordered on the spiritual, and he told his readers he felt "a kind of unrighteousness at being whole and 'clean'; I experienced an acute feeling of spiritual need to be no better off than the leper."

Quite accurately, he knew that "in real life I am a 'sprint' martyr; the long steady pull is not for me. I tire of too much goodness, and wish to dart off and chase a rabbit." He abandoned his rabbit-chasing days five years later, when he landed with American soldiers in North Africa. That he was later killed was a direct result of his having taken up the long, steady pull.

Lance Bertelsen (essay date 1989)

SOURCE: "San Pietro and the 'Art' of War," in *Southwest Review*, Vol. 24, No. 3, Spring, 1989, pp. 230-256.

[*In the following essay, Bertelsen discusses the literary and cinematic influences of Pyle's "The Death of Captain Waskow," and parallels similarities between Pyle's piece and John Huston's war film San Pietro.*]

"In this war I have known a lot of officers who were loved and respected by the soldiers under them. But never have I crossed the trail of any man as beloved as Capt. Henry T. Waskow of Belton, Texas." So begins Ernie Pyle's most famous World War II dispatch, **"The Death of Captain Waskow"**—a piece that describes the reactions of troops from the 36th "Texas" Division to the death of a young officer during the Italian campaign of 1943-44.

Pyle, the renowned American war journalist, had joined the 36th near the end of the battle for San Pietro Infine. It had been a cruel battle. Committed to suicidal frontal attacks on well-entrenched Germans in the town and surrounding hills, the troops of the 36th responded with good spirit and determination, but were slaughtered by the score in the terraced olive groves and high rock ridges that marked the southern entrance to the Liri Valley.

Documentary footage in the National Archives shows Pyle interviewing troops near San Pietro on 16 December 1943. It was probably that night he encountered Captain Waskow's dead body. Several days later, back in Caserta, depressed and possibly hung over, he wrote the dispatch that would gain him national fame and secure his place as the greatest American journalist of the war.

The battle for San Pietro Infine was a relatively small operation tucked between the bloody landings at Salerno and the muddy stalemate at Monte Cassino. Yet, typical of the bizarre transactions of war, it inspired two of the great documentary works of art to emerge from World War II. Pyle's article—which appeared in newspapers across the U.S.A. on 10 January 1944—was the first. The second was a film called *San Pietro* by John Huston and photographers from the U.S. Army Signal Corps. Huston had already directed the now classic version of *The Maltese Falcon,* and would later direct such films as *The Treasure of the Sierra Madre, The African Queen,* and *The Red Badge of Courage,* but in the winter of 1943 he was a captain assigned to document, in his own words, "the triumphal entry of the American forces into Rome." It didn't work out that way. Instead, Huston and his crew produced one of the most harrowing visions of modern infantry warfare ever filmed: a documentary that conveys the raw repetitive grind of battle and the grim vulnerability of the men who fought it with a respect and bitterness unprecedented in the history of film.

World War II was more than any previous war an event for the camera and news dispatch. It was the war that began during the documentary movement of the 1930s and early 1940s and that drew heavily upon its techniques and resources. In **"The Death of Captain Waskow"** and *San Pietro* the results of this legacy are evident. Both works present themselves as factual records of real events, yet are deeply and allusively informed by literary and cinematic tradition. Both comment on the stoic dignity of man, yet deplore the heartbreaking conditions that evoke it.

And both focus not on the grand invasions and the daring raids, the D-Days and Ploestis, but on a single minor battle fought for an obscure Italian town by troops from a former Texas National Guard unit.

I

The 36th Division's road to San Pietro had not been easy. Trained in Texas, Massachusetts, and North Africa, but untried in battle, it struggled through the Salerno landings, where it produced in PFC Charles ("Commando") Kelly the first Medal of Honor winner in the European theatre. It also produced, after a time, one of the better novels of World War II, Harry Brown's slender, understated *A Walk in the Sun;* a book that in turn inspired the World War II combat movie of the same name.

The 36th's casualty figures at Salerno were terrible. After a month in action, 1800 of its men were dead, wounded, or missing. In his diary account of the aftermath of Salerno, the 36th's commander, General Fred Walker, registered a kind of shocked fascination with the dynamics of body collection and burial: "Bodies brought to the grave were laid, side by side, along the trench . . . they were in various stages of decomposition and lay in eerie, grotesque postures. . . . After all proper records were made, the body was wrapped in a bedsack or other material and laid in the trench." Walker's morbid focus on the mechanics of body disposal may serve to symbolize a qualitative and quantitative shift in American perception that occurred almost as soon as the 36th Division hit the beaches of Italy—a transformation that would come to obsess John Huston and Ernie Pyle. Something horrible was happening to American troops on the peninsula; for the first time in the war they were becoming massively expendable in a dirty, costly, extremely frustrating infantry campaign.

During October and early November 1943 the lost men of the Texas Division were replaced by other uniformed human beings, and on 15 November the 36th was again sent into the line. It rained continuously during this operation. "The men are soaked to the skin," Walker wrote, "and their uniforms are covered with mud up to their waists. They are cold and have no opportunity to dry their clothing or have hot meals. . . . all front line battalions have to be supplied by men who carry what is needed by hand up the side of the mountain through the mud and rain." Ernie Pyle, about this time, noted that "men were exhausted, and their feet were broken out, and infirmities such as arthritis, hernia or heart weakness would leap to the fore on those man-killing climbs."

About the time this redeployment was taking place, John Huston arrived in Caserta. It was early December and the Texas Division's 143rd Infantry Regiment, to which Huston would eventually be attached, was preparing to attack San Pietro and the surrounding hills. Both Pyle and Huston had an eye for landscape, and the landscapes at the entrance to the Liri Valley were spectacular and horrific. "The country is shockingly beautiful," Pyle wrote, "and just as shockingly hard to capture from the enemy. The hills rise to high ridges of almost solid rock.

You can't go around them through the flat, peaceful valleys, because the Germans look down upon you and would let you have it." Huston, characteristically, took an even more ironic view of war's effect on the pastoral. The opening shots of *San Pietro*—a black and white film—show scene after scene of farmland ravaged by war: shattered trees, shell craters, scorched earth. Accompanied by a solemn organ, Huston recites a tourbook description: "In winter the highest peaks of the Liri range ascend into the snows, but the valley floor with its olive groves and ancient vines, its crops of wheat and corn, is green the year around [dramatic pause]. That is, in normal times [shattered trees]. Last year was a bad year for grapes and olives [ravaged fields] and the fall planting was late—many fields lay fallow [shell craters and stagnant water]."

Huston's grim paradox set the tone for the rest of the film; a film that, above all else, is about the vanity of human constructions in a world gone mad with destruction—plow shares beaten into swords and olive branches pounded by artillery. The ancient village of San Pietro, which "for 700 years has stood at the threshold of Liri Valley, welcoming the traveler," is simply one more pathetic victim. In an extremely sardonic passage, Huston's camera surveys the town's devastated buildings and monuments, while his voice drones on, flat and knowing: "the stones of its walls were quarried out of the hills [piles of rubble] . . . population fourteen hundred and twelve at the last census [deserted houses] . . . patron saint, Peter [close-up of blasted icon] . . . point of interest, St. Peter's, 1438 [destroyed church] . . . note interesting treatment of chancel [interior shot panning over shattered dome and roof]." In these establishing shots, Huston's solemn narration and the funereal organ conspire to say what remains unsaid: this is to be a film about a world of death.

The German defenses facing the 36th provided the killing power. Huston describes them in some detail, but perhaps an even better sense of their impregnability is conveyed by Robert Wagner in his history of the 36th in Italy, *The Texas Army:* "German defenses, organized in depth, extended from the orchard covered terraces east of S. Pietro and across the mile-wide valley west to M. Lungo. . . . These emplacements, nearly impervious to constant Allied artillery fire and to attacks by fighter bombers, were deep pits covered by three layers of logs and further protected by earth and rocks. Each had a single opening, just large enough for a man to crawl through. The T-Patchers [36th division troops] had first to penetrate a field of 'S' mines, then barbed wire, and still more 'S' mines. If these outer defenses were pierced, the enemy could still rain down artillery, mortar, and heavy machine gun fire without danger to his own troops, hidden in their shelters." Huston adds one extra detail: when stepped on, the 'S' mines bounced to groin level, then exploded.

The fluctuating mixture of sympathy and subversion notable in the film's establishing shots also colors the treatment of the soldiers who will fight the battle. Despite the dark ironies of the landscape, early in the film Huston constructs a generalized, heroic image of the infantry. Footage of soldiers fixing bayonets and moving out is backed by martial music as Huston recites a paean to the infantry's role in taking and holding ground: "that was for the infantry to do, employing those weapons that confine and destroy life in narrow trenches, caves, and fighting holes. It was up to the man with the rifle, the man under fire from all weapons, the man whose way all our weapons—land, air, and sea—serve only to prepare. It was up to the foot soldier." But as the moment of actual attack approaches, the soldiers of the 143rd regiment are strongly individualized. They are shown separately, full face, close up—smiling, talking, worrying, their eyes full of deference and humor and fear—in a way that makes disturbingly clear their humanity and the non-military aspect of their being. "Of the original force to establish the beachhead at Salerno," Huston says of these men, "the 143rd had since been all but a fortnight in action, under extremely bitter weather conditions. At Salerno, at the Volturno crossing, it had taken mortal punishment. The task ahead promised no less bloodshed, yet it was undertaken in good spirits and high confidence."

The job faced by the T-Patchers was simple, direct, and brutal. After an attack by allied Italian forces on Mt. Lungo failed—Huston shows Italian bodies being carried downhill and loaded on a truck—the 2nd and 3rd battalions of the 143rd infantry were committed to a direct frontal assault across the olive groves to the northeast of San Pietro. At the same time, the 1st battalion of the 143rd was to climb and seize Mt. Sammucro (Hill 1205), which towered above the olive groves.

"In good spirits and high confidence," reported Huston, the 143rd prepared to attack on 8 December 1943. To prepare the viewer, Huston records an intense night artillery bombardment that fades into an early morning scene of widely spaced troops advancing cautiously through sodden olive groves. "It had rained most of the night and was raining at H-hour when the 2nd and 3rd battalions crossed the line of departure" runs the simple narration, but the sequences that follow are some of the most striking of the battle.

The initial shots are taken from the flank. A blustery wind shakes the olive branches, and the troops wear raincoats as they move forward hunched against the weather. A sense of wetness, coldness, fear, and inevitability pervades these shots. There are no heroic speeches or gestures. The troops look like tired workers on their way to hard labor. They have been ordered to assault an impossible objective in miserable weather, and Huston brilliantly conveys their resignation and foreboding as they move to the attack.

In the fourth shot of this sequence, the camera is positioned low behind two soldiers advancing up an incline into heavy smoke. The scene is framed by the trunk of a tree in the right foreground. The soundtrack rumbles with distant mortar explosions and artillery. It is a long take.

The soldier on the far left disappears into the smoke. The soldier on the near right zig-zags slowly up the hill. As the white smoke billows and blows down toward him, his moving figure becomes shadowy and ghost-like, then gradually disappears. A sudden burst of machine gun fire punctuates the soundtrack; the camera pans quickly forty-five degrees to the right and records in a blur what seems to be the death of a third soldier no more than twenty feet from the lens. He falls forward twisting to the left—his feet bounce in the air—and he lies there, on his back, his upper torso hidden behind another tree. His raincoat continues rather pathetically to cover his legs.

Huston has cut the film so that this extraordinary sequence seems to set off the attack. The soundtrack crackles with automatic fire and explosions, and five shots in quick succession show troops running or, more accurately, plodding forward: an officer waving men forward, several riflemen hunched against fire, a machinegun team—the gunner carrying his weapon over his shoulder, his loader with a box of ammunition, and another man without a rifle—all doggedly moving forward through the smoke, past the sometimes unfocused lens of the camera. The drab realism of these scenes—the stolid, mundane materiality of the troops, the awkwardly positioned camera, blurred images, the shock of random death—all serve to convey without narration the sense of monotonous hardship and arbitrary destruction that characterizes infantry warfare.

As the 2nd Battalion's attack bogs down, Huston shifts to a series of extremely close artillery and mortar explosions photographed from beside pinned-down troops. Several soldiers scramble headlong back into declivities, the camera shakes and wobbles from the concussion, sparks and flaming particles from the explosions cascade over their positions. Huston's visual language makes it clear that the attack has failed, and that, given the obstacles faced by the troops, it should have failed. His voice waxes elegiac as he lingers over the pictures of battlefield dead ("men gave their lives in attempts to reach pillboxes and throw hand grenades through the narrow gun openings"). Sorrowful music swells over the bodies. Then a slight pause, a quick fade, and Huston sums up the results of this tactical lesson—"The 3rd battalion was committed."

It is a memorable transition, shaking the audience from comfortable clichés into the brutal repetition of actual warfare. There are none of the rallying speeches, the "college tries," the "doing our duty," the "necessary sacrifices" so familiar from World War II combat films. The 3rd battalion is simply "committed." Again the sodden troops advance through the olive orchards, again they are riddled by defensive fire, again the artillery descends, the camera shudders, the attack fails. The advance, Huston tells us, "never got more than 600 yards past the line of departure."

With the breakdown of the second attack, the first major movement of *San Pietro* is complete, but Huston will not allow the viewer to retreat unmolested. Again the music becomes doleful, but this time it foregrounds not conventional, sanitized pictures of "battlefield dead," but highly disturbing close-ups of bodies being put into white bed sacks (the convenience of zippered body bags being as yet unknown). The dead soldiers' grime contrasts strongly with the whiteness of the sacks. Although we see the gloved hands of the burial detail, Huston keeps the focus unrelentingly on the dead men themselves. The soldiers' faces are only momentarily visible, but their "deadness" and the unwieldy heaviness of the bodies generate a visual combination of horror, solemnity, and matter-of-factness that reinforces the tonal paradoxes of Huston's narration. In the final shot of this sequence, an uncovered soldier lies stiffly on the ground and in a grim conflation of housekeeping and religious tradition a pair of anonymous gloves quickly folds his calloused hands across his body.

There is a remarkable story behind these images. In his autobiography, Huston wrote that he "had interviewed—on camera—a number of men who were to take part in the battle. Some of the things they said were quite eloquent: they were fighting for what the future might hold for them, their country and the world."

> Later you saw these same men dead. Before placing the bodies in coffins for burial, the procedure was to lay them in a row in their bedrolls, make positive identification—where possible—then cover them. At that point it was necessary to lift the body up, and I had my cameras so placed that the faces of the dead came right to the lens. In the uncut version I had their living voices speaking over their dead faces about their hopes for the future.
>
> Considering the emotional effect it would have on the families of these men, and also how American audiences of the time might react to it, we later decided not to include this material.

Thus, seemingly, was lost a sequence that must have been unprecedented in its power and horror—"their living voices speaking over their dead faces." The description recalls the final scenes of later, fictional World War II movies in which the dead comrades appear as ghosts or close-up portraits just before the credits roll—except, in Huston's version, the dead faces and live voices are those of actual combat men. Whether or not such scenes ever actually existed, Huston's retrospective invocation of the motif suggests the kind of emotional effect he was striving for in the film and provides his interpretation of the symbolic and physical relationship binding living and dead on the battlefield—a theme central to Pyle's **"The Death of Captain Waskow."** In the final version of *San Pietro*, however, this gruesome juxtaposition does not survive. What remains are silent, strongly evocative close-ups of the 143rd before the attack, and pictures of their dead bodies being put into sacks after it.

II

At 5:00 P.M. on 7 December—thirteen hours and twenty minutes before the 2nd and 3rd Battalions attacked across the olive groves—the 1st Battalion had begun climbing Mt. Sammucro. By 6:00 the following morning, fighting in fog and darkness, they had seized Hill 1205 from the Germans in what Huston calls "a brilliant success." Then began a series of intense German counterattacks under incessant artillery bombardment that during the next week would decimate both the 1st Battalion and the German attackers. Huston's film represents these fights with the same close-up accuracy and intensity that characterized the scenes on the valley floor. The setting is different—jagged rocks and scrub brush instead of olive groves—but for sheer intimacy of detail, for realistic renditions of how infantrymen under fire move across rocky slopes, for what might be called the violent choreography of ground warfare, these sequences rival those of the 2nd and 3rd battalions' initial attack.

Leading B Company during this action was Captain Henry T. Waskow of Belton, Texas. He survived the initial assault on Mt. Sammucro and by 14 December his company (or what was left of it) was in reserve, carrying supplies and ammunition. Captain Joel Westbrook, the assistant S-3 for the 1st Battalion, wrote that Waskow "was ordered to attack a German OP that had come in behind us and was directing very accurate fire on our rear. Henry just had one platoon left. So naturally he took it. Tidwell, his orderly, told me how it happened. Very simple. A mortar shell, just like any other, laid open his abdomen. He didn't have to live very long." Later, the orderly, PFC Riley M. Tidwell, brought Waskow's body down the mountain lashed to the back of a mule. At the bottom of the trail was Ernie Pyle. With grim ambiguity he wrote several days later, "never have I crossed the trail of any man as beloved as Capt. Henry T. Waskow of Belton, Texas."

In the years before World War II, Pyle had been a traveling writer of local-color columns—a kind of Charles Kuralt in print. In the war dispatches this experience is evident not only in his well-known tendency to identify a soldier's hometown (and sometimes street address), but in his sharp insight into regional and class-based speech and behavior patterns. In **"The Death of Captain Waskow"**—despite its poignance—Pyle cannot help sardonically punning on wild West phrases and turning Texas icons into Italian realities. In the phrase "never have I crossed the trail" Pyle seems to be playing grimly with Texas iconography and dialect. Likewise, the traditional Western body-lashed-to-the-back-of-a-mule motif becomes a brutal actuality in Italy: "their heads hanging down on the left side of the mule, their stiffened legs sticking out awkwardly from the other side, bobbing up and down as the mule walked." But it is in the speech and gestures of the soldiers who gather round Waskow's body—and in the mood of the landscape that holds them—that Pyle finds the aesthetic heart of his most memorable dispatch.

World War II produced a lot of dead bodies—but bodies that were not yet fully dead for the people who survived. Voices *do* speak over dead faces, but they are the voices of others. Such voices—the voices of B Company, 1st Battalion, 143rd Regiment, 36th Division, recorded after the fall of San Pietro—are the central subject of Ernie Pyle's **"The Death of Captain Waskow."**

"I was at the foot of the trail the night they brought Capt. Waskow's body down," Pyle wrote. "The moon was nearly full at the time, and you could see far up the trail, and even part way across the valley below. Soldiers made shadows in the moonlight as they walked. . . . Dead men had been coming down the mountain all evening, lashed to the backs of mules." The "valley below" contained San Pietro and the terraced olive orchards. The dead men coming down the mountain all evening and the soldiers who made shadows as they walked were men of the 143rd enacting a surrealistic vision of the soldier's Psalm: "Yea, though I walk through the valley of the shadow of death . . ."

In this eerie nightscape, cold dead men are taken off the mules by scared living men and laid "in the shadow of the low stone wall alongside the road." Captain Waskow's body, along with four others, is placed "in the shadow beside the low stone wall" until finally "there were five lying end to end in a long row, alongside the road."

The unburdened mules move "off to their olive orchards," leaving the burden to the living men. They gradually move close to Captain Waskow's body. "Not so much to look," wrote Pyle, "as to say something in finality to him, and to themselves. I stood close by and I could hear." This is what he heard:

> One soldier came and looked down, and he said out loud, "God damn it." That's all he said, and then he walked away. Another one came. He said, "God damn it to hell anyway." He looked down for a few last moments, and then he turned and left.

> Another man came; I think he was an officer. It was hard to tell officers from men in the half light, for all were bearded and grimy dirty. The man looked down into the dead captain's face, and then he spoke directly to him, as though he were alive. He said: "I'm sorry, old man."

> Then a soldier came and stood beside the officer, and bent over, and he too spoke to his dead captain, not in a whisper but awfully tenderly, and he said:

> "I sure am sorry, sir."

> Then the first man squatted down, and he reached down and took the dead hand, and he sat there for a full five minutes, holding the dead hand in his own and looking intently into the dead face, and he never uttered a sound all the time he sat there.

> And finally he put the hand down, and then reached up and gently straightened the points of the captain's shirt collar, and then he sort of rearranged the tattered edges of his uniform around the wound. And then he got up and walked away down the road in the moonlight, all alone.

The incremental repetition, the alternations of speech and silence, the tonal variations between "men" and officers, the symbolic coalescence of natural imagery and biblical allusion, all offer grist to the mill of literary criticism. But for the common reader and viewer—the people back home for whom Pyle wrote and Huston photographed—this passage was wrenching because its dialogue at once overthrew and reinforced the strongest kind of popular ethical and cultural identifications. First, and most obviously, Pyle does something that even today is rare in syndicated newspaper columns: he uses one of the strongest forms of profanity in the language, a form extremely rare in literature of the 1940s and one that would not be allowed in films for another twenty years, and then intensifies it by adding "to hell." And then, miraculously, he makes the audience accept it, indeed embrace it, as a kind of prayer—"anyway." As far as I can discover, none of his readers complained about the profanity (although the *Arkansas Democrat* deleted it). This is an extraordinary fact: a transformation or momentary suspension or inversion of cultural norms in the readers that duplicates, as it records, the transforming effect of war on combat men.

Pyle's more conventional appeal to the popular cultural norms and models is his sincere adaptation of speech patterns associated with various "types" in Hollywood movies. The profane soldiers seem "toned up" versions of the tough-guy-with-a-deeply-sympathetic-heart most often played by John Wayne (though Robert Taylor in *Bataan*—the most popular combat movie of 1943—also comes to mind). The officer with the stiff-upper-lip and quite upper-class "I'm sorry, old man" seems an Errol Flynn type, deeply distressed yet under control. But most poignant is the last voice—"the Kid's"—and its shy, sincere, and still respectful "I sure am sorry, sir." The speech pattern is unmistakably Robert Walker's—an actor who played just such a character in *Bataan* and reprised it in many movies, including *Thirty Seconds over Tokyo*. The scene then closes with a quasi-religious, and totally silent, meditation by a soldier who holds the captain's hand and arranges his tattered clothes; at once a battlefield *Pieta* and an image that finds an abbreviated but disturbingly real parallel in Huston's film.

"The Death of Captain Waskow" eventually achieved cinematic form in *The Story of GI Joe* (1945), probably the best combat movie to emerge from World War II. Created primarily from Pyle's dispatches and employing Pyle as a technical adviser, it starred Robert Mitchum as "Capt. Bill Walker" who dies on a mountain in Italy and is lamented by his troops in a precise rendition (minus the profanity) of the scene over Waskow's body. So strong was the "Walker-Waskow" identification (although Joel Westbrook tells me that Waskow was much more a disciplinarian than "Walker") that in 1945 Mitchum went on a promotional tour with Riley Tidwell, the soldier who had brought Waskow's body down from Mt. Sammucro.

But Pyle's column is interesting not only for its manipulation of the popular expectations and norms of its audience. It is also significant because it re-enacts, in what seems to be me to be a quite unconscious, uncannily accurate, and absolutely material way, the conventions of a very powerful literary tradition: the pastoral elegy lamenting the death of a young "shepherd." In using the term "unconscious" I do not intend to imply that Pyle didn't know what a pastoral elegy was or that he had never read one, but simply to suggest that in reporting on the death of Waskow, in a dispatch written from the combat zone under a deadline, he would have scarcely had the time or inclination consciously to pattern his work after this form. What seems more likely, and indeed more interesting, is that the parallels are due to an intertextuality occurring not so much because Pyle had internalized the conventions of the genre but because the elements that make up the genre—men caring for other men and for allegorical "flocks" in a rural setting; the premature death of a beloved young shepherd; the natural environment as a symbolic mourner; a series of human (or divine) mourners speaking to or about the dead man); the questioning of divine providence; the "decking" or beautifying of the body or hearse; the consolation and mourners' movement back into life—all are to be found, with brutal repetition, in the world of men and death that is the battlefield.

Captain Waskow is unmistakably the "good shepherd," the officer loved and respected by his men:

> He was very young, only in his middle twenties, but he carried in him a sincerity and gentleness that made people want to be guided by him.

> "After my own father, he came next," a sergeant told me.

> "He always looked after us," a soldier said. "He'd go to bat for us every time."

> "I've never knowed him to do anything unfair," another one said.

The night they bring his body down, nature puts on mourning; the moonlight throws deep shadows; the atmosphere is hushed and eerie. After the body is laid next to the low stone wall, the grieving soldiers form a kind of procession: each says his piece with the clipped anger or reticence or sorrow of a combat man. Then one man silently arranges Waskow's uniform in a last act of respect, and walks away.

This elegiac structure is infused by the 23rd Psalm, informing the valley of shadows and death that was the Liri. The 23rd Psalm is a pastoral poem, one that takes as its subject the potential death of a human shepherd and his prayer to his Shepherd, the Lord, for protection. The two texts—the one a well known psalm and the other an elegiac sequence recreating itself out of the raw material of men in combat—coalesce in a short description that, as a letter to the editor of *Time* put it, "I don't think any American could read . . . dry-eyed."

But in war, as in the pastoral elegy, mourning must be abbreviated, consolation implicit, and the transition to life immediate. In Milton's *Lycidas,* the mourner "rose and twitch'd his mantle blue / To-morrow to fresh woods, and pastures new"; in Pyle's dispatch, "we lay down on the straw in the cowshed, and pretty soon we were all asleep." In the closing lines of *San Pietro,* Huston's biblical cadences likewise advocate consolation and the resumption of life: "the people prayed to their patron saint to intercede with God on behalf of those who came to deliver them and passed on to the north with the passing battle." But Huston's closing also reminds us that while the villagers may resume life, the soldiers only resume combat. St. Peter would have to "intercede" for many.

The fight for San Pietro continued for several days after Henry Waskow's death. Huston's film portrays the entire battle (or series of battles): the futile tank assault and renewed infantry attacks of 15-16 December ("I had never seen so many dead," Huston wrote, "all around were the dead. I remember remarking to someone that we had seen more dead that day than living"), the crucial seizure of Mt. Lungo, the fall of San Pietro, and the return of the civilian population. As Huston assembled the film, each of these actions is punctuated by images of the dead: a dead soldier's hair blows in the wind as he seems to look from his foxhole at the troops advancing into San Pietro; long lines of Italian gravediggers labor to complete a large field of fresh graves; a dead woman is slowly dug from a booby-trapped house as her relatives weep (in a particularly graphic sequence, her husband reaches out to touch her face and comes away with blood on his hand). After he returned to New York, Huston called the mountains and valleys of central Italy "a dead man's world": a combat environment whose grinding rapacity and difficult landscape combined to produce a literal "population" of undisposed dead bodies. It is an image that haunts Huston's *San Pietro*—as it had haunted Pyle's dispatch on the death of Captain Waskow.

Back in the U.S.A., Pyle's dispatch was an enormous success, appearing in newspapers across the country, taking up the entire front page of the Washington *News* (the issue sold out), reprinted in *Time Magazine,* and evantually contributing to his Pulitzer prize later that year.

But the brass didn't like *San Pietro*. After its first screening, several high-ranking officers complained about the film, and a spokesman for the War Department labelled it "anti-war." Huston replied dramatically that if he ever made a film that was pro-war, "I hoped someone would take me out and shoot me." The film was temporarily suppressed by the War Department, then rescued by General George C. Marshall—and some judicious cutting. The approved thirty-minute version was released to the general public in early 1945.

San Pietro is thus the "official" version of Huston's original film. This may help to explain the rather too upbeat ending of smiling children and new agricultural cultivation "as the battle passed over and beyond San Pietro westward"—to fresh woods and pastures new. Of course there would be smiling children (whom Huston records beautifully) and new cultivation, but there would also be fighting and dying at the Rapido River and on the miserable slopes below Monte Cassino. Huston reminds the viewer, over a series of shots of the 143rd resting after the battle, that many of the soldiers "you see alive here have since joined the ranks of their brothers in arms who fell at San Pietro." But the strong visual reassertion of the non-ironic pastoral, with the Mormon Tabernacle Choir soaring in the background, seems somehow false and out of place. It is a conventional theatrical touch—and there are others in the film.

The careful viewer will notice a remarkable number of left-handed soldiers, and even a bolt action rifle with the bolt on the left side. These shots have been reversed following the Hollywood prescription that the good guys must always attack in the same direction so as not to confuse the audience. (The wounded and the dead are always removed in the opposite direction.) General Mark Clark's high-flown preface, full of heroic phrasing but spoken out of the side of his mouth, rings at once false (in its intent) and true (in what it reveals about the distance between heroic words and reality). And the background music, although sometimes effective, too often sounds trite and theatrical.

Yet the boys who fought the war and died at San Pietro were often trite and theatrical—products of their culture, of patriotic truisms and Hollywood sentiment, of Mom and Dad and apple pie. Here is what Captain Henry T. Waskow wrote to his family:

> If you read this, I will have died in defense of my country and all that it stands for—the most honorable and distinguished death a man can die. It was not because I was willing to die for my country, however—I wanted to live for it—just as any other person wants to do. It is foolish and foolhardy to want to die for one's country, but to live for it is something else.
>
> To live for one's country is to my mind to live a life of service; to—in a small way—to help a fellow man occasionally along the way, and generally to be useful and to serve. It also means to me to rise up in all our wrath and with overwhelming power to crush any oppressor of human rights. . . .
>
> Try to live a life of service—to help someone wherever you are or whatever you may be—take it from me, you can get happiness out of that, more than anything in life.

In this sincere mixture of patriotic sentiment, high-flown morality, proverbial wisdom, and common sense reasoning resides one part of one man killed on one mountain during one battle in Italy in 1943. We hear that hope for "what the future might hold for them, their country and the world" that Huston remembered from T-Patchers he interviewed and then deleted when confronted by their dead faces. We find the goodness of intent and the pastoral care that Pyle memorializes in his prose. We do not find the sordidness, the cruelty, the pettiness, the selfish-

ness that are also part of combat—nor do we find them in Huston's and Pyle's representations. But perhaps Huston and Pyle, in their mixing of the grim and the poignant, in their balancing comradeship and consolation and horror and waste, were closer to the truth of World War II than we in the post-Viet Nam era are willing to admit. The product of a central Texas town, and, as the cliché might continue, a thousand American towns, Henry T. Waskow's is the voice that inspired the voices of **"The Death of Captain Waskow"**; the voice missing from *San Pietro*: the living voice speaking over the dead face.

III

Of all human activities, combat is perhaps the easiest to fictionalize and the hardest to represent accurately. It is the subject of the first great epic of Western culture, yet today is an experience so extreme and so foreign to everyday life that even the best representations seem somehow impotent. One can sit in a modern movie theatre with a large screen and THX sound and experience tension, noise, flash, and chaos—but never feel heat, blast, and fatigue. One can read excellent descriptions of men under fire, but never feel that absolute chill that comes from the realization that someone is trying to kill *you*.

And then there is the rhetoric of war writing—the set of literary and historical conventions that shape an author's conception of an "attack" or a "retreat" even before writing or filming begins. John Keegan, in *The Face of Battle,* and Paul Fussell, in a series of essays on World War II literature and photography, have tellingly explored such conventions as they affect the writing of military history and belles lettres. They have done what seems to me something very much worth doing: they have tried to discover in the representations of battle those cultural norms and ideological motivations that separate the mediation from the fact. In the historian Keegan's case, the primary motivation has been to get closer to the fact; in the critic Fussell's case, the motivation has been to attempt to understand the purpose and dynamics of the mediation.

Both, I think, have contributed markedly to our ability to understand what goes on when war is represented in various media. But to say that we can at least distinguish the conventions at work in a representation, although we can never get back to the fact, is itself misleading. For as the Pyle article shows, sometimes life—or at least, Pyle's version of life—unconsciously enacts the structures of art. And often, as in the case of troops in Viet Nam "John Wayning It," life consciously imitates fictional representation. Most commonly, however, representational precedents allow (or force) us to see and frame events in life that we have merely looked at before. I recently stumbled upon a germane example of this phenomenon in the February 7, 1944 issue of *Time Magazine*—the issue that carried the letter (quoted above) praising Pyle's column. Seventeen pages farther on—in the "World Battlefront" section—was a report about the 36th's infamous attack across the Rapido River. Illustrating it was a photograph that showed four soldiers looking sadly at a "dead comrade in Italy." The photograph could have been an illustration for **"The Death of Captain Waskow"**—and I'm sure that in part it was. The AP photographer had obviously read the column and begun to look for such a shot; the editor at *Time* had read the column and decided to print the photograph. The fact that the picture accompanies a report on the 36th Division only adds to its strong evocative and "artistic" value—yet it is a picture of real combat soldiers looking at a real dead body in a way that certainly was repeated day after day in the combat zone.

In a sense, John Huston was doing precisely the same thing at this time as the AP photographer. With a model of the battle of San Pietro framed in his mind, he was shooting the footage that eventually became the film, *San Pietro*. For despite the extraordinary realism of the film, its battle action seems to have been almost entirely reënacted. According to Eric Ambler, he and Huston did not even arrive at the town of San Pietro until the final day of the battle, probably 16 December 1943. They saw plenty of dead and were mortared by the retreating Germans, but got little in the way of useable footage. They did, according to Ambler, take some close-ups of Texas troops—he calls them "Rangers"—"waiting to leapfrog through after some troops ahead of them had started the attack," and it may have been this film that Huston was remembering when he talked about interviewing soldiers before the battle. The bulk of action in the film, however, was restaged between late December and late February using troops from the 36th Division (and possibly other units).

The hours of unedited footage in the National Archives provide a good sense of how Huston went about the filming. Several scenes—including a number that survive in the final cut—appear on two or more reels and indicate that once a scene was set up, several cameramen would record the action simultaneously from different angles. For example, a scene showing a medic approaching three "wounded" soldiers among the boulders on Mt. Sammucro appears on both reel ADC 750 (the shot that appears in the final cut) and ADC 582 (from a vantage point farther to the right). Likewise the scene of the machine gun crew plodding to the attack appears on two reels; the out-of-focus footage (which appears in the final cut) on ADC 750, and focussed footage on ADC 588. Perhaps the best record of the actual filming occurs on reel ADC 581 during a scene in which a farm building is "cleared" by soldiers who toss smoke grenades into it and then enter the smoking building as if looking for enemy troops. (This scene does not appear in the final cut.) During one sequence, in which a camera continued to roll after the "action" had stopped, we see a soldier in a knit cap come into the frame and attempt to kick a smoking grenade away from the door while the troops stand around watching. Behind the building a second cameraman is visible, and as the soldier who kicked the grenade moves away from the building a third cameraman comes into view on the right. The shots taken from the other two camera angles appear on reels ADC 583 and ADC 587.

Captain Joel Westbrook—who in Henry Waskow lost not only a fellow officer but a very close friend—was assigned after the battle to help facilitate Huston's filming. He recalls that he and Huston would go over maps together, with Westbrook describing parts of the battle and Huston asking if they could be re-created. Huston would then be assigned troops, and move to the designated area. Westbrook recalls making sure that troops throwing hand grenades were given relatively safe concussion grenades rather than the fragmentation type; indeed, in several of the outtakes we can see small explosive charges being tossed in front of troops to simulate enemy shelling. (In the final version of the film, only the subsequent explosion and troop reaction appear.) Westbrook does not, however, remember the exact dates when the filming occurred. He believes that it was sometime in late December or early January, before the T-Patchers returned to the line for the ill-fated attack across the Rapido River on 20-22 January 1944. The dates assigned to the various reels in the National Archives card catalogue are only vaguely accurate, but several slates appear in the footage itself. One indicates that the scenes of women washing clothes in San Pietro were taken on 3 January 1944. Two different slates show that on 31 December Huston was filming in the American cemetery at Capriati. A final slate indicates that Huston was filming destroyed tanks and Italian civilians (both scenes in the final version) in or near San Pietro on 22 January 1944. By this time, many of the 36th Division troops who had restaged the attack scenes were dead or dying on the Rapido.

What the unedited footage does not contain, interestingly, are four of the five brilliant close-ups that define the humanity of the troops before the attack and any scenes of bodies being put into bed sacks. The sources of this footage remain uncertain. Almost all of the other scenes in the final version of the film appear somewhere in the unedited footage, even the stunning sequence of the soldier going down in the initial attack. In light of this evidence, Huston's statement that "for purposes of continuity a few of these scenes were shot before and after the actual battle" but all "within range of enemy small arms or artillery fire," which is appended to the end of *San Pietro,* is patently false. The picture was filmed *primarily* after the battle and, as Westbrook remarked, "maybe in range of very long-range artillery fire."

But the more important question has to do with the effect of this information on the viewer. Westbrook, for example, despite his intimate knowledge of the filming and the battle, nevertheless contends that *San Pietro* is an essentially accurate rendition of the fighting. James Agee, admittedly a Huston partisan, found the film "magnificent"—as have almost all film critics and military historians since. Because "actual" ground combat footage with any degree of coherence is extremely hard to obtain, a high percentage of World War II "combat" film purporting to show infantry warfare is either long-range or restaged action. The final test for representations of something as horrifically confusing as battle, then, would seem to be accuracy of effect rather than authenticity of material.

In Huston's film and Pyle's dispatch, this accuracy begins with a focus on living men becoming dead bodies in powerfully understated moments of transition. There is a striking poem by Richard Wilbur (who joined the 36th Division outside Cervaro) that describes a rope-twirling, knife-throwing soldier, "violent, neat, and practiced," killed by enemy fire. Reminiscent of the machine-gunned soldier in *San Pietro,* his body "turned / To clumsy dirt before it fell." The poet, amazed and stunned at the change, can only ask: "And what to say of him, God knows. / Such violence. And such repose" ("Tywater," 17-18). This is the massive perplexity at death so evident in renditions of what happened at San Pietro. Young men, so immediately alive, just dead. Joel Westbrook on his way up Hill 1205 encountered a group of dead paratroopers, "caught on their way up to reinforce the First. Splendid, husky young men. They seemed just barely dead. You thought, such healthy men you could shake them a little and they would come alive again." So too with Pyle's Henry Waskow, so too with the images of Huston's film; the grimy quick become the grimy dead, but remain inextricably and inexpressibly linked with the living. This is what less accurate representations of infantry warfare neglect; not death, but the dead and their eloquently unspeakable presence. Killing people, as a Viet Nam veteran and colleague succinctly pointed out to me, doesn't mean that they go away. The physical bodies stay right there, dead, and yet in imagination so alive, to be lugged around, to be worked with, to be talked about, until Graves Registration gets them out of sight. Huston and Pyle both knew this, and constructed memorable representations from their knowledge.

Yet one senses that even this vision is not enough; that no matter how accurate a literary or cinematic representation of battle might seem, the basic otherness of the environment and situation will always distance the noncombatant from the reality of even the most mundane and familiar occurrences in it. Somehow living for days in a muddy Italian foxhole just can't seem as truly miserable and debilitating as doing the same thing in a ditch in one's backyard. Bill Mauldin, a friend of Pyle's and one of the great recorders of American combat in Italy, recognized this problem and wrote some darkly humorous instructions for civilians who want to know what it's "really" like to be a combat infantryman:

> Dig a hole in your backyard while it is raining. Sit in the hole until the water climbs up around your ankles. Pour cold mud down your shirt collar. Sit there for forty-eight hours, and, so there is no danger of your dozing off, imagine a guy is sneaking around waiting for a chance to club you on the head or set your house on fire.

> Get out of the hole, fill a suitcase full of rocks, pick it up, put a shotgun in your other hand, and walk on the muddiest road you can find. Fall flat on your face every few minutes as you imagine big meteors streaking down to sock you.

> After ten or twelve miles (remember—you are still carrying the shotgun and suitcase) start sneaking through the wet brush. Imagine that somebody has booby-trapped your route with rattlesnakes which will bite you if you step on them. Give some friend a rifle and have him blast in your direction once in a while.

> Snoop around until you find a bull. Try to figure out a way to sneak around him without letting him see you. When he does see you, run like hell all the way back to your hole in the back yard, drop the suitcase and shotgun, and get in.

> If you repeat this performance every three days for several months you may begin to understand why an infantryman sometimes gets out of breath. But you still won't understand how he feels when things get tough.

We may never understand how he feels "when things get tough"—something, I think, Pyle and Huston both implicitly recognized in their representations of what happened at San Pietro. There is a lapidary paragraph by Louis Simpson, the poet and former infantryman, that stands as a small monument to the problem of representing what is beyond representation and giving voice to those who have experienced the unspeakable. It is thus inscribed:

> To a foot-soldier, war is almost entirely physical. That is why some men, when they think about war, fall silent. Language seems a betrayal of physical life and a betrayal of those who have experienced it absolutely—the dead.

David Nichols (essay date 1989)

SOURCE: A biographical essay in *Ernie's America: The Best of Ernie Pyle's 1930s Travel Dispatches,* edited with an introduction by David Nichols, Random House, 1989, pp. xvii-l.

[*In the following essay, Nichols provides an overview of Pyle's career.*]

Rare is the American who has not dreamed of dropping whatever he is doing and hitting the road. The dream of unrestrained movement is a distinctly American one, an inheritance bequeathed to subsequent generations by those restless souls who populated the American continent. Travel—away from here, toward a vague and distant destination—is part of our national folklore.

Economic hardship has been a common inducement. Steinbeck's Okies traveled west on Route 66 toward what they hoped would be a better life. Others have had a more spiritual motive: the outer journey has been a mere symbol for the inner, the road a means of finding themselves. Still others have traveled to escape themselves, flight on the open road promising to postpone, if not forestall, some rigorous self-examination.

Motives aside, many are the Americans who could say with Huckleberry Finn, "I reckon I got to light out for the

Territory," and do so, hoping in the American way for some transformation, only to be disappointed with the results. Such came to be the case with Ernie Pyle, who, hopeful and excited, set out from Washington, in late summer of 1935, on a big adventure.

Pyle's bosses at Scripps Howard Newspapers had relieved him of what had become an onerous routine—the managing editorship of the *Washington Daily News*—and were permitting him to go where he pleased and write about what he pleased. There was one stipulation: that he produce six pieces a week, each about a thousand words, for distribution to the twenty-four Scripps Howard papers. Driving a Ford coupe, Pyle and his wife, Jerry, took a leisurely journey through the Northeast and into Nova Scotia, Ontario, and Quebec provinces. Then they crossed back into the United States and traveled through Minnesota, Iowa, and Indiana.

During that time, my father, about to turn ten years old, followed Ernie and Jerry's every move in the pages of the Scripps Howard *Indianapolis Times,* now defunct but then very much alive and delivered to Coats' Garage at Templeton, Indiana, each afternoon by the Indianapolis-to-Chicago Greyhound bus. "Delivered" doesn't quite tell the story. Unfailingly, the driver merely slowed, opened the door, and heaved the rolled newspaper in the direction of the office door. If a curly-haired kid named George Nichols was there to catch it, fine. If not, the brown wrapper wouldn't keep the paper from being torn on the paving stones or soaked in a puddle. But he was usually there, waiting. Meeting the Greyhound assured George first crack at Ernie Pyle's column, which fascinated him. Pyle, after all, was on the move, visiting places my father could only dream of. Where had Pyle been today? What had he seen? With whom had he talked along the way?

The boyhood my father was living in Benton County, in and about the village of Templeton, was much like that Pyle had experienced a quarter century before in Vermillion County, Indiana, fifty miles to the southwest. Like Pyle as a boy and later as an adult, my father was hopelessly afflicted with wanderlust. He wanted to break away from his small town and see what there was to see beyond the corn prairie.

The *Indianapolis Times* subscription belonged to my grandparents, who daily read the news about what Roosevelt was up to, what new New Deal scheme was afoot to help people like themselves, people bent on working for a living but who found themselves frustrated and wary of the future. After digesting the news from Washington, my grandparents turned to Pyle's column, which ran under the standing head HOOSIER VAGABOND. While there's no record of what they thought of Pyle's pieces, they must have enjoyed them, because they kept reading. Whatever their quotient of wanderlust, my grandparents had a good deal more on their minds than travel. They had three children to feed and clothe, and times were tough.

My grandfather was a college history professor, recently out of work, a condition he shared with twenty-five percent of his working-age countrymen. (Another twenty-five percent were "underemployed.") Having looked for other jobs and received no offers, my grandfather had moved the family back to Templeton, his childhood home, where rents were cheap and the soil fertile. The family gardened in the summer and lived through the winter on the canned vegetables. A friendly grocer extended credit for meat and staples.

By the time Pyle finished his first trip as a roving reporter, eight weeks and six thousand miles after he began, the fall term at Templeton School was well under way, and my father and his wanderlust were imprisoned for another nine months in the small brick schoolhouse. When the winter term began, the relentless wind—"the wind of futility" Pyle had so evocatively described on his September pass through the Midwest—was bitter cold and dusting snow through the cornstalks at the edge of town. But by then Pyle was on another trip, this time through the South and Southwest and into Mexico. My father's only escape from school and Templeton and that cold wind of futility was each day's edition of the *Indianapolis Times*.

My father and his parents were but three of the thousands of readers who traveled vicariously with Ernie Pyle over the next seven years, following him to every state in the Union at least three times, crossing the American continent with him thirty-five times, journeying to Canada, Alaska, Hawaii, Mexico, Central and South America, and eventually to England in 1940, where Pyle wrote about the German bombings of London and other cities. On the one hand, it was a hard, relentless job, as Pyle often said in his column, but on the other, it was the acting out of a distinctly American fantasy. And while Pyle was sometimes at a loss to see this, readers like my father never were.

REPORTER FROM HOME

It is impossible to reintroduce Ernie Pyle's largely forgotten travel writings without talking about Pyle the war correspondent. Pyle's journalistic reputation is justly based on his front-line dispatches during World War II, when he lived almost exclusively with the infantry in North Africa, Europe, and the Pacific. So sympathetic and affectionate was his portrait of the infantryman—so adept was he at articulating the frustrations, occasional elations, and constant home-yearnings of men whose lives were lived and lost at the whim of others—that his death assured him a permanent place in postwar mythology. It was a martyr's place, no less, because Pyle needn't have gone to war at all. A profound need to be useful in a time of national crisis was his reason for subjecting himself to dangers he admitted frightened him. When he was killed by a Japanese sniper on the island of Ie Shima, near Okinawa, in April of 1945, civilians and servicemen alike grieved as though they'd lost a personal friend.

Some of his wartime readers had never heard of Pyle before he showed up in North Africa and began filing dispatches datelined WITH THE AMERICAN FORCES IN ALGIERS. It may or may not have occurred to them to wonder how he had acquired the understanding of America and Americans so evident in his columns. But those who had read Pyle before the war knew exactly where those kernels of insight so liberally sprinkled in Pyle's dispatches came from. They knew they derived from years of travel in America before the war sent people off in all directions.

Pyle, in fact, was uniquely equipped to bring the reality of the war and the American men fighting it home to the American people. Few correspondents had traveled so widely in their native country, absorbing regional nuance and making the acquaintance of so many Americans. When Pyle arrived in a new war theater, he could readily describe the countryside in terms of its counterpart in the United States. When a soldier told him about his home, Pyle could resurrect a mental picture of the territory: he'd been there, likely as not more than once. Thus was Pyle able to link the prewar man with the soldier he had become, surrounded now by foreign people and cultures, existing day to day in a world turned upside down, his identity shored up by fond memories of home and a longing to return there.

Pyle's readers appreciated this. Physically insulated from the battles being fought in Europe and the Pacific—but not from home-front deprivations and long, hard hours of work in defense industries—those stateside had to exert considerable imagination to conceive of how these men were living (and dying) so far away, and Pyle's writing helped them do so. It also served to unite, albeit in print, those at war and those at home.

The Pyle pieces that follow will explain a great deal about how Pyle was able to do what he did so well during the war. Present here are the same reporting and writing skills that made him the most popular war correspondent in American newspapers: the intimate approach, the insistence on portraying the people behind the headlines, the physical description that enabled the reader to experience to the fullest what Pyle had experienced, the carefully selected detail. This is not the stuff of ordinary newspaper reporting, but it was the essence of Ernie Pyle's work.

The war changed Ernie Pyle, just as it changed the soldiers he wrote about. The man who wrote the travel dispatches collected here was big-hearted and compassionate; he was also hard-edged and hard-drinking, profane and irreverent. So was Pyle the war correspondent. But there was a difference. At war Pyle was a man connected with his times, engaged and tuned in and daily seeking to evoke such from his readers. During the thirties, Pyle was disengaged and tuned out, seeking to divert his readers' attention from what was bothering them—and him. And those things were not, as we'll see, one and the same.

THE AGENDA

It's worth sorting out just who Ernie Pyle was and how he happened to be at large in America between 1935 and early 1942.

Pyle's roving-reporter pieces answered a need for lighter reading fare in some American newspapers at a critical time in the nation's history, but it would be a mistake to suggest that Pyle had perceived this need and had sought to fill it. Neither he nor his Scripps Howard superiors had given much thought to how they would "market" his work to those twenty-four Scripps Howard editors in places as disparate as New York and Indianapolis, Fort Worth and Knoxville, Albuquerque and Evansville. The Pyle travel column would be included with other material in the company's feature service, Scripps Howard Newspaper Alliance, wired daily to the chain's papers, and would compete for space just as any other feature did.

Pyle's bosses were willing to shelve any concerns they had about this new enterprise and let him have his way for a while. His enthusiasm was infectious, and they knew that was generally an indicator of good things to come. They knew him to be a dependable and resourceful sort, a hard worker, and they didn't want to lose him. But lose him they would if they insisted he continue as managing editor of the *Washington Daily News*. For his part, Ernie wanted to give the roving column a try and see what would turn up. Regardless of how his pieces fared elsewhere in the chain, he knew they would run in the *Daily News*. And besides, his agenda was far more personal than professional. Though he saw the travel column as a challenge, he saw it even more as a means of escape.

Ernie's personal agenda wasn't enough, however. There had to be something more, and it came in the form of a public agenda supplied not by corporate headquarters in New York, nor by Scripps Howard Newspaper Alliance in Washington, but by the chain's editors in all those distant cities—and by their often-vocal subscribers. Returning from a meeting of Scripps Howard editors in June of 1936, Frank Ford, editor of the *Evansville Press,* wrote an encouraging letter to Ernie's parents, Will and Maria Pyle. The editors had discussed the travel column, Ford said, and "almost without exception the editors reported the same experience we have had on the *Press*. At first they used a few of the articles. Then readers started calling up and writing in about them, until they were practically forced to use them daily, regardless of how badly the space was needed for other things. Right now, on the *Press,* if we were to omit even one of them indignant subscribers would call in by the dozen." Ford added, "I think most of the editors would agree with me that Ernie's daily column is more widely read than anything else in the paper."

Ernie's column soon became a daily habit with many editors and their phone-calling and letter-writing readers, who saw his pieces as the perfect antidote to the "too-heavy grist of political, economic, and international news" of the day, as one editor put it. It was refreshing, this "gentle wholesomeness and wide-eyed country-boy absorption with homely but essential trivia," as another wrote. "Escape" was the operative word—escape for Pyle and for his readers, most of whom faced hard times.

There was a depression on, after all—the Great Depression, one of the biggest economic and social catastrophes in American history—and what to do about it was a source of bitter controversy. Americans' enthusiasm for politics has been at best inconstant, but in these years virtually everyone had an opinion about how to get the country moving again, and with good reason. This calamity had affected almost everyone, from the wealthiest industrialist to the poorest day laborer. After the prosperity of the 1920s, the 1930s had been a bitter shock: something had gone terribly wrong with the dream. Bitterness and anxiety were playing themselves out daily in newspapers nationwide.

Pyle knew all about this. The Depression had entered its third year and the American electorate's patience with President Herbert Hoover was all but shot when Pyle became managing editor of the *Daily News* in 1932, just as Hoover and Franklin Roosevelt were campaigning for the presidency. From his vantage point in the newsroom, Pyle saw the American people's hopes rise with Roosevelt in office, only to dip again when the economy failed to revive during the first years of the New Deal. He saw accounts of labor strife, bank closings, the rise of right- and left-wing pressures alike. He saw photographs of unemployed men standing in long lines, seeking work or a bowl of soup and a slice of bread—pictures of men in business suits selling apples for a nickel on street corners. And frankly, none of it interested him much. It was important stuff, of course, and it had to receive prominent play in the paper, but politics, economics, and all the attendant wrangling left him flat. So, for that matter, did newspaper management.

Only reluctantly had Pyle accepted the managing editorship. He had been Scripps Howard's aviation editor and columnist from 1928 through 1932. As a lifelong admirer of men of action, Pyle had been perfectly suited to convey to an equally admiring public news of the pilots, their "ships," and the fledgling airlines that employed both. He had thoroughly enjoyed his first attempt at personal journalism and his first experience with insider reporting—becoming intimately involved with a group of people and then explaining that group to outsiders, just as he would do with the infantry during the war. In those years he had developed a highly readable style, intimate and anecdotal, and the column had enjoyed extraordinary success in the *Daily News* and later in other Scripps Howard papers. Pyle's readers had been an expressive lot and had sent letters from all over the country when a column had especially touched them.

By 1932, aviation was no longer the rough-and-tumble business it had once been. Much of its early pioneering spirit had given way to a more businesslike approach, its

randomness to regulation. The old romance was waning. Even so, Pyle had been reluctant to give it up, and even more reluctant to return to the copy desk, where he'd spent most of his early newspaper career. A facile copy editor and a good headline writer, he hated doing both. He had accepted the position because during the Depression it made sense to take a job his bosses badly wanted him to take.

His decision dismayed aviation readers. "Sorry to read you are leaving—seems like losing an old friend," wrote one. Another closed his letter with a cautionary note that proved prophetic. "Please don't forget the old aviation column, however," he wrote, "and also don't forget that work behind the desk without air is bad."

There followed three difficult years of trying to put out a daily newspaper on the tightest of budgets, haggling with upper management for meager pay increases for his staff only to have them taken away when the economy worsened. He had done a good job of it. In his three years as managing editor, Pyle had fired only one employee, an incompetent copy boy. A diplomat, he could extract hard work from his people under circumstances that tried everyone's patience. But working every day in the noisy, congested newsroom, breathing air thick with tobacco smoke, a fair portion of which was his, Pyle had longed for release. Work behind a desk without air truly *was* bad. So was hard drink, consumed at the regular intervals and in the fantastic quantities Ernie, Jerry, and their friends were accustomed to in these years.

This was an era when heavy drinking was as essential a part of being a newspaperman as speedy two-fingered typing. Ernie and Jerry had been drinking to excess for years, but his stint as managing editor had been an especially stressful time, and now they were drinking more than ever. Although both were alcoholics by 1935, Ernie's nights of "alcoholic insanity," as one *Daily News* associate called them, were offset by his having to be at work the next morning. Jerry had no such check on her drinking. She was a recluse, spending her days alone in their shabby apartment, reading books, writing poetry, playing the piano, having a drink or two at lunch—anything to take the edge off the despair she kept tacitly at bay.

Pyle worried about Jerry, and she about him. He feared he was a burned-out newspaper hack at age thirty-four. The job aged them both, Jerry no less than Ernie, for it was up to her to soothe his sagging emotions. When Pyle had been slow to recover from influenza in December of 1934, the *Daily News* had granted him a leave of absence, and he and Jerry had left Washington for an auto tour of the West and Southwest. The trip had been redemptive. Pyle returned to Washington convinced that travel had to figure prominently in his life, just as he'd thought it would during his years at Indiana University. He wrote a series of eleven articles about his trip for the paper, and one of his bosses said the pieces had "a Mark Twain quality that knocked my eye out." Ernie decided that never again could he allow his writing skills to go unsummoned.

Here, too, the trip had made him question his staying in Washington. It had been a good city to be young in, but those wide-open spaces out West exerted a powerful pull. The small towns were a welcome change, too. Washington had become too big, too busy, too congested with New Dealers trying to save the world. And he knew that as long as he stayed in the city, his social circle would continue to consist mostly of newspaper people, and that the drinking would go on and on. It was time for a change.

Such was Pyle's personal agenda in early August 1935, when, doubtless hungover after a rousing farewell party, he and Jerry locked their apartment door, put a few bags in the trunk of the car, and drove their Ford coupe out of Washington and onto the open road. Pyle had no way of knowing that his personal agenda would mesh nicely with the public agenda editors and their readers would set for him in the months and years to come. Nor would he have cared. For now, just getting out of town was enough.

NO EASY JOB

Americans born around the turn of the century had grown up with the automobile. Pyle was eight years old when Henry Ford introduced the Model T, an adolescent when Ford began mass-producing his car for the common man on an assembly line. By the time Pyle began his roving-reporter assignment, the automobile had gone a long way toward transforming American life and the American countryside.

Even a decade earlier, Pyle's travel assignment would have been a terrific hardship. Roads had been either haphazardly marked or not marked at all, their quality a study in diversity. Roadside accommodations had been bleak or nonexistent, and the cars themselves had been too uncomfortable for anything but local travel. Drivers had justly considered motoring a perilous undertaking. Traffic on any thoroughfare had been constantly assaulted by traffic on intersecting roads. Americans had just begun getting used to automobiles in any number, and drivers' safety habits still left much to be desired. Night driving of any distance had been especially dangerous.

By 1935 things were much improved, but driving long distances was still altogether more rigorous than it is today, all the more so in Pyle's case because of the frequency with which he traveled. Roads were still of uneven quality; interstates, with their limited access, were years in the future. Cars of the day were more comfortable than their predecessors but still lacked such amenities as automatic transmissions, air conditioning, and comfortable seats. Pyle was a short, skinny man, and after a long day of motoring cross-country, he often ached from the car's constant bumping over rough back roads. He never knew whether the hotel bed he would sleep in that night would be comfortable or as bumpy as that day's roads. Ernie and Jerry weren't fussy about food, and they were fortunate in this: the quality of roadside restaurants varied as widely as the quality of the roads themselves. And these were the least of their difficulties.

Having already sustained a daily column for almost four years, Ernie knew something of the difficulty of turning out an appealing piece on deadline. But this was harder by far than the aviation column. Here there was no focus, no network of contacts to tie into. Nor were there any economies of effort. Pyle's every travel column was the result of his effort and his alone, not an elaboration of an item someone had phoned into his desk at the *Daily News*. Six pieces a week—six thousand words—is a lot of copy, the product of hours of labor at the typewriter. Consider, too, the travel and interviewing time, and it's no wonder Pyle was defensive when his friends accused him of being permanently on vacation. Even so, the fruitfulness of Pyle's efforts was at one with the difficulty of getting there, because getting there, wherever that was, always became part of the story. Ernie considered what happened along the way to be worth writing about, and his readers agreed.

Network radio had come into its own by the mid-1930s, and national magazines were abundant, but the mass-market economy, slowed now by the Depression, had yet to work its leveling effect on American regions. America was a teeming patchwork of local variety, its regional distinctions potent. The day of a television set in every home was still decades off, and people in one region were still curious about how people lived elsewhere. To the observant and curious visitor, local color and custom abounded. The continental United States was a big place, three quarters the size of Europe. There was lots of ground for Pyle to cover and lots of people to meet.

Local editors could be counted on for tips, and so could readers, who sent Pyle letters and postcards by the score. He filed reader suggestions by state in a little wooden box he carried in the car. Mostly, though, Pyle found his columns by chance. He rarely took notes, rarely conducted anything approximating a formal interview. Where he went and when were almost always up to him. He would collect material for a week or so, then find a congenial hotel in which to write. There followed a hellish several days of frantic composition, revising and retyping, keeping carbons for his files, and sending the originals to Scripps Howard Newspaper Alliance. With few exceptions, Ernie dispatched his pieces via first-class mail. In seven years, not a single one was lost.

NOSTALGIA

In 1893, seven years before Pyle's birth, the historian Frederick Jackson Turner had declared the American frontier closed and with it the first period of American history. But in Pyle's fanciful imagination—and to a lesser extent in actual fact—the American West was still frontier country. During his travel years, Pyle returned again and again to Arizona, New Mexico, Texas, Utah, Wyoming, and Colorado, their big skies and vast, thinly populated spaces a delightful contrast to the crowded

East, which he had grown to dislike intensely. "Am I glad to get West again!" he wrote a friend from Seattle in the spring of 1937. "The three months in the East damn near killed me (literally)—too many things to do, too many people to see, too much of everything. When I crossed the Mississippi River I felt as though I'd shed a big burden."

It was in the West—the most fabled of American regions, object of our national restlessness and our search for a better, less restricted life—that Pyle felt the freedom he'd hoped for. A child of the midlands, he longed for drama in terrain, nature writ large. The far-reaching horizons of the desert country and the sheer rugged beauty of the mountain country inspired in him a sense of independence and well-being. It also fueled his yearning for a mythic past, the lawless, excessive, hard-driving Old West of the frontier, known to men of his grandfather's generation but alive now mostly in legend and in the romantic imaginations of men like himself.

True, he loved the land and the freedom implicit in its openness. He liked Westerners for their democratic sensibilities, their friendliness and general companionability. In this they were like the rural Midwesterners he had grown up with, not at all like Easterners, for whom class lines were sharply drawn and forever the object of hushed speculation. But the greater part of Pyle's attraction to the West was pure nostalgia. He was a man approaching middle age who believed he'd lived his life one step removed from dramas spectacular beyond imagination. Missing World War I because his parents wanted him to finish high school had been an especially bitter disappointment, all the more so because his closest neighborhood friend had gone to the war.

People for whom the past exerts such a bittersweet tug harbor the sense that time has betrayed them by positioning them in such prosaic circumstances as the present. They reluctantly content themselves with searches for others' imperfect memories and the discovery of a few relics here and there. So it was with Pyle and the West and, to a lesser extent, Alaska. Many times in the following pages occur sentiments much like these from a column on Virginia City, Nevada, atop the Comstock Lode, "the richest vein of ore ever found in America." Virginia City's glory days were past by the time Pyle arrived in November of 1937.

> I wanted to be impressed, and excited, when I came around the bend and saw this sight of my grandfather's day. But I don't even have that privilege. The skeleton is there, but progress has slipped inside the bones and made a mundane stirring. . . .
>
> Why, I wonder, can't an old place really die? Why can't it lie down amid its old drama and wrap its romantic robes about it and pose there, unstirring and ghostlike, for the trembling contemplation of us latecomers?

Pyle's nostalgia found its best expression in the West, but it was by no means limited to that region. Nostalgia, in fact, was endemic to the whole roving-column enterprise. "American roads have always been more about the past and future than about the present," Phil Patton has written. Pyle's avoidance of the big cities and his fondness for small towns and the open countryside was in itself evocative of the recent past, though less obviously so.

As a boy, growing up on a farm a few miles outside Dana, Indiana—population about a thousand—Ernie had been a restless child, anxious for an expanded life. Early on he had decided that most of what interested him was happening elsewhere, and that he wanted badly to be a part of it. Arriving in Washington to work on the *Daily News* in 1923, after a few months of reporting on a newspaper in La Porte, Indiana, Pyle had been pleased not only to have a job in the nation's capital, but to leave the Midwest behind as well. Washington represented all the expanded possibilities he'd hoped for. Now in his midthirties, Ernie entertained the notion that what he'd left behind had a validity all its own, though he would never have dreamed of returning to the farm or settling in a small town. In reality, what he had left behind had changed dramatically, and he knew this.

By 1935, America was primarily an urban-industrial nation, but the folk memory of a recent past lived on farms and in small towns was still vivid, all the more so during the Depression. For no matter how elementary was unemployed workers' understanding of economics, they soon learned that their misfortune in these hard times was largely outside their control, the result of their dependence on a system that had gone awry. The temptation to romanticize the past in agrarian America was hard to resist. (Conveniently overlooked in these moments of reverie was the truth that rural America was beset with problems all its own in the Depression years, and had been for well over a decade.) Living in a city often meant surrendering the close personal contact with friends, neighbors, and family that had marked their early years. Thus Ernie's datelines from small, out-of-the-way places were themselves a pastoral look back. When Pyle wrote about his family on the farm in Indiana, he chronicled the near-term American past, still recognizable but changed forever. And his readers, most of whom lived in cities, responded warmly. One wrote Pyle's mother in 1939, "I hope that you may sometimes think, as is true, that through your son you have a part in bringing interest, entertainment, education, and a greater faith in the goodness of people to so many who read his column. It seems to me you have contributed largely to the world."

In any but its mildest form, nostalgia is at cross purposes with life as it's lived. Ernie was pensive about the changing American countryside, but he was still very much the individualist who as a boy longed to shed the restrictions of country life. Thus many of the people whose stories Pyle told were a bit offbeat, living slightly apart from, if not exactly contrary to, the mainstream. This was no accident. For in Pyle's view, character proceeded from eccentricity. The greater the likelihood of an individual's neighbors considering him to be an oddball, the greater his character quotient. When Pyle wrote about people on the road, he defined their character as the sum total of observable details of personal thought, circumstance, or action, and he piled these on at great length. Some were revealing, some not, but all spoke to Pyle's incomplete understanding of character—an understanding based on externalities. He once wrote a column about the world bowling champion, a man who was "intelligent and friendly and a gentleman, but he is not colorful. He doesn't brag or say odd things that make a man interesting in print." Pyle searched out people sufficiently odd to be interesting in print.

The routineness, the banality, of most people's lives struck Ernie and Jerry as the equivalent of premature death. In a 1935 piece on movies versus real life, Pyle wrote:

> Of course, characters on the screen are made to suffer their tragedies, just as we humans do. But their suffering is so dramatic and romantic, while ours here on the globe is the dull, achy kind that embitters and wastes, with so little drama to soften it.

Why in real life, he asked, can't we humans "just go stare out a window and bow our heads and look grave and heartbroken for a few seconds, denoting a long period of grief and yearning, and not have to go through the actual months and years of it?" For Pyle's part, a "flash of happiness" would be preferable to "happiness strung out," because then "there is no dulling." He concluded:

> Yes, just wake me up for the peaks and the valleys, just the tops and the bottoms of them, and please have the anesthetist ready when we come to the plains, and the long bright days when nothing happens.

During his travel years, Pyle went a long way toward acting on these sentiments. Forever on the move, he sought the peaks and valleys, a journalistic outsider who arrived and departed quickly. In New Mexico, an isolated family so enjoyed a visit from the Pyles they begged them to stay. "But we had engagements ahead and we had to run away, as we always have to run away," Ernie wrote.

THE TRAVELING LIFE

Although the 1930s were a time of unusually strong community sentiment among the American people, the Pyles shared in this not at all. They had friends from all walks of life, but their rootlessness allowed them to control their interaction with other people to an unhealthy degree. They were without the scrutiny that close friends and family, living nearby, can bring to bear on misguided ideas and actions. Ernie and Jerry created for themselves an insular life on the road, neatly contained and free of obligations other than maintaining the column. "Stability cloaks you with a thousand little personal responsibilities, and we have been able to flee from them," Ernie wrote of their traveling life.

It was a manageable existence—bags systematically packed in the trunk, hotels picked according to a scheme Pyle worked out—and despite its being premised on constant movement, it had a quirky rhythm, broken only by periodic drinking bouts and frequent ailments, the alcohol often contributing to the illness. Ernie and Jerry were aware of what was happening in the country, but their traveling life protected them from most of the details. They were out of touch with the world around them and eventually with each other. On a 1937 trip to Alaska, Pyle wrote his college friend Paige Cavanaugh, "I haven't had any mail for three weeks, and haven't seen a newspaper or heard a radio for a week, so I don't know what's going on in the world and furthermore don't give a shit." Even when he was getting mail, reading newspapers, and listening to the radio, Pyle showed little interest in the big events that shaped his times.

Though their origins were common enough—his in rural Indiana, hers in small-town Minnesota—Ernie and Jerry had consciously distanced themselves from middle-class America for most of their adult lives. When they were married by a justice of the peace in July of 1925, they didn't tell their Washington friends; they simply moved in together and told everyone they were "shacking up"—everyone, that is, except their parents. Jerry even substantiated the fiction by refusing to wear a wedding ring until she was in her early forties.

Even as youthful puckishness goes, this was bold for the times and an indication of the extent to which the Pyles saw themselves as immune to middle-class pieties and expectations. Though they were without the smugness that so often attends success, the very idea of success was something they made fun of. The way they had lived in Washington reflected this. Their priorities had been to pay the rent, send a little money home to their parents, buy food (not much, for neither cared about eating), and spend the balance on liquor and tobacco. Clothes, furniture, having a family—none of it interested them. Their outlook on life, fatalistic and frankly self-indulgent, was primarily a product of Jerry's manic swings and Ernie's emotional pliability, which rendered him all too vulnerable to her moodiness.

Ernie and Jerry were both master dissemblers who, for the most part, had the good sense and good taste to keep their contempt for convention to themselves. Most everyone they met genuinely liked them, particularly Ernie, who, though shy, had an easygoing, democratizing manner. This spilled over into the column and accounted in no small part for its success. "I find that kids, Civil War veterans, capitalists, professional men, and WPA workers all read everything you write," the editor of the *Rocky Mountain News* told Pyle in a letter. And from the editor of the *Oklahoma News* came this: "[Readers] say, 'Ernie talks our language.' That, I think, is the . . . key to the column's success. It's folksy, human and as unsophisticated as nine out of ten readers"—a compliment, apparently.

What the Oklahoma editor mistook for a lack of sophistication in the writing was actually a savvy bit of calculation on Pyle's part. Because the subject matter of the column was in constant flux, Pyle himself was the only link between daily installments. He understood this. He knew his popularity was based upon his readers' illusion that they knew him personally, and his approach to the column fostered the perception. The voice of the travel columns was a carefully developed product that owed its variety to the demands of the marketplace and to the rigorous nature of the assignment itself. And though it shared much with Pyle, it belied much, too.

Most human-interest columnists today produce three or four pieces a week and draw their material primarily from the local. Pyle operated nationally and published six times a week. Column material was abundant, particularly early on, but six thousand words a week was a tall order. Because he had to allow for travel time and the occasional unproductive segment of a trip, Pyle often resorted to personal essays to keep the column going.

The essay persona was that of a Chaplinesque character forever beguiled by faulty zippers, lingering colds, errant drivers, dreams of glory as a race car driver, and snake phobia. Here was a likeable reporter with an uncannily good ear for American idiom, an endearingly self-effacing manner, and a good sense of humor (laconic, in the Midwestern way)—a man for whom the American romance was alive and well, the Depression be damned. "We must print [the] bad news—but fortunate is the newspaper publisher who can balance that bad news with your wholesome and cheerful account of your journeyings," the editor of the *Memphis Press-Scimitar* told Ernie.

Pyle was often not so temperate in his private correspondence. Here the column persona gave way to the more acerbic side of his personality. From the Yukon, Pyle wrote Cavanaugh:

> [Alaska is] too damn cold for me, even in June. It's just like Hollywood—warm for about three hours in the middle of the day, and the rest of the time you freeze your balls off. Haven't had a comfortable day since I left Seattle two and a half weeks ago. I'm a hot-country man. . . .

Mostly, Pyle's columns were characterized by a moderate voice, but sometimes he let fly at people he clearly disliked—auto mechanics were frequent targets—or disapproved of. Here he is on Americans living and working in the Panama Canal Zone:

> One of their own, who sees them clearly, has called them "stall-fed." They have surrendered the important quality of egotism—the eternal conviction that you could do it better than the other guy. They have given up all personal ambition, natural instincts of competition, all the lovely mystery of life, for a security that gives them a life of calm and a vague discontent.

That last clause is interesting: *for a security that gives them a life of calm and a vague discontent.* It describes with some disdain the aspirations of the very audience for which Pyle was writing: Depression-bound stay-at-homes who looked to his column for a vicarious lift from their troubled circumstances. For many Americans in the Depression years, security was a much-sought-after commodity in whose name they would have happily endured discontent, vague or otherwise. His bohemian posturing aside, Pyle's restlessness was forever at war with his own deep need for security. Every so often he needed to trumpet his disdain for the latter, as if seeing it in print would confirm his defiance of it.

THE CURSE

For Pyle motion was an end in itself, a trait he shared with millions of his countrymen. Unlike most of them, though, he had the means to realize his restive dream, and increasingly it became a curse. The pressures increased with the column's success; what had begun for him as a flight from encroaching obligations and responsibilities had become a tremendous burden. Editors began to vie for his circulation-building presence in their areas, just as military units would compete for his morale-building attention during the war. Five Scripps Howard editors in Ohio sent a joint telegram to Pyle's superiors in Washington in June of 1938:

> OHIO SERIES BY ERNIE PYLE WOULD BE OF VITAL IMPORTANCE IN DEVELOPING VACATION READING TO HELP HOLD CIRCULATION IN THE OHIO INDUSTRIAL CITIES PARTICULARLY HARD HIT BY THE DEPRESSION. . . . PLEASE <u>GIVE THIS IMMEDIATE</u> <u>URGENT CONSIDERATION</u> BECAUSE ERNIE PYLE IN OHIO WOULD BE A PRACTICAL ASSET WHICH COULD NOT BE EQUALED BY ERNIE PYLE IN NEW ENGLAND, SOUTH AMERICA OR ANY OTHER REMOTE PARTS.

Pyle went, begrudgingly.

Readers, too, applied pressure. They wrote him long, appreciative letters, some pouring out their problems, some enclosing tips for future columns, a few chiding him for his not-always-perfect grammar or his occasional use of mild profanity in the column. Whatever the content of the letter, Pyle believed its author deserved an answer. At first he responded to reader mail himself, but later he hired a secretary in Washington to answer the letters. More problematic were those readers who showed up to meet him in person. "We fled San Diego yesterday," Pyle wrote his friend Paige Cavanaugh in October 1939.

> . . . I am disillusioned with fame. Not disillusioned, for I never had illusions about it, but I'm badly frightened. For in San Diego, Mr. Pyle is not second even to God, and the clamor that was set up down there really got me panicky, and we almost went under for the third time under the tidal wave of dinners and drinks and visitors and people who "just want to shake hands" and you know. . . . The whole thing, Mr. Cavanaugh, is something that

I do not want anything of, and why can't a fellow just quietly make an honest living?

Readers in the Southwest reciprocated Pyle's enthusiasm for their region with enthusiasm for him and his column. On stops in Deming, Silver City, and Lordsburg, New Mexico—all within the circulation area of the *El Paso Herald-Post*—Pyle couldn't leave his hotel room or eat in the coffee shop without fans crowding around him, all expressing pleasure in his work. Pyle wrote Lee Miller, his editor:

> I know it must sound awful to you for a guy like me to say this, but we actually know what it is to have to eat in our rooms and sneak out the back way. I'm not trying to overtoot my own horn and I certainly couldn't have the courage to be so immodest to anyone else, but I am just trying to show you that the powers-that-be have no idea what a hold the column really has—and what a basis for selling it if they were interested.

Pyle was alternately pushing for and retreating from syndication outside the Scripps Howard chain, but he was always cranky over whichever way management was leaning at the moment. Already a celebrity, he knew the pressures on him would redouble with increased circulation; on the other hand, as he told Miller, "I'd gaily take a little more money if I could get it, but even that isn't on my mind, for we're able to save some as it is. I guess I'm just like an old screwball I wrote about up at Silver City—all I really want is to be appreciated."

Appreciated by the masses, he might have added, for just as Pyle had learned how intoxicating constant travel is, he was learning how addictive is the attention of strangers. Never mind how "panicky" this made him, or how fame was something he wanted nothing of. Pyle knew perfectly well that a man whose name and picture appeared above a daily newspaper column—especially one that touched as many responsive chords as his did—had no basis for bemoaning his inability to "just quietly make an honest living." He also knew that he had given up any semblance of a normal life for an enterprise that was getting way out of hand.

PARTING

When Ernie and Jerry said goodbye to each other at the Toledo railroad station in April of 1937—she bound for Washington to close out their apartment and put their furniture in storage, he to Alaska for three months of hard travel—both were sad, as Pyle said in the column. Though he believed the Alaska trip would be too much of a hardship for Jerry, the prospect of a three-month separation from her was a difficult one for Ernie: Jerry had been a big help to him on the road, just as she had been during their Washington days. She had helped him overcome his melancholy over the column's not being well received one place or another, or over his inability to get a particular piece just right.

Jerry was an extremely literate person, a good critic, and a shrewd judge of character. She was also an ideal traveling companion for Ernie in that she talked very little (thus giving him time to think as he drove), made few demands on his schedule, and could generally be counted on to retype his columns once he'd pencil-edited the drafts. This is not to say she was passive; on the contrary, she exerted a powerful influence over Ernie and his sensibilities. But she had no career aspirations of her own—none that she voiced, anyway. Pyle's readers knew her not as Jerry but as "That Girl who rides with me," which sounds condescending and offhand, but which was actually a bow to Jerry's demand for privacy. She had no desire to be known through the pages of a newspaper.

Jerry wasn't particularly interested in the traveling life, but this didn't alarm Ernie. As he saw it, life anywhere—their old life in Washington included—held very little for her. Jerry was chronically uninterested in anything but reading, writing poetry, working crossword puzzles, and playing the piano. With the exception of the piano, her interests were mobile enough: couldn't she read *The New Yorker* or work crossword puzzles in Garden City, Kansas, every bit as well as she could in Washington? It was all right that she didn't accompany him to interviews—she was forever waiting in a hotel room or in the car—or share in the romance of the open road. The traveling life was still better than sitting alone in an apartment all day, dwelling upon whatever it was she dwelled upon.

As it turned out, Jerry didn't agree. And although they traveled together periodically in subsequent years, their parting in Toledo was the beginning of ten years of being more apart than together, with Pyle either traveling around the United States or reporting from war zones thousands of miles away. It was also the beginning of Jerry's descent into a hellish spiral of depression and drug addiction.

THE CRACK-UP

One expects to return home at the end of a journey, but where was home for Jerry? A changing woman, she lacked so much as a permanent address against which to measure the scope and nature of the changes. Her life was without context, anything or anyone to divert her attention outward, away from the churning emotions that so frequently kept her in the darkest of troubled states.

Living with her mother in Minnesota or her sister in Denver, staying with friends in Washington or Albuquerque, Jerry's mental health badly deteriorated. Already an alcoholic, she became addicted to Benzedrine, an amphetamine, which, mixed with alcohol, gave her a short-term synergistic high and unnatural vigor, after which she would be listless and without appetite for days. Add this cross-addiction to her longtime dependence on caffeine and nicotine and her lack of interest in food or exercise, and it takes little imagination to see that Jerry was physically and psychologically headed for disaster. But Ernie missed or ignored a great many signs of what was to come.

After all, it's difficult to comprehend the depth of another's despair when you're forever lighting out for the territory. Out of personal preference and professional necessity, Pyle was long accustomed to ignoring suffering around him. As we have seen, he moved quickly in and out of the lives of the people he encountered on the road, quick to sense where the story lay and quick to move on. Now he moved in and out of Jerry's life, too, seeing her when he could, traveling with her when she was able or willing to ride along, but always, always on the move. Just as he had fled Washington to avoid the debilitating complexities of the managing editor job, now he fled Jerry to escape the seeming hopelessness of her condition and what it implied for both their futures. He had so arranged his life that his personal compulsions took on the force of necessity: there was *always* the column to think about.

A deeply intuitive man capable of expressing what he saw or felt clearly and powerfully, Pyle was nonetheless badly confused about intimacy—its meaning, what it demands of those who share in it—just as he was confused about character and what it comprises. He once wrote, "We have worked up a whole new continent-wide list of intimate friends, and consequently we keep up a personal correspondence with about three hundred people." It's impossible to maintain a personal correspondence with three hundred people, or even half that many, but the statement reveals much about Pyle. Like most of us, he was an uneven sort, operating at some remove from his deeper self. Constant travel only abetted this. A man spread too thinly over too great an area, he was incapable of the depth of understanding, the jumps of creative intuition, that Jerry's situation called for.

Ernie had long worried that Jerry's not having a permanent interest in something that at least marginally involved other people would lead to problems. His sense of all this was vague but nonetheless prescient. For as Ernie's popularity grew, Jerry's feelings were mixed. Much as she believed he deserved the recognition and was glad he was getting it, Jerry clearly resented the extent to which Ernie's readers and the editors who ran his column had taken her place in his life.

He was no longer hers. She no longer exerted a major claim on his attention. "I'm just a pawn in the great newspaper game," she wrote a friend. Sure, his letters were profusely sentimental, yearning for the old days when they were always together, but he chose to live his life away from her. Oh, she understood the reasons, and they made sense enough. Yes, she could rejoin him on the road anytime she wished, and he'd be glad of it; but except for certain spectacular instances when she became too sick to care for herself, it was the road and the column and all those readers who held sway. Though Ernie seemed genuinely delighted at their reunions, he also seemed to have gotten along well enough without her in the interim. She could hardly say the same for herself.

In the best of circumstances, marriage is a complex web of interdependency, hard to sort out; in difficult circumstances, it virtually defies scrutiny—certainly from without and often from within, too. But that complex web becomes a hopeless tangle when asked to accommodate mental illness, multiple addictions, and sexual dysfunction. According to Lee Miller, Pyle's editor, "during some of their years together [Ernie and Jerry's] was a nonphysical union, due to a functional incapacity on Ernie's part. . . ." Pyle was impotent and had been since early in the travel years. When they traveled together, Ernie and Jerry slept in twin beds, except in those rare instances when only a double bed was available—and then both slept poorly.

Ernie's problem further compounded Jerry's troubles, especially when, lonely and depressed, she decided that having a child would answer her emotional needs. She apparently had some doubt about whether her husband's impotence was organic or emotional, a reaction to her, perhaps, or a general fear of intimacy. When Pyle answered her letter about wanting a child, he told Jerry that it would be irresponsible for people their age—forty-one—to have a baby; and further, "I *can't* give you a child, as you know. I haven't been lying when I've told you that the power of sex had gone from me."

Traveling together through New Mexico during the summer of 1940, Ernie and Jerry had to part ways when they received news that Jerry's mother had broken her shoulder and needed Jerry to look after her. Ernie took her to the airport. "We are wandering people," he wrote in the column, "and fate hurls us about to odd destinations. We don't know when we will see each other again. When she got on the plane, we both felt a kind of futility, a small desire to travel again, for a little, in the same direction." They *were* traveling in the same direction, toward mutual disaster, and it came in the early spring of 1941, when Ernie returned from three months in bomb-torn England.

The trip had been a great success for Pyle and the column. It had revived his flagging spirits and had given his writing new energy and increased circulation. There was also the pleasure of returning to a real home: the Pyles had built a house—the first and only one they would ever own—on what was then the outskirts of Albuquerque, and Jerry had seen to its decoration during Ernie's absence. She had looked forward to his homecoming after a long absence on a trip that had horrified her. But there was to be no break from the pressure, no quiet pleasure in their new house with its wonderful view of the mesa. Pyle had to rent a hotel room in which to write by day, so many were the friends stopping by to see him after his long trip. After a short time at Albuquerque, he had to hit the road again to keep the column going: his editors didn't want to lose the new subscribers the column had gained during Ernie's time overseas.

There followed a tortuous year during which Jerry, alone, tried to kill herself by turning on all the gas jets on the stove and closing herself off in the kitchen, and during which, also alone, she almost bled to death in her bed when a stomach ulcer, irritated by alcohol and poor diet, hemorrhaged. On both occasions Ernie dropped the column and stayed at home to care for her. Continuity is the lifeblood of any column, particularly one as personal as Ernie's, but his Scripps Howard superiors were understanding, although many papers outside the chain dropped Pyle for other features during his protracted leaves.

Ernie resumed the column in December 1941, the week after the Japanese attack on Pearl Harbor and the American declaration of war on Japan. Jerry's stomach had healed, and her health continued to improve under the watchful eye of a private nurse Ernie had hired—or so the nurse and Ernie thought. His letters tell the story. "I've talked with Albuquerque every night for the last four nights—one night twice," Pyle wrote to Cavanaugh on March 19, 1942:

> Jerry has been put under opiates for three days. Nurses around the clock again. Just went clear to pot again the last couple of weeks. Fooling everybody in the daytime, and drinking all night apparently. The nurse told me she carried from her room *ten* empty quart [bourbon] bottles at the end of one week!

Pyle felt himself thinning out, the roving-reporter adventure gone pale; his writing lacked the verve of the earlier years and was now a flat recitation of a city or a region's vital statistics or tourist appeal. Increasingly he relied on his column persona to carry the daily installment, but it, too, had thinned, its tone becoming desperately chatty. Pyle had found the traveling life held endless banality, just as the everyday, rooted life did. Now no amount of road noise could diminish the hum between his ears. Alone, he had much time to think about himself and Jerry—their onetime life together and their lives apart, the wreckage of it all.

Ernie had hopefully sought treatment for his impotence from a group of San Diego urologists in the spring of 1942. This, too, was a disaster and left him convinced his sex life was over forever. The treatments were "agonizing and cruel" and yielded no results. Bitter, he wrote Cavanaugh, "The doctors all say, 'Now get lots of intercourse.' Which is like W. C. Fields' sure cure for insomnia—'Get lots of sleep.'"

Jerry was a difficult person, dismissive in her dogmatic way of others' attempts to scrutinize her. And yet, she reached out for help in her own tortured fashion, assuring Ernie that at last she was on the way to recovery, that she had regained some of her earlier resilience and composure and could begin to put herself back together. There was a time when Ernie would have been only too happy to hear this, only too willing to believe it. But now he was beyond ignoring the reality of their lives by pining for the time when Jerry's inner life had been more in check and his limited powers of comprehension less taxed. Now, in March 1942, he voiced to friends his doubts about Jerry's ever recovering.

After a month of exchanging tortured letters and phone calls with Jerry, Ernie was on the verge of collapse himself. He dropped the column—forever, he thought, or at least until the war was over—and returned to Albuquerque. On April 14, Ernie and Jerry were divorced. Both regretted the move, and yet neither could think of any other solution. Ernie hoped the shock of the divorce would force Jerry to right her life. Remarriage was a possibility, assuming she got busy and solved her problems. Meanwhile, they continued to live together in the house in Albuquerque, and Ernie continued to look after her. Her condition worsened. Jerry, Ernie wrote Cavanaugh on May 5,

> has been in a Christ-awful shape this week. Nurse and doctor here almost constantly. Part of it is genuine, part of it self-induced. She hasn't had any Benzedrine since January, but yesterday she pleaded with the doctor and cried like a baby for some. It was so pitiful I couldn't even stay in the room. He told her no, that she had to face it this time right out of her own soul. And she is much better this morning, although still very depressed. She just can't accept the fact that we are divorced and that I'm going away again.

Again leaving Jerry in the care of private nurses, Pyle traveled to Washington to discuss his future with Scripps Howard management, which wanted him to start writing again, perhaps take another foreign trip. Shortly, the government would cease to draft men thirty-seven and older, but for now Pyle was eligible for service. He took the Army physical and was declared 1-A. Meanwhile, the Army's having delayed his induction, he prepared to travel to Britain, this time to report on the training of American troops. While the government processed his travel request, Ernie worked on the copy desk of the *Washington Daily News*. He wrote to Jerry on May 8 that his friends and former colleagues in Washington were "under the impression that I've gone all to pieces, and damned if they haven't got me about half convinced of it myself." His letter to Jerry continued:

> I feel that if I could just run back to Albuquerque and start a life of utter simplicity I would be happy. But I guess I can't, and I have determined not to come back until you have won your great fight. I can't tell you the sadness and almost overwhelming frenzy and depression I've been in these three days; and the feeling that I couldn't live unless I came back to you; but I won't, darling, I'm determined that even should I go clear under, I will not come running back until you have had a chance to do your job under these new conditions. I am confident that you can and will do it; otherwise I would be utterly insane with despair.

Nineteen days later, Jerry's sister and brother-in-law, with the support of Ernie and other family members, took her by train to a sanitarium at Pueblo, Colorado. Jerry was sedated to the point of unconsciousness. Ernie's travel plans were firm by mid-June, and he arrived in New York to await a plane to Ireland. From the Hotel Algonquin, he wrote Jerry a farewell note. The date was June 18, 1942.

Darling—

I am taking off within the hour. I came here because I couldn't stand to go to the Piccadilly without you. I am not excited about going, but do feel a last-minute sense of fatalism or something. I am all alone. Be my old Jerry when I come back. I love you.

Ernie

THE STEADYING POINT

Pyle's was a generation born to calamity. Many a young man born at the turn of the century had fought in World War I, had difficulty finding employment upon his return, had struggled to raise a family during the Depression, and now, in early middle age, watched as a son or sons left home to fight in yet another global war. Pyle had shared in none of this. His parents had blocked his joining the Army during the first war, and he had been steadily and profitably employed throughout the Depression. Because they had no children, Ernie and Jerry were spared both the expense of raising a family and worry over how sons would fare in what promised to be another long, bloody war.

In his seven years of travel, Pyle had stiffly resisted doing pieces on serious matters. Apart from a series on the Dust Bowl and one on public relief in the small town of North Platte, Nebraska, Pyle's dispatches had been mostly free of any but casual references to the economic disasters visited upon millions of Americans in the 1930s. When his editors suggested the North Platte series, Ernie bristled. "I don't like that idea, it sounds too important!" he complained to Cavanaugh.

In the range of options open to him, in his freedom to indulge his restlessness, and in his disconnectedness from community ties, Pyle shared little with his countrymen. By the time America entered the war he was a man so out of step with the times that he despaired of ever finding a place again. In the American way he had equated movement with growth, and circumstances had proved the fallacy of the notion. "Being on the move is no substitute for feeling," Eudora Welty has written. "Nothing is. And no love or insight can be at work in a shifting and never-defined position, where eye, mind, and heart have never willingly focused on a steadying point." The war was to be Pyle's steadying point, and love and insight the hallmarks of his writing. What would make Pyle's war reportage of enduring value would be his decision—and it would be his alone to make—to stop fleeing unpleasantness. In his years as a war correspondent, Pyle would still be on the move, but now the movement would have meaning: the link between the columns would no longer be Pyle and his restlessness but the war and the changes it worked in the men who fought it.

Much as he was a case of arrested maturation, badly as he needed a moral education, Pyle had nonetheless developed considerable skill as an observer and writer. Soon

he would find both personal and professional salvation through service to his countrymen, by plying his skills on behalf of the all-consuming effort in which they were engaged. He would become for the first time in his life morally connected to an undertaking of great moment, and he would enjoy the sensation. The war would strike him as an unqualified disaster, not like the great bombing of London on the night of December 30, 1940, had struck him—as something out of a show. Pyle had watched the bombing from the balcony outside his hotel room, and it had all

> seemed more like something put on just to look at; like some ultimate Billy Rose extravagance, at last attaining to such proportions of Rose giganticism that it passed beyond the realm of human credence— but still remained a form of entertainment.

Curious sentiments, those, considering that down below people were burning to death and others were losing everything they owned. It was not the sort of thing he could have written after even a month of living with the infantry in North Africa, so quickly would experience burn away his romantic understanding of war.

Like so many Americans, Pyle had been painfully slow to respond to the gravity of events overseas. The war that was now to claim his attention and eventually his life had for so long been an abstraction, something real enough but remote from his personal experience, just as the Depression had been. The man who had been in Death Valley looking for the castle-like home of a desert recluse the day German troops marched into Austria would soon be with American men as they marched into North Africa—and thence to Sicily, mainland Italy, France, and the Pacific.

And Pyle would be especially good at describing a particular kind of soldier with a particular kind of American past. Throughout the war he would insist that a goodly number of the men he wrote about derived their strength of purpose from an upbringing close to nature or from the ties of a small community. His fondest profiles would be of men fresh from the country or small towns, unsullied by the fractiousness and wise-guy posturing of the big cities. It wouldn't be that these men were necessarily better soldiers than their city counterparts, or even better human beings; but they would strike him as somehow more *American,* or at least closer to what an American ought to be, anyhow.

Such sentiments would hardly be unique to Pyle. The celebration of rural and small-town values and people would be a set theme in much World War II feature writing. But Pyle's affection for such men would be neither a stylistic crutch nor a jaundiced bow to wartime convention. It would be heartfelt, an outgrowth of his own rural past and his years of prewar travel in the United States. Main Street may have been dead, as Bernard De Voto had declared in 1940, but it was to have a bright future in the nation's wartime mythology. And Pyle would have much to do with its resurrection.

A FAMILIAR VOICE

Like millions of men his age and older, my father went abroad during World War II, and my grandparents, still subscribing to the *Indianapolis Times,* continued to read Pyle's column. Now they relied on Pyle for news of a different sort: they wanted to know how young men like George and other boys from the neighborhood were getting along all those thousands of miles away. Sure, George wrote letters home, but the letters were censored. And the frontline news dispatches—with their breathless leads and action-packed headlines—said so little about the men themselves. Pyle bridged the gap, daily telling the folks at home what was happening to their loved ones across the seas. He told them their young men were changed forever, coarsened by what they had seen and done. Pyle's was the sort of copy few censors bothered to hack away at; in their eyes it was pretty benign stuff. But it had a potency all its own, as thirteen million daily readers could attest.

My father's being overseas didn't prevent his reading Ernie Pyle. By arrangement with Scripps Howard's United Features, Pyle's column ran daily in *Stars and Stripes,* the newspaper for service personnel. While stateside readers read about the boys overseas, the boys overseas read about themselves. Almost always they were pleased with what they read: here was a guy willing to share their fate, not because he had to—he was too old for this crap, anyway—but because he wanted to, felt somehow he *had* to.

A fair number of these young men had read Pyle's column before the war. They were happy to still get their daily dose of Ernie Pyle. It was ironic, though. Pyle's column had inspired in many of them, like my father, a desire to see the country. And what happened? The world went to hell, the Army latched onto them, and their first real taste of travel was to war in Europe or the Pacific. Well, anyway, it was good to read Pyle just the same. His was a familiar voice, sort of like getting a letter from home.

EPILOGUE

Ernie and Jerry were remarried by proxy in early 1943, while Ernie covered the infantry in North Africa. As she had during their travel years, Jerry continued to move in and out of extended periods of depression. Sometimes she wrote Ernie several long, loving letters over a two-week period; at other times she wouldn't write for months. Her drug abuse and heavy drinking continued.

Ernie made two trips home during the war. And in both cases he met with crushing pressure from friends and strangers alike. When he came home for the last time, in September of 1944, his emotions were "wrung and drained" after covering the Normandy invasions and the liberation of Paris. "My spirit is wobbly and my mind is confused," he wrote before leaving France. "All of a sudden it seemed to me that if I heard one more shot or saw one more dead man, I would go off my nut."

Shortly after he arrived in Albuquerque, he returned from the dentist's office one day to a scene as bloody as many he had seen at war. Jerry had locked herself in the bathroom and had tried to commit suicide by stabbing herself numerous times in the throat with a pair of long-bladed scissors. Ernie broke down the door to discover Jerry standing before the sink, the bathroom awash in blood. He held her as a surgeon cleaned and sutured her many wounds. Surprisingly, given their severity, Jerry's physical wounds healed quickly, though her emotional ones never would.

Still badly shaken by Jerry's suicide attempt, wanting to stay home but drawn back to war to finish the work he had begun, Ernie began his long journey to the Pacific Theater on January 1, 1945. He died instantly when a sniper's machine-gun bullet pierced his left temple the morning of April 18, on the small island of Ie Shima, near Okinawa. He was buried in a shallow grave between the bodies of two soldiers. According to the newspapers, "That Girl" took the news bravely, but in truth she lost all will to live.

Jerry flew to Washington that summer to accept Ernie's posthumous Medal for Merit, jointly awarded by the Army and the Navy, and to see a preview of Lester Cowan's film *The Story of GI Joe,* based on Ernie's dispatches and with Burgess Meredith playing Ernie. Seeing Washington again undoubtedly increased Jerry's pain. There were surely many memories of meeting and falling in love with Ernie half a lifetime ago. The candlelight dinners in their first apartment. Parties with the crazy newspaper gang and the airmail pilots from National Airport and Bolling Field. Fires in the fireplace on a winter's evening as she talked Ernie through another blue period. How hysterically they'd laughed about the uniformed chauffeur's having to deliver the White House Christmas card to their shabby little apartment. And that Christmas Ernie had surprised her with a brand-new piano, a baby grand, with a big red ribbon tied around it— the elaborate ruse he'd concocted to get her out of the apartment so the deliverymen could wrestle the piano into the living room. And then his somewhat sheepish announcement that he'd bought it on time. But the payments weren't too much, he'd said, and the dealer would take it back if they were unable to pay. She'd tried to object, really tried to give him hell for that, but she hadn't been able to conceal her pleasure—a baby grand of her own!

During the fall of 1945, not long after her forty-fifth birthday, Jerry, more emaciated than ever, contracted influenza. A short time later her kidneys stopped working. She died of uremic poisoning the morning of November 23 at St. Joseph's Hospital in Albuquerque, where the good sisters of St. Joseph had befriended her during the lonely years when Ernie was overseas, even allowing her to live for a time in a cottage on the hospital grounds. Perhaps it was from watching them that Jerry had decided she wanted to learn to pray, a notion she had mentioned in a letter to Ernie shortly before he was killed and which he had been at a loss to understand. When the sisters of St. Joseph gathered for chapel the evening of November 23, they likely prayed that their troubled friend had finally come to peace, and that her wish had been granted.

All too often our perception of the Great Depression is one of unmitigated gloom, a notion helped along by those duotone archival photos that appear in magazines and on book covers, the tinge of brown accentuating the period's distance from the Kodachrome present. What we forget is that amidst the suffering, everyday life went on, though greatly altered in many cases. We forget that these years were also a time of celebration of things and places American.

The Great Depression was the most amply documented period in American history. Writers and photographers, some on their own and others employed by the federal government, took to the road in unprecedented numbers to record in words and pictures the pulse of America during a troubling time. In its subject matter and tone, Pyle's travel work closely parallels some of the entries in the Federal Writers' Project *American Guide* series and the life-history interviews Ann Banks collected in *First Person America*; but with few exceptions the Depression in the pages that follow is a mere backdrop.

For my part, I'm glad Pyle chose not to write directly about the Depression and its victims during these years; I'm glad he wasn't out jamming a thermometer down the throats of the people he came across. We're the richer for that escapist agenda of his, for while part of the America he wrote about has long since passed into memory, we still have a vivid picture of it in his writings.

As I see it, this book amounts to a documentary look at America during an important time in its history. I believe Pyle's dispatches can add to our understanding of the era just prior to America's coming to the fore of world leadership, the time before the war that changed the world forever. During his travel years, Pyle consistently wrote the kinds of stories more conventional journalists ignored. We're left with a richly descriptive record that tells us much about the rhythm and tone of American life in the 1930s, through the attack on Pearl Harbor and America's entrance into World War II. It's a highly selective record, for reasons I've discussed, but a rich one nonetheless. Almost fifty years later his rendition of people and places casually encountered is still exciting.

Many mornings over the years I've worked on this book I've awakened with a vividly familiar picture of a place or a person in my mind. One was a vision of New York City on a freezing winter evening, just as the neon signs were coming on. I was looking out the window of a hotel room, watching the colors explode in the darkness. Another was of lushly forested mountains, their green tops lost in rain clouds. Yet another was the face of an old black man, seated in a restaurant booth, talking about his not having had the chance to meet Franklin Roosevelt.

Sometimes I was momentarily at a loss to distinguish whether the vision was mine or Pyle's. Invariably I concluded that I was dreaming of a scene from a Pyle piece I'd read the evening before, probably for the third or fourth time. But there were times the illusion persisted that I'd been to this or that place, experienced the very thing I saw in the dream, met that exact person and had that conversation with him.

Morning torpor accounts for some of the confusion, but the greater explanation lies in Pyle's considerable narrative gift. The people and places in his word portraits stick with me and have a way of planting themselves in my conscious mind at unlikely moments. It's snowing outside my window as I write, and I'm thinking of Pyle's description of a snowstorm in the Cumberland Mountains. In a way I can't quite explain, I'm curiously animated recalling his lines. And my animation has to do with that American restlessness I spoke of earlier, a vague discontent with here and now that would be nicely eased by lighting out for the territory.

I'm going to do just that. My father and I are going to pick up what was once Route 66 in Illinois and drive to California—the southern route, through Missouri, Oklahoma, Texas, New Mexico, and Arizona. America has been my home for thirty-two years, but what I've seen of the country has been limited to what little you can see from the window of an airliner at thirty thousand feet, or through the windshield of a car on the interstates that so often circumscribe the indigenous.

One of Pyle's biggest gripes was that from what his contemporaries read in the newspapers or heard on the radio, they could easily get the idea that American life centered in New York and Washington and sometimes Los Angeles—that nothing in between mattered. At great cost to himself, Pyle worked hard arguing for the specificity of person and place as an important part of our American past and present. And today that's more important than ever. Meager assumptions are what we get from most media reports about what's going on "out there." I'd be hard pressed to prove it, but I suspect our immersion in this so-called information age has more blunted than enhanced our sense of the country's teeming diversity of geography, local custom, and individual character.

I have a hunch vestiges of the country Pyle described are still out there, and I want to see them. Reading his pieces over and over—sifting, selecting, editing—I came to realize the extent to which I've been affected by those meager assumptions I speak of. I realized, too, how deeply set in me is the American romance of movement—not as a way of life, but as a periodic tonic. It's more than time to get out of town, clear my head, and listen to a few American voices speaking unself-consciously in their American places.

So we're going to take the back roads, my father and I, and eat in small-town diners and maybe sleep in some of the remaining tourist cabins. It will be a leisurely trip.

We're going to fixate upon the journey itself, not the destination. I'm going to take a copy of this manuscript along and refer to it as we go. I want to measure the country as it is now against Pyle's rendering of it almost half a century ago. I guess that will make this doubly a book of nostalgia—mine and Pyle's. That's fine with me; my restlessness can always use a little structure.

My father tells me old Route 66 will be hard to find. Interstates have replaced most of the old route, sometimes overlapping the same right-of-way, in other places taking a whole new course. Sections of the old pavement remain, but it will likely take some doing to stay on course. We'll probably have to ask questions of many strangers.

FURTHER READING

Biography

Lord Halifax. "A Tribute to Ernie Pyle" from *The American Speeches of Lord Halifax,* pp. 409-10. New York: Oxford University Press, 1947.
> A brief account of the single meeting of Lord Halifax with Ernie Pyle.

McNamara, John. Chapter 13: "Worm's Eye View of the World," from *Extra! U.S. War Correspondents in Action,* pp. 178-92. Boston: Houghton Mifflin Company, 1945.
> Patriotic, war-story biography.

Miller, Lee G. *The Story of Ernie Pyle*. New York: The Viking Press, 1950.
> Biography by a longtime friend of Pyle's, who worked with him at the *Washington News,* based primarily on Pyle's private correspondence.

Painton, Frederick C. "The Hoosier Letter-Writer" from *More Post Biographies, Articles of Enduring Interest about Famous Journalists and Journals and Other Subjects Journalistic*, ed. by John E. Drewry, pp. 274-88. Athens: University of Georgia Press, 1947.
> An elegiac biography that includes numerous quotations from prominent people, including Franklin Delano Roosevelt, on Pyle's death.

Tobin, James. Ernie Pyle's War: America's Eyewitness to World War II. New York: Free Press, 1997, 312 p.
> Chronicle of Pyle's experiences as a war correspondent.

Criticism

Butcher, Fanny. Review of *Brave Men* in *The Chicago Tribune* (November 26, 1944).
> Warm, patriotic review.

> **The following source published by Gale contain additional coverage of Pyle's life and works:** *Dictionary of Literary Biography,* **Vol. 29.**

Arnold Schoenberg

1874-1951

(Full name Arnold Franz Walter Schoenberg) Austrian-born American composer and nonfiction writer.

INTRODUCTION

One of the most significant composers of modern symphonic music, Schoenberg led the avant-garde movement away from classical conventions of melody and harmony during the early twentieth century. Experimenting with serial composition, he devised a method of writing music using a twelve-tone scale, creating works known for their dissonance and unconventional formal qualities. He was also a highly influential teacher, counting among his most celebrated students Alban Berg and Anton Webern, who along with him were known as the Second Viennese School of composers.

Biographical Information

The son of a Viennese shoemaker, Schoenberg had little formal musical training, but learned to play the violin, viola, and cello. In his early twenties he worked as a conductor, arranger, and musical director in Vienna and Berlin, then took up teaching, which would be the often precarious way he would make his living for the rest of his life. Influenced by such composers as Richard Wagner and Gustav Mahler, who became a mentor of his, as well as by new trends in visual arts, he devoted himself to discovering innovative approaches to music, participating in subscription-only musical societies where the work of radical composers such as himself would be assured a fair hearing. In 1933, Schoenberg was fired from his position as a composition instructor at the Prussian Academy of Arts in Berlin because of his Jewish ancestry. He then emigrated to the United States, supporting himself as a lecturer at the University of Southern California and the University of California at Los Angeles while continuing to work on his musical compositions.

Major Works

Critics note aspects of Romanticism in Schoenberg's early musical works, such as *Verklärte Nacht* (1899), written for string sextet, and the cantata *Gurrelieder* (1901-13). Later moving away from conventional musical techniques, he entered what critics regard as his Expressionist period, with works including *Erwartung* (1909) and *Pierrot lunaire* (1912). Convinced that the traditional diatonic musical scale was obsolete, he began experimenting with serialism, eventually inventing a system that used all twelve half-steps in the musical scale, which he introduced in the early 1920s with composi-

tions such as his *Piano Suite*, Op. 25 (1921-23) and *Wind Quintet* (1924). Schoenberg wrote the texts for many of his vocal works, notably the opera *Moses und Aron* (1930-2) and the cantata *A Survivor from Warsaw* (1947), as well as providing program notes for some of his instrumental pieces. He set forth his ideas about music in prose works such as *Harmonielehre* (1911) and *Models for Beginners in Composition* (1942) and the essays collected in *Style and Idea* (1950).

Critical Reception

Because most of Schoenberg's work violated fundamental norms for music of his time, it encountered tremendous resistance from audiences and critics who found it alienating and incomprehensible. These negative reactions still endure. However, he established a lasting and wide-ranging influence among the serious students of new music who were best prepared to understand and appreciate him, and his innovations had a profound influence on later composers such as John Cage, Marc Blitzstein, and Milton Babbitt.

PRINCIPAL WORKS

Harmonielehre (nonfiction) 1911
Models for Beginners in Composition (nonfiction) 1942
Style and Idea (essays) 1950
Structural Functions of Harmony (nonfiction) 1954
†*Briefe* (letters) 1958
Preliminary Exercises in Counterpoint (nonfiction) 1963
Fundamentals of Musical Compositon (nonfiction) 1964
Arnold Schoenberg Self-Portrait: A Collection of Articles, Program Notes, and Letters by the Composer About His Own Works (prose and letters) 1988

*Abridged edition published as *Theory of Harmony*, 1948.
†Enlarged edition published as *Letters*, 1964.

CRITICISM

Paul Rosenfeld (essay date 1928)

SOURCE: "Schoenberg and Varèse," in *Musical Impressions: Selections from Paul Rosenfeld's Criticism*, edited by Herbert A. Leibowitz, Hill and Wang, 1969, pp. 77-81.

[*In the following essay, originally published in 1928, Rosenfeld discusses the connection between Schoenberg and Edgard Varèse.*]

. . . [They] played Europe and the New World off against each other at the International Guild. Schoenberg's *Serenade* began the program; Varèse's *Intégrales* ended it, and the interval was broad as the sea. It was delicate lacework sound against brute shrilling jagged music. It was the latest ghostly flowering of the romantic tradition against a polyphony not of lines, but of metallic cubical volumes. It was, essentially, the thinking introverted solitary against mass movement in which the individual goes lost; for the reason either piece did its author uncommon justice. Few works of Schoenberg traverse less writing for the eye than this new one, and breathe more thoroughly. The march which leads on the *Serenade* and then leads it off again may ultimately belong to the company of Schoenberg's paper pieces. But the rest of the little movements, the minuet, the variations, and the setting of Petrarch's sonnet Number 217, the "Dance Scene" and the "Song without Words," flow lightly; and bring within their small compass and in the familiar character of the *Serenade* a very personal quality of sound. The mood is serener than it was in *Pierrot Lunaire,* and the movement less languorous and less explosive. Nonetheless, the piece's quality is similarly half painful, half dreamy; characteristically Schoenbergian; the tone eerie and *sotto voce;* the structure submitted to intense concentration. The nervous, excited strumming of the mandoline and guitar called for by the

score has correspondences throughout the form. And like so much of Schoenberg the *Serenade* is fundamentally Brahmsian in feeling. The conservatism of the structure, the frequency of rhythmic repetitions, the symmetrical formation of motifs, themes, and entire sections, has been marked by the German aestheticians. Perfectly apparent to the layman is the brooding romanticism of the *melos,* particularly in the "Song without Words," and the spook-romanticism of the loose-jointed periods of the minuet and "Dance Scene." The characteristic undulant movement, the lyrical upheavals of the line, true, have been compressed by this ultramodern into minute spaces; stand immeasurably tightened, curtailed, and broken up. But they exist in Schoenberg as essentially as in Schumann, Wagner, and Brahms. That is the German, apparently, and the European in touch with a past. Schoenberg is the carrier-on, the continuator of his predecessors' line of advance. Despite the architectural preoccupation distinguishing him from the great mass of his artistic ancestors, from Brahms, even, Schoenberg is the romanticist of to-day; as Stravinsky justly if unkindly denominated him. He is the singer *par excellence* of the individual, the proud, solitary, brooding soul; the lover *par excellence* of the singular, the *raffiné,* the precious in musical expression; of the strange and unwonted in harmony and mood. The sudden entirely unheralded high F, *pianpianissimo,* which squeaks in the singer's voice toward the close of the song *Herzgewächse:* what is it but a very extreme example of Schoenberg's characteristic processes? To a degree the *Serenade* approaches the humanistic ideal a little more closely than *Pierrot Lunaire* and *Herzgewächse,* less descriptive and macabre and perverse as it is. But the divergence is insignificant. Jewelry and feeling of rarity remain; and with those aspects of romanticism, its more permanent attractive ones. Like his masters, Schoenberg is busied in a rigorous search for his own truth, for his own naturalness, and uncompromisingly bends the inherited means of music to parallel his way of feeling. The *Serenade* is the work of a truthseeker, not satisfied with conventions, and actively developing the suppleness, copiousness, and precision of his medium. To be sure, there is a novelty in Schoen-berg's approach. His touch is less warm, his emotional frontage narrower than the great romanticists'. He is the man of his hour, and that hour is a difficult and tortured one, less communicable than its forerunners, isolating its members in moody loneliness and semimystical adventure. Schoenberg's music sounds as exquisite, shadowy, and remote as Paul Klee's painting looks. Brahms shudders like a ghost. But the ghost has the old gravity and sentiment, and wears Wagnerian plumes, besides.

Passing from the *Serenade* to *Intégrales* is like passing from the I-ness to the it-ness of things; from a hypersensitive unworldly feeling to a sense of strident material power; and from a traditional expression to one which is independent, and rooted as largely in life as in Berlioz and Stravinsky. Varèse stems from the fat European soil quite as directly as Schoenberg does. The serious approach, the scientific curiosity, of what of the nineteenth century remained on the Continent, is active in him and his audacious art. Besides Varèse is somewhat of a romanticist. For all his extreme aural sensitivity to the ordinary phenomena and perception of the prodigious symphony of the city and port of New York, he has a tendency to seize upon life in terms of the monstrous and the elemental. *Amériques,* the first of his characteristic "machines," resembles Brontosaurus, the nasty hungry *Fresser,* waddling filthy, stinking, and trumpeting through a mesozoic swamp. Fafner was an elf in comparison. That is the Berlioz influence: it is significant that Varèse first appeared before the American public in the capacity of conductor of the Frenchman's prodigious *Requiem.* But his romantic aspects are balanced by more humanistic ones. Varèse has derived his idiom through direct perception, and used it in interests other than those of descriptivity. He has never imitated the sounds of the city in his works, as he is frequently supposed to have done. His music is much more in the nature of penetration. He will tell you how much the symphony of New York differs from that of Paris: Paris' being noisier, a succession of shrill, brittle hissing sounds, New York's on the contrary, quieter, for the mere reason that it is incessant, enveloping the New Yorker's existence as the rivers the island of Manhattan. He works with those sonorities merely because he has come into relation with American life, and found corresponding rhythms set free within himself. It is probable that at the moments in which Varèse is compelled to give form to his feelings about life, sensations received from the thick current of natural sound in which we dwell, push out from the storehouses of the brain as organic portions of an idea.

His feeling is equally preponderantly unromantic. It is much more a feeling of life massed. There are those who will say, of course, that *Intégrales* is merely cubical music. To a definite degree, Varèse's polyphony is different from the fundamentally linear polyphony of Stravinsky's art. His music is built more vertically, moves more to solid masses of sound, and is very rigorously held in them. Even the climaxes do not break the cubism of form. The most powerful pronouncements merely force sound into the air with sudden violence, like the masses of two impenetrable bodies in collision. The hardness of edge and impersonality of the material itself, the balance of brass, percussion and woodwind, the piercing golden screams, sudden stops and lacunae, extremely rapid *crescendi* and *diminuendi,* contribute to the squareness. The memorable evening of its baptism, *Intégrales* resembled nothing so much as shining cubes of freshest brass and steel set in abrupt pulsing motion. But for us, they were not merely metallic. They were the tremendous masses of American life, crowds, city piles, colossal organizations; suddenly set moving, swinging, throbbing by the poet's dream; and glowing with a clean, daring, audacious, and majestic life. Human power exulted anew in them. Majestic skyscraper chords, grandly resisting and moving volumes, ruddy sonorities, and mastered ferocious outbursts cried it forth. For the first time in modern music, more fully even than in the first section of *Le Sacre,* one heard an equivalent Wotan's spear music. But this time, it had something to do not with the hegemony of romantic Germany, but with the vast forms of the democratic, communistic new world.

Without the juxtaposition of the **Serenade,** *Intégrales* would have been a great experience adding to a growing prestige. But that evening the Atlantic rolled. The opposition of the two works precluded such concepts as "Schoenberg's music" and "music by Varèse." One saw two kinds of music, apart as two continents, and based a thousand leagues from each other. Far to the east one saw romanticism rooted in the individualism of western Europe, romanticism that indeed was the gentle old European life. And close, there lay the new humanism, the hard, general spirit, rooted in the massive communal countries: Russia and the United States, itself an integral portion of all one meant saying "the new world" and "America."

Paul Rosenfeld (essay date 1936)

SOURCE: "Gurrelieder," in *Musical Impressions: Selections from Paul Rosenfeld's Criticism,* edited by Herbert A. Leibowitz, Hill and Wang, 1969, pp. 71-77.

[*In the following essay, originally published in 1936, Rosenfeld discusses Schoenberg's* Gurrelieder.]

An artist's expression infrequently is completely individualized by the time of his twenty-seventh year, and that of Schoenberg was not exceptional. When in 1900 he began to set the poetic cycle which the seraph of Danish literature, Jens Peter Jacobsen, had formed from the legend of King Waldemar I of Denmark and the fair Tove and called the songs of Gurre, the castle with which the legend associated their tragic love, the future heresiarch still was, regularly enough, under the domination of the expressions of his immediate predecessors. These were the Wagnerian, the Straussian, the Brahmsian, and the Mahleresque. His setting of **Gurrelieder** for giant orchestra, choruses, and solo voices thus is largely traditional; like the youthful work of other gifted composers, say, the Wagner of *The Flying Dutchman,* the Strauss of *Don Juan,* the Stravinsky of *L'Oiseau de Feu.* The giant cantata recalls the general romanticism of the late nineteenth century, in particular the rapture and the harmonic system of Wagner, the vasty means of Mahler's choral symphonies and something of his melodic architectural form, Strauss's beefy contrapuntal effects and dramatic emphasis, and Brahms's rich Lieder style. It actually is a sort of Wagnerian music drama cast with Strauss's and Mahler's symphonic means in the form of a song cycle, for soloists and chorus, preceded by a prelude and inclusive of two sizable orchestral transitions, and not without distinct Brahmsian characteristics.

One tenor represents Waldemar, another Klaus the fool. The soprano represents Tove; the mezzo the little wood dove; the bass the peasant; the four-part male chorus, Waldemar's ghostly henchmen. The work falls into three parts, lightly corresponding to the three parts of a symphony and the acts of an opera. The first includes the songs of Waldemar and Tove expressing their longing for each other, the songs vocal of their joy in reunion, their nocturnal dialogue and premonitions of death and of resurrection, and finally, after the first orchestral interlude, the song of the wood dove lamenting the death of Tove at the hands of the jealous queen. The second part contains Waldemar's denunciation and rejection of God. The third embodies the demonic nocturnal hunt to which Waldemar and his henchmen have been condemned, the choruses of the men interspersed by the song of the frightened peasant, the jittery soliloquy of the fool, the ghostly Waldemar's expression of his sense of the dead Tove in the voice of the woods, in the regard of the lake, in the laughing light of the stars: and finally the play of the summer wind and the resurrection of the lovers in the life of nature.

The composer of **Dreimals Sieben Lieder des Pierrot Lunaire** is nonetheless clearly heralded, nay actually present, in **Gurrelieder;** as definitely present there as the composer of *Die Walküre* in *Der Fliegende Holländer,* the composer of *Don Quixote* in *Don Juan,* the composer of *Les Noces* in *L'Oiseau de Feu.* The work, naturally enough, is unequal. The first four songs in the first part have far less quality than the later ones; and pages such as that of Waldemar's blasphemy, the macabre hunting chorus, and the final salutation of the sunrise, reveal more of ambition and striving than of power. The dreaminess and the sweetness of some of the music is occasionally cloying. And still, for all its weaknesses, its Wagnerian, Straussian, Brahmsian echoes, **Gurrelieder** is a creation, the sonorous, sumptuously colored embodiment of an original idea, full of glowing poetic music, and doubtless has a future. The conception, to begin with, is a formal one. Each of the nineteen songs composing the whole, a simple or double Lied form, is built up structurally from its own melodic germ and is organically related to the rest by the cyclic use of themes, by contrasts of tonality and character, and by orchestral transitions of various length. The work actually concludes with the chord in the tonality with which it began. And Schoenberg's form is already distinctive: and when we speak of his form as being already distinctive, we are referring to the form of the older, the main part of the **Gurrelieder,** written between 1900 and 1902, and not that of the close of the last section, including the **Sprechstimme,** the melodic use of the celesta, and the high, shrill, piercing sonorities; for that dates from 1910 and is therefore contemporaneous with the **Three Pieces,** Opus 11, and the work of the middle Schoenberg. Here, in the earliest parts of the score, we find him melodic and contrapuntal to a degree, even on the simplest and most Wagnerian pages. While his harmony is fairly Wagnerian, it is anything but slavishly so, displaying a considerable sensitivity. As for his melodic line, it frequently leaps over wide intervals, as in Tove's third song, and skips about nervously in the songs of the peasant and the fool. Instrumental sonorities are often used thematically, from Tove's second song onward. The instruments themselves frequently are employed soloistically, and examples of

the oppositions of the sonorities of various orchestral families are anything but uncommon. And the individualized constituent forms and the grand one they build up communicate individual moods and an individual experience. If these moods and this experience are "romantic"; if **Gurrelieder,** like *Tristan,* constitutes with surging, rapturous, and dreamy page after page a "climate of love," it does so unhackneyedly. The erotic moods are tenderer, more penetrating and spiritualized than Wagner's relatively simple ones. Schoenberg's heroine, too, possibly in conformity with Jacobsen's idea, is much more feminine and shy than Wagner's heroic *amorosa.* The range of the moods also includes such fantastic and original variants as those of the bedeviled peasant, the dislocated and grotesque agonies of the fool, the Puckish humors of the "Summer Wind's Wild Chase." The very implicit experience, the vision of a vital progress by stages of personal love and personal loss to a selfless victorious absorption in the divine breath, the "life" of nature, while essentially romantic, is individual. And while the entire expression, like Wagner's, is rapturous and subjectively lyrical, it is rapturous to the verge of the ecstatic; and its psychographical and subjective lyricism borders on expressionism, on the ecstatically confessional. And it is a magical score, rich in the elusively mysterious, sensuous, melting, and bewitching sort of expressions which, drawn with a fineness no completely waking condition can achieve, flow from some enchantment in the subject itself and, abundant in the music of Schumann, of Wagner, of Debussy, are called poetical.

Need it be asseverated that these distinctive characteristics of **Gurrelieder** are the germs of those completely distinguishing and characterizing the later work, at least that part of it previous to the systematization of the twelve-tone technique? The plasticity of the **Gurrelieder**—what is it but the adumbration of the extraordinary plasticity of those later works, indicative of an intuition always connected with a form-feeling that works itself out with utter relentlessness, compression, and logicality, whether in the molds of the Lied form or in those of contrapuntal forms, the passacaglia, the canon, the inverted canon, or the *motus cancrizans?* The harmonic sensitivity, what is that but the indication of the sensitivity that was to produce the bewitching harmonic beauty of the characteristic atonal pieces, the third of the **Five Pieces for Orchestra,** "Der Wechselnder Akkord" in especial. The wide leaps and skips of the melodic line, are they indeed anything but the annunciation of the melodic line of the scherzo of the first **Kammersymphonie** and of **Das Buch der Hängenden Gärten,** the chamber operas, the song **Herzgewächse,** the **Three Times Seven Songs of Pierrot Lunaire?** For us, they are nothing if not prophetic; and for us, the thematic use of instrumental sonorities is equally so; also the soloistic use of instruments, triumphant first in the **Kammersymphonie** and then in all Schoenberg's instrumental pieces. And the oppositions of the sonorities of various instrumental families seem anticipatory of one of the traits of style most distinctly Schoenbergian. Equally so is the feeling communicated by **Gurrelieder.** The feelings expressed by the later music are those of exquisite, idealistic, not so largely neurotic as neurodynamic modern people—people who make tremendously prompt, deep, intense nervous responses. Tove herself is but an earlier version of the exquisite essence figuring in *Pierrot* as *eine weisse Wäscherin*. And the ideas which compose and relate these essences are those of the erotic experience. More consistently and continually than any other contemporary composer of worth, Schoenberg is the musician of the exquisite, the deep, and also the bitter and painful erotic adventure: a circumstance which connects his art with that of Beardsley, of Strindberg, of Rodin, and that of other great "decadents." Opus 15, the cycle of songs on poems derived from *Das Buch der Hängenden Gärten* by Stefan George, creates a "climate of love" even more subtly, more poignantly and inclusively than *Gurrelieder*. The monodrama *Erwartung* brings to biting, almost madly intense, expression the experience of the modern woman who, wandering beyond the walls of her little garden in search of her lover, finds him dead for the sake of another. And the other little music drama, *Die Glückliche Hand*—the hand of Venus—conveys the experience of an enamored artist who, physically disgusting to his partner, is crushed by her efforts to escape him. The *Serenade,* Opus 24, also expresses, with the help of the words of Petrarch, the experience of the rejected lover. Again, the moods of the later Schoenberg include many that, extensions of the tortured ones of the latter sections of *Gurrelieder,* approach the extreme of uneasiness, of torment and dolor; and the cantata's peasant, Klaus the fool, and the Puckish summer wind attain a kind of apotheosis in the extremely bizarre moods of the "youthful idealist," the moon-drunken dandy Pierrot Lunaire of the fantastic twenty-one songs. The later forms of expression are also extremely ecstatic, almost supremely so, and supremely confessional. Psychographical, subjectively lyrical music would seem to reach its most exalted pitch in these works: they make the composer seem one determined not to shrink from the most audacious articulations of inner movements, those of the unconscious itself, and the ultimate secrets of his own soul. And the whole of the later music, with its many passages of the purest lyrical expansion—for all its inclusion of pages of paper music—constitutes the most poetic, glamorous music produced by any living composer. That poetry is a fragile one, an exquisite one, a sort of expression of the gleaming, evanescent moment of feeling. *Pierrot Lunaire,* which contains this "Celtic magic" perhaps more abundantly than any other one of Schoenberg's works—it is perhaps its apex and one of those of modern music—may even seem, with its elusive lights, surges, ecstasies, aromas, a sort of Chinese jar filled with conserved flower petals, and thus something of an anomaly in the present world. But it is not certain that succeeding times will find it so and may not conceive it as the crystallization of the finest Viennese, the *fin-de-siècle* European sensibility, and find the place of the composer close to that of the other exquisite musical poets, Schumann, Wagner, Chopin, and Debussy.

Indeed so clear a prefigurement of the composer of all these magical pieces does *Gurrelieder* give that it is difficult to understand how musicians whose interest in their art is a serious one could have contrived to assist at the first American performance of the revelatory piece, under Stokowski's baton early in 1932, and continue, for all the grossness of the production, unconvinced of the integrity of Schoenberg's entire output up to the time of his systematization of the twelve-tone technique. That they should have come away as puzzled by the system-making Schoenberg as they were before they heard the cantata, is not a wonder. For *Gurrelieder* casts no light on him. But that it should have failed to make them conscious of the one man present from first to last in all of Schoenberg's pieces confessing the dominance of sensibility, and failed to make them recognize in the later atonal works, up to the *Serenade* and the Suite, Opus 25, the logical developments of the germs stirring in this first experiment with the larger means if not the larger forms, verges upon the miraculous. For us, Schoenberg's declaration at the time of the first performances of his songs on George's poems is unsurprising: "In these Lieder I have succeeded for the first time in approaching an ideal of expression and form that have hovered before me for years. Hitherto, I had merely not sufficient strength and sureness to realize that ideal. Now, however, I . . . have definitely started on my journey." For if we ourselves see anything in Schoenberg's career, it is nothing if not the development of a man according to the law of life which compels us, if we would live and grow, to become ever more fully and nakedly what we essentially are.

Roger Sessions (essay date 1952)

SOURCE: "Some Notes on Schoenberg and the 'Method of Composing with Twelve Tone'," in *Roger Sessions on Music: Collected Essays,* edited by Edward T. Cone, Princeton University Press, 1952, pp. 370-5.

[*In the following essay, originally published in* The Score *in 1952, Sessions analyzes Schoenberg's twelve-tone compositional method.*]

Arnold Schoenberg sometimes said, "A Chinese philosopher speaks, of course, Chinese; the question is, what does he say?" The application of this to Schoenberg's music is quite clear. The notoriety which has, for decades, surrounded what he persisted in calling his "method of composing with twelve tones," has not only obscured his real significance, but, by focusing attention on the *means* rather than on the music itself, has often seemed a barrier impeding a direct approach to the latter. To some extent it has even, rather curiously, distorted the view of Schoenberg's historical achievement, of which the discovery of the twelve-tone method is only one phase.

Schoenberg's priority in the discovery of the "method" is assured, and he set great store by the fact of priority itself. One can understand why. He had the rare but often painful honor of remaining a "controversial" figure even to the time of his death at the age of seventy-six; the still more painful experience of seeing even his disciples used as weapons against him—a situation from which both Berg and Webern would have been the first to recoil. It can easily have seemed to him that this priority, being tangible, was at least historically a precious asset.

The significant fact is that—paradoxically—were the question of priority really important, the event itself would have little value. Once, for instance, we were taught that Mozart introduced the clarinet into the orchestra. Later, one learned that other composers had used the clarinet before him; this fact, however, did not diminish in the least either Mozart's stature, or the historical importance of his immense contribution to the development of the clarinet. If the formulation of the twelve-tone method seems likely, in future estimates of Schoenberg, to assume a less central significance than it has done up till now, this is not because the system itself is insignificant, but because Schoenberg was a great composer, because his music, historically and otherwise, is greater than any system or technique.

For Schoenberg, far from being a mere "chef d'école," of whatever stature, embodied, more than any other musician of his time, one of the great critical moments of musical history. Dodecaphony—here used to mean simply the independence of the twelve notes of the chromatic scale—is the result of an impulse which has been inherent in Western music at least from the moment that musicians began to combine voices simultaneously. As students of music history we have become familiar both with the processes involved and the reasons generally adduced for them. At one period it is a matter of avoiding the tritone; at another, the strengthening of the cadence. Later, as forms become vaster and more complex, harmonies are thrown into relief by means of "secondary dominants"; the resources, both harmonic and linear, of the minor mode are made available within a predominantly major mode, and vice versa; and finally individual tones are raised or lowered, throwing the notes which follow into greater relief, and giving rise to sonorities previously unknown. Whatever their motivation, these processes are all in one way or another expressions of what may be called the chromatic impulse. Throughout the eighteenth and nineteenth centuries their use increased constantly, and penetrated more and more into the heart of the musical vocabulary. What began, in each case, as a means of emphasizing large musical design, later developed into an expressive resource, bringing contrast into the modelling of musical detail. Thus the "chromatic harmony" of Wagner and Liszt was born; harmony based largely on "alterations" which modified the ordinary "root chords," which tended to challenge the compelling force of the relationships between these chords, frequently superseded such relationships, and finally undermined, or at least, qualified, the unity based on tonic, dominant, and subdominant.

The process is one through which every vital inflection, every nuance, gradually imposes itself and demands development. The ear of the composer, in other terms, lin-

gers over arresting or expressive detail, and follows the train of thought or impulse incited by it.

This story has been told often enough; but it still has to be re-told and re-pondered, since it relates a development that leads to the very center of the contemporary musical problem. The processes of impulse just described in purely harmonic terms, constitute, of course, only one phase of an integral musical impulse which embraces all elements, melodic and rhythmic as well.

Perhaps we should recall here what is meant by a musical problem. This must not be envisaged in technical terms alone. It is an *expressive* crisis that arises and demands solution. The technical solution is ex post facto, so to speak; the concept of technique, in fact, has to do with solutions, not with crises or problems as such. Furthermore, a genuine problem is the affair not so much of an individual composer as of music itself. It is a turning point in the development of the human spirit, and represents either the opening up of a new vein, or the exhaustion of an old one. Thus it does not lend itself to easy definition in words. How much easier, in fact, to take the technical ideas out of their context and define them, as it were, in the raw state—a process that actually reduces to absurdity any technical concept whatever.

The truly immense achievement of Schoenberg lies in the fact that his artistic career embodies and summarizes a fundamental musical crisis. More than any other composer he led the crisis to its culmination. He accomplished this by living it through to its furthest implications. But he also found technical means which could enable composers of his own and later generations to seek and find solutions. He opened up a new vein, towards which music had been tending; and the twelve-tone method is in essence the tool through which this vein can be exploited. Its discovery was a historical necessity; had it not been Schoenberg who formulated it, others would have done so, though possibly in a much slower and more laborious manner.

Nothing could be more wrong, in fact, or more unjust to Schoenberg and to his memory, than to regard the twelve-tone method as essentially limited to a single group or a single *Weltanschauung*. In too many quarters, friendly and hostile alike, a kind of orthodoxy has grown up—a convenience since orthodoxy offers both a safe refuge and an easy point of attack. But not only is dodecaphony constantly in process of development; precisely because it is a living process and not a dogma, it means something different, and shows a different aspect, in every individual personality. It has often been remarked that composers who, in the midst of their careers, adopt the twelve-tone method, do not essentially change their styles; they continue writing the music that is conspicuously their own—not less but, let us hope, more so for having been enriched by new elements.

What is the twelve-tone method, then? Obviously, within the limits of a short article one cannot give an adequate account of it and all that it implies, or can imply. Primarily it is a means through which the twelve notes of the chromatic scale—which, unlike the diatonic scale, is uniform and therefore neutral in harmonic implication—can be organized into a basic pattern capable of supplying the impulse toward extended musical development; and which, through the recurrence of the relationships implied in it, makes possible a unity, not unlike that yielded by the principle of tonality, which is implicit in the material premises on which a musical work is based.

The tone-series plays, in dodecaphonic music, somewhat the role played by the diatonic scale in music of the pretonal period. It is, naturally, not an identical role; the series differs from the scale in that it has an independent design, and thus a distinct character of its own—it represents a personal choice, that is, on the part of the composer. Instead of accepting it as a predetermined datum, the latter is guided by his own musical impulse in constructing it; it will, in other words, inevitably bear the stamp of his personality, and, as his command of the technique increases, it will more and more be penetrated by his musical thought. The composer's relationship to the series and to its treatment, in fact, is exactly the same as it is to any technique which he adopts. He will—as in any other technique—achieve spontaneity in proportion to the degree of mastery which he achieves; he will learn the resources of the technique through practice, and will formulate his own principles in accordance with his own needs. As with every other technique, he will heed, modify, or ignore the rules insofar as real musical necessities demand; there is no need to insist on this point. But he will be successful in this respect only in proportion to his mastery of, and insight into, the materials themselves.

It is necessary to emphasize these points because they have been so often misunderstood, and because this misunderstanding has interfered with the appreciation of Schoenberg's real achievement. He has, for instance, always opposed the use of the term "atonality," and this term, like the undue public emphasis given to the twelve-tone method in discussing his music, has for too long stood between the public and the music itself. The objection is that "atonality" is essentially a negative term, but also that it has led even sympathetic listeners to a forced effort to distrust all sensations which could be construed as "tonal"—and therefore to seek the real meaning of the music in some abstract concept which has little to do with what they hear. To be sure, dodecaphonic music cannot be analyzed in terms of tonality; and even areas in the music which one seems to hear in some sense "tonally," derive this quasi-tonal implication from relationships which, as can easily be seen, are inherent in music itself and are the product of no particular period or technique. A fifth remains a fifth, a third a third, in the twentieth as surely as in the fourteenth century. These relationships are felt, today as always, even though no way has yet been found by which the enlarged vocabulary of today can be systematized in a theoretical sense; and it is quite possible that no such systematization will be possible for some time to come.

What Schoenberg achieved, then, with the formulation of the twelve-tone method, was to show his followers a way toward the practical organization of materials. The true significance of the twelve-tone method, and of Schoenberg's immense achievement, cannot possibly be understood if more than this is demanded of it. No doubt, as music continues to develop, the "twelve-tone system" also will evolve—possibly though not necessarily into something quite different from its present form. The more it develops, however, the richer Schoenberg's achievement will have proven to be. For it is, precisely, *not* a new harmonic system: it does not seek to contradict or deny, but to make possible the exploitation of new resources. Its significance is the greater precisely for the fact of being something far more unpretentious, but at the same time far more vital, than a new harmonic theory or a new aesthetic principle could possibly be.

Walter and Alexander Goehr (essay date 1957)

SOURCE: "Arnold Schönberg's Development towards the Twelve-Note System," *The New York Review of Books,* Vol. IV, No. 6, April 22, 1965, pp. 76-93.

[*In the following essay, which was originally published in 1957, the Goehrs recount Schoenberg's development of his twelve-tone compositional method.*]

Although the conditions and problems facing a creative artist vary in different times, an ethnic culture imposes a certain common tradition and leads to a fundamental similarity of outlook. An understanding of the roots and historical development of a culture is essential for an assessment of any individual artist. Assuming this fact, the opportunity is given of seeing the comparative value, the parallels and divergences of individual composers, seemingly unrelated, in a logical and responsible manner. For example, Brahms and Wagner were for decades believed to be antipodes, while we today, in comparative detachment, are able to see the affinities in the common national character of their work.

The German school of music at the threshold of the twentieth century based its teaching upon the study of German music from J. S. Bach to the romantic masters, virtually neglecting earlier music or that of other nationalities. The melodic and rhythmic idiosyncrasies, the harmonic subtleties and the freedom of expression attained by these composers were measured by comparison with arbitrary prototypes of so-called normality (or regularity) created by the theorists. Mastery over technical material was obtained by a study of traditional harmony and academic counterpoint, based upon Fux rather than upon Palestrina and his Italian and Flemish predecessors. Although the music of France, Russia and other nations was studied, a fundamental schism had developed between the outlook of German musicians and those of other national schools. Heinrich Schenker, in his illuminating article 'Rameau or Beethoven' (*Das Meisterwerk in der Musik III,* München, 1930), heads his article with a quotation from a letter of

C. P. E. Bach: 'You may loudly proclaim that the fundamentals of the art of my father and myself are anti-Rameau.' This divergence of attitude continued and grew, and even when German composers were influenced by the works of other national schools, their attitude remained (and remains) sharply differentiated. The very nature of the German tradition and method is a dialectical one and its development is one whereby each successive composer builds upon the technical achievements of his precedessors. There was little place for eclecticism. French composers, eclectic by nature, were much more open to newly discovered technical possibilities and to influence from hitherto unknown types of music. The German remained comparatively little affected by the new experiences made possible by a rapidly improving system of communication and the consequent opportunities for cultural exchange with remote regions of the earth. The teachings of Vincent d'Indy and Paul Dukas illustrate the eclectic and experimental tendency. The influence upon Debussy of Eastern music at the Paris World Exhibition is well known. The differences in method between the two traditions is clearly seen at times when Debussy and Schönberg work with similar musical material, but with utterly different approaches and results. The German attitude of mind, one that can hardly be found in any other cultural sphere of the West, results in a cumulative style steadily and logically progressing to great subtlety and complexity.

One must remember that the German musical language was already in a state of advanced development at the time when Schönberg entered the field. Brahms and Wagner, the former with a subtle juxtaposition of new asymmetries of form and rhythm beneath a surface of the traditional, the latter with his liquidation of the old formal divisions and functions into a dramatically coherent whole, founded the style which composers like Wolf, Mahler, Reger and Strauss developed towards a flowering in the art of music completely original in its plasticity and powers of free and largely asymmetric construction. The developments of Wolf and Mahler in the elaboration of the melodic line (continuing what Wagner had begun) and the widespread adoption of Brahms' great developments in the variation of harmony, brought the musical language to a point at which Schönberg's principles of 'varied repetition' and 'musical prose' can be considered a realistic assessment of the musical style of the time. It is our purpose to demonstrate the processes by which Arnold Schönberg, in the period of his creative life until 1923, was to bring this musical language towards its logical conclusion and subsequent, seemingly revolutionary, development.

Development of artistic style stipulates a dual process: on the one hand, an accumulation of increasingly varied elements, an extension of the means of relating previously unrelated material and consequently, a persistent replacement of comparative regularity and symmetry by asymmetry and irregularity. On the other hand, it stipulates (and this must be particularly emphasised) restriction, reduction and simplification, seemingly retrogressive habits, and the deliberate neglect or sublimation of traditional elements arising from new æsthetic considerations. There results a positive process of addition and accumulation in the creative mind and imagination and a quasi-negative restriction determined by choice and individual preference. When we consider the various facets of the progress of Schönberg's music, we see that the balance between these two contrasting elements of development more than anything else distinguish him from his contemporaries and mark him as a great composer. The farther his style progressed (seemingly away from the German past), the more he concerned himself with analysis and thought upon the fundamental problems inherent in classical and romantic German music. His particular path as an innovator was largely achieved by his more than usual powers of perception to understand and analyse the problems which had faced Mozart, Beethoven, Brahms and many others. Although his musical language was from the beginning one of great originality, the technical means which he used were, to a great extent, derived from the processes of his predecessors in German music. Aware of the continuous striving towards a new musical language, Schönberg wrote in a letter at the time of the completion of *Das Buch der hängenden Gärten,* Op. 15: 'I have succeeded for the first time in approaching an ideal of expression and form that had hovered before me for some years. . . . I may confess to having broken off the bonds of a bygone æsthetic . . . ' (quoted by Dika Newlin in *Bruckner, Mahler, Schönberg,* New York, 1947). Seemingly contradictory is the famous sentence in his article **'Brahms the Progressive'** in *Style and Idea* (London, 1951): 'Analysts of my music will have to realise how much I personally owe to Mozart. People who looked unbelievingly at me, thinking that I made a poor joke, will now understand why I called myself a pupil of Mozart, must now understand my reasons.' These two quotations (and many similar ones can be found in Schönberg's writings and sayings) are characteristic of the duality of his purpose and his development.

In attempting to trace the continuity of musical thought employed in Schönberg's compositions from the *Gurrelieder* (1901) to the Serenade, Op. 24 (1923), we shall deal separately with the different aspects of construction: first, with his treatment and subsequent dissolution of the functions of tonal harmony; then with the significance of his return to the use of counterpoint; and finally, with the character of his rhythm and with other elements which contribute to his conception of form and the novelty of his expression.

Throughout his life, Schönberg occupied his mind with the problems of tonal harmonic structure (*Harmonielehre,* Vienna, 1911, *Structural Functions of Harmony,* pub. posthumously 1954). His system of describing structural harmonic processes may be said to be based on the progressive theories of Simon Sechter, who was Bruckner's teacher and the master with whom Franz Schubert had decided to study counterpoint a few weeks before Schubert's death. In his *Die richtige Folge der Grundharmonien* (Leipzig, 1853), Sechter greatly extended the harmonic vocabulary by acknowledging, describing and analysing chords and harmonic progressions which, although used for a long time by individual composers (even as early as J. S. Bach) for certain purposes of expression, had not previously been granted a theoretically clarified inclusion in the system of tonal harmony.

Schönberg (as others before him and with him) developed the theory of harmony, following Sechter's pattern of incorporating into the system of functional harmony increasingly complex harmonic phenomena which appeared in the works of contemporary composers, sometimes for reasons of freer part-writing and sometimes with the aim of achieving ever more subtle expression. At the beginning of the century, composers like Reger, Mahler and Strauss wrote in an idiom which went very far in the elaboration of harmony and, while adhering to the basically diatonic construction of tonal harmony, included in their vocabulary more and more chords of a chromatic character or chordal combinations of intervals not primarily connected with diatonic harmony (intervals of the whole-tone scale, chords built on fourths, combination of tritone with other intervals, etc.). Some of the harmonies used (especially passing chords in vast prolongations) are of a nature only loosely connected with the idea of diatonic harmony. Schönberg, feeling that here the limits of tonal harmonic analysis were reached, started calling certain types of chords 'roving harmonies'. He saw in these novel chordal phenomena, quite rightly, the source of astonishing new developments and, at the same time, the danger of over-development and of obscuring the basic cadential structure. Wagner had already seen this danger and after *Tristan and Isolde* largely withdrew from the advanced position he had established. Some of these new harmonic happenings in the works of Reger, Strauss (in *Elektra* and *Salome*) and Mahler (particularly in the Seventh and Ninth Symphonies) met with very severe censure from the more conservative contemporary critics and some novel management of chords which Schönberg used in his early works was strongly criticised, e.g. the inversion of the chord of the ninth in **Verklärte Nacht** and the use of the *Quartenharmonien* (chords built on fourths) in the first Chamber Symphony, Op. 9.

Schönberg's use of the whole-tone scale can be compared to good advantage with the practice of Debussy. We find in Debussy's works passages which are almost entirely built, harmonically and melodically, on elements of the whole-tone scale. His predominantly vertical approach to harmony, which takes the actual character of the sound as a basis for the unity of the harmonic structure, has led to very impressive innovations and has influenced many of Debussy's contemporaries (and even composers up to the present time). Schönberg uses the whole-tone scale in a completely different way. In the Chamber Symphony, Op. 9, written in 1906, the fundamental structure is considerably influenced throughout the work by the partially whole-tone character of the first subject, but nevertheless all appearances and developments of these whole-tone elements are strictly subordinated to the functional plan of harmony which binds together the whole work. Furthermore, Schönberg uses many other methods of harmonic form-building (*Quartenharmonien,* varied sequences etc.) which, although apparently complete innovations, are also fitted into the plan of the whole harmonic layout in the manner of the German tradition of composition, and his ability to connect seemingly heterogeneous elements into one logical whole shows him clearly as a follower of Brahms and particularly of the later Beethoven. No such over-all construction can be detected in composers of different traditions, as for example—Debussy.

The Chamber Symphony, Op. 9, is of the greatest significance when showing Schönberg's progress in the harmonic sphere. We cannot, within the scope of this article, describe in detail the complete freedom and mastery Schönberg achieved in this idiom, using all kinds of means in expanded tonality, creating a structure unparalleled by previous music in its variety and subtlety of harmonic form-building, but we want to mention his use of free and more varied relationship of consonance and dissonance. Through his use of the widely leaping and internally varied melodic lines which were his heritage from Wagner and Wolf, he created a new and striking independence between horizontal melody and vertical chord. The result appears to approach in certain places some form of polytonality. Schönberg in subsequent works made considerable use of this and even applied, instead of polyphony in single lines, a technique of passing chord anticipations and suspensions to whole complexes of chord movement. It may be defined, to use the term of Joseph Schillinger, as 'Strata Harmony'. If we compare movement to a succession of vertical straight lines, we see in the application of this technique that these lines become distended and, as it were, distorted. This led to a weakening in the effect of the functional harmonic structure. Thus the technique, grown from humble beginnings where composers ornamented and contrapuntally prolonged their cadences, now brought music to the point where these cadences had been decorated and disguised to such an extent that in many cases they completely disappeared from view, or rather from hearing. Schönberg's use of roving harmonies, his contrapuntal prolongations and the all-important obscuring of the cadences, led him imperceptibly to a position where he had to withdraw key signatures, which became obsolete and gave a false impression of the harmonic structure (starting with the last movement of the Second String Quartet). This was a step towards that 'mythical' atonality which was attributed to Schönberg, yet it was the logical dialectical development of his technique.

It is, of course, an error to see the so-called 'atonal' works as representing some entirely new concept which fell from heaven. Schönberg had stretched the harmonic structure to a point at which the fundamental harmonies and cadence points no longer had full functional significance either aurally or intellectually. For a time he was still prepared to use the technique of harmonic composition which became completely free, and relied more and more on his individual powers of imagination. It is indeed true to say that in works such as the Five Orchestral Pieces, Op. 16, or *Erwartung,* Op. 17, although the overall harmonies might still be analysed according to the principles of tonal structure, the overlapping and frequent use of the neighbour-note technique, combined with the propensity of octave displacement, although completely coherent, make the works practically free of a felt tonality. Even as early as the Three Piano Pieces, Op. 11, we see, as it were in embryo, the kind of technique which he later brings to fruition. In the second half of the first piece, the subject is varied by a replacement of its smaller intervals, the ninth replaces the second, the eleventh the third, etc. In observing this octave displacement, one can understand better the characteristic sound of this music. Whereas in music from Bach to Brahms, the octave had played a most important part in the harmonic and melodic structure, the development of chromatic elaboration and the whole system of extended harmony show us these new intervallic progressions as well as many fourths and a great insistence on the old bogey, the tritone, taking a preponderance of emphasis in the melody and harmony. The traditional functions of a harmonic structure could no longer be said to apply to Schönberg's music. Sooner or later the composer had to face the problem of finding other form-giving elements to substitute for the lessened harmonic functions. From this time onwards, the analysis of his music in terms of fundamental harmony, which had generally been the satisfactory method up to this time, must of necessity be insufficient, artificial and contrived. One need only examine Hindemith's attempt to analyse the third piano piece from Op. 11 to see how little it helps towards an understanding of the musical structure.

It will now be necessary to occupy ourselves with the analysis of those elements which Schönberg found satisfactory to introduce into his work as substitutes for functional harmonic structure, and all subjects which will be discussed in the further part of our enquiry must be understood as such. The development of his counterpoint, his rhythmic practice and other new elements which he saw fit to introduce into his music, will be assessed primarily according to the purpose with which they were introduced, namely, the substitution of form-giving elements for the faded ones of tonal harmony. Schönberg's progress from *Pelleas and Melisande,* Op. 5 (1902-3), to the Serenade, Op. 24 (1923), the point at which he introduced the twelve-note technique, can now be seen as the gradual introduction of such new elements, in their elaboration breaking more and more into the domain of the functional harmonic structure. Certainly the most significant among these elements is Schönberg's reintroduction into his music, at the most fundamental level, of the principles of counterpoint.

During the nineteenth century the German composer's approach to counterpoint underwent a considerable change. Although Beethoven, especially towards the end of his life, and later, to a lesser degree, Reger and Mahler, made considerable use of counterpoint and concerned themselves with the problem of integrating it with their basically homophonic styles, the romantic followers of Beethoven (Weber, Mendelssohn, Schumann and also Brahms) tended to give up the procedures of real counterpoint and to replace them with a harmonically inspired polyphony. With Wagner, who most clearly represented the spirit of the nineteenth century, the polyphonic texture developed still farther away from the original contrapuntal methods, even remembering that the point of departure was not a strict modal style of counterpoint but the well-developed harmonic style of the seventeenth-and eighteenth-century German contrapuntalists. Strict counterpoint was the product of a musical age which thought not in the major-minor tonic system but in a system of authentic and transposed modes, the fundamental difference being that the modal form had a wider degree of possibilities for cadencing. Schönberg realised that with the disappearance of a valid tonal centre, the possibilities for introducing a freer approach to the cadence again existed, in fact his adoption of the twelve-note technique placed him under the obligation of regarding all twelve chromatic notes as equally valid for cadencing, i.e. a dodecatonic system. But at the period in his work before the twelve-note system had crystallised, we see him introducing the elements of a strict contrapuntal practice into the gradually dissolving tonal framework.

In treating the development of music of this period, T. Wiesengrund-Adorno observes that in harmonies composed of an unusual combination of intervals, the single note becomes less integrated in the unity of the chord. In a series of such chords, these comparatively loose notes lend themselves more easily to polyphonic treatment than they would do in more simple diatonic progressions. Chord progressions of relatively constant and similar tensions (according to Schönberg's theory, dissonances are equal to heightened consonances) demand new means of counteracting the greyness and uniformity of harmonic texture. Schönberg felt the need to reintroduce elements of strict counterpoint into his music. There are many examples of this in such works as the Five Orchestral Pieces, the opera, *Die glückliche Hand* and *Pierrot Lunaire.* For example, in the first movement of the Five Orchestral Pieces at Fig. 10, the trumpet plays a *cantus firmus*-like motif of ten bars in minims. This motif enters simultaneously in crotchets in the trombone part while at the same time the violins and violas play the motif as a canon at the octave in quavers. Eight bars later the strings bring a four-part canon of the motif at only a quaver's distance. Such adaptation of the principles of imitation to form the musical basis of the texture is one of the more simple examples of Schönberg's contrapuntal practices. He took the devices known to contrapuntalists farther than did even Bach in his most strict contrapuntal compositions. Besides making continous use of prolongation and contraction, canon, *fugato, passacaglia* and other contrapuntal forms, he introduced inversion, *cancrizans* and quite a number of even more obscure contrapuntal practices which had not been in use since works such as the *Musikalisches Opfer* and the *Hammerklavier* Sonata. In the times of Bach and Beethoven, the strict contrapuntal devices had been modified according to the principles of tonality. While this was essential for the expressiveness and perfection of the harmonic style, the musical form-giving significance of real counterpoint was weakened. For example, in Beethoven's Op. 135 Quartet, the interversions of the three-note motif are only of limited significance, the musical structure being achieved by other means. For Schönberg, such procedure had far more importance in that he treated the contrapuntal devices as form-giving elements in themselves. In doing this, he certainly made a major formal innovation within the principles of musical structure of his time, as such contrapuntal methods had hardly been used for three hundred years. Even now, only a few specialists know in any satisfactory detail the methods and procedures of the composers of early contrapuntal schools.

Schönberg went very far in the emphasis on counterpoint. His music was impelled more and more by purely contrapuntal means, rather than by a fusion of harmony with counterpoint, so that in certain passages he factually endangered the primarily harmonic validity apparent in the post-Wagnerian musical language. In this, he went farther than Mahler, who had also been working in this direction. Thus, comparing the *Adagio* of the Tenth Symphony, sketches of which were published after Mahler's death, with the first or last movements of his Ninth Symphony, which in its finished state it would no doubt have resembled, we see that Mahler still conceived his work in the first instance vertically and later dissolved it into polyphonic texture. But even in a work as early as Schönberg's Chamber Symphony, Op. 9, although it is still to a great extent conditioned by functional harmonic construction, many passages are no longer harmonically conceived, to such an extent are they primarily contrapuntal. The introduction of this rigid contrapuntal practice not only realised vertical combinations which were to become Schönberg's normal in later times, but also tended towards the even further liquidation and invalidity of other traditional formal principles. In the final works of this period the whole texture becomes so detailed, so attenuated and fragmentary, that harmonic development as it had been understood ever since the time of Bach virtually disappeared.

Among the younger generation, there is frequent criticism of Schönberg's seeming lack of method in rhythmic construction. This criticism, made especially by non-German musicians, is based on a completely erroneous comparison between the characteristics of Schönberg's German cultural tradition and those of other national schools. We do not wish to minimise the validity of Stravinsky's rhythmic methods or the other forms of rhythmic construction resulting from stricter attention to the combination of numerical values. On the contrary, one may sympathise and find a development of this long-neglected aspect of musical composition desirable. But it is valueless to criticise a composer from a viewpoint he did not share and consequently could not consider. The thinking which led Messiaen and his school to their adoption of rhythmic composition and eventually to serial forms of

rhythmic construction, could only have been alien to Schönberg even if known to him. It is important to remember that German music had always been rather simple in its rhythms—Luther's hymns had been a typically Protestant simplification of the subtle style of Gregorian chant. One need only look at the simple metres of German poetry of the Middle Ages, which always had a far more limited range of rhythmical interests than did that of other nations. The essence of German music can be found in rhythms of more or less regular patterns within binary and ternary forms. It was these, and not the more varied rhythms of the South or of the Slavs, which were in use in Germany throughout most of its musical history. The Germans wholeheartedly accepted the simple peasant dances of their own and neighbouring countries, and the March and *Ländler* form the main source of rhythmical inspiration in German music. (The other characteristic ingredient of German music, the sentimental song, is to be found at a very early date in the *Locheimer Liederbuch;* its simple and primitive rhythm and its free layout became the main source of the characteristic singing melodies of the German slow movement.)

In the late eighteenth and early nineteenth centuries, the German composers developed a refined and subtle manner of using the few rhythmic elements which were known to them. The most astonishing examples are Haydn and above all Mozart, who brought to perfection a technique of composing with varied bar- and phrase-lengths. In doing this, they accorded with modern concepts concerning the nature of rhythm. Matila C. Ghyka, in his *Essai sur le Rythme* (Paris, 1938), quotes several remarkable definitions of rhythm, among them: 'Rhythm is in time what symmetry is in the Platonic sense, viz. the proportional arrangements of elements in space' (E. d'Eichtal). Again, Professor Sonnenschein (*What is Rhythm?* Oxford, 1925): 'Rhythm is that property of a sequence of events in time, which produces on the mind of the observer the impression of a proportion between the durations of the several events or groups of events of which the sequence is composed.' If we agree with these definitions or with the definition of James Joyce that rhythm is the relation of the parts to the whole, we find that in the music of the time of Mozart and Haydn, many elements contributed to the expression of the rhythmic structure. In a deceptively simple manner, Mozart manages to create a form which is built of asymmetric quantities. We find examples of the contractions and prolongations expressed not only in the juxtaposition of rhythmic elements, but also in the closely calculated interchanges of different types of musical texture (diatonic scales, chromatic scales, *arpeggios,* etc). Alban Berg in his article 'Why is the music of Schönberg so hard to understand?' draws attention to this characteristic of Mozart's music. He quotes the nineteenth-century German theorist, Büssler: 'The greatest masters of form cherish free and bold constructions and rebel against being squeezed into confines of even-numbered bar groups.' This method was further developed in the nineteenth century. The English writer C. F. Abdy Williams (*The Rhythm of Modern Music,* London, 1909) devotes a great deal of space to the analysis of the music of Brahms and others from this viewpoint. Wagner with the free declamatory style in his *Musikdrama* also contributed greatly to the freeing of the musical construction from the 'prison' of the regular bar groups.

Schönberg was particularly interested in these rhythmic methods and created forms in which the music became almost totally free of metre. In this way he composed *Pierrot Lunaire, Erwartung,* Four Orchestral Songs, Op. 22, and *Die glückliche Hand,* among other works. Later, with his adoption of twelve-note technique, it is a matter of great interest that he tended to abandon this style of 'musical prose' and in such works as the Piano Suite and the last two String Quartets, wrote phrases of varied lengths within a simple, almost static, rhythmical form. Here he is most closely allied to the eighteenth century. Whether this was a satisfactory development of the early twelve-note technique could be disputed, and it is certainly a proof of the clear-sightedness and the genius of Schönberg that during the last years of his life he returned to the richer rhythmical structure of the works which he had written just before the adoption of the twelve-note system.

These rhythmic developments went hand in hand with Schönberg's development of the free-moving melody. Schubert, Schumann and Wagner had contributed towards a melody of great subjective expression. Schönberg, after Wagner and Hugo Wolf, introduced the wide spans of series of compound intervals into his melodies. Although chromatic elements, variations of character and creation of interval-contrasts are already well developed by Wagner in the singing line of the parts of *Brünnhilde* and *Isolde,* Schönberg's freeing of the octave led to a melos in which intervals appear as a result of melodic, as opposed to harmonic, elaborations and octave displacements. The abundance of passing notes and rhythmic decoration, in relation to the structural movement of harmony, which was a well-known characteristic of post-Wagnerian style, led Schönberg to a form of melody which, for the sake of tension and variety, carefully avoids the notes sounding in the supporting harmony and gets more and more shy of repeating notes.

Schönberg continued the endeavours of composers of the nineteenth century to expand and extend the existing forms of music. He went farther than Mahler, who had considerably developed traditional forms. At the turn of the century, the discovery by Freud of the existence of free associations and the consequent feeling for less logically and more subjectively connected associations in art had the greatest significance for the development of Expressionism. They led Schönberg to a greater degree of formal detail, an increasing amount of variation and a tendency to compress the single ideas of a piece into shorter spaces of time. In the first Chamber Symphony, although he is still working within a traditional form derived from the one-movement symphonic structure probably invented by Liszt, he liquidates many elements of this form and resorts frequently to a method which can

be considered an equivalent to free association (Schönberg liked to call these passages, which one can already find in Mahler, *Inselbildung*). Gradually, his habit of rarely repeating any subject, even in a varied form, led to the difficulty of understanding Schönberg's music. This is certainly the underlying reason why the works of Schönberg are, and probably will continue to be, more difficult for the ordinary listener to appreciate than the music of Webern, Berg and other contemporary composers. Schönberg himself seemed conscious of, and disturbed by, this fact, and he adopted many methods, some successful, some less so, in his efforts to overcome these difficulties. Many of the innovations he introduced, culminating in that of the twelve-note technique, were designed to clarify and illuminate the highly individual development of his musical thinking. He dispenses with colour for its own sake and in his instrumentation uses the orchestra to bring the important lines of his musical argument into greater relief. At the same time he invented a new type of the application of orchestral colour, the *Klangfarbenmelodie* or melody of 'timbres', first to be found in a systematic application in the third of his Five Orchestral Pieces, *Farben.* The musical argument of this piece is carried by changes of emphasis in instrumental groups, creating an entirely new kind of expression. In the fifth piece, *Das obligate Rezitativ,* the instrumentation is used to give the melody a constantly changing colour. (This technique is obviously an extension of the Wagnerian *ewige Melodie.*) The result of this experiment is that the natural connections and logical developments in his music can sometimes be more easily understood by the ear than by the eye.

As we have shown with the development of his harmony and counterpoint, when Schönberg's works were no longer effectively bound by traditional structural forms, he was faced with the problem of finding suitable new forms. In his Six Little Piano Pieces, Op. 19, he attempted to restrict himself to the exposition and variation of one single idea. The best example is the last piece, allegedly inspired by Mahler's funeral, in which the alternation of chords and fragments of motifs, probably derived from the memory of bells, constitute the piece. In these pieces, Schönberg attempts something fundamentally different from the short pieces of Berg and Webern. Whereas Berg in his Clarinet Pieces tended to contract what had been large forms and Webern in many of his short pieces used traditional formal principles, which found here the utmost concentration imaginable, Schönberg made his ideas suitable to the limitations of a completely integrated short form. Later, when he attempted larger forms again, we find a seemingly chaotic juxtaposition of such short forms, and it is in these works that the most daring and far-developed examples of Schönberg's personal, essentially expressionistic, art are to be found. Yet they remain valid as a perfect development of the characteristic integration of form and content.

In order to conclude this part of the discussion, we shall examine a work which may be regarded as typical of the most advanced and most individual Schönberg ever reached: the monodrama in one act *Erwartung*. Unfortunately it is not possible here to go into sufficient detail to clarify all our opinions, but it is hoped that it will be sufficient to justify our argument.

The first reaction upon hearing *Erwartung* is the very antithesis of the experience when listening to the perfection and apparent Apollonian symmetry of the eighteenth-century classicists. That particular effect upon the listener of classical music at its zenith was obtained by a skilful balance of asymmetries and variants which was so well realised that it resulted in the illusion of perfect symmetry. The style of Schönberg's music tended to cover the well-calculated proportions in its texture which has, as has that of Wagner, an appearance of almost continuous unbroken movement. In *Erwartung* we experience a sense of being overwhelmed and lost in a maze of variation and juxtaposition of elements which are hardly memorable and result in a seeming structural incoherence. But as we know the composition better, we find that all these variants and 'free associations' are well moulded into an overall shape and can be understood in a similar way to the works in the style of the preceding post-Wagnerian era. Though the chordal structure is complex and the individual parts are heavily doubled in augmented fourths, sevenths, etc. (which in this case tend to loosen the vertical coherence), an arc is circumscribed and the basic tonal principle of movement away from and towards a point or centre is retained. The technique of the work does not in itself seem to be a new departure. The basic idea for such immensely long and involved tonal structures had already been developed by Wagner, Mahler and Strauss. The novelty of the aural harmony results from the development described above. One feels that Schönberg here already starts 'composing with notes'; that is, that he tended to replace triads as the functional agents with the identity of individual tones.

The music of *Erwartung* falls into two parts. The overall 'top line' (Schenker might have called it *Urlinie*), whether expressed by the voice or by the instruments, is clearly delineated, although it cannot everywhere be found in the apparent main themes and motifs of the music. The first section commences with a progression from G sharp via B natural to C sharp at the beginning of the composition and closes at bar 270 at the words 'Nun küss ich mich an dir zum Tode'. The climax is reached at bar 194, at the cry 'Hilfe', an accent and leap down directly from the highest note of the voice part (B natural) to C sharp above middle C, a fall of well nigh two octaves. The second part proceeds from bar 270 to the end. The general division is a dramatic one; the first half consisting of the Search and Discovery of the lover's body and the subsequent dementia; the second part of a kind of *Liebestod* sung by the women in a fervid state of anguish and jealousy of the other 'She' (Death, who has taken her lover).

The orchestral introduction of four bars makes a clear movement from G sharp through B natural to C sharp (quasi-dominant/tonic). It is repeated in a contracted

form, this time moving to the leading note C natural-B sharp); the soprano enters for the first time on C sharp. The first scene, as it were in closed form, is clearly founded on a structure in which the notes C sharp and G sharp are predominant. To add to the illusion of a closed form, many of the chords are retained literally and appear throughout the scene. Practically all important structural notes, the notes which begin and end all phrases, are C sharp and its neighbour notes. There is a movement towards an emphasis on the semi-tone below at bar 29 *et seq.*, but a clear return to the quasi-tonic of C sharp in the *codetta* of the scene, bar 35 *et seq.* In the following scenes there is a gradual heightening of tension. Twice high B flats in bars 153 and 179 lead to the cry 'Hilfe' in bar 190 on the high B natural which falls back to C sharp. This is the over-all climax and highest point of the melodic line. From here the melody falls, often in long leaps, back to the C sharp in bar 270. (It is interesting to observe the parallel of the falling minor sixth (A-C sharp) in bars 194 and 270, obviously characteristic as a cadential movement as well as a psychological weakening, a premonition of death.).

The second half commences from G sharp (the first note of bar 273 and 274) and moves up to the B flat of bar 313, cadencing back to G sharp at bar 317, just before the extraordinary bars where the voice sings the words 'Oh, der Mond schwankt. . . . ' From here, the music falls again with greatly augmenting note values, to the dramatic point in bar 350 'für mich ist kein Platz da. . . .' The final section, which seems to act as a kind of spiritual resolution, lowers the tension by the introduction of chords of whole tone triads, which move in regular manner and, turning, reach again a section in which a C sharp seems to take its important position, introduced as a pedal in bar 416 and remaining a key note of the voice part, especially at the cadencing on 'dir entgegen . . . ' in bars 422-3. The C sharp disappears completely in bar 424, allowing the bass to make a determined step towards B natural. The final solution comes in the contra bassoon's C sharp in the middle of bar 425, introduced most characteristically by the last melodic phrase of the opera. The voice, which had again taken the G sharp (quasidominant) at bar 424, continues in bar 425 to the last utterance and reaches by a tritonus step the G sharp, slightly later than the C sharp bass has been established by the bassoon. The oblique vertical resolution of the harmony is characteristic of Schönberg's methods. It is also not without importance that three trombones have the triad A, C sharp, F natural at the point where the contra bassoon reaches the C sharp in the higher octave.

It might seem that an analysis which is made in the ways briefly indicated above would have but limited validity in this type of music. Yet we feel that the replacing of a harmonically valid form by an overall melodic one, though it could not have the significance of the old forms, nevertheless enabled the composer to differentiate between sections which return to their starting-point and those which move away from it. This is of the greatest importance towards an understanding of the subsequent revolution in the manner of composing music. The position may be compared to that reached by Joyce in *Finnegan's Wake*. In this work, the author could hold the thread through the maze of images, diversions, etc., only by continuous and relatively unvaried repetition of the so-called story (the death and rebirth). The conclusion reached is that the method of free association could no longer in itself prove to be a satisfactory manner of creation. The artists concerned seem to have realised that to create wider and more variegated forms they needed some valid structural principle, which would enable them to give more finite form to the perpetual variants their expression demanded.

After the astonishing realisation of the last works described, it became apparent to Schönberg that to continue his musical creation he had now constantly and intellectually to develop the composition with twelve notes. He saw clearly that for a time he would have to apply this entirely new method to forms much less elaborate than those he had used before. He made concessions in using older and simpler forms which he had discarded for quite a time. Even the regular sonata form and the form of the classical variations were used again and again, but filled with the completely new content resulting from his now strict use of the twelve-note system. Although the last period of Schönberg's musical creation (which does not come within the scope of this article) must be considered quite as important as the earlier periods, and he achieved works which can in every way stand comparison with his earlier achievements, perhaps even in some cases surpassing them, the line of development in this last period is not as clearly definable as it had been earlier. While endeavouring to give older forms new content, Schönberg creates intermittently works which might at first sight appear to continue directly the style of the great expressionist compositions like *Pierrot Lunaire, Die glückliche Hand* and *Erwartung*—for example, *Ode to Napoleon, A Survivor from Warsaw* and especially parts of his opera, *Moses and Aaron*. But when observed and analysed in more detail, these works, although in effect and texture frequently reminiscent of works of an earlier period, speak in a completely new musical language and the use of the twelve-note system is here, quite naturally and logically, freer and less strict than in those works based on older forms (which, for want of a better word, may be described as 'neo-classicist'). Schönberg also, in some of the masterpieces of the last period (e.g. Orchestral Variations, Op. 31, and particularly *Moses and Aaron*), combines new forms, which he went on creating in direct continuation of his expressionist period, with more stylised classical sections. The introduction and the extraordinary finale of the Orchestral Variations, Op. 31, are much nearer to this free expression than the variations themselves, which are kept to a large extent within the classical frame. And in the opera, *Moses and Aaron,* for dramatic and other reasons—some of the material had been sketched many years earlier, during Schönberg's expressionist period—free forms, with all the manifold applications of *Inselbildungen* and purely linear-based formulations (as explained in our analysis of *Erwartung*)

alternate with the more consolidated and simplified forms of the dance movements. Schönberg's treatment of harmony and counterpoint certainly went into a period of great simplification as soon as he had decided to compose in the strict twelve-note system. Harmonically, this system gave him security in its definite application, and in counterpoint he was no longer hampered by the unclear position in which the polyphonic style had been ever since the introduction of tonal and later functional harmony. In fact, only then did counterpoint regain the freedom and expression which it had had at the time of the early Flemish and Italian schools.

Schönberg's rhythm (except in those few compositions in which he kept very close to traditional dance or *Lied* forms) and basic adherence to musical prose was not developed much farther in his last period. Here and there a simplification may be observed, but seldom a further refinement. The tonal works of the last period need not be discussed here, as they were written partly for teaching purposes or as commissions for certain American institutions. And Schönberg has told us that several of these compositions, especially the very beautiful second Chamber Symphony, were based on material invented in his youth.

Schönberg was a master of German music. Even the fact that he spent the later part of his life in America in no way changed his determination to follow to the end logically and methodically what he felt was the right way (although living in America had considerably changed the style and attitude of many composers, e.g. Hindemith and Bartók). We should like to see in Schönberg's last achievement, the opera, *Moses and Aaron,* on which he worked practically all his life, the climax of his musical creation. Unfortunately he did not live to finish this work. The short experience we have of the opera (it has been performed only once so far, in 1954) gives us the impression that this is a work of supreme inspiration, perhaps Schönberg's greatest. Quite new experiences in sound, harmony and rhythm take us by surprise in the famous dances from the opera. The rhythm especially, as never before in Schönberg's works, moves in an orbit not far from Stravinsky's, and the whole expression is far more striking than in any of Schönberg's works after *Erwartung*.

We are not here concerned with the fact that Schönberg's work will always be much more difficult for the listener and the student than the works of his pupils and other contemporary composers. We do not think that this fact has anything to do with the greatness of his inspiration and fulfilment. It will always be amazing to observe the particular intellectual quality of Schönberg's compositions, their fast-moving sequence of thought and invention, their most imaginative colours of orchestration and the sometimes harsh and insistent reiteration of strong sounds and expressions. Just as we must recognise that Wagner's work, although prepared by many major innovators, was the culmination of nineteenth-century German music, we must without doubt recognise that

Schönberg's achievements—his compositions, his teachings, his writings—as well as his personal seriousness and belief in his mission, make him surely the greatest and most important musician of the first half of the twentieth-century.

Virgil Thomson (essay date 1965)

SOURCE: "How Dead is Arnold Schoenberg?," in *The New York Review of Books,* April 22, 1965, pp. 6-8.

[*In the following essay, Thomson reviews* Arnold Schoenberg Letters, *finding notable the book's portrayal of Schoenberg as an artist.*]

In 1910 Arnold Schoenberg, then thirty-five, began to keep copies of all the letters he wrote. Many of these were about business—teaching jobs, the publication of his works, specifications for performance. He would seem around that time to have arrived at a decision to organize his career on a long-line view involving the dual prospect of his continuing evolution as a composer—for he was clearly not one to have shot his bolt by thirty—and of his counting on pedagogy, for which he had a true vocation, as his chief support.

His plan was to become a private teacher (*privatdozent*) at the Academy of Music and Fine Arts in Vienna, avoiding by the modesty of such a post both the anti-Semitic attacks and the anti-modernist attacks that he felt would make it impossible for him to be offered a staff appointment. Actually he was offered a staff appointment two years later; but by that time he had got what he could out of Vienna and removed to the more lively music and art center that was Berlin.

The Vienna plan of 1910 had been calculated to play down his own music and call attention to his qualities as a teacher by bringing to the notice of the academic authorities the work of two pupils, Alban Berg and Erwin Stein.

> Perhaps after all the two men in whose hands the Conservatoire's destiny lies, can be brought to realize who I am, what a teacher the Conservatoire would deprive itself of, and how ungifted it would be to take on someone else when I am to be had for the asking. And alas I am to be had!!!

But no sooner was he had than he found a way, always his preoccupation, of leaving Vienna. For though he naturally loved his native city, he suffered from its perfidy toward music. And indeed Vienna is a bitch. Her treatment of Mozart and Schubert proved that. And even those who led her on a leash—Beethoven, say, and Brahms—got little profit out of their dominance, save in the latter case a certain satisfaction from administering through a henchman on the press local defeats to Wagner and to Bruckner.

Schoenberg at twenty-six, in 1901, had moved to Berlin, but two years later he was back home. The 1910 dis-placement lasted five years, till 1915, when he was obliged to return for mobilization. He was then forty. At fifty he left Vienna again, this time for good, to accept a teaching post in Berlin at the Prussian Academy of Arts. By then he was world-famous, but he was still poor. And he had come to insist in the hearing of all not only on his skill as a teacher but on his absolute authenticity as a composer. He left no slighting remark of foe or friend unprotested.

"I am much too important," he wrote in 1923 to Paul Stefan, "for others to need to compare themselves to me." Further, "I thoroughly detest criticism and have only contempt for anyone who finds the slightest fault with anything I publish." These are the words of one who has long since lost youth's bravado, who has been critically flayed and left with no skin at all to cover his nerve ends.

Except for his usual reaction to critical attacks, mostly foreign by this time, the years from 1926 to '33 seem to have been his least painful. He was an honored artist well paid; and he worked for only six months a year, these of his choosing. This freedom allowed him to spend winters South, eventually in Catalonia, where he found relief from a growing respiratory weakness.

The letters from this time are those of almost any successful musician. To conductors and impresarios he itemizes everything, exactly how his works are to be played and exactly what circumstances he will not tolerate. To enemies and to friends he draws an indictment for every rumored slight, then offers full forgiveness if they will admit him right. In fact, he is right; he has had to be. After all the persecutions and misunderstandings he has suffered, he cannot bother to blame himself for anything. He protests, though, against all who refuse him understanding and honor and against all anti-Semitism, especially the anti-Semitism of Jews who descend to that level in refusing his music. For in success he still must fight; fighting has become a conditioned reflex. And he cannot quite relax enough, even with time and money, for going on with the two great opera-oratorios, *Moses and Aaron* and *Jacob's Ladder*. Indeed, he did not ever finish them. For he was tired; his health was undermined; and soon he was to be a refugee.

From the summer of 1933, when he left Germany for good, till his death in 1951, he wrote a great deal of music and did untold amounts of teaching in the Los Angeles region, where he had gone for his health in the fall of '34 and where UCLA picked him up cheap at sixty, then at seventy threw him on the scrap heap with a pension of thirty-eight dollars a month for feeding a family of five. America, no less than Austria, be it said, behaved like a bitch. And though he found here through Germanic connections publishers for his work, money dispensers such as the Guggenheim Foundation could not see their way to helping him.

The sweetness and the bitterness of Schoenberg's American letters are ever so touching. The European correspondence rings like a knell, for he never ceases to sing out that save for himself and his pupils music is dead. In America he fancies for a moment that his teaching can bring it to life. Then come the disillusionments, first that the basic teaching is too poor for him to build on (he can thus teach only the simplest elements) and second that American music has detached itself from the Germanic stem. He despises equally the reactionary programs of Toscanini and the heretical modernisms of Koussevitsky, neither of whom plays his works. And in his mouth the word Russian has become an injury.

"Fundamentally," he writes in 1949 to his brother-in-law Rudolf Kolisch,

> I agree with your analysis of musical life here. It really is a fact that the public lets its leaders drive it unresistingly into their commercial racket and doesn't do a thing to take the leadership out of their hands and force them to do their job on other principles. But over against this apathy there is a great activity on the part of American composers, la Boulanger's pupils, the imitators of Stravinsky, Hindemith, and now Bartók as well. These people regard musical life as a market they mean to conquer [in contrast to his own Germanic view of it as a religion] and they are all sure they will do it with ease in the colony that Europe amounts to for them. They have taken over American life lock, stock and barrel, at least in the schools of music. The only person who can get an appointment in a university music department is one who has taken his degree at one of them, and even the pupils are recruited and scholarships awarded to them in order to have the next generation in the bag. The tendency is to suppress European influences and encourage nationalistic methods of composition constructed on the pattern adopted in Russia and other such places.

He is quite right, of course; and the shoe pinches. The only advantage he can see is that

> the public is at the moment more inclined to accept my music, and actually I did foresee that these people, so chaotically writing dissonances and that rough, illiterate stuff of theirs, would actually open the public's eyes, or rather ears, to the fact that there happen to be more organized ways of writing a piece, and that the public would come to feel that what is in my music is after all a different sort of thing.

The basis of Schoenberg's claim had not before been that he was doing "a different sort of thing," but rather that he was doing the same thing Bach and Brahms had done, and even Mozart, and that any novelty involved was merely a technical device for continuing classical music-writing into modern times. He did not consider himself different from the earlier German masters (for him the only ones one need take seriously) or from living ones either, but merely, as regards the latter, a better workman. But in America's wider musical horizon, which included (along with Germany) France, Italy, Russia, and the Orient, he felt obliged to assert his distinction as a difference in kind. His neighbor in Hollywood, Igor Stravinsky, was doing in fact just that, had been doing so ever since he had observed it being done in Paris by Pablo Picasso. In Picasso's assumption geniuses were a species, with only a few available, and with consequently the right to a very high price. Poor Schoenberg, who for all his artist's pride was humble before talent, even student talent, may not have been considered eligible for the big money simply because he naively believed that professional skill and an artist's integrity were enough. In any case, never in his published letters or other writing did he lay claim to special inspiration, to divine guidance, to a genius's birthright, or to any form of charismatic leadership.

But in America he felt impotent and outraged that music should be taking off without his consent, that pregnancy should not await the doctor. Indeed he tended to consider all such independences as irresponsible and as probably a plot against his music. Another plot, indeed, where there already had been so many! And so he came to view our movement as the work of men differing from him not only in degree but also in kind. And the integrity represented by himself and his pupils he ended by denying to almost everybody else.

Yet he remained a fine companion; there was no deception in him. And he went on writing letters to everyone in praise of the artists he had loved—in painting, Wassily Kandinsky and Oskar Kokoschka, in architecture Adolf Loos, in music Gustav Mahler, Anton von Webern, and Alban Berg. For himself he demanded honor and begged money. He despised the State of Israel for trying to create a music "that disavows my achievements"; then later he aspired to citizenship and offered to revise the whole of music education there.

The self-portrait that is distilled from these letters is that of a consecrated artist, cunning, companionable, loyal, indefatigable, generous, persistent, affectionate, comical, easily wounded, and demanding, but not the least bit greedy. That artist we know from his music to have been a Romantic one; but he was too sagacious for that, too realistic. And he was too preoccupied with the straightforward in life ever to have become aware, even, of the great dream-doctor Sigmund Freud, though they were contemporaneous in Vienna, with neither of them exactly ignorant about contemporary thought.

We know him for a Germanic artist too, for whom every major decision was a square antithesis, an either-or, for whom a certain degree of introversion was esteemed man's highest expressive state (*inwardness* is the translation word for what must have been *innigkeit*), and for whom our century's outbreak of musical energies represented only a series of colonial revolutions to be suppressed, floods to be dammed, drained off, and channelized, naturally by himself acting alone. The dream is unbelievable, but in today's world not far from having come true, like Dr. Freud's sexual revolution.

Schoenberg's music and teaching are at present a world influence of incomparable magnitude. Nor have the vigor and charm of his personality ever been in doubt. Nevertheless his work is still not popular. Like the music of Bruckner and of Mahler and, until in recent decades only, that of Brahms, it has the savor rather of a cause than of plain nourishment. Mozart, Beethoven, and Schubert, in the past; Debussy and Stravinsky in our time, have been as clear to us as Santa Claus. Not so Arnold Schoenberg, at least not yet. But the man has long been precious to those who knew him; and now the letters, with their punctilious indignation and casual buffoonery, their passionate friendships and irascible complaints, their detailed accountings and their Olympian self-regard, their undying optimism under the most humiliating poverty and disregard, have given us a man that many will come to love and laugh at and get angry at and cherish, just as if he were still with us.

And perhaps he is. In Vienna, certainly, Mozart still walks beside one, Beethoven is at his window, and Schubert is drinking and writing songs in any tavern. The whole career of Arnold Schoenberg resists historical pinning down. Not in the Vienna of 1874, where he was born, nor in that of 1900, where he was virtually unnoticed, nor in Berlin of the early Teens and late Twenties, where he was a power, nor in the Hollywood of '34 to '51, where he was merely beloved, in none of these places did he sum up a time. He slipped into and out of them all, just being Arnold Schoenberg, and everywhere except in Berlin being roundly persecuted for that. Even today I would not be too sure he is not writing music over many a student's shoulder and putting in many a violation of his own famous method just to plague its more pompous practitioners.

Certainly he is being a plague to Igor Stravinsky, whose adoption of that method after the master's death has left him in a situation almost as skinless as that of Schoenberg in life. Certain known attacks on Stravinsky's music there, none of them published here, have obliged him, as a confessed Schoenbergian, to take cognizance of these with what grace he can muster, which is considerable. Reviewing the Letters last October in the London *Observer,* he accepted their strictures with a gallant *mea culpa* and paid higher praise to their author than he has ever paid, I think, to any other musician.

"The lenses of Schoenberg's conscience," he said, "were the most powerful of the musicians of the era, and not only in music." Also, "the Letters are an autobiography . . . the most consistently honest in existence by a great composer." Actually Stravinsky's exit from a seeming impasse has been ever so skillful and handsome. And its warmth of phrase is such as to make one forget almost that the gesture was imposed. Imposed by what? Simply by the fact that a great and living master had been resoundingly slapped by a dead one.

As for how dead Arnold Schoenberg really is, let us not hazard a guess. The Viennese composers have never rested easy.

Richard Huggett (essay date 1967)

SOURCE: "Orgy in Covent Garden," in *Saturday Book,* Vol. 27, 1967, pp. 146-61.

[*In the following essay, Huggett recounts a performance of* Moses and Aaron *in Covent Garden.*]

On the first day's rehearsal I asked the stage manager if there was a chance of getting free tickets for any of the six scheduled performances of **Moses and Aaron**. He nodded with weary resignation: 'For this old thing?' he replied. 'Don't worry; they'll be giving them away in hundreds. Nobody will come. You'll see.'

His words summed up the general atmosphere of gloom and despondency. Schoenberg, undoubtedly the most non-popular composer of the day, was the darling of a small clique of intellectual musicians, but the general public didn't know his music or want to know. He had invented twelve-tone serial music, that strange and inaccessible world of sound, and **Moses and Aaron** was regarded as the supreme achievement in that world. Schoenberg died in 1951, leaving **Moses and Aaron** unfinished. Berlin and Zürich had recently presented the two acts of the opera cautiously stylised in production, but these had seemed to confirm what Schoenberg had always said—that it was unstageable.

The prevailing feeling in the Covent Garden company was that here was one of those rather tiresome and boring acts of piety which state-endowed theatres occasionally feel they have to perform to justify their position. 'They've got to do stuff like this,' it was explained to me, 'otherwise they get their grant cut.' The expectation was that there would be a small amount of respectful attention from the intellectual Press, a fair-sized audience on the first night consisting of the critics, the regular first-nighters and those peculiar people who actually *like* Schoenberg, a chorus of reverent hallelujahs from the critics, and total indifference from the public, who would be merely waiting for Callas in *Tosca.* For the remaining performances there would be five empty houses. The company could then breathe a long sigh of relief, their painful duty done, and the whole production would be quietly dropped and forgotten.

Just how wrong can you be? Who could have known that **Moses and Aaron** would be the most spectacular smash-hit of the season, that tickets would become the hottest black-market property in London, hotter than Olivier's *Othello,* hotter than Fonteyn/Nureyev, hotter even than Callas? Who could have forseen the orgy of newspaper vulgarity it would provoke? Who could have known that it would be the most joked-about, talked-of event of the season, that all-night queues would be fighting for the few standing tickets, that questions would be asked about it in Parliament? Nobody could have foreseen any of this, neither Sir David Webster, nor William Beresford, the press officer, nor Georg Solti, the conductor, nor Peter

Hall, the producer, nor any of the three hundred singers, actors, dancers, guardsmen and animals involved.

It wasn't only that the company didn't think it would be a success. They didn't even like it, neither principals, chorus nor orchestra. The chorus really hated it, for the burden on their shoulders had been by far the heaviest. For nearly a year, working overtime under the loving but relentless discipline of their chorus-master, Douglas Robinson, they had sweated and groaned and cursed over those complex twelve-tone rhythms and those outlandish atonal harmonies, surely the most difficult choral music ever written. Now, at the end of a long and exhausting season, they were tired and irritable. In time many came to like it more, or at least to dislike it less, for increased mastery over the score revealed unsuspected beauties, and, by the end of the season, Schoenberg had made many converts.

The instigator and prime mover behind the venture was Georg Solti, who, since he had heard a recording in 1961, had conceived a passionate desire to stage **Moses and Aaron** at Covent Garden. By early 1964 the production was ready to be set up and several important decisions had been made. It would be cast entirely from the resident company; no need to import expensive foreign stars. It would be sung in English, and David Rudkin, author of *Afore Night Come,* was commissioned to prepare a translation of Schoenberg's libretto. And, since the theatrical problems were as complex as the musical, it seemed logical to engage a team of theatrical experts. Peter Hall was approached; the idea appealed to him, and he agreed, bringing a trio of Aldwych Theatre associates: Clifford Williams and Guy Wolfenden to assist in the direction, and John Bury to design the set and costumes. Peter Hall was no stranger to opera production. He had produced John Gardner's *The Moon and Sixpence* at Sadler's Wells some years before.

All were in agreement on one important point. The stylisation of the two continental productions would not work. The staging must be as realistic as was permitted by the resources of the Royal Opera House and the restrictions of the Lord Chamberlain. In view of the excessive demands made by the libretto this decision was not lightly taken; but Schoenberg had wanted realism and the instructions in the score had been specific.

> After the procession the slaughtermen kill the beasts, throw hunks of meat to the crowd . . . wine streams forth everywhere, general drunkenness, heavy stone jars are hurled around . . . four naked virgins strip before the Calf, the Priests seize their throats, plunge the knife into their hearts . . . a naked youth darts forward, seizes girl, rips the clothes from her . . . naked people shrieking and screaming run past the altar. . . .

Nevertheless, Peter Hall was to insist repeatedly that this was *not* a sensational opera.

Rather than impose a further physical burden on the long-suffering chorus, it was resolved to engage a special team of actors and actresses to cope with the more strenuous aspects of the orgy scene. Over a period of many weeks hundreds of actors auditioned in the Amphitheatre Crush Bar at the Opera House. Divided into groups of six, they improvised energetically such diverse scenes as the building of the pyramids, the crossing of the Red Sea, and the ritual sacrifices round the Golden Calf. From these forty were chosen. They were a strangely assorted group, widely differing in age, colour, nationality and theatrical experience. Almost all of them, however, had one thing in common: they had not acted in an opera before.

Even for Covent Garden, which is accustomed to mounting its operas on a grand scale, **Moses and Aaron** was going to be exceptionally lavish, and the statistics cautiously released by the press office had a Cecil B. de Mille flavour . . . 150 chorus, 40 actors, 40 guardsmen, 20 children, 20 dancers, 12 animals; the total number involved including the principals would be just short of three hundred. It was a pity that no mention was made of the amount of timber in John Bury's set or the amount of towellene required for three hundred costumes.

On May 10, 1965, the rehearsals started in the London Opera Centre. This enormous building, formerly a cinema, lies halfway down the Commercial Road, sandwiched between building sites, docks and factories. It is not an attractive district. The Centre houses the Opera School, a recording studio, a huge workshop, paint-dock and scenery-store, and a vast rehearsal room the size of Covent Garden's stage. A steep metal ramp covered the entire floor of what had been the stalls—this was John Bury's set in embryo. Rows of tiered seats covered what had been the stage. The actors sat on the ramp and the chorus on the seats, gazing at each other in mutual curiosity. Peter Hall climbed on to a nearby stone altar.

He called everybody on to the ramp and grouped them round the various steps, rostra and altars. 'Now in this scene,' he explained, 'Moses and Aaron appear at the back of the stage and move across and then down centre. You must all turn and see them, and there is going to be a blinding sun which shines down on top of you. You're terrifically excited by it, and you're all in ecstasy. So let's start.'

Georg Solti, in purple shirt and sun-glasses, started to conduct. John Constable, the repetiteur, started to play on the Bechstein grand. Forbes Robinson and Richard Lewis, as Moses and Aaron respectively, appeared and moved down into the mob at a stately pace. Singers screamed out their welcoming chorus of joy, dancers twisted and gyrated, actors shuddered and reacted with ecstasy. It was all very impressive.

'Please remember,' said Peter Hall when we had finished, 'that I simply can't give you all individual directions for every moment of the play or we'll be here for two years not two months. You will all have to improvise, and I'd much rather you overdid it and forced me to cut you down, than underdid it and compelled me to call for some action. I shall have to rely on you all to use your imagination and initiative.'

We did it again and again, and at 1.30 we broke for lunch. The basement canteen was a large one but it wasn't used to dealing with crowds like this, which were to throng it thrice daily. During these long, hot, sunny lunch-hours the pubs and cafés within a mile radius were crowded with singers and actors, to the polite bewilderment of the locals.

In 'The Prospect of Whitby' a group of choristers, safe from the ears of authority, were complaining loud and long. It became speedily clear to anybody who happened to be listening that although a few English, Scots and foreign singers had infiltrated their sacred ranks, the great bulk of the Covent Garden chorus were Welsh. With all those Dais, Owens, Morgans, Griffiths, Blodwens and Gwyneths, the Rhondda valley reigned supreme. 'You can keep this bloody opera, man. . . . But it's not music, whatever *they* say; where's the bloody tune? . . . You can't sing it. . . . My voice is cracking, I can feel it. . . . Nobody will come, only a bunch of short-arsed phoneys. . . . Give me *Faust* any day, give me *Carmen,* now there's *real* music. . . . One good thing, man, we'll never have to do it again. . . . Oh, it's back to Cardiff for me, man, I'm telling you. . . . ' The voices floated musically over the beer tankards and hot sausage rolls.

That evening, with the opera company performing *Otello* at Covent Garden, the actors had the Opera Centre to themselves. Grouped comfortably round the Bechstein they listened to John Constable playing Act 2 while Peter Hall gave a running commentary on the action. 'This is where the Golden Calf is dragged on . . . this is where you get drunk . . . this is where the animals are slaughtered and you all eat the bloody meat . . . this is where the naked youth sacrifices the naked girl. Schoenberg says in the score that they must be as naked as the conventions of the stage permit. This is where the Golden Calf is destroyed and somebody runs on and says, "Cave, Moses is coming," and you all run off.

'Now I want you to hear the same music in full score because it sounds so different from the piano.' He put on the record. The music sounded unbelievably ugly, harsh and ear-tingling. 'It's terrific stuff this,' he smiled, 'it's the most gut-stirring music ever written and it starts where the *Rite of Spring* leaves off. But don't forget, this is not a sensational opera, and I don't want Fleet Street to get the idea that there's nothing to it but a long sexual orgy. So please don't talk about it.'

Over the next four hot dusty weeks the singers, actors, and a special contingent of Scots Guardsmen, looking uncomfortably out of place in their army blazers and winkle-pickers, sweated it out, and what slowly took shape was not only the production but the nature of the problems involved. The basic difficulty in opera production never changes. By its very nature opera is a highly artificial art-form. A realistic opera, strictly speaking, is a contradiction. But somewhere down the line there is a compromise where the conflicting demands of drama and music can in part be satisfied.

From the start Peter Hall decided that this was not to be one of those productions in which the singers contented themselves merely with singing and left all the acting to the actors. This was to be total theatre. Actors were to sing, or, at least, seem to. Singers were to act, or seem to act. 'I want you all to do everything with such conviction,' he said, 'that the audience must be incapable of deciding who are the actors and who are the singers.'

The actors were given copies of the libretto and instructed to learn the words of the choruses so that they could silently mouth them to give the illusion that they were singing—a process known in the profession as 'goldfishing'. But they really would join the spoken and shouted choruses, and long exhausting rehearsals were held so that their shouting synchronised with that of the chorus. As for the singers joining in the acting, this wasn't so easy. Many singers, especially the older ones in the chorus, are hidebound by the long-established formal conventions of opera, as any theatre producer has found to his cost, and most of them are happiest when standing centre-stage with their eyes firmly fixed on the conductor. It would be necessary to coax them with subtlety and cunning. So it can be seen that Peter Hall's major problem wasn't so much theatrical as diplomatic.

The invention of television has made things easier, for closed-circuit TV enables the conductor to be seen on any number of monitor sets placed in the wings. Singers can turn left, right and even upstage and still see him. Even so, there were difficulties. 'Ladies, I want you all to move down right and kneel behind the altar,' Peter Hall would say. A howl of dismay would rise. 'But, Mr Hall, we can't see the conductor. How can we sing if . . . '

'All right, don't worry, we'll sort it out. . . . Now, you gentlemen, would you move away down left? . . . Thanks. . . . Now, ladies, can you see Mr Solti?'

'Thank you, yes we can.'

'Good. Now, gentlemen, I want you to cross the stage. . . .'

'But, Mr Hall, if they do that we can't see anything. . . .'

'Please don't panic, ladies, we'll sort it out. Actors, I want you to rush down and mingle with the ladies here. . . .'

'But, Mr Hall, I don't want to be awkward but I really can't sing with all them actors rushing between us. Upsets me, it does, and we can't see Mr Solti. Really, I've never had to go through anything like this before.'

'Don't worry, ladies, please don't panic. We'll get it all sorted out.'

The pledge of secrecy made on the first day didn't last long, but this surprised nobody. A secret shared by three hundred people has, one supposes, a limited term of life. For the first month the outside world knew little about what was happening in the Commercial Road, and nothing appeared in the papers apart from the formal announcement, with cast lists, that the opera was to be presented in June and July. But by early June whispers were heard in Fleet Street that something interesting was happening in the Opera Centre. The *Evening Standard* was the first in the field. A photographer was sent to investigate and take rehearsal pictures. Next day a picture of Yvonne Minton, Morag Noble, Elaine Blighton and Elizabeth Bainbridge was published with the caption ORGY IN COMMERCIAL ROAD. The story went on to say that these ladies were to sing the parts of the four naked virgins.

The secret was out. Every newspaper editor loves an orgy, and when a few days later the Press was formally invited to take pictures of the animals on hire from Chessington Zoo who were making their first appearance in rehearsals, an army of photographers and reporters turned up. An event which ordinarily would have caused only a ripple of interest in Fleet Street was now covered by every paper in the country. While six donkeys, goats, kids, three horses, a camel and a Highland Shetland bull were ceremoniously paraded across the stage, the cameras clicked and flashed excitedly. (The bull, it later transpired, was actually a cow, and had to withdraw from the 1966 revival owing to pregnancy.)

At the beginning of June the company moved into the Royal Opera House for the last weeks of rehearsals. Every morning an army of blue-denimed stage-hands erected John Bury's set and every afternoon they removed it. New props appeared daily: a huge unfinished statue of Moses, a section of a pyramid, hundreds of gold trinkets and jewels, the Golden Calf mounted on rollers, the animals' carcasses and the blood-stained meat. This had to be eaten; it looked disgustingly realistic and tasted—disgusting.

Finally the Sacred Phalluses appeared. The High Priests bring these on to the stage during the climax of the orgy scene and give them to the six dancing boys, who strap them on and perform a very sensual, phallic dance. Out of the depths of hiserotic imagination John Bury had produced what looked rather like carnival hats: they were long and pointed, they were painted with cheerful, multi-coloured stripes, and they had little paper tassels attached to the point. The actors thought they were very funny and charming; but not the chorus.

The first distant rumblings of mutiny were heard. From canteen, pub and dressing-room outraged chapel-going voices could be heard complaining with high moral fervour. 'I know he's a clever young man and all that but

. . . those phalluses aren't very *nice,* are they? . . . obscene, I'd say . . . disgusting, I call it . . . downright immoral . . . my wife's coming and my married daughter and they'll want to know what they are, well, it's going to be a bit embarrassing having to explain, isn't it?' Fortunately, the voices of Morality and Good Taste were overruled. John Bury's phalluses stayed and were greatly admired.

A source of more open mutiny was the blood. This had been cleverly faked by the ever-resourceful property department who, after several false starts, had produced a liquid which had the right colour and consistency and looked horribly realistic (the recipe was and still is a closely guarded secret). It was warm and smelly and the taste of it on the tongue and the feel of it on the skin was literally sickening. Buckets of it had to be thrown over the company, actors and chorus had to wallow in it, lick it, drink it, and smear it on their faces and near-naked bodies.

This sort of thing is one of the less attractive aspects of theatrical life; actors are frequently required to undergo unpleasant ordeals like this; they are used to it and can take it in their stride. But the chorus found it more difficult. 'Don't come near me with that, young man,' snarled one elderly female chorister, as she saw the blood bowl approaching. 'Mr Hall, I'm not having that stuff on my face and that's flat . . . it makes me sick . . . I won't be able to sing.' Protests rose from all sides.

There was physical danger, too. John Bury's steeply sloping metal ramp was very slippery, especially when covered with blood and wine. Bruises, grazes, cuts, strained tendons began to occur with alarming frequency, and one unlucky dancer almost wrenched his big toe off when he caught it in a narrow slit near the footlights. The ramp was then covered with a variety of substances including sand, and little lumps of hard cork. The final surface was not comfortable either for rape or dying, but at least there was no more slipping.

Meanwhile on the other side of Floral Street the wardrobe department was busily turning out three hundred biblical costumes which had to be ragged, torn and stained with blood and muck. 'You don't call *those* costumes, I hope,' said Wardrobe contemptuously. For people whose expert skill enables them to produce anything from Salvador Dali creations for *Salome* to gorgeous Regency gowns for Callas or the incredibly elaborate eighteenth-century dresses for *Rosenkavalier,* these loincloths, these strips of black towellene, were a frustrating anti-climax. Wardrobe looked a little happier when the four high priests came for their fitting: they were to be dressed in white-and-gold robes with gold turban and scarlet waistband which looked rather splendid. But these had to be dirtied in their turn till they looked as drab as the others.

The Press was now becoming deeply interested in the goings-on, and the most extraordinary rumours began to circulate. Is it true, asked Fleet Street indignantly, that the animals are to be killed and a fresh bunch led to the slaughter at every performance? Nonsense, said the Royal Opera House, firmly. In fact the only casualty during the whole venture was the camel who was led on to the stage during one particularly hectic rehearsal, surveyed the proceedings with unutterable contempt, deposited his candid opinion of **Moses and Aaron** on to the floor, slipped on it as he was led across, and crashed through the ramp on to the stage floor some fifteen feet beneath. Bleating piteously, his head and hump could be seen projecting through the hole. The risk of the same thing happening during a performance was too great: he was clearly not satisfied with his part, so he was released from his contract and returned to Chessington Zoo.

Is it true, asked Fleet Street excitedly, that four girls from a Soho strip-club are to be engaged to replace the four virgins? No comment, said Covent Garden primly. But now it can safely be revealed that the four ladies of the Opera company had not been happy about stripping off and singing their extremely difficult quartet with their backs to the conductor. Peter Hall invited four girls from the highly respectable Astor Club to watch a rehearsal and asked them if they would like to muck in? They would and they did. Thenceforth it was they who were stripped by the high priests, raped, and ritually sacrificed, while the four ladies sang their quartet from the safety of the wings. Peter Hall has always believed in specialisation where possible.

Is it true, asked Fleet Street apprehensively, that the Lord Chamberlain, perturbed by the rumours, was going to send a representative to the public dress-rehearsal and that even at this late stage the entire production might be forcibly abandoned if what he saw exceeded the legal definition of decency? Not true, retorted Covent Garden, for only that very morning Sir David Webster had received a letter in which the Lord Chamberlain had expressed his complete trust in the discretion and good taste of the Royal Opera House management.

Is it true, asked Fleet Street lasciviously, that people are going to run about in the orgy scene *completely naked*? You can come and see for yourselves on the first night, replied Covent Garden loftily. In the final week Fleet Street stepped up the pressure and proceeded to give Covent Garden the full gutter-press treatment. It was gripped by such a **Moses and Aaron** frenzy that it seemed nothing else was happening in the world; whenever you opened a paper there were pictures, stories, interviews, cartoons, gossip, rumours, each sillier than the last. ORGY NIGHT AT THE OPERA. . . . NAKED VIRGINS SHOCK CAST. . . . PUBLIC WILL NOT STAND FOR THIS ORGY. . . . REMARKABLE ORGY BUT DO WE WANT TO PAY FOR THIS? screamed the headlines. In a last-minute attempt to damp the fires of sensationalism Peter Hall announced: 'Don't get the wrong idea; my orgy is quite tame.' Reporters and photographers, rigidly excluded from rehearsals and frustrated by Sergeant Martin and his vigilant front-of-house staff from infiltrating the theatre, fell back on the time-honoured practice of haunting the stage-door and the Nag's Head opposite, taking pictures of the company as they went in and out, and furtively begging for inside information.

It was this which led to one outbreak of violence. A photographer from one of the national papers was attempting to take a picture of the four strip-club girls when his operation was interrupted by one of the singers who suddenly charged angrily at him. 'This is a serious work of art,' he cried angrily. 'You're just cheapening and vulgarising it.' The photographer stated that he was only doing his job; an argument rose; tempers were lost. The singer seized the camera and attempted to destroy it; the photographer clung to it like a limpet; they scuffled and grappled all the way down Floral Street, and were stopped only by the chance appearance of an astonished Sir David Webster who had just stepped out for lunch. The singer was calmed and the photographer was placated: apologies were exchanged and they parted calmly if not amicably. Happily for all, the editor of the newspaper was persuaded not to print this story.

But it wasn't all strippers and orgies. The Friends of Covent Garden assembled one Sunday evening at the Opera House to hear a symposium on the opera and extracts from the score. So many turned up that the amphitheatre and gallery had to be opened to accommodate them. Forbes Robinson and Richard Lewis sang extracts, and those who spoke on different aspects of the opera included Georg Solti, Peter Hall, John Bury and Egon Wellesz, a former pupil and friend of the composer. Solti ended by saying, 'This is difficult music, very difficult. But if you listen hard it becomes easy. Soon it becomes like Mozart opera.'

The public dress-rehearsal was held on Saturday morning, June 26, and was well received. Amongst the invited audience was Frau Gertrude Schoenberg, the composer's widow, who said, 'What a pity my Arnold is not alive to see this; he would have liked to see it done like this.' When Peter Hall was introduced to her he asked: 'I hope you don't feel that we have gone too far.' 'On the contrary, young man,' she replied firmly, 'in my opinion you have not gone far enough.' She thought that the orgy scene was tame but a move in the right direction.

This was not the opinion of some of the Friends of Covent Garden who had been present: they thought the production was 'sickening' . . . 'excessive' . . . 'horrible'. . . . 'They've gone too far,' said one to the *Evening Standard*. 'Everything was just thrown at you. There's no subtlety. It was revolting.' One anonymous correspondent seemed to agree with this. He wrote to Peter Hall saying he was disgusted at the things which were being done in his name and would call down the vengeance of heaven on the entire venture. It was signed *'God'*.

The night of the première arrived, Monday, June 28, 1965. It was a perfect summer's evening, hot and dry. By six-thirty the streets round the Opera House were jammed with people and slow-moving traffic, not only singers and audience, but sight-seers, first-night celebrity-spotters, ticket-scalpers (one pair of stalls was sold for £100), and the general public who wanted to see what was going to happen and to be there when it did. Was it imagination or was there an unusually large contingent of policemen on duty, walking down Floral Street, grouped round the stage-door, and guarding the front entrance? Probably there was, for a rumour was circulating that a hostile demonstration was being planned and that the evening might end in a riot.

Who could be planning this? one wondered. The Friends of Glyndebourne, perhaps? One thought of all the famous riots of musical history: *Tannhäuser, Electra, Salome, Rite of Spring*. Was *Moses and Aaron* to be added to this distinguished list? Would women stand and scream that they had been insulted? Would they throw things on to the stage? There was an electric tension in the air, a terrifying sense of expectancy and foreboding, 'I've never known anything like it,' said the oldest stage-hand gloomily. For once one felt glad that Bow Street police station was so near.

The first-night audience included not only many international celebrities and all fashionable London but operatic administrators from all over the world, anxious to see if a realistic *Moses and Aaron* was a practical proposition. They did not have to wait long for an answer. Few people, least of all the singers, realised how short the opera is. Even with a long interval it scarcely lasts two hours, and by 9.25 history had been made. From every point of view the performance was superb: the musical and technical difficulties which had made the final week's rehearsals so stormy and frustrating all melted away as if by magic. Forbes Robinson and Richard Lewis and all the other principals gave magnificently assured performances, and the Lost Tribes of Egypt sang and acted with a passionate fervour which fully justified their reputation as one of the finest operatic choruses in the world. Welsh puritanism and middle-class inhibitions were flung aside; they threw themselves into the orgy scene, blood, phalluses and all, with an abandon which astonished and delighted everybody.

At the end the audience, which had been on the edge of its seats with excitement, cheered for twenty minutes. If anybody had come to make trouble they clearly stayed to applaud, for not a single hostile note marred this glorious sound. It was a very gratifying, very emotional experience for everybody concerned. This was the final accolade. Here was an unknown and difficult opera performed by the resident company without a single international star name, and their reward for a year's hard work was a standing ovation which even Callas might envy.

The evening finished with an orgy of another sort in the Crush Bar for the company and several hundreds of Covent Garden's most intimate personal friends. Large quantities of delicious cold food and *vin rosé* were consumed, and the feasting continued into the small hours,

by which time early editions of the papers were available. Fleet Street had gone hysterical with joy; it was a paen of triumph . . . ORGY NIGHT AT THE OPERA. . . . THAT WAS QUITE AN ORGY FOR 31/6. . . . AN ORGY BUT NOT EROTIC. . . . HURRAH FOR THIS FIRST-CLASS ORGY. Later, the Sundays, weeklies, monthlies and quarterlies had their reservations, but by and large one thing emerged clearly: Georg Solti's dream had come true. He and Peter Hall had been proved triumphantly in the right. Never again would *Moses and Aaron* be regarded as unstageable.

Two days after the final performance the full company and orchestra conducted by Georg Solti gave a special concert performance at the Proms. From the back of the promenade I looked at their familiar and well-loved faces, now looking strangely different in their white ties, dinner-jackets and long evening gowns. The blood-stained desert seemed a hundred miles and a thousand years away. They sang better than ever, and the listeners, released from the distraction of stage spectacle, were able to concentrate on the music as never before. It was a profoundly moving experience. I remembered how ugly and meaningless the music had seemed when I had first heard it. But I had heard it every day for three months, and familiarity had bred understanding and love. Now my ear could accept Schoenberg's atonal harmonies so completely that I wondered how I could ever have found them difficult. I remembered that Solti had said, 'Soon it will be easy, like Mozart opera,' and he was quite right. But I felt I could almost go further. Now, large portions of it were easy—like Gilbert and Sullivan.

George Steiner (essay date 1967)

SOURCE: "Schoenberg's Moses and Aaron," in *Language and Silence: Essays on Language, Literature, and the Inhuman,* Atheneum, 1967, pp. 127-39.

[*In the following essay, Steiner analyzes the relationship between music and language in Schoenberg's* Moses and Aaron.]

It is difficult to conceive of a work in which music and language interact more closely than in Arnold Schoenberg's *Moses und Aron*. (The German title has an advantage of which Schoenberg, half in humor, half in superstition, was aware: its twelve letters are a symbolic counterpart to the twelve tones which form a basic set in serial composition.) It is, therefore, impertinent to write about the opera if one is unable to analyze its powerful, intensely original musical structure. This analysis has been undertaken by several musicologists and students of Schoenberg. One would wish that the intrinsic difficulty of the subject had not been aggravated by the "initiate" technicality of their approach. This is especially true of the account of the music written by Milton Babbit and issued with the only recording so far available of *Moses and Aaron* (Columbia K-31-241).

If I write this program note, it is because the great majority of those in the audience at Covent Garden will be in my position; they do not have the training or knowledge needed to grasp the technical unfolding of the score. The demands made are, in fact, severely beyond those required by a classical composition, or even by the orchestral density of Mahler. Together we shall have to take comfort in Schoenberg's frequent admonition:

> I cannot often enough warn against the overrating of analysis since it invariably leads to what I have always fought against: the knowledge of how something is *made;* whereas I have always tried to promote the knowledge of what something *is.*

And one recalls Kierkegaard's observation at the outset of his discussion of *Don Giovanni:*

> though I feel that music is an art which to the highest degree requires experience to justify one in having an opinion about it, still I comfort myself . . . with the paradox that, even in ignorance and mere intimations, there is also a kind of experience.

In the case of **Moses and Aaron** I would go further. It belongs to that very small group of operas which embody so radical and comprehensive an act of imagination, of dramatic and philosophic argument articulated by poetic and musical means, that there are aspects of it which go well beyond the normal analysis of an operatic score. It belongs not only to the history of modern music—in a critical way, as it exemplifies the application of Schoenberg's principles on a large, partly conventional scale—but to the history of the modern theater, of modern theology, of the relationship between Judaism and the European crisis. These aspects do not define or in any way exhaust the meaning of the work; that meaning is fundamentally musical. But an account of them may prove helpful to those who approach the work for the first time, and who would place it in its historical and emotional context. Like other very great and difficult works of art, Schoenberg's opera goes decisively outside the confines of its *genre* while giving to that *genre* a new and seemingly obvious fulfillment.

In a letter to Alban Berg of October 16, 1933, when he had just returned formally to Judaism in the face of Nazi anti-Semitism, Schoenberg wrote:

> As you have doubtless realised, my return to the Jewish religion took place long ago and is indeed demonstrated in some of my published work (*"Thou shalt not, thou must"*) as well as in **Moses and Aaron,** of which you have known since 1928, but which dates from at least five years earlier; but especially in my drama **The Biblical Way** which was also conceived in 1922 or '23 at the latest.

Der Biblische Weg remains unpublished; but what is known about it points clearly to the theme of the opera. It tells of a Zionist visionary, in whose name, Max Arun, there may be a foreshadowing of Moses and Aaron, who fails to achieve his goal through human imperfection.

Equally relevant is the other piece referred to by Schoenberg, the second of the **Four Pieces** for mixed chorus, op. 27. Written in 1925, it sets to music the prohibition of Mosaic law against the making of images. "An image asks for names. . . . Thou shalt believe in the Spirit; thou must, chosen one." This injunction, expressed in a cadenced prose which anticipates the "spoken song" of the opera, summarizes the central dramatic idea and conflict of **Moses and Aaron**. But Schoenberg's interest in the musical statement of religious thought and in the dramatic idiom of the Old Testament goes back even further: to **Die Jakobsleiter,** an oratorio left incomplete in 1917.

This concern persisted throughout Schoenberg's later work: in the **Kol Nidre** of 1938, in the brief, harrowing cantata *A Survivor from Warsaw* (1947), in the setting of Psalm 130 (1950), in Schoenberg's final opus, the unfinished **Modern Psalms**. The last words he set to music were: "And yet I pray as all that lives prays." Thus **Moses and Aaron** is thematically and psychologically related to an entire set of works in which Schoenberg sought to express his highly individual, though at the same time profoundly Judaic concept of identity, of the act of spiritual creation, and of the dialogue—so inherent in music—between the song of man and the silences of God. The opera is both Schoenberg's *magnum opus* (what T. W. Adorno calls his *"Hauptwerk quand-même"*) and a composition rooted in the logic and development of his entire musical thought.

Schoenberg began writing **Moses and Aaron** in Berlin in May 1930; he completed Act II in Barcelona on March 10, 1932. Roberto Gerhard, in whose Barcelona flat Schoenberg often worked, tells an instructive anecdote. Schoenberg did not mind friends chatting in the room, even when he was engaged on the fantastically complex score; what he could not tolerate were sudden spells of quiet. The dates of composition are, of course, important. On the one hand they mark Schoenberg's hard-fought professional acceptance, as Ferruccio Busoni's successor at the Prussian Academy of Arts. But they also mark bouts of illness which led Schoenberg to seek refuge in a southern climate, and, above all, the rise of the Nazi menace. A year after he had completed Act II, Schoenberg was compelled to leave Berlin and start a life of exile.

He did not live to complete the opera or hear it performed. An extract was given in concert form at Darmstadt on July 2, 1951 (plans for a production at the *Maggio Musicale* in Florence fell through). Schoenberg died less than a fortnight later. The first complete concert program was given at the Musikhalle in Hamburg under the direction of Hans Rosbaud in March 1954. On June 16, 1957, Rosbaud directed the stage *première* of **Moses und Aron** at the Stadttheater in Zurich. This was followed by a Berlin production under Hermann Scherchen in October 1959. Since that time there have been few major opera houses in Europe or the United States which have not expressed the hope of producing the work, and retreated before its formidable demands.

Karl Wörner says that *Moses and Aaron* "is without precedent." This is not so: as opera, it is related to Wagner's *Parsifal,* and there are orchestral anticipations both in Mahler and in Schoenberg's own earlier compositions and in his short operas, *Erwartung* and *Die Glückliche Hand*. But it is technically more demanding than any other major opera, and the quality of the religious-philosophic conflict requires from the performers and producer an unusual range of insight and sympathy. Schoenberg has deliberately used a *genre* saturated with nineteenth-century values of unreality and modish display to express an ultimate seriousness. In so doing he reopened the entire question of opera.

The libretto is organized wholly in terms of musical form and development (if serial music anticipates electronic music it is in the totality of control which the composer aims at in every aspect of the musical experience). As Schoenberg remarked: "It is only while I'm composing that the text becomes definite, sometimes even after composition." Nevertheless, the book of *Moses and Aaron* is itself of great fascination. Schoenberg has a distinctive style which one sees in his paintings and theoretical writings no less than in his music. He worked in large strokes, and achieved an effect of clarity and abstract energy by leaving out syntactical qualifications or half-tones. Like much in Schoenberg's musical texts and literary tastes, the libretto shows traces of German expressionism, and of the sources of expressionism. Characteristically, Strindberg plays a part: Schoenberg knew *Wrestling Jacob* when he planned *Die Jakobsleiter,* and was aware of Strindberg's *Moses* when writing his own very different treatment of the theme.

The idiom used in *Moses and Aaron* is highly personal. It is kept apart from the rhythms and tonality of the Luther Bible. Schoenberg wrote to Berg on August 5, 1930: "I am of the opinion that the language of the Bible is medieval German, which, being obscure to us, should be used at most to give colour; and that is something I don't need." Above all, each German word, whether in *Sprechgesang,* in direct song or choral declaration, is uniquely and precisely fitted to the musical context. The words are no less *durchkomponiert* ("fully composed, musicalised") than are the notes. This is what makes any decision to produce *Moses and Aaron* in English so wrong-headed. To alter the words—their cadence, stress, tonalities—as must be done in translation, is tantamount to altering the key relations or orchestration in a piece of classical music. Moreover, there is no need to subvert Schoenberg in this way: the story of *Exodus* is known to everyone, and Schoenberg's presentation of the plot is utterly lucid. A brief outline would have given an English-speaking audience all the help it wants.

The relationship of language to music in *Moses and Aaron* is unlike that in any other opera. The problem of that relationship, of how to apportion the stress between word and musical tone, of whether the ideal libretto should not be weak precisely in order to mark the distance between music drama and the spoken play, under-

lies the whole history of opera. As Joseph Kerman has shown, it is the problematic achievement of Wagner, the late Verdi, and twentieth-century operatic composers to have given the libretto a new seriousness. Hence the marked affinity to modern literature and psychological argument in the operas of Janácek, Berg, and Stravinsky. Hence the ironic allegoric treatment of the debate between poet and composer in Richard Strauss's *Capriccio.*

But *Moses and Aaron* goes much deeper. It belongs to that group of works produced in the twentieth century, and crucial to our present aesthetics, which have their own possibility as essential theme. I mean that it asks of itself—as Kafka does of fiction, as Klee asks of visual form—whether the thing can be done at all, whether there are modes of communication adequate. Kierkegaard wrote of Mozart: "The happy characteristic that belongs to every classic, that which makes it classic and immortal, is the absolute harmony of the two forces, form and content." One would say of modern art that what makes it such and unmistakable to our sensibility is the frequent dissonance between moral, psychological content and traditional form. Being a drama of non-communication, of the primal resistance of intuitive or revealed insight to verbal and plastic incarnation (the refusal of the Word to be made flesh), *Moses and Aaron* is, on one vital plane, an opera about opera. It is a demonstration of the impossibility of finding an exhaustive accord between language and music, between sensual embodiment and the enormous urgency and purity of intended meaning. By making the dramatic conflict one between a man who speaks and a man who sings, Schoenberg has argued to the limit the paradoxical convention, the compromise with the unreal, inherent in all opera.

The paradox is resolved in defeat, in a great cry of necessary silence. This alone makes it difficult to think of a serious opera coming after or going beyond *Moses and Aaron*. But that was exactly Schoenberg's own problem as a post-Wagnerian, and as an heir to Mahler in artistic morality even more than in orchestral technique. Like Mahler, he was proposing to aggravate, in the literal sense, the easy coexistence, the *libertinage* between music and public which obtained in the opera house at the turn of the century and which Strauss, for all his musical integrity, never refuted. As Adorno notes, *Moses and Aaron* can be approached in the same spirit as a major cantata of Bach. But unlike Bach, it is a work which at every moment calls to account its own validity and expressive means.

The motif of a sharp conflict between Moses and Aaron is, of course, present in the Pentateuch. It may well be that later priestly editors, with their particular professional association with Aaron's priesthood, smoothed away some of the grimmer evidence, and obscured the full, murderous consequences of the clash. Schoenberg made of this archaic, hidden antagonism a conflict of ultimate moral and personal values, of irreconcilable formulations or metaphors of man's confrontation with God. Working on the principle—discernible at the roots of

Greek tragic drama—that fundamental human conflict is internal, that dramatic dialogue is in the final analysis between self and self, Schoenberg gathered the entire force of collision into a single consciousness.

This is the drama of Moses. Aaron is one of the possibilities, the most seductive, the most humane, of Moses' self-betrayals. He is Moses' voice when that voice yields to imperfect truth and to the music of compromise. Schoenberg remarked in 1933: "My Moses more resembles—of course only in outward respect—Michelangelo's. He is not human at all." So far as the harsh, larger-than-life stature of the personage goes, this may be so. But the poignancy of the opera, its precise focus of emotion and suffering, comes above all from Moses' humanity, from that in him which is riven and inarticulate. It is not of the fiercely contained eloquence of Michelangelo's statue that one thinks when listening to **Moses and Aaron,** but of Alban Berg's *Wozzeck* (written just before Schoenberg started composing his own opera). Moses and Wozzeck are both brilliant studies in dramatic contradiction, operatic figures unable to articulate with their own voices the fullness of their needs and perceptions. In both cases the music takes over where the human voice is strangled or where it retreats into desperate silence.

Schoenberg admitted to Berg: "Everything I have written has a certain inner likeness to myself." This is obviously true of Moses, and it is here that Michelangelo's figure, which fascinated Freud in a similar way, may be relevant. To any Jew initiating a great movement of spirit or radical doctrine in a profoundly hostile environment, leading a small group of disciples, some of them perhaps recalcitrant or ungrateful, to the promised land of a new metaphysic or aesthetic medium, the archetype of Moses would have a natural significance. By introducing into music, whose classical development and modes seemed to embody the very genius of the Christian and Germanic tradition, a new syntax, an uncompromisingly rational and apparently dissonant ideal, Schoenberg was performing an act of great psychological boldness and complexity. Going far beyond Mahler, he was asserting a revolutionary—to its enemies an alien, Jewish—presence in the world of Bach and Wagner. Thus the twelve-tone system is related, in point of sensibility and psychological context, to the imaginative radicalism, to the "subversiveness" of Cantor's mathematics or Wittgenstein's epistemology.

Like Freud, Schoenberg saw himself as a pioneer and teacher, reviled by the vast majority of his contemporaries, driven into solitude by his own unbending genius, gathering a small band around him and going forward, in exile, to a new world of meaning and vital possibility. In Moses' bitter cry that his lessons are not being understood, that his vision is being distorted even by those nearest him, one hears Schoenberg's own inevitable moments of discouragement and angry loneliness. And there is almost too apt an analogy in the fact that he died on the threshold of acceptance, before his stature had been widely acknowledged, before he could complete **Moses and Aaron** or hear any of it performed.

Except for one moment (I, 2, bars 208-217)—and I have never understood just why it should be at *this* particular point in the opera—Moses does not sing. He speaks in a highly cadenced, formal discourse, his voice loud and bitter against the fluencies of the music and, in particular, against Aaron's soaring tenor. (The parodistic yet profoundly engaged treatment of Aaron's vocal score seems to be full of references to traditional operatic *bel canto* and the ideal of the Wagnerian *Heldentenor*.) The fact that the protagonist of a grand opera should not sing is a powerful theatrical stoke, even more "shocking" than the long silence of Aeschylus' Cassandra or the abrupt, single intervention of the mute Pylades in *The Libation Bearers*. But it is also much more than that.

Moses' incapacity to give expressive form (music) to his vision, to make revelation communicable and thus translate his individual communion with God into a community of belief in Israel, is the tragic subject of the opera. Aaron's contrasting eloquence, his instantaneous translation—hence traduction—of Moses' abstract, hidden meaning into sensuous form (the singing voice), dooms the two men to irreconcilable conflict. Moses cannot do without Aaron; Aaron is the tongue which God has placed into his own inarticulate mouth. But Aaron diminishes or betrays Moses' thought, that in him which is immediate revelation, in the very act of communicating it to other men. As in Wittgenstein's philosophy, there is in **Moses and Aaron** a radical consideration of silence, an inquiry into the ultimately tragic gap between what is apprehended and that which can be said. Words distort; eloquent words distort absolutely.

This is implicit in the first lines of the opera spoken by Moses against the background of the orchestral opening and the murmur of the six solo voices which portray the Burning Bush. The fact that Moses so often speaks simultaneously with Aaron's song, or that we hear his voice in conflict with the orchestra, points to Schoenberg's essential design. Moses' words are internal, they are his thought, clear and integral only before it moves outward into the betrayal of speech.

Moses addresses his God as "omnipresent, invisible, and inconceivable." *Unvorstellbar,* that which cannot be imagined, conceived, or represented (*vorstellen* means, precisely, to enact, to mime, to dramatize concretely), is the key word of the opera. God is *because* He is incommensurate to human imagining, because no symbolic representation available to man can realize even the minutest fraction of His inconceivable omnipresence. To know this, to serve a Deity so intangible to human mimesis, is the unique, magnificent destiny which Moses envisions for his people. It is also a fearful destiny. As the Voice out of the Burning Bush proclaims:

> This people is chosen
> before all others,

to be the people of the only God,
that it should know Him
and be wholly His;
that it undergo all trials
conceivable to thought
over the millennia.

The last two lines are eloquently ambiguous: the words can also be read to mean: "all trials to which this thought—of a God invisible and inconceivable—may be exposed."

Aaron enters and the misunderstanding between the two brothers is immediate and fatal. Aaron rejoices in the proud uniqueness of Israel's mission, in the grandeur of a God so much more powerful and demanding than all other gods (these other gods continue to be real to Aaron). He exults in *imagining* such a God, in finding words and poetic symbols by which to make Him present to His people. Yet even as he sings, Moses cries out: "No image can give you an image of the unimaginable." And when Aaron elaborates, with a rich ease of perception mirrored in the music, the notion of a God who will punish and reward His people according to their deserts, Moses proclaims a Kierkegaardian God, infinitely, scandalously transcending any human sense of cause and effect:

> Inconceivable because invisible;
> because immeasurable;
> because everlasting;
> because eternal;
> because omnipresent;
> because omnipotent.

To which litany of abstraction, of inexpressible apprehension, Aaron responds with the joyous assurance that God shall bring wonders to pass on behalf of His enslaved people.

He does. Confronted with the rebellious bewilderment of the Jews, with their call for visible signs of the new revelation, Moses retreats into his own inarticulateness. It is Aaron who proclaims himself the word and the deed. It is he who casts Moses' rod to the ground where it turns into a serpent, and shows Moses' hand to be leprous and then miraculously restored. During the entire last part of the Act, Moses is silent. It is Aaron who proclaims the doom of Pharaoh and the covenant of the Promised Land. Fired by his eloquence, the people of Israel march forth and the music is exultant with Aaron's certitude. It is through him that God appears to be speaking.

In one sense, in one possible idiom, He is. Moses' understanding of God is much more authentic, much deeper; but it is essentially mute or accessible only to very few. Without Aaron, God's purpose cannot be accomplished; through Aaron it is perverted. That is the tragic paradox of the drama, the metaphysical scandal which springs from the fact that the categories of God are not parallel or commensurate to those of man.

Act II centers on the Golden Calf. With Moses' long absence on Sinai, the Elders and the people have grown rebellious and afraid. The invisibility of God has become an intolerable anguish. Aaron yields to the voices that cry out for an image, for something that eye and hand can grasp in the act of worship. On the darkening stage the Golden Calf shines forth.

What follows is one of the most astonishing pieces of music written in the twentieth century. As musical analysts point out, it is a symphony in five movements with solo voices and choruses. The orchestration is so intricate yet dramatic in its statements and suggestions that it seems incredible that Schoenberg should have *heard* it all inside him, that he should have known exactly (if he did) how these fantastic instrumental and rhythmic combinations would work without, in fact, ever hearing a note played. The pageant of the Golden Calf makes the utmost demands on orchestras, singers, and dancers. Rearing horses, treasure-laden camels, and Four Naked Virgins are requirements which even the most resourceful of opera houses find difficult to meet.

What Schoenberg had in mind is something very different from an ordinary operatic ballet. It is a total dramatic integration of voice, bodily motion, and orchestral development. Even the most frenzied moments of the idolatrous, sexual orgy are plotted in terms of a rigorous, immensely subtle musical structure. As Schoenberg wrote to Webern:

> I wanted to leave as little as possible to those new despots of the theatrical art, the producers, and even to envisage the choreography as far as I'm able to. . . . You know I'm not at all keen on the dance. . . . Anyway so far I've succeeded in thinking out movements such as at least enter into a different territory of expression from the caperings of common-or-garden ballet.

But these "caperings" are not wholly irrelevant. In Schoenberg's treatment of the Golden Calf, as in so much of **Moses and Aaron,** there is a revaluation—either straightforward or parodistic—of the conventions of opera. Are these conventions applicable to the modern circumstance? How much seriousness can they sustain? Thus the Golden Calf is both the logical culmination of, and a covert satire on, that catalogue of orgiastic ballets and ritual dances which is one of the distinctive traits of grand opera from Massenet's *Hérodiade* to *Tannhäuser,* from *Aïda* and *Samson et Dalila* to *Parsifal* and *Salome.* Schoenberg is fully aware of the dual quality of the scene. It is at the same time supremely serious and ironic in its exhaustive use of the convention:

> In the treatment of this scene, which actually represents the very core of my thought, I went pretty much to the limit, and this too is probably where my piece is most *operatic;* as indeed it must be.

With the return of Moses—his indistinct, terrifying figure looms suddenly on the horizon and is seen by one of the exhausted revelers—the drama moves swiftly to its climax. At a glance from Moses, the Golden Calf vanishes:

Begone, you that are the image of the fact that
what is measureless cannot be bounded in an image.

The two brothers confront each other on the empty stage.
And once more it is Aaron who has the better of the
argument. He has given the people an image so that Israel
may live and not fall into despair. He loves the people
and knows that the demands of abstraction and inwardness which Moses makes upon the human spirit are beyond the power of ordinary men. Moses loves an idea, an
absolute vision, relentless in its purity. He would make of
Israel the hollow, tormented vessel of an inconceivable
presence. No people can endure such a task. Even the
Tables of the Law which Moses has brought from the
mountain are only an image, a palpable symbol of hidden
authority.

Baffled, incensed by Aaron's argument, Moses smashes
the Tables. Aaron accuses him of faint-heartedness. The
tribes of Israel shall continue their march to the Promised
Land whether or not they have grasped the full meaning
of God's revelation. As if to confirm his words, the Chorus resumes its march across the stage. It is led by a pillar
of fire, and Aaron goes forth glorying in the visible
wonder of God.

Moses is left alone. Is Aaron right? Must the inconceivable, unimaginable, unrepresentable reality of God diminish to mere symbol, to the tangible artifice of
miracle? In that case all he has thought and said (the two
are identical to Moses) has been madness. The very attempt to express his vision was a crime. The orchestra
falls silent as the unison violins play a retrograde inversion of the basic twelve-tone set. Moses cries out, "O
word, thou word that I lack!" and sinks to the ground,
broken.

This is one of the most moving, dramatic moments in the
history of opera and of the modern theater. With its implicit allusion to the *Logos,* to the Word that is yet to
come but which lies beyond speech, it gathers into one
action both the claims of music to be the most complete
idiom, the carrier of transcendent energies, and all that is
felt in twentieth-century art and philosophy about the gap
between meaning and communication. But Moses' defeat
also has a more specific, historical bearing, which may help
us understand why Schoenberg did not complete the opera.

The letters of 1932 and 1933 show that he had every intention of doing so. As late as November 1948, Schoenberg
could write: "I should really best like to finish *Die
Jakobsleiter* and *Moses and Aaron*" What intervened?

There is evidence that Schoenberg found it difficult to
give the third Act a coherent dramatic shape. He wrote to
Walter Eidlitz on March 15, 1933, that he had re-cast
Aaron's Death for the fourth time "because of some almost incomprehensible contradictions in the Bible." As it
stands, the text of Act III is a curious torso, both repetitive and moving. Once more, Moses and Aaron, now in
chains, state their opposite conceptions of idea and image. But Moses no longer addresses his brother directly.
He is speaking to the Jewish people as it prepares to
enter into the mire and compromise of history. He proph-
esies that Jews will prosper only so long as they dwell in
the stern wilderness of the spirit, in the presence of the
One and Inconceivable God. If they forget their great act
of renunciation and seek an ordinary haven in the world,
they will have failed and their suffering shall be the
greater. Salvation lies in apartness. The Jew is himself
when he is a stranger.

Freed of his chains, Aaron falls dead at Moses' feet. (Is
there here, one wonders, a reminiscence of Hunding's
death when Wotan glances at him in scorn?) As we have
no music to accompany the words, it is difficult to judge
their effect. But the third Act is essentially static. There
is no dramatic justification for Moses' triumph over a
prostrate Aaron. Much is missing.

But the real impediment probably lay deeper. As Adorno
remarks, *Moses and Aaron* was "a preventive action
against the looming of Nazism." But even as Schoenberg
worked on the score, Nazism was moving rapidly to its
triumph. The words *Volk* and *Führer* figure prominently
in the opera; they designate its supreme historical values,
Israel and Moses. Now they were wrested out of
Schoenberg's grasp by the million voices bawling them at
Nuremberg. How could he continue to set them to music?
As he labored on the third Act in March 1933, Schoenberg
must have known that the culture in which he had hammered
out his vision of a new music, and for whose opera houses
he had conceived *Moses and Aaron,* was heading for ruin
or exile—as was his own personal life.

It is this which gives the end of Act II its tremendous
authority and logic. The events that were now to come to
pass in Europe were, quite literally, beyond words, too
inhuman for that defining act of humane consciousness
which is speech. Moses' despairing cry, his collapse into
silence, is a recognition—such as we find also in Kafka,
in Broch, in Adamov—that words have failed us, that art
can neither stem barbarism nor convey experience when
experience grows unspeakable. Thus *Moses and Aaron*
is, despite its formal incompletion, a work of marvelous
finality. There was no more to be said.

Roger Sessions (essay date 1972)

SOURCE: "Schoenberg in the United States," in *Roger
Sessions on Music: Collected Essays,* edited by Edward
T. Cone, Princeton University Press, 1972, pp. 353-69.

[*In the following essay, Sessions surveys Schoenberg's
music influenced by American music and culture.*]

In any survey of Schoenberg's work one fact must be
emphasized above all: that no younger composer writes
quite the same music as he would have written had
Schoenberg's music not existed. The influence of an artist is not, even during his lifetime, confined to his dis-

ciples or even to those who have felt the direct impact of his work. It is filtered through to the humblest participant, first in the work of other original artists who have absorbed and reinterpreted it for their own purposes; then through the work of hundreds of lesser individuals, who unconsciously reflect the new tendencies even when they are opposed to them. For genuinely new ideas determine the battlegrounds on which their opponents are forced to attack. In the very process of combat the latter undergo decisive experiences which help to carry the new ideas forward.

In Schoenberg's case this process is clear. The appearance, around 1911, of his first completely characteristic works, and of his *Harmonielehre,* marks the approximate beginning of the years that were decisive in the formation of contemporary music. True, these works—both music and book—only carried to more radical conclusions tendencies already present in the music of the time; these manifestations, then hailed as revolutionary, seem to us now more like footnotes and queries to established modes of thought than integral and challenging steps toward new ones. What was new in Debussy and Ravel and Scriabin seemed more fundamental and far-reaching than it does today.

But in the Three Piano Pieces, op. 11, and the Five Orchestral Pieces, op. 16, a much more thorough-going challenge became evident. What led in Wagner to an enlargement of musical resources, in Debussy and Scriabin to the cultivation of special and restricted corners, here openly insists that new resources, having multiplied to an overwhelming extent, demand a logic of their own, depriving the earlier principles of their validity even in music of a relatively conventional type. The *Harmonielehre,* which exerted its influence on some of the least likely persons, raised the same questions in the realm of theory, deducing them from the very logic of previous practice. The musical status quo has never completely recovered from the blow.

In 1933 Schoenberg came to the United States and ten years later became an American citizen. In the country to which he came, musical activity is intense on many levels, and despite many necessary reservations the development within the last generation has been phenomenal. Musical education has penetrated everywhere; both the general level and the quality of instruction available on the highest level of all have risen to a degree amazing to all who confronted the musical conditions of thirty-five years ago. American composers of serious intent have begun to appear in considerable numbers, and to achieve an influence and recognition undreamed by their predecessors; moreover, they have become aware of themselves, of their inner and outer problems, and better equipped to face these. Above all it has become evident that musical talent, the raw material from which musical culture grows, is strikingly abundant.

It is, however, clear that the institutional structure of music in the United States has not yet been established in definitive outlines. The relationship between the art and the business of music, and of both of these with the "public"; the role and direction of musical education; the influence of radio, gramophone, and amateur musical activities—these are questions which in the United States are still fundamentally unsettled. There is similar confusion as to what we may call the structure of musical effort: the respective roles in musical culture and production of the composer, performer, critic, and scholar.

These latter observations are true of course not only of the United States but of modern civilization in general. But conditions here differ from those elsewhere in the fact that whereas elsewhere the forces of opposition are those of an established cultural tradition, here there is a perceptible undertow in the growing musical consciousness of a culture still in the making. It is this which keeps the musical life of the country in a state of constant change and flux, and which makes the situation chaotic but far from hopeless.

It is not surprising therefore that Schoenberg should have found himself in a quite new relationship to his environment and that his impact should have taken on a new significance. I do not mean to minimize the importance of either the revolutionary or the specifically Viennese Schoenberg. The former has already affected the course of music in a profound sense, and though possibly the first full impact of a composer's work is the most immediately powerful one—think of the *Eroica,* of *Tristan,* in contrast to the last quartets or *Parsifal*—nevertheless with the constant ripening of his art, the latter imposes itself in another, more gradual and more definitely constructive, sense. But that is a task for the composer's successors, and is even independent of his purely historical importance.

As for Vienna, Schoenberg has outlived it as he has outlived Alban Berg. Had he not done so his position might be today less evident than it is. There are other musicians from Central, also from Western and Eastern, Europe, whose impact has been purely provincial; they have conceived their mission as that of winning spheres of influence for their own native background; and have found—by an inexorable law of human polarization—the most sympathetic acclaim often in circles most tenacious in the pursuit of an American "national" style. Undeniably Schoenberg is a product of Vienna, and of a Viennese tradition with which he is as deeply imbued as anyone living. But it is characteristic of the man, the situation, and possibly of the Viennese tradition itself that his impact on the United States has been that of a third Schoenberg—one by no means unknown in Europe nor difficult to find for those who sought him, but one often obscured in the heat of controversy and the battle positions which his followers were led to assume in his behalf. For in coming to the United States, he left the scene of his most bitter struggles; he came with the prestige of a fighter of distant and only dimly understood battles, with the respect and admiration of a few to whom the battles were neither so distant nor so dimly understood.

Others recognized the achievement of the composer of *Verklärte Nacht* and other early works, and were ready to acclaim him as at least an asset to American musical life.

He taught and lectured in Boston and New York and finally was appointed Professor of Music, first at the University of Southern California, later at the University of California in Los Angeles. His music received sporadic performances; he found himself frequently quoted, frequently in demand as a writer and lecturer. His main influence, however, has been exerted through his teaching, the musicians with whom he has come in contact, and finally the series of works composed in the years since he has lived in the United States—works which in my opinion represent a separate phase and a new level in his music as a whole.

These works include a Suite for strings, written in 1934; the Fourth String Quartet written in 1936 and performed by the Kolisch Quartet in 1937; the Violin Concerto, performed in 1940 by Louis Krasner with the Philadelphia Orchestra; a second Chamber Symphony; a setting of the *Kol Nidrei* for chorus and orchestra; Variations on a Recitative for organ, first performed by Carl Weinrich for the United States section of the I.S.C.M. in March, 1944; the Concerto for Piano first performed by Edward Steuermann and the Philadelphia Orchestra in the spring of this year; finally two works shortly to be performed, the *Ode to Napoleon,* after Byron, for *Sprechstimme,* piano and strings, and a Theme and Variations, written originally for band and later arranged for orchestra.

Of these works, the Suite is consciously in an "old style," and the Second Chamber Symphony is the completion of a work left unfinished some forty years earlier. With the latter, the organ Variations have given rise to rumors of a "conservative" trend in Schoenberg's music—a "return" at least to "tonality" and to a more "consonant" style. No doubt, the new Variations and possibly the *Ode,* both shortly to receive their world premières, will add to these rumors which purport to herald a "capitulation" on Schoenberg's part. The organ Variations are extremely freely but none the less unmistakably in the key of D minor, though also influenced by serial thinking; the orchestral Variations are in G minor, signature and all, and definitely in a simpler style. The *Ode to Napoleon,* though still in the twelve-tone system, is superficially more "consonant" than many of Schoenberg's earlier works in that, to a very large extent, its style is characterized by the superimposition of triads and their derivatives. It is, however, doubtful if either the *Ode* or the organ Variations will prove comforting to those who pretend to see any reversal on Schoenberg's part. They are presumably quite as "forbidding" as any of his reputedly "atonal" works.

"Atonality," in fact, is a conception which Schoenberg has never accepted and which has certainly no relationship to the experience of a practiced listener to his music. If "tonality" means anything in other than academic terms

it must certainly denote the *sensation* of relationships between tones, and of functional differences arising from these relationships. The tonic, the leading tone, and so on are sensations habitual in all listeners. In no sense are they mere theoretical abstractions; they are not inextricably bound up with any systematic formula yet established nor are they in the last analysis definable in terms of any such formula alone. The prevailing harmonic concepts or definitions of "tonality" are inadequate not only to the music of contemporary composers, but to many elusive problems in classic music. It should, however, be clear that these inadequacies are in no manner to be conjured away through the adoption of the essentially meaningless term "atonal," any more than the presence or absence of an occasional triad or sixth-chord is of more than incidental significance in determining the characteristics of a style such as Schoenberg's.

I believe that in these works written since 1936 Schoenberg has achieved a freedom and resourcefulness which carries them in this respect far beyond his earlier works, especially those in the twelve-tone technique. Regarding that technique itself much misleading nonsense has been written. I am in no sense a spokesman for it; I have never been attracted to it as a principle of composition. But one must distinguish carefully between technical principles in the abstract, and the works in which they become embodied; even a great work does not validate a dubious principle, nor does a valid principle produce in itself good or even technically convincing work. It would for example be easy, though basically irrelevant, to show that Beethoven's *Heiliger Dankgesang* in the Lydian mode, like most other modern "modal" works, is based on a technically specious conception of the nature and function of the modes. Similarly, assuming the fugue or sonata to have been valid as principles of musical structure, how many grievous sins have been committed in their names!

One can not too often insist that in music it is the composer's inner world of tone and rhythm which matters, and that whatever technical means he chooses in order to give it structure and coherence are subject to no a priori judgment whatever. The essential is that structure and coherence be present; and the demand which art makes on its creator is simply that his technique be sufficiently mastered to become an obedient and flexible instrument in his hands. True, the twelve-tone technique became at one time a fighting slogan; this happened under the stress of combat, the inevitable result of bitter opposition met by Schoenberg and his disciples. Today, however, it is no longer invoked as a universal principle; it is recognized for what it is as a mode of technical procedure, a principle which evolves and becomes modified by practice. Once more—the significance of music springs solely from the composer's imagination and not from ideas about technique. The latter are merely tools which he forges for himself, for his own purposes. They gain what validity they possess from the results, in music, to which they make their imponderable contribution.

In regard to Schoenberg's work it may also be stressed that the twelve-tone technique is a part of the *process* rather than an essential element of the form. It is not essential or even possible for the listener to apprehend it in all its various transformations. He must listen to Schoenberg's music in exactly the same spirit as he listens to any music whatever, and bring to it the same kind of response. If he is fortunate he will from the first discover moments of profound and intense beauty which will tempt him further. He will always find that the music makes the utmost demands on his ear and his musical understanding, and he will probably find that with a little familiarity it begins to impose itself. In any case, esoteric notions or strained efforts will, as in the case of all music, serve as a barrier rather than as an aid to his understanding.

So if in some works of the 1920s one feels a certain tenseness and dogmatic insistence, one must regard that as a necessary phase in Schoenberg's development. At the time he was exploring and mastering the resources of the new technique. In the works of the last ten years one feels no such limitation. The technique is used with the ease of virtuosity, with complete resourcefulness, and with such freedom that it is sometimes difficult to discover. The Fourth Quartet, the Violin and the Piano Concertos are, as far as I can see, his finest achievements of these years, perhaps of his whole work. They are larger in scope, if not in gesture, than the *Ode to Napoleon* or the organ Variations; like these they are in no conceivable wise more "conservative" than the earlier works even though they differ from these in several essential respects.

They differ first of all in their longer and broader lines. This is not simply a question of "continuity"; Schoenberg has always been in this respect a master of form, and in no work known to me can he be accused of a lack of logic. But—with those qualifications and exceptions—the individual details are underlined to a degree that they, rather than the larger lines, seem to bear the main expressive burden. It is a question of emphasis; the "fragmentary" impression that disturbs many listeners results from the fact that every sensation is intensified to the utmost degree. All contrasts are of the sharpest kind, and it is not surprising that they strike the hearer most forcibly, even after familiarity with the work has brought their essential continuity more to the fore. In the later works, above all in the Piano Concerto, the expressive emphasis shifts strikingly to the line as a whole. A sustained melodic line becomes the rule rather than the exception. The melodic style itself has become more concentrated, less extravagant and diffuse in detail. I am tempted to cite examples: the graceful melody which opens the Piano Concerto; the declamatory opening phrase of the slow movement of the Quartet; or the haunting and tender Andante of the Violin Concerto.

The very adoption of the concerto form, with the predominance of one instrument, underlines this tendency. Though Schoenberg's uncompromising polyphony results in a large measure of obbligato treatment of the solo parts, especially in the Piano Concerto, this treatment is nevertheless on the broadest lines, the constant tone quality contributing unmistakably to the architectonics of the works. Equally consistent is the orchestral dress. Though certainly as vivid as in the earlier works, it contrasts strikingly with these in that it, too, is laid out on broader lines. The constant and kaleidoscopic change so characteristic of the Five Orchestral Pieces or the Bach transcriptions, has been superseded by a style in which tone colors, in all their characteristic boldness, remain constant over longer stretches, and are opposed to each other in sharply defined and large-scale contrasts. Needless to say, the instruments are employed with complete freedom from preconceived ideas and with full awareness of the relationship between ends and means. While it makes extreme demands, technical and otherwise, on the performers—the solo parts of both concertos are truly formidable—it does so always with full awareness; the demands lie in the musical ideas themselves and are in no way superimposed on them. They pose new problems for the performers—but they have this in common with much of the best music of every generation.

These works possess other and more elusive characteristics, at some of which I have already hinted in connection with the *Ode to Napoleon*. It is not easy concretely to demonstrate, in the two concertos and the Quartet, a still wider range of harmonic effect—one which includes all the simplest as well as the most complex relationships—or a much vaster harmonic line, at the least suggesting a new tonal principle, powerfully binding like the old but embracing all possible relationships within the chromatic scale. As far as I know, no adequate study has yet been made of Schoenberg's work in its harmonic and tonal aspects—aspects which lie deeper than the twelve-tone system or the individual sonority, and guide the ear of the listener in his real apprehension of the music. The above-mentioned qualities seem to me, however, strikingly present in all of this later music and a most important element in the effect of unity, sweeping movement, and concentration which the works produce. If I express myself cautiously in this regard it is because they raise questions of capital importance, for which nothing less than a painstaking effort of research, and a totally new theoretical formulation, would be necessary. Meanwhile the works are there, with a new challenge, different in kind but perhaps not in importance from that embodied in the Three Piano Pieces and the Five Orchestral Pieces thirty-odd years ago.

The above remarks are at best cursory and convey all too little idea of the works themselves. It goes without saying that performances have been very few, and their real impact limited. The scores are available, however, through the foresight of G. Schirmer, Inc. The enthusiasm of many of the most gifted among young musicians as well as the gradually deepening interest of their elders is one of the striking phenomena of a period in which the prevailing trend seems superficially to be all in the direction of a not entirely genuine "mass appeal," facile and standardized effect, and a kind of hasty shabbiness of conception and workmanship.

As a teacher Schoenberg has fought against these latter tendencies with undiminished energy. Here, too, his influence has been both direct and indirect. In New York and especially in California considerable numbers of Americans have passed under his instruction. At one time he even was in demand among the composers of film music in Hollywood; his demands, however, proved too high, and composers in search of easy formulas of effect withdrew in disappointment. The same thing has happened to those who have gone to Schoenberg in the hopes of learning to compose in the twelve-tone system or in the "modern idiom." Nothing is farther from Schoenberg's ideas than that sort of instruction. He does not, in fact, preoccupy himself with "style" at all, in the usual sense of the word. What concerns him is the musical development, in the most integral sense, of the pupil. He insists on the most rigorous training in harmony and counterpoint; those familiar with his *Harmonielehre* must needs appreciate the extent to which this is true. For one who has never been his pupil, the striking feature of his teaching is precisely that it is systematic without ever becoming a "system" in any closed sense; that it is almost fanatically rigorous in its ceaseless striving after mastery of resource; logical and clear in its presentation of materials, but as free as teaching can be from any essential dogmatic bias. It is based on constant experiment and observation; theoretical comment is offered always in the most pragmatic spirit—as an aid to the clarification of technical problems and not as abstract principle. They are literally, as with many such features in the *Harmonielehre,* the observations of a keen and experienced mind with reference to a specific matter in hand, to which they are completely subordinate.

Musical experience, and development through experience, is Schoenberg's watchword as a teacher. His pupils speak of his boundless love for music—the energy of his enthusiasm for a classic work as he analyzes it in his classes, or of the demands on which he insists in its performance by them. They speak of his tireless energy in asking of them—above all the gifted ones—that they bring into their work the last degree of resourcefulness of which they are capable. It is not surprising that under such instruction they learn to make the greatest demands on themselves, or that their love of music and sense of music is developed both in depth and intensity as a result. It is this which distinguishes Schoenberg's pupils above all—their training is not merely in "craftsmanship" but an integral training of their *musicality,* of ear and of response. The conceptions which they have gained are rounded and definite; they have not only gained tools of composition, but have developed also their own individual sense of the purposes for which these tools are to be used.

In complete agreement they testify to the fact that nothing has been taught them of the twelve-tone system or of "modern" composition as such. Schoenberg's attitude is that musicians must come to these things, too, through development and necessity or not come to them at all. Having given them a basis on which they can develop further, and a sense of the demands of art, he insists that they must find for themselves their path in the contemporary world. He is fond of telling them that there is still much good music to be written in C major, and offering them no encouragement to follow the paths he himself has chosen.

Perhaps it will be seen from this what I meant in speaking at the beginning of this paper of a "third Schoenberg." In his educational tenets he has not, of course, changed through living in the United States. But he has brought these tenets from the principal stronghold of a great and old tradition to a fresh land which is beginning slowly and even cautiously to feel its musical strength. He has given to many young musicians by direct influence, and to others through his disciples, a renewed sense of all that music is and has been, and it is hardly over-bold to foresee that this is going to play its role, perhaps a mighty one, in the musical development of the United States. A small testimony to what this new contact may produce may be seen in a very valuable little book—***Models for Beginners in Composition***—which Schoenberg prepared for students in a six-weeks' summer course in California. Certainly the eagerly awaited treatise on counterpoint, and the one also planned on the principles of composition, based on Beethoven's practice, will furnish deeper insights; they cannot fail to prove to be works of capital value. But the little book has for me a special significance as a moving testimony to Schoenberg's relationship to the American musical scene, and his brilliantly successful efforts to come to grips with certain of its problems.

In this essay I have purposely avoided dwelling on the more problematical aspects of Schoenberg and his work; I have made no attempt at an exact or careful estimate. No doubt, Schoenberg is still in many respects a problematical figure, as is every other contemporary master. But it seems more relevant to regard him as a source of energy and impulse; final estimates may well be left to posterity, and the habit of attempting them at every turn is one of the dangerously sterile features of our contemporary culture. It is a symptom of a rather nervous self-consciousness and above all of self-distrust.

What is essential now is to recognize the need our world has for the qualities that Schoenberg possesses, and how admirably he supplies our need. In a world-wide condition in which the rewards of facile mediocrity and of compromise are greater than ever, and in which one hears an ever-insistent demand that music and the other arts devote themselves to the task of furnishing bread and circuses to an economically or politically pliable multitude, the musical world yet celebrates in sincere homage the seventieth birthday of an artist who not only, in the face of the most bitter and persistent opposition, scorn and neglect, has always gone his own way in uncompromising integrity and independence, but who has been and is still the most dangerous enemy of the musical status quo. This takes place in spite of the fact that his work is all too seldom performed, that it is exacting in the extreme, and is virtually unknown except to a very few who have made the attempt really to penetrate its secrets. It is in the last analysis an act of gratitude to one who has, so much more than any other individual, been one of the masculine forces that have shaped the music of our time, even that music which seems farthest from his own. It is not only a tribute to a truly great musician, but a hopeful sign that art on the highest level may still survive the bewilderments and the terrors of a mighty world crisis, of which so much is still ahead of us, and which contains so many imponderables.

Alan Lessem (essay date 1974)

SOURCE: "Schönberg and the Crisis of Expressionism," in *Music & Letters,* Vol. 55, No. 4, October, 1974, pp. 429-36.

[*In the following essay, Lessem associates Schoenberg's creative crisis with the early-twentieth-century Expressionist movement.*]

In Arnold Schönberg's published writings, as well as those of Webern and Berg, there is no lack of reference to the decisiveness of the year 1908, in which he took the first steps in what has subsequently been described as 'free atonal' composition. Since then, too, there has been much wrangling over the implications of 'atonality', abstractly considered, but less willingness to explore some of the broader issues of the crisis into which Schönberg and his pupils were plunged—a crisis which has its place in the social and intellectual history of our century.

In pre-War Vienna the perilous closeness of political and moral collapse (and an inevitable general hardening to the pursuit of new enterprise) brought with it a heightened awareness, on the part of thinking men, of the phenomenon of social stagnation and disintegration. Hugo von Hoffmansthal described this phenomenon as "das Gleitende" (the "slipping away" of the world); its most pervasive symptoms were an abnormal cultivation of the self, a pre-occupation with the expressions of psychic disturbance and a guilt-ridden sexuality. Superficially this aspect of the *Zeitgeist* is reflected in the texts of Schönberg's *Erwartung* and *Die glückliche Hand,* but it is necessary to distinguish those who, struggling with a sense of impotence, responded to their age with a melancholy or ironic scepticism (Hermann Bahr, Arthur Schnitzler, Robert Musil) from those who, on the other hand, sought to confront it with an ethical opposition, animated not by parochial reaction but by the traditional precepts of European humanism.

Among the most intransigent in the struggle against decadence was the satirist and polemicist Karl Kraus. In his own journal *Die Fackel* (founded 1899) he exposed and condemned abuses of language so evident in the inflated stylishness and superfluous phraseology of the Viennese *feuilletonistes.* An affinity of temperament between Kraus and Schönberg drew them, from time to time, together. In the dedication which the composer sent to Kraus with a copy of his *Harmonielehre* (1911) he wrote: "I have learnt more perhaps from you than one can learn if one is to remain independent". At the very outset of his book he had attacked the mental indolence that, in his time, canonized its prejudices in art under the name of *Schönheitsgesetze* (laws of beauty) and refused to recognize, for fear of disturbing a false equilibrium, the relativity of such 'laws' to history. Another name that appears in the *Harmonielehre* is that of the architect Adolph Loos, with whom Schönberg was personally associated for many years. Round the turn of the century Loos campaigned as a journalist against the pseudo-historicism prevalent in the architecture of Vienna, directing his attack primarily at the decorative art of *Jugendstil* which, since the Secession of 1897, was widely considered as setting the tone of fashionably modern taste. In his essay 'Ornament and Crime' (1908) he presented his views concisely: "As ornament is no longer a natural product of our civilization, it accordingly represents backwardness or degeneration . . . Lack of ornament is a sign of spiritual strength".

Loos was a pioneer in the new trend towards functionalism in architecture and handicrafts. Similarly, Schönberg made it clear to the readers of his *Harmonielehre* that his concern was not with 'æsthetics' but with skills comparable to those of a good cabinet maker:

> Spareness of material! that is, in truth, artistic economy; to use only the means that are indispensably necessary to the production of a particular result. All else is purposeless and hence clumsy. Nothing can be beautiful if it is not organic.

To Schönberg and like-minded thinkers the general Viennese taste for *Schmuck* (ornament) was a form of intellectual dishonesty, in that a pretentious parade of effects was allowed to conceal a real poverty of substance. It was a means, merely, of affecting an equivocal pose and impeded what Schönberg took to be a proper communication of ideas. With regard to this problem he wrote: "Great art must proceed to precision and brevity . . . This is what musical prose should be—a direct and straightforward presentation of ideas, without mere padding and empty repetitions".

Paradoxically, however, the desire for a "direct presentation of ideas" would pose a very real threat to the forms which had conventionally mediated them. For in the philosophy and practice of art it had been commonly understood that immediately perceived reality is, as such, not an æsthetic phenomenon, and to become so must be mediated through some form of representation (Hegel's *Schein*). The challenge, for Schönberg and his contemporaries, was to discover how expression and form could be properly conciliated without resorting to the gratuitous solution provided by mere compromise. As Schönberg put it: "I believe it won't do: to toy with freedom while one is still bound to the unfree". For those who met only indifference to the urgency of this issue, it became necessary, for the sake of 'truthfulness', to contemplate the risk of going beyond entrenched norms of æsthetic mediation. Art had to become 'Expressionistic'.

The music of Schönberg's crucial period, which extended from 1908 to the composition of the first twelve-note works, was shaped, as he noted some years later, by powerful and pervasive subjective impulses: "In my first works of the new style I was guided, in the shaping of forms, by exceptionally strong forces of expression (*Ausdrucksgewalten*), both with regard to particulars and to the whole". Further, he allowed himself to believe that the intensity of the subjective demand would, of necessity, generate artistic forms that were appropriate to it. Intuition, fired by necessity and rarely disturbed by conscious reflection, could be trusted to do its own work. In close accord, the painter Wassily Kandinsky described "inner necessity" as a fundamental shaping force; indeed, the affirmation of its intuitive rightness was as widespread in the early years of this century as it had been over a hundred years earlier. Then, the rebellious attitudes of J.-J. Rousseau, evident too in German *Empfindsamkeit*, came as a reaction to eighteenth-century intellectualism. Similarly, the rationalistic and mechanistic modes of thinking which, as methodological procedure, dominated the latter part of the nineteenth century, seemed to those who became heir to it to exclude a wholeness of spirit and to deny the significance of temporal flux and its necessarily non-conceptual expression. Joining in the protest, after Nietzsche, were proponents of a *Lebensphilosophie*—prominently Wilhelm Dilthey and Henri Bergson; further corroboration for irrational modes of cognition was given in the phenomenology of Edmund Husserl. "Vital experience" came to be interpreted, in Bergson's sense, as the unique and the irreversible. It was to be valued as a means of bridging the gap between the metaphysical and the physical, between universals and particulars.

In Germany a fresh burst of activity in the arts, literature and drama carried with it a new set of attitudes which, achieving some degree of coherence between about 1910 and 1925, has retrospectively been referred to as Expressionism. The Expressionists believed themselves to be caught in a malaise of degenerate cultural and intellectual life, and hence the importance attached by them to a new content, one that would signify a rebirth of moral and spiritual values. Expressionism was never a conscious grouping or movement that could be defined by any kind of common programme, but poets, dramatists and painters were drawn together in their rejection of the methods of Naturalism, and also set themselves apart from Impression and Symbolism by refusing the refuge offered by the temple of art. A commitment to intuition, they believed, would lead them back to an essential humanity which both materialism and æstheticism had by-passed. Refusing all compromise, they pledged themselves to a constantly self-renewing sensibility while acknowledging, too, that anxiety was the price to be paid for continuing

exploration with unforeseeable results. There were differences among them, but all seemed to have agreed on Kandinsky's warning against an over-evaluation of formal convention made without reference to that which animates it: namely, inner content. Believing himself to be peculiarly sensitive to what he described as the "Abstract Spirit" of his time, Kandinsky hailed the approach of a new era in which the sensuous properties of art would find their proper place as an expression of spiritual values. There is, too, an echo of the theories of early Romanticism in the primary place Kandinsky gave to music as 'pure' expression; his desire was to achieve, for painting, the emancipation from ordinary signification already attained by music.

Schönberg and Kandinsky first met at a holiday resort— a meeting recollected by Kandinsky in a letter to the composer of 1 July 1936. No date is mentioned for the meeting, which probably took place round 1909 or 1910. The men may have met by chance, but Willi Reich, in his recent biography, suggests that they were brought together by Kandinsky's reading of an excerpt from the *Harmonielehre,* from which he then quoted in his *Über das Geistige in der Kunst* of 1912. The published correspondence between the two testifies to the close mutual interest in one another's work during 1911-12—an interest renewed by Schönberg in 1922 but suspended a year later as a result of Kandinsky's alleged anti-Semitism. Schönberg's essay **'Das Verhältnis zum Text'** was published in Kandinsky's almanach *Der Blaue Reiter* (1912). In it he praised Kandinsky's book 'On the Spiritual in Art' and expressed enthusiasm over the promised emancipation of the "painting of the future" from the externals of ordinary subject-matter. In his own book Kandinsky equated Schönberg's renunciation of tonality with the aims of the new movement: namely, the liberation of art from conventional aids to perception and cognition: "His music leads us to where musical experience is a matter not of the ear, but of the soul—and from this point begins the music of the future". The goal of contemporary artists, Franz Marc insisted, was "to create *symbols* for their age, symbols for the altars of a new spiritual religion. The artist as technician will simply vanish behind such works". The parallel with Schönberg is important. For it is the voice of this new generation that speaks, in particular, in the third scene of **Die glückliche Hand,** where the efforts of worker-technicians (and even of the protagonist himself) to create a merely decorative art (*Schmuck*) are scorned and rejected.

An affinity between Schönberg's objectives and those of the Expressionists has been suggested in much of the critical literature. Certainly, the desire of the time for *Ausdruckswahrheit* was one that he shared. All that was not essential to it, including, and in particular, what Kandinsky described as "conventional beauty", had to be sacrificed. Art historians have, of course, recognized the roots of this desire for 'naked' expression in early Romanticism, and have queried the independence of Expressionism as a category of style. One need only cite, in support of this historical link, Arnold Hauser's description of the essence of Romanticism and compare it with an 'Expressionist' programme attached to Schönberg's music by a contemporaneous critic:

> Romantic art is the first to consist in the 'human document', the screaming confession, the open wound laid bare.
>
> Schönberg, indomitable, offers himself to the whole world with all his private dæmons. Indeed, in a virtual frenzy of confession, he tears open his breast to show the stigmata . . . The blood of his wounds becomes sound.

Expressionism, to be sure, did tend towards *Sturm und Drang* histrionicism; how one prefers to respond to that aspect of it is a matter of taste (and it does seem that our contemporary taste has decreed against works like *Die glückliche Hand*). But it would not be fair to brand the Expressionists as self-indulgent, for it was precisely the self-indulgence of the etiolated æstheticism in which late Romanticism had foundered that they rejected. The stand that Schönberg took, with Kandinsky, against an 'empty' beauty (one devoid of content) was one that alienated him from even the once well-disposed among his critics. In 1911 Richard Specht claimed that he had now only 'contempt' for the praiseworthy sophistication of melodic and harmonic resources achieved in works prior to 1908. Adolph Weissmann described his 'Expressionism' as a capitulation to immediate and local excitation, by-passing any corporeal frame of reference and sacrificing art to spirituality. Arnold Schering believed that such impulses would lead to a kind of *Übermusik* or even *Anti-Musik*. Paul Bekker, though more sympathetic than others, nevertheless drew similar conclusions:

> The music of the nineteenth century, as it developed from the classical art, was shaped by the urge towards representation, a corporealization of the process of feeling. . . . But here lies the chasm. Schönberg's music does not illustrate, it does not represent. It lives in a strange, unknown dimension of feeling, in which the corporeal, the firm outline of the artistic object, no longer exists.

To suggest, as Bekker does, a 'chasm' separating Schönberg from the nineteenth century is, surely, to overstate the historical argument, for already in that century the problem of 'representation' within a classical frame of reference became a central one. The historical development would rather seem to be one in which the rebellion of Romantic transcendentalism against the æsthetic immanence of classicism culminated ultimately in, as it were, a total mobilization: art against art. The resulting crisis has been discussed by T. Wiesengrund-Adorno, who argues that feeling 'truly' expressed can no longer recognize the autonomy of art. In Expressionism art survives only in threatening to cancel itself out:

> The essential, disrupting moment is for [Schönberg] the function of musical expression. Passions are no longer simulated; rather does his music record, untransposed, the impulses of the unconscious, its

shocks and traumas. The seismographic registration of traumatic shocks becomes, at the same time, the law of the form of the music.

To identify form and expression absolutely, as Adorno seems to do, would be to postulate an extreme nominalism and also to suggest an absence of working procedure in the music. Recent attempts to seek out and define the characteristics of Expressionism in music have stumbled against this problem, and have not passed beyond merely descriptive determinations which rely heavily on reference by negation. Most problematic is the negation implicit in Karl Wörner's *Momentform,* signifying as it does the absence of any kind of repetition or systematically conceived relationship between formal parts. Wörner's term is, of course, self-contradictory, as form has to do with relationships. Furthermore, Schönberg, who always subjected any consideration of isolated particularities to the criterion expressed by the word *Zusammenhang* (formal connectedness), would surely have rejected the implications of *Momentform* as irrelevant to his concerns. While granting, with Bekker and Adorno, that it was characteristic of Expressionism to insist on the precedence of 'spirit' over 'art', one would nevertheless expect the absence of means of formal organization to be apparent rather than real. The source of these means derived, as Schönberg frequently asserted, from an almost somnambulistic intuition; thus the formal relationships created by them, rather than sounding on the surface of the music, will be found to exist buried in its deeper tissues. They are the subconscious controlling forces from which stems the logic of all dreams and visions.

Yet for much of the music of this century the metaphor of the dream and its wider implications needs to be thoroughly explored. Psychologists have attributed the extraordinary, hallucinatory vividness of dream images to the deeply buried 'syntax' that creates them. Schönberg stressed, often enough, the hidden, compulsive logic that underlay the operation of his musical fantasy. In common with some of his contemporaries, he believed that a return to the deeper recesses of the psyche would not only tap afresh the sources of artistic inspiration but would also lead away from the senses towards what he described, in a letter to Nicholas Slonimsky, as a "higher and better order". It may be suggested, then, that his surrender to an untrammelled fantasy during the 'free atonal' period represented an evolutionary retreat from what he saw as a blind alley of over-refinement, the retreat being made in the hope of an advance in a new direction. Arthur Koestler has described such action as *reculer pour mieux sauter*—"a favourite gambit in the grand strategy of the evolutionary process". He believes that it has played as important a part in the history of human endeavour as it has in biology. While the parallel with biology must remain hypothetical, it may become a useful one in elucidating the phenomenon of so-called 'primitivism' in early twentieth-century music, art and drama. It seems no accident that, contemporaneously with Schönberg, composers such as Stravinsky, Bartók and Ives found inspiration in elements that precede or underlie the civilized superstructure of culture.

Musical fantasy was once described by Schönberg as "a dream of future fulfilment", promising a liberation from the limitations of ordinary sense-experience. The monodrama *Erwartung* can be viewed as an allegory of such an 'expectation', perhaps by necessity nocturnal and experienced only in a state of hallucination. In *Die Jakobsleiter,* 'One Wrestling', having abandoned old laws, awaits the intuition of new laws, and the archangel Gabriel speaks of a necessary blindness. In *Pierrot lunaire* the blindness is that of a pathetic (and again nocturnal) clown who is the *alter ego* of the Romantic hero; here the artistic conventions of the past, rejected by Expressionism as being no longer authentic, are momentarily restored and vindicated through the spirit of irony. Through the War years, the crisis of form, to which was linked a crisis of personal belief, remained unresolved. The Rilke poems chosen by Schönberg for his orchestral songs of Op. 22 give voice to his own anxious expectations; the poem entitled 'Alle welche dich suchen', for example, ends with the plea, "Gib deinen Gesetzen recht, die von Geschlecht zu Geschlecht sichtbarer sind". In *Die Jakobsleiter* the Biblical ladder becomes a symbol of evolving life in its struggle to overcome mere existence. Gabriel makes the 'dissolution' of life and its illusions a condition for entry into the spiritual domain where the 'laws' are to be found; the music, with its high degree of textual integration, its clarity of line and thematic work, points to the imminence of such laws. Most significantly, an emerging principle of organization, described some years ago by Winfried Zillig, yields strict formal recurrences and pitch symmetries which should be associated, in the text, with the concept of a transcendent order. Schönberg's secrecy with regard to the development and consolidation of his twelve-note method was surely motivated, not by narrow pride, but by a natural reluctance to allow the method to be evaluated *in abstracto,* that is, without relation to the human and spiritual experience out of which it evolved.

Robert Craft (essay date 1975)

SOURCE: "Towards Schoenberg," in *Current Convictions: Views and Reviews,* Alfred A. Knopf, 1975, pp. 195-210.

[*In the following essay Craft evaluates and edition of* Style and Idea, *then reviews Charles Rosen's* Arnold Schoenberg.]

The best of Arnold Schoenberg's occasional writings on music [*Style and Idea: Selected Writings of Arnold Schoenberg,*] are as richly instructive as his theoretical and didactic ones. Like them, too, many of the essays depend on examples printed in music type, which sets Schoenberg apart from other composer-writers, such as Berlioz, whose many verbal talents the creator of *Pierrot Lunaire* lacks, or Schumann or Debussy, who are simply

more enjoyable to read. But the substance of the musical journalism of these three is less profound than that of *Style and Idea,* and the rewards of Schoenberg's book warrant the greater effort it requires, especially in the chapters "Twelve-Tone Composition" and "Theory and Composition." Yet even these are not difficult for anyone conversant with the general principles of musical forms and of such basic devices of harmony and counterpoint as chord inversion and canon. Finally, Schoenberg's own chronological and autobiographical account of the evolution of atonality and twelve-tone composition is still the most accessible.

. . . . .

By contrast, the reader who will profit most from Charles Rosen's *Arnold Schoenberg* is one with prior knowledge of the composer, which may raise a question about the market for the Modern Masters series. Laymen have apparently not complained of obstacles of a specialist nature in the monographs on poets, philosophers, psychologists, sociologists, political activists—with which the collection has thus far been overbalanced at the expense of those on artists and cinematographers (the latter now possessing the widest of all powers to influence). But who except musicians will be able to follow Mr. Rosen's exposition of Schoenberg's serial system, though this is admirably lucid as well as free from the diagrammatic and numerical sigla that limit to initiates the readership of most new publications on the subject?

The reasons why the Modern Masters volume is sometimes more difficult to digest than that of Schoenberg on Schoenberg are that the composer did not understand his work in the same way ("I see things that at the time of composing [were] still unknown to me"), that he did not write about his later and more complex developments, and that because of the recent exponential increase in the quantity and sophistication of Schoenberg studies, a musicologist of Mr. Rosen's caliber must contend with a multitude of new material. In short, the contemporary scholar is obliged to keep in perspective a greatly expanded view of his subject, as well as, in Mr. Rosen's case, to concentrate it into the abbreviated format prescribed for Modern Masters. Owing to this last circumstance, too, Mr. Rosen could not afford to spell out any step that might be taken for granted. Having said this, however, one must add that a characteristic of all of Charles Rosen's criticism is his directness in identifying and confronting central issues.

. . . . .

The editorial decisions in publishing an enlarged edition of *Style and Idea* involved questions of selection, of sequence, and of language—the last in problems of translation as well as in the possible correction of the author's grammar and vocabulary (for instance, by putting within brackets an obviously intended word after the one Schoenberg actually used). The book's solutions to all three problems are disappointing. Too many of the additions do not enhance the picture of Schoenberg, while some of them, such as the causeries on national music, which expose his chauvinism and egomania, are damaging:

> Wagner's music was not only the best and most significant of its age . . . but it was also the music of 1870 Germany, who conquered the world of her friends and enemies through all her achievements. . . . ;

> [In the 1914-1918 war] the battle against German music . . . was primarily a battle against my own music. . . .

Not against that of Richard Strauss? Was Schoenberg already in 1914 regarded as a threat of European proportions? Of Italian national music in the 1920s, he remarks that it was

> written on higher orders (whereas I, in my reactionary way, [stuck] to writing [my music] on orders from The Most High) . . .

which illustrates how his wit in his writing sometimes comes through as arrogance.

The new volume also makes available some of Schoenberg's criticism of his contemporaries, but none of it resounds to his credit. In particular, the article on an early opera by Krenek could have awaited a future "Complete Writings." Nor does a piece that accuses Webern of brainpicking, written two months before Schoenberg's death, increase the author's stature, though it does reveal that he withheld his discovery of the twelve-tone concept (early 1920s) from his pupil. Elsewhere in the book Schoenberg mentions that he confided in Webern about the use of a twelve-tone *theme* in **Jacob's Ladder** (1917), which is not the same thing, of course; but the editor should have referred the reader to the other article in both cases, and should have partially balanced Schoenberg's late view of Webern by including the 1947 preface to the latter's Concerto for Nine Instruments—a brief statement, yet one that emphasizes the solidarity between the two men.

. . . . .

On the other hand, the essays on Bach, Brahms, Liszt, and Mahler, containing Schoenberg's most valuable criticism, might have been more effectively placed nearer the beginning of the book. It was in the masters of the past that Schoenberg found his own principles, and his illustrations of transcendent musical laws in Bach and Brahms provide an excellent introduction to the continuation of them in his own art. Furthermore, his hubris is less obtrusive while he is observing, for example, that the first three movements of the *Pastorale* Symphony employ almost no minor chords, and that one of Beethoven's means of avoiding the minor was

> by leaving many sections in unison unaccompanied, where the melody is understood without the harmony[;]

or when he is ferreting out the psychological weakness in Liszt that partly explains the failure of his music:

> He, for whom the poet stood foremost, suppressed the poet in himself by letting other poets talk him into too much. He, who felt form as formalism, created a far worse formalism—one which is uninhabitable, because in his forms invented by the intellect no living being has ever dwelt . . . ;

or when he is absorbed in the notion that Karl Philipp Emanuel Bach, and not Johann Sebastian, must have devised the "Royal Theme" of the *Musical Offering*—as a joke to prevent the elder Bach from displaying his contrapuntal versatility:

> In the *Art of the Fugue* a minor triad offered many contrapuntal openings, [but] the Royal Theme, also a minor triad, did not admit one single canonic imitation. All the miracles that the *Musical Offering* presents are achieved by counter-subjects, counter-melodies, and other external additions.

The editor of **Style and Idea** might in some cases have sacrificed literalism for exactness of meaning. Thus "pitch" could have been substituted for Schoenberg's ambiguous "tone," when the more clearly defining word is what he means. But in a construction such as "By avoiding the establishment of a key modulation is excluded," not to have inserted a bracketed comma after "key" is inexcusable. Finally, whatever Schoenberg's shortcomings as a writer, the only truly mystifying verbiage in the book is contributed by its editor, who nevertheless maligns the composer's English:

> Despite the advice of some of his American pupils, the present writer included, [Schoenberg] doggedly pursued his own path.

The reader will appreciate this doggedness when he tries to penetrate the editor's statement that

> Although the present volume contains most of Schoenberg's longer articles in both German and English, no more than a small portion of his other writings appear [*sic*] herein.

But the present volume does not contain *any* article in German. And what can possibly be meant by the claim:

> Published articles . . . have been used as the basic material in Schoenberg's own English wherever possible, supplemented by manuscripts, in various stages of completion, which often serve to illuminate certain points which do not exist elsewhere.

If a point does not exist elsewhere, how can it be illuminated anywhere? And does "wherever possible" refer to the intelligibility of the composer's English or to the fact that some of the originals were in German? Passages such as these arouse the reader's suspicion that in the comment,

[Schoenberg] had little use for a grammatically correct, so-called polished style of writing that would not [*sic*] clearly present his ideas,

the editor is speaking not for Schoenberg but for himself.

. . . . .

The most personal of the pieces appearing in English for the first time is Schoenberg's circular letter to friends in Europe after nearly a year (the winter of 1933-34) as a refugee in the United States. His grumblings about the musical and other miseries of America are surprisingly good-humored—compared, that is, to most of his other references to the struggles of his life. Undoubtedly Schoenberg did provoke more relentless opposition than any other major composer, and his belief in and assertion of his genius not only are excusable but were indispensable. Yet to be constantly reminded of his heroic persistence and matchless achievements ("One of the greatest virtues of my music is that . . .") eventually dampens the sympathy of the reader, who begins to feel that Schoenberg should have found consolation in the certainty of having determined the course of music in his time, as well as realized that the hostility he aroused was commensurate to his importance. "It was as if he saw that the controversial nature of his work was central to its significance," Mr. Rosen remarks, but though the composer unquestionably did see this, he seems to have been unable to accept it.

In fact the resistance to Schoenberg's music is perfectly understandable, and his own wishful explanation—that bad performances were to blame and that, if heard as intended, the music would win acceptance—indicates only one of the causes. Good readings of at least some of his music are no longer uncommon, after all, yet its audience appeal has not grown proportionately. As Mr. Rosen says, "Better performances do not make difficult music popular"; and Schoenberg's creations *are* more complex, densely packed, faster moving for their contents than those of any of his contemporaries.

Some listeners would add that Schoenberg's expression is more intense and disturbing, and that his art lacks emotional diversity, its domain being that of the macabre and of the more ingrown manifestations of middle-European expressionism—to which those who are most familiar with the music might rejoin that it is also euphoric (the Orchestra Variations), sweet (the Serenade), and not without an "Apollonian" side (the composer's own adjective for his Septet). But in his first chapter, Mr. Rosen examines such attempts at affective attributing and justly concludes that they are based on incomprehension:

> did [Schoenberg] go so far in the destruction of the tonal system that had ruled Western music for centuries in the interest of giving form to an anxiety that was part of his public as well as his private universe?

The misunderstanding inherent in these questions—the reason why they ought not to be answered—is that they suggest that a style is a simple vehicle for expressing a meaning or an emotion; they turn the style into a pure form and the emotion into a pure significance. But a form and its meaning cannot be divided so simply, above all in a work of music.

At last it seems generally to be accepted that Schoenberg's compositions of the years 1909-1913, together with some of his serial pieces of the 1920s and later, are the fulcrum of twentieth-century music. This is not an aesthetic judgment, of course, yet Mr. Rosen leaves no doubt that, of contemporary composers, Schoenberg alone satisfies the condition of true originality, which requires the exploration of a self-created universe coherent and rich enough to offer possibilities beyond the development of an individual manner.

As for the Schoenberg influence, Mr. Rosen is too conservative in estimating that it has now "surpassed that of Bartók and even perhaps of Stravinsky," since, soon after Schoenberg's death, his influence already included Stravinsky. But does Schoenberg (or Bartók, or Stravinsky) still exert any direct influence on most new music being composed today, except in the sense that this music could not have existed without his (and their) innovations? Not insofar as resemblances are concerned, at any rate, or the extension of traditions, the Schoenberg "school," except as a subject of academic study, now appearing to be defunct, bypassed by others arising from different directions.

. . . . .

Anyone who knows or has read Charles Rosen recognizes the awesomeness of his intellect. For those who may not be aware of his prodigal gifts, it should be said that Mr. Rosen is a polymath who could contribute to at least three other categories of the Modern Masters series—linguistics, painting, literature. Furthermore, he always treats the most highly developed aspects of his subjects, and in language of such precision and elegance as virtually to defy both paraphrasing (which explains why no summary of his *Arnold Schoenberg* is attempted here) and quotation (most of his arguments being too tightly embedded in contexts to be successfully extracted). When an aperçu can be detached, however, it promises to stand by itself for as long as any writing on the second Viennese school:

> [The] miniatures of Webern, Berg, and Schoenberg do not diminish the emotions they express but enlarge them, as if fragments of feeling were blown up by a powerful microscope.

Mr. Rosen's *Arnold Schoenberg* is one of the most brilliant monographs ever to be published on any composer, let alone on the most difficult master of the present age. It is also the first essay on Schoenberg that is beyond partisanship, as well as the first to place him in the perspective of four centuries of European music. Being concerned primarily with the exposition of musical ideas and artistic logic, Mr. Rosen provides only incidental bits of biography. Nor is his book essentially a work of criticism, though it contains critical insights of a very high order—on style, above all, which will not surprise anyone who has read Mr. Rosen's *The Classical Style.*

Still less is *Arnold Schoenberg* a "survey" of the music. Mr. Rosen concentrates on a few works, mainly of the period immediately before World War I—more on these, in any case, than on the serial pieces of the two decades following it. This focus is now widely shared, yet some of the comments on the serial music could provoke controversy, such as the claim for the Third Quartet as a more "ambitious and in some ways [more] fully achieved" creation than the Orchestra Variations (which is given only two paragraphs). The other most controversial matter is not new but a seemingly permanent part of all discussion of Schoenberg: the assumptions that "harmony is conveyed" as powerfully along a musical line as it is by "a simultaneous chord," that "harmonic tension" can be "displaced" to "the melodic line," and that "harmonic dissonance [can] be reconstructed by shape and texture." These are now accepted *ex hypothesi* by perhaps a majority of listeners, though some continue to regard them as incapable of proof.

. . . . .

Having said this much, the reviewer can do little more than add a few footnotes of his own, and perhaps help in some trivial tidying up for future editions—since, as if in compensation for the elevation of the discourse, the text does contain a number of minor errors. Thus the chronology of the Paris and Vienna concerts mentioned on page 5 should be reversed. And surely *Histoire du Soldat* has been mistakenly included in a list of works exemplifying "the evocation of the elegant surface of the past." Also, it is not true that *Erwartung* requires "numerous rapid and expensive changes of scene." Actually there are four, staged on a single set, taking place in or around a forest at night, and requiring only a few props—moon, bench, pasteboard house, corpse (optional).

Mr. Rosen is somewhat careless, too, in defining octave transposition as "the shifting of one or more notes of a melody to a higher or lower register" (only of a melody?), and canon as "a form in which every voice sings the same line but enters at a different moment" (and never at different pitches?). And his description of the *Sprechstimme* part in *Pierrot Lunaire* as having "a certain improvised freedom of pitch" is insufficient, since it neglects to mention that Schoenberg insisted that the performer follow at least the direction of the notated interval.

Occasionally, too, Mr. Rosen overstates, not in his theses but in the illustration of them. This is hardly of any consequence when, apropos the deployment of the orchestra in *Erwartung,* he writes that

sixteen first violins and fourteen seconds are called for but used all at once only at a very few points.

(Actually all thirty of them play together in 127 out of 426 measures, or for nearly a third of the time.) Nor is the exaggeration serious when, in the demonstration of his argument that "pitch is . . . not by any means always the most important [element]," Mr. Rosen asserts that in the third piece of *Pierrot Lunaire*

> the clarinet part could be transposed a half-step up or down while the other instruments remain at the correct pitch, and (although some effect would be lost) the music would still make sense; but if the dynamics are not respected, the music becomes totally absurd and makes no sense at all.

Not *much* sense, but certainly *some,* as old recordings with practically no range of highs and lows tend to prove. If a clarinet in B flat were substituted for the one in A, however, "some effect would be lost" only on a listener who had not heard the music before, since anyone even slightly acquainted with it would experience acute discomfort, at least in measures 6-9, where, debatably, the pitches are more important than the dynamics.

. . . . .

But a similar magnification of fact also occurs in connection with one of the book's principal subjects, the "saturation of [the chromatic] musical space" in *Erwartung*. "Tonality contained within itself the element of its own destruction," Mr. Rosen writes. One part of this element is modulation, the transition from one key to another, or

> the setting up of a second triad as a sort of polarized force or anti-tonic against the tonic; the second triad functions as a subsidiary tonic in that part of the piece where it holds sway, and acts as a means of creating tension. Since dissonance is the essential expressive element of music, and modulation is dissonance on a large scale, it makes expression *for the first time an element of the total structure.* The concept of modulation was eventually to prove the powerful force that corrupted tonality.

Another part, or aspect, of the same thing is chromaticism, the use of the subdivisions, or semitone intervals, of the diatonic scale. Chromaticism, Mr. Rosen observes,

> contains a kind of magnetic impulse to fill out the space. . . .

> Most composers must have been aware of the tendency to fill out the chromatic space as a kind of gravitational force. . . .

> The tendency to fill out the chromatic space becomes naturally more marked by the middle of the nineteenth century. . . .

> It was Schoenberg's genius to have recognized almost unconsciously the dispossession of the principal means of musical expression by the new

force of what had been a subordinate and contributing element.

This is true, but the illustration that follows overlooks a detail which spoils the perfection of the case. "The last page of *Erwartung*," Mr. Rosen says, consists of

> massed chromatic movement at different speeds, both up and down. . . . [The] low woodwinds begin, triple *pianissimo,* a rising chromatic series of six-note chords. The other instruments enter with similar chords moving up or down the chromatic scale . . . with the dynamics remaining between triple and quadruple *pianissimo.*

In fact, however, the basses begin at a louder dynamic level than that, and they are clearly intended to stand out. ("Schoenberg never abandoned [the] hierarchy of principal and subordinate voices," Mr. Rosen remarks, in connection with another work, and the distinction is "rigidly enforced by the dynamics.") Moreover, the basses descend not chromatically, but in whole-tone scales (in thirds with the contrabassoon), which are in contrast to chromatic movement. Finally, by rounding out two full octaves, these scales provide a residual sense of a traditional species of cadence.

. . . . .

The core of *Arnold Schoenberg* is a discussion of *Erwartung,* perhaps the most radical of all musical creations, as well as, in the opinion of many, the composer's highest achievement. "This quintessential expressionist work," as Mr. Rosen writes, is a "well-attested miracle, inexplicable and incontrovertible." Few would demur, while, concerning the intractability of the piece to traditional analysis, no one could. Schoenberg himself described one of the chief difficulties:

> A great number of more-than-five-tone [-pitch] chords . . . have not [*sic*] yet been systematically investigated. It can be maintained neither that they belong to a tonality, nor that they point toward one. And conversely . . . no proof has yet been brought that these properties are entirely lacking.

And Mr. Rosen observes:

> Almost all of the chords in *Erwartung* have six notes. . . . [The] six-note chord is generally made up of two three-note chords outlining the seventh, e.g., a fourth above an augmented fourth. . . .

But to give any more of this analysis would require the quotation of Mr. Rosen's musical examples, so it must suffice to say that his exegesis of the chordal structure of the work is the most convincing that has so far been made.

The listener with no experience of *Erwartung*'s harmonic language nevertheless senses its consistency. But he apprehends the form of the piece at a different level from that of chordal relationships. Mr. Rosen states that

It is in the field of rhythm that the large form of *Erwartung* is most immediately perceptible . . . [the] contrast between passages with a marked *ostinato* effect and those with no repeating figures of any kind [being] the chief instrument in the definition of the dramatic action of the mono-drama.

This is indisputable, but it overlooks still another rhythmic factor, and one that must be counted among the score's most innovatory features: the unprecedented fluidity of tempo. In fact the tempo changes every three to four measures (on an average), when not actually in flux (accelerating or decelerating; also—a novelty far ahead of its time—individual sections or groups of instruments sometimes play "out of tempo," faster than the orchestra as a whole).

Erwartung also has "a shape related to the libretto," as Mr. Rosen acknowledges, but apart from rhythmic delineation, he does not say what this is. Perhaps a layman might describe it as a progression from sudden changes of direction and mood, new starts and resolutions—conveyed, to some extent, by a fragmentary, recitative style—to longer lines and more songlike passages in the later portions of the work. And, in correspondence to this, the same listener would probably retain an impression of an over-all increase in orchestral density and volume from a single instrument at the beginning to that "saturation of musical space" at the end, this being parallel to the greater intimacy of the musical dimensions in the first scenes as compared to the broader, more "open" final one. And the hypothetical listener would very likely have had a sense of increasing movement from the more static earlier scenes to the last one, in which the majority of fast-tempo passages occur. But all of this is only to say that Schoenberg's music drama, like numerous operas by other composers, intensifies as it develops.

. . . . .

"There is no fully developed sense of key anywhere in *Erwartung*," Mr. Rosen remarks, and it might be added that whatever *un*developed sense of key it may contain is at best ambiguous, ephemeral, and probably illusory, affirmable only during some of the *ostinati* and in melodic phrases, for although melody and harmony are never completely detachable, spacing (as at 418) can make them more so. But other elements than the harmonic must be considered, especially since one of them, as Mr. Rosen rightly maintains, is even more important. "Form was as basically thematic for Schoenberg as it was for most nineteenth-century composers," he writes.

> The really revolutionary art was less the destruction of the tonal frame with the *George-Lieder* of 1909 than the renunciation of thematic form as well with *Erwartung* in the same year. In this work Schoenberg did away with all the traditional means in which music was supposed to make itself intelligible: repetition of themes, integrity and discursive transformation of clearly recognizable

motifs, harmonic structure based on a framework of tonality.

The statement is unchallengeable, except, possibly, that it does not allow for elasticity among other arbiters of the "clearly recognizable," and that the "traditional means" to intelligibility, not completely itemized in this quotation, should also include such small features as the use of sequences. But in spite of Schoenberg's renunciation of "thematic form," does not comprehension increase with the recognition of recurring thematic figures? Here Mr. Rosen has not completely overcome the long-standing predicament that the lack of well-defined terms has created for all musicians. Thus his definition of a motif as "a succession, generally short, with a latent power of development, of creating a larger continuity" is more precise than his description of a melody as "a definable shape, an arabesque"—only that?—"with a quasi-dramatic structure of tension and resolution." As Mr. Rosen says:

> Both motif and melody are *tonal* forms. The power of development and variation that lies in a motif is given by the context of tonality. . . . The structure of melody is equally tonal: a melody is intended above all to be memorable, and its mnemonic powers comes [*sic*] from the adherence of its line to tonal functions. . . . Motif generates melody: that is the traditional relation between them. . . .

But since motifs and melodies are also found in atonal music, the statement reveals one reason why they are more difficult to remember in Schoenberg than in Beethoven—namely, that the contexts of atonal harmony are infinitely more complex and difficult to perceive than tonal ones.

This explains why the historical significance of *Erwartung* can be regarded as greater than that of Schoenberg's twelve-tone compositions, which "required a mimesis of tonal melody." For *Erwartung* is

> "athematic" or "nonmotivic" in the sense that understanding and appreciating it does not require recognizing the motifs from one part of the work to another as all music from Bach to Stravinsky demands. . . .

This statement, too, is unexceptionable: *Erwartung* can be appreciated independently of the recognition of motifs. Yet the musical experience is deepened by an awareness of the motivic relationships—which will differ from one listener to another because of the "developing variation" (Schoenberg's term for a principle of all of his music), the transformation, and even the mergers to which the motifs are subjected. An interval is inverted, or replaced by a slightly larger one—on the grounds that contour is more important than exact distance (as in the case of the *Sprechstimme* part in *Pierrot Lunaire*). Also, at least one motif in *Erwartung* is as short as a single interval, the minor third that occurs three times in the first melodic passage (bassoon to oboe) and obsessively after that, especially in the vocal part.

These comments are merely a part of one reader's marginalia. Now it must be said that with this book Charles Rosen not only has created impossibly high standards for the Modern Masters series but also has notched the profession of writing about music to a level that no colleague can readily approach. His *Arnold Schoenberg* is indispensable to anyone seeking to understand the crucial musical ideas of the first three decades of the twentieth century.

Josef Rufer (essay date 1977)

SOURCE: "Schönberg—Yesterday, Today, and Tomorrow," in *Breaking the Sound Barrier: A Critical Anthology of the New Music,* edited by Gregory Battcock and translated by William Drabkin, E. P. Dutton, 1981, pp. 316-30.

[*In the following essay, originally published in* Perspectives of New Music *in 1977, Rufer examines the relevance of Schoenberg's music and theory to contemporary audiences.*]

Anyone for whom music is not merely a gourmet's treat, but an art that consists essentially of ideas, will want to provide himself from time to time with an overview of the state and development of the music of our time. And he will probably surrender, at first, to the confusing aspects of mutually contradictory or overlapping tendencies, directions, and opinions with which we are confronted verbally as well as musically. Tonal music versus nontonal music, polytonal versus twelve tone, serial versus aleatory—or whatever the latest rage is called (although often it is no longer the latest rage by the time it is disseminated): are these concepts reducible in any way to a common denominator: music? Music, which is the resounding of the spirit, the documentation of creative fantasy, and which (as Schönberg profoundly expressed) depicts the unconscious nature of these and other worlds; are we not merely talking around it when we seize it and try to bring ourselves closer with the aid of stylistic and technical terms, when we establish, as criteria for evaluation, such completely external characteristics as style and itemized contents, the recognition of which is certainly not art? Unfortunately, such superficial judgments have become increasingly common. That these remain superficial in nature can be recognized with a minimum of knowledge. And so music is no longer weighed, but labeled and catalogued instead. The newer, the better—this has become the sole criterion. It is the same hectic stampede forward that we have been able to observe for a long time in painting and literature. It destroys the spiritual continuity and organic growth from yesterday to today. It consciously rules out even tradition, and thus the confrontation with tradition that had always been the unquestioned custom in the past, with every master of every era. Hence there follows a paucity of tradition and consequently the loss of all standards of measure. The only standard that remains, then, is the obsession with being modern or ultramodern: originality at any price, even at that of music itself. But are tradition and originality actually incompatible opposites? Before we attempt to find an answer to this question, which might provide a way out of today's dilemma, let me address myself to the other side of this issue of the deterioration of musical culture—the effect on the listener. The present method of labeling music obviates all need to arrive at one's own judgment. Even before hearing a piece the listener knows whether or not he is going to like it, depending on his own attitudes, tastes, and demands—in short, on his own musical education as a prerequisite to these things. This education is the basis of all musical culture per se, and I should not be so presumptuous in speaking of its deterioration had not truly qualified people been warning of it for quite some time. In his *Zeitgemässe Glossen für Erziehung zur Musik* and again in a later communication, *Über das humanistische Gymnasium* (1945), Richard Strauss called for a comprehensive reform of the musical education of our youth, the concert- and operagoers of the future. He wrote: "Wherein consists the so-called artistic enjoyment for the majority of these listeners? In a purely sensuous 'feast for the ears,' in no way impaired by understanding." Strauss went on to compare the "so-called appreciative audience" with the ten-year-old child who watches a performance of *Wallenstein* in Chinese translation, and then he states clearly what is to be done:

> When the graduate is able to read Homer or Horace in the original, once he is in a position to understand *Wahlverwandtschaften* or *Faust* as an Englishman can understand *Hamlet*, once he also understands a Beethoven symphony, a Mozart quintet, or a *Meistersinger* or *Tristan* prelude in all its profoundness, and has learned to appreciate the architecture of these sound structures in their full magnitude and to read the language of these musical symbols, then will his intellectual preparation have acquired all of the fundamentals that can enable him to accomplish the most, in accordance with his natural abilities. Only then will the humanistic high school have fulfilled its obligations in the shaping of a spiritual, artistic person.

Here in Vienna in 1919, long before Strauss—and encompassing all the arts—the great architect Adolf Loos, in his *Richtlinien für ein Kunstamt,* had already pointed out to the Austrian government its great responsibility in checking the cultural deterioration, which was already evident then. He assigned the task of writing the section on music in this publication to Arnold Schönberg, who began his contribution as follows:

> The most important task of the music faculty is the preservation of the German nation's superiority in music, a superiority rooted in the giftedness of its people. This would seem to be owing to the fact that the German elementary school teacher of earlier times was invariably a music teacher as well: and that even in the smallest village he was active as such, creating a reservoir vast enough to satisfy the needs of the highest strata of society. With the establishment of the modern elementary school,

musical training was reduced to a barely sufficient vocal training. And in another hundred years we will have lost our superiority.

These warnings went unheeded, and until now nothing has been done to alter the situation. The consequences began to be felt as early as around 1900, at first with some isolated scandals concerning concert performances of the music of Schönberg and his circle—at that time still tonal music! This must be kept in mind; more than any subsequent resistance to non-tonal music, this pins down precisely when and where the rift occurred before the beginnings of current new music, and why it widened: to the extent, namely, that knowledge as well as feeling for tradition was lost. First, among the listeners, the audience. Further—and we have come that far today—among those composers of today's avant-garde for whom tradition was never a vital concept, in other words something productive, which has been for all masters the self-evident point of departure for creative enterprise and not merely an obstacle to that originality at any price, which for them became the sole evaluative criterion. They had not learned it any other way; perhaps they did not want to learn it at all. For had they taken a look at Schönberg's *Harmonielehre* (which is in fact a part of a master's theory of composition), then they might have opened their eyes and ears to the fact that this revolutionary, in 1911, having just realized his first keen visions outside the realm of tonality, wrote a tonal harmony text in which one reads:

> Moreover it is sad that the notion that nowadays one may write anything one pleases prevents so many young people from first learning something worth respecting, and from understanding the classics and acquiring some culture. For in the past one could write whatever one pleased, but it just was not good. Only the masters could never write as they felt like; they had to do the inevitable: the accomplishment of their mission. To prepare for this with all diligence and amid a thousand doubts—whether having a thousand scruples will suffice, whether one has understood correctly what a higher power has commissioned—this is reserved for those who have the courage and the fervor to bear the consequences, like an awesome burden loaded upon their shoulders against their will. This is a far cry from the willfulness of a method—and more courageous.

That was a warning and a confession at the same time, uttered by Schönberg the revolutionary at the very moment when he himself had seemed to throw all tradition overboard, the first step beyond the confines of tonality—note that I use the expression "seemed to"! Because tradition for him was something indispensable, experienced, alive: the sum of everything new in the creative work of the old masters—the link between the new and what had been previously created; the precondition for anything new. For, in his words, "all music is new insofar as it is the product of a truly creative spirit. Bach is as new today as ever—a continuous revelation."

With these words Schönberg destroyed the opposition between tradition and progress. Likewise, I am free of any suspicion of advocating that the future imitate the past—that it take the comfortable path of traditionalism, which must be held in sharp contradistinction to tradition. For the former transmits only the scheme or prescription by which music is *made:* the artistic, which Schönberg abhorred exceedingly and against which he constantly warned his students. He merely taught them at all times to recognize "what music *is,*" above all through the works of Bach, Beethoven, Mozart, and Brahms, hence in a continuously self-rejuvenating tradition. On the other hand, he would never have shown anyone how to compose "modern." In this connection it is essential to emphasize this once and for all.

In his lecture **"Brahms the Progressive,"** written in 1947 on the fiftieth anniversary of Brahms's death, Schönberg said:

> Anyone who analyzes my music will realize how much I am personally indebted to Mozart. People who looked at me with disbelief, thinking that I was making a poor joke when I called myself a "pupil of Mozart" will then understand my reasons. This will help them, not to grasp my music but to understand Mozart. And it will show young composers what is essential, what must be learned from the great masters, and how to bear this teaching in mind without sacrificing their own personality.

Can the meaning and function of tradition be outlined more clearly? And the word *personality* here stands for individual style, for being original against one's will, for the unconscious aspect of creative expression.

The musical public was scandalized at Schönberg's originality at the very beginning, during the tonal period (which lasted until 1908), without feeling or recognizing the natural increase of its innate affinity with tradition—this originality *in statu nascendi,* which unfolded unconsciously and imperceptibly from one work to the next. And it is precisely in these tonal works of Schönberg that there lies the key to his later works; to his unbridled unconscious, which represents the roots of an originality that is genuine for this very reason; and to his extremely sensitive feeling for structure [*Formgefühl*], with which his imagination moved resiliently between the Scylla of tradition and the Charybdis of its visions and of its inner compulsion to bring law and freedom, always represented anew in each work, to harmonic resolution. From the first work to the last, this bears the stamp of what we understand and treasure in the concept of *classical.*

At the end of his life, Schönberg deplored his status with the public:

> Those of my works which would have interested them (namely, those which they regarded as atonal and interesting) they did not wish to hear; and those works which are not called atonal, because they are less dissonant, are not interesting enough for these people, who do not know them at all. . . . I am convinced that the works of my last period would at least gain the respect they deserve if the public had the opportunity to do justice to the works of my earlier periods.

Whether yesterday, today, or tomorrow—whether tonal, atonal, or twelve tone—Schönberg remained the same: a composer whose sole endeavor was to make music. The principle by which it is made, the style—these were always questions of secondary importance to him. For this reason he loved and treasured to the end his early tonal works (something we ought to remember with due respect); thus at the high point of his twelve-tone period (after 1934) he returned to composing several significant tonal works (It goes without saying that these are also hardly known). When news of this reached Europe, after the last war, it was generally reported that "Schönberg had contritely returned to tonality." I recall a telephone call from Furtwängler, who wanted to know more details about this; but anyone knowing Schönberg would have hardly needed to hear his reply:

> Fate directed me along a more difficult road. But there has always been within me a burning desire to return to the earlier style, and from time to time I yield to this desire. And so it happens that at times I write tonal music. For me, stylistic differences of this sort have no special significance. I do not know which of my compositions are better; I like them all, for I liked them as I wrote them.

And so it seems appropriate now to investigate the creative synthesis of originality and tradition which the composer realized ever since his early tonal period; to investigate the New, which still remained hidden here in tonal guise, yet at the time was perceived by the public as new and produced a vehement shock wave; and to trace the tradition that accommodated itself to the New without losing any of its own spiritual identity—indeed, to see itself newly affirmed in its rejuvenation.

The fertile soil in which this grew was Mozart and Beethoven, whose quartets young Schönberg played with his friends in the early 1890s, and Wagner and Brahms, the antipodes about which Viennese families were split. Yet Schönberg at that time sensed the fascination of *Tristan* as much as the constructive forces—the New— that he discerned in the music of Brahms. Both were models to which he dedicated himself, without sacrificing himself to them.

"Schönberg yesterday" conceptually encompasses his entire life and work—which is to say that it includes a yesteryear and a yester-yesteryear. This yester-yesteryear, the first tonal period, began with songs. Strictly tonal, they testify to his schooling in classical models— for example, with the structured bass lines in the counterpoint of Brahms's piano music—as well as in increasingly stronger individual modulations in successive songs. Germs of a development important for the future are found everywhere, still more or less hidden in conventions dictated by tradition. A striking example of this is *Erwartung* from opus 2. Right at the beginning, the daring chord E-flat-A-D-G-flat-C-flat stands embedded between two E-flat-major triads. But it is not there merely on account of its daring, that is, for it sonic effect. Rather, it is encircled by the voice, which builds it up melodically, thereby illustrating its many facets and establishing an entirely new element of tension in E-flat major. In what follows, freely varied and sequenced, this chord then constitutes the germ cell of the middle section, so that the entire song is built upon and developed from this one chord formation, borne by a stupendous feeling for structure. Already here we can see the compositional foundation upon which he experiences tonality and its carrying capacity, pursuing its subtlest ramifications to the limit. Moreover, it is the same feeling for structure, the same manner of thinking and forming music, that Schönberg applied twenty-five years later to composition with twelve tones that are related only to one another (rather than to a fundamental tone), in which a work is invented and developed from a single underlying construction.

In the melodic aspects of the string sextet *Verklärte Nacht* one can already find Schönberg's characteristic alternation between chromatic passages and those involving wide melodic skips. At the time it made listening more difficult, like constant variations in the repetition of musical ideas, like the rhythmically artful "hamming-up" of the stereotyped metric articulation ("In a given phrase there exists only one strong beat"), or asymmetric melodic construction, that is, the departure from four-bar regularity (which, like the rhyming of "heart" with "part" and "love" with "dove," made understanding and perception easier), and the turning toward something that Schönberg likened to "metrical prose" in contrast to rhyme, a trend in musical development that was already perceivable in Reger.

And of course the rich harmony that was already considered "new" by listeners of the day. The Tonkünstlerverein in Vienna, to which Schönberg had submitted the sextet for performance, rejected it on the grounds that it contained an inversion of the ninth-chord that could not exist, namely one with the ninth in the bass. Schönberg took this in good humor, realizing that one "could not perform what does not exist."

The next composition, the tone poem *Pelleas und Melisande* (1902), represents a further leap forward in the realm of harmony. In one place the basic tonality of D minor is extended by chainlike sequences piled on top of one another in contrary motion, resulting in six-part whole-tone chords. These suspend the tonality momentarily and at the same time prepare the way for the first chords in fourths, which Schönberg created here, independently of Debussy and Scriabin. And this was in 1902! Years later, the composer admitted that he had hesitated to write down these harmonies, but that they had forced themselves on him against his will (!), as a particular expression of a mood, with such clarity that he

was unable to reject this inspiration. But if these new harmonies in Debussy and Scriabin are purely impressionistic and motivelike, respectively, in Schönberg they are a means of expression constructively embedded in the tonality. Despite this Schönberg hesitated in the face of such an unusual idea and cautiously probed, in keeping with his deep sense of responsibility.

Schönberg's feeling for structure, which developed from traditional practice, secured him even then and not only in his own musical ventures; but it grew just as the classical models themselves had developed. A page from the composer's *Nachlass* describes how he had fitted content and organization in Maeterlinck's drama into a purely musical four-movement framework. In composing his First String Quartet in D Minor, he followed the formal organization of Beethoven's *Eroica* Symphony, especially in the layout of the development section. The single-movement format of the quartet was retained in his next work, the First Chamber Symphony in E Major, except that now the content and its presentation force an imaginative new formal conception: the first movement, in sonata form, has its reprise only at the end of the work, and thereby frames the middle part, which consists of scherzo, development section, and slow movement. To this is added a new melodic-thematic development: the whole-tone and quartal harmony of *Pelleas* is now linearized as well, opening up entirely new areas that result in new grammatical modes of expression. And one more thing becomes clear: This is not chromatically "softened-up" music. On the contrary, the new harmonies do not explode the tonality, but render it even firmer. Once more, Schönberg tamed the centrifugal forces in a sovereign manner, producing the most extreme concentration of tonality extracted with the greatest harmonic enrichment up until the Second String Quartet in F-sharp Minor. That work—in 1908—marked the end of the tonal period of creativity and, at the same time, the climax; but also, in the last movement, the organically necessitated transition to music without a key signature. The first movement is still clearly in F-sharp minor. In the second and third (the single-movement form is abandoned in favor of the classical separation of movements) the structural cohesiveness of the basic tonality becomes increasingly questionable, and in the last movement Schönberg takes the revolutionary step forward by omitting the key signature altogether—a historic moment in music, which now looks upon new territories and dreams of new worlds. Once again, to be sure, with supreme power the music returns to tonality, as both movement and piece end in F-sharp major. But something truly unheard-of had already occurred—the step beyond the boundaries of tonality was irreversible, and its crisis could no longer be ignored; precisely because Schönberg tried simply everything in his power in order to overcome this crisis.

To this Finale, like the third movement, words are added in the form of a song: Stefan George's poem "Entrückung," which significantly opens with the words, "I sense air from other planets." This is preceded by a brief instrumental introduction, which is also interesting because Schönberg designated it as the first example of what he called *Klangfarbenmelodie* [tone-color melody]. It expresses the feeling of weightless hovering, which the poet utters in words and which is transformed into music here—written in 1908, a glance into the then still utopian future—truly creative vision!

And that was yester-yesteryear. Yesteryear followed immediately and—as we recognize today—entirely organically: the period of free atonality. With a single blow Schönberg opened up new worlds of musical means of expression, inviting boundless freedom and fully unfettered music-making. And here Schönberg's total genius manifested itself: instinctively, with uncanny sureness, and with the sense of duty of a true artist, he avoided these dangers. Of course he was aware of having exceeded the limits of an aesthetic that had been valid until that time, but he considered himself all the more sure of the language he had built on the foundations of a tradition that was part of his flesh and blood. Very likely he saw himself face to face with sheer, limitless freedom, yet he never let this degenerate into chaos. But that is precisely what he was accused of. He was reviled as the destroyer of tradition—without his accusers recognizing traditions themselves. Professionals and public alike reacted with an outrage of unimaginable vehemence. But Schönberg remained unperturbed. He had arrived at a decision: either to retreat within the confines of tonality, accepting it as an ostensible law of nature and thus sacrificing the veracity of his music; or to believe in the infallibility of the logic of his musical thinking and to fulfill the task assigned to him by fate—despite all the consequences for his bare existence, which for years meant extreme poverty and complete isolation. This posture grew out of a deep religious sense and remained undaunted by the heavy blows from the political and artistic world, which accompanied him until death.

But at that time he replied to his adversaries:

> What I did was neither revolutionary nor anarchical. . . . Never was it the intention or effect of the new art to displace, let alone to destroy, the old. On the contrary, no one loves his predecessors more deeply, intimately, and respectfully than the artist who creates truly new things. For reverence is class-consciousness, and love the sense of belonging together.

What Schönberg composed during the period of free atonality, which lasted about fifteen years, was controlled exclusively by his profound sense of structure, schooled by the models of the old masters. With what sovereignty this occurred is immediately recognizable in the first of the Three Piano Pieces opus 11, which ushered in the new era. It is sixty-four measures long and in strict two-part song form. The eleven-measure theme, itself divisible into three parrts, and its five-measure resolution are followed by a varied repetition, again sixteen measures long. Then, for contrast, a loosely constructed middle section—once more sixteen measures in length—is followed by the fifteen-measure reprise. The sixteenth measure is missing here to compensate for an extra measure inserted before the middle section—an extraordinary structural subtlety!

But his other works of the period are also, in this respect, abundant with links to tradition; in fact, far more than the obvious classical and preclassical forms, as are found in *Pierrot lunaire,* or the artful six-part canons of the choruses in *Die glückliche Hand*. What an abundance of new concepts of form were produced and developed, for example, from the new discoveries and their novel manner of presentation in *Das Buch der hängenden Gärten,* a song cycle on poems of Stefan George; or in the Five Orchestral Pieces opus 16—consider only the third of these, whose musical idea was labeled "changing chord" by the composer; or the Six Little Piano Pieces opus 19, each in the form of a musical aphorism, again a new idea conceived by Schönberg.

I have used the term *originality* several times to mean an apparent contradiction of tradition. Doubtless, there exists from time immemorial a tendency to overrate this term. Its use is especially questionable when it does not refer, spontaneously, to the originality of ideas but to that of workmanlike technique, that is, to purely external ability. Regarding this matter, I found a scrap of paper in Schönberg's *Nachlass* on which some remarks were outlined, dating from the time when *Pierrot lunaire* was composed; and this underscores their importance, because *Pierrot* is to this day regarded among the most original works of the new music: "The originality craze is degenerating into vogue. Artists seek nothing but more newness. And find it!! But surely they are not all geniuses?!? Therefore: newness (originality) not the decisive factor of genius. Only one of its most common symptoms." From this we can infer that Schönberg never once searched for originality. Rather—recall his assertion regarding the chords in fourths in *Pelleas*—it had intruded "against his will"—unconsciously. The unconscious dominated his creativity everywhere and at all times, and what he produced thereby he esteemed more highly and more profoundly in each case. "When more happens than one can imagine," he said, "then it can only happen unconsciously."

Yesteryear became yesterday; it was fifty years ago that Schönberg, with his **"Method of Composition with Twelve Tones Related Only to One Another,"** succeeded in finding a firm basis on which to construct nontonal music. He was now (as he wrote to J. M. Hauer in 1923) "in a position to compose without hesitation and with imagination, as one does in childhood, and yet work under a precisely defined aesthetic control."

The public's reaction was predictable: Schönberg was now decried as a musical design engineer. He was convicted for all time. The catchword was unsurpassable as an argument. For it relieved everyone of having a personal opinion beyond the slogan "we said it all along" and of the responsibility of listening to these musical designs and coming to grips with them. Had those who had been chosen to be musicians and musical scholars done so at the time, they could have found the path to the music that lay within and behind these designs. Had they but heeded what Schönberg indicated—both orally and in writing—in the way of advice to his students, friends, and anyone who cared to listen: that it was a matter of twelve-tone *compositions,* not *twelve-tone* compositions, that is, of intellectual, sonic, and musical substances; that these were works of a musical conception and not mathematical designs; and that twelve-tone music certainly requires no more design work than is demanded by what is known as "motivic work" in tonal music. Moreover, to what extent is design to be looked upon with such contempt? Surely augmentation and diminution, inversion, and other mirror forms of counterpoint need not be taken entirely as phantoms, especially if the other voices simultaneously contribute to the thematic material. "But," wrote Schönberg to his brother-in-law, violinist Rudolf Kolisch, "although I am not ashamed of a solid design basis in a composition even where I have consciously produced it—where, in other words, it is less valid than in the places where it was conceived instinctively and subconsciously—still, I do not wish to be regarded as a design engineer because of a little serial combination, since that would signify too little reciprocal accomplishment on my part."

"What can be designed with these twelve tones," he stated on another occasion, "depends on the inventive powers of the individual. Expression is limited only by the creative ability and personality of the composer." For Schönberg, the twelve-tone method of composition was "rather a method of a workmanlike nature, which could exercise a decisive influence on neither the structure nor the character of a work. This is a question of the treatment of the material, in the sense of a characteristic refinement of its stipulations, which determines the form. As such, however, it is of a very great importance."

And here, within the scope of our topic "Schönberg yesterday, today, and tomorrow," we must address ourselves to a fundamental misconception concerning his twelve-tone method of composition: the mechanical transfer of the concept of the row [*Reihenidee*] to all the elements involved in the creation of music—rhythm, dynamics, tone color, and so on—as has been practiced in so-called serial music. Whoever rejects this procedure and denies it the name music is comparable to, and thus apparently branded as, an arch-opponent of Schönberg, in a parallelism as illogical as it is superfluous. In so doing, one forgets or neglects only that the premises in the two cases are fundamentally different. Underlying serial music is a conscious intellectual effort, an artistic manipulation by which an idea—that of Schönberg—is taken over mechanically. Underlying Schönberg's twelve-tone music, however, is a musical *inspiration,* thus an unconscious act. For the tendency toward dodecaphony was intuitive and, long before its recognition and formulation by Schönberg, was clearly recognizable in the music of Reger, Hindemith, Bartók and—last, but not least—Schönberg and Berg. Schönberg did nothing but "hear

out" the inspirations of this genre with all their possibilities of development. And he did this not for the sake of effect or of being original but out of a necessity: to compensate for the loss of the supremely structural functions of tonality. He himself used the term *necessity* in this connection. For the transfer of the row concept to all other parameters of music, there was no such necessity; on the other hand, only this necessity legitimizes, in the realm of art, what would otherwise remain arbitrariness, or at best exhibitionistic contrivance.

Hand in hand with this misconception there goes another: the conscious and radical rejection of all tradition on the part of serial composers. In sharp contrast to this, Schönberg's theory demands the complete mastery of classical and preclassical compositional techniques as an unconditional prerequisite for composition with twelve tones. But here the boundaries are clearly drawn, as the incompatibility and, moreover, the contradiction between serial and twelve-tone music are apparent. To this it must be added marginally that the welfare of music is in no way dependent on the use of Schönbergian methods; that these in no way will guarantee the quality of a work; and that most twelve-tone works—written and as yet unwritten all over the world—may be just as dubious as is most tonal music at all times. Value is determined neither by style nor by label, but by whether the music says something; whether we are moved, stirred, or inspired by it. This is the gist of Schönberg's saying that the difference between old and new music is smaller than the difference between good and bad music. And in justifying the necessity of the development toward non-tonal music by the richness of its combinations, ideas, and tone pictures, which a priori predestined it to a higher level, he closes with the characteristic sentence: "But everything depends not on material, but on genius, as is always true in Art."

That his genius developed in the fertile soil of the German musical tradition is not only evident in his music but also in numerous self-critical documents. In Schönberg's *Nachlass* I found a penciled remark on a yellowed sheet of paper, probably dating from World War I, at which time German music was boycotted abroad:

> Whenever I think about music, nothing ever comes to mind—whether intentionally or unintentionally—but German music. Whoever is its opponent will often have to take the responsibility for utter starvation before this knowledge becomes natural to him. But German music thrives in times of hunger; deprived of nourishment, its silent power will create and fill banquet halls in eternity. And it will always be reaching toward Heaven, where rampant inferiority boasts artistry.

More than a decade later, during the composing of *Moses und Aron,* Schönberg commented on his deep identification with German music in a paper titled **"Nationale Musik":**

> The fact that no one has yet recognized this is due not only to the difficulty of my music but also, and to a greater extent, to the laziness and

arrogance of those who sit in judgment. For it is quite apparent. But I will say it once more myself: my teachers were Bach and Mozart primarily, and Beethoven, Brahms, and Wagner secondarily.

And then, having summarized what he learned from these masters—it turns unwittingly into an embracing composition method in key words—he continued:

> I have never closed my ears to anyone, and therefore can safely say that my originality derives from having imitated immediately whatever good I saw, even when I did not see it in others at first. I might add that, often enough, I saw it first in myself. For I have not stood still with what I perceived: I acquired it in order to possess it; I developed and expanded it, and it led me to new things. I am convinced that people will some day recognize how intimately this New is related to the very best of what was given to us as models. I claim credit for having composed truly new music, which, since it is founded on tradition, is destined to become tradition.

But no one paid any attention to him. That was yesterday, more than forty years ago. His name and his music seemed to fall into oblivion after 1933. In the 1930s the young Dallapiccola, who made an effort to learn something about Schönberg and his twelve-tone music, was advised not to waste his time on something that had been considered passé for a long time. The surprise was all the greater when the free world became accessible to us once again in 1945: Schönberg's ideas, in the meantime, had found resonance everywhere, especially among young people, all over Europe, in all corners of the earth. Today Schönberg has become the center of musical development in twentieth-century music, which does not mean that he is universally understood and accepted. That will still require considerable time, and today nothing is in shorter supply than time. But there exists no composer of yesterday, today, or tommorrow who can avoid coming to grips with Schönberg. It can be said, without exaggeration, that not only Alban Berg and Anton Webern would not be what they are without him, but also Luigi Dallapiccola, Ernst Krenek, Hans Werner Henze, Giselher Klebe, Wolfgang Fortner, Luigi Nono, and Pierre Boulez, the last of whom (as H. H. Stuckenschmidt wrote):

> with unsuspecting naïvaté wrote his *Schönberg est mort* and then, as a conductor, took ten years to acquaint himself with what he had defamed, as the rebel disciple who had betrayed Schönberg. As once before, namely Hindemith in the 1920s, so the admittedly defenseless Webern, who lost his life in 1945, was crowned a sort of antipope to Schönberg, commensurate with his boundless admiration of the master. The idea that Webern's music, in its essential forms, is thinkable without Schönberg is as absurd for any knowledgeable person as that a pupil could have a formal influence on his teacher. But the power of fanfare, with which nearly every adherent to the Boulez-Stockhausen generation blared out Webern's simple

countenance, is leveled, both quantitatively and qualitatively, at their own standard-bearer. It does not diminish Webern's greatness to assert objectively that, in his work and specifically in his adoption of the twelve-tone technique, the elements are a simplification of Schönberg *ad usum delphini*.

This also is part of the picture "Schönberg today," and I could not have expressed it any better. The noise from the fanfare has long since faded away. Perhaps it was needed to chase away the great shadows that lay beneath this generation. Tomorrow and the future will bring new sounds, probably without fanfare. But they will, as before, encircle the focal point called Schönberg and, we hope, understand him as a great living tradition. And out of this recognition, the strength will be drawn for future developments. Until then Schönberg will have the last word, as is the case here and now.

Around 1930 he had an interview with Dr. Eberhard Preussner and Dr. Heinrich Strobel on the Berlin radio network. May his concluding remarks from then be also those of today:

> . . . Herr Strobel, do not underestimate the extent of the circle that has formed around me. It will expand out of the thirst for knowledge of an idealistic younger generation, which feels itself drawn more to the mysterious than to the everyday. But however this may turn out, I can only think and say what my mission prescribes. Gentlemen, do not call that arrogance; I would rather have had greater success. It is in no way my wish to stand on a pedestal as a stylite. As long as I am permitted to consider my thinking and imagination as correct, I will not be able to believe anything except that my ideas must be thought out and expressed, even if they cannot be understood. I personally do not believe that my ideas are so utterly unintelligible. But let us consider: should great incontestable ideas, like those of a Kant, not be permitted to be thought or expressed, simply because to this day honest people must admit that they cannot follow them? To whomever the Lord God has given the mission to say unpopular things, he has lent the power to resign himself to the fact that it is invariably the others who are understood.

Lucy S. Dawidowicz (essay date 1977)

SOURCE: "Arnold Schoenberg: A Search for Jewish Identity," in *The Jewish Presence: Essays on Identity and History,* Holt, Rinehart and Winston, 1977, pp. 32-45.

[*In the following essay, Dawidowicz concludes that* Moses and Aaron *is "the vehicle through which Schoenberg asserted his Jewishness."*]

In December 1966, more than fifteen years after the composer's death, Arnold Schoenberg's unfinished opera ***Moses and Aaron*** was given a belated American premiere by the Opera Company of Boston. The occasion was full of ironies. The performance, which took place in

America's historic citadel of high culture, was staged in a shabby one-time movie palace; the impresario was Missouri-born and Arkansas-reared; the work itself, a twelve-tone opera glorifying Jewish monotheism, was written by a Jew who had become a Lutheran but returned to Judaism. As a further affront to Boston's traditions, the opera contained an orgy scene which, in another day, would certainly have been banned.

Producing *Moses and Aaron* demands immense resources. Sarah Caldwell, the artistic director whose previous productions of other seldom-heard works have put Boston on the national operatic map, assembled for *Moses and Aaron* a cast which included two stars—a bass-baritone for the role of Moses (Donald Gramm, one of the Metropolitan Opera's best acting singers) and a tenor to sing Aaron (Richard Lewis, who sang the role in the British production of 1965); twenty singing principals; a chorus of fifty-five sopranos, mezzos, and altos; forty-eight actors and dancers; and members of the Boston Symphony Orchestra under the direction of Osbourne McConathy. What with seventy Elders, twelve Tribal Chieftains, four Naked Virgins (not to speak of the Golden Calf), and who knows how many supernumeraries, it is no surprise the production cost $300,000. (Boston has a tradition of sorts for big musical settings: In 1869, to celebrate the National Peace Jubilee, 10,000 singers, 1,000 musicians, and 100 firemen beating anvils with sledgehammers performed the "Anvil Chorus" from *Il Trovatore*.)

Both the libretto and the music of *Moses and Aaron* are fully Schoenberg's creation. As to the music, it is a complex contrapuntal composition whose absorbing twelve-tone structure and atonality serve to enhance and amplify the terror and awe of the libretto. The opera opens with God's summons to Moses before the Burning Bush, as told in Exodus 3-4. The Voice from the Burning Bush (sung by six solo voices behind the stage and a six-part speaking chorus) calls Moses to bring the Israelites the message of the One God and to lead them to freedom. Moses pleads that he is unfit; because he is slow of speech and of a slow tongue, the people will not believe him. God promises that He will perform wondrous things to convince the people of Moses's message. Aaron will be Moses's spokesman to the people.

In the next scene the brothers confront one another (Exod. 4:27-28). Text and music stress the discrepancy between word and image, thought and feeling, idea and myth. Moses speaks earnestly, in inflected, accented speech (*Sprechstimme*), while Aaron sings sensuous floating melodies, florid, with a hint of the cantorial. Aaron fails utterly to understand the new and religiously revolutionary basis of Moses's monotheism—that man's reward lies in his freedom to act righteously. Instead, he translates this idea back to the pagan concepts of reward for obedience to the gods and punishment for disobedience.

In the third scene, against nervous orchestral runs, the Israelites exchange fearsome rumors about the impending arrival of Moses and Aaron. The intricate contrapuntal choral composition gives expression to their fears and superstitions, and to the divisions among them. In the closing scene of Act I, Moses and Aaron bring God's message (Exod. 4:29-31). The Israelites at first mock the new God who cannot be seen or heard. As Moses despairs of his ability to communicate his message, Aaron performs "the signs in the sight of the people." He turns Moses's rod into a serpent, and back into a rod; Moses's hand becomes leprous and then whole again; the Nile waters turn into blood. (In the Boston production, all these actions were pantomimed.) "And the people believed." The act closes with a rapturous hymnal chorus in march tempo as the Israelites go off into the desert wasteland: "We are His chosen folk before all others, / We are the chosen ones, / Him alone to worship, / Him alone to serve."

Between the end of Act I and the choral interlude that precedes Act II, the Jews have left Egypt, crossed the Red Sea, and journeyed into the desert. Moses has ascended Mount Sinai (Exod. 24:18). The Israelites fear that Moses and his God have abandoned them. The small chorus whispers its anxiety in hushed tones: "Where is Moses? Where is his God?" The musical theme recalls God's promise to Moses, but its repetitive syncopated staccato heightens doubt and insecurity.

Act II opens to show the disarray in the Israelite camp in the forty days since Moses's ascent. Violence and lewdness prevail; the seventy Elders can no longer exercise authority. The people turn on them savagely, demanding their old gods back. The fearful elders turn to Aaron for direction. Unsure of himself, he yields quickly.

The jubilation begins, introduced by great fanfares. The Golden Calf (Exod. 32:3-6) is brought onstage. The stupendous scene of "The Golden Calf and the Altar" is, according to Karl Wörner's analysis, a symphony in five movements for solo voices and choruses. It opens with a ritualistic dance of the slaughterers who prepare the animal sacrifices; then follow worshipful processions of the sick, the poor, and the old. The music has an eerie, abnormal character. Fanfares introduce the tribal leaders who come to pay homage to the Golden Calf. The tempo accelerates. When a youth exhorts the Israelites to remember their religion of freedom and to destroy "the image of temporality," the tribal leaders murder him, to a fury of brass and drums. Then a gentle swaying dance tempo is heard as the people begin to exchange gifts and kindnesses. But coarseness and drunkenness soon overtake them. The priestly ritual begins: the four Naked Virgins give themselves to the embrace of the priests, who then sacrifice them upon the altar to the Golden Calf. Music and action intensify in a frenzy of syncopated tension, ending in a percussive, delirious finale.

As the killing, self-destruction, and sexual debauchery come to an end and the sacrificial fires are extinguished, a voice from afar proclaims that Moses is descending from the mountain. Moses appears and destroys the

Golden Calf with these words: "Begone, you image of powerlessness to enclose the boundless in an image finite!" The brothers confront each other. Moses demands an explanation. Aaron justifies himself: he loves his people—"I live just for them and want to sustain them." Moses insists that his love is for the idea of the One God. Aaron answers that the common people can comprehend only part of that idea, the perceivable part, that they need feeling and hope. Moses refuses to "debase" his idea; he will remain faithful to it, as it is set forth in the tablets. Aaron counters that the tablets, too, are images, "just part of the whole idea." At that, Moses smashes the tablets. (In Exod. 32:19-20, Moses smashes the tablets first, then destroys the Golden Calf.) In despair, he asks God to relieve him of his mission as Aaron chides him for faint-heartedness. Then the pillar of fire by night and the pillar of cloud by day appear, and the people follow them in religious ecstasy. Aaron explains that "the Infinite thus shows not Himself, but shows the way to Him and the way to the Promised Land." Once again believing in, and reconciled to, their chosenness, the Israelites sing the marchlike hymn with which Act I closed. But Moses sinks to the ground, despairing of the possibility of expressing the idea of the inconceivable God. The violins sustain taut legatos of unbearable poignancy as Moses cries out in defeat, "O word, thou word, that I lack!"

Schoenberg's text for the unfinished third act departs rather drastically from the biblical original. Aaron, a prisoner in chains, is dragged in by soldiers. Moses calls him to account for having betrayed God's word, wrought miracles, believed in the physical reality of a land flowing with milk and honey, and given the people false gods. Now, Moses charges, Aaron has disobeyed God's word by smiting the rock, instead of speaking to it, to make the waters of Meribah flow. (In a letter to Walter Eidlitz in 1933, Schoenberg complained about "incomprehensible contradictions in the Bible" which made it difficult for him to complete the act. He was referring to the variants in Exod. 19:5-6 and Num. 20:7-12.) When the soldiers ask to kill Aaron, Moses orders them to "set him free, and if he can,/he shall live." But Aaron, freed, falls dead.

There is in Schoenberg's *Moses and Aaron* an almost uncanny intuition of the meaning of biblical Judaism and of Moses's historic role as the founder of Israelite monotheism. It is doubtful whether Schoenberg read any serious scholarly literature on the subject; in any case, much of what was then available had been written under the influence of Wellhausen and the higher critics who dated Israel's ethical monotheism from the later period of classical prophecy. Schoenberg's artistic conception, on the other hand, is essentially traditionalist (and quite in accord with recent archaeological findings and modern scholarship), and it is thus interesting to speculate on how he arrived at his position. He was quite obviously not a fundamentalist, of either a Jewish or a Christian variety, and he had been remote from traditional Jewish thought. Is this operatic exaltation of monotheism and condemnation of idolatry to be seen then as a confession of Jewish identity? Or did he perhaps undertake it as a celebration of Jewish morality at a time when European society was poised at the brink of pagan violence and destruction?

Schoenberg completed the first two acts of *Moses and Aaron* in March 1932. While he was still at work on the third act, the Reichstag passed the Enabling Act (March 23, 1933), which gave Hitler and the National Socialists the power to enact any legislation at will. A month later, the Jews were driven by Nazi law from their positions in government and cultural institutions. Dismissed from his post at the Prussian Academy of Arts, Schoenberg left Berlin for America. On July 24, 1933, in a simple ceremony at the Liberal Synagogue of Paris, he was readmitted to the Jewish community. (His two witnesses were David Marianoff, Albert Einstein's son-in-law, and Marc Chagall.) On October 16, 1933, he wrote to Alban Berg: "As you have doubtless realized, my return to the Jewish religion took place long ago and is indeed demonstrated in some of my published work . . . and in *Moses and Aaron*. . . ."

Schoenberg himself considered his return to Judaism to be a political rather than a religious act. Yet such matters are seldom as simple as one would like to believe; indeed, the complex twists of Schoenberg's own life would indicate that religion and politics cannot in his case be easily separated, and that faith and identity, self-esteem and group pride, all played a part in the formulation of his final intellectual and emotional position.

Arnold Schoenberg was born in Leopoldstadt, Vienna's Jewish quarter, on September 13, 1874. His father, Samuel, a shopkeeper, had come from Pressburg, now Bratislava, the stronghold of Jewish Orthodoxy in Hungary. No doubt Samuel Schoenberg had brought some Jewish traditions and practices with him when he migrated to the big city. Until his death in 1889, when Arnold was fifteen, the family still observed the Jewish holidays, according to Gertrud Schoenberg, the composer's widow, with whom I spoke in California in 1966. It is unlikely that Schoenberg himself had any Jewish education.

At the age of seventeen, Schoenberg began working in a bank, and at the same time continued his self-education in music and composition. Around 1895, as a cellist in an amateur student orchestra in Vienna, he met the conductor Alexander von Zemlinsky, who became interested in his compositions. In 1901, Schoenberg married Zemlinsky's sister Mathilde (she died in 1923).

In 1898, at twenty-four, to his family's deep shock, Schoenberg became a Lutheran. No one knows exactly why he converted. His cousin, Hans Nachod, says that Schoenberg was persuaded to make the move by a singer friend, but Gertrud Schoenberg probably was closer to the truth in maintaining that his conversion was prompted by cultural rather than by religious motives. It was, she said, "quite a usual procedure for educated Jews, as the belief in assimilation at this time flourished."

Schoenberg's parents had come to Vienna during the great Jewish migration from the hinterlands of Galicia, Hungary, and Bohemia after the enactment of the 1867 Constitution, which erased the legal inequities under which Jews had suffered. In thirty years, from 1860 to 1890, the Jewish population of Vienna rose from 1 to 12 percent. Jews flocked to the *gymnasia* and the universities, where they were overwhelmingly concentrated in the faculties of law and medicine. They also went into journalism—en masse, it seemed to the Austrians. Yet although (or because) Jews shaped Vienna's literary and artistic tastes, anti-Semitism continued to prevail in most professional, academic, and government circles, even before Karl Lueger became *Burgermeister* and Christian Socialism a vehicle for political anti-Semitism. At a time when a birth certificate should have sufficed, many positions still required proof of baptism. Freud, for example, a *privatdozent* for seventeen years, was kept from being appointed at the University of Vienna, according to Ernest Jones, by "the anti-Semitic attitude of official quarters. . . ."

The keys to musical Vienna were similarly held by men who did not like to open doors to Jews. Mahler's baptism, in 1897, constituted his ticket of admission to the directorship of the Vienna Opera. It seems entirely likely that Schoenberg, too, became a Christian in order to have easier access to important musical institutions and influential musicians. Perhaps, like others of his generation and upbringing who stood neither here nor there in their Jewishness, he was attracted to what must have seemed the dazzlingly brilliant cultural life of the non-Jewish and ex-Jewish intellectuals, poets, composers, and artists. (Schoenberg was also a painter, active in the Expressionist movement and a participant in the *Blaue Reiter* exhibition of 1912.) Among themselves, young Jewish cosmopolitans often attributed Vienna's accelerating anti-Semitism to the bearded traditionalist Jews who had migrated from the Galician towns and villages with their baggage of poverty, Orthodoxy, and Yiddish. For many, the baptismal waters represented a means of escaping identification with these Jews.

Religion—Judaism or Evangelical Lutheranism—meant little to Schoenberg in the time following his conversion. One of his biographers has characterized it as a period of "positivistic atheism." Later he developed an interest in Swedenborgian ideas. Schoenberg himself described this process in a letter to the German poet Richard Dehmel on December 13, 1912:

> For a long time I have been wanting to write an oratorio on the following subject: modern man, having passed through materialism, socialism, and anarchy, and despite having been an atheist, still having in him some residue of ancient faith (in the form of superstition), wrestles with God (see also Strindberg's "Jacob Wrestling") and finally succeeds in finding God and becoming religious.

Dehmel could not provide the poetic text Schoenberg wanted. Eventually, using Balzac's now quite unknown theosophical novel, *Seraphita,* Schoenberg began composing both text and music for the oratorio, *Die Jakobsleiter*. The work contained suggestions of ideas he was later to use in *Moses and Aaron:* "this Either and this Or," "instincts" versus "commandments," spirit versus matter. But Schoenberg never finished *Die Jakobsleiter*. For one thing he was drafted into Franz Josef's army, where he became a *Kapellmeister*. Later, groping his way back toward Judaism, and more rigorous in his religious thinking, he may have become uneasy with alien and pseudoliterary texts and have decided to turn to more appropriate and authentic ones.

In 1922 a small incident set Schoenberg on an irrevocable course back to Jewishness and Judaism. At a resort in Mattsee near Salzburg, where he had gone to spend the summer, he was told that Jews were not welcome. He came to realize that the Christian promise to accept Jews at the price of assimilation (read: conversion) was a fraud. "For I have at last learnt the lesson that has been forced upon me during this year and I shall never forget it," he wrote to Wassily Kandinsky. "It is that I am not a German, not a European, indeed perhaps scarcely even a human being (at least, the Europeans prefer the worst of their race to me), but I am a Jew."

In a second letter to Kandinsky on May 4, 1923, in which he referred to "that man Hitler" who would make no exception even for a "good" Jew like himself, Schoenberg prophesied that though the anti-Semites would try to "exterminate" Einstein, Mahler, and himself, they would not succeed with those "much tougher elements thanks to whose endurance Jewry has maintained itself unaided against the whole of mankind for twenty centuries. For these are evidently so constituted that they can accomplish the task that their God has imposed on them: to survive in exile, uncorrupted and unbroken, until the hour of salvation comes!"

Thereafter, Schoenberg's immersion in Jewish themes seemed inevitable. Until his death in 1951, Jewish subject matter continued to attract him. During 1926 and 1927 he worked on a play, *Der biblische Weg,* which he said had been "conceived in 1922 or '23 at the latest"— that is, at the very time his self-esteem rebelled at German anti-Semitism. The drama, never published, was, in his own words, "a very up-to-date treatment of the story of how the Jews became a people." Its protagonist, Max Aruns (Moses and Aaron in one), attempts to unite his people and lead them to the fulfillment of their God-given mission. But dissidents beat him to death, and his leadership falls to another. *Der biblische Weg* foreshadowed the dramatic core and conflict of *Moses and Aaron*. Thus, Asseino (from "Sinai"?), the spokesman of traditional Jewry, speaks to Max Aruns:

> Max Aruns, you want to be Moses and Aaron in one person! Moses, to whom God gave the idea but denied the gift of speech; and Aaron, who could not grasp the idea but could formulate it and move the masses.

Thenceforth, the idea of an opera about Moses and Aaron seized Schoenberg's imagination. On April 10, 1930, he wrote to Alban Berg that after a year of "very strenuous work," he needed a holiday and he was playing tennis instead of working. (Oscar Levant said Schoenberg once told him that if he had not been a composer, he would have liked to have been a champion tennis player.) At the end of the letter, he said he would like best to do an opera: " . . . perhaps I shall do *Moses and Aaron*." By August 1930 he was already at work on it. He completed the second act just as National Socialism stood at Germany's threshold.

Theodor W. Adorno has suggested that the composition of *Moses and Aaron* was Schoenberg's defense against the rise of Hitler. (Hence the fall of the Third Reich eliminated the need to complete the opera.) This must surely have been a major motive. The figure of Moses served to reinforce Schoenberg's Jewish self-esteem, to strengthen his rejection of the world that National Socialism was then fashioning in Europe, a world governed by paganism, violence, and bloodshed. (Something akin to this motive probably animated Freud's interests in Moses as well.) It has also been suggested that Schoenberg saw himself as a revolutionary herald of a new musical system—atonality—and identified his own lack of popular success with Moses's failure to communicate with the people. I myself, however, prefer to think that Schoenberg intended *Moses and Aaron* as a challenge—musically, philosophically, politically, and culturally—to Wagner's *Parsifal*, the only other religious music drama to which it might legitimately be compared.

The two operas are total opposites. Musically, Wagner was the last great Romantic, while Schoenberg, the great adversary of Romanticism, advocated musical cerebralism and classicism. Philosophically, or theologically, *Moses and Aaron* and *Parsifal* appear to represent the antagonism between Judaism and Christianity, between monotheism and trinitarianism. *Parsifal,* Wagner's version of the legend of the Holy Grail, glorifies compassion and repentance through Christ. It is religious drama in that it leads from conflict to a renewal of faith and a restatement of religious values.

Yet notwithstanding its exaltation of Christianity, *Parsifal* remains pseudoreligious; it is not genuinely Christian. Wagner hardly identified himself as a Christian, in part because he could not accept Christianity's Jewish origins: "For us it is sufficient to derive the ruin of the Christian religion from its drawing upon Judaism for the elaboration of its dogma." Rather, he defined the Holy Grail as the spiritual aspect of the Nibelungen hoard, Amfortas with the German kaiser, Parsifal with Siegfried. He wrote once that "the abstract highest God of the Germans, Wotan, did not really need to yield place to the God of the Christians; rather could he be completely identified with him. . . . Christianity has been unable in our day to extirpate the local native gods." Thus, Wagner's Christianity turns out to be Teutonic paganism; as others have pointed out, *Parsifal* is not a religious Christian drama but the fifth opera in the Ring, welding Teutonic paganism, medieval Christianity, and modern German nationalism into one romantic *Gesamtkunstwerk,* a stage-consecrational-festival play.

It is, I think, plausible that Schoenberg felt the need to define himself in opposition to this kind of German Christianity, which was, at different levels of consciousness, inextricably associated with paganism and idolatry. Perhaps, in *Moses and Aaron,* he wished not only to surpass Wagner as a composer but also to distinguish himself decisively from the Wagner who was a Christian-pagan, German nationalist, and anti-Semite, and from the rising Nazi culture that Wagner would have applauded. Thus, *Moses and Aaron,* the vehicle through which Schoenberg asserted his Jewishness, comes to symbolize the antithesis of everything that *Parsifal* represents, a reassertion of the intrinsic and superior value of Jewish monotheism—in itself, for Schoenberg, the purest concept of belief.

Carl Dalhaus (essay date 1978)

SOURCE: "Schoenberg's aesthetic theology," in *Schoenberg and the New Music,* translated by Derrick Puffett and Alfred Clayton, Cambridge University Press, 1987, pp. 81-93.

[In the following essay, which was originally published in 1978, Dalhaus discusses Schoenberg's essays that reveal the aesthetic sense upon which he based his musical compositions.]

I

In 'My Evolution' (1949), his draft of an inner biography, Schoenberg wrote: 'This is also the place to speak of the miraculous contributions of the subconscious. I am convinced that in the works of the great masters many miracles can be discovered, the extreme profundity and prophetic foresight of which seem superhuman.' Then, using a music example, Schoenberg demonstrates a latent connection between contrasting themes in the Op. 9 Chamber Symphony 'solely in order to illustrate the power behind the human mind, which produces miracles for which we do not deserve credit.'

Dubious though the thematic connection which Schoenberg thought he had discovered in his work decades later may seem, it is unusual and characteristic that the inspiration that he felt had been conferred on him did not consist of a theme, but rather of a connection between themes. The inspired idea, in the face of which Schoenberg felt moved to make use of the language of art religion, occurred unconsciously, remained initially latent and manifested itself in a relationship and not a substance. The idea which assumes concrete form in a work such as the Chamber Symphony is thus realised less in the musical shapes that make up the surface than in the tissue of relationships which, hidden beneath, connect the ideas with one another.

The principle on which the interconnection of themes in the Chamber Symphony is based is that of 'contrasting derivation'. It was formulated by Arnold Schmitz in 1923 with regard to Beethoven sonata movements. And the very fact that both Schmitz's analyses and those of Schoenberg contain certain questionable features, and yet were produced independently of each other, enables us to see them all the more clearly as the expression of a tendency characteristic of the time, which transcends their inherent differences: the tendency to regard hidden connections as being the most important and convincing ones.

Yet the most striking thing about the quotation from Schoenberg's **'My Evolution'** is the seemingly self-evident manner with which, in one and the same sentence, there is talk of the workings of the 'subconscious' and of a 'miracle', with the result that categories taken from religion and from psychology or depth psychology intermingle as if they were interchangeable.

It would be completely unjustified to dismiss the word 'miracle' as being a mere metaphor lacking religious substance. In the essay **'Composition with Twelve Notes'** from the year 1935 Schoenberg makes use of the language of aesthetic theology in a way which requires us to take him at his word, and with a seriousness and an insistence which prevent us from suspecting his manner of expressing himself of being pardonable pseudo-religious rhetoric:

> To understand the very nature of creation one must acknowledge that there was no light before the Lord said: 'Let there be Light'. And since there was not yet light, the Lord's omniscience embraced a vision of it which only His omnipotence could call forth. We poor human beings, when we refer to one of the better minds among us as a creator, should never forget what a creator is in reality. A creator has a vision of something which has not existed before this vision. And a creator has the power to bring his vision to life, the power to realise it.

This mingling of religious and psychological categories, which irritates in the 1949 **'My Evolution',** reaches back in Schoenberg's thinking at least to the year 1911. In the essay **'Franz Liszt's Work and Being',** 'faith', which Schoenberg contrasts sharply with mere 'conviction', moves close to 'instinctive life':

> Liszt's importance lies in the one place where great men's importance can lie: in faith. Fanatical faith, of the kind that creates a radical distinction between normal men and those it impels. Normal men *possess* a conviction; great men are *possessed* by a faith. . . . But the work, the perfected work of the great artist, is produced, above all, by his instincts; and the sharper ear he has for what they say, the more immediate the expression he can give

them, the greater his work is. That is exactly the relationship, or perhaps it is even more direct, between faith—faith independent of reason—and instinctive life.

The Romantic religion of art to which Schoenberg subscribed whole-heartedly—a religion of art which his opposite Stravinsky felt to be inadmissible and dishonest, as regards both religion and aesthetics—was rooted in an assumption which seemed as natural to nineteenth-century Protestant theology as it seems suspect to that of the twentieth century: the assumption that the substance of religion consisted in subjective emotion, which one could then interpret as the guarantee of religious truth, as in the case of Schleiermacher, or as the source of religious illusions, as in the case of Feuerbach, but which in any case formed the starting-point of both apologetics and polemics. Theology was—contrary to the name, which it continued to bear—anthropocentric.

However, it is not the business of a historian to subject the roots of religion in subjective emotion to theological criticism for which he is not qualified. What matters is to recognise that the art religion which spread in the aesthetics, and particularly in the popular aesthetics, of the nineteenth century was a variant of the religion of emotion which was considered to be legitimate theology by Protestantism of the time. Dogmatism, the decline of which seemed inexorable, was replaced by philosophy of religion, and this finally turned into psychology of religion. Thus it is not surprising that the basis of art religion changed progressively from Wackenroder's emotional devotion via Schopenhauer's metaphysics of the will to Sigmund Freud's psychology of the instincts, which was adopted by Schoenberg.

If as a result of this the proximity of 'faith' and 'instinctive life' in Schoenberg's thinking is capable of being interpreted in the context of the history of ideas, then the aesthetically decisive factor lies in the conviction that the idea of a musical work, in which a composer's 'instinctive life' manifests itself, consists primarily of relationships, and indeed of relationships which in essence remain latent. In Schoenberg's thinking there is a configuration of three factors: faith, to which reason cannot attain; the urge which emanates from the expressive need of the subconscious; and the expression of a musical work idea less in terms of themes than in terms of thematic relationships which are not capable of being perceived directly and which, precisely for that reason, seem all the more convincing. The configuration proves difficult to explicate inasmuch as to concentrate on one of the factors to the detriment of the others—be it the theological, the psychological or the aesthetic, compositional—technical component—would be one-sided, inadequate or heavy-handed.

The extent to which the aesthetic categories of the eighteenth, nineteenth and twentieth centuries are secularised theological concepts has never been underestimated. As a result, the fact that the reverse of the consecration of the profane, which one calls art religion, is a deconsecration of the sacred, led to a situation where the various interpretations of the phenomenon veered from one extreme to the other. Because of its legal origins, the term 'secularisation' was associated with the idea of taking other people's property; but this did not stop the view that the acquisition was illegitimate from being countered by the opposing view that the transformation was legitimate because it was a historically necessary formal change. While on the one hand the art religion of the nineteenth century could be suspected of investing the musical expression of earthly and sometimes all-too-human emotions with a metaphysical dignity which was a mere aesthetic illusion, on the other hand Richard Wagner claimed, in commenting on *Parsifal,* nothing less than that the substance of religion, which had petrified in the form of ecclesiastical Christianity, should be saved and incorporated by art as the living manifestation of the spirit of the age.

A belief in origins which considers the primary ownership of a thing to be the only legitimate one is the antithesis of a philosophy of history aimed at the future which adheres to the possibility that the real substance, or at least the part relevant to the present, which lies concealed in theological ideas and concepts, can be brought out into the open by translation into the realms of aesthetics, psychology or politics; and that this secularisation does not represent an illegitimate appropriation, but the fulfilment of a promise contained in the religious categories. To translate them into another language is to establish their true meaning.

Yet Schoenberg's texts cannot be interpreted unequivocally in either way, and, in any case, it is probable that similar formulations from the turn of the century have to be assessed differently from those of the last few decades. Whether Schoenberg, like Freud, conceived of psychological categories as being the roots of religious ones, or whether he simply regarded the subconscious as a place where religion manifests itself without being psychologically reducible must remain in the balance, at least for the time being.

In general one can interpret the process that one calls secularisation in at least four ways: first, as the questionable appropriation and transformation of theological substance; secondly, as historical evolution, to which as a historian one already accords a claim to validity, without openly coming to a conclusion, in that one concedes continuity to the process—and in the language of historians that virtually amounts to historical legitimacy; thirdly, as a structural analogy in which the direction of the transfer—for example, between depth psychology and theology—remains just as open to question as does its legality; and fourthly, as a metaphorical interpretation, the substantiality of which depends on how close to the truth one considers an 'unreal', poetic language to be.

To apply the various schemes of interpretation available in hermeneutics to Schoenberg's art-religious confessions would not be impossible, though it would be like going for a walk in a labyrinth, the exit of which is very difficult to find indeed.

II

Schoenberg's output consists to roughly equal extents of vocal and of instrumental works. Yet his aesthetic theory—sometimes at odds with his compositional practice—is one-sidedly determined by instrumental music. Schoenberg's claim, in his essay on **'The Relationship to the Text'**, that, when composing a song, he permitted himself to be led solely by the initial sound of the poem, turns out to be all the more revealing in the context of the history of ideas on account of the fact that an analysis of the George songs proves it to be blatantly untrue. However implausible the idea may seem, faced with a work like **Erwartung,** that in the period of early atonality the text was merely a means of building large-scale forms without the support of tonality, it does tally with the fact that dodecaphony, the primary function of which Schoenberg considered to be the purely musical foundation of larger forms, at first formed the basis, on the whole, of instrumental works.

Thus the fact that instrumental music, particularly in the form of a discourse based on musical logic, represented what Schoenberg considered to be 'real' music is doubtless connected with the influence of Schopenhauer's metaphysics of absolute music, a metaphysics which, transmitted by Wagner and Nietzsche, had around 1900 become the aesthetics of all German composers from Strauss and Mahler to Schoenberg and Pfitzner. Yet if one is not afraid of a hypothesis for which there is no tangible documentary evidence, one can also reconstruct a link back to the time around 1800, which, even though Schoenberg may not have been aware of it, makes his aesthetics appear more comprehensible.

The 'vision' which, in Schoenberg's words, characterises a musical 'creation' that may be referred to as such without arrogance or blasphemy is the outline of a distinct world of one's own. Mahler, for example, spoke of a 'world' constructed by a symphony 'with all the technical means at one's disposal'. That music is 'a world of its own' was however the fundamental idea with which, in 1799, Ludwig Tieck, in his *Phantasien über die Kunst,* founded the Romantic metaphysics of music, which was in essence an aesthetic of instrumental music, or, to be more precise, an aesthetic of the symphony as the paradigm of large-scale instrumental music. That aesthetic theology, which was centred on the concept of musical creativity, believed it had found its proper subject in instrumental and not in vocal music was by no means an accident, as can be shown by a short digression into the history of ideas.

The claim that man, God's likeness, is an 'alter deus' as a poet and only as a poet, who does not imitate but creates, had been advanced as early as 1561 by Julius Caesar Scaliger, the compiler of Renaissance poetics. But the idea, as Hans Blumenberg pointed out, first acquired philosophical substance and historical importance in the eighteenth century, when it combined with Leibniz's idea of the possible worlds to form a configuration from which emanated the idea, crucial to modern poetics, that a poet is the creator of another, that is, of a possible world. Johann Jakob Breitinger's *Critische Dichtkunst* of 1740, as Oskar Walzel realised, puts 'Leibniz's idea of the possible worlds to aesthetic use'.

But the concept of the creative formed an exclusive antithesis to the traditional imitative principle moulded by Aristotelian philosophy. Planning a world of one's own could not be reconciled with imitating nature as it is—be it the empirical appearance or the metaphysical essence of nature.

Yet vocal music—to return to the starting-point of the argument—had since the sixteenth century been declared to be the imitation of that which was expressed by the text. Instrumental music without a text, the content of which remained imprecise as long as it did not regress to primitive tone painting, seemed both to the sixteenth-century humanist and to the eighteenth-century encyclopaedist to be an inferior kind of vocal music, to say nothing of more negative ways of describing it.

But from 1800 onwards there is a gradual change in the order of precedence of the genres. If for thousands of years the lack of a text had been regarded as a deficiency in music defined in principle by harmony, rhythm and language, then this was reversed in the writings of E. T. A. Hoffmann and Eduard Hanslick, where the text appears as an 'extra musical' addition to a tonal art whose 'real' being manifested itself in 'pure' instrumental music. Yet there is, it seems, a close and direct connection between the change of paradigms in music aesthetics from vocal to instrumental music, and the transition from the imitative principle to the idea of the creative. If vocal music in general remains an imitation formally dependent on a text or on the contents of a text, then instrumental music, inasmuch as it aspires to the heights of the symphonic style, can be understood as the construction of a world of its own. In the symphony the composer adopts a claim which had previously been made for the poet: the claim that a poet, as opposed to a painter or a sculptor, does not imitate the real world but founds a possible one. (Scaliger spoke of 'condere' as opposed to 'narrare'.)

But if one acknowledges the connection which existed between the emancipation of instrumental music and the use in music aesthetics of the poetological idea of the creative, then it becomes clear why it was instrumental music, which had liberated itself from poetry, that Tieck called 'poetic'. Poetry, understood in the sense in which Breitinger had formulated it, was the paradigm of the generation of a personal, possible world; and music became 'poetic' in advancing a similar claim and substantiating it convincingly in works such as Beethoven's symphonies and Bach's fugues—which Goethe felt to be a musical symbol of a possible world prior to the creation of the real world.

Tieck's metaphysics of instrumental music were adapted by Schopenhauer, and Schopenhauer's philosophy was in turn adapted by Schoenberg. It is hardly possible to deny that the aesthetic theology implied or encapsulated therein, the conjunction of the concept of the creative and that of large-scale instrumental music, had a far-reaching influence on Schoenberg's thinking, with the result that in spite of the oblique relationship between aesthetic theory and compositional practice—a practice in which there can be no talk of instrumental music ranking lower or of a secondary role for the texts—we must expect to find traces of metaphysical dogma.

III

It would not be an exaggeration to call early atonality, which Schoenberg embarked upon with 'fear and trembling' and in full awareness of an irrevocable quality which was difficult to bear, a state of emergency in the precise sense that a state of emergency is the opposite of a state of affairs in which the law prevails. Yet the emancipation of the dissonance, which was not so much a qualitative leap logically resulting from what had gone before as an arbitrary act, was not at all the mere abolition of an old law and the introduction of a new one. The critics who raised a hue and cry about anarchy did indeed touch upon an essential aspect of the process, the significance of which they vaguely perceived, even though their aesthetic judgment failed to assess it correctly.

The concept of the state of emergency means that Schoenberg claimed that the suspension of the existing musical order, which he accomplished in the final movement of Op. 10, defined a historical state whose advent would turn out to be irrevocable, no matter how one looked at it. Schoenberg took a decision whose seriousness—and the fact is nothing short of self-evident—no one at the time who was musically competent could afford to disregard. Before embarking on an interpretation of history which concerned itself with continuity and discontinuity, one would first of all have to find a reason for the fact that even bitter opponents perceived Schoenberg's decision to be an act of incalculable significance, an event which, even a decade and a half later, could only be circumvented, so it was thought, by countering it with an equally abrupt decision in favour of neoclassicism, the supposedly necessary next step, with which Schoenberg's expressionist atonality was so to speak to be relegated to a past which was of no concern to the present.

To say that Schoenberg owed to the resounding success of the **Gurrelieder** a reputation which could not simply be destroyed by claiming that Opp. 10 and 11 were insignificant sectarian aberrations is of course true to a certain extent, though it does not explain everything. One of the reasons why the transition to atonality was taken seriously at all, that is, in the sense of a catastrophe, was, apart from the respect which was Schoenberg's due, a mode of thought no doubt typical of the nineteenth and early twentieth centuries: the tendency, which ran counter to the dominant belief in progress, to look upon approaching events as being both the road to impending disaster and unavoidable.

Yet the fact remains—and to have to admit this is rather difficult for a historian—that it is, strictly speaking, impossible to give a reason for Schoenberg's decision of 1907. Those who speak of historical necessity, of the dictates of the historical moment which Schoenberg obeyed, make the event appear more harmless than it actually was. The suspension of the existing order, the proclamation of the musical state of emergency, was an act of violence. And thus the theories with which Schoenberg attempted to justify the emancipation of the dissonance are characterised by a helplessness which prevents us from taking them at their word as being motives for compositional decisions. The same holds true, a decade and a half later, for the step to 'composition with twelve notes related only to one another'. Dodecaphony did not acquire the power which caused it to spread irresistibly, even if with some delay, on account of the arguments on which it was based. The reasons for its validity were always rather weak, both in the case of Schoenberg, and later in that of Adorno, who mistrusted it anyway. And even the works in which it manifested itself were, considering its subsequent influence, evidently not the decisive factor, despite their undoubted quality. Either, as in the case of Berg, the technique was unmistakably of secondary importance, one means amongst many with which Berg took precautionary measures within the works themselves. Or, as in the case of Webern, it produced a conflict between latent structure and expressive gesture which led to an open controversy in Webern reception. Or again, as in Schoenberg's late works, dodecaphony remained one of several possibilities, the common and all-embracing principle of which was developing variation.

Apart from this, the attempt to explain in terms of the philosophy of history Schoenberg's power to take decisions, that is, to interpret the diktat of the individual as that of history, is questionable inasmuch as the concept of the 'one' history which the philosophy of history assumes to exist is doubtful and may be suspected of being a myth. What really happens are histories—in the plural: at different places and under diverging circumstances. 'History' in the singular is a fiction.

But insofar as neither a diktat of history, nor the unavoidable logic of apologetic arguments, nor even the compelling evidence that we are dealing with technical preconditions to which important works owe their aesthetic life, is able to provide truthful reasons for the steps to atonality and dodecaphony, then the problem of authority, which arose nonetheless in the case of the one decision as in that of the other, comes to the fore with the clarity it requires, even if a solution is at present hardly in sight.

The authority which Schoenberg claimed for himself and which his contemporaries also accorded him through the tone they assumed, both in their polemics and in their apologias, was rooted in the emphatic awareness of a calling based on the feeling of being a tool. One would not want to deny the obvious fact that Schoenberg's interpretation of himself was determined by a concept of genius which was of Romantic origin, though this is not a sufficient explanation. It is far more the case that the moral pathos which marks Schoenberg's musical poetics, and even technical statements such as those about musical prose—a pathos which was completely foreign to the nineteenth-century concept of genius—bears unmistakably prophetic traits, in the original, authentic sense, that is, that prophecy is directed less at the future and at its impending calamities than at the present and its corrupt depravity. Schoenberg, from a position of extreme vulnerability, is continually sitting in judgment over his contemporaries, whose artistic shortcomings he deciphers as moral ones in an essay such as **'Opinion or Insight?'** of 1925.

The fact that anarchical and law-giving tendencies or instincts conflicted in Schoenberg's thinking, forming a complicated configuration which forces one to read him twice if one wishes to understand him, has never been underestimated, and for this reason the phrase 'conservative revolutionary' seemed appropriate. An attempt to uncover the common root from which both the rebellious and the dictatorial traits emanated cannot content itself with pointing to the stereotype of revolutionary dialectics, in which there is a transition or sudden reversal from the one to the other. Rather, the state of emergency which Schoenberg induced with atonality, and the renewed state of legality which he hoped to constitute by means of dodecaphony, were similar in character, in that their substance consisted in an act of decision and not in a systematic web of argument or historical derivation. Schoenberg, if one is not afraid of applying the notorious phrase to him, was a musical decisionist.

The concept of an authority which is prophetic and moral, which judges and which simply decides and does not engage in argument, is so unusual in aesthetics, however, that at first one involuntarily feels that the religious pathos—despite the tradition which sees an artistic genius as a *homo a deo excitatus*—has been assumed illegitimately. The claim that only theological language can enable one to deal with Schoenberg's irritating decisionism in an appropriate manner is in fact based on nothing but the observation that the other languages taken over by aesthetics have failed when faced with this phenomenon. The striking contrast between the compelling fact of Schoenberg's authority and the weakness and inadequacy of compositional-technical or historical-philosophical explanations forces one to have recourse to theological categories, which do at least make some kind of orientation possible. One may then continue to argue endlessly about their logical status—about whether they are legitimate or illegitimate examples of secularisation, whether they are structural analogies without claims to historical origins and continuity, or whether they are merely metaphors whose sole function consists in maintaining the awareness of an unresolved problem.

IV

The analyses of Classical and Romantic works which Schoenberg published and the commentaries which he added to them are based on an unusual concept of tradition which cannot be properly understood as the adherence to an agreed position, nor as the reconstruction of an original state of affairs, nor as the redefinition and appropriation of the ideas of others. Schoenberg offended generally accepted opinion when interpreting the works of others hardly less than when planning his own. He did not think seriously about the possibility or impossibility of understanding the past as it really was; historical authenticity was of little interest to him. The charge that his method of analysis was nothing more than a reflection of his own ideas and problems in the works of others he would rightly have considered narrow-minded and rejected accordingly.

The aesthetics of reception, which in the past few decades have become the scholarly fashion, have made art historians aware of a problem which conveys a feeling of the unfathomable: the problem that the meaning of a work which has come down to us from the past cannot be classified with sufficient exactitude and clarity as the intention of the author or as the embodiment of its contemporaries' views, nor as the result or even the quintessence of reception history, nor yet as an objective substance inherent in the object itself which is independent of the history of its genesis or influence.

An author does not need to know what he is doing; and that he is a privileged interpreter of his own works is a view which was long ago consigned to the scrapheap of outmoded prejudices, with the result that one almost feels provoked to resurrect it a little. The views of contemporaries prove to be a doubtful court of appeal, for what was put in words almost always seems narrow and biased, and the special kind of empathy which contemporaries have and which later generations do not have was either not expressed at all or only expressed inadequately. The documents of reception history are either few and far between and inconsequential, or, if many of them have come down to us, paint a confusing picture; and they seldom permit the abstraction of a result in which inner connections are perceivable, even in the case of unrestrained dialectical interpretation. And finally the idea that a work has an objective, clearly defined meaning *per se* which reception more or less approaches, independent of its author's intentions and the perceptions of the audience, is, as 'substantialism', suspected of being metaphysical. (Of course, the empiricists' premiss that metaphysics are *a priori* unscientific is itself unscientific because it is dogmatic.)

It seems then that Schoenberg shared none of the opposing convictions in the controversy sketched above, but rather that he took his bearings tacitly from a concept of tradition which is far removed from present-day thinking and whose essence can most nearly be elucidated by looking at the theological source contained in the aesthetic transformation, albeit in concealed form.

If one is not afraid of crude simplification one may assume that there is a distinction which is as self-evident in theology as it is initially disconcerting in aesthetics: the distinction between the meaning that a tradition or a work conveys and the substance on which it is based.

The belief that the revelation on Mount Sinai did not put into words a distinct, clearly defined meaning, but that 'meaning' is a category which first constitutes itself in the countless refracted forms in which revelation discloses itself to the human mind—in other words, that an undivided other world of meaning manifests itself in a divided real world of meaning—belonged, as Gershom Scholem has shown, to the fundamental principles of Torah exegesis in Jewish mysticism of the Middle Ages and the early Modern Age. Revelation is not in itself a comprehensible message, but becomes one only in the reflections which it experiences in human consciousness. And there is no limit to their number.

The changes which aesthetic 'substantialism' (let us not abandon the concept as such) experiences when it is subjected to a theologically-based interpretation are far-reaching. On the one hand, instead of a hard and fast meaning which reception may or may not elucidate, one assumes that there is merely a possibility of meaning which can be updated in various directions. But on the other hand—and this circumvents a dilemma of reception aesthetics—the substratum on which the constitution of meaning is based is not conceived of as a dead letter which only reception can fill with life borrowed from the subject, but appears as an energy which imbues all forms of appropriation.

The mystical exegesis of revelation and the concept of tradition in modern reception aesthetics—which, it is true, do not seem to be aware of the theological implications or structural analogies—share the fundamental assumption that meaning handed down from the past can be experienced only via a third party, and not directly. The utopian dream of a congeniality which provides direct access to it turns out to be an illusion, the reason being an inadequate model, that of a message between subjects engaged in conversation. Furthermore it belongs to the realm of mystical dialectics to accord the same validity to interpretations which are obviously incompatible simply because no one can know whether or not an exegesis unacceptable under certain circumstances will, under quite different premises, turn out to be true in the near or distant future. And finally the fact that in the case of equally valid but conflicting interpretations we are still dealing with interpretations of one and the same thing forces us to assume the presence of a substance in which is rooted the identity of the object, which in extreme versions of reception aesthetics is on the point of dissolving into thin air; of a substance which can only consist of the mere letter of the text or over and above that in an energy effective therein, though not in an unalterable sense, if, that is, one is prepared to accept the assumptions that form the common feature of the mystical exegesis of a text and modern reception aesthetics.

That the idea of a primaeval energy, which only constitutes itself as meaning or a message in a multitude of refractions, could be turned from theological to aesthetic use was only possible because Schoenberg, in the analysis of the works of others as in the design of his own, proceeded from the concept of a formal idea whose essence lies beyond the real tonal forms and the connections created between them. In order not to understand Schoenberg too quickly, and that means, wrongly, one has to become aware of the fact that his method of analysis, if pursued to its logical conclusion, dissolves musical works into a system of relationships in which—contrary to hidebound prejudice—not even interval structures form a clear, unalterable substance. What holds a movement together from within is intangible and cannot be written down, for—to put it in its ideal form—it is an embodiment of relationships between variants or manifestations of thematic material which can be divided into an unlimited number of constituent parts and whose every feature can be varied.

But if one now allows that it is on the one hand not enough to speak solely of relationships and of connections which as it were are suspended in thin air, and that the substance, in which the inner unity is founded, cannot on the other hand be pinned down, then there remains only a single solution: that Schoenberg presupposed as a foundation an energy which, as we have seen, he determined in theological-aesthetic terms when at one and the same time stating that it emanated from the 'subconscious' and that it was brought about by a 'miracle'. The idea of tradition on which his analyses of Classical and Romantic works were tacitly based thus belongs to the same theological-aesthetic configuration in which ideas about 'belief' and 'instinctive life', about the latent character of what is structurally important, and about the primacy of the tissue of relationships over the fashioning of forms were also rooted and where they found the place which permits their significance as part of the systematic coherence of Schoenberg's thinking to become clearly apparent.

Peter Stadlen (essay date 1981)

SOURCE: "Schoenberg's Speech-Song," in *Music & Letters,* edited by Edward Olleson and Nigel Fortune, Vol. 62, No. 1, January, 1981, pp. 1-11.

[In the following essay, Stadlen examines Schoenberg's use of "speech-song," a compositional technique of using "spoken note with fixed durations and pitches," in Pierrot Lunaire.]

If *Pierrot lunaire* has never had quite the success which that work of genius surely deserves, the reason is above all the confusion that has resulted from the vocal mixture known as speech-song. It was not, as Erwin Stein claimed, Schoenberg's invention. Rudolph Stephan has reminded us that spoken notes with fixed durations and pitches were first used in Humperdinck's melodrama *Die Königskinder*. His belief that Schoenberg is likely to have attended one of the Vienna performances of 1897 is supported by the fact that a song composed in 1899 is marked 'less sung than declaimed, to be performed in a descriptive manner'. It will not do, on the other hand, to trace Schoenberg's use of speech-song to his connections with Wolzogen's 'Überbrettl'. This Berlin cabaret did not feature the genre of the *diseuse,* and Schoenberg did not start his engagement there until December 1901, that is to say after he had composed his 'Brettl Lieder'; they are to be sung, and he received the texts around Christmas 1900. Yet by that time he had already conceived of the essence of the melodrama in the **Gurrelieder**.

The melody of **Pierrot,** Schoenberg says in his preface, is not meant to be sung, but must be transformed, 'with due regard to the pitches indicated', into a speech-melody. The artist

> needs to be acutely aware of the difference between sung sounds and spoken sounds: the sung sound maintains a constant pitch; the spoken sound starts off at a given pitch but instantly leaves it by rising or falling.

This formulation of an undoubted phonetic fact is to blame, if generations of 'speech-singers' have failed to realize an amalgam of speech impressions and fixed pitch—precisely because they have attempted to follow Schoenberg's instructions. True, pitches never remain stationary in the course of speaking, and each syllable does, of course, start with a definite frequency; but it is wrong to conclude from this that the initial frequency of a syllable occupies a privileged position. Neither at the start of a syllable nor at any other moment of its duration can the pitch be perceived as unequivocally as in the case of a sung note. The ear must be content to establish a kind of average pitch," and it will succeed best in this with short, staccato notes, for instance in a particularly incredulous 'really?'. Close scrutiny may reveal this to comprise a tenth—rather unexpectedly, because an interval produced in this way tends to be veiled through the musically undemonstrative voice-production of speech.

In **Pierrot** reciters have always found it easiest to reproduce the prescribed pitches without singing them where it is a matter of short notes and wide leaps, for instance 'Erinn'rung mordend!' in 'Nacht', precisely because in such cases there is no time for the change of gear that Schoenberg, in his instructions, demands for every single note. Ethnic groups do exist whose speech-sounds are sometimes longer than many of their singing notes, but in European languages the reverse is clearly true. In **Pierrot** it is above all the long notes, as Boulez has observed, that cause the difficulties. Not only does Schoenberg's faulty analysis tempt speakers to render the notated pitches unambiguous by simply singing them, correctly or incorrectly; in order to minimize that initial impression and to restore the speech character, there follows a glissando. This brings us to Schoenberg's second error: the pitch curves of natural speech cannot be slowed down without leading to a kind of howling which is utterly dissimilar to speech and often will add an unintended and misleading nuance to the poetics of the work. These unauthentic glissandi, moreover, as distinct from the few expressly notated in the score, have a tendency to land well below the next note, a fault that leads to a further, equally regrettable glissando in the opposite direction. Most awkward, however, is the shifting of the pitch impressions as a result of these ups and downs—always provided, of course, that the rendering of the notated pitches was really intended at all.

Such doubts may seem absurd, given the musically highly significant role that is assigned to the recitation in *Pierrot* and to the spoken choruses in *Die glückliche Hand*. In *Pierrot* the speaking voice is given vital thematic tasks, for instance in 'Parodie', where it forms canons at the unison or at the octave with various instruments, or again in 'Oh alter Duft', where it doubles an instrumental line, as had already occurred in *Gurrelieder*. There are, furthermore, those cases of self-contained phrases when some notes are sung and others spoken: in *Pierrot* bar 10 of 'Mondestrunken', bar 35 of 'Colombine', bars 16-18 of 'Dandy', bar 13 of 'Gebet an Pierrot'; in *Die glückliche Hand* bar 8 in the first tenor part. Finally, at the start of the latter the polyphonic section consists of singing, sonorous speaking and whispering. One may well wonder how Schoenberg imagined whispered pitches to be realized; but that he intended these, too, may be deduced from the fact that one of the whispered passages, bar 30 of 'Dandy', is notated without pitch differences.

Verbal instructions as to pitch occur in both works, however. In *Pierrot* one finds at bar 10 of 'Madonna' the instruction 'very high', in the male voices of *Die glückliche Hand* in the whispered bar 9 'with some tone, high', and in the spoken bar 216 'higher than the female voices'. Schoenberg would hardly have made these entries had he taken it for granted that the pitches he had indicated would be observed. This raises the question whether these entries were made at the time of composition or at a later stage. The 'very high' in 'Madonna' is found in both *Pierrot* autographs, but this does not prove that the entry dates from the time when the piece was first written down, on 9 May 1912. For although the manuscript that eventually served as the printer's copy appears to have been largely the one used during the composition, the 'Madonna' pages belong to those that Rufer has declared to be not in Schoenberg's hand. Given Schoenberg's Berlin-Zehlendorf stamp at the end of the piece, it could have been written down at any time before the end of May 1913. The other autograph certainly dates from a time after the work's completion, since the pieces are written in two groups of eleven and ten respectively, each group on music paper of the same size but not in the sequence in which they were composed. Admittedly, the sequence here is not the final one either, which seems to imply that the manuscript was written before the first performances in the autumn of 1912—unless, to be sure, the sequence on those occasions was not the definitive one.

The verbal instructions in *Die glückliche Hand* are found not only in the fair copy, finished on 20 November 1913, but also in a working autograph. Although this working score was not completed until 18 November of that year, its first page (which contains bar 9) bears the note: 'started Friday 9 September 1910'. In the margin Schoenberg wrote, clearly at the same time as (almost) everything on the page: '[the notes with crossed stems] must be spoken at exactly the prescribed time and sustained as indicated; the pitch is to be realized approximately through speech'. Apart from the sketchy style of these remarks, other features suggest that this page of the manuscript—interrupted as we know for a long time—may have been written substantially earlier than the fair copy, perhaps really in 1910. All instruments are written at pitch, whereas the fair copy and the published score employ the conventional transpositions; and one finds here the method, later abandoned, of distinguishing spoken from sung passages, not only by the crossing of stems but also—as is specially pointed out in a marginal note—by underlinings of different thickness.

One cannot dismiss the possibility that as early as the time of conception of *Pierrot,* or even perhaps of *Die glückliche Hand,* Schoenberg was capable of disloyalty towards the pitches of his speech-song. Such an assumption is further supported by the remark found as a footnote to 'Gebet an Pierrot', the first piece to be composed (12 March 1912) and originally intended to open the cycle: 'The recitation must just hint at the pitch'. The blatant contrast between this indifferent attitude to the realization of the pitches and, on the other hand, their minutely differentiated elaboration and integration into the composition suggests a conflict, from the very beginning, in Schoenberg's mind between a desire for speech character and another, seemingly incompatible desire for an exact rendering of the notes. It is little wonder if the confusion caused by such a conflict continues to make itself felt time and again.

It is noteworthy that the *Gurrelieder* score, sent before 16 July 1912 to Vienna for facsimile publication, contains no instructions for the execution of the speech-song part. It seems, moreover, that Alban Berg, who coached the speaker of the first performance in Vienna on 23 February 1913—he had worked since 1909 under Schoenberg's supervision on the piano reduction—had at first no doubts that the part was musically unambiguous. At least he implies as much in his letter to Schoenberg of 13 January 1913, when he asks: 'Does it suffice if one achieves the closest possible approximation to the pitch?'. No less remarkable is Schoenberg's reply:

> Here [in the speaking part of the *Gurrelieder*] the pitch notation is certainly not to be taken as seriously as in the *Pierrot* melodramas. The result

here should on no account be such a song-like speech-melody as in the latter . . . the pitches are merely to be regarded as differences of register, which is to say that the passage in question (!!! not the individual note) is to be spoken higher or lower, respectively. But no interval proportions!

It is hard to avoid the impression that this radical denunciation of the pitches in *Gurrelieder* mirrors Schoenberg's disappointment when, for the first time, he was confronted with the reality of his speech-song during the 25 *Pierrot* rehearsals and the ensuing tour with his first soloist, Albertine Zehme (26 August to 8 December 1912). He must have been particularly anxious to eliminate this problem in the *Gurrelieder* since there was the danger that in a tonal work, as distinct from the atonal *Pierrot,* identifiable but wrongly reproduced pitches could sound like wrong notes. On the other hand, in the letter to Berg the taboo on a singing mode of speech is not yet extended to include *Pierrot;* with regard to this work it appears for the first time in the preface sent separately to Vienna on 31 January 1914, in time to be printed. The warning next appears, emphatically, in the published score of *Die glückliche Hand* (1917)—'a "singing" manner of speech must be avoided'—though it is not yet found among the instructions on the first page of the autograph fair copy.

On the other hand, both the 'to be taken seriously' in Schoenberg's letter of 1913 and the 'with due regard to the pitches' in the printed *Pierrot* preface sound more confident than the earlier 'approximately' and 'hinted at' ('andeutungsweise', admittedly also found in the *Spielanweisungen* of the published score of *Die glückliche Hand*). Again, 'to be taken seriously' sounds more definite than the formulation found in draft—left incomplete and heavily crossed out—in the printer's manuscript of *Pierrot,* sent to Vienna before December 1913: 'the pitches observe their mutual relations as indicated'. The same wording appears in modified form about a year later on the first page of the fair copy of *Die glückliche Hand:* 'The pitches, but in particular the relations between the individual pitches, are to be rendered accordingly'. An apologetic nuance in 'but in particular' is unmistakable; it sounds like resigning oneself to what is possible, if what had originally been intended should turn out to be impossible.

The speech-song confusion is mirrored most vividly in a footnote to bar 214 of *Die glückliche Hand,* both in the fair copy and the printed score and in Steuermann's piano reduction (1923). Here the speaking chorus of six men and six women receives the following instructions:

> the three-note chords are meant to indicate that the passages in question are to be spoken on pitches that lie within the corresponding registers of the singers so that, as it were, chords result. This refers always to the phrase in question (even if the chords are no longer notated) and is suspended by the instruction 'unisono'.

For this footnote to make sense, it has to be assumed that everywhere else in the speech-song parts Schoenberg expected the notated pitches to be strictly observed. Yet it is precisely in the bars marked 'unisono' that one finds in the (fully notated) tenor parts the already mentioned instruction 'higher than the female voices', which implies a doubt whether the written notes will be realized. In such a case it is unavoidable that chords will result, as it is in the many other cases where the same notes are given to more than one member of the chorus. For how can a group of singers sing a phrase 'unisono' if they do not know on what pitches they are to agree? And on what pitches can they agree if not on those which they find in their parts?

In the course of an historic contest in the house of Alma Mahler in 1922, Schoenberg came down on the side of the predominantly spoken delivery of the actress Erika Wagner-Stiedry and decided against the predominantly sung interpretation—later censured in several letters—by Marya Freund. Milhaud, who conducted the second of these performances (Schoenberg himself was in charge of the first), wrote later that Marya Freund 'if anything erred on the side of observing [the notes] too carefully'; by this he probably meant, not that she sang too correctly, but that her delivery was too reminiscent of singing, for it was just this that Schoenberg later reproached her with. No one who has heard a brazenly sung performance will deny that this does substantially detract from the *Pierrot* ambience. When Milhaud adds that in his view there exists no final solution of this problem, one may suspect that the existence of a problem was discussed in the course of that evening.

Also problem-ridden is the attitude of Erwin Stein, whose *Pierrot* performance with Frau Wagner-Stiedry in 1920 had been expressly sanctioned by the composer and who in those years belonged to the innermost Schoenberg circle. Yet in two articles of 1927 and 1928 Stein declared that in the speech-song of *Pierrot* the initial pitches are so short as to be irrelevant for the formation of harmony. This new twist served to justify and elaborate on the wording of the previously mentioned footnote to *Die glückliche Hand*—'to be spoken on pitches that lie within the corresponding registers'. The reciter, we now read,

> must not only transpose her part regardless of the accompaniment, just to suit the register of her voice; she must also reduce the individual intervals in accordance with her vocal compass; what matters are merely the proportions of the melodic line, that is to say, as long as a fifth represents a larger leap than a fourth, and so on.

One may well doubt whether Schoenberg and Stein tried to think this through to the end. Did they really expect the reciter to establish the ratio between her own speaking compass and a generally valid, average vocal compass, so that in due course she would be able to multiply each occurring interval by this complex fraction? None of this was evident when I took the piano part in the *Pierrot* performances that Stein conducted in England in 1942. On the contrary, he tried his utmost during rehearsals to get the speaker, Hedli Anderson, to render the pitches correctly.

That same year, 1942, saw the release of Schoenberg's own *Pierrot* recording with Frau Wagner-Stiedry, whose interpretation almost always ignores the pitches and quite often even goes against the direction of the melody as notated. Nonetheless, one reads of a letter to Schoenberg in which Stein describes how he had defended this interpretation in a discussion with the English musicians Walter Legge and Cecil Gray. And one is incredulous when he goes on to report Karl Rankl's delight with Hedli Anderson's nearly note-perfect rendering: are, then, he asks, the prescribed pitches in *Pierrot* to be observed?

Yet if Stein, in his articles, still grants a measure of validity at least to the pitch contours, Schoenberg in 1949 went so far as to claim that after all the reciter in *Pierrot* 'never sings the theme, but, at most, speaks against it, while the themes (and everything else of musical importance) happen in the instruments'—unmindful that prior to 1914 he had added the annotation to 'Eine blasse Wäscherin': 'here the recitation must definitely sound like an accompaniment to the instruments; they are the main parts and the voice is subsidiary'. This can only mean that in all other pieces the opposite is the case. Not many months later he insisted that the *Pierrot* poems 'must be *spoken* without fixed pitch'; and in 1950 he declared in a letter, after complaining about the 'wrong melodies' produced by the speaker in a recording of *Gurrelieder,* that there no melodies at all are intended, for otherwise he would surely have written them down—precisely as if he had forgotten that that was just what he had in fact done.

The wheel comes full circle in January 1951 when he writes to the Stiedrys—as he had done 38 years earlier to Berg—'as against *Pierrot,* there are no pitches here [i.e. in the melodrama of the *Gurrelieder*]'. Yet a year or two after Schoenberg's death Rudolf Kolisch, his brother-in-law, told me that towards the end of his life Schoenberg had repeatedly declared that in *Pierrot* the notated pitches need to be avoided because they do not fit the music. Considered jointly, what these two edicts amount to is that in *Pierrot* Schoenberg was prepared to accept any pitches whatsoever, with the sole exception of those which he had actually composed.

A variant of the disavowal reported by Kolisch is already found in a footnote to the score of *Moses und Aron:* 'Here, as everywhere else, please never sing the speech notes! They do not correspond to the rows!' Referring as it does to the chorus in bar 752 of Act I, this remark would seem to come rather late in the day; it also contradicts the prefatory instruction to the chorus comprising the Voice from the Burning Bush, not, admittedly, to sing the notes but to speak them with the 'closest possible approximation of the indicated heights'. This, in turn, does not agree with the cryptic statement that in Moses's spoken part 'the pitch differences are merely intended to characterize the declamation'.

It is true that in *Moses und Aron* (1930-32), as distinct from the earlier works that contain speech-song, there are indications in the compositional style itself that the speech-song parts were not conceived in a uniform manner. On the one hand, the chorus contains, time and again, diatonic and even triadic formations that could not possibly have been intended as such, since in the context of this score they would amount to at least as drastic a stylistic contradiction as are the dissonant melodies which Schoenberg, I believe, dreaded in the *Gurrelieder* in 1913. On the other hand, such a view of speech notes as representing no more than approximate indications of the speaking register contrasts with the once again very precise elaboration of other spoken episodes, both of the chorus and, above all, in the part of Moses. The latter, moreover, contains some passages—as *Pierrot* had done already—where the notes are written without heads but merely with stems (e.g. Act II, bars 1003, 1010-11, 1019), proving an obviously intended contrast with most bars in the part. Yet again Aron, a sung part, is offered the choice of speaking some notes, in which case, though, they have to be played by an instrument (bars 1043-7); this may well mean that Schoenberg assumed at that time that the frequencies of the spoken pitches could not be perceived as such.

These obvious inner contradictions in Schoenberg's attitude eventually brought about a radical solution. Whereas in *Kol Nidre* of 1938 the recitation of the Rabbi—in so far as notes are used at all—is still notated on the usual five lines (as also in the *De Profundis* of 1950, perhaps because here the same voices alternate between singing and speaking), in the *Ode to Napoleon* (1942), *A Survivor from Warsaw* (1947) and *Modern Psalm* (1950) Schoenberg places the notes at varying distances above or below a single line. Significantly, he applied the same procedure to the originally still fully notated speech lines of *Die Jakobsleiter* when, in 1944, he temporarily resumed work on the oratorio, left unfinished in 1922—almost as if he wanted to make it clear that he had never wanted those sour pitches. In spite of this, however, he uses extra stave-lines and—height of absurdity—accidentals, so that here again some twelve to fourteen pitches are not so much indicated by the notation but can be read into it, though the intervals as assumed here are considerably narrower than those of the chromatic scale since they are supposed to fit into the narrower range of speech.

With this, Schoenberg finally reveals his basic misconception—going back fifteen years and implied by Erwin Stein's articles—that as a consequence of the speaking range being narrower than that of the singing voice, spoken sounds have a lesser pitch tolerance than sung sounds. In fact the opposite is the case: in comparison with a singer, a speaker has at his disposal a greater variety of sounds all of which may be heard as the same pitch, precisely because—as noted earlier—a spoken pitch impression results from the vague, hardly predictable average of a frequency curve. And not only does the speaker operate with a larger number of single-pitch frequency impressions than the singer; the difference between his one 'note' and the next is less distinct.

All this suggests that at some level or other of his consciousness Schoenberg did intend the notated pitches to emerge as speechsong pitches, but that with characteristic stubbornness he was prepared to sacrifice an essential aspect of his composition for the sake of an interpretative nuance. But such a sacrifice was not really necessary. The difference between singing and speaking is by no means, as Schoenberg assumed, restricted to the contrast between steady and sliding pitch. It also depends—and not least—on tone production, i.e. the distribution, density and strength of those bands of the frequency spectrum that function as vocal formants. In singing, vowels preserve their timbre, whereas in the course of speech there is a continual interchange of various diphthongs and triphthongs. While a singing voice could hardly produce the rapid pitch curves of realistic, natural speech, it is perfectly possible for the speaking voice to maintain a given pitch for substantially longer periods than are usual in everyday speech. Schoenberg, in fact, did not desire a realistic speaking for his melodramatic style but repeatedly demanded a kind of declamation: Stein talks of 'elevated speech' and Schoenberg, in the *Pierrot* preface, of 'speech that contributes to a musical form'. But evidently Schoenberg failed to take into consideration the fact that the elevated speech of auctioneers, priests and tragedians (to take a grouping used by phoneticians) not only exaggerates the ups and downs of speech but will also occasionally prolong a given pitch unnaturally. If this goes unnoticed in most cases, the reason is that the notes of such a sequence only very rarely belong to the chromatic scale.

There remains the question why such virtually fixed pitches still do not sound as if they were being sung. The answer is that, somewhat ironically, the impression of singing in fact results from the minute fluctuations of pitch that comprise vibrato. A voice production avoiding vibrato has enabled Marie-Thérèse Escribano, and to some extent Helga Pilarczyk earlier, to convey in recorded performances of *Pierrot* the prescribed pitches without violating the taboo on singing. There remain, to be sure, problems of range and of notes that are too long after all. These have to be shortened unless they happen to end on one of the 'musical' consonants l, m or n on which it is possible to linger, even though Stein—that is to say, Schoenberg—explicitly prohibited such compromises.

Nonetheless, it is this technique that renders possible a realization of Schoenberg's grandiose *Pierrot* that is by and large authentic—and not only musically. Schoenberg, it is true, noted in his diary at the time of composition: 'Here the sounds acquire an all-but-animalic immediacy

in expressing sensuous and spiritual emotions'. Yet it seems that this was meant to relate to the expressionist style of the music rather than to the execution of the speech-song. At least, one may conclude as much from his letter to the Stiedrys dated August 1940, where he writes: ' . . . this time I intend to catch perfectly that light, ironical, satirical tone in which the piece was actually conceived'. This is confirmed by Steuermann's story of Schoenberg's reaction when the first-ever speaker showed a tendency to play the tragic heroine and grow too tearful in 'Der kranke Mond': 'Don't despair, Frau Zehme, there is after all such a thing as Life Insurance!'

Had Schoenberg been aware that an effective method exists of realizing speech-song, he would presumably never have become enmeshed in the contradictions set out above. Nor would he, in *Moses und Aron,* ever have written those tonal chorus passages which have now become realizable and thus render the work, strictly speaking, impossible to perform. Finally, in the *Ode to Napoleon, A Survivor from Warsaw* and *Modern Psalm* he would have composed the speaker's part in as unambiguously precise a manner as he evidently had conceived it.

Jean Christensen (essay date 1984)

SOURCE: "The Spiritual and The Material in Schoenberg's Thinking," in *Music & Letters,* Vol. 65, No. 4, October, 1984, pp. 337-44.

[*In the following essay, Christensen explains the system of philosophy underlying all of Schoenberg's work.*]

Preserved in the archive of the Arnold Schoenberg Institute in Los Angeles is a collection of some 200 items, mostly unpublished and undescribed, consisting of drafts, sketches and casual notes left over when Schoenberg's more finished writings were selected for publication towards the end of his life and after his death. They are not in their original condition. Many hands have sifted through them searching for items of specific interest. Eventually what order remained was obliterated when the archivist, the late Clara Steuermann, dismantled Schoenberg's binders and folders as a consequence of her decision to preserve ideas rather than artefacts. But the composer's own annotations make it possible to restore his ordering and, to a large extent, to reconstruct his design.

During his last stay in Germany, in the late summer and autumn of 1932, Schoenberg sorted his already extensive collection of personal papers according to chronology, form and content. The organization emerged readily from the recurrent subject-matter and concerns contained in this rich fund of ideas and observations from which he drew and to which he added continuously. Individual documents were assigned to various classifications, and an additional system of numbering provided cross-references between categories, enabling him to plot interrelationships between ideas in different areas.

This comprehensive enterprise, more like a filing system than a simple method for clearing one's desk, is characteristic of Schoenberg's temperament. A demonstration of his dedication to the internal logic of his own ideas is a plan for an autobiography designed to reveal the coherence of his intellectual world. From the earliest dated document of 1924 it is already clear that this was to be no factual narrative, and on its revision in 1932 the title **'Biography in Encounters'** (**'Lebensgeschichte in Begegnungen'**) was added.

> I have for a long time been planning to write an autobiography that will be accomplished, as far as my memory allows, by presenting all the persons with whom I have been in contact, in so far as they and their relationship to me are of interest, as they showed themselves to me and by describing precisely the relationship between them and myself. This is of course not primarily an act of revenge, rather it is a system which I expect will open my memory. [As I proceed,] the links between different persons and separate events will emerge; in such a way I believe that I will be able to be as truthful as is possible, whereas I should certainly fail in an attempt at a chronological account. . . .
>
> I will prepare a filing system of envelopes or small manila folders and gradually collect notes which I shall write as they occur to me, without forcing anything, without any programme. I will read through these notes frequently, make comments on persons and events at the relevant places and eventually come to the point where I can give some sections a finished shape.

The autobiography was to have been a record of his thought, of the transitions that marked the stages of his intellectual development. In one of the early documents (*c.* 1932) he wrote a brief outline of his spiritual itinerary:

> How I became a musician
> How I became a Christian
> How I became a Brahmsian
> How I became a Wagnerian

The project was continued in America. At some time in the mid 1940s Schoenberg wrote a series of headings, distributed over a number of pages, each with subsequent additions of relevant names and dates (not included here): 'My friendships . . . Publishers . . . My relations . . . Musicians, painters, poets . . . Writers . . . Music critics and theorists . . . Conductors . . . Rabbi . . . University . . . Scientists . . . Thieves . . . Rogues . . . Patrons . . . Students . . . Orchestras . . . Performers. . . .'

Schoenberg's lifelong concern to preserve coherence and consistency in his ideas and activities is nowhere more succinctly stated than it is in the draft of a letter to Willem Mengelberg discussing his role as co-chairman of the proposed Mahler Society:

> I can work in one way only: with total personal commitment. Consequently, everything that hap-

pens must be my own work, my responsibility, and carry my personal stamp throughout. Impersonal attitudes should not be expected of me; people have the right to demand that I take a personal standpoint, and I have the duty to do so.

The 'personal stamp' that informs all of Schoenberg's writings, from his most ambitious projects to even the more ephemeral and circumstantial notes in the Los Angeles papers, was the product of a consistent personal philosophy at whose heart lies the concept of an opposition between the spiritual and the material. This religious/philosophical idea, expressed for the first time in explicit form in *Die Jakobsleiter* (c. 1915-22), structured all his thinking. According to the two categories of spirit and matter he evaluated persons and events and created a scheme of divisions which, though flexible and never doctrinaire, was the source of his unfailing idealism. He made use of them when defining the principles of his ethics, when explaining his hierarchical model of human existence, when evaluating cultural activities and when developing his ideas about the nature of art, about the obligations of artists and about the relationship between beauty and truth, progress and tradition. In each of these areas the dual categories of spirit and matter were his touchstones.

The two categories are seen with particular clarity in a fairly complete draft of 1931-2 for the text of a choral work. The first of its three verses comprises a strophe and an anti-strophe focusing respectively on the qualities that belong to the material and to the spiritual.

> Man is evil!
> He not only defends himself
> but also attacks;
> he not only searches for what is right
> but also reaches for power;
> he strives not only for what is necessary
> but also for the superfluous;
> he not only defends his own interests
> but also desires the hurt of his opponent;
> he wants not only to preserve his self-esteem
> but also to oppress his fellow man.
>
> [Man is good!]
> He is not subservient to dark instincts
> but is capable of telling good from evil.
> He can forget evil, think about good.
> He searches for what is new, reaches out for what
> 　is great.
> He not only fights for himself and his belongings
> but promotes ideas, sacrifices himself for them.
> He saves not only himself by flight.
> but also covers your retreat.
> He is not only a friend in good fortune
> but is also concerned about the suffering of
> 　others.

The text immediately demonstrates Schoenberg's procedure for testing a cultural phenomenon: he first draws the balance between the material and the spiritual elements involved and then determines its place within his scheme. In its unmediated confrontation between the two extremes of his universe the choral text presents in starkest contrast the outer limits of the hierarchy of human attitudes that had been developed in detail in *Die Jakobsleiter,* with its distinct classes of 'progressing' characters and its list of 46 types of 'lost souls', the latter subdivided into a dozen or so main groups according to degrees of materialistic preoccupation. The scheme takes the form of a pyramid rising from the low region of material concerns to the elevated sphere of spiritual achievement. At the top are the few capable of approaching the highest revelations. At the bottom are the many who, at best, glimpse the divine truth only fleetingly. In between is a profusion of 'stages' distinguished by the varying intensity with which the protagonists engage in the battle against materialism. Indifference is culpable, but the spiritual awareness of those on the lower levels can be raised by those above.

> Apathy is the most primitive kind of resistance. This is the condition of unorganic matter, which can be organized—given organs—by subjecting it to strong emotional shocks.

Consequently, Schoenberg's view, though uncompromising, is essentially optimistic and non-élitist: education and the arts are the means for creating a progressively intellectual milieu. Thus his evaluation of the results of his own teaching in America is one of satisfaction:

> Out of 1,000 students not one will become a great master; but quite a few will become able connoisseurs, good teachers, good friends of the arts . . .

He was active in a number of societies for the promotion of the arts, and a draft survives of plans for an 'Alliance for the Protection of Intellectual Culture' ('Schutzbund für geistige Kultur'). This provides further gradations within the upper levels of his hierarchical pyramid. There are students and friends of the arts, willing to make sacrifices for the sake of 'intellectual culture'. On a higher level are 'teachers and reproducers', actively concerned in the struggle to raise spiritual standards. The highest class comprises 'creative scientists and artists', the devoted seekers after truth. The 'Alliance' is Schoenberg's ideal model for cultural progress:

> Culture . . . tempers everything that would be too hot or too cold if left to primeval, savage instincts; it avails itself of elemental forces only in exceptional situations, cases for which society has as yet not found a different solution.

The conviction in the possibility and necessity of progress lies at the root of Schoenberg's refusal to tolerate uninformed criticism.

> I find applause and hissing equally embarrassing and humiliating . . . not least for the audience itself; it should beware of giving vent to its inability to judge, since that would only reveal its own cowardice and its lack of responsibility . . .

His vehement response to criticism, predictably well-represented in the Los Angeles documents, was not merely a matter of injured pride; first and foremost it reflects his belief that critics have the obligation to keep abreast of artists and other explorers in order to be the first to comprehend new ideas and communicate them to the public. When they excuse themselves from their task by arguing for outdated aesthetics they shirk their responsibility. On occasion they even have the presumption to state flatly that they 'do not understand' new works—and this they do 'with pride! not with embarrassment; with no sense of shame'.

The chief responsibility for sustaining the battle against materialism, however, must be waged not by critics but by artists, those in search of the highest revelations, and no one reaped sharper criticism than fellow composers who betrayed their deepest obligations. The full weight of sarcasm fell on Richard Strauss, who in Schoenberg's opinion openly exploited the low, materialistic concerns of his audiences. In response to a comment by Strauss to the effect that 'in each of my works there must be a melody which can be understood by the most stupid fellow in the hall' he noted:

> One would like to believe that Strauss has a hard time placing himself on the level of the most stupid fellow: but if one takes a look at these melodies, one has to admit that he has succeeded in doing so. And it gives the impression of being done quite naturally.
>
> One yields to practical necessities; he identifies concessions with practical necessity. Genius has the boldness to dispense with conventions in pursuit of inner necessities; he has the effrontery to dispense with the conventional necessities of his tiny ego. This confusion is typical of the pur-veyor of kitsch in the face of ideas. Problems arise for him and are solved by him in the same way: he misunderstands them. But it cannot be disputed that he has dealt with them: he has hidden them under a coating of sugar icing, so that the public sees only the greatness of his world, the world of a *Marzipanmeister.*

The commentary ends: 'This is not the way of thinking of a man whom God has given a mission.'

Schoenberg's concept of the artist's vocation is unyielding: liberating man's divine spirit is the one worthy goal of artistic creations; concessions to materialism are unacceptable. The artist who sacrifices truth for grandeur, popularity, charm or beauty betrays his commitment. The conflict between truth and beauty was of vital importance to Schoenberg. This central theme of *Moses und Aron* was already present in the earliest sketches for *Die Jakobsleiter* in the persons of the two main characters, 'The Chosen One', who searches for a hidden truth, and 'The Called One', whose goal is sensuous beauty. Schoenberg's delineation of the relative value of truth and beauty is that of an artist to whom the process of artistic creativity is a way of participating in the universal struggle between matter and spirit. In this interpretation, beauty is but the occasional by-product of the search for ultimate truth; and it is a dubious quality that readily partakes of the nature of matter. As a late note (in English) on performance practices states: 'The most beautiful tone is often only the result of superficiality joined with sentimentality.'

Schoenberg's musical theories and compositional practices were consistent with his philosophy. A small notebook from the American years contains a hasty but resolute draft (in English) for an essay on the 'mutual relations between beauty and logic in music' describing his creative approach in terms of a quest for truth, a tenacious testing of materials:

> [The essay's] main purpose shall be to dethrone beauty as much as possible as a serious factor in the creation [of] music. It shall be assumed that it [is] neither the aim of a composer to produce beauty nor is a feeling of beauty a producing 'agence' [sic] in his imagination. It might and often does occur that in spite of an occupation in quite a different direction the complete work produces a feeling of beauty in a listener.

> But the main problem of a composer is: expression and presentation of musical ideas, the right organization which is based on musical logic, and what one calls form in music is not a preconceived shape in which music has to be filled in.

> Musical ideas are such combinations of tones, rhythms and harmonies, which require a treatment like the main thesis of a philosophical or [space left open] subject. It arises [sic] a question, puts up a problem, which in the course of the piece has to be answered, resolved, carried through. It has to be carried through many contradictionary [sic] situations, it has to be developed by drawing consequences from what it postulates, has to be checked in many cases, and all this might lead to a conclusion . . .

Another draft, entitled 'Some Ideas about the Establishment of a Modern Theory of Composition' ('Einige Ideen zur Begründung einer modernen Kompositionslehre'), explains the origins of his artistic tools with a characteristically direct comparison between the problems of verbal and musical communication; the need for artistic creativity arises at the precise moment when a person wants to refer to something that transcends the sphere of ordinary, circumstantial matters.

> In the case of simple events, happy or sad experiences the like of which everybody knows, the strictly historical enumeration of the facts is enough for me, mostly by stating the facts alone, as one does in such instances as births, engagements, deaths and so on.

> I need to make further demands on my presentation only when the event I want to communicate is complex, unusual, or when I want to attain the effects that lie outside the material sphere . . . In

this case the prevailing concern is for the best, the most effective disposition, for structure; this requires consideration alongside, if not priority over, the material facts. In this case I am obliged to depart in some degree from the pure truth; I can no longer be content with representing things and events as they are, as they happened; I must change the sequence of events; things that are too light I must colour darker, tint dark hues lighter; I must represent insignificant elements more modestly and allow essential elements more room, pride of place and the external attributes of a more important appearance. I will often have to separate and dissociate elements that in real life were connected; conversely, I have to associate elements where I need to do so for my particular effect. Thus I distance myself from ordinary facts, dispense with them, place myself—the narrator—above them . . . This big step away from the imitation of nature is the first step in art . . .

This view dictated all Schoenberg's artistic practices. In his paintings he frequently disregarded the outward appearance of his subjects—the details of their material form—in order to capture an inner truth, their spiritual reality.

> I have, on the one hand, a poor memory for what people look like, but I could (formerly), on the other hand, with a few lines draw a person's face after having seen him once. I was unable to explain this contradiction until I discovered that it is connected with another ability: I can imitate the vision [*Blick*] of most people! And that is because *I only look people in the eyes* (so that I often would not know whether somebody has a moustache or not). This is also the reason why my drawings got worse after the first few lines; that is, when I started adding details.

As a composer he followed comparable procedures. When setting texts to music, for instance, he rigorously refused to let words, even his own, determine the expressive features of the musical setting, since music can capture a truth which is beyond words. Noticing that a large part of the public feels more comfortable when the understanding of a musical work is facilitated by a text, he complained:

> My music has never been liked unless there was a text to it.—As for ***Pierrot Lunaire***, after a while people so liked the text that they did not even let themselves be distracted by my music.

In the large religious works the characters closest to truth do not communicate with words: in ***Die Jakobsleiter*** the Soul's words dissolve into ecstatic, textless vocalise as she is liberated from her material body and approaches the divine light, and in ***Moses und Aron*** the prophet lacks Aaron's command of language.

To Schoenberg the sole concern of serious music was that spiritual reality which notes can express. Indeed, one of the most personal features of his compositional technique, those unmediated, often abrupt and extremely demanding transitions that characterize his musical style, is dictated by his determination to dispense with circumstantial matters and penetrate to the essential. He selected this feature for special consideration in a 'brief self-characterization' written for the *Herder Konversationslexikon:*

> As a composer: Continuation of artistic procedures that have been passed down, in an effort to achieve the most intensive use of musical space (in the smallest space the greatest content).

Perhaps the most interesting aspect of Schoenberg's philosophy is its close correlation with his compositional working procedures. In his sketchbooks for *Die Jakobsleiter,* for instance, there are two predominant types of sketches. One consists of notations written down in broad outline, leaving space open for filling in details and often continuing for pages with all its main features present in next-to-final shape. In this manner the sketch catches the essence of an idea, neglecting details of its materialization. The other type is written down in fairly complete form but not continued or expanded *in situ.* When it eventually reappears in a later draft it is often found in a new context but with all elements of its original form retained. For Schoenberg, then, these sketches represented inspired ideas, particles of ultimate truth, which once found or revealed could neither be altered nor lose validity. In the letter to Mengelberg already quoted he wrote:

> For me there is only the music paper on which I write my music, which therefore has to be right. I think *once*—thoroughly, and nothing of what I write is then open to change later on.

To capture those moments of truth when the spirit escapes from its material prison was the lasting goal of Schoenberg's artistry, the one which, he felt, applied to all genuine works of art from all ages:

> There is only one direct way to perpetuate the past, tradition, the thinking of our predecessors: to begin all over again, as if everything that went before were false; once again to enter into contact with the essence of things and not just to proceed with the technique of elaborating on given materials.

This vision, acquired early in life and defined in philosophical terms in maturity, inspired that unity of his work to which he refers in a note written when he was about 54:

> To be quite precise, I have been saying the same thing for about 25 years (if not more), only I am constantly saying it better.

Schoenberg was never the strict, systematic philosopher, though he frequently referred to philosophical literature in his writings and possessed a number of treatises. His personal approach to the laws and resources of human knowledge was largely an offshoot of nineteenth-century idealism, itself characterized by the categoric distinction

between mind and matter and the prominent place accorded ethics in its scheme of things, the opposition between reason and desires. Though for the most part rejected by present-day philosophy, this 'categoric' conceptual scheme was for Schoenberg an inspiring and organizing force in a rich creative life. His own system served his personal interpretation of the human condition; it was his means of exposing inertia and generating creativity. His categories did not constitute a rigid set of separate pigeon-holes but served as guidelines for his intuition, allowing him to evaluate a variety of phenomena against a single basic ideal without neglecting contradictions and ambivalences. A seeker of eternal truth, he accepted the relative and often paradoxical nature of human knowledge. And he believed that the highest revelations elude verbal formulations. As he once put it:

> Should an author ever try to say anything about his work?
>
> If something remains to be said, why is it not in the work itself?
>
> If nothing remains to be said: what is there to talk about?

Robert P. Morgan (essay date 1984)

SOURCE: "Secret Languages: The Roots of Musical Modernism," in *Modernism: Challenges and Perspectives,* edited by Monique Chefdor, Ricardo Quinones and Albert Wachtel, University of Illinois Press, 1986, pp. 33-50.

[*In the following essay, originally published in* Critical Inquiry *in 1984, Morgan associates Schoenberg's development of atonal music with a "crisis in language" that occurred in the early twentieth century.*]

> In der modernen Prosa sprechen wir eine Sprache, die wir mit dem Gefühle nicht verstehen. . . . Wir können nach unserer innersten Empfindung in dieser Sprache gewissermassen nicht mitsprechen, denn es ist uns unmöglich, nach dieser Empfindung in ihr zu *erfinden;* wir können unsere Empfindungen in *ihr* nur dem Verstande, nicht aber dem zuversichtlich verstehenden Gefühle mittheilen. . . . In der modernen Sprache kann nicht *gedichtet* werden, d.h. . . . eine dichterische Absicht kann in ihr verwirklicht, sondern eben nur *als solche* ausgesprochen werden.

> (In modern prose we speak a language we do not understand with the feeling. . . . we cannot discourse in this language according to our innermost emotion, for it is impossible to *invent* in it according to that emotion; in *it,* we can only impart our emotions to the understanding, but not to the implicitly understood feeling. . . . In modern speech no *poesis* is possible, that is to say, poetic aim cannot be realized therein, but only spoken out *as such.*)

> Seitdem nun die modernen europäischen Sprachen . . . mit immer ersichtlicherer Tendenz ihrer rein

Konventionellen Ausbildung folgten, entwickelte sich andererseits die Musik zu einem bisher der Welt unbekannten Vermögen des Ausdruckes. Es ist, als ob das durch die Kompression seitens der konventionellen Civilization gesteigerte rein menschliche Gefühl sich einen Ausweg zur Geltendmachung seiner ihm eigenthümlichen Sprachgesetze gesucht hätte, durch welche es, frei vom Zwange der logischen Denkgesetze, sich selbst verständlich sich ausdrüken könnte.

(Now, ever since the modern European languages . . . have followed this conventional drift to a more and more obvious tendency, music, on the other hand, has been developing a power of expression unknown to the world before. It is as though the purely human feeling, intensified by the pressure of a conventional civilization, has been seeking an outlet for the operation of its own peculiar laws of speech; an outlet through which, unfettered by the laws of logical thought, it might express itself intelligibly to itself.)

In reading recent literature on the history and aesthetics of Western music, one consistently encounters references to the "language" of this music, especially with regard to the practice of eighteenth- and nineteenth-century tonality. Although the word "language" is used metaphorically in such cases, the metaphor seems remarkably apt (and convenient), and this no doubt accounts for its persistence. When applied to twentieth-century music, however, the sense of the term—and thus the nature of the metaphor—requires significant adjustment. For here, unlike the case in earlier Western music, one is unable to find that most characteristic feature of all natural languages, the universal acceptance of an enduring set of formal conventions evident throughout a given linguistic domain. Attempts, as in Donald Mitchell's *The Language of Modern Music,* to define a twentieth-century musical mainstream (in Mitchell's case, Schoenbergian dodecaphony), elevating its technical and systematic foundation to the status of a uniquely "proper" language for the age, appear seriously misguided and in flagrant opposition to the actual course of twentieth-century musical developments. Musical modernism is marked, above all, by its "linguistic plurality" and by the failure of any one language to assume a dominant position.

This plurality and the significant transformations in musical structure, expression, and intent it reflects form interesting parallels with characteristic features of the modernist movement in general; and it is primarily these connections that I wish to explore here. That such parallels exist is hardly surprising, since music—or perhaps more accurately the *idea* of music—is intimately tied to certain basic conceptions underlying the modernist revolution. Indeed, musical developments of the critical years around the turn of the century mirror with particular clarity the general intellectual and artistic climate of the period as a whole.

Although considerable controversy persists concerning both the nature and chronology of modernism, there seems to be widespread agreement that it incorporated a wish to turn away from concrete, everyday reality, to break out of the routine of ordinary actions in the hope of attaining a more personal and idealized vision of reality. There were of course precedents for this attitude in romanticism, but its artistic manifestations began to take on uniquely modern colorations toward the end of the century. In particular, there is a prevalent move away from realism and naturalism toward a new and radical abstractionism, evident not only in a turn toward less representational modes in the visual arts but in new attitudes toward language in literature and, as we shall see, in music (by metaphorical extension) as well.

It is frequently noted that a "crisis in language" accompanied the profound changes in human consciousness everywhere evident near the turn of the century. As the nature of reality itself became problematic—or at least suspect, distrusted for its imposition of limits upon individual imagination—so necessarily did the relationship of language to reality. Thus the later nineteenth century increasingly questioned the adequacy of an essentially standardized form of "classical" writing—writing that, even though often in "elevated" form, bore a close connection to ordinary discourse—as an effective vehicle for artistic expression. Indeed, it was precisely the mutually shared, conventional aspects of language that came to be most deeply distrusted for their failure to mirror the more subjective, obscure, and improbable manifestations of a transcendent reality—or rather realities, the plural reflecting an insistence upon the optional and provisional nature of human experience. Language in its normal manifestations, with its conventionalized vocabulary and standardized rules for syntactical combination, proved inadequate for an artistic sensibility insisting upon, in Nietzsche's words, "a world of abnormally drawn perspectives."

This dissatisfaction with "normal" language received its classic statement through Hofmannsthal's Lord Chandos. Writing in 1902, Hofmannsthal conveys through the figure of the aristocratic Chandos the loss of an encompassing framework within which the various objects of external reality are connected with one another and integrated with the internal reality of human feelings. Chandos's world has become one of disparate, disconnected fragments, resistant to the abstractions of ordinary language. It is a world characterized by "a sort of feverish thought, but thought in a material that is more immediate, more fluid and more intense than that of language." Chandos longs for a new language in which "not a single word is known to me, a language in which mute objects speak to me and in which perhaps one day, in the grave, I will give account of myself before an unknown judge." The content and forms of art thus shift away from exterior reality, which no longer provides a stable, "given" material, toward language itself—to "pure" language in a sense closely related to the symbolists' "pure" poetry. "No artist tolerates reality," Nietzsche proclaimed; and, according to Flaubert, he should write "a book about nothing, a book without external attachments, which would hold itself together by itself through the internal force of its style."

It is more than coincidental, I think, that both Nietzsche and Hofmannsthal were intensely musical and intimately involved with music. For both, music provided a sort of idealized model for the reformulation of art and language. Indeed, music acquired the status of a central symbolic image for many of the principal artistic concerns of the years immediately preceding and following the turn of the century. Walter Pater provided perhaps the strongest statement (certainly the most famous) in asserting (in 1873) that "all art constantly aspires towards the condition of music." Removed from ordinary reality by its nonsubstantive and nondesignative nature, music offered the age an ideal embodiment of the notion that art is pure form, and thus pure language. Pater's is only one of a series of such pronouncements appearing in the aesthetic literature of the period, e.g., in Verlaine's "De la musique avant toute chose," or in Valéry's "Reprendre à la musique leur bien." Music, with its apparent indifference to external reality, comes to be viewed as the purest manifestation of human thought—as a "language" capable of producing the sort of "immediacy, fluidity and intensity" that Hofmannsthal found missing in ordinary words.

The tendency to propose music as a model for artistic intentions and aspirations is equally evident among painters. Delacroix, for example, stressed "the music of a picture"; and Gauguin, when questioned concerning the meaning of one of his paintings ("Where are we going . . ."), said that it should be understood as "music without a libretto." But perhaps the most fully developed argument for a musical "basis" for painting appeared in Kandinsky's writings from the early years of the present century, in which he calls for the creation of a "pure painting" independent of external reality. Kandinsky repeatedly evokes music as an ideal for a more abstract, "object-free" art: "After music, painting will be the second of the arts . . . [it] will attain to the higher level of pure art, upon which music has already stood for several centuries." Similarly: "Music, which externally is completely emancipated from nature, does not need to borrow external forms from anywhere in order to create its language. Painting today is still almost entirely dependent upon natural forms, upon forms borrowed from nature. And its task today is to examine its forces and its materials, to become acquainted with them, as music has long since done, and to attempt to use these materials and forces in a purely painterly way for the purpose of creation." Indeed, Kandinsky goes so far as to envision the eventual development of a *malerische Generalbass* and a *Harmonielehre der Malerei* (i.e., theories of figured bass and of harmony for painting).

The idea of music as a uniquely privileged medium able to penetrate to the essence of reality and thus express things inaccessible to language as such has a history extending back at least to the turn of the nineteenth century. Its definitive philosophical statement was supplied by Schopenhauer, in whose formulation it became a cornerstone of the aesthetics of romanticism. Writing in 1819, in *The World as Will and Idea,* he praises music above all other arts as a "universal language" capable of expressing, "in a homogeneous material, mere tone, and with the greatest determinateness and truth, the inner nature, the in-itself of the world." Unlike the other arts, it is not a "copy of the phenomenon, or more accurately, the adequate objectivity of will, but is the direct copy of the will itself, and therefore exhibits itself as the metaphysical to everything physical in the world." The composer thus becomes in Schopenhauer's eyes a sort of clairvoyant, privy to truths hidden from ordinary beings: he "reveals the inner nature of the world, and expresses the deepest wisdom in a language which his reason does not understand; as a person under the influence of mesmerism tells things of which he has no conception when he awakes."

This view reflects, and presupposes, a uniquely modern and Western conception of music as an autonomous art, freed from the verbal texts to which it had traditionally been attached and upon which its meaning and significance had always depended. Schopenhauer is explicit on the point that only *instrumental* music enjoys the special powers he ascribes to the art: "It is precisely this universality, which belongs exclusively to it, together with the greatest determinateness, that give music the high worth which it has as the panacea for all our woes. Thus, if music is too closely united with the words, and tries to form itself according to the events, it is striving to speak a language which is not its own." It was not until the eighteenth century, however, that instrumental music gradually began to emerge as an equal partner to vocal music; and thus only then could such a "pure" music be taken seriously, and questions arise as to what this textless music might be "saying." Already by the early years of the nineteenth century the prevailing attitude toward instrumental music had completely changed. For many it had become the only true music, the only form in which music could attain its highest and purest expression. Wilhelm Wackenroder, writing at the end of the eighteenth century, praises music above all other arts, for "it speaks a language we do not know in ordinary life, which we have learned, we know not where or how, and which one can only take to be the language of angels."

Yet though many thus viewed the insubstantiality of musical material—its "purity"—as sufficient to justify its role as a model for artistic regeneration, for the composer matters were by no means so simple. Indeed, by the end of the century a crisis had developed in musical language as shattering as that in the language of literature. To the composer, the idea that music offered a "pure material" must have seemed grotesquely naive. Far from supplying a sort of *tabula rasa* on which could be inscribed, free from all external interference, the "hidden hieroglyphics" of uninhibited fantasy, music in fact came tied to a remarkably fixed system of built-in conventions and constraints. Not by chance, this system began to be theoretically codified at just the time that instrumental music began to break away from its vocal-linguistic heritage. It was as if music, suddenly removed from the semantic and syntactic foundation previously supplied by language, had to discover its own grammar. With Rameau's *Traité de l'harmonie* of 1722 as the most conspicuous initiator, the history of modern Western music theory represents a concerted effort to map out the coordinates of a new and autonomous musical system capable of matching the logical coherence and expressive power of language itself. If music was to be a world removed from ordinary reality (in Wackenroder's phrase, *eine abgesonderte Welt*), it was nevertheless to be a world of reason, logic, and systemization.

This increasingly systematic conception of musical structure was bound to take its toll. As the nineteenth century progressed, a growing number of composers felt that musical language was becoming frozen in the conventions of an overly standardized harmonic vocabulary and a formal framework too heavily bound to empty symmetrical regularities. By the middle of the century, Wagner was already acutely conscious of the delimiting nature of the inherited style. His inclination to dissolve tonality through chromatic saturation of the triadic substructure, producing almost constant harmonic ambiguity, is one well-known symptom of this concern, as is his dissatisfaction with what he had come to view as the meaningless periodicities of "quadratic compositional construction." Wagner wanted music to become "endless melody," free to develop continuously according to its own inner impulses rather than to the "outward forms" of an imposed convention.

Intensifying the growing discontent with a musical language that, flattened out under the weight of its own habits, seemed to be rapidly losing its former expressive power was the dramatic growth of "lighter" music during this period. The nineteenth century gave birth to a veritable industry for the production of music for instruction and household entertainment—not popular music, but so-called "salon" music pretending to a degree of technical complexity and emotional depth designed to satisfy the cultural ambitions of a growing middle class. Such music was turned out in increasing volume throughout the nineteenth century as part of the burgeoning publishing and printing business. Compositions were often offered in periodic series on a subscription basis, and many of the better-known composers of the day provided songs, piano pieces, etc., for such purposes on commission. The degree of banality and sentimentality in these pieces, suitable for unsophisticated yet "aspiring" music lovers, was necessarily high. Hanslick, writing in the 1860s, commented on the phenomenon: "By far the largest portion of the music published here [in Vienna] consists of little dances, practice pieces, and the basest kind of brilliant piano music, which makes no secret of its spiritual and technical poverty."

A sense of malaise thus developed in the musical world paralleling that found in the other arts of the period. For the composer committed to a similar quest for "spiritual-

ity," the inherited language of music seemed no "purer" than the languages of such "representational" artistic modes as painting and literature. It was equally burdened with a system of conventions that, trivialized through overuse and exploitation, had been rendered unresponsive to the more immediate and intuitive dimensions of human experience. Trapped under syntactical and formal constraints rooted in the past, the composer was as much the prisoner of an "external" reality as was the poet or painter. He might well have echoed Nietzsche's famous remark: "I fear we shall never be rid of God, so long as we still believe in grammar."

Debussy, writing in the early years of the new century, expresses the dilemma in a typically witty, yet revealing, manner in ridiculing the ossified formal prescriptions of the classical-romantic symphony (a genre generally held to be the highest manifestation of absolute music):

> The first section is the customary presentation of a theme on which the composer proposes to work; then begins the necessary dismemberment; the second section seems to take place in an experimental laboratory; the third section cheers up a little in a quite childish way interspersed with deeply sentimental phrases during which the chant withdraws as is more seemly; but it reappears and the dismemberment goes on; the professional gentlemen, obviously interested, mop their brows and the audience calls for the composer. But the composer does not appear. He is engaged in listening modestly to the voice of tradition which prevents him, it seems to me, from hearing the voice that speaks within him.

The inner voice has become the important one for Debussy, as well as for many others of his generation. One can already recognize the condition in Wagner, who praises Liszt's symphonic poems, for example, precisely for "those individual peculiarities of view that made their creation possible." It is what is individual and unique, rather than general and conventional, that now matters.

Yet even Wagner, certainly among the most radical composers of the later nineteenth century, remained faithful to a latent foundation of traditional tonal and formal principles. The triad remains for him an always implicit, and usually explicit, structural norm, even when the underlying diatonic basis is obscured by his richly chromatic textures; and so does the dominant-to-tonic harmonic progression, the main key-defining agent in the classical canon. Moreover, the same is true of all of his contemporaries, and even of the earlier Debussy. Thus Ferruccio Busoni, writing in 1906, can look back over the entire nineteenth century (and specifically to late Beethoven, which he takes as representative of the extremes of musical freedom attained during the century) and comment (in his *New Aesthetic of Music,* perhaps the first conscious—or self-conscious—manifesto of musical modernism) on the ultimate failure of even its most progressive figures to achieve a radical break with the past:

Such lust of liberation filled Beethoven, the romantic revolutionary, that he ascended one short step on the way leading music back to its loftier self—a short step in the great task, a wide step in his own path. He did not quite reach absolute music, but in certain moments he divined it, as in the introduction to the fugue of the Sonata for Hammerklavier. Indeed, all composers have drawn nearest the true nature of music in preparatory and intermediate passages (preludes and transitions), where they felt at liberty to disregard symmetrical proportions, and unconsciously drew free breath.

Busoni's words again recall Nietzsche's aphorism about God and grammar: the apparent order and logical precision of standardized language is distrusted as bearing false witness to an increasingly unstable world of "degrees and many refinements of relationships." As if in response to this view, which I take to be fundamental to all the main currents of modernism (for "grammar" can be replaced by "conventional tonal structure," by "traditional modes of visual representation," etc.), the major progressive composers of the first decade of the new century undertook a radical dismantling of the established syntax of Western music. This move "beyond tonality" was remarkably widespread (although it assumed very different forms in different composers). It profoundly altered the face of music and supplied the technical foundation for musical modernism.

Although the technical consequences of this musical revolution are, I believe, ultimately comprehensible only within the context of the broader cultural crisis I have focused upon up to now, they are themselves of considerable interest and significance. I will thus turn now to consider some of the more specialized developments in musical language that occurred during the first decade of the century. It will be useful to treat these in rather general terms, for they are thus applicable to a wide range of composers (including Debussy, Scriabin, Stravinsky, Schoenberg, and Bartók) who in other respects might seem to have relatively little in common. Of course these technical developments did not come about instantaneously; they had an extended history. But the final step was taken only after the turn of the century; and in this instance this step produced a difference in kind rather than simply another one of degree.

One way to view the revolution in musical language during these years is as a transformation in the relationship between compositional foreground and compositional background—that is, between the musical surface and its formal substructure. (I have already made tacit use of this distinction in discussing the music of Wagner.) Music is above all an art of ornament and elaboration; and it must maintain a subtle, and often fragile, relationship between its variegated embellishments and the simpler, stricter, and more solid supporting framework that holds these embellishments together and supplies their foundation. Indeed, a striking feature of the foreground-background relation is the mutual dependence of the two. The underlying framework is often not sounded at all, but must be deduced from the implications of the foreground; while the foreground, though actually sounded, owes its "grammatical" meaning solely to its connection with a "virtual" background. The history of Western music theory can be read as an attempt to codify a set of rules for, on the one hand, approved background relationships and, on the other, permissible foreground divergences. To take a few relatively simple examples applying mainly to "local" levels of structure, such theoretical concepts as consonance, diatonicism, triad, and fundamental progression belong to background phenomena, while those of dissonance, chromaticism, and auxiliary tones belong to the foreground.

Since at any given moment the background elements are not necessarily present on the surface, their proper apperception must depend upon strong conventions concerning what is "normal" and thus structural, as opposed to what is "abnormal" and thus superficial and ornamental. All Western music, at least since the Renaissance, displays a more or less complex interaction between foreground and background structures. Although the degree to which these levels can depart from one another has varied considerably from style to style, it is characteristic of the post-Renaissance period as a whole that a sufficient balance is maintained to ensure that the underlying structure is never seriously threatened. During the nineteenth century, however, this balance begins noticeably to waver. Since the background represents what is essentially fixed and unchanging, while the foreground contains what is unique, individual, and characteristic in a composition, it is not surprising that an age of such marked individualism should produce a radical shift in the foreground-background dialectic, tilting the balance heavily toward the surface. The growth of chromaticism, an emphasis on novel dissonances, an ever-greater exploitation of motivic and thematic elements at the expense of architectural ones—all this reflects a significant structural realignment. By the latter part of the century such technical innovations often make it extremely difficult to hear an implied background at all through the heavy accumulations of wayward foreground detail. The latter becomes so complex, so laden with multiple, entangled, and often contradictory layers of implication that the underlying structure (to the extent that one can still be inferred) is brought to the edge of collapse.

The more adventurous composers of the nineteenth century countered the problem largely by structuring the foreground features of their compositions at the expense of background ones. The various techniques of thematic transformation evident in Liszt, Wagner, and other composers of the period serve to hold together through surface correspondences extended spans of music whose background structures have been seriously weakened. Similarly, lengthy symphonic movements are often organized according to shifting and opposed key areas that, according to conventional background criteria, form dissonant relationships applicable only to local formal contexts (e.g., the C/B dichotomy in Strauss's *Also Sprach Zarathustra*).

Yet even in such extreme instances, traditional background structures continue to exert a strong influence. Despite the often exotic surface peculiarities, the music maintains at least a latent reference to the standardized grammar of Western tonality. The triad still represents the sole harmonic norm (no matter how rarely a pure triad may appear); and the traditional dominant-to-tonic progression still retains its key-defining function (though it may now appear more by implication than by actual statement).

Nevertheless, the growing strain brought on by the conflicting claims of foreground and background in complex European music reached a crisis point by the end of the century. If, on the one hand, the substructure became too obscure, the "meaning" of the foreground was apt to seem unclear; whereas if the substructure was rendered too clearly audible, the luxurious surface detail so typical of fin-de-siècle textures tended to sound like nothing more than "junk"—i.e., decoration in the worst sense of the term. One notes the latter problem, it seems to me, to some degree in even the greatest composers of the turn of the century. It is especially evident in such figures as Reger and Franck, who attempted to reconcile a classicizing tendency with a penchant for the most progressive technical procedures of the day. Thus Reger's complex modulations and intensely chromatic voice-leading are contained within a highly regular phrase structure with cadential points defined by blatantly unambiguous dominant-tonic progressions. The heightened chromatic motion on the surface seems to have no influence upon the substructure, which sounds through with schematic clarity. Both surface and background take on the aspect of cliché: the surface, because it acquires the attributes of a momentary decoration without wider repercussions; the background, because it provides a too "easy" (because too obviously conventional) resolution for the entangled interrelationships suggested by the surface. But it is not only in Reger that one hears the problem: the specter of kitsch looms over even the greatest achievements of an age in which music threatened literally to become pure ornament.

A solution demanded a major restructuring of the received musical language. In the broadest terms, it involved a projection of musical phenomena previously considered to belong solely to the foreground—elements that are ephemeral, passing, structurally unessential, and thus, in a sense, accidental (the "chance" results of voice leading, etc.)—onto the structural background. I have already noted a tendency in this direction in nineteenth-century music, in the increasing emphasis on individual foreground features. Nevertheless, the moment when agreed-upon background relationships no longer supplied even an implicit matrix for controlling the confusion of surface detail marked a fundamental turn in the history of compositional thought. A fixed and conventional conception of musical structure gave way to one that was variable, contingent, and contextual—dependent upon the specific attributes of the particular composition. Those qualities of uniqueness and individuality, of the ephemeral and accidental, that had previously marked the foreground alone now characterized the background as well.

The final, conclusive break occurred in the first decade of the century, in Scriabin, Debussy, Schoenberg, and Stravinsky, as well as others. Significantly, the leaders in this musical revolution were themselves all nurtured within the tonal tradition and produced in their earlier careers compositions written according to more or less traditional tonal assumptions. The rift with the past led to different responses, but the particular solution of each composer can be largely understood as a direct outgrowth of the stylistic evolution of his earlier music and thus of a particular orientation toward tonality.

It will be helpful to consider briefly two composers who arrived at radically different solutions to this common problem: Scriabin and Schoenberg. Scriabin's early music seems remarkable mainly for its conservatism, its unequivocal harmonic relationships ordered within an essentially conventional larger tonal context. Yet as in much music of the later nineteenth century (Scriabin was born in 1872 and his first mature works began to appear in the 1890s), the harmonic structure is covered with a dense network of auxiliary tones that, although clearly subordinate (there is never any doubt about the triadic background), resolve only with the greatest reluctance. The obvious disparity between the rich accretions of surface detail and the all-too-apparent harmonic underpinnings produces formal-expressive problems similar to the ones noted in Reger. Only in Scriabin the dissonances are prolonged over such long spans that the whole structure seems to float precariously over the delicately maintained chordal foundation; and in the later 1890s and early 1900s, the complex surface sonorities are increasingly emphasized at the expense of their background supports. When triadic resolutions do occur, they sound more and more like perfunctory nods to tradition, dictated solely by protocol. The heart of the music has been displaced from the substructure to the surface, so that the resolutions sound like a breach of faith.

Scriabin's own particular development of extended chromaticism and delayed resolution is closely tied to his use of elaborate dominant type sonorities. The dominant seventh is the one chordal type within the traditional vocabulary whose tonal function is, at least under normal circumstances, unambiguous, and which is thus able to define a key area entirely by itself. By focusing upon elaborations of such harmonies in his earlier music, Scriabin was able to preserve at least some degree of tonal definition; despite the increasing avoidance of resolution, one is usually able to infer what the resolution *should* be. Moreover, up until about 1907 tonal resolutions do ultimately occur, although they may be delayed right up to the final measure. The moment arrives in Scriabin's evolution, however, when the dominant-type sonorities completely lose their functional subordination to an inferred background tonic. The dominant, one might say, has moved deeper into the structural background to become an "absolute" sonority in its own right, with a meaning no longer dependent upon its relationship to a simpler, more stable structure. The dominant-type harmony, in fact, assumes the role of a center, or tonic, itself; but it is a new kind of unstable tonic, whose priority must be contextually defined within each composition.

Significantly, Scriabin referred to this new tonic sonority as the "mystic chord," for to him it was the source of previously unimagined musical power. Moreover, he conceived of it as built up of intervals of a fourth, thus distinguishing it from previous harmonic norms. Yet the chord can just as readily be viewed as a series of thirds, in which case it conforms to traditional conceptions of triadic extension. What was actually novel about the chord, then, was not so much its internal structure, or even the way it sounds in isolation, but its functional location in the background. There it shed its traditional grammatical meaning, acquiring a new and seemingly inscrutable one more in keeping with Scriabin's growing mystical orientation. Only through such drastic structural means could music become more responsive to those transcendent and visionary claims that increasingly occupied the composer from about 1908 to 1915, the final years of his brief life.

Schoenberg's development, though different in many ways, reveals significant parallels with Scriabin's. In his earlier works, too, the surface elaborations of a still basically tonal language are stressed to a point that eventually brings about the latter's dissolution. But Schoenberg's chromaticism is the product of rich webs of thematic and motivic development that bury the structural background under a complex, thickly woven contrapuntal overlay. Whereas in Scriabin the harmonic background moves slowly and projects its triadic nature with relative clarity, in Schoenberg's music of the early 1900s the density and speed of the counterpoint produce a constantly shifting harmonic basis that at every moment appears ready to dissolve the argument into complete tonal uncertainty. Dominant-type harmonies, though still present, are increasingly de-emphasized as too suggestive of unwanted conventional resolutions. The stress is on highly varied dissonant complexes, which sound like opaque, heavily refracted distortions of the traditional harmonic functions that were fast becoming grammatical impossibilities, or at least embarrassments, to Schoenberg's ears. The final resolutions in the op. 8 orchestral songs, for example, or those of the Second String Quartet and *Kammersymphonie,* are still triadic; but they seem like reluctant tributes to a remote and distrusted authority.

Schoenberg's theoretical writings also reflect his new conception of foreground-background relationships. In a famous passage in his *Harmonielehre,* first published in 1911, he points to several momentary vertical structures cut out of compositions by Bach and Mozart, claiming to show that the sort of complex and highly differentiated dissonant harmonic structures found in his own work were already present in music of the eighteenth century. What for Bach and Mozart were passing "accidents," the

result of surface contrapuntal elaborations firmly tied to an unmistakably inferrable triadic background, have become for Schoenberg absolute entities warranting theoretical investigation and explanation in their own right.

In Schoenberg's music, as in Scriabin's, the moment at which the latent background completely receded, leaving virtually no trace, is approached gradually, almost imperceptibly; but sometime around 1907-8 a final margin was irreparably traversed. Despite this step-by-step evolution, the consequences were fundamental. Schoenberg's own awareness of having made a critical turn is apparent in the preface to his song cycle *Das Buch der hängenden Gärten* (generally considered to be the first major composition in the new style): "For the first time I have been successful in coming near an ideal of expression and form which I had had in mind for years. . . . Now that I have finally embarked upon this path I am conscious that I have broken all barriers of a past aesthetic." And later he remarked of the last two movements of his Second String Quartet, a work briefly predating the cycle: "No longer could the great variety of dissonant sonorities be balanced out through occasional insertion of such tonal chords as one normally uses to express a tonality"; it was no longer "appropriate to force the motion into the Procrustean bed of tonality."

Schoenberg thus sacrificed a traditional background in order to allow the compositional foreground to speak more freely, unencumbered by the constraints of a conventional syntax. Here, finally, was a music that could communicate directly, unmediated by external controls, and that was thus actually able to approach that "purity" of language so indiscriminately attributed to music in general by those working in the other arts. Yet the price to be paid was severe: Schoenberg's newly liberated foreground projected a "language" that no one, not even the composer himself, could understand, at least in the sense that one had always been able to "understand" traditional tonal music. As the composer himself remarked in his *Harmonielehre,* referring to the advanced harmonic constructions found in music of the century's first decade: "Why it is as it is, and why it is correct, I am at the moment unable to say."

There can be no coincidence, certainly, in the fact that Schoenberg's final break with traditional tonality initiated the most productive period of his creative life. Within a two-year span from 1907 to 1909 he completed seven major compositions, including such extended works as the Second String Quartet, op. 10, *Das Buch der hängenden Gärten,* op. 15, the Five Orchestral Pieces, op. 16, and *Erwartung,* op. 17. The sense of a release, of a newly won freedom suddenly available beyond the "barriers of a past aesthetic," is evident in both the quantity and character of this music. Yet Schoenberg, working at the outer edges of what then seemed musically possible (at least to one committed to the notion of a continuously evolving tradition), increasingly felt the strain of operating at such disorienting heights, where only his unconscious, intuitive feeling for what was musically valid could serve him as guide. After the brief period of unprecedented productivity coinciding with the first explorations of the atonal terrain, Schoenberg's output decreased dramatically, coming to a virtual halt by 1916. For seven years thereafter no new compositions were published; and when new works began to appear again in 1923, they revealed a composer embarked upon a radically different course. In the intervening years Schoenberg had evolved a new musical system intended to replace tonality, one that—like tonality—would provide a method for consciously determining compositional choices.

This was the twelve-tone system, which Schoenberg envisioned as supplying the basis for a new "musical language," the *lingua franca* of a new stage in musical history. For despite the revolutionary character of many aspects of his thought, Schoenberg remained committed to the idea that this next stage would share with past ones a dependence upon a set of widely accepted compositional conventions, within whose terms all composers could shape their own personal statements. As a consequence, he came to view his own earlier atonal works as representatives of an essentially transitional phase of music history. Writing in 1932 on the historical necessity of the twelve-tone system, he commented upon his atonal work:

> The first compositions in this new style were written by me around 1908. . . . From the very beginnings such compositions differed from all preceding music, not only harmonically but also melodically, thematically, and motivically. But the foremost characteristic of these pieces in *statu nascendi* were their extreme expressiveness and their extraordinary brevity. . . . Thus, subconsciously, consequences were drawn from an innovation which, like every innovation, destroys while it produces. New colorful harmony was offered; but much was lost. . . . Fulfillment of all formal functions—comparable to the effect of punctuation in the construction of sentences, of subdivision into paragraphs, and of fusion into chapters—could scarcely be assured with chords whose constructive values had not as yet been explored. Hence it seemed at first impossible to compose pieces of complicated organization or of great length. . . . the conviction that these new sounds obey the laws of nature and of our manner of thinking—the conviction that order, logic, comprehensibility and form cannot be present without obedience to such laws—forces the composer along the road of exploration. He must find, if not laws or values, at least ways to justify the dissonant character of these harmonies and their successions.

Schoenberg's change of attitude was by no means exceptional. Following World War I, Western composers generally tended to pull back from the heady, more experimental atmosphere of the prewar years. Manifestations of a new point of view were everywhere evident: e.g., in the simpler, more objective and more "everyday" type of music fostered by Satie and *Les Six,* and in the various

moves toward a "new classicism" by such otherwise diverse figures as Stravinsky, Bartók, and Hindemith. Yet what seems in retrospect most telling about all of these developments was their failure to produce a new set of musical procedures even remotely comparable—in terms of commonality, of reflecting a consensus—to those of traditional tonality. Thus the twelve-tone system, though indisputably one of the most remarkable and influential technical achievements of twentieth-century music, has remained an essentially provisional method, occasionally employed by many composers but consistently used by relatively few. Nor did the widespread neoclassical turn of the between-the-war years produce an even marginally unified technical orientation; rather, it gave rise to a series of strongly personal and thus divergent and idiosyncratic reformulations of technical and stylistic traits drawn from virtually the entire range of Western music history. Cocteau's famous "call to order," which reverberated throughout the postwar period, remained in this respect largely unanswered.

From the present perspective, then, it would appear that the most important historical moment in defining the main coordinates of twentieth-century music was the widespread break from traditional tonality that occurred during the first decade of the century. From this moment springs the unprecedented stylistic, technical, and expressive variety of the music of the modern age—in short, what I have previously referred to as its linguistic plurality. Despite the numerous attempts that have been—and continue to be—made to offer a systematic account of Schoenberg's prewar music, the true force and significance of this music lies, it seems to me, precisely in its determination to speak in an unknown and enigmatic tongue that largely defies rational comprehension.

This may help explain the unique position this music continues to occupy in our consciousness. Along with other composers of the time (one thinks also, inevitably, of the Stravinsky of the *Rite of Spring*), Schoenberg set the essential tone of music in the modern age. He attempted to transform musical language from a public vehicle, susceptible to comprehension by ordinary people (but thereby also limited to more or less ordinary statement), to a private one capable of speaking the unspeakable. Music became an incantation, a language of ritual that, just because of its inscrutability, revealed secrets hidden from normal understanding.

The fifteen songs of **Das Buch der hängenden Gärten** are settings of poems drawn from the volume of that title by Stefan George, who himself favored "a language inaccessible to the profane multitude." George's distinct elitism equally colors Schoenberg's aesthetic. (The composer once commented: "If it is art, it is not for all; and if it is for all, it is not art.") But Schoenberg's elitism can be understood in part as an understandable reaction against a musical language that had lost its fundamental expressive core and thus its capacity to challenge, to illuminate, and to astonish. The composers of the first decade of the century undertook to revive musical language by reinventing it. They tried to disengage musical sounds from their inherited attachments, to set them free from conventional associations in pursuit of what Schoenberg (along with Kandinsky) called the "spiritual." In sober retrospect, they may seem to have failed; yet theirs was a brave and exhilarating effort that fundamentally altered the nature of musical discourse.

Joan Allen Smith (essay date 1986)

SOURCE: "The Twelve Tone Method," in *Schoenberg and His Circle: A Viennese Portrait*, Schirmer Books, 1986, pp. 183-218.

[*In the following essay, Smith provides an overview of Schoenberg's twelve-tone method.*]

Several Viennese composers outside of the Schoenberg circle were concerned with repeated pitch structures and some even with the concept of chromatic completion (the structurally geared use of all twelve pitch classes) coincidentally with Schoenberg. However, the idea of an ordering within the twelve-tone set, and the application of the four systematic operations of transposition, inversion, retrogression, and retrograde-inversion, which brought about a musically constructive method for twelve-tone composition, were Schoenberg's alone. They did not come to him in a single insight but rather developed slowly over a number of years.

The composer probably most concerned, besides Schoenberg, with finding a substitute for the long-range structural functions of tonal harmony was Anton Webern. Of all of Schoenberg's pupils, he was the most noticeably experimental, and in many ways Webern seemed musically less tied to the past and more willing than Schoenberg himself to carry theoretical ideas to their logical extreme. However, it was always Schoenberg who saw the far-reaching implications of compositional trends, and it was Berg, of the three most closely tied to past ideas, who many years later performed the feat of adapting the twelve-tone method to his tonally oriented style while still expanding the limits of the method far beyond Webern's rather conventional serial techniques.

Recalling the developmental period, from about 1906 to 1923, Webern, in "The Path to Twelve-Note Composition," and Schoenberg, in various sources, remember many of the same points as being important.

> (Webern) In 1906, Schoenberg came back from a stay in the country, bringing the Chamber Symphony. It made a colossal impression. I'd been his pupil for three years, and immediately felt "You must write something like that, too!" Under the influence of the work I wrote a sonata movement the very next day. In that movement I reached the farthest limits of tonality.

> (Schoenberg) Fall 1906 Webern returned from vacation, sees Chamber Symphony (written

Rottach-Egern), says had thought about how modern music should look. Sees Chamber Symphony fulfills that idea.

> 1907 new style. Told Webern about short pieces. One of the piano pieces should consist of only 3-4 measures. Webern starts writing shorter and shorter pieces. Follows all my developments. Always tries to surpass everything (exaggerates).

> (Webern) What happened? I can only relate something from my own experience; about 1911 I wrote the "Bagatelles for String Quartet" (Opus 9), all very short pieces, lasting a couple of min-utes—perhaps the shortest music so far. Here I had the feeling, "When all twelve notes have gone by, the piece is over." Much later I discovered that all this was a part of the necessary development.

The Bagatelles for String Quartet, in common with other Webern works of the period, are significant in that they serve as a bridge between the earlier atonal music and that of the twelve-tone period. In these works, concern for a twelve-pitch organization is already evident. Many pieces (in the Bagatelles, all except the fifth piece) begin with a statement of the chromatic collection, without repetition of pitches. Although the remainder of the piece can often be divided into statements of this collection that roughly correspond to phrasing, these divisions contain numerous repeated pitches. The collection is always unordered, and most significant, it does not constitute the primary structural stratagem of the piece. This continues to focus upon the factors characteristic of earlier atonal works. As is interesting to note, with regard to Webern's feeling that "when all twelve notes have gone by, the piece is over," the introductory presentation of the chromatic collection is sometimes quite different from what follows; sometimes it is set off as an introduction, and often there is a quality of display about it. When the score reverts to the old motivic way of doing things, it is easy to speculate that Webern simply didn't know what else to do. Schoenberg described this and related problems in an essay, **"Composition with Twelve Tones (1)"**:

> The first compositions in this new style were written by me around 1908 and, soon afterwards, by my pupils, Anton von Webern and Alban Berg. From the very beginning such compositions differed from all preceding music, not only harmonically but also melodically, thematically, and motivally. But the foremost characteristics of these pieces *in statu nascendi* were their extreme brevity. At that time, neither I nor my pupils were conscious of the reasons for these features. Later I discovered that our sense of form was right when it forced us to counterbalance extreme emotionality with extraordinary shortness. Thus, subconsciously, consequences were drawn from an innovation which, like every innovation, destroys while it produces. New colourful harmony was offered; but much was lost.

> Formerly the harmony had served not only as a source of beauty, but, more important, as a means

of distinguishing the features of the form. For instance, only a consonance was considered suitable for an ending. Establishing functions demanded different successions of harmonies than roving functions; a bridge, a transition, demanded other successions than a codetta; harmonic variation could be executed intelligently and logically only with due consideration of the fundamental meaning of the harmonies. Fulfilment of all these functions—comparable to the effect of punctuation in the construction of sentences, of subdivision into paragraphs, and of fusion into chapters—could scarcely be assured with chords whose constructive values had not as yet been explored. Hence, it seemed at first impossible to compose pieces of complicated organization or of great length.

A little later I discovered how to construct larger forms by following a text or a poem.

This problem was of course eventually solved by Schoenberg's four operations (transposition, inversion, retrograde, and retrograde-inversion). In fact, a principal contribution of these operations was that they allowed the piece to continue, and in so doing, made possible a revival of large-scale traditional forms.

In an essay published posthumously, Schoenberg relates his excitement about *Jakobsleiter:*

Ever since 1906-8, when I had started writing compositions which led to the abandonment of tonality, I had been busy finding methods to replace the structural functions of harmony. Nevertheless, my first distinct step toward this goal occurred only in 1915. I had made plans for a great symphony of which *Die Jakobsleiter* should be the last movement. I had sketched many themes, among them one for a scherzo which consisted of all the twelve tones.

But in the manuscript notes, the competition with Webern comes through:

1914(15) I start a symphony. Wrote about it to Webern. Mention singing *without* words (**Jakobsleiter**). Mention Scherzo theme including all 12 tones. After 1915, Webern seems to have used 12 tones in some of his compositions,—*without telling me.*

Webern jealous about Berg. Had suggested to me to tell Berg he (in about 1908 or 9) should not work in the new style—he has no right to do it—it does not fit to his style—but it fitted to Webern's!!!

Webern commited at this period (1908-1918) many acts of infidelity with the intention of making himself the innovator.

The gradual move toward a twelve-tone composition seems to have gone on steadily with both composers. Webern described one of his Goethe songs, "Gleich und Gleich," from 1916, as follows:

My Goethe song, "Gleich und Gleich" (Four Songs Op. 12, No. 4, composed in 1917) begins as follows: G sharp-A-D sharp-G, then a chord E-C-B flat-D, then F sharp-B-F-C sharp. That makes twelve notes: none is repeated. At that time we were not conscious of the law, but had been sensing it for a long time. One day Schoenberg intuitively discovered the law that underlies twelve-note composition. An inevitable development of this law was that one gave the succession of twelve notes a *particular order.*

Webern begins this piece, as he describes, with a statement of the chromatic collection partitioned into tetrachords. The remainder of the piece is divisible into sections in which the entire collection is in most cases represented. These sections correspond largely to the phrase divisions of the piece. It is the tetrachordal division, however, rather than the twelve-tone nature of it, that evokes the motivic material of the piece, and it is clear that at this point (1916) Webern had no idea of twelve-tone ordering as an organizational means for nontonal music.

Theodor Adorno suggests a problem of Webern's abbreviated works which begins to be solved in the Opus 12 songs:

With the Songs Op. 12 an almost unnoticeable change begins. Webern's music secretly expands: in his own way he is mastering the solution which Schoenberg first displayed in *Pierrot lunaire* and the Songs Op. 22: that one cannot persist with the method of absolute purity [clarity] without music being spiritually reduced to physical deterioration. The new expansion is only hinted at; the first and last of the songs are still aphoristically short, but they do breathe a little, and the two middle songs . . . have well developed vocal lines, though certainly of a subtle character in which the earlier process of splitting-up is still maintained.

This point is reminiscent of certain issues suggested by Adolf Loos:

Twenty-six years ago I maintained that ornament would disappear from articles of use as man develops. . . . But I never meant that decoration should be ruthlessly and systematically done away with. . . . Only when time has made it disappear, can it never be applied again. Just as man will never go back to tattooing his face.

Loos believed that absence of decoration was a sign of cultural advancement. A strong believer in the reflection by art of its time, he did not himself eliminate all decoration from his own work. Even in cases where the beauty of his materials was itself decorative, he employed carving to accent the line of a chest or friezes to outline the top of a wall. But for Webern, the situation was somewhat different. Music, unlike architecture, usually lacks external function, and Webern, in perhaps going too far in the direction of clarity, endangered that essential filigree which, although in the foreground of musical structure, is nonetheless an inherent, essential aspect of its character. There is a point at which, in music and the painterly arts, too much clarity jeopardizes depth of expression.

The law that until all twelve pitch classes have occurred none may be repeated—a law essential to twelve-tone structure in that it creates a contextual framework within which repetition may occur—is described by Schoenberg in his same manuscript notes:

> [1921] Found out that the greater distance between a tone and its repetition can be produced if 12 tones lie between. Started 12-tone composition. Told Erwin Stein I had now a way I wanted to keep secret from all my imitators, because I am annoyed by them: I even do not know any more what is mine and what is their's [*sic*].

Between 1920 and the meeting of 1923, in which he revealed the method to his students, Schoenberg worked out the several consequences of ordering all twelve pitch classes and incorporated his findings into several pieces.

In the Five Piano Pieces, Op. 23; the Serenade, Op. 24; and the Piano Suite, Op. 25, Schoenberg experimented with various aspects of what was to be the method long before the twelve-tone method itself crystallized. George Perle has succinctly described the complex interrelationships of these pieces:

> In Opus 23, No. 1, pitch or pitch-class order is exploited as a separable referential component, as it is to some degree in Schoenberg's earlier atonal compositions, but far more pronouncedly and extensively. The pitch and pitch-class order of the initial melodic figure in the second number of the same opus is so pervasive that one may already speak of it as an ordered set, but it is not the only source of pitch-class relations. Both movements were completed in July, 1920. Around the same time Schoenberg commenced the Variations movement of Opus 24, the earliest example of an entire movement exclusively based on a totally ordered—though not yet twelve-tone—series. The first consistently twelve-tone piece, Opus 25, No. 1, was composed in July of the following year.

Perle goes on to call our attention to an important sketch for a twelve-tone "passacaglia," dated 5 March 1920, four months prior to any of the works described above, which already contains a chart from an all-combinatorial twelve-tone set:

> In the compositional sketches the row does not serve merely as a special sort of "theme," as in the passacaglia on a twelve-tone row in the first act (completed in the previous summer) of *Wozzeck*. Every harmonic and melodic element participates in the unfolding of one or another serially generated hexachord. The idea of a twelve-tone *system,* in which every pitch component is derived from an ordered twelve-tone series, was thus already formulated in these sketches, before Schoenberg had taken the first step along the irregular path he

followed for almost three years before definitively arriving at the same result with his resumption of the composition of Opus 25.

The first totally twelve-tone work of some length was the Wind Quintet, composed in 1923 and 1924. Schoenberg has described the freedom provided by his method:

> The construction of a basic set of twelve tones derives from the intention to postpone the repetition of every tone as long as possible. . . .
>
> The other function is the unifying effect of the set. Through the necessity of using besides the basic set, its retrograde, its inversion, and its retrograde inversion, the repetition of tones will occur oftener than expected. But every tone appears always in the neighbourhood of two other tones in an unchanging combination which produces an intimate relationship most similar to the relationship of a third and a fifth to its root. It is, of course, a mere relation, but its recurrence can produce psychological effects of a great resemblance to those closer relations.
>
> Such features will appear in every motif, in every theme, in every melody and, though rhythm and phrasing might make it distinctly another melody, it will still have some relationship with all the rest. The unification is here also the result of the relation to a common factor.

The implications of the twelve-tone method were most completely understood by Schoenberg's more intellectual students. Max Deutsch and Felix Greissle, who both taught the method for many years, and Erwin Ratz, who was a scholar, all knew Schoenberg's music intimately and could follow his musical development in great detail. Their knowledge of the twelve-tone method is organic and invaluable. Humphrey Searle, a pupil of Webern rather than Schoenberg, came to Vienna after Schoenberg had already moved to the United States but had the opportunity to observe Webern's compositional technique. Of the performers included in this chapter, those of the Kolisch Quartet, especially Rudolf Kolisch, engaged in exhaustive analytical labors and therefore had an intimate acquaintance with the method. Their concerns focus upon the interpretive problems of twelve-tone music.

> EUGEN LEHNER: I don't know who coined the phrase "It's not the answer that matters but the right question is what matters." But I would really, if nobody else claims the authorship, then I would rather attribute it to Schoenberg. That was what Schoenberg was about—to find the right question, not the answer. He was not interested in the answer but the question he was interested in. And that's the reason he would not supply an answer if somebody asked about something he did, because, "That's your worry." So, I would say, I wish nobody would claim it so that I can attribute it to Schoenberg. . . . And that was the essence of Schoenberg as intellectual, as the egghead. And that's the reason, whatever he heard, whatever

snatch remark, he worked on it. It bothered him and occupied him until he could formulate the right proof.

OSKAR KOKOSCHKA: Webern was an outspoken puritan. He reduced even what he learned from Schoenberg. Schoenberg was already reducing the material to the essential, but he—in just five sounds, he wrote music. He gave what Schoenberg wanted. . . . Schoenberg wanted to reduce [to] the essentials.

MAX DEUTSCH: You have some pages in the *Harmonielehre* where you can find he was under the impression to find out something very exceptional. When he wrote *Jakobsleiter* . . . for the first time in the history of music, you have a chord with twelve tones—all the twelve tones are in it. . . . That was the first moment he had the twelve tones together. You have a kind of discord in *Erwartung*. You have it too in *Glückliche Hand*, but not in this way. I mean, . . . without the octave and not doubled. For the first time in this place in *Jakobsleiter*.

LEHNER: *Pierrot lunaire* as a twelve-tone piece. In other words, it's so close to it—to total organization—that it is just one step off it, and why should we believe that Schoenberg, with his incredibly keen intellect and his superhuman sense of curiosity, was not aware of that? Certainly he formulated, "What makes music get away from a tonal center? Obviously, the equal importance of all the notes, so there is no tonal center and no more gravitating force." . . . Of course, if we could consciously force our whole musical thinking [so] that this balance is kept perfect, no predominance of any single note which could possibly exert a gravitation, then that would be the ideal of atonal music. . . . Then, of course, we must organize it so that there is a perfect balance—take care that no note happens more often before the other notes are out. So therefore,— . . . remember that's a conjecture on my part—the idea of the twelve-tone must have been born [at] this moment when he realized what makes music lose tonality, the tonal effects. And the next step was probably a conscious step: if the equality of the existing twelve notes in our Western system brings that, then we must organize it so that we make sure that there is no tonal center. And indeed, if I could accept my own supposition, and if you go through such a piece . . . like the Wind Quintet, then you will see how true it is. But then, fortunately for posterity, this phase didn't last, because Schoenberg was the same naïve, inspired artist like all the great composers were. So, fortunately, . . . no matter what his intention was, when he sat down and the inspiration came, he was just writing music, very much to his astonishment, because it always turned out differently than what he expected.

Schoenberg might have continued to keep his secret had it not been for the publications of another composer, Josef Matthias Hauer. Hauer, who began writing a kind of twelve-tone music around 1908, organized the possible combinations of the twelve pitch classes into groups, called *Tropen,* which formed the material for the composition. Hauer began publishing articles about this method in 1919. Schoenberg did not like to read articles and seems not to have read these until several years later, although some of his students, including Kolisch, had seen the articles. He himself had met Hauer through Adolf Loos. It was the fear that he would be considered a follower of Hauer and not himself the originator of the twelve-tone method which prompted him to announce the method publicly. Schoenberg's attitude toward Hauer varied but was always formal and courteous. Although Hauer was more a theoretic realizer than a composer, several of his pieces were performed in concerts of the Verein für musikalische Privataufführungen.

In June of 1921, the Verein held a competition for chamber music works. The judges for this event were listed as Schoenberg, Berg, Webern, Stein, and Steuermann, although it is doubtful that Schoenberg and Stein actually took part in the deliberations, being away from Vienna for the entire summer. Fritz Heinrich Klein, a pupil of Berg, entered under a pseudonym a piece entitled *Die Maschine: Eine extonale Selbstsatire,* a work that experimented with various unusual twentieth-century compositional techniques; these were itemized on the title page of the piece:

> This work contains:
>
> 1) A twelve-beat "rhythmic theme";
> 2) A twelve-different-note "pattern theme";
> 3) a twelve-different-interval "interval theme";
> 4) a "neutral scale" constructed from alternating minor and major seconds;
> 5) a "combination theme" constructed from nos. 2, 3, and 4;
> 6) the largest chord in music: the "mother chord" consisting of twelve different pitches and also twelve different intervals, derived from the "pyramid chord" (twelve intervals arranged according to size);
> 7) the "mirror construction" and the "clef register" of a theme, as well as its "systematic symmetry," and
> 8) the mathematical-contrapuntal development of ideas 1 to 7.

This piece, which utilized a kind of chromatic completion including the all-interval set discovered by Klein and used by Berg in his first twelve-tone works. "Schliesse mir die Augen beide" and the *Lyric Suite,* eventually won the competition. It thus seems unlikely that Schoenberg would not have seen the piece. A copy of the score containing the following inscription was found in Schoenberg's library:

> It is the same Machine which found itself (as a score for chamber orchestra) in the summer of 1921 in your beloved hands, on the occasion of the competition of the Society f. P. M. P. . . .

Beneath this, Schoenberg added the following note:

Not correct. In Webern's hands, who told me about it but was not able to interest me in it. I doubt if I had this in my hands, but more especially that I looked at it, and certainly that I knew what it represented.

In any case, he has fundamentally nothing in common with twelve-tone composition: a compositional means which had its discrete pre-cursor in "working with tones," which I used for two or three years without discovering the twelve as the ultimate necessity.

Schoenberg's concern to prove the twelve-tone method entirely the necessary and inevitable consequence of his own musical development and so irrevocably tied to historical context is not evidence that he was uninfluenced by this and other early twelve-tone or serial experiments. Schoenberg's highly developed curiosity and his tendency to impose himself upon the activities of his students and associates would in fact suggest the opposite. There is no reason to believe that Schoenberg's own eventual method was not influenced by the work of those around him, although such influence may have been unconscious. Schoenberg preferred to consider himself influenced by Mozart and other great composers of the past, a view attributable to his own sense of uniqueness and a necessity to set himself apart. Whatever the effects of these other early ventures, Schoenberg's method does indeed possess important features that go far beyond the developments discussed above and that were for Schoenberg himself of basic importance.

The aspects of twelve-tone writing that Schoenberg took most seriously—the concept of chromatic completion and the ordering of pitch classes within the set—are missing in Hauer's method. As Schoenberg described it:

> In using Hauer's *Tropen,* one could not even postpone the reappearance of a tone for as long as possible. Hauer mixes *Tropen,* that is sets of six tones, according to his own taste or feeling of form (which only he himself possesses); there is certainly no such function of logic as in the method described here.

Although Schoenberg himself was not fully aware of the totality of implications inherent in his method either at the time of its inception or later, it is nevertheless true that the Schoenbergian twelve-tone idea embodies a richness of combinational and derivational possibilities related to its special properties that is unavailable in other similar but less refined approaches.

In February of 1923, after learning about Hauer's publications, Schoenberg called together about twenty of his students and friends and explained to them his method of twelve-tone composition. Felix Greissle, who was present at the meeting, recalled it as follows:

> He all of a sudden called all of his students and friends together, you see, and we had a meeting at which there were present Alban Berg, Anton

Webern, Egon Wellesz, Steuermann, Erwin Stein, and many others, and there he began to develop the twelve-tone theory; in other words, he explained to us the four forms of the row, and he also showed us certain fragments he had composed this way—a piano piece, I remember . . . —we all tried to understand and I think we came pretty close to what he meant except there was one person who resisted—who resisted more by being silent and not saying anything, and that was Anton Webern. He was the one who resisted most. At one point, when Schoenberg said, "There I used the row transposition and transposed it into the tritone," so Webern said, "Why?" Schoenberg looked at him and said, "I don't know," and then Webern burst out, "Ah, ah!," because Webern was waiting for some intuitive sign in the whole matter and this was it, you see.

Considering that Webern undoubtedly was already very aware of the ramifications of eliminating tonal structure and even of the concept of chromatic completion (although probably not of the structural possibilities of chromatic ordering), it is interesting that, according to Greissle, he more than Berg had difficulty in accepting the twelve-tone method as outlined in this initial meeting. It seems likely that it was the very concept of ordering within the set, together with the seemingly mechanical operations implied by that ordering, that caused Webern some concern. Only with familiarity and practice would it have been possible for the operations of the twelve-tone method, which must first have seemed so mathematical and artificial, to have been handled with the ease and custom of the often equally mechanical operations (such as modulation, progression, and cadence) that long use of the tonal system had by then made second nature. This view is supported by Schoenberg's recollection of the meeting:

> In 1924 [actually 1923] I had become aware that Hauer had also written 12 tone music. Up to this time I had kept it a secret that I do it. But in order to make clear that I had not been influenced by Hauer, but had gone my own way, I called a meeting of all my students and friends where I explained this new method and the way which I had gone.

> Curiously, when I had shown the four basic forms, Webern confessed that he had written also something in 12 tones (probably suggested by the scherzo of my symphony of 1915) and he said: "I never knew, what to do after the 12 tones" meaning that the 3 inversions now could follow and the transpositions. One thing had become clear to all of them:

> That the permanent use of only *one* 12-tone set in one work was something quite different from everything else others might have attempted. My way meant: *Unity.* My way derived from compositional necessities.

Although Schoenberg explained the method to his pupils in this meeting, he did not especially encourage them to use it in their own compositions. (At the same time, he expected it from Berg and Webern.) He mentioned it rarely in lessons with his students and resisted talking about either the method or about his own compositions in front of them. This reticence could be explained by his strong reluctance to interfere with the direction of his pupils and by his conviction that the twelve-tone method arose out of historical necessity:

> In the last hundred years, the concept of harmony has changed tremendously through the development of chromaticism. The idea that one basic tone, the root, dominated the construction of chords and regulated their succession—the concept of *tonality*—had to develop first into the concept of *extended tonality*. Very soon it became doubtful whether such a root still remained the centre to which every harmony and harmonic succession must be referred. Furthermore, it became doubtful whether a tonic appearing at the beginning, at the end, or at any other point really had a constructive meaning. Richard Wagner's harmony had promoted a change in the logic and constructive power of harmony. One of its consequences was the so-called *impressionistic* use of harmonies, especially practised by Debussy. His harmonies, without constructive meaning, often served the colouristic purpose of expressing moods and pictures. Moods and pictures, though extra-musical, thus became constructive elements, incorporated in the musical functions; they produced a sort of emotional comprehensibility. In this way, tonality was already dethroned in practice, if not in theory. This alone would perhaps not have caused a radical change in compositional technique. However, such a change became necessary when there occurred simultaneously a development which ended in what I call the *emancipation of the dissonance*.

Although Berg appears to have been less concerned than either Schoenberg or Webern with the compositional problems leading to the development of the twelve-tone method, it is possible that he was more intimately involved than was Webern in its beginnings. This alternative is suggested in a letter from Berg to his wife, dated 1 April 1923:

> Schoenberg was very nice and once more very friendly to me. But alas at the expense of other friends who (according to him) whenever he talked about his achievements in musical theory would always say: "Yes, I've done that too." As he doesn't expect this sort of thing from me, he wants to show me all his secrets in his new works.

It is not conclusively established by any textual evidence in the work of Berg that he was familiar with the details of twelve-tone composition before Schoenberg explained it to his followers. Although many passages in *Wozzeck* suggest an awareness of the concept of twelve-tone completion albeit within an otherwise tonalistic context, there is no indication that Berg was consistently attempting a substitution for the articulative possibilities of the tonal center. His experiment with the abbreviated style of Schoenberg's Opus 19 and many of Webern's pre-twelve-tone works was confined to the Clarinet Pieces,

Op. 5, and the *Altenberg Lieder*. Even after taking up the twelve-tone method, Berg never completely abandoned tonal concepts, preferring instead to suit the twelve-tone method to his own tonally-enhanced ideas in a way that went far beyond Schoenberg's adaption of tonally associated formal structures to twelve-tone composition. In his use of the twelve-tone idea, Berg never strictly adhered to the Schoenbergian method, using more than one set in a composition (something not done by Schoenberg) and, especially in the case of *Lulu,* interpolating passages of material that cannot strictly be termed twelve-tone at all.

Schoenberg accepted Berg's independent use of the method:

> I have to admit that Alban Berg, who was perhaps the least orthodox of us three—Webern, Berg and I—in his operas mixed pieces or parts of pieces of a distinct tonality with those which were distinctly non-tonal. He explained this, apologetically, by contending that as an opera composer he could not, for reasons of dramatic expression and characterization, renounce the contrast furnished by a change from major to minor.

> Though he was right as a composer, he was wrong theoretically. I have proved in my operas **Von Heute auf Morgen** and **Moses und Aron** that every expression and characterization can be produced with the style of free dissonance.

Berg may not have understood fully or cared about the theories motivating the genesis of the twelve-tone idea but rather adhered to it in his position of Schoenberg disciple or for other, also personal, reasons. His adoption of the twelve-tone method at a time when he was at the height of his success as a composer was made possible through his great originality and compositional flexibility. Although the twelve-tone method may not have been adopted with the same urgent necessity by Berg as by Schoenberg and Webern, it is perhaps in Berg's music that the twelve-tone method is used in the most refined and original manner, even if the composer himself may not have come to it spontaneously and from necessity. Certainly, as a composer, Berg was very conscious of the need to remain independent of the opinions of his mentor, as he stated repeatedly in his correspondence. It seems unlikely that he would have embraced the twelve-tone method purely from a loyalty to Schoenberg if he in fact failed to appreciate its possibilities.

> MAX DEUTSCH: You know the score of **Glückliche Hand?** That is the most important work of our century. The row technique is in it. So, . . . in 1923, when he came back from Amsterdam, he called us for [an] appointment for a meeting in Mödling, . . . in the Bernhardgasse 6 in Mödling. And he spoke the first words, . . . "I finally have found out that the new technique is the completion with twelve tones of the chromatic scale, but these twelve tones in interdependence from what"—that is, those were Schoenberg's words, and he added, "And with that, our music," he means Austrian music, "they have for fifty years the leadership."

That was the words of Schoenberg. . . .

JOAN ALLEN SMITH: Before this time, had he said anything to you about it?

DEUTSCH: Never! . . . Nothing! 1923, he told it and he wrote it down. That is the truth!

SMITH: Who was at the meeting where Schoenberg disclosed the twelve-tone method?

FELIX GREISSLE: . . . [People] close to Schoenberg like Wellesz, who had at one time studied a little with Schoenberg but then was not so close any more. . . . Then [Oskar] Adler was there. He was a friend of Schoenberg's youth—a doctor, a medical doctor—played the viola marvelously, and he was at the same time very much occupied with theosophy and astrology. He was a very unusual man. He was there. . . . George Szell composed at that time, but he was not there. Szell was in the other camp. Ja, Hauer, he was not on that day there, but a little later, he invited Hauer on one Sunday and again a lot of friends, and he said, you know, he and Hauer had found from another side almost the same thing, and he was very—and he acknowledged it very much. He did it also, you see—he wouldn't have done it, it would have looked bad, but if he did it openly and friendly, it looked much better. Hauer behaved badly, very badly. I never understood why he gave Hauer so much importance, because Hauer was a very bad composer—he was a terrible composer. . . .

SMITH: But Hauer did get the idea first, didn't he?

GREISSLE: Ja, he did it but it was absolutely— the genesis was so different. It was put together almost mechanically, you see, and with Schoenberg it was the result of coming to it through composition—Hauer through speculation. There was an enormous difference between the two. . . . Hauer was—I found him mediocre, really very stupid. You know, there is an excellent portrait of Hauer. There's a novel by Werfel, *Verdi*, and in there, I think in the fourth or fifth chapter, comes a German composer who befriends Verdi, and this is a portrait of Hauer—an excellent portrait of Hauer. I was there when Hauer was invited by Mrs. Mahler, who was married to Werfel at that time, and Hauer . . . started immediately talking about twelve tone and he never stopped. He wore everybody out. And Werfel was there and he listened. . . . And he wrote and the portrait is very good— better than almost anything else Werfel ever did.

SMITH: Did you have any idea that Schoenberg was working on something new before this meeting with the students?

ERWIN RATZ: Oh yes, he entertained ideas of it for many years. We see it in the works—what is the oratorio called?

SMITH: *Jakobsleiter*.
RATZ: Yes, yes. These ideas were already in preparation for a long time. It didn't happen overnight. Schoenberg had for many years—already during the war he was occupied with these ideas. The real revelation was . . . 1923. . . .

SMITH: I wonder if Schoenberg ever talked about this new thing to you while he was thinking about it.

RATZ: No, he spoke first about it after it was completely worked out. After he [had written] his first composition—that was the Suite, the Piano Suite, then he showed us the thing.

SMITH: At this meeting with the students, was everyone enthusiastic about it or did it seem very difficult?

RATZ: They really weren't students. There were— yes, I was also studying at the university at that time, but it was a matter of people who had a private interest. They had heard nothing about twelve tone. There was then the later circle of students, to some extent the older ones—there were Berg, Webern, Polnauer, and so forth.

SMITH: So then did he present this to you as something he had already thought out completely?

RUDOLF KOLISCH: Ja.

SMITH: Do you think he ever discussed his ideas with anyone during this period? It was all by himself? Not with Berg or Webern?

KOLISCH: No. In fact, it was only as a *fait accompli*. It was even presented in a very strange and solemn way. He called us all together, you know. It was Mödling. And he told us that he— but I don't know whether he called it—probably not discovery or invention, but he said he had found something which would assure the hegemony of German music for centuries. . . . Ja. That is true. That he really said, but . . . it's very strange, no? Don't you find it strange? . . . The particular perspective of assuring that the—

SMITH: How did people react? Was everyone very excited in a positive way?

KOLISCH: Well, there was only the small circle of his, you know. All of us were of course very excited about it. None of us had any idea what it really was.

SMITH: Did everyone accept it immediately and start working on his own piece or were there people who were skeptical?

KOLISCH: Well, there was no model yet at this time. There was no model which to follow. Of course I knew already. I had been thinking about it because I was in touch with Hauer. Hauer showed me his tropes, you know?

SMITH: And this was independently that you were in touch with Hauer? Did you perform his music?

KOLISCH: Also I did—as much as one could call

it—. It was really more demonstrations of the principle than music.

SMITH: Did Hauer himself consider them mere demonstrations or did he consider them important pieces?

KOLISCH: That is hard to say. Certainly important. He considered it important—very—completely convinced of—the importance of himself and of—and, in a way, it was important. But, whereas Schoenberg always emphasized the—what happened apart from this category, Hauer was completely absorbed in it. . . . The principle is the same, only Schoenberg composed music and used this—ja?—as a method of composition, whereas Hauer composed tropes—twelve-tone rows.

SMITH: Was Hauer at this meeting?

KOLISCH: No.

SMITH: He did meet with Schoenberg several times, didn't he?

KOLISCH: Oh yes. They were friends. . . . And Schoenberg took him completely seriously.

HANS CURJEL: I was in Donaueschingen, the music festival, in '24; there Schoenberg was playing his Serenade and in the same program was Hauer—not the same evening. And they met at Donaueschingen, and I remember there was a big discussion in a café . . . with Schoenberg and Hauer, and the atmosphere was not too friendly—was not at all too friendly.

SMITH: Do you remember what was said?

CURJEL: It was a discussion about how near Hauer and Schoenberg were, and everybody—Hauer said, "I am the inventor" and Schoenberg said, "I am the inventor."

SMITH: And they argued there in the café?

CURJEL: Yes, it was very lively. There were Schoenberg, Hauer, Hindemith, and a few people—two or three—and I.

GREISSLE: I think he must have made up his mind not to tell anybody. He had a reason later to do it. And the reason was that he—I told you that he didn't read any books about music and so on. But he came across an article of Hauer, and then he saw all of a sudden. So he invited all his pupils and friends, and he told us what twelve tone was. He explained it. We were in part puzzled and part surprised. I was not because I knew already that there was something, and even that it was twelve tone. And there were degrees of acceptance, and there was one who couldn't accept it so easily. Guess who?

SMITH: Perhaps Berg?

GREISSLE: No. Berg didn't have a hard time at all. Berg accepted it only in part, huh? He had a

twelve-tone row and he made a, as he called it, a palette of colors. And he used it in different combinations, but he was not twelve-tone. Almost never twelve-tone with him. No, Webern had a hard time—terribly hard time. . . .

SMITH: Do you think he accepted it because he decided eventually that it was the right thing to do?

GREISSLE: Ja. That it was the right thing to do. Oh, yes, of course, yes. Naturally. The only thing is that Webern did nothing of which he wasn't sure that Schoenberg would approve of it. Webern was never independent—his whole life, he wasn't independent. Wait a minute, from 1933 to 1938, ja. In 1933, Schoenberg left Germany and came to this country, and I lived very close to Webern. So I saw him almost every day, and I saw the dependence. I don't blame him for it, you know. I mean, still he was a great composer. Well let's say—I don't like to use the word "great" easily. He used to write Schoenberg in Los Angeles, and Schoenberg never answered letters very frequently, and the longer Webern would have to wait for an answer the more angry he got and the more things he found that weren't so bad about the Nazis and so on. And Schoenberg wrote a letter and he got the letter and everything was all right. . . . Webern was sometimes towards friends very open and his innermost thoughts would just spill out. But between thought and action is an enormous difference. And that was there, you see; he never would have done anything against Schoenberg. But he was hurt if Schoenberg didn't write him—he was deeply hurt because everything—his belief in himself depended on how Schoenberg [saw him]. . . . And of course, when he said something uncontrolled, it didn't mean that he actually thought it.

SMITH: Well, do you think that it would have been possible for Webern to decide against writing twelve-tone?

GREISSLE: No, no, impossible! Totally impossible.

SMITH: Webern seems very remote to me. Was he that way in person? Was he very restrained?

KOLISCH: Ja, ja, he was that. He was even inhibited. But enormously strong—very strong person. . . .

SMITH: One of the impressions that I have definitely received is that he changed his mind frequently.

KOLISCH: Entirely wrong. . . . I know no other person who—who changed his mind so little. . . .

SMITH: Did Schoenberg appreciate Webern's work?

KOLISCH: Oh, ja.

SMITH: But Schoenberg was never influenced by what other people were composing. Do you believe that Webern was himself influenced much by Schoenberg?

KOLISCH: Well, completely. . . .

SMITH: Then how can you say that he was a strong person when he was so completely influenced?

KOLISCH: You see, he established his own orbit—ja?—around the planet. The planet was still in the center.

SMITH: Did Schoenberg ever discuss twelve-tone music?

RATZ: Well, you see, I was there when he gave his first lecture on twelve-tone music. He called his group of students together and said he would like to talk about these new principles. . . . Schoenberg always refused to do twelve-tone analyses. He said it was a purely technical matter which isn't anyone's business, and it certainly has nothing to do with art; it's as if someone wanted to develop a philosophy of C-major.

CLARA STEUERMANN: My husband told me that when the first performances of *Gurrelieder* were being prepared and a whole group of them traveled together, I forget which city it was, but they went together to hear the performance and to hear the rehearsals. And at one of the rehearsals—they were having difficulty at the time because this chorus in the last part, the voices were not finding their pitches. And so there was Schoenberg sitting with—I don't know, Jalowetz, Erwin Stein, Steuermann, and whoever else was there, and Schoenberg was sort of thinking out loud and said, "I wonder what I could do, what instrument I could use to reinforce the voices to help them to find their pitches." And Steuermann, who was then a very young man, and who had not been with Schoenberg very long, sort of said under his breath "harp," because it occurred to him that after all the harp has a sort of indeterminate quality and would blend with the voices. Whereupon, Schoenberg turned around and said, "Why did you say that? How did you think of that? How did you know what was in my mind?" He was very disturbed because apparently he had also thought of using harp, so he was not at all charmed by the idea that someone else could have that idea also. So it seems scarcely possible to me that, with something like this twelve-tone idea, he would have discussed it *a priori* with any one of his students. Now, my husband did say that he had a feeling that Webern may have begun to sense certain implications of the consequences of atonal writing. But as far as I know from anyone connected with it, there is no question whatever that this was indeed Schoenberg's unique intellectual property at the time that he presented it.

BRUNO SEIDLHOFER: Berg was, in my opinion, by far the most musically gifted of the three. He obeyed; Schoenberg was a god to him. Even when one talked with him—ah, Schoenberg, ah, whatever Schoenberg said, that was it. . . . Also other people said that who knew Schoenberg—. He had an enormous will, had Schoenberg—influence! He was a great man. He was above all many-sided, I think; he painted fantastically well also, and he composed very well, but unfortunately, its grounding on a twelve-tone basis shifted everything off-balance. I don't think much of it.

SMITH: So you think that Berg really didn't want to do twelve-tone composition?

STEFAN ASKENASE: He would never have invented it. That is sure, because Schoenberg was a very strong personality and he was very much influenced by him. If he had not been influenced—let's say even if he had been living in the same period and had not met Schoenberg, I don't think he would have become a twelve-tone composer. That's my feeling.

SMITH: Do you think that this relationship with Schoenberg was a bad thing for Berg?

ASKENASE: As I said, . . . he could see that it was—well, I can't say a bad thing, but something—etwas was ihn belastete. He had the feeling of a weight—something that [weighed] on him.

SOMA MORGENSTERN: Alban usually—all of his life, most of his works he did on vacation in the country. He composed—very few things composed in Vienna. The most of the work he did on vacation.

SMITH: What did he do when he was in Vienna?

MORGENSTERN: Oh, he was teaching, he was working continuously, but he didn't do the first version, you know. But he worked in Vienna. But the very first composition, he always made on vacation.

SMITH: When you first began to play twelve-tone works, did you approach the music in the same way more or less that you would have approached a tonal work?

KOLISCH: Yes.

SMITH: And when Schoenberg would rehearse you, did he rehearse in the same way that he had rehearsed tonal music?

KOLISCH: Ja. He even refused to let us in on the secrets, you know? You already knew that. . . .

SMITH: Why do you think he had this attitude?

KOLISCH: Well, he had it mainly because this method for composing was so much misunderstood and taken as . . . a system and a recipe for composing . . . It was not necessary with us, of course. It was an error, which he admitted. It was, you know, a principle which he really carried through. He did not talk about it—and much later, you know, and not very deeply. And you know he never taught it . . .

never even wrote it.

SMITH: I understand that Schoenberg was very particular in his rehearsals.

EUGEN LEHNER: Very, ja. Especially when he was younger. And naturally, when he dealt with music which he understood. His later music, he obviously didn't understand.

SMITH: What do you mean by that?

LEHNER: . . . I maintain that all these things that Schoenberg did that were rationalized, it was only [*ex*] *post facto,* not before the fact. . . . I see an incredible resemblance between Bruckner and Schoenberg, even physical. . . . Both were the same naïve, inspired composers who, when the inspiration came, they just sat down and they were writing with an incredible speed music. But then, when the final double bar came, then the difference set in. The Austrian peasant, the Catholic Austrian peasant [Bruckner], when he finally did the final double bar, knelt down and thanked the Lord that he deemed his body right to be his mouthpiece. The intellectual Jewish Schoenberg did the same, but something else happened to it. He was too curious. When he, next day, when he surveyed what he did, he was astonished. "What the hell did I do here? What does it mean? That's not what I wanted to write. Why did I do it?" . . . That's how I feel it must have happened. And then, out of his intellectualism, the rationalization and the theories, building theories, came into the picture. But [*ex*] *post facto.* And the more, I have an indirect indication of it when I see certain compositions. When I take a piece like the Wind Quintet. It's worthwhile studying this fact because you see that is a piece that I have the impression that was written with premeditation. Because that was just about when circumstances forced him to formulate, unfortunately much too prematurely, a theory about the twelve-tone. . . . Well anyway, when circumstances forced him, very, very prematurely, to formulate the theory of it, then I think the Wind Quintet must have been the piece to which he sat down with that in mind, you know, to prove it. Because, if you study it, you can see the really practically infantile simplicity and completely guileless proceeding—how he applied that.

SMITH: When you say, "forced by circumstances," are you speaking of Hauer's activities?

LEHNER: Partly that and partly also the interests of all his—don't forget that Schoenberg was a passionate teacher. Don't forget that Berg and Webern, they were more than pupils, they were absolutely dependent on Schoenberg. . . . Schoenberg was absolutely the most essential part of their lives. . . . So it's easy to imagine how such a person, when he hits upon a fascinating idea, that he was unable to keep it for himself and not theoreticize and talk about it endlessly and formulate it and so on.

SMITH: After he started writing twelve-tone music,

was his approach to analysis of twelve-tone music very similar to his analysis of tonal music?

GREISSLE: . . . I can't tell you. First of all, you see, the analysis of a piece always depends upon what the piece is. So, if it is like other music, then it [the analysis] will be like [that] of other music. You mean, did he follow the same principles? Yes, of course. And always—it was frequently—almost always—the interaction between the theme or the melodic line of the harmony, you see, which in twelve-tone counterpoint didn't count so much any more, but all that was going on, what the events forced the composer to do.

SMITH: Have you seen many of Schoenberg's sketches?

DEUTSCH: Frankly, no. But I can tell you something which happened with me and him alone. One day, after the war—1918, 1919—I was very—because I was an injured soldier, he asked me to come to Mödling. I was alone with him. He had something to tell me concerning his son. I was the teacher of his son. But not a musical teacher—in Latin and Greek, in *mathematique* and so on. He chose me for his tutor. The other story! He was alone in his room, and suddenly, he rises up and goes to his armoire, took out a score. . . . I was the first man to see the score of the *Jakobsleiter.* . . . And I have seen, in this first page, corrections. I had not—I was not able—I was so emotional for that that I cannot ask him, so he told me, "Very good, huh?" That's all. I was so emotional. And that is what I have seen of his own works. Nothing—I am not Webern, and not Berg. And none of the others have seen it.

SMITH: Did Schoenberg ever discuss his sketches and unfinished pieces with other people or was he very private?

GREISSLE: Occasionally he did, yes. Occasionally he did and he even told us what he had done and why he had done it. I heard quite a lot about the Serenade. And—he showed us at one time the slow movement of the Suite for clarinets, strings, and piano. . . .

SMITH: Did you ever have a chance to find out how Schoenberg himself went about writing a piece?

GREISSLE: Ja, at one time, he said how he invented it. This was much later. At one time, there was a contract at Universal Edition that some of his works had to appear in transcriptions. And we all got it distributed among us, and Steuermann got *Die glückliche Hand* and *Erwartung.* Jalowetz got the *Pelleas und Melisande,* and I got . . . the Second String Quartet. The First String Quartet, nobody wanted it I think. And when I worked on it, I had to show him every movement, and when it came to the second movement, he looked and I said to him, "I don't know how you wrote this. . . ." So he said to me, "The first time I had in mind nothing but the motion. Something was moving in eighths, and fast eighths, and only out of this motion, the theme finally evolved, and when I had the theme, it was a regular composition." He said it's the piece that was one he always wanted to write and never succeeded. . . . I think that the work came to him as a whole concept, so that he didn't make any mistake when he worked on it because this was always in his mind somehow. But, it went from measure to measure. I never saw him. I lived in the house, and I saw how he worked for instance on the woodwind quintet, and it was from measure to measure. In the evening, he stopped and it continued there and he never—oh, he did a little erasing once in awhile when he wrote something down wrong but very little only—only when there was a slip of the pencil. Otherwise, it came out of his mind. He was at that time already—when he was at the last movement, he knew the row in all its forms by heart. He didn't have to write it down again. Webern never knew. Webern always had to write it down.

SMITH: Did Schoenberg make charts of the different set forms?

GREISSLE: In the beginning, he made a chart for himself. And then, when he started working he knew it by heart. Webern never knew it by heart. Webern used too many forms, too many forms—four or five transpositions and so on for one small piece. I always remember Webern's big boards on the piano. . . . And there were all the rows in all their forms. In the middle, was a small sheet of music paper. There were four notes, and it was the composition. And when I visited him three days later, there were two more notes. And, look, one shouldn't make any jokes about somebody. It is none of our business how he does it. The result is what counts. And the result was there, but it was very hard for Webern—very difficult. It was not difficult for Schoenberg. Schoenberg really wrote with comparative ease. When he had a problem, it was certainly not a problem because he was not able to put it down on paper. Never. This was never true. Schoenberg, of all the musicians I have met in my life, had the greatest technique—fantastic technique—with greatest ease! . . .

SMITH: I know that there are some sketches in the Schoenberg collection. Would you say that in these sketchbooks the materials are quite well developed when they are first written down.

GREISSLE: Sketches? Very little—almost immediately the whole piece. And I said because he had this idea in total of something—of a Gestalt of a whole piece—and he worked from there, the sketches were in his mind. . . . The image was there already. He didn't need to sketch.

LEHNER: Once, we spent a summer with Steuermann and Kolisch . . . down in the mountains in a village, and we analyzed the whole Third Quartet, bar by bar, note to note, and in these nearly thousand bars, to our great satisfaction, we found two places where there is a misprint or, if not a misprint, Schoenberg made a grave mistake . . . So, no sooner we came to Berlin, the first time we went to Schoenberg, we . . . showed it to him. "Is that a misprint?" . . . I don't know the notes; let's say it was an F-sharp into an F-natural and a B-flat instead of a B-natural. . . . And so he called his wife to bring the manuscript. So she found the manuscript. " . . . That's correct; it is F-sharp." "And this other place?" "No, no, that's correct." So, we said, "Oh, it's not a misprint, then it's a mistake, because it must be an F-natural and a B-flat." And then we explained to him and I don't know, that's the third transposition and that is the fifth note. . . . And Schoenberg gets mad—red in the face! "You want to say—if I hear an F-sharp, I will write an F-sharp. If I hear an F-natural, I will write an F-natural. Just because of your stupid . . . theory, are you telling to me what I should write?"

BENAR HEIFETZ: You know, everybody thinks about Schoenberg, his kind of composing—twelve-tone system—was far away from the music but it's not true. He could sit the whole evening and listen to a Beethoven quartet or a Mozart quartet, and we always have to know it because he really loved it. . . . So, since Schoenberg still was in Vienna, we were very close together. We came always together; he was very *gastfreundlich*. He was a wonderful host, and I remember the way he used to say—we were all very arrogant because, under Schoenberg and Alban Berg, nobody could compose so—but he always said, "There is no bad composition. If the composer doesn't have talent, he knows how to write. He has a gift to write. Sometimes he does it, he has a talent but he doesn't know how to write. So every composition has something good." You wouldn't believe that Schoenberg would say this. And, for instance, he always used to ask us, "Why don't you play [an] Edvard Grieg quartet?" "Schoenberg, how could we play such music today?" And he said, "You know, I always hear the way he composed it, and when he composed it, the harmonies were absolutely new to us." So he was very gracious and very—he hated the world because they hated him. He was suspicious and very stubborn.

HUMPHREY SEARLE: I think the interesting thing was that he [Webern] didn't feel that atonal music and twelve-tone music were a break from the past; they were sort of a continuation of it. That was sort of his point of view.

SMITH: At the time that it all happened, did you feel that this was a development—a natural development—out of what he had been doing before, or that this was something new—that it was more like an invention?

KOLISCH: Ja, it appeared as something new. We could not see this from this perspective yet. That appeared really as something very fundamentally drastic.

OSKAR KOKOSCHKA: [About twelve-tone music] And that we knew, so there was no discussion. The past was active at that time still. For us, it was the past. It was out of discussion. We talked about when he wrote something—this passage, whether it expresses what he meant to do—about such things we were talking—would it be better in that way or in that way and so on. But mostly, they played. Bach he played. He liked Bach very much. . . . These tendencies like Poulenc or like the Russian [Prokofiev], that wasn't clean for us. Purist he was in that way, and me too, of course, and that's why we liked each other, because we were both in different ways common. . . .

SMITH: When you came back in 1924, Schoenberg had already developed the twelve-tone method. Did he talk to you about this or did you have any feelings about it at the time?

KOKOSCHKA: We all thought it's *the* music, so there was no dispute about it. It was just *the* fact. All the others were behind and didn't understand it, so we thought. . . . But we all agreed that the late Beethoven was the tower. We even thought Schoenberg was building on the late Beethoven, and not only building on it but now trying to open our ears for Beethoven. That's what we thought, at least I understood it in that way. As a nonmusician, I didn't care for these fights between the musicians—didn't know even about it. I only knew that Alban Berg, for example—and I think Schoenberg thought the same way—that he wanted to be on the safe side, so he was inclined to be the bridge between the past and this new music. Just as I thought new painting is when you paint what you really see and not what you have learned or routine or convention—what you really not only see but in a way feel as the expression of the period in which you live—the *Geist,* the spirit, of the period—so he thought he reflects in his music the spirit of his time and all the others didn't. . . . We were like *Auswanderer* . . . like immigrants, but in your own town. Of course afterwards, they discovered that we had been the real ones, but it's always the same.

David Hamilton (essay date 1989)

SOURCE: "Schoenberg's First Opera," in *The Opera Quarterly,* Vol. 6, No. 3, Spring, 1989, pp. 48-58.

[*In the following essay, Hamilton concludes that Schoenberg's opera* Erwartung, *while highly original, owes more to the influence of his contemporaries than to his later, more radical, atonal music.*]

Each of Arnold Schoenberg's four operas is *sui generis.* The first two one-acters, **Erwartung** (1909) and **Die glückliche Hand** (1910-1913), stem from his most experimental period and break new ground both musically and dramatically. The former is an intense, apparently freely associative psychological drama, the latter an autobiographical allegory with a more self-evident musical structure. The one-act comedy **Von heute auf morgen** (1928-1929), the first opera written using the twelve-tone technique, belongs theatrically to the *Zeitoper* tradition.

The libretto by Gertrude Schoenberg, the composer's second wife (under the pseudonym "Max Bionda"), was, like that of Strauss's *Intermezzo,* suggested by an incident from contemporary life—in this case, the domestic affairs of Schoenberg's colleague Franz Schreker; formally, it reflects the neoclassical practice characteristic of the contemporaneous instrumental music. Finally, the two-act torso of the incomplete **Moses und Aron** (1930-1932), a profound and disturbed exploration of the impossibility of communicating great truths, religious and otherwise, presents an equally clearly articulated musical design.

Besides the sheer practical difficulty of these operas, two world wars and the consequences of Nazi racial and artistic policies also militated against frequent productions and inhibited the growth of any continuous performing tradition for Schoenberg's operas. The first two did not reach the stage until 1924 and accumulated relatively few productions in the years remaining before Hitler's advent (most notably, as a double bill at Berlin's Kroll Opera in 1930). *Erwartung* has acquired some currency since 1950, both in concert form and as part of "contemporary" double and triple bills, while the progress of **Die glückliche Hand** has been impeded by its obscurer dramatic character and by Schoenberg's elaborately specific staging and lighting conceptions. **Von heute auf morgen** came before the public more rapidly (Frankfurt, 1930), but has been seen only rarely since; perhaps the current revival of interest in *Zeitoper* will bring it up for reappraisal, though past verdicts on the stageworthiness of its comedy have been less than encouraging. **Moses und Aron,** not available for performance as long as Schoenberg lived and hoped to compose music for the brief final act, was first heard in concert form in 1954 and staged in Zurich three years later. Since then it has become established in the international repertory (lately and conspicuously at the Salzburg Festival); the New York stage premiere is promised in 1989 by the New York City Opera.

By the time this article appears in print, *Erwartung* will have received its New York stage premiere (at the Metropolitan Opera), and, as a favored item in Hildegard Behren's repertory for orchestral-concert engagements in the 1980s, has been heard if not seen in other American cities. Within the context of Schoenberg's compositional development it has long held a special place as the most extended and "athematic" example of his "atonal" style; though recent studies have revealed a multitude of subsurface motivic and harmonic connections, its uniqueness subsists. Less often has it been viewed in the perspective of general operatic history, in which regard its designation as a "monodrama" is immediately a red herring. The standard music-historical reference books tell us that a "monodrama" was a melodrama—a theatrical work *spoken* over musical accompaniment—for a single character.

The sketchy historical record indicates that the designation, like the subject matter itself, originated with the text's author, Marie Pappenheim (1882-1966). Some fifty years after the event, the musicologist Helmut Kirchmeyer recorded her account of *Erwartung*'s origins: "On a summer holiday in Steinakirchen in lower Austria, where Stein, Berg, Mopp, and other artists were staying near the Schoenberg and Zemlinsky families, Schoenberg suddenly challenged the young poetess: 'Then write me an opera libretto, young lady. . . . Write whatever you wish, I need a libretto.' Marie Pappenheim responded: 'I certainly cannot write a libretto, at most I could write a monodrama.'" According to Kirchmeyer, Pappenheim then believed that she had invented the word monodrama (presumably intending it to denote a "one-character drama") and was thus unaware of its music-historical background. Schoenberg may have been similarly ignorant, though he definitely knew the then-still-active tradition of *melo*drama, exemplified by such recitations with music as Strauss's *Enoch Arden* (1897) and Max von Schillings's *Hexenlied* (1904) and, in the theater, by the more specifically notated *Sprechgesang* in the first version (1897) of Humperdinck's *Königskinder,* which he emulated in the final part of **Gurre-Lieder** and would develop to powerful effect in **Pierrot lunaire**. However, *Erwartung* is *sung* throughout.

Here is the rest of what Pappenheim told Kirchmeyer about the opera's origins:

> Two days later, Marie Pappenheim went to friends at Traunkirchen, and there wrote the libretto for **Erwartung**. She had experienced the forest a year earlier in Ischl, where every night around 10:30 she had to go through a stretch of dark forest on her way home; therein she found the plot of the drama. . . . Lying in the grass, she wrote in pencil on large sheets of paper, and made no copy; she hardly read through what she had written, and expected that Schoenberg, whom she did not yet know very well, would surely make proposals for changes. . . . Three weeks later, she returned to Steinakirchen, firmly believing that her poem was no opera libretto. But Schoenberg took it from her page by page (she wanted to correct it), and composed it immediately.

In 1909 Pappenheim was a medical student in Vienna, interested in literature and the arts; some of her poems were published in Karl Kraus's *Die Fackel.* At this point she was not entirely confident of her literary abilities, as her letter of 3 October to Schoenberg at Steinakirchen suggests: "I am writing out the final alterations on a separate piece of paper. Naturally I don't want you to have to work any more. I have shown it to no one, not even Zemlinsky. Certainly it does not please *me.* I did not write earlier, as I was very agitated. Now I am 50 percent better. That you have already finished gives me new courage." Although her medical degree, conferred the following year, was in skin diseases, Pappenheim's older brother Martin was a psychiatrist, and both must have been well aware of the psychoanalytic movement—indeed, their second cousin Berta Pappenheim had been the pseudonymous "Anna O" of a historically central analysis by Josef Breuer, described in Freud and Breuer's 1895 *Studies in Hysteria.*

The single character of **Erwartung** is an unnamed woman; searching in a forest for her lover, she is gripped in rapid alternation by violent apprehension and rapt reminiscence. Progressively, fear gains the upper hand, and after three relatively short scenes in the forest she emerges in a clearing before a house, dress torn, hair in disarray, face and hands bleeding. Here she discovers a body, which turns out to be that of her lover—the only event in the drama that takes place outside of her mind (or does it?). Following this traumatic identification, her mind careens through states of increasing bitterness and suspicion, alighting upon past hints that the lover might have been betraying her with another woman. Her final words may imply that she now denies the reality of his death:

> Oh, bist du da . . .
> Ich suchte . . .
>
> Oh, are you there . . .
> I was looking . . .

In fact, the reality of the entire action is ambiguous, at the least. At the time of the Kroll Opera performances Schoenberg noted that "the whole drama *can* be understood as a nightmare of anxiety [*Angsttraum*]." In a roughly contemporaneous essay he wrote: "In **Erwartung** the aim is to represent in *slow motion* everything that occurs during a single second of maximum spiritual excitement, stretching it out to half an hour." Subsequent writers have speculated that the protagonist herself may have murdered the man out of jealousy, prior to the opera's beginning, and is returning to the scene of the crime. These interpretations are not, of course, incompatible.

The woman's situation in part parallels that of Isolde, but filtered through the distorting mirror of intense psychological stress. At measures 237-42 she retrospectively imagines the reunion she had expected with her absent lover, reminding us of Isolde and Tristan in act 2 of Wagner's opera:

> Der Abend war so voll Frieden . . .
> Ich schaute und wartete . . .
> Über die Gartenmauer dir entgegen . . .
> so niedrig ist sie . . .
> Und dann winkten wir beide . . .
>
> The evening was so peaceful . . .
> I looked and waited . . .
> Across the garden wall, toward you . . .
> so low it is . . .
> And then we both waved . . .

By the time of this fleeting vision, however, she is virtually in the position of Isolde in act 3, who came "to die with Tristan true" but found him at the point of death. Pappenheim's woman accuses her lover of depriving her of "the favor of being allowed to die with you" ("Oh! nicht einmal die Gnade, mit dir sterben zu dürfen"; mm. 351-56). Near the end of **Erwartung** (mm. 401-09), *Tristan*'s central imagery of night and day, light and darkness, is particularly conspicuous:

Das Licht wird für alle kommen . . .
aber ich allein in meiner Nacht? . . .
Der Morgen trennt uns . . . immer der Morgen . . .
So schwer küsst du zum Abschied . . .
Wieder ein ewiger Tag des Wartens . . .

The light will come for everyone . . .
but I, alone in my night? . . .
The morning separates us . . . always
    the morning . . .
So heavily you kiss me farewell . . .
Yet another endless day of waiting . . .

Moreover, the characterization of the "other woman" as "die Frau mit den weissen Armen" recalls an element of the Tristan legend, albeit one not used by Wagner, the rival Iseult of the White Hands.

This should occasion no surprise, for Wagner's opera—its words as well as its music—was the governing image of sexual passion in the culture that brought forth *Erwartung*. Even closer than *Tristan* to the world·of abnormal psychology that Pappenheim's libretto inhabits were the then-new one-act operas of Richard Strauss. Especially if she were herself the cause of his death, *Erwartung*'s protagonist apostrophizing her lover's corpse resembles Salome, and their lines once almost converge: "Was soll ich allein hier tun?" (mm. 392-93) echoes Salome's "Was soll ich jetzt tun, Jochanaan?" The moon that literally presides over *Salome*'s action is also on hand at the beginning of *Erwartung,* vanishing in the second scene and reappearing in the third. *Elektra,* first performed in Vienna the preceding March, finds further echoes; Hofmannsthal's drama deals more directly with its characters' neurotic concerns than does *Salome,* in which Wilde's penchant for ornamental verbiage and parallel structure gets in the way of psychological truth.

But the *Elektra* libretto, too, is structured and "artificial" by comparison to Pappenheim's erratically gushing stream of incomplete sentences and freeassociative phrases, as her protagonist's mind darts between past and present, desire and fear. What she gave Schoenberg was truly not a libretto, but instead an interior monologue, with no distance, none of the objectivity required by a drama of characters who must display external selves to each other and to the spectator. In previous operas that objectivity occasionally gives way to the special, close-up focus of the soliloquy or scene, but in *Erwartung* that focus is both normative and exclusive, persisting for the entire opera. Nor does Pappenheim's libretto indulge in artifices of verbal structure and parallelism. Its imagery, however conditioned by the period of its origin, offers itself as symptomatic rather than symbolic, as raw mental data rather than metaphor.

Schoenberg's response to this unique text was equally extraordinary. In 1946 he wrote that "I personally belong to those who generally write very fast, whether it is 'cerebral' counterpoint or 'spontaneous' melody," and he cited *Erwartung* as an example, claiming that he wrote its nearly thirty minutes of music in just fourteen days. The first page of the composition draft in short score (see illustration) is dated 27 August 1909, and the end of the work 12 September, which actually makes a total of seventeen days; the manuscript full score was finished a few weeks later, on 4 October. As Charles Rosen has observed, when Schoenberg "lost the thread of a piece, he could almost never pick it up again without disaster," and fortunately no Austrian equivalent of Coleridge's "person on business from Porlock" interrupted this period of extreme concentration, though in 1940 Schoenberg told his class at UCLA that "when he was about halfway through, he found something in the text that didn't seem to fit the rest, so lost a whole day correcting that. He had to write to Marie P. about it and wait for her answer." According to Josef Rufer, Pappenheim's manuscript text includes "many cuts and alterations in Schoenberg's handwriting, and several musical sketches at various points in the text."

As already noted, *Erwartung*'s reputation as "athematic" and "atonal" has eventually yielded to analytic efforts; certain motivic cells (among them tri-tone-plus-semitone, minor-third-plus-semitone) pervade the texture both horizontally and vertically. Occasional suggestions of Schoenberg's favored D minor come to a head near the end in the quotation from the song "Am Wegrand" (originally in that key), at "Tausend Menschen ziehn vorüber" (m. 411). The motivic and harmonic correspondences are close enough to the surface to bring about consistency, yet too ephemeral to afford the security—the formal bearings, the sense of location within the piece's progress—we are accustomed to receive from explicit themes and from procedures such as repetitions and symmetries, abjured in the music of *Erwartung*.

This is intentional, of course, and appropriate to an opera in which the time scale is not realistic, but purely psychological: to a mind at sea, buffeted by conflicting impressions of nature and spontaneous irruptions from the subconscious, the flow of consciousness is constantly unordered and surprising. Schoenberg has captured this with remarkable fidelity, so that even after repeated hearings we can hardly help experiencing the music's progression as still startling. (This characteristic definitely complicates performance. In a recent conversation James Levine reported—and concurred with—Pierre Boulez's view that *Erwartung* is one of the two most challenging pieces to conduct from memory, because there is no ordered repetition of elements.) That music influences our perception of time is a truism; *Erwartung*'s aggressively heterogeneous aspect effectively numbs the listener's ability to measure the passage of time.

Erwartung isn't formless, but the dimensions of the formal units are small—as brief as a few measures each—and they aren't articulated in traditional ways, via cadences or symmetries. That many of these segments center around a leading melodic component should help, but will do so only if the performance is really well prepared;

too often, those melodic components fail to emerge from the orchestral polyphony, despite the cautionary *Hauptstimme* markings in Schoenberg's full score. Again, the performance difficulty is a necessary consequence of the special expressive task Schoenberg has undertaken. For maximum timbral diversity he generally uses the large orchestra as a repository from which to draw ever-fresh chamber ensembles for successive formal units. The players must therefore continually readjust to "new" colleagues with whom they are playing and trying to balance lines—quite a contrast to conventionally scored repertory, whose relatively standardized orchestra-tional practices (not to mention, in most cases, the works themselves) they have long since internalized.

Yet, for all its originality, Schoenberg's first opera remains fundamentally within the operatic aesthetic promulgated by Wagner in doctrine and example, and subscribed to in the present century by Strauss and Berg among others (though rejected by Debussy and Stravinsky): structural and emotional weight concentrated in the orchestra, formal units linked to yield an uninterrupted composition, intensively motivic textures, the strong didactic intent inherited from Beethoven's high ethical concerns. Its three successors would further extend that tradition, if each in a specific direction.

Robin Gail Schulze (essay date 1992)

SOURCE: "Design in Motion: Words, Music, and the Search for Coherence in the Works of Virginia Woolf and Arnold Schoenberg," in *Studies in the Literary Imagination,* Vol. XXV, No. 2, Fall, 1992, pp. 5-22

[*In the following essay, Schulze examines the influence of Schoenberg's musical theory on the works of Virginia Woolf.*]

Academics, alas, can be surprisingly narrow-minded. Shaped by our institutions, we have a tendency to divide ideas into neat little teachable, publishable packages, defining ourselves and our thoughts in terms of time periods, genres, continents, languages, theories, departments, and disciplines. Such separations certainly make the work of knowing easier, but they often lead us to read only part of a complex story. The period now roughly defined as "modern," from the late 1800s to the Second World War, happily and frustratingly resists every arbitrary boundary the academy attempts to draw. Modernism, modernist literature, call it what you will, occurs in vastly different forms in many different countries. Authors borrow freely from other arts and across disciplines, experimenting in a variety of languages and media. Poetry becomes prose, literature becomes music, music mimics painting, American writers live in England, France, Italy, and Germany, and the "beginning" and "end" of modernist writing remain tantalizingly elusive and ambiguous. T.S. Eliot's poetry speaks to the slipperiness of academic distinctions. His poems serve scholars as examples of both British and American verse, his

plays appear in both drama and poetry courses, his work is read as both staunchly elitist and decadently subversive, he remains a Monarchist Anglican from London and a rebel from St. Louis, Missouri. Attempting to determine the general tendencies of such a lively period and such perplexing authors boggles the mind. To think about the "modern period" at all, one must think broadly and widely, just the sort of thing that we scholars seem to hate most.

The fact remains, however, that thinking broadly and widely is just what many modernist authors did best. Fed up with the conventions governing their work and their lives, they wandered across boundaries of time and place, borrowing from sister arts, rummaging the cupboards of the distant past, exploring non-western cultures, casting and recasting themselves and their art in an ongoing intellectual journey that demanded and valued change. One of the most vigorous such explorers of the modern period was Virginia Woolf. Like many of her modernist colleagues, Woolf did not divide her life into disciplines. Hungry for new forms that would not duplicate past repressions, Woolf embarked on an experimental interdisciplinary voyage that eventually led her to consider words as music.

It is certainly nothing new to say that from 1925 to 1931, roughly the years between her completion of *Mrs. Dalloway* and her creation of *The Waves,* Virginia Woolf became increasingly dissatisfied with the conventional form of the novel. Woolf's criticism, letters, and diaries of the period all reveal her growing distaste for the constraints of chronological plot—this happened, then that happened—and detailed narrative. In her much-quoted 1925 essay, "Modern Fiction," Woolf paused to consider her artistic development in light of her paunchier Victorian contemporaries. Leveling her pen at the literary abuses of Arnold Bennett and the "materialist" school, Woolf's now famous commentary shows her deepening sense that the novel must evolve to fit the fragmentation of the time.

> Whether we call it life or spirit, truth or reality, this, the essential thing, has moved off, or on, and refuses to be contained any longer in such ill-fitting vestments as we provide. Nevertheless, we go on perseveringly, conscientiously, constructing our two and thirty chapters after a design which more and more ceases to resemble the vision in our minds. So much of the enormous labour of proving the solidity, the likeness to life, of the story is not merely labour thrown away but labour misplaced to the extent of obscuring and blotting out the light of the conception. The writer seems constrained, not by his own free will but by some powerful and unscrupulous tyrant who has him in thrall to provide a plot, to provide comedy, tragedy, love interest, and an air of probability embalming the whole so impeccable that if all his figures were to come to life they would find themselves dressed down to the last button of their coats in the fashion of the hour. The tyrant is obeyed; the novel is done to a turn. But sometimes, more and more

often as time goes by, we suspect a momentary
doubt, a spasm of rebellion, as the pages fill themselves in the customary way. Is life like this? Must
novels be like this? (*The Common Reader*)

Clearly, the answer from Woolf's perspective is no, novels need not be "like this," they need not adhere to a
single chronological narrative full of boring details that
leave the characters more dead than alive. Woolf pictures
Bennett and company as vassals of an autocratic dictator
who insists that there must be *one* kind of order, *one*
definition of "real," *one* plot to govern the whole. "Done
to a turn," such novels follow a given recipe to perfection, but they result in a monotonous mental meatloaf.
Woolf continues:

> Look within and life, it seems, is very far from
> being "like this." Examine for a moment an
> ordinary mind on an ordinary day. The mind
> receives a myriad impressions—trivial, fantastic,
> evanescent, or engraved with the sharpness of
> steel. From all sides they come, an incessant
> shower of innumerable atoms; and as they fall, as
> they shape themselves into the life of Monday or
> Tuesday, the accent falls differently from of old;
> the moment of importance came not here but there;
> so that if a writer were a free man and not a slave,
> if he could write what he chose, not what he must,
> if he could base his work upon his own feeling
> and not upon convention, there would be no plot,
> no comedy, no tragedy, no love interest or
> catastrophe in the accepted style, and perhaps not
> a single button sewn on as the Bond Street tailors
> would have it.

Using Bennett as a foil, Woolf throws off her chains only
to face a further dilemma in the question of form. Given
Woolf's picture of "life going on," how does the author
ever shape such fragmentary experience into a "novel"?
The work Woolf pictures as a replacement for Bennett's
(and by implication, to some extent, her own) misguided
efforts, is a study in negativity. The perfect novel has no
plot, no comedy, no tragedy, no love interest, no catastrophe, no solidity. Woolf distinctly lists the conventions
that authors must abandon, but offers little concrete advice about what a potentially liberating new order might
look like. Woolf's essay ends on a vague note of "anything goes." "Nothing," she writes, "no 'method,' no
experiment, even of the wildest—is forbidden, but only
falsity and pretence." Woolf couches her affirmation of
experimentation in negative terms. Her amorphous proto-
novel remains a matter of "what if," a consummation that,
sensing its difficulties, Woolf herself appears hesitant to
enact and equally unwilling to prescribe.

1925 thus found Woolf in a quandary. On the one hand,
she believed that the imposition of a causal chronological
system upon the random play of experience was a potentially deadly thing. On the other hand, she recognized the
enduring need for some kind of artistic order to generate
meaning and save the author from utter chaos. The problem Woolf faced was to create a new, more protean form
that could move beyond complete negativity without du-
plicating the oppressive sins of novels past. In response

to the problem, Woolf produced increasingly experimental novels that comment on their own creation. In *Mrs.
Dalloway,* the conflict Woolf creates between Dr.
Holmes and Septimus Smith mirrors to the letter the conflict between Bennett's solid autocratic realism and a liberated art of a "myriad impressions." A lover of rational
systems, Dr. Holmes, as Septimus notes, reflects "human
nature," that part of us that wants desperately to believe
that life operates according to a prescribed pattern, that
every effect has a discernible cause, that order and normalcy can be discovered and maintained. Septimus, on
the other hand, remains open to an incessant shower of
innumerable atoms that score upon his consciousness.
Past, present, and future meld together; dogs become
men; the dead peer out from behind bushes; nothing can
control the flood of life coming in. Septimus lives in a
state of imaginative freefall, his thoughts the embodiment
of Woolf's plotless, conventionless, non-chronological
fiction.

Septimus, however, is also mad as a hatter—a state, as
Woolf well knew, incompatible with writing a good
book. His visionary nature leaves him unable to communicate, and he ends his life by leaping out a window to
avoid the ministrations of the ever persistent Holmes.
Septimus' flight from the window constitutes an image of
artistic liberation, but Woolf sees such complete freedom
as ending in isolation and death. Woolf kills off
Septimus, an act that reflects her own reluctance to reject
completely the Bennettian constraints on the novel.

Indeed, the form of *Mrs. Dalloway* mirrors the anxious
nature of its content. Periodically throughout the book,
Woolf throws off the control of causal plot and retreats
into moments of mind-time where the flow of events
ceases. During segments of mind-time, Woolf sets various time streams loose at once, either in the mind of one
character, who retreats into internal solioquy, collapsing
past, present and future, or in the simultaneous perspectives given by several characters recording a single moment. The result of either technique is that plot time
stands still; Woolf replaces conventional chronological
narrative with a simultaneous internalized expression of
"life going on."

Yet for all of its experimental tendencies, *Mrs. Dalloway,*
by Woolf's definition, remains a conventional novel.
Mrs. Dalloway has a plot, a love interest, and an omniscient narrator who gives play to a privileged authorial
perspective. Woolf grounds *Mrs. Dalloway* solidly in the
world of causal events. Despite Clarissa Dalloway's de-
tours into mind-time, her day moves from morning to
night with steady regularity, a progress marked by Big
Ben, who tolls ominously in the background, "first a
warning, musical; then the hour irrevocable," an image of
inescapable chronology. The novel begins in the middle
of June; the War is over; Clarissa is over fifty; she has
lived in Westminster for over twenty years; it is Wednesday morning, 10:30 a.m. Woolf endows *Mrs. Dalloway*
with a distinct "air of probability," a particular time and
a definite place, rooted in the tradition of the "one plot."

Mrs. Dalloway, then, poses a serious question for Woolf as an artist. How does one write a novel without becoming either a Septimus or a Holmes? To record life as a series of jumbled impressions that score upon the mind poses the threat of literary madness. To record life as a plot, however, makes the author into a Holmes, a mononarrative bully who insists that everything cohere in a particular way. Woolf's response to the problem reveals the working of a distinctly interdisciplinary mind. In *To the Lighthouse* Woolf turns her attention to the visual arts in the work of Lily Briscoe, projecting a new aesthetic order to counter Bennett's autocratic reign. For all her grace and elegance, Mrs. Ramsay takes the place of Dr. Holmes. A purveyor of comfort, a singer of lullabies, a constant reassuring force, Mrs. Ramsay embodies a Victorian confidence in "ideal completeness," or, as Woolf put it in her essay "How it Strikes a Contemporary," "the conviction that life is of a certain quality" (*The Common Reader*). Shore-bound and short-sighted in both a literal and figurative sense, Mrs. Ramsay's brand of order is safe, but limited. Lily's canvas, however, poses a distinctly different kind of coherence. Abstract rather than mimetic, Lily's work moves away from a conventional, representational form. Like Woolf's projected prefect book, Lily's painting does not succumb to an air of probability or a wealth of stultifying detail. Like Woolf's projected perfect author, Lily records atoms as they score upon her consciousness, creting a simultaneous expression of "life going on." Confident in Lily's experiment, Woolf successfully kills off Mrs. Ramsay without any fear of impending chaos. *To the Lighthouse* ends with Lily's triumphant claim, "I have had my vision."

Woolf thus closes *To the Lighthouse* with a statement of faith that the artist can offer a new form to capture the essence of "life going on." In spite of Lily Briscoe's triumph, however, *To the Lighthouse* again reflects Woolf's definition of a conventional novel. Woolf herself speculated that the critics would find *To the Lighthouse* "sentimental" and "Victorian" (*The Diary of Virginia Woolf* III). The book has a definite beginning and a definite end, held together by the steady chronological progress of Lily's artistic process. Where Lily achieves a simultaneous record of atoms, Woolf stays rooted in the realm of causal teleological chronology, the world of the "one plot" and the omniscient narrator. The most adventurous part of Woolf's novel shows her persistent fear of the potential chaos behind a frame of causal plot. In "Time Passes" Woolf collapses time into a formless pool, relegating "events," such as Mrs. Ramsay's death, to sentence-long afterthoughts separated from the rest of the text by brackets. A stab in the direction of Woolf's perfect book, "Time Passes" has no plot, no love interest, at times, no characters at all. Yet "Time Passes" is also a space of things unmade rather than made. Woolf pictures the text in which night and day, month and year, run shapelessly together as the potential space of "idiot games," mad Septimus-like ramblings that can only reflect the chaos they wish to record. At the end of "Time Passes," Woolf retreats back into the realm of conventional causal chronology, forming a protective frame around the disruptive, achronological space within. Formally, *To the Lighthouse* struggles against the abstract experimental possibilities posed by Lily's picture.

Woolf's reluctance to look to the visual arts as a sustaining experimental model, however, perhaps reflects the fact that Lily's picture, too, presents problems in terms of Woolf's perfect book. Woolf closes her novel with Lily's "vision," and the atoms of experience stand ordered in one particular way. Lily finishes her painting and sets down her brush, Mr. Ramsay reaches the lighthouse. The form of the book implies that Lily's ordering task ends and that, behind the mask of metanarrative coherence, there lies a particular single set of atoms to be seen. Her vision is static rather than changing, an end point of causal chronology that contradicts Woolf's professed artistic ideal of art as continuous process, "life going on." Lily's new order threatens the birth of a new dictator. Lily herself notes the similarity between her task and that of Mrs. Ramsay.

> This, that, and the other; herself and Charles Tansley and the breaking wave; Mrs. Ramsay bringing them together; Mrs. Ramsay saying, "Life stand still here"; Mrs. Ramsay making of the moment something permanent (as in another sphere Lily herself tried to make of the moment something permanent)—this was of the nature of a revelation. In the midst of chaos there was shape; this eternal passing and flowing (she looked at the clouds going and the leaves shaking) was struck into stability. Life stand still here, Mrs. Ramsay said. "Mrs. Ramsay! Mrs. Ramsay!" she repeated. She owed it all to her.

Both Mrs. Ramsay and Lily Briscoe seek to make the moment something permanent. Lily, like Mrs. Ramsay, wants to shape the flow of chaos, the clouds going and the leaves shaking, into something fixed and lasting. Woolf thus grappled with the fact that a picture, while creating a moment of simultaneity, can never sustain simultaneous expression over time.

Faced with a further crisis of form, Woolf longed, as she wrote in her diary, not for the visual arts, but for poetry and music, for a compact, nonchronological, simultaneous expression of "life going on" to take the place of Holmes's restrictions and Lily's vision. In 1928 Woolf set to work crafting *The Waves,* and from the very start of her experiment Woolf felt she was making something different. "Never in my life," she wrote in her diary,

> did I attack such a vague yet elaborate design; whenever I make a mark I have to think of its relation to a dozen others and though I could go on ahead easily enough, I am always stopping to consider the whole effect. . . . I am not quite satisfied with this method . . . yet I can't at the moment devise anything which keeps so close to the original design & admits to movement. (*The Diary of Virginia Woolf* III,)

Woolf thus conceived of *The Waves* not as a sequence of events or a causal thread, but as an intricate interconnected whole, a pattern of particles that had to be considered both backwards and forwards during its creation, each mark in relation to a dozen others rather than simply the one that came before.

Woolf envisioned the book not as a story, but as a "shape," a "design," or, Woolf's most popular metaphor, a "method." As in *To the Lighthouse,* the characters in *The Waves* comment on the artistic experiment at hand. Like Mrs. Ramsay and Lily Briscoe, the voices Woolf presents attempt to order a world of random experience with varying degrees of success. Woolf constructs six "characters" that represent competing systems of imposed conscious order. Neville, Louis, Bernard, Susan, Jinny, Rhoda—each voice constructs an internal narrative that shapes the self and orders experience. Jinny, Susan, Neville, and Louis all choose to define themselves and interpret experience through a single artificial system. Each of the four selects a single "story," a single end to life which serves as a buttress against the waves. As Rhoda says, Jinny, Louis, Neville, and Susan choose to live life "wholly, indivisibly, and without caring in the moment." Louis is the man of business who "forms unalterable conclusions upon the true nature of what is to be known." Neville is the limited poet who clings to the words and the myths of the past, believing that "change is no longer possible." Susan chooses a life of unchanging "natural happiness"; Jinny cries her single sexual call of "come, come, come." Adopting distinctly chronological, teleological views of existence, all four see the end of life even as they live the beginning. All four characters, however, also suffer for their imposed stability. Louis, Neville, Susan, and Jinny lead ordered and focused lives, but they become the static, constricted, dull victims of their own narrow interpretations of self and experience. The imposition of a single narrative upon random experience creates order and meaning, but, like Bennett's solid narrative, it ultimately destroys life.

Along with her four failed, or anchored "characters," however, Woolf presents two protean figures in *The Waves* who remain open to random experience, Rhoda and the author, Bernard. Both Rhoda and Bernard exist without unifying singular stories to govern their lives. Rhoda lives in the crushing waves of experience without a narrative anchor to shape her self and stabilize the atoms that score upon her consciousness. "I cannot make one moment merge in the next," she says, "to me they are all violent, all separate." Unable to form fictions, to string experience together with "like and like and like," Rhoda collapses into the disordered realm of her own dreams, eventually choosing death as a release from chaos.

Like Rhoda, Bernard the author exists without a stultifying imposed mono-narrative. Yet, unlike Rhoda, Bernard has the ability to create meaning. Bernard spins stories and makes phrases. Where Rhoda cannot make one moment merge with the next, Bernard sees endless se-

quences. Drawing images together in an alphabetized notebook, Bernard effectively orders experience within the pages of a never-ending fictional catalogue, pellet by pellet of bread, drop by drop of water, moments and fragments linked together in a creative and active chain. For Bernard, life is a story that he never stops telling himself, an ever-changing artistic process. Bernard states:

> I took my mind, my being, the old dejected, almost inanimate object and lashed it about among these odds and ends, sticks and straws, detestable little bits of wreckage, flotsam and jetsam, floating on the oily surface. I jumped up, I said, 'Fight.' 'Fight,' I repeated. It is the effort and the struggle, it is the perpetual warfare, it is the shattering and piecing together—this is the daily battle, defeat or victory, the absorbing pursuit. The trees, scattered, put on order; the thick green of the leaves thinned itself to a dancing light. I netted them under with a sudden phrase. I retrieved them from formlessness with words.

Faced with a choice between fiction and emptiness, Bernard consciously embraces fiction. The process of putting together ends only with the end of life itself.

Thus, Woolf gives us one consciousness that manages to stay afloat in the waves without submitting to the paralysis of mono-narrative or the terror of chaos. Bernard escapes both forms of death by approaching life as a protean artistic process. His stories offer a theoretical alternative to both Bennettian constraints and experimental lunacy, a changing artistic order that offers coherence yet insists that there is no one true story, no one final vision. Yet *The Waves* is not merely a triumph of theory, it is a triumph of form. Woolf's design successfully mimics in structure what Bernard preaches in content. Throughout *The Waves,* Woolf clearly rejects both the chronological plot and the omniscient narrator. Woolf crafts the entire book into a series of nine time pools in which her six voices register experience simultaneously in the same, utterly consistent, narrative voice. Within the pools the six voices chart six perspectives, six different versions of "life going on." No one voice gives the "privileged perspective," no one acts as the governing omniscient consciousness, no one offers a restrictive true story. Within the time pools, causal chronology ceases; Jinny speaks, Susan speaks, Rhoda speaks, Neville speaks, Bernard speaks, Louis speaks—Woolf's six voices form a changing pattern that she orders and reorders from pool to pool. Woolf thus creates a clear "method" that substitutes for the stultifying coherence of causal chronological plot. Woolf's continuously reordered time pools stress the fact that artistic coherence is a matter of process rather than product, a necessary ongoing linking and relinking of random particles to form an endless number of stories rather than a single story.

For such formal and theoretical experiments, Woolf frequently earns the critical label, "postmodern." Drawing on the old notion that modernist writers value unity, coherence, completeness, and authority, critics find

Woolf's antiauthoritarian aesthetics of process and Bernard's acceptance of meaning as multiple to be sure signs of her subversive difference. Such critics "rescue" Woolf from the oppressive modernist canon by enshrining her as a postmodern author ahead of her time. Yet Woolf's ever-shifting stance and attention to process rather than product do not necessarily indicate a "postmodern" approach. Such provisionalizing strategies are a hallmark of works of modernist music. Looking again across disciplines, *The Waves* reveals a musical sensibility common to that of many twentieth-century composers, particularly that of the founding father of atonal expression, Arnold Schoenberg. Schoenberg's push toward new forms in music—his ultimate rejection of functional tonality and his creation of the method of composing with twelve tones—resembles, in both rhetoric and ideology, Woolf's rejection of chronological causal narrative and her subsequent creation of a "design in motion" to hold the text of *The Waves* together. Broadening the scope of critical vision to include modernist music suggests that Woolf conceived of *The Waves,* like *To the Lighthouse,* in a distinctly interdisciplinary context.

Indeed, there is a good deal of evidence to suggest that Woolf's aesthetic longing for music during the creation of *The Waves* was not simply an idle wish. As Quentin Bell notes in his biography of Woolf, Leonard Woolf began working as a record critic for *The Nation* in 1927, roughly the time that Virginia Woolf first began to conceptualize *The Waves* (*Virginia Woolf: A Biography*). To assist Leonard's new post, the Woolfs purchased the finest gramophone money could buy and, as Bell notes, Woolf became immersed in a flood of music that accompanied her own creation. Bell claims that Woolf, who had a "fairly catholic taste" in music, developed a particular preference for Beethoven's late string quartets, quartets that test the very boundaries of tonal music, quartets of "rhythmic violence" and complex chromaticism that prefigure many of Schoenberg's techniques. Schoenberg himself presents Beethoven's late quartets as an antecedent to his own more radical systems in his widely read essay **"Composition with Twelve Tones"** (*Style and Idea*).

Also during the composition of *The Waves,* Woolf met Ethel Smyth, Britain's foremost female composer. Energetic and aggressive, Smyth stormed into Woolf's life and the two quickly became friends and eventually, lovers. Entirely conversant with the modern music scene throughout Europe, Smyth was friends with the great conductors Bruno Walter and Thomas Beecham, both of whom she petitioned frequently for aid in getting her works performed. As Louise Collis notes in her biography of Smyth, *Impetuous Heart,* Smyth also knew well the work of Schoenberg, whose music she disliked and used as a frequent point of negative comparison with her own compositions. Given Smyth's consistent desire to talk about herself and her work, Woolf gained a great deal of information (as much unsolicited as requested) about both musicians and musical forms. Woolf attended Smyth's rehearsals at the BBC and listened to her broadcasts on the radio (Collis 123). Woolf's letters and diaries are filled with comments such as the one she wrote to Smyth on February 27, 1930: "I want to talk and talk and talk—About music" (*The Letters of Virginia Woolf* IV).

Given the cultural climate of England at the time, it appears that Woolf would have had ample opportunity to fulfill her desire to "talk about music," particularly avant-garde music. The late 1920's were a time of increasing difficulty for modern composers working in proto-fascist countries. Schoenberg's work, scorned by the Viennese public and rejected by the cultural elite, remained virtually unplayed in Europe in the years between the wars. Ironically, however, Schoenberg's music gained some exposure in England, a country traditionally musically conservative. As early as 1921, Edward Clark, the head of the BBC Music Department, made a policy of broadcasting concerts of new music to the British public that was being repressed and ignored throughout Europe. As British musicologist Leo Black notes with gratitude, Clark was almost single-handedly responsible for creating a public forum for the work of Schoenberg and his circle:

> Edward Clark, who left the BBC in 1936, should have a key place in any history of twentieth-century British music. It was he who knew everything that was going on in the world of contemporary music—particularly in Europe—and everybody who was engaged in it. The BBC was involved from the 1920's onwards in the hazardous enterprise of introducing to the British listeners Schoenberg and Webern as well as Bartok and Stravinsky.

Clark, a composer himself, was Schoenberg's only English-speaking pupil before the First World War, and he took it as a personal trust to bring Schoenberg's compositions to the British public at a time when virtually no one else was listening. The results, by today's standards, were amazing. On January 28, 1928, Schoenberg came to Queen's Hall in London to conduct a concert of his own works. The hall was packed to overflowing; the concert was relayed, thanks to Clark, to all British radio stations. After the concert, Schoenberg was greeted by a cheering crowd of hundreds of British followers who waited outside in the streets until the concert was finished. Clark generated a level of public acceptance for Schoenberg's music in the late twenties that Schoenberg was never to see again.

Thinking in such a musical and historical context, the potential similarities between Woolf's and Schoenberg's experiments come into focus. Schoenberg, like Woolf, was a rather cautious innovator who balked at the constraints of conventional tonal music even while he clung to hierarchical tonal systems to order his art. Functional tonal music is directed music, music with a destination, a home base, a tonic key that serves as an anchor for the harmonic motion of a particular piece. Tonal music operates through a strict hierarchical system: dominant triads

(triads built on the fifth of the scale) resolve to tonic triads; subdominant triads (triads built on the fourth note of the scale) resolve to dominant traids; median triads (triads built on the sixth scale degree) resolve to subdominant triads; and so on. All tones have a particular function and an acknowledged proper direction, tending toward tonic through a carefully mapped set of harmonic relationships or "progressions." Translated into literary terms, tonal music has a causal chronology, a series of tonal events (this leads to that) dictated by an exacting conventional system, a specific teleology that imposes a "one true story" that orders all tonal materials. Tonal music implies the expectation and fulfillment of a single impressed rubric.

In the late nineteenth and early twentieth centuries, composers such as Wagner and Mahler began to experiment with breaking the constraints of conventional tonal music. Increased chromaticism, lengthy excursions from tonic through remote key areas, prolonged cadences that evade a return to tonic and destabilize tonal expectations—Wagner and Mahler's tonal innovations led to richly chromatic compositions that Schoenberg and his contemporaries labeled products of "extended tonality." Like Wagner and Mahler, Schoenberg began his career writing lush chromatic music that, for all its complexity and extended techniques, was distinctly tonal in conception.

Yet like Woolf, Schoenberg soon became dissatisfied with the conventional restraints of his task. Schoenberg longed to be rid of the causal, chronological "one plot" of functional tonality. Schoenberg's early work, like Woolf's, was motivated by a clash between a musical Septimus, who wished to break the bonds of tonal music, and a musical Holmes, who insisted that the system of tonal hierarchy stay in place. The result was a radically extended tonality, moments of densely chromatic, virtually atonal, music held together by an imposed tonal superstructure—music, like Woolf's novels prior to *The Waves,* at war with itself.

In Schoenberg's case, however, the pull of the musical Septimus was too great to resist. In 1908, Schoenberg broke free from tonal conventions and began to write music that consciously defeated tonal expectations. Schoenberg's **Second String Quartet,** generally considered the first truly atonal utterance in Western music, bids farewell to a coherent tonal base. As Schoenberg notes in **My Evolution,**

> In the first and second movements there are many sections in which the individual parts proceed regardless of whether or not their meeting results in codified harmonies. Still, here, and also in the third and fourth movements, the key is presented distinctly at all the main dividing points of the formal organization. Yet the overwhelming multitude of dissonances cannot be balanced any longer by occasional returns to such tonal triads as represent a key. It seemed inadequate to force a movement into the Procrustean bed of a tonality

without supporting it by harmonic progressions that pertain to it. This was my concern, and it should have occupied the mind of all my contemporaries also. That I was the first to venture the decisive step will not be considered universally a merit—a fact I regret but have to ignore.

Leaving functional tonality behind, Schoenberg reconceptualized the musical universe as a world of atoms scoring, a vast unrelated pool of potential tones outside the constraints of an imposed hierarchy. Stripping away conventions, Schoenberg reached the musical equivalent of the atomistic space behind Bennett's Victorian metanarrative of "ideal completeness."

In 1909, Schoenberg took a further step into chaos and composed **Erwartung,** an operatic mono-drama that has since its inception plagued musicologists who relish the challenge of discerning hidden orders. Within **Erwartung,** Schoenberg pushes atonal expression to its furthest limits, generating the musical equivalent of Woolf's perfectly negative book. **Erwartung** contains no classical formal structures, no motivic recurrences, no rhythmic patterns, no themes, no clear repetition of any kind. To save himself from utter disorder, Schoenberg ties **Erwartung** together with the thin thread of a text, an imposed literary plot to substitute for the missing musical plot of functional tonality. Schoenberg, like Woolf, realized that Septimus alone could not create art. Afraid of the implications of his own formless rambling, Schoenberg retreated into his study and emerged, eleven years later, with a new, more protean, technique for ordering tones.

Schoenberg's method of composing with twelve tones was the result of his withdrawal, a carefully controlled musical technique designed to generate purely non-hierarchical, atonal, acausal music that utterly defeats, through a coherent system, all tonal expectations. Schoenberg's method divides the octave, not into a diatonic key presentation of eight notes, but into twelve equal half steps. Twelve-tone music consists of varied presentations of a basic "tone row," a set of twelve different notes that forms a complete egalitarian expression of all musical material contained in the octave. The twelve notes in the row are sounded twelve at a time, without repetition of any one note, a technique that leads to the highest possible chromatic density and completely disorganizes the tonal expectations of the listener. Schoenberg varies presentations of the tone row from set to set through the musical techniques of "inversion" (the row turned upside down), retrograde (the row presented backwards), retrograde inversion (upside down and backwards), and pure transposition. Yet from presentation to presentation, the row always consists of twelve half steps, taken twelve at a time, without repetition. In twelve-tone music there are no "leading tones," no fifths or fourths, no one note leads or tends toward any other. No one note is more important than any other.

Thus Schoenberg's twelve-tone music replaces functional tonality with a tightly-ordered chromatic barrage that overturns the very idea of directional dissonance and consonance. Twelve-tone music disrupts the causal hierarchical "plot" of tonal music and allows for, as Schoenberg put it, "the emancipation of the dissonance." Schoenberg writes in **"Composition with Twelve Tones,"**

> But while a "tonal" composer still has to lead his parts into consonances or catalogued dissonances, a composer with twelve independent tones apparently possesses the kind of freedom which many would characterize by saying: "everything is allowed." "Everything" has always been allowed to two kinds of artists: to masters on the one hand, and to ignoramuses on the other.

Schoenberg, thus, saw his technique as a highly complex, protean structure that defeated tonal causality without succumbing to chaos.

Working across disciplinary boundaries, I believe that Woolf's "method" for composing *The Waves,* her "design in motion," shows some striking similarities to Schoenberg's method of composing with twelve tones. Translating *The Waves* into musical terms, Woolf's rejection of a single causal chronological plot (this leads to that), her rejection of the "one true story," leads her to write fiction which is basically "atonal" in conception. Like Schoenberg, Woolf abandons the causal impetus of her art and creates a form which defeats both chronological causality and functional hierarchy. In place of the causal stream of tonal music, Woolf presents six voices, the rough equivalent of a Schoenbergian "tone row," that are ordered and ordered again. Woolf discards a single plot in favor of a process of, as Schoenberg put it, "continuous variation" that disrupts the idea of any one proper musical movement.

Woolf essentially creates pools of six voices taken six at a time in a shifting array that defeats expectations and prohibits the question "what happens next?" Woolf's "row," her ever-changing pattern of six particles, has the same destabilizing effect on Woolf's fiction as the tone row has on Schoenberg's music. Six characters, offering six perspectives, six at a time, defeats the idea of any one privileged perspective or, in musical terms, any one privileged harmonic base. Woolf's serial presentation of voices defeats the convention of the omniscient narrator in the same way that Schoenberg's serial presentation of tones defeats a tonic key. Woolf's voice pools are adirectional spaces of simultaneous presentation that provide for the emancipation of all perspectives, a literary corollary to Schoenberg's "emancipation of the dissonance." *The Waves* uses distinctly Schoenbergian serial techniques to disrupt the ideas of the "one true story." The antiauthoritarian, ever-changing presentation of voices that lies at the heart of Schoenberg's twelve-tone music is also the motivating force behind Woolf's *The Waves.*

Reading Woolf's words as music, the very first "movement" of *The Waves* shows an attention to ordered disruption worthy of the best of serial composers. The order of voices in the opening of the first voice pool of *The Waves* reads as follows:

Bernard-Susan-Rhoda-Neville-Jinny-Louis

Bernard-Susan-Louis-Rhoda-Neville-Jinny

Susan-Rhoda-Louis-Neville-Jinny-Bernard

In the opening of her first movement, Woolf presents all six of her voices, six at a time, without repeating any one voice until the entire set has been used. No one presentation of the voice row is privileged, no one voice is privileged. Woolf's organization disrupts standard narrative expectations. All the voices seem equally important, all the visions of the childhood equally true. The ever-changing non-causal array defeats the wish for a stable chronological narrative with a definite direction. Woolf's presentation guarantees that, in Bernard's terms, "there is nothing one can fish up in a spoon; nothing one can call an even." In musical terms, nothing you can walk out humming. Although Woolf, like most serial composers, does indeed deviate from the strict row presentation set out in the opening movement (voices repeat, interruptions intervene) at many points in *The Waves,* the patterns of carefully controlled rotation remains the same. "Neville, Susan, Louis, Jinny, Rhoda and a thousand others," says Bernard at the end of *The Waves,*

> How impossible to order them rightly; to detach one separately, or to give the effect of the whole—again like music. . . . Each played his own tune, fiddle, flute, trumpet, drum or whatever the instrument might be.

Woolf's six voices sound as distinct musical tones, each different, each separate, each playing his or her own tune. Yet each adds to a musically conceived simultaneous serial whole.

This essay thus ends with a web of probability rather than an actual proof of influence. Yet I think that the ideological similarity between Woolf's and Schoenberg's work is helpful in defining the period and the sensibility we loosely term as "modern." Both Woolf and Schoenberg inherit a late-Victorian abyss. They each look out into the random sea of particles behind the metanarrative coherence of a bygone age and realize that art must order the world in a new way without becoming a new dictator. Both respond to a late-Victorian confusion and artistic breakdown by creating protean artistic systems to substitute for the loss of old beliefs. Both create controlled forms, born of artistic confidence, that assert the beauty of artistic process over potential chaos or static product.

Given the work of Woolf and Schoenberg, the "modern" period may be seen as one of provisionalizing action rather than formalist oppression. Perhaps Woolf herself says it best in "A Sketch of the Past."

It is the rapture I get when in writing I seem to be discovering what belongs to what; making a scheme come right; making a character come together. From this I reach what I might call a philosophy; at any rate it is a constant idea of mine; that behind the cotton wool is hidden a pattern; that we—I mean all human beings—are connected with this; that the whole world is a work of art; that we are parts of the work of art. *Hamlet* or a Beethoven quartet is the truth about this vast mass that we call the world. But there is no Shakespeare; there is no Beethoven; certainly and emphatically there is no God; we are the words; we are the music; we are the thing itself.

For modernists like Schoenberg and Woolf, art is the thing that "makes it come right." There is no pattern behind the cotton wool, no God, no ultimate Beethoven, no cosmic Shakespeare to order this vast mass that we call the world; the patterns we make on our side of the carpet are pure imposition. Yet, without the one God, the one order, the world becomes our palette, our keyboard, our stage—a place where beautiful patterns can be made and made again.

Michael Gilbert (essay date 1994)

SOURCE: "'Ich habe von einen Esel gelernt': Eisler Pro and Contra Schönberg," in *High and Low Cultures: German Attempts at Mediation,* edited by Reinhold Grimm and Jost Hermand, The University of Wisconsin Press, 1994, pp. 59-73.

[*In the following essay, Gilbert discusses the relationship between Schoenberg and Hanns Eisler.*]

I

In a series of conversations with GDR scholar/journalist Hans Bunge, published under the title *Fragen Sie mehr über Brecht* (an allusion to a passage in which Eisler states: "Fragen Sie nicht so viel über Schönberg—Fragen Sie bitte mehr über Brecht!"), composer Hanns Eisler mentions a cantata text which he presumably talked his friend and collaborator Bertolt Brecht into writing on the occasion of Arnold Schönberg's seventy-second birthday in 1947, and for which he, Eisler, evidently prepared at least a few musical sketches. Eisler had previously referred to this intriguing birthday present in a brief article "Brecht und die Musik" (written for a special issue of the journal *Sinn und Form* in 1957), in which the story behind the cantata is explained. In the article, Eisler notes that the text was based on Schönberg's own description of an incident in which he was able to climb a steep grade in spite of heart condition by emulating the serpentine manner in which a donkey made it to the top. As related by Eisler, the end of Schönberg's story went as follows:

> Da habe ich ihm [dem Esel] das nachgemacht, und so kann ich sagen: ich habe von einem Esel gelernt.

Interestingly, this anecdote reportedly dates from the first occasion on which Eisler introduced his friend Brecht to Schönberg, something which made Eisler very nervous, given Brecht's reputation for "behaving badly" (Eisler's words). In any case, the cantata title "Ich habe von einem Esel gelernt" is clearly intended as a provocatively humorous comment on Eisler's difficult but close relationship with Schönberg and his music.

In his conversations with Bunge, Eisler also emphasizes the fact that the text had never been located again (that is, as of the late 1950s and early 1960s, when Bunge conducted the interviews) though the composer was convinced that Schönberg's widow could find it if she only looked hard enough. In any event, since that time the birthday cantata has not been found—neither the text nor the musical sketches; Joachim Lucchesi and Ronald Shull's recent exhaustive documentation volume *Musik bei Brecht* (1988) makes no reference to it at all. But whether the cantata ever turns up or not, its title—"I learned from an ass"—remains and serves to represent the essential two-sidedness of Hanns Eisler's relationship with his teacher/mentor Arnold Schönberg, the point being that Eisler *did* learn from Schönberg. Indeed, he learned a great deal and seldom failed to acknowledge the enormous debt of gratitude he owed to his former teacher both musically and personally, even if he regarded Schönberg politically and ideologically to be an *Esel.*

Before addressing Eisler's association with Schönberg and its aftermath, some preliminary theoretical consideration should be given to the matter of "mediation between high and low culture" specifically in reference to the art of music. Musical culture represents a particularly significant example of this issue, for in no other (traditional) art form has the modern split between high and low culture assumed such extreme proportions, and created such devisiveness among producers and consumers of culture, as in the case of music. Moreover, this state of affairs has everything to do with the difficulty Eisler experienced in coming to terms with both the musical-artistic and ideological stance of his teacher Schönberg; indeed, this is what eventually caused Eisler to seek a very different path from that of his mentor, one which, in many respects, represents an attempt at mediation. The various dimensions of that attempt and the question of how successful Eisler was in his efforts to mediate or reconcile the so-called "new music" and workers' culture, the bourgeois avant-garde and socialist *Volkstümlichkeit,* constitutes the core of the following discussion.

First, however, the thesis stated above merits elaboration and closer examination: Why is music the example *par excellence* of the high/low culture phenomenon? One key aspect of this is the fact that even before the advent of what, properly speaking, constitutes musical modernity—i.e., the dissolution of traditional form, abandonment of traditional principles of harmony and tonality, etc.—in fact, beginning as early as the mid-19th century, the art of music, especially in the German tradition, comes to be celebrated by many for its presumed "lack of content" (*Inhaltslosigkeit*). This is a perspective which found its best-known defender in the Viennese music critic Eduard Hanslick (in particular, with his book *Vom Musikalisch-Schönen* [*On the Musically Beautiful,* 1854]). Without delving into the often overstated absolute vs. programmatic music debate of the later 19th century, we may say that the issue pertinent to the emergent high/low culture split is that the ideological underpinnings of musical modernity are already contained in this perception of music as the quintessentially autonomous art form, one essentially disinterested regarding reality and existing in a world of its own as "absolute sounding form." The notions of Hanslick and others in his camp were subsequently institutionalized and/or radicalized (aesthetically speaking) in the early 20th century, yielding a doctrine of esoteric, avant-garde, high-cultural formal experimentation. By the 1920s, this segment of musical culture had come to be referred to generally as "die neue Musik," and Arnold Schönberg and his so-called "New Viennese School"—consisting primarily of himself and his pupils Alban Berg, Anton von Webern, *and* Hanns Eisler (frequently overlooked in this context because of his later conflict with Schönberg)—counted themselves among its most prominent and pioneering representatives. In considering the outlook of the musical avant-garde of that time, it is intriguing to note that, in defending their modernist agenda, certain key figures in the *pictorial* arts—for example, painter Wassily Kandinsky—appeal in their writings to music as the quintessentially modern medium of artistic expression, one which by its very nature is (presumably) "abstract" and, at least in the minds of those in the tradition of Hanslick, consists of little or nothing more than its own virtually infinite permutations of pitch, rhythm, and timbre: what one could call "sound for sound's sake."

While this factor alone cannot account for the extreme gap between high and low musical culture which manifests itself even before the end of World War I, the modernist sensibilities of the elite musical-cultural avant-garde of the time, drawing on the *Autonomieästhetik* of the preceding era, certainly help to explain why Schönberg, as of 1930, could legitimately claim that he no longer had a public at all: "called upon to say something about my public, I have to confess: I do not believe I have one." Eisler, similarly, could legitimately state that modern music (that is, "die neue Musik") was an art that "nobody wanted." In his words, "hardly any other form of art leads the phantom existence that modern music does. . . . of all the arts, it is *music* which most emphatically expresses the dissolution of bourgeois culture."

Eisler's concern about this "dying patient" (he likens modern art music to a death rattle) centered around his perception of a fundamental loss of "community" (*Gemeinschaft*) and the extreme isolation of serious music: "Der Musiker, der seine Kunst liebt und dem sie zwingendstes Bedürfnis ist, wird mit Entsetzen die völlige Isoliertheit seiner Kunst erkennen." And while

Eisler approached this matter of music's concrete social function (i.e., the apparent loss of such a function) from the basis of his ever-deepening political convictions as a Marxist, composers and critics from across the political spectrum (except for those like Schönberg, who didn't seem terribly concerned about the lack of an audience) engaged in a debate about a genuine crisis in the art of music that fills the musical journals of the Weimar years and continues on into the post-World War II era. It was this situation that led composer Ernst Krenek, for example, to remark that music in the modern era had lost its "intrinsic value," by which he meant "its ability to appear as an obviously necessary element of human life, something which the public demands and which is offered spontaneously"; while Paul Hindemith, a leading figure of the so-called *Gemeinschaftsmusik* movement, observed in the journal *Melos* in 1929: "Der Musiker hat es heute schwer. Schwerer vielleicht als zu irgend einer anderen Zeit. Was uns alle angeht ist dies: wie und was müssen wir schreiben, um ein grösseres neues Publikum zu bekommen; und wo ist dieses Publikum?" Indeed, virtually every composer working from that point on, assuming that he/she was interested in any sort of more broadly based "musical community," has been confronted with this extreme high/low culture split in the realm of musical culture, and has engaged in various attempts at mediation, either for the sake of survival or, in the case of those with a more politicized agenda, for the sake of being able to contribute something of "intrinsic value" to society (to borrow Krenek's phrase).

In summarizing this first consideration with regard to the roots of the extraordinary high/low culture problem in music, it is fair to say that, as great a gap as there may be between high and low literature, or high and low art, the high end of the spectrum in those instances has been assimilated into the bourgeois cultural mainstream to a far greater degree than high modernist music (something which, moreover, appears to be true to only a slightly lesser extent of Western European culture than of American culture). In other words, it is not at all uncommon that the same people who decorate their walls with the art of Picasso or even Jackson Pollock (indeed, whose business spaces are often replete with abstract designs, and housed in the most modern architecture) and who appreciate the writings of Joyce and Kafka, Stevens and Ginsberg, are by and large skeptical of, or even averse to, modern art music. Another aspect of this is the fact that the works of modern music that *have* succeeded in making it into the mainstream concert repertoire (for example, early and "neoclassical" Stravinsky, or Berg's quasi-Romantic Violin Concerto, or the folk-idiom based works of Béla Bartók) are precisely those which are not as far removed from traditional musical values. In comparison, much of what Arnold Schönberg or Anton von Webern wrote in the 1920s is still distinctly too "far out" for many audiences. By the same token, modern art attracts hordes of people to museums and commands exorbitant prices on the art market, while at the same time the programming of so-called "avant-garde" music is in all but academic communities (in which modernism has typically been canonized if not enshrined) or the most advanced centers of culture (Berlin, Paris, New York, etc.) still a serious financial risk for musical ensembles, most of which are already in debt.

Another related dimension of this situation is the fact that musical life in our time has broken down into a multiplicity of subcultures to a degree unprecedented among the arts. With slight exaggeration, one could argue that the defenders or representatives of the high-cultural musical avant-garde may as well be dealing with an entirely different medium than those who perform rock or produce music video, to say nothing of the fabricators of "Muzak"; or one thinks, for example, of the phenomenon of "formatting" in musical broadcasting on radio. In that sense, one can truly no longer speak of music, but only of music*s,* a phenomenon which also reflects the advanced commodification of our culture, specifically, the development and cultivation of different markets for those different musics. The essential point to be emphasized here with respect to "attempts at mediation" is this: in such a cultural-ideological climate, attempts at mediation between high and low culture are inherently difficult, perhaps even impossible; in the context of advanced or radical cultural pluralism, it is very difficult to define any longer what constitutes "intrinsic value" as Krenek spoke of it as late as the 1920s; and, in any case, such attempts at mediation are courageous, requiring a great deal of vision, determination, and (perhaps) idealism. One of the points I wish to make about Hanns Eisler is precisely this: as worthy as his attempts at mediation often were— Eisler wrote much good music—his greatest legacy may well be the vision he left behind of a new *intrinsically mediated* musical culture that didn't yet and perhaps couldn't yet exist.

I turn now to a second preliminary consideration with regard to the dimensions of the high/low culture situation in music, and, by way of that, to the story of Eisler's association with Schönberg, his subsequent break with him, and his efforts to find some socially productive middle ground between high and low musical culture. Hanns Eisler was born in 1898, the same year as Brecht, into a national-cultural tradition (Viennese/Austrian/German) at a critical moment in its historical development: namely, on the threshold of cultural modernity. The emphasis here is on the phrase "national-cultural tradition," for art music, from the point of view of Austrian/German national-cultural identity (and/or national-cultural ideology) was not merely perceived as high culture, but rather as *highest* culture, the supreme achievement of German intellectual and cultural life and, in the minds of some (young Thomas Mann, for instance) as its very soul or essence. Many factors contribute to this prominence of (high) music in the German tradition; not least of all it has to do with the uniquely difficult and repressed development of modern German civilization, that peculiarly German "Missverhältnis von Geist und Macht." From the perspective of cultural philosophy and ideology, it is clearly linked as well to the legacy of German Romanticism, extending back at least as far as E. T. A. Hoffmann

and culminating in Richard Wagner's reception of Schopenhauer, in which music becomes the supreme art precisely because it is supremely ineffable. As Isolde says in her grand apotheosis at the end of Wagner's *Tristan:* "höchste Lust, unbewusst"—those three words, for better or worse, suggest the sublime (and sublimely irrational) position occupied by music in the German national artistic canon and consciousness. Another way to put it would be to say that the familiar characterization of Germany in the 19th century as "the land of poets and thinkers" ("das Land der Dichter und Denker") is, with all due apologies to Madame de Stäel, essentially misguided; it was above all the land of musicians and composers, where poets and thinkers were preoccupied with music to a degree not found in other European cultures. Indeed, as far as high musical culture in the era of Romantic nationalism is concerned, one could easily speak in terms of a "German century" extending from Beethoven to Mahler.

How does this tie in with Eisler's work with Schönberg and the former's subsequent attempts at mediation? The point is that Eisler was born into a national-cultural tradition in which the very concept of music (specifically, musical high culture) was laden with extraordinary cultural-historical and ideological baggage. Around the turn of the century—one thinks of Thomas Mann, Hofmannsthal, Nietzsche, the phenomenon of Wagnerism, the sheerly monumental "musical-philosophical edifices" *(Gedankengebäude)* of Gustav Mahler and Richard Strauss—high music had become the object of a veritable national-mythological-intellectual cult. It is therefore necessary to keep in perspective that Eisler's break with Schönberg as of 1926 was not merely a personal act of rebellion by an outspoken and at times impudent pupil, but rather a conscious act of outright sacrilege. Schönberg, after all, in spite of his radical technical innovations, was rooted as deeply as one could possibly have been in that great tradition of German music, and was in that sense truly a conservative if not reactionary figure (something the sophisticated, critically-minded pupil Eisler realized from early on). To Schönberg, a work like Eisler's "Zeitungsausschnitte" (newspaper clippings) of 1925-26 (with which, in the words of Albercht Betz, Eisler "bid good riddance to the lyricism of the concert hall"), to say nothing of his efforts to reconcile Schönberg's compositional standards with socialist political ideals, represented nothing less than the debasement of art, or, in the parlance of the young, apolitical Thomas Mann (whether Schönberg would actually have spoken in such terms or not), the ultimate corruption of culture by mere "civilization." This, too, was part of the burden with which Eisler was dealing in being an Austrian-German, *and* a socialist, *and* composing in the wake of Schönberg's advance into musical modernism, in his efforts to mediate between high and low musical culture. To reenforce this observation from another angle, one could well argue that mediation between high and low musical culture was easier (that is, intrinsically less of a challenge) for an American composer like George Gershwin (given the more democratic, pluralistic cultural ideal of America and the pervasiveness of indigenous popular traditions such as jazz and spiritual music), or even for an Eastern European composer like Bartók, whose musical identity as a Hungarian national was strongly linked to popular folk tradition. Obviously, such traditions existed in Germany as well, but apart from the fact that they became virtually impossible for Eisler and others to draw on in the wake of National Socialism, Eisler was rooted and educated overwhelmingly in the high cultural tradition, meaning the extraordinary achievements of Beethoven, Schubert, Brahms, Bruckner, Wagner, Mahler, and all of the others: i.e., music as *highest* culture. That represented an additional complication and, in the end, had at least something to do (I suspect) with the relative effectiveness of Eisler's attempts at mediation.

II

The story of Eisler's apprenticeship to Arnold Schönberg is related in several standard sources (most notably, the Eisler biographies of Fritz Hennenberg and Albrecht Betz) and need not be related in detail here. (Another crucial source for this are Eisler's many documented conversations; he liked to talk.) It should therefore suffice to highlight the most essential chapters in this story vis-à-vis Eisler's eventual attempt to mediate between high and low musical culture.

By the time Eisler came to Schönberg as a pupil at the New Viennese Conservatory in 1919 on a tuition-free basis (a matter which from the outset complicated things emotionally for Eisler in dealing with Schönberg), Eisler had already developed a keen interest in socialism, partly for personal reasons (his mother had a working-class background). He began working with workers' choruses that same year and taught at the Verein für volkstümliche Musikpflege, a kind of musical *Volksschule* for working-class people. In general, from early on, Eisler had a tendency to be very outspoken (also quite witty) and politically inclined. He also had a serious critical interest in literature (his early poetic sources were writers such as Klabund, Morgenstern, Trakl, and even Rilke) and composed an antiwar oratorio ("Gegen den Krieg") already during his school days, one reflecting his pacifist inclinations. In addition, as of the time he entered the conservatory, his older brother and sister (Gerhart and Elfriede, the later Ruth Fischer) had already embarked on their long, problematic careers as professional socialist revolutionaries; the tendency toward political radicalism clearly ran in the family. Thus, without citing further evidence, given Schönberg's emphatic political conservatism, it is clear that the Eisler-Schönberg connection was from the very outset a *Spannungsverhältnis*.

It is also noteworthy that Eisler's apprenticeship with Schönberg dates from precisely that point in Schönberg's career at which he embarked on the twelve-tone (dodecaphonic) method of composition (ca. 1922-23, beginning with the op. 24 Serenade), a new, daring, untried proposition—and in the end, Eisler's skepticism about the potential of this latest musical experiment of the bourgeois avant-garde was among the things that led Schönberg to feel so betrayed when they had their great falling-out in 1926. At the same time, this strong sense of personal betrayal on Schönberg's part cannot be understood without reference to the fact that their personal relationship was fairly close and rather father/son-like in nature. Consequently, it is not surprising that, later in his life, Eisler humbly acknowledged how Schönberg had reacted with such "generosity" at the time of their break, in response to his own "ungrateful, rebellious, irritable, crude, and insulting" behavior (Eisler's own words).

Examining the Eisler-Schönberg connection from a more positive angle, Eisler clearly had in Schönberg a gifted and very strict teacher with the highest technical standards. In reflecting on this in the latter years of his life, Eisler wrote:

> Das Hauptsächliche, was ich Schönberg verdanke, ist, ich glaube, ein richtiges Verständnis der musikalischen Tradition der Klassiker. Ich kann sagen, dass ich überhaupt erst dort musikalisches Verständnis und Denken gelernt habe. . . . Dann lernte ich bei Schönberg etwas, was heute gar nicht mehr richtig verstanden wird: Redlichkeit in der Musik, Verantwortlichkeit . . . und das Fehlen von jeder Angeberei. . . . Diese unerbittliche Strenge, dieses Streben nach musikalischer Wahrheit . . . die strenge, saubere, ehrliche Handwerkslehre, die Schönberg gab . . . das ist eben eine grosse geschichtliche Leistung von Schönberg.

Indeed, for all of his innovations as a composer, Schönberg the teacher and theoretician was tradition-minded to the nth degree: instruction consisted largely of analysis of the works of the great German canon—Bach, Mozart, Beethoven, Schubert, Brahms, etc.—but absolutely nothing modern. There was, interestingly enough, some common ground between Eisler and his teacher musically; above all, both shared an affinity to the "logic and clarity" of the work of Johannes Brahms, in particular his chamber music.

Eisler's early work in the shadow of Schönberg included some atonal and twelve-tone writing, also the use of *Sprechstimme,* a Schönbergian technique; and the young composer was quickly recognized for his talent, receiving, for example, the prestigious Kunstpreis der Stadt Wien in 1925 for his Piano Sonata op. 1. From there, he went on to have numerous successes at so-called "new music festivals" such as those held at Donaueschingen and at Baden-Baden, one of the most important forums for the "neue Musik" movement at that time, as well as abroad. His first regular teaching appointment was in Berlin, at a private conservatory.

Given the personal and professional support Schönberg had given him (at no charge), it was a reasonably nasty affair when Eisler finally parted company with his teacher in 1926. The essential problem, notwithstanding the personal dimensions to this, was that Eisler could no longer take Schönberg's political attitudes seriously—or, rather, his *apolitical* attitudes—for even if he had monarchist sympathies, Schönberg was more than anything else a classic *Unpolitischer.* Above all, Eisler had become convinced that something had to be done about the extreme isolation of modern (high) music and its creators, which in his judgment rendered music impotent as a means of social and cultural regeneration and change. In the words of Albrecht Betz, "in short, it was the fact that music turned a deaf ear to the conflicts of the times, its social confrontations, that disturbed him and made him want to break away from Arnold Schönberg." With that, Eisler emancipated himself and embarked on his journey to create "socially and politically useful" music. His intent was to restore some social purpose or function to an art which he regarded as inherently communal (going back to the dawn of civilization), but to do this without abandoning the sophisticated compositional standards and techniques to which he had been held by his teacher Schönberg—or, for that matter, neglecting the historical reality of musical modernity. It would be fair to say that, if some of Eisler's music was less than great, it was very seldom less than impectably composed and logically conceived, just as it possessed genuine historical integrity, something which would have been unthinkable without Schönberg's influence and the kind of rigorous training he received under his tutelage. There is much of Schönberg which therefore remained *aufgehoben* in Eisler's music—as different as much of that music was on the surface, most notably in its distinct lack of sentimentality or subjective emotionality, either in music or choice of text, and its more restrained application of modernist compositional techniques.

Just as the Eisler-Schönberg story has been told in detail elsewhere, the development of Eisler's career has been extensively documented and discussed. Hence, it should suffice here to outline the major phases of his life and work, although it is true that Eisler's name (in contrast to those of Schönberg's other two pupils, Alban Berg and Anton von Webern) is still found primarily in the footnotes of music history books, if it is to be found at all. This, of course, is the price he paid for breaking company with Schönberg and becoming a "socialist composer." Following this brief overview, a series of key issues pertinent to the question of mediation between high and low culture will be addressed as they relate to Eisler's music. Finally, by way of concluding, a few remarks will be made concerning the last phase of Eisler's career: in particular, the impact of Schönberg's death on Eisler, who at the time (1951) was coming to grips with the repressive Stalinist cultural climate of the early GDR.

As noted above, Eisler's break with Arnold Schönberg came in 1926, not long after his relocation to Berlin. Later that same year, he applied for membership in the KPD (German Communist Party), and by 1927 his involvement in the *Arbeitermusikbewegung* (leftist workers' music movement) had also increased significantly. Eisler became a musical columnist for *Die Rote Fahne,* worked with the agitprop group "Das Rote Sprachrohr," and taught music at the Marxist Workers' School in Ber-

lin beginning in 1928. This was during the time when his future collaborator Bertolt Brecht was still working with left-liberal composer Kurt Weill (as well as, for a brief time, Paul Hindemith)—which is to underscore the fact that when Brecht turned to Eisler as of 1930, he encountered someone who had a head start on him both politically and aesthetically. (This is not the place to go into Eisler's influence on Brecht, but it is worth noting the decisive influence Eisler had on Brecht's political and intellectual/artistic development at this early stage of their association.)

The next few years leading up to Eisler's exile from Germany witnessed the first of several productive periods of collaboration with Brecht, resulting in, among other works, the Lehrstück *Die Massnahme* (1930), the film *Kuhle Wampe* (1932), and the play with music *Die Mutter* (likewise 1932). While in exile, Eisler became deeply committed to the antifascist cultural "Volksfront" (popular front) concept; indeed, he represents a far better example of that ideal than Brecht, as Eisler maintained close ties to many people and groups whom Brecht rejected or from whom he remained quite distant—most notably, Thomas Mann, with whom Eisler enjoyed a warm personal friendship; the Horkheimer-Adorno circle, about which Brecht was very skeptical; and, of course, Arnold Schönberg himself. In 1935-1936, Eisler made the first of several trips to the United States and began teaching at the New School for Social Research in New York City. He moved to the U.S. "to stay" in 1938, but not before he encountered considerable difficulty obtaining a visa and a residency permit—a matter in which Thomas Mann personally intervened. Eventually, like so many other German exiles, and after further problems with U.S. immigration authorities, he wound up in Hollywood in 1942 and remained there until 1948. Prior to his relocation to California, Eisler had begun one of his most important projects, a book on film music *(Composing for the Film)* that was supported by a grant from the Rockefeller Foundation. While the juxtaposition of the names Rockefeller and Eisler may seem a bit amusing, the project resulted in a volume now considered a classic in its field, as well as a remarkable piece of instrumental music, "14 Ways of Describing Rain," composed for the Joris Ivens documentary film *Rain* (1940).

Interestingly, the music Eisler wrote during the Hollywood years consisted largely of songs—lieder in the great German tradition of lieder—at times, quite personal and rather lyrical, though inevitably resistant to undue sentimentality. There were, for example, the *Hollywood Elegies,* the *Anakreon-Fragmente* (based on Mörike's translations) and the set of *Hölderlinfragmente,* written, as Eisler put it, "für die Schublade," in the darkest days of exile (1943). but he also wrote a fair amount of stage music, keeping up with Brecht's prolific output during those years: in particular, scores for *Furcht und Elend des Dritten Reiches, Schweyk im Zweiten Weltkrieg, Leben des Galilei,* and the film score for *Hangmen Also Die.* Most of these were composed for voices and small orchestra or chamber ensemble, yielding that kind of antisentimental musical transparency which both he and Brecht preferred (a style often referred to as "Brechtian music"). Apart from his impeccable musical logic, the most distinctive hallmarks of Eisler's style, consistent with his rational, politicized, anti-Romantic outlook, are his economy of musical means, transparency of texture, predominance of the text/vocal line (i.e., the distinct primacy of the text), and general conciseness of form.

In 1948, facing deportation in the wake of the HUAC witch-hunt, Eisler left for Europe, following a gala farewell concert in his honor in New York City sponsored by the likes of Leonard Bernstein, Aaron Copland, Randall Thompson, Roy Harris, Roger Sessions, and Walter Piston—in short, the entire progressive American musical elite of the 1940s. His travel paper arrangements were, once again, looked after by Thomas Mann, who in this instance went far out on a limb to assist him. As of 1949, he was back in Berlin; he began lecturing at the Humboldt Universität and settled in Berlin/GDR the following year. It was at this time that he became known as the composer of the GDR national anthem "Auferstanden aus Ruinen" (text by Johannes R. Becher).

The next and final chapter—life under Stalinism—was not unlike what Brecht experienced, but it took a greater toll on Eisler. In particular, in the wake of the controversy over his libretto for an opera based on the Faust legend, a project of tremendous personal and artistic significance to the composer, Eisler spent most of the years 1953-1954 in Vienna, while Brecht, back in Berlin at the Berliner Ensemble, was genuinely concerned that his friend and chief musical collaborator might not return. The remainder of Eisler's life was spent in a fairly privileged position within the framework of GDR culture but, nevertheless, in a continuous *Spannungsverhältnis*—a veritable cultural-political tug-of-war—with the Stalinist cultural bureaucracy. As Wolf Biermann has pointed out, in spite of what they made of him—a *Staatskomponist*— the Stalinists generally considered his aesthetic inclinations too modern, too critical, too reminiscent of "late-bourgeois decadence"; in other words, in spite of the way his music was promoted, he was in fact more tolerated than liked, which to an extent was true of Bertolt Brecht and his work with the Berliner Ensemble as well. Eisler's last years saw the completion of some of his best-known works: a set of some forty songs to texts by Kurt Tucholsky, the *Deutsche Sinfonie* (based on poetry by Brecht), and his *Requiem* for Lenin. His last work, which bears the title *Ernste Gesänge,* is set for baritone and string orchestra, with (adapted) texts by Hölderlin, Leopardi, and Stephan Hermlin. He died on 6 September 1962.

This latter period in Eisler's life and work will be taken up again at the conclusion of my discussion. However, as noted above, a series of key issues pertinent to the matter of mediation between high and low culture as it relates to Eisler's music must first be considered. These are five: (1) the impact of fascism on Eisler's attitudes as a composer and his role in the so-called Expressionism debate;

(2) Eisler's emphasis on the primacy of vocal music and the implications thereof for his compositional aesthetic; (3) the matter of subjectivity and emotionality in Eisler's music vis-à-vis his attempt to mediate between high and low musical culture; (4) aesthetic mediation in relation to Eisler's pronounced emphasis on the building of a new musical culture; and (5) mediation in relation to the general issue of political or politicized art, as exemplified by Eisler's music.

First, in understanding the path Eisler took that lay somewhere between the Schönbergian and post-Schönbergian avant-garde, on the one hand, and popular and/or traditional means of musical expression, on the other, it is crucial to remember that, within the framework of leftist cultural debates of the exile period, Eisler, together with Ernst Bloch, Brecht, and others, was an outspoken defender of musical and cultural modernism. Specifically, Eisler emphasized the need for an explicitly *antifascist* aesthetic: that is to say, one that would counter the cultural conservatism of Nazism, and one with a dialectical conception of music history: "wir [leben] nicht nur in einer Fäulniszeit . . . , sondern in einer dialektisch übergehenden, in einer Zeit und Gesellschaft, die von der künftigen schwanger ist." In this sense, Eisler, like Bloch, saw an element of *anticipation* in the music of Arnold Schönberg; or, as he stated elsewhere about his former teacher: "Aus der Geschichte der Musik ist er nicht wegzudenken. Verfall und Niedergang des Bürgertums, gewiss; aber welch eine Abendröte!"

Second, from early on, in his critical writings and in his work as a composer, Eisler stressed the inherent conceptual clarity and the consequently enhanced functionality or utility of music with text. In other words, he stressed the need, as he perceived it, to reestablish the primacy of vocal music in opposition to instrumental-symphonic music as it had prevailed in the preceding era. The crucial point to be emphasized here is that Eisler, the defender of musical modernism (on the one hand, against the conservative "aesthetic barbarism" of the Nazis, and, on the other, against Stalinist anti-modernism), relied to a considerable extent upon text to "ground" his works conceptually and ideologically, in conjunction with his efforts to "refunction" modern musical culture. Initially, around the time of his break with Schönberg (c. 1925-1928), he did so partly to make a critical statement about the poetic inclinations of Schönberg and his "high modern" music; but later, in connection with an explicitly socialist agenda, text played a crucial role in helping Eisler achieve the compositional balance he sought in terms of aesthetic mediation. Eisler had exceptionally high musical values (a legacy of his studies with Schönberg); given his sense of history, he simply would not have resorted to writing epigonal *Schlag*. The textual foundation, as advanced or "difficult" as the music may have been at times, provided an immediate route of access for his listeners to the content he sought to convey. Thus, the textual dimension was crucial to Eisler's efforts at mediation; without it, working in a purely instrumental medium, he would have faced a far greater, if not insurmountable, challenge in attempting to reconcile form and content. Tellingly, his output of instrumental music is very limited compared to his output of songs, choruses, and other vocal works.

With regard to the third issue, of subjectivity and emotionality in both high and low music, it should be noted that, from early on, Eisler was distinctly *dis*inclined toward post-Wagnerian musical grandiloquence as exemplified by composers such as Strauss, Mahler, etc.—as well as the early works of Schönberg. As noted above, he was "attracted more to Brahms's academic stringency." The pertinence of this aesthetic outlook for his subsequent attempts at mediation is that, in attempting to mediate the gap between high and low cultures, Eisler sought to counter the excessive subjectivity and emotionality associated with the former (which had reached a peak around the time he was born) without embracing the sheer banality or "canned" emotionality of the latter. One of the factors at work here was the advent of modern mass-cultural pop musical "hits". But Eisler was also turned off by the "low" music of the preceding era—for example, 19th-century ballad songs, sentimental male chorus numbers, etc., due to their prevalence in the old workers' choruses, all of which he saw as a means of perpetuating "musikalische Dummheit" or "Barbarei in der Musik," and of perpetuating, along with this, the oppression of the working class. In short, in Eisler's case, mediation also represented a quest for some kind of musical middle ground in which emotion is contained or "packaged" more responsibly than in either the high(est) or low(est) traditions/forms of musical culture. In this respect, he was fairly successful in much of his music—the primary reason why he became Brecht's composer of choice, even though Eisler felt Brecht went too far at times in his insistence on "rationality in music." While the following generalization is true to a greater or lesser extent depending upon the specific piece or type of piece involved (with Eisler's works forming a continuum ranging from hard-core *Kampflieder* to lyrical *Elegien*), it may nevertheless be said that the best of his music is sophisticated yet accessible, multilayered but transparent, and, generally, emotionally restrained without denying the significance of emotion as an intrinsic factor in the way music operates, and in people's response to it.

Fourth, related to Eisler's quest for "musical intelligence" as an aspect of aesthetic mediation was his recurrent emphasis on the need to eliminate "musical illiteracy," and to build a new musical culture upon new social foundations. In other words, the pedagogical factor and instinct behind Eisler's work are exceptionally important; figuratively speaking, one could look at his compositions as the musical equivalents of Brecht's concept of *Lehrstück*. Like Arnold Schönberg, he was throughout his life a composer, theoretician, *and* teacher; and much of the extensive body of critical writing he left behind has an implicit pedagogical function, directed as it is towards stimulating people to rethink their traditional musical assumptions and values. The "new musical culture" Eisler envisioned could simply not be realized by

resorting to the standards of contemporary low musical culture; but it was just as unthinkable on the basis of modernist, avant-garde high cultural music alone. In other words, Eisler harbored no illusions about whether or not the masses were ready for Schönberg; clearly, they were not:

> Eine Milliarde Arbeiter und Bauern . . . werden vorläufig mit Schönberg nichts oder nur sehr wenig anfangen können. Sie haben andere und dringlichere Aufgaben. Auf dem Gebiet der Musik ist es die Liquidierung des Musikanalphabetismus. Erst nach solcher Liquidierung und erst nachdem auch die kompliziertesten Werke der Klassiker volkstümlich geworden sind [!], kann Schönberg wieder neu zur Diskussion gestellt werden.

However, to this position statement Eisler added: "Über das Resultat einer solchen Diskussion bin ich nicht ohne Optimismus."

Finally, the matter of "political art." Here, it is crucial to emphasize that, while ultimately the political agenda was primary to Eisler, he never consented to the abandonment of high artistic standards; that is to say, Eisler's approach to "mediation" is intrinsically a question of how to create good art which at the same time is politically effective (or, as Brecht would have said, art with genuine *Gebrauchswert*). This is not intended as an apology for Eisler's political views, nor is it said to appease those who as yet maintain that art and politics (let alone music and politics) do not mix. Rather, the point is that, like his friend Brecht, Eisler saw in his work something born of the necessity of a difficult time; in considering the judgments of others about his music, he would undoubtedly have endorsed Brecht's poetic plea "Gedenkt unsrer / Mit Nachsicht."

Breaking with his mentor in 1926, Eisler set out to be Schönberg's antithesis, though having assimilated a great deal of Schönberg's musical thinking and values. But, in true dialectical fashion, what he ultimately sought to create and be was the valid synthesis of the two; the concept of dialectical synthesis seems useful in considering the matter of mediation in Eisler's case. In the end, Eisler was not able fully to realize the aesthetic solution he was after; it remained a vision, as is evident from the final, at times difficult, chapter in his life and work.

III

Schönberg's death in 1951 had a profound personal impact on Eisler. As he wrote at the time:

> Mit Schönberg ist die spätbürgerliche Musik gestorben. Er war ein Genie, der [*sic*] den Weg der bürgerlichen Kunst bis zum Ende gegangen ist. Neben ihm können nur bestehen: Bartók . . . und Strawinsky.

And further:

> Der Tod Schönbergs hat mich aufs tiefste erschüttert. Es war gar nicht leicht, bei ihm zu

lernen, denn vieles durfte man nicht lernen, und es war schwierig, gegen einen solchen Meister zu bestehen.

By some remarkable coincidence, if Eisler is to be believed, the death of Arnold Schönberg on 13 July 1951 coincided precisely with Eisler's completion of the first draft of his controversial opera libretto *Johann Faustus,* and the conjunction of these two events serves as fruitful basis upon which to conclude my discussion.

In a sense, Eisler set out to accomplish via his *Johann Faustus* opera what Thomas Mann had previously envisioned through the character Leverkühn in his *Faustus* novel, which Eisler so deeply admired; indeed, Eisler quotes from the novel in a statement to West German musicians written in 1951, in which he attempts to clarify what he, the new socialist composer, was attempting to achieve:

> Es geht um sehr viel, um das, was Thomas Mann den 'Durchbruch' nennt. Ich will die schöne Stelle aus seinem *Doktor Faustus* hierher setzen: 'Die ganze Lebensstimmung der Kunst, glauben Sie mir, wird sich ändern. Es ist unvermeidlich, und es ist ein Glück. Viel melancholische Ambition wird von ihr abfallen. Wir stellen es uns nur mit Mühe vor, und doch wird es das geben und wird das Natürliche sein: eine Kunst ohne Leiden, seelisch gesund, eine Kunst, mit der Menschheit auf Du und Du.

Elsewhere, in his "Notes on the *Faustus* Project," Eisler laid out the extraordinary task he perceived to have before him at this moment in history:

> Mit meiner Oper hoffe ich einen neuen Weg gehen zu können, der uns aus dieser Verwirrtheit herausbringt. Ich kann das nur tun, wenn ich nicht experimentiere, wie mein Freund Brecht, oder gar provoziere und schockiere, wie es ebenfalls Brecht liegt, sondern indem ich mit einer reifen, runden, gültigen Leistung komme; sie muss begriffen werden von den unerfahrenen Ohren und den erfahrensten, und der Text muss begriffen werden von den Unerfahrensten und den Gebildetesten. Die Schwierigkeiten dieser Aufgabe sind enorm.

In his efforts to realize this ambitious concept of a "new path," Eisler had at least two major things working against him: a Stalinist cultural bureaucracy which lacked his depth of sophistication and a dialectical perspective on musical history and aesthetics; and, arguably, his own idealism and ambition, i.e., the sheer magnitude of the task which he had set for himself. It is therefore not surprising that, in the decade or so that followed, leading up to the composer's death in 1962, the *Johann Faustus* project was shelved. As far as we know, not one note of music for the opera was ever written, and whether the work could ever have lived up to Eisler's extraordinary expectations of ushering in a new, intrinsically mediated, musical culture—of a highly refined culture but, nevertheless, "eine Musik mit der Menschheit auf Du und Du"—necessarily remains a matter of speculation.

On this final point, some element of skepticism or reservation seems prudent, as worthy and noble as Eisler's aspirations otherwise may have been. In conclusion, it may fairly be said that Eisler, like his contemporary and compatriot Johannes R. Becher, died with a dream of "künftige Vollendung"; his concept of a new synthesis inherently mediating "Musik mit der Menschheit auf Du und Du" ultimately remained a vision. It appears that Eisler himself realized that his outlook was somehow *unzeitgemäss,* out of synch with historical, political, and cultural reality. Perhaps this is what he had in mind when adapting Hölderlin's poem "Der Gang aufs Land" for his final work, the *Ernste Gesänge:* the movement in question, entitled "Komm! ins Offene, Freund" (the opening words of the poem), contains the revealing lines "aber kommen doch auch der segenbringenden Schwalben / Immer einige noch, ehe der Sommer, ins Land." But this is not to diminish the historical significance of Hanns Eisler, Arnold Schönberg's forgotten pupil. Having learned from an *Esel-Meister* (which is explicitly not to say: "ein *Meister-Esel*"), he left behind a remarkable legacy of his own, as one who sought to create a mediated, "spiritually healthy," musical culture—a legacy that has been grossly underappreciated and unjustifiably marginalized in the annals of modern music history.

Daniel C. Melnick (essay date 1994)

SOURCE: "Music and the Modern Imagination: Nietzsche and Schoenberg," in *Fullness of Dissonance: Modern Fiction and the Aesthetics of Music,* Associated University Presses, 1994, pp. 44-58.

[*In the following essay, Melnick explores the wider applications of Schoenberg's atonality and Friedrich Nietzche's theory of music to modern art and literature.*]

Nietzsche is the conclusive nineteenth-century figure for the study of music's tie to modernism, and in this regard he is, next to Beethoven, the most significant, not only for his influence on individual novelists like Proust, Lawrence, and Mann, but for his seminal ideas about dissonance and its tie to listening and reading, and to modern existence itself.

One key to Nietzsche's ideas about music is suggested by his late reflections "contra Wagner," his postulating there that his own writings rather than Wagner's operas were the true focus of his early conceptions of music in *The Birth of Tragedy.* Here, as well as in his 1886 preface to his early work, and in *The Wagner Case,* Nietzsche's late comments abrasively confront and—in their athletic vigor—triumph over what he saw as the decadence of Wagner's operas, the music's "surrender" to passive "impotence" and "hatred against life." Wagner's listener becomes a central target of this critique: His listener is numbed to independent perception, to the needed, tragic and playful questioning. The operas achieve "effects . . . in the service, the slavery, of poses" in order "to give the people satisfaction," to "impress" them, so that ultimately the listener is "comforted metaphysically." The effect, then, of Wagner's art is one of "surrender," of "floating," of "hebetation" on the passive "mass, on the immature, on the blasé, on the sick, on the idiots, on Wagnerians."

The rhetorical thrust of Nietzsche's critique of the listener's "surrender" in Wagner is to call for an alternative way of engaging aesthetic experience based on radical doubt about ordinary habits of perceiving works of art. Theodor Adorno helps us to describe that doubt. A consenting passivity in the music listener, he writes, "serves the status quo, which could be changed only by people who, instead of confirming themselves and the world, would reflect critically on the world and on themselves." In Nietzsche's work, music—revalued as a metaphor—can become an instrument to identify and stimulate that active, critically reflective doubt.

Before we examine the conception of music to be found in *The Birth of Tragedy* and elsewhere, let me describe generally the nature of Nietzschean doubt in music. Rather than a Wagnerian, manipulative cynicism that, to Nietzsche, seems to secure and reinforce a passivity in the "spectator," Nietzsche desires a "pessimism of strength," which can arise from the musical experience and which comprehends as well as confirms "the fullness of existence." Both in aesthetic experience and in "life," consciousness and language—through which it knows itself—are redefined as activities filled with imaginative potentiality, a play of possibilities continually on the verge of coming into being. Arising from this redefinition of consciousness are critical recognitions both of the disfiguring and imprisoning hold which cliché can have over perception and of the relative "fictiveness" of "truth." Yet Nietzsche's radical and affirming pessimism emerges from, and itself yields, a sense of the overabundance and vitality of consciousness.

As we read Nietzsche's own texts, we confront a rhetoric—or really a process—which has an impact not unlike that detected by listeners as diverse as Tovey, Mann, Bloch, and Barthes in Beethoven's late works: We experience a disruption of complaisant "certainties" which is not cynical but rather looses in us a creative process and potentiality. The radical doubt with which Nietzsche assaults the reader compels in him a sense of the open-ended abundance of fiction, so that the text becomes, finally, the scene of intense activity in the reader. What such a text requires is embodied and defined by an important entry (no.310) on the wave and "we who will" from *The Gay Science*. This passage takes up a key image of sea and swimmer/navigator which has recurred in the texts on music I have examined, and it is akin also to another passage in Nietzsche's work—on the image of woman stirring the menaced recognition of life as a fiction, amid "the flaming surf"—which Derrida takes up in *Spurs* as part of his critical performance on Nietzsche.

> How greedily this wave approaches, as if there were some objective to be reached! How with awe-inspiring haste it crawls into the inmost nooks of the rocky cliff! It seems that it wants to anticipate somebody; it seems that something is hidden there, something of value, high value.
>
> And now it comes back, a little more slowly, still quite white with excitement—is it disappointed? But already another wave is approaching, still greedier and wilder than the first, and its soul too seems to be full of secrets and the lust to dig up treasures. Thus live the waves—thus we who will.

This destabilizing metaphorical leap from the waves to the way we live evokes how the shore of our consciousness is confronted by an overfull, vertiginous choice of imaginative possibility; the leaping vigor of Nietzsche's own text aims to provoke "us," his readers, with a wrenched and greedy liberation from habitual thinking, with "waves" of self-questioning and freedom. "The danger for the reader," David Allison suggests, "ultimately lies in the dispossession of his own identity and the loss of his conventional world." Nietzsche's texts confront the bourgeois "self" in the reader with its tendency to identify with the power of the will, and they stir a transformation of that tendency by means of their critical and satiric instability. To engage the aphoristic attack particularly of his late style, its hyperbole, parody, and oxymoronic ambiguity—in short, to read Nietzsche—is, finally, to engage an intimate assault on and opening up of consciousness.

The distinction between the perceiving consciousness—with its manifestation in "style"—and the perceived "world" is erased for Nietzsche; both present themselves as a "play of appearances," an interactive abundance of fictions, finally as "waves" of language. They emerge so partly because the habitual fictions or codes—which form how and what we know—are subject to the workings of desire, to our creative will (as Gilles Deleuze argues in his discussion of Nietzsche's politics of desire). What results is a suspension of consciousness and the world *as fictions*, as "texts." Nietzsche's notion of self-overcoming mirrors this conception of consciousness, for it celebrates a process of the provisional, committed creation and testing of versions of selves. The idea of how "overcoming" operates illuminates the workings of Nietzsche's own text—and of modern narrative, I would add—on and for the reader. The process of testing and creating selves is the process into which the modern novel initiates the reader; such fiction self-consciously promises and welcomes the playful vitality of the process as it affirms its tragic endlessness and uncertainty. To read such a text is to navigate the disaster of modernity, to preserve access to creative freedom, and to resist the totalizing structures—or horizon—of assurance; "reading," Derrida suggests about this Nietzschean strategy, "is to perforate such an horizon or the hermeneutic sail." Nietzsche's text powerfully invites this critical engagement as it eludes definitive interpretation.

Nietzsche's link to the assumptions underlying Deconstruction is worth examining here and can help us to understand some of the implications of Nietzsche's thought for dissonant narrative and for modernism itself. The work of Paul de Man, for example, offers a sometimes discomfiting appropriation of Nietzsche along with, indeed, a panoply of pre-, proto-, and postmodernisms. The dense, obscure abstraction of de Man's discourse, even the brief early invocations of racist elitism, and then the later risk of solipsism in his interpretations—all bespeak the tense importation into his work of certain, at times deformed, practices of modernism. The tortuous abstraction in de Man's presentation of these various strands of thought enacts the dilemma of a critical practice on the edge of nihilism; the agony of its circuitous refusal to affirm anything beyond its own practice in language mirrors the agony of a disappearing humanism in the aftermath of modernity.

Several essays of de Man take up Nietzsche's thought, most notably in *Allegories of Reading,* in which the emphasis is on exposing the disordered freedom of consciousness at work particularly in the most prescriptive Nietzschean rhetoric and texts. This approach to Nietzsche grows from de Man's allegiance to two contradictory strains in modernist thinking: One is concerned with the agonized risk and fertility of a freed, open-ended consciousness, and the other is concerned with the purely linguistic autonomy of modernist form.

About the first, more clearly Nietzschean conception, de Man develops an idea of reading—and interpretation—as an opportunity to circumvent the "self" and the "self"-deception or "blindness" assumed by the reader's "knowledge" and values, his epistemological and methodological perspective. In this way, de Man argues for literature's power to enact and achieve the Nietzschean insight in *Ecce Homo* that "to become what one is, one must not have the faintest notion what one is." "The text," de Man writes in *Blindness and Insight,* "brings the reader back to what he might have been before he shaped himself into a particular self." In this derivative conception, the reader experiences a version of Binneswanger's "fall upwards," an always incomplete and unstable process, a movement out of the structured representations of empirical or metaphysical "reality" onto the plain of freed, imaginative consciousness. Particularly modern literature offers the moments of "unbearable" pressure in this way to renew alternative selves, to activate the imagination.

Simultaneously at work, however, in de Man's conception is a contradictory assumption that abjures all ethical resonance in literature. De Man emphasizes that literary language does not "represent" reality or any access to "meaning," but is rather a projection of purely fictive possibility, empirical only in rejecting the claims of "presence" and certainty as meaningless. In various essays, de Man adapts and indeed reduces ideas of music developed by Rousseau or Rilke or Nietzsche to a demonstration that literature—specifically a musicalized literature—demystifies and negates all "truth" claims in a process of continual, fictive construction and deconstruction. Human reality, whether critical, creative, or empirical, becomes in de Man's hands, a shallow, debased version of the scene and drama Nietzsche brilliantly describes, as follows: "Truth" is

> a mobile army of metaphors, metonyms, and anthropomorphisms—in short, a sum of human relations, which have been enhanced, transposed, and embellished poetically and rhetorically and which after long use seem firm, cannonical, and obligatory to a people: truths are illusions about which one has forgotten that this is what they are.

De Man, however, in emphasizing a quasi-tragic reduction of literature into pure figuration, solely into the language of tropes, "isolates too purifyingly" (as Harold Bloom suggests) "the trope from the topos or commonplace that generates it." De Man's tendency is to withdraw from the Nietzschean insistence on truth as a struggling "sum of human relations," of "people," yet "these are," as Jonathan Arac writes, exactly "the elements, less than the figures, from which to construct a history of the contingencies that have put us in the odd place that we are."

It is in a struggle to understand "the odd place that we are" that Nietzsche himself creates a rhetoric to explore the sense of the endless multiplicity, contradiction, and nontruth of "truth." In this way, he offers us a prototype for modern narrative texts. Given the skepticism and freedom at work in such texts, the critical Nietzschean aim becomes to envision—as Erich Heller writes, echoing Zarathustra—what it is like to perceive and live without belief in truth, again not cynically, but with the awareness that "truth" is a function of will, judgment, self-critical sublimation, and choice.

II

We can now return to the issue of the activity—as opposed to the passivity—of the aesthetic consciousness and to Nietzsche's use of the dissonant metaphor to characterize that activity. It is Nietzsche's development of that analogy which explains and prefigures the musicality—the dissonance—of the modern novel.

Nietzsche takes up the matter of music in *The Birth of Tragedy from the Spirit of Music* and then implicitly in *Thus Spoke Zarathustra.* The latter work unfolds on many levels under the aegis of the musical metaphor: "Perhaps the whole of Zarathustra may be reckoned as music," Nietzsche writes in *Ecce Homo,* and he adds a salient point about the Dionysian listener/reader: "Certainly a rebirth of the art of *hearing* was among its preconditions." Nietzsche's 1886 introduction to *The Birth of Tragedy* also reminds us of Zarathustra's tie to the work of 1872.

In this early major text, he presents the fundamental idea that Greek tragedy emerged from the tension between the Apollonian and the Dionysian: the former manifests itself as the perfected, dream-like heroic forms of tragedy, which imagine the desired ideals in "existence," and the latter is the Dionysian, "choric" response embodying the audience's emotional reaction to tragedy, the force of their awed, enraged, and immense desire for the perfected Apollonian forms. To maintain the balance between Apollo and Dionysus, is the process—and finally the ascetic ideal of "overcoming"—at the core of Nietzsche's vision generally, as Arthur Danto argues. Here, in Greek tragedy, the disillusioning, anarchic, "tragic insight" of the musical, Dionysian imagination—with its capacious desire for and summoning up of Apollonian forms—is the choric audience's recognition that beautiful Apollo is but a fiction yet, as such, a crucial source of the "multifarious diversity" seen as fictions, as metaphors. Here the perceiver's recognition (like the creator's) denies all certainty of self, of subject, and of audience itself, in other words, moves away from the lyric ideal toward the model of dissonance. Nietzsche's conception of dissonance provides a key analysis of this Dionysian response of the perceiver in tragic art. The passage on dissonance occurs at the end of *The Birth of Tragedy,* after his celebration of the Dionysian vision he has already located in Wagner; it is one of the moments in the text when, in retrospect, we see Nietzsche wrest himself free of his anxious projection of a Nietzschean image onto Wagner's operas. Now he links musical dissonance to the phenomenon in Greek tragedy of facing the terrible, out of an over-fullness of life, and of having the capacity to render and to affirm it as part of the abundance of life.

Here, the Dionysian is not seen as rooted in a Schopenhauerian "metaphysical solace" which substitutes the presence and witness of irrational "truth" for a Socratic "rationalization" of the "truth." Rather, Nietzsche's redefinition now insists that the Dionysian is an aesthetic activity, above all a process involving the listener/reader in a journey of engagement, the destination of which is unknown:

> Existence and the world seem justified only as an aesthetic phenomenon. In this sense, it is precisely the tragic myth that has to convince us that even the ugly and disharmonic are part of an artistic game that will in the eternal amplitude of its pleasure plays with itself. But this primordial phenomenon of Dionysian art is difficult to grasp, and there is only one direct way to make it intelligible and grasp it immediately: through the wonderful significance of *musical dissonance. . . .* The joy aroused by the tragic myth has the same origin as the joyous sensation of dissonance in music. The Dionysian, with its primordial joy experienced even in pain, is the common source of music and tragic myth.

Musical dissonance becomes here a metaphor for the creative process activated within the freed consciousness (a "singing Socrates" indeed). Dissonance—the ambiguous movement away from and between tonal "certainties"—exists in a state of suspension, of striving beyond "heard harmony" toward its negation, the powerful, unheard creative silence which each of the writers studied

here finds and celebrates in Beethoven. Dissonance—which longs "to get beyond all hearing"—"reveals to us the playful construction and destruction of the individual world as the overflow of a primordial delight."

Nietzsche here moves beyond affirming the solemn myth in Wagner which holds the listener in the grasp of "metaphysical solace" and "surrender." To see this feature of the text most clearly, Walter Kaufmann shows, *The Birth of Tragedy* should be read in conjunction with excised portions and notes and particularly with the contemporaneous fragment "On Music and Words" (appended to Carl Dahlhaus's *Between Romanticism and Modernism*), a fragment which, as Dahlhaus indicates, "contains the outlines of Nietzsche's later critique of Wagner." Read in this way, *The Birth of Tragedy* "explodes" the limitations of its sporadic, lyrical, "Wagnerian" affirmations, of the text's "authority," so that the Dionysian *process* at work here is shown to concern not a mythic presence but the disordered freedom of consciousness. This movement redefining the Dionysian not as solemn, irrational "truth" but as a process, finally, of liberation, is carried further in the 1886 preface criticizing the turgid lack of musicality in *The Birth of Tragedy* (which was, after all, his Ph.D. thesis). The Preface avows the need to "dance," to "learn to laugh" as essential to the nature of music, to Dionysian "play." The rhetoric of modern narrative is forecast by this rhetoric of the 1886 preface, with its own experimental "dance" intermingling "critical irony and tragic gaiety, earned by that irony," very much like the autobiographical, literary strategy of *Ecce Homo* as Altieri describes it (such an aesthetic strategy pervades Nietzsche, as Alexander Nehamas shows).

Modern consciousness and narrative, and finally history itself (as Foucault suggests about Nietzsche) can all be understood as emanations of such dissonance. The link for Nietzsche between a dissonant aesthetic and ethic becomes evident here, and we can now also begin to see the connection between Dionysian dissonance and other keys to Nietzsche's thought—the idea of self-overcoming, as I noted earlier, and that of the eternal return. These Nietzschean ideas link together, as Kathleen Higgins has argued, to convey a "simultaneous awareness of past and present [finally projecting] a sense of the whole in which the present moment is the immediately experienced part." She explains, using and then moving beyond a Zuckerkandlian perspective, that Nietzsche reveals how "we enjoy the fullness of the present musical moment, even if it is dissonant, not for its own efficiency in moving towards the evident musical goal, but for its own surprising presence." Pierre Klossowski similarly and even more insistently shows that this network of linkages (eternal return, self-overcoming, and, I would add, musical dissonance) shares an ethic and aesthetic which, above all, posit the flux of *multiplicity* in selves and events. Nietzsche's tragic affirmation of that multiplicity is nowhere more evident than in his embrace of *amor fati,* of the eternally recurrent process by which the encompassing flux of image and experience is tested and affirmed, now, as it were, intrinsically worthy of fated reperformance. This notion of the embrace of multiplicity and "reperformance" points again to the connection I am exploring between Dionysian dissonance and the modern novel; for, in this regard, the eternal return and dissonance provide a model for reading itself. The engagement, testing, and affirmation of the ever-changing, clashing, and unfolding waves of multiplicity define that opportunity and operation of reading modern narrative. (Claude Lévesque speaks in similar terms of the tie, in the century since Nietzsche, between dissonance and aesthetic language generally.)

III

The connection between Dionysian dissonance and the modern novel can be illustrated in D. H. Lawrence's vision, in *Aaron's Rod,* which we saw presents an image of Beethoven as well, or later in *Apocalypse,* which is in part a lapsed, English "nonconformist's" variation on themes from Nietzsche's *Genealogy of Morals.* In this, his last prophetic essay, Lawrence defines and presents the Dionysian as a dynamic "seeing through" the veil of the conventional, the forced pose, the "known," the empirical; in pre-Socratic Greece, for example, "'the cold,' 'the moist,' 'the hot,' 'the dry,' were things in themselves, realities, gods, *theoi.*" What is seen in the Dionysian perspective is a great flux of "life's" images, both agonized and beneficient, all filled not with materialist presence but with imaginative desire, with the "gods"—that is, with the "primordial delight" of imaginative consciousness. And in Lawrence's Nietzschean vision such creative delight exists in opposition to the "evasion" insisted on by the author of Revelations, with John's "proud impotence" so like the resentment and solace the Wagnerian listener is confronted with.

> By the very frenzy with which the Apocalypse destroys the sun and the stars, the world. . . . we can see how deeply the apocalyptists are yearning for the sun and the stars and the earth and the waters of the earth, for nobility and lordship and might, and scarlet and gold spendour, for passionate love, and a proper unison with men, apart from this sealing business. What man most passionately wants is his living wholeness and his living unison, not his own isolate salvation of his 'soul.' . . . We ought to dance with rapture that we should be alive and in the flesh, and part of the living, incarnate cosmos.

The Dionysian is a means of ascertaining neither revenge nor false solace nor mechanistic truth. Rather it is the process of creating a world of yearned-for, imaginative truth, an earth whose soil is meaning, in which it is not only dirt but the stuff of significance into which one thrusts one's hands. Such are the images Lawrence offers in *Apocalypse,* as does Joyce in Stephen's epiphany at the end of chapter IV of *A Portrait of the Artist as a Young Man.*

What is the bearing of Dionysian dissonance on the rhetoric of such images in modern fiction? For the freed, creative, Dionysian consciousness, language becomes the scene, indeed the very process of tapping the capacity for imaging, for the metamorphosis of selves and of meanings. A result is the layering and complicating of modern narrative—its freeing from convention, its opening up to ambiguity. Language as dissonance formulates its images as freely created fictions. Particularly for the novelist with a consciousness of this fictiveness, language displaces its own self-destruction through its abundant waves of imaginative energy, the process of its dissonance. Finally, the "sinister resonance" of a work like Conrad's *Heart of Darkness* ("dwelling on the ear after the last note had been struck") is a metaphor imaging that freed critical and creative novelistic consciousness, above all, in the reader.

The "wisdom" resonating in dissonant fiction is particularly the awareness that, as modern fiction activates creative freedom *in the reader,* a profound risk is involved, which Lawrence and the novelists who play out the Nietzschean logic recognize. When Lawrence, for example, introduces the fertile image of Dionysis in his theoretical essays or of "Osiris cut to pieces" in his late *The Man Who Died,* the texts also simultaneously dramatize the potential despair in the object of Dionysian metamorphosis. Particularly, Lawrence's late fable takes up the notion, which Nietzsche also voices in *Zarathustra,* of imagining for Jesus a final human trajectory, a full, agonized fall to sensuous earth. Resurrected, he is repelled by being worshipped by his followers, disappears to Egypt, and takes a Dionysian part there in the rite of a priestess of "Isis in Search" of dismembered Osiris.

> She was looking for fragments of the dead Osiris, dead and scattered asunder, dead, torn apart, and thrown in fragments over the wide world. . . . [S]he must gather him together and fold her arms around the re-assembled body till it became warm again, and roused to life, and could embrace her, and could fecundate her womb. . . . [S]he had not [yet] found the last reality, the final clue to him, that alone could bring him really back for her.

The fleeing, alienated Jesus, she finds, is this realization of Osiris. In a prose of intentional uncontrol that characteristically forces together incantation and an exposing objectivity, Lawrence allows Jesus momentarily to know (both sexually and spiritually) his nakedness: "If I am naked enough for this contact, I have not died in vain." Lawrence insists always here on the naked as the operative term and concept; his emphasis is above all on the vulnerable, the unmoored and stripped down, the fated transiency, the naked circling in death of Jesus. This metamorphosis in a continual death and stripping of former selves takes him out again at the fable's end, past Isis, navigating still further in death: "Let the boat carry me."

Jesus in *The Man Who Died* experiences the risk and fate embodied in the image of Osiris—and of Dionysus and, indeed, of Orpheus—another dismembered god. This new, final, open-ended fable of Jesus contains precisely the challenge of dissonance to his hearer/reader, that the orphic song contains—and the same danger of dismembered, constantly disappearing and reassembling consciousness. An endless metamorphosis, charged with desire, in the midst of dying selves—Blanchot explains in "Orpheus' Gaze"—constitutes the knotted and paradoxical effect for the reader as for character and creator in twentieth-century narrative; "in his song . . . Orpheus is the dismembered, endlessly dying Orpheus his song has created. The song cannot do without desire and lost Eurydice and dismembered Orpheus." The "song-text" which emerges for Lawrence and other modern novelists is composed of Dionysian dissonance. "Dissonance takes root in this nether region," Claude Lévesque concludes in "Language to the Limit," a region

> where resounds endlessly the mute scream let out by Dionysus. . . . Why be astonished that man, at the point of not being able to know and to bear it anymore, in appealing to the other, takes on the colossal and intolerable voice of the scream?

In dissonant narrative, we hear—and see bared in the text and in ourselves—the potential despair in the object of Dionysian metamorphosis: It is the yearned-for release, both endless rupture and healing, compounded of the promise and the void of creative desire. These antinomies are best defined and understood through an examination of the crucial modern composer in the mode of dissonance, Arnold Schoenberg.

IV

The example of Schoenberg's music can further clarify the risks and opportunities for the perceiver in a musicalized text. In this composer's work, we hear a full, uncentering "roaring" of "unearthly" dissonance, to use images from the George poem sung in the finale of Schoenberg's second string quartet (1911); in that movement, as the strings violently disassemble a primitive scale of half-tones and the soprano offers a twelve tone melody as she sings of "breath[ing] the air of another planet," the listener hears a historic welcome of the free play of dissonance in music. Indeed, the dissonance of this final movement of the 1911 quartet—not the serial controls of his later music—embodies the aesthetic of dissonance I explore and most clearly parallels the aims of modernist narrative. Schoenberg's dissonance achieves an intentionally difficult negation of music's grounding, commonly received, tonal conventions, a negation that becomes the only certainty left to assume (as Charles Rosen suggests). Such dissonance—typical of Schoenberg's reimagining of the entire range of musical conventions—achieves its creative negation above all, as Rosen and Adorno indicate, *in the context* of the common musical language—that is, above all as opposition. Schoenberg drives to its logical conclusion the subversions propounded by the irony and ironic beauty of Mahler's symphonies; by Debussy's nuanced, synaesthetic, sometimes violent freeing of tonal centers from clichéd stability, even by Brahms, as he follows a Beethovenian logic of freed formal experiment, breaking

atrophied lyric conventions in favor of developing a "musical prose," as Schoenberg suggests in *Style and Idea*. The severe and radical logic in Schoenberg's music is an indication that—like Beethoven before him, only more "absolutely"—Schoenberg must attempt to explode the compulsively and falsely "affirming" stasis of the common language in order to emancipate the creative imaginative potentiality of language itself; both Rosen and Carl Dahlhaus emphasize that this "emancipation of the dissonance" is, as Dahlhaus writes, "the reason why tonality had been renounced."

Schoenberg's aim is, then, to give his musical language the guise and substance of freedom, of a freed, continual becoming, shaped though it need be, by opposition and negativity. By exposing what Webern calls "the chasms in cliché," this difficult, disruptive, continual negation in the dissonant language becomes in part a protest against those too-easy, preformed, subjective affirmations to which the listener could otherwise surrender. Nietzsche's prescription for a dissonant aesthetic consciousness is fulfilled here, for—as Stanley Cavell points out— Schoenberg understood the dangerous necessity of dissonant composition: "that taste must be defeated," music "discomposed," in order to fulfill "the essential moral motive" of modern art. Adorno describes this necessity in *Philosophy of Modern Music* when he analyzes what I am calling the Dionysian or dissonant consciousness in Schoenberg's music. The bourgeois illusion of individual subjective affirmation—the "illusion of authenticity"—is, Adorno writes, "sacrificed" because it is "incompatible with the state of that consciousness which has been driven so far towards individuation by the liberal order, to the point that this consciousness negates the order which had advanced it thus far." Schoenberg's dissonant language presents that negation "as its goal. It is the surviving message of despair from the shipwrecked."

Here we directly face the notion of the risk to the perceiver of dissonance. Schoenberg's listener is thrust into the activity of perceiving this new language of dissonance as a radical event in the language of consciousness itself. Its alienation and liberation of the "perceptual" process aims at straining the potentiality of tonality, of the order of consciousness and language exercised now in revolt at the outer limits of their capacity; the "fictive" creations of dissonance are radical particularly in that they demand an openness to negation in the listener. Schoenberg's self-consciousness about this demand on his diminished audience for the "new music" in Vienna helps to raise the issue of the performative impact of dissonance on the perceiver. By continually reenacting the "shipwreck" of modern consciousness (the casting out onto the waves of negation), the rhetorical strategy of Schoenberg's desperate negation leads the perceiver to engage a risktaking, aesthetic and ethical challenge, one suggested by the antinomies which Adorno, Rosen, Dahlhaus, and others explore: that challenge is to encounter dissonant negation *as the form,* the language and activity ("not mere contemplation" as Adorno says in

Prisms, "but praxis") which embodies and achieves the survival of a freed consciousness in the modern period.

Jean-François Lyotard's critique of Schoenberg—in "Several Silences"—questions this freedom achieved by the composer's dissonant strategy (and his critique finds echoes in Jacques Attali's argument, in James Winn's contrasting of Schoenberg's "subjectivity" with Stravinsky's rhetoricity, and in certain criticisms of Adorno's "atonal philosophy" mounted, for example, by John Shepard et al.). Lyotard would abjure what he sees as Schoenberg's puritanical seeking of "the tragic" and of a "therapeutics" in which music is a "discourse" of stigmatizing negativity and "control." Instead, Lyotard would embrace an aesthetic of "circulation by chance," a "free wandering" suggested teasingly by images of Mao's noisy swimming in the Yangste and of Cage's play with noise and silence. Yet where Lyotard hears in Schoenberg's dissonance a holding aloof from the free play of cultural sounds, there is as accurately a refusal to wrest apart—indeed an insistence on the link between—freedom and critical consciousness; and where he hears a "liquefying" or "dememorizing" of "domination" in Cagean play, there coexists in such play also an ornamental, "aestheticized subjectivity" (as Dahlhaus suggests in *Schoenberg*), a postmodern forgetting and erasure—like plastic surgery—of the scars in twentieth-century history and culture, to use an image from Kroker and Cook's *The Postmodern Scene.*

Schoenberg's art provides a revelatory model for modern fiction and particularly for its modernist aim: to prompt the perceiver first to imagine a disintegration of consciousness, a tearing apart of received, assumed "expressivity," a movement into contradiction, obliquity, parody, and silence, so that **Moses and Aaron** ends incomplete, fractured, its sung speech splintering into silence: "O word that I lack." Yet, simultaneously, as the act of imagining can negate the processes of consciousness, Schoenberg's music offers a paradigmatic model for dissonant narrative which conveys within that negation a liberating attitude toward consciousness. Torn from the moribund habits of ordinary, habitual consciousness, the reader of the modern novel is challenged to engage the liberated fullness of fictive form within the suspension and negation of the habitual modes of perception. The "fullness" of alienation within the dissonant fiction of Proust, Mann, and Joyce achieves above all a full, imaginative, and critical freedom within the suspension of consciousness as a fiction—abundant, multifarious, playful, alien, and distressed.

Philippe Lacoue-Labarthe (essay date 1994)

SOURCE: "The Caesura of Religion," in *Opera Through Other Eyes,* edited by David J. Levin, Stanford University Press, 1994, pp. 45-77.

[*In the following essay, Lacoue-Labarthe discusses the religious undercurrents in Schoenberg's work.*]

No doubt, it is not impossible to say that Wagner fundamentally *saturated* opera. A proof of this, which is nonetheless indirect, is that everything which followed without exempting itself from the exorbitant ambition he had imposed upon the form carries the stigmata of the end. This may be in the nostalgic and relatively comfortable mode to which the late Strauss resigned himself, a mode that in short ended his career with an adieu, more disenchanted than really melancholic, to the two genres in which, as he well recognized, a limit had been reached (this is why the so-called *Four Last Songs,* if only because they return to the "law of genre," that is, to a pre-Mahlerian state of the *Lied,* have a meaning analogous to the autoreflection "in the manner of" which orders *Capriccio*). But it may also be in the mode of redundancy, and thus of oversaturation, for which the early Strauss was renowned (or the Schönberg of the **Gurrelieder**) and in which the Puccini of *Turandot* pathetically exhausted himself. But then again, it may be in the more equivocal and more subtle (more "French") mode of destructuration à la Debussy. Or finally, it may be in the style of properly modern radicality, the style of violent rupture and incompleteness, of "failure": Berg's *Lulu,* Schönberg's **Moses and Aaron**. And here, it is incontestable, things are much more grave. One might say, not only because it raises the ante where the means of expression are concerned (a move that Nietzsche had already denounced as an art subordinated to the search for effects), but rather because of its *systematic* character, in the strict sense of the term, that Wagner's work left to its posterity a task every bit as impossible as the one left by German Idealism (Hegel) to its great followers in philosophy: to continue that which is finished. Thus, just as one may speak of the "Hegelian closure" of philosophy, one might speak of the Wagnerian closure of opera and even of art itself, or as they said at the time, of *great art,* for such was the "ambition" of art. As a result of their anti-Hegelianism, what Wagner's writings and *The Birth of Tragedy* most clearly show is that in wishing to overcome [*überwinden*] opera and all its "culture," Wagner devotes himself with the *Gesamtkunstwerk* to a totalizing sublation, to an *Aufhebung* of all the arts, and to a *restoration* of "great art" which is all the more powerful for being all the more modern (with other technical means, in effect): a restoration of Greek tragedy, of course. At the same time, if the other arts were able to take another direction, and allowed themselves to be guided from the outset by another concept of "great" and another intuition of "art," opera, itself a recent art though it would wish itself ancient, suffered severely from such a declaration of completion. In fact, it was unable to recover from it, or only did so poorly.

Here *saturate* means simply: too much music or, if one prefers, despite the paradox, too much "Italianism" and too much credit accorded the *prima la musica.* In short it is the belief in music's "sublational" capacity (or, as he would say, its "synthesizing" capacity) that destroys for Wagner any chance of acceding to "totality" and binds him to musical saturation, condemning him to choose sides in what is after all nothing but the classical dilemma of opera. Saturation is a false totalization, at least insofar as it testifies to the false character of any will to totalization, be it conceptual or not. On this point at least, though for entirely different reasons, Heidegger and Adorno agree with one another, and both of them attribute the responsibility for this unrestrained, "infinite" melocentrism to Schopenhauer, to the metaphysics of "feeling" and the "unconscious" (to the vague mysticism, Adorno says, of "thalassal regression"). Wagner definitively considered nothing but the problem of opera and did so to the nearly exclusive benefit of music and not to that of theater, where, in relation to the Italian apparatus, his innovations are rather slim. Or to put it otherwise: as a *Dichterkomponist* (a monstrous term, as Adorno remarks), Wagner confused language with "words" and music with the essence of language, its origin and its assumption. In the demonstration which he conducts in the "Music Drama" chapter of *In Search of Wagner*, Adorno cites some passages that are in this sense damning:

> Science has laid bare to us the organism of language, but what she showed us was a dead organism, which only the poet's utmost can bring to life again, namely, by suturing the wounds with which the anatomic scalpel has gashed the body of language and by breathing into it the breath that may animate it with living motion. This breath, however, is—music. . . .
>
> The necessary bestowal from within oneself, the seed that can only in the most ardent transports of love condense itself from its noblest forces—which grows only in order to be released, i.e. to be released for the purposes of fertilization, indeed which is in and of itself [*an sich*] this more or less materialized drive—this procreative seed is the poetic intention, which brings to the gloriously loving woman, Music, the stuff for bearing.

Despite their erotico-dialectical pathos (the same pathos, though less rigorous, or, as Adorno would say, more "voluptuous" than that which governs the opening paragraphs of *The Birth of Tragedy*), texts of this genre have at least one merit: they reveal the reason why all operas that have seriously tried to resist Wagnerian saturation, leaving aside those that have deliberately renounced totalization (this is above all true of Berg), have taken the form of a sort of "performative" meditation on the essence of language (of speech) in its relation to music, and thus on the very nature of the opera form. In Strauss, who is the most belated and no doubt the most "informed," the protocol, under its slightly belabored eighteenth-century elegance, is relatively coarse, even if it gives ample evidence of a certain intelligence about what is at stake. But finally it is a bit disarming to take as one's subject the *Querelle des Bouffons* or that of the Piccinists and the Gluckists, for with an opera in opera or about opera (*Ariadne, Capriccio*) one remains in the simple register of the *mise en abîme* and citation. In the end, one does not choose at all; with an emphatic wink one leaves the generic conflict of opera in suspense. By contrast, in Berg (Wozzeck, the "poor creature," is the interdiction of

eloquence and music, and consequently is interdiction itself) and above all in Schönberg, the problem is touched upon with an entirely different profundity, and with an entirely different acuity.

Above all in Schönberg: it is well known that this problem is the very subject of *Moses and Aaron* and, what is more essential, that it is constitutive of the opera's treatment. The opposition of speech and singing (or, more exactly, of *Sprechgesang* and *Gesang*) which, no matter what Adorno says, very rigorously transposes the biblical opposition of Moses' stammering and Aaron's eloquence into the register of the work—and here the very question of the prohibition of (re)presentation, which thus is *also* the subject of the opera, is condensed—leads the opera to put its own principle into question with great lucidity. And consequently it reopens the scar that Wagner, by musical saturation, had intended to suture definitively in a sort of hyperbolic assumption of opera itself. Now what Adorno, who is in fact one of the few who have confronted Schönberg's *oeuvre désoeuvrée*, "saves" from *Moses,* despite his vigilance with respect to Wagnerism, is precisely musical saturation. In the final pages of his great essay of 1963, "Sakrales Fragment: Über Schönberg's *Moses und Aron*," Adorno remarks that Schönberg, who evidently does not order his work according to a serialist dramaturgy of opera, also does not order his work according to a dramaturgy of the Wagnerian type (if a traditional model is still operative, it would be that of oratorio). This prevents nothing: when Adorno wants to justify what he calls the "success" of *Moses,* what he brings forward is the work's "power," and does so all the more because this power accords with the metaphysical (or religious) aims of the work. Now with what does this power or, and this amounts to the same thing, this "monumentality of tone" have to do? Not with simplicity, at least not immediately, but rather "with everything which is gathered together in this music and which occupies the musical space." Adorno comments:

> In no other work does Schönberg so consistently and with such facility follow the rule that the compositional effort—that is to say, in the first place the sheer quantity of simultaneous events—should correspond to the content of the music, of the events to be represented. In *Moses* he takes this to extremes. Nowhere else is there so much music, almost in the literal sense of so many notes, as here *ad majorem Dei gloriam*. The sheer density of the construction becomes the medium in which the ineffable can manifest itself without usurpation. For it is this that can be wholly and convincingly created in the material by Schönberg's own musical consciousness.

Once again the style of this saturation is not Wagnerian, if only because the writing is too complex and because it no longer orders itself according to the imperative of a *melos*. But all the same, it is a saturation. And it is linked to a religious or metaphysical content as its most adequate mode of expression. It is as if in the end *Moses and Aaron* were nothing other than the negative (in the photographic sense) of *Parsifal*, thus accomplishing, in a paradoxical manner, the project of the total work. And in fact, this is virtually what we read in Adorno's final remarks:

> By conceptualizing this we have probably arrived at the full measure of Schönberg's success in his biblical opera. It is intensified by what seems at first to stand in its way: the inordinate complexity of the music. This leads to the liberation of Schönberg's supreme talent, his gift for combination, his precise grasp of distinct but simultaneous events. The idea of unity in diversity becomes a sensuous musical reality in him. He was able not just to imagine, but actually to invent complexes of opposed extremes, which yet occur simultaneously. In this respect he represents the culmination of the tradition in which every detail is composed. This talent reveals his metaphysical ingenuity. The unity of what he had imagined truly does justice to the idea which forms the subject of the text. The striking effect and the unity of the disparate are one and the same. Hence the simplicity of the end result. The complexity is nowhere suppressed, but is so shaped as to become transparent. If everything in the score is clearly heard, its very clarity means that it is heard as a synthesis.

In its near clarity (and yet . . .), one sees that this description could apply to Wagner. In any case, the possibility of a synthetic perception, the unified (and thus totalizing) character of music, the adequation of such a unity to the "idea" of the text (to its metaphysical significance), "obligation" itself, these are all incontestably principles which pertain to Wagnerian aesthetics. Thus we are confronted with a question, and one which is not without consequences: How is it that the shadow of Wagner can continue to cloud the hope, which was as much Schönberg's as Adorno's, to put an end—lucidly—to Wagnerism? Which is to say, to the worst (the most disastrous) conception of "great art"?

If there is any chance of making sense of this, we must reread "Sakrales Fragment."

At the end of his analysis, that is, just before the Benjaminian *Rettung* of the work which neatly finishes the essay on Schönberg, we find this statement (Adorno, who, without ever mentioning the word, has cataloged the reasons for the failure of *Moses,* has just indicated that in the end, Schönberg was the victim of the bourgeois illusion of the "immortality of art," of the belief in genius— that metaphysical transfiguration of bourgeois individualism—indeed, of the absence of doubt as to the reality of greatness; or to put it otherwise, that he was the victim of his own renunciation of "that extreme of the aesthetic, the sole legitimation of art," and he continues):

> In Schönberg's fragmentary main works—the term 'main work' is itself symptomatic—there is something of the spirit that Huxley castigated in one of his early novels. The greatness, universal validity, totality of the masters and masterpieces

of yore—all this can be regained if only you are strong enough and have the genius. This has something of the outlook that plays off Michelangelo against Picasso. Such blindness about the philosophy of history has causes rooted in the philosophy of history itself. They are to be found in the feeling of an inadequate sense of authority, the shadow-side of modern individuation. To overcome this blindness would mean relativizing the idea of great art even though great art alone can provide the aesthetic seriousness in whose absence authentic works can no longer be written. Schönberg has actually rendered visible one of the antinomies of art itself. The most powerful argument in his favour is that he introduced this antinomy, which is anything but peculiar to him, into the innermost recesses of his own *oeuvre*. It is not to be overcome simply by an act of will or by virtue of the power of his own works. The fallacy that it is necessary to negotiate or depict the most rarefied contents in order to produce the greatest works of art—a fallacy which puts an end to the Hegelian aesthetics—derives from the same misconception. The elusive content is to be captured by chaining it to the subject matter which, according to tradition, it once inhabited. A futile endeavor. The prohibition on graven images which Schönberg heeded as few others have done, nevertheless extends further than even he imagined. To thematize great subjects directly today means projecting their image after the event. But this in turn inevitably means that, disguised as themselves, they fail to make contact with the work of art. (translation slightly modified)

Schönberg's merit, which all the same no longer permits one to "save" the work, is thus to have "rendered visible one of the antinomies of art itself" (and not just, as one might think, an antinomy of the art of the "bourgeois era" and of the epoch of individuation, even if it has devolved to properly modern art to manifest it). This antinomy is very simple, and is without resolution: "great art" *is* and *cannot be* (or can no longer be) the guarantee, indeed, the norm of authenticity in art. The notion of "great art," which alone provides "the aesthetic seriousness in whose absence authentic works can no longer be written," must be "relativized." But one does not relativize the absolute. "Great art" remains the norm—just as, for reasons that are hardly different, it was for Hegel and Schelling, for Nietzsche, for Heidegger—but it is a ruinous norm for all art which would submit itself to this category. This is why "great art," the will to "great art" is the impossibility of art. This contradiction is at the very heart of Schönberg's work, and especially of *Moses,* and we will see that it is this which makes for its "greatness," beyond its "intention." In its *Wahrheitsgehalt,* as Benjamin said: in its truth content.

This is, at bottom, what defines the essence of art, at least of modern art: it is only itself in the impossibility of effecting that which founds its authenticity. It does not follow from this that one must renounce apprehending "the most rarefied contents" (the spiritual contents, as Hegel said, the metaphysical as such, for this is and has always been "the high"). But it does follow, on the other hand, that one must renounce "negotiating or depicting [*darstellen*] the most rarefied contents." If one credits Adorno, here, with the greatest lucidity (and the allusion to Hegel cannot but lead one to do so), what is seen as the "error" is exactly what Heidegger, in the first version of his lectures *The Origin of the Work of Art,* denounced as the "remarkable fatality" to which "all meditation about art and the work of art, every theory of art and all aesthetics" is submitted, from the Greeks at least to Hegel, which is to say, to us: the artwork "always allows itself *also* to be considered as a fabricated thing [*ein Zeugwerk,* an allusion to the Platonico-Aristotelian misinterpretation of *tekhne*], presenting a 'spiritual content.' Thus art becomes the presentation of something supersensible in a palpable material submitted to a form." Now because of Schönberg but also beyond him, Adorno refers this questioning of *Darstellung*—art is not *essentially* (re)presentation—to the biblical prohibition of representation—to the "iconoclastic prescription," as Jean-Joseph Goux says—which "Schönberg heeded as few others have done," and which "extends further than even he imagined." It goes without saying that here all comparison with the Heideggerian procedure ends. If there is indeed something which Heidegger could not—or rather would not—recognize, even if his thought and the deconstruction of Hegelian aesthetics ought to have forced him to do so, it is that one might refer the problematic of *Darstellung* to such an origin. But Adorno had every reason to do just this. And so it is that he affirms, in a mode that Heidegger would probably have impugned, that all that is left is to "conceive" the "trace" of these "great contents" today, which brings us back all the same to modern art, to an art in which, by tradition, the content was attached to certain subjects. All of which amounts to saying that great contents "fail to make contact with the work of art."

Here it is clear that we have touched the problem of the "end of art." Since Hegel, the end of art signifies the birth of aesthetics (the philosophy or science of art, or even the simple "reflection" on art) no matter where one situates the event: in the decline of the Greek fifth century, as Heidegger above all would be tempted to think, or in the exhaustion of Christian art. (In the meantime, the question is relatively secondary: in both cases, the end of art means in reality the end of religion, and this is the essential point.) In his manner, Adorno remains faithful to this determination: no doubt there was once "great art," which is to say that "great contents" were once able to supply matter to artworks. But that all that remains is to conceive the trace of this—and this makes all the difference—in no way suffices to define the program of an aesthetics. The reason is simply that "great contents" do not belong *essentially* to the work of art. If one must maintain the project of an aesthetics—and it is well known that Adorno, perhaps against Heidegger, will resolutely devote himself to this—this will not reduce itself to end, as is the case in Hegel and also, though in a more complex fashion, in Heidegger, as a nostalgia for a religion, which is to say, a community.

This is why it is not at all a matter of indifference that this bundle of questions—at once very close to and very far from Heideggerian questions, but near at least in that it is the enclosing domination of Hegelian aesthetics that is abjured—should thus present all the marks of a philosophical reflection on the essence, the history, and the destination of art even as it proceeds both very rigorously and very loyally in its interpretation of *Moses*. This is an artwork, and not just any artwork, in its intentions, in what lies beyond its intentions, and in the failure or success of the two, which carries or at least allows one to assemble such a bundle of questions. All things being equal, Schönberg is for Adorno what Schiller, for example, is for Hegel, Wagner for the early Nietzsche, and Hölderlin for Heidegger: the offering of a work which explicitly thematizes the question of its own possibility as a work—this makes it modern—and which thereby carries in itself, as its most intimate subject, the question of the essence of art. Such works necessitate a philosophical decision as to the future of art or its chances today—which is to say, from now on. Schiller sanctions the end of art (its "death"), but Wagner is the hope of a rebirth. And Hölderlin, always on the condition that we do not envisage his final dereliction, is the hope of "another beginning."

Thus the question is to know exactly what *Moses and Aaron* offers to Adorno (to the continuing project of aesthetics).

The response to this question lies entirely in the title Adorno gives to his essay: "Sakrales Fragment."

Despite the peremptory (and perhaps uselessly romantic) declaration that virtually opens the essay, according to which "everything is in pieces, fragmentary, like the Tablets of the Law which Moses smashed," this title is not justified solely by the fact that *Moses and Aaron* is unfinished. This would hardly explain the fact that, despite appearances, the simplest meaning of the word "fragment" is in the end not at all the meaning retained by Adorno. The reference here to the Tablets is in reality not formal; it is even less formalist, in the genre of a more or less subtle *mise en abîme*. As it appears a bit further on, only the word "sacred" is able to explain the "fragment," and it is to the meta-romantic speculation of Benjamin that one must connect the following corrective:

> Important works of art are the ones that aim for an extreme; they are destroyed in the process and their broken outlines survive as the ciphers of a supreme, unnameable truth. It is in this positive sense that *Moses und Aron* is a fragment and it would not be extravagant to attempt to explain why it was left incomplete by arguing that it could not be completed.

No doubt there is still something of the *mise en abîme* in this final formula. But the *mise en abîme* is necessary here because it is nothing other than the effect of the *reflection* that structures *Moses and Aaron*. And it is difficult to see how an art that takes itself as its own object, being constrained to put its own possibility to the test, might escape from it.

The Benjaminian hermeneutic principle that Adorno obeys obliges him in effect to perform a double reading.

On the one hand he locates, as the very *intention* that presides over the work, what he calls the "fundamental experience" of *Moses*: that of properly *meta-physical* heroism (more so, it would seem, than that of "religious" heroism). In applying himself to the beginning of the *Pieces for Choir,* op. 27: "Heroic, those who accomplish acts for which they are lacking in courage," Adorno designates the subject of *Moses* as the pure contradiction of a (consequently impossible) task, the task of being "the mouthpiece of the Almighty." This task is defined in a strictly Hegelian manner if one remembers the *Lectures on the Philosophy of Religion* where Hegel says that Moses has nothing other than "the value of an organ" "over there" (in the Orient, I suppose). Moreover, "contradiction" is defined in the Hegelian lexicon as the contradiction of the finite and the infinite: the absolute—rather than God, for what is at stake in Schönberg's libretto is "thought" and not faith—evades finite beings with which it is incommensurable.

> [According to Moses,] to act as the mouthpiece of the Almighty is blasphemy for mortal man. Schönberg must have touched on this theme even before *Die Jakobsleiter,* when he composed a setting for Rilke's poem in the songs Opus 22: "All who attempt to find you, they tempt you / And they who thus find you, they bind you / to image and gesture." Thus God, the Absolute, eludes finite beings. Where they desire to name him, because they must, they betray him. But if they keep silent about him, they acquiesce in their own impotence and sin against the other, no less binding, commandment to name him. They lose heart because they are not up to the task which they are otherwise enjoined to attempt. (trans. slightly modified)

And it is, moreover, to this contradiction that Adorno refers Moses' exclamation, at which point the music composed by Schönberg interrupts itself. For Adorno, this is the point where the work itself is condemned to fragmentation:

> At the end of Act II of the biblical opera, in the final sentence which has become music, Moses breaks down and laments, 'O word, thou word that I lack.' The insoluble contradiction which Schönberg has taken as his project and which is attested by the entire tradition of tragedy, is also the contradiction of the actual work. If it is obvious that Schönberg felt himself to be a courageous man and that he invested much of himself in Moses, this implies that he advanced to the threshold of self-knowledge about his own project. He must have grasped the fact that its absolute metaphysical content would prevent it from becoming an aesthetic totality. But by the same token he refused to accept anything less.

Now this contradiction, which Adorno very strangely calls "tragic" (I will come back to this), is not simply the subject of the work. Adorno insists a great deal on this: it is indeed the contradiction of the work itself, that is, "the fact that its absolute metaphysical content would prevent it from becoming an aesthetic totality." Thus the essential and not accidental incompleteness of *Moses*. This incompleteness is inscribed, at bottom, in Moses' very first words, which Adorno has no need to recall: "Unique, eternal, omnipresent, invisible, and unrepresentable God."

But, Adorno remarks, "tragic" is not an adequate adjective. And suddenly the structure of the *mise en abîme* (the impossibility that the "work reflects as properly its own") is insufficient to open an adequate access to the work, for it is too premeditated: "The impossibility which appears intrinsic to the work is, in reality, an impossibility which was not intended. It is well known that great works can be recognized by the gap between their aim and their actual achievement."

This is why, on the other hand, with all due respect this time to the "truth content"—to that very thing, Benjamin would say, which constitutes the work as an "object of knowledge"—Adorno invokes a second, more essential reason for the incompleteness of *Moses,* for its impossibility. This reason is the end of art, that is, the end of the possibility of "great art":

> The impossibility we have in mind is historical: that of sacred art today and the idea of the binding, canonical, all-inclusive work that Schönberg aspired to. The desire to outdo every form of subjectivity meant that he had subjectively to create a powerful, dominant self amidst all the feeble ones. An immense gulf opens up between the trans-subjective, the transcendentally valid that is linked to the Torah, on the one hand, and the free aesthetic act which created the work on the other. This contradiction becomes fused with the one which forms the theme of the work and directly constitutes its impossibility. Theologians have complained that the designation of monotheism as 'thought'—that is, something which is only subjectively intended—diminishes the idea of transcendence in the text, since every thought is in a sense transcendental. Nevertheless, a truth manifests itself in this, however clumsily it is expressed: the absolute was not present in the work other than as a subjective intention—or idea, as the philosophers would say. By conjuring up the Absolute, and hence making it dependent on the conjurer, Schönberg ensured that the work could not make it real.

Whence Adorno's thesis, if I may drily summarize it: in its intention, *Moses* is a "sacred opera"; but because "cultic music cannot be willed" and because "the problematic character of a religious art that single-handedly tears itself free from its epoch" cannot efface itself (trans. modified), *Moses* is in truth a "sacred fragment."

It is not my intention to critique this thesis. It is perfectly solid, and takes its authority from precise and reliable historical and sociological considerations. It is supported by extremely fine textual and musical analyses, and the whole thing has the weight of self-evidence. Nevertheless, I believe it is possible to put this thesis to the test of an "aesthetic" category to which Adorno, at least here, does not make the slightest allusion although everything in his text calls for it, and does so constantly: the category of the *sublime.*

If I was astonished a moment ago that Adorno could describe as tragic the contradiction of the finite and the infinite, which according to him is the subject of *Moses,* this is because this contradiction in Hegel—and this contradiction as Adorno himself envisions it—is nothing other than that of "sublimity," which, as is well known, defines the properly Jewish moment of religion. Moreover, at least since Kant, the Mosaic utterance (the Law, but above all the prohibition of representation) has been presented as the paradigm of the sublime utterance. And it is probably the case that since Michelangelo, if we correctly interpret what Freud wished to say, the *figure* of Moses, as paradoxical as this might seem, has been taken as the emblematic figure of the sublime. The sublime, in the tradition of the sublime, is overdetermined by the biblical reference. And everything takes place as if Adorno did not want to hear a word of this.

Here things necessarily take a turn: though he manifests the will to exceed the Hegelian determination of "great art," and thus of the beautiful—of the sensual presentation that is adequate to a spiritual content, to an Idea, which is for Hegel the (Greek) truth of the (Jewish) sublime, that is, of the affirmation of the fundamental inadequation of the sensual and the Idea, or of the incommensurability of the finite and the infinite, whence the prohibition of representation precisely originates—and given that he sketches this gesture vis-à-vis Hegel and, behind him, vis-à-vis the whole philosophical tradition since Plato, insofar as it thinks the beautiful as the *eidetic* apprehension of being (and Adorno has a very clear consciousness, for example, of the "figurative character of all European art," including music, if only because of the invention of the *stilo rappresentativo* and of *musica ficta*), how is it that Adorno was unable to see or did not want to see that in reality Schönberg's endeavor expressly inscribes itself in the canonical tradition of the sublime? This would have in no way prevented him from producing the demonstration that he produces and which is incontestable because the contradiction of *Moses* is in fact incontestable. But this would have permitted him, perhaps, to reach another "truth" of *Moses* or to attempt a *Rettung* which would not be solely aesthetic, that is, imprisoned by the principle of adequation and judging the "failure" or "success" of the work solely from the viewpoint of the beautiful. That is, definitively, judging from the Hegelian point of view.

For, if there is no "critique" to be made, there is all the same a "reproach" to be offered. I will try briefly to explain myself.

One can begin again with this: if Adorno were attentive to the problematic of the sublime—if only he had remembered that Kant offers the prohibition of representation itself as the privileged example of the sublime—he would have been able to maintain his analysis without any essential modifications. In any case, it is the Hegel of the considerations on Judaism and sublimity which props up Adorno's procedure here, whether he knows this or not, and these considerations presuppose the "Analytic of the Sublime." Thus with one stroke he could have returned to all the analyses of purportedly sublime works or works recognized as sublime which, since Kant and Schiller, generally agree with one another in thinking that there is no possible sublime presentation—or, *a fortiori,* figuration—and thus that the question of the very possibility of a sublime art always arises, at least as long as we continue to define art by (re)presentation. To take an example which Adorno could not but be aware of, this is exactly the difficulty Freud encounters when, on the basis of Schillerian aesthetics (the essay "Grace and Dignity"), he tackles Michelangelo's figure of Moses: not only does he remain perplexed as to the meaning of the figure, but in fact he wonders whether in the end it is still art, that is, if it is "successful" (and it is a "limit," he thinks).

At the same time, one cannot forget that, as regards Kant, leaving out that which arises from nature's sublime (and which poses altogether different problems), the only examples of the sublime given by the *Third Critique* are examples of sublime *utterances* (as is traditional since Longinus), of which the most important are not poetic utterances but are, rather, prescriptive utterances and more specifically prohibitions, precisely like the Mosaic Law. Thus Kant speaks of "abstract (or restrictive) representation," indeed, of "negative representation." And because it also bears on representation or figuration, the Mosaic utterance, in its sublime simplicity (it is a purely negative commandment), is evidently a meta-sublime utterance, if I may use this term: it tells the truth of the sublime in a sublime manner: that there is no possible presentation of the meta-physical or of the absolute. *Mutatis mutandis,* this is a bit like the exclamation "O word, thou word that I lack," which for Adorno completes Schönberg's *Moses.* But above all, and one must not forget this, Kant says that inasmuch as a "presentation of the sublime" can belong to the fine arts (and one can well imagine why he remains extremely circumspect on this point), the only three modes or genres that one can rigorously recognize as "sublime genres" are (sacred) oratorio, the didactic (that is, philosophical) poem, and verse tragedy (*Critique of Judgment*).

Now it is precisely these three genres of the art of the sublime—if such a thing exists or can exist—that *Moses* works together jointly, for it is simultaneously oratorio ("sacred" as Adorno says), philosophical poem (whose subject is nothing less than the absolute itself), and, I will come to this, tragedy (in verse). It is, at least, *if we abstract from the opera form.* And this is why I ask the question whether Adorno, beyond his critique of the opera as such, might not have been able to accede to another "truth" of the work.

That *Moses* is an opera, this is particularly difficult to dispute. From the dramaturgical point of view, it has all the faults of the genre: among other things, I am thinking of the episode of worshipping the Golden Calf, which Adorno considers admirable from the viewpoint of musical composition, but which, in the style of an "obligatory ballet" (in the second act, of course), lacks nothing of the lascivious absurdity of the "flower maidens" in *Parsifal*. But it is already less difficult to dispute that the dramaturgical principles which he obeys are those of the Wagnerian music-drama. Even if *Moses* can be understood as an anti-*Parsifal* (which would thus retain all that is essential from that against which it protests), it does not seem to me that one might affirm without further consideration, as does Adorno, that Schönberg has the same attitude toward the biblical text that Wagner has toward the myths that he reelaborates, even if Adorno's argumentation appears from the outset unimpeachable and is difficult to resume. Adorno conducts his demonstration in the following manner:

> With the vestiges of a naivety which is perhaps indispensible [Schönberg] puts his trust in proven methods. Not that he is tempted to resort to formulae in order to revive or renew sacred music. But he does strive for a balance between the pure musical development and the desire for monumentality, much as Wagner had done. He too extended his critique of the musical theatre to the bounds of what was possible in his day. But at the same time he wanted the larger-than-life as evidence of the sacred. He deluded himself into believing that he would find it in myths. They are inaccessible to the subjective imagination that aspires to the monumental while suspending the traditional canon of forms which alone would create it. *Moses und Aron* is traditional in the sense that it follows the methods of Wagnerian dramaturgy without a hiatus. It relates to the biblical narrative in just the same way as the music of the *Ring* or *Parsifal* relate to their underlying texts. The central problem is to find musical and dramatic methods whereby to represent the idea of the sacred—that is to say, not a mythical but an anti-mythical event.

There is no doubt that *Moses* represents a compromise, nor is it doubtful that, as Adorno insists a bit further on, the musical language that Schönberg wanted to enlist in the service of monumentality, subject to dramaturgical constraints that are contrary to him, ruins itself as such: "The new language of music, entirely renovated to its innermost core, speaks as if it were still the old one." And it is true that the "unified pathos" of the work, a pathos which hardly suits "the specifically Jewish inflection" of Moses, causes the musical elaboration, because of this exterior fact, to disavow "the over-specific idea of the work as a whole": "The aesthetic drive towards sensuous expression works to the detriment of what that drive brings into being." Is the dramaturgical model on which Schönberg bases his work that of Wagner?

Adorno points out this contradiction: a mythical dramaturgy with antimythical aims is only in effect a contradiction under two conditions: on the one hand the dramatic action must be of a mythical type, which is not to say that the myth must supply the material for the libretto, but—this at least is the solution Wagner found—that the scenic acts, indeed all the signifiers and mythical cells, must be constantly musically overdetermined (hence, the *Leitmotiv*). This is not at all the case in Schönberg. (To put it otherwise, Schönberg no doubt aims for a "music-drama," in the broad sense of the term, yet all the same he does not respect Wagnerian dramaturgy.) And on the other hand, it is necessary that opera should wish itself, as Adorno says, a "sacred opera," which *Parsifal* manifestly wanted to be.

Now it is exactly on this point that Schönberg's lucidity is greatest. His religious intentions, his search for a "great sacred art" are undeniable. Equally undeniable is his determination to write an anti-*Parsifal* (at bottom, this imposed itself). At the time when *Moses* was in the works, this determination is indissolubly artistic, philosophical, and political. All the same, he renounced this determination, and not just at any time, but in 1933 precisely. On this point Adorno says what must be said, and not just in any way, though his remarks appear a bit short.

Perhaps it is the case that in all of his argumentation—and this would be at the very least my hypothesis—Adorno twice allows himself to get carried away: the first time by the Wagnero-Nietzschean determination of music-drama, conceived as "new tragedy" or as "modern tragedy," the second time by the Hegelian determination of tragedy.

Hegel defines tragedy, or more exactly the tragic scenario, as "the struggle of new gods against ancient gods." This is obviously the kind of scenario that Adorno rediscovers in *Moses*: the struggle of monotheism, as he says, against the gods of the tribe. Now as this is also, *mutatis mutandis,* the Wagnerian scenario (that of the *Ring* or of *Parsifal*), it is easy to see how the assimilation of the two is possible. (And this was surely the case, in one way or another, for Schönberg. Even if his true subject lay elsewhere—for as Adorno sees very well, it had to do with the very possibility of art—the rivalry with Wagner, and with Wagnerism, weighed on him with too great a force. Here I must admit that I am allowing myself to be guided by the admirable filmic version of *Moses* by Jean-Marie Straub and Danièle Huillet, for one must recognize that it is their dramaturgical intuition that is, as it happens, decisive. They stage the first two acts, but not that which remains of the third, in a Greek fashion, even if it is, for this production, actually the Roman theater of Alba Fucense in the Abruzzi region. In its original intention, in fact, *Moses* is a tragedy.)

But to continue from this point and think that an identity of scenario implies an identity of function, this is a great step. In the direct line of the Nietzsche of *The Birth of*

Tragedy, but equally that of the Hegel who analyzes tragedy as a "religious" work of art (which is also to say, a political work of art), Adorno spontaneously thinks of tragedy from the starting point of the chorus, and of the chorus as the bearer of "religion" itself, not so much as fervor or belief, but as being-in-community. The chorus is not the people, or the representative of the people (of the spectators); but it is all the same the index that tragedy is originally a common or communitarian work of art, that it is community in and through the work, that is, a work without an individual or singular subject. That all "great art" is in the last resort the creation of a people, this is a dogma of German aesthetics from Hegel to Heidegger. And despite everything—I mean: despite "critical theory"—Adorno accepts this dogma right up to the moment in which it is revealed that the failure of a music which "extends a hand to the cult" with such force and determination has to do with the fact that such a music, not-withstanding the affirmation of the "obligatory character" of its content, fails in being "substantial" in the Hegelian sense, because it is too "willed." An art can only attain greatness if the subject which carries it is—Adorno of course does not say: the people—society. This is why at bottom Adorno condenses all the questions of *Moses* in this question, itself of a transcendental sort: How is a cultic music simply possible outside of any cult? This is also to say, outside of any religious belonging and of any faith, and above all outside of all (social effectiveness of the cultic. I attach here, with no commentary, the two following pieces:

> The impossibility of the sacred work of art becomes increasingly evident the more the work insists on its claim to be one without invoking the support of any outside authority. With the modesty characteristic of the greatest emotional integrity, Schönberg ventured into this realm. The objection that the individual is no longer capable of the subjective piety which the biblical story calls for misses the mark. Bruckner was presumably a believer in an anachronistic sense and as musically inspired as any composer can be. Yet the Promised Land remained closed to him, and perhaps even to the Beethoven of the *Missa Solemnis*. The impossibility we are speaking of extends right into the objective preconditions of the form. Sacred works of art—and the fact that *Moses und Aron* was written as an opera does not disqualify it from being one—claim that their substance is valid and binding, beyond all yearning and subjective expression. The very choice of canonical biblical events implies such a claim. It is certainly implicit in the pathos of the music of *Moses und Aron*, whose intensity gives reality to a communal 'we' at every moment, a collective consciousness that takes precedence over every individual feeling, something of the order of the togetherness of a congregation. Were it otherwise, the predominance of the choruses would scarcely be imaginable. Without this transindividual element or, in other words, if it were merely a case of what is known as religious lyric poetry, the music would simply accompany the events or illustrate them. The compulsion to introduce into the music a sense of

its own intellectual situation, to organize it in such a way that it expresses the underlying foundation of the events described, in short, its high aesthetic seriousness forces it into a collective stance. It must of necessity extend a hand to the cult if it is not entirely to fail its own intention. But cultic music cannot simply be willed. Anyone who goes in search of it compromises the very concept. (translation slightly modified)

We may legitimately ask what produced the conception of this work in the light of such immense difficulties, which may be compared to those experienced twenty years before in connection with *Die Jakobsleiter*. It is not the product of that misconceived monumentality, that unlegitimated gesture of authority which marks so much of the pictorial arts of the nineteenth century, from Puvis de Chavannes down to Marées. Of course it was Schönberg's own individual make-up that provided the critical impetus. His parents do not seem to have been orthodox in their beliefs, but it may be supposed that the descendant of a family of Bratislava Jews living in the Leopoldstadt, and anything but fully emancipated, was not wholly free of that subterranean mystical tradition to be found in many of his contemporaries of similar origins, men such as Kraus, Kafka and Mahler.

The Enlightenment displaced the theological heritage, shifting it on to the plane of the apocryphal, as we can infer from Schönberg's own autobiographical remarks. In particular, superstition survived tenaciously in his life and he often reflected on it. It is doubtless an instance of secularized mysticism. The experience of pre-fascist Germany, in which he rediscovered his Jewish roots, must have released this repressed dimension of his nature. *Moses und Aron* was composed directly before the outbreak of the Third Reich, probably as a defensive reaction to what was about to sweep over him. Later, even after Hitler's fall, he did not return to the score.

It is hardly doubtful that a question of the transcendental type is fundamental to *Moses*, and it would probably have been difficult for it to be otherwise if one considers that which in the German tradition regularly associated Kant and the figure of Moses ("Kant is the Moses of our nation," said Hölderlin). But it is perhaps not so certain that this question bears on the possibility of a sacred art in the final analysis.

In reality Adorno's demonstration is only possible inasmuch as it attaches itself almost exclusively to the music and remains perfectly indifferent to the rest, which is to say, if you will, to the text. This will not in any way be reduced to the libretto, but implies, beyond the scenario itself (in its strange loyalty to the biblical text, which Adorno greatly underestimates all the same), the dramaturgical structures which this scenario induces (for example, the chorus, which is in effect the people, is not Greek at all and in no way has a relation of the tragic type to the protagonists, despite immediate appearances) and, above all, the poem. Now not only does Adorno pay no attention to the text of Act III, under the pretext that it is not set to music (even so, this is decisive for the meaning that Schönberg expressly wished to confer upon the work, which thus concludes, as it is effectively written, with a pardon), but he systematically minimizes the problem of the relation between thought and language, a relation which is central, by assigning it to an inevitably subjective and profane ("heretical") interpretation of revelation, even though it is perhaps here that the transcendental question is articulated for Moses himself.

This exclusive attention accorded the music verifies itself in a privileged manner in the final *Rettung,* which is entirely given over to demonstrating the "success" of the work, which is to say, its adequation, despite the fundamental contradiction between intention and composition which subtends the opera. All of this comes down to displaying an internal adequation of the musical texture itself (identified *in fine* with the final accomplishment, by way of musical genius, of the passage to monotheism), which properly redeems the fault that had consisted in making *musica ficta* serve against the figure. And it is such an adequation which fundamentally re-establishes, beyond the peripeteias of "great art" in the bourgeois era, the enigmatic but unseverable link between music and Jewishness.

At the same time, if one pays attention this time to the critical aspect of the analysis, it is still this exclusive attention to the music which explains that besides the main grievance (music would be the image of that which eludes all images), one of the major accusations bears on the "unified pathos" of the work. As Adorno very clearly indicates, the incrimination does not take aim only at the "factitious" character of pathos, which arises because the religious content has lost all "substantiality." As a result of this, the "new language," withdrawing from itself, "speaks as if it were still the old one," according to a compromise of the Wagnerian type between monumentality and musical modernity, which authorizes Adorno to speak of the strangely "traditional" effect of *Moses.* Nor does it take aim only at the insufficient differentiation of the couple formed by Moses and Aaron, the one who speaks and the one who sings, due this time to the "imitative" over-determination of the music. Moses, says Adorno, should not speak, for in the Bible he stutters. He adds that "it highlights the crisis of an art which makes use of this text purely as art and of its own free will." But it essentially aims for obedience to the Wagnerian principle of the unity of language, which "cannot accommodate what the subject matter requires above all: the strict separation of Moses' monotheism from the realm of myth, the regression to the tribal gods. The pathos of the music is identical in both." And it is here, moreover, that Adorno puts his fundamental hermeneutic principle into play, one which is borrowed once again from Benjamin, this time from the Benjamin of the celebrated essay "Goethe's *Elective Affinities.*" For he explains that if one wishes to break the "vicious circle" of "entrapment in the coils of myth" which alone justifies the unity of language and technique in Wagner, "the caesura was to be deci-

sive." But, he remarks, "the rupture was to become music." This is evidently not the case:

> The undifferentiated unity from which the ruthless process of integration allows nothing to be exempted comes into collision with the idea of the One itself. Moses and the Dance round the Golden Calf actually speak the same language in the opera, although the latter must aim to distinguish between them. This brings us close to the source of traditionalism in Schönberg, an issue which has only started to become visible in recent decades and especially since his death. In his eyes the idea of musical vocabulary as the organ of meaning was still instinctive and unquestioned. This vocabulary imagined itself able to articulate everything at any time. But this assumption was shaken by Schönberg's own innovations.

To put it in other words, Schönberg betrays his own modernism. He bases his work on the codified syntax of tonality while his atonality would demand that he break it, in conformity with the subject of the work (which would thus be, one must believe: how is it that only atonal music is adequate to the monotheistic idea?). Because of this, Schönberg would be a victim of his epoch, exactly as Schiller was for Hegel. He would succumb to the bourgeois idea of genius, which is to say—but Adorno, precisely, does not say this and probably could not say this, at least not as crudely—of the sublime. But all the same, it is this which is at stake; the lexicon does not fool us:

> This introduces a fictional element into the actual construction which so energetically opposes one. The situation points back to an illusion from which the bourgeois spirit has never been able to free itself: that of the unhistorical immortality of art. It forms a perfect complement to that decorative stance from which the Schönbergian innovations had effected their escape. The belief in genius, that metaphysical transfiguration of bourgeois individualism, does not allow any doubt to arise that great men can achieve great things at any time and that the greatest achievements are always available to them. No doubt can be permitted to impugn the category of greatness, not even for Schönberg. A justified scepticism towards that belief, which is based on a naive view of culture as a whole, is to be found in that specialization which Schönberg rightly opposed on the grounds that it acquiesced in the division of labor and renounced that extreme of the aesthetic, the sole legitimation of art.

A verdict without appeal, but which is all the same astonishing on the part of someone who bases his work on the *past* existence of a "great sacred art" in order to condemn any and all factitious "restorations," as if at the same time, to put it by way of a shortcut, the sublime (grandeur) were a bourgeois invention and "great sacred art" were not a retrospective illusion—a projection—of the educated German bourgeoisie from Hegel to Heidegger, or from Kant to Adorno himself. That "aesthetic extremism" should be "the sole legitimation of art" for us, today, this is not doubtful. Who knows if this was not the case for Sophocles, or for Bach? And who knows if it is not precisely this that Wagner betrayed with his "compromises," but not Schönberg, who, as a victim of the bourgeois mythology of art—as Adorno is right to emphasize—all the same chose to abandon (one can suppose: knowing full well the cause of his decision) *Moses,* to *interrupt* it, rather than present supplementary evidence for the re-mythologization of art and of religion.

In any case, the question remains: What exactly does Adorno mean when he declares that the rupture (or the caesura) should have made "itself music"? It is easy to see that what is incriminated here is the too powerful homogeneity of the music, its flawless density which paradoxically (or, rather, dialectically) "redeems" or "saves" it as music to the detriment of the work itself in its project, that is, as a "sacred opera." The opposition of the *Sprechgesang* and the *melos,* to put it otherwise, does not "caesure" the continuity of the musical discourse, nor therefore does it bring out the monotheistic idea. The unity of language is pagan, idolatrous. But is the caesura simply a matter of differentiation internal to language—indeed, of the clear-cut opposition of voices? In what sense, at bottom, does Adorno understand "caesura"? And, an inseparable question: Why does he make so little of the interruption of the work—apparently accidental, "empirical," but does one ever know?—and above all, why does he make so little of the very strange mode in which this interruption comes about? I do not at all wish to suggest that the interruption *is* the caesura, but perhaps rather that the caesura, more inaudible to Adorno's ear than it is invisible to his eyes, masks itself in the interruption—which, from then on, would no longer be thinkable as interruption.

Here of course we must credit Adorno, in an analogous manner to that which he uses with the word *Rettung,* for using the word *caesura* in the enlarged but rigorous sense which Benjamin gives it in his essay on Goethe, where it is the technical term forged by Hölderlin for his structural theory of tragedy which is elevated to the level of a general critical (or aesthetic) concept: all works are organized as such from the starting point of the caesura inasmuch as the caesura is the hiatus, the suspension or the "anti-rhythmic" interruption which is not only necessary, as in metrics, to the articulation and the equilibrium of verse (of the phrase and, by extension, of what one might call the work phrase), but, more essentially, the place whence that which Hölderlin calls "pure speech" surges forth. The caesura, to put it otherwise, is the liberation by default—but a non-negative default—of the meaning itself or of the truth of the work. And from the critical point of view, it is only the caesura that indicates, in the work, the place that one must reach in order to accede to the *Wahrheitsgehalt.*

On the basis of this hermeneutic model, Adorno is right to look for the caesura in *Moses,* as in any supposedly great work. Perhaps his only fault is to look for it, by "melocentrism," only in the music. For if one takes stock

of what Schönberg effectively *wrote,* one can just as well construct the hypothesis that it is at the very place where the music—but not the work—interrupts itself, that is, precisely where Moses proclaims that the word (speech) fails him: "O Wort, du Wort, das mir fehlt!"

Indeed, it is well known that up until the end of the second act Schönberg *simultaneously* composed the libretto and the score. And that at the moment when he was to begin composing the third act—whether it is an accidental cause or not does not matter here—abruptly and without giving any indication exactly why, he only wrote the text of one scene, the scene where Moses, who reaffirms his "idea," pardons Aaron or at least orders that he not be executed. And here again it is necessary to recognize that the dramaturgical choice of Straub and Huillet is particularly illuminating: for not only do they play this merely spoken scene in the unbearable silence which succeeds the unfurling of the music, a silence that Adorno analyzes so well, but they have it played in a place other than that which, since the outset, was properly the stage or the theater. They do this in such a way that it is not only the tragic apparatus as Adorno understands it that collapses in a single stroke, but the entire apparatus which kept *Moses* within the frame of opera or music-drama. And it is here, probably, that religion is interrupted.

If such an indication is fair, if, dramaturgically, one must take into account this rupture or this hiatus and the passage to simple speech—for such is the enigma of that which remains of Schönberg's work—then there is indeed a caesura, and it clarifies the truth of the work in another way. In particular, it no longer permits one to refer the difference in enunciation between the two protagonists to Schönberg's submission to the imperatives of *musica ficta* (and of Wagnerian dramaturgy). It is from this principle that the music must despoil itself and remain nothing other than naked speech.

Beyond its structural function, in Hölderlin the caesura signifies—and it is because of this that it holds Benjamin's attention—the interruption *necessary* for tragic truth to appear, which is to say, the necessary separation, the necessary cut which must (but in the sense of a *sollen*) produce itself in the process of infinite collusion between the human and the divine which is the tragic flaw itself, hubris. The tragic separation, the uncoupling of God and man (which Hölderlin interprets as *katharsis*), thus signifies the law of finitude, which is to say, the impossibility of the immediate: "For mortals just as for immortals, the immediate is prohibited." An immediate interpretation of the divine (Oedipus) is no more possible than an immediate identification with the divine (Antigone). Mediation is the law [*Gesetz*], a law, moreover, that Hölderlin thinks in a rigorously Kantian fashion (as when he speaks of the "categorical diversion" of the divine which brings about the imperative obligation for man to return toward the earth).

From here on, according to this model—and according to the logic of the extension of the concept inaugurated by

Benjamin and apparently recognized by Adorno himself—why should we not think that insofar as it strikes and suspends the music in the course of a brief and dry scene, the caesura in *Moses* brutally makes it appear that Moses, the inflexible guardian of the Law and the defender of his own great—of his own sublime—conception of God, is also the one who by virtue of immoderation wants to be the too immediate interpreter of God: the mouth or the organ of the absolute, the very voice of God as its truth. This is why in never ceasing to proclaim the unrepresentability of God, indeed his ineffability, neither will he cease (on the same ground of *musica ficta* where Aaron moves around in all his ease) from striving to sing and not to confine himself strictly to speech, as if, by the effect of a compromise induced by his rivalry with Aaron, he were secretly tempted by the idea of a possible presentation (a sublime presentation, according to the rules of his great eloquence) of the true God, of the unpresentable itself. To the point where, for lack of speech or a word, in the despairing recognition of this lack—and here, precisely at this phrase the caesura is situated—he is swallowed up by his own great audacity and the music interrupts itself. By this one may understand why, in the only scene of the final act, all "sobriety" as Hölderlin would have said, Moses grants his pardon, which is to say that he renounces murder. Thus is verified the profound insight that underlies Freud's *Moses and Monotheism,* according to which the prohibition of representation is nothing other than the prohibition of murder.

Such is the reason for which that which interrupts itself along with the music, that which is "caesured," is religion itself, if religion is defined as the belief in a possible (re)presentation of the divine, that is, if religion is unthinkable without an art or as an art (which, happily, does not mean—"we have passed this step"—that art would be unthinkable without religion or as religion). What is at stake here, in the interruption of that which was without a doubt at the outset the project of a "sacred opera," is the very thing that Adorno considers beyond doubt for Schönberg: the figurativity of music. But in order to recognize this, it would have been necessary for Adorno to have been ready to *read Moses,* and not simply to hear it. Or it would have been necessary perhaps for him to have been able to recognize, in according more credit (or confidence) to Schönberg, the limits of his own musical mysticism.

At one moment in his analysis, Adorno notes this:

> Schönberg's own need to express is one that rejects mediation and convention and therefore one which names its object directly. Its secret model is that of revealing the Name. Whatever subjective motive lay behind Schönberg's choice of a religious work, it possessed an objective aspect from the very outset—a purely musical one in the first instance.

But is it not the same Adorno who had written some years earlier:

> The language of music is quite different from the language of intentionality. It contains a theological dimension. What it has to say is simultaneously revealed and concealed. Its Idea is the divine Name which has been given shape. It is demythologized prayer, rid of efficacious magic. It is the human attempt, doomed as ever, to name the Name, not to communicate meanings.

For Adorno as for Schönberg, music in its very intention would, in short, come under the horizon of that which Benjamin called "pure language," which is perhaps not without a rapport to that which Hölderlin, on the subject of the caesura, called "pure speech." But the Name, as Adorno well knows, is unpronounceable—and music is a vain prayer, the sublime as such, according to its most tried and true code since Kant: "[Music's] Idea is the divine Name which has been given shape." An art (of the) beyond (of) signification, which is to say, (of the) beyond (of) representation. All the same, under the "O Wort, du Wort, das mir fehlt!" that Moses proclaims in the last burst of music, it is not prohibited to hear resonating an "O Name, du Name, der mir fehlt!" As when Kant takes as his major example of the sublime utterance the very prohibition of representation (the Mosaic law), this is in reality a meta-sublime utterance which tells in a sublime manner—and the passage to the naked word in Act III of *Moses* is absolutely sublime—the truth of the sublime, itself sublime. Ultimate paradox: the naked word—the language of signification itself—comes to tell of the impossible beyond signification, something which Benjamin would not have denied, and to signify the transcendental illusion of expression. This is why *Moses* is not "successful." It is "unsaveable" if for Adorno "to save" never means anything other than to consider artworks according to the scale of adequation, which is to say, of beauty: the religious gesture par excellence. Now what *Moses* says precisely, but despite itself—and one must well imagine Schönberg constrained and forced, which is after all the lot of every modern artist—is that art is religion in the limits of simple inadequation; probably the end, in every sense, of religion. Or to be more just: the caesura of religion.

Michael Strasser (essay date 1995)

SOURCE: "'A Survivor from Warsaw' as Personal Parable," in *Music & Letters,* Vol. 76, No. 1, February, 1995, pp. 52-63.

[*In the following essay, Strasser contends that* A Survivor from Warsaw *is the story of Schoenberg's experiences as a Jew.*]

Arnold Schoenberg's *A Survivor from Warsaw*, Op. 46, is undoubtedly one of his most immediately powerful expressions and, in terms of public acceptance, one of the more successful of his later works. Widely and justifiably viewed as a fitting memorial to the millions of Jews who lost their lives during World War II, *A Survivor from Warsaw* can also be considered as a musical and literary testament to Schoenberg's own spiritual struggle—a personal parable of his experiences as a Jew.

The idea for a work honouring the Jewish victims of Nazi Germany was apparently suggested to Schoenberg in early 1947 by Corinne Chochem, a dancer of Russian origin who had organized programmes of Jewish dances in New York in the 1930s and was co-author of a book containing music, choreography and photographs illustrating dances performed by Palestinian Jews. In her first extant letter to Schoenberg, dated 2 April 1947, she informs him:

> I have written to New York for a correct translation of the song 'I Believe the Messiah Will Come' but as yet have not received it.
>
> I am enclosing the music and words to a Partisan Song that was sung by the Vilna Ghetto. I was able to find many verses both in English and in Hebrew, as well as in Yiddish. I am sending you the English words only and if you are interested I will also send you the Hebrew. Two versions of this melody with very slight variation have appeared in different publications and I am submitting both.
>
> Thank you so much for your co-operation and understanding and please call on me for whatever additional help I can give you.

The first extant letter from Schoenberg to Chochem was written some three weeks later (20 April 1947), and it is in this letter that we find the first reference to the work that became *A Survivor from Warsaw*:

> I think it is the best to tell you at once the fee I want to receive for a composition of 6-9 minutes for small orchestra and chorus, perhaps also one or more soloists on the melodie [*sic*] you gave me.
>
> I plan to make it this scene—which you described—in the Warsaw Ghetto, how the doomed Jews started singing, before going to die.
>
> My fee should be $1000.00 (one thousand) for which I sell you the right to make and sell records.
>
> I hope you do not find this fee extravagant. It is not, because I got for a piece of 4 1/2 minutes for my prelude to the Genesis from Mr. Shilkret $1500.00.
>
> I hope, when you agree to pay this sum to receive also the translations.

From these two letters we can assume that Chochem had approached Schoenberg about the possibility of composing a work that would describe a scene similar to that which is represented in *A Survivor from Warsaw*. She evidently envisaged a piece that would use a pre-existing song—possibly one or both of the two mentioned in her letter of 2 April. Schoenberg's request for translations indicates that, at this early stage, he was thinking along the same lines.

Chochem's handwritten reply, dated simply 'Monday', must have been written on 21 April. immediately after she received Schoenberg's letter.

> Thank you very kindly for your prompt reply.
>
> We really should have talked over the financial arrangements at our first meeting, but I was sure Dr. Toch had explained to you my financial capacity. I wish I were in the position of a wealthy patron. However, my recognition and awareness as to what such an album would be to Jewish cultural life and to the musical world in general is greater than my ability to pay adequately. Unless the composers are willing to help me carry this project through I may have to stop right there.
>
> You have no idea how anxious I am to have your cooperation . . . Would it be alright if I send you $200 and on completion $300 additional? Would you perhaps wish to make just one side of a record (12 inches)?
>
> I am planning to go to San Francisco for a while and would like to meet with you before I do so— If you can possibly see me—I will be glad to come to your house.

In addition to signalling the alarm she felt over the size of Schoenberg's requested fee, Chochem's letter reveals that she was planning to issue a gramophone album of new works by several composers, one of whom was possibly Ernst Toch, who also apparently introduced her to Schoenberg. Perhaps Chochem had conceived of a collection of pieces based on Jewish melodies; or she may have intended to pay homage to Jewish victims of World War II. In any case, she may have been influenced in her plans by the *Genesis Suite* commissioned by Nathaniel Shilkret in 1944, for which Schoenberg, Stravinsky and Toch, among others, had contributed movements.

Two days later (23 April 1947), Schoenberg again wrote to Chochem, explaining that his time was principally devoted to finishing several projects left uncompleted when he retired, stating that when he took on other work he could only do it to earn extra income 'because my grocer and the State (asking taxes) demand it'. In response to Chochem's appeal to his generosity in helping her complete her project, Schoenberg pointedly argued that 'I have done throughout my whole life so much for idealistic ends (and so little has to be [*sic*] returned to me in kind) that I have done my duty'. He refused to reduce his fee, but offered to accept an initial payment of $500, with the balance in monthly instalments paid 'by the recording company'. If she was able to make the necessary financial arrangements, Schoenberg reminded Chochem that he 'would like to have as soon as possible the story and the translation of the text'.

There is no further extant correspondence between Chochem and Schoenberg, and it appears that Chochem abandoned her ambitious scheme. Schoenberg, however, was apparently inspired by their discussions to pursue the idea of a work based on the events of the Holocaust and proceeded on his own. In the first week of July, he received a letter (dated 1 July) from the Koussevitzky Music Foundation, reminding him that the Foundation was still interested in commissioning an orchestral work. Schoenberg wrote back on 7 July 1947:

> It is a co-incidence.
>
> A little more than a month ago I had started a composition for orchestra and had planned to ask the Koussevitzky Foundation whether the commission for a work like that is still in force.
>
> You will understand that my answer to your letter from July 1, 1947 is: yes. I accept with pleasure the renewal of the commission and will try to finish this composition in about two or (perhaps: I never know) six weeks.
>
> But at the same time I would like to tell you, that I have not yet decided upon the definite form of the piece. My original plan was to write it for a small group of about 24 musicians, one or two 'speakers' and a mens [sic] choir of an adequate size. It is still in my hands to make it a 'symphonic poem' for standard orchestra without speakers and choir—if the commission demands this.
>
> I must receive your answer as soon as possible, because I would like to make now a definite decision.

A week later (14 July 1947), Margaret Grant, Executive Secretary of the Foundation, wrote to assure Schoenberg that he had the freedom to cast the work as he saw fit:

> It is true that a 'symphonic poem' for standard orchestra might be easier to perform and would probably be heard more frequently. Nevertheless, Dr. Koussevitzky feels that it is importnat for you to have complete liberty to choose, and that it would be most interesting to have from you a composition such as you have described.

Schoenberg's letter implies that he had begun working on his new piece in June, but according to annotations on the autograph score the actual composition took only thirteen days (11-23 August 1947). On 24 August 1947, Schoenberg wrote to Koussevitzky:

> I am happy to inform you that the piece you commissioned for the Koussevitzky Foundation is finished . . .
>
> I could not change the piece into a symphonic poem as I had hoped to do. It would not have been the same thing, I wanted to express. But, though I employ one narrator and a mens [sic] choir, I could at least eliminate the second speaker—it required many changes!
>
> I don't know whether you are aquainted [sic] with the fact that for more than twenty years I abandonned [sic] the habit of writing a conventional score but used a manner of condensation by avoiding transposition in clarinets, horns etc.

> But since my illness three years ago I am suffering from a nervous eye trouble which prevents small writing. I was forced to have a special music paper made for me and this is why my manuscript might surprise you. You will understand that as long as this illness lasts I am unable to write music in another manner—but these manuscripts always contain—except for possible errores [sic]—all I can say, in music at least.
>
> In addition to the musical manuscript I send you the manuscript of the text . . .

Schoenberg closed his letter by asking Koussevitzky to send his commissioning fee 'as soon as possible, because I am in the hands of terrible crooks: publishers, recording companies etc.' In December 1947, under the composer's direction. René Leibowitz prepared a full orchestral score of the work from Schoenberg's 'condensed' (particelle) autograph score.

Except for a brief statement in Koussevitzky's first letter to Schoenberg concerning the commission (1 April 1944) which notes that the composer 'retains all rights to the composition', there is no discussion of performance rights in the extant correspondence between Schoenberg and the Koussevitzky Foundation. One might reasonably assume, however, that the completed work would have been given its première by the Boston Symphony Orchestra, as had been the case with all but one of the orchestral works commissioned by the Foundation between its establishment in 1942 and 1947. But in fact *A Survivor from Warsaw* was first heard not in Boston or in any other major centre but in the provincial south-western city of Albuquerque, New Mexico.

On 12 March 1948, Schoenberg received a letter from Kurt Frederick, conductor of the Albuquerque Civic Orchestra, who, as part of his efforts to promote twentieth-century music, had previously contacted Schoenberg about securing performance materials for *Pierrot lunaire:*

> Just recently I heard that you wrote a composition for a men's chorus and small orchestra. This is to ask whether it would be possible for me to obtain the score, and whether, if the composition does not prove too difficult, there would be a chance of our performing it in Albuquerque?

Schoenberg sent a copy of the score to Frederick on 20 March 1948. In a follow-up letter dated 23 March 1948, Richard Hoffmann, who was serving as Schoenberg's assistant at the time, informed Frederick: 'In the event that you perform the cantata, Mr. Schoenberg, in place of accepting a performance fee, agrees that you give him the copyright parts'.

Frederick, recognizing the implications of Schoenberg's request, quickly wrote to Hoffmann (26 March 1948) to ask for clarification:

> There was one point in your letter which I did not understand. It was in connection with the right of

performance of the 'Survivor'. Did you mean that I ought to copy the orchestra material and send it to Mr. Schoenberg after the performance instead of paying a fee for the performance? And if so, does that mean that Albuquerque would have the first performance of this composition? This would be, of course, a tremendous boost for our young orchestra, and would make my work in behalf of contemporary good music much easier. I also have no doubt that in this case I could meet our board's opposition against performances of modern music easily.

Please answer soon.

Hoffman's reply (31 March 1948) reassured Frederick that

> the matter stands just as you describe in your letter . . . Yes it means that you would give the work its first performance, but, Mr. Schoenberg would like to draw your attention to the fact that copyists consider their work of great importance and charge accordingly!

Schoenberg's awarding of the première of his new composition to Frederick and his amateur orchestra raised eyebrows in some quarters. Ross Parmenter, writing in the *New York Times* in advance of the première, noted:

> Arnold Schoenberg has never been prolific. A world premiere of one of his new works is news. It is doubly so when he bestows it unexpectedly on an out-of-the-way amateur organization. And that is what he has done . . .

> Having been commissioned by the Koussevitzky Music Foundation, the work was expected to be played for the first time by the Boston Symphony. The Albuquerque premiere was a surprise even to Serge Koussevitzky, who said he was very 'pleased' when the news was relayed to him last week.

The première of *A Survivor from Warsaw,* originally scheduled for 7 September 1948, did not take place until the orchestra's second concert of the season on 4 November 1948 at the University of New Mexico in Albuquerque under Frederick's direction. Immediately after the performance, Frederick wrote to Schoenberg

> to thank you for having allowed me to perform *A Survivor from Warsaw* in Albuquerque. The study of this work was a great experience for me and for every single one of the performers.

> I would like to tell you who the performers were. The orchestra, an amateur organization, consisted of lawyers, doctors, secretaries, high school and university students, railroad engineers, etc. Besides our community chorus and the university chorus, a chorus from Estancia asked for the honor of singing the 'Sch'me jisroel'. Estancia is a community of about 1000 inhabitants, predominantly farmers. The singers from Estancia had to drive 120 miles to come to rehearsals and to the performance in Albuquerque. I have never before

experienced the devotion with which the above groups studied your composition. I doubt that any professional organization could have shown as much enthusiasm.

> The performance was a tremendous success. The audience of over 1600 was shaken by the composition and applauded until we repeated the performance. This happened in a town, which a few years ago was considered to be a small 'Railroad Town'.

Schoenberg's reply, dated 12 November 1948, indicates his pleasure at hearing of the successful première of his new work. It also offers some insight into why he was willing to trust Frederick with the first performance:

> Your enthusiasm and capacity seems to have produced a miracle, about which not only Albuquerque, but probably the whole of Amerika [sic] 'kopfstehen wird'.

> I am very glad that I had the good sense to give you the performance in this small city and I did so, especially on the basis of your personal data. They convinced me that you are a real Viennese musician of the best tradition, but simultaneously with modernistic spirit which in Vienna is not so rare as the conservative party in Vienna would like to make believe.

> I thank you most cordially.

. . . . .

The emotional impact that *A Survivor from Warsaw* had on the performers and audience at the Albuquerque première has not dimmed with time. The source of the work's effect on audiences is not difficult to fathom, for the event to which it bears witness—the brutal and systematic annihilation of most of Europe's Jewish population—is a crime unparalleled in the annals of human history. To audiences of the late 1940s and the 1950s, for whom the bitter experiences of world war were still vivid, *A Survivor from Warsaw* must have carried a special meaning. Today, when the passage of time has, for many, dulled the sense of shock and outrage that the revelation of Nazi barbarism once provoked—when even the word 'holocaust' has seemingly lost its power to evoke the terror of the death camps—Schoenberg's composition continues to serve as an eloquent reminder of the enormity of the crime that took place half a century ago.

The reports of mass murder that began to filter out of Germany during the war must have shocked Schoenberg, but they certainly came as no surprise. As early as 1923, he foresaw the consequences of German anti-Semitism. In a letter to Wassily Kandinsky dated 4 May of that year, he asked: 'But what is anti-Semitism to lead to if not to acts of violence? Is it so difficult to imagine that?' His growing interest in the Jewish nationalist movement and his increasing concern over the fate of German Jews led him to draft a forceful and detailed plan of action just before he left France for the United States in October 1933. He asserted that it was his intention

> to engage in large scale propaganda among all of Jewry in the United States and also later to other countries, designed first of all to get them to produce the financial means sufficient to pay for the gradual emigration of the Jews from Germany. I propose to move the Jewish community to its very depths by a graphic description of what lies in store for the German Jews, unless they receive help within the next two or three months.

Schoenberg specified exactly how he intended to accomplish this goal (indicating, as Alexander Ringer points out, an understanding of the power of propaganda rivalling that of Joseph Goebbels or Frank Capra) and then revealed how important this campaign was to him: 'I offer the sacrifice of my art to the Jewish cause. And I bring my offer enthusiastically, because for me nothing stands above my people.' Considering Schoenberg's deeply held views about his role as an artist, this statement serves as the best possible indication of the depth of his commitment to the cause of Jewish survival.

In spite of his efforts, Schoenberg was frustrated in his attempts to awaken public awareness to the dangerous situation. By 1938, when he wrote **'A Four-Point Program for Jewry'** (a document characterized by Ringer as 'Schoenberg's political testament'), he realized that the growing spectre of war meant that the Nazi contagion would very likely spread across Europe. Within the next year, he must also have realized that his terrible vision was becoming reality and that there was no longer anything he could do to help.

One can only begin to imagine the anguish Schoenberg must have felt during the war years. For him the tragedy took on a personal meaning when he discovered shortly after Hitler was defeated that his brother Heinrich had not survived. Later, he learnt that a cousin, Arthur Schönberg, had also perished. Without doubt, there were others among his circle of friends and acquaintances who were lost.

On the surface, it appears only natural that Schoenberg would seek to memorialize the Jewish victims of Nazism and that such a musical tribute would be deeply expressive. That *A Survivor from Warsaw* succeeds at this level is attested to by its reception at the first performance. I feel, however, that the work held a deeper, personal meaning for its composer and that much of the emotional impact of the work arises from the fact that Schoenberg saw in this tragic and inspiring story a parallel to the events of his own spiritual struggle.

. . . . .

This correspondence between the text and musical structure of *A Survivor from Warsaw* and Schoenberg's own experience has been overlooked by commentators, who have focused on the historical aspects of the story, espe-

cially its supposed connection with the Jewish uprising which took place in the Warsaw ghetto during the spring of 1943. Michael Steinberg, for example, in a *Boston Globe* review of a 1969 performance of *A Survivor from Warsaw* by the Boston Symphony Orchestra, described the work as

> a short, intensely concentrated music drama whose subject is an episode in the battle that began [on] April 19, 1943, in the Warsaw ghetto. A survivor tells the story of a group of Jews, who, at the moment of their deportation to the death camp, suddenly, in a last flaring of spirit and faith, burst into singing the prayer *Shema Yisroel*.

The title of the work is partly responsible for the tendency for writers to link the story to the Warsaw revolt. The narrator's reference to living in the sewers also plays a role in creating the impression that Warsaw is the setting, since it is well known that the sewers were used by the Jewish resistance fighters.

In fact, the events described in *A Survivor from Warsaw* have no specific relationship to the 1943 battle. The setting of the story is not Warsaw but a concentration camp. There are several clues to this fact in the narration. First, the narrator states that 'the day began as usual', thus implying that the prisoners were used to a routine such as one would find in a camp. The trumpets sound reveille, and the prisoners are awakened from an uneasy sleep. They come out of what are apparently barracks of some kind, and one of the prisoners urges the others to hurry. 'Get out! The sergeant will be furious!' This sergeant is obviously someone who is well known to the inmates; the narrator tells us that 'they fear the sergeant'. A further indication that the story is set in a concentration camp is the *Feldwebel*'s statement, 'In einer Minute will ich wissen, wie viele ich zur Gaskammer abliefere!' The decision as to who would be sent to the gas chamber was one made at the camps, not at deportation sites. It is highly unlikely that Schoenberg would have used the term *Gaskammer* as a synonym for *Konzentrationslager*, especially considering the care with which he handled other details of the text.

It is quite possible, however, that even though it is set in a concentration camp, the story of *A Survivor from Warsaw* is actually based on an event that took place in Warsaw. Rene Leibowitz, who undoubtedly discussed the work with Schoenberg during the period when he was copying the orchestral score, wrote that Schoenberg based the text on a story related to him by a young man who had escaped from the Warsaw ghetto. This could very well be true, and should not automatically be viewed as contradicting the evidence of Corinne Chochem's role in presenting the subject to Schoenberg. After all, the composer indicated at the head of the score that the text was 'based partly upon reports which I have received directly or indirectly'. But by the time he composed *A Survivor from Warsaw* he had moved away from the depiction of any specific event. This tragic story had become for him a symbol—a parable—of his own spiritual struggle and that of his people throughout history.

The evidence suggests that when Schoenberg constructed his text he sought to dissociate the story from a specific incident, deliberately obscuring details of time and place in order to emphasize its symbolic character. As noted above, the scene is not Warsaw but an anonymous concentration camp. Precise time references have been removed as well. One early sketch of the narrator's text begins: "I cannot remember all that happened *the last day* [my italics] before I lived underground, in the sewers of Warsaw'. In the final version of the text, in which the narrator states simply, 'I have no recollection how I got underground to live in the sewers of Warsaw for so long a time', the listener no longer knows exactly when the events of the story took place.

Thus, the final version of the text is constructed in such a way as to blur the background, thereby throwing the central event of the story into sharper focus. The narrator's recollection of events mirrors this emphasis; he is very vague about how he arrived in the sewers of Warsaw, but he remembers the events leading up to the singing of the 'Shema Yisroel'—wherever and whenever they took place—in great detail.

. . . . .

The key to understanding *A Survivor from Warsaw* lies in the second sentence of the text: 'I remember only the grandiose moment when they all started to sing, as if prearranged, the old prayer they had neglected for so many years—the forgotten creed!' Surely no witness would have reported an incident to Schoenberg in such terms. The words are entirely his, and they reflect his perception of the elemental truth contained in the reports that he heard.

Let us remember the events of the story. The prisoners are run out of their barracks into the pre-dawn darkness. They have not slept; they are worried about their families. They are shouted at, beaten, and then ordered to count off so that they can be sent to the gas chamber. In a sense, they are told to organize their own execution. Every action taken by the Nazis against them has been coldly calculated to rob them of their humanity—simply because they are Jews. Finally, at the point at which they face the ultimate humiliation and the ultimate horror—at the point when one would expect them to break—their Jewishness becomes a positive, defiant force. This is what gives the climactic moment of the work its power; this is what Schoenberg recognized to be the essence of the reports he had received; and this is what moved him so profoundly—for he saw this story as an analogue to his own experience.

Schoenberg converted early in life to the Protestant faith. Like so many other Austrian Jews, he was moved by a desire to enter into the mainstream of Viennese life, and saw his conversion as a passport to acceptability. How-

ever, amid a rising tide of anti-Semitism and the growth of Jewish consciousness personified by the writings of, among others, Theodore Herzl and the activities of Benno Straucher, Schoenberg found it harder to avoid confronting the issue of his Jewishness. Ringer states that

> When, three years after [World War I] in what was ostensibly a liberal republic, Schoenberg and his family found that Jews could no longer vacation in an Austrian resort of their choice, the composer, struck to the heart, diverted himself of whatever illusions he had left about any possible benefits of assimilation and conversion and with typical vigor and determination plunged headlong into his personal search for constructive answers to the Jewish question.

Over the next decade, Schoenberg and all other German and Austrian Jews were faced with ever more humiliating reminders of their deteriorating position. The situation grew increasingly intolerable for Schoenberg after he moved to Berlin in 1925. Finally, in September 1932, in the face of growing Nazi political power and the increasing arrogance of the 'swastika-swaggerers and pogromists', as he had previously described Hitler and his thugs, Schoenberg wrote the following in a letter to Alban Berg: 'I've had it hammered into me so loudly and so long that only by being deaf to begin with could I have failed to understand it. And its a long time now since it wrung any regrets from me. Today I'm proud to call myself a Jew. . . .' The correlation between this statement with what happens in *A Survivor from Warsaw* is striking and not at all coincidental. Like the condemned Jews in that work, Schoenberg finally rebelled against the humiliations heaped upon him and forcefully reasserted his Jewish identity.

The relationship between Schoenberg's cantata and his Jewish consciousness has a spiritual as well as a nationalistic or racial dimension. Schoenberg's characterization of the 'Shema Yisroel' as 'the old prayer they had neglected for so many years—the forgotten creed' is a crystallization of his belief that European Jews, intent on assimilation, had rejected their heritage—their one source of strength. In 1933 he stated this explicitly: 'In the diaspora the idol worship of our host nations has uprooted us and deprived us of our faith . . . we must surrender once again to our faith . . . it alone ensures our viability and justifies our existence'. The connection between this statement and the message of *Moses und Aron* is obvious, and in this sense *A Survivor from Warsaw* is closely associated with Schoenberg's opera. The later work provides a modern parable of the Jewish people once again embracing the role that the inconceivable God has set out for them and realizing anew the special nature of their life 'in the desert'.

One other issue should be addressed before aspects of the work's musical structure are discussed. If Schoenberg's purpose in writing this cantata was to focus on the larger issues of his own experience and that of his people, then why did he state that his survivor was from Warsaw? As shown above, the construction of the text indicates that he wanted to obscure the background of his story; yet he must have known that listeners would link the name of Warsaw and the reference to the sewers with the heroic battle fought there by Jewish resistance fighters. Even if the evidence suggests that the events upon which Schoenberg based his story may have actually taken place in Warsaw, he could easily have stated that the survivor was from Berlin, Kraków, Amsterdam or any of the thousands of other cities and towns from which Jews were expelled, thereby further distancing his tale from a specific event. But the Warsaw uprising had a special significance for Schoenberg, as it must for all Jews—for there, they fought back. While not the only instance of armed Jewish resistance during the war, the Warsaw ghetto uprising was the largest and best-known revolt, and it has come to be universally regarded as an inspiring symbol of the indestructability of the human spirit in the face of unspeakable brutality and overwhelming odds.

As early as 1923, Schoenberg foresaw the importance of armed struggle when he wrote that the ultimate 're-establishment of a Jewish State can come about only in the manner that has characterized similar events throughout history: not through words and moralizing but through the success of arms and a happy combination of interests'. And, a decade later, in a letter to Jakob Klatzkin dated 13 June 1933 he expressed this sentiment even more forcefully:

> The timid will never be able to make the sacrifices required by courage and self-denial. Those unwilling to risk life and property won't be able to participate in our struggle for liberation. We must succeed in persuading Jewish youth of the necessity of this struggle completely and without qualifications.

These two passages illustrate Schoenberg's support for the affirmative, militant Zionism advocated by Vladimir Jabotinsky. He undoubtedly saw in the Warsaw uprising a useful example of what it would take for the Jews finally to acquire and maintain a land of their own. He may have been moved to include an oblique reference to the rebellion in his text, but again, I do not believe that he ever intended that this reference be taken as the central point of the work.

. . . . .

The cantata can be divided into two distinct sections. The first, lasting some 80 bars, consists of the narrator's account of the events leading up to the singing of the 'Shema Yisroel'. The setting of the prayer itself comprises the second section. Although this second part is only nineteen bars long, the intensity of the musical and dramatic expression serves to negate any sense of structural imbalance between it and the much longer narrative section.

The entire piece is based on twelve-note techniques, and the musical materials remain the same throughout, but the two sections are organized according to widely differing principles. The second section is built around the 'Shema' melody, and it thus contrasts with the narrative section, which contains relatively little sustained melodic material. Christian Martin Schmidt has suggested that the two sections are representative of different periods in Schoenberg's compositional development: the first, 'athematic', reflects a return to the techniques of the composer's so-called atonal period; the second, with its clear reliance on the 'Shema' theme, can be seen as representative of the later twelve-note period.

The narrative section does indeed seem to recall the techniques that Schoenberg used in the decade or so before the discovery of the twelve-note method. Schmidt notes in particular the pervasive use of augmented triads as a kind of 'harmonic pedal', recalling that Schoenberg had used similar extended 'harmonic pedals' in a number of works from this period, including the first of the *Fünf Orchesterstücke,* Op. 16, *Die glückliche Hand,* Op. 18, and the last of the *Kleine Stücke für Kammerorchester,* dating from 1910.

The presence of a sustained melodic line in the second section of the cantata is the feature that most distinguishes it from the narrative. Beginning in bar 80, the 'Shema' melody becomes the framework around which the rest of the piece is constructed. Augmented triads no longer pervade the texture in their role as a 'harmonic pedal'. Programmatic elements that had been used extensively in the first section (the trumpet fanfare, military drum, and fifes—represented by flutes and piccolo) are also absent in this section. The texture becomes much thicker, and there is a greater reliance on horizontal realization of various set forms.

This symbolic progression in *A Survivor from Warsaw* from the procedures of *c.* 1910 to those characteristic of 'classic' twelve-note technique is not surprising if one sees the work as representative of Schoenberg's own spiritual struggle. There was always a strong connection between the spiritual and creative aspects of his life, a connection borne out in the opening paragraphs of '**Composition with Twelve Tones**':

> To understand the very nature of creation one must acknowledge that there was no light before the Lord said: 'Let there be light.' And since there was not yet light, the Lord's omniscience embraced a version of it which only His omnipotence could call forth.
>
> We poor human beings, when we refer to one of the better minds among us as a creator, should never forget what a creator is in reality.
>
> A creator has a vision of something which has not existed before this vision.
>
> And a creator has the power to bring his vision to life, the power to realize it.
>
> In fact, the concept of creator and creation should

be formed in harmony with the Divine Model; inspiration and perfection, wish and fulfillment, will and accomplishment coincide spontaneously and simultaneously.

Although Schoenberg continues by admitting that it is difficult, if not impossible, for a human creator to imitate the perfection of the Divine Model, he clearly viewed his creative work as a spiritual activity. He saw a parallel between the struggles of his creative life and those of his personal spiritual life. He considered his discovery of the twelve-note method as a vision—a divine revelation that was perhaps as significant and meaningful as his reconciliation with his Jewish faith and heritage.

The connection between these two decisive events in Schoenberg's life is further strengthened by the fact that they occurred in close chronological proximity. Schoenberg first mentioned his work with twelve-note procedures to Joseph Rufer in the summer of 1921, but, as revealed in a letter to Nicolas Slonimsky dated 3 June 1937, there followed a period of experimentation before he fully realized the implications of his discovery. During this same period, the issue of his Jewishness had also been very much on Schoenberg's mind. On 20 April 1923, he wrote in a letter to Kandinsky that

> . . . I have at last learnt the lesson that has been forced upon me during this year, and I shall never forget it. It is that I am not a German, not a European, indeed perhaps scarcely even a human being (at least, the Europeans prefer the worst of their race to me), but I am a Jew.
>
> I am content that it should be so! Today I no longer wish to be an exception; I have no objection at all to being lumped together with all the rest.

Again, one finds a parallel between the sentiments expressed in this letter and the climactic moment in *A Survivor from Warsaw*—'the grandiose moment when they started to sing' the 'Shema Yisroel'. The change in musical style that occurs at exactly that point in the score underlines the deep connection Schoenberg felt between his spiritual reawakening and his discovery of the twelve-note method.

A Survivor from Warsaw stands as a moving tribute to the millions of European Jews who suffered and died at the hands of Nazi Germany. As such, it has stirred audiences from the time of its first performances in 1948. Much of the work's power, however, emanates from the deeper significance that it held for its creator. I am convinced that Schoenberg saw in this story of a small group of condemned Jewish prisoners both a striking crystallization of his own inner struggle with his Jewishness and a modern parable confirming the message of *Moses und Aron:* God has a special role for His Chosen People, and that only by acknowledging and accepting the uniqueness of their status can the Jews endure and triumph over the adversities that confront them. *A Survivor from Warsaw* symbolizes the religious and nationalistic ideals of its composer, and ranks with *Moses und Aron, Die*

Jakobsleiter and the three psalm settings of Op. 50 as one of the most profoundly spiritual of Schoenberg's musical expressions.

FURTHER READING

Bibliography

Christensen, Jean and Jesper. *From Arnold Schoenberg's Literary Legacy: A Catalog of Neglected Items.* Warren: Harmonie Park Press, 1988, 164 p.
    Includes previously uncataloged manuscripts from the Arnold Schoenberg Institute archives.

Biography

The Berg-Schoenberg Correspondence: Selected Letters, edited by Juliane Brand, Christopher Hailey, and Donald Harris. New York: W. W. Norton, 1987, 497 p.
    Documents Schoenberg's relationship with the composer Alban Berg.

Ennulat, Egbert M. *Arnold Schoenberg Correspondence: A Collection of Translated and Annotated Letters Exchanged with Guido Adler, Pablo Casals, Emanuel Feuermann, and Olin Downes.* Metuchen: Scarecrow Press, 1991, 320 p.
    Selected letters spanning four decades of Schoenberg's career.

Kallir, Jane. *Arnold Schoenberg's Vienna.* New York: Galerie St. Etienne, 1984, 120 p.
    Focuses on Schoenberg's work as a painter.

Newlin, Dika. *Schoenberg Remembered: Diaries and Recollections (1938-76).* New York: Pendragon Press, 1980, 369 p.
    Reminiscences by one of Schoenberg's American students.

Reich, Willi. *Schoenberg: A Critical Biography.* New York: Praeger Publishers, 1971, 268 p.
    Originally published in Austria; written with the cooperation of Schoenberg's widow.

Criticism

Bailey, Walter B. *Programmatic Elements in the Works of Schoenberg.* Ann Arbor: UMI Research Press, 1984, 188 p.
    Examines Schoenberg's relationship to program music.

Berg, Alban. "Why Is Schoenberg's Music So Hard to Understand?" In *Contemporary Composers on Contemporary Music*, edited by Elliot Schwartz and

Barney Childs, pp. 59-71. New York: Holt, Rinehart, and Winston, 1967.
Defense of Schoenberg by one of his most famous students.

Carpenter, Patricia. "Musical Form and Musical Idea: Reflections on a Theme of Schoenberg, Hanslick, and Kant." In *Music and Civilization: Essays in Honor of Paul Henry Lang*, edited by Edmond Strainchamps and Maria Rika Maniates in collaboration with Christopher Hatch. New York: W. W. Norton, 1984, pp. 394-427.
Discusses Schoenberg's theories about how music works.

Cherlin, Michael. "Schoenberg and *Das Unheimliche*: Spectres of Tonality." *The Journal of Musicology* 11, No. 3 (Summer 1993): 357-373.
Analyzes "uncanny" elements in Schoenberg's twelve-tone compositions.

Cone, Edward T. "Sound and Syntax: An Introduction to Schoenberg's Harmony." In *Music: A View from Delft*, pp. 249-66. Chicago: University of Chicago Press, 1989.
Close reading of tonal patterns in Schoenberg's musical scores.

Crawford, John C., and Dorothy L. Crawford. "Arnold Schoenberg." In *Expressionism in Twentieth-Century Music*, pp. 65-94. Bloomington: Indiana University Press, 1993.
Examines Schoenberg's Expressionist period.

Dahlhaus, Carl. *Schoenberg and the New Music*. Cambridge: Cambridge University Press, 1987, 305 p.
Essays about Schoenberg and other avant-garde composers.

Frisch, Walter. *The Early Works of Arnold Schoenberg, 1893-1908*. Berkeley: University of California Press, 1993, 328 p.
Includes discussion of Schoenberg's theoretical writings.

Haimo, Ethan. *Schoenberg's Serial Odyessy: The Evolution of His Twelve-Tone Method, 1914-1928*. Oxford: Clarendon Press, 1990, 192 p.
Close study of key musical texts from this period.

MacDonald, Malcolm. *Schoenberg*. London: J. M. Dent and Sons, 1976, 289 p.
Introductory survey of the composer's life and music.

Neighbour, Oliver. "Arnold Schoenberg." In *The New Grove Second Viennese School: Schoenberg, Webern, Berg*, by Oliver Neighbour, Paul Griffiths, and George Perle, pp. 1-88. New York: W. W. Norton, 1983.
Basic information about Schoenberg derived from *The New Grove Dictionary of Music and Musicians*.

Perspectives on Schoenberg and Stravinsky, edited by Benjamin Boretz and Edward T. Cone. New York: W. W. Norton, 1983, 284 p.
Includes essays by Schoenberg and contemporary American composers.

Ribe, Neil M. "Atonal Music and Its Limits." *Commentary* 84, No. 5 (November 1987): 49-54.
Discusses the place of atonalism in the contemporary canon of modern music.

Rosen, Charles. *Arnold Schoenberg*. New York: Viking Press, 1975, 113 p.
Critical examination of Schoenberg's works.

Schoenberg, edited by Merle Armitage. New York: G. Schirmer, 1937, 319 p.
Includes writings about Schoenberg by Leopold Stokowski, Roger Sessions, Franz Werfel, Otto Klemperer, and Berthold Viertel.

Sterne, Colin C. *Arnold Schoenberg, the Composer as Numerologist*. Lewiston: Edwin Mellen Press, 1993, 231 p.
Proposes that Schoenberg used numerology as a composition tool.

Studies in the Schoenbergian Movement in Vienna and the United States: Essays in Honor of Marcel Dick, edited by Anne Trenkamp and John G. Suess. Lewiston: Edwin Mellen Press, 1990, 315 p.
Includes essays about Schoenberg and the Second Viennese School.

Wellesz, Egon. *Arnold Schönberg*. London: J. M. Dent and Sons, 1925, 159 p.
Early study of Schoenberg's life and works.

Twentieth-Century Literary Criticism

Cumulative Indexes
Volumes 1-75

How to Use This Index

The main references

> Calvino, Italo
> 1923–1985 .... CLC 5, 8, 11, 22, 33, 39,
> 73; SSC 3

list all author entries in the following Gale Literary Criticism series:

BLC = *Black Literature Criticism*
CLC = *Contemporary Literary Criticism*
CLR = *Children's Literature Review*
CMLC = *Classical and Medieval Literature Criticism*
DA = *DISCovering Authors*
DAB = *DISCovering Authors: British*
DAC = *DISCovering Authors: Canadian*
DAM = *DISCovering Authors: Modules*
    DRAM: *Dramatists Module;* *MST*: *Most-Studied Authors Module;*
    MULT: *Multicultural Authors Module;* *NOV*: *Novelists Module;*
    POET: *Poets Module;* *POP*: *Popular Fiction and Genre Authors Module*
DC = *Drama Criticism*
HLC = *Hispanic Literature Criticism*
LC = *Literature Criticism from 1400 to 1800*
NCLC = *Nineteenth-Century Literature Criticism*
PC = *Poetry Criticism*
SSC = *Short Story Criticism*
TCLC = *Twentieth-Century Literary Criticism*
WLC = *World Literature Criticism, 1500 to the Present*

The cross-references

> See also CANR 23; CA 85-88;
> obituary CA116

list all author entries in the following Gale biographical and literary sources:

AAYA = *Authors & Artists for Young Adults*
AITN = *Authors in the News*
BEST = *Bestsellers*
BW = *Black Writers*
CA = *Contemporary Authors*
CAAS = *Contemporary Authors Autobiography Series*
CABS = *Contemporary Authors Bibliographical Series*
CANR = *Contemporary Authors New Revision Series*
CAP = *Contemporary Authors Permanent Series*
CDALB = *Concise Dictionary of American Literary Biography*
CDBLB = *Concise Dictionary of British Literary Biography*
DLB = *Dictionary of Literary Biography*
DLBD = *Dictionary of Literary Biography Documentary Series*
DLBY = *Dictionary of Literary Biography Yearbook*
HW = *Hispanic Writers*
JRDA = *Junior DISCovering Authors*
MAICYA = *Major Authors and Illustrators for Children and Young Adults*
MTCW = *Major 20th-Century Writers*
NNAL = *Native North American Literature*
SAAS = *Something about the Author Autobiography Series*
SATA = *Something about the Author*
YABC = *Yesterday's Authors of Books for Children*

Literary Criticism Series
Cumulative Author Index

Aleshkovsky, Yuz .... CLC 44
  See also Aleshkovsky, Joseph
Alexander, Lloyd (Chudley) 1924- ... CLC 35
  See also AAYA 1; CA 1-4R; CANR 1, 24, 38,
    55; CLR 1, 5; DLB 52; JRDA; MAICYA;
    MTCW; SAAS 19; SATA 3, 49, 81
Alexie, Sherman (Joseph, Jr.) 1966- CLC 96;
  DAM MULT
  See also CA 138; DLB 175; NNAL
Alfau, Felipe 1902- .... CLC 66
  See also CA 137
Alger, Horatio, Jr. 1832-1899 .... NCLC 8
  See also DLB 42; SATA 16
Algren, Nelson 1909-1981 .... CLC 4, 10, 33
  See also CA 13-16R; 103; CANR 20, 61;
    CDALB 1941-1968; DLB 9; DLBY 81, 82;
    MTCW
Ali, Ahmed 1910- .... CLC 69
  See also CA 25-28R; CANR 15, 34
Alighieri, Dante 1265-1321 ...... CMLC 3, 18;
  WLCS
Allan, John B.
  See Westlake, Donald E(dwin)
Allan, Sidney
  See Hartmann, Sadakichi
Allan, Sydney
  See Hartmann, Sadakichi
Allen, Edward 1948- .... CLC 59
Allen, Paula Gunn 1939- .... CLC 84; DAM
  MULT
  See also CA 112; 143; DLB 175; NNAL
Allen, Roland
  See Ayckbourn, Alan
Allen, Sarah A.
  See Hopkins, Pauline Elizabeth
Allen, Sidney H.
  See Hartmann, Sadakichi
Allen, Woody 1935- CLC 16, 52; DAM POP
  See also AAYA 10; CA 33-36R; CANR 27, 38;
    DLB 44; MTCW
Allende, Isabel 1942- . CLC 39, 57, 97; DAM
  MULT, NOV; HLC; WLCS
  See also AAYA 18; CA 125; 130; CANR 51;
    DLB 145; HW; INT 130; MTCW
Alleyn, Ellen
  See Rossetti, Christina (Georgina)
Allingham, Margery (Louise) 1904-1966 C L C
  19
  See also CA 5-8R; 25-28R; CANR 4, 58; DLB
    77; MTCW
Allingham, William 1824-1889 ...... NCLC 25
  See also DLB 35
Allison, Dorothy E. 1949- .... CLC 78
  See also CA 140
Allston, Washington 1779-1843 .... NCLC 2
  See also DLB 1
Almedingen, E. M. .... CLC 12
  See also Almedingen, Martha Edith von
  See also SATA 3
Almedingen, Martha Edith von 1898-1971
  See Almedingen, E. M.
  See also CA 1-4R; CANR 1
Almqvist, Carl Jonas Love 1793-1866 N C L C
  42
Alonso, Damaso 1898-1990 .... CLC 14
  See also CA 110; 131; 130; DLB 108; HW
Alov
  See Gogol, Nikolai (Vasilyevich)
Alta 1942- .... CLC 19
  See also CA 57-60
Alter, Robert B(ernard) 1935- .... CLC 34
  See also CA 49-52; CANR 1, 47
Alther, Lisa 1944- .... CLC 7, 41
  See also CA 65-68; CANR 12, 30, 51; MTCW
Altman, Robert 1925- .... CLC 16
  See also CA 73-76; CANR 43
Alvarez, A(lfred) 1929- .... CLC 5, 13

  See also CA 1-4R; CANR 3, 33; DLB 14, 40
Alvarez, Alejandro Rodriguez 1903-1965
  See Casona, Alejandro
  See also CA 131; 93-96; HW
Alvarez, Julia 1950- .... CLC 93
  See also CA 147
Alvaro, Corrado 1896-1956 .... TCLC 60
Amado, Jorge 1912- CLC 13, 40; DAM MULT,
  NOV; HLC
  See also CA 77-80; CANR 35; DLB 113;
    MTCW
Ambler, Eric 1909- .... CLC 4, 6, 9
  See also CA 9-12R; CANR 7, 38; DLB 77;
    MTCW
Amichai, Yehuda 1924- .... CLC 9, 22, 57
  See also CA 85-88; CANR 46, 60; MTCW
Amichai, Yehudah
  See Amichai, Yehuda
Amiel, Henri Frederic 1821-1881 .... NCLC 4
Amis, Kingsley (William) 1922-1995 CLC 1, 2,
  3, 5, 8, 13, 40, 44; DA; DAB; DAC; DAM
  MST, NOV
  See also AITN 2; CA 9-12R; 150; CANR 8, 28,
    54; CDBLB 1945-1960; DLB 15, 27, 100,
    139; DLBY 96; INT CANR-8; MTCW
Amis, Martin (Louis) 1949- CLC 4, 9, 38, 62,
  101
  See also BEST 90:3; CA 65-68; CANR 8, 27,
    54; DLB 14; INT CANR-27
Ammons, A(rchie) R(andolph) 1926- CLC 2, 3,
  5, 8, 9, 25, 57; DAM POET; PC 16
  See also AITN 1; CA 9-12R; CANR 6, 36, 51;
    DLB 5, 165; MTCW
Amo, Tauraatua i
  See Adams, Henry (Brooks)
Anand, Mulk Raj 1905- .. CLC 23, 93; DAM
  NOV
  See also CA 65-68; CANR 32; MTCW
Anatol
  See Schnitzler, Arthur
Anaximander c. 610B.C.-c. 546B.C. CMLC 22
Anaya, Rudolfo A(lfonso) 1937- ..... CLC 23;
  DAM MULT, NOV; HLC
  See also AAYA 20; CA 45-48; CAAS 4; CANR
    1, 32, 51; DLB 82; HW 1; MTCW
Andersen, Hans Christian 1805-1875 NCLC 7;
  DA; DAB; DAC; DAM MST, POP; SSC
  6; WLC
  See also CLR 6; MAICYA; YABC 1
Anderson, C. Farley
  See Mencken, H(enry) L(ouis); Nathan, George
    Jean
Anderson, Jessica (Margaret) Queale 1916-
  CLC 37
  See also CA 9-12R; CANR 4, 62
Anderson, Jon (Victor) 1940- .. CLC 9; DAM
  POET
  See also CA 25-28R; CANR 20
Anderson, Lindsay (Gordon) 1923-1994 C L C
  20
  See also CA 125; 128; 146
Anderson, Maxwell 1888-1959 TCLC 2; DAM
  DRAM
  See also CA 105; 152; DLB 7
Anderson, Poul (William) 1926- .... CLC 15
  See also AAYA 5; CA 1-4R; CAAS 2; CANR
    2, 15, 34; DLB 8; INT CANR-15; MTCW;
    SATA 90; SATA-Brief 39
Anderson, Robert (Woodruff) 1917- CLC 23;
  DAM DRAM
  See also AITN 1; CA 21-24R; CANR 32; DLB
    7
Anderson, Sherwood 1876-1941 TCLC 1, 10,
  24; DA; DAB; DAC; DAM MST, NOV;
  SSC 1; WLC
  See also CA 104; 121; CANR 61; CDALB
    1917-1929; DLB 4, 9, 86; DLBD 1; MTCW

Andier, Pierre
  See Desnos, Robert
Andouard
  See Giraudoux, (Hippolyte) Jean
Andrade, Carlos Drummond de .... CLC 18
  See also Drummond de Andrade, Carlos
Andrade, Mario de 1893-1945 .... TCLC 43
Andreae, Johann V(alentin) 1586-1654 LC 32
  See also DLB 164
Andreas-Salome, Lou 1861-1937 ... TCLC 56
  See also DLB 66
Andress, Lesley
  See Sanders, Lawrence
Andrewes, Lancelot 1555-1626 .... LC 5
  See also DLB 151, 172
Andrews, Cicily Fairfield
  See West, Rebecca
Andrews, Elton V.
  See Pohl, Frederik
Andreyev, Leonid (Nikolaevich) 1871-1919
  TCLC 3
  See also CA 104
Andric, Ivo 1892-1975 .... CLC 8
  See also CA 81-84; 57-60; CANR 43, 60; DLB
    147; MTCW
Androvar
  See Prado (Calvo), Pedro
Angelique, Pierre
  See Bataille, Georges
Angell, Roger 1920- .... CLC 26
  See also CA 57-60; CANR 13, 44; DLB 171
Angelou, Maya 1928- CLC 12, 35, 64, 77; BLC;
  DA; DAB; DAC; DAM MST, MULT,
  POET, POP; WLCS
  See also AAYA 7, 20; BW 2; CA 65-68; CANR
    19, 42; DLB 38; MTCW; SATA 49
Annensky, Innokenty (Fyodorovich) 1856-1909
  TCLC 14
  See also CA 110; 155
Annunzio, Gabriele d'
  See D'Annunzio, Gabriele
Anodos
  See Coleridge, Mary E(lizabeth)
Anon, Charles Robert
  See Pessoa, Fernando (Antonio Nogueira)
Anouilh, Jean (Marie Lucien Pierre) 1910-1987
  CLC 1, 3, 8, 13, 40, 50; DAM DRAM
  See also CA 17-20R; 123; CANR 32; MTCW
Anthony, Florence
  See Ai
Anthony, John
  See Ciardi, John (Anthony)
Anthony, Peter
  See Shaffer, Anthony (Joshua); Shaffer, Peter
    (Levin)
Anthony, Piers 1934- .... CLC 35; DAM POP
  See also AAYA 11; CA 21-24R; CANR 28, 56;
    DLB 8; MTCW; SAAS 22; SATA 84
Antoine, Marc
  See Proust, (Valentin-Louis-George-Eugene-)
    Marcel
Antoninus, Brother
  See Everson, William (Oliver)
Antonioni, Michelangelo 1912- .... CLC 20
  See also CA 73-76; CANR 45
Antschel, Paul 1920-1970
  See Celan, Paul
  See also CA 85-88; CANR 33, 61; MTCW
Anwar, Chairil 1922-1949 .... TCLC 22
  See also CA 121
Apollinaire, Guillaume 1880-1918 TCLC 3, 8,
  51; DAM POET; PC 7
  See also Kostrowitzki, Wilhelm Apollinaris de
  See also CA 152
Appelfeld, Aharon 1932- .... CLC 23, 47
  See also CA 112; 133
Apple, Max (Isaac) 1941- .... CLC 9, 33

See also CA 81-84; CANR 19, 54; DLB 130

Appleman, Philip (Dean) 1926- .... **CLC 51**
　　See also CA 13-16R; CAAS 18; CANR 6, 29,
　　56

Appleton, Lawrence
　　See Lovecraft, H(oward) P(hillips)

Apteryx
　　See Eliot, T(homas) S(tearns)

Apuleius, (Lucius Madaurensis) 125(?)-175(?)
　　CMLC 1

Aquin, Hubert 1929-1977 .... **CLC 15**
　　See also CA 105; DLB 53

Aragon, Louis 1897-1982 .. **CLC 3, 22; DAM
　　NOV, POET**
　　See also CA 69-72; 108; CANR 28; DLB 72;
　　MTCW

Arany, Janos 1817-1882 .... **NCLC 34**

Arbuthnot, John 1667-1735 .... **LC 1**
　　See also DLB 101

Archer, Herbert Winslow
　　See Mencken, H(enry) L(ouis)

Archer, Jeffrey (Howard) 1940- ..... **CLC 28;
　　DAM POP**
　　See also AAYA 16; BEST 89:3; CA 77-80;
　　CANR 22, 52; INT CANR-22

Archer, Jules 1915- .... **CLC 12**
　　See also CA 9-12R; CANR 6; SAAS 5; SATA
　　4, 85

Archer, Lee
　　See Ellison, Harlan (Jay)

Arden, John 1930-**CLC 6, 13, 15; DAM DRAM**
　　See also CA 13-16R; CAAS 4; CANR 31; DLB
　　13; MTCW

Arenas, Reinaldo 1943-1990 . **CLC 41; DAM
　　MULT; HLC**
　　See also CA 124; 128; 133; DLB 145; HW

Arendt, Hannah 1906-1975 .... **CLC 66, 98**
　　See also CA 17-20R; 61-64; CANR 26, 60;
　　MTCW

Aretino, Pietro 1492-1556 .... **LC 12**

Arghezi, Tudor .... **CLC 80**
　　See also Theodorescu, Ion N.

Arguedas, Jose Maria 1911-1969**CLC 10, 18**
　　See also CA 89-92; DLB 113; HW

Argueta, Manlio 1936- .... **CLC 31**
　　See also CA 131; DLB 145; HW

Ariosto, Ludovico 1474-1533 .... **LC 6**

Aristides
　　See Epstein, Joseph

Aristophanes 450B.C.-385B.C.**CMLC 4; DA;
　　DAB; DAC; DAM DRAM, MST; DC 2;
　　WLCS**
　　See also DLB 176

Arlt, Roberto (Godofredo Christophersen)
　　1900-1942**TCLC 29; DAM MULT; HLC**
　　See also CA 123; 131; HW

Armah, Ayi Kwei 1939-**CLC 5, 33; BLC; DAM
　　MULT, POET**
　　See also BW 1; CA 61-64; CANR 21; DLB 117;
　　MTCW

Armatrading, Joan 1950- .... **CLC 17**
　　See also CA 114

Arnette, Robert
　　See Silverberg, Robert

**Arnim, Achim von (Ludwig Joachim von
　　Arnim)** 1781-1831 ...... **NCLC 5; SSC 29**
　　See also DLB 90

Arnim, Bettina von 1785-1859 .... **NCLC 38**
　　See also DLB 90

Arnold, Matthew 1822-1888**NCLC 6, 29; DA;
　　DAB; DAC; DAM MST, POET; PC 5;
　　WLC**
　　See also CDBLB 1832-1890; DLB 32, 57

Arnold, Thomas 1795-1842 .... **NCLC 18**
　　See also DLB 55

Arnow, Harriette (Louisa) Simpson 1908-1986
　　CLC 2, 7, 18

See also CA 9-12R; 118; CANR 14; DLB 6;
　　MTCW; SATA 42; SATA-Obit 47

Arp, Hans
　　See Arp, Jean

Arp, Jean 1887-1966 .... **CLC 5**
　　See also CA 81-84; 25-28R; CANR 42

Arrabal
　　See Arrabal, Fernando

Arrabal, Fernando 1932-.... **CLC 2, 9, 18, 58**
　　See also CA 9-12R; CANR 15

Arrick, Fran .... **CLC 30**
　　See also Gaberman, Judie Angell

Artaud, Antonin (Marie Joseph) 1896-1948
　　TCLC 3, 36; DAM DRAM
　　See also CA 104; 149

Arthur, Ruth M(abel) 1905-1979 ...... **CLC 12**
　　See also CA 9-12R; 85-88; CANR 4; SATA 7,
　　26

Artsybashev, Mikhail (Petrovich) 1878-1927
　　TCLC 31

Arundel, Honor (Morfydd) 1919-1973**CLC 17**
　　See also CA 21-22; 41-44R; CAP 2; CLR 35;
　　SATA 4; SATA-Obit 24

Arzner, Dorothy 1897-1979 .... **CLC 98**

Asch, Sholem 1880-1957 .... **TCLC 3**
　　See also CA 105

Ash, Shalom
　　See Asch, Sholem

Ashbery, John (Lawrence) 1927-**CLC 2, 3, 4,
　　6, 9, 13, 15, 25, 41, 77; DAM POET**
　　See also CA 5-8R; CANR 9, 37; DLB 5, 165;
　　DLBY 81; INT CANR-9; MTCW

Ashdown, Clifford
　　See Freeman, R(ichard) Austin

Ashe, Gordon
　　See Creasey, John

Ashton-Warner, Sylvia (Constance) 1908-1984
　　CLC 19
　　See also CA 69-72; 112; CANR 29; MTCW

Asimov, Isaac 1920-1992 **CLC 1, 3, 9, 19, 26,
　　76, 92; DAM POP**
　　See also AAYA 13; BEST 90:2; CA 1-4R; 137;
　　CANR 2, 19, 36, 60; CLR 12; DLB 8; DLBY
　　92; INT CANR-19; JRDA; MAICYA;
　　MTCW; SATA 1, 26, 74

Assis, Joaquim Maria Machado de
　　See Machado de Assis, Joaquim Maria

Astley, Thea (Beatrice May) 1925- ... **CLC 41**
　　See also CA 65-68; CANR 11, 43

Aston, James
　　See White, T(erence) H(anbury)

Asturias, Miguel Angel 1899-1974 **CLC 3, 8,
　　13; DAM MULT, NOV; HLC**
　　See also CA 25-28; 49-52; CANR 32; CAP 2;
　　DLB 113; HW; MTCW

Atares, Carlos Saura
　　See Saura (Atares), Carlos

Atheling, William
　　See Pound, Ezra (Weston Loomis)

Atheling, William, Jr.
　　See Blish, James (Benjamin)

Atherton, Gertrude (Franklin Horn) 1857-1948
　　TCLC 2
　　See also CA 104; 155; DLB 9, 78

Atherton, Lucius
　　See Masters, Edgar Lee

Atkins, Jack
　　See Harris, Mark

Atkinson, Kate .... **CLC 99**

Attaway, William (Alexander) 1911-1986
　　CLC 92; BLC; DAM MULT
　　See also BW 2; CA 143; DLB 76

Atticus
　　See Fleming, Ian (Lancaster)

Atwood, Margaret (Eleanor) 1939-**CLC 2, 3,
　　4, 8, 13, 15, 25, 44, 84; DA; DAB; DAC;
　　DAM MST, NOV, POET; PC 8; SSC 2;**

WLC
　　See also AAYA 12; BEST 89:2; CA 49-52;
　　CANR 3, 24, 33, 59; DLB 53; INT CANR-
　　24; MTCW; SATA 50

Aubigny, Pierre d'
　　See Mencken, H(enry) L(ouis)

Aubin, Penelope 1685-1731(?) .... **LC 9**
　　See also DLB 39

Auchincloss, Louis (Stanton) 1917-**CLC 4, 6,
　　9, 18, 45; DAM NOV; SSC 22**
　　See also CA 1-4R; CANR 6, 29, 55; DLB 2;
　　DLBY 80; INT CANR-29; MTCW

Auden, W(ystan) H(ugh) 1907-1973**CLC 1, 2,
　　3, 4, 6, 9, 11, 14, 43; DA; DAB; DAC; DAM
　　DRAM, MST, POET; PC 1; WLC**
　　See also AAYA 18; CA 9-12R; 45-48; CANR
　　5, 61; CDBLB 1914-1945; DLB 10, 20;
　　MTCW

Audiberti, Jacques 1900-1965**CLC 38; DAM
　　DRAM**
　　See also CA 25-28R

Audubon, John James 1785-1851 .. **NCLC 47**

Auel, Jean M(arie) 1936-**CLC 31; DAM POP**
　　See also AAYA 7; BEST 90:4; CA 103; CANR
　　21; INT CANR-21; SATA 91

Auerbach, Erich 1892-1957............ **TCLC 43**
　　See also CA 118; 155

Augier, Emile 1820-1889 .... **NCLC 31**

August, John
　　See De Voto, Bernard (Augustine)

Augustine, St. 354-430 .... **CMLC 6; DAB**

Aurelius
　　See Bourne, Randolph S(illiman)

Aurobindo, Sri 1872-1950 .... **TCLC 63**

Austen, Jane 1775-1817 **NCLC 1, 13, 19, 33,
　　51; DA; DAB; DAC; DAM MST, NOV;
　　WLC**
　　See also AAYA 19; CDBLB 1789-1832; DLB
　　116

Auster, Paul 1947- .... **CLC 47**
　　See also CA 69-72; CANR 23, 52

Austin, Frank
　　See Faust, Frederick (Schiller)

Austin, Mary (Hunter) 1868-1934 . **TCLC 25**
　　See also CA 109; DLB 9, 78

Autran Dourado, Waldomiro
　　See Dourado, (Waldomiro Freitas) Autran

Averroes 1126-1198 .... **CMLC 7**
　　See also DLB 115

Avicenna 980-1037 .... **CMLC 16**
　　See also DLB 115

Avison, Margaret 1918- **CLC 2, 4, 97; DAC;
　　DAM POET**
　　See also CA 17-20R; DLB 53; MTCW

Axton, David
　　See Koontz, Dean R(ay)

Ayckbourn, Alan 1939- **CLC 5, 8, 18, 33, 74;
　　DAB; DAM DRAM**
　　See also CA 21-24R; CANR 31, 59; DLB 13;
　　MTCW

Aydy, Catherine
　　See Tennant, Emma (Christina)

Ayme, Marcel (Andre) 1902-1967 .... **CLC 11**
　　See also CA 89-92; CLR 25; DLB 72; SATA 91

Ayrton, Michael 1921-1975 .... **CLC 7**
　　See also CA 5-8R; 61-64; CANR 9, 21

Azorin .... **CLC 11**
　　See also Martinez Ruiz, Jose

Azuela, Mariano 1873-1952 . **TCLC 3; DAM
　　MULT; HLC**
　　See also CA 104; 131; HW; MTCW

Baastad, Babbis Friis
　　See Friis-Baastad, Babbis Ellinor

Bab
　　See Gilbert, W(illiam) S(chwenck)

Babbis, Eleanor
　　See Friis-Baastad, Babbis Ellinor

Babel, Isaac
 See Babel, Isaak (Emmanuilovich)
Babel, Isaak (Emmanuilovich) 1894-1941(?)
 TCLC 2, 13; SSC 16
 See also CA 104; 155
Babits, Mihaly 1883-1941 .... **TCLC 14**
 See also CA 114
Babur 1483-1530 .... **LC 18**
Bacchelli, Riccardo 1891-1985 .... **CLC 19**
 See also CA 29-32R; 117
Bach, Richard (David) 1936- **CLC 14; DAM NOV, POP**
 See also AITN 1; BEST 89:2; CA 9-12R; CANR 18; MTCW; SATA 13
Bachman, Richard
 See King, Stephen (Edwin)
Bachmann, Ingeborg 1926-1973 .... **CLC 69**
 See also CA 93-96; 45-48; DLB 85
Bacon, Francis 1561-1626 .... **LC 18, 32**
 See also CDBLB Before 1660; DLB 151
Bacon, Roger 1214(?)-1292 .... **CMLC 14**
 See also DLB 115
Bacovia, George .... **TCLC 24**
 See also Vasiliu, Gheorghe
Badanes, Jerome 1937- .... **CLC 59**
Bagehot, Walter 1826-1877 .... **NCLC 10**
 See also DLB 55
Bagnold, Enid 1889-1981 .... **CLC 25; DAM DRAM**
 See also CA 5-8R; 103; CANR 5, 40; DLB 13, 160; MAICYA; SATA 1, 25
Bagritsky, Eduard 1895-1934 .... **TCLC 60**
Bagrjana, Elisaveta
 See Belcheva, Elisaveta
Bagryana, Elisaveta .... **CLC 10**
 See also Belcheva, Elisaveta
 See also DLB 147
Bailey, Paul 1937- .... **CLC 45**
 See also CA 21-24R; CANR 16, 62; DLB 14
Baillie, Joanna 1762-1851 .... **NCLC 2**
 See also DLB 93
Bainbridge, Beryl (Margaret) 1933-**CLC 4, 5, 8, 10, 14, 18, 22, 62; DAM NOV**
 See also CA 21-24R; CANR 24, 55; DLB 14; MTCW
Baker, Elliott 1922- .... **CLC 8**
 See also CA 45-48; CANR 2
Baker, Jean H. .... **TCLC 3, 10**
 See also Russell, George William
Baker, Nicholson 1957- **CLC 61; DAM POP**
 See also CA 135
Baker, Ray Stannard 1870-1946 .... **TCLC 47**
 See also CA 118
Baker, Russell (Wayne) 1925- .... **CLC 31**
 See also BEST 89:4; CA 57-60; CANR 11, 41, 59; MTCW
Bakhtin, M.
 See Bakhtin, Mikhail Mikhailovich
Bakhtin, M. M.
 See Bakhtin, Mikhail Mikhailovich
Bakhtin, Mikhail
 See Bakhtin, Mikhail Mikhailovich
Bakhtin, Mikhail Mikhailovich 1895-1975
 CLC 83
 See also CA 128; 113
Bakshi, Ralph 1938(?)- .... **CLC 26**
 See also CA 112; 138
Bakunin, Mikhail (Alexandrovich) 1814-1876
 NCLC 25, 58
Baldwin, James (Arthur) 1924-1987**CLC 1, 2, 3, 4, 5, 8, 13, 15, 17, 42, 50, 67, 90; BLC; DA; DAB; DAC; DAM MST, MULT, NOV, POP; DC 1; SSC 10; WLC**
 See also AAYA 4; BW 1; CA 1-4R; 124; CABS 1; CANR 3, 24; CDALB 1941-1968; DLB 2, 7, 33; DLBY 87; MTCW; SATA 9; SATA-Obit 54

Ballard, J(ames) G(raham) 1930-**CLC 3, 6, 14, 36; DAM NOV, POP; SSC 1**
 See also AAYA 3; CA 5-8R; CANR 15, 39; DLB 14; MTCW; SATA 93
Balmont, Konstantin (Dmitriyevich) 1867-1943
 TCLC 11
 See also CA 109; 155
Balzac, Honore de 1799-1850**NCLC 5, 35, 53; DA; DAB; DAC; DAM MST, NOV; SSC 5; WLC**
 See also DLB 119
Bambara, Toni Cade 1939-1995 **CLC 19, 88; BLC; DA; DAC; DAM MST, MULT; WLCS**
 See also AAYA 5; BW 2; CA 29-32R; 150; CANR 24, 49; DLB 38; MTCW
Bamdad, A.
 See Shamlu, Ahmad
Banat, D. R.
 See Bradbury, Ray (Douglas)
Bancroft, Laura
 See Baum, L(yman) Frank
Banim, John 1798-1842 .... **NCLC 13**
 See also DLB 116, 158, 159
Banim, Michael 1796-1874 .... **NCLC 13**
 See also DLB 158, 159
Banjo, The
 See Paterson, A(ndrew) B(arton)
Banks, Iain
 See Banks, Iain M(enzies)
Banks, Iain M(enzies) 1954- .... **CLC 34**
 See also CA 123; 128; CANR 61; INT 128
Banks, Lynne Reid .... **CLC 23**
 See also Reid Banks, Lynne
 See also AAYA 6
Banks, Russell 1940- .... **CLC 37, 72**
 See also CA 65-68; CAAS 15; CANR 19, 52; DLB 130
Banville, John 1945- .... **CLC 46**
 See also CA 117; 128; DLB 14; INT 128
Banville, Theodore (Faullain) de 1832-1891
 NCLC 9
Baraka, Amiri 1934-**CLC 1, 2, 3, 5, 10, 14, 33; BLC; DA; DAC; DAM MST, MULT, POET, POP; DC 6; PC 4; WLCS**
 See also BW 2; CA 21-24R; CABS 3; CANR 27, 38, 61; CDALB 1941-1968; DLB 5, 7, 16, 38; DLBD 8; MTCW
Barbauld, Anna Laetitia 1743-1825**NCLC 50**
 See also DLB 107, 109, 142, 158
Barbellion, W. N. P. .... **TCLC 24**
 See also Cummings, Bruce F(rederick)
Barbera, Jack (Vincent) 1945- .... **CLC 44**
 See also CA 110; CANR 45
Barbey d'Aurevilly, Jules Amedee 1808-1889
 NCLC 1; SSC 17
 See also DLB 119
Barbusse, Henri 1873-1935 .... **TCLC 5**
 See also CA 105; 154; DLB 65
Barclay, Bill
 See Moorcock, Michael (John)
Barclay, William Ewert
 See Moorcock, Michael (John)
Barea, Arturo 1897-1957 .... **TCLC 14**
 See also CA 111
Barfoot, Joan 1946- .... **CLC 18**
 See also CA 105
Baring, Maurice 1874-1945 .... **TCLC 8**
 See also CA 105; DLB 34
Barker, Clive 1952- .... **CLC 52; DAM POP**
 See also AAYA 10; BEST 90:3; CA 121; 129; INT 129; MTCW
Barker, George Granville 1913-1991 **CLC 8, 48; DAM POET**
 See also CA 9-12R; 135; CANR 7, 38; DLB 20; MTCW

Barker, Harley Granville
 See Granville-Barker, Harley
 See also DLB 10
Barker, Howard 1946- .... **CLC 37**
 See also CA 102; DLB 13
Barker, Pat(ricia) 1943- .... **CLC 32, 94**
 See also CA 117; 122; CANR 50; INT 122
Barlow, Joel 1754-1812 .... **NCLC 23**
 See also DLB 37
Barnard, Mary (Ethel) 1909- .... **CLC 48**
 See also CA 21-22; CAP 2
Barnes, Djuna 1892-1982**CLC 3, 4, 8, 11, 29; SSC 3**
 See also CA 9-12R; 107; CANR 16, 55; DLB 4, 9, 45; MTCW
Barnes, Julian (Patrick) 1946-**CLC 42; DAB**
 See also CA 102; CANR 19, 54; DLBY 93
Barnes, Peter 1931- .... **CLC 5, 56**
 See also CA 65-68; CAAS 12; CANR 33, 34; DLB 13; MTCW
Baroja (y Nessi), Pio 1872-1956**TCLC 8; HLC**
 See also CA 104
Baron, David
 See Pinter, Harold
Baron Corvo
 See Rolfe, Frederick (William Serafino Austin Lewis Mary)
Barondess, Sue K(aufman) 1926-1977 **CLC 8**
 See also CA 1-4R; 69-72; CANR 1
Baron de Teive
 See Pessoa, Fernando (Antonio Nogueira)
Barres, Maurice 1862-1923 .... **TCLC 47**
 See also DLB 123
Barreto, Afonso Henrique de Lima
 See Lima Barreto, Afonso Henrique de
Barrett, (Roger) Syd 1946- .... **CLC 35**
Barrett, William (Christopher) 1913-1992
 CLC 27
 See also CA 13-16R; 139; CANR 11; INT CANR-11
Barrie, J(ames) M(atthew) 1860-1937 **TCLC 2; DAB; DAM DRAM**
 See also CA 104; 136; CDBLB 1890-1914; CLR 16; DLB 10, 141, 156; MAICYA; YABC 1
Barrington, Michael
 See Moorcock, Michael (John)
Barrol, Grady
 See Bograd, Larry
Barry, Mike
 See Malzberg, Barry N(athaniel)
Barry, Philip 1896-1949 .... **TCLC 11**
 See also CA 109; DLB 7
Bart, Andre Schwarz
 See Schwarz-Bart, Andre
Barth, John (Simmons) 1930-**CLC 1, 2, 3, 5, 7, 9, 10, 14, 27, 51, 89; DAM NOV; SSC 10**
 See also AITN 1, 2; CA 1-4R; CABS 1; CANR 5, 23, 49; DLB 2; MTCW
Barthelme, Donald 1931-1989**CLC 1, 2, 3, 5, 6, 8, 13, 23, 46, 59; DAM NOV; SSC 2**
 See also CA 21-24R; 129; CANR 20, 58; DLB 2; DLBY 80, 89; MTCW; SATA 7; SATA-Obit 62
Barthelme, Frederick 1943- .... **CLC 36**
 See also CA 114; 122; DLBY 85; INT 122
Barthes, Roland (Gerard) 1915-1980**CLC 24, 83**
 See also CA 130; 97-100; MTCW
Barzun, Jacques (Martin) 1907- .... **CLC 51**
 See also CA 61-64; CANR 22
Bashevis, Isaac
 See Singer, Isaac Bashevis
Bashkirtseff, Marie 1859-1884 ...... **NCLC 27**
Basho
 See Matsuo Basho

See Bennett, Hal
See also BW 1; CA 97-100
Bennett, Hal .... **CLC 5**
See also Bennett, George Harold
See also DLB 33
Bennett, Jay 1912- .... **CLC 35**
See also AAYA 10; CA 69-72; CANR 11, 42;
JRDA; SAAS 4; SATA 41, 87; SATA-Brief
27
Bennett, Louise (Simone) 1919-**CLC 28; BLC;
DAM MULT**
See also BW 2; CA 151; DLB 117
Benson, E(dward) F(rederic) 1867-1940
TCLC 27
See also CA 114; 157; DLB 135, 153
Benson, Jackson J. 1930- .... **CLC 34**
See also CA 25-28R; DLB 111
Benson, Sally 1900-1972 .... **CLC 17**
See also CA 19-20; 37-40R; CAP 1; SATA 1,
35; SATA-Obit 27
Benson, Stella 1892-1933 .... **TCLC 17**
See also CA 117; 155; DLB 36, 162
Bentham, Jeremy 1748-1832 .... **NCLC 38**
See also DLB 107, 158
Bentley, E(dmund) C(lerihew) 1875-1956
TCLC 12
See also CA 108; DLB 70
Bentley, Eric (Russell) 1916- .... **CLC 24**
See also CA 5-8R; CANR 6; INT CANR-6
Beranger, Pierre Jean de 1780-1857**NCLC 34**
Berdyaev, Nicolas
See Berdyaev, Nikolai (Aleksandrovich)
Berdyaev, Nikolai (Aleksandrovich) 1874-1948
TCLC 67
See also CA 120; 157
Berdyayev, Nikolai (Aleksandrovich)
See Berdyaev, Nikolai (Aleksandrovich)
Berendt, John (Lawrence) 1939- ...... **CLC 86**
See also CA 146
Berger, Colonel
See Malraux, (Georges-)Andre
Berger, John (Peter) 1926- ....**CLC 2, 19**
See also CA 81-84; CANR 51; DLB 14
Berger, Melvin H. 1927- .... **CLC 12**
See also CA 5-8R; CANR 4; CLR 32; SAAS 2;
SATA 5, 88
Berger, Thomas (Louis) 1924-**CLC 3, 5, 8, 11,
18, 38; DAM NOV**
See also CA 1-4R; CANR 5, 28, 51; DLB 2;
DLBY 80; INT CANR-28; MTCW
Bergman, (Ernst) Ingmar 1918- **CLC 16, 72**
See also CA 81-84; CANR 33
Bergson, Henri 1859-1941 .... **TCLC 32**
Bergstein, Eleanor 1938- .... **CLC 4**
See also CA 53-56; CANR 5
Berkoff, Steven 1937- .... **CLC 56**
See also CA 104
Bermant, Chaim (Icyk) 1929- .... **CLC 40**
See also CA 57-60; CANR 6, 31, 57
Bern, Victoria
See Fisher, M(ary) F(rances) K(ennedy)
Bernanos, (Paul Louis) Georges 1888-1948
TCLC 3
See also CA 104; 130; DLB 72
Bernard, April 1956- .... **CLC 59**
See also CA 131
Berne, Victoria
See Fisher, M(ary) F(rances) K(ennedy)
Bernhard, Thomas 1931-1989 **CLC 3, 32, 61**
See also CA 85-88; 127; CANR 32, 57; DLB
85, 124; MTCW
Bernhardt, Sarah (Henriette Rosine) 1844-1923
TCLC 75
See also CA 157
Berriault, Gina 1926- .... **CLC 54**
See also CA 116; 129; DLB 130
Berrigan, Daniel 1921- .... **CLC 4**

See also CA 33-36R; CAAS 1; CANR 11, 43;
DLB 5
Berrigan, Edmund Joseph Michael, Jr. 1934-
1983
See Berrigan, Ted
See also CA 61-64; 110; CANR 14
Berrigan, Ted .... **CLC 37**
See also Berrigan, Edmund Joseph Michael, Jr.
See also DLB 5, 169
Berry, Charles Edward Anderson 1931-
See Berry, Chuck
See also CA 115
Berry, Chuck .... **CLC 17**
See also Berry, Charles Edward Anderson
Berry, Jonas
See Ashbery, John (Lawrence)
Berry, Wendell (Erdman) 1934- **CLC 4, 6, 8,
27, 46; DAM POET**
See also AITN 1; CA 73-76; CANR 50; DLB 5,
6
Berryman, John 1914-1972**CLC 1, 2, 3, 4, 6, 8,
10, 13, 25, 62; DAM POET**
See also CA 13-16; 33-36R; CABS 2; CANR
35; CAP 1; CDALB 1941-1968; DLB 48;
MTCW
Bertolucci, Bernardo 1940- .... **CLC 16**
See also CA 106
Berton, Pierre (Francis De Marigny) 1920-
CLC 104
See also CA 1-4R; CANR 2, 56; DLB 68
Bertrand, Aloysius 1807-1841 .... **NCLC 31**
Bertran de Born c. 1140-1215 .... **CMLC 5**
Besant, Annie (Wood) 1847-1933 .... **TCLC 9**
See also CA 105
Bessie, Alvah 1904-1985 .... **CLC 23**
See also CA 5-8R; 116; CANR 2; DLB 26
Bethlen, T. D.
See Silverberg, Robert
Beti, Mongo ...... **CLC 27; BLC; DAM MULT**
See also Biyidi, Alexandre
Betjeman, John 1906-1984 **CLC 2, 6, 10, 34,
43; DAB; DAM MST, POET**
See also CA 9-12R; 112; CANR 33, 56; CDBLB
1945-1960; DLB 20; DLBY 84; MTCW
Bettelheim, Bruno 1903-1990 .... **CLC 79**
See also CA 81-84; 131; CANR 23, 61; MTCW
Betti, Ugo 1892-1953 .... **TCLC 5**
See also CA 104; 155
Betts, Doris (Waugh) 1932- ...... **CLC 3, 6, 28**
See also CA 13-16R; CANR 9; DLBY 82; INT
CANR-9
Bevan, Alistair
See Roberts, Keith (John Kingston)
Bialik, Chaim Nachman 1873-1934**TCLC 25**
Bickerstaff, Isaac
See Swift, Jonathan
Bidart, Frank 1939- .... **CLC 33**
See also CA 140
Bienek, Horst 1930- .... **CLC 7, 11**
See also CA 73-76; DLB 75
Bierce, Ambrose (Gwinett) 1842-1914(?)
**TCLC 1, 7, 44; DA; DAC; DAM MST; SSC
9; WLC**
See also CA 104; 139; CDALB 1865-1917;
DLB 11, 12, 23, 71, 74
Biggers, Earl Derr 1884-1933 .... **TCLC 65**
See also CA 108; 153
Billings, Josh
See Shaw, Henry Wheeler
Billington, (Lady) Rachel (Mary) 1942- **C L C
43**
See also AITN 2; CA 33-36R; CANR 44
Binyon, T(imothy) J(ohn) 1936- .... **CLC 34**
See also CA 111; CANR 28
Bioy Casares, Adolfo 1914-**CLC 4, 8, 13, 88;
DAM MULT; HLC; SSC 17**
See also CA 29-32R; CANR 19, 43; DLB 113;

HW; MTCW
Bird, Cordwainer
See Ellison, Harlan (Jay)
Bird, Robert Montgomery 1806-1854**NCLC 1**
Birney, (Alfred) Earle 1904- **CLC 1, 4, 6, 11;
DAC; DAM MST, POET**
See also CA 1-4R; CANR 5, 20; DLB 88;
MTCW
Bishop, Elizabeth 1911-1979 **CLC 1, 4, 9, 13,
15, 32; DA; DAC; DAM MST, POET; PC
3**
See also CA 5-8R; 89-92; CABS 2; CANR 26,
61; CDALB 1968-1988; DLB 5, 169;
MTCW; SATA-Obit 24
Bishop, John 1935- .... **CLC 10**
See also CA 105
Bissett, Bill 1939- .... **CLC 18; PC 14**
See also CA 69-72; CAAS 19; CANR 15; DLB
53; MTCW
Bitov, Andrei (Georgievich) 1937- ... **CLC 57**
See also CA 142
Biyidi, Alexandre 1932-
See Beti, Mongo
See also BW 1; CA 114; 124; MTCW
Bjarme, Brynjolf
See Ibsen, Henrik (Johan)
Bjornson, Bjornstjerne (Martinius) 1832-1910
TCLC 7, 37
See also CA 104
Black, Robert
See Holdstock, Robert P.
Blackburn, Paul 1926-1971 .... **CLC 9, 43**
See also CA 81-84; 33-36R; CANR 34; DLB
16; DLBY 81
Black Elk 1863-1950 **TCLC 33; DAM MULT**
See also CA 144; NNAL
Black Hobart
See Sanders, (James) Ed(ward)
Blacklin, Malcolm
See Chambers, Aidan
Blackmore, R(ichard) D(oddridge) 1825-1900
TCLC 27
See also CA 120; DLB 18
Blackmur, R(ichard) P(almer) 1904-1965
CLC 2, 24
See also CA 11-12; 25-28R; CAP 1; DLB 63
Black Tarantula
See Acker, Kathy
Blackwood, Algernon (Henry) 1869-1951
TCLC 5
See also CA 105; 150; DLB 153, 156, 178
Blackwood, Caroline 1931-1996**CLC 6, 9, 100**
See also CA 85-88; 151; CANR 32, 61; DLB
14; MTCW
Blade, Alexander
See Hamilton, Edmond; Silverberg, Robert
Blaga, Lucian 1895-1961 .... **CLC 75**
Blair, Eric (Arthur) 1903-1950
See Orwell, George
See also CA 104; 132; DA; DAB; DAC; DAM
MST, NOV; MTCW; SATA 29
Blais, Marie-Claire 1939-**CLC 2, 4, 6, 13, 22;
DAC; DAM MST**
See also CA 21-24R; CAAS 4; CANR 38; DLB
53; MTCW
Blaise, Clark 1940- .... **CLC 29**
See also AITN 2; CA 53-56; CAAS 3; CANR
5; DLB 53
Blake, Fairley
See De Voto, Bernard (Augustine)
Blake, Nicholas
See Day Lewis, C(ecil)
See also DLB 77
Blake, William 1757-1827 . **NCLC 13, 37, 57;
DA; DAB; DAC; DAM MST, POET; PC
12; WLC**
See also CDBLB 1789-1832; DLB 93, 163;

MAICYA; SATA 30

Blake, William J(ames) 1894-1969 ...... **PC 12**
See also CA 5-8R; 25-28R

Blasco Ibanez, Vicente 1867-1928 **TCLC 12;
DAM NOV**
See also CA 110; 131; HW; MTCW

Blatty, William Peter 1928-**CLC 2; DAM POP**
See also CA 5-8R; CANR 9

Bleeck, Oliver
See Thomas, Ross (Elmore)

Blessing, Lee 1949- .... **CLC 54**

Blish, James (Benjamin) 1921-1975 . **CLC 14**
See also CA 1-4R; 57-60; CANR 3; DLB 8;
MTCW; SATA 66

Bliss, Reginald
See Wells, H(erbert) G(eorge)

Blixen, Karen (Christentze Dinesen) 1885-1962
See Dinesen, Isak
See also CA 25-28; CANR 22, 50; CAP 2;
MTCW; SATA 44

Bloch, Robert (Albert) 1917-1994 .... **CLC 33**
See also CA 5-8R; 146; CAAS 20; CANR 5;
DLB 44; INT CANR-5; SATA 12; SATA-Obit
82

Blok, Alexander (Alexandrovich) 1880-1921
TCLC 5
See also CA 104

Blom, Jan
See Breytenbach, Breyten

Bloom, Harold 1930- .... **CLC 24, 103**
See also CA 13-16R; CANR 39; DLB 67

Bloomfield, Aurelius
See Bourne, Randolph S(illiman)

Blount, Roy (Alton), Jr. 1941- .... **CLC 38**
See also CA 53-56; CANR 10, 28, 61; INT
CANR-28; MTCW

Bloy, Leon 1846-1917 .... **TCLC 22**
See also CA 121; DLB 123

Blume, Judy (Sussman) 1938- ... **CLC 12, 30;
DAM NOV, POP**
See also AAYA 3; CA 29-32R; CANR 13, 37;
CLR 2, 15; DLB 52; JRDA; MAICYA;
MTCW; SATA 2, 31, 79

Blunden, Edmund (Charles) 1896-1974 **C L C
2, 56**
See also CA 17-18; 45-48; CANR 54; CAP 2;
DLB 20, 100, 155; MTCW

Bly, Robert (Elwood) 1926-**CLC 1, 2, 5, 10, 15,
38; DAM POET**
See also CA 5-8R; CANR 41; DLB 5; MTCW

Boas, Franz 1858-1942 .... **TCLC 56**
See also CA 115

Bobette
See Simenon, Georges (Jacques Christian)

Boccaccio, Giovanni 1313-1375 ... **CMLC 13;
SSC 10**

Bochco, Steven 1943- .... **CLC 35**
See also AAYA 11; CA 124; 138

Bodenheim, Maxwell 1892-1954 .... **TCLC 44**
See also CA 110; DLB 9, 45

Bodker, Cecil 1927- .... **CLC 21**
See also CA 73-76; CANR 13, 44; CLR 23;
MAICYA; SATA 14

Boell, Heinrich (Theodor) 1917-1985 **CLC 2,
3, 6, 9, 11, 15, 27, 32, 72; DA; DAB; DAC;
DAM MST, NOV; SSC 23; WLC**
See also CA 21-24R; 116; CANR 24; DLB 69;
DLBY 85; MTCW

Boerne, Alfred
See Doeblin, Alfred

Boethius 480(?)-524(?) .... **CMLC 15**
See also DLB 115

Bogan, Louise 1897-1970 . **CLC 4, 39, 46, 93;
DAM POET; PC 12**
See also CA 73-76; 25-28R; CANR 33; DLB
45, 169; MTCW

Bogarde, Dirk .... **CLC 19**

See also Van Den Bogarde, Derek Jules Gaspard
Ulric Niven
See also DLB 14

Bogosian, Eric 1953- .... **CLC 45**
See also CA 138

Bograd, Larry 1953- .... **CLC 35**
See also CA 93-96; CANR 57; SAAS 21; SATA
33, 89

Boiardo, Matteo Maria 1441-1494 .... **LC 6**

Boileau-Despreaux, Nicolas 1636-1711 . **LC 3**

Bojer, Johan 1872-1959 .... **TCLC 64**

Boland, Eavan (Aisling) 1944- .. **CLC 40, 67;
DAM POET**
See also CA 143; CANR 61; DLB 40

Bolt, Lee
See Faust, Frederick (Schiller)

Bolt, Robert (Oxton) 1924-1995**CLC 14; DAM
DRAM**
See also CA 17-20R; 147; CANR 35; DLB 13;
MTCW

Bombet, Louis-Alexandre-Cesar
See Stendhal

Bomkauf
See Kaufman, Bob (Garnell)

Bonaventura .... **NCLC 35**
See also DLB 90

Bond, Edward 1934- **CLC 4, 6, 13, 23; DAM
DRAM**
See also CA 25-28R; CANR 38; DLB 13;
MTCW

Bonham, Frank 1914-1989 .... **CLC 12**
See also AAYA 1; CA 9-12R; CANR 4, 36;
JRDA; MAICYA; SAAS 3; SATA 1, 49;
SATA-Obit 62

Bonnefoy, Yves 1923- ... **CLC 9, 15, 58; DAM
MST, POET**
See also CA 85-88; CANR 33; MTCW

Bontemps, Arna(ud Wendell) 1902-1973**C L C
1, 18; BLC; DAM MULT, NOV, POET**
See also BW 1; CA 1-4R; 41-44R; CANR 4,
35; CLR 6; DLB 48, 51; JRDA; MAICYA;
MTCW; SATA 2, 44; SATA-Obit 24

Booth, Martin 1944- .... **CLC 13**
See also CA 93-96; CAAS 2

Booth, Philip 1925- .... **CLC 23**
See also CA 5-8R; CANR 5; DLBY 82

Booth, Wayne C(layson) 1921- .... **CLC 24**
See also CA 1-4R; CAAS 5; CANR 3, 43; DLB
67

Borchert, Wolfgang 1921-1947 .... **TCLC 5**
See also CA 104; DLB 69, 124

Borel, Petrus 1809-1859 .... **NCLC 41**

Borges, Jorge Luis 1899-1986**CLC 1, 2, 3, 4, 6,
8, 9, 10, 13, 19, 44, 48, 83; DA; DAB; DAC;
DAM MST, MULT; HLC; SSC 4; WLC**
See also AAYA 19; CA 21-24R; CANR 19, 33;
DLB 113; DLBY 86; HW; MTCW

Borowski, Tadeusz 1922-1951 .... **TCLC 9**
See also CA 106; 154

Borrow, George (Henry) 1803-1881 **NCLC 9**
See also DLB 21, 55, 166

Bosman, Herman Charles 1905-1951 **T C L C
49**
See also Malan, Herman
See also CA 160

Bosschere, Jean de 1878(?)-1953 ... **TCLC 19**
See also CA 115

Boswell, James 1740-1795 . **LC 4; DA; DAB;
DAC; DAM MST; WLC**
See also CDBLB 1660-1789; DLB 104, 142

Bottoms, David 1949- .... **CLC 53**
See also CA 105; CANR 22; DLB 120; DLBY
83

Boucicault, Dion 1820-1890 .... **NCLC 41**

Boucolon, Maryse 1937(?)-
See Conde, Maryse
See also CA 110; CANR 30, 53

Bourget, Paul (Charles Joseph) 1852-1935
TCLC 12
See also CA 107; DLB 123

Bourjaily, Vance (Nye) 1922- .... **CLC 8, 62**
See also CA 1-4R; CAAS 1; CANR 2; DLB 2,
143

Bourne, Randolph S(illiman) 1886-1918
TCLC 16
See also CA 117; 155; DLB 63

Bova, Ben(jamin William) 1932- ...... **CLC 45**
See also AAYA 16; CA 5-8R; CAAS 18; CANR
11, 56; CLR 3; DLBY 81; INT CANR-11;
MAICYA; MTCW; SATA 6, 68

Bowen, Elizabeth (Dorothea Cole) 1899-1973
**CLC 1, 3, 6, 11, 15, 22; DAM NOV; SSC 3,
28**
See also CA 17-18; 41-44R; CANR 35; CAP 2;
CDBLB 1945-1960; DLB 15, 162; MTCW

Bowering, George 1935- .... **CLC 15, 47**
See also CA 21-24R; CAAS 16; CANR 10; DLB
53

Bowering, Marilyn R(uthe) 1949- .... **CLC 32**
See also CA 101; CANR 49

Bowers, Edgar 1924- .... **CLC 9**
See also CA 5-8R; CANR 24; DLB 5

Bowie, David .... **CLC 17**
See also Jones, David Robert

Bowles, Jane (Sydney) 1917-1973 **CLC 3, 68**
See also CA 19-20; 41-44R; CAP 2

Bowles, Paul (Frederick) 1910- **CLC 1, 2, 19,
53; SSC 3**
See also CA 1-4R; CAAS 1; CANR 1, 19, 50;
DLB 5, 6; MTCW

Box, Edgar
See Vidal, Gore

Boyd, Nancy
See Millay, Edna St. Vincent

Boyd, William 1952- .... **CLC 28, 53, 70**
See also CA 114; 120; CANR 51

Boyle, Kay 1902-1992**CLC 1, 5, 19, 58; SSC 5**
See also CA 13-16R; 140; CAAS 1; CANR 29,
61; DLB 4, 9, 48, 86; DLBY 93; MTCW

Boyle, Mark
See Kienzle, William X(avier)

Boyle, Patrick 1905-1982 .... **CLC 19**
See also CA 127

Boyle, T. C. 1948-
See Boyle, T(homas) Coraghessan

Boyle, T(homas) Coraghessan 1948-**CLC 36,
55, 90; DAM POP; SSC 16**
See also BEST 90:4; CA 120; CANR 44; DLBY
86

Boz
See Dickens, Charles (John Huffam)

Brackenridge, Hugh Henry 1748-1816**N C L C
7**
See also DLB 11, 37

Bradbury, Edward P.
See Moorcock, Michael (John)

Bradbury, Malcolm (Stanley) 1932- **CLC 32,
61; DAM NOV**
See also CA 1-4R; CANR 1, 33; DLB 14;
MTCW

Bradbury, Ray (Douglas) 1920-**CLC 1, 3, 10,
15, 42, 98; DA; DAB; DAC; DAM MST,
NOV, POP; SSC 29; WLC**
See also AAYA 15; AITN 1, 2; CA 1-4R; CANR
2, 30; CDALB 1968-1988; DLB 2, 8;
MTCW; SATA 11, 64

Bradford, Gamaliel 1863-1932 ...... **TCLC 36**
See also CA 160; DLB 17

Bradley, David (Henry, Jr.) 1950- .. **CLC 23;
BLC; DAM MULT**
See also BW 1; CA 104; CANR 26; DLB 33

Bradley, John Ed(mund, Jr.) 1958- .. **CLC 55**
See also CA 139

Bradley, Marion Zimmer 1930-**CLC 30; DAM**

See also CA 113; 153; DLB 70

Childress, Alice 1920-1994 **CLC 12, 15, 86, 96; BLC; DAM DRAM, MULT, NOV; DC 4**
See also AAYA 8; BW 2; CA 45-48; 146; CANR 3, 27, 50; CLR 14; DLB 7, 38; JRDA; MAICYA; MTCW; SATA 7, 48, 81

Chin, Frank (Chew, Jr.) 1940- .... **DC 7**
See also CA 33-36R; DAM MULT

Chislett, (Margaret) Anne 1943- ...... **CLC 34**
See also CA 151

Chitty, Thomas Willes 1926- .... **CLC 11**
See also Hinde, Thomas
See also CA 5-8R

Chivers, Thomas Holley 1809-1858 **NCLC 49**
See also DLB 3

Chomette, Rene Lucien 1898-1981
See Clair, Rene
See also CA 103

Chopin, Kate **TCLC 5, 14; DA; DAB; SSC 8; WLCS**
See also Chopin, Katherine
See also CDALB 1865-1917; DLB 12, 78

Chopin, Katherine 1851-1904
See Chopin, Kate
See also CA 104; 122; DAC; DAM MST, NOV

Chretien de Troyes c. 12th cent. -.. **CMLC 10**

Christie
See Ichikawa, Kon

Christie, Agatha (Mary Clarissa) 1890-1976 **CLC 1, 6, 8, 12, 39, 48; DAB; DAC; DAM NOV**
See also AAYA 9; AITN 1, 2; CA 17-20R; 61-64; CANR 10, 37; CDBLB 1914-1945; DLB 13, 77; MTCW; SATA 36

Christie, (Ann) Philippa
See Pearce, Philippa
See also CA 5-8R; CANR 4

Christine de Pizan 1365(?)-1431(?) .... **LC 9**

Chubb, Elmer
See Masters, Edgar Lee

Chulkov, Mikhail Dmitrievich 1743-1792 **LC 2**
See also DLB 150

Churchill, Caryl 1938- ..... **CLC 31, 55; DC 5**
See also CA 102; CANR 22, 46; DLB 13; MTCW

Churchill, Charles 1731-1764 .... **LC 3**
See also DLB 109

Chute, Carolyn 1947- .... **CLC 39**
See also CA 123

Ciardi, John (Anthony) 1916-1986 . **CLC 10, 40, 44; DAM POET**
See also CA 5-8R; 118; CAAS 2; CANR 5, 33; CLR 19; DLB 5; DLBY 86; INT CANR-5; MAICYA; MTCW; SATA 1, 65; SATA-Obit 46

Cicero, Marcus Tullius 106B.C.-43B.C. **CMLC 3**

Cimino, Michael 1943- .... **CLC 16**
See also CA 105

Cioran, E(mil) M. 1911-1995 .... **CLC 64**
See also CA 25-28R; 149

Cisneros, Sandra 1954- **CLC 69; DAM MULT; HLC**
See also AAYA 9; CA 131; DLB 122, 152; HW

Cixous, Helene 1937- .... **CLC 92**
See also CA 126; CANR 55; DLB 83; MTCW

Clair, Rene .... **CLC 20**
See also Chomette, Rene Lucien

Clampitt, Amy 1920-1994 ..... **CLC 32; PC 19**
See also CA 110; 146; CANR 29; DLB 105

Clancy, Thomas L., Jr. 1947-
See Clancy, Tom
See also CA 125; 131; CANR 62; INT 131; MTCW

Clancy, Tom .... **CLC 45; DAM NOV, POP**
See also Clancy, Thomas L., Jr.
See also AAYA 9; BEST 89:1, 90:1

Clare, John 1793-1864 **NCLC 9; DAB; DAM POET**
See also DLB 55, 96

Clarin
See Alas (y Urena), Leopoldo (Enrique Garcia)

Clark, Al C.
See Goines, Donald

Clark, (Robert) Brian 1932- .... **CLC 29**
See also CA 41-44R

Clark, Curt
See Westlake, Donald E(dwin)

Clark, Eleanor 1913-1996 .... **CLC 5, 19**
See also CA 9-12R; 151; CANR 41; DLB 6

Clark, J. P.
See Clark, John Pepper
See also DLB 117

Clark, John Pepper 1935- ...... **CLC 38; BLC; DAM DRAM, MULT; DC 5**
See also Clark, J. P.
See also BW 1; CA 65-68; CANR 16

Clark, M. R.
See Clark, Mavis Thorpe

Clark, Mavis Thorpe 1909- .... **CLC 12**
See also CA 57-60; CANR 8, 37; CLR 30; MAICYA; SAAS 5; SATA 8, 74

Clark, Walter Van Tilburg 1909-1971 **CLC 28**
See also CA 9-12R; 33-36R; DLB 9; SATA 8

Clarke, Arthur C(harles) 1917- **CLC 1, 4, 13, 18, 35; DAM POP; SSC 3**
See also AAYA 4; CA 1-4R; CANR 2, 28, 55; JRDA; MAICYA; MTCW; SATA 13, 70

Clarke, Austin 1896-1974 .... **CLC 6, 9; DAM POET**
See also CA 29-32; 49-52; CAP 2; DLB 10, 20

Clarke, Austin C(hesterfield) 1934- **CLC 8, 53; BLC; DAC; DAM MULT**
See also BW 1; CA 25-28R; CAAS 16; CANR 14, 32; DLB 53, 125

Clarke, Gillian 1937- .... **CLC 61**
See also CA 106; DLB 40

Clarke, Marcus (Andrew Hislop) 1846-1881 **NCLC 19**

Clarke, Shirley 1925- .... **CLC 16**

Clash, The
See Headon, (Nicky) Topper; Jones, Mick; Simonon, Paul; Strummer, Joe

Claudel, Paul (Louis Charles Marie) 1868-1955 **TCLC 2, 10**
See also CA 104

Clavell, James (duMaresq) 1925-1994 **CLC 6, 25, 87; DAM NOV, POP**
See also CA 25-28R; 146; CANR 26, 48; MTCW

Cleaver, (Leroy) Eldridge 1935- ..... **CLC 30; BLC; DAM MULT**
See also BW 1; CA 21-24R; CANR 16

Cleese, John (Marwood) 1939- .... **CLC 21**
See also Monty Python
See also CA 112; 116; CANR 35; MTCW

Cleishbotham, Jebediah
See Scott, Walter

Cleland, John 1710-1789 .... **LC 2**
See also DLB 39

Clemens, Samuel Langhorne 1835-1910
See Twain, Mark
See also CA 104; 135; CDALB 1865-1917; DA; DAB; DAC; DAM MST, NOV; DLB 11, 12, 23, 64, 74; JRDA; MAICYA; YABC 2

Cleophil
See Congreve, William

Clerihew, E.
See Bentley, E(dmund) C(lerihew)

Clerk, N. W.
See Lewis, C(live) S(taples)

Cliff, Jimmy .... **CLC 21**
See also Chambers, James

Clifton, (Thelma) Lucille 1936- **CLC 19, 66;**

BLC; DAM MULT, POET; PC 17
See also BW 2; CA 49-52; CANR 2, 24, 42; CLR 5; DLB 5, 41; MAICYA; MTCW; SATA 20, 69

Clinton, Dirk
See Silverberg, Robert

Clough, Arthur Hugh 1819-1861 ... **NCLC 27**
See also DLB 32

Clutha, Janet Paterson Frame 1924-
See Frame, Janet
See also CA 1-4R; CANR 2, 36; MTCW

Clyne, Terence
See Blatty, William Peter

Cobalt, Martin
See Mayne, William (James Carter)

Cobbett, William 1763-1835 .... **NCLC 49**
See also DLB 43, 107, 158

Coburn, D(onald) L(ee) 1938- .... **CLC 10**
See also CA 89-92

Cocteau, Jean (Maurice Eugene Clement) 1889-1963 **CLC 1, 8, 15, 16, 43; DA; DAB; DAC; DAM DRAM, MST, NOV; WLC**
See also CA 25-28; CANR 40; CAP 2; DLB 65; MTCW

Codrescu, Andrei 1946- **CLC 46; DAM POET**
See also CA 33-36R; CAAS 19; CANR 13, 34, 53

Coe, Max
See Bourne, Randolph S(illiman)

Coe, Tucker
See Westlake, Donald E(dwin)

Coetzee, J(ohn) M(ichael) 1940- **CLC 23, 33, 66; DAM NOV**
See also CA 77-80; CANR 41, 54; MTCW

Coffey, Brian
See Koontz, Dean R(ay)

Cohan, George M(ichael) 1878-1942 **TCLC 60**
See also CA 157

Cohen, Arthur A(llen) 1928-1986 . **CLC 7, 31**
See also CA 1-4R; 120; CANR 1, 17, 42; DLB 28

Cohen, Leonard (Norman) 1934- **CLC 3, 38; DAC; DAM MST**
See also CA 21-24R; CANR 14; DLB 53; MTCW

Cohen, Matt 1942- .... **CLC 19; DAC**
See also CA 61-64; CAAS 18; CANR 40; DLB 53

Cohen-Solal, Annie 19(?)- .... **CLC 50**

Colegate, Isabel 1931- .... **CLC 36**
See also CA 17-20R; CANR 8, 22; DLB 14; INT CANR-22; MTCW

Coleman, Emmett
See Reed, Ishmael

Coleridge, M. E.
See Coleridge, Mary E(lizabeth)

Coleridge, Mary E(lizabeth) 1861-1907 **TCLC 73**
See also CA 116; DLB 19, 98

Coleridge, Samuel Taylor 1772-1834 **NCLC 9, 54; DA; DAB; DAC; DAM MST, POET; PC 11; WLC**
See also CDBLB 1789-1832; DLB 93, 107

Coleridge, Sara 1802-1852 .... **NCLC 31**

Coles, Don 1928- .... **CLC 46**
See also CA 115; CANR 38

Colette, (Sidonie-Gabrielle) 1873-1954 **T C L C 1, 5, 16; DAM NOV; SSC 10**
See also CA 104; 131; DLB 65; MTCW

Collett, (Jacobine) Camilla (Wergeland) 1813-1895 .... **NCLC 22**

Collier, Christopher 1930- .... **CLC 30**
See also AAYA 13; CA 33-36R; CANR 13, 33; JRDA; MAICYA; SATA 16, 70

Collier, James L(incoln) 1928- **CLC 30; DAM POP**
See also AAYA 13; CA 9-12R; CANR 4, 33,

Author Index

See also CA 49-52; CANR 2, 53

Epstein, Jacob 1956- .... **CLC 19**
See also CA 114

Epstein, Joseph 1937- .... **CLC 39**
See also CA 112; 119; CANR 50

Epstein, Leslie 1938- .... **CLC 27**
See also CA 73-76; CAAS 12; CANR 23

Equiano, Olaudah 1745(?)-1797**LC 16; BLC; DAM MULT**
See also DLB 37, 50

ER .... **TCLC 33**
See also CA 160; DLB 85

Erasmus, Desiderius 1469(?)-1536 ...... **LC 16**

Erdman, Paul E(mil) 1932- .... **CLC 25**
See also AITN 1; CA 61-64; CANR 13, 43

Erdrich, Louise 1954- ..... **CLC 39, 54; DAM MULT, NOV, POP**
See also AAYA 10; BEST 89:1; CA 114; CANR 41, 62; DLB 152, 175; MTCW; NNAL; SATA 94

Erenburg, Ilya (Grigoryevich)
See Ehrenburg, Ilya (Grigoryevich)

Erickson, Stephen Michael 1950-
See Erickson, Steve
See also CA 129

Erickson, Steve 1950- .... **CLC 64**
See also Erickson, Stephen Michael
See also CANR 60

Ericson, Walter
See Fast, Howard (Melvin)

Eriksson, Buntel
See Bergman, (Ernst) Ingmar

Ernaux, Annie 1940- .... **CLC 88**
See also CA 147

Eschenbach, Wolfram von
See Wolfram von Eschenbach

Eseki, Bruno
See Mphahlcle, Ezekiel

Esenin, Sergei (Alexandrovich) 1895-1925 **TCLC 4**
See also CA 104

Eshleman, Clayton 1935- .... **CLC 7**
See also CA 33-36R; CAAS 6; DLB 5

Espriella, Don Manuel Alvarez
See Southey, Robert

Espriu, Salvador 1913-1985 .... **CLC 9**
See also CA 154; 115; DLB 134

Espronceda, Jose de 1808-1842 ..... **NCLC 39**

Esse, James
See Stephens, James

Esterbrook, Tom
See Hubbard, L(afayette) Ron(ald)

Estleman, Loren D. 1952-**CLC 48; DAM NOV, POP**
See also CA 85-88; CANR 27; INT CANR-27; MTCW

Eugenides, Jeffrey 1960(?)- .... **CLC 81**
See also CA 144

Euripides c. 485B.C.-406B.C.**CMLC 23; DA; DAB; DAC; DAM DRAM, MST; DC 4; WLCS**
See also DLB 176

Evan, Evin
See Faust, Frederick (Schiller)

Evans, Evan
See Faust, Frederick (Schiller)

Evans, Marian
See Eliot, George

Evans, Mary Ann
See Eliot, George

Evarts, Esther
See Benson, Sally

Everett, Percival L. 1956- .... **CLC 57**
See also BW 2; CA 129

Everson, R(onald) G(ilmour) 1903- . **CLC 27**
See also CA 17-20R; DLB 88

Everson, William (Oliver) 1912-1994 **CLC 1,**
5, 14
See also CA 9-12R; 145; CANR 20; DLB 5, 16; MTCW

Evtushenko, Evgenii Aleksandrovich
See Yevtushenko, Yevgeny (Alexandrovich)

Ewart, Gavin (Buchanan) 1916-1995**CLC 13, 46**
See also CA 89-92; 150; CANR 17, 46; DLB 40; MTCW

Ewers, Hanns Heinz 1871-1943 ..... **TCLC 12**
See also CA 109; 149

Ewing, Frederick R.
See Sturgeon, Theodore (Hamilton)

Exley, Frederick (Earl) 1929-1992 **CLC 6, 11**
See also AITN 2; CA 81-84; 138; DLB 143; DLBY 81

Eynhardt, Guillermo
See Quiroga, Horacio (Sylvestre)

Ezekiel, Nissim 1924- .... **CLC 61**
See also CA 61-64

Ezekiel, Tish O'Dowd 1943- .... **CLC 34**
See also CA 129

Fadeyev, A.
See Bulgya, Alexander Alexandrovich

Fadeyev, Alexander .... **TCLC 53**
See also Bulgya, Alexander Alexandrovich

Fagen, Donald 1948- .... **CLC 26**

Fainzilberg, Ilya Arnoldovich 1897-1937
See Ilf, Ilya
See also CA 120

Fair, Ronald L. 1932- .... **CLC 18**
See also BW 1; CA 69-72; CANR 25; DLB 33

Fairbairn, Roger
See Carr, John Dickson

Fairbairns, Zoe (Ann) 1948- .... **CLC 32**
See also CA 103; CANR 21

Falco, Gian
See Papini, Giovanni

Falconer, James
See Kirkup, James

Falconer, Kenneth
See Kornbluth, C(yril) M.

Falkland, Samuel
See Heijermans, Herman

Fallaci, Oriana 1930- .... **CLC 11**
See also CA 77-80; CANR 15, 58; MTCW

Faludy, George 1913- .... **CLC 42**
See also CA 21-24R

Faludy, Gyoergy
See Faludy, George

Fanon, Frantz 1925-1961**CLC 74; BLC; DAM MULT**
See also BW 1; CA 116; 89-92

Fanshawe, Ann 1625-1680 .... **LC 11**

Fante, John (Thomas) 1911-1983 ..... **CLC 60**
See also CA 69-72; 109; CANR 23; DLB 130; DLBY 83

Farah, Nuruddin 1945- **CLC 53; BLC; DAM MULT**
See also BW 2; CA 106; DLB 125

Fargue, Leon-Paul 1876(?)-1947 ... **TCLC 11**
See also CA 109

Farigoule, Louis
See Romains, Jules

Farina, Richard 1936(?)-1966 .... **CLC 9**
See also CA 81-84; 25-28R

Farley, Walter (Lorimer) 1915-1989 **CLC 17**
See also CA 17-20R; CANR 8, 29; DLB 22; JRDA; MAICYA; SATA 2, 43

Farmer, Philip Jose 1918- ....**CLC 1, 19**
See also CA 1-4R; CANR 4, 35; DLB 8; MTCW; SATA 93

Farquhar, George 1677-1707 ...**LC 21; DAM DRAM**
See also DLB 84

Farrell, J(ames) G(ordon) 1935-1979 **CLC 6**
See also CA 73-76; 89-92; CANR 36; DLB 14;
MTCW

Farrell, James T(homas) 1904-1979**CLC 1, 4, 8, 11, 66; SSC 28**
See also CA 5-8R; 89-92; CANR 9, 61; DLB 4, 9, 86; DLBD 2; MTCW

Farren, Richard J.
See Betjeman, John

Farren, Richard M.
See Betjeman, John

Fassbinder, Rainer Werner 1946-1982**CLC 20**
See also CA 93-96; 106; CANR 31

Fast, Howard (Melvin) 1914- **CLC 23; DAM NOV**
See also AAYA 16; CA 1-4R; CAAS 18; CANR 1, 33, 54; DLB 9; INT CANR-33; SATA 7

Faulcon, Robert
See Holdstock, Robert P.

Faulkner, William (Cuthbert) 1897-1962**CLC 1, 3, 6, 8, 9, 11, 14, 18, 28, 52, 68; DA; DAB; DAC; DAM MST, NOV; SSC 1; WLC**
See also AAYA 7; CA 81-84; CANR 33; CDALB 1929-1941; DLB 9, 11, 44, 102; DLBD 2; DLBY 86; MTCW

Fauset, Jessie Redmon 1884(?)-1961**CLC 19, 54; BLC; DAM MULT**
See also BW 1; CA 109; DLB 51

Faust, Frederick (Schiller) 1892-1944(?)
TCLC 49; DAM POP
See also CA 108; 152

Faust, Irvin 1924- .... **CLC 8**
See also CA 33-36R; CANR 28; DLB 2, 28; DLBY 80

Fawkes, Guy
See Benchley, Robert (Charles)

Fearing, Kenneth (Flexner) 1902-1961 . **C L C 51**
See also CA 93-96; CANR 59; DLB 9

Fecamps, Elise
See Creasey, John

Federman, Raymond 1928- .... **CLC 6, 47**
See also CA 17-20R; CAAS 8; CANR 10, 43; DLBY 80

Federspiel, J(uerg) F. 1931- .... **CLC 42**
See also CA 146

Feiffer, Jules (Ralph) 1929- ..... **CLC 2, 8, 64; DAM DRAM**
See also AAYA 3; CA 17-20R; CANR 30, 59; DLB 7, 44; INT CANR-30; MTCW; SATA 8, 61

Feige, Hermann Albert Otto Maximilian
See Traven, B.

Feinberg, David B. 1956-1994 .... **CLC 59**
See also CA 135; 147

Feinstein, Elaine 1930- .... **CLC 36**
See also CA 69-72; CAAS 1; CANR 31; DLB 14, 40; MTCW

Feldman, Irving (Mordecai) 1928- ..... **CLC 7**
See also CA 1-4R; CANR 1; DLB 169

Felix-Tchicaya, Gerald
See Tchicaya, Gerald Felix

Fellini, Federico 1920-1993 .... **CLC 16, 85**
See also CA 65-68; 143; CANR 33

Felsen, Henry Gregor 1916- .... **CLC 17**
See also CA 1-4R; CANR 1; SAAS 2; SATA 1

Fenton, James Martin 1949- .... **CLC 32**
See also CA 102; DLB 40

Ferber, Edna 1887-1968 .... **CLC 18, 93**
See also AITN 1; CA 5-8R; 25-28R; DLB 9, 28, 86; MTCW; SATA 7

Ferguson, Helen
See Kavan, Anna

Ferguson, Samuel 1810-1886 .... **NCLC 33**
See also DLB 32

Fergusson, Robert 1750-1774 .... **LC 29**
See also DLB 109

Ferling, Lawrence
See Ferlinghetti, Lawrence (Monsanto)

See also Barker, Harley Granville
See also CA 104

Grass, Guenter (Wilhelm) 1927-**CLC 1, 2, 4, 6, 11, 15, 22, 32, 49, 88; DA; DAB; DAC; DAM MST, NOV; WLC**
See also CA 13-16R; CANR 20; DLB 75, 124; MTCW

Gratton, Thomas
See Hulme, T(homas) E(rnest)

Grau, Shirley Ann 1929-.. **CLC 4, 9; SSC 15**
See also CA 89-92; CANR 22; DLB 2; INT CANR-22; MTCW

Gravel, Fern
See Hall, James Norman

Graver, Elizabeth 1964- .... **CLC 70**
See also CA 135

Graves, Richard Perceval 1945- .... **CLC 44**
See also CA 65-68; CANR 9, 26, 51

Graves, Robert (von Ranke) 1895-1985 **C L C 1, 2, 6, 11, 39, 44, 45; DAB; DAC; DAM MST, POET; PC 6**
See also CA 5-8R; 117; CANR 5, 36; CDBLB 1914-1945; DLB 20, 100; DLBY 85; MTCW; SATA 45

Graves, Valerie
See Bradley, Marion Zimmer

Gray, Alasdair (James) 1934- .... **CLC 41**
See also CA 126; CANR 47; INT 126; MTCW

Gray, Amlin 1946- .... **CLC 29**
See also CA 138

Gray, Francine du Plessix 1930- ..... **CLC 22; DAM NOV**
See also BEST 90:3; CA 61-64; CAAS 2; CANR 11, 33; INT CANR-11; MTCW

Gray, John (Henry) 1866-1934 ...... **TCLC 19**
See also CA 119

Gray, Simon (James Holliday) 1936- **CLC 9, 14, 36**
See also AITN 1; CA 21-24R; CAAS 3; CANR 32; DLB 13; MTCW

Gray, Spalding 1941-**CLC 49; DAM POP; DC 7**
See also CA 128

Gray, Thomas 1716-1771**LC 4, 40; DA; DAB; DAC; DAM MST; PC 2; WLC**
See also CDBLB 1660-1789; DLB 109

Grayson, David
See Baker, Ray Stannard

Grayson, Richard (A.) 1951- .... **CLC 38**
See also CA 85-88; CANR 14, 31, 57

Greeley, Andrew M(oran) 1928- ..... **CLC 28; DAM POP**
See also CA 5-8R; CAAS 7; CANR 7, 43; MTCW

Green, Anna Katharine 1846-1935 **TCLC 63**
See also CA 112; 159

Green, Brian
See Card, Orson Scott

Green, Hannah
See Greenberg, Joanne (Goldenberg)

Green, Hannah 1927(?)-1996 .... **CLC 3**
See also CA 73-76; CANR 59

Green, Henry 1905-1973 .... **CLC 2, 13, 97**
See also Yorke, Henry Vincent
See also DLB 15

Green, Julian (Hartridge) 1900-
See Green, Julien
See also CA 21-24R; CANR 33; DLB 4, 72; MTCW

Green, Julien .... **CLC 3, 11, 77**
See also Green, Julian (Hartridge)

Green, Paul (Eliot) 1894-1981**CLC 25; DAM DRAM**
See also AITN 1; CA 5-8R; 103; CANR 3; DLB 7, 9; DLBY 81

Greenberg, Ivan 1908-1973
See Rahv, Philip

See also CA 85-88

Greenberg, Joanne (Goldenberg) 1932- **C L C 7, 30**
See also AAYA 12; CA 5-8R; CANR 14, 32; SATA 25

Greenberg, Richard 1959(?)- .... **CLC 57**
See also CA 138

Greene, Bette 1934- .... **CLC 30**
See also AAYA 7; CA 53-56; CANR 4; CLR 2; JRDA; MAICYA; SAAS 16; SATA 8

Greene, Gael .... **CLC 8**
See also CA 13-16R; CANR 10

Greene, Graham (Henry) 1904-1991**CLC 1, 3, 6, 9, 14, 18, 27, 37, 70, 72; DA; DAB; DAC; DAM MST, NOV; SSC 29; WLC**
See also AITN 2; CA 13-16R; 133; CANR 35, 61; CDBLB 1945-1960; DLB 13, 15, 77, 100, 162; DLBY 91; MTCW; SATA 20

Greer, Richard
See Silverberg, Robert

Gregor, Arthur 1923- .... **CLC 9**
See also CA 25-28R; CAAS 10; CANR 11; SATA 36

Gregor, Lee
See Pohl, Frederik

Gregory, Isabella Augusta (Persse) 1852-1932 **TCLC 1**
See also CA 104; DLB 10

Gregory, J. Dennis
See Williams, John A(lfred)

Grendon, Stephen
See Derleth, August (William)

Grenville, Kate 1950- .... **CLC 61**
See also CA 118; CANR 53

Grenville, Pelham
See Wodehouse, P(elham) G(renville)

Greve, Felix Paul (Berthold Friedrich) 1879-1948
See Grove, Frederick Philip
See also CA 104; 141; DAC; DAM MST

Grey, Zane 1872-1939 .. **TCLC 6; DAM POP**
See also CA 104; 132; DLB 9; MTCW

Grieg, (Johan) Nordahl (Brun) 1902-1943 **TCLC 10**
See also CA 107

Grieve, C(hristopher) M(urray) 1892-1978 **CLC 11, 19; DAM POET**
See also MacDiarmid, Hugh; Pteleon
See also CA 5-8R; 85-88; CANR 33; MTCW

Griffin, Gerald 1803-1840 .... **NCLC 7**
See also DLB 159

Griffin, John Howard 1920-1980 ..... **CLC 68**
See also AITN 1; CA 1-4R; 101; CANR 2

Griffin, Peter 1942- .... **CLC 39**
See also CA 136

Griffith, D(avid Lewelyn) W(ark) 1875(?)-1948 **TCLC 68**
See also CA 119; 150

Griffith, Lawrence
See Griffith, D(avid Lewelyn) W(ark)

Griffiths, Trevor 1935- .... **CLC 13, 52**
See also CA 97-100; CANR 45; DLB 13

Grigson, Geoffrey (Edward Harvey) 1905-1985 **CLC 7, 39**
See also CA 25-28R; 118; CANR 20, 33; DLB 27; MTCW

Grillparzer, Franz 1791-1872 .... **NCLC 1**
See also DLB 133

Grimble, Reverend Charles James
See Eliot, T(homas) S(tearns)

Grimke, Charlotte L(ottie) Forten 1837(?)-1914
See Forten, Charlotte L.
See also BW 1; CA 117; 124; DAM MULT, POET

Grimm, Jacob Ludwig Karl 1785-1863**NCLC 3**
See also DLB 90; MAICYA; SATA 22

Grimm, Wilhelm Karl 1786-1859 .... **NCLC 3**
See also DLB 90; MAICYA; SATA 22

Grimmelshausen, Johann Jakob Christoffel von 1621-1676 .... **LC 6**
See also DLB 168

Grindel, Eugene 1895-1952
See Eluard, Paul
See also CA 104

Grisham, John 1955- .... **CLC 84; DAM POP**
See also AAYA 14; CA 138; CANR 47

Grossman, David 1954- .... **CLC 67**
See also CA 138

Grossman, Vasily (Semenovich) 1905-1964 **CLC 41**
See also CA 124; 130; MTCW

Grove, Frederick Philip .... **TCLC 4**
See also Greve, Felix Paul (Berthold Friedrich)
See also DLB 92

Grubb
See Crumb, R(obert)

Grumbach, Doris (Isaac) 1918-**CLC 13, 22, 64**
See also CA 5-8R; CAAS 2; CANR 9, 42; INT CANR-9

Grundtvig, Nicolai Frederik Severin 1783-1872 **NCLC 1**

Grunge
See Crumb, R(obert)

Grunwald, Lisa 1959- .... **CLC 44**
See also CA 120

Guare, John 1938- . **CLC 8, 14, 29, 67; DAM DRAM**
See also CA 73-76; CANR 21; DLB 7; MTCW

Gudjonsson, Halldor Kiljan 1902-
See Laxness, Halldor
See also CA 103

Guenter, Erich
See Eich, Guenter

Guest, Barbara 1920- .... **CLC 34**
See also CA 25-28R; CANR 11, 44; DLB 5

Guest, Judith (Ann) 1936- **CLC 8, 30; DAM NOV, POP**
See also AAYA 7; CA 77-80; CANR 15; INT CANR-15; MTCW

Guevara, Che .... **CLC 87; HLC**
See also Guevara (Serna), Ernesto

Guevara (Serna), Ernesto 1928-1967
See Guevara, Che
See also CA 127; 111; CANR 56; DAM MULT; HW

Guild, Nicholas M. 1944- .... **CLC 33**
See also CA 93-96

Guillemin, Jacques
See Sartre, Jean-Paul

Guillen, Jorge 1893-1984 .... **CLC 11; DAM MULT, POET**
See also CA 89-92; 112; DLB 108; HW

Guillen, Nicolas (Cristobal) 1902-1989 **C L C 48, 79; BLC; DAM MST, MULT, POET; HLC**
See also BW 2; CA 116; 125; 129; HW

Guillevic, (Eugene) 1907- .... **CLC 33**
See also CA 93-96

Guillois
See Desnos, Robert

Guillois, Valentin
See Desnos, Robert

Guiney, Louise Imogen 1861-1920 **TCLC 41**
See also CA 160; DLB 54

Guiraldes, Ricardo (Guillermo) 1886-1927 **TCLC 39**
See also CA 131; HW; MTCW

Gumilev, Nikolai Stephanovich 1886-1921 **TCLC 60**

Gunesekera, Romesh 1954- .... **CLC 91**
See also CA 159

Gunn, Bill .... **CLC 5**
See also Gunn, William Harrison

Harris, George Washington 1814-1869 **NCLC 23**
See also DLB 3, 11

Harris, Joel Chandler 1848-1908 ... **TCLC 2; SSC 19**
See also CA 104; 137; DLB 11, 23, 42, 78, 91; MAICYA; YABC 1

Harris, John (Wyndham Parkes Lucas) Beynon 1903-1969
See Wyndham, John
See also CA 102; 89-92

Harris, MacDonald .... **CLC 9**
See also Heiney, Donald (William)

Harris, Mark 1922- .... **CLC 19**
See also CA 5-8R; CAAS 3; CANR 2, 55; DLB 2; DLBY 80

Harris, (Theodore) Wilson 1921- ..... **CLC 25**
See also BW 2; CA 65-68; CAAS 16; CANR 11, 27; DLB 117; MTCW

Harrison, Elizabeth Cavanna 1909-
See Cavanna, Betty
See also CA 9-12R; CANR 6, 27

Harrison, Harry (Max) 1925- .... **CLC 42**
See also CA 1-4R; CANR 5, 21; DLB 8; SATA 4

Harrison, James (Thomas) 1937- **CLC 6, 14, 33, 66; SSC 19**
See also CA 13-16R; CANR 8, 51; DLBY 82; INT CANR-8

Harrison, Jim
See Harrison, James (Thomas)

Harrison, Kathryn 1961- .... **CLC 70**
See also CA 144

Harrison, Tony 1937- .... **CLC 43**
See also CA 65-68; CANR 44; DLB 40; MTCW

Harriss, Will(ard Irvin) 1922- .... **CLC 34**
See also CA 111

Harson, Sley
See Ellison, Harlan (Jay)

Hart, Ellis
See Ellison, Harlan (Jay)

Hart, Josephine 1942(?)- **CLC 70; DAM POP**
See also CA 138

Hart, Moss 1904-1961 **CLC 66; DAM DRAM**
See also CA 109; 89-92; DLB 7

Harte, (Francis) Bret(t) 1836(?)-1902 **TCLC 1, 25; DA; DAC; DAM MST; SSC 8; WLC**
See also CA 104; 140; CDALB 1865-1917; DLB 12, 64, 74, 79; SATA 26

Hartley, L(eslie) P(oles) 1895-1972 **CLC 2, 22**
See also CA 45-48; 37-40R; CANR 33; DLB 15, 139; MTCW

Hartman, Geoffrey H. 1929- .... **CLC 27**
See also CA 117; 125; DLB 67

Hartmann, Sadakichi 1867-1944 ... **TCLC 73**
See also CA 157; DLB 54

Hartmann von Aue c. 1160-c. 1205 **CMLC 15**
See also DLB 138

Hartmann von Aue 1170-1210 ...... **CMLC 15**

Haruf, Kent 1943- .... **CLC 34**
See also CA 149

Harwood, Ronald 1934- .... **CLC 32; DAM DRAM, MST**
See also CA 1-4R; CANR 4, 55; DLB 13

Hasek, Jaroslav (Matej Frantisek) 1883-1923 **TCLC 4**
See also CA 104; 129; MTCW

Hass, Robert 1941- ... **CLC 18, 39, 99; PC 16**
See also CA 111; CANR 30, 50; DLB 105; SATA 94

Hastings, Hudson
See Kuttner, Henry

Hastings, Selina .... **CLC 44**

Hathorne, John 1641-1717 .... **LC 38**

Hatteras, Amelia
See Mencken, H(enry) L(ouis)

Hatteras, Owen .... **TCLC 18**
See also Mencken, H(enry) L(ouis); Nathan, George Jean

Hauptmann, Gerhart (Johann Robert) 1862-1946 .... **TCLC 4; DAM DRAM**
See also CA 104; 153; DLB 66, 118

Havel, Vaclav 1936- ... **CLC 25, 58, 65; DAM DRAM; DC 6**
See also CA 104; CANR 36; MTCW

Haviaras, Stratis .... **CLC 33**
See also Chaviaras, Strates

Hawes, Stephen 1475(?)-1523(?) .... **LC 17**

Hawkes, John (Clendennin Burne, Jr.) 1925- **CLC 1, 2, 3, 4, 7, 9, 14, 15, 27, 49**
See also CA 1-4R; CANR 2, 47; DLB 2, 7; DLBY 80; MTCW

Hawking, S. W.
See Hawking, Stephen W(illiam)

Hawking, Stephen W(illiam) 1942- .. **CLC 63**
See also AAYA 13; BEST 89:1; CA 126; 129; CANR 48

Hawthorne, Julian 1846-1934 .... **TCLC 25**

Hawthorne, Nathaniel 1804-1864 **NCLC 39; DA; DAB; DAC; DAM MST, NOV; SSC 29; WLC**
See also AAYA 18; CDALB 1640-1865; DLB 1, 74; YABC 2

Haxton, Josephine Ayres 1921-
See Douglas, Ellen
See also CA 115; CANR 41

Hayaseca y Eizaguirre, Jorge
See Echegaray (y Eizaguirre), Jose (Maria Waldo)

Hayashi Fumiko 1904-1951 .... **TCLC 27**
See also DLB 180

Haycraft, Anna
See Ellis, Alice Thomas
See also CA 122

Hayden, Robert E(arl) 1913-1980 . **CLC 5, 9, 14, 37; BLC; DA; DAC; DAM MST, MULT, POET; PC 6**
See also BW 1; CA 69-72; 97-100; CABS 2; CANR 24; CDALB 1941-1968; DLB 5, 76; MTCW; SATA 19; SATA-Obit 26

Hayford, J(oseph) E(phraim) Casely
See Casely-Hayford, J(oseph) E(phraim)

Hayman, Ronald 1932- .... **CLC 44**
See also CA 25-28R; CANR 18, 50; DLB 155

Haywood, Eliza (Fowler) 1693(?)-1756 **LC 1**

Hazlitt, William 1778-1830 .... **NCLC 29**
See also DLB 110, 158

Hazzard, Shirley 1931- .... **CLC 18**
See also CA 9-12R; CANR 4; DLBY 82; MTCW

Head, Bessie 1937-1986 ... **CLC 25, 67; BLC; DAM MULT**
See also BW 2; CA 29-32R; 119; CANR 25; DLB 117; MTCW

Headon, (Nicky) Topper 1956(?)- ..... **CLC 30**

Heaney, Seamus (Justin) 1939- **CLC 5, 7, 14, 25, 37, 74, 91; DAB; DAM POET; PC 18; WLCS**
See also CA 85-88; CANR 25, 48; CDBLB 1960 to Present; DLB 40; DLBY 95; MTCW

Hearn, (Patricio) Lafcadio (Tessima Carlos) 1850-1904 .... **TCLC 9**
See also CA 105; DLB 12, 78

Hearne, Vicki 1946- .... **CLC 56**
See also CA 139

Hearon, Shelby 1931- .... **CLC 63**
See also AITN 2; CA 25-28R; CANR 18, 48

Heat-Moon, William Least .... **CLC 29**
See also Trogdon, William (Lewis)
See also AAYA 9

Hebbel, Friedrich 1813-1863 **NCLC 43; DAM DRAM**
See also DLB 129

Hebert, Anne 1916- **CLC 4, 13, 29; DAC; DAM MST, POET**
See also CA 85-88; DLB 68; MTCW

Hecht, Anthony (Evan) 1923- **CLC 8, 13, 19; DAM POET**
See also CA 9-12R; CANR 6; DLB 5, 169

Hecht, Ben 1894-1964 .... **CLC 8**
See also CA 85-88; DLB 7, 9, 25, 26, 28, 86

Hedayat, Sadeq 1903-1951 .... **TCLC 21**
See also CA 120

Hegel, Georg Wilhelm Friedrich 1770-1831 **NCLC 46**
See also DLB 90

Heidegger, Martin 1889-1976 .... **CLC 24**
See also CA 81-84; 65-68; CANR 34; MTCW

Heidenstam, (Carl Gustaf) Verner von 1859-1940 .... **TCLC 5**
See also CA 104

Heifner, Jack 1946- .... **CLC 11**
See also CA 105; CANR 47

Heijermans, Herman 1864-1924 .... **TCLC 24**
See also CA 123

Heilbrun, Carolyn G(old) 1926- .... **CLC 25**
See also CA 45-48; CANR 1, 28, 58

Heine, Heinrich 1797-1856 .... **NCLC 4, 54**
See also DLB 90

Heinemann, Larry (Curtiss) 1944- ... **CLC 50**
See also CA 110; CAAS 21; CANR 31; DLBD 9; INT CANR-31

Heiney, Donald (William) 1921-1993
See Harris, MacDonald
See also CA 1-4R; 142; CANR 3, 58

Heinlein, Robert A(nson) 1907-1988 **CLC 1, 3, 8, 14, 26, 55; DAM POP**
See also AAYA 17; CA 1-4R; 125; CANR 1, 20, 53; DLB 8; JRDA; MAICYA; MTCW; SATA 9, 69; SATA-Obit 56

Helforth, John
See Doolittle, Hilda

Hellenhofferu, Vojtech Kapristian z
See Hasek, Jaroslav (Matej Frantisek)

Heller, Joseph 1923- **CLC 1, 3, 5, 8, 11, 36, 63; DA; DAB; DAC; DAM MST, NOV, POP; WLC**
See also AITN 1; CA 5-8R; CABS 1; CANR 8, 42; DLB 2, 28; DLBY 80; INT CANR-8; MTCW

Hellman, Lillian (Florence) 1906-1984 **CLC 2, 4, 8, 14, 18, 34, 44, 52; DAM DRAM; DC 1**
See also AITN 1, 2; CA 13-16R; 112; CANR 33; DLB 7; DLBY 84; MTCW

Helprin, Mark 1947- **CLC 7, 10, 22, 32; DAM NOV, POP**
See also CA 81-84; CANR 47; DLBY 85; MTCW

Helvetius, Claude-Adrien 1715-1771 .. **LC 26**

Helyar, Jane Penelope Josephine 1933-
See Poole, Josephine
See also CA 21-24R; CANR 10, 26; SATA 82

Hemans, Felicia 1793-1835 .... **NCLC 29**
See also DLB 96

Hemingway, Ernest (Miller) 1899-1961 **C L C 1, 3, 6, 8, 10, 13, 19, 30, 34, 39, 41, 44, 50, 61, 80; DA; DAB; DAC; DAM MST, NOV; SSC 25; WLC**
See also AAYA 19; CA 77-80; CANR 34; CDALB 1917-1929; DLB 4, 9, 102; DLBD 1, 15, 16; DLBY 81, 87, 96; MTCW

Hempel, Amy 1951- .... **CLC 39**
See also CA 118; 137

Henderson, F. C.
See Mencken, H(enry) L(ouis)

Henderson, Sylvia
See Ashton-Warner, Sylvia (Constance)

Henderson, Zenna (Chlarson) 1917-1983 **SSC 29**
See also CA 1-4R; 133; CANR 1; DLB 8; SATA 5

MULT, POET
See also AAYA 2; BW 2; CA 33-36R; CANR 25; CLR 10; DLB 38; MAICYA; MTCW; SATA 4

Jordan, Pat(rick M.) 1941- .... **CLC 37**
See also CA 33-36R

Jorgensen, Ivar
See Ellison, Harlan (Jay)

Jorgenson, Ivar
See Silverberg, Robert

Josephus, Flavius c. 37-100 .... **CMLC 13**

Josipovici, Gabriel 1940- .... **CLC 6, 43**
See also CA 37-40R; CAAS 8; CANR 47; DLB 14

Joubert, Joseph 1754-1824 .... **NCLC 9**

Jouve, Pierre Jean 1887-1976 .... **CLC 47**
See also CA 65-68

Joyce, James (Augustine Aloysius) 1882-1941
TCLC 3, 8, 16, 35, 52; DA; DAB; DAC; DAM MST, NOV, POET; SSC 26; WLC
See also CA 104; 126; CDBLB 1914-1945; DLB 10, 19, 36, 162; MTCW

Jozsef, Attila 1905-1937 .... **TCLC 22**
See also CA 116

Juana Ines de la Cruz 1651(?)-1695 ...... **LC 5**

Judd, Cyril
See Kornbluth, C(yril) M.; Pohl, Frederik

Julian of Norwich 1342(?)-1416(?) .... **LC 6**
See also DLB 146

Juniper, Alex
See Hospital, Janette Turner

Junius
See Luxemburg, Rosa

Just, Ward (Swift) 1935- .... **CLC 4, 27**
See also CA 25-28R; CANR 32; INT CANR-32

Justice, Donald (Rodney) 1925- .. **CLC 6, 19, 102; DAM POET**
See also CA 5-8R; CANR 26, 54; DLBY 83; INT CANR-26

Juvenal c. 55-c. 127 .... **CMLC 8**

Juvenis
See Bourne, Randolph S(illiman)

Kacew, Romain 1914-1980
See Gary, Romain
See also CA 108; 102

Kadare, Ismail 1936- .... **CLC 52**

Kadohata, Cynthia .... **CLC 59**
See also CA 140

Kafka, Franz 1883-1924 **TCLC 2, 6, 13, 29, 47, 53; DA; DAB; DAC; DAM MST, NOV; SSC 29; WLC**
See also CA 105; 126; DLB 81; MTCW

Kahanovitsch, Pinkhes
See Der Nister

Kahn, Roger 1927- .... **CLC 30**
See also CA 25-28R; CANR 44; DLB 171; SATA 37

Kain, Saul
See Sassoon, Siegfried (Lorraine)

Kaiser, Georg 1878-1945 .... **TCLC 9**
See also CA 106; DLB 124

Kaletski, Alexander 1946- .... **CLC 39**
See also CA 118; 143

Kalidasa fl. c. 400- .... **CMLC 9**

Kallman, Chester (Simon) 1921-1975 **CLC 2**
See also CA 45-48; 53-56; CANR 3

Kaminsky, Melvin 1926-
See Brooks, Mel
See also CA 65-68; CANR 16

Kaminsky, Stuart M(elvin) 1934- ..... **CLC 59**
See also CA 73-76; CANR 29, 53

Kane, Francis
See Robbins, Harold

Kane, Paul
See Simon, Paul (Frederick)

Kane, Wilson

See Bloch, Robert (Albert)

Kanin, Garson 1912- .... **CLC 22**
See also AITN 1; CA 5-8R; CANR 7; DLB 7

Kaniuk, Yoram 1930- .... **CLC 19**
See also CA 134

Kant, Immanuel 1724-1804 .... **NCLC 27**
See also DLB 94

Kantor, MacKinlay 1904-1977 .... **CLC 7**
See also CA 61-64; 73-76; CANR 60; DLB 9, 102

Kaplan, David Michael 1946- .... **CLC 50**

Kaplan, James 1951- .... **CLC 59**
See also CA 135

Karageorge, Michael
See Anderson, Poul (William)

Karamzin, Nikolai Mikhailovich 1766-1826
NCLC 3
See also DLB 150

Karapanou, Margarita 1946- .... **CLC 13**
See also CA 101

Karinthy, Frigyes 1887-1938 .... **TCLC 47**

Karl, Frederick R(obert) 1927- .... **CLC 34**
See also CA 5-8R; CANR 3, 44

Kastel, Warren
See Silverberg, Robert

Kataev, Evgeny Petrovich 1903-1942
See Petrov, Evgeny
See also CA 120

Kataphusin
See Ruskin, John

Katz, Steve 1935- .... **CLC 47**
See also CA 25-28R; CAAS 14; CANR 12; DLBY 83

Kauffman, Janet 1945- .... **CLC 42**
See also CA 117; CANR 43; DLBY 86

Kaufman, Bob (Garnell) 1925-1986 . **CLC 49**
See also BW 1; CA 41-44R; 118; CANR 22; DLB 16, 41

Kaufman, George S. 1889-1961 **CLC 38; DAM DRAM**
See also CA 108; 93-96; DLB 7; INT 108

Kaufman, Sue .... **CLC 3, 8**
See also Barondess, Sue K(aufman)

Kavafis, Konstantinos Petrou 1863-1933
See Cavafy, C(onstantine) P(eter)
See also CA 104

Kavan, Anna 1901-1968 .... **CLC 5, 13, 82**
See also CA 5-8R; CANR 6, 57; MTCW

Kavanagh, Dan
See Barnes, Julian (Patrick)

Kavanagh, Patrick (Joseph) 1904-1967 **C L C 22**
See also CA 123; 25-28R; DLB 15, 20; MTCW

Kawabata, Yasunari 1899-1972 **CLC 2, 5, 9, 18; DAM MULT; SSC 17**
See also CA 93-96; 33-36R; DLB 180

Kaye, M(ary) M(argaret) 1909- .... **CLC 28**
See also CA 89-92; CANR 24, 60; MTCW; SATA 62

Kaye, Mollie
See Kaye, M(ary) M(argaret)

Kaye-Smith, Sheila 1887-1956 .... **TCLC 20**
See also CA 118; DLB 36

Kaymor, Patrice Maguilene
See Senghor, Leopold Sedar

Kazan, Elia 1909- .... **CLC 6, 16, 63**
See also CA 21-24R; CANR 32

Kazantzakis, Nikos 1883(?)-1957 **TCLC 2, 5, 33**
See also CA 105; 132; MTCW

Kazin, Alfred 1915- .... **CLC 34, 38**
See also CA 1-4R; CAAS 7; CANR 1, 45; DLB 67

Keane, Mary Nesta (Skrine) 1904-1996
See Keane, Molly
See also CA 108; 114; 151

Keane, Molly .... **CLC 31**

See also Keane, Mary Nesta (Skrine)
See also INT 114

Keates, Jonathan 19(?)- .... **CLC 34**

Keaton, Buster 1895-1966 .... **CLC 20**

Keats, John 1795-1821 . **NCLC 8; DA; DAB; DAC; DAM MST, POET; PC 1; WLC**
See also CDBLB 1789-1832; DLB 96, 110

Keene, Donald 1922- .... **CLC 34**
See also CA 1-4R; CANR 5

Keillor, Garrison .... **CLC 40**
See also Keillor, Gary (Edward)
See also AAYA 2; BEST 89:3; DLBY 87; SATA 58

Keillor, Gary (Edward) 1942-
See Keillor, Garrison
See also CA 111; 117; CANR 36, 59; DAM POP; MTCW

Keith, Michael
See Hubbard, L(afayette) Ron(ald)

Keller, Gottfried 1819-1890 **NCLC 2; SSC 26**
See also DLB 129

Kellerman, Jonathan 1949- ... **CLC 44; DAM POP**
See also BEST 90:1; CA 106; CANR 29, 51; INT CANR-29

Kelley, William Melvin 1937- .... **CLC 22**
See also BW 1; CA 77-80; CANR 27; DLB 33

Kellogg, Marjorie 1922- .... **CLC 2**
See also CA 81-84

Kellow, Kathleen
See Hibbert, Eleanor Alice Burford

Kelly, M(ilton) T(erry) 1947- .... **CLC 55**
See also CA 97-100; CAAS 22; CANR 19, 43

Kelman, James 1946- .... **CLC 58, 86**
See also CA 148

Kemal, Yashar 1923- .... **CLC 14, 29**
See also CA 89-92; CANR 44

Kemble, Fanny 1809-1893 .... **NCLC 18**
See also DLB 32

Kemelman, Harry 1908-1996 .... **CLC 2**
See also AITN 1; CA 9-12R; 155; CANR 6; DLB 28

Kempe, Margery 1373(?)-1440(?) .... **LC 6**
See also DLB 146

Kempis, Thomas a 1380-1471 .... **LC 11**

Kendall, Henry 1839-1882 .... **NCLC 12**

Keneally, Thomas (Michael) 1935- **CLC 5, 8, 10, 14, 19, 27, 43; DAM NOV**
See also CA 85-88; CANR 10, 50; MTCW

Kennedy, Adrienne (Lita) 1931- ..... **CLC 66; BLC; DAM MULT; DC 5**
See also BW 2; CA 103; CAAS 20; CABS 3; CANR 26, 53; DLB 38

Kennedy, John Pendleton 1795-1870 **NCLC 2**
See also DLB 3

Kennedy, Joseph Charles 1929-
See Kennedy, X. J.
See also CA 1-4R; CANR 4, 30, 40; SATA 14, 86

Kennedy, William 1928- .. **CLC 6, 28, 34, 53; DAM NOV**
See also AAYA 1; CA 85-88; CANR 14, 31; DLB 143; DLBY 85; INT CANR-31; MTCW; SATA 57

Kennedy, X. J. .... **CLC 8, 42**
See also Kennedy, Joseph Charles
See also CAAS 9; CLR 27; DLB 5; SAAS 22

Kenny, Maurice (Francis) 1929- ..... **CLC 87; DAM MULT**
See also CA 144; CAAS 22; DLB 175; NNAL

Kent, Kelvin
See Kuttner, Henry

Kenton, Maxwell
See Southern, Terry

Kenyon, Robert O.
See Kuttner, Henry

Kerouac, Jack .... **CLC 1, 2, 3, 5, 14, 29, 61**

See also Kerouac, Jean-Louis Lebris de
See also CDALB 1941-1968; DLB 2, 16; DLBD 3; DLBY 95
Kerouac, Jean-Louis Lebris de 1922-1969
See Kerouac, Jack
See also AITN 1; CA 5-8R; 25-28R; CANR 26, 54; DA; DAB; DAC; DAM MST, NOV, POET, POP; MTCW; WLC
Kerr, Jean 1923- .... **CLC 22**
See also CA 5-8R; CANR 7; INT CANR-7
Kerr, M. E. .... **CLC 12, 35**
See also Meaker, Marijane (Agnes)
See also AAYA 2; CLR 29; SAAS 1
Kerr, Robert .... **CLC 55**
Kerrigan, (Thomas) Anthony 1918-**CLC 4, 6**
See also CA 49-52; CAAS 11; CANR 4
Kerry, Lois
See Duncan, Lois
Kesey, Ken (Elton) 1935- **CLC 1, 3, 6, 11, 46, 64; DA; DAB; DAC; DAM MST, NOV, POP; WLC**
See also CA 1-4R; CANR 22, 38; CDALB 1968-1988; DLB 2, 16; MTCW; SATA 66
Kesselring, Joseph (Otto) 1902-1967**CLC 45; DAM DRAM, MST**
See also CA 150
Kessler, Jascha (Frederick) 1929- ...... **CLC 4**
See also CA 17-20R; CANR 8, 48
Kettelkamp, Larry (Dale) 1933- .... **CLC 12**
See also CA 29-32R; CANR 16; SAAS 3; SATA 2
Key, Ellen 1849-1926 .... **TCLC 65**
Keyber, Conny
See Fielding, Henry
Keyes, Daniel 1927-**CLC 80; DA; DAC; DAM MST, NOV**
See also CA 17-20R; CANR 10, 26, 54; SATA 37
Keynes, John Maynard 1883-1946 **TCLC 64**
See also CA 114; DLBD 10
Khanshendel, Chiron
See Rose, Wendy
Khayyam, Omar 1048-1131**CMLC 11; DAM POET; PC 8**
Kherdian, David 1931-...................... **CLC 6, 9**
See also CA 21-24R; CAAS 2; CANR 39; CLR 24; JRDA; MAICYA; SATA 16, 74
Khlebnikov, Velimir .... **TCLC 20**
See also Khlebnikov, Viktor Vladimirovich
Khlebnikov, Viktor Vladimirovich 1885-1922
See Khlebnikov, Velimir
See also CA 117
Khodasevich, Vladislav (Felitsianovich) 1886-1939 .... **TCLC 15**
See also CA 115
Kielland, Alexander Lange 1849-1906**T C L C 5**
See also CA 104
Kiely, Benedict 1919- .... **CLC 23, 43**
See also CA 1-4R; CANR 2; DLB 15
Kienzle, William X(avier) 1928- ..... **CLC 25; DAM POP**
See also CA 93-96; CAAS 1; CANR 9, 31, 59; INT CANR-31; MTCW
Kierkegaard, Soren 1813-1855 ...... **NCLC 34**
Killens, John Oliver 1916-1987 .... **CLC 10**
See also BW 2; CA 77-80; 123; CAAS 2; CANR 26; DLB 33
Killigrew, Anne 1660-1685 .... **LC 4**
See also DLB 131
Kim
See Simenon, Georges (Jacques Christian)
Kincaid, Jamaica 1949- .. **CLC 43, 68; BLC; DAM MULT, NOV**
See also AAYA 13; BW 2; CA 125; CANR 47, 59; DLB 157
King, Francis (Henry) 1923-**CLC 8, 53; DAM**

NOV
See also CA 1-4R; CANR 1, 33; DLB 15, 139; MTCW
King, Martin Luther, Jr. 1929-1968 **CLC 83; BLC; DA; DAB; DAC; DAM MST, MULT; WLCS**
See also BW 2; CA 25-28; CANR 27, 44; CAP 2; MTCW; SATA 14
King, Stephen (Edwin) 1947-**CLC 12, 26, 37, 61; DAM NOV, POP; SSC 17**
See also AAYA 1, 17; BEST 90:1; CA 61-64; CANR 1, 30, 52; DLB 143; DLBY 80; JRDA; MTCW; SATA 9, 55
King, Steve
See King, Stephen (Edwin)
King, Thomas 1943- ... **CLC 89; DAC; DAM MULT**
See also CA 144; DLB 175; NNAL
Kingman, Lee .... **CLC 17**
See also Natti, (Mary) Lee
See also SAAS 3; SATA 1, 67
Kingsley, Charles 1819-1875 .... **NCLC 35**
See also DLB 21, 32, 163; YABC 2
Kingsley, Sidney 1906-1995 .... **CLC 44**
See also CA 85-88; 147; DLB 7
Kingsolver, Barbara 1955-**CLC 55, 81; DAM POP**
See also AAYA 15; CA 129; 134; CANR 60; INT 134
Kingston, Maxine (Ting Ting) Hong 1940-**CLC 12, 19, 58; DAM MULT, NOV; WLCS**
See also AAYA 8; CA 69-72; CANR 13, 38; DLB 173; DLBY 80; INT CANR-13; MTCW; SATA 53
Kinnell, Galway 1927- **CLC 1, 2, 3, 5, 13, 29**
See also CA 9-12R; CANR 10, 34; DLB 5; DLBY 87; INT CANR-34; MTCW
Kinsella, Thomas 1928- .... **CLC 4, 19**
See also CA 17-20R; CANR 15; DLB 27; MTCW
Kinsella, W(illiam) P(atrick) 1935- . **CLC 27, 43; DAC; DAM NOV, POP**
See also AAYA 7; CA 97-100; CAAS 7; CANR 21, 35; INT CANR-21; MTCW
Kipling, (Joseph) Rudyard 1865-1936 **T C L C 8, 17; DA; DAB; DAC; DAM MST, POET; PC 3; SSC 5; WLC**
See also CA 105; 120; CANR 33; CDBLB 1890-1914; CLR 39; DLB 19, 34, 141, 156; MAICYA; MTCW; YABC 2
Kirkup, James 1918- .... **CLC 1**
See also CA 1-4R; CAAS 4; CANR 2; DLB 27; SATA 12
Kirkwood, James 1930(?)-1989 .... **CLC 9**
See also AITN 2; CA 1-4R; 128; CANR 6, 40
Kirshner, Sidney
See Kingsley, Sidney
Kis, Danilo 1935-1989 .... **CLC 57**
See also CA 109; 118; 129; CANR 61; DLB 181; MTCW
Kivi, Aleksis 1834-1872 .... **NCLC 30**
Kizer, Carolyn (Ashley) 1925-**CLC 15, 39, 80; DAM POET**
See also CA 65-68; CAAS 5; CANR 24; DLB 5, 169
Klabund 1890-1928 .... **TCLC 44**
See also DLB 66
Klappert, Peter 1942- .... **CLC 57**
See also CA 33-36R; DLB 5
Klein, A(braham) M(oses) 1909-1972**CLC 19; DAB; DAC; DAM MST**
See also CA 101; 37-40R; DLB 68
Klein, Norma 1938-1989 .... **CLC 30**
See also AAYA 2; CA 41-44R; 128; CANR 15, 37; CLR 2, 19; INT CANR-15; JRDA; MAICYA; SAAS 1; SATA 7, 57

Klein, T(heodore) E(ibon) D(onald) 1947-**CLC 34**
See also CA 119; CANR 44
Kleist, Heinrich von 1777-1811 **NCLC 2, 37; DAM DRAM; SSC 22**
See also DLB 90
Klima, Ivan 1931- .... **CLC 56; DAM NOV**
See also CA 25-28R; CANR 17, 50
Klimentov, Andrei Platonovich 1899-1951
See Platonov, Andrei
See also CA 108
Klinger, Friedrich Maximilian von 1752-1831 **NCLC 1**
See also DLB 94
Klingsor the Magician
See Hartmann, Sadakichi
Klopstock, Friedrich Gottlieb 1724-1803 **NCLC 11**
See also DLB 97
Knapp, Caroline 1959-...................... **CLC 99**
See also CA 154
Knebel, Fletcher 1911-1993 .... **CLC 14**
See also AITN 1; CA 1-4R; 140; CAAS 3; CANR 1, 36; SATA 36; SATA-Obit 75
Knickerbocker, Diedrich
See Irving, Washington
Knight, Etheridge 1931-1991 **CLC 40; BLC; DAM POET; PC 14**
See also BW 1; CA 21-24R; 133; CANR 23; DLB 41
Knight, Sarah Kemble 1666-1727 .... **LC 7**
See also DLB 24
Knister, Raymond 1899-1932 .... **TCLC 56**
See also DLB 68
Knowles, John 1926- . **CLC 1, 4, 10, 26; DA; DAC; DAM MST, NOV**
See also AAYA 10; CA 17-20R; CANR 40; CDALB 1968-1988; DLB 6; MTCW; SATA 8, 89
Knox, Calvin M.
See Silverberg, Robert
Knox, John c. 1505-1572 .... **LC 37**
See also DLB 132
Knye, Cassandra
See Disch, Thomas M(ichael)
Koch, C(hristopher) J(ohn) 1932- .... **CLC 42**
See also CA 127
Koch, Christopher
See Koch, C(hristopher) J(ohn)
Koch, Kenneth 1925- ..... **CLC 5, 8, 44; DAM POET**
See also CA 1-4R; CANR 6, 36, 57; DLB 5; INT CANR-36; SATA 65
Kochanowski, Jan 1530-1584 .... **LC 10**
Kock, Charles Paul de 1794-1871 . **NCLC 16**
Koda Shigeyuki 1867-1947
See Rohan, Koda
See also CA 121
Koestler, Arthur 1905-1983**CLC 1, 3, 6, 8, 15, 33**
See also CA 1-4R; 109; CANR 1, 33; CDBLB 1945-1960; DLBY 83; MTCW
Kogawa, Joy Nozomi 1935- .. **CLC 78; DAC; DAM MST, MULT**
See also CA 101; CANR 19, 62
Kohout, Pavel 1928- .... **CLC 13**
See also CA 45-48; CANR 3
Koizumi, Yakumo
See Hearn, (Patricio) Lafcadio (Tessima Carlos)
Kolmar, Gertrud 1894-1943 .... **TCLC 40**
Komunyakaa, Yusef 1947- .... **CLC 86, 94**
See also CA 147; DLB 120
Konrad, George
See Konrad, Gyoergy
Konrad, Gyoergy 1933- .... **CLC 4, 10, 73**
See also CA 85-88
Konwicki, Tadeusz 1926- .... **CLC 8, 28, 54**

See also CA 101; CAAS 9; CANR 39, 59; MTCW

Koontz, Dean R(ay) 1945- ..... **CLC 78; DAM NOV, POP**
See also AAYA 9; BEST 89:3, 90:2; CA 108; CANR 19, 36, 52; MTCW; SATA 92

Kopit, Arthur (Lee) 1937-**CLC 1, 18, 33; DAM DRAM**
See also AITN 1; CA 81-84; CABS 3; DLB 7; MTCW

Kops, Bernard 1926- .... **CLC 4**
See also CA 5-8R; DLB 13

Kornbluth, C(yril) M. 1923-1958 .... **TCLC 8**
See also CA 105; 160; DLB 8

Korolenko, V. G.
See Korolenko, Vladimir Galaktionovich

Korolenko, Vladimir
See Korolenko, Vladimir Galaktionovich

Korolenko, Vladimir G.
See Korolenko, Vladimir Galaktionovich

Korolenko, Vladimir Galaktionovich 1853-1921 .... **TCLC 22**
See also CA 121

Korzybski, Alfred (Habdank Skarbek) 1879-1950 .... **TCLC 61**
See also CA 123; 160

Kosinski, Jerzy (Nikodem) 1933-1991**CLC 1, 2, 3, 6, 10, 15, 53, 70; DAM NOV**
See also CA 17-20R; 134; CANR 9, 46; DLB 2; DLBY 82; MTCW

Kostelanetz, Richard (Cory) 1940- ..**CLC 28**
See also CA 13-16R; CAAS 8; CANR 38

Kostrowitzki, Wilhelm Apollinaris de 1880-1918
See Apollinaire, Guillaume
See also CA 104

Kotlowitz, Robert 1924- .... **CLC 4**
See also CA 33-36R; CANR 36

Kotzebue, August (Friedrich Ferdinand) von 1761-1819 .... **NCLC 25**
See also DLB 94

Kotzwinkle, William 1938- ..... **CLC 5, 14, 35**
See also CA 45-48; CANR 3, 44; CLR 6; DLB 173; MAICYA; SATA 24, 70

Kowna, Stancy
See Szymborska, Wislawa

Kozol, Jonathan 1936- .... **CLC 17**
See also CA 61-64; CANR 16, 45

Kozoll, Michael 1940(?)- .... **CLC 35**

Kramer, Kathryn 19(?)- .... **CLC 34**

Kramer, Larry 1935- .... **CLC 42; DAM POP**
See also CA 124; 126; CANR 60

Krasicki, Ignacy 1735-1801 .... **NCLC 8**

Krasinski, Zygmunt 1812-1859 .... **NCLC 4**

Kraus, Karl 1874-1936 .... **TCLC 5**
See also CA 104; DLB 118

Kreve (Mickevicius), Vincas 1882-1954**TCLC 27**

Kristeva, Julia 1941- .... **CLC 77**
See also CA 154

Kristofferson, Kris 1936- .... **CLC 26**
See also CA 104

Krizanc, John 1956- .... **CLC 57**

Krleza, Miroslav 1893-1981 .... **CLC 8**
See also CA 97-100; 105; CANR 50; DLB 147

Kroetsch, Robert 1927-**CLC 5, 23, 57; DAC; DAM POET**
See also CA 17-20R; CANR 8, 38; DLB 53; MTCW

Kroetz, Franz
See Kroetz, Franz Xaver

Kroetz, Franz Xaver 1946- .... **CLC 41**
See also CA 130

Kroker, Arthur 1945- .... **CLC 77**

Kropotkin, Peter (Aleksieevich) 1842-1921 **TCLC 36**
See also CA 119

Krotkov, Yuri 1917- .... **CLC 19**
See also CA 102

Krumb
See Crumb, R(obert)

Krumgold, Joseph (Quincy) 1908-1980 **C L C 12**
See also CA 9-12R; 101; CANR 7; MAICYA; SATA 1, 48; SATA-Obit 23

Krumwitz
See Crumb, R(obert)

Krutch, Joseph Wood 1893-1970 ...... **CLC 24**
See also CA 1-4R; 25-28R; CANR 4; DLB 63

Krutzch, Gus
See Eliot, T(homas) S(tearns)

Krylov, Ivan Andreevich 1768(?)-1844**N C L C 1**
See also DLB 150

Kubin, Alfred (Leopold Isidor) 1877-1959 **TCLC 23**
See also CA 112; 149; DLB 81

Kubrick, Stanley 1928- .... **CLC 16**
See also CA 81-84; CANR 33; DLB 26

Kumin, Maxine (Winokur) 1925- **CLC 5, 13, 28; DAM POET; PC 15**
See also AITN 2; CA 1-4R; CAAS 8; CANR 1, 21; DLB 5; MTCW; SATA 12

Kundera, Milan 1929- . **CLC 4, 9, 19, 32, 68; DAM NOV; SSC 24**
See also AAYA 2; CA 85-88; CANR 19, 52; MTCW

Kunene, Mazisi (Raymond) 1930- .... **CLC 85**
See also BW 1; CA 125; DLB 117

Kunitz, Stanley (Jasspon) 1905-**CLC 6, 11, 14; PC 19**
See also CA 41-44R; CANR 26, 57; DLB 48; INT CANR-26; MTCW

Kunze, Reiner 1933- .... **CLC 10**
See also CA 93-96; DLB 75

Kuprin, Aleksandr Ivanovich 1870-1938 **TCLC 5**
See also CA 104

Kureishi, Hanif 1954(?)- .... **CLC 64**
See also CA 139

Kurosawa, Akira 1910-**CLC 16; DAM MULT**
See also AAYA 11; CA 101; CANR 46

Kushner, Tony 1957(?)-**CLC 81; DAM DRAM**
See also CA 144

Kuttner, Henry 1915-1958 .... **TCLC 10**
See also Vance, Jack
See also CA 107; 157; DLB 8

Kuzma, Greg 1944- .... **CLC 7**
See also CA 33-36R

Kuzmin, Mikhail 1872(?)-1936 ...... **TCLC 40**

Kyd, Thomas 1558-1594**LC 22; DAM DRAM; DC 3**
See also DLB 62

Kyprianos, Iossif
See Samarakis, Antonis

La Bruyere, Jean de 1645-1696 .... **LC 17**

Lacan, Jacques (Marie Emile) 1901-1981 **CLC 75**
See also CA 121; 104

Laclos, Pierre Ambroise Francois Choderlos de 1741-1803 .... **NCLC 4**

La Colere, Francois
See Aragon, Louis

Lacolere, Francois
See Aragon, Louis

La Deshabilleuse
See Simenon, Georges (Jacques Christian)

Lady Gregory
See Gregory, Isabella Augusta (Persse)

Lady of Quality, A
See Bagnold, Enid

La Fayette, Marie (Madelaine Pioche de la Vergne Comtes 1634-1693 .... **LC 2**

Lafayette, Rene

See Hubbard, L(afayette) Ron(ald)

Laforgue, Jules 1860-1887**NCLC 5, 53; PC 14; SSC 20**

Lagerkvist, Paer (Fabian) 1891-1974 **CLC 7, 10, 13, 54; DAM DRAM, NOV**
See also Lagerkvist, Par
See also CA 85-88; 49-52; MTCW

Lagerkvist, Par .... **SSC 12**
See also Lagerkvist, Paer (Fabian)

Lagerloef, Selma (Ottiliana Lovisa) 1858-1940 **TCLC 4, 36**
See also Lagerlof, Selma (Ottiliana Lovisa)
See also CA 108; SATA 15

Lagerlof, Selma (Ottiliana Lovisa)
See Lagerloef, Selma (Ottiliana Lovisa)
See also CLR 7; SATA 15

La Guma, (Justin) Alex(ander) 1925-1985 **CLC 19; DAM NOV**
See also BW 1; CA 49-52; 118; CANR 25; DLB 117; MTCW

Laidlaw, A. K.
See Grieve, C(hristopher) M(urray)

Lainez, Manuel Mujica
See Mujica Lainez, Manuel
See also HW

Laing, R(onald) D(avid) 1927-1989 .. **CLC 95**
See also CA 107; 129; CANR 34; MTCW

Lamartine, Alphonse (Marie Louis Prat) de 1790-1869**NCLC 11; DAM POET; PC 16**

Lamb, Charles 1775-1834 ..... **NCLC 10; DA; DAB; DAC; DAM MST; WLC**
See also CDBLB 1789-1832; DLB 93, 107, 163; SATA 17

Lamb, Lady Caroline 1785-1828 ... **NCLC 38**
See also DLB 116

Lamming, George (William) 1927- **CLC 2, 4, 66; BLC; DAM MULT**
See also BW 2; CA 85-88; CANR 26; DLB 125; MTCW

L'Amour, Louis (Dearborn) 1908-1988 **C L C 25, 55; DAM NOV, POP**
See also AAYA 16; AITN 2; BEST 89.2; CA 1-4R; 125; CANR 3, 25, 40; DLBY 80; MTCW

Lampedusa, Giuseppe (Tomasi) di 1896-1957 **TCLC 13**
See also Tomasi di Lampedusa, Giuseppe
See also DLB 177

Lampman, Archibald 1861-1899 ... **NCLC 25**
See also DLB 92

Lancaster, Bruce 1896-1963 .... **CLC 36**
See also CA 9-10; CAP 1; SATA 9

Lanchester, John .... **CLC 99**

Landau, Mark Alexandrovich
See Aldanov, Mark (Alexandrovich)

Landau-Aldanov, Mark Alexandrovich
See Aldanov, Mark (Alexandrovich)

Landis, Jerry
See Simon, Paul (Frederick)

Landis, John 1950- .... **CLC 26**
See also CA 112; 122

Landolfi, Tommaso 1908-1979 .... **CLC 11, 49**
See also CA 127; 117; DLB 177

Landon, Letitia Elizabeth 1802-1838 **N C L C 15**
See also DLB 96

Landor, Walter Savage 1775-1864 **NCLC 14**
See also DLB 93, 107

Landwirth, Heinz 1927-
See Lind, Jakov
See also CA 9-12R; CANR 7

Lane, Patrick 1939- ... **CLC 25; DAM POET**
See also CA 97-100; CANR 54; DLB 53; INT 97-100

Lang, Andrew 1844-1912 .... **TCLC 16**
See also CA 114; 137; DLB 98, 141, 184; MAICYA; SATA 16

Lang, Fritz 1890-1976 .... **CLC 20, 103**

See also CA 77-80; 69-72; CANR 30

Lange, John
See Crichton, (John) Michael

Langer, Elinor 1939- .... CLC 34
See also CA 121

Langland, William 1330(?)-1400(?)... **LC 19;**
DA; DAB; DAC; DAM MST, POET
See also DLB 146

Langstaff, Launcelot
See Irving, Washington

Lanier, Sidney 1842-1881 ..... **NCLC 6; DAM**
POET
See also DLB 64; DLBD 13; MAICYA; SATA 18

Lanyer, Aemilia 1569-1645 .... **LC 10, 30**
See also DLB 121

Lao Tzu .... **CMLC 7**

Lapine, James (Elliot) 1949- .... CLC 39
See also CA 123; 130; CANR 54; INT 130

Larbaud, Valery (Nicolas) 1881-1957**TCLC 9**
See also CA 106; 152

Lardner, Ring
See Lardner, Ring(gold) W(ilmer)

Lardner, Ring W., Jr.
See Lardner, Ring(gold) W(ilmer)

Lardner, Ring(gold) W(ilmer) 1885-1933
TCLC 2, 14
See also CA 104; 131; CDALB 1917-1929;
DLB 11, 25, 86; DLBD 16; MTCW

Laredo, Betty
See Codrescu, Andrei

Larkin, Maia
See Wojciechowska, Maia (Teresa)

Larkin, Philip (Arthur) 1922-1985**CLC 3, 5, 8,**
9, 13, 18, 33, 39, 64; DAB; DAM MST,
POET
See also CA 5-8R; 117; CANR 24, 62; CDBLB
1960 to Present; DLB 27; MTCW

Larra (y Sanchez de Castro), Mariano Jose de
1809-1837 .... NCLC 17

Larsen, Eric 1941- .... CLC 55
See also CA 132

Larsen, Nella 1891-1964**CLC 37; BLC; DAM**
MULT
See also BW 1; CA 125; DLB 51

Larson, Charles R(aymond) 1938- ... CLC 31
See also CA 53-56; CANR 4

Larson, Jonathan 1961(?)-1996 .... CLC 99

Las Casas, Bartolome de 1474-1566 ... LC 31

Lasch, Christopher 1932-1994 .... CLC 102
See also CA 73-76; 144; CANR 25; MTCW

Lasker-Schueler, Else 1869-1945 ... TCLC 57
See also DLB 66, 124

Latham, Jean Lee 1902- .... CLC 12
See also AITN 1; CA 5-8R; CANR 7; MAICYA;
SATA 2, 68

Latham, Mavis
See Clark, Mavis Thorpe

Lathen, Emma .... CLC 2
See also Hennissart, Martha; Latsis, Mary J(ane)

Lathrop, Francis
See Leiber, Fritz (Reuter, Jr.)

Latsis, Mary J(ane)
See Lathen, Emma
See also CA 85-88

Lattimore, Richmond (Alexander) 1906-1984
CLC 3
See also CA 1-4R; 112; CANR 1

Laughlin, James 1914- .... CLC 49
See also CA 21-24R; CAAS 22; CANR 9, 47;
DLB 48; DLBY 96

Laurence, (Jean) Margaret (Wemyss) 1926-
1987 .. **CLC 3, 6, 13, 50, 62; DAC; DAM**
MST; SSC 7
See also CA 5-8R; 121; CANR 33; DLB 53;
MTCW; SATA-Obit 50

Laurent, Antoine 1952- .... CLC 50

Lauscher, Hermann
See Hesse, Hermann

Lautreamont, Comte de 1846-1870**NCLC 12;**
SSC 14

Laverty, Donald
See Blish, James (Benjamin)

Lavin, Mary 1912-1996**CLC 4, 18, 99; SSC 4**
See also CA 9-12R; 151; CANR 33; DLB 15;
MTCW

Lavond, Paul Dennis
See Kornbluth, C(yril) M.; Pohl, Frederik

Lawler, Raymond Evenor 1922- .... CLC 58
See also CA 103

Lawrence, D(avid) H(erbert Richards) 1885-
1930**TCLC 2, 9, 16, 33, 48, 61; DA; DAB;**
DAC; DAM MST, NOV, POET; SSC 4, 19;
WLC
See also CA 104; 121; CDBLB 1914-1945;
DLB 10, 19, 36, 98, 162; MTCW

Lawrence, T(homas) E(dward) 1888-1935
TCLC 18
See also Dale, Colin
See also CA 115

Lawrence of Arabia
See Lawrence, T(homas) E(dward)

Lawson, Henry (Archibald Hertzberg) 1867-
1922 .... **TCLC 27; SSC 18**
See also CA 120

Lawton, Dennis
See Faust, Frederick (Schiller)

Laxness, Halldor .... CLC 25
See also Gudjonsson, Halldor Kiljan

Layamon fl. c. 1200- .... **CMLC 10**
See also DLB 146

Laye, Camara 1928-1980 .. **CLC 4, 38; BLC;**
DAM MULT
See also BW 1; CA 85-88; 97-100; CANR 25;
MTCW

Layton, Irving (Peter) 1912-**CLC 2, 15; DAC;**
DAM MST, POET
See also CA 1-4R; CANR 2, 33, 43; DLB 88;
MTCW

Lazarus, Emma 1849-1887 .... NCLC 8

Lazarus, Felix
See Cable, George Washington

Lazarus, Henry
See Slavitt, David R(ytman)

Lea, Joan
See Neufeld, John (Arthur)

Leacock, Stephen (Butler) 1869-1944**TCLC 2;**
DAC; DAM MST
See also CA 104; 141; DLB 92

Lear, Edward 1812-1888 .... NCLC 3
See also CLR 1; DLB 32, 163, 166; MAICYA;
SATA 18

Lear, Norman (Milton) 1922- .... CLC 12
See also CA 73-76

Leavis, F(rank) R(aymond) 1895-1978**CLC 24**
See also CA 21-24R; 77-80; CANR 44; MTCW

Leavitt, David 1961- ..... **CLC 34; DAM POP**
See also CA 116; 122; CANR 50, 62; DLB 130;
INT 122

Leblanc, Maurice (Marie Emile) 1864-1941
TCLC 49
See also CA 110

Lebowitz, Fran(ces Ann) 1951(?)-**CLC 11, 36**
See also CA 81-84; CANR 14, 60; INT CANR-
14; MTCW

Lebrecht, Peter
See Tieck, (Johann) Ludwig

le Carre, John .... **CLC 3, 5, 9, 15, 28**
See also Cornwell, David (John Moore)
See also BEST 89:4; CDBLB 1960 to Present;
DLB 87

Le Clezio, J(ean) M(arie) G(ustave) 1940-
CLC 31
See also CA 116; 128; DLB 83

Leconte de Lisle, Charles-Marie-Rene 1818-
1894 .... **NCLC 29**

Le Coq, Monsieur
See Simenon, Georges (Jacques Christian)

Leduc, Violette 1907-1972 .... CLC 22
See also CA 13-14; 33-36R; CAP 1

Ledwidge, Francis 1887(?)-1917 .... TCLC 23
See also CA 123; DLB 20

Lee, Andrea 1953-**CLC 36; BLC; DAM MULT**
See also BW 1; CA 125

Lee, Andrew
See Auchincloss, Louis (Stanton)

Lee, Chang-rae 1965- .... CLC 91
See also CA 148

Lee, Don L. .... CLC 2
See also Madhubuti, Haki R.

Lee, George W(ashington) 1894-1976**CLC 52;**
BLC; DAM MULT
See also BW 1; CA 125; DLB 51

Lee, (Nelle) Harper 1926- .. **CLC 12, 60; DA;**
DAB; DAC; DAM MST, NOV; WLC
See also AAYA 13; CA 13-16R; CANR 51;
CDALB 1941-1968; DLB 6; MTCW; SATA
11

Lee, Helen Elaine 1959(?)- .... CLC 86
See also CA 148

Lee, Julian
See Latham, Jean Lee

Lee, Larry
See Lee, Lawrence

Lee, Laurie 1914-1997 **CLC 90; DAB; DAM**
POP
See also CA 77-80; 158; CANR 33; DLB 27;
MTCW

Lee, Lawrence 1941-1990 .... CLC 34
See also CA 131; CANR 43

Lee, Manfred B(ennington) 1905-1971**CLC 11**
See also Queen, Ellery
See also CA 1-4R; 29-32R; CANR 2; DLB 137

Lee, Stan 1922- .... CLC 17
See also AAYA 5; CA 108; 111; INT 111

Lee, Tanith 1947- .... CLC 46
See also AAYA 15; CA 37-40R; CANR 53;
SATA 8, 88

Lee, Vernon .... TCLC 5
See also Paget, Violet
See also DLB 57, 153, 156, 174, 178

Lee, William
See Burroughs, William S(eward)

Lee, Willy
See Burroughs, William S(eward)

Lee-Hamilton, Eugene (Jacob) 1845-1907
TCLC 22
See also CA 117

Leet, Judith 1935- .... CLC 11

Le Fanu, Joseph Sheridan 1814-1873**NCLC 9,**
58; DAM POP; SSC 14
See also DLB 21, 70, 159, 178

Leffland, Ella 1931- .... CLC 19
See also CA 29-32R; CANR 35; DLBY 84; INT
CANR-35; SATA 65

Leger, Alexis
See Leger, (Marie-Rene Auguste) Alexis Saint-
Leger

Leger, (Marie-Rene Auguste) Alexis Saint-
Leger 1887-1975 **CLC 11; DAM POET**
See also Perse, St.-John
See also CA 13-16R; 61-64; CANR 43; MTCW

Leger, Saintleger
See Leger, (Marie-Rene Auguste) Alexis Saint-
Leger

Le Guin, Ursula K(roeber) 1929- **CLC 8, 13,**
22, 45, 71; DAB; DAC; DAM MST, POP;
SSC 12
See also AAYA 9; AITN 1; CA 21-24R; CANR
9, 32, 52; CDALB 1968-1988; CLR 3, 28;
DLB 8, 52; INT CANR-32; JRDA; MAICYA;

Lyre, Pinchbeck
See Sassoon, Siegfried (Lorraine)
Lytle, Andrew (Nelson) 1902-1995 ... **CLC 22**
See also CA 9-12R; 150; DLB 6; DLBY 95
Lyttelton, George 1709-1773 .... **LC 10**
Maas, Peter 1929- .... **CLC 29**
See also CA 93-96; INT 93-96
Macaulay, Rose 1881-1958 .... **TCLC 7, 44**
See also CA 104; DLB 36
Macaulay, Thomas Babington 1800-1859
NCLC 42
See also CDBLB 1832-1890; DLB 32, 55
MacBeth, George (Mann) 1932-1992 **CLC 2, 5, 9**
See also CA 25-28R; 136; CANR 61; DLB 40;
MTCW; SATA 4; SATA-Obit 70
MacCaig, Norman (Alexander) 1910- **CLC 36;
DAB; DAM POET**
See also CA 9-12R; CANR 3, 34; DLB 27
MacCarthy, (Sir Charles Otto) Desmond 1877-
1952 .... **TCLC 36**
MacDiarmid, Hugh **CLC 2, 4, 11, 19, 63; PC 9**
See also Grieve, C(hristopher) M(urray)
See also CDBLB 1945-1960; DLB 20
MacDonald, Anson
See Heinlein, Robert A(nson)
Macdonald, Cynthia 1928- .... **CLC 13, 19**
See also CA 49-52; CANR 4, 44; DLB 105
MacDonald, George 1824-1905 .... **TCLC 9**
See also CA 106; 137; DLB 18, 163, 178;
MAICYA; SATA 33
Macdonald, John
See Millar, Kenneth
MacDonald, John D(ann) 1916-1986 **CLC 3, 27, 44; DAM NOV, POP**
See also CA 1-4R; 121; CANR 1, 19, 60; DLB
8; DLBY 86; MTCW
Macdonald, John Ross
See Millar, Kenneth
Macdonald, Ross .... **CLC 1, 2, 3, 14, 34, 41**
See also Millar, Kenneth
See also DLBD 6
MacDougal, John
See Blish, James (Benjamin)
MacEwen, Gwendolyn (Margaret) 1941-1987
CLC 13, 55
See also CA 9-12R; 124; CANR 7, 22; DLB
53; SATA 50; SATA-Obit 55
Macha, Karel Hynek 1810-1846 .... **NCLC 46**
Machado (y Ruiz), Antonio 1875-1939 **TCLC 3**
See also CA 104; DLB 108
Machado de Assis, Joaquim Maria 1839-1908
TCLC 10; BLC; SSC 24
See also CA 107; 153
Machen, Arthur .... **TCLC 4; SSC 20**
See also Jones, Arthur Llewellyn
See also DLB 36, 156, 178
Machiavelli, Niccolo 1469-1527 **LC 8, 36; DA;
DAB; DAC; DAM MST; WLCS**
MacInnes, Colin 1914-1976 .... **CLC 4, 23**
See also CA 69-72; 65-68; CANR 21; DLB 14;
MTCW
MacInnes, Helen (Clark) 1907-1985 **CLC 27, 39; DAM POP**
See also CA 1-4R; 117; CANR 1, 28, 58; DLB
87; MTCW; SATA 22; SATA-Obit 44
Mackay, Mary 1855-1924
See Corelli, Marie
See also CA 118
Mackenzie, Compton (Edward Montague)
1883-1972 .... **CLC 18**
See also CA 21-22; 37-40R; CAP 2; DLB 34,
100
Mackenzie, Henry 1745-1831 .... **NCLC 41**
See also DLB 39
Mackintosh, Elizabeth 1896(?)-1952

See Tey, Josephine
See also CA 110
MacLaren, James
See Grieve, C(hristopher) M(urray)
Mac Laverty, Bernard 1942- .... **CLC 31**
See also CA 116; 118; CANR 43; INT 118
MacLean, Alistair (Stuart) 1922(?)-1987 **CLC
3, 13, 50, 63; DAM POP**
See also CA 57-60; 121; CANR 28, 61; MTCW;
SATA 23; SATA-Obit 50
Maclean, Norman (Fitzroy) 1902-1990 **CLC
78; DAM POP; SSC 13**
See also CA 102; 132; CANR 49
MacLeish, Archibald 1892-1982 **CLC 3, 8, 14,
68; DAM POET**
See also CA 9-12R; 106; CANR 33; DLB 4, 7,
45; DLBY 82; MTCW
MacLennan, (John) Hugh 1907-1990 **CLC 2,
14, 92; DAC; DAM MST**
See also CA 5-8R; 142; CANR 33; DLB 68;
MTCW
MacLeod, Alistair 1936- **CLC 56; DAC; DAM
MST**
See also CA 123; DLB 60
Macleod, Fiona
See Sharp, William
MacNeice, (Frederick) Louis 1907-1963 **CLC
1, 4, 10, 53; DAB; DAM POET**
See also CA 85-88; CANR 61; DLB 10, 20;
MTCW
MacNeill, Dand
See Fraser, George MacDonald
Macpherson, James 1736-1796 .... **LC 29**
See also DLB 109
Macpherson, (Jean) Jay 1931- .... **CLC 14**
See also CA 5-8R; DLB 53
MacShane, Frank 1927- .... **CLC 39**
See also CA 9-12R; CANR 3, 33; DLB 111
Macumber, Mari
See Sandoz, Mari(e Susette)
Madach, Imre 1823-1864 .... **NCLC 19**
Madden, (Jerry) David 1933- .... **CLC 5, 15**
See also CA 1-4R; CAAS 3; CANR 4, 45; DLB
6; MTCW
Maddern, Al(an)
See Ellison, Harlan (Jay)
Madhubuti, Haki R. 1942- **CLC 6, 73; BLC;
DAM MULT, POET; PC 5**
See also Lee, Don L.
See also BW 2; CA 73-76; CANR 24, 51; DLB
5, 41; DLBD 8
Maepenn, Hugh
See Kuttner, Henry
Maepenn, K. H.
See Kuttner, Henry
Maeterlinck, Maurice 1862-1949 ... **TCLC 3;
DAM DRAM**
See also CA 104; 136; SATA 66
Maginn, William 1794-1842 .... **NCLC 8**
See also DLB 110, 159
Mahapatra, Jayanta 1928- .... **CLC 33; DAM
MULT**
See also CA 73-76; CAAS 9; CANR 15, 33
Mahfouz, Naguib (Abdel Aziz Al-Sabilgi)
1911(?)-
See Mahfuz, Najib
See also BEST 89:2; CA 128; CANR 55; DAM
NOV; MTCW
Mahfuz, Najib .... **CLC 52, 55**
See also Mahfouz, Naguib (Abdel Aziz Al-
Sabilgi)
See also DLBY 88
Mahon, Derek 1941- .... **CLC 27**
See also CA 113; 128; DLB 40
Mailer, Norman 1923- **CLC 1, 2, 3, 4, 5, 8, 11,
14, 28, 39, 74; DA; DAB; DAC; DAM MST,
NOV, POP**

See also AITN 2; CA 9-12R; CABS 1; CANR
28; CDALB 1968-1988; DLB 2, 16, 28;
DLBD 3; DLBY 80, 83; MTCW
Maillet, Antonine 1929- .... **CLC 54; DAC**
See also CA 115; 120; CANR 46; DLB 60; INT
120
Mais, Roger 1905-1955 .... **TCLC 8**
See also BW 1; CA 105; 124; DLB 125; MTCW
Maistre, Joseph de 1753-1821 .... **NCLC 37**
Maitland, Frederic 1850-1906 .... **TCLC 65**
Maitland, Sara (Louise) 1950- .... **CLC 49**
See also CA 69-72; CANR 13, 59
Major, Clarence 1936- **CLC 3, 19, 48; BLC;
DAM MULT**
See also BW 2; CA 21-24R; CAAS 6; CANR
13, 25, 53; DLB 33
Major, Kevin (Gerald) 1949- .. **CLC 26; DAC**
See also AAYA 16; CA 97-100; CANR 21, 38;
CLR 11; DLB 60; INT CANR-21; JRDA;
MAICYA; SATA 32, 82
Maki, James
See Ozu, Yasujiro
Malabaila, Damiano
See Levi, Primo
Malamud, Bernard 1914-1986 **CLC 1, 2, 3, 5,
8, 9, 11, 18, 27, 44, 78, 85; DA; DAB; DAC;
DAM MST, NOV, POP; SSC 15; WLC**
See also AAYA 16; CA 5-8R; 118; CABS 1;
CANR 28, 62; CDALB 1941-1968; DLB 2,
28, 152; DLBY 80, 86; MTCW
Malan, Herman
See Bosman, Herman Charles; Bosman, Herman
Charles
Malaparte, Curzio 1898-1957 .... **TCLC 52**
Malcolm, Dan
See Silverberg, Robert
Malcolm X .... **CLC 82; BLC; WLCS**
See also Little, Malcolm
Malherbe, Francois de 1555-1628 .... **LC 5**
Mallarme, Stephane 1842-1898 **NCLC 4, 41;
DAM POET; PC 4**
Mallet-Joris, Francoise 1930- .... **CLC 11**
See also CA 65-68; CANR 17; DLB 83
Malley, Ern
See McAuley, James Phillip
Mallowan, Agatha Christie
See Christie, Agatha (Mary Clarissa)
Maloff, Saul 1922- .... **CLC 5**
See also CA 33-36R
Malone, Louis
See MacNeice, (Frederick) Louis
Malone, Michael (Christopher) 1942- **CLC 43**
See also CA 77-80; CANR 14, 32, 57
Malory, (Sir) Thomas 1410(?)-1471(?) **LC 11;
DA; DAB; DAC; DAM MST; WLCS**
See also CDBLB Before 1660; DLB 146; SATA
59; SATA-Brief 33
Malouf, (George Joseph) David 1934- **CLC 28,
86**
See also CA 124; CANR 50
Malraux, (Georges-)Andre 1901-1976 **CLC 1,
4, 9, 13, 15, 57; DAM NOV**
See also CA 21-22; 69-72; CANR 34, 58; CAP
2; DLB 72; MTCW
Malzberg, Barry N(athaniel) 1939- ... **CLC 7**
See also CA 61-64; CAAS 4; CANR 16; DLB
8
Mamet, David (Alan) 1947- **CLC 9, 15, 34, 46,
91; DAM DRAM; DC 4**
See also AAYA 3; CA 81-84; CABS 3; CANR
15, 41; DLB 7; MTCW
Mamoulian, Rouben (Zachary) 1897-1987
CLC 16
See also CA 25-28R; 124
Mandelstam, Osip (Emilievich) 1891(?)-1938(?)
TCLC 2, 6; PC 14
See also CA 104; 150

Mander, (Mary) Jane 1877-1949 ... **TCLC 31**
Mandeville, John fl. 1350- .... **CMLC 19**
See also DLB 146
Mandiargues, Andre Pieyre de .... **CLC 41**
See also Pieyre de Mandiargues, Andre
See also DLB 83
Mandrake, Ethel Belle
See Thurman, Wallace (Henry)
Mangan, James Clarence 1803-1849**NCLC 27**
Maniere, J.-E.
See Giraudoux, (Hippolyte) Jean
Manley, (Mary) Delariviere 1672(?)-1724**L C 1**
See also DLB 39, 80
Mann, Abel
See Creasey, John
Mann, Emily 1952- ....**DC 7**
See also CA 130; CANR 55
Mann, (Luiz) Heinrich 1871-1950 ... **TCLC 9**
See also CA 106; DLB 66
Mann, (Paul) Thomas 1875-1955 **TCLC 2, 8, 14, 21, 35, 44, 60; DA; DAB; DAC; DAM MST, NOV; SSC 5; WLC**
See also CA 104; 128; DLB 66; MTCW
Mannheim, Karl 1893-1947 .... **TCLC 65**
Manning, David
See Faust, Frederick (Schiller)
Manning, Frederic 1887(?)-1935 ... **TCLC 25**
See also CA 124
Manning, Olivia 1915-1980 .... **CLC 5, 19**
See also CA 5-8R; 101; CANR 29; MTCW
Mano, D. Keith 1942- .... **CLC 2, 10**
See also CA 25-28R; CAAS 6; CANR 26, 57; DLB 6
Mansfield, Katherine**TCLC 2, 8, 39; DAB; SSC 9, 23; WLC**
See also Beauchamp, Kathleen Mansfield
See also DLB 162
Manso, Peter 1940- .... **CLC 39**
See also CA 29-32R; CANR 44
Mantecon, Juan Jimenez
See Jimenez (Mantecon), Juan Ramon
Manton, Peter
See Creasey, John
Man Without a Spleen, A
See Chekhov, Anton (Pavlovich)
Manzoni, Alessandro 1785-1873 .... **NCLC 29**
Mapu, Abraham (ben Jekutiel) 1808-1867 **NCLC 18**
Mara, Sally
See Queneau, Raymond
Marat, Jean Paul 1743-1793 ....**LC 10**
Marcel, Gabriel Honore 1889-1973 . **CLC 15**
See also CA 102; 45-48; MTCW
Marchbanks, Samuel
See Davies, (William) Robertson
Marchi, Giacomo
See Bassani, Giorgio
Margulies, Donald .... **CLC 76**
Marie de France c. 12th cent. - .... **CMLC 8**
Marie de l'Incarnation 1599-1672 ......**LC 10**
Marier, Captain Victor
See Griffith, D(avid Lewelyn) W(ark)
Mariner, Scott
See Pohl, Frederik
Marinetti, Filippo Tommaso 1876-1944**TCLC 10**
See also CA 107; DLB 114
Marivaux, Pierre Carlet de Chamblain de 1688-1763 .... **LC 4; DC 7**
Markandaya, Kamala .... **CLC 8, 38**
See also Taylor, Kamala (Purnaiya)
Markfield, Wallace 1926- .... **CLC 8**
See also CA 69-72; CAAS 3; DLB 2, 28
Markham, Edwin 1852-1940 .... **TCLC 47**
See also CA 160; DLB 54
Markham, Robert

See Amis, Kingsley (William)
Marks, J
See Highwater, Jamake (Mamake)
Marks-Highwater, J
See Highwater, Jamake (Mamake)
Markson, David M(errill) 1927- .... **CLC 67**
See also CA 49-52; CANR 1
Marley, Bob .... **CLC 17**
See also Marley, Robert Nesta
Marley, Robert Nesta 1945-1981
See Marley, Bob
See also CA 107; 103
Marlowe, Christopher 1564-1593**LC 22; DA; DAB; DAC; DAM DRAM, MST; DC 1; WLC**
See also CDBLB Before 1660; DLB 62
Marlowe, Stephen 1928-
See Queen, Ellery
See also CA 13-16R; CANR 6, 55
Marmontel, Jean-Francois 1723-1799 .. **LC 2**
Marquand, John P(hillips) 1893-1960**CLC 2, 10**
See also CA 85-88; DLB 9, 102
Marques, Rene 1919-1979 ..... **CLC 96; DAM MULT; HLC**
See also CA 97-100; 85-88; DLB 113; HW
Marquez, Gabriel (Jose) Garcia
See Garcia Marquez, Gabriel (Jose)
Marquis, Don(ald Robert Perry) 1878-1937 **TCLC 7**
See also CA 104; DLB 11, 25
Marric, J. J.
See Creasey, John
Marrow, Bernard
See Moore, Brian
Marryat, Frederick 1792-1848 .... **NCLC 3**
See also DLB 21, 163
Marsden, James
See Creasey, John
Marsh, (Edith) Ngaio 1899-1982 **CLC 7, 53; DAM POP**
See also CA 9-12R; CANR 6, 58; DLB 77; MTCW
Marshall, Garry 1934- .... **CLC 17**
See also AAYA 3; CA 111; SATA 60
Marshall, Paule 1929-**CLC 27, 72; BLC; DAM MULT; SSC 3**
See also BW 2; CA 77-80; CANR 25; DLB 157; MTCW
Marsten, Richard
See Hunter, Evan
Marston, John 1576-1634**LC 33; DAM DRAM**
See also DLB 58, 172
Martha, Henry
See Harris, Mark
Marti, Jose 1853-1895**NCLC 63; DAM MULT; HLC**
Martial c. 40-c. 104 .... **PC 10**
Martin, Ken
See Hubbard, L(afayette) Ron(ald)
Martin, Richard
See Creasey, John
Martin, Steve 1945- .... **CLC 30**
See also CA 97-100; CANR 30; MTCW
Martin, Valerie 1948- .... **CLC 89**
See also BEST 90:2; CA 85-88; CANR 49
Martin, Violet Florence 1862-1915 **TCLC 51**
Martin, Webber
See Silverberg, Robert
Martindale, Patrick Victor
See White, Patrick (Victor Martindale)
Martin du Gard, Roger 1881-1958 **TCLC 24**
See also CA 118; DLB 65
Martineau, Harriet 1802-1876 .... **NCLC 26**
See also DLB 21, 55, 159, 163, 166; YABC 2
Martines, Julia
See O'Faolain, Julia

Martinez, Enrique Gonzalez
See Gonzalez Martinez, Enrique
Martinez, Jacinto Benavente y
See Benavente (y Martinez), Jacinto
Martinez Ruiz, Jose 1873-1967
See Azorin; Ruiz, Jose Martinez
See also CA 93-96; HW
Martinez Sierra, Gregorio 1881-1947**TCLC 6**
See also CA 115
Martinez Sierra, Maria (de la O'LeJarraga) 1874-1974 .... **TCLC 6**
See also CA 115
Martinsen, Martin
See Follett, Ken(neth Martin)
Martinson, Harry (Edmund) 1904-1978**C L C 14**
See also CA 77-80; CANR 34
Marut, Ret
See Traven, B.
Marut, Robert
See Traven, B.
Marvell, Andrew 1621-1678**LC 4; DA; DAB; DAC; DAM MST, POET; PC 10; WLC**
See also CDBLB 1660-1789; DLB 131
Marx, Karl (Heinrich) 1818-1883 . **NCLC 17**
See also DLB 129
Masaoka Shiki .... **TCLC 18**
See also Masaoka Tsunenori
Masaoka Tsunenori 1867-1902
See Masaoka Shiki
See also CA 117
Masefield, John (Edward) 1878-1967**CLC 11, 47; DAM POET**
See also CA 19-20; 25-28R; CANR 33; CAP 2; CDBLB 1890-1914; DLB 10, 19, 153, 160; MTCW; SATA 19
Maso, Carole 19(?)- .... **CLC 44**
Mason, Bobbie Ann 1940-**CLC 28, 43, 82; SSC 4**
See also AAYA 5; CA 53-56; CANR 11, 31, 58; DLB 173; DLBY 87; INT CANR-31; MTCW
Mason, Ernst
See Pohl, Frederik
Mason, Lee W.
See Malzberg, Barry N(athaniel)
Mason, Nick 1945- .... **CLC 35**
Mason, Tally
See Derleth, August (William)
Mass, William
See Gibson, William
Masters, Edgar Lee 1868-1950 **TCLC 2, 25; DA; DAC; DAM MST, POET; PC 1; WLCS**
See also CA 104; 133; CDALB 1865-1917; DLB 54; MTCW
Masters, Hilary 1928- .... **CLC 48**
See also CA 25-28R; CANR 13, 47
Mastrosimone, William 19(?)- .... **CLC 36**
Mathe, Albert
See Camus, Albert
Mather, Cotton 1663-1728 .... **LC 38**
See also CDALB 1640-1865; DLB 24, 30, 140
Mather, Increase 1639-1723 .... **LC 38**
See also DLB 24
Matheson, Richard Burton 1926- ..... **CLC 37**
See also CA 97-100; DLB 8, 44; INT 97-100
Mathews, Harry 1930- .... **CLC 6, 52**
See also CA 21-24R; CAAS 6; CANR 18, 40
Mathews, John Joseph 1894-1979 .. **CLC 84; DAM MULT**
See also CA 19-20; 142; CANR 45; CAP 2; DLB 175; NNAL
Mathias, Roland (Glyn) 1915- .... **CLC 45**
See also CA 97-100; CANR 19, 41; DLB 27
Matsuo Basho 1644-1694 .... **PC 3**
See also DAM POET

See Bakhtin, Mikhail Mikhailovich

Meged, Aharon
See Megged, Aharon

Meged, Aron
See Megged, Aharon

Megged, Aharon 1920- .... CLC 9
See also CA 49-52; CAAS 13; CANR 1

Mehta, Ved (Parkash) 1934- .... CLC 37
See also CA 1-4R; CANR 2, 23; MTCW

Melanter
See Blackmore, R(ichard) D(oddridge)

Melikow, Loris
See Hofmannsthal, Hugo von

Melmoth, Sebastian
See Wilde, Oscar (Fingal O'Flahertie Wills)

Meltzer, Milton 1915- .... CLC 26
See also AAYA 8; CA 13-16R; CANR 38; CLR 13; DLB 61; JRDA; MAICYA; SAAS 1; SATA 1, 50, 80

Melville, Herman 1819-1891NCLC 3, 12, 29, 45, 49; DA; DAB; DAC; DAM MST, NOV; SSC 1, 17; WLC
See also CDALB 1640-1865; DLB 3, 74; SATA 59

Menander c. 342B.C.-c. 292B.C. .... CMLC 9; DAM DRAM; DC 3
See also DLB 176

Mencken, H(enry) L(ouis) 1880-1956 T C L C 13
See also CA 105; 125; CDALB 1917-1929; DLB 11, 29, 63, 137; MTCW

Mendelsohn, Jane 1965(?)- .... CLC 99
See also CA 154

Mercer, David 1928-1980CLC 5; DAM DRAM
See also CA 9-12R; 102; CANR 23; DLB 13; MTCW

Merchant, Paul
See Ellison, Harlan (Jay)

Meredith, George 1828-1909 . TCLC 17, 43; DAM POET
See also CA 117; 153; CDBLB 1832-1890; DLB 18, 35, 57, 159

Meredith, William (Morris) 1919-CLC 4, 13, 22, 55; DAM POET
See also CA 9-12R; CAAS 14; CANR 6, 40; DLB 5

Merezhkovsky, Dmitry Sergeyevich 1865-1941 TCLC 29

Merimee, Prosper 1803-1870NCLC 6, 65; SSC 7
See also DLB 119

Merkin, Daphne 1954- .... CLC 44
See also CA 123

Merlin, Arthur
See Blish, James (Benjamin)

Merrill, James (Ingram) 1926-1995CLC 2, 3, 6, 8, 13, 18, 34, 91; DAM POET
See also CA 13-16R; 147; CANR 10, 49; DLB 5, 165; DLBY 85; INT CANR-10; MTCW

Merriman, Alex
See Silverberg, Robert

Merritt, E. B.
See Waddington, Miriam

Merton, Thomas 1915-1968 CLC 1, 3, 11, 34, 83; PC 10
See also CA 5-8R; 25-28R; CANR 22, 53; DLB 48; DLBY 81; MTCW

Merwin, W(illiam) S(tanley) 1927- CLC 1, 2, 3, 5, 8, 13, 18, 45, 88; DAM POET
See also CA 13-16R; CANR 15, 51; DLB 5, 169; INT CANR-15; MTCW

Metcalf, John 1938- .... CLC 37
See also CA 113; DLB 60

Metcalf, Suzanne
See Baum, L(yman) Frank

Mew, Charlotte (Mary) 1870-1928 .. TCLC 8
See also CA 105; DLB 19, 135

Mewshaw, Michael 1943- .... CLC 9
See also CA 53-56; CANR 7, 47; DLBY 80

Meyer, June
See Jordan, June

Meyer, Lynn
See Slavitt, David R(ytman)

Meyer-Meyrink, Gustav 1868-1932
See Meyrink, Gustav
See also CA 117

Meyers, Jeffrey 1939- .... CLC 39
See also CA 73-76; CANR 54; DLB 111

Meynell, Alice (Christina Gertrude Thompson) 1847-1922 .... TCLC 6
See also CA 104; DLB 19, 98

Meyrink, Gustav .... TCLC 21
See also Meyer-Meyrink, Gustav
See also DLB 81

Michaels, Leonard 1933- CLC 6, 25; SSC 16
See also CA 61-64; CANR 21, 62; DLB 130; MTCW

Michaux, Henri 1899-1984 .... CLC 8, 19
See also CA 85-88; 114

Micheaux, Oscar 1884-1951 .... TCLC 76
See also DLB 50

Michelangelo 1475-1564 .... LC 12

Michelet, Jules 1798-1874 .... NCLC 31

Michener, James A(lbert) 1907(?)- CLC 1, 5, 11, 29, 60; DAM NOV, POP
See also AITN 1; BEST 90:1; CA 5-8R; CANR 21, 45; DLB 6; MTCW

Mickiewicz, Adam 1798-1855 .... NCLC 3

Middleton, Christopher 1926- .... CLC 13
See also CA 13-16R; CANR 29, 54; DLB 40

Middleton, Richard (Barham) 1882-1911 TCLC 56
See also DLB 156

Middleton, Stanley 1919- .... CLC 7, 38
See also CA 25-28R; CAAS 23; CANR 21, 46; DLB 14

Middleton, Thomas 1580-1627 LC 33; DAM DRAM, MST; DC 5
See also DLB 58

Migueis, Jose Rodrigues 1901- .... CLC 10

Mikszath, Kalman 1847-1910 .... TCLC 31

Miles, Jack .... CLC 100

Miles, Josephine (Louise) 1911-1985CLC 1, 2, 14, 34, 39; DAM POET
See also CA 1-4R; 116; CANR 2, 55; DLB 48

Militant
See Sandburg, Carl (August)

Mill, John Stuart 1806-1873 .... NCLC 11, 58
See also CDBLB 1832-1890; DLB 55

Millar, Kenneth 1915-1983 .... CLC 14; DAM POP
See also Macdonald, Ross
See also CA 9-12R; 110; CANR 16; DLB 2; DLBD 6; DLBY 83; MTCW

Millay, E. Vincent
See Millay, Edna St. Vincent

Millay, Edna St. Vincent 1892-1950 TCLC 4, 49; DA; DAB; DAC; DAM MST, POET; PC 6; WLCS
See also CA 104; 130; CDALB 1917-1929; DLB 45; MTCW

Miller, Arthur 1915-CLC 1, 2, 6, 10, 15, 26, 47, 78; DA; DAB; DAC; DAM DRAM, MST; DC 1; WLC
See also AAYA 15; AITN 1; CA 1-4R; CABS 3; CANR 2, 30, 54; CDALB 1941-1968; DLB 7; MTCW

Miller, Henry (Valentine) 1891-1980CLC 1, 2, 4, 9, 14, 43, 84; DA; DAB; DAC; DAM MST, NOV; WLC
See also CA 9-12R; 97-100; CANR 33; CDALB 1929-1941; DLB 4, 9; DLBY 80; MTCW

Miller, Jason 1939(?)- .... CLC 2
See also AITN 1; CA 73-76; DLB 7

Miller, Sue 1943- .... CLC 44; DAM POP
See also BEST 90:3; CA 139; CANR 59; DLB 143

Miller, Walter M(ichael, Jr.) 1923-CLC 4, 30
See also CA 85-88; DLB 8

Millett, Kate 1934- .... CLC 67
See also AITN 1; CA 73-76; CANR 32, 53; MTCW

Millhauser, Steven 1943- .... CLC 21, 54
See also CA 110; 111; DLB 2; INT 111

Millin, Sarah Gertrude 1889-1968 ... CLC 49
See also CA 102; 93-96

Milne, A(lan) A(lexander) 1882-1956TCLC 6; DAB; DAC; DAM MST
See also CA 104; 133; CLR 1, 26; DLB 10, 77, 100, 160; MAICYA; MTCW; YABC 1

Milner, Ron(ald) 1938- CLC 56; BLC; DAM MULT
See also AITN 1; BW 1; CA 73-76; CANR 24; DLB 38; MTCW

Milnes, Richard Monckton 1809-1885 N C L C 61
See also DLB 32, 184

Milosz, Czeslaw 1911- CLC 5, 11, 22, 31, 56, 82; DAM MST, POET; PC 8; WLCS
See also CA 81-84; CANR 23, 51; MTCW

Milton, John 1608-1674 ..... LC 9; DA; DAB; DAC; DAM MST, POET; PC 19; WLC
See also CDBLB 1660-1789; DLB 131, 151

Min, Anchee 1957- .... CLC 86
See also CA 146

Minehaha, Cornelius
See Wedekind, (Benjamin) Frank(lin)

Miner, Valerie 1947- .... CLC 40
See also CA 97-100; CANR 59

Minimo, Duca
See D'Annunzio, Gabriele

Minot, Susan 1956- .... CLC 44
See also CA 134

Minus, Ed 1938- .... CLC 39

Miranda, Javier
See Bioy Casares, Adolfo

Mirbeau, Octave 1848-1917 .... TCLC 55
See also DLB 123

Miro (Ferrer), Gabriel (Francisco Victor) 1879-1930 .... TCLC 5
See also CA 104

Mishima, Yukio 1925-1970CLC 2, 4, 6, 9, 27; DC 1; SSC 4
See also Hiraoka, Kimitake
See also DLB 182

Mistral, Frederic 1830-1914........... TCLC 51
See also CA 122

Mistral, Gabriela .... TCLC 2; HLC
See also Godoy Alcayaga, Lucila

Mistry, Rohinton 1952- .... CLC 71; DAC
See also CA 141

Mitchell, Clyde
See Ellison, Harlan (Jay); Silverberg, Robert

Mitchell, James Leslie 1901-1935
See Gibbon, Lewis Grassic
See also CA 104; DLB 15

Mitchell, Joni 1943- .... CLC 12
See also CA 112

Mitchell, Joseph (Quincy) 1908-1996CLC 98
See also CA 77-80; 152; DLBY 96

Mitchell, Margaret (Munnerlyn) 1900-1949 TCLC 11; DAM NOV, POP
See also CA 109; 125; CANR 55; DLB 9; MTCW

Mitchell, Peggy
See Mitchell, Margaret (Munnerlyn)

Mitchell, S(ilas) Weir 1829-1914 ... TCLC 36

Mitchell, W(illiam) O(rmond) 1914-CLC 25; DAC; DAM MST
See also CA 77-80; CANR 15, 43; DLB 88

Mitford, Mary Russell 1787-1855 ... NCLC 4

Roussel, Raymond 1877-1933 .... **TCLC 20**
See also CA 117
Rovit, Earl (Herbert) 1927- .... **CLC 7**
See also CA 5-8R; CANR 12
Rowe, Nicholas 1674-1718 .... **LC 8**
See also DLB 84
Rowley, Ames Dorrance
See Lovecraft, H(oward) P(hillips)
Rowson, Susanna Haswell 1762(?)-1824
NCLC 5
See also DLB 37
Roy, Gabrielle 1909-1983 **CLC 10, 14; DAB;
DAC; DAM MST**
See also CA 53-56; 110; CANR 5, 61; DLB 68;
MTCW
Rozewicz, Tadeusz 1921- .. **CLC 9, 23; DAM
POET**
See also CA 108; CANR 36; MTCW
Ruark, Gibbons 1941- .... **CLC 3**
See also CA 33-36R; CAAS 23; CANR 14, 31,
57; DLB 120
Rubens, Bernice (Ruth) 1923- .... **CLC 19, 31**
See also CA 25-28R; CANR 33; DLB 14;
MTCW
Rubin, Harold
See Robbins, Harold
Rudkin, (James) David 1936- .... **CLC 14**
See also CA 89-92; DLB 13
Rudnik, Raphael 1933- .... **CLC 7**
See also CA 29-32R
Ruffian, M.
See Hasek, Jaroslav (Matej Frantisek)
Ruiz, Jose Martinez .... **CLC 11**
See also Martinez Ruiz, Jose
Rukeyser, Muriel 1913-1980 **CLC 6, 10, 15, 27;
DAM POET; PC 12**
See also CA 5-8R; 93-96; CANR 26, 60; DLB
48; MTCW; SATA-Obit 22
Rule, Jane (Vance) 1931- .... **CLC 27**
See also CA 25-28R; CAAS 18; CANR 12; DLB
60
Rulfo, Juan 1918-1986 ...... **CLC 8, 80; DAM
MULT; HLC; SSC 25**
See also CA 85-88; 118; CANR 26; DLB 113;
HW; MTCW
Rumi, Jalal al-Din 1297-1373 .... **CMLC 20**
Runeberg, Johan 1804-1877 .... **NCLC 41**
Runyon, (Alfred) Damon 1884(?)-1946 **T C L C
10**
See also CA 107; DLB 11, 86, 171
Rush, Norman 1933- .... **CLC 44**
See also CA 121; 126; INT 126
Rushdie, (Ahmed) Salman 1947- **CLC 23, 31,
55, 100; DAB; DAC; DAM MST, NOV,
POP; WLCS**
See also BEST 89:3; CA 108; 111; CANR 33,
56; INT 111; MTCW
Rushforth, Peter (Scott) 1945- .... **CLC 19**
See also CA 101
Ruskin, John 1819-1900 .... **TCLC 63**
See also CA 114; 129; CDBLB 1832-1890;
DLB 55, 163; SATA 24
Russ, Joanna 1937- .... **CLC 15**
See also CA 25-28R; CANR 11, 31; DLB 8;
MTCW
Russell, George William 1867-1935
See Baker, Jean H.
See also CA 104; 153; CDBLB 1890-1914;
DAM POET
Russell, (Henry) Ken(neth Alfred) 1927- **C L C
16**
See also CA 105
Russell, Willy 1947- .... **CLC 60**
Rutherford, Mark .... **TCLC 25**
See also White, William Hale
See also DLB 18
Ruyslinck, Ward 1929- .... **CLC 14**

See also Belser, Reimond Karel Maria de
Ryan, Cornelius (John) 1920-1974 ..... **CLC 7**
See also CA 69-72; 53-56; CANR 38
Ryan, Michael 1946- .... **CLC 65**
See also CA 49-52; DLBY 82
Ryan, Tim
See Dent, Lester
Rybakov, Anatoli (Naumovich) 1911-**CLC 23,
53**
See also CA 126; 135; SATA 79
Ryder, Jonathan
See Ludlum, Robert
Ryga, George 1932-1987**CLC 14; DAC; DAM
MST**
See also CA 101; 124; CANR 43; DLB 60
S. H.
See Hartmann, Sadakichi
S. S.
See Sassoon, Siegfried (Lorraine)
Saba, Umberto 1883-1957 .... **TCLC 33**
See also CA 144; DLB 114
Sabatini, Rafael 1875-1950 .... **TCLC 47**
Sabato, Ernesto (R.) 1911-**CLC 10, 23; DAM
MULT; HLC**
See also CA 97-100; CANR 32; DLB 145; HW;
MTCW
Sacastru, Martin
See Bioy Casares, Adolfo
Sacher-Masoch, Leopold von 1836(?)-1895
NCLC 31
Sachs, Marilyn (Stickle) 1927- .... **CLC 35**
See also AAYA 2; CA 17-20R; CANR 13, 47;
CLR 2; JRDA; MAICYA; SAAS 2; SATA 3,
68
Sachs, Nelly 1891-1970 .... **CLC 14, 98**
See also CA 17-18; 25-28R; CAP 2
Sackler, Howard (Oliver) 1929-1982 **CLC 14**
See also CA 61-64; 108; CANR 30; DLB 7
Sacks, Oliver (Wolf) 1933- .... **CLC 67**
See also CA 53-56; CANR 28, 50; INT CANR-
28; MTCW
Sadakichi
See Hartmann, Sadakichi
Sade, Donatien Alphonse Francois Comte 1740-
1814 .... **NCLC 47**
Sadoff, Ira 1945- .... **CLC 9**
See also CA 53-56; CANR 5, 21; DLB 120
Saetone
See Camus, Albert
Safire, William 1929- .... **CLC 10**
See also CA 17-20R; CANR 31, 54
Sagan, Carl (Edward) 1934-1996 ..... **CLC 30**
See also AAYA 2; CA 25-28R; 155; CANR 11,
36; MTCW; SATA 58; SATA-Obit 94
Sagan, Francoise .... **CLC 3, 6, 9, 17, 36**
See also Quoirez, Francoise
See also DLB 83
Sahgal, Nayantara (Pandit) 1927- .... **CLC 41**
See also CA 9-12R; CANR 11
Saint, H(arry) F. 1941- .... **CLC 50**
See also CA 127
St. Aubin de Teran, Lisa 1953-
See Teran, Lisa St. Aubin de
See also CA 118; 126; INT 126
Saint Birgitta of Sweden c. 1303-1373**C M L C
24**
Sainte-Beuve, Charles Augustin 1804-1869
NCLC 5
**Saint-Exupery, Antoine (Jean Baptiste Marie
Roger) de** 1900-1944**TCLC 2, 56; DAM
NOV; WLC**
See also CA 108; 132; CLR 10; DLB 72;
MAICYA; MTCW; SATA 20
St. John, David
See Hunt, E(verette) Howard, (Jr.)
Saint-John Perse
See Leger, (Marie-Rene Auguste) Alexis Saint-

Leger
Saintsbury, George (Edward Bateman) 1845-
1933 .... **TCLC 31**
See also CA 160; DLB 57, 149
Sait Faik .... **TCLC 23**
See also Abasiyanik, Sait Faik
Saki .... **TCLC 3; SSC 12**
See also Munro, H(ector) H(ugh)
Sala, George Augustus .... **NCLC 46**
Salama, Hannu 1936- .... **CLC 18**
Salamanca, J(ack) R(ichard) 1922-**CLC 4, 15**
See also CA 25-28R
Sale, J. Kirkpatrick
See Sale, Kirkpatrick
Sale, Kirkpatrick 1937- .... **CLC 68**
See also CA 13-16R; CANR 10
Salinas, Luis Omar 1937- ...... **CLC 90; DAM
MULT; HLC**
See also CA 131; DLB 82; HW
Salinas (y Serrano), Pedro 1891(?)-1951
TCLC 17
See also CA 117; DLB 134
Salinger, J(erome) D(avid) 1919-**CLC 1, 3, 8,
12, 55, 56; DA; DAB; DAC; DAM MST,
NOV, POP; SSC 2, 28; WLC**
See also AAYA 2; CA 5-8R; CANR 39; CDALB
1941-1968; CLR 18; DLB 2, 102, 173;
MAICYA; MTCW; SATA 67
Salisbury, John
See Caute, David
Salter, James 1925- .... **CLC 7, 52, 59**
See also CA 73-76; DLB 130
Saltus, Edgar (Everton) 1855-1921 . **TCLC 8**
See also CA 105
Saltykov, Mikhail Evgrafovich 1826-1889
NCLC 16
Samarakis, Antonis 1919- .... **CLC 5**
See also CA 25-28R; CAAS 16; CANR 36
Sanchez, Florencio 1875-1910 .... **TCLC 37**
See also CA 153; HW
Sanchez, Luis Rafael 1936- .... **CLC 23**
See also CA 128; DLB 145; HW
Sanchez, Sonia 1934- ..... **CLC 5; BLC; DAM
MULT; PC 9**
See also BW 2; CA 33-36R; CANR 24, 49; CLR
18; DLB 41; DLBD 8; MAICYA; MTCW;
SATA 22
Sand, George 1804-1876**NCLC 2, 42, 57; DA;
DAB; DAC; DAM MST, NOV; WLC**
See also DLB 119
Sandburg, Carl (August) 1878-1967**CLC 1, 4,
10, 15, 35; DA; DAB; DAC; DAM MST,
POET; PC 2; WLC**
See also CA 5-8R; 25-28R; CANR 35; CDALB
1865-1917; DLB 17, 54; MAICYA; MTCW;
SATA 8
Sandburg, Charles
See Sandburg, Carl (August)
Sandburg, Charles A.
See Sandburg, Carl (August)
Sanders, (James) Ed(ward) 1939- .... **CLC 53**
See also CA 13-16R; CAAS 21; CANR 13, 44;
DLB 16
Sanders, Lawrence 1920-**CLC 41; DAM POP**
See also BEST 89:4; CA 81-84; CANR 33, 62;
MTCW
Sanders, Noah
See Blount, Roy (Alton), Jr.
Sanders, Winston P.
See Anderson, Poul (William)
Sandoz, Mari(e Susette) 1896-1966 .. **CLC 28**
See also CA 1-4R; 25-28R; CANR 17; DLB 9;
MTCW; SATA 5
Saner, Reg(inald Anthony) 1931- .... **CLC 9**
See also CA 65-68
Sannazaro, Jacopo 1456(?)-1530 .... **LC 8**
Sansom, William 1912-1976 **CLC 2, 6; DAM**

Shue, Larry 1946-1985**CLC 52; DAM DRAM**
See also CA 145; 117
Shu-Jen, Chou 1881-1936
See Lu Hsun
See also CA 104
Shulman, Alix Kates 1932- .... **CLC 2, 10**
See also CA 29-32R; CANR 43; SATA 7
Shuster, Joe 1914- .... **CLC 21**
Shute, Nevil .... **CLC 30**
See also Norway, Nevil Shute
Shuttle, Penelope (Diane) 1947- .... **CLC 7**
See also CA 93-96; CANR 39; DLB 14, 40
Sidney, Mary 1561-1621 .... **LC 19, 39**
Sidney, Sir Philip 1554-1586 **LC 19, 39; DA;**
DAB; DAC; DAM MST, POET
See also CDBLB Before 1660; DLB 167
Siegel, Jerome 1914-1996 .... **CLC 21**
See also CA 116; 151
Siegel, Jerry
See Siegel, Jerome
Sienkiewicz, Henryk (Adam Alexander Pius)
1846-1916 .... **TCLC 3**
See also CA 104; 134
Sierra, Gregorio Martinez
See Martinez Sierra, Gregorio
Sierra, Maria (de la O'LeJarraga) Martinez
See Martinez Sierra, Maria (de la O'LeJarraga)
Sigal, Clancy 1926- .... **CLC 7**
See also CA 1-4R
Sigourney, Lydia Howard (Huntley) 1791-1865
NCLC 21
See also DLB 1, 42, 73
Siguenza y Gongora, Carlos de 1645-1700**L C**
8
Sigurjonsson, Johann 1880-1919 ... **TCLC 27**
Sikelianos, Angelos 1884-1951 .... **TCLC 39**
Silkin, Jon 1930- .... **CLC 2, 6, 43**
See also CA 5-8R; CAAS 5; DLB 27
Silko, Leslie (Marmon) 1948-**CLC 23, 74; DA;**
DAC; DAM MST, MULT, POP; WLCS
See also AAYA 14; CA 115; 122; CANR 45;
DLB 143, 175; NNAL
Sillanpaa, Frans Eemil 1888-1964 ... **CLC 19**
See also CA 129; 93-96; MTCW
Sillitoe, Alan 1928- ... **CLC 1, 3, 6, 10, 19, 57**
See also AITN 1; CA 9-12R; CAAS 2; CANR
8, 26, 55; CDBLB 1960 to Present; DLB 14,
139; MTCW; SATA 61
Silone, Ignazio 1900-1978 .... **CLC 4**
See also CA 25-28; 81-84; CANR 34; CAP 2;
MTCW
Silver, Joan Micklin 1935- .... **CLC 20**
See also CA 114; 121; INT 121
Silver, Nicholas
See Faust, Frederick (Schiller)
Silverberg, Robert 1935- **CLC 7; DAM POP**
See also CA 1-4R; CAAS 3; CANR 1, 20, 36;
DLB 8; INT CANR-20; MAICYA; MTCW;
SATA 13, 91
Silverstein, Alvin 1933- .... **CLC 17**
See also CA 49-52; CANR 2; CLR 25; JRDA;
MAICYA; SATA 8, 69
Silverstein, Virginia B(arbara Opshelor) 1937-
CLC 17
See also CA 49-52; CANR 2; CLR 25; JRDA;
MAICYA; SATA 8, 69
Sim, Georges
See Simenon, Georges (Jacques Christian)
Simak, Clifford D(onald) 1904-1988**CLC 1, 55**
See also CA 1-4R; 125; CANR 1, 35; DLB 8;
MTCW; SATA-Obit 56
Simenon, Georges (Jacques Christian) 1903-
1989 .. **CLC 1, 2, 3, 8, 18, 47; DAM POP**
See also CA 85-88; 129; CANR 35; DLB 72;
DLBY 89; MTCW
Simic, Charles 1938- .... **CLC 6, 9, 22, 49, 68;**
DAM POET

See also CA 29-32R; CAAS 4; CANR 12, 33,
52, 61; DLB 105
Simmel, Georg 1858-1918 .... **TCLC 64**
See also CA 157
Simmons, Charles (Paul) 1924- .... **CLC 57**
See also CA 89-92; INT 89-92
Simmons, Dan 1948- ..... **CLC 44; DAM POP**
See also AAYA 16; CA 138; CANR 53
Simmons, James (Stewart Alexander) 1933-
CLC 43
See also CA 105; CAAS 21; DLB 40
Simms, William Gilmore 1806-1870 **NCLC 3**
See also DLB 3, 30, 59, 73
Simon, Carly 1945- .... **CLC 26**
See also CA 105
Simon, Claude 1913- **CLC 4, 9, 15, 39; DAM**
NOV
See also CA 89-92; CANR 33; DLB 83; MTCW
Simon, (Marvin) Neil 1927-**CLC 6, 11, 31, 39,**
70; DAM DRAM
See also AITN 1; CA 21-24R; CANR 26, 54;
DLB 7; MTCW
Simon, Paul (Frederick) 1941(?)- ..... **CLC 17**
See also CA 116; 153
Simonon, Paul 1956(?)- .... **CLC 30**
Simpson, Harriette
See Arnow, Harriette (Louisa) Simpson
Simpson, Louis (Aston Marantz) 1923-**CLC 4,**
7, 9, 32; DAM POET
See also CA 1-4R; CAAS 4; CANR 1, 61; DLB
5; MTCW
Simpson, Mona (Elizabeth) 1957- .... **CLC 44**
See also CA 122; 135
Simpson, N(orman) F(rederick) 1919-**CLC 29**
See also CA 13-16R; DLB 13
Sinclair, Andrew (Annandale) 1935-. **CLC 2,**
14
See also CA 9-12R; CAAS 5; CANR 14, 38;
DLB 14; MTCW
Sinclair, Emil
See Hesse, Hermann
Sinclair, Iain 1943- .... **CLC 76**
See also CA 132
Sinclair, Iain MacGregor
See Sinclair, Iain
Sinclair, Irene
See Griffith, D(avid Lewelyn) W(ark)
Sinclair, Mary Amelia St. Clair 1865(?)-1946
See Sinclair, May
See also CA 104
Sinclair, May .... **TCLC 3, 11**
See also Sinclair, Mary Amelia St. Clair
See also DLB 36, 135
Sinclair, Roy
See Griffith, D(avid Lewelyn) W(ark)
Sinclair, Upton (Beall) 1878-1968 **CLC 1, 11,**
15, 63; DA; DAB; DAC; DAM MST, NOV;
WLC
See also CA 5-8R; 25-28R; CANR 7; CDALB
1929-1941; DLB 9; INT CANR-7; MTCW;
SATA 9
Singer, Isaac
See Singer, Isaac Bashevis
Singer, Isaac Bashevis 1904-1991**CLC 1, 3, 6,**
9, 11, 15, 23, 38, 69; DA; DAB; DAC; DAM
MST, NOV; SSC 3; WLC
See also AITN 1, 2; CA 1-4R; 134; CANR 1,
39; CDALB 1941-1968; CLR 1; DLB 6, 28,
52; DLBY 91; JRDA; MAICYA; MTCW;
SATA 3, 27; SATA-Obit 68
Singer, Israel Joshua 1893-1944 .... **TCLC 33**
Singh, Khushwant 1915- .... **CLC 11**
See also CA 9-12R; CAAS 9; CANR 6
Singleton, Ann
See Benedict, Ruth (Fulton)
Sinjohn, John
See Galsworthy, John

Sinyavsky, Andrei (Donatevich) 1925-1997
CLC 8
See also CA 85-88; 159
Sirin, V.
See Nabokov, Vladimir (Vladimirovich)
Sissman, L(ouis) E(dward) 1928-1976**CLC 9,**
18
See also CA 21-24R; 65-68; CANR 13; DLB 5
Sisson, C(harles) H(ubert) 1914- .... **CLC 8**
See also CA 1-4R; CAAS 3; CANR 3, 48; DLB
27
Sitwell, Dame Edith 1887-1964 **CLC 2, 9, 67;**
DAM POET; PC 3
See also CA 9-12R; CANR 35; CDBLB 1945-
1960; DLB 20; MTCW
Siwaarmill, H. P.
See Sharp, William
Sjoewall, Maj 1935- .... **CLC 7**
See also CA 65-68
Sjowall, Maj
See Sjoewall, Maj
Skelton, Robin 1925-1997 .... **CLC 13**
See also AITN 2; CA 5-8R; 160; CAAS 5;
CANR 28; DLB 27, 53
Skolimowski, Jerzy 1938- .... **CLC 20**
See also CA 128
Skram, Amalie (Bertha) 1847-1905**TCLC 25**
Skvorecky, Josef (Vaclav) 1924- **CLC 15, 39,**
69; DAC; DAM NOV
See also CA 61-64; CAAS 1; CANR 10, 34;
MTCW
Slade, Bernard .... **CLC 11, 46**
See also Newbound, Bernard Slade
See also CAAS 9; DLB 53
Slaughter, Carolyn 1946- .... **CLC 56**
See also CA 85-88
Slaughter, Frank G(ill) 1908- .... **CLC 29**
See also AITN 2; CA 5-8R; CANR 5; INT
CANR-5
Slavitt, David R(ytman) 1935- ...... **CLC 5, 14**
See also CA 21-24R; CAAS 3; CANR 41; DLB
5, 6
Slesinger, Tess 1905-1945 .... **TCLC 10**
See also CA 107; DLB 102
Slessor, Kenneth 1901-1971 .... **CLC 14**
See also CA 102; 89-92
Slowacki, Juliusz 1809-1849 .... **NCLC 15**
Smart, Christopher 1722-1771 .. **LC 3; DAM**
POET; PC 13
See also DLB 109
Smart, Elizabeth 1913-1986 .... **CLC 54**
See also CA 81-84; 118; DLB 88
Smiley, Jane (Graves) 1949-**CLC 53, 76; DAM**
POP
See also CA 104; CANR 30, 50; INT CANR-
30
Smith, A(rthur) J(ames) M(arshall) 1902-1980
CLC 15; DAC
See also CA 1-4R; 102; CANR 4; DLB 88
Smith, Adam 1723-1790 .... **LC 36**
See also DLB 104
Smith, Alexander 1829-1867 .... **NCLC 59**
See also DLB 32, 55
Smith, Anna Deavere 1950- .... **CLC 86**
See also CA 133
Smith, Betty (Wehner) 1896-1972 .... **CLC 19**
See also CA 5-8R; 33-36R; DLBY 82; SATA 6
Smith, Charlotte (Turner) 1749-1806 **N C L C**
23
See also DLB 39, 109
Smith, Clark Ashton 1893-1961 .... **CLC 43**
See also CA 143
Smith, Dave .... **CLC 22, 42**
See also Smith, David (Jeddie)
See also CAAS 7; DLB 5
Smith, David (Jeddie) 1942-
See Smith, Dave

See also CA 5-8R; 112; CANR 31; DLB 9, 48, 102; DLBY 84; SATA 2; SATA-Obit 36

Sturgeon, Theodore (Hamilton) 1918-1985 **CLC 22, 39**
See also Queen, Ellery
See also CA 81-84; 116; CANR 32; DLB 8; DLBY 85; MTCW

Sturges, Preston 1898-1959 .... **TCLC 48**
See also CA 114; 149; DLB 26

Styron, William 1925- **CLC 1, 3, 5, 11, 15, 60; DAM NOV, POP; SSC 25**
See also BEST 90:4; CA 5-8R; CANR 6, 33; CDALB 1968-1988; DLB 2, 143; DLBY 80; INT CANR-6; MTCW

Suarez Lynch, B.
See Bioy Casares, Adolfo; Borges, Jorge Luis

Su Chien 1884-1918
See Su Man-shu
See also CA 123

Suckow, Ruth 1892-1960 .... **SSC 18**
See also CA 113; DLB 9, 102

Sudermann, Hermann 1857-1928 .. **TCLC 15**
See also CA 107; DLB 118

Sue, Eugene 1804-1857 .... **NCLC 1**
See also DLB 119

Sueskind, Patrick 1949- .... **CLC 44**
See also Suskind, Patrick

Sukenick, Ronald 1932- .... **CLC 3, 4, 6, 48**
See also CA 25-28R; CAAS 8; CANR 32; DLB 173; DLBY 81

Suknaski, Andrew 1942- .... **CLC 19**
See also CA 101; DLB 53

Sullivan, Vernon
See Vian, Boris

Sully Prudhomme 1839-1907 .... **TCLC 31**

Su Man-shu .... **TCLC 24**
See also Su Chien

Summerforest, Ivy B.
See Kirkup, James

Summers, Andrew James 1942- .... **CLC 26**

Summers, Andy
See Summers, Andrew James

Summers, Hollis (Spurgeon, Jr.) 1916- **CLC 10**
See also CA 5-8R; CANR 3; DLB 6

Summers, (Alphonsus Joseph-Mary Augustus) Montague 1880-1948 .... **TCLC 16**
See also CA 118

Sumner, Gordon Matthew 1951- ...... **CLC 26**

Surtees, Robert Smith 1803-1864 .. **NCLC 14**
See also DLB 21

Susann, Jacqueline 1921-1974 .... **CLC 3**
See also AITN 1; CA 65-68; 53-56; MTCW

Su Shih 1036-1101 .... **CMLC 15**

Suskind, Patrick
See Sueskind, Patrick
See also CA 145

Sutcliff, Rosemary 1920-1992 **CLC 26; DAB; DAC; DAM MST, POP**
See also AAYA 10; CA 5-8R; 139; CANR 37; CLR 1, 37; JRDA; MAICYA; SATA 6, 44, 78; SATA-Obit 73

Sutro, Alfred 1863-1933 .... **TCLC 6**
See also CA 105; DLB 10

Sutton, Henry
See Slavitt, David R(ytman)

Svevo, Italo 1861-1928 . **TCLC 2, 35; SSC 25**
See also Schmitz, Aron Hector

Swados, Elizabeth (A.) 1951- .... **CLC 12**
See also CA 97-100; CANR 49; INT 97-100

Swados, Harvey 1920-1972 .... **CLC 5**
See also CA 5-8R; 37-40R; CANR 6; DLB 2

Swan, Gladys 1934- .... **CLC 69**
See also CA 101; CANR 17, 39

Swarthout, Glendon (Fred) 1918-1992 **CLC 35**
See also CA 1-4R; 139; CANR 1, 47; SATA 26

Sweet, Sarah C.
See Jewett, (Theodora) Sarah Orne

Swenson, May 1919-1989 **CLC 4, 14, 61; DA; DAB; DAC; DAM MST, POET; PC 14**
See also CA 5-8R; 130; CANR 36, 61; DLB 5; MTCW; SATA 15

Swift, Augustus
See Lovecraft, H(oward) P(hillips)

Swift, Graham (Colin) 1949- ...... **CLC 41, 88**
See also CA 117; 122; CANR 46

Swift, Jonathan 1667-1745 **LC 1; DA; DAB; DAC; DAM MST, NOV, POET; PC 9; WLC**
See also CDBLB 1660-1789; DLB 39, 95, 101; SATA 19

Swinburne, Algernon Charles 1837-1909 **TCLC 8, 36; DA; DAB; DAC; DAM MST, POET; WLC**
See also CA 105; 140; CDBLB 1832-1890; DLB 35, 57

Swinfen, Ann .... **CLC 34**

Swinnerton, Frank Arthur 1884-1982 **CLC 31**
See also CA 108; DLB 34

Swithen, John
See King, Stephen (Edwin)

Sylvia
See Ashton-Warner, Sylvia (Constance)

Symmes, Robert Edward
See Duncan, Robert (Edward)

Symonds, John Addington 1840-1893 **NCLC 34**
See also DLB 57, 144

Symons, Arthur 1865-1945 .... **TCLC 11**
See also CA 107; DLB 19, 57, 149

Symons, Julian (Gustave) 1912-1994 **CLC 2, 14, 32**
See also CA 49-52; 147; CAAS 3; CANR 3, 33, 59; DLB 87, 155; DLBY 92; MTCW

Synge, (Edmund) J(ohn) M(illington) 1871-1909 ... **TCLC 6, 37; DAM DRAM; DC 2**
See also CA 104; 141; CDBLB 1890-1914; DLB 10, 19

Syruc, J.
See Milosz, Czeslaw

Szirtes, George 1948- .... **CLC 46**
See also CA 109; CANR 27, 61

Szymborska, Wislawa 1923- .... **CLC 99**
See also CA 154; DLBY 96

T. O., Nik
See Annensky, Innokenty (Fyodorovich)

Tabori, George 1914- .... **CLC 19**
See also CA 49-52; CANR 4

Tagore, Rabindranath 1861-1941 **TCLC 3, 53; DAM DRAM, POET; PC 8**
See also CA 104; 120; MTCW

Taine, Hippolyte Adolphe 1828-1893 . **NCLC 15**

Talese, Gay 1932- .... **CLC 37**
See also AITN 1; CA 1-4R; CANR 9, 58; INT CANR-9; MTCW

Tallent, Elizabeth (Ann) 1954- .... **CLC 45**
See also CA 117; DLB 130

Tally, Ted 1952- .... **CLC 42**
See also CA 120; 124; INT 124

Tamayo y Baus, Manuel 1829-1898 **NCLC 1**

Tammsaare, A(nton) H(ansen) 1878-1940 **TCLC 27**

Tam'si, Tchicaya U
See Tchicaya, Gerald Felix

Tan, Amy (Ruth) 1952- **CLC 59; DAM MULT, NOV, POP**
See also AAYA 9; BEST 89:3; CA 136; CANR 54; DLB 173; SATA 75

Tandem, Felix
See Spitteler, Carl (Friedrich Georg)

Tanizaki, Jun'ichiro 1886-1965 **CLC 8, 14, 28; SSC 21**
See also CA 93-96; 25-28R; DLB 180

Tanner, William

See Amis, Kingsley (William)

Tao Lao
See Storni, Alfonsina

Tarassoff, Lev
See Troyat, Henri

Tarbell, Ida M(inerva) 1857-1944 . **TCLC 40**
See also CA 122; DLB 47

Tarkington, (Newton) Booth 1869-1946 **TCLC 9**
See also CA 110; 143; DLB 9, 102; SATA 17

Tarkovsky, Andrei (Arsenyevich) 1932-1986 **CLC 75**
See also CA 127

Tartt, Donna 1964(?)- .... **CLC 76**
See also CA 142

Tasso, Torquato 1544-1595 .... **LC 5**

Tate, (John Orley) Allen 1899-1979 **CLC 2, 4, 6, 9, 11, 14, 24**
See also CA 5-8R; 85-88; CANR 32; DLB 4, 45, 63; MTCW

Tate, Ellalice
See Hibbert, Eleanor Alice Burford

Tate, James (Vincent) 1943- ..... **CLC 2, 6, 25**
See also CA 21-24R; CANR 29, 57; DLB 5, 169

Tavel, Ronald 1940- .... **CLC 6**
See also CA 21-24R; CANR 33

Taylor, C(ecil) P(hilip) 1929-1981 .... **CLC 27**
See also CA 25-28R; 105; CANR 47

Taylor, Edward 1642(?)-1729 ..... **LC 11; DA; DAB; DAC; DAM MST, POET**
See also DLB 24

Taylor, Eleanor Ross 1920- .... **CLC 5**
See also CA 81-84

Taylor, Elizabeth 1912-1975 ..... **CLC 2, 4, 29**
See also CA 13-16R; CANR 9; DLB 139; MTCW; SATA 13

Taylor, Frederick Winslow 1856-1915 **TCLC 76**

Taylor, Henry (Splawn) 1942- .... **CLC 44**
See also CA 33-36R; CAAS 7; CANR 31; DLB 5

Taylor, Kamala (Purnaiya) 1924-
See Markandaya, Kamala
See also CA 77-80

Taylor, Mildred D. .... **CLC 21**
See also AAYA 10; BW 1; CA 85-88; CANR 25; CLR 9; DLB 52; JRDA; MAICYA; SAAS 5; SATA 15, 70

Taylor, Peter (Hillsman) 1917-1994 **CLC 1, 4, 18, 37, 44, 50, 71; SSC 10**
See also CA 13-16R; 147; CANR 9, 50; DLBY 81, 94; INT CANR-9; MTCW

Taylor, Robert Lewis 1912- .... **CLC 14**
See also CA 1-4R; CANR 3; SATA 10

Tchekhov, Anton
See Chekhov, Anton (Pavlovich)

Tchicaya, Gerald Felix 1931-1988 .. **CLC 101**
See also CA 129; 125

Tchicaya U Tam'si
See Tchicaya, Gerald Felix

Teasdale, Sara 1884-1933 .... **TCLC 4**
See also CA 104; DLB 45; SATA 32

Tegner, Esaias 1782-1846 .... **NCLC 2**

Teilhard de Chardin, (Marie Joseph) Pierre 1881-1955 .... **TCLC 9**
See also CA 105

Temple, Ann
See Mortimer, Penelope (Ruth)

Tennant, Emma (Christina) 1937- **CLC 13, 52**
See also CA 65-68; CAAS 9; CANR 10, 38, 59; DLB 14

Tenneshaw, S. M.
See Silverberg, Robert

Tennyson, Alfred 1809-1892 ... **NCLC 30, 65; DA; DAB; DAC; DAM MST, POET; PC 6; WLC**

See also CDBLB 1832-1890; DLB 32
Teran, Lisa St. Aubin de .... CLC 36
    See also St. Aubin de Teran, Lisa
Terence 195(?)B.C.-159B.C. **CMLC 14; DC 7**
Teresa de Jesus, St. 1515-1582 .... **LC 18**
Terkel, Louis 1912-
    See Terkel, Studs
    See also CA 57-60; CANR 18, 45; MTCW
Terkel, Studs .... **CLC 38**
    See also Terkel, Louis
    See also AITN 1
Terry, C. V.
    See Slaughter, Frank G(ill)
Terry, Megan 1932- .... CLC 19
    See also CA 77-80; CABS 3; CANR 43; DLB 7
Tertz, Abram
    See Sinyavsky, Andrei (Donatevich)
Tesich, Steve 1943(?)-1996 .... **CLC 40, 69**
    See also CA 105; 152; DLBY 83
Teternikov, Fyodor Kuzmich 1863-1927
    See Sologub, Fyodor
    See also CA 104
Tevis, Walter 1928-1984 .... CLC 42
    See also CA 113
Tey, Josephine .... TCLC 14
    See also Mackintosh, Elizabeth
    See also DLB 77
Thackeray, William Makepeace 1811-1863
    **NCLC 5, 14, 22, 43; DA; DAB; DAC; DAM
    MST, NOV; WLC**
    See also CDBLB 1832-1890; DLB 21, 55, 159,
    163; SATA 23
Thakura, Ravindranatha
    See Tagore, Rabindranath
Tharoor, Shashi 1956- .... CLC 70
    See also CA 141
Thelwell, Michael Miles 1939- .... CLC 22
    See also BW 2; CA 101
Theobald, Lewis, Jr.
    See Lovecraft, H(oward) P(hillips)
Theodorescu, Ion N. 1880-1967
    See Arghezi, Tudor
    See also CA 116
Theriault, Yves 1915-1983 .... **CLC 79; DAC;
    DAM MST**
    See also CA 102; DLB 88
Theroux, Alexander (Louis) 1939- CLC 2, 25
    See also CA 85-88; CANR 20
Theroux, Paul (Edward) 1941- **CLC 5, 8, 11,
    15, 28, 46; DAM POP**
    See also BEST 89:4; CA 33-36R; CANR 20,
    45; DLB 2; MTCW; SATA 44
Thesen, Sharon 1946- .... CLC 56
Thevenin, Denis
    See Duhamel, Georges
Thibault, Jacques Anatole Francois 1844-1924
    See France, Anatole
    See also CA 106; 127; DAM NOV; MTCW
Thiele, Colin (Milton) 1920- .... CLC 17
    See also CA 29-32R; CANR 12, 28, 53; CLR
    27; MAICYA; SAAS 2; SATA 14, 72
Thomas, Audrey (Callahan) 1935- CLC 7, 13,
    37; SSC 20
    See also AITN 2; CA 21-24R; CAAS 19; CANR
    36, 58; DLB 60; MTCW
Thomas, D(onald) M(ichael) 1935- . **CLC 13,
    22, 31**
    See also CA 61-64; CAAS 11; CANR 17, 45;
    CDBLB 1960 to Present; DLB 40; INT
    CANR-17; MTCW
Thomas, Dylan (Marlais) 1914-1953**TCLC 1,
    8, 45; DA; DAB; DAC; DAM DRAM,
    MST, POET; PC 2; SSC 3; WLC**
    See also CA 104; 120; CDBLB 1945-1960;
    DLB 13, 20, 139; MTCW; SATA 60
Thomas, (Philip) Edward 1878-1917 . **T C L C
    10; DAM POET**

See also CA 106; 153; DLB 19
Thomas, Joyce Carol 1938- .... **CLC 35**
    See also AAYA 12; BW 2; CA 113; 116; CANR
    48; CLR 19; DLB 33; INT 116; JRDA;
    MAICYA; MTCW; SAAS 7; SATA 40, 78
Thomas, Lewis 1913-1993 .... **CLC 35**
    See also CA 85-88; 143; CANR 38, 60; MTCW
Thomas, Paul
    See Mann, (Paul) Thomas
Thomas, Piri 1928- .... **CLC 17**
    See also CA 73-76; HW
Thomas, R(onald) S(tuart) 1913- CLC 6, 13,
    48; DAB; DAM POET
    See also CA 89-92; CAAS 4; CANR 30;
    CDBLB 1960 to Present; DLB 27; MTCW
Thomas, Ross (Elmore) 1926-1995 ... CLC 39
    See also CA 33-36R; 150; CANR 22
Thompson, Francis Clegg
    See Mencken, H(enry) L(ouis)
Thompson, Francis Joseph 1859-1907**TCLC 4**
    See also CA 104; CDBLB 1890-1914; DLB 19
Thompson, Hunter S(tockton) 1939-. **CLC 9,
    17, 40, 104; DAM POP**
    See also BEST 89:1; CA 17-20R; CANR 23,
    46; MTCW
Thompson, James Myers
    See Thompson, Jim (Myers)
Thompson, Jim (Myers) 1906-1977(?)**CLC 69**
    See also CA 140
Thompson, Judith .... CLC 39
Thomson, James 1700-1748 ... **LC 16, 29, 40;
    DAM POET**
    See also DLB 95
Thomson, James 1834-1882 **NCLC 18; DAM
    POET**
    See also DLB 35
Thoreau, Henry David 1817-1862**NCLC 7, 21,
    61; DA; DAB; DAC; DAM MST; WLC**
    See also CDALB 1640-1865; DLB 1
Thornton, Hall
    See Silverberg, Robert
Thucydides c. 455B.C.-399B.C. .... **CMLC 17**
    See also DLB 176
Thurber, James (Grover) 1894-1961. **CLC 5,
    11, 25; DA; DAB; DAC; DAM DRAM,
    MST, NOV; SSC 1**
    See also CA 73-76; CANR 17, 39; CDALB
    1929-1941; DLB 4, 11, 22, 102; MAICYA;
    MTCW; SATA 13
Thurman, Wallace (Henry) 1902-1934**T C L C
    6; BLC; DAM MULT**
    See also BW 1; CA 104; 124; DLB 51
Ticheburn, Cheviot
    See Ainsworth, William Harrison
Tieck, (Johann) Ludwig 1773-1853 **NCLC 5,
    46**
    See also DLB 90
Tiger, Derry
    See Ellison, Harlan (Jay)
Tilghman, Christopher 1948(?)- .... **CLC 65**
    See also CA 159
Tillinghast, Richard (Williford) 1940-**CLC 29**
    See also CA 29-32R; CAAS 23; CANR 26, 51
Timrod, Henry 1828-1867 .... **NCLC 25**
    See also DLB 3
Tindall, Gillian 1938- .... CLC 7
    See also CA 21-24R; CANR 11
Tiptree, James, Jr. .... **CLC 48, 50**
    See also Sheldon, Alice Hastings Bradley
    See also DLB 8
Titmarsh, Michael Angelo
    See Thackeray, William Makepeace
**Tocqueville, Alexis (Charles Henri Maurice
    Clerel Comte)** 1805-1859 ...**NCLC 7, 63**
Tolkien, J(ohn) R(onald) R(euel) 1892-1973
    **CLC 1, 2, 3, 8, 12, 38; DA; DAB; DAC;
    DAM MST, NOV, POP; WLC**

See also AAYA 10; AITN 1; CA 17-18; 45-48;
    CANR 36; CAP 2; CDBLB 1914-1945; DLB
    15, 160; JRDA; MAICYA; MTCW; SATA 2,
    32; SATA-Obit 24
Toller, Ernst 1893-1939 .... **TCLC 10**
    See also CA 107; DLB 124
Tolson, M. B.
    See Tolson, Melvin B(eaunorus)
Tolson, Melvin B(eaunorus) 1898(?)-1966
    CLC 36; BLC; DAM MULT, POET
    See also BW 1; CA 124; 89-92; DLB 48, 76
Tolstoi, Aleksei Nikolaevich
    See Tolstoy, Alexey Nikolaevich
Tolstoy, Alexey Nikolaevich 1882-1945**T C L C
    18**
    See also CA 107; 158
Tolstoy, Count Leo
    See Tolstoy, Leo (Nikolaevich)
Tolstoy, Leo (Nikolaevich) 1828-1910**TCLC 4,
    11, 17, 28, 44; DA; DAB; DAC; DAM MST,
    NOV; SSC 9; WLC**
    See also CA 104; 123; SATA 26
Tomasi di Lampedusa, Giuseppe 1896-1957
    See Lampedusa, Giuseppe (Tomasi) di
    See also CA 111
Tomlin, Lily .... CLC 17
    See also Tomlin, Mary Jean
Tomlin, Mary Jean 1939(?)-
    See Tomlin, Lily
    See also CA 117
Tomlinson, (Alfred) Charles 1927-**CLC 2, 4, 6,
    13, 45; DAM POET; PC 17**
    See also CA 5-8R; CANR 33; DLB 40
Tomlinson, H(enry) M(ajor) 1873-1958**T C L C
    71**
    See also CA 118; DLB 36, 100
Tonson, Jacob
    See Bennett, (Enoch) Arnold
Toole, John Kennedy 1937-1969 **CLC 19, 64**
    See also CA 104; DLBY 81
Toomer, Jean 1894-1967 ....**CLC 1, 4, 13, 22;
    BLC; DAM MULT; PC 7; SSC 1; WLCS**
    See also BW 1; CA 85-88; CDALB 1917-1929;
    DLB 45, 51; MTCW
Torley, Luke
    See Blish, James (Benjamin)
Tornimparte, Alessandra
    See Ginzburg, Natalia
Torre, Raoul della
    See Mencken, H(enry) L(ouis)
Torrey, E(dwin) Fuller 1937- .... CLC 34
    See also CA 119
Torsvan, Ben Traven
    See Traven, B.
Torsvan, Benno Traven
    See Traven, B.
Torsvan, Berick Traven
    See Traven, B.
Torsvan, Berwick Traven
    See Traven, B.
Torsvan, Bruno Traven
    See Traven, B.
Torsvan, Traven
    See Traven, B.
Tournier, Michel (Edouard) 1924-**CLC 6, 23,
    36, 95**
    See also CA 49-52; CANR 3, 36; DLB 83;
    MTCW; SATA 23
Tournimparte, Alessandra
    See Ginzburg, Natalia
Towers, Ivar
    See Kornbluth, C(yril) M.
Towne, Robert (Burton) 1936(?)- ..... **CLC 87**
    See also CA 108; DLB 44
Townsend, Sue 1946- .... **CLC 61; DAB; DAC**
    See also CA 119; 127; INT 127; MTCW; SATA
    55, 93; SATA-Brief 48

Townshend, Peter (Dennis Blandford) 1945-
    CLC 17, 42
    See also CA 107
Tozzi, Federigo 1883-1920 .... TCLC 31
    See also CA 160
Traill, Catharine Parr 1802-1899 .. NCLC 31
    See also DLB 99
Trakl, Georg 1887-1914 .... TCLC 5
    See also CA 104
Transtroemer, Tomas (Goesta) 1931-CLC 52,
    65; DAM POET
    See also CA 117; 129; CAAS 17
Transtromer, Tomas Gosta
    See Transtroemer, Tomas (Goesta)
Traven, B. (?)-1969 .... CLC 8, 11
    See also CA 19-20; 25-28R; CAP 2; DLB 9,
    56; MTCW
Treitel, Jonathan 1959- .... CLC 70
Tremain, Rose 1943- .... CLC 42
    See also CA 97-100; CANR 44; DLB 14
Tremblay, Michel 1942- CLC 29, 102; DAC;
    DAM MST
    See also CA 116; 128; DLB 60; MTCW
Trevanian .... CLC 29
    See also Whitaker, Rod(ney)
Trevor, Glen
    See Hilton, James
Trevor, William 1928- . CLC 7, 9, 14, 25, 71;
    SSC 21
    See also Cox, William Trevor
    See also DLB 14, 139
Trifonov, Yuri (Valentinovich) 1925-1981
    CLC 45
    See also CA 126; 103; MTCW
Trilling, Lionel 1905-1975 ...... CLC 9, 11, 24
    See also CA 9-12R; 61-64; CANR 10; DLB 28,
    63; INT CANR-10; MTCW
Trimball, W. H.
    See Mencken, H(enry) L(ouis)
Tristan
    See Gomez de la Serna, Ramon
Tristram
    See Housman, A(lfred) E(dward)
Trogdon, William (Lewis) 1939-
    See Heat-Moon, William Least
    See also CA 115; 119; CANR 47; INT 119
Trollope, Anthony 1815-1882NCLC 6, 33; DA;
    DAB; DAC; DAM MST, NOV; SSC 28;
    WLC
    See also CDBLB 1832-1890; DLB 21, 57, 159;
    SATA 22
Trollope, Frances 1779-1863 .... NCLC 30
    See also DLB 21, 166
Trotsky, Leon 1879-1940 .... TCLC 22
    See also CA 118
Trotter (Cockburn), Catharine 1679-1749L C
    8
    See also DLB 84
Trout, Kilgore
    See Farmer, Philip Jose
Trow, George W. S. 1943- .... CLC 52
    See also CA 126
Troyat, Henri 1911- .... CLC 23 `
    See also CA 45-48; CANR 2, 33; MTCW
Trudeau, G(arretson) B(eekman) 1948-
    See Trudeau, Garry B.
    See also CA 81-84; CANR 31; SATA 35
Trudeau, Garry B. .... CLC 12
    See also Trudeau, G(arretson) B(eekman)
    See also AAYA 10; AITN 2
Truffaut, Francois 1932-1984 .. CLC 20, 101
    See also CA 81-84; 113; CANR 34
Trumbo, Dalton 1905-1976 .... CLC 19
    See also CA 21-24R; 69-72; CANR 10; DLB
    26
Trumbull, John 1750-1831 .... NCLC 30
    See also DLB 31

Trundlett, Helen B.
    See Eliot, T(homas) S(tearns)
Tryon, Thomas 1926-1991 . CLC 3, 11; DAM
    POP
    See also AITN 1; CA 29-32R; 135; CANR 32;
    MTCW
Tryon, Tom
    See Tryon, Thomas
Ts'ao Hsueh-ch'in 1715(?)-1763 .... LC 1
Tsushima, Shuji 1909-1948
    See Dazai, Osamu
    See also CA 107
Tsvetaeva (Efron), Marina (Ivanovna) 1892-
    1941 .... TCLC 7, 35; PC 14
    See also CA 104; 128; MTCW
Tuck, Lily 1938- .... CLC 70
    See also CA 139
Tu Fu 712-770.. PC 9
    See also DAM MULT
Tunis, John R(oberts) 1889-1975 ...... CLC 12
    See also CA 61-64; CANR 62; DLB 22, 171;
    JRDA; MAICYA; SATA 37; SATA-Brief 30
Tuohy, Frank .... CLC 37
    See also Tuohy, John Francis
    See also DLB 14, 139
Tuohy, John Francis 1925-
    See Tuohy, Frank
    See also CA 5-8R; CANR 3, 47
Turco, Lewis (Putnam) 1934- ...... CLC 11, 63
    See also CA 13-16R; CAAS 22; CANR 24, 51;
    DLBY 84
Turgenev, Ivan 1818-1883 .... NCLC 21; DA;
    DAB; DAC; DAM MST, NOV; DC 7; SSC
    7; WLC
Turgot, Anne-Robert-Jacques 1727-1781 L C
    26
Turner, Frederick 1943- .... CLC 48
    See also CA 73-76; CAAS 10; CANR 12, 30,
    56; DLB 40
Tutu, Desmond M(pilo) 1931- CLC 80; BLC;
    DAM MULT
    See also BW 1; CA 125
Tutuola, Amos 1920-1997CLC 5, 14, 29; BLC;
    DAM MULT
    See also BW 2; CA 9-12R; 159; CANR 27; DLB
    125; MTCW
Twain, Mark TCLC 6, 12, 19, 36, 48, 59; SSC
    26; WLC
    See also Clemens, Samuel Langhorne
    See also AAYA 20; DLB 11, 12, 23, 64, 74
Tyler, Anne 1941- . CLC 7, 11, 18, 28, 44, 59,
    103; DAM NOV, POP
    See also AAYA 18; BEST 89:1; CA 9-12R;
    CANR 11, 33, 53; DLB 6, 143; DLBY 82;
    MTCW; SATA 7, 90
Tyler, Royall 1757-1826 .... NCLC 3
    See also DLB 37
Tynan, Katharine 1861-1931 .... TCLC 3
    See also CA 104; DLB 153
Tyutchev, Fyodor 1803-1873 .... NCLC 34
Tzara, Tristan 1896-1963 ...... CLC 47; DAM
    POET
    See also Rosenfeld, Samuel; Rosenstock, Sami;
    Rosenstock, Samuel
    See also CA 153
Uhry, Alfred 1936- ... CLC 55; DAM DRAM,
    POP
    See also CA 127; 133; INT 133
Ulf, Haerved
    See Strindberg, (Johan) August
Ulf, Harved
    See Strindberg, (Johan) August
Ulibarri, Sabine R(eyes) 1919-CLC 83; DAM
    MULT
    See also CA 131; DLB 82; HW
Unamuno (y Jugo), Miguel de 1864-1936
    TCLC 2, 9; DAM MULT, NOV; HLC; SSC

11
    See also CA 104; 131; DLB 108; HW; MTCW
Undercliffe, Errol
    See Campbell, (John) Ramsey
Underwood, Miles
    See Glassco, John
Undset, Sigrid 1882-1949TCLC 3; DA; DAB;
    DAC; DAM MST, NOV; WLC
    See also CA 104; 129; MTCW
Ungaretti, Giuseppe 1888-1970CLC 7, 11, 15
    See also CA 19-20; 25-28R; CAP 2; DLB 114
Unger, Douglas 1952- .... CLC 34
    See also CA 130
Unsworth, Barry (Forster) 1930- ..... CLC 76
    See also CA 25-28R; CANR 30, 54
Updike, John (Hoyer) 1932-CLC 1, 2, 3, 5, 7,
    9, 13, 15, 23, 34, 43, 70; DA; DAB; DAC;
    DAM MST, NOV, POET, POP; SSC 13, 27;
    WLC
    See also CA 1-4R; CABS 1; CANR 4, 33, 51;
    CDALB 1968-1988; DLB 2, 5, 143; DLBD
    3; DLBY 80, 82; MTCW
Upshaw, Margaret Mitchell
    See Mitchell, Margaret (Munnerlyn)
Upton, Mark
    See Sanders, Lawrence
Urdang, Constance (Henriette) 1922-CLC 47
    See also CA 21-24R; CANR 9, 24
Uriel, Henry
    See Faust, Frederick (Schiller)
Uris, Leon (Marcus) 1924- CLC 7, 32; DAM
    NOV, POP
    See also AITN 1, 2; BEST 89:2; CA 1-4R;
    CANR 1, 40; MTCW; SATA 49
Urmuz
    See Codrescu, Andrei
Urquhart, Jane 1949- .... CLC 90; DAC
    See also CA 113; CANR 32
Ustinov, Peter (Alexander) 1921- .... CLC 1
    See also AITN 1; CA 13-16R; CANR 25, 51;
    DLB 13
U Tam'si, Gerald Felix Tchicaya
    See Tchicaya, Gerald Felix
U Tam'si, Tchicaya
    See Tchicaya, Gerald Felix
Vaculik, Ludvik 1926- .... CLC 7
    See also CA 53-56
Vaihinger, Hans 1852-1933 .... TCLC 71
    See also CA 116
Valdez, Luis (Miguel) 1940- ..CLC 84; DAM
    MULT; HLC
    See also CA 101; CANR 32; DLB 122; HW
Valenzuela, Luisa 1938- CLC 31, 104; DAM
    MULT; SSC 14
    See also CA 101; CANR 32; DLB 113; HW
Valera y Alcala-Galiano, Juan 1824-1905
    TCLC 10
    See also CA 106
Valery, (Ambroise) Paul (Toussaint Jules) 1871-
    1945 ..... TCLC 4, 15; DAM POET; PC 9
    See also CA 104; 122; MTCW
Valle-Inclan, Ramon (Maria) del 1866-1936
    TCLC 5; DAM MULT; HLC
    See also CA 106; 153; DLB 134
Vallejo, Antonio Buero
    See Buero Vallejo, Antonio
Vallejo, Cesar (Abraham) 1892-1938TCLC 3,
    56; DAM MULT; HLC
    See also CA 105; 153; HW
Vallette, Marguerite Eymery
    See Rachilde
Valle Y Pena, Ramon del
    See Valle-Inclan, Ramon (Maria) del
Van Ash, Cay 1918- .... CLC 34
Vanbrugh, Sir John 1664-1726 LC 21; DAM
    DRAM
    See also DLB 80

Literary Criticism Series
Cumulative Topic Index

This index lists all topic entries in Gale's *Classical and Medieval Literature Criticism, Contemporary Literary Criticism, Literature Criticism from 1400 to 1800, Nineteenth-Century Literature Criticism,* and *Twentieth-Century Literary Criticism.*

Topic Index

Topic Index

Twentieth-Century Literary Criticism
Cumulative Nationality Index

Nationality Index

TCLC-75 Title Index

Title Index